Contents

Implementation Handbook
for the Convention
on the
Rights of the Child

Implementation Handbook

for the Convention on the

Rights

of the

Child

prepared for UNICEF

by Rachel Hodgkin and Peter Newell

United Nations Children's Fund

ISBN 92-806-3337-6
Sales No. E.97.XX.SWZ.2

UNICEF, UNICEF House,
Three United Nations Plaza,
New York, NY 10017, USA

UNICEF Regional Office for Europe
Palais des Nations
1211 Geneva 10, Switzerland

Cover photographs (left to right) : UNICEF/5376/Isaac; UNICEF/94-0971/Craig; UNICEF/95-1185/Pirozzi; UNICEF/HQ96-0224/Toutounji; UNICEF/3933/90/Sprague.

Inside photographs: p. XX, UNICEF/97-0507/Murray-Lee; p. 18, UNICEF/DOI94-0989/Press; p. 36, UNICEF/97-0484/Murray-Lee; p. 50, UNICEF/5131/Isaac; p. 84, UNICEF/Noorani; p. 118, UNICEF/DOI94-0876/Lemoyne; p. 144, UNICEF/DOI95-0488/Ayisi; p. 196, UNICEF/DOI93-1185/Horner; p. 210, UNICEF/5391/Isaac; p. 224, UNICEF/97-0494/Murray-Lee; p. 256, UNICEF/2133/Murray-Lee; p. 268, UNICEF/90-0017/Tolmie; p. 280, UNICEF/3200/Bregnard; p. 368, UNICEF/5761/Goodsmith; p. 390, UNICEF/DOI94-1186/Pirozzi; p. 538, UNICEF/93-BOU1005/Press; p. 558, UNICEF/HQ96-0245/Toutounji; p. 574, UNICEF/4404Z/Murray-Lee; p. 584, UNICEF/HQ97-0279/Noorani.

Designed by Philippe Terrigeol
Typeset and printed on chlorine-free paper
by Atar SA, Geneva, Switzerland
January 1998

Foreword

The nearly universal ratification of the Convention on the Rights of the Child is a remarkable achievement. The fact that virtually every country in the world has committed itself to a code of binding obligations towards its children gives us tremendous hope for the future and puts children's rights at the cutting edge of the global struggle for human rights. It also places a tremendous responsibility on governments and civil society to live up to these commitments.

The United Nations Children's Fund is mandated to advocate for the protection of children's rights, to help meet their basic needs and to expand their opportunities to reach their full potential. We are guided in doing this by the provisions and principles of the Convention on the Rights of the Child. Of course achieving this mission requires concrete actions with direct impact on children. As part of our effort to help turn words into action, UNICEF is pleased to publish this Handbook on implementation of the Convention on the Rights of the Child. The Handbook is intended to advance the efforts of governments, NGOs, and United Nations organizations in making human rights a reality for each and every child on this planet.

It is our hope that the Handbook will be used as a reference in the day-to-day practical process of improving the quality of children's lives. It has been structured in a way that allows users to easily consult those chapters most relevant to their work and has been written in clear language which should be accessible to all.

We believe that the Implementation Handbook is an important tool which will assist UNICEF and its partners in the collective endeavour to promote and protect children's rights.

Carol Bellamy
Executive Director
UNICEF

Preface

As the first three chairpersons of the Committee on the Rights of the Child, we welcome the preparation and publication of this Implementation Handbook for the Convention on the Rights of the Child.

The Handbook provides a detailed reference for the implementation of law, policy and practice to promote and protect the rights of children. The Handbook brings together under each article of the Convention an analysis of the Committee's growing interpretation during its first six years and the examination of the first 68 Initial Reports of States Parties. It places these in the context of key comments, decisions and reports of the other treaty bodies and relevant United Nations bodies.

The Handbook also provides a concise description of the role, powers and procedures, and developing activities of the Committee and its appendices include a guide to related United Nations bodies and the texts of key international instruments.

We hope that the Handbook will be widely used by all those involved in promoting the fullest possible implementation of the Convention – governments and governmental agencies, UNICEF and other United Nations organizations and bodies, international, regional and national NGOs and others.

As the Committee noted in the report of its second session in 1992, its members are "solely accountable to the children of the world". We hope this Handbook will help to bring the Convention alive and encourage all those working with and for children to see implementation as more than a formal process. We hope it will be seen as the vivid and exciting process of working to improve the lives of the world's children.

Hoda Badran
Chairperson
1991-1995

Akila Belembaogo
Chairperson
1995-1997

Sandra Mason
Chairperson
1997-Present

Acknowledgements

The idea of this Handbook was born in conversations with past and present members of the Committee on the Rights of the Child and with Bilge Ogün Bassani, Deputy Regional Director of UNICEF's Regional Office for Europe in Geneva. We are grateful for the considerable support and assistance we have received throughout the preparation of the Handbook from André Roberfroid, Regional Director; Ms. Bassani; and from Lesley Miller, Child Rights Project Officer, UNICEF Regional Office for Europe.

Omissions and mistakes which remain are entirely our responsibility. We very much hope that those who use the Handbook will provide comments to UNICEF, to ensure that future editions are improved.

First and foremost, we gratefully acknowledge the contribution of current and former members of the Committee on the Rights of the Child:

Hoda Badran

Akila Belembaogo

Flora Eufemio

Thomas Hammarberg

Judith Karp

Yuri Kolosov

Sandra Mason

Swithun Mombeshora

Marta Santos Pais

Marilia Sardenberg

We also acknowledge the significant contribution of the following:

The Office of the High Commissioner for Human Rights, in particular: Helga Klein, Support Services Branch, Soussan Raadi-Azarakhchi and Paolo David, Secretariat to the Committee on the Rights of the Child.

Those from all over the world who were asked to review all or part of various drafts of the Handbook, and who have provided encouragement and comments:

Birgit Arellano, Rädda Barnen International Department

Ulla Armyr, Rädda Barnen International Department

Carlos Arnaldo, Free Flow of Information and Communication Research, UNESCO

Mark A. Belsey, Health Consultant

Julie Bissland, Refugee Women and Children, UNHCR

Paul Bloem, Adolescent Health, WHO

Neil Boothby, Senior Co-ordinator Refugee Children, UNHCR

Denis Broun, Health Section, UNICEF-New York

Nigel Cantwell, UNICEF International Child Development Centre, Florence

Geert Cappelaere, Children's Rights Centre, University of Gent

Eva Clärhall, Rädda Barnen International Department

David Clark, Nutrition Section, UNICEF-New York

Shalini Dewan, Publications Section, UNICEF-New York

Bruce Dick, Health Section, UNICEF-New York

Abdel Wahed El Abassi, Health Section, UNICEF-Mali

Carl von Essen, Rädda Barnen International Department

Preeti Ghelano, National Children's Bureau, UK

Målfrid Grude Flekkøy, former Ombudsman for Children, Norway

Kimberly Gamble-Payne, Regional Office for Eastern and Southern Africa, UNICEF

Savitri Gooneskere, School of Law, University of Colombo

Christina Gynnå Oguz, Demand Reduction Section, UN Drug Control Programme

Ian Hassall, Former Commissioner for Children, New Zealand

James R.Himes, UNICEF International Child Development Centre, Florence

Caroline Hunt, Human Rights Unit, UNHCR

Rachel Hurst, Disabled Peoples' International

Urban Jonsson, Regional Office for South Asia, UNICEF

June Kane, Consultant, UNICEF

Gerison Lansdown, Children's Rights Office, UK

Janis Marshall, Human Rights Unit, UNHCR

Kathleen Marshall, Centre for the Child and Society, University of Glasgow

Marta Mauras, Regional Office for Latin America and the Caribbean, UNICEF

Sarah McNeill, Unlimited Productions, UK

Vitit Muntarbhorn, Chulalongkorn University, Thailand

Marjorie Newman-Williams, Programme Division, UNICEF-New York

Yoshie Noguchi, International Labour Standards Department, International Labour Office

Alfhild Petrén, Rädda Barnen International Department

Rebeca Rios-Kohn, Office of Evaluation, Policy and Planning, UNICEF-New York

Philippa Russell, Council for Disabled Children, UK

Hélène Sackstein, NGO Group for the Convention on the Rights of the Child

Ben Schonveld, World Organisation Against Torture (OMCT)

Robert Smith, UK Committee for UNICEF

Rodolfo Stavenhagen, Department of Social Sciences, El Colegio de Mexico, Mexico

Laura Theytaz-Bergman, NGO Group for the Convention on the Rights of the Child

Trond Waage, Ombudsman for Children, Norway

Those who have helped with editing and style issues and verifying quotations, including in UNICEF-New York, Vicky Haeri and Susan Mann; in UNICEF-Geneva, Hélène Martin and in London, Miranda Horobin.

Those who have helped with research, including in UNICEF-Geneva, Peggy Creese, Research and Documentation Centre and Beatrice Baglietto, Child Rights Section; in London, Alexandra McLeod, United Nations Office and Information Centre; in Florence, Patricia Light and the remarkable range of publications of the International Child Development Centre.

Rachel Hodgkin and Peter Newell
London, 15 October 1997

Rachel Hodgkin and **Peter Newell,** who were commissioned by UNICEF to prepare the Implementation Handbook, are long-term advocates for and commentators on the human rights of children, in the United Kingdom and internationally; both work as consultants for UNICEF. In 1996 they carried out an inquiry in the United Kingdom and wrote a report on *Effective Government Structures for Children* for the Gulbenkian Foundation (with an international dimension supported by UNICEF). They live in London and have three young children.

Rachel Hodgkin is principal policy officer for the National Children's Bureau, based in London, and clerk to the All Party Parliamentary Group for Children. Previously she helped set up and subsequently worked at the Children's Legal Centre, a centre for children's rights advocacy in the United Kingdom. She is on the Executive Board of the UK Committee for UNICEF and worked as special adviser to UNICEF Geneva in its development with the Council of Europe of a European Strategy for Children.

Peter Newell chairs the Council of the Children's Rights Development Unit in the United Kingdom, and co-edited the Unit's major publication, the *UK Agenda for Children*, an analysis of action required to bring law, policy and practice into line with the Convention on the Rights of the Child. Previously he wrote *The UN Convention and Children's Rights in the UK*, published by the National Children's Bureau, and co-authored a detailed feasibility study on establishing a children's rights commissioner. He is Coordinator of "EPOCH – End Physical Punishment of Children", a UK-based campaign, and of the international network, EPOCH-WORLDWIDE.

Introduction

Aims and structure

The *Handbook* aims to be a practical tool for implementation, explaining and illustrating the implications of each article of the Convention on the Rights of the Child and their interconnections.

Under each article the Handbook brings together, analyzes and summarizes:

- comments and recommendations of the Committee on the Rights of the Child, recognized as the highest authority for interpretation of the Convention, from the official reports of its first 15 sessions (1991 to January 1997), and relevant extracts from the Committee's reporting guidelines. In particular, it analyzes the Committee's "Concluding Observations" on the first 68 Initial Reports submitted by States Parties. When the Committee is speaking as the Committee (for example in its Concluding Observations and in official reports of its sessions and of the General Discussions which it has convened on topics related to the Convention), the special significance of the Committee's comments are highlighted in the text in blue (individual Committee members are also quoted, but the quotations are not highlighted, as they do not carry the same authority);

- illustrative comments from the *Travaux préparatoires* of the Convention, the reports of the sessions of the Working Group which drafted the Convention;

- reservations and declarations made by States when ratifying or acceding to the Convention;

- relevant provisions from other international instruments, for example from the Universal Declaration of Human Rights and the two Covenants, on Civil and Political Rights and on Economic, Social and Cultural Rights (many of the Convention's articles have their origin in these instruments), other Declarations and Conventions, United Nations rules and guidelines on juvenile justice, the Standard Minimum Rules on the Equalization of Opportunities for Persons with Disabilities, Conventions of the International Labour Organization (ILO) and the Hague Conventions;

- relevant General Comments from other "Treaty Bodies", the Committees responsible for supervising implementation of other international instruments including, in particular, the Human Rights Committee (responsible for the Covenant on Civil and Political Rights) and the Committee on Economic, Social and Cultural Rights (responsible for the Covenant on Economic, Social and Cultural Rights);

- comments from the *Manual on Human Rights Reporting*, the 1997 edition of which includes a chapter by the first Rapporteur to the Committee on the Rights of the Child, Marta Santos Pais, on the Convention;

- comments and recommendations from other key United Nations bodies and agencies, and conclusions and recommendations of global conferences on human rights and social development.

The *Handbook* does not include analysis of regional human rights instruments, nor does it cover international or regional legal case law.

The role and activities of the Committee on the Rights of the Child and the reporting obligations of States Parties under the Convention are covered under the relevant Convention articles – articles 43 and 44.

The *Handbook* is not intended as a guide to the progress of implementation in individual countries. The purpose of quoting the Committee's comments and recommendations to States, and the purpose of the boxed examples from Initial Reports and other sources, is to illustrate and expand interpretation of the Convention.

Those who wish to analyze progress in particular States are encouraged to obtain the Initial Report and subsequent Periodic Reports of the State, together with the records of the Committee's examination of these reports, and its Concluding Observations.

The section on each article in the *Handbook* is structured to include:

- a concise summary of the article's implications and its relationship with other articles;

- relevant extracts from the *Guidelines for Initial Reports* and the *Guidelines for Periodic Reports* prepared by the Committee on the Rights of the Child (the full text of the *Guidelines for Periodic Reports* is also included in Appendix 3, page 604);

- detailed consideration of the background to and implications of individual elements of the article;

- occasional boxed examples from States Parties' Initial Reports and other official reports and recommendations (the *Handbook* has not attempted to analyze reports and other information provided by non-governmental organizations). These boxes are not intended necessarily to denote good or best practice, but to illustrate and illuminate issues raised by the article. The examples used have not been evaluated, and may not even describe current practice;

- a concluding "Implementation Checklist": this emphasizes that the articles of the Convention are interdependent and identifies other closely related articles. The Checklist poses questions designed to be used to investigate progress towards implementation.

- the appendices include the full texts of the Convention on the Rights of the Child and other key instruments, and of the Committee's *Guidelines for Periodic Reports*. In addition there is a guide to United Nations and United Nations-related agencies, and a bibliography.

How to use the "Implementation Checklists"

The Checklists have no official status. Each Checklist has been drafted to help all those involved in implementation – Governments, UNICEF and other United Nations agencies and international bodies, NGOs and others – to investigate the implications of the article for law, policy and practice and to promote and evaluate progress towards implementation.

The Checklists concern implementation, not reporting. They should not be confused with the official *Guidelines* for reporting prepared by the Committee on the Rights of the Child to advise States Parties in the preparation of Initial and Periodic Reports under the Convention (relevant extracts from these Guidelines are included under each article in the *Handbook*).

Each Checklist includes a reminder that no article should be considered in isolation – that the Convention is indivisible and its articles interdependent. The Checklists emphasize that in implementing each article, regard should be paid to the "general principles" highlighted by the Committee on the Rights of the Child and that other articles which are particularly closely related should be identified.

Each Checklist starts with a standard set of questions about general measures of implementation for the article in question: have the responsible government departments and other agencies been identified and appropriately coordinated, has there been a comprehensive review and adoption of an implementation strategy, budgetary analysis and allocation of resources, development of monitoring and evaluation and necessary training and so on. Further questions relate to the detail of implementation.

The questions are drafted so that they can be answered "YES", "NO", "PARTIALLY" or "DON'T KNOW" (insufficient information available to assess implementation). Answering "yes" or "no" to the questions which make up each Checklist does not necessarily indicate compliance or non-compliance with the Convention.

The Checklists can be used as the basis from which to develop more detailed and sensitive checklists for national or local use. Beyond the basic "YES", "NO" or "DON'T KNOW" answers, the questions provide a framework for collecting together the relevant information to build up a full analysis of and commentary on implementation.

So if the answer to a Checklist question is "YES", a summary could follow of the relevant law, policy and practice, and references to more detailed information which confirms the realization of the particular right for all relevant children. If "NO", an outline of the situation, and a summary of action required for compliance could be made. The answer "PARTIALLY" would be accompanied by information on the state of implementation, and on further action required. If the answer is "DON'T KNOW", there could be a summary of available information and an outline of the gaps in information which make it impossible to determine the state of implementation of the particular right.

Help develop the Implementation Checklists

Users are encouraged to help with the development of the Implementation Checklists, by sending comments and proposed additions to UNICEF:

**Implementation Handbook,
Programme Section, UNICEF,
Regional Office for Europe, Palais des Nations,
CH-1211 Geneva 10, Switzerland**

Explanation

of references

Abbreviated references are included in the text throughout, with a bibliography giving full references, and a list of the international instruments referred to, in Appendix 1, page 591. Commonly used acronyms are explained on page 681.

Official reports of the Committee on the Rights of the Child

The following abbreviated versions of references to certain series of the Official Reports of the Committee on the Rights of the Child are used:

Guidelines for Initial Reports; *Guidelines for Periodic Reports*: these are the guidelines prepared by the Committee for States Parties on the reports to be submitted under the Convention. The full titles are:

General Guidelines regarding the form and contents of initial reports to be submitted by States Parties under article 44, paragraph 1(a), of the Convention, (CRC/C/5, 15 October 1991);

General Guidelines regarding the form and contents of periodic reports to be submitted by States Parties under article 44, paragraph 1(b), of the Convention, (CRC/C/58, 20 November 1996).

IR: Initial Report – the report which States Parties must submit within two years of ratifying the Convention. (States must subsequently submit Periodic Reports, five years after the date on which their Initial Report was due. No periodic reports had been examined by the Committee before publication of this *Handbook*.)

IRCO: Initial Report Concluding Observations. Thus "Nigeria IRCO, Add.61, para. 39" refers to paragraph 39 of the Committee's Concluding Observations on Nigeria's Initial Report; "Add.61" comes from the full official reference "CRC/C/15/Add.61".

Also **IR Prelim. Obs.**: Initial Report Preliminary Observations (the Committee sometimes issues these when it wishes a State to submit further information). All Concluding Observations and Preliminary Observations on States Parties' Initial Reports are in the series "CRC/C/15/Add. ...".

SR: Summary Record of sessions of the Committee on the Rights of the Child, mostly of discussions between State Party representatives and the Committee, in each case identifying the State concerned (all Summary Records of Committee sessions are in the series "CRC/C/SR. ...").

Session reports: an official report is published following each of the sessions of the Committee on the Rights of the Child. In the *Handbook* the full reference is given, for example *Report on the fifth session, January 1994, CRC/C/24, pp. 38-43.*

(Within the United Nations documentation system, special symbols have been established for each of the human rights Treaty Bodies. Thus the reference for all Committee on the Rights of the Child documents begins "CRC/C/...". An explanation of all United Nations human rights document symbols is available from the Office of the High Commissioner for Human Rights.)

Other key documents

Other key documents frequently referred to include:

Reservations, Declarations and Objections relating to the Convention on the Rights of the Child. This document is regularly updated. The version referred to in the text is CRC/C/2/Rev.5, 30 July 1996.

Compilation of General Comments and General Recommendations adopted by Human Rights Treaty Bodies. This document is regularly updated. The version referred to in the text is HRI/GEN/1/Rev.2, 29 March 1996.

Travaux préparatoires: As yet, all reports of the "open-ended Working Group" which drafted the Convention on the Rights of the Child have not been published. The Working Group was set up by the United Nations Commission on Human Rights in 1979. Edited extracts from the official reports were published in 1992 in *The United Nations Convention on the Rights of the Child, A Guide to the "Travaux préparatoires"*, compiled and edited by Sharon Detrick, Martinus Nijhoff. Where extracts from the *Travaux préparatoires* are quoted in the *Handbook*, the reference to the official United Nations document and also the book reference are given.

Manual on Human Rights Reporting: a first edition, covering major international human rights instruments but not the Convention on the Rights of the Child, was jointly published by the United Nations Centre for Human Rights and the United Nations Institute for Training and Research (UNITAR) in 1991. A new edition, published in 1997, includes a section on "The Convention on the Rights of the Child" by Marta Santos Pais, who was first Rapporteur of the Committee on the Rights of the Child (this edition is jointly published by the Office of the High Commissioner for Human Rights, Geneva; United Nations Institute for Training and Research (UNITAR); United Nations Staff College Project, Turin; United Nations, Geneva, 1997). In the *Handbook*, the two editions are referred to as the *Manual on Human Rights Reporting*, 1991, and the *Manual on Human Rights Reporting*, 1997.

How to get the Committee's reports

The Office of the High Commissioner for Human Rights is the Secretariat for the Committee on behalf of the Secretary-General. Summary records are prepared for all public and some private meetings of the Committee (all meetings are held in public unless the Committee decides otherwise). The Initial and Periodic Reports of States Parties, Concluding Observations of the Committee, summary records and reports on the Committee's sessions are generally made available in the Committee's three working languages (English, French and Spanish; although summary records are not generally translated into Spanish); in addition the Committee may decide to make particular documents available in one or more of the other "official" languages of the Convention (Arabic, Chinese and Russian).

The Committee's official documents are available from:

Secretariat to the Committee on the Rights of the Child,
Office of the High Commissioner for Human Rights
Room D.205, Palais des Nations, 8-14 Avenue de la Paix,
1211 Geneva 10, Switzerland
(ph. 00 41 22 917 1234; fax 00 41 22 917 0123);

and from the Distribution and Sales Section,
Palais des Nations, 8-14 Avenue de la Paix, 1211 Geneva 10, Switzerland

They are also available electronically:
http: //www.unhchr.ch

Definition
of a child

article

1

Text of Article 1

For the purposes of the present Convention, a child means every human being below the age of 18 years unless, under the law applicable to the child, majority is attained earlier.

Article 1 of the Convention on the Rights of the Child defines "child" for the purposes of the Convention as every human being below the age of 18. The wording leaves the starting point of childhood open. Is it birth, conception, or somewhere in between? Had the Convention taken a position on abortion and related issues, universal ratification would have been threatened. For the purposes of the Convention, childhood ends at the 18th birthday unless, in a particular State, majority is achieved earlier.

Setting an age for the acquisition of certain rights or for the loss of certain protections is a complex matter. It balances the concept of the child as a subject of rights whose evolving capacities must be respected (acknowledged in articles 5 and 14) with the concept of the State's obligation to provide special protection. On some issues, the Convention sets a clear line: no capital punishment or life imprisonment without the possibility of release for those under the age of 18 (article 37); no recruitment into the armed forces or direct participation in hostilities for those under the age of 15 (article 38). On other issues, States are required to set minimum ages: for employment (article 32) and for criminal responsibility (article 40). The requirement to make primary education compulsory also implies setting an age (article 28).

The Committee on the Rights of the Child has emphasized that when States define minimum ages in legislation, they must do so in the context of the basic principles within the Convention, in particular the principle of non-discrimination (article 2, for example challenging different marriage ages for boys and girls), as well as the principles of best interests of the child (article 3) and the right to life and maximum survival and development (article 6). There must be respect for the child's "evolving capacities" (article 5). And there should be consistency, for example, in the ages set for the completion of compulsory education and for admission to employment.

In its reporting guidelines, the Committee asks for information on any minimum ages set in legislation for various purposes. In comments, it has urged that protective minimum ages should be raised, in particular those for sexual consent, admission to employment and criminal responsibility. ■

Summary

Extracts from
Committee on the Rights of the Child
Guidelines for Reports to be submitted by States Parties under the Convention

For full text of *Guidelines for Periodic Reports*, see Appendix 3, page 604.

Guidelines for Initial Reports

"Definition of the child

Under this section, States Parties are requested to provide relevant information, pursuant to article 1 of the Convention, concerning the definition of a child under their laws and regulations. In particular, States Parties are requested to provide information on the age of attainment of majority and on the legal minimum ages established for various purposes, including, inter alia, legal or medical counselling without parental consent, end of compulsory education, part-time employment, full-time employment, hazardous employment, sexual consent, marriage, voluntary enlistment into the armed forces, conscription into the armed forces, voluntarily giving testimony in court, criminal liability, deprivation of liberty, imprisonment and consumption of alcohol or other controlled substances."

(CRC/C/5, para. 12)

Guidelines for Periodic Reports

"II. DEFINITION OF THE CHILD (art.1)

Under this section, States Parties are requested to provide relevant information with respect to article 1 of the Convention, including on:

Any differences between national legislation and the Convention on the definition of the child;

The minimum legal age defined by the national legislation for the following:
Legal and medical counselling without parental consent;
Medical treatment or surgery without parental consent;
End of compulsory education;
Admission to employment or work, including hazardous work, part-time and full-time work;
Marriage;
Sexual consent;
Voluntary enlistment in the armed forces;
Conscription into the armed forces;
Participation in hostilities;
Criminal responsibility;
Deprivation of liberty, including by arrest, detention and imprisonment, inter alia in the areas of administration of justice, asylum-seeking and placement of children in welfare and health institutions;
Capital punishment and life imprisonment;
Giving testimony in court, in civil and criminal cases;
Lodging complaints and seeking redress before a court or other relevant authority without parental consent;
Participating in administrative and judicial proceedings affecting the child;
Giving consent to change of identity, including change of name, modification of family relations, adoption, guardianship;
Having access to information concerning the biological family;
Legal capacity to inherit, to conduct property transactions;
To create and join associations;
Choosing a religion or attending religious school teaching;
Consumption of alcohol and other controlled substances;

Starting point of childhood for purposes of Convention

Neither the 1924 nor the 1959 Declaration of the Rights of the Child define the beginning or end of childhood. But the Convention's Preamble draws attention to the statement in the Preamble to the 1959 Declaration "that the child, by reason of his physical and mental immaturity needs special safeguards and care, including appropriate legal protection, *before as well as after birth*" (editors' emphasis).

As mentioned previously, the wording of article 1 of the Convention avoids setting a starting point for childhood. The intention of those who drafted the article was to avoid taking a position on abortion and other pre-birth issues, which would have threatened the Convention's universal acceptance. Thus the *Manual on Human Rights Reporting,* 1997 advises: "The wording of article 1 does not specifically address the question of the moment at which 'childhood' should be considered to begin, thus intentionally avoiding, in view of the prevailing diversity of national legal solutions, a single solution common to all States.

"By avoiding a clear reference to either birth or the moment of conception, the Convention endorses a flexible and open solution, leaving to the national legislation the specification of the moment when childhood or life begins." (*Manual*, p. 413)

The preambular statement from the 1959 Declaration, quoted above, caused difficulties within the Working Group that drafted the Convention. In order to reach consensus, the Group agreed that a statement should be placed in the *travaux préparatoires* to the effect that "In adopting this preambular paragraph, the Working Group does not intend to prejudice the interpretation of article 1 or any other provision of the Convention by States Parties" (E/CN.4/1989/48, pp. 8-15, Detrick, p. 110).

Thus, the Convention leaves individual States to balance for themselves the conflicting rights and interests involved in issues such as abortion and family planning. And it is relevant to note that article 41 emphasizes that the Convention does not interfere with any domestic legislation (or applicable international law) "more conducive to the realization of the rights of the child..."

Obviously most of the articles of the Convention can apply to the child only after birth. Various States have, however, found it necessary to lodge declarations or reservations underlining their own particular legislative and/or other attitudes to the unborn child, in particular in relation to the child's "inherent right to life" and the State's obligation to "ensure to the maximum extent possible the survival and development of the child" under article 6.

For example, Argentina stated: "Concerning article 1 of the Convention, the Argentine Republic declares that the article must be interpreted to the effect that a child means every human being from the moment of conception up to the age of 18" (CRC/C/2/Rev.5, p. 12). This reflects the Argentinean Civil Code, which states: "Human existence begins from conception in the womb; and a person may acquire certain antenatal rights, as if he had already been born. These rights remain irrevocably acquired if those conceived in the womb are born alive, even though only for moments after being separated from their mother" (Argentina IR, para. 39).

The Holy See, in its declaration, "recognizes that the Convention represents an enactment of principles previously adopted by the United Nations and, once effective as a ratified instrument, will safeguard the rights of the child before as well as after birth, as expressly affirmed in the Declaration of the Rights of the Child and restated in the ninth preambular paragraph of the Convention. The Holy See remains confident that the ninth preambular paragraph will serve as the perspective through which the rest of the Convention will be interpreted, in conformity with article 31 of the Vienna Convention on the Law of Treaties of 23 May 1969." (CRC/C/2/Rev.5, p. 20)

The United Kingdom, in contrast, declared that it "interprets the Convention as applicable only following a live birth." (CRC/C/2/Rev.5, p. 33)

The Committee on the Rights of the Child has suggested that reservations to preserve State laws on abortion are unnecessary. But the Committee has commented adversely on high rates of abortion, on the use of abortion as a method of family planning and on "clandestine" abortions, and has encouraged measures to reduce the incidence of abortion. For further discussion see article 6 (page 88).

China made the following reservation: "The People's Republic of China shall fulfil its obligations provided by article 6 of the Convention to the extent that the Convention is consistent with the provisions of article 25 concerning family planning of the Constitution of the People's Republic of China and with the provisions of article 2 of the Law of Minor Children of the People's Republic of China." (CRC/C/2/Rev.5, p. 15)

The Committee, consistent with its general practice of urging all States to withdraw reservations, commented:

"In the light of the discussion in the Committee on the question of the continuing need for the State Party's reservation to article 6 of the Convention and the information provided by the State Party that it is open to considering making adjustments in regard to its reservation, the Committee encourages the State Party to review its reservation to the Convention with a view to its withdrawal." (China IRCO, Add.56, para. 24)

Luxembourg stated: "The Government of Luxembourg declares that article 6 of the present Convention presents no obstacle to implementation of the provisions of Luxembourg legislation concerning sex information, the prevention of back-street abortion and the regulation of pregnancy termination." (CRC/C/2/Rev.5, p. 24)

Other States have declared that they would interpret article 1 in conformity with their own legislation or constitutions (e.g. see CRC/C/2/Rev.5: Botswana, p. 15; Indonesia, p. 21; Malaysia, p. 24).

The end of childhood

For the purposes of the Convention on the Rights of the Child, childhood ends and majority is achieved at the 18th birthday "unless, under the law applicable to the child, majority is attained earlier". Thus the Convention is more prescriptive, but not inflexible, about defining for its purposes the end of childhood.

During discussion of Yemen's Initial Report, a Committee member noted that article 1 "might create confusion since it stated that 'a child means every human being below the age of eighteen years unless, under the law applicable to the child, majority is attained earlier'. The actual meaning of the article was that the child should be protected at least up to the age of 18, but that, since the child was also a subject of law, it was possible for him to be allowed some autonomy before the age of 18. That was why article 1 of the Convention remained relatively open. However the Convention was quite strict on some points, especially the death penalty, which it explicitly prohibited for anyone under 18 years of age..." (Yemen, SR.262, para. 10)

The *Manual on Human Rights Reporting*, 1997 refers to the age of 18 as "a general upper benchmark":
"This age limit should thus be used by States Parties as a rule and a reference for the establishment of any other particular age for any specific purpose or activity. This provision further stresses the need for States Parties to ensure special protection to every child below such a limit.

"While setting a general upper limit at 18, article 1 allows for the child's majority to be attained earlier under the law applicable to the child. Such expression should in no way be interpreted as a general escape clause, nor should it allow ages to be established which might be contrary to the principles and provisions of the Convention..." (*Manual*, p. 414)

In a relevant General Comment on a provision concerning child protection in the International Covenant on Civil and Political Rights, the Human Rights Committee emphasizes that protective ages must not be set "unreasonably low", and that in any case a State Party cannot absolve itself under the Covenant from obligations to children under 18 years old, even if they have reached the age of majority under domestic law.

Article 24 of the Covenant recognizes the right of every child, without any discrimination, to receive from his family, society and the State the protection required by his or her status as "a minor". The Covenant does not define "minor", nor does it indicate the age at which a child should attain majority. The 1989 General Comment by the Human Rights Committee states: "This is to be determined by each State Party in the light of the relevant social and cultural conditions. In this respect, States should indicate in their reports the age at which the child attains his majority in civil matters and assumes criminal responsibility. States should also indicate the age at which a child is legally entitled to work and the age at which he is treated as an adult under labour law. States should further indicate the age at which a child is considered adult for the purposes of article 10, paragraphs 2 and 3 [which cover separate treatment for juvenile offenders]. However, the Committee notes that the age for the above purposes should not be set unreasonably low and that in any case a State Party cannot absolve itself from its obligations under the Covenant regarding persons under the age of 18, notwithstanding that they have reached the age of majority under domestic law." (Human Rights Committee, General Comment 17, HRI/GEN/1/Rev.2, p. 24)

During the drafting of the Convention on the Rights of the Child, some States' representatives argued unsuccessfully for an age lower than 18 to be set. However, the view that the age should be set high to afford greater protection prevailed (see E/CN.4/L.1542, pp. 5-6, Detrick, pp. 115-116). The text allows States in which majority is attained before the age of 18 to substitute a lower age for particular purposes – provided doing so is consistent with the whole of the Convention, and in particular with its general principles. Equally, the Convention itself does not insist that States with higher ages of majority should lower them,

acknowledging that the definition in article 1 is "for the purposes of the Convention". All the rights in the Convention must apply to all under 18 years old, unless majority is attained earlier.

It was clear from discussions in the Working Group drafting the Convention that there is no generally agreed upon definition of majority in use, and that in some cases majority can be attained for some purposes by satisfying criteria other than age (for example status of marriage, acquisition of "sufficient understanding"). Reference was made to the fact that the concept of majority age "varied widely between countries and also within national legislation, according to whether the civil, penal, political or other aspects of majority were at issue" (E/CN.4/L.1542, pp. 5-6, Detrick, p. 116). Such differences have been fully illustrated in the Initial Reports of States Parties and in discussions between States' representatives and the Committee on the Rights of the Child.

Some States made declarations with regard to the age of majority. For example, Cuba declared "that in Cuba, under the domestic legislation in force, majority is not attained at 18 years of age for purposes of the full exercise of civic rights". And Liechtenstein noted, "According to the legislation of the Principality of Liechtenstein children come of age at 20 years. However, the Liechtenstein law provides for the possibility to prolong or to shorten the duration of minority." (CRC/C/2/Rev.5, pp. 16 and 23)

Defining specific minimum ages in legislation

The following section discusses briefly the various issues raised by the Committee's *Guidelines for Initial and Periodic Reports* (see box, page 2) in relation to article 1 and the definition

---

Ages of majority

According to its Initial Report, Burkina Faso's legal code sets the age of majority at 20 (even though the age of majority for criminal matters is 18). The minimum age for marriage is 20 for boys and 19 for girls, although a judge may make derogation down to 18 for boys and 15 for girls (Burkina Faso IR, paras. 7,11,13). When asked about this by the Committee on the Rights of the Child, a representative from Burkina Faso was reported as saying: "While the Convention set the age of majority at 18, his Government considered that the country did not have a sufficient economic structure to enable children to accept such a responsibility before the age of 20." (Burkina Faso SR.136, para. 3)

Bolivian law defines juveniles (or child and adolescent) as being between birth and the age of 21 (save for those who marry at 18, who reach majority at that age). Thus "legal counselling without parental consent for the initiation of legal proceedings may not take place below the age of 21 years, when the majority is reached" (Bolivia IR, paras. 15 and 18).

of the child. Both *Guidelines* request information on "the minimum legal age defined by the national legislation" for various purposes (many of the issues covered relate to other articles in the Convention; further interpretation and discussion will be found in the sections of this *Handbook* on those articles). The *Guidelines for Periodic Reports* also requests information on "any differences between national legislation and the Convention on the definition of the child". In most societies, until they ratified the Convention, there had been no comprehensive consideration of the various laws defining childhood. Article 1 provokes such a review of all relevant legislation in each State Party.

The request for information on minimum legal ages does not imply that the Convention requires a specific age to be set in each case. The Committee is simply seeking information on how domestic law defines the child. In general, minimum ages that are protective should be set as high as possible (for example protecting children from hazardous labour, custodial sentences or involvement in armed conflict). Other minimum ages relate to the child gaining autonomy and to the need for the State to respect the child's civil rights and evolving capacities.

Respect for Convention's general principles

The Committee has emphasized that in setting minimum ages States must have regard to the entire Convention and in particular to its general principles. There must be no discrimination, the child's best interests must be a primary consideration and the child's maximum survival and development must be ensured. For example, the Committee noted:

"... there is a need to consider seriously questions relating to the legal definition of the child, in particular the minimum age for marriage, employment, military service and testimony before a court. It appears that these provisions do not sufficiently take into consideration the principles of the best interest of the child and non-discrimination" (El Salvador IRCO, Add.9, para. 10; see also Sudan IRCO, Add.10, para. 18).

"... The Committee notes in particular the lack of conformity of legislative provisions in matters relating to the legal definition of the child. The early and lower marriageable age for girls compared with boys raises serious questions as to its compatibility with the Convention, in particular article 2. The discrepancy between the age for completion of compulsory education and the minimum age for admission to employment is another matter of concern. The lack of a minimum age below which children are presumed not to have the

capacity to infringe penal law is also noted with concern...
"The Committee recommends that legislative measures be taken to establish a definition of the child in the light of the Convention, including with a view to ensuring an equal age for marriage for girls and boys in the light of article 2, a minimum age of criminal responsibility in the light of article 40, paragraph 3(a), and an equal age of completion of compulsory education and minimum age for admission to employment, in the light of articles 28, 29, and 32..." (Senegal IRCO, Add.44, paras. 11 and 25)

The importance of the non-discrimination principle (article 2) in relation to the definition of the child is stressed in the Committee's *Guidelines for Periodic Reports*, which asks specifically for information "in cases where there is a difference in the legislation between girls and boys, including in relation to marriage and sexual consent, the extent to which article 2 of the Convention has been given consideration"; and also "in cases where the criteria of puberty is used under criminal law, the extent to which this provision is differently applied to girls and boys, and whether the principles and provisions of the Convention are taken into consideration" (para. 24; see box on page 2).

The Committee has frequently expressed concern if a State has a lower minimum age for the marriage of girls than for boys. Marriage age is of particular significance because in many countries upon marrying children are assumed to acquire majority and thus to lose their protective rights under the Convention (see below, page 9).

During discussion of Senegal's Initial Report, a Committee member commented on this form of discrimination against girls: "It was argued by some countries that a low marriage age for girls was an advantage because it would legitimize the relationship in case of pregnancy, but, in the Committee's view, that was not a very strong argument when set against the negative consequences in later life." (Senegal SR.248, para. 11)

More generally, the Committee has noted that physical development – puberty – is not a reliable guide to the transition from childhood to adulthood. In comments to individual States, the Committee has recommended that certain protective minimum ages should be raised – particularly those relating to sexual consent, access to employment and criminal responsibility (for Committee comments, see below, pages 9 and 12, and also article 34, page 455; article 32, page 427; and article 40, page 539).

As the *Manual on Human Rights Reporting, 1997*, states: "It would be in fact unrealistic to set a single uniform age for all these possible purposes which would apply in all countries in the world. Yet, in the light of the principles and provisions of the Convention, such limits cannot be set at an unreasonably low level or on the basis of arbitrary criteria. They particularly have to take the best interests of the child as a primary consideration, pursuant to article 3, and never give rise to discrimination as determined by article 2. Moreover, in the light of article 41, the most conducive solution for the child should always prevail, which would always prevent lowering the minimum level of protection provided by the Convention as a whole or depriving from all meaningful content the obligations arising therefrom. In this spirit, the Committee has often expressed its deep concern in relation to national legal texts where the attainment of the age of puberty is used as a criterion in civil and criminal matters. Based on a subjective, purely physical and often vague concept, serious consequences may be applied to children, particularly girls as in the case of the assessment of the minimum age for criminal responsibility." (*Manual*, p. 414-415)

Some of the minimum ages the Committee seeks information on in the *Guidelines* relate to children's acquisition of autonomous rights: rights to take actions and make decisions on their own behalf (for example to obtain legal and medical counselling and to consent to medical treatment or surgery without parental consent; to create and join associations, choose a religion, give consent to adoption; and to changes of identity).

The Convention does not provide direction on the specific age, or ages, at which children should acquire such rights, but it does provide a framework of principles. Under article 12, children capable of forming views have the right to express their views freely in all matters affecting them. Their views must be given "due weight in accordance with the age and maturity of the child". And the Convention emphasizes the importance of respecting children's "evolving capacities" (article 5, see page 78; also article 14, see page 180). In some States, in addition to setting in legislation certain ages for the acquisition of particular rights, the flexible concept of the child's evolving capacities has been reflected by the inclusion in the law of a general principle: that children acquire rights to make decisions for themselves on certain matters once they have acquired "sufficient understanding" (see page 8). The advantage of such formulas is that they avoid rigid age barriers; the disadvantage is that

they leave judgements on when children have acquired sufficient understanding to adults, who may not respect the concept of evolving capacities.

Some minimum ages relate both to increased autonomy and to protection. For example, the child's right to seek legal and medical counselling and to lodge complaints without parental consent, and to give testimony in court, may be crucial to protection from abuse within the family. It is not in the child's interests that a minimum age should be defined for such purposes.

The list of minimum legal ages the Committee requests information on in its *Guidelines* is by no means comprehensive. During consideration of Initial Reports from States Parties, the following additional age-related issues were raised: voting age and the minimum age for standing in elections; age at which a child can independently acquire a passport; age limitations on access to certain media (films, videos, etc.); age at which a child can join a religious order or community for life.

In relation to monitoring implementation of the whole Convention, the Committee has suggested

"that the collection and analysis of statistical data by age group be guided by the provisions of article 1 of the Convention... "
(UK dependent territory: Hong Kong IRCO, Add.63, para. 22).

This comment underlines the importance of collecting consistent data on all children up to 18.

The following section covers the various issues listed in the *Guidelines* that the Committee seeks information about under article 1.

Legal or medical counselling without parental consent

While the *Guidelines* seeks information on any "minimum legal age defined by the national legislation", the Convention provides no support for setting a minimum age below which the child cannot seek and receive independent legal or medical counselling. The purpose of the question is to determine which, if any, children are excluded from this right. The right to seek advice does not in itself imply a right to make decisions, which would be dependent on the child's evolving capacities.

Legal counselling The child's right to receive legal counselling without parental consent is clearly vital to the enforcement of many rights guaranteed under the Convention, including some where the child's interests are distinct from, or may even be in conflict with, those of the parents: for example, in cases of violence to children, including sexual abuse, within the family and in institutions; in cases of dispute over children's rights to a name or a nationality; in cases involving separation from parents, family reunification, illicit transfer and abduction, adoption, exploitation in employment and other forms of exploitation.

The child's own right to legal assistance when alleged as or accused of having infringed the penal law is referred to in article 40(2)(b)(ii). Similarly, the child whose liberty is restricted has the right to "prompt access to legal and other appropriate assistance..." under article 37(d). It is also necessary for children to be able to receive legal counselling when exercising their right to be heard in "any judicial and administrative proceedings affecting the child..." (article 12(2)), and to participate in proceedings relating to separation from parents under article 9.

Medical counselling The child's right to receive medical counselling without parental consent is vital in cases in which the child's views and/or interests are distinct from, or may be in conflict with, those of parents – for example

cases of violence and abuse by parents and other family members; cases involving child/parent conflicts over access to health services and treatment decisions, and the adolescent child's access to family planning education and services. The child's right to advice and counselling is distinct from consideration of the age at which the child may acquire an independent right to consent to medical treatment – see below.

Article 24(2)(e) requires States to take appropriate measures to ensure that children as well as parents "are informed, have access to education and are supported in the use of basic knowledge of child health and nutrition, the advantages of breastfeeding, hygiene and environmental sanitation and the prevention of accidents".

Medical treatment or surgery without parental consent

Some countries have set an age at which a child can give valid consent, or withhold consent, to medical treatment. Legislation in other countries provides that children acquire independent rights to consent and to withhold consent once they are judged to have "sufficient understanding" (see

Medical advice and consent for minors

France's Initial Report indicates that French law permits minors of either sex to have access to contraception and to be supplied with contraceptives on an anonymous basis. A recent law provides for minors, at their request, to be tested and treated for sexually transmitted diseases free of charge and anonymously in authorized locations. The law requires that a female below the age of majority consent to voluntary interruption of pregnancy and such consent be given without her parent present (France IR, paras. 154-156).

The United Kingdom's Initial Report states that under the Children Act 1989, a child can refuse to consent to a psychiatric or medical examination or other assessment in child protection proceedings if he or she is judged to be of "sufficient understanding". Following the *Gillick* case in 1985, under common law children of any age have had the right to give consent to clinical care and treatment provided they have the maturity to understand the implications of the proposed care and treatment. A more recent case held that the courts have jurisdiction to override a child's refusal of treatment when that refusal threatens the child's life (UK IR, para. 66).

In Sweden, "Contraception guidance is provided for children and young persons without parents being informed of the children so desiring. Allowance is made, however, for each child's level of maturity. Parents also remain uninformed of an abortion performed on a minor, if the child objects to their being thus informed and there is a presumption that the minor will suffer considerable harm if the information is divulged to the custodian" (Sweden IR, para. 46).

Norway's Initial Report states that "Doctors shall provide information about the condition, illness and treatment to their patients aged 12 years or older... Children between 12 and 16 years may request the doctor not to give specific information to their parents. Such a request shall be complied with if the doctor finds that the children's wishes should be respected. The child's degree of maturity is a factor in this evaluation" (Norway IR, para. 73).

Finnish legislation provides for children of sufficient maturity to make their own medical decisions (medical personnel assess maturity in the given situation); if a child aged 12 or more refuses psychiatric care, any decision on involuntary treatment must be submitted to the Provincial Court and the child has the right to appeal (Finland IR, paras. 36 and 37).

box opposite); in some cases, legislation also defines a minimum age at which maturity should be assumed.

In some countries, legislation enables courts to intervene and order medical treatment of a child in cases where a parent has refused consent, perhaps on cultural or religious grounds (this intervention would be justified under the Convention by article 3(1) and (2)).

When compulsory education ends

Article 28(1) (a) and (b) require States to achieve the child's right to education "progressively and on the basis of equal opportunity"; primary education must be compulsory, and the development of different forms of secondary education must be encouraged and made "available and accessible to every child". The ages of primary and secondary education are not defined by the Convention (see article 28, page 369). Article 32 requires States to protect the child from any work that is likely to interfere with the child's education. The Committee on the Rights of the Child has indicated the need to coordinate the age at which compulsory education ends with the age for access to full-time employment; and the *Guidelines for Periodic Reports* reinforces this, asking, "How the minimum age for employment relates to the age of completion of compulsory schooling, how it affects the right of the child to education and how relevant international instruments are taken into account" (see also article 32, page 439). In several cases, the Committee has expressed concern at "discrepancies" between the ages and proposed "an equal age" (see page 439).

Admission to employment or work, including hazardous work, part-time and full-time work

Article 32 requires States to protect children from "any work that is likely to be hazardous or to interfere with the child's education", to "provide for a minimum age or minimum ages for admission to employment" and to "provide for appropriate regulation of the hours and conditions of employment". The Committee on the Rights of the Child has in several cases recommended that minimum ages should be raised, and, further, has frequently recommended that States should ratify the relevant International Labour Organization's Conventions on minimum ages for employment (see article 32, page 438). As noted above, the Committee has proposed that there should be an "equal age" for the time when compulsory education ends and the admission to full-time employment begins.

Sexual consent

In most countries, a minimum age is set below which children are judged incapable of consenting to any form of sexual activity with others. The definition of sexual abuse and exploitation includes not only conduct involving violence or other forms of coercion, but also all sexual conduct with a child below a certain age, even when it was or appeared to be consensual (see also article 19, page 241 and article 34, page 462). Consequently sexual intercourse with a child below the age of consent renders the perpetrator liable to the charge of rape.

The Committee on the Rights of the Child has emphasized the importance of setting a minimum age below which a child's consent is not to be considered valid:

"The Committee also expresses its concern that the age of sexual maturity has not been fixed, which threatens the protection of children from possible exploitation in the use of pornographic materials." (Sweden IRCO, Add.2, para. 8)

The Committee has proposed to various countries that the age set should be raised.

It is assumed that the status of marriage implies an ability to consent to sex with one's partner. The Committee has expressed consistent concern at the young age at which marriage is permitted in some States and at the discrimination inherent in setting a lower age for girls than for boys (see below, page 10). The *Guidelines for Periodic Reports* asks whether the non-discrimination requirements of the Convention's article 2 have been given ample consideration "in cases where there is a difference in the legislation between girls and boys, including in relation to marriage and sexual consent..."

During discussion of Uruguay's Initial Report, a Committee member noted that the age of consent was fixed at 14 years for boys and 12 years for girls; the Convention did not countenance a distinction of that nature (Uruguay SR.326, para. 18).

The Committee has not as yet commented on issues of discrimination that may be raised where different ages of consent are set for different forms of sexual activity (for example heterosexual and homosexual activities). Nor has it commented on the provision in some States of a higher age of consent where the partner is in a position of trust or authority over the child (see page 463).

Marriage

In many societies, an age is set when children may marry without parental consent (usually the age of majority), and a lower age is set when they may marry with parental consent. In some societies, marriage is permitted in exceptional cases at an earlier age with the permission of a court or

article 1

other authority, for example when a girl is pregnant or has a child. The Committee on the Elimination of Discrimination against Women has proposed in a General Recommendation that the minimum age for marriage should be 18 years old (see below).

The Committee on the Rights of the Child has emphasized that the age of marriage for both girls and boys must be the same to conform with article 2 of the Convention and that ages should not be set too low (implying in its comments that 14 years old is too low) to conform with other general principles such as the best interests of the child and the right to maximum survival and development:

"The Committee is concerned that the national legislation establishes a different minimum age for marriage between boys and girls and that it authorizes the marriages of girls as young as 14 years of age who have obtained parental consent from the father or the mother. Such situations may raise the question of compatibility with the principles of non-discrimination and the best interests of the child, in particular as these children will be considered as adults and therefore no longer eligible for the protection afforded by the Convention." (Madagascar IRCO, Add.26, para. 9)

"The Committee wishes to express its general concern that the State Party does not appear to have fully taken into account the provisions of the Convention, including its general principles, as reflected in its articles 2, 3, 6, and 12, in the legislative and other measures relevant to children in Paraguay. In this connection, the Committee notes that the low marriageable age for girls, presently standing at 12, and the fact that this age is lower for girls than boys are incompatible with the provisions of the Convention, including those of its article 2..." (Paraguay Prelim. Obs., Add.27, para. 7. See also Nicaragua IRCO, Add.36, para. 13; Yemen IRCO, Add.47, para. 7)

The Committee has also expressed concern about discriminatory situations in which different laws may provide different marriage ages within one State – thus asserting its view that the general principles of the Convention should override the cultural and religious background to such discrimination:

"The Committee is worried about the existence of disparities concerning the three different laws (Sri Lankan, Kandyan and Muslim) regulating the minimum age for marriage. These legislations establish different minimum ages for marriage between boys and girls and authorize the marriages of girls as young as 12 years of age who have obtained parental consent from the parents. Such situations may raise the question of compatibility with the

principles of non-discrimination and the best interests of the child..."

The Committee

"strongly recommends that consideration should be given to raising and standardizing the age for contracting marriage in all communities..." (Sri Lanka IRCO, Add.40, paras. 11 and 28)

The Universal Declaration of Human Rights, in article 16, states that men and women "of full age" have the right to marry and to found a family. The Convention on Consent to Marriage, Minimum Age for Marriage and Registration of Marriages 1962 notes this in its Preamble and goes on to reaffirm that all States should take all appropriate measures to eliminate completely child marriages and the betrothal of young girls before the age of puberty. Its article 2 requires State Parties to "take legislative action to specify a minimum age for marriage. No marriage shall be legally entered into by any person under this age, except where a competent authority has granted a dispensation as to age, for serious reasons, in the interests of the intending spouses."

Thus this Convention does not set a minimum age for marriage. But a General Assembly Recommendation on Consent to Marriage, Minimum Age for Marriage and Registration of Marriages 1965 proposes in Principle II that the minimum age prescribed in law "in any case shall not be less than fifteen years of age".

In 1993 the Committee on the Elimination of Discrimination against Women (CEDAW) made a General Recommendation on "Equality in marriage and family relations", which proposes that the minimum age for marriage should be 18 for both women and men. Within the Recommendation, CEDAW analyzes three articles in the Convention on the Elimination of All Forms of Discrimination against Women that have special significance for the status of women in the family, as a contribution to International Year of the Family (1994). Article 16 of the Convention requires States to take all appropriate measures to eliminate discrimination against women in all matters relating to marriage and family relations. Paragraph 2 requires that "The betrothal and the marriage of a child shall have no legal effect, and all necessary action, including legislation, shall be taken to specify a minimum age for marriage and to make the registration of marriages in an official registry compulsory."

CEDAW comments: "In the Vienna Declaration and Programme of Action adopted by the World Conference on Human Rights, held at Vienna from 14 to 25 June 1993, States are urged to

Defining minimum ages

In Nicaragua, a boy over 15 years old and a girl over 14 may marry without the authorization of their parents or guardians (Nicaragua IR, para. 78). In discussions with government representatives, a Committee member commented: "It was not the purpose of the Convention to impose the same age limit in all areas of life and indeed it explicitly recognized that, for example, the minimum age of employment should not be the same as the minimum age at which the death penalty could be imposed. Nevertheless, the Convention imposed certain basic reference points which needed to be taken into account in the revision of the existing minimum ages under Nicaraguan law. For example, the different minimum ages for marriage and majority for boys and girls appeared to violate article 2 of the Convention and the Nicaraguan Constitution, both of which prohibited discrimination on grounds of sex. The earlier marriage age for girls had been justified by reference to the tendency for girls to reach physical maturity at an earlier age, while other equally important psychological and emotional factors had been ignored." (Nicaragua SR.212, para. 24)

During discussions with Jordan, a Committee member commented:
"... in setting marriageable ages, it was important to take into account a young person's mental and emotional maturity as well as their physical maturity, particularly in the case of girls, who matured physically at an earlier age than boys. It was that global view of maturity that the Convention required in order to satisfy one of its fundamental principles, namely, that every child should be treated equally, with no discrimination on the basis of gender." (Jordan SR.144, para. 25)

repeal existing laws and regulations and to remove customs and practices which discriminate against and cause harm to the girl child. Article 16(2) and the provisions of the Convention on the Rights of the Child preclude States Parties from permitting or giving validity to a marriage between persons who have not attained their majority. In the context of the Convention on the Rights of the Child, "a child means every human being below the age of 18 years unless, under the law applicable to the child, majority is attained earlier".

"Notwithstanding this definition, and bearing in mind the provisions of the Vienna Declaration, the Committee considers that the minimum age for marriage should be 18 years for both man and woman. When men and women marry, they assume important responsibilities. Consequently, marriage should not be permitted before they have attained full maturity and capacity to act. According to the World Health Organization, when minors, particularly girls, marry and have children, their health can be adversely affected and their education is impeded. As a result their economic autonomy is restricted...

"Some countries provide for different ages for marriage for men and women. As such provisions assume incorrectly that women have a different rate of intellectual development from men, or that their stage of physical and intellectual development at marriage is immaterial, these provisions

should be abolished. In other countries, the betrothal of girls or undertakings by family members on their behalf is permitted. Such measures contravene not only the Convention, but also a woman's right freely to choose her partner.

"States Parties should also require the registration of all marriages whether contracted civilly or according to custom or religious law. The State can thereby ensure compliance with the Convention and establish equality between partners, a minimum age for marriage, prohibition of bigamy and polygamy and the protection of the rights of children." (Committee on the Elimination of Discrimination against Women, General Recommendation 21, HRI/GEN/1/Rev.2, p. 126)

Voluntary enlistment and conscription into armed forces; participation in hostilities

Article 38 of the Convention on the Rights of the Child requires States to refrain from recruiting into their armed forces anyone who has not attained the age of 15, and, in recruiting children between the ages of 15 and 18, "to give priority to those who are oldest". In addition States Parties must "take all feasible measures to ensure that persons who have not attained the age of fifteen years do not take a direct part in hostilities".

The Committee on the Rights of the Child has commended States that have set a higher age limit on recruitment than 15 and that have ratified the Additional Protocols to the Geneva Conventions. The Committee has stated clearly that it believes there should be no involvement in hostilities and no recruitment into the armed forces of anyone under 18 years old (for further discussion and details of the proposed Optional Protocol to the Convention on the Rights of the Child, see article 38, page 523).

Criminal responsibility

Article 40(3)(a) of the Convention on the Rights of the Child requires "the establishment of a minimum age below which children shall be presumed not to have the capacity to infringe the penal law".

The report of the Committee's October 1995 General Discussion on juvenile justice stated:

"It was particularly felt that the general principles of the Convention had not been adequately reflected in national legislation or practice. In relation to non-discrimination, particular concern was expressed about instances where criteria of a subjective and arbitrary nature (such as with regard to the attainment of puberty, the age of discernment or the personality of the child) still prevailed in the assessment of the criminal responsibility of children and in deciding upon the measures applicable to them." (Report on the tenth session, CRC/C/46, p. 36)

It is clear, from the Initial Reports of States Parties and the reports of discussions with the Committee, that the definition of the age of criminal responsibility is often blurred. In some States, it appears, paradoxically, that children can be liable under criminal law for major offences at a younger age than they can be liable for minor offences.

The Committee has, in several cases, underlined that a minimum age must be defined in legislation. For many States, the Committee has urged that the age should be raised, and the Committee has welcomed proposals to set the age at 18. The Committee has also indicated that the age of criminal responsibility must be consistent throughout a State's jurisdiction. The United Nations Standard Minimum Rules for the Administration of Juvenile Justice, the "Beijing Rules", proposes in rule 4: "In those legal systems recognizing the concept of the age of criminal responsibility for juveniles, the beginning of that age shall not be fixed at too low an age level, bearing in mind the facts of emotional, mental and intellectual maturity" (for further discussion and text of the Committee's comments, see article 40, page 550).

Deprivation of liberty; imprisonment

Article 37(b) requires that "no child shall be deprived of his or her liberty unlawfully or arbi-

trarily. The arrest, detention or imprisonment of a child shall be in conformity with the law and shall be used only as a measure of last resort and for the shortest appropriate period of time". While the Convention on the Rights of the Child sets no lower age limit on restriction of liberty, it is clear from the Committee's comments that it believes that the minimum age should be set in relation to the other basic principles of the Convention, and in particular to articles 2, 3 and 6; and the Committee has expressed concern at the restriction of the liberty of young children. In article 9, the principle that a child shall only be separated from his or her parents when such separation "is necessary for the best interests of the child" places further limits on restriction of liberty away from the family.

The *Guidelines for Periodic Reports* expands on the information requested: that it should cover the minimum legal age defined in the national legislation for "Deprivation of liberty, including by arrest, detention and imprisonment, *inter alia* in the areas of administration of justice, asylum-seeking and placement of children in welfare and health institutions" (para. 24; see also article 37, page 496), emphasizing that article 37 applies to any restriction of liberty of the child, not just to that occurring within the penal system.

Capital punishment and life imprisonment

Article 37(a) of the Convention on the Rights of the Child bars the imposition of capital punishment and life imprisonment without the possibility of release for offences committed before the age of 18. In several cases, the Committee has expressed concern at breaches of this clear prohibition. In addition, the Committee has expressed concern at situations in which the law technically still allows capital punishment of those under the age of 18, although the sentence is not applied in practice, and at situations where suspended sentences of death are permitted for under-18s (see article 37, page 494).

Giving testimony in court, in civil and criminal cases

Article 12(2) requires that the child shall have the opportunity to be heard in any judicial and administrative proceedings that affect him or her. Here again, the Convention does not suggest that a minimum age be set; the Committee seeks information through the *Guidelines* on whether children below a certain age are barred from being heard in either civil or criminal cases.

Civil cases involving children include those concerned with custody and the upbringing of children, including separation from parents, adoption and so forth.

Criminal cases involving children include those in which the child gives evidence, including when the child is being prosecuted for a criminal offence; cases in which others are being prosecuted for offences against the child; and cases involving other parties when the child is a witness. In relation to children alleged as or accused of having infringed the penal law, under article 40(2)(b)(iv) they must not be compelled to give testimony.

The Committee has noted the importance of enabling children to give evidence in cases involving the prevention of violence and exploitation, including the sexual exploitation of children. It has commended States that have made special arrangements to hear evidence from children in such cases (see article 19, page 252).

El Salvador's Initial Report notes that minors under the age of 14 may not testify in civil cases; judges may, at their discretion however, take into account the testimony of minors under 14 in criminal cases (El Salvador IR, paras. 39-40). During discussions with government representatives, a member of the Committee on the Rights of the Child "was concerned to note that while children under the age of 14 were not allowed to testify in civil cases, their testimony might be admitted in criminal cases if the judge saw fit. To what extent were the best interests of the child being taken into consideration in deciding whether the child's views should be listened to or not?" (El Salvador SR.86, para. 28)

The Committee commented:

"...the Committee feels that there is a need to consider seriously questions relating to the legal definition of the child, in particular the minimum age for marriage, employment, military service and testimony before a court. It appears that these provisions do not sufficiently take into consideration the principles of the best interest of the child and non-discrimination." (El Salvador IRCO, Add.9, para. 10)

Lodging complaints and seeking redress without parental consent before a court or other authority

The Committee on the Rights of the Child has indicated that the full implementation of article 12 requires the child to have access to complaints procedures (see page 155). The child's ability to lodge complaints and seek redress without parental consent before a court is particularly important in relation to complaints concerning violence or exploitation, including sexual exploitation, within the family. There is no suggestion in the Convention that children below a certain age should not be able to lodge complaints or apply to courts or other bodies for redress, with or without parental consent; any decision to exclude a child from such rights would have to be made in the context of the general principles including non-discrimination and best interests.

Participating in administrative and judicial procedures affecting the child

As noted above, article 12(2) of the Convention on the Rights of the Child requires that the child is provided with an opportunity to be heard in any judicial and administrative proceedings affecting him or her. The Convention sets no age limit on this right (see article 12, page 150).

Giving consent to change of identity, including change of name, modification of family relations, adoption, guardianship

Article 8 of the Convention requires respect for the right of the child to preserve his or her identity, including nationality, name and family relations. The Convention does not suggest that there should be a minimum age for recognition of this right. It appears that very few States have defined in legislation arrangements for the child's consent in relation to all aspects of changing identity.

The request for information on these individual aspects of change of identity is included in the *Guidelines for Periodic Reports*, but was not in the *Guidelines for Initial Reports,* so few Initial Reports have included comprehensive information and there has been little discussion with the Committee. Many States did indicate in Initial Reports that they have established an age at which the child has a right to consent or refuse consent to his or her adoption. The Committee has welcomed moves to reduce the age at which the child's consent is required for adoption, for example from 15 in Belgium (see article 21, page 273).

Having access to information about the child's biological family

Article 7 of the Convention on the Rights of the Child requires that the child have "as far as possible, the right to know ... his or her parents". The right to knowledge of biological parents is of particular importance to adopted children and children born through artificial means of conception. In many States, legislation places limits both on the information made available to the child and the age at which any information is available to the child. Implementation of this right depends on sufficient information being included in the registration of the child's birth and whether the information is made accessible to the child (see article 7, page 104). In many States adopted children up to the age of 18 do not have a right of access to information about their biological parents, likely to amount to a breach of article 7.

The *Guidelines for Periodic Reports*, in addition to seeking information on the minimum age defined in legislation for the child's access to this information, also asks in its section on adoption (para. 83) for information on "the effects of adoption on the rights of the child, particularly his or her civil rights, including the child's identity and the right of the child to know his or her biological parents."

Legal capacity to inherit, to conduct property transactions

In some States the capacity to inherit and to conduct property transactions is achieved only with majority and/or on marriage; in others, various ages are set in legislation. Where minimum ages are set, they should be consistent with the Convention's general principles, in particular of non-discrimination and the best interests of the child.

The Committee on the Elimination of Discrimination against Women (CEDAW), in a General Recommendation, noted that, in many countries, law and practice concerning inheritance and property result in serious discrimination against women: "...Women may receive a smaller share of the husband's or father's property at his death than would widowers and sons" (Committee on the Elimination of Discrimination against Women, General Recommendation 21, HRI/GEN/1/Rev.2, p. 126). Such discrimination may also affect those under 18 years old, in which case it raises an issue under the Convention on the Rights of the Child. The Committee on the Rights of the Child has commented on discrimination in inheritance:

"...The Committee notes in particular the lack of conformity of legislative provisions concerning non-discrimination including in relation to marriage, inheritance and parental property." (Nepal IRCO, Add.57, para. 10)

Legal capacity to create or join associations

The child's right to freedom of association is recognized in the Convention on the Rights of the Child under article 15, and the Committee has emphasized that this right is linked to articles 12 and 13 in realizing the child's rights to participation.

Some States indicated in their Initial Reports that there is an age below which children are not permitted to join associations or to do so without the agreement of their parents. The Convention provides no support for arbitrary limitations on the child's right to freedom of association (see article 15, page 192).

Choosing a religion; attending religious education in school

Article 14 requires respect for the child's right to freedom of thought, conscience and religion. Few States as yet have legislation specifically upholding the child's right to freedom of religion, but in some States an age is specified when decisions concerning religious upbringing and education transfer from the parent to the child. In States in which religious education is allowed in schools, there may be provisions in legislation allowing students to opt out of particular religious teaching and/or worship, and/or giving them a right to alternative teaching. Article 14(2) requires States to respect the rights and duties of parents "to provide direction to the child in the exercise of his or her right in a manner consistent with the evolving capacities of the child" (see article 14, page 180).

Consumption of alcohol and other controlled substances

Article 33 requires States to take "all appropriate measures, including legislative, administrative, social and educational measures, to protect children from the illicit use of narcotic drugs and psychotropic substances as defined in the relevant international treaties... " Many States have made it an offence to sell alcohol and tobacco products and any other controlled substances to children below a certain age. The setting of such ages should be related to the basic principles of articles 2, 3 and 6 (see article 33, page 445).

Implementation Checklist

● *General measures of implementation*

Have appropriate general measures of implementation been taken in relation to article 1, including

☐ identification and coordination of the responsible departments and agencies at all levels of government (definition of the child in article 1 is relevant to **all government departments**)

☐ identification of relevant non-governmental organizations/civil society partners?

☐ a comprehensive review to ensure that all legislation, policy and practice is compatible with the article, for all children in all parts of the jurisdiction?

☐ adoption of a strategy to secure full implementation

    ☐ which includes where necessary the identification of goals and indicators of progress?

    ☐ which does not affect any provisions which are more conducive to the rights of the child?

    ☐ which recognizes other relevant international standards?

    ☐ which involves where necessary international cooperation?

(Such measures may be a part of an overall governmental strategy for implementing the Convention as a whole).

☐ budgetary analysis and allocation of necessary resources?

☐ development of mechanisms for monitoring and evaluation?

☐ making the implications of article 1 widely known to adults and children?

☐ development of appropriate training and awareness-raising (in relation to article 1 likely to include the **training of all those working with or for children, and education for parenting**)?

● *Specific issues in implementing article 1*

☐ Does the State define childhood for the purposes of the Convention as beginning

    ☐ at birth?

    ☐ for some purposes before birth?

☐ Does a child acquire all adult rights by his or her 18th birthday or earlier?

Do all children acquire the right to vote and to stand for election

    ☐ at 18?

    ☐ before 18?

Are protective minimum ages defined in legislation for the following:

    ☐ beginning and end of compulsory education?

    ☐ admission to employment, including

        ☐ hazardous work?

        ☐ part-time work?

☐ full-time work?
☐ giving a valid consent to sexual activities?
☐ marriage?
☐ access to certain categories of violent/pornographic media?
☐ buying/consuming alcohol or other controlled substances?
☐ voluntary enlistment in the armed forces?
☐ conscription into the armed forces?
☐ participation in hostilities?
☐ criminal responsibility?
☐ deprivation of liberty in any situation, including in the juvenile justice system; immigration, including asylum-seeking; and in education, welfare and health institutions?
☐ capital punishment and life imprisonment?

☐ Is any general principle established in legislation that once a child has acquired "sufficient understanding", he or she acquires certain rights of decision making?
☐ Are there mechanisms for assessing the capacity/competence of a child?
☐ Can a child appeal against such assessments?
☐ Are there other ways in which legislation respects the concept of the child's "evolving capacities"?

Do children acquire rights, either at prescribed ages, or in defined circumstances, for
☐ getting legal and medical counselling without parental consent?
☐ having medical treatment or surgery without parental consent?
  giving testimony in court
  ☐ in civil cases?
  ☐ in criminal cases?
☐ leaving home without parental consent?
☐ choosing residence and contact arrangements when parents separate?
☐ acquiring a passport?
☐ lodging complaints and seeking redress before a court or other relevant authority without parental consent?
☐ participating in administrative and judicial proceedings affecting the child?
☐ giving consent to change of identity, including
☐ change of name?
☐ nationality?
☐ modification of family relations?
☐ adoption?
☐ guardianship?
☐ having access to information concerning his or her biological origins (e.g. in cases of adoption, artificial forms of conception, etc.)?
☐ having legal capacity to inherit?
☐ conducting property transactions?

☐ creating and joining associations?

☐ choosing a religion?

☐ choosing to attend/not attend religious education in school?

☐ joining a religious community?

☐ Where such minimum ages are defined in legislation, have they been reviewed in the light of the Convention's basic principles, in particular of non-discrimination, best interests of the child and right to maximum survival and development (articles 2, 3, and 6)?

☐ Do the legal provisions relating to the attainment of majority, acquisition of specific rights at a particular age or set minimum ages, as mentioned above, apply to all children without discrimination on any ground?

Reminder : **The Convention is indivisible and its articles are interdependent. The definition of the child in article 1 is relevant to the implementation of each article of the Convention.**

Particular regard should be paid to:
The general principles

Article 2: all rights to be recognized for each child in the jurisdiction without discrimination on any ground

Article 3(1): the best interests of the child to be a primary consideration in all actions concerning children

Article 6: right to life and maximum possible survival and development

Article 12: respect for the child's views in all matters affecting the child; opportunity to be heard in any judicial or administrative proceedings affecting the child

Closely related articles

Articles whose implementation is particularly related to that of article 1 include:

Article 5: respect for the child's "evolving capacities" (also article 14(2))

Article 24: access to medical advice and counselling; consent to treatment

Article 28: ages for compulsory education

Article 32: setting of ages for admission to employment

Article 34: age of sexual consent

Article 37: no capital punishment or life imprisonment for offences committed below the age of 18

Article 38: minimum age for recruitment into armed forces and participation in hostilities

Article 40: age of criminal responsibility

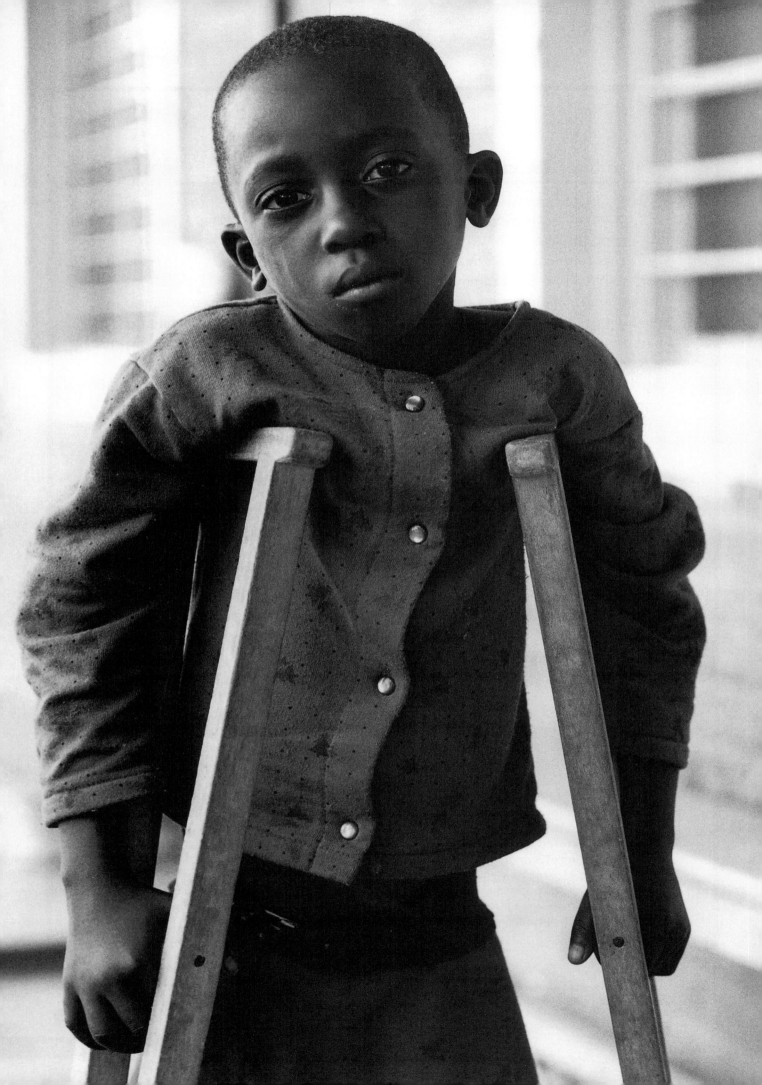

Non-discrimination

Text of Article 2

1. States Parties shall respect and ensure the rights set forth in the present Convention to each child within their jurisdiction without discrimination of any kind, irrespective of the child's or his or her parent's or legal guardian's race, colour, sex, language, religion, political or other opinion, national, ethnic or social origin, property, disability, birth or other status.

2. States Parties shall take all appropriate measures to ensure that the child is protected against all forms of discrimination or punishment on the basis of the status, activities, expressed opinions, or beliefs of the child's parents, legal guardians, or family members.

The first paragraph of article 2, along with article 3(2) and article 4, sets out the fundamental obligations of States Parties in relation to the rights outlined in the remainder of the Convention on the Rights of the Child – to "respect and ensure" all the rights in the Convention to all children in their jurisdiction without discrimination of any kind. "Non-discrimination" has been identified by the Committee on the Rights of the Child as a general principle of fundamental importance for implementation of the whole Convention. The Committee has emphasized the importance of collecting disaggregated data in order to monitor the extent of discrimination.

In a relevant General Comment, the Human Rights Committee proposes that the term "discrimination" should be understood to imply "any distinction, exclusion, restriction or preference which is based on any ground such as race, colour, sex, language, religion, political or other opinion, national or social origin, property, birth or other status, and which has the purpose or effect of nullifying or impairing the recognition, enjoyment or exercise by all persons, on an equal footing, of all rights and freedoms."

The non-discrimination principle does not bar affirmative action, the legitimate differentiation in treatment of individual children; a Human Rights Committee General Comment emphasizes that States will often have to take affirmative action to diminish or eliminate conditions that cause or help to perpetuate discrimination. In its Preamble, the Convention on the Rights of the Child recognizes that "in all countries in the world, there are children living in exceptionally difficult conditions, and that such children need special consideration…". In this respect, the Committee on the Rights of the Child has consistently underlined the need to give special attention to disadvantaged and vulnerable groups.

Summary

The implications of discrimination in relation to particular rights of the child are covered in this *Implementation Handbook* under the other corresponding Convention articles. Certain articles set out special provisions for children particularly prone to forms of discrimination, for example, disabled children (article 23), and refugee children (article 22). Because discrimination is at the root of various forms of child exploitation, other articles to protect the child call for action that involves challenging discrimination.

Paragraph 2 of article 2 asserts the need to protect children from all forms of discrimination or punishment on the basis of the status or activities of their parents and others close to them. ■

Extracts from
Committee on the Rights of the Child
Guidelines for Reports to be submitted by States Parties under the Convention

For full text of *Guidelines for Periodic Reports*, see Appendix 3, page 604.

Guidelines for Initial Reports

"General principles

Relevant information, including the principal legislative, judicial, administrative or other measures in force or foreseen, factors and difficulties encountered and progress achieved in implementing the provisions of the Convention, and implementation priorities and specific goals for the future should be provided in respect of:

(a) Non-discrimination (article 2);

...

In addition, States Parties are encouraged to provide relevant information on the application of these principles in the implementation of articles listed elsewhere in these guidelines."

(CRC/C/5, paras. 13 and 14)

Guidelines for Periodic Reports

"III. GENERAL PRINCIPLES

A. Non-discrimination (art. 2)

Reports should indicate whether the principle of non-discrimination is included as a binding principle in the Constitution or in domestic legislation specifically for children and whether all the possible grounds for discrimination spelled out in article 2 of the Convention are reflected in such legal provisions. Reports should further indicate the measures adopted to ensure the rights set forth in the Convention to each child under the jurisdiction of the State without discrimination of any kind, including non-nationals, refugees and asylum-seekers.

Information should be provided on steps taken to ensure that discrimination is prevented and combated, both in law and practice, including discrimination on the basis of race, colour, sex, language, religion, political or other opinion, national, ethnic or social origin, property, disability, birth or other status of the child, his/her parents or legal guardians.

Please indicate the specific measures adopted to reduce economic, social and geographical disparities, including between rural and urban areas, to prevent discrimination against the most disadvantaged groups of children, including children belonging to minorities or indigenous communities, disabled children, children born out of wedlock, children who are non-nationals, migrants, displaced, refugees or asylum-seekers, and children who are living and/or working on the streets.

Please provide information on the specific measures taken to eliminate discrimination against girls and when appropriate indicate measures adopted as a follow-up to the Fourth World Conference on Women.

Please indicate measures taken to collect disaggregated data for the various groups of children mentioned above.

What measures have been taken to prevent and eliminate attitudes to and prejudice against children contributing to social or ethnic tension, racism and xenophobia?

Information should also be provided on the measures pursuant to article 2, paragraph 2 taken to ensure that the child is protected against all forms of discrimination or punishment on the basis of the status, activities, expressed opinions or beliefs of the child's parents, legal guardians or family members.

Please indicate major problems encountered in implementing the provisions of article 2 and plans to solve these problems, as well as any evaluation of progress in preventing and combating all forms of discrimination, including those arising from negative traditional practices."

(CRC/C/58, paras. 25 - 32. The following paragraphs of the *Guidelines for Periodic Reports* are also relevant to reporting under this article: 24, 64, 65, 74, 76, 80,, 87, 92, 93, 106, 109, 115, 118, 120, 128, 132, 138, 143, 152, 159, 161, 164, 166; for full text of *Guidelines*, see Appendix 3, page 604.)

Definition of "discrimination"

The term "discrimination" is not defined in the Convention, nor is it defined in the International Covenant on Civil and Political Rights, which includes a similar non-discrimination principle. The Committee on the Rights of the Child has asserted the fundamental importance of article 2 and raises the issue of non-discrimination in its consideration of each State Party report. The Committee has not, as of September 1997, issued any interpretative General Comment on the issue. The Human Rights Committee, however, which oversees the Covenant, has issued a General Comment proposing a definition of discrimination.

Under article 2 of the Covenant on Civil and Political Rights, "Each State Party to the present Covenant undertakes to respect and to ensure to all individuals within its territory and subject to its jurisdiction the rights recognized in the present Covenant, without distinction of any kind, such as race, colour, sex, language, religion, political or other opinion, national or social origin, property, birth or other status".

Article 24(1) of the Covenant also requires that "Every child shall have, without any discrimination as to race, colour, sex, language, religion, national or social origin, property or birth, the right to such measures of protection as are required by his status as a minor, on the part of his family, society and the State..."

And the Covenant's article 26 states: "All persons are equal before the law and are entitled without any discrimination to the equal protection of the law. In this respect, the law shall prohibit any discrimination and guarantee to all persons equal and effective protection against discrimination on any ground such as race, colour, sex, language, religion, political or other opinion, national or social origin, property, birth or other status."

The Human Rights Committee, in a 1989 General Comment, emphasizes that "non-discrimination, together with equality before the law and equal protection of the law without any discrimination, constitute a basic and general principle relating to the protection of human rights". The Human Rights Committee quotes article 1 of the International Convention on the Elimination of All Forms of Racial Discrimination, which says that the term "racial discrimination" shall mean "any distinction, exclusion, restriction or preference based on race, colour, descent or national or ethnic origin which has the purpose or effect of nullifying or impairing the recognition, enjoyment or exercise, on an equal footing, of human rights and fundamental freedoms in the political, economic, social, cultural or any other field of public life." Article 1 of the Convention on the Elimination of All Forms of Discrimination against Women uses a similar definition.

While these Conventions deal only with cases of discrimination on specific grounds, the Human Rights Committee notes that "the term 'discrimination' as used in the Covenant should be understood to imply any distinction, exclusion, restriction or preference which is based on any ground such as race, colour, sex, language, religion, political or other opinion, national or social origin, property, birth or other status, and which has the purpose or effect of nullifying or impairing the recognition, enjoyment or exercize by all persons, on an equal footing, of all rights and freedoms".

In relation to discrimination against children and the Covenant, the same Human Rights Committee General Comment states: "The Covenant requires that children should be protected against discrimination on any grounds such as race, colour, sex, language, religion, national or social origin, property or birth. In this connection, the Committee notes that, whereas non-discrimination in the enjoyment of the rights provided for in the Covenant also stems, in the case of children, from article 2 and their equality before the law from article 26, the non-discrimination clause contained in article 24 relates specifically to the measures of protection referred to in that provision. Reports by States Parties should indicate how legislation and practice ensure that measures of protection are aimed at removing all discrimination in every field, including inheritance, particularly as between children who are nationals and children who are aliens, or as between legitimate children and children born out of wedlock."

The Human Rights Committee goes on to emphasize that the "enjoyment of rights and freedoms on an equal footing, however, does not mean identical treatment in every instance". The principle of equality sometimes requires States Parties "to take affirmative action in order to diminish or eliminate conditions which cause or help to perpetuate discrimination prohibited by the Covenant." And finally, it states that "not every differentiation of treatment will constitute discrimination, if the criteria for such differentiation are reasonable and objective and if the aim is to achieve a purpose which is legitimate under the Covenant" (Human Rights Committee, General Comment 18, HRI/GEN/1/Rev.2, p. 26).

"States Parties shall respect and ensure the rights set forth in the present Convention ..."

The language of article 2 itself and its interpretation by the Committee on the Rights of the Child emphasize that the obligation of States Parties to prevent discrimination is an active one, requiring, like other aspects of implementation, a range of measures that include review, strategic planning, legislation, monitoring, awareness-raising, education and information campaigns, and evaluation of measures taken to reduce disparities.

A commentary published in the *Bulletin of Human Rights* asserts that in terms of international law, the obligation "to respect" requires States "to refrain from any actions which would violate any of the rights of the child under the Convention ... The obligation 'to ensure' goes well beyond that of 'to respect', since it implies an affirmative obligation on the part of the State to take whatever measures are necessary to enable individuals to enjoy and exercise the relevant rights" (*Bulletin of Human Rights*, 91/2, "The legal framework of the Convention on the Rights of the Child", Philip Alston, p. 5).

An "active" approach to implementing the principle

The Committee on the Rights of the Child has constantly stressed the need for an "active" approach to implementation and in particular to non-discrimination. It underscored this point in its comments on the first Initial Report submitted to it:

"The Committee emphasizes that the principle of non-discrimination, as provided for under article 2 of the Convention, must be vigorously applied, and that a more active approach should be taken to eliminate discrimination against certain groups of children, most notably girl children" (Bolivia IRCO, Add.1, para. 14. See also, e.g. Egypt IRCO, Add.5, para. 12; Philippines IRCO, Add.29, para. 23; UK IRCO, Add.34, para. 12).

The implementation of article 2 must be integrated into the implementation of all other articles – ensuring that all the rights mentioned are available to all children without discrimination of any kind:

"The Committee is also concerned that the general principles of the Convention, as laid down in its articles 2, 3, 6 and 12, are not being applied and duly integrated into the implementation of all articles of the Convention. Concern is expressed at the status and situation of girl children and the insufficiency of measures to prevent and combat discrimination practised against them. Of equal concern to the Committee is the apparent absence of pro-active measures to combat discrimination against disabled children, children belonging to ethnic minorities and children born out of wedlock." (Nigeria IRCO, Add.61, para. 12)

Reviewing legislation and writing non-discrimination principle into legislation

The Committee on the Rights of the Child has indicated that, as with the other articles identified as general principles, the non-discrimination principle should be written into legislation as well as into any national policies on children and implementation. And it has emphasized that there should be the possibility to challenge discrimination before the courts:

"[the Committee] ... regrets that there is no provision in the national legislation relating to the best interests of the child or the prohibition of discrimination against children ... "Principles relating to the best interests of the child and the prohibition of discrimination in relation to children should be incorporated into domestic law, and it should be possible to invoke them before the courts." (Mexico IRCO, Add.13, paras. 7, 15. See also Indonesia IRCO,

Add.25, para. 18; Denmark IRCO, Add.33, para. 24; Canada IRCO, Add.37, para. 11; Sri Lanka IRCO, Add.40, para. 25; Senegal IRCO, Add.44, para. 25; Finland IRCO, Add.53, para. 13)

The *Guidelines for Periodic Reports* asks whether non-discrimination is included as a binding principle in the Constitution or in domestic legislation specifically for children "and whether all the possible grounds for discrimination spelled out in article 2 of the Convention are reflected in such legal provisions". In some States, a non-discrimination clause is written into the Constitution and therefore applies to all children. In others, non-discrimination principles are included in human rights legislation with reference to children. The Convention, like other human rights instruments, does not require States to have a Constitution. But where there is a Constitution, its provisions must be consistent with the Convention, or, in the terms of article 41, must be more conducive to the realization of the rights of the child.

discrimination by gender is legislation defining different minimum ages for boys and girls to marry (for further discussion, see article 1, page 9); another example is the discrimination inherent in some State legislation dealing with children of married parents and those born out of wedlock, referred to as non-marital children.

On occasion, the Committee has proposed the introduction of legislation to challenge discrimination on a particular ground or to ensure that non-discrimination legislation is in force throughout the jurisdiction, as in the case of the United Kingdom:

"The Committee recommends that race relations legislation be introduced in Northern Ireland as a matter of urgency and is encouraged by the information presented by the delegation of the State Party regarding the Government's intention to follow up on this matter." (UK IRCO, Add.34, para. 28)

The Committee has emphasized that the principle of non-discrimination applies equally to private

Protection against discrimination on the grounds of age

Certain human rights laws in the provinces of Canada have outlawed discrimination based on age (with some exceptions), according to information in Canada's Initial Report. Until 1992, New Brunswick's Human Rights Act covered discrimination on grounds of age for those aged 19 or above only; following revision, children are covered against discrimination on the grounds of age. In Nova Scotia, the Human Rights Act was revised in 1991, and the prohibition on discrimination on the basis of age was expanded to cover all age groups. The Initial Report states that the Act does, however, allow for exceptions so that children can be conferred some appropriate benefit or protection with respect to services or facilities (Canada IR, paras. 1034, 1126).

The Committee has also emphasized the need for States to review their Constitutions and all existing legislation to ensure that these do not involve discrimination; often, in the same comments, the Committee has drawn attention to a particular example of existing discrimination in legislation:

"The State Party should pursue its efforts with a view to fully reflecting in its legislation and practice the provisions and principles of the Convention, in particular the principles of non-discrimination, the best interests of the child and the right of the child to freely express his or her views. In this regard, the Committee recommends that existing legislation be modified to fully ensure equal treatment between children born in and out of wedlock." (Italy IRCO, Add.41, para. 16; see also Germany IRCO, Add.43, para. 28)

In examining Initial Reports the Committee frequently comes across instances in which some forms of discrimination are written into existing legislation. A particularly common example of

institutions and individuals as well as to the State, and that this must be reflected in legislation:

*"The Committee notes with concern that the legislative measures taken to prevent and eliminate any form of discrimination in the light of article 2 of the Convention are insufficient. It notes in this regard that, according to section 23 of the Constitution, the principle of non-discrimination does not apply to private professionals or institutions; the same provision allows for derogation in important areas such as adoption, marriage, divorce and other matters of personal law and prevents, inter alia, girls from having inheritance rights. In addition, it allows for discrimination on the basis of race in relation to the minimum age for marriage, inheritance and children born out of wedlock. The Committee further notes in this regard the different minimum ages for marriage for girls and boys in the legislation...
"...Particular attention should be paid to ensuring effective implementation of the principle of non-discrimination, including by*

revising relevant constitutional provisions, as well as other legislative texts reflecting any kind of discrimination such as on the basis of gender, race, birth or marital status." (Zimbabwe IRCO, Add.55, paras. 12 and 22)

Other active measures to challenge discrimination

The Committee on the Rights of the Child recognizes that the reflection of the principle of non-discrimination in the law, while fundamental to implementation, is not in itself sufficient; other strategies are needed to implement the principle, in particular to challenge traditional and other discriminatory attitudes and customs:

"The Committee notes that, although Egyptian laws and regulations guarantee equality between the sexes, there is in reality still a pattern of disparity between boys and girls, in particular as far as access to education is concerned." (Egypt IRCO, Add.5, para. 6)

"The Committee is concerned that, although the National Charter guarantees equality between the sexes in Jordan, discriminatory attitudes and prejudices are still vivid within the society, and that there are still disparities in practice ..." (Jordan IRCO, Add.21, para. 11)

During discussions with Mongolia, a Committee member stated: "... the Committee was often told that a country was free of discrimination, but such assertions meant only that the law prohibited discrimination. The Committee wanted to encourage an additional effort to improve the situation of some groups of children in Mongolia

which might suffer de facto..." (Mongolia SR.265, paras. 31 and 32).

In a meeting with Indonesian representatives, a Committee member stressed the importance of affirmative action: "Discrimination always existed between different groups of children in practice. In formulating its questions, the Committee had had in mind not only the legal aspects but the actual measures taken by the Indonesian authorities to ensure that those groups of children which tended in every society to be handicapped or discriminated against in some way were given the possibility to enjoy fully the rights which should be given to all children." (Indonesia SR.80, para. 31)

The Committee has identified traditional attitudes and customs that perpetuate discrimination in many societies, whether the discrimination is reflected in legislation or not:

"The Committee is also preoccupied by the widespread discriminatory attitudes towards girls and disabled children..." (El Salvador IRCO, Add.9, para. 12)

"...Other difficulties noted by the Committee relate to ... the existence of traditional customs and values which, for instance, have delayed efforts to combat discrimination against girls...

"The Committee is deeply concerned at the situation of girl children, both as regards the effect of legislation in place, measures adopted and practices and customs which serve to

---

Between law and reality

In some cases, States themselves have identified the persistence of discrimination through traditional customs: "...non-discrimination is a general principle of the law of the protection of children in Madagascar. Between law and fact, however, lies an area of loopholes, confusion and practice based on actual social life. Some traditions, particularly in rural areas, are still very strong and will disappear completely only if coordinated information and civic and moral education activities are carried out. There are still traditional 'rejections', a customary means of exclusion that has particularly adverse effects. The village community, the *fokonolona*, the family group or simply the parents may reject a child because of the conditions in which his birth took place (born a twin, born on an unlucky day, born with certain deformities that are regarded as a threat to the social group, born in abnormal conditions, etc.). The lawmakers have tried to combat such rejections by prohibiting the rejection of minors ... It is not obvious, however, that this prohibition has had tangible results. Rejection of children has definitely been on the decline, but basically as a result of the dedicated work of NGOs, religious missions and welfare organizations which contact families and take in children in danger of rejection." (Madagascar IR, paras. 14 and 15)

During discussions with the Committee on the Rights of the Child, the Madagascar representative responded: "It had been asked what steps were being taken to change the attitude of parents to those children traditionally believed to be unlucky. No official measures had been adopted. Efforts in that direction were being made by religious organizations and other NGOs, and children were taught in primary schools not to reject others; but no official attempt had as yet been made to educate parents ..." (Madagascar SR.164, para. 20)

---

discriminate against girl children, such as early marriage, and the insufficient attention accorded to their schooling." (Pakistan IRCO, Add.18, paras. 8 and 16)

"The Committee is also concerned about the persistence of some discriminatory social attitudes towards vulnerable groups of children, including those born out of wedlock and disabled children." (Burkina Faso IRCO, Add.19, para. 9)

"... The Committee is also concerned that lasting prejudices and traditional beliefs affect certain groups of children, including disabled children and children born on a certain day of the week (considered to bring bad luck), preventing them from fully enjoying the rights recognized by the Convention." (Madagascar IRCO, Add.26, para. 8)

"The Committee is concerned that traditional attitudes prevailing in the country may not be conducive to the realization of the general principles of the Convention, in particular as regards the persistence of gender stereotypes and the existing role distribution between boys and girls, the abusive sexual practices which might affect very young girls and the discriminatory attitude towards certain categories of particularly vulnerable children such as young single mothers, disabled children, children affected by HIV/AIDS or Rastafarian children." (Jamaica IRCO, Add.32, para. 11. See also, for example, Jordan IRCO, Add.21, para. 8; Honduras IRCO, Add.24, para. 11; Colombia IRCO, Add.30, para. 12)

In comments on Initial Reports, the Committee has proposed various forms of action, including:

- studies of discrimination – the Committee's *Guidelines for Periodic Reports* emphazises throughout the importance of collecting disaggregated statistics and other information in order to identify discrimination in access to rights (see article 4, page 68, for details);
- development of comprehensive strategies;
- information and awareness-raising campaigns, including public campaigns to challenge discriminatory attitudes and practices – a "comprehensive and integrated public information campaign";
- involvement of political, religious and community leaders in influencing attitudes and discouraging discrimination.

For example:

"Strategies and educational programmes along with the adequate dissemination of information should be undertaken in order to counter certain prejudices which affect children negatively, such as gender-based discrimination (known as 'machismo') and discrimination against disabled children (specially in rural areas)..." (El Salvador IRCO, Add.9, para. 18)

"The Committee suggests that the Government develop public campaigns on the rights of the child with a view to effectively addressing the problem of persisting discriminatory attitudes and practices against particular groups of children such as girl children, children belonging to a minority or indigenous group and poor children. It is also suggested that further proactive measures be developed to improve the status of these groups of children." (Nicaragua IRCO, Add.36, para. 31)

"In order to effectively combat persisting discriminatory attitudes and negative traditions affecting girls, the Committee encourages the State Party to launch a comprehensive and integrated public information campaign aimed at promoting children's rights within the society, and particularly within the family." (Nepal IRCO, Add.57, para. 26)

"...it is suggested that political, religious and community leaders should be encouraged to take an active role in supporting efforts to eradicate traditional practices or customs which discriminate against children, particularly the girl child, or are harmful to the health and welfare of children..." (Pakistan IRCO, Add.18, para. 27. See also: Namibia IRCO, Add.14, paras. 15 and 19; Colombia Prelim. Obs. Add.15, para. 15 and Colombia IRCO, Add.30, para. 21; Honduras IRCO, Add.24, para. 24; Jamaica IRCO, Add.32, para. 22; Republic of Korea IRCO, Add.51, para. 20; Finland IRCO, Add.53, para. 25; Lebanon IRCO, Add.54, para. 26; China IRCO, Add.56, para. 34; Morocco IRCO, Add.60, para. 25)

Implementation "irrespective of budgetary constraints"

The Committee has emphasized that implementation of the general principles in articles 2 and 3 of the Convention must not be "made dependent on budgetary constraints." In practice, poverty is clearly a major cause of discrimination affecting children. The Committee's intention is to ensure that non-discrimination and the best interests of children are primary considerations in setting budgets and allocating available resources. In its *Guidelines for Periodic Reports* the Committee asks for information on "The measures taken to ensure that children, particularly those belonging to the most disadvantaged groups, are protected against the adverse effects of economic policies, including the reduction of budgetary allocations in the social sector" (para. 20).

The Committee consistently emphasizes the need for affirmative action – positive discrimination – on behalf of disadvantaged and vulnerable groups:

"... the Committee notes that the application of this and the other general principles of the Convention cannot be dependent upon

budgetary resources. With regard to budgetary priorities in the allocation of available resources, the State Party should be guided by the principle of the best interest of the child, as provided for in article 3 of the Convention, particularly as this applies to the most vulnerable groups of children, such as girl children, indigenous children, and children living in poverty, including abandoned children" (Bolivia IRCO, Add.1, para. 14).

"The Committee is concerned that proper attention has not yet been given to the implementation of the general principles of the Convention, particularly its articles 2, 3, and 12. The Committee reiterates that the implementation of these principles is not to be made dependent on budgetary constraints" (Indonesia IRCO, Add.25, para. 11; see also France IRCO, Add.20, para. 19).

Monitoring and evaluation

It is essential to monitor the realization of all rights within the Convention for all children, without discrimination. Thus the monitoring process and the indicators used must be sensitive to the various issues specifically mentioned in the article: race, colour, sex, language, religion, political or other opinion, national, ethnic or social origin, property, disability, birth or other status. As the wording indicates, the list is not exhaustive but merely illustrative, and States must consider other grounds that might cause discrimination. The *Guidelines for Periodic Reports* requests disaggregated data under many articles, for example by age, gender, region, rural/urban area, social and ethnic origin (for full list of disaggregated data requested by the Committee, see article 4, page 68). The purpose is to ensure that States Parties have sufficient information to judge whether there is discrimination in implementing the article or provision concerned.

The consideration of the implications of each and every article must include the consideration of possible discrimination against individual children or groups of children. Article 2 highlights the "double jeopardy" many children face, discriminated against not only on the grounds of their age and status but also on the grounds of their sex or race or disability.

In addition, the Committee on the Rights of the Child has suggested that strategies to combat discrimination should be evaluated:

"The Committee would like to suggest that further consideration be given to evaluating the effectiveness of measures to raise awareness for the prevention and combating of discrimination and promoting tolerance, particularly with respect to discrimination on the grounds of gender, ethnic origin, discrimination against disabled children and children

born out of wedlock" (UK dependent territory: Hong Kong IRCO, Add.63, para. 24).

"...to each child within their jurisdiction..."

Article 2 emphasizes that all the rights in the Convention on the Rights of the Child must apply to all children in the State, including visitors, refugees and those in the State illegally.

The Committee on the Rights of the Child has on several occasions raised the issue of alien children and pointed out that the Convention accords them equal rights:

"The Committee notes that all children who have had their asylum requests rejected but remain in the country have had their rights to health care and education provided de facto but not de jure. It is the view of the Committee that such services should be provided as a matter of principle according to the letter and spirit of articles 2 and 3 of the Convention." (Norway IRCO, Add.23, para. 12)

"...with regard to the provision of health and education services to children in asylum-seeking situations, the Committee wishes to draw attention to the provisions of article 2 of the Convention which state, inter alia, that 'States Parties shall respect and ensure the rights set forth in the present Convention to each child within their jurisdiction'." (Denmark IRCO, Add.33, para. 30)

"The Committee is concerned about the application of the law and policy concerning children seeking asylum, including unaccompanied children. It is particularly concerned that unaccompanied minors who have had their asylum request rejected, but who can remain in the country until they are 18 years old, may be deprived of an identity and denied the full enjoyment of their rights, including health care and education. Such a situation, in the view of the Committee, raises concern as to its compatibility with articles 2 and 3 of the Convention." (Belgium IRCO, Add.38, para. 9)

"The principle of non-discrimination should be fully implemented by the State Party; ... the rights of illegal immigrant children and non-accompanied children be fully protected." (Portugal IRCO, Add.45, para. 21)

In States with semi-autonomous provinces and territories, the Committee has stressed that differences in legislation or other factors must not cause discrimination in the enjoyment of the rights in the Convention for children depending on where they live.

In discussions with Canadian Government representatives, a Committee member stated that "under article 2 States Parties were required to 'respect and ensure' the rights of children under the terms of the Convention, irrespective of factors such as race, sex, or 'other status'. He took that as implying that the Federal Government was obliged to ensure that equal protection was given to the rights of children in all the different provinces and territories. The Committee had been entrusted with the task of monitoring progress made by States Parties in the implementation of the Convention and was therefore obliged to ensure that the Convention was applied throughout Canada, irrespective of regional differences." (Canada SR.214, para. 45)

The Committee commented to Canada:

"...Disparities between provincial or territorial legislation and practices which affect the implementation of the Convention are a matter of concern to the Committee. It seems, for instance, that the definition of the legal status of the children born out of wedlock being a matter of provincial responsibility may lead to different levels of legal protection of such children in various parts of the country." (Canada IRCO, Add.37, para. 9)

The Committee has also emphasized among general concerns about discrimination that, for example, children of migrant workers, non-nationals, illegal immigrant children and children of minorities or indigenous communities must enjoy the rights guaranteed by the Convention without discrimination:

"While the Committee takes note of the delegation's statement that the rights of the child as contained in the Convention are not in contradiction with the Constitution, it is concerned that national legislation does not appear to ensure that all children, including non-nationals, are protected by the rights guaranteed in the Convention." (Indonesia Prelim. Obs., Add.7, para. 8)

"The Committee expresses its concern at the unequal distribution of the national wealth in the country and the disparities and discrepancies in the enforcement of the rights provided for under the Convention between the different regions of the country, to the detriment of rural children and children belonging to minorities or indigenous communities." (Mexico IRCO, Add.13, para. 9)

"With regard to article 2 of the Convention, the Committee notes with concern that the principle of non-discrimination is not fully implemented for girls, disabled children and illegal immigrant children, non-accompanied children and children living in rural areas, especially in the fields of education and health." (Portugal IRCO, Add.45, para. 13)

The Committee has also noted more general discrimination existing between regions within a State, which is not caused by legislative differences:

"The Committee expresses its concern at the existing geographical and social disparities in the enjoyment of the rights provided for under the Convention." (Chile IRCO, Add.22, para. 13)

"The Committee is also concerned about persisting and significant economic and social disparities between the northern and southern parts of the country, which bear a negative impact on the situation of children." (Italy IRCO, Add.41, para. 10)

"The Committee is concerned about the prevailing disparities between urban and rural areas and between regions in relation to the provision of and access to social services, including education, health and social security." (China IRCO, Add.56, para. 11)

"...without discrimination of any kind, irrespective of the child's or his or her parent's or legal guardian's race, colour, sex, language, religion, political or other opinion, national, ethnic or social origin, property, disability, birth or other status"

The grounds for discrimination specifically mentioned in article 2 of the Convention on the Rights of the Child with the addition of ethnic origin and disability are similar to those stated in the International Covenants on Civil and Political Rights and on Economic, Social and Cultural Rights (article 2 in each Covenant). The Committee has identified numerous grounds for discrimination in its examination of States Parties' reports (see box, page 28). Other Convention articles highlight groups of children who may also suffer particular forms of discrimination, for example children without families (article 20), refugee children (article 22), disabled children (article 23), children of minorities or indigenous communities (article 30), children suffering economic and other exploitation (articles 32, 34, 36), children involved in the juvenile justice system and children whose liberty is restricted (articles 37 and 40), and children in situations of armed conflict (article 38). A discussion of gender discrimination follows and also appears in this *Handbook* under other relevant articles of the Convention.

Discrimination against girls
The Committee has paid particular attention to the issue of discrimination against girls. The

Grounds for discrimination against children

The following grounds for discrimination and groups affected by discrimination have been identified by the Committee in its examination of the first 68 Initial Reports (they are listed in no particular order of significance):

gender, including
    marriage age of girls and of boys
    inheritance rights of girls and of boys
disability
race, xenophobia and racism
ethnic origin
language
children not registered at birth
children born a twin
children born on an unlucky day
children born in abnormal conditions
orphans
place of residence
    distinctions between different provinces/territories, etc.
    rural (including rural exodus)
    urban
    children in remote areas
    displaced children
    homeless children
    abandoned children
    children placed in alternative care
        ethnic minority children placed in alternative care
    institutionalized children
    children living and/or working in the streets
children involved in juvenile justice system
    in particular, children whose liberty is restricted
children affected by armed conflict
working children
children subjected to violence
child beggars
children affected by HIV/AIDS
children of parents with HIV/AIDS
young single mothers
minorities, including
    Roma children/gypsies/travellers/nomadic children
    children of indigenous communities
non-nationals, including
    immigrant children
        illegal immigrants
        children of migrant workers
        refugees/asylum-seekers
            including unaccompanied refugees
children affected by natural disasters
children living in poverty/extreme poverty
unequal distribution of national wealth
social status/social disadvantage/social disparities
children affected by economic problems/changes
economic status of parents causing racial segregation at school
parental property
parents' religion
non-marital children (children born out of wedlock)
children of single-parent families
children of incestuous unions
children of marriages between people of different ethnic/religious groups or nationalities

Guidelines for Periodic Reports asks for information on "the specific measures taken to eliminate discrimination against girls and when appropriate indicate measures adopted as a follow-up to the Fourth World Conference on Women" (para. 28).

The Committee held a General Discussion on the girl child, in January 1995, intended to prepare the Committee to contribute to the Fourth World Conference on Women: Action for Equality, Development and Peace, held at Beijing in September 1995. A recommendation adopted by the Committee, on "Participation and contribution" to the Beijing Conference, reaffirmed

"the importance of the Convention on the Rights of the Child and of its implementation process in decisively improving the situation of girls around the world and ensuring the full realization of their fundamental rights".

The Committee recalled that the Convention on the Rights of the Child and the Convention on the Elimination of All Forms of Discrimination against Women

"have a complementary and mutually reinforcing nature",

and recommended that

"they should be an essential framework for a forward-looking strategy to promote and protect the fundamental rights of girls and women and decisively eradicate inequality and discrimination."

The Committee decided to contribute fully to the World Conference and to submit the results of the General Discussion (*Report on the eighth session, January 1995, CRC/C/38, p. 3*).

The General Discussion report notes that because the Convention on the Rights of the Child is the most widely ratified human rights instrument,

"it was undoubtedly also the most widely accepted framework for action in favour of the fundamental rights of girls. There was an undeniable commitment on the part of the international community to use the provisions of the Convention as an agenda for action to identify persisting forms of inequality and discrimination against the girl child, to abolish practices and traditions detrimental to the enjoyment of their rights and to define a real forward-looking strategy to promote and protect those rights."

The General Discussion report states:

"Addressing the questions of inequality and discrimination on the basis of gender did not imply that they had to be seen in a complete isolation, as if girls were a special group entitled to special rights. In fact, girls are simply human beings who should be seen as individuals and not just as daughters, sisters, wives or

mothers, and who should fully enjoy the fundamental rights inherent to their human dignity... Within the larger movement for the realization of women's rights, history had clearly shown that it was essential to focus on the girl child in order to break down the cycle of harmful traditions and prejudices against women. Only through a comprehensive strategy to promote and protect the rights of girls, starting with the younger generation, would it be possible to build a shared and lasting approach and a wide movement of advocacy and awareness aimed at promoting the self-esteem of women and allowing for the acquisition of skills which will prepare them to participate actively in decisions and activities affecting them. Such an approach must be based on the recognition of human rights as a universal and unquestionable reality, free from gender bias...."

During the Discussion,

"mention was made of the State Party reports submitted to the Committee and to the full picture they provided of the situation of girls around the world. Several States had identified persistent traditions and prejudices as a main difficulty affecting the enjoyment of girls' fundamental rights. Discrimination often arose from the way roles were traditionally distributed within the family. Girls often shared the responsibilities of the household, taking care of younger siblings and refused access to education and participation in social life. The son preference, historically rooted in the patriarchal system, often manifested itself by neglect, less food and little health care. Such a situation of inferiority often favoured violence and sexual abuse within the family, as well as problems associated with early pregnancy and marriage. In some cases it had led to such traditional practices as female circumcision and forced marriage. Reports had also indicated that the situation of the girl was of particular concern in rural or remote areas under the strong influence of community and religious leaders and aggravated by the persistence of harmful traditions and beliefs."

The Committee noted that in its Concluding Observations, it had recommended:

"that a comprehensive strategy be formulated and effectively implemented to create awareness and understanding of the principles and provisions of the Convention; launch educational programmes to eradicate all forms of discrimination against the girl child; and encourage the participation of all segments of society, including non-governmental organizations. In this connection, the Committee had further suggested that customary, religious and community leaders may be systematically involved in the steps undertaken to overcome

the negative influences of traditions and customs."

Other recommendations the Committee noted included:

- ● ensuring girls effective access to the educational and vocational system, to enhance their rate of school attendance and reduce the drop-out rate;
- ● eliminating stereotypes in educational materials and training all those involved in the educational system about the Convention;
- ● incorporating the Convention in school and training curricula;
- ● eradicating degrading and exploitative images of girls and women in the media and advertising.

The Committee also noted that *"legislative measures send a formal message that traditions and customs contrary to the rights of the child will no longer be accepted, create a meaningful deterrent and clearly contribute to changing attitudes. The Committee had often recommended, in the light of article 2 of the Convention, that national legislation of States Parties should clearly recognize the principle of equality before the law and forbid gender discrimination, while providing for effective protection and remedies in case of non-respect. There was also a need to reflect in the legislation the prohibition of harmful traditional practices, such as genital mutilation and forced marriage, and any other form of violence against girls, including sexual abuse.*

"The Committee had also identified certain areas where law reform should be undertaken, in both the civil and penal spheres, such as the minimum age for marriage and the linking of the age of criminal responsibility to the attainment of puberty. In several States the minimum age for marriage was different for girls and boys. To explain this, States had often argued that girls attain physical maturity earlier. However, maturity cannot be identified simply as physical development; social and mental development also had to be taken into account. Moreover, on the basis of such criteria, girls are considered as adults before the law upon marriage, thereby being deprived of the comprehensive protection of the Convention. It was noted that the final document of the Cairo Conference on Population and Development (A.CONF.171/13) has recently encouraged governments to raise the minimum age at marriage, and the Special Rapporteur on violence against women in her preliminary report to the Commission on Human Rights recognized that the age of marriage is a factor contributing to the violation of women's rights (E/CN.4/1995/42)."

The Committee expressed concern at the situation of specific vulnerable groups of girls, including those affected by armed conflict and refugee children:

"in view of the prevailing circumstances of emergency surrounding them, such girls do not really have any time to enjoy their childhood, and the traditional inferiority affecting girls' lives is seriously aggravated. Sexual violence and abuse and economic exploitation often occur, education is not perceived as a priority when urgent basic needs must be met, forced and early marriage is seen as a protective measure. And although dramatically affected by emergency situations, girls often cannot voice their fear and insecurity or share their hopes and feelings."

There was further concern about the situation of working girls:

"Girls below the age of 15 often do the same household work as adult women; such labour is not regarded as 'real work' and is therefore never reflected in the statistical data. To free girls from this cycle they must have the equal chances and equal treatment, with special emphasis on education."

The Discussion concluded that there was an urgent need to gather gender-disaggregated data,

"in a comprehensive and integrated manner, at the international, regional, national and local levels, with a view to assessing the prevailing reality affecting girls, identifying persisting problems and challenging the prevalence of invisibility, which in turn allows for the perpetuation of vulnerability" (Report on the eighth session, January 1995, CRC/C/38, pp. 47-52).

The Platform for Action unanimously adopted by representatives from 189 countries at the Fourth World Conference on Women (Beijing, September 1995) includes a detailed section on "Strategic Objectives and Actions" for the girl child (section L, p. 145, et seq.).

Legitimate forms of discrimination

As indicated above (page 22), the bar on discrimination of any kind does not outlaw legitimate differentiation between children in implementation – for example to respect the "evolving capacities" of children and to give priority, "special consideration" or affirmative action to children living in exceptionally difficult conditions.

The Convention's Preamble recognizes that "in all countries in the world, there are children living in exceptionally difficult conditions, and that such children need special consideration". This sentiment is echoed in the World Declaration on the Survival, Protection and Development of Children, agreed to at the World Summit for

Children in 1990. The Declaration placed in this category, as examples, children who are "victims of apartheid and foreign occupation; orphans and street children and children of migrant workers; the displaced children and victims of natural and man-made disasters; the disabled and the abused, the socially disadvantaged and the exploited..." (para. 20(7)). The list was developed in the Plan of Action for implementing the Declaration, and individual countries that have developed "national plans of action" have also used the concept.

Inevitably, the category of children living in exceptionally difficult conditions includes children with widely different problems requiring widely different remedies. The situation of such children is best defined in terms of discrimination in the realization and enjoyment of various rights in the Convention.

The *Guidelines for Periodic Reports* seeks information on "the specific measures adopted to reduce economic, social and geographical disparities, including between rural and urban areas, to prevent discrimination against the most disadvantaged groups of children, including children belonging to minorities or indigenous communities, disabled children, children born out of wedlock, children who are non-nationals, migrants, displaced, refugees or asylum-seekers, and children who are living and/or working on the streets". The *Guidelines* also asks, under various articles, for information on special or specific measures adopted for disadvantaged children.

The Committee on the Rights of the Child has frequently commented on the need to identify the most vulnerable and disadvantaged children in a State, has expressed concern about their situation and has recommended action to ensure that such children enjoy their rights under the Convention:

"... the Committee notes with concern the disparities in the status and treatment of children in Bolivia conforming to distinctions based on race, sex, language and ethnic or social origin. Vulnerable groups of children, including girl children, indigenous children and children living in poverty, are particularly disadvantaged in their access to adequate health and educational facilities and are the primary victims of such abuses as sale and trafficking, child labour and sexual and other forms of exploitation. The diminished level of protection for girl children inherent in the lower minimum age for marriage is discriminatory and, as a result, deprives this group of children of the benefit of other protections afforded by the Convention." (Bolivia IRCO, Add.1, para. 9)

"The Committee is concerned that society is not sufficiently sensitive to the needs and situation of children from particularly vulnerable and disadvantaged groups, such as the disabled, in the light of article 2 of the Convention." (Russian Federation IRCO, Add.4, para. 9)

"In the light of the discussions and taking into account the situation of children in El Salvador, the Committee recommends that urgent measures be adopted for the protection of children belonging to vulnerable groups, in particular displaced and refugee children, disabled and homeless children, as well as children subject to abuse or violence within the family. Such measures should encompass social assistance and rehabilitation programmes oriented towards those groups of children and be undertaken, with the cooperation and support of the relevant United Nations agencies and international organizations, in the spirit of article 45(b) of the Convention." (El Salvador IRCO, Add.9, para. 19. See also Costa Rica IRCO, Add.11, para. 9; Mexico IRCO, Add.13, para. 18; Belarus IRCO, Add.17, para. 7; Canada IRCO, Add.37, para. 17; Italy IRCO, Add.41, para. 11; Yemen IRCO, Add.47, para. 9)

Children living and/or working on the street Most, if not all, States Parties have reported, or acknowledged during discussion with the Committee on the Rights of the Child, that they have some children living and/or working on the streets. Their situation, being among the most disadvantaged and vulnerable children, has been a major issue of concern and a focus for recommendations by the Committee (see also article 9, page 121, and article 20, page 263).

In the Report on its sixth (special) session, the Committee noted resolution 1994/93 of the Commission on Human Rights on "The plight of street children":

"In particular, it welcomed the statement by the Commission that strict compliance with the provisions of the Convention on the Rights of the Child would constitute a significant step towards solving the problems in this connection. It also welcomed the fact that the Commission commended the Committee 'for the attention it pays in its monitoring activities to the situation of children who, to survive, are forced to live and work in the streets'. Furthermore, the Committee noted that the Commission reiterated its invitation to the Committee to consider the possibility of a general comment thereon... In its discussion the Committee also pointed out that the term 'street children' may not clearly define the nature or the causes of the violations these children suffer. It is in fact an expression that covers a diversity of situations affecting

article 2

children. Some work in the street but have homes, others are abandoned or for other reasons become homeless, others again have escaped abuse, some are pushed into prostitution or drug abuse. Another concern about the term was that it was understood in some societies to be stigmatizing and discriminatory. The Committee, therefore, had endeavoured to use more appropriate terminology.

"Recollection was made of an earlier discussion about the drafting by the Committee of general comments on the Convention. In view of the present heavy work-load of the Committee and the fact that some further experience ought to be assembled before the provisions and principles of the Convention would be interpreted in the form of general comments, it was agreed that the issue of general comments would be considered at a later stage of its activities." (Report on sixth (special) session, April 1994, CRC/C/29, p. 31)

The Committee recommended to Mexico:

"...that urgent measures be adopted to combat discrimination against children belonging to the most vulnerable groups, in particular children subject to abuse or violence within the family, children living and/or working in the streets and children belonging to indigenous communities, including measures to eliminate and prevent discriminatory attitudes and prejudices such as those based on gender." (Mexico IRCO, Add.13, para. 18)

"The Committee is worried about the large number of children who have been forced, in order to survive, to live and/or work in the street." (Indonesia IRCO, Add.25, para. 16)

"The large and growing number of children who, due to rural exodus, extreme poverty, abandonment, as well as situations of violence within the family, are forced to live and/or work in the streets, are deprived of their fundamental rights and exposed to various forms of exploitation, is a matter of deep concern." (Philippines IRCO, Add.29, para. 16)

On occasion the Committee has proposed a "comprehensive study":

"The Committee recommends that measures be taken to give appropriate support to all children living at risk, especially children living on the streets. The Committee suggests that a comprehensive study be undertaken by the authorities so that they may be in a position to promote and implement policies and programmes." (Portugal IRCO, Add.45, para. 24)

Protection of child from discrimination or punishment on basis of status, activities, expressed opinions or beliefs of child's parents, guardians or family members: article 2(2)

It is doubtful whether the very wide potential implications of this provision have been sufficiently considered during the preparation and consideration of Initial Reports by States Parties. Paragraph 1 of article 2 lists as grounds for discrimination "the child's **or his or her parent's or legal guardian's** race, colour, sex..." [bold face supplied by editors]. Paragraph 2 adds protection against "all forms of discrimination or

---

Children living and/or working on the street

One Committee member, during discussions with government representatives from El Salvador, commented "on the term 'street children', which he found demeaning, he said that it was important to look for alternative terminology that was less conducive to discrimination" (El Salvador SR.86, para. 33).

Mexico's Initial Report revealed that the economic and social crisis of the 1980s in that country "resulted in a large number of children being obliged to live on the streets, working as bootblacks, matchboys, windscreen washers, peddlers etc., or begging in order to eke out a living. Street children are to be found throughout the nation". The Programme for Juveniles in Special Circumstances aims to prevent minors from being driven onto the streets, to promote changes in the behaviour of homeless children and children on the streets and to re-integrate minors into their families.

In Mexico "street children are classified as follows:
(a) children on the streets: involved in semi-employed activities to assist their families; irregular school attendance. About 90 per cent of all street children are thought to come into this category;
(b) homeless children: live on the streets and are separated from their families. Ten per cent of all street children come under this heading;
(c) minors at risk: their economic and social situation, and consequently their family situation, are precarious; at risk of being driven out of the family home" (Mexico IR, paras. 297-299, 302).

The child – an easy target for discrimination

A commentary in the *Bulletin of Human Rights* suggests that paragraph 2 of article 2 of the Convention on the Rights of the Child makes an important contribution to international human rights law "by emphasizing that the protection accorded to the child should clearly include all situations in which the child is, or risks, being discriminated against or punished on the basis of the attributes or behaviour of other persons. There is no shortage, either in the annals of each country's own domestic experience or in terms of problems raised in international human rights bodies, of cases in which children have suffered physically, mentally and in other ways as a result of actions for which they personally bore no responsibility whatsoever. Children are often easy targets, in many cases more so than their parents, family members or guardians. Moreover, discriminating against or punishing a child is an effective way of 'killing two birds with one stone'. The child suffers directly, but the parents or others responsible for the child also suffer, albeit perhaps indirectly. Paragraph 2 of this article [article 2] is specifically intended to address such practices and to make clear that they are entirely unacceptable under international law" (*Bulletin of Human Rights* 91/2, Philip Alston, "The legal framework of the Convention on the Rights of the Child", p. 7).

punishment on the basis of the status, activities, expressed opinions, or beliefs of the child's parents, legal guardians, or family members". Paragraph 1 concerns discrimination only in relation to the enjoyment of rights in the Convention; paragraph 2 requires action against "all forms of discrimination", and is not confined to the issues raised by the Convention.

In its examination of reports, the Committee has noted a variety of examples of the child suffering discrimination covered by paragraph 2 (see box above, page 22).

Implementation requires States to ensure that any existing Constitution, relevant legislation, court decisions and administrative policy and practice comply with this principle. For example, are "all appropriate measures" taken to protect children from discrimination or punishment when their parents are subject to action on the grounds of criminal behaviour or immigration status? (In addition, article 9 emphasizes that children must be separated from their parents only when separation is necessary for the best interests of the child; see page 121). Are children penalized because of their parents' marital status? Does the State have the means to intervene on behalf of children whose rights (for example to health care) are threatened because of the extreme religious beliefs of their parents? Do policy and practice in institutions ensure that brothers and sisters are not victimized because of the behaviour of a sibling?

Discrimination on the grounds of "family status"

Canada's Initial Report gives details of the protection against discrimination provided by both federal and provincial legislation. Interestingly, in relation to article 2(2) of the Convention on the Rights of the Child, "family status" is included as a prohibited ground for discrimination in the federal Canadian Human Rights Act; children who suffer discrimination as a result of their family status can make a complaint under the Act (Canada IR, para. 61). Among Canadian provinces, the Saskatchewan Human Rights Code protects everyone, including children, from discrimination "on the basis of race, colour, creed, religion, sex, sexual orientation, family status, marital status, disability (mental and physical), age (between the ages of 18 and 64), nationality, ancestry, place of origin and receipt of public assistance". Family status was added in 1993, "defined as 'being in a parent and child relationship'. This provision will prevent people with children from being discriminated against on that basis in employment, housing or public services. Experience in other jurisdictions has been that this provision is most frequently used when families are renting housing" (Canada IR, paras. 534-535). New Brunswick's Human Rights Act does not generally prohibit discrimination against a child because of the status, activities, opinions or non-religious beliefs of his or her parents, guardians or family members, but the Initial Report indicates that the Human Rights Commission does interpret the Act as prohibiting discrimination based on race, colour, religion, and so forth, of parents, guardians or family members (Canada IR, para. 1032).

Implementation Checklist

• General measures of implementation

Have appropriate general measures of implementation been taken in relation to article 2, including

☐ identification and coordination of the responsible departments and agencies at all levels of government (the principle of non-discrimination in article 2 is relevant to **all government departments**)?

☐ identification of relevant non-governmental organizations/civil society partners?

☐ a comprehensive review to ensure that all legislation, policy and practice is compatible with the article, for all children in all parts of the jurisdiction?

☐ adoption of a strategy to secure full implementation

    ☐ which includes where necessary the identification of goals and indicators of progress?

    ☐ which does not affect any provisions which are more conducive to the rights of the child?

    ☐ which recognizes other relevant international standards?

    ☐ which involves where necessary international cooperation?

(Such measures may be part of an overall governmental strategy for implementing the Convention as a whole).

☐ budgetary analysis and allocation of necessary resources?

☐ development of mechanisms for monitoring and evaluation?

☐ making the implications of article 2 widely known to adults and children?

☐ development of appropriate training and awareness-raising?

• Specific issues in implementing article 2

☐ Is the Convention's principle of non-discrimination with special reference to children included in the constitution, if any, and in legislation?

☐ Are rights recognized for all children in the jurisdiction, without discrimination, including

    ☐ non-nationals?

    ☐ refugees?

    ☐ illegal immigrants?

☐ Has the State identified particularly disadvantaged and vulnerable groups of children?

☐ Has the State developed appropriate priorities, targets and programmes of affirmative action to reduce discrimination against disadvantaged and vulnerable groups?

Does legislation, policy and practice in the State ensure that there is no discrimination against children on the grounds of the child's or his/her parent's/guardian's

    ☐ race?

    ☐ colour?

How to use the checklists, *see page XVII*

      ☐ gender?
      ☐ language?
      ☐ religion?
      ☐ political or other opinion?
      ☐ national origin?
      ☐ social origin?
      ☐ ethnic origin?
      ☐ property?
      ☐ disability?
      ☐ birth?
      ☐ other status?
      (for a full list of grounds of discrimination identified by the Committee on the Rights of the Child, see box, page ...)

☐ Is disaggregated data collected to enable effective monitoring of potential discrimination on all of these grounds in the enjoyment of rights, and discrimination between children in different regions, and rural and urban areas?

☐ Has the State developed in relation to girls an implementation strategy for the Platform for Action adopted at the Fourth World Conference on Women?

☐ Does monitoring of the realization of each right guaranteed in the Convention include consideration of the principle of non-discrimination?

Does legislation, policy and practice in the State ensure that the child is protected against all forms of discrimination or punishment on the basis of the child's parent's, legal guardian's or family members'

      ☐ status, including marital status?
      ☐ activities?
      ☐ expressed opinions?
      ☐ beliefs?

Reminder: **The Convention is indivisible and its articles interdependent. Article 2, the non-discrimination principle, has been identified as a general principle by the Committee on the Rights of the Child, and needs to be applied to all other articles.**

Particular regard should be paid to:
The other general principles

Article 3(1): the best interests of the child to be a primary consideration in all actions concerning children

Article 6: right to life and maximum possible survival and development

Article 12: respect for the child's views in all matters affecting the child; opportunity to be heard in any judicial or administrative proceedings affecting the child.

Best interests of the child

Text of Article 3

1. In all actions concerning children, whether undertaken by public or private social welfare institutions, courts of law, administrative authorities or legislative bodies, the best interests of the child shall be a primary consideration.

2. States Parties undertake to ensure the child such protection and care as is necessary for his or her well-being, taking into account the rights and duties of his or her parents, legal guardians, or other individuals legally responsible for him or her, and, to this end, shall take all appropriate legislative and administrative measures.

3. States Parties shall ensure that the institutions, services and facilities responsible for the care or protection of children shall conform with the standards established by competent authorities, particularly in the areas of safety, health, in the number and suitability of their staff, as well as competent supervision.

The Committee on the Rights of the Child has highlighted article 3(1), that the best interests of the child shall be a primary consideration in all actions concerning children, as one of the general principles of the Convention on the Rights of the Child, alongside articles 2, 6 and 12. The principle was first seen in the 1959 Declaration of the Rights of the Child. Interpretations of the best interests of children cannot trump or override any of the other rights guaranteed by other articles in the Convention. The concept acquires particular significance in situations where other more specific provisions of the Convention do not apply. Article 3(1) emphasizes that governments and public and private bodies must ascertain the impact on children of their actions, in order to ensure that the best interests of the child are a primary consideration, giving proper priority to children and building child-friendly societies.

Within the Convention itself, the concept is also evident in other articles, providing obligations to consider the best interests of individual children in particular situations in relation to

● separation from parents: The child shall not be separated from his or her parents against his or her will "except when competent authorities subject to judicial review determine, in accordance with applicable law and procedures, that such separation is necessary for the best interests of the child"; and States must respect the right of the child to maintain personal relations and direct contact with both parents on a

Summary

regular basis "except if it is contrary to the child's best interests" (article 9(1) and (3));

- parental responsibilities: Both parents have primary responsibility for the upbringing of their child and "the best interests of the child will be their basic concern" (article 18);
- deprivation of family environment: Children temporarily or permanently deprived of their family environment "or in whose own best interests cannot be allowed to remain in that environment", are entitled to special protection and assistance (article 20);
- adoption: States should ensure that "the best interests of the child shall be the paramount consideration" (article 21);
- restriction of liberty: Children who are deprived of liberty must be separated from adults "unless it is considered in the child's best interest not to do so" (article 37(c));

- court hearings of penal matters involving a juvenile: Parents or legal guardians should be present "unless it is considered not to be in the best interest of the child" (article 40(2)(b)(iii)).

The second and third paragraphs of article 3 are also of great significance. Article 3(2) outlines an active overall obligation of States, ensuring the necessary protection and care for the child's well-being in all circumstances, while respecting the rights and duties of parents. Together with article 2(1) and article 4, article 3(2) sets out the overall obligations of the State.

Article 3(3) requires that standards be established by "competent bodies" for all institutions, services and facilities for children, and that the State ensures that the standards are complied with. ∎

Extracts from
Committee on the Rights of the Child
Guidelines for Reports to be submitted by States Parties under the Convention

For full text of *Guidelines for Periodic Reports*, see Appendix 3, page 604.

Guidelines for Initial Reports

"General principles

Relevant information, including the principal legislative, judicial, administrative or other measures in force or foreseen, factors and difficulties encountered and progress achieved in implementing the provisions of the Convention, and implementation priorities and specific goals for the future should be provided in respect of:

...

(b) Best interests of the child (article 3);

...

In addition, States Parties are encouraged to provide relevant information on the application of these principles in the implementation of articles listed elsewhere in these guidelines."

(CRC/C/5, paras. 13 and 14)

Guidelines for Periodic Reports

"III. GENERAL PRINCIPLES

...

B. Best interests of the child (art. 3)

Reports should indicate whether the principle of the best interests of the child and the need for it to be a primary consideration in all actions concerning children is reflected in the Constitution and relevant national legislation and regulations.

Please provide information on the consideration given to this principle by courts of law, administrative authorities or legislative bodies, as well as by public or private social welfare agencies.

Please provide information on how the best interests of the child have been given primary consideration in family life, school life, social life and in areas such as:

> *Budgetary allocations, including at the central, regional and local levels, and where appropriate at the federal and provincial levels, and within governmental departments;*
>
> *Planning and development policies, including housing, transport and environmental policies;*
>
> *Adoption;*
>
> *Immigration, asylum-seeking and refugee procedures;*
>
> *The administration of juvenile justice;*
>
> *The placement and care of children in institutions;*
>
> *Social security.*

Information should be included on the measures taken in the light of article 3, paragraph 2, including of a legislative and administrative nature, to ensure children such protection and care as is necessary for their well-being.

Information should also be provided on the steps taken pursuant to article 3, paragraph 3, to establish appropriate standards for all public and private institutions, services and facilities responsible for the care and protection of children and to ensure that they conform with such standards, particularly in the areas of safety, health, number and suitability of their staff, as well as competent supervision.

In the light of the legislative and administrative measures taken to ensure the consideration of the best interests of the child, please indicate the main problems remaining in this respect.

Please indicate in what ways the principle of the 'best interests of the child' is made part of the training of professionals dealing with children's rights."

(CRC/C/58, paras. 33 - 39. The following paragraphs of the *Guidelines for Periodic Reports* are also relevant to reporting under this article: 20, 64, 65, 74, 76, 80, 87, 93, 101, 106, 114, 115, 118, 120, 128, 132, 138, 143, 152, 159, 161, 164, 166; for full text of *Guidelines*, see Appendix 3, page 604.)

Article 3(1)

The concept of the "best interests" of children has been the subject of more academic analysis than any other concept included in the Convention on the Rights of the Child. In many cases, its inclusion in national legislation pre-dates ratification of the Convention, and the concept is by no means new to international human rights instruments. The 1959 Declaration of the Rights of the Child uses it in Principle 2: "The child shall enjoy special protection, and shall be given opportunities and facilities, by law and by other means, to enable him to develop physically, mentally, morally, spiritually and socially in a healthy and normal manner and in conditions of freedom and dignity. In the enactment of laws for this purpose, the best interests of the child shall be the paramount consideration."

The principle is included in two articles of the 1979 Convention on the Elimination of All Forms of Discrimination against Women and in the Declaration on Social and Legal Principles relating to the Protection and Welfare of Children, with Special Reference to Foster Placement and Adoption Nationally and Internationally.

The principle does not appear in either of the International Covenants, but the Human Rights Committee, in two of its General Comments on interpretation of the International Covenant on Civil and Political Rights, has referred to the child's interest being "paramount" in cases of parental separation or divorce (Human Rights Committee General Comments 17 and 19, HRI/GEN/1/Rev.2, pp. 25 and 30).

In relation to refugees, the Executive Committee of the United Nations High Commissioner for Refugees has formally stressed "that all action taken on behalf of refugee children must be guided by the principle of the best interests of the child as well as by the principle of family unity" (see article 22, page 284).

"In all actions concerning children, whether undertaken by public or private social welfare institutions, courts of law, administrative authorities or legislative bodies..."

The wording of the principle indicates that its scope is very wide, going beyond State-initiated actions to cover private bodies too, and embracing all actions concerning children as a group.

In its reporting *Guidelines* and in its examination of States Parties' reports, the Committee on the Rights of the Child has emphasized that consideration of the best interests of the child should be built into national plans and policies for children and into the workings of parliaments and government, nationally and locally, including, in particular, in relation to budgeting and allocation of resources at all levels. The assessment of child impact and building the results into the development of law, policy and practice thus becomes an obligation.

"...the best interests of the child..."

The Working Group drafting the Convention did not discuss any further definition of "best interests", and the Committee on the Rights of the Child has not as yet attempted to propose criteria by which the best interests of the child should be judged in general or in relation to particular circumstances, aside from emphasizing that the general values and principles of the Convention should be applied to the context in question.

The Committee has repeatedly stressed that the Convention should be considered as a whole and has emphasized its interrelationships, in particular between those articles it has elevated to the status of general principles (articles 2, 3, 6 and 12). Thus, the principles of non-discrimination, maximum survival and development, and respect for the views of the child must all be relevant to determining what are the best interests of a child in a particular situation, as well as to determining the best interests of children as a group. And consideration of best interests must embrace both short- and long-term considerations for the child. Any interpretation of best interests must be consistent with the spirit of the entire Convention – and in particular with its emphasis on the child as an individual with views and feelings of his or her own and the child as the subject of civil and political rights as well as special protections. States Parties cannot interpret best interests in an overly culturally relativist way and cannot use their interpretation of "best interests" to deny rights now guaranteed to children by the Convention, for example to protection against traditional practices and violent punishments (see pages 334 and 242).

The Committee has stressed that the principle should be applied along with the other general principles in all those instances in which the Convention does not set a precise standard. One example, in relation to the definition of the child, is that the Convention requires that a minimum age of criminal responsibility be set (article 40(3)(a)). In determining the age, the principles of non-discrimination, best interests and maximum survival and development should all be applied (see also article 1, page 12, and article 40, page 550).

The Committee has proposed consideration of the best interests and other general principles in relation to many issues. For example:

"...the Committee feels that there is a need to consider seriously questions relating to the legal definition of the child, in particular the minimum age for marriage, employment, military service and testimony before a court. It appears that these provisions do not sufficiently take into consideration the principles of the best interest of the child and non-discrimination." (El Salvador IRCO, Add.9, para. 10; see also Sri Lanka IRCO, Add.40, para. 11)

"... Of equal concern to the Committee is the insufficient consideration of the principle of the best interests of the child to tackle situations of detention, institutionalization, abandonment of children and as well as in relation to the right of the child to testify in court." (Bulgaria IRCO, Add.66, para. 12)

(See also further Committee comments on significance of all the identified general principles under article 2, page 22; article 4, page 60; article 6, page 87; and article 12, page 152.)

"...shall be a primary consideration"

The wording indicates that the best interests of the child will not always be the single, overriding factor to be considered; there may be competing or conflicting human rights interests, for example between individual children, between different groups of children and between children and adults. The child's interests, however, must be the subject of active consideration. It needs to be demonstrated that children's interests have been explored and taken into account as a primary consideration.

Some debate took place in the Working Group drafting the Convention, and proposals were made that the article should refer to the child's best interests as **the** primary consideration" or "the paramount consideration". These proposals were rejected. The very wide umbrella-like coverage of article 3(1) – "in all actions concerning children" – includes actions in which other parties may have equal claims to have their interests considered. (E/CN.4/L.1575, pp. 3-7, Detrick, pp. 132 and 133)

Where the phrase "best interests" is used elsewhere in the Convention (see above, page 37), the focus is on deciding appropriate action for individual children in particular circumstances and requires determination of the best interests of individual children. In such situations, the child's interests are the paramount consideration (as stated explicitly in relation to adoption in article 21; see page 272).

A guiding principle in implementation: requirement to assess "child impact" in government

The Committee on the Rights of the Child has emphasized that article 3(1) is fundamental to the overall duty to undertake all appropriate measures to implement the Convention for all children under article 4. For example:

"...the best interests of the child must be a guiding principle in the application of the Convention." (Mexico IRCO, Add.13, para. 16)

"[The Committee] also emphasizes the value of adopting a comprehensive approach to the implementation of the rights of the child which is both effective and consistent with the provisions and general principles of the Convention, particularly the best interests of the child and non-discrimination which apply irrespective of budgetary resources." (France IRCO, Add.20, para. 19)

"... the Committee wishes to emphasize the importance of the provisions of article 3 of the Convention, relating to the best interests of the child, in guiding deliberations and decisions on policy, including with regard to the allocation of human and economic resources for the implementation of the rights guaranteed under the Convention..." (Paraguay Prelim. Obs., Add.27, para. 9)

"With regard to the implementation of article 4 of the Convention, the Committee would like to suggest that the general principles of the Convention, particularly the provisions of its article 3, relating to the best interests of the child, should guide the determination of policy-making at both the central and local levels of government..." (UK IRCO, Add.34, para. 24. See also Lebanon IRCO, Add.54, para. 35; Zimbabwe IRCO, Add.55, para. 29, etc.)

Where a plan of action for children is proposed, the "best interests" principle should be fully integrated. Integration of the principle must imply the development of mechanisms to assess the impact of government actions on children and to incorporate the results of the assessment in policy development :

"It is also recommended that the State Party prepare, as a matter of priority, a national plan of action for children. The Committee would like to see the provisions and principles of the Convention fully integrated into this plan, particularly its articles 2, 3, 4, 6 and 12." (Belarus IRCO, Add.17, para. 11)

In relation to the vital issue of resource allocation, the best interests principle demands first that within the overall central government budget, and regional and local budgets, there be an adequate allocation for children (for further discussion, see article 4, page 63). There must therefore be sufficient analyses of relevant budgets to determine the proportion and amount allocated to children. In considering priorities in resource allocation, both between and within services at the national and local level, best interests must be a primary consideration. The non-discrimination principle is also important; but as emphasized under article 2 (page 30), the non-discrimination principle allows for positive discrimination – that is, affirmative action – on behalf of particularly disadvantaged or vulnerable groups of children. Thus, the setting of priorities and targeting within resource allocation is vital to reducing discrimination in overall implementation.

The Committee has paid increasing attention to the importance of budget analysis in its examination of reports and in its discussions with representatives of States Parties. Its *Guidelines for Periodic Reports* seeks information on: the proportion of the budget devoted to social expenditure for children at all levels; budget trends; the "arrangements for budgetary analysis enabling the amount and proportion spent on children to be clearly identified"; and "the steps taken to ensure that all competent national, regional and local authorities are guided by the best interests of the child in their budgetary decisions and evaluate the priority given to children in their policy-making" (para. 20):

"...With regard to budgetary priorities in the allocation of available resources, the State Party should be guided by the principle of the best interest of the child, as provided for in article 3 of the Convention, particularly as this applies to the most vulnerable groups of children, such as girl children, indigenous children, and children living in poverty, including abandoned children." (Bolivia IRCO, Add.1, para. 14)

"The best interests of the child is a guiding principle in the implementation of the Convention, including its article 4, and, in this connection, the Committee notes the importance of the implementation of that principle, ensuring that the maximum extent of resources are made available for children's programmes, in reviewing budget allocations to the social sector, both at the federal and provincial levels." (Pakistan IRCO, Add.18, para. 26)

"The Committee recommends that the State Party, in the light of articles 3 and 4 of the Convention, undertake all appropriate measures to the maximum extent of the available resources to ensure that sufficient budgetary allocation is provided to services for children, particularly in the areas of education and health, and that particular attention is paid to the protection of the rights of children belonging to vulnerable groups." (Colombia IRCO, Add.30, para. 16; see also, e.g. Nepal IRCO, Add.57, para. 30)

Similarly, the impact on children of economic adjustment policies and budgetary cuts must be considered in the light of the best interests principle and other basic principles. This consideration is also highlighted in the *Guidelines for Periodic Reports*: "The measures taken to ensure that children, particularly those belonging to the most disadvantaged groups, are protected against the adverse effects of economic policies, including the reduction of budgetary allocations in the social sector" (para. 20).

The Committee has commented, for example, that

"...the Government should ensure that spending cuts carried out by municipalities are effected with due regard for the best interests of children, particularly those from the most vulnerable groups..." (Sweden IRCO, Add.2, para. 10)

"With respect to economic adjustment policies, the Committee recommends that the Government undertake a thorough review of the impact of these policies with a view to identifying ways to ensure adequate protection for children, in particular the disadvantaged and vulnerable ones, in the light of articles 2, 3 and 4 of the Convention." (Costa Rica IRCO, Add.11, para. 13)

"...Budgetary allocations for the implementation of economic, social and cultural rights should be ensured during the period of transition to market economy to the maximum extent of available resources and in the light of the best interests of the child." (Ukraine IRCO, Add.42, para. 20)

The Committee looks for processes which ensure that the best interests of children are considered in policy formulation, and it has begun systematically to promote the concept of child impact assessment (see also article 4, page 66):

"In the light of the provisions of article 3 of the Convention, the Committee is of the view that the Government has not yet fully developed a procedure to ensure that the 'best interests of the child' guide the decision-making process. Consideration of the impact of various policy options on the enjoyment of the rights of the child should form an integral part of this process." (Nigeria IRCO, Add.61, para. 13)

During discussion of Senegal's Initial Report, a Committee member noted that the principle of the best interests of the child was both broader and deeper than the issue of custody in divorce cases. "That notion – a cornerstone of the Convention – meant that, when conflicts of interest arose, the best interests of the child should be the primary consideration. In the legal, judicial and administrative spheres, such an approach called for the creation of a new set of decision-making procedures. UNICEF was, for instance, exploring the use of 'child-impact analyses', which would assess the effect of a decision on a child before that decision had been taken..." (Senegal SR.248, para. 43)

The concept of the child's best interests should not be viewed merely legalistically, but should be a primary consideration in all actions concerning children, a Committee member commented during discussion of Hong Kong's Initial Report: "It was not always easy to define what was in the best interests of the child, particularly where those interests might conflict with others. The approach taken by some countries was to try to find out, before any decision was taken, what would be the impact on the child of each of the various options..." (UK dependent territory: Hong Kong SR.329, para. 81)

The Committee went on to comment in its Concluding Observations:

"The Committee is concerned that insufficient measures have been taken to ensure the fullest implementation of the general principles of the Convention, in particular those contained in articles 3 and 12, especially in the choice, formulation and application of policy measures to promote and protect the rights of the child. In this regard it is noted that a system for integrating a child impact analysis into policy formulation and decision-making has not yet been put into place...

"The implementation of the principles and provisions of the Convention requires that priority be given to children's issues, particularly in the light of the principle of the 'best interests of the child' and of the fact that Governments have, in international forums, agreed to the principle of 'First Call for Children', including in the final document adopted by the World Conference on Human Rights. It is recommended, therefore, that in the

formulation of policy options and proposals there should be an accompanying assessment of its impact on children so that decision makers can be better advised when formulating policy as to its effect on the rights of the child." (UK dependent territory:Hong Kong IRCO, Add.63, paras. 13 and 20)

The best interests principle should guide the deliberations of parliaments as well as the policies of governments:

"The Committee also welcomes the decision taken by the Government to submit an annual report to the Parliamentary Assemblies on the implementation of the Convention and on its policies in relation to the situation of children in the world. This procedure will contribute to emphasizing the importance of the principle of the best interests of the child, which is a primary consideration to be taken into account in all actions concerning children, including those undertaken by legislative bodies." (France IRCO, Add.20, para. 6)

"The Committee recommends that special efforts should be made by the Government in order to fully harmonize the existing legislation with the provisions of the Convention and in the light of its general principles as well as to ensure that the best interests of the child, as stipulated in article 3 of the Convention, be a primary consideration in all actions concerning children, including those undertaken by Parliament." (Chile IRCO, Add.22, para. 14)

Best interests principle to be reflected in legislation

The Committee has indicated that it expects the best interests principle to be written into legislation in a way that enables it to be invoked before the courts. For example, the Committee

"...regrets that there is no provision in the national legislation relating to the best interests of the child or the prohibition of discrimination against children." (Mexico IRCO, Add.13, para. 7)

"... Principles relating to the best interests of the child and prohibition of discrimination in relation to children should be incorporated into domestic law, and it should be possible to invoke them before the courts." (Indonesia IRCO, Add.25, para. 18. See also Denmark IRCO, Add.33, para. 24; Canada IRCO, Add.37, para. 11; Sri Lanka IRCO, Add.40, para. 25; Germany IRCO, Add.43, para. 16)

When a best interests principle is already reflected in national legislation, it is generally in relation to decision-making about individual children, in which the child is the primary, or a primary, subject or object – for example in family proceedings following separation or divorce of parents, in adoption and in state intervention to protect children from ill-treatment. It is much less common to find the principle in legislation covering other "actions" that concern groups of children or all children but may not be specifically directed at children. The principle should apply, for example, to policy-making on employment, planning, transport and so on. Even within services whose major purpose is children's development, for example education or health, the principle is often not written into the legislative framework. Thus, in relation to the United Kingdom, the Committee noted its concern

"...about the apparent insufficiency of measures taken to ensure the implementation of the general principles of the Convention, namely the provisions of its articles 2, 3, 6, and 12. In this connection, the Committee observes in particular that the principle of the best interests of the child appears not to be reflected in legislation in such areas as health, education and social security which have a bearing on the respect for the rights of the child." (UK IRCO, Add.34, para. 11)

In some countries, the principle is written, in some form, into the Constitution. Thus according to Colombia's Initial Report, article 44 of the Colombian Constitution recognizes in its last paragraph the higher interest of the child by the provision: "The rights of children take precedence over the rights of other persons." (Colombia IR, para. 61). But in discussions with Colombian government representatives and in its Preliminary Observations, the Committee expressed concern over

"... the significant gap between the laws adopted to promote and protect the rights of the child and the practical application of those laws to the actual situation of a great number of children in Colombia." (Colombia Prelim. Obs., Add.15, para. 6)

Not subject to derogation

The Committee has emphasized that the general principles of the Convention on the Rights of the Child are not subject to derogation in times of emergency. For example, in the report of its General Discussion on children in armed conflicts the Committee commented that none of the general provisions in articles 2, 3 and 4 *"admit a derogation in time of war or emergency." (Report on second session, September - October 1992, CRC/C/10, para. 67)*

"Fundamental importance" of article 3(2)

A commentary published in the *Bulletin of Human Rights* emphasizes the "fundamental importance" of paragraph 2 of article 3: "Its significance derives in the first place from its position as an umbrella provision directed at ensuring, through one means or another, the well-being of the child. Secondly, its comprehensiveness means that it constitutes an important reference point in interpreting the general or overall obligations of governments in the light of the more specific obligations contained in the remaining parts of the Convention. The obligation which is explicit in the undertaking 'to ensure the child such protection and care as is necessary for his or her well-being' is an unqualified one. While the next phrase makes it subject to the need to take account of the rights and duties of other entities, the obligation of the State Party, albeit as a last resort, is very clearly spelled out. The verb used to describe the obligation ('to ensure') is very strong and encompasses both passive and active (including pro-active) obligations. The terms 'protection and care' must also be read expansively, since their objective is not stated in limited or negative terms (such as 'to protect the child from harm') but rather in relation to the comprehensive ideal of ensuring the child's 'well-being'..." (*Bulletin of Human Rights* 91/2, "The Legal framework of the Convention on the Rights of the Child", Philip Alston, p. 9)

States to ensure necessary protection and care for the child, taking account of rights and duties of parents and others legally responsible: article 3(2)

States must ensure necessary protection and care for all children in their jurisdiction. They must take account of the rights and duties of parents and others legally responsible for the child. But there are many aspects of "care and protection" that individual parents cannot provide – for example protection against environmental pollution or traffic accidents. And where individual families are unable or unwilling to protect the child, the State must provide a "safety net," ensuring the child's well-being in all circumstances. Often, the obligations of State and parent are closely related – for example the State is required to make available compulsory free primary education; parents have a duty to ensure education in line with the child's best interests.

The Committee on the Rights of the Child has very frequently referred to circumstances in which the State is failing to adequately provide for particular groups of vulnerable children. The most common category are children living and/or working on the street, identified as existing in significant numbers in most States. Article 3(2) makes clear that, notwithstanding the rights and duties of parents and any others legally responsible, the State has an active obligation to ensure such children's well-being. This general obligation is linked to its obligations under the other general principles of the Convention in articles 2, 6, and 12 and to any relevant specific obligations – for example to provide "appropriate assistance to parents and legal guardians" in their child-rearing responsibilities under article 18(2), to provide "special protection and assistance" to children deprived of their family environment (article 20(1)), to recognize the rights of children to benefit from social security and to an adequate standard of living (articles 26 and 27) and to protect children from all forms of violence and exploitation (articles 19, 32, 33, 34, 35, 36).

Similarly, in times of economic recession or crisis, or of environmental disaster or armed conflict this overriding active obligation comes into play, linked to other more specific provisions. In order to be able to fulfil its obligations, the State must ensure that it knows, as far as possible, when a child's well-being is threatened and additional State action is required. The Committee has frequently expressed concern as to whether the most disadvantaged children in a State have been identified

"... in order to ensure that adequate safety nets are in place to prevent a deterioration of the rights they are entitled to under the Convention..."

The Committee recommended

"... that programmes be carefully targeted to the needs of both rural and urban children and that adequate social safety nets are in place for the most disadvantaged groups of children." (Belarus IRCO, Add.17, paras. 7 and 15)

The Committee has welcomed the inclusion of a legislative duty reflecting that of paragraph 2 of article 3:

"[The Committee] particularly welcomes the inclusion in the Constitution of a provision directly based on article 3, paragraph 2, of the Convention..." (Iceland IRCO, Add.50, para. 5)

The requirement to take account of the rights and responsibilities of parents and others legally responsible does not prevent the State on occasion from having to intervene without their agreement. The article, together with article 9 in particular (see page 121), covers situations in which parents and others threaten the well-being of individual children, through child abuse or neglect, for example.

Institutions, services and facilities for care or protection of children must conform with established standards: article 3(3)

Standards must be established for institutions, services and facilities for children, and the State must ensure that the standards are complied with through appropriate monitoring. Other articles refer to particular services that States Parties should ensure are available; for example "for the care of children" (under article 18(2) and (3)), alternative care provided for children deprived of their family environment (article 20), care for disabled children (article 23), rehabilitative care (article 39) and institutional and other care related to the juvenile justice system (article 40). There should also be health and educational institutions providing care or protection.

The provision covers not only state-provided institutions, services and facilities but also all those "responsible" for the care or protection of children. In many countries, much of the non-family care of children is provided by voluntary or private bodies, and in some States policies of privatization of services are taking more institutions out of direct State control. Article 3(3) requires standards to be established for all such

institutions, services and facilities by competent bodies. Together with the non-discrimination principle in article 2, the standards must be consistent and conform to the rest of the Convention.

The provision does not provide an exhaustive list of the areas in which standards must be established but it does mention "particularly in the areas of safety, health, in the number and suitability of their staff, as well as competent supervision." In addition, services and institutions providing care and protection must comply with all other provisions of the Convention, respecting, for example, the principles of non-discrimination and best interests and the right of children to have their views and other civil rights respected and to be protected from all forms of violence and exploitation (articles 2, 3, 12, 13, 14, 15, 16, 19, 32-37). In addition, article 25 (see page 341) sets out the right of a child who has been placed for care, protection or treatment "to a periodic review of the treatment provided to the child and all other circumstances relevant to his or her placement."

Implementation of article 3(3) requires a comprehensive review of the legislative framework applying to all such institutions and services, whether run directly by the State, or by voluntary and private bodies. The review needs to cover all services – care, including foster care and daycare, health, education, penal institutions and so on. Consistent standards should be applied to all, with adequate independent inspection and monitoring. In institutions, widespread abuse of children, both physical and sexual, has been uncovered in recent years in many States, emphasizing the lack of appropriate safe-guards, including independent inspection and effective complaint procedures.

Disaster response

Perhaps as a result of the Chernobyl disaster, the Belarus Rights of the Child Act includes a provision in its article 28 for "Rights of children who are victims of natural calamities or accidents or disasters". The State must provide such children with "prompt free assistance, take urgent measures to remove them from the danger zone, take care of reuniting them with their families and provide the necessary medical help, including in other countries. In the event of the loss of their parents, these children shall be afforded the same social protection as any child who has been deprived of parental care" (Belarus IR, para. 102).

Paraguay's National Constitution (1992) includes an article on the protection of the child (article 53): "The family, society and the State shall have the duty to guarantee the child full and harmonious development and full enjoyment of his rights, and shall protect him against neglect, malnutrition, violence, abuse, trafficking and exploitation. All persons shall have the right to demand that the competent authority complies with these guarantees and punishes those who infringe them" (Paraguay IR, para. 27).

The Committee on the Rights of the Child has frequently commented on inadequate monitoring and supervision, in particular of institutions, and has also commented on the over-use of institutional placement (see article 20, page 260):

"The Committee recommends that alternatives to institutionalization in boarding schools, such as foster care, should be actively sought. The Committee also recommends the further training of personnel in all institutions, such as social, legal or educational workers. An important part of such training should be to emphasize the promotion and protection of the child's sense of dignity and the issue of child neglect and maltreatment. Mechanisms to evaluate the ongoing training of personnel dealing with children are also required." (Russian Federation IRCO, Add.4, para. 19)

"The Committee encourages the State Party to address the situation of children in institutions, with a view to envisaging and making available possible alternatives to institutional care and to establishing effective monitoring mechanisms of the realization of the rights of the child placed in an institution." (Poland IRCO, Add.31, para. 34. See also Nicaragua IRCO, Add.36, para. 18; China IRCO, Add.56, para. 18)

On several occasions, the Committee has noted its concern at ill-treatment of children in institutions or alternative care:

"The Committee is very much alarmed at reports it has received of the ill-treatment of children in detention centres. In view of the seriousness of such alleged violations, the Committee is concerned about the insufficient training provided to law enforcement officials and personnel of detention centres on the provisions and principles of the Convention and other relevant international instruments..." (Paraguay Prelim. Obs., Add.27, para. 13)

"The Committee regrets that appropriate measures have not yet been taken to effectively prevent and combat ill-treatment of children in schools or in institutions where children may be placed...
"The Committee also recommends the establishment of effective monitoring mechanisms of the realization of the rights of the child placed in an institution." (Ukraine IRCO, Add.42, paras. 14 and 27)

"The Committee recommends that the system of foster care be carefully monitored in order to eliminate any possible acts of abuse against the children placed in such care." (Croatia IRCO, Add.52, para. 25)

Implementation Handbook for the Convention on the Rights of the Child

Implementation Checklist

● *General measures of implementation*

Have appropriate general measures of implementation been taken in relation to article 3, including

☐ identification and coordination of the responsible departments and agencies at all levels of government (implementation of article 3 is relevant to a**ll departments of government**)?

☐ identification of relevant non-governmental organizations/civil society partners?

☐ a comprehensive review to ensure that all legislation, policy and practice is compatible with the article, for all children in all parts of the jurisdiction?

☐ adoption of a strategy to secure full implementation

    ☐ which includes where necessary the identification of goals and indicators of progress?

    ☐ which does not affect any provisions which are more conducive to the rights of the child?

    ☐ which recognizes other relevant international standards?

    ☐ which involves where necessary international cooperation?

(Such measures may be part of an overall governmental strategy for implementing the Convention as a whole).

☐ budgetary analysis and allocation of necessary resources?

☐ development of mechanisms for monitoring and evaluation?

☐ making the implications of article 3 widely known to adults and children?

☐ development of appropriate training and awareness-raising **for all those working with or for children**?

● *Specific issues in implementing article 3*

Article 3(1)

Is the principle that the best interests of the child shall be a primary consideration in all actions concerning children reflected in

    ☐ the Constitution (if any)?

    relevant legislation applying to

        ☐ public social welfare institutions?

        ☐ private social welfare institutions?

        ☐ courts of law?

        ☐ administrative authorities?

        ☐ legislative bodies?

Is consideration of the best interests of affected children – child impact assessment – required in legislation, administrative decision-making, and policy and practice at all levels of government concerning

- ☐ budget allocations to the social sector and to children, and between and within departments of government?
- ☐ social security?
- ☐ planning and development?
- ☐ the environment?
- ☐ housing?
- ☐ transport?
- ☐ health?
- ☐ education?
- ☐ employment?
- ☐ administration of juvenile justice?
- ☐ the criminal law (e.g. the effects of the sentencing of parents on children, etc.)?
- ☐ nationality and immigration, including asylum-seeking?
- ☐ any rules governing alternative care, including institutions for children?
- ☐ Are there legislative provisions relating to children in which the best interests of the child are to be the "paramount" rather than primary consideration?
- ☐ Where legislation requires determination of the best interests of a child in particular circumstances, have criteria been adopted for the purpose which are compatible with the principles of the Convention?

Article 3(2)
- ☐ Does legislation require the State to provide such care and protection as is necessary for the well-being of any child in cases where it is not otherwise being provided?
- ☐ Does legislation provide for such care and protection at times of national disaster?
- ☐ Is there adequate monitoring to determine whether this provision is fully implemented for all children?

Article 3(3)
Has the State reviewed all institutions, services and facilities, both public and private, responsible for the care or protection of children to ensure that formal standards are established covering

- ☐ safety?
- ☐ health?
- ☐ protection of children from all forms of violence and abuse?
- ☐ the number and suitability of staff?
- ☐ conformity with all provisions of the Convention?
- ☐ independent inspection and supervision?

Reminder: The Convention is indivisible and its articles are interdependent. Article 3(1) has been identified by the Committee on the Rights of the Child as a general principle of relevance to implementation of the whole Convention. Article 3(2) provides States with a general obligation to ensure necessary protection and care for the child's well-being.

Particular regard should be paid to:
Other general principles

Article 2: all rights to be recognized for each child in jurisdiction without discrimination on any ground
Article 6: right to life and maximum possible survival and development
Article 12: respect for the child's views in all matters affecting the child; opportunity to be heard in any judicial or administrative proceedings affecting the child

Other articles requiring specific consideration
of the child's best interests

Article 9: separation from parents
Article 18: parental responsibilities for their children
Article 20: deprivation of family environment
Article 21: adoption
Article 37(c): separation from adults in detention
Article 40(2)(b)(iii): presence of parents at court hearings of penal matters involving a juvenile

Article 3(3)
Article 3(3) is relevant to the provision of all institutions, services and facilities for children, for example all forms of alternative care (articles 18, 20, 21, 22, 23 and 39), health care (article 24), education (article 28), and juvenile justice (articles 37 and 40)

Implementation of rights in the Convention

article

4

Text of Article 4

States Parties shall undertake all appropriate legislative, administrative, and other measures for the implementation of the rights recognized in the present Convention. With regard to economic, social and cultural rights, States Parties shall undertake such measures to the maximum extent of their available resources and, where needed, within the framework of international cooperation.

Article 4 sets out States' overall obligations to implement all the rights in the Convention on the Rights of the Child. They must take "all appropriate legislative, administrative, and other measures". Only in relation to economic, social and cultural rights, is there the qualification that such measures shall be undertaken to the maximum extent of their available resources and, where needed, within the framework of international cooperation. Other general implementation obligations on States Parties are provided by article 2 (to respect and ensure the rights in the Convention to all children without discrimination, see page 19), and article 3(2) (to "undertake to ensure the child such protection and care as is necessary for his or her well-being...", see page 44).

While emphasizing that there is no favoured legislative or administrative model for implementation, the Committee on the Rights of the Child has proposed a wide range of strategies to ensure Governments give appropriate priority and attention to children in order to implement the whole Convention effectively. From the beginning, in its *Guidelines for Initial Reports,* the Committee has emphasized the particular importance of ensuring that all domestic legislation is compatible with the Convention and that there is appropriate coordination of policy affecting children within and between all levels of government. The *Guidelines for Periodic Reports* seeks detailed information on a wide range of measures, including legislative and administrative ones.

Other Treaty Bodies have made relevant General Comments about the overall obligations of States Parties in relation to other instruments, quoted below.

In its *Guidelines* (see box), the Committee has linked, under the heading "General Measures of Implementation", the obligations of article 4 with those of article 42, to make the provisions and principles of the Convention widely known to adults and children (see page 561), and also with the requirement in article 44(6), to make reports under the Convention widely known (see page 582).

Neither the Convention itself nor the Committee defines which of the articles include civil and political rights and which are economic, social or cultural rights. It is clear that almost all articles include elements which amount to civil or political rights. ∎

Summary

Extracts from
Committee on the Rights of the Child
Guidelines for Reports to be submitted by States Parties under the Convention

For full text of *Guidelines for Periodic Reports*, see Appendix 3, page 604 .

Guidelines for Initial Reports

"General measures of implementation

Under this section, States Parties are requested to provide relevant information pursuant to article 4 of the Convention, including information on:

(a) The measures taken to harmonize national law and policy with the provisions of the Convention; and

(b) Existing or planned mechanisms at national or local level for coordinating policies relating to children and for monitoring the implementation of the Convention.

In addition, States Parties are requested to describe the measures that have been taken or are foreseen, pursuant to article 42 of the Convention, to make the principles and provisions of the Convention widely known, by appropriate and active means, to adults and children alike.

States Parties are also requested to describe those measures undertaken or foreseen, pursuant to article 44, paragraph 6, of the Convention, to make their reports widely available to the public at large in their own countries."

(CRC/C/5, paras. 9 - 11)

Guidelines for Periodic Reports

"I. GENERAL MEASURES OF IMPLEMENTATION (arts.4, 42 and 44, paragraph 6 of the Convention)

In the spirit of the World Conference on Human Rights, which encouraged States to consider reviewing any reservation with a view to withdrawing it (see A/CONF.157/23, II, paras. 5 and 46), please indicate whether the Government considers it necessary to maintain the reservations it has made, if any, or has the intention of withdrawing them.

*States Parties are requested to provide relevant information pursuant to **article 4** of the Convention, including information on the measures adopted to bring national legislation and practice into full conformity with the principles and provisions of the Convention, together with details of:*

> *Any comprehensive review of the domestic legislation to ensure compliance with the Convention;*

> *Any new laws or codes adopted, as well as amendments introduced into domestic legislation to ensure implementation of the Convention.*

> *Please indicate the status of the Convention in domestic law:*

> *With respect to recognition in the Constitution or other national legislation of the rights set forth in the Convention;*

> *With respect to the possibility for the provisions of the Convention to be directly invoked before the courts and applied by the national authorities;*

> *In the event of a conflict with national legislation.*

*In the light of **article 41** of the Convention, please indicate any provisions of the national legislation which are more conducive to the realization of the rights of the child.*

Please provide information on judicial decisions applying the principles and provisions of the Convention.

Please provide information on remedies available in cases of violation of the rights recognized by the Convention.

Please indicate any steps taken or envisaged to adopt a comprehensive national strategy for children in the framework of the Convention, such as a national plan of action on children's rights and relevant goals established.

Please provide information on existing or planned mechanisms at the national, regional and local levels, and when relevant at the federal and provincial levels, for ensuring implementation of the Convention, for coordinating policies relevant to children and for monitoring progress achieved, including information on:

The governmental departments competent in the areas covered by the Convention, the steps taken to ensure the effective coordination of their activities, as well as to monitor the progress made by them;

The steps taken to ensure effective coordination of activities between central, regional and local authorities, and where relevant between federal and provincial authorities;

Any governmental institutions created to promote the rights of the child and monitor implementation, and how they relate to non-governmental organizations;

Any independent body established to promote and protect the rights of the child, such as an Ombudsperson or Commissioner;

The measures taken to ensure the systematic gathering of data on children and their fundamental rights and to assess existing trends at the national, regional and local levels, and where appropriate at the federal and provincial levels, as well as the steps taken to develop mechanisms for the identification and gathering of appropriate indicators, statistics, relevant research and other relevant information as a basis for policy-making in the field of children's rights;

The steps taken to ensure a periodic evaluation of progress in the implementation of the Convention at the national, regional and local levels, and where appropriate at the federal and provincial levels, including through the preparation of any periodic report by the Government to the Parliament.

Please indicate any initiatives taken in cooperation with the civil society (for example, professional groups, non-governmental organizations) and any mechanisms developed to evaluate progress achieved.

Using indicators or target figures where necessary, please indicate the measures undertaken to ensure the implementation at the national, regional and local levels, and where relevant at the federal and provincial levels, of the economic, social and cultural rights of children to the maximum extent of available resources, including:

The steps undertaken to ensure coordination between economic and social policies;

The proportion of the budget devoted to social expenditures for children, including health, welfare and education, at the central, regional and local levels, and where appropriate at the federal and provincial levels;

The budget trends over the period covered by the report;

Arrangements for budgetary analysis enabling the amount and proportion spent on children to be clearly identified;

The steps taken to ensure that all competent national, regional and local authorities are guided by the best interests of the child in their budgetary decisions and evaluate the priority given to children in their policy-making;

The measures taken to ensure that disparities between different regions and groups of children are bridged in relation to the provision of social services;

The measures taken to ensure that children, particularly those belonging to the most disadvantaged groups, are protected against the adverse effects of economic policies, including the reduction of budgetary allocations in the social sector.

Please indicate the extent to which international cooperation relevant to the State Party is designed to foster the implementation of the Convention, including economic, social and cultural rights of children. Please indicate the proportion of international aid at the multilateral and bilateral levels allocated to programmes for children and the promotion of their rights and, where appropriate, the assistance received from regional and international financial institutions. Please also indicate the percentage of international cooperation contributed during the reporting period in the total government budget, as well as the percentages of such cooperation respectively allocated to the health sector, to the education sector, to the social sector and to other sectors. Please further indicate any relevant measures adopted as a follow-up to the Declaration and Programme of Action of the World Summit for Social Development."

(CRC/C/58, paras. 11-21. The following paragraphs of the *Guidelines for Periodic Reports* are also relevant to reporting under this article: introduction, paras. 3 and 5; for full text of *Guidelines*, see Appendix 3, page 604.)

General measures of implementation

As a Committee member commented in 1995 during examination of Canada's Initial Report: "... given the wide range of different administrative and legislative systems among the [then] 174 States Parties, the Committee was in no position to specify particular solutions. Indeed, a degree of diversity in the mechanisms set up to implement the Convention might lead to a degree of competition, which could be very beneficial. The important point was that the Convention should be the main benchmark and inspiration of action at the provincial and central levels..." (Canada SR.214, para. 54)

In determining measures for implementation, States Parties must respect the general principles identified by the Committee in articles 2, 3(1) and 6. The Committee has particularly emphasized the best interests principle.

Following its General Discussion on economic exploitation of children (4 October 1993), the Committee adopted a set of general recommendations designed to improve the system of prevention, protection and rehabilitation regarding children in situations of economic exploitation. These asserted the importance of the overall framework provided by the Convention's general principles, and made comments of general relevance on key measures of implementation:

"Here, as elsewhere, the Convention calls upon States Parties to take action through the establishment, in conformity with its principles and provisions, of an adequate legal framework and necessary mechanisms of implementation..."

The Committee went on to stress the importance of

"periodic assessment and evaluation of progress achieved in the implementation of the Convention. This monitoring activity will enable States Parties to review their laws and policies on a regular basis and to focus on areas where further or other action is required."

It also recommended

"the establishment of a national mechanism for coordinating policies and monitoring the implementation of the Convention on the Rights of the Child... Such a coordinating mechanism (as is the case of a National Committee or National Commission on the Rights of the Child), being composed of the various competent entities at the country level, is in a position to ensure a global and multidisciplinary approach to the implementation of the Convention and to promote an effective interaction and complementarity of the activities

developed. Furthermore, it may facilitate the gathering of all relevant information, enable a systematic and accurate evaluation of the reality and pave the way for the consideration of new strategies for the promotion and protection of the rights of the child, including in the field of protection from economic exploitation..." (Report on the fifth session, January 1994, CRC/C/24, pp. 38 - 43)

Each of the International Covenants has articles similar to article 4 of the Convention on the Rights of the Child, setting out overall implementation obligations; and the responsible Treaty Bodies have developed relevant General Comments.

Article 2 of the International Covenant on Civil and Political Rights, on implementation, includes as its first paragraph the non-discrimination principle, equivalent to article 2(1) of the Convention. Paragraph 2 states: "Where not already provided for by existing legislative or other measures, each State Party to the present Covenant undertakes to take the necessary steps, in accordance with its constitutional processes and with the provisions of the present Covenant, to adopt such legislative or other measures as may be necessary to give effect to the rights recognized in the present Covenant." Paragraph 3 requires States Parties to the Covenant to ensure an "effective remedy" for any person whose rights or freedoms as recognized by the Covenant are violated. There is no parallel to this provision in the Convention, but in its *Guidelines for Periodic Reports,* the Committee requests information "on remedies available in cases of violation of the rights recognized by the Convention" (para. 16).

In an early General Comment, the Human Rights Committee noted that article 2 of the Covenant on Civil and Political Rights "generally leaves it to the State Parties concerned to choose their method of implementation in their territories, within the framework set out in that article. It recognizes, in particular, that the implementation does not depend solely on constitutional or legislative enactments, which in themselves are often not *per se* sufficient. The [Human Rights] Committee considers it necessary to draw the attention of States Parties to the fact that the obligation under the Covenant is not confined to the respect of human rights, but that States Parties have also undertaken to ensure the enjoyment of these rights to all individuals under their jurisdiction. This aspect calls for specific activities by the States Parties to enable individuals to enjoy their rights..." The General Comment goes on to emphasize the importance of ensuring that individuals know what their rights are – an obligation included in the Convention on the Rights of the Child in article 42 (see page 561) (Human Rights Committee General Comment 3, 1981, HRI/GEN/Rev.2, p. 4).

"With regard to economic, social and cultural rights, States Parties shall undertake such measures to the maximum extent of their available resources..."

During the drafting of the Convention, an early version of what was to become article 4 qualified States Parties' obligations by including the phrase "in accordance with their available resources". A number of delegates proposed its deletion, on the grounds that the civil and political rights guaranteed in the International Covenant on Civil and Political Rights were not subject to the availability of resources, and that Covenant's standards should not be limited in the new Convention. But some delegates argued for the retention of the qualification (E/CN.4/1989/48, pp. 30-31, Detrick, p. 155). The compromise proposal that was accepted differentiates civil and political rights from economic, social and cultural rights. States Parties are to undertake "all appropriate legislative, administrative and other measures" for the implementation of all rights recognized in the Convention. But in relation to economic, social and cultural rights, these measures are to be undertaken "to the maximum extent of their available resources and, where needed, within the framework of international cooperation".

Progressive implementation: General Comment of the Committee on Economic, Social and Cultural Rights

The concept of progressive realization of economic, social and cultural rights is reflected in paragraph 1 of article 2 of the International Covenant on Economic, Social and Cultural Rights: "Each State Party to the present Covenant undertakes to take steps, individually and through international assistance and cooperation, especially economic and technical, to the maximum of its available resources, with a view to achieving progressively the full realization of the rights recognized in the present Covenant by all appropriate means, including particularly the adoption of legislative measures." Paragraph 2 provides the principle of non-discrimination. Paragraph 3 states: "Developing countries, with due regard to human rights and their national economy, may determine to what extent they would guarantee the economic rights recognized in the present Covenant to non-nationals."

The Committee on Economic, Social and Cultural Rights made a detailed General Comment on "The nature of States Parties' obligations" in 1990. Those relating to the adoption of legal measures are quoted below (page 57). As regards progressive realization through the maximum of available resources, the Committee stated: "The concept of progressive realization constitutes a recognition of the fact that full realization of all economic, social and cultural rights will generally not be able to be achieved in a short period of time. In this sense the obligation differs significantly from that contained in article 2 of the International Covenant on Civil and Political Rights which embodies an immediate obligation to respect and ensure all of the relevant rights. Nevertheless, the fact that realization over time, or in other words progressively, is foreseen under the Covenant should not be misinterpreted as depriving the obligation of all meaningful content. It is on the one hand a necessary flexibility device, reflecting the realities of the real world and the difficulties involved for any country in ensuring full realization of economic, social and cultural rights. On the other hand, the phrase must be read in the light of the overall objective, indeed the *raison d'être* of the Covenant which is to establish clear obligations for States Parties in respect of the full realization of the rights in question. It thus imposes an obligation to move as expeditiously and effectively as possible towards that goal. Moreover, any deliberately retrogressive measures in that regard would require the most careful consideration and would need to be fully justified by reference to the totality of the rights provided for in the Covenant and in the context of the full use of the maximum available resources...

"...the Committee is of the view that a minimum core obligation to ensure the satisfaction of, at the very least, minimum essential levels of each of the rights is incumbent upon every State Party. Thus, for example, a State Party in which any significant number of individuals is deprived of essential foodstuffs, of essential primary health care, of basic shelter and housing, or of the most basic forms of education is, *prima facie*, failing to discharge its obligations under the Covenant. If the Covenant were to be read in such a way as not to establish such a minimum core obligation, it would be largely deprived of its *raison d'être*. By the same token, it must be noted that any assessment as to whether a State has discharged its minimum core obligation must also take account of resource constraints applying within the country concerned. Article 2(1) obligates each State Party to take the necessary steps "to the maximum of its available resources". In order for

Defining "available resources"

Resources to implement the Convention may be divided into three categories:

- **human resources** – "people": the capacities, actions, time and energy of individuals and communities;
- **economic resources** – "things": both financial inputs, which can be budgeted for, and materials, which are purchased. These also include material inputs donated in kind, such as food and building supplies;
- **organizational resources** – the "enabling environment": formal and informal arrangements between people and the procedures by which actions are structured in society. These include the amounts and distribution of power and political commitment, which permit the effective use of human and economic resources.

The above resources may be further classified into two main forms of **stocks** and **flows**. "Stocks", also referred to as "assets" or "endowments", are the accumulated pools of value that society has at its disposal, to conserve or to use for different purposes. They provide the basis for present and future economic activity, establishing the range of possibilities open to society. "Flows" are the actual expenditure or use of those resources, either through direct consumption or application (for instance, eating a meal or installing a handpump) or through transactions or exchanges in the market place...

From the perspective of child rights, society's "stocks" are crucial. Sufficient endowments must remain available to invest in and support actions to meet the needs of future generations. Such an intergenerational perspective underlines the importance of long-term investment, building of human capacity, conservation of natural resources and empowerment of organizations and communities to enable actions in the future – as an **obligation**, not merely as an optional use of present efforts.

The relationship between these categories may be described by the following table:

Type	Stocks	Flows
Human resources	Skills, professionalism Motivation, will power Aspirations, "vision" Knowledge, experience Desire, commitment Energy	Skilled, manual and intellectual work or labour Struggle, threat, negotiation, dialogue Exchange of information and experience
Economic resources	Land, natural resources Physical infrastructure (roads, electricity, water) Equipment, tools Assets, savings Technology, information	Budget, expenditure Credit Supplies Interest Profit
Organizational resources	Administrative structures, norms, procedures Laws and regulations Professional organization Political power, leadership, control Political organization Local organizations and committees Service organizations Family, clans	Decisions Participation Mobilization Management Regulation Monitoring Training

(From "Resources and Child Rights: an Economic Perspective", David Parker, in *Implementing the Convention on the Rights of the Child: Resource Mobilization in Low-income Countries*, edited by James R. Himes, UNICEF International Child Development Centre, Martinus Nijhoff, 1995, pp. 35-37)

a State Party to be able to attribute its failure to meet at least its minimum core obligations to a lack of available resources, it must demonstrate that every effort has been made to use all resources that are at its disposition in an effort to satisfy, as a matter of priority, those minimum obligations.

"The Committee wishes to emphasize, however, that even where the available resources are demonstrably inadequate, the obligation remains for a State Party to strive to ensure the widest possible enjoyment of the relevant rights under the prevailing circumstances. Moreover, the obligations to monitor the extent of the realization, or more especially of the non-realization, of economic, social and cultural rights, and to devise strategies and programmes for their promotion, are not in any way eliminated as a result of resource constraints..." (Committee on Economic, Social and Cultural Rights, General Comment 3, HRI/GEN/1/Rev.2, pp. 57-58)

The approach of the Committee on Economic, Social and Cultural Rights to the concept of "the maximum of available resources" is applicable to interpretation of article 4 of the Convention on the Rights of the Child. The identification of "minimum core obligation to ensure the satisfaction of, at the very least, minimum essential levels of each of the rights" for children has been further developed recently under the "20:20 initiative", designed by the main United Nations agencies and recommended in the Programme of Action of the World Summit for Social Development in 1995. This proposes a compact between donor and developing countries to meet basic human development targets worldwide (see box, page 72).

"Available resources"

As the box opposite describes, the "available resources" which can be harnessed within a State for the implementation of rights extend well beyond financial resources; there are also human and organizational resources.

"all appropriate ... legislative ... measures"

The Convention proposes that States should undertake "legislative, administrative, and other measures" to implement all the rights it contains – including economic, social and cultural rights. Thus, as regards legal implementation, there is no question of the Convention being divided into two categories of rights – social/economic/cultural and civil/political – with only the latter being implemented as legally enforceable rights.

The Convention does not identify which of its rights are "economic, social, and cultural", but the *Guidelines* for both Initial and Periodic Reports group articles 7, 8, 13 - 17 and 37(a) under the heading "Civil Rights and Freedoms." However, the *Guidelines for Periodic Reports* indicates that these are not the only civil rights guaranteed under the Convention. In fact, it is clear that almost all other articles include at least elements that constitute civil/political rights. And legislation is an essential element in their implementation.

Although lack of available resources may restrict full implementation of some Convention rights, and no law on its own can make poverty or unacceptable inequalities disappear, this does not mean that economic, social and cultural rights cannot be defined in legislation or are non-justiciable. The Convention requires States, for example, to define a period of compulsory, free education, ages for admission to employment, and so on. Rights can be drafted as goals towards which the State undertakes to work; or the legislation can expressly include the principle of "the maximum extent of available resources". Where the Convention is self-executing some States have held that its economic rights are non-justiciable, but others have, for example, applied the "standstill" principle, whereby economic entitlements under international treaties must not fall below the level in operation at the date of ratification.

The importance of legislative measures to implement such rights was stressed in the General Comment of the Committee on Economic, Social and Cultural Rights quoted above. Paragraph 1 of article 2 of the International Covenant on Economic, Social and Cultural Rights requires that: "Each State Party to the present Covenant undertakes to take steps, individually and through international assistance and cooperation, especially economic and technical, to the maximum of its available resources, with a view to achieving progressively the full realization of the rights recognized in the present Covenant by all appropriate means, including particularly the adoption of legislative measures." Article 2 of the International Covenant on Civil and Political Rights, on the other hand, requires States to "adopt such legislative or other measures as may be necessary to give effect to the rights in the present Covenant" and to ensure an "effective remedy" is available when such rights are violated.

The Committee on Economic, Social and Cultural Rights comments: "Article 2 is of particular importance to a full understanding of the Covenant and must be seen as having a dynamic relationship with all of the other provisions of the

article 4

Covenant. It describes the nature of the general legal obligations undertaken by States Parties to the Covenant. Those obligations include both what may be termed (following the work of the International Law Commission) obligations of conduct and obligations of result. While great emphasis has sometimes been placed on the difference between the formulations used in this provision and that contained in the equivalent article 2 of the International Covenant on Civil and Political Rights, it is not always recognized that there are also significant similarities. In particular, while the Covenant provides for progressive realization and acknowledges the constraints due to the limits of available resources, it also imposes various obligations that are of immediate effect. Of these, two are of particular importance in understanding the precise nature of States Parties obligations. One of these, which is dealt with in a separate General Comment ... is the 'undertaking to guarantee' that relevant rights 'will be exercised without discrimination' ...

"The other is the undertaking in article 2(1) 'to take steps', which, in itself, is not qualified or limited by other considerations. The full meaning of the phrase can also be gauged by noting some of the different language versions. In English the undertaking is 'to take steps', in French it is 'to act' (*s' engage à agir*) and in Spanish it is 'to adopt measures' (*a adoptar medidas*). Thus, while the full realization of the relevant rights may be achieved progressively, steps towards that goal must be taken within a reasonably short term after the Covenant's entry into force for the States concerned. Such steps should be deliberate, concrete, and targeted as clearly as possible towards meeting the obligations recognized in the Covenant.

"The means which should be used in order to satisfy the obligation to take steps are stated in article 2(1) to be 'all appropriate means, including in particular the adoption of legislative measures'. The Committee recognizes that in many instances legislation is highly desirable and in some cases may even be indispensable. For example, it may be difficult to combat discrimination effectively in the absence of a sound legislative foundation for the necessary measures. In fields such as health, the protection of children and mothers, and education, as well as in respect of the matters dealt with in articles 6 to 9 [employment and social security rights] legislation may also be an indispensable element for many purposes.

"Among the measures which might be considered appropriate, in addition to legislation, is the provision of judicial remedies with respect to rights which may, in accordance with the nation-al legal system, be considered justiciable. The Committee notes, for example that the enjoyment of the rights recognized, without discrimination, will often be appropriately promoted, in part, through the provision of judicial or other effective remedies. Indeed those States Parties which are also parties to the International Covenant on Civil and Political Rights are already obligated (by virtue of articles 2(1), 2(3), 3 and 26 of that Covenant) to ensure that any person whose rights or freedoms (including the right to equality and non-discrimination) recognized in that Covenant are violated, 'shall have an effective remedy' (article 2(3)(a)). In addition, there are a number of other provisions, including articles 3, 7(a)(i), 8, 10(3), 13(2)(a), 13(3), 13(4) and 15(3) which would seem to be capable of immediate application by judicial and other organs in many national legal systems. Any suggestion that the provisions indicated are inherently non-self-executing would seem to be difficult to sustain."

Some of the provisions in the articles referred to here also appear in the Convention on the Rights of the Child. The Covenant's article 10(3) provides for special protection and assistance for children without discrimination, for their protection from economic and social exploitation, for their employment in harmful work to be punishable by law and for age limits for paid employment of children. Article 13(2)(a) of the Covenant provides for free compulsory primary education and 13(3) and (4) include rights to set up private schools along the lines of article 29(2) of the Convention on the Rights of the Child.

The Committee on Economic, Social and Cultural Rights goes on to comment: "Where specific policies aimed directly at the realization of the rights recognized in the Covenant have been adopted in legislative form, the Committee would wish to be informed, *inter alia*, as to whether such laws create any right of action on behalf of individuals or groups who feel that their rights are not being fully realized. In cases where constitutional recognition has been accorded to specific economic, social and cultural rights, or where the provisions of the Covenant have been incorporated directly into national law, the Committee would wish to receive information as to the extent to which these rights are considered to be justiciable (i.e. able to be invoked before the courts). The Committee would also wish to receive specific information as to any instances in which existing constitutional provisions relating to economic, social and cultural rights have been weakened or significantly changed." (Committee on Economic, Social and Cultural Rights, General Comment 3, HRI/GEN/1/Rev.2, p.55)

Ensuring all legislation is fully compatible with the Convention

The Committee on the Rights of the Child has emphasized in examining all Initial Reports that an essential aspect of implementation is ensuring that all legislation is "fully compatible" with the provisions and principles of the Convention, requiring a comprehensive review of all legislation (where necessary, it has proposed that countries should seek technical assistance within the framework of international cooperation). For example:

"The Committee believes that there is need of a comprehensive review of the domestic legislation to bring it into line with the provisions of the Convention, to ensure that all children subject to the jurisdiction of Indonesia are adequately protected by the rights guaranteed under the Convention, and to provide the basis for specifically targeted strategies as well as for monitoring progress made." (Indonesia IRCO, Add.25, para. 8)

"The Committee also welcomes the political commitment within the country to improve the situation of children, which finds expression notably through the setting up of an Inter-ministerial Legal Committee to review national legislation and its compatibility with the provisions of the Convention, through the establishment of Committees on the rights of the child at the national, regional, zonal and woreda levels, as well as through the adoption of a National Plan of Action and the establishment of a Ministerial Committee to monitor its implementation." (Ethiopia IRCO, Add.67, para. 5)

Similarly, in comments on other Initial Reports:
"The Committee is concerned about the insufficient steps taken in the framework of legal reform to bring existing legislation into full conformity with the Convention..." (Jordan IRCO, Add.21, para. 10)

With reference to Jamaica, the Committee expressed concern
"that in the framework of the legislative reform under way, a number of areas remain where national legislation has not yet been brought into full conformity with the provisions of the Convention..." (Jamaica IRCO, Add.32, para. 7)

"The Committee recommends that legislative measures be undertaken to ensure that national legislation conforms with the provisions of the Convention..." (Mauritius IRCO, Add.64, para. 22)

Reviews of legislation should be comprehensive:
"The Committee recommends that a comprehensive review of the domestic legal framework be undertaken. Such a review requires that the provisions and principles of the Con-

vention serve as both its guide and support and that it encompass not only national but also local-level legislative and administrative measures impacting on the rights of the child." (China IRCO, Add.56, para. 25)

"... it is also suggested that steps be taken to reflect and duly take into account in national legislation the holistic and comprehensive approach to the implementation of the rights of the child recommended by the Committee..." (UK dependent territory: Hong Kong IRCO, Add.63, para. 20)

Commission to review legislation

Uruguay's Initial Report describes the Commission created in 1990 to revise legislation concerning the country's minors, and to bring it into line with international developments. The Commission included representatives of official agencies responsible for children's affairs, academics and associations of legal professionals. It created "a forum for discussion and analysis which spent almost three years drafting the new Children's Code. With this initiative the Uruguayan State inaugurated a new era in the drafting of legislation with the direct involvement of non-governmental organizations in the debate to allow them to make their views known and enhance the proposed legislation" (Uruguay IR, para. 65).

Any systems of "customary" or regional or local law must also be reviewed and made compatible with the Convention:

"The Committee also recommends that the State Party, in undertaking a comprehensive review of the national legal framework and its conformity with the principles and provisions of the Convention, should also take into account the compatibility of the system of customary law and regional and local laws with the articles of the Convention." (Nigeria IRCO, Add.61, para. 27)

Even in States such as Chile, where the Convention is self-executing (see below), the Government was recommended by the Committee to *"fully harmonize the existing legislation with the provisions of the Convention..."* (Chile IRCO, Add.22, para. 14)

And the Committee has emphasized, in its concerns about Mexico:

"...Mere reference in the report to the Convention as being the 'Supreme Law of the Land', pursuant to article 133 of the Constitution, should not preclude the Government

from taking the necessary steps to fully harmonize national legislation with the provisions of the Convention, namely in the light of article 4 of the Convention." (Mexico IRCO, Add.13, para. 7)

Canada's Initial Report indicates that international conventions on human rights do not automatically become part of Canada's domestic law, but Canadian courts frequently refer to them in interpreting and applying domestic law, and in particular to the Canadian Charter of Rights and Freedoms (Canada IR, para. 28). In its Concluding Observations on Canada, the Committee recommended that

"In view of the fact that the Convention can only be referred to before the courts as a means of interpretation of national legislation, further steps be taken to ensure the effective implementation of the Convention at the national level..." (Canada IRCO, Add.37, para. 23)

The Committee has also commented on situations in which the legal status of the Convention appears unclear, for example in the case of France because of particular court decisions (France IRCO, Add.20, para. 12; see also France SR.139, paras. 14 and 39, etc.).

Importance of reflecting the Convention's general principles in legislation

In particular, the Committee has emphasized the importance of ensuring that domestic law reflects the identified "general principles" in the Convention (articles 2, 3, 6 and 12):

"The Committee would like to suggest that greater priority be given to incorporating the general principles of the Convention, especially the provisions of its article 3, relating to the best interests of the child, and article 12, concerning the child's right to make their views known and to have those views given due weight, in the legislative and administrative measures and in policies undertaken to implement the rights of the child." (UK IRCO, Add.34, para. 27)

"... the Committee also wishes to emphasize the importance of taking action to ensure that the general principles of the Convention, particularly those relating to non-discrimination, the best interests of the child and the respect for the views of the child as guaranteed under articles 2, 3 and 12 respectively, are reflected in domestic law..." (Canada IRCO, Add.37, para. 23)

The Committee has stressed that it should be possible to invoke the general principles of the Convention before the courts:

"The Committee recommends that the State Party harmonize its national legislation with the provisions and principles of the Convention. Principles relating to the best interests of the child and the prohibition of discrimination in relation to children should be reflected in domestic law, and it should be possible to invoke them before the courts." (Sri Lanka IRCO, Add.40, para. 25)

Incorporation of Convention in domestic law

The Committee on the Rights of the Child has promoted the incorporation of the Convention into domestic law:

"The Committee welcomes the incorporation of the Convention on the Rights of the Child, as well as other human rights treaties ratified by Argentina, into the domestic legal system and the high legal status attributed to them by virtue of which they are given precedence over national laws." (Argentina IRCO, Add.35, para. 6)

"The Committee notes with satisfaction that the Convention, as well as other international treaties dealing with human rights, are incorporated into domestic law, and that article 13 of the Constitution states that human rights provisions of the Constitution are to be interpreted in line with international human rights instruments ratified by Ethiopia." (Ethiopia IRCO, Add.67, para. 4)

"The Committee notes with appreciation that the Convention is fully incorporated into domestic law, and that the Civil Code and the Code of Criminal Procedure expressly provide that their provisions shall not apply in case they conflict with a provision of an international Convention in force in Syria..." (Syrian Arab Republic IRCO, Add.70, para. 3)

The Committee has welcomed situations, as for example in Chile (see also Burkina Faso SR.135, para. 14) where
"...the Convention on the Rights of the Child is self-executing in the State Party, and ... its provisions may be, and in practice have been, invoked before the courts." (Chile IRCO, Add.22, para. 4)

It has also commended situations in which the Convention clearly takes precedence over domestic law where they conflict. In Belgium, domestic courts have quoted articles of the Convention, including articles 3 and 9. In addition, the country's highest court had "unequivocally asserted the primacy of international treaty law over domestic provisions, even those enacted subsequently" (Belgium SR.222, paras. 10-14). The Committee commented:

"The Committee welcomes the fact that the Convention is self-executing and that its provisions may be, and in practice have been in several instances, invoked before the court. It *also notes with satisfaction the fact that Belgium applies the principle of the primacy of international human rights standards over national legislation in case of conflict of law."* (Belgium IRCO, Add.38, para. 6)

The Constitution of the Republic of Bulgaria (1991) states: "The international instruments ratified in the manner established by the Constitution, promulgated and entered into force in the Republic of Bulgaria, shall be part of the country's domestic law. They shall enjoy superiority over such norms of domestic law that contradict them" (Bulgaria IR, para. 2). The Committee commented:

"The Committee welcomes the fact that according to the Constitution international instruments ratified by Bulgaria are part of the country's domestic law and enjoy superiority over norms of domestic law that contradict them." (Bulgaria IRCO, Add.66, para. 4)

Developing consolidated statutes for the rights of the child

The Committee on the Rights of the Child has commended the existence in some countries of consolidated acts on the rights of the child – noting it as a positive aspect in Belarus, for example (Belarus IRCO, Add.17, para. 3) – and has encouraged moves towards such statutes in other states. Among its recommendations to Burkina Faso, it proposed special efforts

"to pursue the process of bringing the existing legislation into line with the provisions of the Convention and to take fully into account the interests of the child in the course of drafting new legislation, including through the possibility of considering a comprehensive legislative act on the rights of the child..." (Burkina Faso IRCO, Add.19, para. 15)

"The Committee also recommends that the State Party adopt all the necessary measures to ensure that its national legislation fully conforms to the Convention. In this regard, and in recognition of the importance of ensuring an integrated legal approach to children's rights in the light of the principles and provisions of the Convention, the Committee encourages the State Party to pursue its efforts aimed at the adoption of a Code on Children and Adolescents." (Guatemala IRCO, Add.58, para. 25)

"The Committee welcomes the adoption of a national Charter on Children's Rights but recommends that it be given the status of law and its provisions, where necessary, raised to the standards of the Convention." (Sri Lanka IRCO, Add.40, para. 27)

Rights of the child in constitutions

Many countries have constitutions that appear to meet various requirements of the Convention, in so far as they guarantee all citizens – including children – specific rights and freedoms. However, this is generally an illusion, since in practice children manifestly cannot claim these rights on an equal basis with adults – first because domestic law may contradict the rights (for example, children of compulsory school age do not have freedom of movement; in law young children are not permitted to have sexual relationships or enter into financial contracts; children cannot vote, and so on) and, second, because constitutions themselves often explicitly uphold parents' rights to bring up and educate their children as they see fit, without reference to the child's own rights.

Because of children's physical, emotional and economic dependence on adults, they may deserve special measures of protection within the

Ethiopia's draft Constitution

According to the Initial Report, Ethiopia's draft (1995) Constitution has a distinct section on the rights of the child. Article 36 includes:

"1. Every child has the following rights:

(a) the right to life;

(b) the right to obtain name and nationality;

(c) the right to know and be cared for by his parents or legal guardians;

(d) the right to be protected from labour exploitation and not to be forced to undertake work that may harm his education, health and well-being;

(e) the right to be free from harsh or inhuman punishments that may be inflicted on his body, in schools or child care institutions.

"2. Child care should always be a priority consideration of the Government, private charity organizations or courts or administrative authorities or legislative organs, when any measure affecting children is to be taken.

"3. Juvenile delinquents or children under the care of rehabilitation centres or children growing up in Government aid or children under the care of the Government or private orphanages shall be segregated from adults.

"4. Children born out of wedlock have equal status and rights to children born in wedlock.

"5. Special protection shall be given by law to orphans; systems by which children could be adopted should be facilitated and the establishment of institutions for the care and education of the child shall be encouraged."

(Ethiopia IR, para. 19)

constitution; and because the future prosperity of the State depends on them, it is also in the State's interest to accord them special constitutional rights.

The Committee has welcomed instances in which existing or new constitutions have incorporated special sections on children, reflecting at least some of the Convention's principles. Commenting on Nepal's Initial Report,

"The Committee notes the efforts made by the Government in the field of law reform, especially the adoption of a new Constitution – with a special section to ensure the rights of the child – and the Children's Act which covers many areas concerning children's rights..." (Nepal IRCO, Add.57, para. 3)

The Committee commented to Norway:

"In case the Government of Norway should decide to amend its Constitution to include a special provision on the incorporation of certain human rights treaties in its Constitution, the Committee would like to encourage the incorporation of a reference to the Convention on the Rights of the Child." (Norway IRCO, Add.23, para. 14)

"all appropriate ... administrative, and other measures ..."

The Committee's *Guidelines for Periodic Reports* asks in particular for information on existing or planned mechanisms at national or local level for coordinating policies relating to children and for monitoring the implementation of the Convention (para. 18).

A "comprehensive national strategy" for children

The Committee on the Rights of the Child, often quoting the principle of "first call for children", promoted at the World Summit for Children, has emphasized that children must be accorded a high, or higher, priority. In stressing the need for a comprehensive approach to the implementation of children's rights, the Committee has frequently promoted the need for a national policy or plan of action reflecting not only the World Summit goals but also the implementation of the whole Convention. The Plan of Action for implementing the World Summit Declaration spells out in some detail what National Plans of Action should contain (Plan of Action, para. 34). The Committee's *Guidelines for Periodic Reports* asks for information on "any steps taken or envisaged to adopt a comprehensive national strategy for children in the framework of the Convention..." (para. 17)):

"The Committee encourages the State Party to undertake a thorough review of its national plan of action on children. It is recommended that the goals of the plan should be achieved, measurably, within a specific timeframe, and that the Convention on the Rights of the Child be fully integrated into the plan." (Pakistan IRCO, Add.18, para. 24)

"The Committee, in taking note of the activities undertaken throughout the State Party to develop and implement outlines for the follow-up to the World Summit for Children, recommends that future outlines, development plans, programmes or plans of action on the rights of the child be prepared on the basis of all the provisions and principles of the Convention." (China IRCO, Add.56, para. 27)

"The Committee recommends that children's issues be accorded a higher priority in the State Party. It is the Committee's view that the development of a global and national policy on children must be attended to urgently..." (Guatemala IRCO, Add.58, para. 25. See also Bulgaria IRCO, Add.66, para. 9; New Zealand IRCO, Add.71, paras. 9 and 22)

The Vienna Declaration and Programme of Action adopted by the World Conference on Human Rights in 1993 urged all nations "to undertake measures to the maximum extent of their available resources, with the support of international cooperation, to achieve the goals in the World Summit Plan of Action. The Conference calls on States to integrate the Convention on the Rights of the Child into their national action plans..." (A/CONF.157/23 para 47). (For a summary of reviews of National Programmes of Action (NPAs), see *Implementing the Convention on the Rights of the Child, Resource Mobilization in Low-Income Countries*, ed. James R. Himes, UNICEF International Child Development Centre, Martinus Nijhoff, 1995, pp. 56 et seq.)

Such plans, together with the process of implementation, should pay particular attention to the general principles of the Convention on the Rights of the Child:

"It is the Committee's view that further efforts must be undertaken to ensure that the general principles of the Convention, in particular 'the best interests of the child' and the participation of children, not only guide policy discus-sions and formulation, and decision-making, but also are integrated into the development and implementation of all projects and programmes." (Nigeria IRCO, Add.61, para. 32)

The Standard Rules on the Equalization of Opportunities for Persons with Disabilities emphasizes that "the needs and concerns of persons with disabilities should be incorporated into general development plans and not be treated separately" (rule 14.3).

Budgeting and budgetary analysis

The Committee has emphasized that States' obligation to implement economic, social and cultural rights "to the maximum extent of their available resources" implies adequate budgetary analysis. The *Guidelines for Periodic Reports* seeks information on:

- the steps undertaken to ensure coordination between economic and social policies;
- the proportion of the budget devoted to social expenditures for children, including health, welfare and education at the central, regional and local levels, and where appropriate at the federal and provincial levels;
- the budget trends over the period covered by the report;
- the steps taken to ensure that all competent national, regional and local authorities are guided by the best interests of the child in their budgetary decisions and to evaluate the priority given to children in their policymaking;
- the measures taken to ensure that disparities between different regions and groups of children are bridged in relation to the provision of social services;
- the measures taken to ensure that children, particularly those belonging to the most disadvantaged groups, are protected against the adverse effects of economic policies, including the reduction of budgetary allocations in the social sector.

It is extremely rare for children to be as visible in the economic policies of government as the *Guidelines for Periodic Reports* implies they should be. Most government departments have no idea what proportion of their budget is spent on children, few know what impact their expenditure has on children. The Committee has emphasized that monitoring and evaluation in this sphere, as in all others, is essential for any effective strategies:

"The Committee also suggests that the State Party undertake a study on the impact on children and their families of the economic reform process that has been ongoing during the last several years in terms of its impact on government budgetary resources available for support services, as well as on the impact of unemployment and changed conditions of employment on children, young persons and their families. Conclusions from such a study could be a useful starting point for developing a comprehensive strategy for future action." (New Zealand IRCO, Add.71, para. 26. See also Russian Federation IRCO, Add.4, para. 16;

Romania IRCO, Add.16, para. 12; Nigeria IRCO, Add.61, para. 28)

The Committee has made various consistent comments on budgetary issues in its examination of States Parties' reports. The overall proportion of national and local budgets allocated to social programmes must be adequate, and there must be sufficient budgetary provision to protect and promote children's rights. Lack of available resources cannot be used as a reason for not establishing social security programmes and social safety nets:

"The Committee wishes to emphasize that the general lack of financial resources cannot be used as a justification for neglecting to establish social security programmes and social safety nets to protect the most vulnerable groups of children. Accordingly, it is the opinion of the Committee that a serious review should be undertaken to determine the consistency of the economic and social policies being developed with the State Party's obligations under the Convention, in particular articles 26 and 27, especially with respect to the establishment or improvement of social security programmes and other social protection." (Nigeria IRCO, Add.61, para. 33)

The Committee has been highly sensitive to the impact on children of the world recession, economic adjustments and cutbacks that occurred during the first half of the 1990s. In a statement made by the Committee following its General Discussion on economic exploitation of children (4 October 1993) it expressed overall concern at the effects on children of programmes of economic reform and resolved to invite international financial institutions, including the World Bank and the International Monetary Fund, to a discussion about the need to protect the rights of the child:

"When analyzing States' reports, the Committee noted that groups of children in both poor and rich countries have been victimized by sweeping measures to curb inflation and encourage economic growth. Social allocations have been cut in drastic proportion. "This has caused new poverty. Groups of vulnerable children, in particular, have been made to suffer: the girl child, the disabled, minority ethnic groups, orphans, displaced and refugee children. "Political leaders who met three years ago for the World Summit for Children stated that measures for structural adjustment should be undertaken without undermining the well-being of children. "The Convention on the Rights of the Child states that Governments should implement the economic, social and cultural rights of the child 'to the maximum extent of their

article 4

available resources'. The Committee is not convinced that any Government fully lives up to that ambition today.

"There is an urgent need for a discussion on how children can be protected in programmes of economic reform. International, regional and national financial institutions have a role to play in this endeavour." (Report on the fourth session, September - October 1993, CRC/C/20, Annex VI, p. 57)

States must minimize the negative effects of structural adjustment programmes, transition to a market economy and any spending cuts on children; and the needs of the most vulnerable groups of children must be given priority:

"...the Government should ensure that spending cuts carried out by municipalities are effected with due regard for the best interests of children, particularly those from the most vulnerable groups..." (Sweden IRCO, Add.2, para. 10)

"The Committee urges the Government of Peru to take all the necessary steps to minimize the negative impact of the structural adjustment policies on the situation of children. The authorities should, in the light of articles 3 and 4 of the Convention, undertake all appropriate measures to the maximum extent of their available resources to ensure that sufficient resources are allocated to children..." (Peru IRCO, Add.8, para. 19).

"With respect to article 4 of the Convention, the Committee is concerned about the adequacy of measures taken to ensure the implementation of economic, social and cultural rights to the maximum extent of available resources. It appears to the Committee that insufficient expenditure is allocated to the social sector both within the State Party and within the context of international development aid; the Committee wonders whether sufficient consideration has been given to the enjoyment of fundamental rights by children belonging to the most vulnerable groups in society." (UK IRCO, Add.34, para. 9)

"...Budgetary allocations for the implementation of economic, social and cultural rights should be ensured during the period of transition to market economy to the maximum extent of available resources and in the light of the best interests of the child." (Ukraine IRCO, Add.42, para. 20)

During discussion of Peru's Initial Report, a Committee member was reported as commenting: "... in times of economic crisis, economists often recommended budget cuts, which mainly affected allocations for the poor, the young, education and health care. It was said that such a course would stimulate the economy and the

population would eventually benefit. The problem with such an approach was that it undermined the whole concept of the rights of the child. The reference in article 4 of the Convention to the obligation on the part of States Parties to undertake the relevant measures to the maximum extent of their available resources meant that current policies must give priority to children." (Peru SR.82, para. 34)

National bodies concerned with overall budgeting must be linked directly to those developing policy for children and implementation of the Convention:

"The Committee also recommends that, in the light of article 4 of the Convention, priority be given in budget allocations to the realization of the economic, social and cultural rights of children, with particular emphasis on health and education, and on the enjoyment of these rights by children belonging to the most disadvantaged groups. In this regard, the Committee suggests that the ministries responsible for overall planning and budgeting be fully involved in the activities of the Higher Committee on Child Welfare and the National Committee on Children, with a view to ensuring a direct and immediate budgetary impact of their decisions." (Syrian Arab Republic IRCO, Add.70, para. 26)

The general principles of the Convention must be applied to allocation of resources and budgeting, including the best interests principle, and the principle of non-discrimination – for example, in disparities between regions, rural/urban areas:

"The best interests of the child is a guiding principle in the implementation of the Convention, including its article 4, and in this connection, the Committee notes the importance of the implementation of that principle, ensuring that the maximum extent of resources are made available for children's programmes, in reviewing budget allocations to the social sector, both at the federal and provincial level." (Pakistan IRCO, Add.18, para. 26)

"...within the framework of the application of article 4 of the Convention, relating to the allocation of resources to the maximum extent possible, the Committee is concerned about the insufficient portion of the national and local-level budgets allocated to social and human needs, especially with regard to responding to the situation of the most vulnerable groups of children. In this connection, the Committee wishes to emphasize the importance of the provisions of article 3 of the Convention, relating to the best interests of the child, in guiding deliberations and decisions on policy, including with regard to the allocation of human and economic resources for the implementation of the rights guaran-

teed under the Convention." (Paraguay Prelim. Obs., Add.27, para. 9)

"With respect to article 4 of the Convention, it is the Committee's opinion that sufficient budgetary provision must be made to respond to national and local priorities for the protection and promotion of children's rights. While noting the trend towards decentralizing the provision of services to the municipal level as a means of promoting greater popular participation, the Committee emphasizes that such a policy must be designed to overcome and remedy existing disparities between the regions and rural/urban areas..." (Guatemala IRCO, Add.58, para. 31. See also Spain IRCO, Add.28, para. 14; Philippines IRCO, Add.29, para. 21; China IRCO, Add.56, para. 31; Nepal IRCO, Add.57, para. 30; Mauritius IRCO, Add.64, para. 26; Panama IRCO, Add.68, para. 28; Myanmar IRCO, Add.69, para. 32; New Zealand IRCO, Add.71, para. 26)

Effective coordination

One of the most common "subjects of concern" expressed by the Committee in its Concluding Observations on States Parties' Initial Reports has been a lack of coordination, and it has made frequent recommendations for "effective coordination". One product of coordination across government is the comprehensive national strategy or plan of action for children (see above, page 62). This then in turn becomes the framework for coordinated action for the realization of children's rights:

"The Committee recommends that the State Party strengthen coordination between the various governmental mechanisms involved in children's rights, at both the national and local levels, with a view to developing a comprehensive policy on children and ensuring effective evaluation of the implementation of the Convention in the country." (Mauritius IRCO, Add.64, para. 23)

The Committee has referred to lack of coordination between government departments and ministries and other governmental bodies, between federal or central government and provincial, regional or local government, between government and public and private bodies, including non-governmental organizations dealing with human rights and children's rights, and between such bodies themselves.

For example:

"Coordination between the various governmental agencies involved in the implementation of the Convention and its monitoring should be ensured, and efforts should be made towards closer cooperation with non-governmental organizations." (Philippines IRCO, Add.29, para. 19)

To Argentina, the Committee noted:

"The Committee is concerned that sufficient administrative and other measures seem not to have been taken to facilitate an effective coordination of the implementation of the Convention on local, regional and national levels".

The Committee recommended better coordination between existing mechanisms and institutions, and

"increased coordination between efforts undertaken at the local and provincial level

---

Coordinating committees – two examples

In Bulgaria, the functions of the Committee for Young People and Children are: "(a) to develop the State's policy towards children and young people by working to make protection of children into a priority of State policy; (b) to elaborate and submit to the Government draft acts and programmes for the development and protection of children. The Committee for Young People and Children also distributes the subsidies approved by the State budget for implementing the State's policy with respect to children." (Bulgaria IR, para. 17)

In Ethiopia, a National Inter-Ministerial Committee was formed in 1994 to monitor implementation of the Convention. It consists of members from the Ministries of Labour, Health, Education, Information, Justice, Culture and Sports, the Police Commission and the Children's, Youth and Family Welfare Organization (CYFWO). The Committee is chaired by the Ministry of Labour and Social Affairs, and CYFWO acts as secretariat. Similar committees have been formed in most of the regional, zonal and "woreda" administrations, and regional administrations have taken steps to set up similar committees at community level. The CYFWO is a semi-autonomous government agency within the Ministry of Labour and Social Affairs, which works closely with non-governmental organizations. Its objectives are:

"to make government institutions and the society at large aware of the special needs of children;

to encourage, coordinate and supervise, by following up their well-being, all efforts made for the attainment of an all-round physical, mental and emotional development of children" (Ethiopia IR, paras. 24-26).

with those taken at the national level."
(Argentina IRCO, Add.35, paras. 9 and 15. See
also Canada IRCO, Add.37, para. 20; Nepal IRCO,
Add.57, para. 28; UK dependent territory: Hong
kong IRCO, Add.63, paras. 12 and 22; Syrian Arab
Republic IRCO, Add.70, para. 21)

Permanent government mechanisms

The Committee has made it clear that it sees the
process of implementation as a continuing process requiring "permanent" mechanisms. For
example, in its Concluding Observations on
Germany's Initial Report, it recommended that
the State Party give further consideration

"to the establishment of a permanent and
effective coordination mechanism on the
rights of the child at the Federal, Land and
local levels." (Germany IRCO, Add.43, para. 23)

Similarly to Chile, Canada and others, the Committee suggested:
"... an overall national mechanism be set up
with the mandate to assure continuing supervision and evaluation throughout the country
of the implementation of the Convention,
which is particularly important within the context of the realization by the Government of
the decentralization programme." (Chile IRCO,
Add.22, para. 15)

"The Committee is concerned that sufficient
attention has not been paid to the establishment of a permanent monitoring mechanism
that will enable an effective system of implementation of the Convention in all parts of
the country. Disparities between provincial or
territorial legislation and practices which
affect the implementation of the Convention
are a matter of concern to the Committee."
(Canada IRCO Add.37 para. 9. See also Belgium
IRCO, Add.38, para. 13; Guatemala IRCO, Add.58,
para. 27; Mauritius IRCO, Add.64, para. 22)

Where permanent mechanisms have been established, the Committee has welcomed them. For
example (to Denmark):

"The Committee is encouraged to note the
existence of the Government's Children's Committee, and the Inter-Ministerial Committee
on Children which is composed of civil servants from 16 ministries".

The Committee went on to recommend that the
Convention should be established as the frame-
work for these two bodies (Denmark IRCO,
Add.33, paras. 4 and 17).

On occasion, the Committee has proposed the
establishment of particular mechanisms – for
example an inter-ministerial committee – both to
facilitate coordination and monitoring:

"The Committee emphasizes the importance
and value of setting up a coordinating mechanism with the mandate of determining priorities and regularly monitoring and evaluating

progress in the implementation of the rights
of the child at the federal, provincial and local
levels. As a first step in this direction, the
Committee suggests that the State Party consider the possibility of setting up an interministerial committee or similar body with political
authority to review initially and determine
appropriate action to follow up on the observations made during the constructive dialogue
between the State Party and the Committee."
(Pakistan IRCO, Add.18, para. 25; see also Portugal
IRCO, Add.45, para. 9)

Child impact analysis

The Committee has looked for processes which
ensure that children's interests are considered
in policy formulation, and has begun to propose
that States should adopt a comprehensive system
of "child impact assessment" (see also article 3,
page 41):

"The Committee is concerned that insufficient
measures have been taken to ensure the fullest implementation of the general principles
of the Convention, in particular those contained in articles 3 and 12, especially in the
choice, formulation and application of policy
measures to promote and protect the rights of
the child. In this regard it is noted that a
system for integrating a child impact analysis
into policy formulation and decision-making
has not yet been put into place...
"The implementation of the principles and
provisions of the Convention requires that priority be given to children's issues, particularly
in the light of the principle of the 'best interest of the child' and of the fact that Governments have, in international forums, agreed
to the principle of 'First Call for Children',
including in the final document adopted by
the World Conference on Human Rights. It is
recommended, therefore, that in the formulation of policy options and proposals there
should be an accompanying assessment of its
impact on children so that decision makers
can be better advised when formulating policy as to its effect on the rights of the child."
(UK dependent territory: Hong Kong IRCO,
Add.63, paras. 13 and 20)

To Myanmar, in a comment on budgetary issues,
"... the Committee suggests that the 'child
impact' of decisions taken by the authorities
be assessed on an ongoing basis." (Myanmar
IRCO, Add.69, para. 32)

In comments on New Zealand's Initial Report,

"The Committee notes with interest the
recently established procedure of the State
Party to have an evaluation of the impact on
children of all proposed legislation affecting
children that is submitted to the Cabinet. It

welcomes such a child impact analysis as part of the legislative process." *(New Zealand IRCO, Add.71, para. 4)*

Monitoring of implementation

The Committee has frequently noted that without sufficient data collection, including disaggregated data, it is impossible to assess the extent to which the Convention has been implemented.

In its *Guidelines for Periodic Reports* the Committee asks for detailed statistical and other information under most articles (see box, page 68).

In its comments to Colombia:

"The Committee expresses its concern at the insufficient steps taken to gather relevant information on the implementation of the Convention as well as to ensure an effective monitoring system at the national, regional and local levels."

The Committee went on to recommend

"... that reliable quantitative and qualitative information be systematically collected and analyzed to evaluate progress in the realization of the rights of the child and to monitor closely the situation of marginalized children, including those belonging to the poorest sectors of society and to indigenous groups." (Colombia IRCO, Add.30, paras. 10 and 15)

To Poland, the Committee proposed

"that the State Party undertake to gather all the necessary information on the situation of children in the various areas covered by the Convention, including in relation to those children belonging to the most vulnerable groups. It also suggests that a multidisciplinary monitoring system be established to assess the progress achieved and the difficulties encountered in the realization of the rights recognized by the Convention at the central, regional and local levels, and in particular to monitor regularly the effects of economic change on children. Such a monitoring system should enable the State Party to shape appropriate policies and to combat prevailing disparities and traditional prejudices." (Poland IRCO, Add.31, para. 23)

Similar recommendations are contained in many Concluding Observations. For example:

"The Committee further recommends that the Government of Spain gather all the necessary information in order to have an overall view of the situation in the country and to ensure a comprehensive and multidisciplinary evaluation of progress and difficulties in implementing the Convention. This evaluation should enable it to shape appropriate policies to combat disparities and lasting prejudices." (Spain IRCO, Add.28, para. 13)

"Measures should be taken to strengthen the monitoring mechanisms of the Convention. Qualitative and quantitative data and indicators for evaluating the progress and efficiency of programmes aiming at the full enjoyment of children's rights should be developed...." (Philippines IRCO, Add.29, para. 20)

"...The establishment of a comprehensive network for the collection of data covering all areas of the Convention and taking into account all groups of children within Canadian jurisdiction is recommended." (Canada IRCO, Add.37, para. 20. See also Belgium IRCO, Add.38, para. 14; Tunisia IRCO, Add.39, para. 12; Senegal IRCO, Add.44, para. 10; China IRCO, Add.56, para. 28; Nepal IRCO, Add.57, para. 29; Guatemala IRCO, Add.58, para. 27; Mauritius IRCO, Add.64, para. 24; New Zealand IRCO, Add.71, para. 25)

In several cases, the Committee has proposed that States should seek international cooperation in developing monitoring (for example, to Guatemala, Mauritius etc.; see references above).

In observations concerning Hong Kong, the Committee emphasized that statistics should be collected in accordance with the definition of the child in article 1, for all up to the age of 18:

"... the Committee would like to suggest that the collection and analysis of statistical data by age group be guided by the provisions of article 1 of the Convention..." (UK dependent territory: Hong Kong IRCO, Add.63, para. 22).

The Committee has also proposed independent studies to aid monitoring of implementation, for example in relation to Denmark, where it proposed that the newly-established Children's Council should carry out such studies. (Denmark IRCO, Add.33, para. 20)

Participation of civil society

The Committee has stressed that coordination and action to implement the Convention should extend beyond government to all segments of society. Also, in the Introduction to its *Guidelines for Periodic Reports*, it emphasizes that the process of preparing a report "should encourage and facilitate popular participation and public scrutiny of government policies" (para. 3). It has stressed the importance of the involvement of non-governmental organizations (NGOs) and civil society, and in particular the direct involvement of children and young people (see also article 12, page 154):

"To enhance the effective implementation of the Convention, the Committee suggests that the State Party consider closer coordination with non-governmental organizations at the policy-making level..." (Sweden IRCO, Add.2, para. 10)

Statistical information requested by the Committee on the Rights of the Child in its *Guidelines for Periodic Reports*

In paragraph 7 of the introduction to the *Guidelines for Periodic Reports*, the Committee on the Rights of the Child asks that reports should be accompanied by "detailed statistical information, indicators referred to therein and relevant research... Quantitative information should indicate variations between various areas of the country and within areas and between groups of children and include:

- changes in the status of children;
- variations by age, gender, region, rural/urban area, and social and ethnic group;
- changes in community systems serving children;
- changes in budget allocations and expenditure for sectors serving children;
- changes in the extent of international cooperation received or contributed for the realization of children's rights."

In the *Guidelines*, the Committee asks for further statistical information in relation to the implementation of various articles, as listed below:

Article 2: Measures taken to collect disaggregated data on the most disadvantaged groups of children including: children belonging to minorities or indigenous communities; disabled children; children born out of wedlock; children who are non-nationals; migrants, displaced, refugees or asylum-seekers; and children who are living and/or working on the streets (paras. 27 and 29).

Article 4 (budget): Proportion of budget devoted to social expenditures for children, including health, welfare and education, at the central, regional and local levels, and where appropriate at the federal and provincial levels;

budget trends over period covered by report;

arrangements for budgetary analysis enabling the amount and proportion spent on children to be clearly identified;

measures taken to ensure that disparities between different regions and groups of children are bridged in relation to the provision of social services [implies budgetary analysis];

measures taken to ensure that children, particularly those belonging to the most disadvantaged groups, are protected against the adverse effects of economic policies, including the reduction of budgetary allocations to the social sector;

proportion of international aid at the multilateral and bilateral levels allocated to programmes for children and the promotion of their rights and, where appropriate, the assistance received from regional and international financial institutions;

the percentage of international cooperation contributed during the reporting period in the total government budget, as well as the percentages of such cooperation respectively allocated to the health, education, social and other sectors (paras. 20 and 21).

Article 6: Disaggregated data for deaths and causes of deaths of children, including incidence of suicide (para. 41).

Article 9: Relevant disaggregated information, *inter alia*, in relation to situations of detention, imprisonment, exile, deportation or death causing separation of child from parents (para. 72).

Article 10: Disaggregated information on applications for family reunification and how they are dealt with (para. 74).

Article 11: Data on children concerned in illicit transfer and non-return of children abroad, including by gender, age, national origin, place of residence, family status and relationship with perpetrator of illicit transfer (para. 78).

Article 18(1) and (2): Relevant disaggregated information (for example by gender, age, region, rural/urban areas and social and ethnic origin) on children who have benefited from measures adopted to assist parents/guardians in child-rearing, and on institutions, facilities and services developed for the care of children; also information on resources allocated to them (para. 67).

Article 18(3): Disaggregated information on coverage in relation to services and facilities provided for working parents and financial implications, and on children benefiting from such measures, including by age, gender and national, social and ethnic origin (para. 101).

Article 19: Relevant data on children suffering all forms of violence, abuse, neglect, maltreatment or exploitation including within the family, in institutional or other care (welfare, educational, penal), disaggregated by age, gender, family situation, rural/urban, social and ethnic origin (para. 88; numbers of cases of violence in relation to exploitation also raised in para. 159).

Article 20: Relevant disaggregated data on children deprived of their family environment, including by nature of alternative care provided (para. 81).

Article 21: Relevant disaggregated data on children involved in intercountry adoption, including by age, gender, status of the child, situation of the child's family of origin and of adoption, as well as country of origin and of adoption (para. 85).

Article 22: Disaggregated data on asylum-seeking and refugee children, including numbers going to school and covered by health services, and trained staff handling them (para. 120).

Article 23: System for identification and tracking disabled children; children covered, including by type of disability, the coverage of the assistance provided, programmes and services made available, including in the fields of education, training, care, rehabilitation, employment and recreation, including financial and other resources allocated, data to be disaggregated *inter alia* by gender, age, rural/urban area, and social and ethnic origin (para. 92).

Article 24: Infant and child mortality, including average rates and providing disaggregated data, including by gender, age, region, rural/urban area, ethnic and social origin;

distribution of both general and primary healthcare services in rural and urban areas and balance between preventive and curative health care;

information on children having access to and benefiting from medical assistance and health care, as well as persisting gaps, by gender, age, ethnic and social origin;

disaggregated data on: immunization rates; proportion of children with low birthweight; most common diseases and impact on children; proportion of child population affected by malnutrition (chronic and severe) and lack of clean drinking water; children provided with adequate nutritious food; risks from environmental pollution;

coverage of appropriate pre- and post-natal health care of mothers, rate of mortality and main causes (average and disaggregated *inter alia* by age, gender, region, urban/rural area, social and ethnic origin);

proportion of pregnant women who have access to and benefit from pre- and post-natal health care, trained personnel and hospital care and delivery;

disaggregated data on health education for all segments of society, including, in particular, parents and children;

disaggregated data on the incidence of pregnancy among children, including by age, region, rural/urban area, and social and ethnic origin (para. 95).

prevalence of HIV/AIDS, including incidence among general population and children, coverage of treatment and management of HIV infection and AIDS, in urban and rural areas (para. 96).

assessment of traditional practices prejudicial to children's rights (para. 97).

Article 25: Relevant data on periodic reviews of placement and treatment of children, including in situations of abandonment, disability, asylum-seeking and refugees, including unaccompanied children, and in situations of conflict with the law; disaggregated *inter alia* by age, gender, national, ethnic and social origin, family situation and place of residence, as well as by duration of placement and frequency of its review (para. 87).

Article 26: Disaggregated information concerning coverage and financial implications of children's right to social security, including incidence by age, gender, number of children per family, civil status of the parents, the situation of single parents, and the relationship of social security to unemployment (para. 100).

Article 27(1) - (3): Incidence of "adequate standard of living" among child population, including by gender, age, region, rural/urban area, social and ethnic origin, and family situation;

assistance made available to parents and others to implement right to an adequate standard of living, including budget implications, relationship to cost of living and impact on population (information to be disaggregated where relevant);

population addressed by measures for material assistance and support programmes, in particular nutrition, clothing and housing, including by gender, age, rural/urban area, social and ethnic origin, the proportion of budget allocated, the coverage ensured (para. 103).

Article 27(4): Relevant disaggregated data concerning recovery of maintenance from parents or others having financial responsibility for the child (para. 79).

Article 28: Proportion of overall budget (at the central, regional and local, and where appropriate at the federal and provincial levels) devoted to children and allocated to the various levels of education;

real cost to the family of the child's education and support provided;

measures of sufficiency of teachers, adequacy of educational facilities and accessibility to all children;

rate of illiteracy below and over 18 years, and rate of enrolment in literacy classes, including by age, gender, region, rural/urban area and social and ethnic origin;

other relevant disaggregated data on children concerned including on education outcomes;

proportion of children enrolled in primary education, and who complete primary education, as well as any relevant disaggregated data including by age, gender, region, urban/rural area, national, social and ethnic origin, service coverage and budgetary allocation;

concerning secondary education, disaggregated data on children enrolled, financial assistance provided and budget allocated;

rate of access to higher education, disaggregated by age, gender and national, social and ethnic origin;

relevant disaggregated data on availability and accessibility of educational and vocational information and guidance;

disaggregated data on drop-out rates and measures to reduce them, school attendance and retention, and children excluded from school;

disaggregated data on children who do not enjoy the right to education and circumstances in which children are temporarily or permanently excluded from school; for example disability, deprivation of liberty, pregnancy, HIV/AIDS infection (paras. 106-108).

Article 30: Relevant disaggregated data on children belonging to ethnic, religious or linguistic minorities and who are indigenous and on children affected by measures adopted to protect their rights (para. 166).

Article 31: Disaggregated data on implementation of children's rights to leisure, play, recreation, cultural activities and so on (para. 118).

Article 32: Relevant disaggregated data on children involved in child labour, including by age, gender, region, rural/urban area and social and ethnic origin, as well as on infringements observed by inspectors and sanctions applied (para. 154).

Article 33: Any relevant disaggregated data on the incidence of drug abuse among children and their involvement in illicit production and trafficking;

Relevant disaggregated data on the use by children of alcohol, tobacco and other substances that may be prejudicial to their health and may be available, with or without restriction, to adults (paras. 156 and 157).

Article 34: Relevant disaggregated data on children involved in sexual exploitation, including number of cases of commercial sexual exploitation and sexual abuse (para. 159).

Article 35: Relevant disaggregated data on children involved, including numbers of cases of sale of children, and abduction of children (paras. 162, 159).

Article 36: Relevant disaggregated data on children involved in the measures adopted to protect children from all forms of exploitation prejudicial to children's welfare (para. 164).

Article 37(b)-(d): Alternatives to deprivation of liberty, frequency with which they are used and disaggregated data on the children concerned;

disaggregated data on all children deprived of their liberty – unlawfully, arbitrarily and within the law – and on the reasons for and period of deprivation of liberty;

details of cases concerning children who have been deprived of their liberty, including the percentage of cases in which legal or other assistance has been provided, and in which the legality of the deprivation of liberty has been challenged before an appropriate authority, together with the results of such challenges (paras. 139, 141 and 145).

Article 38: Where relevant, proportion of children participating in hostilities, including by age, gender and social and ethnic origin;

proportion of children being recruited or voluntarily enlisted into armed forces, including by age, gender and social and ethnic origin;

children involved in humanitarian assistance and relief programmes;

also number of child casualties due to armed conflict, as well as the number of children displaced by armed conflict (paras. 124-127).

Article 39: Numbers of children who received physical and/or psychological treatment as a consequence of armed conflict (para. 130);

measures to promote physical and psychological recovery and social re-integration of children involved with the system of administration of juvenile justice, and disaggregated data on the children concerned (para. 150).

also on children concerned in rehabilitative measures for child victims of sexual abuse and exploitation (para. 159).

Article 40: Disaggregated data on the children alleged as, accused of or recognized as having infringed the penal law, *inter alia* by age, gender, region, rural/urban area, national, social and ethnic origin, offence and disposition made available (para. 137).

"The Committee recommends that support should be given to local and other non-governmental organizations for the mobilization of work on the rights of the child. The Committee also recommends the active participation of non-governmental organizations as well as children and youth groups in changing and influencing attitudes for the better implementation of the rights of the child." (Russian Federation IRCO, Add.4, para. 17)

"The Committee recognizes the importance of the annual meeting held between the public authorities and the non-governmental community on the anniversary of the adoption of the Convention on the Rights of the Child by the General Assembly of the United Nations. The Committee stresses the value of such a meeting in launching a fruitful dialogue between the Government and the 'civil society', as well as in ensuring a serious evaluation of the governmental policies adopted for the promotion and protection of the rights of the child." (France IRCO, Add.20, para. 5)

"The participation of children themselves in the promotion of the rights of the child is of great importance, especially at the community level." (Ukraine IRCO, Add.42, para. 21)

"The Committee welcomes the readiness of the State Party to collaborate with the non-governmental organization community,

including children's organizations, which was reflected in the drafting process of the Government's report and in the presence during the dialogue of a child representative of a non-governmental organization." (Nepal IRCO, Add.57, para. 7. See also Spain IRCO, Add.28, para. 17; Madagascar IRCO, Add.26, para. 19; Denmark IRCO, Add.33, para. 18; Portugal IRCO, Add.45, para. 11; UK dependent territory: Hong Kong IRCO, Add.63, para. 21; Panama IRCO, Add.68, para. 6)

Awareness-raising and training

The Committee has linked the obligation under article 42, to make the provisions and principles of the Convention widely known to adults and children alike, to article 4. In the overall process of awareness-raising, the Committee has emphasized the importance of incorporating the Convention in the school curriculum as well as in training for those working with and for children (for discussion, see article 42, page 564).

Accountability to Parliament

The Committee has also commended the idea of a periodic report to Parliament (see *Guidelines for Periodic Reports*, para. 18):

"The Committee also welcomes the decision taken by the Government to submit an annual report to the Parliamentary Assemblies on the implementation of the Convention and on its

The world's first children's commissioner

Norway's Initial Report describes the establishment in 1981 and the activities of the world's first Office of Commissioner for Children (or children's ombudsman). Norway has a number of national ombudsman offices: "The position of the Commissioner for Children is rather different from that of the other ombudsmen. The Commissioner for Children does not deal with complaints related to specific areas of law, but serves as spokesman for children's concerns in most aspects of society. The role of the children's ombudsman as a spokesman, and as the person responsible for safeguarding the rights of children, applies to all areas of Norwegian legislation that affect children...".

Main points of the Act and Regulations relating to the Commissioner for Children are:
"(a) The Commissioner shall be an independent spokesman for children in Norway;

(b) The Commissioner has a general mandate to observe and make efforts to improve the living conditions for children between the ages of 0 and 17;

(c) The Commissioner has the right to make his own professional priorities and determine how issues are to be dealt with;

(d) The Commissioner has the right of access to all documents in all matters affecting children that are dealt with by the public authorities. He also has the right of access to all children's institutions".

The report notes that "The only areas that are not the concern of the Commissioner are individual family conflicts and matters that are the subject of legal proceedings. The Commissioner must therefore consider all areas of society, make people aware of any developments that are harmful to children, and propose changes in order to improve the situation of children. The Commissioner must be alert to the consequences and implications of all areas of Norwegian legislation and regulations which may affect children. The Commissioner for Children has no powers of decision, nor does he or she have the right to rescind the decisions of other authorities. In consequence the main instruments at the disposal of the Commissioner are information, acting as spokesman for children, and issuing well-documented statements..." (Norway IR, paras. 34-41)

policies in relation to the situation of children in the world. This procedure will contribute to emphasizing the importance of the principle of the best interests of the child, which is a primary consideration to be taken into account in all actions concerning children, including those undertaken by legislative bodies." (France IRCO, Add.20, para. 6)

In addition, it has consistently proposed that there should be parliamentary debate on States' reports under the Convention and on the Committee's Concluding Observations (see *Guidelines for Periodic Reports*, para. 23, and article 44(6), page 582).

Independent offices to promote and advocate children's rights

The Committee has commended the establishment of independent offices for children – a children's ombudsman, commission or commissioner. Thus in its comments on Norway, it noted

"that Norway was the first country in the world to establish an ombudsman working for the benefit of children. It also notes the spirit of dialogue existing between the Government, the municipalities and the ombudsman and civil society including the non-governmental community." (Norway IRCO, Add.23, para. 3)

The Committee also welcomed the creation by the Government of Denmark of the National Council for Children's Rights, set up for a trial period with a similar role *(Denmark IRCO, Add.33, para. 6)*. In its report on Nicaragua, the Committee stated it

"would also like to express the hope that the Office of an Ombudsman for Children be created with a view to promoting and protecting the rights of the child." (Nicaragua IRCO, Add.36, para. 29)

In its Concluding Observations on Argentina, the Committee proposed monitoring,

"including through an ombudsman" (Argentina IRCO, Add.35, para. 15).

And to Portugal, Guatemala and Bulgaria:
"The Committee welcomes the establishment of an ombudsperson (Proveda de Justiça) and the creation in the ombudsperson's office of a focal point on children's rights." (Portugal IRCO, Add.45, para. 6)

"... the Committee notes with satisfaction the establishment of the Office of the Human Rights Procurator and its Children's Ombudsman." (Guatemala IRCO, Add.58, para. 5)

"While encouraged by the existing national debate, the Committee is worried at the lack of an independent body to monitor observance of human rights, particularly the rights of the child....

"The Committee encourages the State Party to pursue its consideration on the establishment of an independent mechanism to monitor observance of children's rights, such as an Ombudsperson or a National Commission for Children's Rights." (Bulgaria IRCO, Add.66, paras. 10 and 23)

The Committee welcomed the establishment of a general ombudsman in Panama but still proposed a specific post for children:

"The recent establishment of a 'People's Defender' which will monitor the enjoyment of human rights in Panama, including children's rights, is welcomed by the Committee...
"The Committee recommends that the establishment of an independent body, such as an ombudsperson, be given further consideration by the Government..." (Panama IRCO, Add.68, paras. 5 and 24)

The Committee has stressed the importance of independence from government:

"...The Committee also encourages the State Party to consider the establishment of an independent mechanism, such as an Ombudsperson or a human rights commission, to monitor the realization of the rights of the child and to deal with individual complaints relating thereto." (Nepal IRCO, Add.57, para. 29. See also UK dependent territory: Hong Kong IRCO, Add.63, para. 20; Mauritius IRCO, Add.64, para. 25)

And the Committee proposed to New Zealand:
"... that the office of Commissioner for Children be strengthened and that further consideration be given to measures which would give the office increased independence and make it accountable directly to Parliament." (New Zealand IRCO, Add.71, para. 24)

International cooperation for implementation

In its comments on general measures of implementation, the Committee has urged many countries to seek and use international cooperation and technical assistance. It has also encouraged donor countries to ensure that their aid programmes follow the lines of the Convention and establish a clear priority for children. Its *Guidelines for Periodic Reports* asks for information on "the extent to which international cooperation relevant to the State party is designed to foster implementation of the Convention, including economic, social and cultural rights of children." The *Guidelines* requires from donor countries identification of the amount of international aid as a proportion of the total government budget and details of the allocation to health, education and other sectors.

To some States, the Committee has proposed international assistance. For example:

"...To ensure the full implementation of article 4, the Committee recommends that considera- tion be given to the provision of international assistance within the general framework of the Convention." (Guatemala IRCO, Add.58, para. 31)

International assistance should be linked to implementation by both donors and recipients:
"...The Committee is also concerned that the State Party's international cooperation policies do not yet fully give priority to children." (Portugal IRCO, Add.45, para. 12)

"International cooperation resources should be channelled towards the realization of children's rights and effort should be pursued to reduce the negative impact of foreign debt and debt servicing on children." (Nepal IRCO, Add.57, para. 30)

"... Moreover, in the light of article 4 of the Convention, international assistance provided to Panama should aim at the promotion of children's rights." (Panama IRCO, Add.68, para. 28)

The 20:20 initiative (see box) has been designed by leading United Nations agencies to promote a collaborative approach to achieving basic human development goals worldwide.

Some 40 governments along with NGOs, United Nations agencies, the World Bank and the International Monetary Fund (IMF) met in Oslo in 1996 to discuss the future of the 20:20 initiative. Although aid to developing countries has reached its lowest level since comparable statistics began in 1951, there are indications that donor and developing countries are devoting increased resources to securing the human development services outlined in 20:20.

The 20:20 initiative – a global compact for human development

A mere $30 billion to $40 billion a year for 10 years is the estimated cost of achieving the follow- ing human development targets worldwide:
- Universal primary education (for girls as well as boys);
- Halving adult illiteracy rates (equalizing the female rate with the male);
- Primary health care for all (including the immunization of children);
- Eliminating severe malnutrition;
- Halving moderate malnutrition rates;
- Providing family planning services for all willing couples;
- Safe drinking water and sanitation for all;
- Credit for all (to ensure self-employment opportunities).

"Developing countries devote on average only 13 per cent of their national budgets ($57 billion a year) to basic human development concerns. They have considerable scope for changing their budget priorities by reducing their military spending (around $125 billion a year), by privatizing their loss-making public enterprises and by giving up some low-priority development projects. It is proposed that they earmark at least 20 per cent of their budgets ($88 billion a year) to human priority concerns. The scope for restructuring will differ from one country to another: the target of 20 per cent only suggests an average pattern.

"Donor countries also have considerable scope for changing the allocation priorities in their aid budgets in the post-cold-war era. On average, bilateral donors allocate only 7 per cent of their aid to the various human priority concerns (basic education, primary health care, mass-coverage water supply systems and family planning services). The problem here is not so much the proportion of aid they give to the social sector (16 per cent on average) as the distribution within the social sec- tor. Less than one-fifth of education aid goes to primary education, and a similar proportion of aid for water supply and sanitation is earmarked for rural areas, with very little for low-cost mass- coverage programmes. If donors also lift their aid allocation for human priority goals to 20 per cent, this would provide $12 billion a year rather than the current $4 billion. Again, the 20 per cent tar- get is an average with some donors having greater scope for restructuring than others.

"Such a 20:20 compact for human development would be based on a sharing of responsibility. Three-fourths of the contributions would come from the developing countries and one-fourth from the donors. No new money is required, because the compact is based on restructuring existing bud- get priorities..."

(From the *Human Development Report 1994*, United Nations Development Programme (UNDP), Oxford University Press, p. 7.)

Implementation Checklist

article 4

● General measures of implementation

Article 4 sets on States Parties overall obligations to implement all the rights in the Convention.

☐ Has there been a comprehensive review to consider what measures are appropriate for implementation of the Convention?

☐ Has there been a comprehensive review of all legislation, including any customary, regional or local law in the State, to ensure compatibility with the Convention?

Are the general principles identified by the Committee reflected in legislation:

☐ Article 2: all rights to be recognized for each child in jurisdiction without discrimination on any ground?

☐ Article 3(1): the best interests of the child to be a primary consideration in all actions concerning children?

☐ Article 6: right to life and maximum possible survival and development?

☐ Article 12: respect for the child's views in all matters affecting the child; opportunity to be heard in any judicial or administrative proceedings affecting the child?

☐ Is it possible to invoke these principles before the courts?

☐ Is the Convention incorporated or self-executing in national law?

☐ Does the Convention take precedence over domestic law when there is a conflict?

☐ Does the Constitution reflect the principles of the Convention, with particular reference to children?

☐ Has a consolidated law on the rights of the child been developed?

☐ Is there a comprehensive national strategy for implementation of the Convention?

☐ Where there is a National Plan or Programme of Action for children, has implementation of all aspects of the Convention been integrated into it?

Has one (or more) permanent mechanism(s) of government been established

    ☐ to ensure appropriate coordination of policy?

    ☐ between provinces/regions, etc.?

    ☐ between central government departments?

    ☐ between central and local government?

    ☐ between economic and social policies?

    ☐ to ensure effective evaluation of policy relating to children?

    ☐ to ensure effective monitoring of implementation?

☐ Are such mechanisms directly linked to the institutions of governments that determine overall policy and budgets in the State?

☐ Is the principle that the best interests of the child should be a primary consideration formally adopted at all levels of policy-making and budgeting?

Is the proportion of the overall budget devoted to social expenditure adequate

    ☐ nationally?

    ☐ regionally/at provincial level?

    ☐ locally?

Is the proportion of social expenditure devoted to children adequate

- ☐ nationally?
- ☐ regionally/at provincial level?
- ☐ locally?

Are permanent arrangements established for budgetary analysis at national and other levels of government to ascertain

- ☐ the proportion of overall budgets devoted to children?
- ☐ any disparities between regions, rural/urban, particular groups of children?
- ☐ the effects of structural readjustment, economic reforms and changes on
  - ☐ all children?
  - ☐ on the most disadvantaged groups of children?
- ☐ the proportion and amount received/given in relation to international cooperation to promote the rights of the child, and allocated to different sectors?

☐ Do the arrangements for monitoring ensure a comprehensive, multidisciplinary assessment of the situation of all children in relation to implementation of the Convention?

☐ Is sufficient disaggregated data collected to enable evaluation of the implementation of the non-discrimination principle?

☐ Are there arrangements to ensure a child impact analysis during policy formulation and decision-making at all levels of government?

☐ Is there a regular report to Parliament on implementation of the Convention?

☐ Are parliamentary mechanisms established to ensure appropriate scrutiny and debate of matters relating to implementation?

☐ Is civil society involved in the process of implementation at all levels, including in particular

- ☐ appropriate non-governmental organizations (NGOs)?
- ☐ children themselves?

☐ Is there a permanent mechanism for consulting on matters relating to implementation with appropriate NGOs and with children themselves?

☐ Has an independent office to promote the rights of children – ombudsman, commissioner – been established?

- ☐ Is its independence from government assured?
- ☐ Does it have appropriate legislative powers, e.g. of investigation?

Reminder : **The Convention is indivisible and its articles are interdependent. Article 4 requires States Parties to take all appropriate legislative, administrative and other measures to implement the rights in the Convention. Thus it relates to all other articles.**

Parental guidance and the child's evolving capacities

article 5

Text of Article 5

States Parties shall respect the responsibilities, rights and duties of parents or, where applicable, the members of the extended family or community as provided for by local custom, legal guardians or other persons legally responsible for the child, to provide, in a manner consistent with the evolving capacities of the child, appropriate direction and guidance in the exercise by the child of the rights recognized in the present Convention.

Article 5, together with article 18 in particular, provides a framework for the relationship between the child, his or her parents and family, and the State. The article provides the Convention on the Rights of the Child with a flexible definition of "family" and introduces to the Convention two vital concepts: parental "responsibilities" and the "evolving capacities" of the child. The article also signals clearly that the Convention regards the child as the active subject of rights, emphasizing the exercise "by the child" of his or her rights.

Summary

In no sense is the Convention "anti-family", nor does it pit children against their parents. On the contrary, the Preamble upholds the family as "the fundamental group of society and the natural environment for the growth and well-being of all its members and particularly children". Several articles emphasize the primary responsibility of parents and place strict limits on State intervention and any separation of children from their parents (articles 3(2), 7, 9, 10, 18); one of the aims for education is the development of respect for the child's parents (article 29). ■

"States Parties shall respect the responsibilities, rights and duties…"

Article 5 introduces to the Convention the concept of parents' and others' "responsibilities" for their children, linking them to parental rights and duties, which are needed to fulfil responsibilities. Article 18 expands on the concept of parental responsibilities (see page 227). In it, States

Parties are required to "use their best endeavours" to ensure recognition of the principle that both parents have common responsibilities for the upbringing and development of the child: "Parents or, as the case may be, legal guardians, have the primary responsibility for the upbringing and development of the child. The best interests of the child will be their basic concern." Beyond this, the Convention does not specifically define "parental responsibilities". But as is the case with the definition of the best interests of the child, the content of the whole Convention is relevant. Parents have responsibilities, in the terms of article 5, to appropriately support "the exercise by the child of the rights recognized in the present Convention".

The *Guidelines for Periodic Reports* seeks information on "the consideration given by law to parental responsibility, including the recognition of the common responsibilities of both parents in the upbringing and development of the child and, that the best interests of the child will be their basic concern. Also indicate how the principles of non-discrimination, respect for the views of the child and the development of the child to the maximum extent, as provided for by the Convention, are taken into account." (para. 65)

The implication is that the concept of parental responsibilities should be reflected and defined in the law, using the framework of the Convention.

During discussion of Belgium's Initial Report, a Committee member pointed out that "article 19 of the Convention encouraged States Parties to adopt appropriate measures to protect children from all forms of violence and abuse. The presentation of evidence against parents and guardians was extremely difficult. Several countries had accordingly begun to define parental responsibility and authority in their civil legislation, including both concepts of dialogue, negotiation and the participation of children in family life with the aim of trying to avert ill-treatment entirely. The Committee believed that the response to abuse should go beyond criminal sanction." (Belgium SR.224, para. 38)

In response, a representative of Belgium said that article 371 of the Civil Code would very shortly be amended: "The old article stated that a child of any age owed honour and respect to his parents. The new article, however, stipulated that a child and his father and mother owed each other mutual respect, whatever their age. In legal terms, the word 'mutual' could imply that certain types of conduct by a parent towards his child were not in conformity with the wording used." (Belgium SR.224, para. 64)

The Committee noted with approval the relevant legislative developments:

"... The Committee particularly welcomes the adoption of a comprehensive legal framework to ensure full conformity with the Convention and ... the revision of article 371 of the Civil Code, which will now provide for 'mutual respect between parents and children'..." (Belgium IRCO, Add.38, para. 5)

The Convention thus challenges concepts that parents have absolute rights over their children, which the Committee has noted are traditional in many societies but already changing to some degree in most. The rights and the duties that parents have derive from their responsibilities for the welfare of the child, that is to act in the best interests of the child:

"The Committee further notes that insufficient attention has been paid to the principle of the best interests of the child both in legislation and practice, as well as to the respect for the views of the child in school, social and family life. In this regard, it is noted that, as recognized by the State Party, the civil rights and freedoms of the child are to be exercised subject to parental consent or discipline, thus raising doubts as to the compatibility of this practice with the Convention, notably articles 5 and 12...

"Appropriate measures should also be adopted by the State Party with a view to ensuring respect for the views of the child in family, school and social life and to promoting the exercise of the rights by the child in a manner consistent with his or her evolving capacities." (Zimbabwe IRCO, Add.55, paras. 16 and 30)

A particular example of the need for State respect for the responsibilities, rights and duties of parents is in relation to children involved with the system of juvenile justice. The United Nations Standard Minimum Rules for the Administration of Juvenile Justice, the "Beijing Rules", requires that parents must be notified about the apprehension of a juvenile and that the child has the right to have his or her parent/guardian present (a right qualified in article 40 of the Convention by the "best interests" principle) and, generally, the right to participate in the proceedings (rules 7(1), 10(1) and 15(2)). Rule 18(2) requires that "No juvenile shall be removed from parental supervision, whether partly or entirely, unless the circumstances of her or his case make this necessary."

"... of parents or, where applicable, the members of the extended family or community as provided for by local custom, legal guardians or other persons legally responsible for the child, ..."

The broad definition of family in the Convention on the Rights of the Child reflects the wide variety of kinship and community arrangements within which children are brought up around the world. The importance of the family is emphasized in the Preamble to the Convention: "... the family, as the fundamental group of society and the natural environment for the growth and well-being of all its members and particularly children, should be afforded the necessary protection and assistance so that it can fully assume its responsibilities within the community", and "... the child, for the full and harmonious development of his or her personality, should grow up in a family environment, in an atmosphere of happiness, love and understanding".

Article 5 acknowledges the extended family, referring not only to parents and others legally responsible but also to the extended family or community where they are recognized by local custom.

The *Guidelines for Periodic Reports* asks for information on "family structures within the society".

In the outline for its General Discussion on "The role of the family in the promotion of the rights of the child", the Committee on the Rights of the Child stated:

"The basic institution in society for the survival, protection and development of the child is the family. When considering the family environment, the Convention reflects different family structures arising from various cultural patterns and emerging familial relationships. In this regard, the Convention refers to the extended family and the community and applies in situations of nuclear family, separated parents, single-parent family, common-law family and adoptive family. Such situations deserve to be studied in the framework of the rights of the child within the family. Relevant measures and remedies have to be identified to protect the integrity of the family (see, in particular, arts. 5, 18 and 19), and to ensure appropriate assistance in the upbringing and development of children." (Report on the fifth session, January 1994, CRC/C/24, Annex V, p. 63)

The International Covenant on Civil and Political Rights upholds, in article 23, the family as "the natural and fundamental group unit of society... entitled to protection by society and the State" and sets out, in article 24, the child's right to "such measures of protection as are required by his status as a minor, on the part of his family, society and the State". In two General Comments in 1989 and 1990, the Human Rights Committee emphasizes the flexible definition of the family, which "is interpreted broadly to include all persons composing it in the society of the State Party concerned" (Human Rights Committee, General Comment 17, HRI/GEN/1/Rev.2, p. 25).

And in General Comment 19 of the Human Rights Committee: "The Committee notes that the concept of the family may differ in some respects from State to State, and even from region to region within a State, and that it is therefore not possible to give the concept a standard definition. However, the Committee emphasizes that, when a group of persons is regarded as a family under the legislation and practice of a State, it must be given the protection referred to in article 23. Consequently, States Parties should report on how the concept and the scope of the family is construed or defined in their own society and legal system. Where diverse concepts of the family, 'nuclear' and 'extended', exist within a State, this should be indicated with an explanation of the degree of protection afforded to each. In view of the existence of various forms of family, such as unmarried couples and their children or single parents and their children, States Parties should also indicate whether and to what extent such types of family and their members are recognized and protected by domestic law and practice." (Human Rights Committee, General Comment 19, HRI/GEN/1/Rev.2, p. 29)

"... to provide, in a manner consistent with the evolving capacities of the child, appropriate direction and guidance in the exercise by the child of the rights recognized in the present Convention"

The wording here emphasizes the child as the subject of the rights recognized in the Convention, referring to the exercise "by the child" of these rights.

When it ratified the Convention on the Rights of the Child, the Holy See made a reservation "... That it interprets the articles of the Convention in a way which safeguards the primary and inalienable rights of parents, in particular in so far as these rights concern education (arts. 13 and 28), religion (art. 14), association with others (art. 15) and privacy (art. 16)", (CRC/C/2/Rev.5, p. 20).

In its Concluding Observations, the Committee expressed concern about the reservation,

"... in particular with respect to the full recognition of the child as a subject of rights."

The Committee went on to recommend

"... that the position of the Holy See with regard to the relationship between articles 5 and 12 of the Convention be clarified. In this respect, it wishes to recall its view that the rights and prerogatives of the parents may not undermine the rights of the child as recognized by the Convention, especially the

right of the child to express his or her own views and that his or her views be given due weight." (Holy See IRCO, Add.46, paras. 7 and 13)

Some other reservations and declarations have underlined parental authority. For example, the Republic of Kiribati stated that it "considers that a child's rights as defined in the Convention, in particular the rights defined in articles 12-16 shall be exercised with respect for parental authority, in accordance with the I-Kiribati customs and traditions regarding the place of the child within and outside the family". Similarly, a declaration from Poland stated that such rights "shall be exercised with respect for parental authority, in accordance with Polish customs and traditions regarding the place of the child within and outside the family".

Singapore made a wider reservation, that the child's rights and in particular those in articles 12 to 17 "shall in accordance with articles 3 and 5 be exercised with respect for the authority of parents, schools and other persons who are entrusted with the care of the child and in the best interests of the child and in accordance with the customs, values and religions of Singapore's multiracial and multi-religious society regarding the place of the child within and outside the family." (CRC/C/2/Rev.5, pp. 23, 29 and 30)

The Committee has frequently expressed concern where countries do not appear to have fully accepted the concept of the child as an active subject of rights, relating this to article 5 and also to articles 12-16:

"The national legislation and practice should take into full consideration, in the light of article 5 of the Convention, the capacity of the child to exercise his or her rights, namely in the field of citizenship." (Mexico IRCO, Add.13, para. 8)

"... the Committee notes that an understanding of children as a subject of rights does not appear to be fully reflected in legislative and other measures in the State Party..." (Nicaragua IRCO, Add.36, para. 9)

"The Committee wishes to emphasize that the Convention provides for the protection and care of children, and in particular for the recognition of the child as the subject of his or her own rights..." (Iceland IRCO, Add.50, para. 13)

"...It is important that awareness be developed of the child as a subject of rights and not only as a recipient of protection..." (China IRCO, Add.56, para. 33)

The Committee has consistently stressed this view of the child during its examination of States Parties' reports. And it has strongly emphasized that upholding the rights of the child within the family is not exercised at the expense of others'

rights, in particular those of parents, but, on the contrary, strengthens the rights of the entire family. Thus, a Committee member said during discussions with Burkina Faso: "... it was important, in striving to implement the Convention's provisions, to promote the true spirit of that instrument to the effect that it was not a question of seeking 'child power' but of showing that upholding the rights of the child strengthened the rights of the entire family, and that, with regard to parenthood, the emphasis should not be on authority but on responsibility." Another member agreed that "it was wrong to interpret the assertion of children's rights as in conflict with those of parents; the rights of the child and of the family went hand in hand" (Burkina Faso SR.136, paras. 51 and 53).

On the same subject, the *Manual on Human Rights Reporting,* 1997 states: "With the Convention, children's rights are given autonomy – not with the intention of affirming them in opposition to the rights of adults or as an alternative to the rights of parents, but in order to bring into the scene a new dimension: the consideration of the perspective of the child within the framework of the essential value of the family. The child is therefore recognized in his or her fundamental dignity and individuality, with the right to be different and diverge in his or her assessment of reality." (*Manual*, p. 445)

The Committee sees the family as crucial to the realization of the child's civil rights. In the outline for its General Discussion on the role of the family in the promotion of the rights of the child, it stated:

"The civil rights of the child begin within the family... The family is an essential agent for creating awareness and preservation of human rights, and respect for human values, cultural identity and heritage, and other civilizations. There is a need to consider appropriate ways of ensuring balance between parental authority and the realization of the rights of the child, including the right to freedom of expression." (Report on the fifth session, January 1994, CRC/C/24, Annex V, p. 63)

At the end of the General Discussion, the Committee reached some preliminary conclusions:

"Traditionally, the child has been seen as a dependent, invisible and passive family member. Only recently has he or she become 'seen' and, furthermore, the movement is growing to give him or her the space to be heard and respected. Dialogue, negotiation, participation have come to the forefront of common action for children.

"The family becomes in turn the ideal framework for the first stage of the democratic experience for each and all of its individual

members, including children. Is this only a dream or should it also be envisaged as a precise and challenging task?"

The Committee affirmed that the Convention is

"... the most appropriate framework in which to consider, and to ensure respect for, the fundamental rights of all family members, in their individuality. Children's rights will gain autonomy, but they will be especially meaningful in the context of the rights of parents and other members of the family to be recognized, to be respected, to be promoted. And this will be the only way to promote the status of, and respect for, the family itself." (Report on the seventh session, September - October 1994, CRC/C/34, para. 183 et seq.)

The *Manual on Human Rights Reporting,* 1997 further stresses the point: "The family is also particularly well-placed to be the first democratic reality the child experiences – a reality shaped by the values of tolerance, understanding, mutual respect and solidarity, which strengthens the

Parental guidance and evolving capacities

The Bulgarian Constitution (1991) proclaims two basic principles: "(a) the child alone exercises his or her own rights depending on his or her developing abilities, and (b) parents and other persons who by law look after the child have the right, responsibility and obligation to provide adequate guidance to the child in such cases where this does not come into conflict with the child's own competence. Thus, Bulgarian legislation entrusts parents to be the legal representatives of their minor children and to provide guidance to their adolescent children only in their best interest.... The law recognizes the competence of adolescents to conduct legal actions 'with the consent of their parents'. From the point of view of their age minors are not permitted to carry out actions of legal consequence. Their legal representatives (parents and guardians) carry out such actions on their behalf... They can, however, act on their own without needing the consent of the parents in 'carrying out ordinary minor deals for satisfying their current needs and in disposing of anything they have acquired through their own labour'... Parental consent is required for children taking jobs if they are under 15; parents, though, are not entitled to any proceeds from their children's earning..." (Bulgaria IR, paras. 93-94, 96)

child's capacity for informed participation in the decision-making process." (*Manual*, p. 446)

Article 5 makes clear that the nature of parental direction and guidance is not unlimited; it must be "appropriate", be consistent with the "evolving capacities of the child" and with the remainder of the Convention. Several States Parties made reservations upholding parental authority (see above, page 70); and others, in their Initial Reports, have referred to the "traditional" authority of parents. Article 5 stresses that parental authority is far from unlimited, and article 18 emphasizes that the child's best interests will be the parents' "basic concern".

In its Initial Report, the United Kingdom suggests that article 19 of the Convention has to be read in conjunction with article 5 and that "appropriate direction and guidance" of the child "include the administration, by the parent, of reasonable and moderate physical chastisement to a child" (UK IR, para. 335). In discussion with United Kingdom Government representatives, a Committee member stated: "There was no place for corporal punishment within the margin of discretion accorded in article 5 to parents in the exercise of their responsibilities. Other countries had found it helpful to incorporate a provision to that effect in their civil law..." (UK SR.205, para. 72)

Similarly, a Committee member noted during discussion of Senegal's Initial Report: "The Committee recognized the existence of traditional attitudes and practices, but firmly believed that those that went against the interests of the child should be abolished. The belief that to spare the rod was to spoil the child was one such attitude: it was preferable to provide guidance than to inflict corporal punishment." (Senegal SR.248, para. 73)

Thus, when reading article 5 in conjunction with article 19, the Committee is clear that parental "guidance" must not take the form of violent or humiliating discipline, as the child must be protected from "all forms of physical or mental violence" while in the care of parents and others. The Committee has consistently upheld the view that corporal punishment is not compatible with the Convention and has recommended its prohibition, including within the family (see article 19, page 242).

Using the concept of "evolving capacities" has avoided the need for the Convention to set arbitrary age limits or definitions of maturity tied to particular issues. The "evolving capacities" of the child is one of the Convention's key concepts – an acknowledgement that children's development towards independent adulthood must be respected and promoted throughout childhood. It is linked to article 12's requirement that the views of children should be given "due weight in accordance with the age and maturity of the child". The concept is repeated in article 14: parents and legal guardians may provide direction to the child, in relation to the child's right to freedom of thought, conscience and religion, in a manner consistent with his or her evolving capacities.

Article 1 defines "child" as every human being below the age of 18 or below the age of majority if achieved earlier (see page 1). At the same time article 5 emphasizes the path to maturity, which must come from increasing exercise of autonomy. Much of the information sought by the Committee in its *Guidelines for Periodic Reports* in relation to article 1 (definition of a child) on any "minimum legal ages" set for various purposes relates to the recognition of the child's growing autonomy and independent exercise of rights: for example legal and medical counselling without parental consent; medical treatment or surgery without parental consent; sexual consent; giving testimony in court; participating in administrative and judicial proceedings, creating and joining associations and so on (see article 1, page 5, for further discussion).

In many countries, children acquire certain rights of self-determination well before the age of majority; they often gain full adult rights on marriage, which in some States is permitted at the age of 14 or 15. In a few countries the concept of "evolving capacities" is further reflected by a general provision in legislation that once children acquire sufficient maturity or understanding, they may make decisions for themselves when there is no specific limitation on doing so set down in the law.

The *Manual on Human Rights Reporting,* 1997 links the concept of "evolving capacities" with articles 12 and 13. Parents are expected to provide appropriate direction and guidance to the child: "But in this endeavour they are required to act in a manner that takes into consideration the evolving capacities of the child, his or her age and maturity. In the light of article 12, a system of shared, positive and responsible dialogue should thus prevail. In fact, parents are particularly well placed to build the capacity of children to intervene in a growing manner in the different stages of decision, to prepare them for responsible life in a free society, informing them, giving the necessary guidance and direction, while assuring children the right to express views freely and to give those views due weight (articles 12 and 13).

Children's opinions will thus be taken into account, although not necessarily endorsed, and children will be given the possibility of understanding the reasons for a different decision being taken. Children will become active partners, with appropriate skills to participate, rather than a passive reflection of parents' wishes." (*Manual*, p. 446)

Preparation for parenthood

As indicated above, the Committee has noted that the traditional view of the child as a "dependent, invisible and passive" member of the family persists in some States. The Committee has highlighted the need to prepare parents for their responsibilities. The *Guidelines for Periodic Reports* seeks information on parenting education programmes and on counselling for parents, and how knowledge about child development and the evolving capacities of the child are conveyed to parents and others responsible for children. In addition, the *Guidelines* requests information on any evaluation of the effectiveness of such educational measures (for further discussion, see article 18, page 228).

The Committee has emphasized the need to prepare parents adequately for their responsibilities (see further comments under article 18, page 228):

"The Committee stresses the need for greater efforts in developing family education and awareness of the common parental responsibilities of both parents in the light of article 18 of the Convention..." (Jamaica IRCO, Add.32, para. 24)

There exists a growing recognition of the importance of early child development within the family for the prevention of violence and other forms of crime, both in childhood and later life. This recognition provides further motivation for developing comprehensive support and education programmes for parenting and preparation for parenthood. For example, the United Nations Guidelines for the Prevention of Juvenile Delinquency, the "Riyadh Guidelines", proposes: "Measures should be taken and programmes developed to provide families with the opportunity to learn about parental roles and obligations as regards child development and child care, promoting positive parent-child relationships, sensitizing parents to the problems of children and young persons and encouraging their involvement in family and community-based activities" (para. 16).

Implementation Checklist

● General measures of implementation

Have appropriate general measures of implementation been taken in relation to article 5 including

☐ identification and coordination of the responsible departments and agencies at all levels of government (article 5 will be particularly relevant to **departments concerned with family law and family support**)?

☐ identification of relevant non-governmental organizations/civil society partners?

☐ a comprehensive review to ensure that all legislation, policy and practice is compatible with the article, for all children in all parts of the jurisdiction?

☐ adoption of a strategy to secure full implementation

    ☐ which includes where necessary the identification of goals and indicators of progress?

    ☐ which does not affect any provisions which are more conducive to the rights of the child?

    ☐ which recognizes other relevant international standards?

    ☐ which involves where necessary international cooperation?

(Such measures may be part of an overall governmental strategy for implementing the Convention as a whole).

☐ budgetary analysis and allocation of necessary resources?

☐ development of mechanisms for monitoring and evaluation?

☐ making the implications of article 5 widely known to adults and children?

☐ development of appropriate training and awareness-raising (in relation to article 5, likely to include **training of all those working with and for families, and education for parenting**)?

● Specific issues in implementing article 5

☐ Does the definition of "family" for the purposes of the realization of the rights of the child correspond with the flexible definition of the Convention?

☐ Is there a detailed legal definition of parental responsibilities, duties and rights?

☐ Has such a definition been reviewed to ensure compatibility with the principles and provisions of the Convention?

☐ Does legislation ensure that direction and guidance provided by parents to their children is in conformity with the principles and provisions of the Convention?

How to use the checklists, *see page XVII*

☐ Are the evolving capacities of the child appropriately respected in the Constitution and in legislation?

☐ Is there a general principle that once a child has acquired "sufficient understanding" in relation to a particular decision on an important matter, he or she is entitled to make the decision for him/herself?

☐ Are information campaigns/education programmes on child development, the evolving capacities of children, etc. available to parents, other caregivers and children, and to those who support them?

☐ Have these campaigns/programmes been evaluated?

Reminder : **The Convention is indivisible and its articles are interdependent. Article 5 should not be considered in isolation. Its flexible definition of the family is relevant to interpretation of other articles. The article asserts the child as an active subject of rights with evolving capacities, relevant to implementation of all other rights, including in particular the child's civil and political rights.**

Particular regard should be paid to:
The general principles

Article 2: all rights to be recognized for each child in jurisdiction without discrimination on any ground
Article 3(1): the best interests of the child to be a primary consideration in all actions concerning children
Article 6: right to life and maximum possible survival and development
Article 12: respect for the child's views in all matters affecting the child; opportunity to be heard in any judicial or administrative proceedings affecting the child

Closely related articles

Articles whose implementation is related to that of article 5 include:

Article 1: definition of the child in legislation and practice must take account of the child's "evolving capacities"
Article 18: parental responsibilities and State support for parenting

Child's right to life and maximum survival and development

article 6

Text of Article 6

1. States Parties recognize that every child has the inherent right to life.

2. States Parties shall ensure to the maximum extent possible the survival and development of the child.

Summary

Article 6 is one of the articles designated by the Committee on the Rights of the Child as a general principle, guaranteeing the child the fundamental right to life, upheld as a universal human rights principle in other instruments, and to survival and development to the maximum extent possible.

The concept of "survival and development" to the maximum extent possible is crucial to the implementation of the whole Convention. The Committee on the Rights of the Child sees development as an holistic concept, and many articles of the Convention specifically refer to the goal of development. Other articles emphasize the key role of parents and the family for child development and the State's obligation to support them. Protection from violence and exploitation is also vital to maximum survival and development. It should be noted that the World Summit for Children and the World Summit for Social Development have set relevant targets and goals. ■

Extracts from
Committee on the Rights of the Child
Guidelines for Reports to be submitted by States Parties under the Convention

For full text of *Guidelines for Periodic Reports*, see Appendix 3, page 604 .

Guidelines for Initial Reports

"General Principles

Relevant information, including the principal legislative, judicial, administrative or other measures in force or foreseen, factors and difficulties encountered and progress achieved in implementing the provisions of the Convention, and implementation priorities and specific goals for the future should be provided in respect of:

> *...*

> > *(c) The right to life, survival and development (article 6);*

> *..."*

In addition, States Parties are encouraged to provide relevant information on the application of these principles in the implementation of articles listed elsewhere in these guidelines."

"Basic health and welfare

Under this section States Parties are requested to provide relevant information, including the principal legislative, judicial, administrative or other measures in force; the institutional infrastructure for implementing policy in this area, particularly monitoring strategies and mechanisms; and factors and difficulties encountered and progress achieved in implementing the relevant provisions of the Convention, in respect of:

> *(a) Survival and development (article 6, para. 2);...".*

(CRC/C/5, paras. 13-14, 19)

Guidelines for Periodic Reports

III. GENERAL PRINCIPLES

"C. The right to life, survival and development (art. 6)

Please describe specific measures taken to guarantee the child's right to life and to create an environment conducive to ensuring to the maximum extent possible the survival and development of the child, including physical, mental, spiritual, moral, psychological and social development, in a manner compatible with human dignity, and to prepare the child for an individual life in a free society.

Information should also be provided on the measures taken to ensure the registration of the deaths of children, the causes of death and, where appropriate, investigation and reporting on such deaths, as well as on the measures adopted to prevent children's suicide and monitor its incidence and to ensure the survival of children at all ages, including adolescents, and the prevention of risks to which that group may be particularly exposed (for example, sexually transmitted diseases, street violence). Please provide relevant disaggregated data, including on the number of suicides among children."

VI. BASIC HEALTH AND WELFARE

"Health and health services (art. 24)

Please indicate the measures adopted pursuant to articles 6 and 24:

> *To recognize and ensure the right of the child to the enjoyment of the highest attainable standard of health and to facilities for treatment and rehabilitation;*

> *To ensure that no child is deprived of his or her right of access to such healthcare services;*

> *To ensure respect for the general principles of the Convention, namely non-discrimination, the best interests of the child, respect for the views of the child and the right to life, and survival and development to the maximum extent possible."*

(CRC/C/58, paras. 40-41, 93. The following paragraphs of the *Guidelines for Periodic Reports* are also relevant to reporting under this article: 64, 74, 76, 80, 101, 106, 115, 118, 120, 128, 132, 138, 143, 147, 152, 159, 161, 164, 166; for full text of *Guidelines*, see Appendix 3, page 604.)

General principle to be reflected in legislation

As with the other identified general principles (articles 2, 3, and 12), the Committee on the Rights of the Child has proposed that article 6 should be reflected in domestic legislation:

"The Committee wishes to express its general concern that the State Party does not appear to have fully taken into account the provisions of the Convention, including its general principles, as reflected in its articles 2, 3, 6 and 12, in the legislative and other measures relevant to children in Paraguay." (Paraguay Prelim. Obs., Add.27, para. 7)

The inherent right to life of the child

The right to life is already upheld as a universal human rights principle in article 3 of the Universal Declaration of Human Rights: "Everyone has the right to life, liberty and security of person". Article 6 of the International Covenant on Civil and Political Rights upholds the same principle: "Every human being has the inherent right to life. This right shall be protected by law. No one shall be arbitrarily deprived of his life" (paragraph 1). The other paragraphs of the article in the Covenant place limitations on the use of the death penalty in those countries that have not abolished it (see below, page 89).

The Human Rights Committee, in a General Comment in 1982 on the right to life, upheld in article 6 of the International Covenant on Civil and Political Rights, notes that the right has too often been narrowly interpreted: "The expression 'inherent right to life' cannot properly be understood in a restrictive manner, and the protection of this right requires that States adopt positive measures. In this connection, the Committee considers that it would be desirable for States Parties to take all possible measures to reduce infant mortality and to increase life expectancy, especially in adopting measures to eliminate malnutrition and epidemics." (Human Rights Committee, General Comment 6, HRI/GEN/1/Rev.2, p. 6)

According to the *Manual on Human Rights Reporting*, 1997 measures taken by States to implement article 6 of the Convention on the Rights of the Child may be "of a positive nature and thus designed to protect life, including by increasing life expectancy, diminishing infant and child mortality, combating diseases and rehabilitating health, providing adequate nutritious foods and clean drinking water. And they may further aim at preventing deprivation of life, namely by prohibiting and preventing death penalty, extra-legal, arbitrary or summary executions or any situation of enforced disappearance. States Parties should therefore refrain from any action that may intentionally take life away, as well as take steps to safeguard life." (*Manual*, p. 424)

Article 24 of the Convention on the Rights of the Child expands on the child's right to health and health services, and specifically requires "appropriate measures ... to diminish infant and child mortality" (Article 24(2)(a), see page 324). The Committee has commended States for reducing mortality rates and has expressed concern whenever rates have risen and at situations in which rates vary in a discriminatory way (for Committee's comments and full discussion, see article 24, page 325).

An early age of marriage – in particular for girls – not only raises an issue of discrimination under article 2 but also threatens the rights of both the child-mother and the new child to life and to maximum survival and development under article 6:

"...It is the Committee's view that the early and lower marriageable age for girls as compared with boys raise the serious questions as to their compatibility with the principles and provisions of the Convention, in particular those laid down in its articles 2, 3 and 6." (Nicaragua IRCO, Add.36, para. 13)

The Platform for Action of the Fourth World Conference on Women, held at Beijing in 1995, indicates that: "More than 15 million girls aged 15 to 19 give birth each year. Motherhood at a very young age entails complications during pregnancy and delivery and a risk of maternal death that is much greater than average. The children of young mothers have higher levels of morbidity and mortality..." (Platform for Action, para. 268)

Definition of the child and the child's right to life

As noted under article 1 (page 3), the Preamble to the Convention on the Rights of the Child recalls the provision in the United Nations Declaration of the Rights of the Child that "the child, by reason of his physical and mental immaturity, needs special safeguards and care, including appropriate legal protection, before as well as after birth." The Working Group drafting the Convention agreed that a statement should be placed in the *travaux préparatoires* to the effect that "In adopting this preambular paragraph, the Working Group does not intend to prejudice the interpretation of article 1 or any other provision of the Convention by States Parties" (E/CN.4/1989/48, pp. 8-15, Detrick, p. 110).

Article 1 deliberately leaves open the starting point of childhood, that is, whether it is conception, birth or sometime in between. Thus, the Convention leaves individual States to balance for themselves the conflicting rights and interests involved in issues such as abortion and family planning, and the Committee on the Rights of the Child has suggested that reservations to preserve State laws on abortion are unnecessary (for details of reservations and discussion, see article 1, page 3).

Croatian Government representatives asked for the advice of the Committee on whether a girl's right to choose an abortion should be limited and whether it should not be obligatory to inform parents. A Committee member responded: "...the Committee could not give a categorical answer to the Croatian question on a girl child's freedom to choose: the State Party should simply try to ensure that the relevant legislation was in keeping with the Convention and, in particular, with articles 3 and 12" (Croatia SR.281, paras. 3 and 5).

The Committee has commented adversely on high rates of abortion and on the use of abortion as a method of family planning, and it has encouraged measures to reduce the incidence of abortion:

"...The Committee also expresses its concern at the frequent recourse to abortion as what appears to be a method of family planning." (Russian Federation IRCO, Add.4, para. 12)

"The Committee considers that greater efforts should be made to provide family education; to develop awareness of the equal responsibilities of parents; to disseminate widely knowledge about modern methods of family planning and, thereby, to reduce the practice of abortion." (Romania IRCO, Add.16, para. 15)

"The Committee expresses its concern at the health status of children, particularly in the aftermath of the Chernobyl nuclear disaster, the apparent priority given to curative health care rather than decentralized preventive health care, the low prevalence of breastfeeding and the high number of abortions." (Belarus IRCO, Add.17, para. 9)

The Committee has also expressed concern at "clandestine" abortions and the negative effects of teenage pregnancies, including on the right to life of young mothers. Nicaragua's Initial Report states that "...clandestine abortions are one of the major causes of maternal mortality, particularly among the very young" (Nicaragua IR, para. 122). A Committee member commented "that under the [Nicaraguan] Penal Code abortion was prohibited except for 'therapeutic reasons'. If the mother was under age or had been the victim of rape, could those be considered legitimate therapeutic grounds for an abortion? Were abortion services available for under-age girls who had been the victims of sexual abuse and, if so, were they free? She suggested that however sensitive the religious and moral issues involved in that area, and despite the fact that abortion was not in itself a good form of family planning, consideration needed to be given to changing some of the prevailing social attitudes to abortion." It was revealed that in Nicaragua 24 per cent of births are to teenage mothers (Nicaragua SR.212, para. 22).

In its Concluding Observations, the Committee stated:

"The Committee is concerned about the relatively high maternal mortality rate, especially as it affects young girls, in Nicaragua. It also notes that clandestine abortions and teenage pregnancies appear to be a serious problem in the country." (Nicaragua IRCO, Add.36, para. 19)

Contentious ethical issues arise in relation to the right to life, which the Committee has not as yet tackled – for example the responsibility to sustain significantly disabled children at birth and to sustain the life of very premature babies. The Standard Rules on the Equalization of Opportunities for Persons with Disabilities requires that "States should ensure that persons with disabilities, particularly infants and children, are provided with the same level of medical care within the same system as other members of society" (rule 2.3). The Rules emphasizes that States have an obligation "to enable persons with disabilities to exercize their rights, including their human, civil and political rights, on an equal basis with other citizens", and to eliminate "any discriminatory provisions against persons with disabilities" (rule 15.1 and 15.2).

Relevant to the principle of non-discrimination and the right to life, some States have introduced laws on abortion that permit termination of pregnancy at a later stage, sometimes up to full term when tests have indicated that the foetus has a disabling impairment.

As medical technology advances, these issues of rights may become more complex and pose a greater number of ethical dilemmas and possible conflicts between the rights of the child and his or her mother.

The death penalty

Article 37(a) of the Convention on the Rights of the Child prohibits capital punishment "for offences committed by persons below eighteen years of age". The Convention's article 6 also asserts this by recognizing every child's right to life and survival.

Article 6 of the International Covenant on Civil and Political Rights says: "Sentence of death shall not be imposed for crimes committed by persons below eighteen years of age and shall not be carried out on pregnant women" (para. 5). A Second Optional Protocol to the Covenant, adopted by the United Nations General Assembly in 1989, aims at the abolition of the death penalty. Under its article 1, no one within the jurisdiction of a State Party to the Protocol may be executed.

The Committee on the Rights of the Child has raised the issue with a number of States Parties and emphasized that it is not enough that the death penalty is not applied to children. Its prohibition regarding children must be confirmed in legislation (see article 37, page 494 for Committee's comments and further discussion).

Armed conflict

Armed conflict poses a threat to the right to life of an increasing number of children. Article 38 of the Convention on the Rights of the Child (see page 511) requires special measures of care and protection for children affected by armed conflict.

The Human Rights Committee, in a General Comment in 1982, comments "The right to life enunciated in article 6 of the Covenant ... is the supreme right from which no derogation is permitted even in times of emergency." The General Comment goes on to emphasize that averting the danger of war and strengthening international peace and security "would constitute the most important condition and guarantee for the safeguarding of the right to life" (Human Rights Committee, General Comment 6, HRI/GEN/1/Rev.2, p. 6).

And in another General Comment in 1984 it emphasizes that "the designing, testing, manufacture, possession and deployment of nuclear weapons are among the greatest threats to the right to life which confront mankind today ... The production, testing, possession, deployment and use of nuclear weapons should be prohibited and recognized as crimes against humanity. The Committee accordingly, in the interest of mankind, calls upon all States, whether parties to the Covenant or not, to take urgent steps, unilaterally and by agreement, to rid the world of this menace." (Human Rights Committee General Comment 14, HRI/GEN/1/Rev.2, p. 18)

Homicide and other violence to children

The obligation under article 6 of the Convention on the Rights of the Child to preserve the life of children and to promote survival and maximum development is expanded upon in many other articles (article 19, protection from all forms of violence; article 37, protection from torture and cruel, inhuman or degrading treatment or punishment; article 38, protection of children affected by armed conflict, and others). In many countries, very young children are the most at risk of homicide (see infanticide below, page 91).

The Committee on the Rights of the Child has asserted the right to life, as well as other provisions, when expressing concern at violence to children by security forces, police and others. For example:

"The Committee expresses its deep concern at the continued violence which has already caused thousands of killings, disappearances and displacements of children and parents. It is therefore necessary that the Peruvian Government and Peruvian society adopt an urgent, effective and fair response to protect the rights of the child." (Peru IRCO, Add.8, para. 7)

"The Committee is deeply alarmed at the persistence of violence against children, including at the reported information on the 84 children killed. The high number of child victims of violence raises serious concern, particularly in view of the ineffectiveness of investigations into crimes committed against children which paves the way for widespread impunity." (Guatemala IRCO, Add.58, para. 20)

"... the Committee is deeply alarmed that the necessary safeguards against the excessive use of force by law enforcement officials or anyone else acting in this capacity are undermined by the provisions of section 73 of the Criminal Code. This may give rise to the violation of children's rights, including their right to life, and leads to impunity for the perpetrators of such violations. Therefore, it is

Urgent action to defend right to life

The Committee on the Rights of the Child has adopted a procedure for taking "urgent action" when alerted to a particular threat to the rights of the child (see also page 578). Up to 1997, each of the two "urgent actions" taken by the Committee related to the right to life. The Committee made an urgent appeal to the Pakistan Government in 1991 concerning a seven-year-old boy allegedly threatened imminently with the death penalty who had been accused of writing blasphemous remarks on the wall of a mosque (Pakistan SR.134, para 4).

The procedure was also invoked in 1991 in relation to Indonesia over an incident in East Timor, as documented in this statement made by a Committee member in the official reports of the Committee:

"In November 1991, the Committee had sent a telegram to the Government of Indonesia in which it expressed its concern regarding a dramatic incident which had taken place in the city of Dili, in East Timor. On 12 November 1991 a peaceful demonstration attended mostly by children had been brutally broken up by Indonesian security forces. Forty-three children, the youngest of whom was 10 years old, had been killed; 26, the youngest of whom was six years old, had disappeared; 37, the youngest of whom was 10 years old, had been injured; and 10, the youngest of whom was 12 years old, had been detained. Admittedly, the Indonesian authorities had taken action against several members of the police; but the situation of the disappeared children had regrettably not been clarified. That dramatic incident raised questions about the training received by members of the security forces and about their excessive use of violence. Mistakes were obviously committed in situations of political strife, but when such mistakes occurred frequently, Governments must respond vigorously. The Committee would have appreciated a reply to its telegram." (Indonesia SR.81, para. 7)

The Indonesian representative responded that he considered the questions about Dili

"... out of order. The Committee on the Rights of the Child was not authorized to address political issues." He also noted that Indonesia had set up a national committee of inquiry (Indonesia SR.81, para. 16).

Committee members emphasized that their questions were not politically inspired; the Committee

"was required to consider the situation of all children under the jurisdiction, whether *de facto* or *de jure*, of a State Party" (Indonesia SR.81, paras. 24 and 25).

In the Committee's Concluding Observations issued a year later, in October 1994, it reiterated:

"The State Party has given assurances that violations similar to those which occurred in November 1991, when security forces used excessive violence against children peacefully demonstrating in Dili, would not occur again. The Committee, however, remains seriously disturbed by the continuing pattern of violation of the right to freedom of assembly and the great number of complaints of ill-treatment of children attributed to the police, security or military personnel, in particular in situations of arrest and detention..." (Indonesia IRCO, Add.25, para. 15)

the view of the Committee that the above-mentioned provisions of the Nigerian Criminal Code are incompatible with the principles and provisions of the Convention." (Nigeria IRCO, Add.61, para. 24)

"Disappearance" of children has caused concern in a number of countries. In 1993, the General Assembly adopted a Declaration on the Protection of All Persons from Enforced Disappearances (A/RES/47/133), noting that any act of enforced disappearance is an offence of human dignity and constitutes a violation of the rules of international law, including "the right not to be subjected to torture and other cruel, inhuman or degrading treatment or punishment. It also violates or constitutes a grave threat to the right to life" (article 1).

Article 20 of the Declaration covers the prevention of the abduction of children of parents subjected to enforced disappearance, and prevention of the abduction of children born during their mother's enforced disappearance.

The Committee commented on these and related issues in its Concluding Observations on Colombia's Initial Report:

"The Committee expresses its grave concern over the life-threatening situation faced by an alarming number of children in Colombia, particularly those who, in order to survive, are working and/or living on the streets. Many of those children are victims of "social cleansing" campaigns and subject to arbitrary arrest and torture and other inhuman or degrading treatment by authorities. They are also subject to coercion, disappearance, trafficking and murder by criminal groups....

"The Committee further recommends that firm measures be taken to ensure the right to survival for all children in Colombia, including those who live in a situation of poverty, who have been abandoned, or those who to survive are forced to live and/or work in the streets. Such measures should aim at the effective protection of children against the occurrence of violence, disappearance, assassination or alleged organ trafficking. Thorough and systematic investigation should be carried out and severe penalties applied to those found responsible for such violations of children's rights. Violations of human rights and children's rights should always be examined by civilian courts under civilian law, not military courts..." (Colombia IRCO, Add.30, paras. 12 and 17; see also Colombia Prelim. Obs., Add.15, paras. 7 and 10)

The Human Rights Committee, in a General Comment, also notes that States should take "specific and effective measures" to prevent the disappearance of individuals: "States should establish effective facilities and procedures to investigate thoroughly cases of missing and disappeared persons in circumstances which may involve a violation of the right to life." (Human Rights Committee General Comment 6, HRI/GEN/1/Rev.2, p. 6)

The right to life of children who live and/or work on the streets may be particularly threatened:

"The Committee further recommends that firm measures be taken to ensure the right of survival of all children in Nepal, including those who live and/or work in the streets..." (Nepal IRCO, Add.57, para. 35)

Infanticide In societies in which boys are valued economically and socially above girls, unequal population figures by gender indicate that infanticide may still be widespread. The Platform for Action adopted at the Fourth World Conference on Women states: "...in many countries available indicators show that the girl child is discriminated against from the earliest stages of life, through her childhood and into adulthood. In some areas of the world, men outnumber women by five in every 100." Among the stated reasons for the discrepancy is preference for a son which results in prenatal sex selection and female infanticide. The Platform for Action proposes elimination of "all forms of discrimination against the girl child and the root causes of son preference, which result in harmful and unethical practices such as prenatal sex selection and female infanticide; this is often compounded by the increasing use of technologies to determine foetal sex, resulting in abortion of female foetuses... Enact and enforce legislation protecting girls from all forms of violence, including female infanticide and prenatal sex selection..." (Fourth World Conference on Women, Beijing, China, September 1995, Platform for Action, paras. 259, 277(c) and 283(d)).

The 1986 report of the Working Group on Traditional Practices Affecting the Health of Women and Children identifies "son preference" as one priority concern, defined as "the preference of parents for male children which often manifests itself in neglect, deprivation or discriminatory treatment of girls to the detriment of their mental and physical health". The Working Group found the practice prevalent in many parts of the world. The report states that "abnormal sex ratios in infant and young child mortality rates, in nutritional status indicators and even population sex ratios show that discriminatory practices are widespread and have serious repercussions". When linked to neglect and discrimination towards female children, "it leads to serious health consequences which account for between 500,000 to one million deaths among female children". The Working Group notes that the availability of amniocentesis and other techniques which enable the sex of the foetus to be determined were leading to selective abortion on grounds of gender in some areas. Its report also notes that "excess female mortality in childhood is an indicator of serious external influences against the normal biological advantages with which nature has endowed the female. Male infants have an inherently greater vulnerability than female infants for many causes of death ... male mortality in childhood is greater than female mortality. The greater the proportion of deaths due to infection and malnutrition, the larger the expected difference becomes." Thus the report emphasizes the importance of recording and analyzing infant and child mortality rates by sex (E/CN.4/1986/42, paras. 149, 150, 164).

In its discussions with representatives of China, a member of the Committee on the Rights of the Child noted: "China had passed important legislation to address the problem of gender discrimination, but the distorted gender ratio was alarming, and had to be seen against a background of late abortions, the abandonment of infants and possible infanticide..." (China SR.299, para. 18)

The Committee followed up the issue in its Concluding Observations:

"While noting the measures taken to confront the problems of discrimination on the grounds of gender and disability, the Committee remains concerned at the persistence of practices leading to cases of selective infanticide...

"It is the Committee's view that family planning policy must be designed to avoid any threat to the life of children, particularly girls. The Committee recommends in this regard that clear guidance be given to the population and the personnel involved in the family-planning policy to ensure that the aims it promotes are in accordance with principles and provisions of the Convention, including those of its article 24. The State Party is urged to take further action for the maintenance of strong and comprehensive measures to combat the abandonment and infanticide of girls as well as the trafficking, sale and kidnapping or abduction of girls." (China IRCO, Add.56, paras. 15 and 36)

The Committee has noted the possible existence of infanticide in a number of countries:

"The Committee is concerned by the reported increase in child abuse, including infanticide, domestic violence and child prostitution ..." (Mauritius IRCO, Add.64, para. 18)

Many legal systems recognize the particular crime of infanticide as a distinctly defined form of homicide with reduced penalties. The ostensible intention is to provide a special defence for mothers suffering psychological trauma as a result of the process of birth. But by denoting a special, and lesser, crime, such laws appear to discriminate against children as victims of homicide.

In addition to girls, disabled children are particularly at risk of infanticide in some countries.

Suicide In its examination of Initial Reports by States Parties, the Committee was concerned to find high, and in some cases increasing, rates of suicide among children in some countries:

"...It is also concerned by the high rates of suicide ... among youth." (Finland IRCO, Add.53, para. 16)

"The increasing incidence of suicide among young people is an additional cause for concern." (Canada IRCO, Add.37, para. 16)

"... adolescent mental health issues, including the problem of youth suicide, is a matter of serious concern to the Committee." (UK dependent territory: Hong Kong IRCO, Add.63, para. 15)

The *Guidelines for Periodic Reports* specifically asks for information on the rates and the prevention of suicide (para. 41). Statistics on suicide from those countries that collect them show wide variations between countries and very much higher suicide rates among young men than among young women (see table in *The Progress of Nations 1996*, UNICEF, 1996, p. 46).

In several cases, the Committee has proposed further studies on the causes and on the effective methods of prevention:

"The Committee suggests that the State Party continue to give priority to studying the possible causes of youth suicide and the characteristics of those who appear to be most at risk and take steps as soon as practicable to put in place additional support and intervention programmes, be it in the field of mental health, education, employment or another field, which could reduce this tragic phenomenon. In this regard, the State Party may want to call on Governments and experts in other countries which also may have experience in dealing with this problem." (New Zealand IRCO, Add.71, para. 28. See also Norway IRCO, Add.23, para. 17; Denmark IRCO, Add.33, para. 21; Sri Lanka IRCO, Add.40, para. 37; Bulgaria IRCO, Add.66, para. 29)

The Committee has also noted that suicide rates may vary between different groups within a society in a discriminatory way, which also requires study. For instance, suicide rates among certain of Canada's indigenous peoples are considerably higher than those of the overall population. Between 1986 and 1990, there was an average of 37 suicides for every 100,000 registered Indian youths aged 10-19, five times greater than the figure among non-Indians (Canada IR, para. 1400).

In discussions with the Committee, Canadian representatives indicated that a report by the Royal Commission on Aboriginal Peoples, entitled "Choosing Life", had suggested that reported figures for suicide among indigenous peoples did not necessarily reflect the true incidence. It further suggested that general figures concealed wide variations among individual Aboriginal communities (Canada SR.216, para. 69).

In its Concluding Observations on Canada, the Committee stated:

"... Research should be developed on the problems relating to the growing rate of

infant mortality and suicide among children within aboriginal communities." (Canada IRCO, Add.37, para. 26)

Investigation and registration of death

In its *Guidelines for Periodic Reports,* the Committee acknowledges the importance of adequate investigation of and reporting on the deaths of all children and the causes of death, as well as the registration of deaths and their causes. Establishing a procedure for investigating all child deaths reduces the possibility of a cover-up of the real causes. In addition, it is acknowledged that because of religious and social attitudes, suicide tends to be underreported in many States. In States that have set up systematic procedures for investigating all child deaths, the experience tends to reveal many more deaths in which some form of violence or neglect is implicated. Adequate investigation also informs preventive strategies, for example support for parents, education and accident prevention.

The United Nations Rules for the Protection of Juveniles Deprived of their Liberty emphasizes the importance of an independent inquiry into the cause of death of any juvenile in detention. In some States, there has been disturbing evidence of violence to and between inmates, as well as high suicide rates. The Rules requires that "Upon the death of a juvenile during the period of deprivation of liberty, the nearest relative should have the right to inspect the death certificate, see the body and determine the method of disposal of the body. Upon the death of a juvenile in detention, there should be an independent inquiry into the causes of death, the report of which should be made accessible to the nearest relative. This inquiry should also be made when the death of a juvenile occurs within six months from the date of his or her release from the detention facility and there is reason to believe that the death is related to the period of detention." (rule 57)

The challenge of development

The World Declaration on the Survival, Protection and Development of Children, adopted at the World Summit in 1990, set out the stark reality of childhood for millions of children "exposed to dangers that hamper their growth and development. They suffer immensely as casualties of war and violence; as victims of racial discrimination, *apartheid*, aggression, foreign occupation and annexation; as refugees and displaced children, forced to abandon their homes and their roots; as disabled; or as victims of neglect, cruelty and exploitation.

"Each day millions of children suffer from the scourges of poverty and economic crisis – from hunger and homelessness, from epidemics and illiteracy, from degradation of the environment. They suffer from the grave effects of the problems of external indebtedness and also from the lack of sustained and sustainable growth in many developing countries, particularly the least developed ones. Each day, 40,000 children die from malnutrition and disease, including acquired immunodeficiency syndrome (AIDS), from the lack of clean water and inadequate sanitation and from the effects of the drug problem..." (World Declaration, paras. 4-6)

At the same Summit, world leaders committed themselves to "work for optimal growth and development in childhood, through measures to eradicate hunger, malnutrition and famine, and thus to relieve millions of children of tragic sufferings in a world that has the means to feed all its citizens". The Plan of Action sets out specific proposals and targets relevant to survival and development (see also article 24, page 321, article 28, page 372).

The Plan noted: "Fortunately, the necessary knowledge and techniques for reaching most of the goals already exist. The financial resources required are modest in relation to the great achievements that beckon. And the most essential factor – the provision to families of the information and services necessary to protect their children – is now within reach in every country and for virtually every community. There is no cause which merits a higher priority than the protection and development of children, on whom the survival, stability and advancement of all nations – and, indeed, of human civilization – depends" (Plan of Action, para. 36).

The World Summit for Social Development (Copenhagen, March 1995) reaffirmed the goals of the World Summit for Children and provided certain new goals, in particular for the eradication of poverty, with special priority for the needs of women and children "who often bear the greatest burden of poverty" (A/CONF.166/9, p. 13).

"...ensure to the maximum extent possible the survival and development of the child"

In its second paragraph, article 6 of the Convention on the Rights of the Child goes beyond the fundamental right to life to promote survival and development "to the maximum extent possible." The concept of "development" is not just about the preparation of the child for adulthood. It is about providing optimal conditions for childhood, for the child's life now.

The Committee on the Rights of the Child has emphasized that it sees child development as an holistic concept, embracing the whole Convention. In the *Guidelines for Periodic Reports*, it asks States to describe measures taken "to create an environment conducive to ensuring to the maximum extent possible the survival and development of the child, including physical, mental, spiritual, moral, psychological and social development, in a manner compatible with human dignity, and to prepare the child for an individual life in a free society" (para. 40).

Many of the obligations of the Convention, including in particular those related to health, adequate standard of living, education, and leisure and play (articles 24, 27, 28, 29 and 31) are relevant to ensuring the maximum development of the child, and individual articles expand on the concept of "development". For instance, under article 27, States Parties recognize "the right of every child to a standard of living adequate for the child's physical, mental, spiritual, moral and

social development". Among the aims of education set out in article 29 is "...The development of the child's personality, talents and mental and physical abilities to their fullest potential..." and preparation of the child for "responsible life in a free society".

The Convention provisions protecting the child from violence and exploitation (in particular articles 19 and 32-39) are as vital to maximum survival and development as those on the provision of services are. Research now testifies to the potentially serious short- and long-term effects on development of all forms of violence, including sexual abuse and exploitation.

The Convention's Preamble upholds the family as the "natural environment for the growth and well-being of all its members and particularly children" and recognizes that the child, "for the full and harmonious development of his or her personality, should grow up in a family environment, in an atmosphere of happiness, love and understanding". Article 5 requires respect for the "evolving capacities of the child" – a key concept of overall development. Article 18 recognizes that parents or legal guardians have the "primary responsibility" for the upbringing and development of the child and requires the State to provide appropriate assistance and under article 20, special protection for those deprived of a family environment. Article 25 requires periodic review of all children placed for care, protection or treatment – an important safeguard for their maximum development. And in relation to disabled children, article 23 requires assistance to be provided "in a manner conducive to the child's achieving the fullest possible social integration and individual development, including his or her cultural and spiritual development."

The Committee expects implementation of all other articles to be carried out with a view to achieving the maximum survival and development of the child – a concept clearly integral to the best interests of the child.

To illustrate the point, a Committee Member commented to Indonesian representatives that "the intention of article 6 was to encourage those in authority to ensure that resources were allocated to the maximum extent possible for the survival and development of the child, including health and education. It was an ambitious article and required more than legal provisions." (Indonesia SR.80, para. 38)

Child development a priority in social policy

In Ethiopia, "the National Social Policy specifically states that priority shall be given and all efforts made for the attainment of the physical, mental and psychological development of children. One of the objectives of the Transitional Government is the reduction of poverty and ensuring better living conditions for the population. To this end, necessary macroeconomic policies that will accelerate the socio-economic development of the country have been issued. The implementation of these policies will contribute to the improvement of basic services such as nutrition, health care, education, sanitation, housing, etc., and thereby ensure the survival and development of Ethiopian children." (Ethiopia IR, para. 58)

Implementation Checklist

article 6

● General measures of implementation

Have appropriate general measures of implementation been taken in relation to article 6 including

☐ identification and coordination of the responsible departments and agencies at all levels of government (article 6 is relevant to **all departments affecting children directly or indirectly**)?

☐ identification of relevant non-governmental organizations/civil society partners?

☐ a comprehensive review to ensure that all legislation, policy and practice is compatible with the article, for all children in all parts of the jurisdiction?

☐ adoption of a strategy to secure full implementation

    ☐ which includes where necessary the identification of goals and indicators of progress?

    ☐ which does not affect any provisions which are more conducive to the rights of the child?

    ☐ which recognizes other relevant international standards?

    ☐ which involves where necessary international cooperation?

(Such measures may be part of an overall governmental strategy for implementing the Convention as a whole).

☐ budgetary analysis and allocation of necessary resources?

☐ development of mechanisms for monitoring and evaluation?

☐ making the implications of article 6 widely known to adults and children?

☐ development of appropriate training and awareness-raising (in relation to article 6 likely to include **all those working with or for children and their families, and education for parenting**)?

● Specific issues in implementing article 6

☐ Is the general principle reflected in article 6 included in the State's legislation?

☐ Have appropriate measures been introduced to reduce rates of infant and child mortality for all sectors of the population?

☐ Have the rates of infant and child mortality consistently decreased over recent years, including disaggregated rates?

☐ Is the rate of abortion recorded and reported, including by age?

☐ Where abortion is permitted, is its use appropriately regulated?

☐ Where abortion is permitted, is there no discriminatory variation in the term at which it is permitted, (e.g. dependent on identification of disability)?

How to use the checklists, *see page XVII*

☐ Is the State satisfied that there is no infanticide, in particular of
    ☐ girls?
    ☐ disabled children?
☐ Is the rate of child pregnancies recorded and reported?
☐ Have appropriate measures been undertaken to reduce the number of child pregnancies?
☐ Are there circumstances in which the death penalty may be applied to children?
☐ Are there appropriate arrangements to ensure the registration of, investigation of and reporting on the deaths of all children and their causes?
☐ Are homicide rates analysed by the age of the victim in order to identify the proportion of children of different age groups who are murdered?
☐ Does the crime of infanticide exist in the legislation of the State?
☐ If so, has it been reviewed in the light of the Convention's principles?
☐ Are suicides by children recorded and reported and the rates analyzed by age?
☐ Have appropriate measures been taken to reduce and prevent suicide by children?

Reminder : **The Convention is indivisible and its articles are interdependent. Article 6 – the child's right to life and to maximum survival and development – has been identified by the Committee as a general principle of relevance to implementation of the whole Convention.**

Particular regard should be paid to:
Other general principles

Article 2: all rights to be recognized for each child in jurisdiction without discrimination on any ground
Article 3(1): the best interests of the child to be a primary consideration in all actions concerning children
Article 12: respect for the child's views in all matters affecting the child; opportunity to be heard in any judicial or administrative proceedings affecting the child

Closely related articles

Articles whose implementation is related to that of article 6 include:

Article 37(a): prohibition of capital punishment
Articles particularly related to the child's right to maximum development include articles 18, 24, 27, 28, 29 and 31)

Birth registration, name, nationality and right to know and be cared for by parents

article 7

Text of Article 7

1. The child shall be registered immediately after birth and shall have the right from birth to a name, the right to acquire a nationality and, as far as possible, the right to know and be cared for by his or her parents.

2. States Parties shall ensure the implementation of these rights in accordance with their national law and their obligations under the relevant international instruments in this field, in particular where the child would otherwise be stateless.

Summary

Article 7 provides for the registration of children and for children's rights to a name and a nationality and to know and be cared for by their parents.

The article reflects the text of article 24(2) and (3) of the International Covenant on Civil and Political Rights: "24(2) Every child shall be registered immediately after birth and shall have a name. (3) Every child has the right to acquire a nationality". The Human Rights Committee General Comment on article 24 of the Covenant notes: "In the Committee's opinion, this provision should be interpreted as being closely linked to the provision concerning the right to special measures of protection and it is designed to promote recognition of the child's legal personality" (Human Rights Committee, General Comment 17, HRI/GEN/1/Rev.2, p. 25).

As the *Manual on Human Rights Reporting*, 1997 notes, article 7 of the Convention on the Rights of the Child also contains a "new right" – the right of the child to know and be cared for by his or her parents (*Manual*, p. 430). The right is qualified by the words "as far as possible". It may not be possible to identify parents, and even when they are known, it may not be in the child's best interests to be cared by them.

Article 7 should be read in conjunction with article 8 (preservation of identity, including nationality, name and family relations), article 9 (separation from parents), article 10 (family reunification) and article 20 (continuity in upbringing of children deprived of their family environment). ■

The child's right to be "registered immediately after birth"

The importance of universal registration

The registration of all children is important for a number of reasons identified by the Committee:

First, registration is the State's first official acknowledgement of the child's existence; it represents a recognition of each child's individual importance to the State and of the child's status under the law. Where children are not registered, they are likely to be less visible, and sometimes less valued, citizens.

The Committee has expressed concern about those countries that failed to ensure universal registration:

"...Such a situation implies the non-recognition of these children as persons before the

Implementation Handbook for the Convention on the Rights of the Child

law, which will affect the level of enjoyment of their fundamental rights and freedoms. In addition, such children are not included in relevant statistical and other information on children and their situation, therefore, cannot be properly monitored." (Madagascar IRCO, Add.26, para. 10)

"The Committee is concerned at the difficulties in ensuring the registration of children after birth, as well as at the problems faced by children who have not been registered in the enjoyment of their fundamental rights and freedoms." (Philippines IRCO, Add.29, para. 11)

"The Committee is concerned at the insufficient steps undertaken to ensure birth registration of children, particularly those living in remote areas, and to the adverse effects arising therefrom for the enjoyment of their fundamental rights." (Nepal IRCO, Add.57, para 16)

If the existence of children is not officially confirmed in the first place, there can be no confidence that their disappearance or death will be recorded either. The Committee expressed concern that in Peru

"...due to the internal violence, several registration centres have been destroyed, adversely affecting the situation of thousands of children who are often left without any identity document, thus running the risk of their being suspected of involvement in terrorist activities."

The Committee recommended that:

"Specific measures should be undertaken to provide undocumented children fleeing zones affected by internal violence with adequate identity documents." (Peru IRCO, Add.8, paras. 8 and 17)

Second, birth registration is an essential element of national planning for children – providing the demographic base on which effective strategies can be built. Without registration, for example, it is unlikely that countries can have an accurate knowledge even of their infant mortality rates, a key indicator for child survival strategies (see also the importance of infant death registration, article 6 page 93). While the costs of securing universal registration may be high, particularly in countries with dispersed rural populations, the benefits are substantial, not least in relation to efficient use of resources.

As the Committee has commented, registration is necessary:

"..to facilitate the effective monitoring of the situation of children and thus assist in the development of suitably appropriate and targeted programmes" (Nicaragua IRCO, Add.36, para. 16).

Obstacles to universal registration

Bolivia acknowledged that despite having some of the strongest legal provisions for compulsory free registration in Latin America, the practice was far from adequate:

"...A great many children are not registered immediately after their birth for various reasons: ignorance of the parents, especially in the rural area, and the lack of the infrastructure for registration in remote localities, registration which is generally in the hands of improvised staff with little training, no knowledge of the law, and unable to speak Spanish, the official language, correctly." (Bolivia IR, para. 79)

"The Committee suggests that special efforts be developed to ensure an effective system of birth registration, in the light of article 7, to ensure the enjoyment of the fundamental rights of the Convention by all children without discrimination and as a meaningful tool to assess prevailing difficulties and to promote progress." (Senegal IRCO, Add.44, para. 22)

"The Committee recommends that special efforts be developed to guarantee an effective system of birth registration, in the light of article 7 of the Convention, to ensure the full enjoyment of their fundamental rights by all children. Such a system would serve as a tool in the collection of statistical data, in the assessment of prevailing difficulties and in the promotion of progress in the implementation of the Convention..." (Ethiopia IRCO Add.67 para 29)

Third, registration is a means of securing children's other rights – such as their identification following war, abandonment or abduction, enabling children to know their parentage (particularly if born out of wedlock), gaining them access to state benefits and protection through legal age limits (for example in employment, recruitment to the armed services or in the juvenile justice system) and reducing the danger of trafficking in babies or of infanticide. The Human Rights Committee General Comment notes: "The main purpose of the obligation to register children after birth is to reduce the danger of abduction, sale of or traffic in children, or of other types of treatment that are incompatible with the enjoyment of the rights provided for in the Covenant. Reports by States Parties should indicate in detail the measures that ensure the immediate registration of children born in their territory."

(Human Rights Committee, General Comment 17, HRI/GEN/1/Rev.2, p. 25).

Honduras reported to the Committee on the Rights of the Child that "As regards children in particular, there is no regulation in Honduran law to preserve their identity in a specific and unconditional way. The result is that there are large numbers of unidentified children. This means that they are civilly non-existent and thus deprived of their names and nationality" (Honduras IR, para. 43). The Committee commented:

"Despite the measures taken by the Government of Honduras to improve and facilitate the registration of children, the Committee remains worried that difficulties persist in providing children in Honduras with the necessary registration certificates and that the absence of such basic documentation detailing the child's age and family affiliations may hamper the implementation of a child's other rights, including his/her access to public health services and to the necessary protection that a child should be accorded under the system of the administration of juvenile justice." (Honduras IRCO, Add.24, para 12)

"The Committee is concerned about the continuing difficulties encountered in ensuring birth registration, particularly of children born out of wedlock..." (Sri Lanka IRCO, Add.40, para. 14)

"Serious concerns remain as to the effectiveness of measures taken to ensure the registration of all children, through the household registry. As acknowledged by the State Party, absence of registration may be due to parents' lack of knowledge of the relevant law and policy and of the negative effects of non-registration on children's legal status. The migration of people from their traditional place of residence may cause similar difficulties. Deficiencies in the registration system lead to children being deprived of basic safeguards for the promotion and protection of their rights, including in the areas of child trafficking, abduction, sale and maltreatment, abuse or neglect...
"...The Committee, while noting that the State Party has adopted measures to reduce the under-reporting of girl children, recommends that urgent measures be taken to develop more widespread awareness of the importance of registration. In the light of recent developments such as population movements within the country, the Committee also recommends that the State Party consider the possibility of reviewing the effectiveness of the existing system of registration." (China IRCO, Add.56, paras. 16 and 37)

"... the Committee recommends that an adequate system of registration of refugee children be established to ensure their rights are protected." (Ethiopia IRCO, Add.67, para. 29)

When and how children should be registered

According to the Convention, the child should be registered "immediately after birth" which implies a defined period of days rather than months. However, if for any reason children are not registered or if their records have been lost, then the omission should be made good by the State.

Universal registration first requires that domestic law makes registration a compulsory duty both of parents and of the relevant administrative authorities, with appropriate sanctions (for example Colombia was asked by a member of the Committee what its sanctions were in cases of non-registration or late registration and how registration was secured, particularly in rural areas and for families displaced by violence (Colombia SR.114, para. 19)). Other persons may also be placed under legal duties to declare births – for example professionals attending the birth or the owners of a house (or captains of ships) in which a birth take place.

Second, the commitment of resources is needed.

The Committee has encouraged flexible methods of registration, for example:

"The Committee encourages the State Party to adopt all appropriate measures to ensure the birth registration of all children, including those born in rural areas and on commercial farms, and encourages the efforts designed to establish registration units at schools and clinics." (Zimbabwe IRCO, Add.55, para. 27)

"Children's birth registration should be given priority to ensure that every child is recognized as a person and enjoys his/her full rights. The Committee encourages further steps to ensure the birth registration of children, including the establishment of mobile registration offices and registration units in schools." (Nepal IRCO, Add.57, para. 31; see also Nicaragua IRCO, Add.36, para. 16, Mongolia IRCO, Add.48, para. 22)

The *Manual on Human Rights Reporting*, 1997 notes: "Birth registration should be ensured by States Parties to every child under their jurisdiction, including to non-nationals, asylum seekers, refugee and stateless children...In some situations, however, practical difficulties may be encountered in the registration of children. States Parties' reports have shown that this is often the case in relation to children born from nomadic groups, in rural or remote areas where birth registration offices may be lacking and access to them may, in view of their distance, pose additional problems to the children's families. Similar problems may arise in situations of emergency, including armed conflicts. In such circumstances, States have to adopt solutions which, being designed to ensure the implementation of this right, are also appropriate to the specific particularities of such situations. In this regard, the establishment of mobile registration offices has often shown to be an effective option." (*Manual*, p. 430)

What details should be registered?

Although the Convention does not specify what must be registered, other rights (to name and nationality, to know parentage, family and identity) imply that registration ought, as a minimum, to include:

- the child's name at birth,
- the child's sex,
- the child's date of birth,
- where the child was born,
- the parents' names and addresses,
- the parents' nationality status.

Other information – for example the parents' occupations, the child's siblings or his or her ethnic status – may also be useful for statistical purposes.

The registration of the baby's parents may prove problematic. It is hard to find reasons, so far as the child is concerned, why the baby's mother should not be registered, although such an omission is permitted in France, to the expressed concern of the Committee (see below, page 105):

The matter of naming the father is more complicated. The State is likely to have an interest in both parents being registered so that they can subsequently be required to maintain the child. For example, Colombian law states: "Every minor has the right to know who are his or her parents. The State has a corresponding duty to give every opportunity for ensuring a responsible primogeniture". Colombian State officials may therefore subpoena a presumed father to agree to recognize a child born outside marriage or may initiate proceedings if he refuses to do this, providing free genetic profiling for this purpose (Colombia IR, paras. 81-4). However, given that birth registers tend to be public documents, the child's right to privacy may be jeopardized, for example in a case where the father has an incestuous relationship with the mother. Belgium reported that it allowed registration of the single filiation from the mother in such circumstances (Belgium IR, para. 124). Under the Convention the child does have a principled right to know this information, but it need not be contained in data found in the public domain. The *Guidelines for Periodic Reports* asks about "the measures adopted to prevent any kind of stigmatization or discrimination of the child" (para. 51).

Examples of early and late registration

An office or a representative of the Civil Register is found in every Costa Rican hospital, so that within a few hours of a hospital birth (over 96 per cent of Costa Rican births are in hospital) the mother is visited and the necessary data taken. Since 1988, an official health booklet has been drawn up on each child. It includes, among other information, the child's fingerprints. This process has made it possible to identify several abandoned babies (Costa Rica IR, paras. 106-7).

Colombia has initiated a register for abandoned children and those caught up in the justice system: "Information was provided on their social background, where possible, as well as the details of any administrative or judicial action. There was also a photograph of each child, which was especially useful in identifying and tracing younger children who were often not certain of their origins." The register has been computerized so that the network of around 300 family welfare centres across Colombia has access to it (Colombia SR.189, para. 25).

The child's right "from birth to a name"

The article specifically provides that the right to a name should be "from birth". States should therefore ensure that abandoned babies and children are always provided with a name; any temptation to use numbers should be resisted – for example in circumstances of mass movement of refugees which include many unaccompanied children.

The Convention does not suggest that children have a right to any particular sort of name. However, a significant number of countries not only make arrangements for children's names to be registered but also prescribe what names are used. For example, article 18 of the American Convention on Human Rights 1969 states: "Every person has the right to a given name and to the surname of his parents or that of one of them. The law shall regulate the manner in which this right shall be ensured for all, by the use of assumed names if necessary."

The intention of such a provision appears relatively uncontroversial and protective of certain categories of children – as the Human Rights Committee General Comment observes "providing for the right to have a name is of special importance in the case of children born out of wedlock" (Human Rights Committee, General Comment 17, HRI/GEN/1/Rev.2, p. 25). However in some circumstances prescriptive laws on names may conflict with the non-discrimination rights under article 2 or with the right to peacefully enjoy minority cultural practices under article 30, for example in cases where minority groups have different naming traditions that do not involve using parental surnames.

In this regard the Committee informed Iceland:

"... the Committee welcomes the legal change abolishing the requirement that a person seeking Icelandic citizenship has to add an Icelandic name to his or her original name." (Iceland IRCO, Add.50, para. 11)

Moreover, where countries go further and enforce a law that the child must, or in some cases must not, bear the father's name, article 3 (concerning the best interests of the child) may have a bearing. For example, Belgium maintains an extremely complicated set of laws relating to the naming of children born in and out of wedlock, including children born of adulterous relationships where the father's name can only be used with the agreement of the woman who was his lawful wife at the time of the conception. Belgium acknowledged the latter rules have been problematic, since they are as much about the "moral interests of the conjugal family" as about the best interests of the child (Belgium IR, para. 123).

The Committee raised the issue with Uruguay:

"In this regard, the Committee is particularly concerned at the persisting discrimination against children born out of wedlock, including in regard to the enjoyment of their civil rights. It notes that the procedure for the determination of their name paves the way for their stigmatization and the impossibility of having access to their origins..." (Uruguay IRCO, Add.62, para. 11).

It would be dangerous to assume that any international or domestic law asserting children's right to their parents' name necessarily represents a provision "more conducive to the realization of the rights of the child" under article 41 of the Convention on the Rights of the Child. Countries should also carefully examine any laws on names for inadvertent breach of articles 2 and 3.

The provisions of article 5 (parental guidance and the child's evolving capacities), article 12 (respect for the child's opinion) and article 19 (protection from harm) should also be considered in relation to naming. The right to a name from birth is unavoidably a matter for adult caregivers or the State; babies can play no part in choosing

their names. However, provision should be made so that children can apply to the appropriate authorities to change their name at a later date. Children's names can also be changed following the remarriage of parents or adoption. In such circumstances, children's rights to identity are also involved (see article 8, page 112).

The Committee took up the point in relation to Yugoslavia:

"The Committee takes note that the principle of respect for the views of the child has been reflected in such situations as the change of name ..." (Federal Republic of Yugoslavia IRCO, Add.49, para. 31)

Although parents are the persons most likely to decide the child's name, consistency with the Convention should not allow this to be an absolute parental right. Domestic laws should have appropriate mechanisms to prevent registration of a name that might make a child an object of ridicule.

The child's right to "acquire a nationality", with particular reference to the State's "obligations under the relevant international instruments, in particular where the child would otherwise be stateless"

Some States confer limited forms of nationality to certain groups of children, for example the children of parents who are not themselves citizens. This appears to be a form of discrimination. The "right to acquire a nationality" implies a right to all the benefits derived from nationality.

This point was taken up by the Committee in relation to Myanmar:

"...It is also seriously concerned by the fact that the Citizenship Act establishes three different categories of citizenship and therefore some categories of children and their parents might be stigmatized and/or denied certain rights.

"In the field of the right to citizenship, the Committee is of the view that the State Party should, in the light of articles 2 (non-discrimination) and 3 (best interests of the child), abolish the categorization of citizens..." (Myanmar IRCO, Add.69, paras. 14 and 34)

The issue of children's nationality is particularly difficult, given the sensitivity of all nations about sovereignty and citizenship, differing legal and religious presumptions on how nationality should be acquired and the ever-increasing anxiety of richer nations to exclude, or to deny citizenship to, poor people from other nations. The drafting of this article and articles 9 (separation from parents) and 10 (family reunification) picks a careful way between these anxieties and the recognition that children should have a right to nationality. Article 7(2) thus provides that: "States Parties shall ensure the implementation of these rights in accordance with their national law and their obligations under the relevant international instruments in this field, in particular where the child would otherwise be stateless."

Nonetheless, a number of reservations or interpretative declarations have been entered to article 7 – by Andorra, Kuwait Liechtenstein, Maldives, Monaco, Singapore, Thailand, Tunisia and the United Kingdom. These countries indicate that their Constitutions or domestic laws relating to nationality may define or restrict the scope of article 7. For example, Kuwait stated: "The State of Kuwait understands the concept of article 7 to signify the right of the child who was born in Kuwait and whose parents are unknown (parentless) to be granted Kuwaiti nationality as stipulated by the Kuwaiti Nationality Laws" (CRC/C/2/Rev.5, p. 23), though in fact stateless children may not necessarily be parentless.

The wording "right to acquire nationality" is taken directly from the International Covenant on Civil and Political Rights (article 24(3)). The General Comment by the Human Rights Committee already quoted states: "Special attention should also be paid, in the context of the protection to be granted to the children, to the right of every child to acquire a nationality, as provided for in article 24, paragraph 3. While the purpose of this provision is to prevent a child from being afforded less protection by society and the State because he is stateless, it does not necessarily make it an obligation for States to give their nationality to every child born in their territory. However, States are required to adopt every appropriate measure, both internally and in cooperation with other States, to ensure that every child has a nationality when he is born. In this connection, no discrimination with regard to the acquisition of nationality should be admissible under internal law as between legitimate children and children born out of wedlock or of stateless parents or based on the nationality status of one or both of the parents. The measures adopted to ensure that children have a nationality should always be referred to in reports by States Parties" (Human Rights Committee, General Comment 17, HRI/GEN/1, Rev.2, p. 25).

The words in article 7(2): "States Parties shall ensure the implementation of these rights in accordance with their national law and their obli-

gations under the relevant international instruments in this field, in particular where the child would otherwise be stateless" refer primarily to the Convention on Reduction of Statelessness 1961, which provides that children should acquire the nationality of the State in which they were born if they are not granted nationality by any other State, or if such children fail to make the proper applications to obtain this right, then they should be entitled to the nationality of one of their parents (subject to certain conditions). Originally it was proposed that the first provision be incorporated into the Convention but difficulties with some national laws made this unacceptable (E/CN.4/L.1542, pp. 6-7; Detrick, pp. 125-129). Article 7(2) represents a compromise between the two positions and is a clear pointer to the provisions of article 41: "Nothing in the present Convention shall affect any provisions which are more conducive to the realization of the rights of the child and which may be contained in ... (b) International law in force for that State."

The Committee on the Rights of the Child has raised concerns about stateless children:

"The Committee is concerned that ... there are still disparities in practice, in particular with regard to...the acquisition of Jordanian nationality. In this last respect, the Committee is concerned that in the light of Jordanian legislation, cases of statelessness might arise..." (Jordan IRCO, Add.21, para. 11)

"The Committee is concerned that the problem of statelessness has not been resolved, in particular with regard to refugee children and children born outside the territory of the Federal Republic of Yugoslavia and subject to its jurisdiction.
"Legislative and other measures should be undertaken to ensure that children are protected from statelessness and that for each child under the jurisdiction of the State, the rights set forth in the Convention are respected and ensured." (Federal Republic of Yugoslavia IRCO, Add.49, paras. 14 and 32)

"The situation of refugee and Syrian-born Kurdish children is a matter of concern to the Committee in the light of article 7 of the Convention. In this regard, the Committee notes the absence of facilities for the registration of refugee children born in Syria, and that Syrian-born, Kurdish children are considered either as foreigners or as maktoumeen (unregistered) by the Syrian authorities and face great administrative and practical difficulties to acquire Syrian nationality, although they have no other nationality at birth.
"...the Committee underlines that the right to be registered and to acquire a nationality shall be guaranteed to all children within the

Syrian Arab Republic's jurisdiction without discrimination of any kind, irrespective, in particular, of the children's or his or her parents' or legal guardians' race, religion or ethnic origin, in line with article 2 of the Convention..."
(Syrian Arab Republic IRCO, Add.70, paras, 15 and 27)

Nationality can be acquired either from parents (*jus sanguinis*) or from place of birth (*jus soli*). Islamic law favours nationality taken from parentage; some countries prohibit dual nationality, so a choice between nationalities may have to be made for children, and some countries have systems that accommodate both parentage and place of birth, sometimes with discriminatory effects. Another potentially discriminatory practice is when the child automatically takes the nationality of the father rather than the mother.

The United Kingdom and Lebanon, for example, were criticized by the Committee:

"...the reservation relating to the application of the Nationality and Immigration Act does not appear to be compatible with the principles and provisions of the Convention ... [the Committee] is concerned about the possible adverse effects on children of the restrictions applied to unmarried fathers in transmitting citizenship to their children, in contradiction of the provisions of articles 7 and 8 of the Convention..." (UK IRCO, Add.34, paras. 7 and 12)

"The Committee is concerned with the apparent discrimination in the granting of nationality to a child of parents of mixed nationality; nationality may only be obtained by a child from her/his Lebanese father but not from the mother and, in the case of unmarried parents, only if the Lebanese father acknowledges the child." (Lebanon IRCO, Add.54, para. 15)

The words "the right to acquire nationality" can be interpreted as being the right "from birth", (Principal 3 of the Declaration of the Rights of the Child 1959 states simply "The child shall be entitled from his birth to a name and a nationality"), but in any event must mean that stateless children should have the right to acquire the nationality of the country in which they have lived for a specified period. The latter provision is important given the growing numbers of stateless, often parentless, children who receive adequate protection from the country in which they live throughout their childhood but then discover that they are unlawful residents at the time of their majority.

This matter was raised with Belgium:

"The Committee is...particularly concerned that unaccompanied minors who have had their asylum request rejected, but who can remain in the country until they are 18 years old, may be deprived of an identity and denied the full enjoyment of their rights ..." (Belgium IRCO, Add.38, para. 9)

Decisions about nationality are often made by parents at the time of the child's birth. Older children, however, should be able to apply on their own behalf to change their nationality.

"as far as possible, the right to know... his or her parents"

Meaning of "parent"

A few decades ago the definition of "parent" was fairly straightforward. There were the "biological" parents, sometimes known as the "natural" or "birth" parents, and there might also be "psychological" or "caring" parents who were those' such as adoptive or foster parents, who acted as the child's primary caregiver throughout his or her infancy.

When article 7 was drafted, it was pointed out that the laws of some countries – for example, the former German Democratic Republic, the United States of America and the former Union of Soviet Socialist Republics – upheld "secret" adoptions whereby adopted children did not have the right to know the identity of their biological parents (E/CN.4/1989, pp. 18-22, Detrick, p. 127). However nowadays the term "biological" parent may have a more complex meaning; for example, where egg donation is concerned, the "parent" could be either the genetic parent (the donor of the egg) or the birth mother.

Countries have entered declarations and reservations in relation to this right:
"The United Kingdom interprets the references in the Convention to 'parents' to mean only those persons who, as a matter of national law, are treated as parents. This includes cases where the law regards a child as having only one parent, for example where a child has been adopted by one person only and in certain cases where a child is conceived other than as a result of sexual intercourse by the woman who gives birth to it and she is treated as the only parent" (CRC/C/2/Rev.2, p. 33).

"In cases of irrevocable adoptions, which are based on the principle of anonymity of such adoptions, and of artificial fertilization, where the physician charged with the operation is required to ensure that the husband and wife, on the one hand, and the donor, on the other, remain unknown to each other, the non-communication of a natural parent's name or natural parents' names to the child is not in contradiction with this provision" (Czech Republic, CRC/C/2/Rev.2, p. 16).

"The Government of Luxembourg believes that article 7 of the Convention presents no obstacle to the legal process in respect of anonymous births, which is deemed to be in the interest of the child, as provided under article 3 of the Convention" (CRC/C/2/Rev.2, p. 24).

"With respect to article 7 of the Convention, the Republic of Poland stipulates that the right of an adopted child to know its natural parents shall be subject to the limitations imposed by binding legal arrangements that enable adoptive parents to maintain the confidentiality of the child's origin" (CRC/C/2/Rev.2, p. 29).

Notwithstanding these reactions, a reasonable assumption is that, as far as the child's right to know his or her parents is concerned, the definition of "parents" includes genetic parents (for medical reasons alone this knowledge is of increasing importance to the child) **and** birth parents, that is the mother who gave birth and the father who claimed paternity through partnership with the mother at the time of birth (or whatever the social definition of father is within the culture: the point being that such social definitions are important to children in terms of their identity). Moreover, a third category, the child's psychological parents – those who cared for the child for significant periods during infancy and childhood – should also logically be included since these persons too are intimately bound up in children's identity and thus their rights under article 8 (see page 111).

Meaning of "as far as possible"

It is necessary to distinguish among situations: First, when a parent **cannot** be identified (for example, when the mother does not know who the father is or when the child has been abandoned). States Parties can do little about this, although legislation under article 2 must ensure that such children are not discriminated against.

Second, when mothers **refuse** to identify fathers (including extreme circumstances, for example in cases of incest or when the father has raped the mother). While mothers could, arguably, be legally required to name the father, it would be difficult to enforce this and conflict could be raised between the mother's rights and the child's rights.

The Committee did however express concern about the situation in France:

"Regarding the right of the child to know his or her origins, including in cases of a mother requesting that her identity remain secret during the birth and declaration of the birth, adoption and medically-assisted procreation, the Committee is concerned that the legislative measures being taken by the State party might not fully reflect the provisions of the

Convention, particularly its general principles." (France IRCO, Add.20, para. 14)

Third, when the State decides that a parent **should not** be identified. For example:

- where adoption law limits the child's entitlement and access to information to know who his or her genetic parents are;

- where the law requires a falsification of paternity on the birth certificate, for example in relation to a child whose father is not the mother's current husband or, as in the case of Uruguay, where the Committee deplored the fact that as regards children born out of wedlock:

  "...when born to a mother or father who is a minor, these children cannot be recognized by that parent." (Uruguay IRCO, Add.62, para. 11)

- with anonymous egg/sperm donation for *in vitro* fertilization, where most countries protect the secrecy of the donor.

The third category includes the most controversial aspects of the interpretation of "as far as possible", appearing to unnecessarily breach children's right to know their genetic parents.

Some States Parties argue that "secret" adoptions (where the child is not entitled to discover his or her genetic parents) are necessary to secure the success of an adoption. However, other countries have pursued policies of open adoptions that have not adversely affected the outcome for the child.

The United Nations Declaration on Social and Legal Principles Relating to the Protection and Welfare of Children with Special Reference to Foster Placement and Adoption Nationally and Internationally provides that "The need of a foster or an adopted child to know about his or her background should be recognized by persons responsible for the child's care unless this is contrary to the child's best interests" (article 9).

Three points should be noted. First, article 7 does not refer to "the best interests of the child," although this was proposed by some delegates in the drafting sessions (E/CN.4/1989/48, pp. 18-22; Detrick, p. 129). The words "as far as possible" appear to provide a much stricter and less subjective qualification than "best interests". The words imply children are entitled to know their parentage if this is possible, even if this is deemed to be against their best interests. But the holistic nature of the Convention suggests that a child who would definitely be harmed by the discovery of his or her parent's identity could be prevented from having this information. This interpretation is supported by the fact that "as far as possible" also covers the child's right to be cared for by his or her parents – and no one could maintain that "as far as possible" in that context does not include consideration of the child's best interests. But it is clear that children's right to know their parentage could only be refused on the grounds of best interests in the most extreme and unambiguous circumstances.

Second, "best interests" is nowhere defined and there are no easy answers as to whether it is more harmful to children's best interests to give them distressing information about their origins or to refuse them this information on the grounds the information might cause them harm.

Third, the Convention's articles 5 (evolving capacities of the child) and 12 (child's opinion) suggest that the determination of what is or is not in the child's best interests so far as knowledge of origins is concerned may not be made just at one point during the child's life. The best interests of a six-year-old in relation to this issue may be quite different from the best interests of a 16-year-old.

This is not to say that adopted children are obliged to contact or even to be told the details of their genetic parents (although it appears to be the accepted practice in most countries that children should know the circumstances of their birth from as early an age as possible). Many children choose not to trace their genetic parents, since the significant parents in their lives are likely to be those who have cared for them and raised them. Nonetheless under the terms of article 7, the State should ensure that information about genetic parents is preserved to be made available to children if possible.

A stronger argument mounted by those countries that maintain secrecy is not about the rights of the child (or of the adopting couple) but about protecting the child's mother from extreme forms of social condemnation (such as ostracism, injury or death). In such instances there are competing rights: children's rights to know their origins and mothers' rights to confidentiality and protection. Article 30 of the Hague Convention on the Protection of Children and Cooperation in respect of Intercountry Adoption 1993 (an international treaty on intercountry adoption, see article 21, page 276) upholds mothers' rights, empowering the State of origin of the child to withhold information about the parents' identity. Those countries that maintain adoption secrecy in order to protect the mother should, nonetheless, have provisions to release information to the receiving authorities or the child, either with the mother's permission or at a time when she will not suffer harm.

Similar arguments prevail over falsifying parentage in cases of adultery. Some countries require that husbands are the lawfully recognized fathers of any children born within that marriage. In many cases this entails the complicity of the mother and is likely to be rather more to the benefit than to the disadvantage of the child. However, there is a difference between individuals lying and States enforcing a lie. In some circumstances both parents will want the true parentage of a child to be declared and may be prevented by the law from doing so.

Regarding the secrecy of egg and sperm donation, two arguments are commonly made. First, that it is not in the best interests of the child to know of his or her artificial conception. This does not seem convincing, however, particularly when advances in medical knowledge reveal how important it is for people know their genetic parentage. Second, it is argued that unless their anonymity is secured donors will be deterred, fearing future embarrassment or even maintenance suits by their biological children. However, legislation can protect a donor parent from maintenance suits and the experience of Sweden (see box on page 107) suggests that donors are not deterred by the possibility of being identified to a resulting child. In any event, the law on artificial forms of fertilization, as with adoption, should be framed to protect the rights and well-being of children, not to meet the needs of childless couples.

The Committee has commented:

"Concerning the right of the child to know his or her origins, the Committee notes the possible contradiction between this provision of the Convention with the policy of the State Party in relation to artificial insemination, namely in keeping the identity of sperm donors secret." (Norway IRCO, Add.23, para. 10)

And the Committee made a similar observation to Denmark (Denmark IRCO, Add.33, para. 11).

"...as far as possible, the right to ... be cared for by his or her parents"

This right must be read in the context of three other articles – article 5, which acknowledges, alongside the primacy of parents, "the members of the extended family or community as provided for by local custom" (see page 77); article 9, which requires that "a child shall not be separated from his or her parents against their will, except when... such separation is necessary for the best interests of the child" (see page 121) and article 18, which endorses the principle that both parents have joint responsibility for caring for their children, appropriately supported by the State (see page 229). Article 27 (requiring States to assist parents in their material responsibilities in relation to caring for children) is also relevant.

The right to be "cared for" by both parents implies a more active involvement in the child's life than simply paying the other parent or the State money to support the child (see article 27(4)). It should be noted that unlike article 5, which refers to the (albeit limited) rights of parents and others, this article is framed in terms of the child's right, not the parents'. (At one stage the drafting of this article included the proposed formulation "The child shall have the right from his birth to know and belong to his parents", but the words "belong to" were considered inappropriate to children's rights (E/CN.4/1989/48, pp. 18-22, Detrick, p. 127)).

This focus on the child's right must cast doubt on the legitimacy of Luxembourg's official declaration that it would maintain its law that says "If at the time of conception, the father or mother was bound in marriage to another person, the natural child may be raised in the conjugal home only with the consent of the spouse of his parent" (CRC/C/2/Rev.5, p 24).

As with children's right to know their parents, the right to be cared for by parents is qualified by the words "as far as possible". The purpose of this proviso is in one sense self-evident. It may not be possible if the parents are dead or have repudiated the child. It also may not be possible when the State authorities have judged that parental care is not in the child's best interests because the parents are abusive or neglectful (see article 9, page 121). However, the onus is on the State to prove this; the right upholds a general principle running through the Convention – that in ordinary circumstances, children are best off with their parents.

Swedish children's rights to know parents

Swedish legislation, as outlined in the Initial Report, contains some of the strongest provisions for enabling children to know their parentage:

"Concerning the right of the child to know who its parents are, mention can be made of the following rules:

(a) If the mother's spouse is not the child's father and paternity cannot be established through confirmation by any man, special provisions of the Code of Parenthood and Guardianship make it the duty of the municipal social welfare committee to try to ascertain who is the child's father. In cases of this kind, it is usually necessary for paternity proceedings to be filed with a court of law.

(b) Under the Insemination Act, a child conceived through artificial insemination is entitled to obtain particulars concerning the donor, providing the child is sufficiently mature. The decision to be made on this point, however, is governed by the child's best interests".

(Sweden IR, para. 61)

The point at which this right becomes most problematic is perhaps when children themselves decide that they would rather not be cared for by parents, although parents and State do not support this. Among the many thousands of homeless children in all countries are those who fall into this category – children who have, in effect, voted with their feet. States need flexible, child-centred procedures where runaway children are concerned. Any automatic return of such children to parents without investigation of the reasons why they ran away and without provision of alternative measures of care, for example, is in conflict with the provisions and principles of the Convention.

Implementation Checklist

article 7

● *General measures of implementation*

Have appropriate general measures of implementation been taken in relation to article 7, including:

☐ identification and coordination of the responsible departments and agencies at all levels of government (article 7 is relevant to the **departments of justice, home affairs, social welfare and health**)?

☐ identification of relevant non-governmental organizations/civil society partners?

☐ a comprehensive review to ensure that all legislation, policy and practice is compatible with the article, for all children in all parts of the jurisdiction?

☐ adoption of a strategy to secure full implementation

☐ which includes where necessary the identification of goals and indicators of progress?

☐ which does not affect any provisions which are more conducive to the rights of the child?

☐ which recognizes other relevant international standards?

☐ which involves where necessary international cooperation?

(Such measures may be part of an overall governmental strategy for implementing the Convention as a whole).

☐ budgetary analysis and allocation of necessary resources?

☐ development of mechanisms for monitoring and evaluation?

☐ making the implications of article 7 widely known to adults and children?

☐ development of appropriate training and awareness-raising (in relation to article 7 likely to include the **training of birth registration officers, social workers, adoption agency staff and medical personnel**)?

● *Specific issues in implementing article 7*

☐ Does domestic law require parents to register children immediately after their birth?

☐ Is the duty to register well publicized?

☐ Is registration free?

☐ Is registration made easy for parents, both in terms of access (for example by providing mobile registration units or using schools) and comprehensibility (for example by use of minority languages or by training registration staff)?

☐ Are all children born within the jurisdiction registered, including those born of non-citizens?

How to use the checklists, *see page XVII*

☐ Where parents fail to register children, is there a duty on the State to secure registration?

Does registration include necessary information for the child to claim his or her rights to:

    ☐ a name?
    ☐ a nationality?
    ☐ knowledge of parentage?

☐ Are arrangements in place to secure the confidentiality of any potentially stigmatizing information on the birth register?

☐ Does domestic law provide for the naming of all children from birth?

☐ Does this law ensure that no children are discriminated against (for example by laws requiring certain forms of naming)?

☐ Are children of appropriate maturity able to apply to change their names?

☐ Are the courts empowered to veto a name that is against the best interests of the child (for example one which could render the child an object of fear or ridicule)?

☐ Does domestic law ensure that all stateless children living within the jurisdiction have a right to acquire the State's nationality?

☐ Has the State ratified The Convention on Reduction of Statelessness 1961?

☐ Is there no discrimination between forms of nationality?

☐ Is there no discrimination in the acquisition of nationality (for example in relation to children born out of wedlock or to rights to acquire the nationality of either parent)?

☐ Are children able to apply to change their nationality?

☐ Does domestic law and administrative practice ensure that the identities of children's parents (including genetic parents, birth mother and caring parents) are accurately recorded and preserved?

☐ Do children have the right to know from the earliest date possible the truth about the particular circumstances of their parenting (for example by adoption or by an artificial form of conception)?

☐ Do all children, including adopted children and children conceived by artificial forms of conception, have the right to know, as far as possible, who their genetic parents are?

☐ Is any refusal of this right based either on the grounds that refusal of information is necessary to protect the child from a likelihood of harm or is necessary to protect the child's parent from a likelihood of harm?

☐ When children are refused the right to know parentage, are they able to reapply at a later date?

☐ Do domestic laws contain a presumption that children should be cared for by their parents?

   ☐ Is this law framed as the child's right?

☐ Where children do not wish to be cared for by parents, is provision made to investigate the reasons why they do not and to provide alternative measures of care while arrangements for their future are being determined?

Reminder : **The Convention is indivisible and its articles are interdependent. Article 7 should not be considered in isolation.**

Particular regard should be paid to:
The general principles

Article 2: all rights to be recognized for each child in jurisdiction without discrimination on any ground

Article 3(1): the best interests of the child to be a primary consideration in all actions concerning children

Article 6: right to life and maximum possible survival and development

Article 12: respect for the child's views in all matters affecting the child; opportunity to be heard in any judicial or administrative proceedings affecting the child.

Closely related articles

Articles whose implementation is related to that of article 7 include:

Article 5: parental guidance and child's evolving capacities

Article 8: preservation of child's identity

Article 9: non-separation from parents except when necessary for best interests

Article 10: international family reunification

Article 11: protection from illicit transfer and non-return of children abroad

Article 16: protection from arbitrary interference in privacy, family and home

Article 18: parents having joint responsibility

Article 20: children deprived of their family environment

Article 21: adoption

Article 22: refugee children

Article 30: children of minorities or indigenous peoples

Article 35: prevention of sale, trafficking and abduction

Preservation of identity

Text of Article 8

1. States Parties undertake to respect the right of the child to preserve his or her identity, including nationality, name and family relations as recognized by law without unlawful interference.

2. Where a child is illegally deprived of some or all of the elements of his or her identity, States Parties shall provide appropriate assistance and protection, with a view to speedily re-establishing his or her identity.

Summary

Article 8 of the Convention on the Rights of the Child concerns the children's rights to identity and their rights to have such identity preserved or, where necessary, re-established by the State.

The article was introduced in the Working Group drafting the Convention by the Argentinean delegate on the grounds that it was necessary to secure the speedy intervention of the State when the child's right to preserve his or her identity had been violated. Argentina was at the time tackling the disappearance of children and babies, which had occurred under the regime of the Argentinean junta during the 1970s and 1980s. While many such children were killed, a number had been adopted by childless couples; active steps were needed to trace these children and establish their true identity (E/CN.4/1986/39, pp. 8-10; Detrick, pp. 292-294). The United Nations General Assembly subsequently adopted a Declaration on the Protection of All Persons from Enforced Disappearance in 1992 (Resolution 47/133).

Although article 8 only describes three aspects of identity – nationality, name and family relations – other articles, such as article 2 (non-discrimination) and article 30 (right to enjoy culture, religion and language), should render unlawful most forms of interference in children's identity. Article 20 also provides that children deprived of their family environment should where possible have continuity of upbringing, particularly with regard to their ethnic, cultural and linguistic background. ∎

Extracts from

Committee on the Rights of the Child

Guidelines for Reports to be submitted by States Parties under the Convention

For full text of *Guidelines for Periodic Reports*, see Appendix 3, page 604.

Guidelines for Initial Reports

"Civil rights and freedoms

Under this section States Parties are requested to provide relevant information, including the principal legislative, judicial, administrative or other measures in force; factors and difficulties encountered and progress achieved in implementing the relevant provisions of the Convention; and implementation priorities and specific goals for the future in respect of:

...(b) Preservation of identity (article 8)."

(CRC/C/5, para. 15)

Guidelines for Periodic Reports

"IV. CIVIL RIGHTS AND FREEDOMS

B. Preservation of identity (Art. 8)

Please indicate the measures adopted to preserve the child's identity and to prevent any unlawful interference. In the case of the illegal deprivation of some or all of the elements of the child's identity, reports should also indicate the measures adopted to provide appropriate assistance and protection to the child and ensure the speedy re-establishment of his or her identity."

(CRC/C/58, para. 54. The following paragraphs of the *Guidelines for Periodic Reports* are also relevant to reporting under this article: 24, 83, 160 and 165; for full text of *Guidelines*, see Appendix 3, page 604.)

Child's right "to preserve his or her identity including nationality, name and family relations as recognized by law without unlawful interference"

The three elements of identity particularly specified are nationality, name and family relations (as recognized by law):

Nationality

Because of religious doctrine and political interests, the rights of children to nationality are not strong under the Convention. The link between nationality and identity is therefore important. A child's "national identity" may be derived from the nationality of his or her parents, suggesting that legislation that prevents children from inheriting the nationality of their parents might not be compatible with the Convention – for example those States that prohibit dual nationality or those States that do not recognize the right of children to inherit the nationality of their unmarried father. On the other hand, the concept of the child's "national identity" can involve identity acquired through residence as well as through birth or parentage, which renders equally questionable legislation that does not allow children to acquire full nationality from significant periods of residence, and those States that, by deporting parents, prevent children from enjoying their national identity acquired from place of birth or residence. These issues, and the Committee's comments, are discussed under articles 7 (see page 102) and 9 (see page 122).

Name

Some States prohibit children's names being changed by their parents (for example on divorce and remarriage), although this tends to be more due to respect for fathers' rights than for children's. It should be noted that most adoption law authorizes a change of name (although some States require consent for any name change by older children, such as the Federal Republic of Yugoslavia (Federal Republic of Yugoslavia IR, para. 48)).

Family relations

The phrase "family relations as recognized by law" is unclear. It emerged from a less than logical series of amendments in the drafting process. The original version from Argentina was "the child has the inalienable right to retain his true and genuine personal, legal and family identity". Some States protested that "family identity" had no meaning in their legal codes, and they proposed a change to "family identity as recognized by law"; others simultaneously proposed changing "family identity" to "family relations". Both changes were accepted, although, in fact, it seems that "as recognized by law" is inappropriate, because Argentina's original point was that identity includes more than just legal forms of identity (E/CN.4/1986/39, pp. 8-10; Detrick, p. 294).

The phrase does however recognize an important principle, which is that a child's identity means more than just knowing who one's parents are (see article 7). Siblings, grandparents and other relatives can be as, or more, important to the child's sense of identity as his or her parents are. Most domestic legal instruments governing, for example, adoption, fostering or divorce arrangements, fail to recognize this fact – children are given legal rights to discover who their biological parents are, or to make applications for contact with them, but rarely do those rights extend to cover other members of the child's biological family.

The concept of "children's identity" has tended to focus on the child's immediate family, but it is increasingly recognized that children have a remarkable capacity to embrace multiple relationships, speak several languages fluently and enjoy a complex, multicultural world. From the secure foundation of an established family environment, children can enjoy complex and subtle relationships with other adults and with a range of cultures, to a much larger degree than is often recognized. Thus children's best interests and senses of identity may be sustained without having to deny them knowledge of their origins, for example after reception into State care, through "secret" adoptions or anonymous egg/sperm donations and so forth (see also article 7, page 106).

Children who live in a different country from that of one or both of their parents are not able to preserve their identity, in terms of family relations. Those countries that maintain long waiting lists for immigrant or emigrant children to be granted permission to join their parents should ensure that such cases are dealt with speedily and with a presumption in favour of the child being allowed to join their parents (see articles 9, 10 and 22).

Additional Protocol 1 to the Geneva Conventions provides for the preservation of the identity of children who have been displaced or evacuated in time of war. The authorities must provide each child with a card to be sent to the Red Cross Central Tracing Committee. The card should include a photograph and details of the child's name, sex, date and place of birth, name of parents and next-of-kin, the child's nationality, native language, religion, home and present addresses, any identifying marks and health details and details of where the child was found and how he or she left the country (Geneva Conventions, Additional Protocol 1, article 78(3)).

Name, nationality and family are only some elements of identity. Other aspects of identity include:

- the child's personal history since birth – where he or she lived, who looked after him or her, why crucial decisions were taken, etc.
- the child's race, culture, religion and language. An "unlawful" interference in this aspect of identity could include:
  - the suppression of minority languages in the education system, state information and the media;
  - State persecution or proscription of the practice of a religion;
  - failure to give adopted, fostered or institutionally placed children the opportunity to enjoy their ethnic, cultural, linguistic or religious heritage.

  The preservation of these aspects of identity is also upheld in article 20 (which provides that when children are without families "due regard shall be paid to the desirability of continuity in the child's upbringing and to the child's ethnic, religious, cultural and linguistic background" see page 264) and article 30 (which upholds the right of children of minority and indigenous communities to enjoy and practice their culture, religion and language, see page 407).
- children's physical appearance, abilities and inclinations (including gender and sexual orientation).

"Preserve"

The word implies both the non-interference in identity and the maintenance of records relating to genealogy, birth registration and details relating to early infancy that the child could not be expected to remember. Some of these are beyond the scope of the State, but measures should be taken to enforce detailed record-keeping (and preservation of records or, in the case of abandoned children, any identifying items) where children are refugees, abandoned, fostered, adopted or taken into the care of the State. Equal care must be taken to ensure such records are confidential – see article 16, page 202.

In that regard the Committee raised concerns with Ukraine:

"The Committee is worried by the high rate of abandonment of children, especially new-born babies, and the lack of a comprehensive strategy to assist vulnerable families. This situation can lead to illegal intercountry adoption or other forms of trafficking and sale of children. In this context the Committee is also concerned about the absence of any law prohibiting the sale and trafficking of children, and the fact that the right of the child to have his/her identity preserved is not guaranteed by the law." (Ukraine IRCO, Add.42, para. 11)

And with Peru:

"The Committee is concerned that, due to the internal violence, several registration centres have been destroyed, adversely affecting the situation of thousands of children who are often left without any identity document, thus running the risk of their being suspected of involvement in terrorist activities...
"Special measures should be undertaken to provide undocumented children fleeing zones affected by internal violence with adequate identity documents." (Peru IRCO, Add.8, paras. 8 and 17)

A right to preservation of identity suggests that the law should place penalties on those who breach it. This certainly is the recommendation of the 1992 Declaration on Enforced Disappearances: "The abduction of children of parents subjected to enforced disappearance or of children born during their mother's enforced disappearance, and the act of altering or suppressing documents attesting to their true identity, shall constitute an extremely serious offence, which shall be punished as such."

"Without unlawful interference"

This suggests that the child's right to preservation of identity can be lawfully violated – a suggestion questioned by some countries when the Convention was being drafted (E/CN.4/1989/48, pp. 55-56; Detrick, pp. 295-6). Certainly when

the State itself is guilty of the violation, the provision could appear to be too weak since the State prescribes the laws. However it should be assumed that the provision includes international law, including the Convention on the Rights of the Child.

The right of a child who has been "illegally deprived of some or all of the elements of his or her identity" to be provided by the State with "appropriate assistance and protection with a view to speedily re-establishing his or her identity"

This right means that the State must recognize the seriousness to children of any deprivation of their identity by dedicating resources to remedy the situation.

"Appropriate assistance"

This could include:

- making available genetic profiling to establish parentage;
- actively tracing relatives or community members of unaccompanied refugee children;
- using the media to advertise missing children and to reunite families (see box);
- ensuring that any child-custody cases where an illegal abduction has been alleged (including those relating to international disputes) are expeditiously dealt with at an appropriately senior level in the judiciary, that is, within days or weeks rather than months (see articles 11, page 139 and 35, page 471);
- ensuring that any changes to a child's identity, such as name, nationality, parental rights of custody, etc., are officially recorded;
- enabling children to have access to the professional files maintained on them (see article 16, page 202);
- ensuring that children in State care are encouraged to practice their religion, culture and language of origin;
- amending nationality laws to allow for a "best interests of children" consideration in issues relating to deportation or family reunification, and speeding up nationality and asylum procedures.

The *Manual on Human Rights Reporting*, 1997 advises that appropriate assistance can include "legislative measures, including in the civil and penal areas – for instance to annul any adoption based on an irregular situation, such as the child's

---

"Children in search of their parents" – a Colombian TV programme

Colombia, with estimates of 18,000 abandoned or disappeared children, has introduced a television programme called "Children in search of their parents". The programme assists children in finding parents with whom they have lost contact (Colombia SR.114, para. 25).

abduction, or to penalize such possible offences... the establishment of mechanisms to re-establish the child's identity, such as a national data bank where changes made in the elements of the identity of children (including the name, nationality and family relations) may be kept and, when appropriate, acceded to" (*Manual,* pp. 432-433).

"Protection"

This includes securing appropriate temporary placement for children while their identify is re-established. It should also involve explaining to the children what is happening and why – ignorance and uncertainty can unnecessarily add to children's insecurity and lack of well-being.

"Speedily re-establishing his or her identity"

The article emphasizes the importance of speed to the child. The "identity" of children is not just a matter of parentage and culture of origin. As children grow they assume the identity of the family or culture in which they live, to a point at which it would be a second deprivation of identity to remove them, and unacceptable in terms of the child's best interests. This is a particularly bitter fact for parents who have been illegally separated from their children, whether they were separated by the State or through abduction by individuals. (It should be noted that Argentina originally proposed the words "In particular, this obligation of the State includes restoring the child to his blood-relations to be brought up", but this proposal did not find acceptance (E/CN.4/1986/39, pp. 8-10; Detrick, pp. 292-4)).

Implementation Checklist

article 8

● General measures of implementation

Have appropriate general measures of implementation been taken in relation to article 8, including

☐ identification and coordination of the responsible departments and agencies at all levels of government (definition of the child in article 8 is relevant to **the departments of justice, home affairs, foreign affairs, public communication and the media, social welfare and education**)?

☐ identification of relevant non-governmental organizations/civil society partners?

☐ a comprehensive review to ensure that all legislation, policy and practice is compatible with the article, for all children in all parts of the jurisdiction?

☐ adoption of a strategy to secure full implementation

    ☐ which includes where necessary the identification of goals and indicators of progress?

    ☐ which does not affect any provisions which are more conducive to the rights of the child?

    ☐ which recognizes other relevant international standards?

    ☐ which involves where necessary international cooperation?

(Such measures may be part of an overall governmental strategy for implementing the Convention as a whole).

☐ budgetary analysis and allocation of necessary resources?

☐ development of mechanisms for monitoring and evaluation?

☐ making the implications of article 8 widely known to adults and children?

☐ development of appropriate training and awareness-raising?

● Specific issues in implementing article 8

☐ Are children able to acquire the nationality of both parents?

☐ Are children able to acquire the nationality of the State in which they have lived for a significant period?

☐ Are they able to live with their parents in their State of nationality?

☐ Are questions of nationality and right to family reunification dealt with speedily?

☐ Are any changes of children's name overseen by a judicial process which gives paramount consideration to the best interests of the child?

☐ Are such changes fully recorded and the records accessible to the child?

☐ Are children able to know and associate with members of their family of origin, so far as this is compatible with their best interests?

☐ Are accurate records kept about the identity, and any changes to the identity, of all children?

☐ Can children apply to have access to these records?

☐ Where parentage is in doubt, are children able to have it established by genetic testing (free of charge if necessary)?

☐ Are other resources provided to trace missing children or missing family members (for example using tracing agencies or the media)?

☐ Are all cases dealt with expeditiously where illegal actions relating to children's identity and family relations are alleged to have occurred?

☐ Is unlawful interference with children's rights to preserve their identity an offence, subject to penalties?

☐ Do education, welfare and justice systems allow the child to enjoy his or her culture, religion and language of origin?

☐ Where children are in the care of the State, are accurate records kept about their family of origin and early childhood?

☐ Do such children have access to these records?

☐ Do placements of children by the State endeavour, where compatible with the child's best interests, to give continuity to the child's ethnic, religious, cultural and linguistic background?

Reminder : **The Convention is indivisible and its articles interdependent. Article 8 should not be considered in isolation. Particular regard should be paid to:**

The general principles:

Article 2: all rights to be recognized for each child in jurisdiction without discrimination on any ground

Article 3(1): the best interests of the child to be a primary consideration in all actions concerning children

Article 6: right to life and maximum possible survival and development

Article 12: respect for the child's views in all matters affecting the child; opportunity to be heard in any judicial or administrative proceedings affecting the child

Closely related articles

Articles whose implementation is related to that of article 8 include:

Article 7: birth registration, right to name and nationality and to know and be cared for by parents

Article 9: non-separation from parents except when necessary in best interests

Article 10: international family reunification

Article 11: protection from illicit transfer and non-return from abroad

Article 16: protection from arbitrary interference in privacy, family and home

Article 18: parents having joint responsibility

Article 20: children deprived of family environment

Article 21: adoption

Article 22: refugee children

Article 30: children of minorities or indigenous peoples

Article 35: prevention of sale, trafficking and abduction of children

Separation from parents

Text of Article 9

1. States Parties shall ensure that a child shall not be separated from his or her parents against their will, except when competent authorities subject to judicial review determine, in accordance with applicable law and procedures, that such separation is necessary for the best interests of the child. Such determination may be necessary in a particular case such as one involving abuse or neglect of the child by the parents, or one where the parents are living separately and a decision must be made as to the child's place of residence.

2. In any proceedings pursuant to paragraph 1 of the present article, all interested parties shall be given an opportunity to participate in the proceedings and make their views known.

3. States Parties shall respect the right of the child who is separated from one or both parents to maintain personal relations and direct contact with both parents on a regular basis, except if it is contrary to the child's best interests.

4. Where such separation results from any action initiated by a State Party, such as the detention, imprisonment, exile, deportation or death (including death arising from any cause while the person is in the custody of the State) of one or both parents or of the child, that State Party shall, upon request, provide the parents, the child or, if appropriate, another member of the family with the essential information concerning the whereabouts of the absent member(s) of the family unless the provision of the information would be detrimental to the well-being of the child. States Parties shall further ensure that the submission of such a request shall of itself entail no adverse consequences for the person(s) concerned.

Summary

Article 9 of the Convention on the Rights of the Child enshrines two essential principles of children's rights: first, that children should not be separated from their parents unless it is necessary for their best interests and, second, that all procedures to separate children from parents on that ground must be fair. It also affirms children's rights to maintain relations and contact with both parents, and places a duty on the State to inform parent and child of the whereabouts of either if the State has caused their separation (for example by deportation or imprisonment).

The basic principles are enshrined in the 1959 Declaration of the Rights of the Child: "The child, for the full and harmonious development of his personality, needs love and understanding. He shall, wherever possible, grow up in the care and under the responsibility of his parents... " (article 6).

The International Covenant on Civil and Political Rights provides "The family is the natural and fundamental group unit of society and is entitled to protection by society and the State" (article 23(1), which is mirrored by article 10 of the International Covenant on Social, Economic and Cultural Rights) and: "No one shall be subjected to arbitrary or unlawful interference with his privacy, family, home or correspondence, nor to unlawful attacks on his honour and reputation. Everyone has the right to the protection of the law against such interference or attacks" (articles 17(1) and (2)). ■

Extracts from
Committee on the Rights of the Child
Guidelines for Reports to be submitted by States Parties under the Convention

For full text of *Guidelines for Periodic Reports*, see Appendix 3, page 604.

Guidelines for Initial Reports

"Family environment and alternative care

Under this section, States Parties are requested to provide relevant information, including the principal legislative, judicial, administrative or other measures in force, particularly how the principles of the "best interests of the child" and "respect for the views of the child" are reflected therein; factors and difficulties encountered and progress achieved in implementing the relevant provisions of the Convention; and implementation priorities and specific goals for the future in respect of:

...(c) Separation from parents (article 9);

In addition, States Parties are requested to provide information on the numbers of children per year within the reporting period in each of the following groups, disaggregated by age group, sex, ethnic or national background and rural or urban environment: homeless children, abused or neglected children taken into protective custody, children placed in foster care, children placed in institutional care, children placed through domestic adoption, children entering the country through intercountry adoption procedures and children leaving the country through intercountry adoption procedures.

States Parties are encouraged to provide additional relevant statistical information and indicators relating to children covered in this section."

(CRC/C/5, paras. 16-18)

Guidelines for Periodic Reports

"V. FAMILY ENVIRONMENT AND ALTERNATIVE CARE

C. Separation from parents (art. 9)

Please indicate the measures adopted, including of a legislative and judicial nature, to ensure that the child is not separated from his or her parents except when such separation is necessary for the best interests of the child, as in cases of abuse or neglect of the child or when the parents live separately and a decision must be made as to the child's place of residence. Please identify the competent authorities intervening in these decisions, the applicable law and procedure and the role of judicial review.

Please provide information on the measures taken pursuant to article 9, paragraph 2 to ensure to all interested parties, including the child, an opportunity to participate in any proceedings and to make their views known.

Please indicate the measure adopted, including of a legislative, judicial and administrative nature, to ensure that the child who is separated from one or both parents has the right to maintain personal relations and direct contacts with both parents on a regular basis, except if it is contrary to the best interests of the child. Please further indicate the extent to which the views of the child are taken into consideration in this regard.

Implementation Handbook for the Convention on the Rights of the Child

The child's right "not to be separated from parents against their will, except when judged ... necessary for the child's best interests"

The words "against their will" refers either to the parents' will or to the parents' and child's will together; the grammar makes clear that it does not mean the child's will alone. And, in one sense, the right of children to parental care is inevitably subject to the "will" of parents. Infants have no power or ability to choose their caregivers. They are dependent on their family, community and the State to make that choice for them. Moreover, even if young children were in a position to "choose" their parents, they could not force them to act as parents against their will. The State can seek to force parents to financially maintain their children, but it cannot compel parents to care for them appropriately.

The article gives two examples of when it may be necessary to separate children from one or both parents: first, when the parents have abused or neglected the child and, second, when parents live apart. A third example was suggested by the United States representative during the drafting of the Convention: "where there is a disagreement between parent(s) and child as to the child's place of residence" (E/1982/12/Add.1, C, pp. 49-55; Detrick, p. 168). This suggestion was dropped on the grounds that an exhaustive list of reasons should not be attempted. The two examples are simply illustrations of cases when separation from parents may occur.

However, the third example given by the United States does raise a profound difficulty for some children – when parents agree between themselves where the child should live, or how parental access should be organized, but when the child is unhappy with the arrangement. Few States make provision for the child in such circumstances, arguing that the State should not interfere in the private arrangements of parents. But if the State accepts that it has a role as arbitrator when there are disputes between husband and wife, then it should accept its role as arbitrator when there is dispute between parent and child – at least to the extent of establishing judicial machinery for the child to make a case for arbitration.

Other aspects of "unnecessary" separation from parents include:

State care Failure to keep children in contact with their parents when they are in state care may occur (for example in institutions, specialist schools and placements for disabled children, street children projects, foster care, "simple adoption" etc.). Often this may be done for the primary convenience of the caregiver, particularly when the child's parents appear to be hostile, disruptive or irrelevant to the child's progress. Arguments are raised that the child needs to "settle in" or that seeing parents upsets the child. However evidence strongly suggests that children are less likely to be reunited with their parents if contact is not maintained with them during the early months of State care. Planning of placements should secure that contact can be easily maintained by the parents, who may be unable to travel distances or visit at set times.

Abandoned, runaway or unaccompanied children living or working on the streets
Parents in extreme circumstances of poverty, violence or armed conflict may abandon their children, or children and parents may simply lose contact with each other as a result of the pressure of such events; sometimes children leave home for the streets because of violence or exploitation by their parents. The result is that most large cities in the world contain populations of chil-

Children in hospital

Costa Rica reported to the Committee in respect of article 9 that its Ministry of Health had drawn up rules to ensure that mothers and newly born babies are lodged together immediately after birth: "The baby had traditionally been kept away from his mother, at least during the first 12 hours... Likewise, in hospitals, the presence of the parents during the hospitalization of their children is permitted and they are encouraged to participate in caring for them during their stay. Until a few years ago, only the mother was permitted to be present but nowadays the presence of either of the two parents is allowed." (Costa Rica IR, para. 151)

dren living independently of their families. State provision for these children should always give them an opportunity of finding and being reunited with their parents and family. For some this may not be possible, but others will have their rights under article 9 breached by assumptions that they are best provided for away from their original family.

Children in hospitals Failure to allow parents to visit and, where appropriate, remain with their children in hospital may occur. Again, this form of separation, more common in industrialized than developing countries, is maintained primarily for the convenience of the staff, although the medical needs of the child patient may be cited. In fact, it is now generally recognized that children's recovery is greatly aided by having parents with them in hospital. Though hospital practice may often be dependent on medical staff and hospital managers, the State has a role in encouraging child-friendly hospitals.

Children of parents in prison

France has set up an interministerial group to look at the question of children whose parents are imprisoned. It is estimated that 140,000 French children are separated from one or both of their parents who are in prison; about 50 children under 18 months old are living with their mothers in prison. The group is considering the issues involved in bringing up children in a prison environment and in their separation from their mothers. (France IR, paras. 258-260)

Parents in prisons The imprisonment of parents, particularly of mothers of dependent young children, is deeply problematic, because the child is being punished along with the parent. While it is argued that the punishment of offenders always has repercussions on innocent relatives, where young children are concerned the effects can be particularly catastrophic to the children and costly to the State (both immediately, in terms of providing for the children's care, and long term, in terms of the social problems arising from early separation). One solution is to accommodate young infants together with their mothers in prison; the other is to find more constructive sanctions. Where possible, the latter course should be adopted. Although babies tend to be unconcerned about where they live so long as they are with their mothers, difficulties must arise about when and if to separate mother and child as the child grows older. Article 2(2) protects children against "all forms of discrimination or punishment on the basis of the status, activities...of the child's parents, legal guardians or family members" (see page 32). Although mothers have been singled out here as being particularly crucial to the development of young children, States should recognize that the imprisonment of fathers can also be very detrimental, depriving children of important role models and often causing the family to become impoverished.

Child offenders Removal of offending children from their families may be judged as necessary in the best interests of the child where judicial authorities are satisfied that the parents have contributed to the criminal activities of the child. However, care orders removing parental rights should not be an automatic part of a sentencing tariff for juvenile offending. Rule 18(2) of the United Nations Standard Minimum Rules for the Administration of Juvenile Justice, the "Beijing Rules", states: "No juvenile shall be removed from parental supervision, whether partly or entirely, unless the circumstances of his or her case make this necessary."

Immigration and deportation Article 10 deals with the limited rights of children to family reunification when they or their parents are (or wish to be) in different countries. When articles 9 and 10 were being drafted the chairman of the Working Group drafting the Convention made a declaration: "It is the understanding of the Working Group that article 6 [now article 9] of this Convention is intended to apply to separations that arise in domestic situations, whereas article 6 *bis* [now article 10] is intended to apply to separations involving different countries and relating to cases of family reunification. Article 6 *bis* [now 10] is not intended to affect the general right of States to establish and regulate their respective immigration laws in accordance with their international obligations". The Chairman's declaration caused some concern. Three State representatives in the Working Group responded by emphasizing that "international obligations" included principles recognized by the international community, particularly human rights and children's rights principles – including, of course, the principles of article 9. The representative of the Federal Republic of Germany "reserved the right to declare that silence in the face of the chairman's declaration did not mean agreement with it" (E/CN.4/1989/48, pp. 32-37; Detrick, pp. 181-2).

Such a declaration is, in any event, no more than a clarification of drafting intentions: though influential it does not carry legal force. The declaration was cited in the defence of Canada during one of that country's oral sessions with the Committee. A Committee member commented in relation to the issues of immigration control and deportation: "Under article 9, States Parties should ensure that there would be no separation unless it was in the best interests of the child concerned and determined by competent authorities subject to judicial review. Concern had been expressed at how a child's best interests were taken into consideration when decisions to deport parents were made. Were family values taken into account by decision-makers? Article 9 also referred to the need for judicial proceedings to give all interested parties the right and opportunity to be heard. It was unclear when and how a child could make his or her views known and with what legal support. Article 12, paragraph 2, established the right of children to be heard in any administrative and judicial proceedings" (Canada SR.216, para. 28).

The Canadian representative argued that: "International law did not provide an express right to family reunification nor did the Convention recognize family reunification as an express right... One issue of concern discussed in the United Nations Working Group on the draft convention in December 1988 had been whether the provision in article 9 concerning non-separation from parents would require States to amend their immigration laws to avoid the separation of children from their parents. The Working Group had requested that a statement should be included in the report on its deliberations to indicate that article 10 on family reunification was the governing matter on that issue. It had been the Working Group's understanding that article 10 was not intended to affect the general right of States to

establish and regulate their respective immigration laws in accordance with their international obligations". However, he did concede that international treaties clearly recognized "the vital importance of family reunification". (Canada SR.216, paras. 47 and 55)

Despite this discussion, the Committee member expressed the view that provisions on family reunification under article 10 should be seen in the light of article 9 (Canada SR.216, para. 84).

Japan entered a reservation on this issue: "The Government of Japan declares that paragraph 1 of article 9 of the Convention on the Rights of the Child be interpreted not to apply to a case where a child is separated from his or her parents as a result of deportation in accordance with its immigration law" (CRC/C/2/Rev.5, p. 22). The Committee had not, as of September 1997, discussed this reservation with the government of Japan.

Armed conflict The separation of parents and children also arises during armed conflict (article 38) or when they have become refugees (article 22). The consequences of civil war or economic breakdown can be devastating to the family unit.

Often, the State government can do little about the upheavals of armed conflict, but if the reins of power are in its hands, it has clear obligations towards children, as the Committee informed Myanmar:

"While welcoming the recent peace agreements between the Government and a great majority of rebel armed groups in the country, the Committee strongly recommends the State Party to prevent any occurrence of forced relocation, displacement and other types of involuntary population movements which deeply affect families and the rights of children. The Committee also recommends that the State party reinforce its central tracing agency to favour family reunification." (Myanmar IRCO, Add.69, para. 40)

Traditions or customs The separation of children and parents because of custom perhaps most commonly occurs when a child is conceived out of wedlock. In the past, many mothers might abandon such children or would be forced to give them up for adoption. These actions still persist in some parts of the world – for example, the Committee said to Sri Lanka:

"...The Committee also encourages the authorities to give full support to mothers of children born out of wedlock wishing to keep their child." (Sri Lanka IRCO, Add.40, para. 34)

Under articles 7 and 18 children have the right to be cared for by both parents, who share common responsibility for their upbringing, development and best interests. Choices and judicial decisions may have to be made about where children live and how much contact they have with the non-resident parent following parental separation. Such decisions ought to be determined solely in accordance with the child's best interests but sometimes are subject to tradition or religious doctrine – for example that adulterous parents forfeit rights of access to children or that children must live with the paternal family upon the death of the father. Such decisions are contrary to the Convention if they are made without reference to the needs and interests of the individual child concerned.

The child's right for any decision that separation from his or her parents is in his or her best interests to:

- **be undertaken by competent authorities;**
- **be subject to judicial review;**
- **be in accordance with applicable law and procedures;**
- **give all interested parties the opportunity to participate and make their views known**

"Competent authorities"

The word "competent" relates to an authorized position rather than to ability; nonetheless such authorities must have skills to determine, on the basis of the evidence, what is in the child's best interests. Such skills could be acquired through formal training (for example, in psychology, social work or children's legal casework) or an equivalent weight of experience (for example, through being a community or religious arbitrator). The State should be able to demonstrate that these authorities are genuinely able to give paramount consideration to the child's best interests, which presupposes a degree of flexibility in the decision. Any inflexible dogma defining "best interests", for example stating that children ought to be with their fathers or mothers, should be regarded as potentially discriminatory and in breach of the Convention. (It is true to say that article 6 of the United Nations Declaration on the Rights of the Child, the precursor of the Convention on the Rights of the Child, did make a statement in favour of keeping, save in exceptional circumstances, children of "tender years" with their mothers. This bias towards giving mothers custody of babies and infants, though common in many countries and an important protection in very patriarchal societies, does not find expression in the Convention).

"Subject to judicial review"

The phrase carries with it a body of expectations about natural justice and fair hearings. These include a requirement that the judge or arbitrator should have no personal interest in the case, should be as well informed as possible about all the circumstances of the case and should be able to give reasons for the final ruling that all sides are heard and that all parties should hear the evidence (which means, if necessary, providing interpretation).

While this part of article 9 was being drafted, country representatives repeatedly emphasized the need to expedite the judicial process so that the "separation period should be made as short as possible under national legislation" (E/1982/12/Add.1, C, pp. 49-55, Detrick, p. 168). Although the need for speed is not explicitly mentioned in the article, it should be assumed to be a necessary component of any judicial review in order to secure compliance with article 8(2) (duty to speedily re-establish child's identity, including family ties).

The article makes no mention of privacy of the proceedings. However article 14(1) of the International Covenant on Civil and Political Rights provides that the public may be excluded from judicial hearings "when the interest of the private lives of the Parties so requires" and that judgements of hearings should generally be made public "except where the interest of juvenile persons otherwise requires or the proceedings concern matrimonial disputes or the guardianship of children". Article 3 of the Convention on the Rights of the Child, relating to the best interests of the child, and article 16 (right to privacy) suggest an assumption that judicial hearings under article 9 should be held in private.

In addition rule 3(2) of the United Nations Standard Minimum Rules for the Administration of Juvenile Justice, the "Beijing Rules", extends the Rules' scope to care and welfare proceedings: "Efforts shall be made to extend the principles embodied in the Rules to all juveniles who are dealt with in welfare and care proceedings." The "Beijing Rules" call for fair hearings with sufficient flexibility to respond to the varying special needs of the children concerned, conducted "in an atmosphere of understanding". The Rules stresses the need for privacy, speed, the child's rights to representation and to the presence of parents, appeal procedures, powers to discontinue proceedings, good record keeping and research-based policy.

A number of Eastern European countries entered reservations to article 9 on the grounds that their social work authorities had powers to take children into care without a court hearing. For example, the Republic of Bosnia and Herzegovina stated that it "reserves the right not to apply paragraph 1 of article 9 of the Convention since the internal legislation of the Republic of Bosnia and Herzegovina provides for the right of the competent authorities (guardianship authorities) to determine on separation of a child from his/her parents without a previous judicial review" (CRC/C/2/Rev.5, p. 14).

The inclusion of care and welfare proceedings in the "Beijing Rules" stresses the point that removing children from their parents is as serious a step as depriving them of their liberty, and merits a fair hearing conducted under the rules of natural justice. This reservation has yet, as of September 1997, to be considered by the Committee.

The Republic of Croatia entered a similar reservation, except that the competent authorities are described as "Centres for Social Work" (CRC/C/2/Rev.5, p. 16). The Committee was told that this reservation was likely to be withdrawn with the implementation of a family law statute introducing family courts (Croatia SR.279, paras. 14 and 27-30). Slovenia used the same wording and also informed the Committee it was intending to withdraw its reservation (CRC/C/2/Rev.5, p. 31; Slovenia SR.337, para. 8). Nonetheless the Committee commented:

"The Committee is of the view that the reservation made by the State Party to article 9, paragraph 1, raises questions about its compatibility with the principles and provisions of the Convention, including the principle of the best interests of the child." (Slovenia IRCO, Add.65, para. 10)

The Federal Republic of Yugoslavia (using the word "ward authorities" for competent authorities) entered a similar reservation, but its circumstances were so parlous at the time of the Committee discussions and considerations that the reservation took a relatively low priority, the Committee simply encouraged it to review the reservation with a view to withdrawal (CRC/C/2/Rev.5, p. 35 and Federal Republic of Yugoslavia IRCO, Add.49, para. 23).

Iceland entered the following reservation: "With respect to article 9, under Icelandic law the administrative authorities can take final decisions in some cases referred to in the article. These decisions are subject to judicial review in the sense that it is a principle of Icelandic law that courts can nullify administrative decisions if they conclude that they are based on unlawful premis-es." Iceland has since indicated to the Committee that its system is under review with a view to withdrawing the reservation, a statement welcomed by the Committee (CRC/C/2/Rev.5, p. 21 and Iceland IRCO, Add.50, para. 4).

"In accordance with applicable law and procedures"

These words again stress the need for legislation governing any procedure where the child is separated from parents against their will, whether it is the State intervening to remove the child or one of the parents seeking custody of the child.

Some States adopt more prescriptive criteria than others for determining what are the best interests of children. Where laws specify grounds for separation, they must be examined carefully for discriminatory application. For example, homelessness or poverty of the parents should not be grounds in themselves for removal of the child, nor should a parent's failure to send the child to school. If these deficiencies are causing the child's development to be impaired, then the State should put its resources into making good the deficiency while maintaining the child in the family. The Committee expressed its concern to Croatia

"that children might be removed from their families because of their health status or the difficult economic situation." (Croatia IRCO, Add. 52, para. 17)

It commented to the United Kingdom:

"...the Committee is concerned that children of certain ethnic minorities appear to be more likely to be placed in care." (UK IRCO, Add.34, para. 12)

And to Belgium:

"...that children belonging to the disadvantaged groups of the population appear more likely to be placed in care. In this regard, the Committee recalls the importance of the family in the upbringing of a child and emphasizes its view that the separation of the child from his or her family must take the child's best interests as a primary consideration." (Belgium IRCO, Add. 38, para. 10)

Finland, on the other hand, reported concern that the pendulum has swung too far in favour of leaving children with biological parents for too long (Finland IR, paras. 299-302; see article 18 page 231).

If, however, laws leave criteria for separation open to judicial discretion so that it is entirely up to the judge to decide what is in the best interests of the child, then the State must be satisfied that judges exercise this discretion objectively.

".. all interested parties shall be given an opportunity to participate in the proceedings and make their views known"

This aspect of a proper judicial review – the need to hear from all relevant parties – is given special emphasis within the Convention for good reasons. It reminds States that both parents must be heard, even when one parent has not had primary care of the child (for example in a case of child neglect by the child's mother, even a non-resident father of the child should be given an opportunity to show he is able and willing to look after the child) or when one parent is out of the country. It also enables other "interested parties" to participate in the proceedings – for example members of the child's extended family, or professionals with a specialist knowledge of the child. "Interested parties" is undefined within the Convention, so that interpretation is left to domestic law or the judge of the case; however, it should be assumed that the widest possible interpretation is needed, since a sound decision on best interests of the child is dependent on having the fullest possible information.

The child, in particular, should not be forgotten. He or she is clearly the most "interested party" involved in the case. Article 12(2) provides that children specifically be given opportunities to be heard directly or through a representative "in any judicial and administrative proceedings affecting the child." Proceedings under article 9 are clearly judicial proceedings affecting the child. Article 12(2) does not specify when the child should be heard directly and when through a representative, but given the general right under 12(1) for children to "express those views freely in all matters affecting the child", it should be assumed that wherever children wish to speak directly to the adjudicators, this should be arranged, but that, in addition, where children are not able to represent their views adequately (through incapacity or because they need an advocate in an adversarial system), appropriate arrangements should be made. However States must recognize that appointing a person to represent the child's best interests is **not** the same as children being given "an opportunity to ... make their views known" (article 9(2)) or "to be heard" (article 12(2)). Professional opinion as to the child's best interests may sometimes conflict with the child's own view of what is best. In such circumstances, States are obliged under the Convention to ensure that the child's views are also heard.

States sometimes specify an age at which children themselves can determine decisions about custody and access (that is, residence and contact), usually with a caveat that the child's decision can be overridden in exceptional circumstances if the child's welfare might actively be harmed by his or her choice. The age appears to range from 7 to 16. Such provisions are not contrary to the Convention. However, provisions that specify an age at which the child's views should be taken into account are questionable, since the expressed views of children of all ages should be considered under article 12 (see page 149).

The child's right "to maintain personal relations and direct contact with both parents on a regular basis" unless contrary to best interests

This right reflects the principle of article 18 that "both parents have common responsibilities for the upbringing and development of the child" (see page 225). States vary as to the care they take in protecting this right of children. The Republic of Korea entered a reservation to the paragraph, without explanation, but told the Committee that it was considering withdrawing the reservation (CRC/C/2/Rev.5, p. 30; Republic of Korea SR.276, para. 14). The Committee nonetheless informed Korea that this reservation

---

The child's or the parent's "right of contact"?

Finland reported to the Committee that its procedure in relation to contact rights had "come under heavy criticism recently, because it does not rest on the principle of protecting the best interest of the child but on the rights of the parents. Sometimes children are forced to see a parent against their will, thus reversing the principle of the Child Protection Act that 'a child shall have the right of access to the parent with whom he or she no longer resides'. On the other hand, authorities cannot easily interfere in situations where the parent residing with the child succeeds in manipulating the child against the other parent – the fear of and resistance to meeting the other parent are in any case real for the child." Finland has set up a working group to look into the issue. (Finland IR, paras. 133-134)

raised questions about its

"...compatibility with the principles and provisions of the Convention, including the principles of the best interests of the child and respect for the views of the child." (Republic of Korea IRCO, Add.51, para. 8)

Too often, children lose the chance to maintain contact with the non-residential parent because of the needs of the residential parent (for example to live at a distance from the other parent) or because of the parents' acrimonious relationship. On the other hand this right of the child can too easily be translated into the right of parents (see box on page 126).

Courts may understandably be reluctant to enforce access if this is likely to have adverse repercussions on the child. But while legislation often decrees that the child's best interests shall be paramount in such decisions, the law does not always make clear that these best interests are generally interpreted as meaning regular contact with both parents. Moreover, States could put more resources into providing practical assistance to children whose parents are in conflict, for example in providing neutral meeting places or the supervision of access.

The right of family members, and specifically parents and children, to be given on request the essential information concerning the whereabouts of a parent or child who has been separated because of an action initiated by the State (for example, detention, imprisonment, exile or death from any cause in custody), unless the provision of information would be detrimental to the well-being of the child

A failure to ensure that parents are told where their children have been detained, or that children are told of the whereabouts of their parents, seems to be an obvious abuse of human rights;

the right and reflects international rules regarding the treatment of prisoners (see article 40, page 539). Circumstances in which provision of information would be detrimental to the child are likely to be rare and exceptional – the presumption should be that children will be more damaged by ignorance of their parents' whereabouts (and equally, that imprisoned children will be more damaged by their parents not being told where they are) than by the discovery of the absent family member's fate, however shocking.

The wording refers only to "essential information concerning the whereabouts", which might be insufficient information in some cases – certainly in the case of death. States should also ensure that family members are given essential information as to cause – why the person has been imprisoned, deported, died in custody and so forth – and other relevant details (for example when they can see the family member or what their legal rights are). The qualification that the information need only be provided "upon request" was specifically sought by some of the State representatives in the drafting group, although it is hard to see how the qualification enhances children's rights (E/CN.4/1983/62, pp. 4-8; Detrick, p. 175). Children and parents should clearly be informed about each other's whereabouts (unless such information is detrimental to the child's well-being) whether or not they have made a request for the information.

The right for requests for such information not to entail "adverse consequences for the person(s) concerned"

This requirement must protect both the person seeking the information and the person to whom the information refers. Again, these are matters of human rights, only needing to be confirmed because of documented cases of abuse. One example where requests for information by the State might unwittingly entail adverse consequences is when inquiries are made about refugee children's relatives, causing unintended repercussions on those relatives.

State assistance for parent-child contact

The Belgium French Community subsidizes "meeting places" for parents to exercise visiting rights in situations where visits are difficult, conflictual or have been suspended for significant periods. The provision of such places are independent of the courts and are as yet only pilot projects. (Belgium IR, para. 194)

Implementation Checklist

article 9

● *General measures of implementation*

Have appropriate general measures of implementation been taken in relation to article 9 including

☐ identification and coordination of the responsible departments and agencies at all levels of government (article 9 is relevant to the **departments of justice (criminal and civil), social welfare, health and education**)?

☐ identification of relevant non-governmental organizations/civil society partners?

☐ a comprehensive review to ensure that all legislation, policy and practice is compatible with the article, for all children in all parts of the jurisdiction?

☐ adoption of a strategy to secure full implementation
    ☐ which includes where necessary the identification of goals and indicators of progress?
    ☐ which does not affect any provisions which are more conducive to the rights of the child?
    ☐ which recognizes other relevant international standards?
    ☐ which involves where necessary international cooperation?
(Such measures may be part of an overall governmental strategy for implementing the Convention as a whole).

☐ budgetary analysis and allocation of necessary resources?

☐ development of mechanisms for monitoring and evaluation?

☐ making the implications of article 9 widely known to adults and children?

☐ development of appropriate training and awareness-raising (in relation to article 9 likely to include the training of the **judiciary, lawyers, social workers, hospital staff and those working in the juvenile justice and immigration systems**)?

● *Specific issues in implementing article 9*

☐ Does the State ensure that parents and children are separated against their will by State authorities only when it is necessary to protect the best interests of the child?

☐ Does domestic law enable judicial intervention on behalf of the child when there is disagreement between the parents and the child as to the child's place of residence or as to access to the child by a parent?

☐ Does the State ensure that contact between parents and children in institutions (such as children's homes or boarding schools) or placements (such as fostercare or respite care for disabled children) is maintained to the maximum extent compatible with the child's best interests?

☐ Do programmes for those children living or working on the streets respect the child's right not to be separated from his or her parents unless it is necessary for his or her best interests?

How to use the checklists, *see page XVII*

- ☐ Are hospitals required or encouraged to make arrangements for parents to be with their children in hospital whenever practicable?
- ☐ Does the criminal justice system have regard for the need for mothers not to be separated from their babies?
- ☐ Does the criminal justice system have regard for the need for parents not to be separated from their children?
- ☐ Does the criminal justice system ensure that juvenile offenders are not separated from their parents except where competent authorities have determined it is necessary for the best interests of the offender?
- ☐ Do laws and procedures governing the deporting of parents under immigration law pay regard to the child's right not to be separated from his or her parents unless necessary for his or her best interests?
- ☐ Do provisions for the family reunification of immigrants and refugees pay regard to the child's rights not to be separated from parents unless necessary for his or her best interests?
- ☐ In times of armed conflict, are forced relocations of civilian populations avoided and all measures adopted for tracing and reuniting children and parents separated by these events?
- ☐ Are measures taken by the State (for example through public education campaigns) to combat traditional customs that separate parents and children unnecessarily?
- ☐ Does the State provide practical or psychological assistance to families in order to prevent unnecessary separation of parents and children?
- ☐ Are all laws specifying the grounds justifying the State in separating children from parents free from discrimination (for example, in relation to families living in poverty or ethnic minority families)?
- ☐ Are all laws specifying the grounds justifying separation from parents free from dogma as to children's best interests (for example, that children are better off with their fathers than their mothers or *vice versa*)?
- ☐ Are all decisions that hold separation from parents necessary for the child's best interests made by authorities competent to determine what these best interests are?
- ☐ Do these authorities have access to all relevant information in this determination?
- ☐ Are these decisions subject to judicial review?
- ☐ Are these cases dealt with speedily?
- ☐ Are children's rights to privacy safeguarded in such cases?
- ☐ Are all relevant people, including the child, able to participate and be heard by those determining these cases?
- ☐ Are there no age limits on the right of the child to participate or be heard?
- ☐ Are the child's views heard if he or she disagrees with the professionals reporting to the court on his or her best interests?
- ☐ Are the proceedings impartial and fair?

How to use the checklists, *see page XVII*

☐ Does the law enshrine the principle that children should, wherever possible, have regular contact with both their parents?

☐ Is practical assistance given to ensure contact is maintained in cases where parents are in conflict?

☐ Does the State provide practical assistance in discovering the whereabouts of parents and children who, for whatever reason, have become separated?

☐ Unless detrimental to children's well-being, are children and parents (and other family members, if appropriate) always informed of the whereabouts of the other in circumstances where they have become separated because of an action of the State (for example, detention, imprisonment, exile or death)?

☐ Are those requesting such information protected from adverse consequences?

Reminder : **The Convention is indivisible and its articles are interdependent. Article 9 should not be considered in isolation.**

Particular regard should be paid to:
The general principles

Article 2: all rights to be recognized for each child in jurisdiction without discrimination on any ground

Article 3(1): the best interests of the child to be a primary consideration in all actions concerning children

Article 6: right to life and maximum possible survival and development

Article 12: respect for the child's views in all matters affecting the child; opportunity to be heard in any judicial or administrative proceedings affecting the child

Closely related articles

Articles whose implementation is related to that of article 9 include:

Article 7: right to know and be cared for by parents

Article 8: right to preservation of identity, including family relations

Article 10: international family reunification

Article 11: protection from illicit transfer and non-return

Article 16: protection from arbitrary interference in privacy, family and home

Article 18: parents having joint responsibility

Article 20: children deprived of their family environment

Article 21: adoption

Article 22: refugee children

Article 24: health services

Article 25: periodic review of treatment when placed by the State away from families

Article 35: prevention of sale, trafficking and abduction of children

Article 37: deprivation of liberty

Article 40: administration of juvenile justice

Implementation Handbook for the Convention on the Rights of the Child

Entering or leaving countries for family reunification

article

10

1. In accordance with the obligations of State Parties under article 9, paragraph 1, applications by a child or his or her parents to enter or leave a State Party for the purpose of family reunification shall be dealt with by the States Parties in a positive, humane and expeditious manner. States Parties shall further ensure that the submission of such a request shall entail no adverse consequences for the applicants and for the members of their family.

2. A child whose parents reside in different States shall have the right to maintain on a regular basis, save in exceptional circumstances, personal relations and direct contacts with both parents. Towards that end and in accordance with the obligation of States Parties under article 9, paragraph 1, States Parties shall respect the right of the child and his or her parents to leave any country, including their own, and to enter their own country. The right to leave any country shall be subject only to such restrictions as are prescribed by law and which are necessary to protect the national security, public order (ordre public), public health or morals or the rights and freedoms of others and are consistent with the other rights recognized in the present Convention.

Summary

Article 10 of the Convention on the Rights of the Child is concerned with rights to "family reunification" of children who are, or whose parents are, involved in entering or leaving a country. The article requires States to deal with family reunification "in a positive, humane and expeditious manner" and to allow parents and children to visit each other if they live in different States. The families primarily affected by article 10 are so-called "economic migrants" and refugees, although it should be noted that the children of refugee parents, or the parents of child refugees, may seek entry for the purposes of family reunification rather than asylum.

While family unity is a fundamental principle of the Convention, the wording of article 10 is notably weaker than that of article 9 in so far as the right to family reunification is not expressly guaranteed (even though article 10 makes an express reference to article 9(1)). The tentative wording of article 10 reflects concerns about immigration control – a cause of great anxiety to richer nations, which are haunted by the spectre of mass migrations of the world's poor.

The article does not directly address the right of children or their parents to "remain" for the purposes of family reunification, taking in the whole question of the deportation of parents. However, by implication, since a deported parent would at once be in a position to wish to re-enter the country, these cases can be assumed to be covered by this article (as well as by article 9, see page 119).

Along with encouraging States to ratify treaties relating to refugees (see article 22, page 281), the Committee recommends that countries ratify the International Convention on the Protection of the Rights of all Migrant Workers and Members of their Families (see Spain IRCO, Add.28, para. 23,

and Belgium IRCO, Add. 38, para. 20). The Convention is relatively new, adopted on December 18, 1990. Its article 44 provides that contracting States should take measures "which they consider appropriate and which are within their powers to facilitate the reunion of migrant workers with their spouses, or with any persons having a relationship with them, which in accordance with the law is the equivalent of marriage, as well as their dependent or single children." Article 22 protects migrant workers from mass expulsion; article 14 protects them from "arbitrary or unlawful interference with his or her privacy, family, home...".
∎

Extracts from
Committee on the Rights of the Child
Guidelines for Reports to be submitted by States Parties under the Convention

For full text of *Guidelines for Periodic Reports*, see Appendix 3, page 604.

Guidelines for Initial Reports

"Family environment and alternative care

Under this section, States Parties are requested to provide relevant information, including the principal legislative, judicial, administrative or other measures in force, particularly how the principles of the "best interests of the child" and "respect for the views of the child" are reflected therein; factors and difficulties encountered and progress achieved in implementing the relevant provisions of the Convention; and implementation priorities and specific goals for the future in respect of:...

(d) Family reunification (article 10).

In addition, States Parties are requested to provide information on the numbers of children per year within the reporting period in each of the following groups, disaggregated by age group, sex, ethnic or national background and rural or urban environment: homeless children, abused or neglected children taken into protective custody, children placed in foster care, children placed in institutional care, children placed through domestic adoption, children entering the country through intercountry adoption procedures and children leaving the country through intercountry adoption procedures.

States Parties are encouraged to provide additional relevant statistical information and indicators relating to children covered in this section."

(CRC/C/5, paras. 16-18)

Guidelines for Periodic Reports

"V. FAMILY ENVIRONMENT AND ALTERNATIVE CARE...

D. Family reunification (art. 10)

Please provide information on the measures adopted to ensure that applications by a child or his or her parents to enter or leave a country for the purpose of family reunification are dealt with by the State in a positive, humane and expeditious manner and that the submission of such a request entails no adverse consequences for the applicants and the members of their family.

Please also indicate how such applications are considered in the light of the Convention and in particular of its general principles of non-discrimination, the best interests of the child, respect for the views of the child, the right to life, and survival and development to the maximum extent possible, including in the case of unaccompanied and asylum seeking children. Disaggregated information should also be provided, including by gender, age, and national and ethnic origin.

Right of child or parent to have any applications "to enter or leave a State Party for the purpose of family reunification" dealt with "in a positive, humane and expeditious manner" by the States Parties

"Positive"

When drafting this article some State representatives were concerned about the interpretation of the word "positive". Two alternatives were proposed – "objective" and "favourable" – and were rejected. "Favourable" was thought to contain too much of an element of prejudgement, whereas "positive", though stronger than "objective", did not assume that the State must agree to the application (E/CN.4/l989/4B, pp. 37-40; Detrick, p. 206). Nonetheless, Japan took pains to enter a declaration that:

"The Government of Japan declares further that the obligation to deal with applications to enter or leave a State Party for the purpose of family reunification 'in a positive, humane and expeditious manner' provided for in paragraph 1 of article 10 of the Convention on the Rights of the Child be interpreted not to affect the outcome of such applications" (CRC/C/2/Rev.5, p. 22).

Because many richer nations have increasingly in recent decades closed their borders to labour migration, family reunion has become the main legal entitlement for the settlement of immigrants. This, in turn, has led to increasingly restrictive conditions being placed on the right to family reunification. Some countries require nationality status before such rights can be secured. Most countries now require applicants to prove that there are sufficient resources to support the immigrant's family members without recourse to public funds. Yet other countries have stricter conditions for foreigners who themselves entered the country for family reunion when they were children. Not all states recognize 16-18 year-olds as children and some countries require children to be "dependent", or the exclusive responsibility of one parent if the parents are separated.

The United Kingdom entered a blanket reservation to enable it to apply immigration legislation as it deems necessary, and it allows children to enter the United Kingdom only if the parent has "sole responsibility" for them or if there are "serious and compelling family and other considerations which make exclusion undesirable...and suitable arrangements have been made for the child's care". (CRC/C/2/Rev.5, p. 33-34) ("Undesirable" has been defined to mean "evidence to show that the child is suffering from conditions in its own country which makes the continuance of its current mode of life intolerable"). The Committee expressed concern about this reservation, commenting that:

"... the reservation relating to the application of the Nationality and Immigration Act does not appear to be compatible with the principles and provisions of the Convention, including those of its articles 2,3,9 and 10".

The Committee suggested that the United Kingdom review its nationality and immigration laws and procedures to ensure their conformity with the principles and provisions of the Convention (UK IRCO, Add.34, paras. 7 and 29).

Liechtenstein "reserves the right to apply the Liechtenstein legislation according to which family reunification for certain categories of foreigners is not guaranteed" (CRC/C/2/Rev.5, p. 24), and Singapore reserved the right to apply its legislation relating to entry and stay in Singapore "as it may deem necessary from time to time" (CRC/C/2/Rev.5, p. 31). These States' reports have yet, as of September 1997, to be considered by the Committee.

Italy, on the other hand, reported to the Committee that its law required that before deportation, enforcement officials should assess the impact on the foreigner's family unit and on his or her obligations and his or her rights in respect of support, instruction and education (Italy IR, para 71).

The Committee expressed concern at the situation in UK dependent territory: Hong Kong

"...with respect to the question of families split between Hong Kong and China, the Committee is concerned that the increase in permits arranged for these children and their families, from 105 to 150, is manifestly insufficient to meet the needs of the estimated 60,000 children currently in China who may have the right of abode in Hong Kong after 1 July 1997."

The Committee recommended that:

"...action should be taken on an urgent basis to reduce the waiting period for family reunification, to raise the quota of permits and to consider other measures to deal with the problems that will arise in the future."
(UK dependent territory: Hong Kong IRCO, Add.63, paras. 14 and 26)

"Humane"

The word "humane" qualifies and strengthens the word "positive". For example, in cases where parents are illegal immigrants but their children have acquired the right to the host country's nationality, it is more humane to allow the family to remain in the country than to deport the parents – even though in both cases the family remains together.

An example of the Committee proposing a humane solution arose in relation to Sri Lanka, when the Committee expressed concern about:

"...the situation of children whose mothers are working abroad, especially in Gulf countries, leaving their children behind. Those children (between 200,000 and 300,000) often live in difficult circumstances and may be subjected to different types of abuse or exploitation."

The proposed solution was not, as might have been expected, to recommend improvements to Sri Lankan services for these motherless children, but, in keeping with article 9

"To avoid the abandonment of children by mothers working abroad, the Committee

suggests that the State Party engage in dialogue with receiving countries to ensure an international agreement that permits migrant workers to take their children abroad. Ratification of the International Convention on the Rights of All Migrant Workers and Members of Their Families should be considered."
(Sri Lanka IRCO Add.40 paras 16 and 33)

Along with the decision being humane, the procedure for making the decision must also be humane. It is essential that immigration processes respect the dignity of the applicants, including the child's dignity. Treatment in detention centres can often be inhumane, as can the investigations by the authorities to authenticate the applications. The Committee has stressed the link between article 10 and article 37 (deprivation of liberty), pointing out that even where applicant children are housed in comfortable surroundings, such as hotels, their liberty is still deprived and their particular needs are not necessarily taken into account (see page 495). Children should not be subjected to investigations that could harm their health (such as bone X-rays to identify their age) or psychological well-being (such as traumatizing interrogations), nor should they be subjected to medical tests without their (or, as appropriate, their parents') consent.

"Expeditious"

All judicial and administrative processes concerning children need to be pursued as quickly as possible. Delay and uncertainty can be extremely prejudicial to children's healthy development. There is a sense in which any period of time is significantly 'longer' in the life of a child than in that of an adult. In immigration cases delays can literally ruin children's chances – for example the long waiting lists of children in the Indian subcontinent seeking the right to join their parents can mean that some pass the key age of 18 while still waiting for their application to be heard.

In its Concluding Observations on Canada, the Committee expressed concern about the position of refugee and immigrant children:

" The Committee recognizes the efforts made by Canada for many years in accepting a large number of refugees and immigrants. Nevertheless, the Committee regrets that the principles of non-discrimination, of the best interests of the child and of the respect for the views of the child have not always been given adequate weight by administrative bodies dealing with the situation of refugee or immigrant children. It is particularly worried ...by the insufficient measures aimed at family reunification with a view to ensuring that it is dealt with in a positive, humane and expeditious manner. The Committee specifically regrets the delays in dealing with reunifica-

tion of the family in cases where one or more members of the family have been considered eligible for refugee status in Canada as well as cases where refugee or immigrant children born in Canada may be separated from their parents facing a deportation order."

The Committee recommended:

"...that the State Party pay particular attention to...the general principles of the Convention, in particular the best interests of the child and respect for his or her views, in all matters relating to the protection of refugee and immigrant children, including in deportation proceedings. The Committee suggests that every feasible measure be taken to facilitate and speed up the reunification of the family in cases where one or more members of the family have been considered eligible for refugee status in Canada. Solutions should also be sought to avoid expulsions causing the separation of families, in the spirit of article 9 of the Convention..." (Canada IRCO, Add.37, paras. 13 and 24)

The Committee also expressed concern over Germany's procedures and treatment of foreign children in need of family reunification:

"The Committee remains concerned about the extent to which account is taken of the special needs and rights of children in asylum-seeking and refugee situations. Procedures governing asylum-seeking children, particularly those relating to family reunification, expulsion of children to safe third countries and the 'airport regulation' give cause for concern. In this respect the Committee notes that the guarantees provided for in the Convention, in particular in its articles 2, 3, 12, 22 and 37(d) do not appear to be complied with, while insufficient attention seems to have been ensured to the implementation of articles 9 and 10 of the Convention...
"The Committee is of the opinion that the issue of asylum-seeking and refugee children deserves further study with a view to its reform in the light of the Convention and of the concerns expressed during the discussion with the Committee ..."
And the Committee also encouraged the involvement of children in these proceedings (Germany IRCO, Add.43, paras. 19, 33 and 29). ("Airport regulation" relates to provisions that penalize companies for allowing passengers to travel without proper visas or entry authorizations.)

Belgium was encouraged by the Committee to

"...ensure that applications for the purpose of family reunification in the case of refugees and migrant workers are dealt with in a positive, humane and expeditious manner." (Belgium IRCO, Add.38, para 19; see also Spain IRCO, Add.28, para. 22)

The Committee also expressed concern that in Norway:

"...the police may not be instructed to delay the expulsion of some members of the family in order to ensure that the whole family remains together and that undue strain on the children is avoided ... it is suggested that solutions should also be sought to avoid expulsions causing separation of families." (Norway IRCO, Add.23, paras. 11 and 24)

Right for such applications to entail "no adverse consequences" for any member of the family

This right relates to those countries where applications to enter or leave have resulted in the applicant or the applicant's family being persecuted or discriminated against. Such treatment is obviously a breach of human rights in all circumstances. The act of making an application should never put an applicant in jeopardy, even though the application may be turned down.

However, where asylum-seeking occurs, the receiving State may unwittingly entail adverse consequences for the child or the child's family by making incautious enquiries; therefore care must be taken not to breach confidentiality in a hazardous manner (see article 22, page 289).

Right of child (save in exceptional circumstances) to maintain, on a regular basis, personal relations and direct contact with both parents where the parents reside in different states

The Hague Convention on the Civil Aspects of International Child Abduction 1980 assists with realizing this right because it allows parents to enforce court orders for access (contact) in the Hague Convention States (see article 11, page 140). But not all parents with access problems in foreign countries have court orders, and only around a quarter of the world's countries have ratified or acceded to the Hague Convention. In such circumstances this right of the child should ensure that States give favourable consideration both to applications for access and applications for entry and exit in order to exercise access.

It is important not to assume that children with refugee status will never be able to return to their State of origin for family visits. Organizing a safe temporary visit may be possible. Evidence of children returning home for the purpose of temporary family reunification should not prejudice their refugee status.

Right of child and parents to leave any country (including their own), subject only to legal restrictions "which are necessary to protect national security, public order (*ordre public*), public health or morals or the rights and freedoms of other and are consistent with the rights of this Convention"

This provision reflects the wording of article 12(2) of the International Covenant on Civil and Political Rights which provides: "Everyone shall be free to leave any country including his own". It was drafted at a time when a number of countries, including many of those in the sphere of the USSR, unreasonably refused to allow citizens to leave the country. This is still the case in certain countries.

The term *ordre public* is used in a number of international treaties; it is said to be more precise than "public order" (E/CN.4/1986/39, pp. 5-8; Detrick, p. 200) but it seems that there are now variety of interpretations of *ordre public* across the world, some of which are more related to economic considerations than to the social ones normally understood by the phrase "public order".

Right of child and parent "to enter their own country"

This right is unqualified by any restrictions. An earlier draft of article 10 proposed that the child be given the right to "return" to his or her country, but this was changed to "enter" to accommodate those circumstances where children were born outside their State of nationality (E/CN.4/1986/39, pp. 5-8; Detrick, p. 201). Article 12(4) of the International Covenant on Civil and Political Rights is the source: "No one shall be arbitrarily deprived of the right to enter his own country."

Implementation Checklist

● *General measures of implementation*

Have appropriate general measures of implementation been taken in relation to article 10 including

☐ identification and coordination of the responsible departments and agencies at all levels of government (article 10 is relevant to the **departments of home affairs, foreign affairs, justice and social welfare**)?

☐ identification of relevant non-governmental organizations/civil society partners?

☐ a comprehensive review to ensure that all legislation, policy and practice is compatible with the article, for all children in all parts of the jurisdiction?

☐ adoption of a strategy to secure full implementation

  ☐ which includes where necessary the identification of goals and indicators of progress?

  ☐ which does not affect any provisions which are more conducive to the rights of the child?

  ☐ which recognizes other relevant international standards?

  ☐ which involves where necessary international cooperation?

  (Such measures may be part of an overall governmental strategy for implementing the Convention as a whole).

☐ budgetary analysis and allocation of necessary resources?

☐ development of mechanisms for monitoring and evaluation?

☐ making the implications of article 10 widely known to adults and children?

☐ development of appropriate training and awareness-raising (in relation to article 10 likely to include **the judiciary, immigration officers and social workers**)?

● *Specific issues in implementing article 10*

Are all applications by parents or children for entry to or exit from the country for the purposes of family reunification dealt with in a

  ☐ positive manner?
  ☐ humane manner?

☐ Are all such applications dealt with as quickly as possible?

☐ Are children and families involved in these applications treated with respect?

☐ Are requests by parents or children not to be deported dealt with in a positive and humane manner?

☐ Does the State recognize the right to family reunification of children who are resident in the country but do not have nationality status or official leave to remain?

☐ Are the views of children taken into account when decisions relating to family reunification are made?

☐ Are applicants and their family members protected from any adverse consequences from making a request to enter or leave the country for family reunification purposes?

☐ Are children permitted entry to the country and/or permission to leave the country in order to visit a parent?

☐ Are parents permitted entry to the country and/or permission to leave the country in order to visit a child?

☐ Subject to the limitations listed in article 10(2), are parents and children entitled to leave the country?

☐ Are parents and children always entitled to enter their own country?

☐ Has the State ratified the International Convention on the Protection of the Rights of All Migrant Workers and Members of their Families?

Reminder: **The Convention is indivisible and its articles are interdependent. Article 10 should not be considered in isolation.**

Particular regard should be paid to:
The general principles

Article 2: all rights to be recognized for each child in jurisdiction without discrimination on any ground

Article 3(1): the best interests of the child to be a primary consideration in all actions concerning children

Article 6: right to life and maximum possible survival and development

Article 12: respect for the child's views in all matters affecting the child; opportunity to be heard in any judicial or administrative proceedings affecting the child

Closely related articles

Articles whose implementation is related to that of article 10 include:

Article 5: parental duties and rights and the child's evolving capacities

Article 7: right to know and be cared for by parents

Article 8: preservation of identity, including family relations

Article 9: non-separation from parents except when necessary for best interests

Article 11: protection from illicit transfer and non-return from abroad

Article 16: protection from arbitrary interference in privacy, family and home

Article 18: parents having joint responsibility

Article 22: refugee children

Article 35: prevention of sale, trafficking and abduction of children

Illicit transfer and non-return of children abroad

Text of Article 11

1. States Parties shall take measures to combat the illicit transfer and non-return of children abroad.

2. To this end, States Parties shall promote the conclusion of bilateral or multilateral agreements or accession to existing agreements.

Summary

Ratifying States have responsibilities under article 11 to prevent children from being wrongfully taken or from being retained outside their jurisdiction, to secure that these children are recovered and to undertake that abducted children brought into their jurisdiction are returned.

The article is primarily concerned with parental abductions or retention. Though the article includes non-parents in its scope, it should be noted that article 35 covers the sale, trafficking and abduction of children. The difference between the two articles is not entirely clear, given that "illicit transfer and non-return of children abroad" is the same thing as "abduction". Broadly speaking, the distinction is one of money – article 11 applies to children taken for personal rather than financial gain, whereas "sale" and "trafficking" has a commercial or sexual motive. Those who abduct children for purely personal motives are usually, though not invariably, parents or other relatives.

The *Manual on Human Right Reporting*, 1997 observes that "children may be abducted by one of the parents and are usually not permitted to return home, even when a previous judicial authority had already decided on the custody and place of residence of the child, as well as on the visiting rights of the parent with whom the child should no longer live. The situation often tends to permanently prevent the child from having access to the parent with whom the child used to live or with whom the child had direct and regular contacts and personal relations (see article 9, paragraph 3 and article 10, paragraph 2). It also shows how important it is to be guided by the best interests of the child and in ensuring, as a general rule, that both parents continue to assume their responsibilities for the upbringing and development of the child, even when separation or divorce has intervened" (*Manual,* p. 451).

The article encourages States to conclude or become parties to multilateral agreements. Principal among these is the Hague Convention on the Civil Aspects of International Child Abduction. ■

Measures to combat illicit transfer and non-return of children abroad

As article 11 acknowledges, a most effective means of implementing its provisions is to sign and implement the relevant international treaties. Of these, the most central is the Hague Convention on the Civil Aspects of International Child Abduction (1980).

The Hague Convention is a global instrument. At the time of writing, a substantial number of countries have ratified the Convention (see box), although there is a significant absence of Middle Eastern and Far Eastern countries. Its provisions, in brief, protect children under the age of 16 who

have been wrongfully (that is, in breach of someone's rights of custody) removed or retained abroad, if the Hague Convention is in force between the two countries involved. In these circumstances the court will normally order such children to be returned promptly to the place where they have habitual residence, when a final decision as to their future can be made. The courts may refuse to order this if the child objects or is at grave risk of harm or has been over a year in the new environment and is settled there – but the court's business is not to investigate the merits of the dispute itself. Each State Party to the Hague Convention has an administrative body called the Central Authority, whose function is to receive and transmit applications under the Convention.

In addition to the Hague Convention, there are regional treaties such as the Inter-American Convention on the International Return of Children, and the European Convention on the Recognition and Enforcement of Decisions Concerning Custody of Children. These can be helpful in augmenting the principles of the Hague Convention, for example by enforcing the details of existing court orders.

Beyond ratifying international treaties, a State should also take other measures to implement article 11. In particular it should secure that

- machinery is in place to speedily put checks on borders and to obtain appropriate court orders when it is suspected that a child is going to be abducted;

- parents are provided with legal aid and financial assistance when it is necessary to pay for the costs of the child's return;

- the judiciary overseeing the law are fully acquainted with the principles of the Hague Convention;

- information is provided from government agencies and State databases to identify the whereabouts of abducted or wrongfully retained children.

The Committee has been relatively silent on the failure of countries to become parties to the Hague Convention and other regional treaties on abduction, though failure to do so could result in a breach of article 11.

Implementation Checklist

article 11

● *General measures of implementation*

Have appropriate general measures of implementation been taken in relation to article 11, including

☐ identification and coordination of the responsible departments and agencies at all levels of government (article 11 is relevant to **departments of home affairs, foreign affairs, justice, social welfare and social security**)?

☐ identification of relevant non-governmental organizations/civil society partners?

☐ a comprehensive review to ensure that all legislation, policy and practice is compatible with the article, for all children in all parts of the jurisdiction?

☐ adoption of a strategy to secure full implementation

    ☐ which includes where necessary the identification of goals and indicators of progress?

    ☐ which does not affect any provisions which are more conducive to the rights of the child?

    ☐ which recognizes other relevant international standards?

    ☐ which involves where necessary international cooperation?

(Such measures may be part of an overall governmental strategy for implementing the Convention as a whole).

☐ budgetary analysis and allocation of necessary resources?

☐ development of mechanisms for monitoring and evaluation?

☐ making the implications of article 11 widely known to adults and children?

☐ development of appropriate training and awareness-raising (in relation to article 11 likely to include the **judiciary, social workers, border officials and the police**)?

● *Specific issues in implementing article 11*

☐ Has the State ratified the Hague Convention on the Civil Aspects of International Child Abduction?

☐ Has the State ratified or acceded to any regional agreements relating to child abduction?

☐ Is the judiciary fully acquainted with the Hague Convention's provisions?

☐ Are effective methods in place to prevent a child from being abducted (e.g. border checks, court orders, confiscation of passports)?

☐ Are parents and children given financial assistance where necessary to exercise their rights under this article and any multilateral agreements?

☐ Are State institutions empowered to release information that will help to trace the whereabouts of abducted children?

Reminder : **The Convention is indivisible and its articles are interdependent. Article 11 should not be considered in isolation.**

Particular regard should be paid to:
The general principles

Article 2: all rights to be recognized for each child in jurisdiction without discrimination on any ground

Article 3(1): the best interests of the child to be a primary consideration in all actions concerning children

Article 6: right to life and maximum possible survival and development

Article 12: respect for the child's views in all matters affecting the child; opportunity to be heard in any judicial or administrative proceedings affecting the child

Closely related articles

Articles whose implementation is related to that of article 11 include:

Article 7: right to be cared for by parents

Article 8: right to preservation of nationality, including nationality and family relations

Article 9: non-separation from parents except in child's best interests; right have contact with both parents on a regular basis

Article 10: right to family reunification

Article 16: protection from arbitrary interference in privacy, family and home

Article 18: both parents having joint responsibility

Article 35: prevention of sale, trafficking and abduction of children

Respect for the views of the child

article 12

Text of Article 12

1. States Parties shall assure to the child who is capable of forming his or her own views the right to express those views freely in all matters affecting the child, the views of the child being given due weight in accordance with the age and maturity of the child.

2. For this purpose, the child shall in particular be provided the opportunity to be heard in any judicial and administrative proceedings affecting the child, either directly, or through a representative or an appropriate body, in a manner consistent with the procedural rules of national law.

The Committee on the Rights of the Child asserted early on the status of article 12 as a general principle of fundamental importance relevant to all aspects of implementation of the Convention on the Rights of the Child and to the interpretation of all other articles.

Paragraph 1 requires States to assure

- that any child capable of forming a view has the right to express views freely in all matters affecting him or her;
- that the child's views are given due weight in accordance with
  - age and
  - maturity.

Paragraph 2 specifically provides the child with the right to be heard in any judicial and administrative proceedings affecting him or her. This covers a very wide range of court hearings and also formal decision-making affecting the child, in for example, education, health, planning, the environment and so on (see page 150).

Summary

The Committee has consistently emphasized that the child must be regarded as an active subject of rights. Article 12, together with the child's right to freedom of expression (article 13), and other civil rights to freedom of thought, conscience and religion (article 14), and freedom of association (article 15) underline children's status as individuals with fundamental human rights, and views and feelings of their own.

The rights of the child set out in the two paragraphs of article 12 do not in themselves amount to a right to self-determination but to involvement in decision-making. The references to the "evolving capacities" of the child, in articles 5 and 14 (pages 75 and 177) do emphasize the need to respect the child's developing capacity for decision making.

Certain other articles include references to children's participation. Article 9(2) refers to the child's right to be heard in relation to proceedings involving separation from his or her parent(s), during which "all interested parties shall be given an opportunity to participate in the proceedings and make their views known" (article 9, page 126). In relation to adoption proceedings, article 21(a) refers to "the informed consent" of the persons concerned (page 273). Every child deprived of his or her liberty has the right under article 37 to challenge the legality of the deprivation before a court or other authority, suggesting a right to initiate court action rather than just to be heard (page 502). And article 40, in relation to children "alleged as, accused of, or recognized as having infringed the penal law," emphasizes the juvenile's right to an active role in the proceedings, but

that he or she must not "be compelled to give testimony or to confess guilt" (article 40(2)(b)(iv), page 548).

The Universal Declaration of Human Rights states: "Everyone has the right to freedom of opinion and expression; this right includes freedom to hold opinions without interference and to seek, receive and impart information and ideas through any media and regardless of frontiers" (article 19). And the International Covenant on Civil and Political Rights states: "Everyone shall have the right to hold opinions without interference" (article 19(1)). The significance of article 12 of the Convention is that it not only requires that children should be assured the right to express their views freely, but also that they should be heard and that their views be given "due weight". ∎

Extracts from
Committee on the Rights of the Child
Guidelines for reports to be submitted by States Parties under the Convention

For full text of *Guidelines for Periodic Reports*, see Appendix 3, page 604.

Guidelines for Initial Reports

"General principles
Relevant information, including the principal legislative, judicial, administrative or other measures in force or foreseen, factors and difficulties encountered and progress achieved in implementing the provisions of the Convention, and implementation priorities and specific goals for the future should be provided in respect of:

....

(d) Respect for the views of the child (article 12).

In addition, States Parties are encouraged to provide relevant information on the application of these principles in the implementation of articles listed elsewhere in these guidelines."
(CRC/C/5, paras. 13 and 14)

Guidelines for Periodic Reports

"III. GENERAL PRINCIPLES

Respect for the views of the child (art. 12)

Reports should indicate how the right of the child to express views freely on all matters affecting him or her, and provision for those views to be given due weight have been incorporated in legislation.

Please provide information on legislative and other measures taken to ensure the right of the child to express views in a manner consistent with his or her evolving capacities, including in:
family life
school life
the administration of juvenile justice
placement and life in institutional and other forms of care
asylum-seeking procedures.

Please indicate the opportunities provided for the child to be heard in judicial and administrative proceedings affecting him or her, as well as the situations in which the child can intervene directly or through a representative or an appropriate body...

Please provide information on any bodies or instances where the child has a right to participate in decision-making, such as schools or local councils.

Please indicate what measures have been taken to raise the awareness of families and the public in general of the need to encourage children to exercise their right to express their views, and to train professionals working with children to encourage children to do so, and to give their views due weight. An indication should be given of the number of hours of child development courses provided for the following staff:

> *Judges in general;*
> *Family court judges;*
> *Juvenile court judges;*
> *Probation officers;*
> *Police officers;*
> *Prison officers;*
> *Teachers;*
> *Health workers;*
> *Other professionals.*

An indication should also be provided of the number of courses about the Convention included in the curriculum of:

> *Law schools;*
> *Teacher training schools;*
> *Medical schools and institutions;*
> *Nursing schools;*
> *Social work schools;*
> *Psychology departments;*
> *Sociology departments.*

Please indicate how the views of the child obtained through public opinion, consultations and assessment of complaints are taken into consideration in the legal provisions, and in policy or judicial decisions."

(CRC/C/58, paras. 42-47. The following paragraphs of the *Guidelines for Periodic Reports* are also relevant to reporting under this article: 24, 64, 65, 69, 70, 74, 76, 80, 83, 87, 88, 93, 101, 106, 109, 113, 115, 118, 120, 128, 132, 133, 138, 143, 152, 153, 159, 161, 164, 166; for full text of *Guidelines*, see Appendix 3, page 604.)

The child as a subject of rights and an active participant

The *Manual on Human Rights Reporting*, 1997 comments: "This article sets one of the fundamental values of the Convention and probably also one of its basic challenges. In essence it affirms that the child is a fully-fledged person having the right to express views in all matters affecting him or her, and having those views heard and given due weight. Thus the child has the right to participate in the decision-making process affecting his or her life, as well as to influence decisions taken in his or her regard...

"At the first sight it might be considered that article 12 is basically addressing the same reality as article 13 on freedom of expression and information. It is true that they are closely connected. But the fact they were both incorporated in the Convention and coexist in an autonomous manner, has to be interpreted as to mean that while article 13 recognizes in a general way freedom of expression, article 12 should prevail in all those cases where the matters at stake affect the child, while stressing the right of the child to be heard and for the child's views to be taken into account." *(Manual,* p. 426)

The 1990 World Summit Declaration declares that children "...must be prepared for responsible life in a free society. They should, from their early years, be encouraged to participate in the cultural life of their societies." And it states: "Among the partnerships we seek, we turn especially to children themselves. We appeal to them to participate in this effort." (World Summit Declaration, paras. 15 and 22)

The Committee on the Rights of the Child has indicated concern about declarations and reservations that appear to challenge full recognition of the child as a subject of rights. For example in ratifying the Convention, Poland made a declaration: "The Republic of Poland considers that a child's rights as defined in the Convention, in particular the rights defined in articles 12 to 16, shall be exercised with respect for parental authority, in accordance with Polish customs and traditions regarding the place of the child within and outside the family" (CRC/C/2/Rev.5, p. 29).

The Committee welcomed Poland's intention to review its declarations and reservations with a view to considering withdrawal. It went on to say

"The Committee is concerned that traditional attitudes still prevailing in the country may not be conducive to the realization of the general principles of the Convention, including, in particular, article 2 (principle of non-discrimination), article 3 (principle of the best interests of the child) and article 12 (respect for the views of the child)." (Poland IRCO, Add.31, paras. 3 and 12)

(For the Committee's comments on similar reservations and declarations, see article 5, page 78).

The Committee has frequently expressed concern where countries do not appear to have fully accepted the concept of the child as an active subject of rights:

"Further efforts are required to ensure the active participation of children and their involvement in all decisions affecting them in the family, at school and in social life, in the light of articles 12, 13 and 15 of the Convention." (Panama IRCO, Add.68, para. 29; for other comments, see article 5, page 79)

And in many cases, the Committee has recommended further action to ensure that children enjoy their civil rights, including the right to participation in decision-making:

"The Committee would like to suggest that further consideration be given to ways of encouraging the expression of views by children and those views being given due weight in the decision-making processes affecting their lives, in particular within school and the local community." (France IRCO, Add.20, para. 23)

"The Committee considers that greater efforts should be made to promote the participation of children in family, school and social life, as well as the effective enjoyment of their fundamental freedoms, including the freedom of opinion, expression and association, which should be subject only to the restrictions provided by the law and which are necessary in a democratic society." (Republic of Korea IRCO, Add.51, para. 26. See also Nicaragua IRCO, Add.36, para. 33; Finland IRCO, Add.53, para. 13; UK dependent territory: Hong Kong IRCO, Add.63, para. 25)

The Committee has welcomed various measures taken by States Parties,

"...to recognize the right of the child to have his or her views heard and taken into account in proceedings affecting the child. Note is taken of the various initiatives to inform children about their rights and to encourage children to express their opinion through special councils established within schools and the local community." (France IRCO, Add.20, para. 7)

Ambitions and fears create challenges

A representative of Argentina, during discussions with the Committee on the Rights of the Child on Argentina's Initial Report, stated: "The ambition remained, however, to do more for children, not just materially but in terms of justice and the relationship of children to society. Where children could be regarded as chattels, subject to exploitation and ill-treatment by adults, no country, no matter how highly developed, could be regarded as being in conformity with the Convention." (Argentina SR.177, para. 39)

France's Initial Report, discussing article 12, states: "The fears raised by this article have served to justify drawing the attention of parents and educators to language and practices that are contrary to the child's interest. A consensus has been established on the following ideas: expressing a point of view is not the same thing as taking a decision. Respecting the child's opinions means listening to them, but not necessarily endorsing them. The adult decision maker's task is to add the child's viewpoint to other elements which might contribute to an enlightened decision. The child's age and maturity are, of course, decisive parameters." (France IR, para. 183)

Many countries have implied in their Initial Reports that implementing children's civil rights is the most challenging aspect of the Convention, a challenge that applies equally to resource-rich countries.

The child who is "capable of forming his or her own views": article 12(1)

Article 12 does not set any lower age limit on children's right to express views freely. It is clear that children can and do form views from a very early age, and the Convention on the Rights of the Child provides no support to those who would impose a lower age limit on the ascertainment or consideration of children's views. And it is important to note, for example, that ascertaining the views of some disabled children may require special consideration.

The *Manual on Human Rights Reporting*, 1997 states: "Pursuant to the provisions of this article, States Parties have a clear and precise obligation to assure to the child the right to have a say in situations that may affect him or her. The child should therefore not be envisaged as a passive human being or allowed to be deprived of such right of intervention, unless he or she would clearly be incapable of forming his or her views. This right should therefore be ensured and respected even in situations where the child would be able to form views and yet be unable to communicate them, or when the child is not yet fully mature or has not yet attained a particular older age, since his or her views are to be taken into consideration 'in accordance with the age and maturity of the child'..." (*Manual*, p. 426)

Some countries reported that they had set a minimum age on the right of the child to be heard, for example in custody proceedings following separation or divorce of parents, but the Convention provides no support for this, and States cannot quote the best interests principle to avoid fulfilling their obligations under article 12.

The "right to express those views freely"

There are no boundaries on the obligation of States Parties to assure the child the right to express views freely. In particular, this emphasizes that there is no area of traditional parental or adult authority – the home or school for example – in which children's views have no place. In article 13 (see page 169) the right is re-stated and developed to include the right to "seek, receive and impart information and ideas of all kinds".

It should be emphasized that article 12 implies no obligation on the child to express views. "Freely" implies without either coercion or constraint:

Practical problems in ascertaining views

Finland noted some of the practical problems that arise when ascertaining the child's views. Although Finnish law provides for children's views to be one of the factors that determines best interests in judicial decisions about where the child lives and other details, "in practice, a number of shortcomings are evident in the ways of ascertaining the child's wishes and opinions in a conflict situation. The current practices have been criticized by several researchers and organizations." No minimum age is attached to the obligation to ascertain the child's views, but that the child should be heard according to his or her level of maturity. The fact that children aged 12 have specially enhanced legal rights (for example to appeal decisions and to refuse custody and access), has led to children under 12 not being heard. The Child Welfare Act requires individual plans to be drawn up on custody: "In the preparation of plans, children must also be heard, if permitted by their age and level of maturity. Studies in recent years, however, show that in non-institutional social work the wishes and opinions of children younger than teenagers are not taken into account sufficiently. Respect for the child's views requires the worker to have the time and the ability to listen to the child and to interpret the child's message. This cannot be achieved by changing the law. It requires changes among those working with children: in their attitudes, training, organization of work, as well as in consultation practices...." (Finland IR, paras. 161 - 165)

Finland reported in discussions with the Committee that retraining aims to "teach social workers to listen not just to children's words, but also to the message they were trying to convey. They had to take account not only of the child's maturity, but also how he had been taught to express himself and the opportunities he had been given to do so". (Finland SR.283, para. 51)

"The child has the right to express views **free-ly**. He or she should therefore not suffer any pressure, constraint or influence that might prevent such expression or indeed even require it." (*Manual on Human Rights Reporting*, 1997, p. 426)

"in all matters affecting the child"

There are few areas of family, community, region, national or international decision-making that do not affect children. When the proposal to include the child's right to express views was first discussed in the Working Group drafting the Convention on the Rights of the Child, the text referred to the right of the child to "express his opinion in matters concerning his own person, and in particular marriage, choice of occupation, medical treatment, education and recreation." But most delegations felt that the matters on which States Parties should enable children to express opinions "should not be subject to the limits of a list, and therefore the list ought to be deleted" (E/CN.4/1349*, p. 3 and E/CN.4/L.1575, pp. 13-14, Detrick, pp. 224 and 225).

The reference to "all matters" shows that the participatory rights are not limited to matters specifically dealt with under the Convention. As the *Manual on Human Rights Reporting,* 1997 comments: "The right recognized in article 12 is to be assured in relation to **all matters** affecting the child. It should apply in all questions, even those that might not be specifically covered by the Convention, whenever those same questions have a particular interest for the child or may affect his or her life...

"The right of the child to express views therefore applies in relation to family matters, for instance in case of adoption, in school life, for instance when a decision of expulsion of the child is under consideration, or in relation to relevant events taking place at the community level, such as when a decision is taken on the location of playgrounds for children or the prevention of traffic accidents is being considered. The intention is therefore to ensure that the views of the child are a relevant factor in all decisions affecting him or her and to stress that no implementation system may be carried out and be effective without the intervention of children in the decisions affecting their lives." (*Manual*, pp. 426-427)

"... the views of the child being given due weight in accordance with the age and maturity of the child"

These words provide an active obligation to listen to children's views and to take them seriously. Again, they are in accordance with the concept of

the evolving capacities of the child, introduced in article 5. In deciding how much weight to give to a child's views in a particular matter, the twin criteria of age and maturity must be considered. Age on its own is not the criterion; the Convention on the Rights of the Child rejects specific age barriers to the significant participation of children in decision-making.

"For this purpose, the child shall in particular be provided the opportunity to be heard in any judicial and administrative proceedings affecting the child": article 12(2)

When originally introduced during the drafting of the Convention on the Rights of the Child, the proposal that children should have a right to be heard in judicial and administrative proceedings was linked to the best interests principle, as the second paragraph of article 3, but it was then moved to take a more logical place with the overall participation principle in what was to become article 12 (E/CN.4/1989/48, pp. 42-45; Detrick, pp. 226 and 227).

The link between the paragraphs indicates that the second paragraph of article 12 applies to children "capable of forming views", again emphasizing that very young children should have the formal right to be heard. The Convention provides no support for a set minimum age. The Committee's *Guidelines for Periodic Reports* asks for information on any minimum ages defined in legislation (see page 5), presumably in order to ascertain whether any children are excluded from this right on the grounds of age. For the child to be "provided the opportunity" suggests an active obligation on the State to offer the child the opportunity to be heard, although, again, it is important to emphasize that there is no requirement that the child express views.

"Any judicial ... proceedings affecting the child" covers a very wide range of court hearings, including all civil proceedings such as divorce, custody, care and adoption proceedings, name-changing, judicial applications relating to place of residence, religion, education, disposal of money and so forth, judicial decision-making on nationality, immigration and refugee status, and criminal proceedings; it also covers States' involvement in international courts. Arguably, it covers criminal prosecutions of the parents, the outcome of which can affect children dramatically.

The reference to "administrative proceedings" broadens the scope still further and certainly includes, for example, formal decision-making in education, health, planning and environmental decisions, social security, child protection, employment and administration of juvenile justice.

The *Manual on Human Rights Reporting*, 1997 emphasizes that the child's right to intervene in judicial or administrative proceedings affecting him or her "should be interpreted in a broad manner so as to include all those situations where the proceedings may affect the child, both when he or she initiates them, for instance by introducing a complaint as a victim of ill treatment, and when the child intervenes as a party to the proceedings, for instance when a decision must be taken on the child's place of residence in view of the separation of the child's parents, or in the case of the change of the child's name." (*Manual*, p. 428)

There is an increasingly recognized need to adapt courts and other formal decision-making bodies to enable children to participate. For court hearings this could include innovations such as more informality in the physical design of the court and the clothing of the judges and lawyers, the video-taping of evidence, sight screens, separate waiting rooms and the special preparation of child witnesses (see also article 19, p. 251).

"either directly, or through a representative or an appropriate body, in a manner consistent with the procedural rules of national law"

States are left with discretion as to how the child's views should be heard; but where procedural rules suggest that this be done through a representative or an appropriate body, the obligation is to transmit the views of the child. This principle should not be confused with the obligation in article 3 to ensure that the best interests of the child are a primary consideration in all actions concerning children.

The *Manual on Human Rights Reporting*, 1997 comments: "The child may be heard in various ways according to this paragraph: directly, through a representative or through an appropriate body. All these forms are possible alternatives, each and every one of them being designed to provide the child the best possible way of expressing his or her views in a free and informed manner. 'Representative' may be a person generally responsible for the child, including parents or legal guardians, but it may also be someone specifically appointed for a particular matter affecting the child – this will be the case when the proceeding concerns a conflict of interests between the child and the parents, as illustrated by article 9 paragraph 1 of the Convention. 'Appropriate body' means any individual or institution, including of a non-govern-

mental nature, which will be in a position to intervene on behalf of the child and be guided by his or her best interests. In some cases, an Ombudsman for children has been established at the national level for this purpose..." (*Manual*, p. 429)

During discussions in the Working Group drafting the Convention on the Rights of the Child, the explanation of the inclusion of the final qualification – "in a manner consistent with the procedural rules of national law" – was "that in case the hearing of the child's opinion required some international legal assistance, the requesting State's procedure should also be taken into account" (E/CN.4/1989/48, pp. 42-45, Detrick, p. 227).

The *Manual on Human Rights Reporting*, 1997 emphasizes:

"The reference to 'procedural rules of national law' is intended to stress the need for the national law to include specific procedures to allow for the implementation of the right as recognized by article 12, and naturally not to be interpreted as a means of allowing possible inadequate solutions contained in the procedural law to prevent the full enjoyment of this fundamental right. In fact, such an interpretation would again be contrary to article 4 of the Convention." (*Manual*, p. 429)

Strategies for implementing participation rights

Right to information – a prerequisite for participation

As the *Manual on Human Rights Reporting*, 1997 makes clear "...the child should be provided with the necessary information about the possible existing options and the consequences arising therefrom. In fact, a decision can only be free once it is also an informed decision." (*Manual*, p. 426)

Article 13 asserts the child's freedom to "seek, receive and impart information and ideas of all kinds..." (see page 169). And, in addition, article 17 asserts the child's general right to information (see page 211). But in relation to the various decision-making arenas in which the child's views could be expressed – the family, school, community, court and so on – there is an implied obligation to ensure that the child is appropriately informed about the circumstances and the options.

Monitoring implementation

The Committee has proposed that States should review the extent of implementation of article 12, which implies asking children themselves about their experiences, and the degree to which their views are heard and respected.

"With respect to the implementation of article 12 of the Convention, the Committee encourages the undertaking of a study, from the perspective of children as bearers of rights, on the subject of children's participation in the family, school and society with a view to the formulation of recommendations on this matter."
(UK dependent territory: Hong Kong IRCO, Add.63, para. 25)

Participation rights without discrimination

In conjunction with the anti-discrimination principle in article 2 (page 19), article 12 emphasizes the equal right of all children to express views freely and have them taken seriously. Thus, for example, the child's language or disability must not impede respect for the article's obligations.

Disabled children's participation without discrimination may require the production of materials in special media and the provision of special technology, interpreters (for example signing for deaf and partially hearing children) and special training, including of other children, parents and other family members, teachers and other adults. The Standard Rules on the Equalization of Opportunities for Persons with Disabilities emphasizes throughout the importance of involving disabled persons and organizations of disabled persons "in all decision-making relating to plans and programmes concerning persons with disabilities or affecting their economic and social status" (rule 14(2)). Rule 18 expands on the role of organizations of persons with disabilities – for example "to identify needs and priorities, to participate in the planning, implementation and evaluation of services and measures concerning the lives of persons with disabilities, and to contribute to public awareness and to advocate change" (rule 18(3)) (see article 23, page 305).

The Platform for Action of the Fourth World Conference on Women states that: "Girls are less encouraged than boys to participate in and learn about the social, economic and political functioning of society, with the result that they are not offered the same opportunities as boys to take part in decision-making processes" (Fourth World Conference on Women, Beijing 1995, Platform for Action, para. 265). This demands educational and other strategies to ensure girls have equal rights to participation and to respect for their views.

With reference to participation in juvenile justice, the Convention on the Rights of the Child explicitly requires the free assistance of an interpreter "if the child cannot understand or speak the language used" (article 40(2)(b)(vi), see page 549).

Implementation not dependent on resources

The Committee on the Rights of the Child has emphasized that implementation of the general principles of the Convention, including article 12,

"cannot be dependent upon budgetary resources." (Bolivia IRCO, Add.1, para. 14; see also Indonesia IRCO, Add.25, para. 11, etc.)

Participation rights to be reflected in domestic legislation

The Committee has underlined that article 12, together with the other articles identified as general principles, should be incorporated into national laws and procedures. To reflect both paragraphs of article 12 in domestic law requires provisions that uphold the right to participation in the informal arena of family life, in alternative care for children deprived of their family environment, in children's school and community life, and specifically in all formal judicial and administrative proceedings affecting the child. The *Manual on Human Rights Reporting,* 1997 comments: "States have to adopt measures to ensure and respect this right. On the one hand, they are naturally required to reflect it in the national legislation, ensuring that there are effective opportunities for children to have a say, to be heard, and thus influence decisions. Law can in fact play an important role both in safeguarding this fundamental right, and in influencing attitudes of the population at large..." (*Manual*, p. 427)

Thus the Committee has frequently recommended that legal reform reflect article 12. For example:

"The Committee would like to suggest that greater priority be given to incorporating the general principles of the Convention, especially the provisions of its article 3, relating to the best interests of the child, and article 12, concerning the child's right to make their views known and to have these views given due weight, in the legislative and administrative measures and in policies undertaken to implement the rights of the child. It is suggested that the State Party consider the possibility of establishing further mechanisms to facilitate the participation of children in decisions affecting them, including within the family and the community." (UK IRCO, Add.34, para. 27. See also for example Belarus IRCO, Add.17, para. 11; Canada IRCO, Add.37, paras. 11 and 23; Italy IRCO, Add.41, para. 9)

Initial Reports show that many countries have incorporated the principle of article 12 into domestic law, at least in relation to certain areas of children's lives and into certain court hearings. In some countries, the Convention has been incorporated into domestic law, or it can be invoked before the courts.

Education, training and other strategies to promote the child's participation

The Committee recognizes that legal frameworks alone will not achieve the necessary changes in attitudes and practice within families, schools or communities. So it has encouraged a variety of other strategies for implementation of article 12, including, in particular, education (proposing as a key strategy the incorporation of the Convention within the school curriculum) and information programmes, and systematic training of all those working with and for children. The *Guidelines for Periodic Reports* seeks information on the awareness-raising of families and the public about the need to encourage children to exercise their right to express their views, and on the training of professionals working with children to do so and to give the views due weight. The *Guidelines* asks specifically about training courses for a wide variety of those working with or for children (para 46).

One Committee member commented, during discussions with China, that "... the Convention's advocacy of the right of children to participate in all aspects of society and express their views demanded not just that children should be trained to act in such a way, but that adults and professionals working with children should be trained to develop participatory attitudes in children" (China SR.299, para. 33).

According to the *Manual on Human Rights Reporting*, 1997 "...information campaigns and the education system are important tools to guide children and enhance their capacity to express views and influence decisions... Similarly, the implementation of this right calls for the training and mobilization of those who live and work with children, preparing them to give children the chance of freely and increasingly participating in society and of gaining democratic skills.

"Moreover, it calls for the establishment of mechanisms where children can experience and enhance their capacity for participation – either through an ongoing process of consultation and exchange within family life, by intervening in schools councils for matters relating to their education, or by influencing life at the community level through their participation in local councils." (*Manual*, pp. 427-428)

Within the overall obligation under the Convention's article 42 to make the principles and provisions widely known by appropriate and active means to adults and children alike, the Committee on the Rights of the Child has stressed participatory rights and the importance of actively involving children themselves in strategies to fulfil article 42 (see page 561). For example:

"The Committee wishes to encourage the State Party to develop further a systematic approach towards increasing public awareness of participatory rights of children, in the light of article 12 of the Convention." (Finland IRCO, Add.53, para. 24)

"The Committee is of the opinion that greater efforts are required to make the provisions and principles of the Convention widely known and understood by adults and children alike, in the light of articles 12 and 42 of the Convention. It encourages the State party to further increase public awareness of the participatory rights of children, as well as to consider incorporating the Convention in the school curriculum." (Nepal IRCO, Add.57, para. 27. See also Cyprus IRCO, Add.59, para. 22; Morocco IRCO, Add.60, para. 18)

Various countries have identified traditional attitudes or practices as an obstacle to the implementation of article 12 and other civil rights of children, and the Committee has underlined the need for educational strategies to combat these:

"Strategies and educational programmes along with the adequate dissemination of information should be undertaken in order to counter certain prejudices which affect children negatively,... to enhance the participation of children, in particular within the family." (El Salvador IRCO, Add.9, para. 18)

"The Committee suggests that serious consideration be given to training in the rights of the child of professional groups working with or for children, including teachers, judges and defensores de familia y de menores. The Committee believes that a new attitude and

Domestic courts use Convention

In Belgium, where the Convention is incorporated in domestic law, courts have given effect to article 12 in relation to divorce and related matters: the Initial Report describes how the Mons Court of Appeal (20 April 1993) recognized the direct effect of article 12 in Belgian law; the court also confirmed a minor's right to intervene in judicial proceedings concerning him or her. An obligation exists in the juvenile court to hear a minor as from the age of 12, even if the child is not a party to a case, when the child's interests are directly involved in disputes between persons vested with parental authority (Belgium IR, paras. 4-7).

approach should be developed, particularly as regards the police and the military, in order to enhance respect for all children, regardless of their social, economic or other background, and to reaffirm the value of their fundamental rights. In this connection, information and training programmes should be strengthened, including at the level of the community and the family, and the rights of the child should be included in the framework of the training curriculum of the professional groups concerned." (Colombia IRCO, Add.30, para. 22)

"The Committee is concerned that some traditional cultural attitudes towards children may hamper the full enjoyment of the rights embodied in the Convention by children in Senegal. An understanding of children as subjects of rights has not yet penetrated all strata of Senegalese society." (Senegal IRCO, Add.44, para. 8. See also Honduras IRCO, Add.24, para. 11; Nigeria IRCO, Add.61, para. 14; UK dependent territory: Hong Kong IRCO, Add.63, para. 13)

Implementation in different settings

Within government, and in overall policy-making

The participation of children at all levels of policy-making has been encouraged by the Committee on the Rights of the Child including government-level arrangements for the implementation of the Convention itself. Commenting on Costa Rica's Initial Report, the Committee

"notes with satisfaction ... efforts to educate children with respect to the Convention and encourage their participation in the imple-

mentation process." (Costa Rica IRCO, Add.11, para. 5)

In 1990, Costa Rica held "children's elections" in which children "expressed their views on what they considered to be the most important rights and which deserved immediate treatment". These views are being channelled into government policy-making (Costa Rica IR, paras. 102 and 103).

In Slovenia (see box opposite, the Committee welcomed

"the establishment of a national children's parliament, which has already had six sessions, and the existence of 'Youth Councils and Child Mayors' meetings'." (Slovenia IRCO, Add.65, para. 7)

And in New Zealand:

"The Committee welcomes the State Party's initiative of convening a 'Youth Parliament' as a means of realizing an important dimension of article 12 of the Convention." (New Zealand IRCO, Add.71, para. 7)

In its *Guidelines for Periodic Reports*, the Committee asks for information on how children's views obtained through public opinion, consultations and assessment of children's complaints are taken into consideration in legal provisions and in policy or judicial decisions (para. 47).

The Committee has emphasized that children should participate in the implementation of article 12 in planning strategies for children's participation:

"With respect to the implementation of articles 12, 13, and 15 of the Convention, the Committee recommends that consideration be given to extending and broadening the involvement of children in the initiatives being undertaken within the State Party to facilitate

To be seen and heard...

A gradual change has occurred in Jamaica: "In recent years, guidance counsellors, parents and teachers have been encouraged to attend seminars and workshops at which the child's right to express himself has been emphasized. This has been an area of weakness in the national administrative arrangements. For many years the principle that 'children should be seen and not heard' in home and school existed, but this is gradually being replaced where children are encouraged to participate at every level and the World Summit for Children has provided an important model to encourage this trend." (Jamaica IR, para. 41)

In Mongolia, the following tasks have been identified that relate to article 12: to improve the skill of the teachers, educationists and parents with regard to respect for the child's right to self-expression and to be heard; to train lawyers, sociologists and others specializing in children's affairs; to institute a centre where children's views and opinions will be evaluated; to improve through the mass media the facilities for the child to express his/her views; to legalize this right of the child through its reflection in legislation related to children; to establish a special children's court (Mongolia IR, para. 83).

Challenging cultural attitudes

In Colombia, asserting children's rights "is rendered difficult by the cultural attitude towards children of both sexes that has prevailed over a long period. Affirmation of the child's right to autonomy and individual development, irrespective of the wishes of his or her parents, relatives, representatives and/or guardians, requires, in considerable sectors of the population, a campaign to make people aware of this question."

Respect for the child's opinion "is something that is not widely recognized in the present Colombian cultural context because children are in many cases not seen as persons capable of interpreting the world and its events on an individual basis and on the basis of their own experience. They tend to be provided with an opinion by their parents, relatives and other adults around them. The awareness creation that must be undertaken to deal with this situation now has a legal basis in the Minors' Code, the relevant provision of which reads as follows: 'Article 10: All minors have the right freely to express their opinion and to know their rights. Consequently, they shall be heard in any judicial or administrative proceedings affecting them, either directly or through a representative, in a manner consistent with the rules in force'." (Colombia IR, paras. 75 and 80)

Honduras reports that its legislation has no provision for hearing or representing the views of the child; however, it intends to remedy this: "In this connection, careful regard will be given to the precocity and premature development of today's children and the fact that a failure to ask the child his or her views may have a negative effect, particularly on the definition of his or her personality." (Honduras IR, para. 36)

School parliaments and children's parliaments

In Slovenia, the Initial Report records that a number of mechanisms have been established to ensure the involvement of children in the decision-making process. In primary schools at all grade levels there were compulsory sessions during which children could present their views and recommendations on activities of concern to them. "In addition all heads of schools were required to organise school parliaments, which had specific duties. At the municipal level, mayors and representatives of school parliaments met every year to discuss issues proposed by schoolchildren. Annual sessions of the Children's Parliament were convened by the National Assembly, with the participation of children's deputies, representatives of all municipalities, NGOs and government ministers. The conclusions of those discussions were subsequently published and the follow-up action taken on the previous year's decisions was evaluated at each session." (Slovenia SR.337, para. 24)

Senegal's Initial Report describes how the institution in the country at both national and local levels of the Children's Parliament reflected the concern of the Senegalese authorities "to ensure that children are fully able to exercise their freedoms as recognized by the Convention. This 'Parliament' has the right to give an advisory opinion on all matters relating to children (legislation, regulations, special events, etc.)." (Senegal IR, para. 59)

children's participation in decisions affecting them." (Nicaragua IRCO, Add.36, para. 33)

Complaints procedures

The Committee on the Rights of the Child sees the provision of effective complaints procedures for children as part of the implementation of article 12 (and has also noted it as an appropriate measure for implementation of article 19, to pro-tect children from all forms of violence and abuse). Children need access to complaints procedures in all aspects of their lives – in the family, in alternative care, in all institutions, and in services and facilities relevant to them. The Committee has expressed concern at the lack of complaints procedures for children, in particular in relation to ill-treatment in institutions and in the family.

Child participation in implementation in Nepal

During preparation of Nepal's Initial Report, a five day Children's National Seminar on the Convention was organized by UNICEF and non-governmental organizations: "During the seminar a group of 30 children, representing different ethnic, religious, geographical and socio-economic backgrounds had a chance to discuss and learn about their rights. The children included child labourers, refugees, disabled children and orphans as well as children from privileged families. One of the main objectives of this seminar was to come up with ways to implement the rights of the child. After the seminar, the children went to their respective villages and cities to interview other children and to observe the state of children there. The children were asked to document ... information about the rights of the child ... in photographs and writing. To ensure even wider participation, announcements were made on TV, radio and in the newspapers, encouraging children throughout the country to send in their impressions on the rights of the child in the form of articles, paintings, poems and songs.

"In April the 30 children returned to the capital for another meeting of the Children's National Seminar on the Convention, this time with another child whom each had chosen during the course of the exercise. The Seminar, whose inaugural function was chaired by a street child and attended by the Speaker of the House of Representatives and other high-ranking government officials, was virtually conducted by the children themselves. They had intensive discussions on the information which they had collected and on the contributions made by other children. They organized a press conference and a discussion session with members of Parliament and the National Planning Commission. The children formed a children's national networking group to promote the rights of the child, and decided to publish a quarterly newspaper to exchange ideas and share experiences. The seminar participants also made comments on the country report". To finalize the report, a working committee of the National Planning Commission was formed, including seven members of the Law Reform Commission, different ministries, NGOs and child representatives.

When Nepalese Government representatives met the Committee in May 1996 to discuss the Initial Report, they were accompanied by a representative of the Bal Chetana Samuha – Child Awareness Group, "a coalition of children, for children and by children for the implementation of the Convention". (Nepal IR, paras. 51-53; Nepal SR.301, paras. 1 and 4)

For example:

"The Committee is concerned about the occurrence of maltreatment and cruelty towards children in and outside the family and suggests that procedures and mechanisms be developed to deal with complaints by children of their maltreatment or of cruelty towards them." (Russian Federation IRCO, Add.4, para. 21. See also Burkina Faso IRCO, Add.19, para. 9; Philippines IRCO, Add.29, para. 25; Senegal IRCO, Add.44, para. 24; China IRCO, Add.56, para. 33)

And the Committee has noted that children need to be able to complain independent of their parents:

"The Committee is concerned that, since children are able to lodge complaints only through their parents or legal guardians, the right to adequate recourse and complaint procedures for children victim of abuse, including sexual abuse, neglect or ill-treatment within their families does not seem to be secured. The Committee is also concerned that the enjoyment by children of their right to partici-pate actively in the promotion of their own rights does not seem to be guaranteed...
"...the Committee recommends that a system of complaints aimed at children victim of any form of violence, abuse, including sexual abuse, neglect, maltreatment or exploitation, even while in the care of their parents, be established, as a means to ensure protection of and respect for their rights." (Ethiopia IRCO, Add.67, paras. 16 and 31)

The report on the Committee's General Discussion on juvenile justice notes that children involved with the juvenile justice system were

"...often denied the right to lodge complaints when they were victims of violation of their fundamental rights, including in cases of ill-treatment and sexual abuse..." (Report on the tenth session, October-November 1995, CRC/C/46, para. 220)

The United Nations Rules for the Protection of Juveniles Deprived of their Liberty, which the Committee has promoted as providing relevant standards for implementation, has various provisions relating to complaints mechanisms (see article 37, page 503). These should clearly be applied to all institutional placements for children.

The Standard Rules on the Equalization of Opportunities for Persons with Disabilities proposes: "15.4. States may consider establishing formal statutory complaints mechanisms in order to protect the interests of persons with disabilities."

In child protection

Article 19 of the Convention on the Rights of the Child sets out various measures for ensuring the protection of the child from all forms of violence and abuse. In each case – and in the planning, implementation and monitoring of child protection systems – respect for the views of the child is important (see article 19, page 237).

Access to an effective complaints procedure is an essential element of child protection, and because of the extent of parental violence and abuse of children, children require access independent of their parents. The *Guidelines for Periodic Reports* asks for information under article 1 (definition of the child) on "the minimum legal age defined by national legislation" for "lodging complaints and seeking redress before a court or other relevant authority without parental consent" (para. 24). The Convention does not support the setting of a minimum age for such purposes; the Committee on the Rights of the Child seeks information on whether any children are excluded from such a right.

The Agenda for Action adopted at the World Congress against Com mercial Sexual Exploitation of Children includes a section encouraging participation, to

"(a) promote the participation of children, including child victims, young people, their families, peers and others who are potential helpers of children so that they are able to express their views and to take action to prevent and protect children from commercial sexual exploitation and to assist child victims to be reintegrated into society; and

(b) identify or establish and support networks of children and young people as advocates of child rights, and include children, according to their evolving capacity, in developing and implementing government and other programmes concerning them" (World Congress Plan of Action, A/51/385, para. 6).

Within the family environment

The Committee on the Rights of the Child has consistently encouraged children's participation in decision-making within the family, proposing that definitions of parents' and other caregivers' responsibilities should include an "article 12

obligation" to hear and take seriously the child's views. In the *Guidelines for Initial Reports*, under the heading of "Family environment and alternative care", the Committee requests States Parties in particular to provide relevant information on how the principles of the "best interests of the child" and "respect for the views of the child" are reflected in legislative, judicial, administrative and other measures in force. (para. 16)

The rights of the child to a name and nationality, and to preservation of identity (articles 7 and 8) require respect for the views of the child.

In October 1994, the Committee held a General Discussion on "The role of the family in the promotion of the rights of the child". One of two main issues addressed was the civil rights and freedoms of the child within the family. In its preliminary conclusions of the Discussion, the Committee stated:

"Traditionally, the child has been seen as a dependent, invisible and passive family member. Only recently has he or she become 'seen' and, furthermore, the movement is growing to give him or her the space to be heard and respected. Dialogue, negotiation, participation have come to the forefront of common action for children. The family becomes in turn the ideal framework for the first stage of the democratic experience for each and all of its individual members, including children. Is this only a dream or should it also be envisaged as a precise and challenging task?" (Report on the seventh session, September/ October 1994, CRC/C/34, paras. 192 and 193)

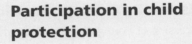

Participation in child protection

The United Kingdom's Initial Report notes that in relation to child protection, whenever the children concerned are considered to have sufficient understanding and are able to express their wishes and feelings and to participate in the process of investigation, assessment, planning and review they should be encouraged to attend "child protection conferences". These are held to decide whether the child is at risk of abuse, and whether or not his or her name should be placed on a local "Child Protection Register". Encouragement of children's participation is included in government guidance on inter-agency cooperation for the protection of children from abuse (UK IR, para. 133).

During discussions on the Initial Report of Pakistan, a Committee member said: "According to article 5 of the Convention, parents had the responsibility, right and duty to provide, in a manner consistent with the evolving capacities of the child, appropriate direction and guidance in the exercise by the child of the rights recognized in the Convention. While the age of a child must be borne in mind, his opinion must also be taken into consideration at all times. That provision was a revolutionary one that must be respected" (Pakistan SR.133, para. 29).

The slogan adopted for the International Year of the Family (1994) was "Building the smallest democracy at the heart of society". And the United Nations body responsible for the Year proposed that families "must become the medium for promoting new values and behaviour consistent with the rights of individual family members, as established by various United Nations instruments" (*Building the smallest democracy at the heart of society*, United Nations Centre for Social Development and Humanitarian Affairs, Vienna, 1991).

As the *Manual on Human Rights Reporting* describes, parents are expected to provide appropriate direction and guidance to the child: "but in this endeavour they are required to act in a manner that takes into consideration the evolving capacities of the child, his or her age and maturity. In the light of article 12, a system of shared, positive and responsible dialogue should thus prevail. In fact, parents are particularly well placed to build the capacity of children to intervene in a growing manner in the different stages of deci-

sion, to prepare them for responsible life in a free society, informing them, giving the necessary guidance and direction, while assuring children the right to express views freely and to give those views due weight (articles 12 and 13). Children's opinions will thus be taken into account, although not necessarily endorsed, and children will be given the possibility of understanding the reasons for a different decision being taken. Children will become active partners, with appropriate skills to participate, rather than a passive reflection of parents' wishes." (*Manual*, p. 446)

In adoption

Relating to adoption, article 12(2) requires that the child is heard in any judicial or administrative proceedings, and article 21(a) refers to the "informed consent" of persons concerned (see also article 21, page 273).

The Committee has stressed that

"In the framework of the adoption process, due consideration should be given to the provisions of article 12 as regards respect for the views of the child." (Costa Rica IRCO, Add.11, para. 14)

In alternative care

Article 20 sets out States' obligation to provide alternative care for children deprived temporarily or permanently of their family environment. The child's participative rights must be protected in all such settings – foster care, *kafalah* of Islamic law, and all kinds of institutions. The Committee's emphasis on the need for legislation and other strategies applies equally to alternative care. In

---

Towards family democratization

During discussion of Portugal's Initial Report, a Government representative indicated that "former family legislation had established a patriarchal and authoritarian family model, which had given the husband authority over his wife and both parents authority over their children. Current family legislation nevertheless provided for an egalitarian family structure, stipulating, for example, that parents should hear their children's view concerning all aspects of family life and should grant autonomy to their children in accordance with the age and maturity of each one. It should be noted that those legislated principles now applied in daily life: a recent poll conducted by the European Values Study Group had determined that parents placed great value on the development of autonomy, personal responsibility and tolerance in their children." (Portugal SR.250, para. 53)

Survey of participation in family life

Uruguay's Initial Report describes the results of a 1993 survey of 409 children and adolescents, conducted by the Uruguay Section of Defence for Children International, of children's experiences of participation within the family: 96.6 per cent of the children interviewed said that their parents showed a readiness to talk with and listen to them; in complete nuclear families 60 per cent replied that their fathers and mothers responded equally to their need for attention. Ninety two per cent of those interviewed stated that the rights which they had identified as most important were those exercised in their family. (Uruguay IR, paras. 130-134)

Parent/child decision-making

Finnish law places an obligation on the parent (custodian) to consult the child on any important question relating to the child before taking a decision. But, its Initial Report comments, in many situations parents are unused to hearing the child's views: "An example is the choice of subjects at school and of career, which have a long-term effect on the child's life. The stated aim of the Comprehensive School Act is to let every child succeed to the best of his or her natural ability. In reality, the custodians wield a lot of authority over the extent to which the child's opinions are heeded in the various stages of his or her education. Under the current law, the choice of subjects at such advanced levels as upper secondary school and vocational school is subject to parental approval, although in practice it is nearly always the children who take their own decisions. This would suggest that the children's right to self-determination should be increased through changing the laws." (Finland IR, para. 168)

In discussions with Finnish government representatives, a Committee member commented that in a number of places in Finland's Initial Report, it was stated that the right of children to participate was guaranteed, provided that the children were "mature": "In her view, that argument was sometimes used to deny children that very right. As she saw it, at every stage of their development children must be given the opportunity to learn participatory skills. In what types of decisions did families allow their children to participate? What kinds of associations were children permitted to form? For example, could they start clubs outside school?" The Finnish representative said that parents were obliged to consult children about decisions affecting them and that "under Finnish law, parents were denied the right to strike their children, and instead had to discuss matters with them, explaining their wishes and expectations." (Finland SR.283, paras. 38 and 54)

addition to the overall right to express views and have them taken seriously (article 12(1)), article 12(2) requires that the child is heard in any judicial or administrative proceedings relating to alternative care. Under article 9(2), in any proceedings to determine that it is necessary to separate a child from his or her parents, "all interested parties" must be given an opportunity to participate (see article 9, page 126).

Under article 25, children placed by the State for care, protection or treatment must have a periodic review; under article 12, children should participate whenever possible in these reviews (see article 25, page 341).

In schools

The Committee has consistently recommended to States Parties that

"further steps be taken to encourage the active participation of children in the schools, as well as outside, in the spirit of article 12 of the Convention." (Argentina IRCO, Add.35, para. 21)

Both paragraphs of article 12 are relevant: the general right of the child to express views freely "in all matters affecting the child", which covers all aspects of school life and decision-making about schooling; and the right to be heard in any "judicial and administrative proceedings affecting the child". For example, "administrative" proceedings might concern choice of school, exclusion from school, formal assessments and so on. There is a need for a legislative framework and procedures that provide for consultation with school students as a group, and also for ascertaining and paying due attention to the views of individual children concerning individual decisions on education (for examples, see box on page 161):

"In relation to the implementation of article 12, the Committee is concerned that insufficient attention has been given to the right of the child to express his/her opinion, including in cases where parents in England and Wales have the possibility of withdrawing their children from parts of the sex education programmes in schools. In this as in other decisions, including exclusion from school, the child is not systematically invited to express his/her opinion and those opinions may not be given due weight, as required under article 12 of the Convention...

"With regard to matters relating to education, the Committee suggests that children's right to appeal against expulsion from school be effectively ensured. It is also suggested that procedures be introduced to ensure that children are provided with the opportunity to express their views on the running of the schools in matters of concern to them..."
(UK IRCO, Add.34, paras. 14 and 32. See also Denmark IRCO, Add.33, para. 24; UK dependent territory: Hong Kong IRCO, Add.63, para. 32)

A particular issue, relevant to articles 12 and 13, is the right of children to organize and contribute to school newspapers and magazines (for discussion, see article 13, page 173).

Participation in state care

France's Initial Report indicates that legislation requires that children over the age of 12 living in social and medico-social facilities and their parents must be involved in the administration of the facility (France IR, para. 81).

The United Kingdom's Initial Report, referring to children in state care, states: "When local authorities are making decisions about children whom they are looking after the Children Act requires them to take account of the children's wishes and feelings. They are required under regulations to tell children what plans they have made about their placement. Before conducting reviews of these arrangements they have to seek and take into account the wishes of the children ... guidance on the conduct of children's homes emphasizes the need to take into account the wishes of the children in the home in the day-to-day running of the home..." (UK IR, paras. 132 and 135).

In child employment

In addition to protective legislation and procedures to prevent exploitation of children in employment (article 32, see also page 427), under article 12, respect is required for the views of the child, and in any judicial or administrative proceedings relating to employment of children, the child has a right to be heard. Children must also have access to complaints procedures relating to employment. Other forms of child labour – forced labour and bonded labour, for example – are breaches of article 12 as well as of other articles of the Convention. However, one of the challenges of ending exploitation of child labour is to ensure that children's often sincere desire to earn money and to help to support the family is also heard and responded to.

In local services, including planning, housing, the environment

The *Manual on Human Rights Reporting*, 1997 uses, as examples of implementation of article 12 at the community level, the involvement of children when decisions are being made about the location of playgrounds or the prevention of traffic accidents, and specifically refers to children's involvement in local councils (*Manual*, p. 427).

The report of the Second United Nations Conference on Human Settlements (Habitat II) states that "Special attention needs to be paid to the participatory processes dealing with the shaping of cities, towns and neighbourhoods; this is in order to secure the living conditions of children and of youth and to make use of their insight, creativity and thoughts on the environment." (United Nations Conference on Human Settlements (Habitat II), A/CONF.165/14, p. 14)

In environmental protection and sustainable development

Article 29 requires that children's education be directed to "the development of respect for the natural environment"; article 24 requires that children are informed (see page 328) about environmental sanitation and it refers to the danger and risks of environmental pollution (see page 326).

Several States Parties have reported, to the Committee, developments in environmental education and the active involvement of children in promoting environmental protection. The direct participation of children was highlighted by the 1992 Earth Summit. The United Nations Conference on Environment and Development produced the Rio Declaration on Environment and Development, in which Principle 21 states: "The creativity, ideals and courage of the youth of the world should be mobilized to forge a global partnership in order to achieve sustainable development and ensure a better future for all." The section of Agenda 21 on "Children and youth in sustainable development" emphasizes that children and youth should participate actively in all relevant decision-making processes, because these processes affect their lives today and have implications for their futures. The objectives include that "Each country should, in consultation with its youth communities, establish a process to promote dialogue between the youth community and Government at all levels, and to establish mechanisms that permit youth access to information and provide them with the opportunity to present their

Consent to employment

According to Belgium's Initial Report, under the Child Labour Act, a competent official must ascertain "whether or not the child consents to perform the activity, the opinion of the child being duly taken into consideration in the light of his age and degree of maturity." (Belgium IR, para. 8)

Participation in schools

Many positive examples of developments or proposals for increasing student participation in the organization of schools and in school life are cited in Initial Reports. France's Initial Report describes the development of a right of representation for students at different levels of the system, starting in the school:

"Within the establishment there is a student council which takes an active part in the life of the establishment;

At the level of the educational district high school councils take part in deliberations and decisions adopted for improving life in high schools;

At the national level, three high school students are elected to sit on the Board of Education and take part in the major discussions on the educational system ...;

The training of representatives has been developed generally throughout the country, with the help of summer universities and training courses;

The establishment of a post of representative of high schools within the Ministry of Education attests to the desire for young people to exercise these new rights to the full ..." (France IR, para. 80)

Chile reported that it was establishing, in standards governing the operation of schools, legal foundations for "student centres", with elected executive boards and class committees, as "a channel through which the concern and needs of young people can be expressed and shared. In this way, the school environment gives students the chance to become used to social interaction and responsibility... Their aim is to act as a forum, and in accordance with the objectives of the establishment and subject to schools' organizational regulations, through which their members can develop their powers of reflection and critical judgement and their willingness to take action, and to prepare them for democratic life and participation in cultural and social exchanges." (Chile IR, paras. 195 and 196)

In Namibia, student representative councils exist "at all levels of schooling" and the Namibian Educational Code of Conduct for Schools states that students have the right to have their opinions taken into consideration in setting school policy regarding discipline and provides grievance and appeals procedures (Namibia IR, paras. 75-78).

In schools in Croatia, "every class had a representative who attended meetings of the teaching staff. While children had little say about curricula, they could express their opinion, a right which they had, in fact, recently exercized in Zagreb, where children had protested at the Ministry of Education against the appointment of a particular school headmaster. Children did not allow adults to treat them as objects." (Croatia SR.281, para. 29)

In Bulgaria, the National Education Act "provides for children over 14 to have their own opinion and preference in choosing a school and type of education when they exercize their right to education. According to the Regulation for the Application of the National Education Act, a student is entitled to express an opinion or put forward proposals before the administration of the school regarding the organization and conduct of its activities, and can elect and be elected in the collective management bodies of the school." (Bulgaria IR, para. 53)

perspectives on government decisions, including the implementation of Agenda 21... Each country and the United Nations should support the promotion and creation of mechanisms to involve youth representation in all United Nations processes in order to influence those processes.

"Children not only will inherit the responsibility of looking after the Earth, but in many developing countries they comprise nearly half the population. Furthermore, children in both developing and industrialized countries are highly vulnerable to the effects of environmental degradation. They

are also highly aware supporters of environmental thinking. The specific interests of children need to be taken fully into account in the participatory process on environment and development in order to safeguard the future sustainability of any actions taken to improve the environment..."

Among activities, Governments should take active steps to "Establish procedures to incorporate children's concerns into all relevant policies and strategies for environment and development at the local, regional and national levels, including those concerning allocation of and entitlement to natural resources, housing and recreation needs, and control of pollution and toxicity in both rural and urban areas" (Agenda 21, chapter 25, Objectives).

In individual health decisions and the planning and provision of health services

The Convention upholds children's rights to participate in decisions about their health and health care, and also in the planning and provision of health services relevant to them (see also article 1, page 8 and article 24, page 323). The *Guidelines for Initial Reports* asks for information on the minimum age at which a child can receive medical counselling without parental consent (para.

12). The *Guidelines for Periodic Reports,* in addition, asks for information about the minimum age for medical treatment or surgery without parental consent (para. 24).

Some countries have set an age from which children are deemed to be able to consent to medical treatment for themselves; in other countries, more in line with the concept of evolving capacities of the child, no age is set but a principle exists that the child acquires the right to make decisions for himself or herself once judged to have "sufficient understanding". In some instances it is linked to a presumption in law that a child of a certain age does have sufficient maturity (see article 1, page 8).

Children's views in planning and neighbourhood administration

In 1989 the Inter-Ministerial Committee on Children in Denmark initiated the "Children as fellow citizens" project, aiming to give children influence in local planning and in the implementation of plans. Five municipalities were chosen to reflect diverse sizes and locations. A project manager was employed in each and local radio and newspapers were used (Denmark IR, paras. 16-19).

Finland's Initial Report emphasizes that the physical environment is in many ways important to children's lives: "The Government has submitted a bill to Parliament on environmental impact assessment... The bill requires that the needs of various Population groups – including those of children – be considered in zoning and in issuing building permits. The environmental impact of building and zoning must be assessed from the children's point of view, and children must be heard both directly and indirectly.

"The Ministry of the Environment has developed means to consciously take into account the needs of children in community planning. The Ministry has participated in a number of experiments where children's points of view have been admitted into the planning process and which aim at creating an environment which is good for children and young people."

The Finnish Ministry of the Environment has produced a handbook for the use of planners and others on the planning of children-friendly living environments. The handbook promotes children as "active users and planners of their environment," and a major non-governmental organization (the Mannerheim League for Child Welfare) has developed proposals for listening to children in environmental decision-making processes and has published a handbook on the subject (Finland IR, paras. 48-50).

In France, children's and young people's councils exist in neighbourhoods as well as communes, departments and regions. The first children's council was set up in 1979. Only recently have they become widespread – increasing from 300 in 1990 to 650 in 1992. A detailed study of the operation and achievements of children's councils was completed in 1993. At that time, inclusion of a module on children's councils in the training course for youth leaders was being discussed (France IR, paras. 82-83).

In 1989 the Norwegian Government adopted National Policy Guidelines to Safeguard the Interests of Children and Adolescents in Planning: "According to the guidelines municipalities shall organize their planning process in such a way that the views of children as affected parties are expressed and so that various groups of children and adolescents are given the opportunity to participate. According to the National Policy Guidelines, the municipalities shall appoint a body to follow up these guidelines." (Norway IR, para. 120)

Spain's children's assemblies

Some autonomous communities in Spain and some local councils have conducted "an experiment of 'child assemblies' to encourage free participation and expression by boys and girls, following democratic procedures like those used by adults, on topics in their local area that interest them.... In general the process of developing such assemblies was launched in school classrooms on the basis of general discussions and elections of pupils' representatives to hold local assemblies. It is in the town halls that such assemblies have generally been held with a view to reproducing as faithfully as possible the sessions ordinarily held there. Although the meetings have been held by children, they have elected mayors, secretaries or parliamentary groups and published records".

According to Spain's Initial Report, the purpose of the children's assembles has been summarized as:

- holding the event in the place where the child is developing – the child's own school, own town hall and own town;
- the drawing of concrete conclusions on how the children actually perceive the realities surrounding them;
- the children's democratic election of their own representatives;
- opportunities for the children to meet and express their own wishes, opinions and needs;
- opportunities for children to get to know the particular formal and political structures in which this type of meeting takes place.

(Spain IR, paras. 118 and 119)

In the media

In the outline for its General Discussion on "The child and the media", the Committee on the Rights of the Child emphasized the importance of the media in offering children the opportunity to express themselves:

"One of the principles of the Convention is that the views of children be heard and given due respect (art. 12). This is also reflected in articles about freedom of expression, thought, conscience and religion (arts. 13–14). It is in the spirit of these provisions that children should not only be able to consume information material but also to participate themselves in the media. This requires that there exist media which communicate with children. The Committee on the Rights of the Child has noted that there have been experiments in several countries to develop child-oriented media; some daily newspapers have special pages for children and radio and television programmes also devote special segments for the young audience. Further efforts are, however, needed..." (Report on the eleventh session, January 1996, Annex IX, CRC/C/50, p. 81)

Following plenary and working group discussion at the Committee's General Discussion various recommendations were proposed for debate, including some relating to children's participation:

"1. Child media. A dossier should be compiled on positive practical experiences of active child participation in the media, such as 'Children's Express' in the United Kingdom and United States.

2. Child forum within Internet. The UNICEF-initiated 'Voices of Youth' at the World Wide Web should be promoted and advertised as a positive facility for international discussion on important issues between young people.

3. Active child libraries. The experience of dynamic child libraries, or child departments within public libraries, should be documented and disseminated.

4. Media education. Knowledge about the media, their impact and functioning should be imparted in schools at all levels. Students should be enabled to relate to and use the media in a participatory manner, as well as to learn how to decode media messages, including in advertising. Good experience in some countries should be made available to others..." (Report on thirteenth session, September-October 1996, General Discussion on "The child and the media", CRC/C/15/Add.65, p. 42 et seq.; see also article 17, page 211).

In asylum-seeking and other immigration procedures

The principles of article 12(1) and (2) should be applied in all immigration procedures including asylum-seeking, in relation to articles 10 and 22.

The 1994 *Refugee children – Guidelines on Protection and Care,* published by the United Nations High Commissioner for Refugees

(UNHCR) emphasizes the importance of the Convention's general principles: non-discrimination, best interests of the child and respect for the views of the child (articles 2, 3 and 12). The *Guidelines* underlines the importance of seeking and taking seriously children's views and feelings, and enabling children to take part in decisions related to asylum-seeking and as refugees (*Refugee children – Guidelines on Protection and Care*, UNHCR, Geneva, p. 23 et seq.). The UNHCR Policy on Refugee Children states: "... Although vulnerable, children are also a resource with much to offer. The potential contributions of children must not be overlooked. They are people in their own right, with suggestions, opinions and abilities to participate in decisions and activities that affect their lives. Efforts on behalf of refugee children fall short if they are perceived only as individuals to be fed, immunized or sheltered, rather than treated as participating members of their community." (UNHCR Executive Committee Document EC/SCP/82, see *Guidelines*, p. 171)

The Committee has commented:

"The Committee recommends that the State Party pay particular attention to the implementation of article 22 of the Convention as well as of the general principles of the Convention, in particular the best interests of the child and respect for his or her views, in all matters relating to the protection of refugee and immigrant children, including in deportation proceedings..." (Canada IRCO, Add.37, para. 24)

Commenting on Germany's Initial Report, the Committee urged that consideration be given to extending and broadening the involvement of children in decisions affecting them,

"including in proceedings relating to family reunification..." (Germany IRCO, Add.43, para. 29)

In the juvenile justice system

In addition to the general principles found in article 12(1) and (2), articles 37 and 40 require legislation and other measures to ensure the child's participation in relation to his or her restriction of liberty and to his or her involvement in the juvenile justice system. Under article 37(d), any child deprived of liberty has the right to prompt access to legal and other assistance as well as the right to challenge the legality of the deprivation of liberty before a court or other competent body (see article 37, page 502). Similarly, under article 40(2)(b), the child alleged as or accused of infringing the penal law has similar rights to legal and other assistance and to participate in a fair hearing, if necessary with the assistance of an interpreter (see article 40, page 547).

The report of the Committee's General Discussion on juvenile justice reviews the Committee's examination of Initial Reports:

"... in relation to the right of the child to participate in proceedings affecting him or her, States Parties' reports had indicated that children were seldom made sufficiently aware of their rights, including the right to assistance from a legal counsel, or of the circumstances surrounding the case or of the measures decided. They were also often denied the right to lodge complaints when they were victims of violation of their fundamental rights, including in cases of ill-treatment and sexual abuse..." (Report on the tenth session, October-November 1995, CRC/C/46, para. 220)

The Committee has raised the issue with some States. For example:

"The Committee expresses its concern regarding the implementation of article 12 of the Convention. The views of the child are not sufficiently taken into account, especially within the family, the school and the juvenile justice system." (Sri Lanka IRCO, Add.40, para. 13)

The United Nations Guidelines on Prevention of Juvenile Delinquency, the "Riyadh Guidelines", in particular emphasizes the importance of participation in prevention as well as planning and implementation: "For the purposes of the interpretation of these guidelines, a child-centred orientation should be pursued. Young persons should have an active role and partnership within society and should not be considered as mere objects of socialization or control" (para. 3). The Guidelines goes on to propose active participation in delinquency prevention policies and processes, and strengthened youth organizations given full participatory status in the management of community affairs (for details, see article 40, page 545).

Implementation Checklist

article 12

● General measures of implementation

Have appropriate general measures of implementation been taken in relation to article 12 including

☐ identification and coordination of the responsible departments and agencies at all levels of government (**all departments affecting children directly or indirectly**)?

☐ identification of relevant non-governmental organizations/civil society partners?

☐ a comprehensive review to ensure that all legislation, policy and practice is compatible with the article, for all children in all parts of the jurisdiction?

☐ adoption of a strategy to secure full implementation

  ☐ which includes where necessary the identification of goals and indicators of progress?

  ☐ which does not affect any provisions which are more conducive to the rights of the child?

  ☐ which recognizes other relevant international standards?

  ☐ which involves where necessary international cooperation?

  (Such measures may be part of an overall governmental strategy for implementing the Convention as a whole).

☐ budgetary analysis and allocation of necessary resources?

☐ development of mechanisms for monitoring and evaluation?

☐ making the implications of article 12 widely known to adults and children?

☐ development of appropriate training and awareness-raising (in relation to article 12 should include training for **all those working with or for children, and parenting education**)?

● Specific issues in implementing article 12

Is the obligation reflected in article 12(1) respected

  ☐ in arrangements for the overall implementation of the Convention?

  ☐ in arrangements for preparing the State's Initial and Periodic Reports under the Convention?

in arrangements for the development of legislation, policy and practice which may affect children

  ☐ in central government?

  ☐ in regional/provincial government?

  ☐ in local government?

How to use the checklists, *see page XVII*

Is an obligation to respect article 12(1) included in legislation applying to

- ☐ the child in the family environment?
- ☐ the process of adoption and adopted children?
- ☐ placement in alternative care and to the child in alternative care, whether provided by the State or by others?
- ☐ all schools and other educational institutions and all educational services affecting children?
- ☐ child protection?
- ☐ health services and institutions?
- ☐ local communities, planning and environmental decision-making affecting children, including in response to the proposals of Agenda 21?
- ☐ child employment and vocational training or guidance?
- ☐ all immigration procedures, including those affecting asylum-seeking children?
- ☐ the child in the juvenile justice system?

☐ Where age limits apply to the laws providing children with an opportunity to express their views and requiring that their views are given due weight, are the limits in accordance with article 12 and other articles ?

☐ Are the rights reflected in article 12 available to all children concerned, including disabled children, without discrimination, where necessary through the provision of interpreters, translations, special materials and technology?

☐ Has there been adaptation to enable children's participation, for example by not using intimidatory and confusing language, and by providing appropriate settings and procedures to enable children to be heard?

☐ Have special arrangements been developed for child witnesses in both civil and criminal proceedings?

Are there no situations in which a child is compelled to

- ☐ express views?
- ☐ give evidence in court or other proceedings?

☐ Does the child in each case have access to adequate information to enable him or her to express informed views and/or to play an informed role in decision-making?

How to use the checklists, *see page XVII*

Are there no matters affecting the child on which the child is, through legislation or otherwise, excluded from

- ☐ expressing views?
- ☐ having those views given due weight?

In relation to paragraph 2 of article 12, are children provided with a right to be heard in all judicial or administrative proceedings affecting them, such as

- ☐ criminal proceedings?
- ☐ civil proceedings?
- ☐ education?
- ☐ health?
- ☐ child protection?
- ☐ placement in alternative care?
- ☐ adoption proiceedings?
- ☐ reviews under article 25?
- ☐ immigration and asylum-seeking?
- ☐ planning, housing and environment?
- ☐ social security?
- ☐ employment?
- ☐ any other?

☐ Has the implementation and use of legislative provisions relating to children's participation been monitored?

☐ Do children have appropriate remedies for breaches of their rights guaranteed by article 12?

Do children have appropriate access to effective complaints procedures in relation to

- ☐ family life, including ill-treatment?
- ☐ alternative care of all kinds?
- ☐ schools and education services?
- ☐ health services and institutions?
- ☐ employment?
- ☐ all forms of detention?
- ☐ all aspects of the juvenile justice system?
- ☐ environmental, planning, housing and transport issues?
- ☐ other services affecting children?

How to use the checklists, *see page XVII*

☐ In each case, do children have access to appropriate advice and advocacy?

Do children have appropriate access to the media and opportunities to participate in the media, particularly

- ☐ radio?
- ☐ print media?
- ☐ television?

☐ Do children have opportunities for training in media skills enabling them to relate to and use the media in a participatory manner?

☐ Are the participatory rights of children within the family promoted through parenting education and preparation for parenthood?

Is training to promote the participatory rights of children provided for

- ☐ judges, including family court and juvenile court judges?
- ☐ probation officers?
- ☐ police officers?
- ☐ prison officers?
- ☐ immigration officers?
- ☐ teachers?
- ☐ health workers?
- ☐ social workers?
- ☐ other professionals?

Reminder : **The Convention is indivisible and its articles are interdependent. Article 12 has been identified by the Committee on the Rights of the Child as a general principle of relevance to implementation of the whole Convention.**

Particular regard should be paid to:
Other general principles

Article 2: all rights to be recognized for each child in jurisdiction without discrimination on any ground

Article 3(1): the best interests of the child to be a primary consideration in all actions concerning children

Article 6: right to life and maximum possible survival and development

All other articles require consideration of the child's right to be heard, and to have his or her views taken seriously. Specifically, the child has a right to be heard in relation to any judicial or administrative proceedings affecting the child, relevant to, for example, articles 9, 10, 21, 25, 37, 40. Also linked to the child's participation rights are articles 13 (freedom of expression), article 14 (freedom of thought, conscience and religion) and article 15 (freedom of association).

Child's right to freedom of expression

article 13

Text of Article 13

1. The child shall have the right to freedom of expression; this right shall include freedom to seek, receive and impart information and ideas of all kinds, regardless of frontiers, either orally, in writing or in print, in the form of art, or through any other media of the child's choice.

2. The exercise of this right may be subject to certain restrictions, but these shall only be such as are provided by law and are necessary:

(a) For respect of the rights or reputations of others; or

(b) For the protection of national security or of public order (ordre public), or of public health or morals.

This is one of a series of articles in the Convention on the Rights of the Child which confirm that civil rights guaranteed for "everyone" in the International Bill of Human Rights do apply to children. The first paragraph sets out the right to freedom of expression – to "seek, receive and impart" information and ideas of all kinds, and the second paragraph limits the restrictions that may be applied to the child's exercise of this right.

The right to freedom of expression is closely linked to the child's right to express views and have them taken seriously under article 12, and to the following two articles: on freedom of thought, conscience and religion and on freedom of association. In addition, article 17 covers the child's access to appropriate information and material. In its examination of reports, the Committee on the Rights of the Child has emphasized that the child is the subject of rights, the possessor of rights, and that the civil rights of children should be recognized explicitly in the law. Article 30 asserts the linked cultural, religious and linguistic rights of the children of minorities and indigenous communities, and article 31, the right of the child to engage in play and recreation and in cultural life and the arts. ■

Summary

The child's right to freedom of expression

The Universal Declaration of Human Rights, in its article 19, guarantees: "Everyone has the right to freedom of opinion and expression; this right includes freedom to hold opinions without interference and to seek, receive and impart information and ideas through any media and regardless of frontiers." Article 19 of the International Covenant on Civil and Political Rights contains similar wording.

In a 1989 General Comment on article 19 of the Covenant, the Human Rights Committee empha-

sizes that children should benefit from civil rights. The Committee pointed out that the rights, providing special protection, set out for children in article 24 of the Covenant, "are not the only ones that the Covenant recognizes for children and that, as individuals, children benefit from all of the civil rights enunciated in the Covenant..." (Human Rights Committee, General Comment 17, HRI/GEN/1/Rev.2, p. 23)

But as the *Manual on Human Rights Reporting*, 1997 comments on children's civil rights: "The prevailing reality was however, and to a certain extent still is, that children, in view of their evolving maturity, are in practice not recognized as having the necessary capacity or competence to exercise them. By their clear incorporation in the Convention, an undeniable statement is made as to their entitlement and ability to fully enjoy such fundamental freedoms." (*Manual*, pp. 433-434)

The *Manual* makes note of the fact that articles 13 to 17 constitute an important chapter of the Convention on the Rights of the Child, indicating the need to envisage the child as an active subject of rights. "States are required to recognize them in the law and to determine therein how their exercise may be ensured. It is therefore not sufficient for the Constitution simply to include them as fundamental rights. In fact, constitutional and/or legal provisions should further indicate how these rights specifically apply to children, which mechanisms have been established to protect them in an effective manner and which remedies are provided in case of their violation." (*Manual*, p. 433)

The Committee on the Rights of the Child has emphasized that, in the case of children, it is not enough that these principles should be reflected in constitutions as applying to "everyone". In its *Guidelines for Periodic Reports,* the Committee requests information on measures taken to ensure that the civil rights, including article 13, "are recognized by law specifically in relation to children", and on how they are implemented in practice. The Committee expects to see the child's right to freedom of expression expressly guaranteed in legislation (and the article requires that any restrictions on the right are set out in legislation – see below). For example, the Committee commented:

"In the light of articles 13, 14 and 15, the Committee is concerned that the State Party has not taken all legal and other appropriate measures to promote and implement those rights ...
"The Committee recommends that the State Party take all appropriate measures, including legal means, to fully implement articles 13, 14 and 15 of the Convention ..." (Myanmar IRCO, Add.69, paras. 16 and 37)

The Committee has frequently commented that the implementation of articles 13 and linked civil rights needs further development. For example:

"With respect to the implementation of articles 12, 13 and 15 of the Convention insufficient attention has been accorded to ensuring the involvement of children in decisions, including within the family, and in administrative and judicial procedures regarding them...
"The Committee notes that provisions of the Convention relating to the participation of children, including its articles 12, 13 and 15, need to be more thoroughly considered and

Monitoring freedom of expression

Uruguay's Initial Report describes a survey by a non-governmental organization of over 400 children, investigating the degree to which their civil rights were respected: "With regard to the right of freedom of expression, 75 per cent answered that their parents discussed with them such matters as moving house, allocation of domestic tasks, television programmes or use of money. Questioned as to whether their parents respected their personal decisions about dress, leisure activities, free time, studies and friends, 85 per cent of the children and adolescents answered in the affirmative. The optional answer that 'no notice is ever taken of my opinion' was recorded in only two per cent of cases. We believe that this information collected by a non-governmental organization constitutes a very clear example of the exercise of the right of freedom of expression by young people and children in Uruguay. The fact that the conceptualization of the child as a subject of rights has been recognized in the family environment constitutes a step towards full acceptance of these rights in all areas of social activity." (Uruguay IR , paras. 133-134)

encouraged. To this end information and awareness campaigns should be developed..." *(Germany IRCO, Add.43, paras. 17 and 29).*

The Committee has proposed monitoring and research to determine to what extent children's civil rights are respected, within and outside the family.

The Committee has encouraged States to look at the implementation of the child's right to freedom of expression in various settings, including within the family. Traditional attitudes towards children and the role they should play in the family, school and society have been identified by the Committee as an impediment to implementation of children's participation in many States (see article 12, page 148 for Committee's comments).

In its outline for the General Discussion on "The role of the family in the promotion of the rights of the child", the Committee commented:

"The civil rights of the child begin within the family ... The family is an essential agent for creating awareness and preservation of human rights, and respect for human values, cultural identity and heritage, and other

civilizations. There is a need to consider appropriate ways of ensuring balance between parental authority and the realization of the rights of the child, including the right to freedom of expression. Corresponding measures to prevent abrogation of these rights of the child within the family should be discussed." (Report on the fifth session, January 1994, Annex V, CRC/C/24, p. 63)

The Committee has also stressed the important role of the media in "offering children the possibility of expressing themselves". Article 17 (see page 211) concerns the role of the mass media and ensuring that the child has access to a wide variety of information and material. In the report of its General Discussion on "The child and the media" the Committee promoted children's participatory rights in relation to the media (see article 12, page 163 and article 17, page 213). The Internet and modern information technology provide children with new opportunities to seek and impart information regardless of frontiers.

Of particular importance to children's freedom of expression is the right to engage in play and recreational activity and to participate freely in cultural life and the arts (see article 31, page 417). Article 30 asserts the particular rights of freedom of expression of children belonging to minorities or indigenous communities to enjoy their own culture, practice and profess their own religion, and use their own language (see article 30, page 407).

Ensuring the freedom of expression rights of disabled children may require special attention. Many provisions in the Standard Rules on the Equalization of Opportunities for Persons with Disabilities are relevant to this, in particular on access to information and communication issues (rule 5), and on cultural activities, recreation and religions (rules 10-12).

The United Nations Rules for the Protection of Juveniles Deprived of their Liberty, which the Committee has promoted as providing relevant standards for implementation, states in rule 13: "Juveniles deprived of their liberty shall not for any reason related to their status be denied the civil, economic, political, social or cultural rights to which they are entitled under national or international law, and which are compatible with the deprivation of liberty, such as social security rights and benefits, freedom of association and, upon reaching the minimum age established by law, the right to marry." Thus aspects of freedom of expression not incompatible with deprivation of liberty must be preserved in all forms of the restriction of liberty.

Restrictions on child's right: article 13(2)

Restrictions on the child's right to freedom of expression are strictly limited by the provisions of paragraph 2 of the article. The restrictions are the same as those applied to "everyone's" freedom of expression in article 19 of the International Covenant on Civil and Political Rights. Any restrictions must be set out in legislation and must be "necessary" for one of the two purposes set out in subparagraphs (a) and (b).

The Committee on the Rights of the Child, in its *Guidelines for Periodic Reports,* requests information on any restrictions applied under article 13. In its examination of States Parties' reports, it has also emphasized the limits on any restrictions on the child's right:

"[The Committee] is also concerned that the authorities seem to give a wide interpretation to limitations for 'lawful purposes' of the exercize of the rights to freedom of religion, expression and assembly, which may prevent the full enjoyment of such rights." (Indonesia IRCO, Add.25, para. 13)

"The Committee considers that greater efforts should be made to promote the participation

of children in family, school and social life, as well as the effective enjoyment of their fundamental freedoms, including the freedom of opinion, expression and association, which should be subject only to the restrictions provided by the law and which are necessary in a democratic society." (Republic of Korea IRCO, Add.51, para. 26)

Article 17(e) of the Convention on the mass media and other information sources, requires States to: "Encourage the development of appropriate guidelines for the protection of the child from information and material injurious to his or her well-being, bearing in mind the provisions of articles 13 and 18." Thus any guidelines must be consistent with the right to freedom of expression and with the restrictions allowed under article 13(2).

One particular issue raised during the drafting of the Convention (and more recently in reservations and declarations made by some States upon ratifying the Convention) concerns the role of parents in relation to children's civil rights, including the right to freedom of expression. During the drafting process, a general proposal that the Convention should confirm explicitly that the civil and political rights accorded to "everyone" in the International Bill of Human Rights do apply to children met with some opposition at first. The need to acknowledge the parents' role was emphasized. An early draft of what was to become article 13 stated: "Nothing in this article shall be interpreted as limiting or otherwise affecting the authority, rights or responsibilities of a parent or other legal guardian of the child." But discussion proceeded to agree that while children might need direction and guidance from parents or guardians in the exercise of these rights, this does not affect the content of the rights themselves, and also that the evolving capacities of the child must be respected (E/CN.4/1986/39 p. 17; E/CN.4/1987/25 pp. 26-27; E/CN.4/1988/28 pp. 9-13; Detrick p. 230 et seq.).

These formulas find general expression in article 5 of the Convention, requiring States to respect the "responsibilities, rights and duties" of parents and others "to provide, in a manner consistent with the evolving capacities of the child, appropriate direction and guidance in the exercise by the child of the rights recognized in the present Convention" (see article 5, page 75). This role for parents is repeated in article 14 (the child's right to freedom of thought, conscience and religion, see page 177) but not in article 13.

On the role of the parents, the *Manual on Human Rights Reporting*, 1997 states: "... as stressed by article 5 of the Convention, parents or others

School magazines

In relation to implementation of articles 12 and 13, Denmark reported that the Ministry of Education had issued a circular providing guidelines on the publication of school magazines, but later abandoned it because "it might give rise to doubts if this circular was in accordance with the Convention" (Denmark IR, paras. 13 and 82).

France's Initial Report describes the encouragement of freedom of expression in schools. The aim of a Decree dated 18 February 1991, relating to the rights and obligations of pupils in public secondary education, and four implementing circulars, was to encourage young high school students to express themselves. The right of publication set out in the law gives high school publications additional support by allowing expression without prior censorship (France IR, para. 80).

responsible for the child, should provide 'direction and guidance' which is appropriate to the child and consistent with the evolving capacities of the child, and with a view to ensuring 'the **exercise by the child** of the rights recognized by the Convention'." (*Manual*, p. 434)

Various States have issued declarations or reservations concerning the relationship between parents and their children's civil rights, which include article 13. When examining Initial Reports, the Committee has consistently asked for a review and withdrawal of reservations; in particular the Committee has expressed concern at reservations that suggest lack of the full recognition of the child as a subject of rights (for further discussion and Committee comments, see article 5, page 78, and article 12, page 148).

Other declarations and reservations relate to potential restrictions on freedom of expression and other civil rights. For example, Algeria made an "interpretative declaration": "Articles 13, 16 and 17 shall be applied while taking account of the interest of the child and the need to safeguard its physical and mental integrity. In this framework, the Algerian government shall interpret the provisions of these articles while taking account of:

The provisions of the Penal Code, in particular those sections relating to breaches of public order, to public decency and to the incitement of minors to immorality and debauchery;

The provisions of Law No. 90-07 of 3 April 1990, comprising the Information Code, and particularly its article 24 stipulating that 'the director of a publication destined for children must be assisted by an educational advisory body';

Article 26 of the same Code, which provides that 'national and foreign periodicals and specialized publications, whatever their nature or purpose, must not contain any illustration, narrative, information or insertion contrary to Islamic morality, national values or human rights or advocate racism, fanaticism and treason... Further such publications must contain no publicity or advertising that may promote violence and delinquency." (CRC/C/2/Rev.5 p. 11)

A reservation made by Austria states: "Article 13 and article 15 of the Convention will be applied provided that they will not affect legal restrictions in accordance with article 10 and article 11 of the European Convention on the Protection of Human Rights and Fundamental Freedoms of 4 November 1950." Belgium made a similar reservation (CRC/C/2/Rev.5, p. 13 and 14). The European Convention has a wider definition of permitted restrictions: article 10(2) – freedom of expression: "The exercise of these freedoms, since it carries with it duties and responsibilities, may be subject to such formalities, conditions, restrictions or penalties as are prescribed by law and are necessary in a democratic society, in the interests of national security, territorial integrity or public safety, for the prevention of disorder or crime, for the protection of health or morals, for the protection of the reputation or rights of others, for preventing the disclosure of information received in confidence, or for maintaining the authority and impartiality of the judiciary."

The Human Rights Committee, in its General Comment on the equivalent article 19 in the International Covenant on Civil and Political Rights, emphasizes that it is the interplay between the principle of freedom of expression and any imposed limitations and restrictions that determines the actual scope of the individual's right. Paragraph 3 of article 19 states that the exercise of the right to freedom of expression "carries with it special duties and responsibilities. It may therefore be subject to certain restrictions, but these shall only be such as are provided by law and are necessary:

(a) For respect of the rights or reputations of others;

(b) For the protection of national security or of public order (*ordre public*), or of public health or morals."

The General Comment states: "Paragraph 3 expressly stresses that the exercise of the right to freedom of expression carries with it special duties and responsibilities and for this reason certain restrictions on the right are permitted which may relate either to the interests of other persons or to those of the community as a whole. However, when a State Party imposes certain restrictions on the exercise of freedom of expression, these may not put in jeopardy the right itself. Paragraph 3 lays down conditions and it is only subject to these conditions that restrictions may be imposed: the restrictions must be 'provided by law'; they may only be imposed for one of the purposes set out in subparagraphs (a) and (b) of paragraph 3; and they must be justified as being 'necessary' for that State Party for one of those purposes." (Human Rights Committee, General Comment 10, HRI/GEN/1/Rev.2, p. 11)

The Human Rights Committee notes that not all countries have provided information in their reports under the Covenant on "all aspects of the freedom of expression. For instance, little attention has so far been given to the fact that, because of the development of modern mass media, effective measures are necessary to prevent such control of the media as would interfere with the right of everyone to freedom of expression in a way that is not provided for in paragraph 3.

"Many State reports confine themselves to mentioning that freedom of expression is guaranteed under the Constitution or the law. However, in order to know the precise regime of freedom of expression in law and in practice, the Committee needs in addition pertinent information about the rules which either define the scope of freedom of expression or which set forth certain restrictions, as well as any other conditions which in practice affect the exercise of this right...." (Human Rights Committee General Comment 10, HRI/GEN/1/Rev.2, p. 11)

Implementation Checklist

article 13

● General measures of implementation

Have appropriate general measures of implementation been taken in relation to article 13, including

☐ identification and coordination of the responsible departments and agencies at all levels of government (article 13 is relevant to **departments of family affairs, welfare, education, media and communication**)?

☐ identification of relevant non-governmental organizations/civil society partners?

☐ a comprehensive review to ensure that all legislation, policy and practice is compatible with the article, for all children in all parts of the jurisdiction?

☐ adoption of a strategy to secure full implementation

　☐ which includes where necessary the identification of goals and indicators of progress?

　☐ which does not affect any provisions which are more conducive to the rights of the child?

　☐ which recognizes other relevant international standards?

　☐ which involves where necessary international cooperation?

(Such measures may be part of an overall governmental strategy for implementing the Convention as a whole).

☐ budgetary analysis and allocation of necessary resources?

☐ development of mechanisms for monitoring and evaluation?

☐ making the implications of article 13 widely known to adults and children?

☐ development of appropriate training and awareness-raising (in relation to article 13 likely to include the training of **all those working with or for children and their families, and parenting education**)?

● Specific issues in implementing article 13

☐ Is the child's right to freedom of expression as guaranteed in article 13 explicitly recognized in legislation?

☐ Does policy and practice actively encourage the child's freedom of expression?

Does law, policy and practice support the child's right to freedom of expression, as set out in article 13, in relation to

　☐ the family?

　☐ alternative care?

　☐ schools?

☐ juvenile justice institutions?

    ☐ the community?

    ☐ the media?

☐ Are the only permitted restrictions on the right to freedom of expression consistent with those set out in paragraph 2 of article 13 and are they defined in legislation?

☐ In particular, are any restrictions on the child's right to contribute to and to publish school and other publications consistent with those set out in paragraph 2?

☐ Are special measures taken to ensure the freedom of expression of disabled children?

☐ Has the State taken any specific measures to encourage and facilitate children's access to the media?

☐ Is there any provision for consideration and resolution of complaints from children regarding breaches of their right to freedom of expression?

Reminder : **The Convention is indivisible and its articles are interdependent. Article 13 should not be considered in isolation.**

Particular regard should be paid to:
The general principles

Article 2: all rights to be recognized for each child in jurisdiction without discrimination on any ground

Article 3(1): the best interests of the child to be a primary consideration in all actions concerning children

Article 6: right to life and maximum possible survival and development

Article 12: respect for the child's views in all matters affecting the child; opportunity to be heard in any judicial or administrative proceedings affecting the child

Closely related articles

Articles whose implementation is related to that of article 13 include:

Article 15: freedom of association

Article 17: access to appropriate information; role of the mass media

Article 29: aims of education

Article 30: cultural, religious and language rights of children of minorities and indigenous communities

Article 31: child's rights to play, to recreation and to participation in cultural life and the arts

Child's right to freedom of thought, conscience and religion

article 14

1. States Parties shall respect the right of the child to freedom of thought, conscience and religion.

2. States Parties shall respect the rights and duties of the parents and, when applicable, legal guardians to provide direction to the child in the exercise of his or her right in a manner consistent with the evolving capacities of the child.

3. Freedom to manifest one's religion or beliefs may be subject only to such limitations as are prescribed by law and are necessary to protect public safety, order, health or morals, or the fundamental rights and freedoms of others.

Summary

Article 14 of the Convention on the Rights of the Child confirms for the child the fundamental civil right to freedom of thought, conscience and religion, which is upheld for "everyone" in the Universal Declaration of Human Rights and the International Covenant on Civil and Political Rights. The second paragraph, echoing article 5 of the Convention, requires respect for the role of parents in providing direction to the child "in a manner consistent with the evolving capacities of the child". The International Covenant requires respect for the liberty of parents to ensure the religious and moral education of their children in conformity with their own convictions, but the emphasis in the Convention on the Rights of the Child is on the freedom of religion of the child, with parental direction consistent with the child's evolving capacities. Paragraph 3 sets out the very limited restrictions allowed on the child's freedom to manifest his or her religion or belief.

The Initial Reports of many States simply record that this right is reflected in their Constitutions and applies equally to children. But the *Guidelines for Periodic Reports* requires information on how it is "recognized by law specifically in relation to children". The Committee has as yet made little comment on the effective implementation of article 14. It is apparent from a range of declarations and reservations that in some States the right of the child to freedom of religion conflicts with tradition and, in some cases, with legislation. Few States appear to have reflected the **child's** right in domestic legislation, and in many, it is parents who determine the child's religion. ■

Extracts from
Committee on the Rights of the Child
Guidelines for Reports to be submitted by States Parties under the Convention

For full text of *Guidelines for Periodic Reports*, see Appendix 3, page 604.

Guidelines for Initial Reports

"Civil rights and freedoms

Under this section States Parties are requested to provide relevant information, including the principal legislative, judicial, administrative or other measures in force; factors and difficulties encountered and progress achieved in implementing the relevant provisions of the Convention; and implementation priorities and specific goals for the future in respect of:

...

(e) Freedom of thought, conscience and religion (article 14);

...".

(CRC/C/5, para. 15)

Guidelines for Periodic Reports

"IV. CIVIL RIGHTS AND FREEDOMS (arts. 7, 8, 13-17 and 37(a))

Under this section, States Parties are requested to provide information on the measures adopted to ensure that the civil rights and freedoms of children set forth in the Convention, in particular those covered by articles 7, 8, 13 to 17 and 37(a), are recognized by law specifically in relation to children and implemented in practice, including by administrative and judicial bodies, at the national, regional and local levels, and where appropriate at the federal and provincial levels.

...

D. Freedom of thought, conscience and religion (art. 14)

Please provide information on the exercise of the right to freedom of thought, conscience and religion by children, and the extent to which the child's evolving capacities are taken into consideration.

Please indicate the measures adopted to ensure the child's freedom to manifest his or her religion or beliefs, including with regard to minorities or indigenous groups. Information should also be provided on measures to ensure respect for the child's rights in relation to any religious teaching in public schools or institutions, as well as on any limitations to which this freedom may be subject in conformity with article 14, paragraph 3."

(CRC/C/58, paras. 48, 56-57. The following paragraphs of the *Guidelines for Periodic Reports* are also relevant to reporting under this article: 24, 81, 165, 166; for full text of *Guidelines*, see Appendix 3, page 604.)

Freedom of thought

Children's right to freedom of thought provokes little controversy or comment in Initial Reports or the Committee. The concept of freedom of thought is linked to the right to form and express views, in article 12. The practical implementation of freedom of thought is related to the freedom to seek, receive and impart information and ideas of all kinds, under article 13; to the child's access to appropriate information, under article 17; and to the child's education, under articles 28 and 29. The child's right to privacy, in article 16, implies that children cannot be forced to reveal their thoughts.

There are no restrictions on the right to freedom of thought. Paragraph 2 requires respect for the rights and duties of parents and others to provide direction to the child in the exercise of the right, consistent with the child's evolving capacities.

Freedom of conscience

Again, the Convention on the Rights of the Child provides no restrictions to the child's right to freedom of conscience, but paragraph 2 of article 14 allows for parents' direction. Issues of conscience might arise, for example, concerning diet, such as vegetarianism, or environmental issues.

One issue of conscience on which there are various human rights recommendations, but no explicit mention in the International Bill of Human Rights or in the Convention, is that of conscientious objection to military service. The Convention, in article 38, prohibits recruitment into the armed forces of anyone under the age of 15. Conscientious objection is a real issue for 15- to 18-year-olds in some countries. In addition, some countries contain militaristic youth organizations and include some form of military training within the education system; if compulsory, these could conflict with article 14.

The Committee on the Rights of the Child has not yet (September 1997) addressed this issue. The first edition of the *Manual on Human Rights Reporting*, 1991, in a commentary on the right to freedom of thought, conscience and religion in article 18 of the International Covenant on Civil and Political Rights, suggests that "the status and position of conscientious objectors should be discussed under this article, and statistical information should be provided regarding the number of persons that applied for the status of, and the number of those that were actually recognized as, conscientious objectors; the reasons given to justify conscientious objection and the rights and duties of conscientious objectors as compared with those persons who serve in the regular military service" (*Manual on Human Rights Reporting*, 1991 p. 108).

The Human Rights Commission has adopted a resolution on respect for conscientious objection to military service (Resolution 1987/46, Human Rights Commission, E/CN.4/1987/60).

Freedom of religion

Article 14 protects the child's right to have a religion, which is an absolute right, and to manifest his or her religion, which may be subject to the very limited restrictions outlined in paragraph 3.

In addition, article 30 of the Convention (see page 407) upholds the right of a child who belongs to an ethnic, religious or linguistic minority or who is indigenous "to profess and

---

Conscientious objection

Finland's Initial Report indicates that its domestic law respects the right of a conscript who has not attained the age of majority to apply for alternative service on the grounds of religious or ethical conviction – and that a custodian's approval is not needed (Finland IR, para. 231).

---

practise his or her own religion ..." And in arranging alternative care, under article 20, States must pay due regard to the child's religious background (see below, page 182).

What freedom of religion means

Article 18(1) of the International Covenant on Civil and Political Rights expands on the right to freedom of religion: "...This right shall include freedom to have or to adopt a religion or belief of his choice, and freedom, either individually or in community with others and in public or private, to manifest his religion or belief in worship, observance, practice and teaching." The second paragraph states "No one shall be subject to coercion which would impair his freedom to have or to adopt a religion or belief of his choice."

The Human Rights Committee issued a lengthy General Comment on article 18 in 1993. It emphasizes that the terms "religion" and "belief" are to be broadly construed, protecting theistic, non-theistic and atheistic beliefs as well as the right not to profess any religion or belief. The article "does not permit any limitations whatsoever on the freedom of thought and conscience or on the freedom to have or adopt a religion or belief of one's choice". No one can be compelled to reveal his adherence to a religion or belief: this is assured by article 18 and by the right to privacy set out in article 17 of the Covenant (Human Rights Committee General Comment 22, HRI/GEN/1/Rev.2, pp. 35-36). The child's right to privacy is echoed in article 16 of the Convention on the Rights of the Child.

The Committee on the Rights of the Child has found that issues affecting the child's privacy may arise in relation to religion in schools. In considering arrangements in Norway to allow opting out of religious education, the Committee raised the need to respect the privacy of the child in relation to his or her religious faith:

"The Committee notes that although an opting-out system exists for children wishing to abstain from compulsory religious education, this requires their parents to submit a formal request exposing the faith of the children

article **14**

Respecting evolving capacities

In Iceland, no one is obliged to belong to a religious denomination. After reaching the age of 16, an individual child can decide whether he or she belongs to a religious denomination and, if so, which one. The opinion of a child aged 12 or over must be considered regarding his or her registration in a religious denomination (Iceland IR, para. 158).

In Denmark, children between 15 and 18 years old may be admitted to or withdrawn from the established church by their custodians, provided they have themselves consented (Denmark IR, para. 96).

In the United Kingdom, "...Where a child is sufficiently mature to make his own determination, the provision that a person with parental responsibility may choose a child's religion must be read in conjunction with the 'Gillick' decision, which established the principle that parental rights yield to the child's right to make his own decisions when he reaches a sufficient understanding and intelligence to be capable of making up his own mind on a matter." (UK IR, para. 172)

In the Republic of Korea, "the Civil Code provides that a person with parental authority has rights and duties to protect and educate his/her child, and guarantees that a parent or legal guardian has freedom to educate his/her child with religious and moral education. It is not deemed natural, however, in the Republic of Korea that the belief of a parent shall be succeeded to by his/her child. Even if students attend schools established by religious organizations, they may have their own respective religion. Any adult or child chooses his/her religion according to his/her own discretion and free intention. However under the current system of deciding schools, from elementary to high school, except private elementary schools, in which students are allocated to the schools located nearest to the student's residence without any consideration on the student's orientation in terms of religion, students' right to enjoy freedom of religion is encroached substantially by receiving religious education they do not want and not receiving what they do want." (Republic of Korea IR, para. 63)

involved and as such may be felt to be an infringement of their right to privacy." (Norway IRCO, Add.23, para. 9)

The child's right and parental direction: article 14(2)

The Convention on the Rights of the Child differs from previous instruments in its treatment of the child's right to freedom of religion *vis-à-vis* his or her parents. For example, in the International Covenant on Civil and Political Rights, paragraph 4 of article 18 refers to the parent-child relationship and requires respect for "the liberty of parents and, when applicable, legal guardians to ensure the religious and moral education of their children in conformity with their own convictions" (see discussion of religious education in schools, below, page 182).

Yet, article 14 of the Convention on the Rights of the Child refers unambiguously to the right of the child to freedom of religion. The second paragraph refers to the "rights and duties" of parents rather than to their "liberty". Similar to the general statement given in article 5, article 14 requires States to "respect the rights and duties of the parents and, when applicable, legal guar-

dians, to provide direction to the child in the exercise of his or her right in a manner consistent with the evolving capacities of the child". But it is the child who exercises the right. Parents can provide direction, but the direction must be consistent with the child's evolving capacities and must be applied in conformity with the whole of the Convention. "Direction" cannot involve, for instance, any form of physical or mental violence (article 19). And the child's views must be taken seriously: article 12 preserves the right of all children who can form views to express their views freely "in all matters affecting the child", which includes matters of religion and choice of religion. And article 13 upholds the child's freedom of expression.

The wording of article 14 and the Convention's general principles certainly do not support the concept of children automatically following their parent's religion until the age of 18, although article 8 (preservation of identity), article 20 (preservation of religion when deprived of family environment), and article 30 (right to practice religion in community with members of the child's group) support children's right to acquire their parents' religion. The Committee's *Guidelines for Periodic Reports* asks about "the

Respecting the child's religious convictions

One State Party acknowledged the dangers of respecting parents' freedom of religion at the expense of children: "The Government of Canada recognizes that care must be taken to ensure that freedom of religion of the parents is not accepted as justification for subjecting children to practices that disregard their religious preferences, involve discrimination on the basis of sex or are harmful to their health or involve abuse or violence." The Initial Report describes a case in which a court declined to make a declaration that a 12-year-old child with leukaemia was in need of protection when she and her parents (who were Jehovah's Witnesses) objected to the administration of blood transfusions on religious grounds. The court also held that an earlier blood transfusion administered against her wishes constituted discrimination on the basis of religion, contrary to section 15 of the Canadian Charter of Rights and Freedoms, and an infringement to her right to security of the person, under section 7 of the Charter. (Canada IR, paras. 114 and 115)

In Belarus, articles in the Rights of the Child Act state that "While having proclaimed the secular nature of education, the State may not, except when inducement to perform religious acts directly threatens the child's life or health or infringes his or her legal rights, interfere with the upbringing of a child on the basis of the particular religious views of the parents or persons acting *in loco parentis* and connected with the observance, outside educational institutions and ... with the child's participation, of religious ceremonies, holidays or traditions." (Belarus IR, para. 44)

child's freedom to manifest his or her religion or beliefs". Under the Convention's article 1 (definition of the child) the *Guidelines* asks for information on any legal minimum age defined in legislation for choosing a religion or attending religious school teaching (see below).

In ratifying the Convention, a number of States made declarations and reservations to article 14 and to other civil rights, several of which related to the role of parents. The Committee has expressed concern at reservations that suggest lack of the full recognition of the child as a subject of rights; and consistent with its general policy, the Committee has urged States to review and withdraw all reservations (for details, see article 5, page 78 and article 12, page 148).

For example, Algeria declared: "The provisions of paragraphs 1 and 2 of article 14 shall be interpreted by the Algerian Government in compliance with the basic foundations of the Algerian legal system, in particular:

● With the Constitution, which stipulates in its article 2 that Islam is the State religion and in its article 35 that there shall be no infringement of the inviolability of the freedom of conviction and the inviolability of the freedom of opinion;

● With Law No. 84-11 of 9 June 1984, comprising the Family Code, which stipulates that a child's education is to take place in accordance with the religion of its father."

(CRC/C/2/Rev.5, p. 10)

In contrast, a declaration from the Netherlands states its understanding that article 14 "is in accordance with the provisions of article 18 of the International Covenant on Civil and Political Rights... and that this article shall include the freedom of a child to have or adopt a religion or belief of his or her choice as soon as the child is capable of making such choice in view of his or her age or maturity" (CRC/C/2/Rev.5, p. 27).

In some States courts have powers to overrule parents who have refused certain types of medical treatment for their children on the grounds of religious conviction. Under the Convention on the Rights of the Child (article 3(2)), it is clear that the State should have such powers of intervention; and under article 12, the child's views should be appropriately respected in any proceedings. Respect for children's refusal of treatment on grounds of their own religious convictions is dependent on their evolving capacities and on consideration of the Convention's general principles (see box above).

When parents disagree over the child's religion

The Convention on the Rights of the Child requires states to recognize the principle that "both parents have common responsibilities for the upbringing and development of the child" (article 18). This must apply to the qualified parental direction that article 14 authorizes in the exercise by the child of his or her right to freedom of religion. Neither parent should have "authority" over such matters. Where there is disagreement and the matter goes to court, the matter should be decided on the basis of the child's right under article 14, with the child's views taken seriously according to his or her age and maturity.

Joining religious orders for life

In Norway, under the 1969 Act Relating to Religious Communities, any person over the age of 15 may join or leave a religious community. In the case of a young child, the parents or legal guardians may decide which religious community the child shall belong to. When a child is 12 years old, he or she has the right to state his or her views in connection with joining or leaving a religious community. Persons under the age of 20 may not vow to belong to a religious order for the rest of their lives; it is prohibited to accept such a vow, if given (Norway IR, para. 150).

The child's right to freedom of religion in alternative care

When children are separated from their families and are in alternative care provided by the State or otherwise, article 14 of the Convention requires that their right to freedom of religion must be maintained. In many countries, religious organizations are prominent in providing alternative care for children. Article 20(3) states that when considering alternative care for a child, "due regard shall be paid to the desirability of continuity in a child's upbringing and to the child's ethnic, religious, cultural and linguistic background" (see article 20, page 264). But inflexible laws requiring that the child should automatically be brought up in the religion of his or her parent(s) are not consistent with article 14.

Religious communities

Under article 14, the ability of children to decide to join or leave a religious community should be subject to parental direction, exercised in accordance with their evolving capacities, and to the particular restrictions in paragraph 3. Some States have legislated on these issues (see box above).

Schooling and freedom of religion

Freedom of religion in the context of compulsory education can be an important issue for children.

The *Guidelines for Periodic Reports* notes: "Information should also be provided on measures to ensure respect for the child's rights in relation to any religious teaching in public schools or institutions, as well as any limitations to which this freedom may be subject in conformity with article 14, paragraph 3" (para. 57).

As noted previously, the International Covenant on Civil and Political Rights requires States (in article 18(4)) to respect "the liberty of parents and, when applicable, legal guardians to ensure the religious and moral education of their children in conformity with their own convictions". In its General Comment on this provision, the Human Rights Committee states: "The Committee is of the view that article 18(4) permits public school instruction in subjects such as the general history of religions and ethics if it is given in a neutral and objective way. The liberty of parents or legal guardians to ensure their children receive a religious and moral education in conformity with their own convictions, set forth in article 18(4), is related to the guarantees of the freedom to teach a religion or belief stated in article 18(1). The Committee notes that public education that includes instruction in a particular religion or belief is inconsistent with article 18(4) unless provision is made for non-discriminatory exemptions or alternatives that would accommodate the wishes of parents and guardians" (Human Rights Committee, General Comment 22, HRI/GEN/1/Rev.2, p. 35).

But the Convention on the Rights of the Child requires that arrangements for moral and religious education be reviewed to ensure respect for the **child's** right to freedom of religion, with parental direction provided in a manner consistent with the child's "evolving capacities".

Some States do not allow religious teaching in state-supported education. In others, there may be religious education and worship or observance in one or more religions. Some States have set an age at which any control of the child's manifestation of religion transfers from parents to the child, although the concept of "evolving capacities" in article 5 and article 14 appears to demand more flexibility.

Another form of discrimination associated with school religion may arise when States provide funding for schooling in certain religions but not others.

Limitations on manifestation of religion: article 14(3)

The limitations allowed by paragraph 3 on the freedom "to manifest one's religion or beliefs" are identical to those in article 18 of the International Covenant on Civil and Political Rights. In its General Comment referred to above, the Human Rights Committee emphasizes that restrictions are permitted "only if limitations are prescribed by law and are necessary to protect public safety, order, health or morals, or the fundamental rights and freedoms of others...In interpreting the scope of permissible

Religion in schools

France's Initial Report indicates that as France is a secular society, there must be complete neutrality in the expression of opinions in the public schools, and any religious or political proselytism is prohibited (France IR, para. 224).

In Denmark, exemption from religious instruction at school for a child aged 15 and above can only occur with the child's consent (Denmark IR, para. 97).

Italian law used to make the teaching of the Catholic religion compulsory in public schools (with the opportunity of exceptions made for non-Catholics). Now, it has been amended to be "more in keeping with the constitutional principles of the secular nature of the State. The new system provides for the possibility that parents and secondary school students may or may not choose religious instruction. However, this possibility, which is being allowed in a school system as rigid as the Italian one, has given rise to heated debate that has also involved the Constitutional Court...

"In its judgements No.203 of 12 April 1989 and No.13 of 11 June 1991, the Constitutional Court stated that students who choose not to have Catholic religious instruction are not required to participate in other school activities. Nevertheless, the Constitutional Court decision does not solve the problem of organizing either religious instruction schedules or the 'replacement' subjects, i.e. the arrangements the school should make for students who choose not to have religious instruction." (Italy IR, paras. 83-86)

In several cases, Canadian courts have held that section 2(a) of the Canadian Charter of Rights and Freedoms which guarantees everyone the right to freedom of conscience and religion is violated by a requirement that public schools conduct religious exercises or give religious instruction, with a preference shown for the Christian religion. Even where there are legal provisions enabling children to opt out of religion in schools, the provisions may not amount to adequate "freedom". In one case, an exemption was available for objecting students, but the Ontario Court of Appeal stated that "the peer pressure and the classroom norms to which children are acutely sensitive, in our opinion, are real and pervasive and operate to compel members of religious minorities to conform with majority religious practices." (Canada IR, para. 112)

Some States' Initial Reports have debated the issue of the extent of parental authority in relation to religious education. For example, the Initial Report of Belgium states: "Exercise of parental authority entails the power to regulate the lives of children. By virtue of this educational power, parents are able to determine the religion in which their children will be brought up. They can choose the type of education to be received by their offspring and can decide whether or not to give them a religious education. This does not mean, however, that parents can impose 'their' convictions on 'their' children. Education is not the same as coercion. Parents can bring up their children according to their convictions, without however indoctrinating them. The difficulty that may arise consists in reconciling the child's right to make philosophical or religious choices with the power of the parents. In the eyes of the legislature, the family is required to play an essential role. A balance of rights and duties in the family cell is vital in order to ensure the stability that is essential for the harmonious development of the young person. However, what is to be done by a school principal who is told by a child that he wants to attend the course in Catholic religion while his parents say that he is to follow the course of non-denominational ethics? There are nowadays signs of a willingness, in some isolated decisions, to authorize minors to act of their own accord when their request relates to a personal right and they are sufficiently old to be assumed capable of judgement." (Belgium IR, para. 140)

In Croatia, in primary schools, parents decide if a child should take religious education. In secondary schools, both the parents and pupil make a statement (Croatia IR, para. 151).

In Germany, at the age of 10, a child must be heard prior to a change in religious denomination; the same applies to the withdrawal of the child from religious instruction in the event that the parents themselves are in disagreement. At the age of 12, a child can no longer be forced to take religious instruction in another denomination against his or her will. At the age of 14, a child has the right to freely choose his or her religious denomination (except that in Bavaria a child may not withdraw from religious instruction in school until he or she attains the age of 18) (Germany IR, para. 13).

limitation clauses, States Parties should proceed from the need to protect the rights guaranteed under the Covenant... Limitations imposed must be established by law and must not be applied in a manner that would vitiate the rights guaranteed in article 18. The Committee observes that paragraph 3 of article 18 is to be strictly interpreted: restrictions are not allowed on grounds not specified there, even if they would be allowed as restrictions to other rights protected in the Covenant, such as national security. Limitations may be applied only for those purposes for which they were prescribed and must be directly related and proportionate to the specific need on which they are predicated. Restrictions may not be imposed for discriminatory purposes or applied in a discriminatory manner..." (Human Rights Committee, General Comment 22, HRI/GEN/1/Rev.2, p. 37)

The Committee on the Rights of the Child has also stressed that the limitations set out in article 14(3) of the Convention on the Rights of the Child are the only ones that may be applied:

"The Committee remains concerned about the actual implementation of the civil rights and freedoms of children. The Committee wishes to emphasize that the implementation of the child's right to freedom of thought, conscience and religion should be ensured in the light of the holistic approach of the Convention and that limitations on the exercise of this right can only be placed in conformity with paragraph 3 of article 14 of the Convention." (China IRCO, Add.56, para. 17)

Discrimination on grounds of religion

Article 2 requires States to respect and ensure the rights in the Convention on the Rights of the Child to each child in their jurisdiction without discrimination of any kind, irrespective of "the child's or his or her parent's or legal guardian's ... religion..." Thus, under article 2 and article 14, the child must not suffer discrimination because of the child's right to have a religion, or to have no religion, nor over the child's right to manifest his or her religion.

In addition, there must be no discrimination affecting the child's enjoyment of any other rights under the Convention on the grounds of the child's, or his or her parent's, religion. And article 2(2) requires States to take all appropriate measures to ensure that the child is protected against all forms of discrimination or punishment on the basis of the status, activities, expressed opinions or beliefs of the child's parents, legal guardians or family members.

The Human Rights Committee, in its General Comment on article 18 of the International Cov-

enant on Civil and Political Rights quoted above, also emphasizes: "The fact that a religion is recognized as a state religion or that it is established as official or traditional or that its followers comprise the majority of the population, shall not result in any impairment of the enjoyment of any of the rights under the Covenant... nor in any discrimination against adherents to other religions or non-believers." (Human Rights Committee, General Comment 22, HRI/GEN/1/Rev.2, pp. 35-38)

When examining Indonesia's Initial Report, a member of the Committee on the Rights of the Child raised allegations made in a recent report of the Special Rapporteur appointed by the Commission on Human Rights on questions relating to religious intolerance, that pressure had been put on members of the Baha'i faith to renounce their religion and that "Baha'i children had reportedly been expelled from school and had their books seized" (Indonesia SR.80, para. 58).

In its Preliminary Observations on Indonesia's Report, and in its Concluding Observations issued a year later, the Committee expressed its concern

"... regarding the implementation of articles 14 and 15 of the Convention. It reiterates that limiting official recognition to certain religions may give rise to practices of discrimination. It is also concerned that the authorities seem to give a wide interpretation to limitations for 'lawful purposes' of the exercise of the rights to freedom of religion, expression and assembly which may prevent the full enjoyment of such rights." (Indonesia IRCO, Add.25, para. 13; see also Indonesia Prelim. Obs., Add.7, paras. 9 and 15)

A reservation by Jordan indicated that it "does not consider itself bound by articles 14, 20 and 21 of the Convention, which grant the child the right to freedom of choice of religion and concern the question of adoption, since they are at variance with the precepts of the tolerant Islamic Shariah" (CRC/C/2/Rev.5, p. 23).

The Committee's Concluding Observations on Jordan's Initial Report stated:

"The Committee expresses concern at the uncertainty in the status of children, and the possible ensuing discrimination, resulting from the coexistence of different personal status regulations according to the child's religion. The Committee takes note of the undertaking in this context by the delegation to provide further information in regard to the rights of children of the Baha'i faith." (Jordan IRCO, Add.21, para. 12)

Article 24(3) requires States to "take all effective and appropriate measures with a view to abolishing traditional practices prejudicial to the health of children". And article 19 requires States to ensure protection from "all forms of physical or mental violence". Practices that stem from or are linked to manifestations and observance of religions must not involve breaches of these or any other articles of the Convention.

Disabled children and freedom of religion

The Standard Rules on the Equalization of Opportunities for Persons with Disabilities includes a section on encouraging measures for equal participation in the religious life of their communities by persons with disabilities (rule 12). It proposes that "States should encourage the distribution of information on disability matters to religious institutions and organizations. States should also encourage religious authorities to include information on disability policies in the training for religious professions, as well as in religious education programmes".

Religion and children deprived of their liberty

The United Nations Rules for the Protection of Juveniles Deprived of their Liberty, which the Committee on the Rights of the Child has commended to States Parties, requires: "...The religious and cultural beliefs, practices and moral concepts of the juvenile should be respected" (rule 4). And in detail it states: "Every juvenile should be allowed to satisfy the needs of his or her religious and spiritual life, in particular by attending the services or meetings provided in the detention facility or by conducting his or her own services and having possession of the necessary books or items of religious observance and instruction of his or her denomination. If a detention facility contains a sufficient number of juveniles of a given religion, one or more qualified representatives of that religion should be appointed or approved and allowed to hold regular services and to pay pastoral visits in private to juveniles at their request. Every juvenile should have the right to receive visits from a qualified representative of any religion of his or her choice, as well as the right not to participate in religious services and freely to decline religious education, counselling or indoctrination." (rule 48)

In its General Comment, quoted above, the Human Rights Committee also emphasized that "persons already subject to certain legitimate constraints, such as prisoners, continue to enjoy their rights to manifest their religion or belief to the fullest extent compatible with the specific nature of the constraint" (Human Rights Committee, General Comment 22, HRI/GEN/1/Rev.2, p. 37).

Implementation Checklist

● General measures of implementation

Have appropriate general measures of implementation been taken in relation to article 14, including

☐ identification and coordination of the responsible departments and agencies at all levels of government (article 14 is particularly relevant to **departments of social welfare and education and to agencies responsible for the State's relations with recognized religions**)?

☐ identification of relevant non-governmental organizations/civil society partners?

☐ a comprehensive review to ensure that all legislation, policy and practice is compatible with the article, for all children in all parts of the jurisdiction?

☐ adoption of a strategy to secure full implementation

    ☐ which includes where necessary the identification of goals and indicators of progress?

    ☐ which does not affect any provisions which are more conducive to the rights of the child?

    ☐ which recognizes other relevant international standards?

    ☐ which involves where necessary international cooperation?

(Such measures may be part of an overall governmental strategy for implementing the Convention as a whole).

☐ budgetary analysis and allocation of necessary resources?

☐ development of mechanisms for monitoring and evaluation?

☐ making the implications of article 14 widely known to adults and children?

☐ development of appropriate training and awareness-raising (in relation to article 14 likely to include the training of **religious groups and all those working with or for children and their families, and parenting education**)?

● Specific issues in implementing article 14

☐ Is the child's right to freedom of thought, conscience and religion, as guaranteed in article 14, explicitly recognized in legislation?

☐ Are there legislative and other arrangements to respect the child's conscientious objection to military service?

☐ Are the only restrictions on the child's right to manifest religion or beliefs consistent with those set out in paragraph 3 of article 14, and are they defined in legislation?

How to use the checklists, *see page XVII*

Does law, policy and practice promote the child's right to freedom of thought, conscience and religion, as set out in article 14, in relation to

- ☐ the child/parent relationship?
- ☐ all forms of alternative care?
- ☐ school?

☐ Does law, policy and practice respect the rights and duties of parents to provide appropriate direction in the exercise by the child of his right as set out in article 14?

☐ If the State has one or more religions recognized in law, does legislation respect the right of the child to have and/or practice another religion or no religion?

☐ Do any restrictions on the right of the child to enter or leave religious communities respect the child's evolving capacities?

Does legislation permit withdrawal from religious education and/or worship in schools at the request of

- ☐ the child?
- ☐ the child's parents?

☐ In such cases, is education and/or arrangements for worship in the religion of the child made available?

☐ Where the State supports the provision of education in different religions, is this done without discrimination?

☐ Is there provision for the consideration and resolution of complaints from children regarding breaches of their rights under article 14?

☐ Have special measures been adopted to ensure the freedom of religion of disabled children?

☐ In relation to children whose liberty is restricted, is rule 48 of the United Nations Rules for the Protection of Children Deprived of their Liberty fulfilled?

How to use the checklists, *see page XVII*

Reminder : **The Convention is indivisible and its articles are interdependent. Article 14 should not be considered in isolation.**

Particular regard should be paid to:
The general principles

Article 2: all rights to be recognized for each child in jurisdiction without discrimination on any ground

Article 3(1): the best interests of the child to be a primary consideration in all actions concerning children

Article 6: right to life and maximum possible survival and development

Article 12: respect for the child's views in all matters affecting the child; opportunity to be heard in any judicial or administrative proceedings affecting the child

Closely related articles

Articles whose implementation is related to that of article 14 include:

Article 8: preservation of identity

Article 13: freedom of expression

Article 15: freedom of association

Article 17: access to appropriate information

Article 20: alternative care – continuity of religion and culture

Articles 28 and 29: rights to education and aims of education

Article 30: rights of children of minorities and indigenous communities

Article 37: restriction of liberty and religious freedom

Article 38: armed conflict and conscientious objection

Child's right to freedom of association and peaceful assembly

Text of Article 15

1. States Parties recognize the rights of the child to freedom of association and to freedom of peaceful assembly.

2. No restrictions may be placed on the exercise of these rights other than those imposed in conformity with the law and which are necessary in a democratic society in the interests of national security or public safety, public order (ordre public), the protection of public health or morals or the protection of the rights and freedoms of others.

Together with articles 12 and 13, the rights to freedom of association and freedom of peaceful assembly promote the child as an active, participating member of society. Article 12 sets out the right of individual children to express their views freely; article 15 adds rights of collective participation.

Previous human rights instruments have promoted these rights for "everyone", and many Initial Reports record that their country's Constitution upholds these rights for "everyone". As with other civil rights, the Committee on the Rights of the Child has encouraged their incorporation into States' own legislation, and the *Guidelines for Periodic Reports* asks for information on the measures adopted to ensure that the rights are "recognized by law specifically in relation to children". Also, under article 1, the *Guidelines* asks whether any minimum age has been defined in legislation concerning the child's right to create or form associations.

The Committee has emphasized that the only restrictions that may be applied are those set out in paragraph 2 of article 15. ∎

Summary

The child's right to freedom of association

Article 20 of the Universal Declaration of Human Rights states: "1. Everyone has the right to freedom of peaceful assembly and association. 2. No one may be compelled to belong to an association." The International Covenant on Civil and Political Rights reasserts these rights in its articles 21 and 22, noting the specific right to form and join trade unions, and applying the limited restrictions as set out in paragraph 2 of article 15 of the Convention on the Rights of the Child. While in many States constitutional principles echoing the international instruments confer a right of association on "everyone", the implications of recognizing this right for children have seldom been explored. The Committee on the Rights of the Child has recommended that the rights for children guaranteed by article 15 should be reflected in legislation. For example:

"The Committee recommends the State Party to consider legal amendments in order to ensure the right to participation of children, including the right to freedom of association and to freedom of peaceful assembly as reflected in article 15 of the Convention."
(Spain IRCO, Add.28, para. 19)

Children's involvement in associations

In France, according to its Initial Report, minors may be active members of an association and can vote in the general assembly and be elected to the board of directors, but they may not hold the offices of president or treasurer, since their legal incapacity precludes them from representing the association in legal proceedings (France IR, paras. 227 and 228).

When Chile prepared its Initial Report in 1993, a bill on community organizations that permitted the formal association of young people from the age of 15 was under consideration. At that stage, the right of children to freely form associations was restricted, as Chilean law did not recognize their legal capacity to perform such civil acts. As a result, children could only join a political party or community youth organization from 18 onwards. In 1990, the Ministry of Education introduced regulations to authorize secondary school students to associate freely in student centres and other student organizations (Chile IR, paras. 24 and 76).

Paraguay's Initial Report describes how "In the political sphere as well as in the spheres of student life and religion, young people are organizing themselves to develop projects to achieve greater participation in areas hitherto restricted to adults. The Federation of Secondary Students has submitted to the Parliamentary Constitutional Affairs Committee the 'student ticket' project, whose aim is to reduce the cost of travel by public transport.

"However students, and in particular secondary school students, encounter problems in forming associations and setting up student centres within the educational centres...." (Paraguay IR, paras. 88-90)

In the Russian Federation, the USSR Associations Act of 1990 was the first legal instrument to specify that children had a right to form associations. According to the Initial Report "In the field of children's organizations, uniformity has given way to variety and pluralism. New types of organization have appeared, voluntary and based on a community of interests – ecological, charitable, cultural etc. ... At the Federal level alone, more than 30 children's organizations are at present registered in Russia... There is a new quality to children's organizations that makes them once again an important factor in the social development of children as free, active citizens of a democratic society and a rapidly changing world..." An Association of Researchers into Children's Trends has been established in the Russian Federation, numbering more than 200 academics and professionals experienced in working with children. Together with the Federation of Children's Organizations, the Association has proposed an outline federal law on children's organizations, movements and associations (Russian Federation IR, paras. 82-85).

Freedom of association implies the right to form associations as well as to join and to leave associations. The Committee has suggested that States should encourage the membership of children in associations:

"...The active participation of children should be encouraged. Similarly, efforts should be undertaken to develop new channels, including membership of associations, through which children may make their views known and have them taken into account." (Jordan IRCO, Add.21, para. 24)

The *Guidelines for Periodic Reports* asks for information on any existing children's organizations, and on the role they play in promoting children's rights. And the Committee has encouraged this:

"...The participation of children themselves in the promotion of the rights of the child is of great importance, especially at the community level." (Ukraine IRCO, Add.42, para. 21)

The Committee has specifically mentioned student organizations in schools and children's organizations in local municipalities. Various Initial Reports have described legislation providing for schools councils and the structures enabling children to have a say in decision-making within their local community (see also article 12, pages 159-160).

During discussions with Italy, a member of the Committee noted that no information on article 15 had been included in its Initial Report: "The provisions of article 15 of the Convention were important, as they affected the ability of children to express their views on decisions of concern to them. She asked whether there were any specific provisions to allow children to form associations, whether there were any school councils or municipal children's organizations or whether the rights of children under article 15 were merely covered by the general constitutional provisions relating to freedom of association." A representative from Italy responded that "The question of freedom of association had not been dealt with in the report because that freedom already existed in Italy. As soon as a child's personality was formed and it was capable of expressing its views, it could both join and form associations and indeed schools encouraged students to do so." (Italy SR.236, paras. 39 and 59)

It should be noted that, in general, the law concerning contracts and administration of organizations may pose obstacles for children below the age of majority or the age of legal capacity acting as directors or trustees of public associations. It seems that few countries have as yet explored this from the perspective of the full implementation of article 15.

During discussions with the representatives of Belarus, the issue of children engaging in political activities was raised. The Belarus Rights of the Child Act in its article 23 covers "the right to join social organizations": "Children have the right to join independent children's organizations provided that the activities of such organizations do not contravene the Constitution and other laws of the Republic of Belarus, violate public order or State security, harm public health or morals or infringe the rights and freedoms of others. Children's organizations shall not engage in political activities." Other articles define youth organizations and state that "young citizens may neither be compelled directly or indirectly to join youth associations nor barred from participating in their activities" (Belarus IR, paras. 45-47). During discussions with the Committee, a Belarus representative explained that citizens were only entitled to express their political views and to exercise the other rights enshrined in the Constitution and national legislation upon reaching the age of majority (18): "It was not a matter of obstructing the expression of political views

but rather banning the activities of children's organizations set up for political purposes." In later discussion one Committee member stated he was unconvinced that youth organizations should be prevented from engaging in political activities: "In that connection, article 15 of the Convention, under which States Parties recognized the rights of the child to freedom of association, placed no restriction on the political activities in which such associations might engage." (Belarus SR.125, para. 13; SR.126, para. 31)

Unlike the International Covenant on Civil and Political Rights, the Convention on the Rights of the Child does not uphold the specific right of children to "form and join trade unions for the protection of his interests" (article 22(1) of the Covenant). But the right is implied in the right to freedom of association, and the limitations in article 15(2) would not justify preventing children from forming or joining unions. Article 32 sets out States' duties to prevent economic and other exploitation in labour (see page 427).

The child's right to freedom of peaceful assembly

The importance of article 15 is its emphasis on children as holders of fundamental civil rights, including the right to engage in peaceful activities as a group.

The article emphasizes children's right to take part in peaceful demonstrations and meetings. When the Committee examined Indonesia's Initial Report, it expressed concern at excessive violence used against children taking part in a peaceful demonstration and commented:

"The State Party has given assurances that violations similar to those which occurred in November 1991, when security forces used excessive violence against children peacefully demonstrating in Dili, would not occur again. The Committee, however, remains seriously disturbed by the continuing pattern of violation of the right to freedom of assembly and the great number of complaints of ill-treatment of children attributed to the police, security or military personnel, in particular in situations of arrest and detention..." (Indonesia IRCO, Add.25, para. 15)

Restrictions on the child's rights: article 15(2)

The Committee on the Rights of the Child has stressed that the rights in article 15 may only be restricted in accordance with paragraph 2 of article 15; restrictions must be defined in legislation

No political associations

A general restriction on children's right to freedom of association is in force in Bulgaria, according to the Initial Report. Children cannot establish or join political parties. "The ban contained in the Political Parties Act on political activity in schools is acting in the same direction. The Political Parties Act permits parties to create their own adolescent organizations for children over 16 years of age. Children at this time do not have their own children's organizations." (Bulgaria IR, para. 80)

and be necessary for one of the specific reasons set out in the article:

"The Committee considers that greater efforts should be made to promote the participation of children in family, school and social life, as well as the effective enjoyment of their fundamental freedoms, including the freedom of opinion, expression and association, which should be subject only to the restrictions provided by the law and which are necessary in a democratic society." (Republic of Korea IRCO, Add.51, para. 26)

In some countries, there are laws limiting children's rights to association and peaceful assembly during certain hours – curfews, often imposed to prevent unaccompanied children from being out of their homes after a certain time in the evening and often related to the age of the child. Such general restrictions on the child's right do not appear to fall within the very limited restrictions allowed in paragraph 2 of article 15.

Unlike article 14, article 15 makes no reference to respecting the rights of parents to provide direction to the child in the exercise of the child's right in a manner consistent with the evolving capacities of the child, but this principle is upheld generally in article 5 (see page 78). Some States indicated in their Initial Reports that there is an age below which children are not permitted to join associations or to do so without the agreement of their parents. The Convention provides no support for arbitrary limitations on the child's right to freedom of association.

Disabled children A particular emphasis of the World Programme of Action Concerning Disabled Persons has been the promotion of the establishment and development of associations of disabled people. The inclusion in the Convention on the Rights of the Child of a specific article on disabled children (article 23), as well as the explicit inclusion of "disability" as one of the grounds of discrimination barred by article 2,

emphasizes the equal right of disabled children to all civil rights, including the right to freedom of association and peaceful assembly. The Standard Rules on the Equalization of Opportunities for Persons with Disabilities contains target areas for equal participation by disabled people, including children; the target areas are relevant to the realization of the rights to freedom of association and freedom of peaceful assembly, in particular rule 5 relating to accessibility both to the physical environment and to information and communication.

Rights for children deprived of their liberty The rights under article 15 for children deprived of their liberty are emphasized in the United Nations Rules for the Protection of Juveniles Deprived of their Liberty, which the Committee has promoted as providing appropriate standards for implementation of the Convention. In general, the Rules requires that "Juveniles deprived of their liberty shall not for any reason related to their status be denied the civil, economic, political, social or cultural rights to which they are entitled under national or international law, and which are compatible with the restriction of liberty, such as social security rights and benefits, freedom of association and, upon reaching the minimum age established by law, the right to marry" (rule 13).

More specifically, the Rules requires that "Every means should be provided to ensure that juveniles have adequate communication with the outside world, which is an integral part of the right to fair and humane treatment and is essential to the preparation of juveniles for their return to society. Juveniles should be allowed to communicate with their families, friends and other persons or representatives of reputable outside organizations, to leave detention facilities for a visit to their home and family and to receive special permission to leave the detention facility for educational, vocational or other important reasons..." (rule 59).

Implementation Checklist

● General measures of implementation

Have appropriate general measures of implementation been taken in relation to article 15 including

☐ identification and coordination of the responsible departments and agencies at all levels of government (article 15 is relevant to **departments of justice, social welfare, education**)?

☐ identification of relevant non-governmental organizations/civil society partners?

☐ a comprehensive review to ensure that all legislation, policy and practice is compatible with the article, for all children in all parts of the jurisdiction?

☐ adoption of a strategy to secure full implementation

　☐ which includes where necessary the identification of goals and indicators of progress?

　☐ which does not affect any provisions which are more conducive to the rights of the child?

　☐ which recognizes other relevant international standards?

　☐ which involves where necessary international cooperation?

(Such measures may be part of an overall governmental strategy for implementing the Convention as a whole).

☐ budgetary analysis and allocation of necessary resources?

☐ development of mechanisms for monitoring and evaluation?

☐ making the implications of article 15 widely known to adults and children?

☐ development of appropriate training and awareness-raising (in relation to article 15 likely to include the training of **all those working with or for children and their families, and parenting education**)?

● Specific issues in implementing article 15

☐ Are the rights of the child to freedom of association and peaceful assembly, as guaranteed in article 15, explicitly recognized in legislation?

☐ Have measures been taken to promote opportunities for children to exercise their rights to freedom of association and peaceful assembly?

☐ Are the only permitted restrictions on these rights consistent with those set out in paragraph 2 of article 15, and are they defined in legislation?

How to use the checklists, *see page XVII*

Does law, policy or practice limit the child's right to freedom of association and peaceful assembly in any circumstances

- ☐ in the community?
- ☐ in school?

Are there any limits on the right of children

- ☐ to form associations?
- ☐ to join or leave associations?

☐ In relation to children in employment, are there any limits on the right of children to form and to join and to leave trades unions?

☐ Have special measures been taken to promote the freedom of association and peaceful assembly of disabled children?

☐ In relation to children whose liberty is restricted, are rules 13 and 59 of the United Nations Rules for the Protection of Juveniles Deprived of their Liberty fulfilled?

☐ Is there provision for the consideration and resolution of complaints from children regarding breaches of their rights under article 15?

Reminder: **The Convention is indivisible and its articles are interdependent. Article 15 should not be considered in isolation.**

Particular regard should be paid to:
The general principles

Article 2: all rights to be recognized for each child in jurisdiction without discrimination on any ground

Article 3(1): the best interests of the child to be a primary consideration in all actions concerning children

Article 6: right to life and maximum possible survival and development

Article 12: respect for the child's views in all matters affecting the child; opportunity to be heard in any judicial or administrative proceedings affecting the child

Closely related articles

Articles whose implementation is related to that of article 15 include:

Article 13: freedom of expression

Article 14: freedom of thought, conscience and religion

Article 29: aims of education

Article 31: child's rights to play, recreation and to participation in cultural life and the arts

Article 32: right of child to join a trade union

Article 37: restriction of liberty and freedom of association

Child's right to privacy

Text of Article 16

1. No child shall be subjected to arbitrary or unlawful interference with his or her privacy, family, home or correspondence, nor to unlawful attacks on his or her honour and reputation.

2. The child has the right to the protection of the law against such interference or attacks.

Article 16 provides for the right of every child to be protected by the law against arbitrary or unlawful interference with his or her privacy, family, home or correspondence as well as against unlawful attacks on his honour and reputation.

Like the previous three articles, article 16 applies specifically to the child a fundamental civil right already established for everyone in the International Bill of Human Rights. Article 12 of the Universal Declaration of Human Rights uses similar wording but without the qualifying "unlawful" before the words "interference" and "attacks". The wording in article 17 of the International Covenant on Civil and Political Rights, ensuring that "no one" is subject to such interference, is otherwise identical to the Convention on the Rights of the Child.

Article 16 must apply to all children without discrimination. The child's privacy is to be protected in all situations, including within the family, alternative care, and all institutions, facilities and services. In addition, the article protects the child's family and home from arbitrary or unlawful interference. The article raises issues concerning the physical environment in which the child lives, the privacy of his or her relationships and communications with others, including rights to confidential advice and counselling, control of access to information stored about the child in records or files, and so on. Inevitably, children's rights to privacy within the family vary according to family structures, living conditions and economic and other factors determining the private space available to the child.

Summary

In addition to article 16, article 40(2)(b)(vii) requires that a child alleged as or accused of having infringed the penal law should "... have his or her privacy fully respected at all stages of the proceedings"; the Committee on the Rights of the Child has suggested this respect should also apply to children in family proceedings and when children are victims of abuse. And the Committee has emphasized the importance of the media respecting children's privacy. ■

Extracts from
Committee on the Rights of the Child
Guidelines for Reports to be submitted by States Parties under the Convention

For full text of *Guidelines for Periodic Reports,* see Appendix 3, page 604.

Guidelines for Initial Reports

"Civil rights and freedoms

Under this section States Parties are requested to provide relevant information, including the principal legislative, judicial, administrative or other measures in force; factors and difficulties encountered and progress achieved in implementing the relevant provisions of the Convention; and implementation priorities and specific goals for the future in respect of:

...

(g) Protection of privacy (article 16);

...".

(CRC/C/5, para. 15)

Guidelines for Periodic Reports

"IV. CIVIL RIGHTS AND FREEDOMS (arts. 7, 8, 13 - 17 and 37(a))

Under this section, States Parties are requested to provide information on the measures adopted to ensure that the civil rights and freedoms of children set forth in the Convention, in particular those covered by articles 7, 8, 13 to 17 and 37(a), are recognized by law specifically in relation to children and implemented in practice, including by administrative and judicial bodies, at the national, regional and local levels, and where appropriate at the federal and provincial levels.

...

F. Protection of privacy (art. 16)

Please indicate the measures adopted to prevent any arbitrary or unlawful interference with the child's privacy, family, home or correspondence, as well as any attack on his or her honour and reputation. Please provide information on the protection provided by the law against such interference or attacks, and the remedies made available to the child. Information should also be provided on specific measures adopted for children placed in institutions for treatment, care or protection, including in judicial or administrative proceedings."

(CRC/C/58, paras. 48 and 59. Paragraph 133 of the *Guidelines for Periodic Reports* is also relevant to reporting under this article; for full text of *Guidelines,* see Appendix 3, page 604.)

...

"No child shall be subjected to arbitrary or unlawful interference with his or her privacy ..."

Some concern arose in the Working Group during the drafting of article 16 in regard to the role of parents, but it was ultimately resolved by the inclusion in the Convention of article 5, which requires respect for parents and legal guardians to provide direction and guidance to the child in the exercise by the child of his or her rights, in a manner consistent with the evolving capacities of the child (for example, see E/CN.4/1987/25, pp. 26 and 27, Detrick, p. 258).

Various States have issued declarations or reservations concerning the relationship between parents and their children's civil rights, mentioning article 16. When examining Initial Reports, the Committee has consistently asked for a review and withdrawal of declarations and reservations; in particular, it has expressed concern at reservations that suggest lack of the full recognition of the child as a subject of rights (for further discussion and Committee comments see article 5, page 78, and article 12, page 148).

The Committee has not provided any detailed comment on the implications of article 16, although it has expressed concern at the lack of the article's reflection in national legislation, along with other civil rights of the child:

"The Committee remains uncertain as to the extent to which the State Party has undertaken measures to ensure that the traditional view of children as mere objects of care has been replaced by an understanding and recognition of the child as a subject of rights. In this regard, clarification is requested as to the applicability of the provisions of the Constitution guaranteeing respect for the civil rights and freedoms of children, including the right to privacy provided for in article 16 of the Convention." (Federal Republic of Yugoslavia IRCO, Add.49, para. 13)

The *Guidelines for Periodic Reports* requests information on how the right guaranteed by article 16 is "recognized by law specifically in relation to children". The Committee on the Rights of the Child has identified certain specific situations in Initial Reports that raise issues under article 16. One example is the provision in one State Party which requires the recording of the child's or his or her parent's religion in relation to religious education in school and in another State Party on children's identity cards (on which ethnic origin is also recorded):

"The Committee notes that although an opting-out system exists for children wishing to abstain from compulsory religious education, this requires their parents to submit a formal request exposing the faith of the children involved and as such may be felt to be an infringement of their right to privacy...
"The Committee suggests that the State Party reconsider its policy on religious education for children in the light of the general principle of non-discrimination and the right to privacy." (Norway IRCO, Add.23, paras. 9 and 23)

"In the field of the right to citizenship, the Committee is of the view that the State Party should, in the light of articles 2 (non-discrimination) and 3 (best interests of the child), abolish the categorization of citizens, as well as mention on the national identity card of the religion and of the ethnic origin of citizens, including children. In the view of the Committee, all possibility of stigmatization and denial of rights recognized by the Convention should be avoided." (Myanmar IRCO, Add.69, para. 34)

Confidential advice for children

The *Guidelines for Periodic Reports*, under article 1 (definition of the child), seeks information on any minimum age defined in legislation for the child to have the right to receive "legal and medical counselling without parental consent",

Privacy in the family

The Initial Report from Belarus indicates that the right to privacy is not reflected in Belarus legislation: "In our view, this right is first of all not adequately defined and, secondly, runs counter to the goal of strengthening the role of family upbringing and shifting the emphasis from social to family upbringing. Thus, the inviolability of the family and home may be considered rather as rights belonging to the parents or persons acting *in loco parentis*. Privacy of the child's correspondence can hardly be guaranteed by law, since this would mean interfering in the relationship between parents and children and limiting adults' formative influence and authority." (Belarus IR, para. 48)

A Committee member noted this paragraph in discussion with government representatives and asked: "Might that not result in interference with the child's privacy?" Belarus representatives indicated in response that they wished to delete this paragraph of the Initial Report; they considered that the private life of a child was a much broader concept than the secrecy of its correspondence and its communications (Belarus SR.124, para. 71; SR.125, para. 9).

Finland's Initial Report notes: "Not much discussion has taken place in Finland on such issues as the parents' right to inspect their children's mail or to listen in to their telephone conversations in order to supervise their doings." But within the education system, Finnish children are guaranteed by law confidential vocational advice (Finland IR, paras. 240 and 241).

and "medical treatment or surgery without parental consent". These involve privacy issues: the right of the child to seek confidential advice on legal and medical matters, and the further right to confidential treatment, including, for example, contraception, and abortion where permitted. The Convention does not support the setting of any arbitrary age below which the child does not have such rights. But article 5 enables parents to provide direction and guidance in a manner consistent with the evolving capacities of the child.

Medical and other professionals often have ethical codes requiring them to respect patient/client confidentiality. When a child is the patient or client, the principles and provisions of the

Child protection and confidentiality

Belgium's Initial Report indicates some potential conflicts in the area of child protection. It says: "Article 458 of the Criminal Code obliges doctors, surgeons, health officers, pharmacists, midwives, and any other persons who, as a result of their trade or profession, are in possession of secrets confided in them, to remain silent about the matters they have learned in the exercise of their profession, except in those cases when they are called upon to testify in court and when the law obliges them to disclose these secrets (contagious diseases and declarations of birth)."

Social workers are also covered by this obligation. But the Initial Report goes on to indicate that respect for professional secrecy is limited by the very purpose of the profession: "The obligation to maintain confidentiality lapses when, despite the advice and support of the medical/social worker, the moral and physical health of the child is seriously endangered. The aim then is to protect the child against his own parents. At this time the medical/social worker does not only have the right to come to the assistance of the child, he even has the duty to do so. In such a case, confidentiality is often wrongly invoked, because the view is taken that the 'client' is the parent. However, professional secrecy is owed to the victim, who is the child... Confidentiality should never be absolute, but relative. It is a means of protecting values, but is not a value in itself." (Belgium IR, paras. 281 and 284-285)

Convention provide a framework for clarifying the child's rights, in particular in relation to his or her parents.

The Report on the International Conference on Population and Development (Cairo, 1994) addresses adolescent sexual and reproductive health issues and, in proposals for action, follows the principles and provisions of the Convention. The Report states: "Recognizing the rights, duties and responsibilities of parents and other persons legally responsible for adolescents to provide, in a manner consistent with the evolving capacities of the adolescent, appropriate direction and guidance in sexual and reproductive matters, countries must ensure that the programmes and attitudes of health-care providers do not restrict the access of adolescents to appropriate services and the information they need, including on sexually transmitted diseases and sexual abuse. In doing so, and in order to, *inter alia*, address sexual abuse, these services must safeguard the rights of adolescents to privacy, confidentiality, respect and informed consent, respecting cultural values and religious beliefs. In this context, countries should, where appropriate, remove legal, regulatory and social barriers to reproductive health information and care for adolescents. ... Adolescents must be fully involved in the planning, implementation and evaluation of such information and services with proper regard for parental guidance and responsibilities" (A/CONF.171/13, paras. 7.41-7.48; also 6.15).

The public advertising of children for fostering or adoption may raise issues of privacy where it involves using photographs and intimate details of children without their informed consent.

In 1988, the Human Rights Committee issued a detailed General Comment on article 17 of the International Covenant on Civil and Political Rights, which concerns the right to privacy. It provides relevant definitions and explanation, in particular that:

- the individual must be protected from interference not only by state authorities but also by others;
- the State must provide legislative and other measures to prohibit such interference;
- interference can only take place in ways defined in law, which must not be arbitrary, must comply with the provisions, aims and objectives of the Covenant, and be reasonable in the particular circumstances;
- the State should enable individuals to complain when they believe their right has been violated and the State should provide appropriate remedies.

The Human Rights Committee emphasizes that States Parties are under a duty themselves not to engage in interference incompatible with article 17 and to provide the legislative framework prohibiting such acts by natural or legal persons. Also, States Parties paid too little attention to the fact that article 17 deals with protection against both unlawful and arbitrary interference: "That means that it is precisely in State legislation above all that provision must be made for the protection of the right set forth in that article... The term 'unlawful' means that no interference can take place except in cases envisaged by the law.

Interference authorized by States can only take place on the basis of law, which itself must comply with the provisions, aims and objectives of the Covenant.

"The expression 'arbitrary interference' is also relevant to the protection of the right provided for in article 17. In the Committee's view, the expression 'arbitrary interference' can also extend to interference provided for under the law. The introduction of the concept of arbitrariness is intended to guarantee that even interference provided for by law should be in accordance with the provisions, aims and objectives of the Covenant and should be, in any event, reasonable in the particular circumstances."

The Human Rights Committee suggests reports should include information on the authorities and organs set up within the legal system of the State that are "competent to authorize interference allowed by the law": "It is also indispensable to have information on the authorities which are entitled to exercise control over such interference with strict regard for the law, and to know in what manner and through which organs persons concerned may complain of a violation of the right provided for in article 17 of the Covenant. States should in their reports make clear the extent to which actual practice conforms to the law. State Party reports should also contain information on complaints lodged in respect of arbitrary or unlawful interference, and the number of any findings in that regard, as well as the remedies provided in such cases."

The Human Rights Committee notes that "As all persons live in society, the protection of privacy is necessarily relative. However, the competent public authorities should only be able to call for such information relating to an individual's private life the knowledge of which is essential in the interests of society as understood by the Convention" (Human Rights Committee, General Comment 16, HRI/GEN/1/Rev.2, pp. 21-23).

Privacy in institutions

The privacy of children in institutions, in particular in residential institutions and custodial institutions, can be particularly threatened by the physical environment and design, by overcrowding, lack of appropriate supervision and so on. (Indeed, Costa Rica's Initial Report identified the closure of large institutions and orphanages as an "essential step" for the protection of children's privacy (Costa Rica IR, paras. 122-4)). Also, the use of video surveillance in institutions can breach children's privacy rights.

Article 16 requires that the child's right to privacy is protected by law. Hence, in institutions there should be minimum requirements on space, including private space, design of toilets and bathrooms, and so on. These issues are covered in the United Nations Rules for the Protection of Juveniles Deprived of their Liberty (see below) and are equally relevant to all institutional placements. Article 3(3) of the Convention on the Rights of the Child requires that institutions, services and facilities responsible for the care or protection of children shall conform with the standards established by competent authorities (see page 45). Standards must reflect the provisions of the Convention, including the child's right to privacy, without discrimination.

Privacy for those whose liberty is restricted
The United Nations Rules for the Protection of Juveniles Deprived of their Liberty has various relevant provisions. First, there is the general principle in rule 13 that states juveniles deprived of their liberty must not be denied any entitlement under national or international law to civil or other rights that are compatible with the deprivation of liberty; in addition, there are specific provisions relating to files (see page 202), design and physical environment, personal effects, visits, correspondence (see page 204) and the conduct of personnel.

The design of detention facilities for juveniles and the physical environment should pay due regard to the juvenile's need for privacy (rule 32); sanitary installations should be so located and of a sufficient standard to enable every juvenile "to comply, as required, with their physical needs in privacy and in a clean and decent manner" (rule 34). Rule 35 states that "The possession of personal effects is a basic element of the right to privacy and essential to the psychological well-being of the juveniles. The right of every juvenile to possess personal effects and to have adequate storage facilities for them should be fully recognized and respected..." Circumstances for visits to the juvenile should "respect the need of the juvenile for privacy, contact and unrestricted communication with the family and the defence counsel" (rule 60). Personnel involved with juveniles deprived of their liberty "should respect the right of the juvenile to privacy and, in particular, should safeguard all confidential matters concerning juveniles or their families learned as a result of their professional capacity" (rule 87(e)).

Privacy in juvenile justice, child protection and other proceedings
In addition to article 16, article 40 requires the privacy of children alleged as or accused of having infringed the penal law "to have his or

No reporting of children's crimes

Uruguay's Initial Report records that article 19 of the Children's Code prohibits the reporting in the news media of crimes committed by children under the age of 18: "The reporting or graphic depiction of crimes committed by children under the age of 18 is absolutely prohibited". Public employees who pass information to the press and the media are liable to fines, which are credited to the Children's Council (since replaced by the National Minors' Institute) (Uruguay IR, para. 143).

her privacy fully respected at all stages of the proceedings".

The United Nations Standard Minimum Rules for the Administration of Juvenile Justice, the "Beijing Rules", expands on the provision in article 40 of the Convention. Rule 8.1 states "The juvenile's right to privacy shall be respected at all stages in order to avoid harm being caused to her or him by undue publicity or by the process of labelling. 2. In principle, no information that may lead to the identification of a juvenile offender shall be published."

The official Commentary to the Rules explains: "Rule 8 stresses the importance of the protection of the juvenile's right to privacy. Young persons are particularly susceptible to stigmatization. Criminological research into labelling processes has provided evidence of the detrimental effects (of different kinds) resulting from the permanent identification of young persons as 'delinquent' or 'criminal'. Rule 8 also stresses the importance of protecting the juvenile from the adverse effects that may result from the publication in the mass media of information about the case (for example the names of young offenders, alleged or convicted). The interest of the individual should be protected and upheld, at least in principle."

Particular protection of the privacy of juveniles is also provided for in article 14 of the International Covenant on Civil and Political Rights, which requires that "any judgement rendered in a criminal case or in a suit at law shall be made public except where the interest of juvenile persons otherwise requires or the proceedings concern matrimonial disputes or the guardianship of children" (article 14(1)).

In the Report of its General Discussion on juvenile justice, the Committee on the Rights of the Child stated:

"The privacy of the child should be fully respected in all stages of the proceedings, including in relation to criminal records and possible reporting by the media." (Report on the tenth session, October - November 1995, CRC/C/46, para. 227)

In the outline prepared for its General Discussion on "The child and the media", the Committee noted the importance of the child's right to privacy in media reporting not only of juvenile justice cases but also of child abuse and family problems (see also below, page 205, and article 17, page 219):

"It is important that the media themselves do not abuse children. The integrity of the child should be protected in reporting about, for instance, involvement in criminal activities, sexual abuse and family problems. Fortunately, the media in some countries have voluntarily agreed to respect guidelines which offer such protection of the privacy of the child; however, such ethical standards are not always adhered to." (Report on the eleventh session, January 1996, CRC/C/50, Annex IX, p. 80)

Among the recommendations that arose during the General Discussion was one that stated specific guidelines should be prepared for reporting on child abuse, "on how to report and at the same time protect the dignity of the children involved. Special emphasis should be placed on the issue of not exposing the identity of the child." (Report on the thirteenth session, September–October 1996, CRC/C/57, para. 256)

Files on children

Most children have some records or reports written about them and stored – in health, education, social services, and juvenile justice systems (see also article 8 – preservation of the child's identity, page 111). Rights to privacy require that legislation should ensure that the child

- knows of the existence of information stored about him or her;
- knows why such information is stored and by whom it is controlled;
- has access to such records, whether stored manually or by electronic means;
- is able to challenge and, if necessary, correct their content, if necessary through recourse to an independent body.

Legislation should limit who else has access to the information stored; such access must not be arbitrary and must be in line with the whole Convention. The child should know who else has access.

The Human Rights Committee, in its General Comment on the similar article on privacy rights in the International Covenant, states: "The gathering and holding of personal information on computers, data banks and other devices, whether by public authorities or private individuals or bodies, must be regulated by law. Effective measures have to be taken by States to ensure that information concerning a person's private life does not reach the hands of persons who are not authorized by law to receive, process and use it, and is never used for purposes incompatible with the Covenant. In order to have the most effective protection of his private life, every individual should have the right to ascertain in an intelligible form, whether, and if so, what personal data is stored in automatic data files, and for what purposes. Every individual should also be able to ascertain which public authorities or private individuals or bodies control or may control their files. If such files contain incorrect personal data or have been collected or processed contrary to the provisions of the law, every individual should have the right to request rectification or elimination." (Human Rights Committee, General Comment 16, HRI/GEN/1/Rev.2, pp. 21-23)

In relation to files used in juvenile justice systems, the "Beijing Rules" (which the Committee has commended as providing appropriate minimum standards) requires in rule 21(1): "Records of juvenile offenders shall be kept strictly confidential and closed to third parties. Access to such records shall be limited to persons directly concerned with the disposition of the case at hand and other duly authorized persons." Rule 21(2): "Records of juvenile offenders shall not be used in adult proceedings in subsequent cases involving the same offender." The official commentary states: "The rule attempts to achieve a balance between conflicting interests connected with records or files: those of the police, prosecution and other authorities in improving control versus the interests of the juvenile offender (see also rule 8). 'Other duly authorized persons' would generally include, among others, researchers."

The United Nations Rules for the Protection of Juveniles Deprived of their Liberty provides more detail: "All reports, including legal records, medical records and records of disciplinary proceedings, and all other documents relating to the form, content and details of treatment, should be placed in a confidential individual file, which should be kept up to date, accessible only to authorized persons and classified in such a way as to be easily understood. Where possible, every juvenile should have the right to contest any fact or opinion contained in his or her file so as to permit rectification of inaccurate, unfounded or unfair statements. In order to exercise this right, there should be procedures that allow an appro-

Who has access to files?

Finland's Initial Report indicated that children in Finland can veto their parents' access to their health files if they are sufficiently mature to understand the matter. This is not the case yet in social welfare files, but the Parliamentary Ombudsman has ruled in favour of a child in a case, so there will be a change in the law governing social work files too (Finland IR, paras. 242 and 245).

In the Province of Quebec in Canada, a child aged 14 or over enjoys access to and disclosure of information about himself or herself in health and social service files, independent of parents (Canada IR, para. 886).

priate third party to have access to and to consult the file on request. Upon release, the records of juveniles shall be sealed, and, at an appropriate time, expunged" (rule 19).

"family"

The term "family" has a broad interpretation under the Convention on the Rights of the Child, including parents "or, where applicable, the members of the extended family or community as provided for by local custom" (article 5), and the Committee has emphasized this interpretation in its examination of States Parties' reports (see article 5, page 77).

In its General Comment on privacy, quoted above, the Human Rights Committee states: "Regarding the term 'family', the objectives of the Covenant require that for purposes of article 17 this term be given a broad interpretation to include all those comprising the family as understood in the society of the State Party concerned..." (Human Rights Committee General Comment 16, HRI/GEN/1/Rev.2, pp. 21 - 23)

Any arrangements permitting interference with a child's family must be set out in the law and must not be arbitrary, must be compatible with the other principles and provisions of the Convention, and must be reasonable in the particular circumstances. Article 9 is especially relevant, setting out the conditions for any separation of the child from his or her parents. The child must have access to a complaints procedure and appropriate remedies in cases of violation of the right.

Article 37(c) of the Convention specifically requires that the child deprived of his or her liberty "shall have the right to maintain contact with his or her family through correspondence and visits, save in exceptional circumstances".

"home"

The Human Rights Committee interprets "home" as follows: "The term 'home' in English ... is to be understood to indicate the place where a person resides or carries out his usual occupation". The Human Rights Committee also notes that "Searches of a person's home should be restricted to a search for necessary evidence and should not be allowed to amount to harassment." (Human Rights Committee General Comment 16, 1988, HRI/GEN/1/Rev.2, pp. 21-23)

Thus "home" will include, for some children, places of alternative care, including various categories of residential institutions, boarding schools, places of detention, long-stay hospitals and so forth.

Any arrangements permitting interference with a child's home, such as searching it, must be set out in the law and must not be arbitrary, must be compatible with the other principles and provisions of the Convention, and must be reasonable in the particular circumstances. Eviction of a family from its home would have to meet these

tests. For children living in alternative care, moves from one "home" to another must not breach the child's right. The child must have access to a complaints procedure and appropriate remedies in cases of violation of the right.

"or correspondence"

All children have the right not to have their correspondence – letters and other forms of communication, including telephone calls – interfered with arbitrarily or unlawfully, in their family or wherever else they may be.

Any arrangements permitting interference with a child's correspondence, such as opening, reading, or limiting it and so forth, must be set out in the law and must not be arbitrary, must be compatible with the other principles and provisions of the Convention and must be reasonable in the particular circumstances. The child must have access to a complaints procedure and appropriate remedies in cases of violation of the right.

The Human Rights Committee commented on the privacy article in the Covenant: "Compliance with article 17 requires that the integrity and confidentiality of correspondence should be guaranteed *de jure* and *de facto*. Correspondence should be delivered to the addressee without interception and without being opened or otherwise read. Surveillance, whether electronic or otherwise, interceptions of telephonic, telegraphic and other forms of communication, wire-tapping and recording of conversations should be prohibited..." (Human Rights Committee, General Comment 16, HRI/GEN/1/Rev.2, pp. 21-23)

As noted above, under article 37 of the Convention on the Rights of the Child, every child deprived of liberty has the right to maintain contact with his or her family through correspondence and visits, save in exceptional circumstances. The United Nations Rules for the Protection of Juveniles Deprived of their Liberty states: "Every juvenile should have the right to communicate in writing or by telephone at least twice a week with the person of his or her choice, unless legally restricted, and should be assisted as necessary in order effectively to enjoy this right. Every juvenile should have the right to receive correspondence" (rule 61).

"nor to unlawful attacks on his or her honour or reputation"

Most, if not all, countries have laws to protect adults from attacks on their honour or reputation

article 16

Parental monitoring

Belgium's Initial Report states: "Regarding privacy and freedom of correspondence, the same principle holds true for everyone: no one has the right to read or intercept correspondence not addressed to him or her. However, some parents and some judges consider that parental authority, entailing the right to bring up and supervise their children, justifies 'censorship' of a minor's correspondence. Some parents take this right as a basis for allowing them to monitor the correspondence and personal relations of their child. They are, however, obliged to use licit means for this purpose. Furthermore, parental authority may and sometimes must yield to the child's right not to be subjected to such interference when the child is capable of due discernment." (Belgium IR, para. 150)

In France, the Postal Services Code specifies that ordinary mail, registered mail or mail of a declared value addressed *poste restante* to non-emancipated minors under 18 years of age may only be delivered to them on presentation of written authorization by their father or mother or guardian (France IR, para. 242).

– both verbal attacks (slander) and attacks in writing and/or through the media (libel). This provision requires that the child should be protected equally under the law. The law must set out the protection, and the child must have an effective remedy in law against those responsible.

The Human Rights Committee comments on the identically worded provision in the International Covenant on Civil and Political Rights: "Article 17 affords protection to personal honour and reputation and States are under an obligation to provide adequate legislation to that end. Provision must also be made for everyone effectively to be able to protect himself against any unlawful attacks that do occur and to have an effective remedy against those responsible." (Human Rights Committee, General Comment 16, HRI/GEN/1/Rev.2, pp. 21-23)

As noted above (page 202), in the report of its 1996 General Discussion on "The child and the media", the Committee on the Rights of the Child expressed concern at images of children – both individual and collective images – portrayed by the media (see also article 17, page 214):

"In their reporting the media give an 'image' of the child; they reflect and influence perceptions about who children are and how they behave. This image could create and convey respect for young people; however, it could also spread prejudices and stereotypes which may have a negative influence on public opinion and politicians. Nuanced and well-informed reporting is to the benefit of the rights of the child..." (Report on the eleventh session, January 1996, CRC/C/50, Annex IX, pp. 80 and 81)

The Committee commented on media attacks on children in Nicaragua:

"The Committee shares the concern expressed by the State Party about the fact that children are often abused in the media to the detriment of their personality and status as minors...
"The Committee recommends that, on an urgent basis, measures be taken to ensure the protection of the child from information and material injurious to his or her well-being and to protect the child's right to privacy, in light of the provisions of articles 16 and 17 of the Convention." (Nicaragua IRCO, Add.36, paras. 17 and 34)

The child's right to the protection of the law against such interference or attacks: article 16(2)

As noted above, in its General Comment, the Human Rights Committee states that interference with the right to privacy can only take place in ways defined in law, which must not be arbitrary, must comply with the provisions, aims and objectives of the Covenant (similarly, in relation to article 16 of the Convention on the Rights of the Child, interference must comply with the principles and provisions of the Convention) and be reasonable in the particular circumstances. In addition the State should enable individuals to complain when they believe their rights have been violated and to have appropriate remedies. (Human Rights Committee General Comment 16, HRI/GEN/1/Rev.2, pp. 21-23)

Implementation Checklist

article **16**

● *General measures of implementation*

Have appropriate general measures of implementation been taken in relation to article 16 including

☐ identification and coordination of the responsible departments and agencies at all levels of government (article 16 is relevant to **departments of social welfare, justice, education, media and communications**)?

☐ identification of relevant non-governmental organizations/civil society partners?

☐ a comprehensive review to ensure that all legislation, policy and practice is compatible with the article, for all children in all parts of the jurisdiction?

☐ adoption of a strategy to secure full implementation

  ☐ which includes where necessary the identification of goals and indicators of progress?

  ☐ which does not affect any provisions which are more conducive to the rights of the child?

  ☐ which recognizes other relevant international standards?

  ☐ which involves where necessary international cooperation?

(Such measures may be part of an overall governmental strategy for implementing the Convention as a whole).

☐ budgetary analysis and allocation of necessary resources?

☐ development of mechanisms for monitoring and evaluation?

☐ making the implications of article 16 widely known to adults and children?

☐ development of appropriate training and awareness-raising (in relation to article 16 likely to include the training of **all those working with or for children and their families, and parenting education**)?

● *Specific issues in implementing article 16*

Does legislation specifically recognize the right of the child to protection from arbitrary or unlawful interference with his or her

  ☐ privacy?

  ☐ family?

  ☐ home?

  ☐ correspondence?

How to use the checklists, *see page XVII*

☐ Does the legislation conform to all the other principles and provisions of the Convention?

Does legislation prevent such interference

　　☐ by State agencies?

　　☐ by others, including private bodies?

☐ Is the only permitted interference with the child's privacy, family, home and correspondence set out in legislation?

Does the legislation in each case ensure that such interference

　　☐ is not arbitrary?

　　☐ conforms with all other principles and provisions of the Convention?

　　☐ is reasonable in the particular circumstances?

☐ Are these legislative protections available to all children without discrimination?

Does the right to protection from arbitrary or unlawful interference with privacy apply to the child

　　☐ in the home?

　　☐ in all forms of alternative care?

　　☐ in schools?

　　☐ in other institutions of all kinds, both state-run and other?

In relation to the child in a residential and/or custodial institution, are there special safeguards of the child's right to privacy in relation to

　　☐ physical environment and design?

　　☐ visits and communication?

　　☐ personal effects?

　　☐ conduct and training of staff?

Does the child have a right to receive confidential counselling without the consent of his/her parents

　　on legal matters

　　　　☐ at any age?

　　　　☐ from a specific age?

　　　　☐ under criteria related to the child's maturity and capacities?

on medical matters

      ☐ at any age?

      ☐ from a specific age?

      ☐ under criteria related to the child's maturity and capacities?

☐ Does legislation protect children from arbitrary and unlawful interference with their family, including members of their extended family?

☐ Does legislation protect children from arbitrary and unlawful interference with their home, including placements in alternative care outside the family home?

Do any limits on the right to protection from arbitrary or unlawful interference with the child's correspondence, including by mail, telephone and all other means, conform with the Convention's principles

      ☐ in the child's home?

      ☐ in alternative care?

      ☐ in institutional care?

      ☐ in places of detention?

Does the child have the following rights in relation to any information kept about him or her in files or records stored either manually or through electronic means

      ☐ to know of the existence of the information?

      ☐ to know of the purpose of collecting and storing it, and who controls it?

      ☐ to have access to it?

      ☐ to be able to challenge and, if necessary, correct anything contained in it?

      ☐ to know in each case who controls access to the information?

      ☐ to know who else has access to the information and for what purpose(s)?

      ☐ to be able to control who else has access to the information?

      ☐ in the event of any dispute over realization of this right, to appeal to an independent body?

☐ In the event of possible violation of any of these rights, does the child have access to an appropriate complaints procedure?

☐ In cases of violation, does the child have appropriate remedies, including compensation?

☐ Are any limitations on any of these rights of the child based only on age and/or lack of maturity and understanding?

How to use the checklists, *see page XVII*

Does legislation guarantee the child's right to privacy, in particular to ensure that nothing which may lead to the child's identification is published in any way, in the case of

☐ children alleged as, accused of, or recognized as having infringed the penal law?

☐ children involved in child protection investigations and proceedings?

☐ children involved in family proceedings?

☐ Is there provision for the consideration and resolution of complaints from children regarding breaches of their rights under article 16?

☐ Does legislation protect the child from unlawful attacks on his or her honour and reputation?

☐ Have appropriate measures been taken to encourage the media to respect children's rights under this article?

Reminder : **The Convention is indivisible and its articles are interdependent. Article 16 should not be considered in isolation.**

Particular regard should be paid to:
The general principles

Article 2: all rights to be recognized for each child in jurisdiction without discrimination on any ground
Article 3(1): the best interests of the child to be a primary consideration in all actions concerning children
Article 6: right to life and maximum possible survival and development
Article 12: respect for the child's views in all matters affecting the child; opportunity to be heard in any judicial or administrative proceedings affecting the child

Closely related articles

Articles whose implementation is related to that of article 16 include:

Article 8: preservation of identity
Article 9: privacy in family proceedings
Article 17: role of the media
Article 19: privacy for victims of violence
Article 20: privacy in alternative care
Article 40: not identifying children involved in juvenile justice system

Child's access to appropriate information

Article 17

Text of Article 17

States Parties recognize the important function performed by the mass media and shall ensure that the child has access to information and material from a diversity of national and international sources, especially those aimed at the promotion of his or her social, spiritual and moral well-being and physical and mental health. To this end, States Parties shall:

(a) Encourage the mass media to disseminate information and material of social and cultural benefit to the child and in accordance with the spirit of article 29;

(b) Encourage international cooperation in the production, exchange and dissemination of such information and material from a diversity of cultural, national and international sources;

(c) Encourage the production and dissemination of children's books;

(d) Encourage the mass media to have particular regard to the linguistic needs of the child who belongs to a minority group or who is indigenous;

(e) Encourage the development of appropriate guidelines for the protection of the child from information and material injurious to his or her well-being, bearing in mind the provisions of articles 13 and 18.

Summary

Article 17 is particularly focused on the role of the mass media in relation to children's rights but includes a general obligation on States Parties to ensure that the child has access to information and material from diverse sources – especially those aimed at promoting well-being and physical and mental health. This is closely linked to the child's right to freedom of expression (article 13), and to maximum development (article 6). The media must be encouraged to disseminate positive material of benefit to the child and in line with the detailed aims for education set out in article 29. The media should also be accessible to the child, promoting and respecting the participatory rights to respect for the views of children (article 12, see page 145). The Committee on the Rights of the Child has noted the key role that the media can play in making the principles and provisions of the Convention on the Rights of the Child widely known to children and adults, in fulfilment of the Convention's article 42 (see page 561). The media can also be crucial in exposing and reporting on breaches of the rights of the child.

During the drafting of the Convention, article 17 started out as a measure simply to protect the child "against any harmful influence that mass media, and in particular the radio, film, television, printed materials and exhibitions, on account of their contents, may exert on his men-

tal and moral development". But early in its discussion, one member of the Working Group suggested that the media did more good than harm and that the article should be phrased in a positive way (E/CN.4/L.1575, pp. 19 and 20, Detrick, p. 279). The final version of the article proposes five actions for States Parties to fulfil in order to achieve the article's overall aim; only the last concerns protecting the child from harmful material. These actions are discussed below. ■

Extracts from
Committee on the Rights of the Child
Guidelines for Reports to be submitted by States Parties under the Convention

For full text of *Guidelines for Periodic Reports*, see Appendix 3, page 604.

Guidelines for Initial Reports

"Civil rights and freedoms

Under this section States Parties are requested to provide relevant information, including the principal legislative, judicial, administrative or other measures in force; factors and difficulties encountered and progress achieved in implementing the relevant provisions of the Convention; and implementation priorities and specific goals for the future in respect of:

...

(d) Access to appropriate information (article 17);

... ".

(CRC/C/5, para. 15)

Guidelines for Periodic Reports

"IV. CIVIL RIGHTS AND FREEDOMS

G. Access to appropriate information (art. 17)

Please provide information on the measures adopted to ensure that children have access from a diversity of national and international sources to information and material aimed at the promotion of the child's social, spiritual and moral well-being and physical and mental health. Please also indicate the measures adopted to encourage:

> *The production and dissemination of children's books, and the dissemination by the mass media of information and material of social and cultural benefit to the child, with particular regard to the linguistic needs of children belonging to a minority group or who are indigenous;*

> *International cooperation in the production, exchange and dissemination of such information and material of social and cultural benefit for the child, in accordance with the spirit of article 29 of the Convention on the aims of education, including any international agreements concluded for that purpose;*

> *The development of appropriate guidelines for the protection of the child from information and material injurious to his or her well-being, as well as from harmful exposure in the mass media, bearing in mind the provisions of articles 13 and 18."*

(CRC/C/58, para. 60. The following paragraphs of the *Guidelines for Periodic Reports* are also relevant to reporting under this article: 22, 23, 55, 133, 159, 161, 164; for full text of *Guidelines*, see Appendix 3, page 604.)

Key roles of the media

The Committee on the Rights of the Child requested one of its members, Thomas Hammarberg, an ex-journalist, to prepare a paper for the General Discussion on "Children, the UN Convention and the Media'.

The paper stated: "The Convention is formally addressed to Governments and does not interfere with independence of the media. Still, it brings an indirect message to media institutions which goes deeper than suggesting that its existence and impact be mentioned. As with human rights in general, the press and other media have essential functions in promoting and protecting rights of the individual, including through monitoring violations and other actions by governments. The rights of the **child** bring particular challenges for the media...". The paper goes on to review the implications of various relevant articles, in particular 12, 13 and 17, emphasizing "two major tendencies in these articles. One is about freedom of expression and the access to the media, the other one is treating the media as an educational tool. Though clearly distinct, the two aspects interrelate." The paper notes that Initial Reports had shown a mixed picture of implementation – several not even mentioning the issues (*Children, the UN Convention and the Media*, paper for General Discussion, 7 October 1996, Thomas Hammarberg).

The "important function performed by the mass media"

In the report of its General Discussion on "The child and the media", the Committee on the Rights of the Child stressed various media roles in relation to full implementation of the Convention on the Rights of the Child, including, but going beyond, the scope of article 17:

"The Committee on the Rights of the Child believes that the media – both written and audiovisual – are highly important in the efforts to make reality [of] the principles and standards of the Convention. The media in many countries have already contributed greatly in creating an awareness of the Convention and its content. The media could also play a pivotal role in monitoring the actual implementation of the rights of the child..."

The Committee also highlighted the importance of children having access to the media:

"Finally, the media is important for offering children the possibility of expressing themselves. One of the principles of the Convention is that the views of children be heard and given due respect (art. 12). This is also reflected in articles about freedom of expression, thought, conscience and religion (art. 13-14). It is in the spirit of these provisions that children should not only be able to consume information material but also to participate themselves in the media. This requires that there exist media which communicate with children. The Committee on the Rights of the Child has noted that there have been experiments in several countries to develop child-oriented media; some daily newspapers have special pages for children and radio and television programmes also devote special segments for the young audience. Further efforts

are, however, needed." (Report on the eleventh session, January 1996, CRC/C/50, Annex IX, pp. 80-81; for the Committee's comments on the potentially harmful influence of the media, see below, page 218)

Following the General Discussion to ensure follow-up, the Committee convened a Working Group, which met at UNESCO headquarters in April 1997 and agreed to put together a "first stage action plan" for the 12 recommendations (see box opposite). Once this was under way, a second stage action could be discussed and planned. The Working Group reported to the Committee in May 1997 (Working Group on Children and the Media: Report to the Committee on the Rights of the Child, High Commissioner for Human Rights/Centre for Human Rights, May 1997).

Ensuring the child "has access to information ... from a diversity of national and international sources" – especially those aimed at promoting well-being and physical and mental health

This section of article 17 provides the overall aim for the five particular strategies outlined in paragraphs (a) to (e). They are related to the child's freedom of expression under article 13(1), which "shall include freedom to seek, receive and impart information and ideas of all kinds, regardless of frontiers, either orally, in writing or in print, in the form of art, or through any other media of the child's choice" (see page 169). They relate to the role of the media in promoting the child's maximum development under article 6,

General Discussion – "The child and the media"

The following recommendations arose during the plenary and working group sessions of the General Discussion:

1. Child media: A dossier should be compiled on positive, practical experiences of active child participation in the media.

2. Child forum within Internet: The UNICEF-initiated "Voices of Youth" on the World Wide Web should be promoted and advertised as a positive facility for international discussion on important issues among young people.

3. Active child libraries: The experience of dynamic child libraries, or child departments within public libraries, should be documented and disseminated.

4. Media education: Knowledge about the media, their impact and their functioning should be imparted in schools at all levels. Students should be enabled to relate to and use the media in a participatory manner, as well as to learn how to decode media messages, including in advertising. Good experiences in some countries should be made available to others.

5. State support to media for children: There is a need for budgetary support to ensure the production and dissemination of children's books, magazines and papers, music, theatre and other artistic expressions for children, as well as child-oriented films and videos. Assistance through international cooperation should also support media and art for children.

6. Constructive agreements with media companies to protect children against harmful influences: Facts should be gathered about various attempts at voluntary agreements with media companies on positive measures, such as not broadcasting violent programmes during certain hours, clear presentations before programmes about their content and the development of technical devices such as 'V-chips', to help consumers to block out certain types of programmes. Likewise, experiences with respect to the introduction of voluntary ethical standards and mechanisms to encourage respect for them should be assembled and evaluated; this should include an analysis of the effectiveness of existing codes of conduct, professional guidelines, press councils, broadcasting councils, press ombudsmen and similar bodies.

7. Comprehensive national plans to empower parents in the media market: Governments should initiate a national discussion on means to promote positive alternatives to the negative tendencies of the media market, to encourage media knowledge and to support parents in their role as guides to their children in relation to electronic and other media. An international workshop should be organized to promote a discussion on this approach.

8. Advice on implementation of article 17 of the Convention on the Rights of the Child: A study should be conducted with the purpose of developing advice to Governments on how they could encourage the development of "guidelines for the protection of the child from information and material injurious to his or her well-being." Such a study should also serve the purpose of assisting the Committee on the Rights of the Child in drafting a General Comment on article 17.

9. Specific guidelines for reporting on child abuse: To encourage further discussion in newsrooms and within the media community as a whole, guidelines should be drafted by appropriate journalism bodies on how to report on abuse of children and at the same time protect the dignity of the children involved. Special emphasis should be placed on the issue of not exposing the identity of the child.

10. Material for journalism education on child rights: Material should be produced to assist journalism and media schools on child rights standards; established procedures for child rights monitoring; existing international, regional and national institutions working with children; as well as basic aspects of child development. The manual planned by the Centre for Human Rights of the United Nations as a tool for journalists' education on human rights should be widely disseminated when it is produced.

11. Network for media watchgroups: The positive work of media watchgroups in various countries should be encouraged and good ideas transferred between countries. The purpose is to give media consumers a voice in the discussion on media ethics and children. A focal point for exchanges should be established.

12. Service to "child rights correspondents": Interested journalists should be invited to sign up on a list of "child rights correspondents". They should be provided regularly with information about important child issues and with interesting reports by others, and be seen as media advisers to the international child rights community.

(Report on the thirteenth session, September-October 1996, CRC/C/57, para. 242 et seq.)

and also to the aims of education (article 29), and the need for health education (article 24). In addition, article 31 states the right of the child to participate freely and fully in cultural and artistic life, and the State's obligation to encourage the provision of appropriate and equal opportunities; here, too, the media can play an important role (see page 417).

The Committee on the Rights of the Child has noted some gaps in children's access to appropriate information, sometimes in particular regions or types of region, for example, rural areas:

"With regard to article 17 of the Convention, the Committee notes that access to appropriate information is not always guaranteed for children, especially those living in rural areas." (Portugal IRCO, Add.45, para. 16)

Children whose liberty is restricted The United Nations Rules for the Protection of Juveniles Deprived of their Liberty highlights access to the media: "Juveniles should have the opportunity to keep themselves informed regularly of the news by reading newspapers, periodicals and other publications, through access to radio and television programmes and motion pictures ..." (rule 62). Special consideration may need to be given to children's access to the media in any institutional placement and in other special circumstances.

"Encourage the mass media to disseminate information and material of social and cultural benefit to the child and in accordance with the spirit of article 29": article 17(a)

Article 29(1) sets out the aims for the education of the child. Article 17 suggests that the content of information and material disseminated by the media should be in accordance with these aims, which are directed to:

● development of the child's personality, talents and mental and physical abilities to their fullest potential;

● development of respect for human rights and fundamental freedoms, and for the principles enshrined in the Charter of the United Nations;

● development of respect for
  ● the child's parents;
  ● the child's cultural identity, language and values;
  ● the national values of:
    ◆ the country in which the child is living;

◆ the country from which he or she may originate;
◆ civilizations different from his or her own;

● preparation of the child for responsible life in a free society, in the spirit of understanding, peace, tolerance, equality of the sexes and friendship among all peoples, ethnic, national and religious groups and persons of indigenous origin;

● development of respect for the natural environment.

(see article 29, page 391).

Promoting understanding, peace and tolerance

The Committee on the Rights of the Child has noted with concern certain instances where the media may be promoting negative attitudes and even hatred of certain groups:

"The Committee is concerned at the information brought to its attention concerning the hostile sentiments apparently broadcast by certain mass media. The Committee is worried about tendencies in the media which may lead to the incitement of hatred against certain ethnic and religious groups. "The Committee is deeply concerned about the absence of pluralism in the activities of the major organs of mass media, limiting the freedom of the child to receive information and the freedom of thought and conscience, as provided for in articles 13 and 14 of the Convention." (Federal Republic of Yugoslavia IRCO, Add.49, paras. 11 and 12)

The Committee has emphasized the responsibility of the media to contribute to fostering "understanding, peace, tolerance,.." and so on, as set out in article 29(1)(d):

"... The Committee observes that the State-controlled mass media, in the interests of healing and building trust within the country, have a role and a responsibility to contribute to the efforts to foster tolerance and understanding between different groups and that the broadcasting of programmes that run counter to this objective should end. The Committee recommends that the securing and dissemination of broader and more diverse sources of information designed for children, including by broadcasting them on the mass media, would assist in ensuring further implementation of the principles and provisions of the Convention, including those of its article 17. It is also suggested that measures should be taken to improve the activities of the mass media in imparting information for children in their own language, including Albanian." (Federal Republic of Yugoslavia IRCO, Add.49, para. 28)

Media standards

Bulgaria's Initial Report suggests that "The opening towards the world through satellite television and video has placed the media and in particular the specialized children's programmes and publications in a very competitive environment. The choice between artistic values and pseudocultural entertainment ever more leans toward the latter. Today's Bulgarian children are characterized by many of the specific cultural indicators of the so called 'TV child' ... After 1989 a true turnaround occurred in the means of mass communications... From a situation of hunger for information society went through a transition to information oversaturation and aggression. There is a similar situation with respect to children's and young people's newspapers and magazines. There appears to be dominant the satisfaction of musical and hedonistic needs, a turning of children's and adolescents' attention to entertainment, fantasy, parapsychology, intersexual relations and sex, erotica and violence. The commercialization of the press and book publishing have created openings for children to have unobstructed access to erotica, pornography, violence and horror as the 'pillars' of mass culture. Certain publications which speculate in sexual problems for commercial purposes are trying to manipulate public opinion. Erotica for its own sake was defined as 'normal' and is presented almost as sexual education about the 'normal things in life' while films containing violence and horror are presented as 'ordinary thrillers'. This has already resulted in negative consequences reflected in the education and behaviour of children." (Bulgaria IR, paras. 67-70)

"The Committee also recommends, in the interests of healing and trust-building within the country and in the spirit of article 17 of the Convention, that the State-controlled mass media should play an active role in the efforts to secure tolerance and understanding between different ethnic groups, and that the broadcasting of programmes which would run counter to this objective come to an end." (Croatia IRCO, Add.52, para. 20)

In 1978, the General Conference of UNESCO proclaimed the Declaration on Fundamental Principles concerning the Contribution of the Mass Media to Strengthening Peace and International Understanding, to the Promotion of Human Rights and to Countering Racialism, Apartheid and Incitement to War.

Promoting equality of the sexes

Another of the aims set out in article 29 is promoting equality of the sexes. The Report of the Committee's General Discussion on the girl child refers to

"the importance of eradicating degrading and exploitative images of girls and women in the media and advertising. The values and models of behaviour that were portrayed contributed to the perpetuation of inequality and inferiority." (Report on the eighth session, January 1995, CRC/C/38, para. 291)

The Platform for Action arising from the 1995 Fourth World Conference on Women has a section on "Women and the media", which both emphasizes the potential of the media for making a far greater contribution to the advancement of women and that "The continued projection of negative and degrading images of women in media communications – electronic, print, visual and audio – must be changed" (The Beijing Declaration and Platform for Action, 1996, paras. 234 and 236). The section on "The girl child" states: "Girls and adolescents may receive a variety of conflicting and confusing messages on their gender roles from their parents, teachers, peers and the media. Women and men need to work together with children and youth to break down persistent gender stereotypes, taking into account the rights of the child and the responsibilities, rights and duties of parents..." (para. 262). Among actions to be taken by Governments is the encouragement by "educational institutions and the media to adopt and project balanced and non-stereotyped images of girls and boys, and work to eliminate child pornography and degrading and violent portrayals of the girl child" (para. 277; also relevant to paragraph (e) of article 17, see below).

Promoting awareness of disability

The Standard Rules on the Equalization of Opportunities for Persons with Disabilities, in rule 1 on "Awareness-raising", proposes: "States should encourage the portrayal of persons with disabilities by the mass media in a positive way; organizations of persons with disabilities should be consulted on this matter." In addition, rule 9 suggests that the media should be encouraged to play an important part in removing negative attitudes "towards marriage, sexuality and parenthood of persons with disabilities, especially of girls and women with disabilities, which still prevail in society."

Prevention of juvenile delinquency

Further advice on the role of the media in the positive socialization of children is given in the

Implementation Handbook for the Convention on the Rights of the Child

United Nations Guidelines for the Prevention of Juvenile Delinquency, the "Riyadh Guidelines", which the Committee on the Rights of the Child has consistently commended as providing appropriate standards for implementation of the Convention on the Rights of the Child. Within the section on "Socialization processes", a sub-section on the mass media reads:

"40. The mass media should be encouraged to ensure that young persons have access to information and material from a diversity of national and international sources.

41. The mass media should be encouraged to portray the positive contribution of young persons to society.

42. The mass media should be encouraged to disseminate information on the existence of services, facilities and opportunities for young persons in society.

43. The mass media generally, and the television and film media in particular, should be encouraged to minimize the level of pornography, drugs and violence portrayed and to display violence and exploitation disfavourably, as well as to avoid demeaning and degrading presentations, especially of children, women and interpersonal relations, and to promote egalitarian principles and roles.

44. The mass media should be aware of its extensive social role and responsibility, as well as its influence, in communications relating to youthful drug and alcohol abuse. It should use its power for drug abuse prevention by relaying consistent messages through a balanced approach. Effective drug awareness campaigns at all levels should be promoted."

Health promotion
In the Convention on the Rights of the Child, another particular reference to children's need for information appears under article 24, in which States Parties are required to take appropriate measures to ensure that parents and children are informed about child health and various specific health issues (article 24(2)(e), see page 328). Here, too, the media can play an important role. For instance:

"... the Committee wishes to encourage the State Party to consider greater use of the media in relation to awareness-raising and education on the dangers of sexual exploitation and abuse and the issues of HIV/AIDS and other sexually transmitted diseases." (Federal Republic of Yugoslavia IRCO, Add.49, para. 41)

"Encourage international cooperation in the production,

exchange and dissemination of such information and material from a diversity of cultural, national and international sources": article 17(b)

This provision reflects a focus on international cooperation to achieve full implementation, found throughout the Convention on the Rights of the Child. It also emphasizes the diversity of material that should be available to the child. Modern technology is dramatically affecting the instant dissemination of information, increasing the potential of the media for education and development, while also raising concerns about the aims and content of some information being made available to children.

"Encourage the production and dissemination of children's books": article 17(c)

Late in the drafting process of article 17, a non-governmental organization proposed that there should be a specific provision to promote children's reading. The International Board on Books for Young People proposed a new subparagraph: "Encourage, at all levels, literacy and the reading habit through children's book production and dissemination, as well as the habit of story-telling" (E/CN.4/1987/25, p. 7; Detrick, p. 287). The provision in subparagraph (c) developed from this proposal.

UNESCO has for many year promoted publication of children's literature, together with the major professional bodies and NGOs.

"Encourage the mass media to have particular regard to the linguistic needs of the child who belongs to a minority group or who is indigenous": article 17(d)

Article 30 (see page 407) requires that the child who belongs to a religious or linguistic minority, or who is indigenous, should not be denied the right to enjoy his or her own culture, to profess and practice his or her own religion or to use his or her own language. The aims of education in article 29 also require respect for varying national values, cultures and languages. Article 17 indicates the important role the mass media should be encouraged to play, for instance through producing material and programmes in minority languages.

In commenting on the need to make the principles and provisions of the Convention on the Rights of the Child well known to adults and children (under article 42, see page 561), the Committee has often emphasized the importance of ensuring translation into minority and indigenous languages, and the particular importance of the media's participation in this task:

"It is the recommendation of the Committee that the principles and provisions of the Convention on the Rights of the Child be widely disseminated throughout the country, including through the mass media, such as radio and television.... The translation of the Convention into the major national minority languages would form an integral part of these dissemination activities." (China IRCO, Add.56, para. 29)

"Encourage the development of appropriate guidelines for the protection of the child from information and material injurious to his or her well-being, bearing in mind the provisions of articles 13 and 18": article 17(e)

Increasing concern exists in many countries about the potential negative effects on children's development, including physical and mental health, of the projection of violence through the mass media. In the report of its General Discussion on "The child and the media", the Committee on the Rights of the Child highlighted this point and other negative aspects of the media (including its portrayal of children and childhood as quoted in relation to article 16, the child's right to privacy, see page 197):

"...Concern has also been expressed about the influence on children of negative aspects of the media, primarily programmes containing brutal violence and pornography. There is discussion in a number of countries about how to protect children from violence on television, in video films and in other modern media. Again, voluntary agreements have been attempted, with varied impact. This particular problem is raised in article 17 of the Convention which recommends that appropriate guidelines be developed 'for the protection of the child from information and material injurious to his or her well-being'.
"Such guidelines have indeed been developed in some countries, with varied results. The United Nations Educational, Scientific and Cultural Organization has recently renewed discussion on this topic." (Report on the eleventh session, January 1996, CRC/C/50, Annex IX, pp. 80-81)

The Convention on the Rights of the Child proposes guidelines, suggesting voluntary rather than legislative controls. In developing guidelines, States Parties must bear in mind the provisions in two other articles:

- the child's right to freedom of expression, which can only be subject to certain limited restrictions, set out in paragraph 2 of article 13 (see page 172);
- parents' primary responsibility for the upbringing and development of the child, with the child's best interests as their basic concern, and the State's obligation to provide appropriate assistance (article 18, see page 225).

Article 5, requiring respect for parents' rights to provide appropriate direction and guidance consistent with the evolving capacities of the child, is also relevant. Ultimately, it is parents and other caregivers who will have primary responsibility for supervising their child's use of the media. The State should assist parents, for example, by ensuring that they have adequate information about the content of television programmes, videos, computer games and so on.

Article 34(b) requires measures to prevent "the exploitative use of children in pornographic performances and materials" (see page 455).

The recommendations which arose from the Committee's General Discussion on "The child and the media" include developing constructive agreements with media companies to protect children against harmful influences, comprehensive plans to empower parents in the media market, training of journalists, and specific guidelines for reporting on child abuse (see box, page 214).

The Committee has noted the absence of adequate protection from potentially injurious material in its examination of various States Parties' reports:

"... national legislation has not yet been brought into full conformity with the provisions of the Convention, including its general principles... In this regard, the Committee's concerns relate in particular to ... the need to protect children against ... harmful information....
"The Committee is concerned that the measures being taken to protect children from information injurious to their well-being are insufficient, in the light of the provisions of article 17 of the Convention." (Jamaica IRCO, Add.32, paras. 7 and 12)

In its Concluding Observations on Canada and Panama, the Committee noted

"... the urgent need to ensure adequate protection of children from harmful information, and particularly from television programmes

inciting or containing violence." (Canada IRCO, Add.37, para. 15)

"...In light of the implementation of article 17 of the Convention, the Committee is also concerned about the need for further measures to protect children from media information and material injurious to their well-being."

The Committee

"... recommends that the State Party reinforce existing measures to protect children from harmful information." (Panama IRCO, Add.68, paras. 16 and 30)

Privacy of the child and the media

One potential threat to the well-being of the child posed by the media relates to the child's right to privacy (see article 16, page 201). In addition, article 40(2)(b)vii) requires respect in media coverage for the privacy of children involved in the juvenile justice system, and the Committee has raised similar concerns about the privacy of child victims of abuse, and of family problems. The Agenda for Action of the World Congress against Commercial Sexual Exploitation of Children (Stockholm 1996) calls on media professionals "to develop strategies which strengthen the role of the media in providing information of the highest quality, reliability and ethical standards concerning all aspects of commercial sexual exploitation of children". It also proposes "voluntary ethical codes of conduct" (A/51/385, p.5, paras. 3(k) and 4(g)).

The media, armed conflict and children

The Graça Machel study on the *Impact of Armed Conflict on Children* indicates that the media is capable of effectively galvanizing international public support for humanitarian action, and that the threat of adverse international publicity may also be positive, holding the potential for keeping some gross violations of human rights in check. "Ultimately, however, while reports of starving children or overcrowded camps for displaced persons may be dramatic, they do little to support efforts for long-term reconstruction and reconciliation." The study also suggests that the media can play an important role by helping readers and viewers to enjoy diversity, "and by promoting the understanding that is needed for peaceful coexistence and the respect that is required for the enjoyment of human rights..." (A/51/306, paras. 28 and 257)

Protection from harmful material

Italy's Initial Report indicates that a new law introduced in 1990 added to the protection of children against harmful broadcasts (Italy IR, paras. 90-92). In discussion with Italian government representatives, a Committee member stated that "there were two aspects to article 17 of the Convention. It required States Parties to adopt guidelines in respect of television programmes and to take concrete action to provide children with alternative programmes. The report referred to the first aspect, but the Committee would appreciate information on the second..., and, in general, on the effectiveness of the voluntary approach to the problem of children and broadcasting" (Italy SR.236, para. 42).

In Hong Kong, the "Fixed Telecommunication Network Service" is fully digital: "This permits the efficient carriage of a wide range of services. Adult and children information services provided on the Service are grouped under special categories. Telephone lines have access to these categories of service only if the registered telephone line users specifically request them. Parents who wish to have access to adult information services but do not wish their children to do so may apply for free-of-charge Personal Identification Numbers. This provides an effective measure to block children's access to information service programmes which their parents consider harmful." (UK dependent territory: Hong Kong IR, para. 42)

China's Initial Report indicates that the State and schools use a variety of methods to prevent "unsuitable material such as violent videos and other unhealthy books and publications" exerting an influence on minors, "the most important being to teach minors, through education and propaganda, to recognize the harmfulness of such material so that they will consciously resist it. The State also uses administrative and judicial procedures to ban and prosecute the unlawful purveying of unsuitable information to minors." (China IR, para. 65)

Implementation Checklist

● General measures of implementation

Have appropriate general measures of implementation been taken in relation to article 17 including

☐ identification and coordination of the responsible departments and agencies at all levels of government (article 17 is relevant to **departments of media and communications, social welfare and education**)?

☐ identification of relevant non-governmental organizations/civil society partners?

☐ a comprehensive review to ensure that all legislation, policy and practice is compatible with the article, for all children in all parts of the jurisdiction?

☐ adoption of a strategy to secure full implementation

    ☐ which includes where necessary the identification of goals and indicators of progress?

    ☐ which does not affect any provisions which are more conducive to the rights of the child?

    ☐ which recognizes other relevant international standards?

    ☐ which involves where necessary international cooperation?

(Such measures may be part of an overall governmental strategy for implementing the Convention as a whole).

☐ budgetary analysis and allocation of necessary resources?

☐ development of mechanisms for monitoring and evaluation?

☐ making the implications of article 17 widely known to adults and children?

☐ development of appropriate training and awareness-raising (in relation to article 17 likely to include the training of **journalists and all those involved in the mass media, and media education,** and developing appropriate **parenting education**)?

● Specific issues in implementing article 17

☐ Has the State taken measures to ensure that all children in the jurisdiction have access to information and material from a diversity of national and international sources, especially those aimed at the promotion of the child's social, spiritual and moral well-being and physical and mental health?

Is such access assured to all children without discrimination, in particular

    ☐ children of minorities and children who are indigenous?

    ☐ disabled children?

☐ children in all categories of institutions, including custodial institutions?

Has the State encouraged the mass media to disseminate information and material of social and cultural benefit to the child, and to promote aims set out in article 29 including

    ☐ development of the child's full potential?

    ☐ development of respect for human rights and fundamental freedoms?

    development of respect for

        ☐ the child's parents?

        ☐ the child's cultural identity, language and values?

        the national values of

☐ the country in which the child is living?

☐ the country from which he or she may originate?

☐ civilizations different from his or her own?

    ☐ preparation of the child for responsible life in a free society?

    ☐ development of respect for the natural environment?

In particular, has the mass media been encouraged to promote

    ☐ understanding and friendship among all peoples, including minorities and indigenous people?

    ☐ equality between the sexes, in line with the proposals of the Platform for Action of the Fourth World Conference on Women?

    ☐ positive portrayal of people with disabilities, in accordance with the Standard Rules on the Equalization of Opportunities for Persons with Disabilities?

    ☐ positive socialization of children, in accordance with the provisions of the UN Guidelines on the Prevention of Juvenile Delinquency?

☐ Does the State encourage international cooperation in the production, exchange and dissemination of such information and material from a diversity of cultural, national and international sources?

☐ Has the State taken measures to encourage the production and dissemination of children's books?

☐ Has the mass media been encouraged to have particular regard for the linguistic needs of children who belong to minorities or are indigenous?

☐ Has the mass media been encouraged to help with health promotion and education?

☐ Has the mass media been encouraged to help disseminate information on the Convention to adults and children?

How to use the checklists, *see page XVII*

☐ Has the State encouraged the development of guidelines and training programmes to promote the participation of children in relation to radio, print media, film and video, the Internet, and other media?

Has the State encouraged the development of guidelines and monitoring procedures for the protection of the child from information and material injurious to his or her well-being in relation to

- ☐ television?
- ☐ radio?
- ☐ film and video?
- ☐ the Internet?
- ☐ other media?

If so, are such guidelines consistent with

- ☐ the child's right to freedom of expression under article 13 and the restrictions allowed on that right set out in paragraph 2?
- ☐ the responsibilities of parents and others and of the State set out in article 18?

☐ Has the State ensured that parents and other carers are provided with sufficient information on the content of media programmes, videos, computer games and so on to enable them to fulfil their responsibilities for the welfare of the child?

☐ Has the State promoted the development of appropriate media education for children?

☐ Has the State encouraged the development of parenting education relating to protection of the child from injurious information and material?

☐ Are there guidelines and other safeguards, including training, to promote respect by the media for the child's right to privacy, and for responsible reporting of abuse, family problems and juvenile justice?

Reminder: **The Convention is indivisible and its articles are interdependent. Article 17 should not be considered in isolation.**

Particular regard should be paid to:
The general principles

Article 2: all rights to be recognized for each child in jurisdiction without discrimination on any ground

Article 3(1): the best interests of the child to be a primary consideration in all actions concerning children

Article 6: right to life and maximum possible survival and development

Article 12: respect for the child's views in all matters affecting the child; opportunity to be heard in any judicial or administrative proceedings affecting the child

Closely related articles

Articles whose implementation is related to that of article 17 include:

Article 5: parental guidance

Article 9: reporting on family proceedings – the child's privacy

Article 13: right to freedom of expression

Article 16: the child's right to privacy

Article 18: primary responsibility of parents

Article 19: reporting on violence and abuse – privacy for child victims

Article 24: health education and promotion

Article 29: aims of education

Article 30: rights of children of minorities and of indigenous communities to enjoy their own culture, religion and language

Article 31: promoting child's right to play, recreation and participation in culture and the arts

Article 34: role of the media in challenging sexual exploitation, including child pornography

Article 36: other forms of exploitation by the media

Article 40: reporting on juvenile justice – privacy for child

Article 42: making the Convention widely known to children and adults

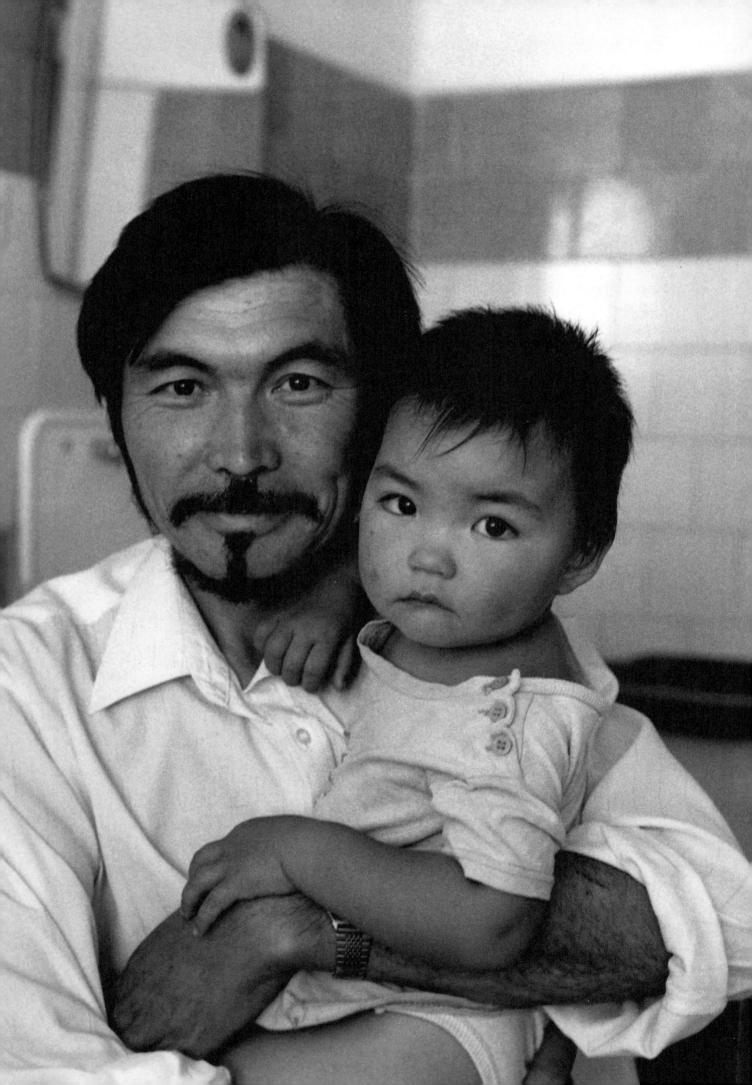

Parents' joint responsibilities assisted by the State

Text of Article 18

1. States Parties shall use their best efforts to ensure recognition of the principle that both parents have common responsibilities for the upbringing and development of the child. Parents or, as the case may be, legal guardians have the primary responsibility for the upbringing and development of the child. The best interests of the child will be their basic concern.

2. For the purpose of guaranteeing and promoting the rights set forth in the present Convention, States Parties shall render appropriate assistance to parents and legal guardians in the performance of their child-rearing responsibilities and shall ensure the development of institutions, facilities and services for the care of children.

3. States Parties shall take all appropriate measures to ensure that children of working parents have the right to benefit from child-care services and facilities for which they are eligible.

Article 18 concerns the balance of responsibilities between the child's parents and the State, and particularly addresses support for parents in the performance of their responsibilities. The article must be read in conjunction with article 5 (parental and family duties and rights, the child's evolving capacities) and articles 3(2) and 27 (the State's responsibility to assist parents in securing that children have adequate protection and care and an adequate standard of living). These four articles of the Convention, taken together, make clear that parents have primary responsibility for the child, but that this responsibility is circumscribed by the child's rights under the Convention (including their best interests) and may be shared with others such as members of the wider family. The State must provide appropriate assistance and, where the parents cannot fulfil their responsibilities, it must step in to ensure that the child's rights and needs are met.

Article 10 of the International Covenant on Economic, Social and Cultural Rights provides that: "The widest possible protection and assistance should be accorded to the family, which is the natural and fundamental group unit of society, particularly for its establishment and while it is responsible for the care and education of dependent children" and "Special measures of protection and assistance should be taken on behalf of all children and young persons without any discrimination". Articles 23 and 24 of the International Covenant on Civil and Political Rights repeat these principles and, in addition, provide: "No one shall be subjected to arbitrary or

Summary

unlawful interference with his privacy, family, home or correspondence" (article 17). The Committee on Economic, Social and Cultural Rights states in a General Comment "In this and other contexts, the term 'family' should be interpreted broadly and in accordance with appropriate local usage" (General Comment 5, HRI/GEN/1/Rev.2, p. 73).

The requirements of the Human Rights Committee are more detailed: "Responsibility for guaranteeing children the necessary protection lies with the family, society and the State. Although the Covenant does not indicate how such responsibility is to be apportioned, it is primarily incumbent

on the family, which is interpreted broadly to include all persons composing it in the society of the State Party concerned, and particularly on the parents, to create conditions to promote the harmonious development of the child's personality and his enjoyment of the rights recognized in the Covenant. However, since it is quite common for the father and mother to be gainfully employed outside the home, reports by States Parties should indicate how society, social institutions and the State are discharging their responsibility to assist the family in ensuring the protection of the child." (Human Rights Committee, General Comment 17, HRI/GEN/I/Rev.2, p. 25)   ■

Extracts from
Committee on the Rights of the Child
Guidelines for Reports to be submitted by States Parties under the Convention

For full text of *Guidelines for Periodic Reports*, see Appendix 3, page 604.

Guidelines for Initial Reports

"Family environment and alternative care

Under this section, States Parties are requested to provide relevant information, including the principal legislative, judicial, administrative or other measures in force, particularly how the principles of the "best interests of the child" and "respect for the views of the child" are reflected therein; factors and difficulties encountered and progress achieved in implementing the relevant provisions of the Convention; and implementation priorities and specific goals for the future in respect of:...

(b) Parental responsibilities (article 18, paras. 1-2)...

...

In addition, States Parties are requested to provide information on the numbers of children per year within the reporting period in each of the following groups, disaggregated by age group, sex, ethnic or national background and rural or urban environment: homeless children, abused or neglected children taken into protective custody, children placed in foster care, children placed in institutional care, children placed through domestic adoption, children entering the country through intercountry adoption procedures and children leaving the country through intercountry adoption procedures.

States Parties are encouraged to provide additional relevant statistical information and indicators relating to children covered in this section.

Basic health and welfare

Under this section, States Parties are requested to provide relevant information, including the principal legislative, judicial, administrative or other measures in force; the institutional infrastructure for implementing policy in this area, particularly monitoring strategies and mechanisms; and factors and difficulties encountered and progress achieved in implementing the relevant provisions of the Convention, in respect of:..

(d)...child-care services and facilities (articles...18, para.3)."

(CRC/C/5, paras. 16-19)

Guidelines for Periodic Reports

"V. FAMILY ENVIRONMENT AND ALTERNATIVE CARE

B. Parental responsibilities (art. 18, paras. 1-2)

Please provide information on the consideration given by law to parental responsibility, including the recognition of the common responsibilities of both parents in the upbringing and development of the child and, that the best interests of the child will be their basic concern. Also indicate how the principles of non-discrimination, respect for the views of the child and the development of the child to the maximum extent, as provided for by the Convention, are taken into account.

Please provide information on the measures adopted to render appropriate assistance to parents and legal guardians in the performance of their child-rearing responsibilities, as well as on the institutions, facilities and services developed for the care of children. Information should also be provided on specific measures adopted for children from single-parent families and belonging to the most disadvantaged groups, including those living in extreme poverty.

Relevant disaggregated information (for example, by gender, age, region, rural/urban areas and social and ethnic origin) should be given on children having benefited from any of these measures and resources allocated to them (at the national, regional and local levels, and where appropriate at the federal and provincial levels). Information should also be provided on progress achieved and difficulties encountered in the implementation of article 18, as well as on the targets set for the future.

VI. BASIC HEALTH AND WELFARE...

C. Social security and child-care services and facilities (arts. 26 and 18, para 3)

Please indicate the measures adopted pursuant to article 18, paragraph 3, and taking into account the provisions of articles 3, 6 and 12 of the Convention, to ensure that children of working parents have the right to benefit from child-care services and facilities for which they are eligible. In this regard, reports should inter alia *provide information on the legislation adopted to recognize this right and ensure its realization, as well as on the coverage with regard to services and facilities, by region and by urban and rural areas, as well as on their financial implications and on the children benefiting from such measures, including by age, gender and national, social and ethnic origin.*

Reports should also provide information on the progress achieved in the implementation of these rights, the difficulties encountered and any targets identified for the future."

(CRC/C/58, paras. 65-67 and 101-2. The following paragraphs of the *Guidelines for Periodic Reports* are also relevant to reporting under this article: 22, 37, 88 and 105; for full text of *Guidelines*, see Appendix 3, page 604.)

"Parents or, as the case may be, legal guardians, have the primary responsibility for the upbringing and development of the child"

Article 18 makes a clear statement supporting the primacy of parents; although elsewhere (articles 5 and 30), the Convention recognizes that family structures vary and that children's wider family, tribe, community or culture can play an important role in the child's upbringing.

In this sense, article 18 is an assertion of parents' rights rather than children's rights. However the assertion is made in relation to the State's powers, not the child's, and the rights themselves are termed responsibilities. Responsibility for the child's "development" suggests a relatively objective measure for assessing parents' exercise of their responsibilities. Development is an extremely wide concept (see article 6, page 94). If children's physical, psychological or intellectu-

al development are being impaired by the avoidable actions of the parents, then the parents can be found to be failing in their responsibilities.

"The best interests of the child will be their basic concern"

When article 18 was being drafted, the delegate from the United States of America commented that it was rather strange to set down responsibilities for private individuals, since the Convention could only be binding on ratifying governments (E/CN.4/1989/48, pp. 50-52; Detrick, p. 270).

The imperative tense used here does at first sight seem odd. How can the State secure that the child's best interests "will be" the parents' basic concern? But the principle does have direct bearing on the actions of States, because it should underpin all legislation on parents' rights. Most nations of the world have a history of laws and customs that assumes parental "ownership" of children – an assumption that parental rights over children could be exercised for the benefit of the parents alone. These laws and customs are now being rethought in many parts of the world. The Convention requires that current legal principles of parental rights be translated into principles of parental responsibilities – the responsibility of parents to act in the best interests of their children.

As has been discussed in relation to article 3 (page 31), "the best interests of the child" are not written in tablets of stone. They will differ from child to child. Parents may have fiercely opposed views on what are a particular child's best interests; professionals, too, may not agree with each other about what is best. The child's rights under the Convention are therefore helpful in making the concept less subjective. Any breach of these rights (including failure to respect children's evolving capacities) is likely to be contrary to the child's best interests.

Parent education

The State also has a duty to advise and educate parents about their responsibilities. Investment in parent education, on a non-compulsory basis, is increasingly recognized as being cost-effective, for example in terms of lowering children's delinquency rates. The United Nations Guidelines on

the Prevention of Juvenile Delinquency (the "Riyadh Guidelines") states: "Measures should be taken and programmes developed to provide families with the opportunity to learn about parental roles and obligations as regards child development and child care, promoting positive parent-child relationships, sensitizing parents to the problems of children and young persons and encouraging their involvement in family and community-based activities." (para 16)

The *Guidelines for Periodic Reports* asks (in relation to article 5): "Please indicate any family counselling services or parental education programmes available, as well as awareness campaigns for parents and children on the rights of the child within family life, and training activities provided to relevant professional groups (for example, social workers) and indicate if any evaluation has been made of their effectiveness. Please also indicate how knowledge and information about child development and the evolving capacities of the child are conveyed to parents or other persons responsible for the child." (para. 63)

The Committee has stressed to many countries the need for parental education measures:

".. the Committee suggests that the State Party undertake measures and programmes to educate the general public on parental responsibilities and to consider the possibility of providing counselling in this regard." (Namibia IRCO, Add.14, para. 22)

"...Greater efforts should be made to provide family life education and develop awareness of the responsibility of the parents. The Committee encourages non-governmental organizations and children and youth groups to pay attention to the need to change attitudes as part of their advocacy action." (Philippines IRCO, Add.29, para. 22)

"As far as protection from ill-treatment is concerned, the Committee recommends that the social preventive approach be strengthened and that further measures be undertaken to educate parents about their responsibilities towards their children, including through the provision of family education, which should emphasize the equal responsibilities of both parents and contribute to the prevention of the use of corporal punishment." (Tunisia IRCO, Add.39, para. 17)

"The Committee is of the opinion that there appears to be a need for more pre-marriage counselling and family-life education programmes, including as a means to prevent family breakdown." (Federal Republic of Yugoslavia IRCO, Add.49, para. 33. See also Romania IRCO, Add.16, para. 15; Honduras IRCO, Add.24, para. 27; UK IRCO, Add.34, para. 30; Bulgaria IRCO, Add.66, para. 28; Panama IRCO, Add.68, para. 30)

Mass parent education

Indonesia launched a programme "BKB" to "empower poor mothers and communities with knowledge and skills allowing them to interact with and provide mental stimulation for the very young child, i.e. the 0-3 year-old child ... Close to 1.3 million mothers in some 18,500 villages have been trained in the programme... the Indonesian approach to early child development is unique in a number of ways. Firstly, it focuses on the 0-3-year-old children rather than the 3-6-year-old children. Secondly, it aims at educating mothers and communities in early child stimulation thus avoiding expensive solutions such as institutions. Thirdly, it is implemented entirely through NGOs and women's group and thus is very much seen as 'belonging' to the community. Fourthly it has successfully combined parental monitoring of physical and mental growth via the introduction of a unique child growth and development chart based on milestones in Indonesian child development. And fifthly, in 1991, President Soeharto elevated the BKB programme to a 'National Movement' thus giving it the highest status and importance possible in Indonesia." (Indonesia IR (vol. 2), paras. 59 and 60)

The Committee observed to the Russian Federation:

"The Committee considers the serious problems of family life in the Russian Federation to be an area of priority concern. The Committee notes with particular concern the tendency towards the breakdown of family culture as regards abandoned children, abortion, the divorce rate, the number of adoptions, the number of children born out of wedlock and recovery of maintenance obligations.

"... greater efforts should be made to provide family life education, to organize discussions on the role of the family in society and to develop awareness of the equal responsibilities of parents." (Russian Federation IRCO, Add.4, paras. 10 and 18)

The State shall use its "best efforts to ensure recognition of the principle that both parents have common responsibilities for the upbringing and development of the child"

Single-parent families

Article 27 calls for appropriate measures to ensure that maintenance is recovered from the parents responsible (in practice, generally from fathers), but "common responsibility" under this article goes beyond financial responsibility. The aim should be that both parents play an active part in their child's upbringing, including the fathers of children born out of wedlock.

Initial Reports from countries across the world document the growing numbers of children living in one-parent families – usually with the mother. The Committee has often expressed concern about the phenomenon, a concern that does not relate to the state of marriage but to the need of children to have both parents actively involved in their upbringing and to the greater likelihood of poverty for children in one-parent families. Marriage relates to childless couples as well as to parents, and a marriage certificate is not needed to ensure the joint partnership of parenthood. Iceland, for example, reported to the Committee that although more than half its children were now born outside marriage, only a fifth were born to parents who were not living together. (Iceland IR, paras. 29-30)

During discussions with Mongolia, a Committee member stated: "Where the best interests of the child were concerned, the Convention did not make any distinctions with regard to the status of the parents – unmarried, divorced, single, etc. The point was that a child's parents, whatever their status, must work for his best interests." (Mongolia SR.265, para. 32) Countries that do not enable fathers of children born outside marriage to assume parental responsibilities under the law risk being in breach of the Convention (bearing in mind that article 9 allows for parents and children to be separated when necessary for the child's best interests).

Growing up in a single-parent family can have a direct impact on the development of children, as Namibia analyzed in its Initial Report (see box).

Absent fathers: repercussions for children

Namibia's Initial Report describes the difficulties faced by female-headed families:

"Female-headed households confront special problems in the area of child-rearing. Women generally have unequal access to the limited opportunities for formal employment in Namibia, partly because of continuing patterns of gender discrimination and partly because wage employment is concentrated in the urban areas. Furthermore, women who are employed are still concentrated in low wage sectors of the economy. Thus, households which depend on a woman's income as a primary source of cash income are typically disadvantaged. The consequences for children are illustrated by the 1990 UNICEF survey, which found that children in households headed by women were more likely to be stunted in growth in all locations surveyed...

"Also, in female-headed households, primary responsibility for the care of young children often falls upon older siblings or grandparents. This contributes to the school drop-out rate for young girls, putting them at an educational disadvantage which tends to help perpetuate women's unequal access to formal employment". A 1990 survey showed that in Namibia female-headed households had particular problems breastfeeding – they often had to introduce solids at an early age, or give up breastfeeding altogether, because of the need to work. For example childhood malnutrition peaks between November and February and May and June, despite the fact that in the latter period food is being harvested, because these are the times women work the hardest planting and harvesting and so have little time to feed their children. (Namibia IR, paras. 140-1, 232-4)

Children from such families are likely to be found in the bottom income groups of all countries, rich and poor. The Committee suggested that Germany, Denmark, Norway and New Zealand make a further study of the situation of single parents. For example:

"The Committee recommends that further steps should be taken to strengthen awareness of the equal responsibilities of parents in child-rearing, in particular in the light of article 18 of the Convention. It is also suggested that the situation of single parents be further studied and that relevant programmes be established to meet their particular needs." (Denmark IRCO, Add.33, para. 26. See also Norway IRCO, Add.23, para. 18; Germany IRCO, Add.43, para. 31; New Zealand IRCO, Add.71, para. 27)

The State can also adopt employment, tax and welfare measures to encourage both parents' active involvement in child rearing. The Committee suggested that

"...appropriate measures be taken to counter the inequalities between men and women with regard to remuneration, since it may be detrimental to the child, in particular in homes headed by a single woman." (Iceland IRCO, Add.50, para. 25)

Social inequalities between men and women may undermine the family as a source of support for children's rights. The Committee encouraged Yemen:

"...to pay special attention to enhancing the role of the family in the promotion of

children's rights, and in this regard stresses the importance of the status of women in family and social life..." (Yemen IRCO, Add.47, para. 16)

The State's "best efforts" to ensure recognition of the joint responsibility of parents should also include educational measures (see page 228 above). The Committee congratulated Germany on the measures it has taken to promote common responsibility:

"Appreciation is expressed of the State Party's acknowledgement of using the Convention on the Rights of the Child as an instrument to sharpen awareness of the responsibilities of persons taking care of children and the need to equalize the responsibilities between parents in bringing up their children..." (Germany IRCO, Add.43, para. 30)

Nigeria was advised:

"...Public awareness and information campaigns must support education and advice on other family matters, including equal parental responsibilities and family planning in order to foster good family practices in line with the principles and provisions of the Convention." (Nigeria IRCO, Add.61, para. 36)

And the United Kingdom:

"The Committee recommends that further measures be undertaken to educate parents about their responsibilities towards their children, including through the provision of family education which should emphasize the equal responsibilities of both parents..." (UK IRCO, Add.34, para. 30)

The Committee spelled out particular concerns relating to teenage mothers. As well as often resulting in lone parenting, teenage pregnancies can blight the health and social expectations of the young mother, who is, of course, a child too under the Convention. The Committee has expressed concern that

"...The high incidence of teenage pregnancies and female-headed households make children particularly vulnerable to sexual abuse, domestic violence, neglect and abandonment, sometimes leading to children becoming involved in activities conflicting with the law." (Jamaica IRCO, Add.32, para. 13)

"...While recognizing that the Government views the problem of teenage pregnancies as a serious one, the Committee suggests that additional efforts, in the form of prevention-oriented programmes which could be part of an educational campaign, are required to reduce the number of teenage pregnancies." (UK IRCO, Add.34, para. 30)

When parents separate

The inequality of parental responsibility in many countries is often highlighted when parents sep-

---

Encouraging fathers' active responsibilities

Italy reported that a recent Italian Constitutional Court ruling "stressed that the balanced development of the child's personality requires the participation of both parents, particularly with regard to emotional and relational aspects. The Constitutional Court has therefore recognized the following rights to which both parents are entitled: the right to take six months of leave, while keeping their post and receiving an allowance equal to 30 per cent of their pay, during the first year of the child's life; the right to take time off when the child is sick, during the first three years; and the right to daily rest to care for the child during his first year of life." (Italy IR, para. 94)

Namibia reported that the "single quarters" provided for male workers in some of the urban areas are gradually being replaced with family housing (Namibia IR, para. 133).

---

arate. A number of countries' Initial Reports revealed legal and social traditions that inflexibly allocate responsibility for child-rearing to either the mother or the father when they separate. Often the formula is that mothers are given initial responsibility for babies, infants and young children but that fathers have subsequent responsibility, and dominant powers generally, to determine the shape of the child's life. Such measures usually represent progress away from a totally patriarchal system – a recognition of the strong bond between mothers and young children which it would be harmful to sever. Nonetheless translating this recognition into an inflexible law can result in a breach of children's rights.

Under the terms of article 18, the law must recognize the principle that **both** parents have **common** responsibility. As is recognized in article 18(2), Government measures should be directed at supporting and promoting the viability of joint parenting. If parents separate, or if they have never lived together, it may be necessary for courts to allocate rights to one or the other parent. (Finland noted: "The common practice of courts to order joint custody, even where the parents are totally unable to agree on anything regarding the child, has come under heavy criticism. At worst, this has left the child in a situation where no solution, even for the most important matters, has been achieved. It may have taken years, for example, for the child to be able to change schools or obtain a passport." (Finland IR, para. 259)) As discussed in relation to article 9 (see page 124) in such circumstances the law should not make inflexible presumptions about which parent takes priority – the grounds for making the decision should focus on the child's best interests.

A Committee member commented in discussion with Belarus that the issue of father's rights was "both controversial and important. In the Committee's view it was not right to equate the child's rights with those of the parents. Its concern was always for the child's interests in all cases, including the situation in which the child was caught in a struggle between the parents." He distinguished between the child's right to see the father and the father's rights: "If the latter, the Committee was not sympathetic." (Belarus SR.125, para. 29)

Article 23(4) of the International Covenant on Civil and Political Rights provides that States Parties "shall take appropriate steps to ensure equality of rights and responsibilities of spouses as to marriage, during marriage and on its dissolution." The Human Rights Committee states in a General Comment "During marriage, the spouses should have equal rights and responsibilities

in the family. This equality extends to all matters arising from their relationship ... Such equality continues to be applicable to arrangements regarding legal separation or dissolution of the marriage ... Thus, any discriminatory treatment in regard to the grounds and procedures for separation or divorce, child custody ... visiting rights or the loss or recovery of parental authority must be prohibited, bearing in mind the paramount interests of the children in this connection." (Human Rights Committee, General Comment 19, HRI/GEN/1/Rev.2, p. 30)

Germany entered a Declaration in relation to article 18(1), which said that this provision did not apply when parents are unmarried or separating "...automatically and without taking into account the best interests of the respective child ... Such an interpretation would be incompatible with article 3(1) of the Convention" (CRC/C/2/Rev.5, p.19). This is undoubtedly the case, as is made clear by article 9 (see page 121). It should, however, be noted how article 9(3) is phrased: "...the right of the child who is separated from one or both parents to maintain personal relations and direct contact with both parents on a regular basis, except if it is contrary to the child's best interests." This, together with article 7 (child's right to know and be cared for by parents) and article 18, implies that the law should presume that, unless it is proved to the contrary, the continued involvement of both parents in the child's life is in his or her best interests.

"For the purpose of guaranteeing and promoting the rights set forth in the present Convention, States Parties shall render appropriate assistance to parents and legal guardians in the performance of their child-rearing responsibilities..."

Paragraph 2 of article 18 emphasizes the State's responsibility to provide appropriate assistance to parents. It reflects the provisions of article 3(2): "States Parties undertake to ensure the child such protection and care as is necessary for his or her well-being, taking into account the rights and duties of his or her parents, legal guardians, or other individuals legally responsible for him or her, and, to this end, shall take all appropriate legislative and administrative measures;" and of article 27(3), as regards the child's right to an adequate standard of living: "States Parties, in accordance with national conditions and within their means, shall take appropriate measures to assist parents and others responsible for the

Government support for parenting

Finland told the Committee on the Rights of the Child: "Part of the cost of the care and maintenance of children is evened out by benefits paid by the State. The underlying idea is that children should not be a considerable financial burden to the family. The State therefore contributes to the general maintenance costs of children, those incurred by the care of small children, disability and illness of a child, as well as to the housing costs of low-income families." Finland has accepted that the State's responsibility for the care of small children should not be limited to day-care provision for working parents: "A new standard was reached in 1990 when parents with small children were given an absolute, statutory right, according to their choice, either to municipal day care for their child or to home care allowance... Under the current legislation, in 1995 a similar right will be extended to all children under the age of four..." (Finland IR, paras. 423 and 411)

child to implement this right." (see pages 44 and 360)

State assistance is obviously appropriate when parents are unable to undertake their child-rearing responsibilities, whether or not this is their fault. As the Committee said:

"Comprehensive measures should be provided for responsible parenthood and for support to needy families, in order to assist them in their child-rearing responsibilities in the light of articles 18 and 27, thus limiting family disruption, reducing the numbers of institutionalized children and limiting the recourse to institutionalization to a measure of last resort." (Italy IRCO, Add.41, para. 17)

Therefore, this implies that the State should assist families identified as at risk of breaking down with any measures that can help the breakdown be avoided, both practical (financial benefits, housing, day care, home helps, equipment and so forth) and psychological (advice, counselling, support networks and so on). The Committee said, in reference to Guatemala:

*"The Committee is concerned at the insufficient support given to families facing severe problems in fulfilling their responsibilities as regards the upbringing of their children...
"The Committee recommends that provision be made for offering social assistance to families to help them with their child-rearing*

responsibilities as laid down in article 18 of the Convention as a means of reducing institutionalization of children..." (Guatemala IRCO, Add.58, paras. 17 and 38)

But beyond targeting support to families "in need", the article enjoins States to recognize their responsibility to assist all parents. Universal services and non-means-tested financial benefits are, as Finland points out (see box), a recognition by the State of its responsibility towards, and interest in, children; such services and benefits are an investment in the country's future. In addition, universal provision is often the most effective form of prevention, in that families at risk are not deterred from receiving the provision because of the stigma attached, or because of ignorance, or because of complications in claiming it.

"For the purpose of guaranteeing and promoting the rights set forth in the present Convention, States Parties shall ... ensure the development of institutions, facilities and services for the care of children"

Relatively few services fall solely within the scope of this right, since article 20 addresses the responsibility of the State to provide for children who cannot live with their families, including provision of suitable institutions; paragraph (3) of article 18 addresses States' duty to secure child services where parents are working (such as day care for infants and after school facilities for older children), and articles 24, 28 and 23 cover health and education services and services for disabled children.

The sorts of services envisaged in article 18(2) include, presumably, community-based initiatives such as centres for mothers with babies and young children, play groups, toy libraries or youth clubs. Additionally, these may contribute to parent education, often on a non-authoritarian basis, and can therefore be of double value to children. Multidisciplinary services such as child guidance or school-based medical staff and advice centres also make an important contribution towards children's care.

Governments often invest in expensive public institutions at the expense of small, locally developed services, although the latter can often be both more economical and more effective in meeting the needs of parents and children. States should be prepared to trust the users of services with capital to develop what they need. It should also be noted that the duty on States under this article is to "ensure the **development** of institutions, facilities and services" which means that the State can never be complacent or inflexible about its delivery of services to children. Constant evaluation of effectiveness and constant resetting of targets are required.

"The State shall take all appropriate measures to ensure that children of working parents have the right to benefit from child-care services and facilities for which they are eligible"

The importance of meeting the needs of children of working parents cannot be overestimated. The provisions of article 3(3) (securing the quality of standards of all facilities for children) were originally drafted specifically in reference to child-care services. This reflects widespread concern about child care for very young children whose developmental needs are for security, consistent individual relationships and one-to-one stimulation.

The needs of older children of working parents are also a matter of concern:

"The Committee notes that the best interest of the child to spend time in his/her family environment may be infringed by the long working hours of parents and that sufficient measures have not been taken to prevent children from being alone at home during their parents' working hours." (Iceland IRCO, Add.50, para. 19)

"The Committee encourages the efforts made to accord high priority to and pursue more intensely the establishment of day-care centres in the community, including as a measure to prevent children being left unattended at home." (UK dependent territory: Hong Kong IRCO, Add.63, para. 28)

Anxieties about day care must be set against the realities of modern life – the economic demands on families that often require one or both parents to work, the new opportunities for women to work outside the narrow domestic sphere and the breakup of extended families (removing a traditional source of child care – the grandparent).

In this context, high-quality, low-cost or free day care and after-school care are essential to protect the needs of children. The Committee noted with interest that as of 1996, every child in Germany will have the legal right to a place in a kindergarten (Germany IRCO, Add.43, para. 12). The Committee has encouraged countries to support further measures to provide child-care services that promote early childhood development and that meet the needs of working mothers:

"The Committee encourages the State Party to further support measures which promote the provision of child-care services and centres for working mothers." (Honduras IRCO, Add.24, para. 27)

"The Committee encourages the State Party to support further measures to promote early childhood development and the provision of child-care services and centres for working mothers." (Jamaica IRCO, Add.32, para. 24)

Interestingly, the Committee recommended to Sri Lanka that:

"... the Ministry of Education should take under its responsibility the establishment and management of preschool facilities." (Sri Lanka IRCO, Add.40, para. 39)

Although the needs of preschool children may not be strictly educational as we commonly think of it, this recommendation underlines the importance of preschool facilities that are more than just containment – the development of infants must be actively encouraged by preschool staff. The World Summit for Children Plan of Action goals include: "Expansion of early childhood development activities, including appropriate low-cost family- and community-based interventions" (World Summit for Children, Declaration and Plan of Action, p.14). Although article 28 of the Convention on the Rights of the Child, on the right to education, does not specifically address preschool education it should be noted that the *Guidelines for Periodic Reports* does ask for information on: "Any system or extensive initiatives by the State to provide early development and education services for young children, especially for young children from disadvantaged social groups" (para 106).

Generous maternity and paternity leave and pay clearly meet the needs of both children and working parents. The Committee commented on this issue to Hong Kong:

"... the extent to which the statutory provisions relating to, inter alia, maternity leave and conditions of employment for nursing mothers are compatible with the principles and provisions of the Convention remains a matter of concern to the Committee."
(UK dependent territory: Hong Kong IRCO, Add.63, para. 16)

Parental leave in Norway

Norway's Initial Report describes its provision for mothers and fathers:

"Parental leaves in connection with the birth (or adoption) of a child have been extended considerably in recent years. In 1986, the period of leave was 18 weeks with full compensation for lost wages; in 1992 it was 35 weeks, or 44 weeks and two days with 80 per cent compensation for lost wages. As of 1 April 1993, the period of leave was extended to 42 weeks with 100 per cent compensation, or 52 weeks with 80 per cent compensation. Three of these weeks must be used by the mother before the birth of the child, otherwise the right to these weeks lapses. There are also lump-sum benefits for women without any leave entitlement who give birth. In 1990, these benefits amounted to NOK [Norwegian Kroner] 8,750; and in 1992, they were NOK 14,825. As of 1 April 1993, these benefits amount to NOK 17,790.

"Four weeks of the new extended leave programme may be used exclusively by the father of the child. The Government wishes to give parents a better opportunity to combine leaves and paid work, and it must be possible to divide leaves between the parents in a manner which is more flexible than has previously been possible. The Government has therefore commissioned a study of a "time account model", which encompasses various means of utilizing some of the weeks of leave for reduced working hours for one or both of the parents...

"Leave with pay is also granted when a child is ill. An employee who is away from work due to the necessary care of an ill child under the age of 12 is entitled to a daily cash allowance for up to 10 days every year, and 15 days per year if the individual has three or more children (30 days for single parents)..." (Norway IR, paras. 341-2 and 344)

Implementation Checklist

article 18

● *General measures of implementation*

Have appropriate general measures of implementation been taken in relation to article 18, including

☐ identification and coordination of the responsible departments and agencies at all levels of government (article 18 is relevant to the **departments of tax and finance, social security, social welfare, employment and education**)?

☐ identification of relevant non-governmental organizations/civil society partners?

☐ a comprehensive review to ensure that all legislation, policy and practice is compatible with the article, for all children in all parts of the jurisdiction?

☐ adoption of a strategy to secure full implementation

    ☐ which includes where necessary the identification of goals and indicators of progress?

    ☐ which does not affect any provisions which are more conducive to the rights of the child?

    ☐ which recognizes other relevant international standards?

    ☐ which involves where necessary international cooperation?

(Such measures may be part of an overall governmental strategy for implementing the Convention as a whole).

☐ budgetary analysis and allocation of necessary resources?

☐ development of mechanisms for monitoring and evaluation?

☐ making the implications of article 18 widely known to adults and children?

☐ development of appropriate training and awareness-raising (in relation to article 18 likely to include the training of **social workers, child guidance staff, community workers, social security officers and those engaged in parent education**)?

● *Specific issues in implementing article 18*

☐ Does legislation support parents' primacy of responsibility for children's upbringing and development?

☐ Is parental responsibility defined in legislation?

☐ Does legislation make clear that the exercise of parental responsibility has the best interests of the child as its basic concern?

☐ Are parents provided with education programmes on the exercise of their responsibilities?

☐ Are laws, administrative systems, tax and welfare measures and public education aimed at supporting both parents' common responsibilities for, and active participation in, their child's upbringing?

☐ Does the law enable fathers of children born outside marriage to assume parental rights and responsibilities (compatible with the child's best interests)?

☐ Is there a presumption in law that children's best interests, unless proved to the contrary, are in maintaining contact with both parents?

article 18

How to use the checklists, *see page XVII*

☐ When parents separate, does legislation ensure that the grounds for allocating parental responsibility are based on the individual child's best interests?
Are all parents provided with the following assistance where necessary:
    ☐ financial support?
    ☐ housing?
    ☐ appropriate child-care equipment?
    ☐ day care and respite care?
    ☐ advice and counselling?

☐ Is good quality day care available for all working parents?
☐ Are parents of disabled children provided with appropriate additional forms of assistance?
☐ Are disabled parents provided with appropriate additional forms of assistance?
☐ Are mothers entitled to maternity leave?
☐ Are fathers entitled to paternity leave?
☐ Are parents entitled to take leave if their child is sick?
☐ Does the State pay for parental leave where necessary?
☐ Does the State encourage employment conditions which assist working parents in the exercise of their parental responsibilities?

Reminder : **The Convention is indivisible and its articles are interdependent. Article 18 should not be considered in isolation.**

Particular regard should be paid to:
The general principles

Article 2: all rights to be recognized for each child in jurisdiction without discrimination on any ground
Article 3(1): the best interests of the child to be a primary consideration in all actions concerning children
Article 6: right to life and maximum possible survival and development
Article 12: respect for the child's views in all matters affecting the child; opportunity to be heard in any judicial or administrative proceedings affecting the child

Closely related articles

Articles whose implementation is related to that of article 18 include:

Article 3(2): State support for children
Article 5: parental responsibilities and child's evolving capacities
Article 9: non-separation from parents except in child's best interests
Article 10: family reunification
Article 16: protection from arbitrary interference with privacy, family and home
Article 27: duty of parents and State to secure an adequate standard of living for the child

Implementation Handbook for the Convention on the Rights of the Child

Child's right to protection from all forms of violence

article

19

Text of Article 19

1. States Parties shall take all appropriate legislative, administrative, social and educational measures to protect the child from all forms of physical or mental violence, injury or abuse, neglect or negligent treatment, maltreatment or exploitation, including sexual abuse, while in the care of parent(s), legal guardian(s) or any other person who has the care of the child.

2. Such protective measures should, as appropriate, include effective procedures for the establishment of social programmes to provide necessary support for the child and for those who have the care of the child, as well as for other forms of prevention and for identification, reporting, referral, investigation, treatment and follow-up of instances of child maltreatment described heretofore, and, as appropriate, for judicial involvement.

Article 19 goes beyond children's rights to protection from what is arbitrarily defined as "abuse" in different societies, and beyond the protection, guaranteed under article 37, from torture and cruel, inhuman or degrading treatment or punishment; article 19 requires children's protection from "all forms of physical or mental violence" while in the care of parents or others. Thus, article 19 asserts children's equal human right to physical and personal integrity. As a principle, it is linked to the right to life and to maximum survival and development guaranteed under article 6 (see page 85).

Article 19 requires states to take a variety of measures – legislative, administrative, social and educational – to protect children from all forms of violence. Paragraph 2 sets out possible protective measures, acknowledging that social and educational measures, and in particular the provision of appropriate support to children and families, are relevant to the protection of the child from violence, abuse and exploitation.

Growing awareness exists in all countries of the extent of violence against children in their homes, in institutions and in the community. Only in the last few decades has the prevalence of deliberate violence to children by parents and other caregivers been widely acknowledged. More recently "discovered" is the widespread sexual abuse of children in the family and in institutions, and also organized sexual abuse, including "sex tourism" and other forms of sexual exploitation (the obligation to protect children from sexual exploitation is further expanded in article 34, see page 455). Along with growing knowledge of the prevalence of violence to children has come growing awareness through research of its dangers and of

Summary

the links between childhood experience of violence and violent and other anti-social behaviour in childhood and later life. In the report of its General Discussion on "Children and armed conflict", the Committee drew attention to the prevention of child abuse and neglect as a "general preventive measure" which could "contribute to the prevention of the future use of violence" (*Report of second session, September-October 1992, CRC/C/10, para. 61*et seq.*).

In its examination of States Parties' reports, the Committee has frequently expressed concern at the prevalence of violence and abuse including sexual abuse, in some cases apparently increasing, and made linked recommendations for a variety of measures. In some cases the Commit-

tee has expressed concern at instances of extreme violence (also raising issues under article 6, see page 89, and article 37, page 491, and often linked to armed conflict, see article 38, page 511).

Many articles need to be considered in the light of article 19. Thus, for example, parents' responsibility to provide "appropriate direction and guidance" to children in exercising their rights under article 5 (see page 80), and the requirement of article 28(2) that school discipline is administered in accordance with the child's human dignity and in conformity with the Convention (see page 383), must both respect the obligation to protect children from "all forms of physical or mental violence". ∎

Extracts from
Committee on the Rights of the Child
Guidelines for Reports to be submitted by States Parties under the Convention

For full text of *Guidelines for Periodic Reports*, see Appendix 3, page 604.

Guidelines for Initial Reports

"Family environment and alternative care

Under this section, States Parties are requested to provide relevant information, including the principal legislative, judicial, administrative or other measures in force, particularly how the principles of the 'best interests of the child' and 'respect for the views of the child' are reflected therein; factors and difficulties encountered and progress achieved in implementing the relevant provisions of the Convention; and implementation priorities and specific goals for the future in respect of:

...

(i) Abuse and neglect (article 19), including physical and psychological recovery and social reintegration (article 39);

...

In addition, States Parties are requested to provide information on the numbers of children per year within the reporting period in each of the following groups, disaggregated by age group, sex, ethnic or national background and rural or urban environment: homeless children, abused or neglected children taken into protective custody, children placed in foster care, children placed in institutional care, children placed through domestic adoption, children entering the country through intercountry adoption procedures and children leaving the country through intercountry adoption procedures.

States Parties are encouraged to provide additional relevant statistical information and indicators relating to children covered in this section."

(CRC/C/5, paras. 16-18)

Guidelines for Periodic Reports

"V. FAMILY ENVIRONMENT AND ALTERNATIVE CARE

...

J. Abuse and neglect (art.19), including physical and psychological recovery and social reintegration (art.39)

*Please indicate all appropriate legislative, administrative, social and educational measures taken **pursuant to article 19** to protect the child from all forms of physical or mental violence, injury or abuse, neglect or negligent treatment, maltreatment or exploitation, including sexual abuse while in the care of parent(s), legal guardian(s) or any other person who has the care of the child. Reports should indicate in particular:*

Whether legislation (criminal and/or family law) includes a prohibition of all forms of physical and mental violence, including corporal punishment, deliberate humiliation, injury, abuse, neglect or exploitation, inter alia within the family, in foster and other forms of care, and in public or private institutions, such as penal institutions and schools;

Other existing legal safeguards relevant to the protection of the child as required by article 19;

Whether complaint procedures have been foreseen and the child can lodge complaints, either directly or through a representative, as well as remedies available (for example, compensation);

The procedures developed for intervention by the authorities in cases where the child requires protection from any form of violence, abuse or negligence, as required by article 19;

The educational and other measures adopted to promote positive and non-violent forms of discipline, care and treatment of the child;

Any information and awareness-raising campaigns to prevent situations of violence, abuse or negligence and to strengthen the system for the child's protection;

Any mechanisms established to monitor the extent of the forms of violence, injury or abuse, neglect, maltreatment or exploitation considered by article 19, including within the family, in institutional or other care, of a welfare, educational or penal nature, and the social and other factors contributing thereto, as well as any evaluation made of the effectiveness of the measures adopted; in this regard disaggregated data should be provided on the children concerned, including by age, gender, family situation, rural/urban, social and ethnic origin.

*With respect to **article 19, paragraph 2**, reports should also provide information inter alia on:*

Effective procedures developed for the establishment of social programmes to provide necessary support for the child and those who have the care of the child, including rehabilitation mechanisms;

Any other forms of prevention;

Effective measures adopted for the identification, reporting, referral, investigation, treatment and follow-up of instances of maltreatment covered by article 19, as well as for judicial involvement;

The existence of any system of mandatory reporting for professional groups working with and for children (for example teachers, medical doctors);

The existence of confidential help lines, advice or counselling for child victims of violence, abuse or neglect or any other form considered by article 19;

The special training provided for relevant professionals.

*Please also indicate the measures adopted **pursuant to article 39** to ensure the physical and psychological recovery and social reintegration of the child victim of any form of neglect, exploitation or abuse referred to in article 19, in an environment which fosters the health, self-respect and dignity of the child. Information should also be provided on the progress achieved, any difficulties encountered and on the targets set for the future.*

Reports should also provide information on the progress achieved in the implementation of these articles, difficulties encountered and targets set for the future."

(CRC/C/58, paras. 88-91. The following paragraphs of the *Guidelines for Periodic Reports* are also relevant to reporting under this article: 60, 61, 109, 158, 159; for full text of *Guidelines*, see Appendix 3, page 604.)

Appropriate legislative, administrative, social and educational measures to protect the child from "all forms of physical or mental violence..."

In its examination of States Parties' reports the Committee on the Rights of the Child has commented on many different forms of violence. In relation in particular to legislation, the Committee has criticized provisions that permit some level of violent punishment of children (see below, page 242). "Mental violence" includes humiliation, harassment, verbal abuse, the effects of isolation and other practices that cause or may result in psychological harm. Research provides growing evidence of the effects on children's mental health of witnessing violence – both family violence within the home and violence in the community, including armed conflict.

The Committee has expressed concern at the level of violence to children, inside and outside the home, and recommended a variety of measures to prevent it. For example:

"The Committee notes that there have been alarming tendencies in recent years on increasing problems concerning vulnerable children, such as discrimination against the girl child and sexual abuse including incest and other forms of violence perpetrated against children. In this connection, the Committee notes that there has not always been adequate enforcement of existing legislation nor have public education activities been sufficiently focused on those problems....
"The Committee encourages the Government to intensify its information and advocacy campaigns at the community and family levels. The Committee therefore suggests that efforts

should be made to widen educational campaigns to focus on gender discrimination and the role of parents, particularly with respect to the prevention of violence and abuse in the family and the problems associated with early marriage and early pregnancy." (Costa Rica IRCO, Add.11, paras. 9 and 16)

"The Committee is concerned about the lack of adequate measures taken by the authorities to evaluate and address the problem of domestic violence.
"A study on the extent and nature of domestic violence is recommended. Appropriate follow-up measures should be envisaged, not least in the field of family education and social support." (Jordan IRCO, Add.21, paras. 15 and 23)

"With respect to child abuse, including sexual abuse, the Committee is seriously alarmed by the prevalence of this type of abuse. The Committee is worried about the fact that no specific rehabilitation measures exist for abused children and that they are treated like delinquents. Corporal punishment also persists in Sri Lankan society and is accepted in schools.
"The Committee recommends that the State Party take measures to combat violence and abuse of children, including sexual abuse and corporal punishment. During the process of reviewing its law on child abuse, the State Party should carefully take into account all the provisions guaranteed by article 19 of the Convention..." (Sri Lanka IRCO, Add.40, paras. 15 and 32. See also Mongolia IRCO, Add.48, paras. 16 and 28; Morocco IRCO, Add.60, paras. 15 and 27; Slovenia IRCO, Add.65, para. 16)

During discussion of Yemen's Initial Report, a Committee member noted that "no country was free of the problem of child abuse. She would like to know whether the assertion that such abuse was not a problem in Yemen was based on research, or on the absence of complaints or reports of abuse. If in fact there were no such complaints or reports, was that because there was no abuse or because society did not concern itself with the problem, and abused children had no remedies?" (Yemen SR.263, para. 9)

"injury or abuse"
The World Health Organization has developed a protocol for the identification and recording of physical abuse (*Protocol for the Study of Interpersonal Physical Abuse of Children*, World Health Organization, 1994), and many societies have their own legal and/or administrative definitions of child abuse – physical, emotional and sexual.

"neglect or negligent treatment"
Neglect may be deliberate or it may be caused by the inability of the parent/family/commu-

---

Legislation not enough

Ethiopia's Initial Report suggests that its existing laws "are by and large compatible with article 19 of the Convention. The problem in this respect is the difficulty of implementing these laws which together with the commitment of the Government require trained manpower and an adequate institutional infrastructure for their effective implementation. In addition, resource limitations, cultural factors and lack of awareness of child rights have had a negative impact on the implementation of existing laws" (Ethiopia IR, para. 224).

nity/State to provide appropriately for the child. Child neglect exists in various forms and to varying degrees in all societies. For example, some countries with highly developed economies and social systems in which employment of women has reached almost the same level as employment of men are now preoccupied with the neglect of very young children by their working parents and with the self-reported "loneliness" of many children. The State's overall obligation to ensure to the maximum extent possible the survival and development of the child (article 6), and its specific obligations to provide appropriate assistance to parents (article 18) together with rights to health care (article 24), to benefit from social security (article 26), to an adequate standard of living (article 27) and to education (article 28) are all particularly relevant to the prevention of neglect.

Reference to "negligent treatment" raises the issue of accidents to children (also raised in article 24(2) (e), see page 328). The developmental state and physical vulnerability of children makes them particularly prone to accidents. While the primary responsibility may be that of parents, state actions are also required to prevent many types of accident. Article 3(2) gives States an over-arching obligation to provide care and protection necessary for the well-being of the child.

"maltreatment or exploitation, including sexual abuse"

The inclusion of these words and of additional articles expanding on sexual and other forms of exploitation (in particular article 32, economic exploitation, page 427; article 34, sexual exploitation, page 455; and article 36, other forms of exploitation, page 481) emphasize the intention of the drafters of the Convention to make the protection implied by article 19 comprehensive. Maltreatment or exploitation covers any other adverse treatment not necessarily involving physical or mental violence or defined as abuse. In most countries, sexual abuse is defined in most countries to include not only violent sexual assaults but also other sexual activity, consensual or not, with children regarded as immature or below a certain defined age of sexual consent. The Committee's *Guidelines* for both Initial and Periodic Reports ask for information under article 1, definition of the child, on any minimum ages for sexual consent defined in legislation; see page 9.

Article 34 emphasizes the international nature of certain kinds of sexual exploitation of children, requiring States to take all appropriate "national, bilateral and multilateral measures to prevent:

(a) The inducement or coercion of a child to engage in any unlawful sexual activity;

(b) The exploitative use of children in prostitution or other unlawful sexual practices;

(c) The exploitative use of children in pornographic performances and materials." (see page 455).

In many cases, the Committee has stressed the need for particular action to combat sexual abuse, including within the family:

"The Committee recommends that the State intensify its action against all violence directed at and ill-treatment of children, in particular sexual abuse. An increased number of programmes should aim at the prevention of sexual misbehaviour towards children. The deep causes of the phenomenon should be seriously looked at. The Committee also recommends the active participation of non-governmental organizations as well as children and youth groups in changing and influencing attitudes in that regard." (Philippines IRCO, Add.29, para. 24)

"The Committee expresses its regret that insufficient measures are being taken to address the problems of child abuse, including sexual abuse..." (Nigeria IRCO, Add.61, para. 19)

"while in the care of parent(s), legal guardian(s) or any other person who has the care of the child"

The scope of article 19 includes what happens within the family home (bearing in mind the

---

Harmful traditional beliefs

During discussions on Jamaica's Initial Report, a government representative stated that "residents of rural areas were often reluctant to report cases of sexual abuse. In some parishes, it was held that sex with a virgin cured venereal disease; that belief was sometimes responsible for the sexual abuse of very small children. Since the mother shared that belief, she would not report the abuse. Such notions, grounded in tradition, were difficult to eradicate. In any event, efforts were under way to revise sexual abuse laws, and the new legislation would in fact be gender-neutral." A Committee member stated that "conducting thorough research and analysis of harmful practices based in tradition often contributed towards reforming the culture; people could change if they were made to understand that their practices were rooted in unsound concepts." (Jamaica SR.197, para. 85)

Convention's wide definition of family; see page 77), and within other "caring" situations – foster care and day care, schools, all institutional settings and so forth. The requirement in article 3(3) for consistent standards and supervision for all institutions, services and facilities is relevant to the prevention of violence to children.

Other articles in the Convention cover in more detail the child's right to protection from forms of violence and exploitation that may take place in these settings or to protection in the wider society, for example from the effects of armed conflict:

- protection of children from traditional practices prejudicial to health (article 24(3), see also page 334);

- sexual exploitation and sexual abuse including "organized" abuse and involvement of children in prostitution and pornography (article 34, see also page 455);

- protection of children from sale, trafficking and abduction (article 35, see also page 471);

- other forms of exploitation (article 36, see also page 481);

- protection from torture and other cruel, inhuman or degrading treatment or punishment (article 37, see page 487);

- effects of armed conflict on children (article 38, see also page 511).

The Committee has also noted that violence and abuse, including within the family, often drives children from their homes:

"The Committee is seriously alarmed by the existence of child abuse (including sexual abuse) and neglect within the family, which often lead to children being abandoned or running away, thus facing the additional risks of violations of their human rights." (Philippines IRCO, Add.29, para. 13)

The child's right to protection from corporal punishment

The Committee on the Rights of the Child has indicated that the Convention on the Rights of the Child requires a review of legislation to ensure that no level of violence to children is condoned. In particular, the Committee has emphasized that corporal punishment in the family, or in schools and other institutions, or in the penal system is incompatible with the Convention.

In the official report of its seventh session in November 1994, the Committee stated:

"In the framework of its mandate, the Committee has paid particular attention to the child's right to physical integrity. In the same spirit, it has stressed that corporal punishment of children is incompatible with the Convention and has often proposed the revision of existing legislation, as well as the development of awareness and educational campaigns, to prevent child abuse and the physical punishment of children." (Report on seventh session, September-October 1994, CRC/C/34, Annex IV, p. 63)

During the Committee's discussions with Burkina Faso, one Committee member said: "In a male-dominated society such as appeared to exist in Burkina Faso, one way of encouraging beneficial change would be for leading personalities in the country, such as political leaders, publicly to make known their abhorrence of the use of violence within the home and their refusal to have recourse to it. A signal of that kind given by respected leaders could be very influential in changing entrenched traditional attitudes, in a way that legal provisions could not do. The Committee considered article 19 of the Convention, on the topic of domestic violence, of great importance in ensuring the protection of children from ill-treatment; its provisions were intended to prompt those in authority in each country to find the most effective way in their own societies to break cycles of violence that were often perpetuated from generation to generation under the cover of tradition and custom." (Burkina Faso SR.136, para. 41)

The Committee has stressed that both legislative and educational measures are needed to change attitudes and practice. It has commended States Parties that have implemented a clear prohibition of corporal punishment within the family as well as in institutions (including Austria, Sweden, Norway, Finland and Cyprus). And it has stressed that the purpose is educational rather than punitive and that such reforms tend to lead to less rather than more prosecutions of parents, because of the change in attitudes that they promote. In most, if not all, States, the law does protect children from serious physical assaults, defined as child abuse or child cruelty. But in many countries, either criminal or civil (family) law, or both, includes specific confirmation of parents', and some other caregivers' and teachers' rights to use violent forms of punishment, often with the stipulation that such punishment must be "reasonable" or "moderate". The Committee has singled out such legislation for particular criticism. Thus, when the Committee examined Spain's Initial Report, it criticized the legal framework:

"...the Committee expresses concern at the wording of article 154 of the Spanish Civil Code which provides that parents 'may administer punishment to their children

reasonably and in moderation', which may be interpreted to allow for actions in contradiction with article 19 of the Convention."

The Committee proposed clear reform:

"...the Committee encourages the Spanish authorities to pursue the law reform to ensure full compliance of the domestic legislation with the provisions of the Convention. In this regard, the Committee recommends that the law reform include the review of the language used in legal provisions and, in particular, the revision of article 154 of the Spanish Civil Code stating that parents 'may administer punishment to their children reasonably and in moderation', in order to bring it into full conformity with article 19." (Spain IRCO, Add.28, paras. 10 and 18)

Similarly, in relation to the United Kingdom's Initial Report:

"The Committee is disturbed about the reports it has received on the physical and sexual abuse of children. In this connection, the Committee is worried about the national legal provisions dealing with reasonable chastisement within the family. The imprecise nature of the expression of reasonable chastisement as contained in these legal provisions may pave the way for it to be interpreted in a subjective and arbitrary manner. Thus, the Committee is concerned that legislative and other measures relating to the physical integrity of children do not appear to be compatible with the provisions and principles of the Convention, including those of its articles 3, 19 and 37. The Committee is equally concerned that privately funded and managed schools are still permitted to administer corporal punishment to children in attendance there which does not appear to be compatible with the provisions of the Convention, including those of its article 28, paragraph 2....

"The Committee is also of the opinion that additional efforts are required to overcome the problem of violence in society. The Committee recommends that physical punishment of children in families be prohibited in the light of the provisions set out in articles 3 and 19 of the Convention. In connection with the child's right to physical integrity, as recognized by the Convention, namely in its articles 19, 28, 29 and 37, and in the light of the best interests of the child, the Committee suggests that the State Party consider the possibility of undertaking additional education campaigns. Such measures would help to change societal attitudes towards the use of physical punishment in the family and foster the acceptance of the legal prohibition of the physical punishment of children." (UK IRCO, Add.34, paras. 16 and 31)

In a concluding statement to the General Discussion on "Children's Rights in the Family", orga-

Sweden's ban on all corporal punishment

Sweden's Initial Report notes: "The basic rights of the child are stated in the Code of Parenthood and Guardianship, chapter 6, section 1 of which lays down as follows: 'A child is entitled to care, security and a good upbringing. A child shall be treated with respect for his person and individuality and may not be subjected to corporal punishment or any other offensive treatment...'" (Sweden IR, para. 52)

nized as the Committee's contribution to the International Year of the Family in October 1994, a Committee member stated, "As for corporal punishment, few countries have clear laws on this question. Certain States have tried to distinguish between the correction of children and excessive violence. In reality the dividing line between the two is artificial. It is very easy to pass from one stage to the other. It is also a question of principle. If it is not permissible to beat an adult, why should it be permissible to do so to a child? One of the contributions of the Convention is to call attention to the contradictions in our attitudes and cultures" (CRC/C/SR.176, 10 October 1994, para. 46).

The Official Report of the Committee's discussion with government representatives about the United Kingdom's Initial Report records that a member of the Committee said: "It was the Committee's experience that difficulties arose whenever a 'reasonable' level of corporal punishment was permitted under a State's internal law. To draw an analogy, no one would argue that a 'reasonable' level of wife-beating should be permitted. His conclusion was that the United Kingdom position represented a vestige of the outdated view that children were in a sense their parents' chattels. In the Scandinavian countries and Austria, stricter legislation had resulted in fewer cases going to court than in the United Kingdom, rather than the reverse. Furthermore, he noted from recent press reports that some judges tended to interpret the legislation fairly liberally: one, for example, had ruled that 15 lashes administered with a leather belt did not constitute excessive punishment. The notion of a permissible level of corporal punishment was thus best avoided." (UK SR.205, para. 63)

The United Kingdom's Initial Report had defended the concept of "reasonable chastisement": "In the United Kingdom Government's view article 19 has to be read in conjunction with article 5 which obliges States to respect a parent's responsibilities to provide appropriate direction and guidance in the exercise by the child of the rights recognized in the present Convention. The Government's view is that appropriate direction and guidance include the administration, by the parent, of reasonable and moderate physical chastisement to a child... Excessive punishment amounting to abuse is, of course, a criminal offence, and so it must remain." (UK IR, para. 335-336)

But in discussion with United Kingdom government representatives, a Committee member stated: "...with regard to corporal punishment within the family the United Kingdom delegation had stated that it was not appropriate to regulate what should be a private matter by means of legislation. It must be borne in mind, however, that article 19 of the Convention required all appropriate measures, including legislative measures, to be taken to protect the child against, *inter alia*, physical violence. A way should thus be found of striking the balance between the responsibilities of the parents and the rights and evolving capacities of the child that was implied in article 5 of the Convention. There was no place for corporal punishment within the margin of discretion accorded in article 5 to parents in the exercise of their responsibilities. Other countries had found it helpful to incorporate a provision to that effect in their civil law..." (UK SR.205, para. 72)

In discussion with Argentina, a Committee member noted "...a slight reservation seemed to have been expressed concerning the extent of the prohibition of (physical) punishment, it being felt that punishment should not exceed certain limits. That seemed to imply that some measure of corporal punishment was permitted. The Committee had in the past discussed that matter with a number of States Parties and drawn the conclusion that, given the categorical wording of article 19 of the Convention, any attempt to define a middle path, by determining how much corporal punishment might be administered to a child, might in some cases serve as an invitation to administer such punishment. Further clarification in the light of article 19 would therefore be welcome."

An Argentinean government representative responded that physical or mental punishment or treatment that showed disrespect for the child was not permitted. The Committee member asked "whether it was permitted by law to hit children, in the civil context of the family. He believed it was important to have a clear legal prohibition, not for purposes of prosecution but to give a signal to society that children should not be subjected to ill-treatment by bigger and older people." The government representative responded: "The 1985 revision of article 268 of the Civil Code prohibited any kind of physical punishment of children. The slightest injury was punishable as an offence. He agreed, however, that from the point of view of the family the message was more important than the penalty, namely, that parents must not exercise their parental and child-rearing function through violence. Nevertheless, family violence did occur and many of the institutions involved in trying to solve the problem were pressing for specific legislation on violence within the family." (Argentina SR.179, paras. 4, 10, 16 and 22)

In its Concluding Observations, the Committee recommended

"...that the State Party considers the possibility of introducing more effective legislation and follow-up mechanisms to prevent violence within the family in the spirit of article 19." (Argentina IRCO, Add.35, para. 20)

During discussion with Germany, a Committee member noted Germany's intention to amend the Civil Code to make a clearer distinction between disciplinary measures that were permitted and those that were prohibited: "However, some countries had found, in attempting to make that distinction, that a certain subjective element was unavoidable. Would it not be preferable simply to prohibit any form of corporal punishment by parents, while at the same time educating them in the use of non-violent alternatives?" (Germany SR.244, para. 66)

The Committee went on to recommend:

"The Committee encourages the State Party to pursue its efforts towards changing attitudes with a view to eradicating all forms of violence against children, including the use of corporal punishment within the family. In this regard, it further encourages that, in the ongoing process of reform of the Civil Code, consideration be given to the incorporation of an absolute ban on corporal punishment." (Germany IRCO, Add.43, para. 30)

During discussion with a Jamaican representative, a member of the Committee suggested that "it would also be useful if the word 'excessive' could be removed from the term 'excessive punishment' in the legislation on the ill-treatment of children" (Jamaica SR.197, para. 7).

The Committee noted another exception allowing for physical punishment in Ethiopia:

"The Committee notes with concern the non-compatibility of certain provisions of domestic law with the principles and rights enshrined in

the Convention, such as ... the provision in the Penal Code for the possibility to sentence children to corporal punishment, [and] the provision in the Civil Code for 'light bodily punishment' as an educative measure within the family....
"...The Committee particularly recommends that ... the sentencing of children to corporal punishment, (and) the 'light bodily punishment' as an educational measure within the family ... be abolished as a matter of priority." (Ethiopia IRCO, Add.67, paras. 13 and 27)

The implication reflected in national attitudes or legislation, that the use of some level of corporal punishment may be in the interests of children, has been dismissed by the Committee in other comments:

"...Abandonment of children, the high rate of child headed families and the persistence of corporal punishment, widely envisaged by parents and teachers as an educational measure, are other subjects of concern to the Committee....
"...The Committee particularly recommends that legislative measures be adopted with a view to ... clearly prohibiting any form of corporal punishment..." (Republic of Korea IRCO, Add.51, paras. 15 and 22)

"...The Committee also expresses its concern at section 7 of the Children's Act which allows parents, members of the family and teachers to beat a child 'if it is thought to be in the interest of the child'...
"The Committee is concerned that appropriate measures have not yet been taken to effectively prevent and combat any form of ill-treatment and corporal punishment of children within the family..." (Nepal IRCO, Add.57, paras. 12 and 19)

To all the States Parties referred to above and to many other countries, the Committee has called for a clear prohibition of all corporal punishment – in the family, in other forms of care, in schools and in the penal system – and has proposed legal reform should be coupled with education campaigns in positive discipline to support parents, teachers and others. For example:

"The Committee expresses its concern at the acceptance in the legislation of the use of corporal punishment in school, as well as within the family. It stresses the incompatibility of corporal punishment, as well as any other form of violence, injury, neglect, abuse or degrading treatment, with the provisions of the Convention, in particular articles 19, 28 paragraph 2 and 37...
"The Committee recommends that the State Party adopt appropriate legislative measures to forbid the use of any form of corporal punishment within the family and in school."

(Zimbabwe IRCO, Add.55, paras. 18 and 31. See also: France IRCO, Add.20, para. 24; Honduras IRCO, Add.24, para. 27; Poland IRCO, Add.31, para. 30; Jamaica IRCO, Add.32. para. 7; Canada IRCO, Add.37, para. 25; Belgium IRCO, Add.38, para. 15; Tunisia IRCO, Add.39, para. 17; Sri Lanka IRCO, Add.40, para. 32; Italy IRCO, Add.41, para. 20; Ukraine IRCO, Add.42, para. 29; Senegal IRCO, Add.44, para. 24; Portugal IRCO, Add.45, para. 23; Lebanon IRCO, Add.54, para. 37; Guatemala IRCO, Add.58, para. 33; Morocco IRCO, Add.60, para. 27; UK dependent territory: Hong Kong IRCO, Add.63, para. 27; Mauritius IRCO, Add.64, para. 31; Bulgaria IRCO, Add.66, para. 30; Panama IRCO, Add.68, para. 30; Syrian Arab Republic IRCO, Add.70, para. 28; New Zealand IRCO, Add.71, para. 29)

The Committee's *Guidelines for Periodic Reports* asks "whether legislation (criminal and/or family law) includes a prohibition of all forms of physical and mental violence, including corporal punishment, deliberate humiliation, injury, abuse, neglect or exploitation, *inter alia* within the family, in foster and other forms of care, and in public or private institutions, such as penal institutions and schools" (para. 88).

In General Comments in 1982 and 1992, the Human Rights Committee, which oversees implementation of the International Covenant on Civil and Political Rights, states that the ban on inhuman or degrading treatment or punishment in article 7 of the Covenant includes corporal punishment: "In the Committee's view, moreover, the prohibition must extend to corporal punishment, including excessive chastisement ordered as punishment for a crime or as an educative or disciplinary measure. It is appropriate to emphasize in this regard that article 7 protects, in particular, children, pupils and patients in teaching and medical institutions" (Human Rights Committee, General Comment 20, HRI/GEN/1/Rev.2, p. 31; see also Human Rights Committee, General Comment 7, which it replaced: HRI/GEN/1/Rev.2, p. 7).

Violence, including corporal punishment, in institutions

Initial Reports to the Committee from various countries have raised the problem of violence to children in institutions, which can take two particular forms:

● "legalized" use (or continued use despite prohibition) of violent and/or humiliating discipline or treatment such as physical punishment, physical restraint, solitary confinement and other forms of isolation, obligations to wear distinctive clothing, reduction of diet, restriction or denial of contact with family members and/or friends, verbal abuse or sarcasm and so on;

- violence, or threats of violence, by children against children, termed "bullying" or "mobbing" in some societies, which can range from teasing and harassment (commonly including racial and sexual harassment) to serious physical assault.

Article 3(3) requires that "institutions, services and facilities responsible for the care or protection of children shall conform with the standards established by competent authorities, particularly in the areas of safety, health, in the number and suitability of their staff, as well as competent supervision". In relation to protection from violence, there should be clear standards established in legislation:

- prohibiting physical punishment and any other inhuman or degrading treatment or punishment (in addition, rules should specify the prohibition of any forms of inhuman or degrading discipline or treatment known to be commonly used);

- requiring clear policies for the prevention of any forms of violence by children against children in institutions;

- ensuring there are clear and well-publicized procedures to enable children to seek confidential advice and to make representations and complaints about their treatment to an independent body with appropriate powers of investigation and recommendation/action. Such procedures should ensure that where necessary children have access to independent advocates or representatives who can advise them and/or act on their behalf; special arrangements may be required to safeguard disabled children (see Standard Rules on the Equalization of Opportunities for Persons with Disabilities, rule 9(4)) and very young children.

In relation to schools, article 28(2) requires that "States Parties shall take all appropriate measures to ensure that school discipline is administered in a manner consistent with the child's human dignity and in conformity with the present Convention". As the Committee has stressed, this includes conformity with article 19, and the protection of children from "all forms of physical or mental violence". Physical punish-

ment and other humiliating punishments amounting to mental violence are thus outlawed. Wherever the reporting process under the Convention has revealed the continued existence of school corporal punishment, the Committee has proposed its abolition (see also article 28, page 383).

In some legal systems, teachers' and other caregivers' existing rights to use physical punishment are derived from their position *in loco parentis*. In others, the independent authority of teachers and others outside the family to use such punishment is explicitly confirmed in the law. Legal reform proposed by the Committee to prohibit physical punishment and other humiliating treatment of children must of course protect all children in all settings – in the home, in other informal settings, in non-institutionalized forms of care (foster care, day care and so forth), and in all institutions.

Corporal punishment in juvenile justice systems

The Committee's examination of States Parties' Initial Reports has found that in some corporal punishment persists as a sentence of the courts for under 18-year-olds. This raises an issue under article 37 as well as article 19, and also conflicts with the United Nations rules and guidelines relating to juvenile justice, which the Committee has consistently promoted as providing relevant standards (see box opposite).

In 1994, an "Expert group meeting on children and juveniles in detention: application of human rights standards" included in its recommendations: "We urge States to adopt all necessary measures to prevent, forbid and eliminate the use of corporal punishment against children" (E/CN.4/1995/100, para. 29).

The Committee on the Rights of the Child has expressed concern at and proposed a ban on corporal punishment in the penal system:

"The Committee notes the non-compatibility of certain areas of national legislation with the provisions and principles of the Convention, including the punishment of flogging."

"The Committee expresses the hope that the review of child-related laws will result in the total abolition of flogging." (Sudan Prelim. Obs., Add.6, para. 7; Sudan IRCO, Add.10, para. 17)

"The Committee is concerned at the present system of juvenile justice, including the lack of a clear legal prohibition of capital punishment, life imprisonment without possibility of release and indeterminate sentencing, as well as at the recourse to whipping as a disciplinary measure for boys." (Zimbabwe IRCO, Add.55, para. 21)

Kindergarten ban in China

In China, school corporal punishment has long been prohibited, and the kindergarten regulations state: "Corporal punishment and disguised corporal punishment of children is strictly prohibited" (China IR, para. 103-104).

Implementation Handbook for the Convention on the Rights of the Child

Corporal punishment and juvenile justice standards

United Nations Standard Minimum Rules for the Administration of Juvenile Justice, the "Beijing Rules": Rule 17.3 (Guiding Principles in Adjudication and Disposition) states: "Juveniles shall not be subject to corporal punishment."

United Nations Rules for the Protection of Juveniles Deprived of their Liberty: Rule 67 states: "...all disciplinary measures constituting cruel, inhumane or degrading treatment shall be strictly prohibited, including corporal punishment..."

United Nations Guidelines for the Prevention of Juvenile Delinquency, the "Riyadh Guidelines": Paragraph 21(h) states that education systems should devote particular attention to "avoidance of harsh disciplinary measures, particularly corporal punishment" and paragraph 54 says "No child or young person should be subjected to harsh or degrading correction or punishment measures at home, in schools or in any other institutions."

The Commission on Crime Prevention and Criminal Justice adopted a resolution in April 1994 specifically stressing the importance of article 19 of the Convention and called on States to take all possible steps to eliminate violence against children in accordance with the Convention (Report on the seventh session, September-October 1994, CRC/C/34, p. 63).

Traditional practices involving violence and/or prejudicial to health

The specific reference to protecting children from traditional practices comes in article 24(3), which obliges States to "take all effective and appropriate measures with a view to abolishing traditional practices prejudicial to the health of children" (see page 334 for further discussion). But traditional practices also need to be reviewed to determine whether they involve any form of physical or mental violence from which children must be protected under article 19.

Suicide and self-harm

Protecting children from self-harm, including suicide and attempted suicide, clearly comes within the ambit of article 19, and also of article 6. Increases in the suicide rate among certain age groups of children in some industrialized countries has caused concern to the Committee, which has proposed research and further action (see article 6, page 92 for further discussion).

Violent images

Concern at the levels of interpersonal violence in Western societies has led to a particular focus on the effect that violent images in the media – in particular on television, in videos and those most recent computer-generated ones – may have on children. The concern is both that frequent exposure to such images may desensitize children to violence, and that they may be encouraged to imitate particular violent behaviour. Article 17(e) requires States Parties to "encourage the development of appropriate guidelines for the protection of the child from information and material injurious to his or her well-being, bearing in mind the provisions of articles 13 and 18" (see article 17, page 218 for further discussion).

Protective and preventive measures: article 19(2)

The second paragraph of article 19 provides a non-exhaustive list of measures that States should take to protect children and to prevent violence.

"...effective procedures for the establishment of social programmes to provide necessary support for the child and for those who have the care of the child, as well as for other forms of prevention..."

These words emphasize the relevance of social conditions to the protection of children from violence and, in particular, to the protection from neglect and negligent treatment, and they link article 19 with other relevant provisions in the Convention on the Rights of the Child, including the overall duty in article 4 (to implement measures "to the maximum extent of available resources"), article 18 (the obligation of States Parties to render appropriate assistance to parents in the performance of their child-rearing responsibilities, and to ensure the development of institutions, facilities and services for the care of children), article 26 (the right of children to benefit from social security) and article 27 (the right of the child to an adequate standard of living).

Specific social programmes promoted by the Committee in its comments on Initial Reports include education/information campaigns on positive non-violent forms of discipline, on the prevention of sexual abuse and exploitation, and on the protection of children from ill-treatment in alternative care and institutions:

Preventing abuse in Sweden

Sweden's Initial Report notes "The best protection against the abuse of children is, of course, to make it easier for parents to be good parents and in this way to prevent the child being neglected and abused. Parental education has an important role to play here, as have various primary and secondary measures of prevention. Open preschool also plays an important part in this connection. The expansion of open preschool has meant the creation, in growing numbers of housing areas, of natural meeting points for parents of very young children... Sweden also has non-institutional mental care services for children and young persons, to which parents and children can turn for support and treatment..." (Sweden IR, para. 127).

"The Committee suggests that measures be adopted by the State Party to provide appropriate assistance to the family in the performance of its child-rearing responsibilities, with a view, inter alia, to preventing domestic violence and abuse, abandonment and institutionalization of children, and to promoting research in these areas." (Uruguay IRCO, Add.62, para. 21)

"Despite the recent increase in the number of social workers employed for child abuse cases, it is the view of the Committee that the caseload of each professional may still be too high and the question of taking additional action to address such matters deserves further study. The Committee encourages the efforts made to accord high priority to and pursue more intensely the establishment of day care

centres in the community, including as a measure to prevent children being left unattended at home. In addition, the Committee encourages the initiative taken to ensure within future reviews of the Family Life Education Programme an assessment of its effectiveness in preventing child abuse." (UK dependent territory: Hong Kong IRCO, Add.63, para. 28)

Many countries have appointed committees or commissions to advise on the prevention of child abuse and other forms of violence, producing recommendations that range over the entire area of social action. In several cases, the Committee has proposed comprehensive studies:

"The Committee suggests that research be undertaken on the issue of child abuse and neglect within the family." (Romania IRCO, Add.16, para. 16)

"A study on the extent and nature of domestic violence is recommended. Appropriate follow-up measures should be envisaged, not least in the field of family education and social support." (Jordan IRCO, Add.21, para. 23)

"In the light of article 19 of the Convention, the Committee further recommends that the Government take all appropriate measures, including of a legislative nature, to combat any form of ill-treatment and sexual abuse of children, including within the family. It suggests, inter alia, that the authorities gather information and initiate a comprehensive study to improve the understanding of the nature and scope of the problem and set up social programmes to prevent all types of child abuse and neglect." (Nepal IRCO, Add.57, para. 34; see also Cyprus IRCO, Add.59, para. 29)

"identification"

A long history exists of denial by adult societies of the extent of violence to children. The first

Improving protection

In Spain, the Office for Juridical Protection of Minors of the Ministry of Social Affairs has launched a project to improve protection of socially disadvantaged children. Its objectives are:

- to facilitate the detection of cases of ill-treatment and/or abandonment and interchange of information on them between professionals and sectors;
- to facilitate the taking of decisions adjusted to the urgency of care and the type of measure to be adopted;
- to facilitate the taking of decisions in situations of presumed need to separate the child from its family;
- to determine the differential impact of the various social measures used on children who have suffered ill-treatment and/or been abandoned;
- to guide the training of the various professionals working in the child protection field.

The Office has also designed data-collection sheets and instruction manuals for use in cases of ill-treatment of children, for the various professional groups involved. (Spain IR, paras. 164 and 165)

step towards effective prevention of violence must be to ensure that all those in contact with children are alerted to the various forms of violence to children and the likely indications of it and that they are informed about appropriate action in conformity with the principles of the Convention. Public information campaigns to increase overall awareness of violence to children are essential and have been proposed by the Committee to many States Parties. For example:

"With reference to the implementation of article 19 of the Convention and the efforts required to prevent and combat the abuse of children, the Committee recommends that consideration be given to the elaboration of a comprehensive and integrated public information campaign, to the undertaking of a review of the national legislative measures in this field and their compliance with the Convention's provisions, as well as to the further development of training programmes for professionals involved in this field of work." (Federal Republic of Yugoslavia IRCO, Add.49, para. 35)

"reporting"

In many countries there are legal obligations to report instances, and/or suspicion of child abuse to appropriate social authorities and/or the police. In some societies, these duties apply to certain professions only (for example, social workers, teachers, doctors and other health workers); in others, they apply to members of the public as well. The Committee's *Guidelines for Periodic Reports* (para. 89) asks for information on "The existence of any system of mandatory reporting for professional groups working with and for children (for example teachers, medical doctors)."

Mandatory reporting also raises potential conflicts with the child's right to confidential advice and counselling, from doctors and others (see article 1, page 7; article 12, page 161; and article 16, page 199). Do children have a right to a completely confidential relationship with, for example, their doctor, lawyer, priest or religious elder? Article 12 suggests that children should have a right to express their views and have them taken seriously in any action proposed or taken in relation to violence towards them, and a formal right to be heard in any administrative procedures. Article 16 asserts the child's right to privacy, which is relevant to the child's right to confidential advice and counselling (see page 199).

Frequently, the Committee has called for children to have access to complaints procedures, including to enable them to report ill-treatment (see below, under "Investigation", page 250).

Need for legal basis for reporting

Social interventions against child abuse and neglect in Korea are at the initial stage of "finding out" according to the Initial Report: "Specialized and active intervention for the prevention and treatment of child abuse by professional personnel has not developed, due to the lack of a legal device to enable professional intervention. Above all, legal institutionalization of reporting child abuse is necessary as the first step towards solving the problem." (Republic of Korea IR, para. 103)

The Committee has noted the traditional attitudes and fears that can deter reporting by both women and children and has proposed awareness-raising and training for those who receive such reports. During discussions with representatives of Jordan, a Committee member acknowledged that social pressures often forced women to keep silent about violence to themselves and their children, since complaints were considered a violation of the privacy of the home and family; the member said "that such assumptions were often shared by the police and the judiciary. In order to change such traditional attitudes and achieve recognition of the fact that treating domestic violence as a private family matter merely tended to perpetuate it, efforts should not only be made to create awareness among the general public but such matters should also be dealt with in the training given to law enforcement officials and the judiciary. The enactment of legislation was not in itself enough to change social realities." (Jordan SR.144, para. 56)

During discussions with Mongolia, a Committee member stated "that there were many countries where information was lacking on acts of violence committed against children within the family. Most often, the members of a family who were victims of such violence remained silent. It was important to do preventive work and to organize public awareness campaigns, in the spirit of article 19 of the Convention." (Mongolia SR.266, para. 12)

In some instances, children and others may face reprisals for reporting:

"The Committee is concerned about the problems associated with ill-treatment, abuse and violence directed towards children in school and in the family, which is reinforced by social custom. In this connection, the Committee notes with concern that child abuse has not

yet been clearly addressed, that adequate legal remedies for abused children do not exist and that there are inadequate safeguards against reprisals against children who report abuse." (Madagascar IRCO, Add.26, para. 11)

"The Committee is deeply concerned about the problems of abuse and violence which persist in the family and society in general. In view of this reality, the adequacy of measures to prevent such abuse and violence, to respond to children's reports of their abuse, to safeguard children who report abuse and to prevent the impunity of those who have committed abuse against children, remain a matter of considerable concern to the Committee." (Nicaragua IRCO, Add.36, para. 22)

"...Finally, the Committee recommends that measures be taken fully to protect professionals who report evidence of sexual abuse to the relevant authorities." (Finland IRCO, Add.53, para. 29)

"referral"

The implication of referral is that the investigation and treatment of violence to children is an issue requiring specialized, trained responses. In systems that require the reporting of child abuse, referral to particular agencies is normally specified, and in many countries there are now detailed administrative procedures for inter-agency collaboration (between social services, education, health, police and prosecution authorities, and including voluntary and private agencies). Such procedures for referral should be in conformity with the Convention, and in particular with article 12.

The Committee has welcomed inter-agency cooperation in child protection:

"... the Committee is encouraged by the steps taken to address the issue of sexual abuse of children, including through the development of the 'Working Together' initiative which advocates and promotes an interdisciplinary approach to addressing this serious problem." (UK IRCO, Add.34, para. 4)

"investigation"

The State should clearly have formal duties, exercised through one or more agencies, to investigate reported instances or allegations of violence to children, in conformity with the Convention's principles.

The *Guidelines for Periodic Reports* asks: "Whether complaints procedures have been foreseen and the child can lodge complaints, either directly or through a representative, as well as remedies available (for example, compensation)" (para. 88). In addition, the *Guidelines* asks for information under article 1 (definition of the child) on "the minimum legal age

defined by national legislation" for "Lodging complaints and seeking redress before a court or other relevant authority without parental consent" (para. 24).

A Committee member noted during discussion of Senegal's Initial Report that the fact that children were not entitled to lodge complaints of abuse was a serious cause of concern "since the child must be treated as a full-fledged subject of law and given the necessary means of defending himself against abuse" (Senegal SR.248, para. 74). The Committee has consistently urged States Parties to develop appropriate complaints procedures to receive complaints from children and others about ill-treatment and other issues, including within the family (see also article 12, page 155):

"The Committee is concerned about the occurrence of maltreatment and cruelty towards children in and outside the family and suggests that procedures and mechanisms be developed to deal with complaints by children of their maltreatment or of cruelty towards them." (Russian Federation IRCO, Add.4, para. 21)

"With reference to the implementation of article 19 of the Convention, the Committee recommends that a system of complaints aimed at children victim of any form of violence, abuse, including sexual abuse, neglect, maltreatment or exploitation, even while in the care of their parents, be established, as a means to ensure protection of and respect for their rights..." (Ethiopia IRCO, Add.67, para. 31. See also Pakistan IRCO, Add.18, para. 28; Burkina Faso IRCO, Add.19, para. 9; China IRCO, Add.56, para. 33)

Under article 6, the Committee has drawn attention to the importance of full investigation of all child deaths (see *Guidelines for Periodic Reports*, para. 41). In countries where a rigorous procedure for such investigations has been implemented, it is less likely that preventable violence to children will go undetected (for discussion, see article 6, page 93).

"treatment and follow-up"

Again, these are specialized functions requiring appropriate training and interdisciplinary cooperation. In addition to the child's rights to health care and relevant services, two other articles of the Convention are relevant:

● the right to periodic review of care and treatment guaranteed by article 25: "States Parties recognize the right of a child who has been placed by the competent authorities for the purposes of care, protection or treatment of his or her physical or mental health to a periodic review of the treatment provided to the child and all other circumstances relevant to his or her placement" (see page 341);

● the obligation to provide rehabilitation for victims, under article 39: "States Parties shall take all appropriate measures to promote physical and psychological recovery and social reintegration of a child victim of: any form of neglect, exploitation, or abuse; torture or any other form of cruel, inhuman or degrading treatment or punishment; or armed conflicts. Such recovery and reintegration shall take place in an environment which fosters the health, self-respect and dignity of the child" (see page 529).

"and, as appropriate, judicial involvement"

The appropriateness, or otherwise, of judicial involvement over instances of violence to children depends on the type and severity of the violence and on the consideration of the Convention's general principles.

The Committee has in some cases expressed concern that lack of prosecution may lead to a feeling of impunity:

"The Committee is also preoccupied by the level of violence and the high incidence of ill-treatment and abuse of children, including cases attributed to the police or military personnel. It notes with concern that the efforts of the Government to combat child abuse and neglect are insufficient, both from the prevention and the sanction point of view... The failure to take effective steps to prosecute and punish those responsible for such violations or to make public decisions taken in this regard, including towards paedophiles, may lead to a feeling in the population that impunity prevails and that it is therefore useless to bring complaints before the competent authorities." (Philippines IRCO, Add.29, para. 14)

In other cases the Committee has generally called for more effective legislation:

"The Committee suggests that the State Party considers the possibility of introducing more effective legislation and follow-up mechanisms to prevent violence within the family in the spirit of article 19." (Argentina IRCO, Add.35, para. 20)

"The Committee welcomes the policy of not allowing corporal punishment in schools or other official institutions and recommends a thorough review of the problem of domestic violence, including the possibility of stricter legislation against all forms of abuse against children in the spirit of article 19 of the Convention, as well as supportive social measures to assist families in crisis." (Lebanon IRCO, Add.54, para. 37)

There are two distinct forms of judicial involvement: to prosecute the perpetrator under the criminal law and to protect the child through various forms of supervision, removal of the perpetrator or placement of the child away from home. In regard to the latter, article 9(1) requires that a child "shall not be separated from his or her parents against their will, except when competent authorities subject to judicial review determine, in accordance with applicable law and procedures, that such separation is necessary for the best interests of the child" (see also page 124). Article 9 indicates in paragraph 1 that one of the circumstances in which such separation may be necessary is a case involving abuse or neglect of a child by his or her parents. When one parent is the alleged abuser, article 9 requires efforts to prevent separation of the child from the other parent.

The Committee has also indicated that the child may suffer from judicial involvement. For example, during discussion of the Initial Report of the Russian Federation, a Committee member was reported as suggesting: "In connection with one particular area of concern which had been raised in the list of issues – that of the increasing number of children suffering from ill-treatment, cruelty and humiliation – she observed that legal measures alone were not sufficient. She had noted that it was intended to strengthen penalties in this respect, but it should be recalled that article 19 placed considerable emphasis on the need for prevention. It might therefore be possible to consider the steps to be taken in order to change attitudes and introduce preventive measures. It would also be interesting to see what role children themselves could play in that respect." (Russian Federation SR.62, para. 42)

While discussing Ukraine's Initial Report, a Committee member noted that the report referred to deprivation of parental rights of persons who mistreated their children or inflicted corporal punishment on them: "In fact, there was no need to adopt such drastic solutions for every case. In his opinion, what the Committee had in mind was a clear signal from the relevant legislation that ill-treatment of children should never take place. If it did occur, the solution in all cases might not be for the child to be taken away from the parents. That might also be contrary to the best interests of the child. Efforts should rather be made to solve the problem within the family, if possible" (Ukraine IR, para. 65).

In deciding whether judicial involvement is appropriate the Convention's general principles come into play, in particular the "best interests" principle (article 3), the right of the child to life

Child abuse victims as witnesses

Legislation in Hong Kong provides for court cases to be given priority in the listings if they involve child abuse victims who have to appear as witnesses: "This facilitates better recall of the events, minimizes trauma and stress and reduces the likelihood of distress. If a delay is unavoidable, a written deposition may be taken from the child by a magistrate". In addition, there are special arrangements for witnesses aged under 14, or under 17 in sexual abuse cases; testimony may be given through closed circuit television from a place outside the courtroom by way of a video-recording of an interview, provided that the witness is available for cross-examination afterwards at the trial (or by a written deposition taken by a magistrate). In addition, the prosecution may issue a notice of transfer to bypass the preliminary hearing before a magistrate and enable the matter to go directly to full trial (UK dependent territory: Hong Kong IR, paras. 60, 34 and 35).

and maximum development (article 6), and the participation of the child in decision-making (article 12). For example:

"It is also the view of the Committee that the best interests of the child should prevail in proceedings concerning child victims of parental abuse, especially in deciding whether parents have the right to represent their child in such cases..." (Nigeria IRCO, Add.61, para. 40)

Recent developments have taken place in a number of countries to safeguard the welfare of child witnesses in cases involving prosecution of adult perpetrators of violence. These include less formal courts and opportunities for children's evidence to be pre-recorded or for children to give evidence or be cross-examined behind screens or through video links. Such provisions are justified in terms of the welfare and best interests of the child but must also comply with the rights of the adult defendants as set out in international law.

The Committee has noted that violations of children's rights under article 19 and other provisions of the Convention should not be investigated by military courts:

"...Violations of human rights and children's rights should always be examined by civilian courts under civilian law, not military courts. The outcome of investigations and cases of convictions should be widely publicized in order to deter future offences and thus combat the perception of impunity." (Colombia IRCO, Add.30, para. 17)

Special training

In addition to its general call for all those working with or for children to receive training in the principles and provisions of the Convention (see article 42, page 561), the Committee has proposed special training in relation to child protection, and the *Guidelines for Periodic Reports* asks for information on "the special training provided for relevant professionals" (para. 89):

"The Committee also recommends that the State Party should develop awareness-raising and training programmes to combat violence against children and prevent their abuse, neglect, abandonment and ill-treatment. Such programmes should be addressed to, inter alia, parents, teachers and law enforcement officials..." (Pakistan IRCO, Add.18, para 28)

"The Committee recommends that the Government of the State Party consider pursuing the measures adopted to fight situations of child ill-treatment. It stresses the importance of ensuring training activities for the professional groups concerned, as well as of developing mediation measures." (Chile IRCO, Add.22, para. 16; see also Mauritius IRCO, Add.64, para. 27)

In its recommendations to Nicaragua, the Committee emphasized the importance of using training to encourage children to defend their own rights, including rights to protection from violence and abuse, proposing

"that the State Party consider using the Convention as a tool for the prevention of violence and abuse. One way to achieve this, the Committee suggests, is by teaching children to defend their rights and for trained individuals working with and for children to transmit the values of the Convention to children. Thus, the Committee recommends that education about the Convention be incorporated into non-formal and formal educational curricula and into training and retraining programmes for professionals working with or for children, including teachers, health workers, social workers, judges and law enforcement officials." (Nicaragua IRCO, Add.36, para. 30)

Implementation Checklist

● *General measures of implementation*

Have appropriate general measures of implementation been taken in relation to article 19 including

☐ identification and coordination of the responsible departments and agencies at all levels of government (article 19 is relevant to **departments of social welfare, justice, health, education**)?

☐ identification of relevant non-governmental organizations/civil society partners?

☐ a comprehensive review to ensure that all legislation, policy and practice is compatible with the article, for all children in all parts of the jurisdiction?

☐ adoption of a strategy to secure full implementation

    ☐ which includes where necessary the identification of goals and indicators of progress?

    ☐ which does not affect any provisions which are more conducive to the rights of the child?

    ☐ which recognizes other relevant international standards?

    ☐ which involves where necessary international cooperation?

(Such measures may be part of an overall governmental strategy for implementing the Convention as a whole).

☐ budgetary analysis and allocation of necessary resources?

☐ development of mechanisms for monitoring and evaluation?

☐ making the implications of article 19 widely known to adults and children?

☐ development of appropriate training and awareness-raising (in relation to article 19 likely to include the training of **all those working in child protection or with or for children and their families, and in parenting education**)?

● *Specific issues in implementing article 19*

☐ Does legislation in the State protect children from all forms of physical or mental violence?

☐ Are there no exceptions or defences available to parents or others in relation to assaults on children?

Does legislation protect all children from any form of corporal punishment

    ☐ in the home?

    in schools

        ☐ state run?

        ☐ private?

in child-care institutions
- ☐ state run?
- ☐ private?
- ☐ in foster care?
- ☐ in other forms of alternative care?

in day care institutions
- ☐ state run?
- ☐ private?
- ☐ other arrangements (e.g. childminding etc.)?

in the penal system
- ☐ as a sentence of the courts?
- ☐ as a punishment in penal institutions?

Does legislation, policy and practice protect all children from
- ☐ ill-treatment and violence, including violence by other children, in schools and all other institutions?
- ☐ traditional practices involving physical or mental violence, or prejudicial to health?

☐ Has the State taken appropriate measures to prevent all forms of violence to children?

Has the State taken appropriate educational and other measures to promote positive, non-violent forms of discipline and treatment
- ☐ in the family?
- ☐ in alternative care?
- ☐ in all institutions which include children?

Do all children in the State have access to effective complaints procedures in relation to ill-treatment
- ☐ while in the care of parents or others legally responsible for them?
- ☐ in all forms of alternative care?
- ☐ in all institutions including schools and custodial institutions?

☐ In cases of ill-treatment, do children have a right to appropriate remedies, including, for example, compensation?

Does legislation in the State require the reporting of all forms of violence and abuse of children to appropriate bodies
- ☐ by certain professional groups?
- ☐ by all citizens?

☐ Have any reporting arrangements/requirements been reviewed in the light of the Convention's principles, including article 12 (respect for the views of the child) and article 16 (the child's right to privacy)?

How to use the checklists, *see page XVII*

Has the State established effective systems for
- [ ] identification of violence, abuse, etc.?
- [ ] reporting?
- [ ] referral?
- [ ] investigation?
- [ ] treatment and follow-up?
- [ ] appropriate judicial involvement?

- [ ] Has the State taken particular measures to identify and respond to sexual abuse within the family and in institutions?
- [ ] Has the State ensured that the principle of respect for the views of the child is observed in child protection procedures and practice?
- [ ] Has the State taken special measures to encourage responsible reporting of child abuse by the mass media?
- [ ] Has the State established or supported confidential helplines, advice or counselling for child victims of violence, abuse or neglect?

Reminder : **The Convention is indivisible and its articles are interdependent. Article 19 should not be considered in isolation.**

Particular regard should be paid to:
The general principles

Article 2: all rights to be recognized for each child in jurisdiction without discrimination on any ground

Article 3(1): the best interests of the child to be a primary consideration in all actions concerning children

Article 6: right to life and maximum possible survival and development

Article 12: respect for the child's views in all matters affecting the child; opportunity to be heard in any judicial or administrative proceedings affecting the child

Closely related articles

Articles whose implementation is related to that of article 19 include:

Article 9: separation from parents following abuse or neglect

Article 18: parental responsibilities

Article 20: alternative care

Article 24(3): protection of children from traditional practices

Article 25: periodic review of placement or treatment

Article 28(2): school discipline without violence

Article 34: protection from sexual exploitation

Article 37: protection from torture and inhuman or degrading treatment or punishment

Article 38: armed conflict

Article 39: rehabilitative care for victims of violence

Children deprived of their family environment

Text of Article 20

1. A child temporarily or permanently deprived of his or her family environment, or in whose own best interests cannot be allowed to remain in that environment, shall be entitled to special protection and assistance provided by the State.

2. States Parties shall in accordance with their national laws ensure alternative care for such a child.

3. Such care could include, inter alia, *foster placement,* kafalah *of Islamic law, adoption or, if necessary, placement in suitable institutions for the care of children. When considering solutions, due regard shall be paid to the desirability of continuity in a child's upbringing and to the child's ethnic, religious, cultural and linguistic background.*

Summary

Article 20 concerns children who are temporarily or permanently unable to live with their families, either because of circumstances such as death, abandonment or displacement, or because the State has determined that they must be removed for their best interests.

Such children are entitled to "special protection and assistance". The method of care for them will depend in part on national traditions (for example Islamic law does not recognize adoption, see article 21, page 271) but must secure the child's rights under the Convention and, in particular, give due regard to the desirability of continuity of upbringing including ethnicity, religion, culture and language (see also article 8 and article 30).

The article principally applies to the social work or welfare departments of government and to social workers, foster caregivers and adoptive parents. Committee members have recommended ratifying States to draw upon the United Nations publication *Human Rights and Social Work: A Manual for Schools of Social Work and the Social Work Profession* (see, for example, Madagascar SR.164, para. 5). This Manual references all the relevant international and regional rights instruments and sets out basic principles and issues, as well as providing training materials in terms of testing questions and case vignettes. The 1986 Declaration on Social and Legal Principles relating to the Protection and Welfare of Children, with Special Reference to Foster Placement and Adoption Nationally and Internationally should also be considered. ■

Extracts from
Committee on the Rights of the Child
Guidelines for Reports to be submitted by States Parties under the Convention

For full text of *Guidelines for Periodic Reports*, see Appendix 3, page 604.

Guidelines for Initial Reports

"Family environment and alternative care

Under this section, States Parties are requested to provide relevant information, including the principal legislative, judicial, administrative or other measures in force, particularly how the principles of the 'best interests of the child' and 'respect for the views of the child' are reflected therein; factors and difficulties encountered and progress achieved in implementing the relevant provisions of the Convention; and implementation priorities and specific goals for the future in respect of:...

...(f) Children deprived of a family environment (article 20);

In addition, States Parties are requested to provide information on the numbers of children per year within the reporting period in each of the following groups, disaggregated by age group, sex, ethnic or national background and rural or urban environment: homeless children, abused or neglected children taken into protective custody, children placed in foster care, children placed in institutional care, children placed through domestic adoption, children entering the country through intercountry adoption procedures and children leaving the country through intercountry adoption procedures.

States Parties are encouraged to provide additional relevant statistical information and indicators relating to children covered in this section."

(CRC/C/5 paras. 16-18)

Guidelines for Periodic Reports

"V. FAMILY ENVIRONMENT AND ALTERNATIVE CARE

G. Children deprived of their family environment (art. 20)

Please indicate the measures adopted to ensure:

> *Special protection and assistance to the child who is temporarily or permanently deprived of his or her family environment or in whose own best interests cannot be allowed to remain in that environment;*

> *Alternative care for such a child, specifying the available forms of such care (inter alia foster placement, kafalah of Islamic law, adoption or if necessary placement in suitable institutions for the care of the child);*

> *That the placement of such a child in suitable institutions will only be used if necessary;*

> *Monitoring of the situation of children placed in alternative care;*

> *Respect for the general principles of the Convention, namely non-discrimination, the bests interests of the child, respect for the views of the child and the right to life, survival and development to the maximum extent.*

Reports should also indicate the extent to which, when such solutions are being considered, due regard is paid to the desirability of continuity in the child's upbringing and to the child's ethnic, religious, cultural and linguistic background. Disaggregated information should be provided on the children concerned by all such measures, including by gender, age, national, social or ethnic origin, language, religion, and by the nature of the measure of alternative care applied.

Reports should also provide information on the progress achieved in the implementation of this article, any difficulties encountered or on targets set for the future."

(CRC/C/58, paras. 80-82. The following paragraphs of the *Guidelines for Periodic Reports* are also relevant to reporting under this article: 35, 37, 43, 59, 86, 87, 165; for full text of *Guidelines*, see Appendix 3, page 604.)

Children who are temporarily or permanently deprived of, or removed in their best interests from, their family environment

It should be noted that this provision refers to family not parents, an important distinction. While it may be in the child's best interests to be removed from his or her parents (see article 9, page 119), the State should first seek placement in the child's wider family, as defined in article 5 (page 77), before looking for alternatives. Children may for example successfully be supported in a family which is run by an older sibling (see box).

Article 4 of the 1986 Declaration on Social and Legal Principles relating to the Protection and Welfare of Children, with Special Reference to Foster Placement and Adoption Nationally and Internationally states: "When care by the child's own parents is unavailable or inappropriate, care by relatives of the child's parents, by another substitute – foster or adoptive – family or, if necessary, by an appropriate institution should be considered." This suggests a hierarchy of options: first, family relatives; second, substitute family through fostering or adoption; and third, an appropriate institution. This approach is reflected in the provisions of article 20 and the rest of the Convention, as well as by comments by the Committee.

Such children shall be "entitled to special protection and assistance"

The use of the word "entitled" stresses the obligation the State has towards children who cannot be cared for by their parents. It goes to the heart of the duty all societies owe children – that if parents cannot meet children's needs then children have a moral claim on the rest of us. Article 3(2) establishes this general obligation: "States Parties undertake to ensure the child such protection and care as is necessary for his or her well-being, taking into account the rights and duties of his or her parents..."

Children who have been deprived of their families often have greater needs than simply the provision of an alternative placement. The loss of family attachments and identity together with the instabilities and disruptions of a new placement can impede their physical, intellectual and emotional development; children in such circumstances are also vulnerable to abuse and exploitation.

Child-headed households

"The child-headed household project was started in 1985 to prevent children in need from institutionalization and to support them to live in their community. They are children and young persons under the age of 20 whose parents are not able to provide proper care, economically and emotionally, because of death, divorce, physical or mental disability or disease. As a result, those children have to be responsible for their family's livelihood. They are provided with livelihood aid, medical aid, educational assistance and appropriate support for clothing, food and transportation. In 1993, there were 7,322 child-headed households with 14,293 members..."

(Republic of Korea IR, para. 134)

Therefore, a concerted effort is needed by professionals and providers across the entire spectrum of services for children. Finland, in its Initial Report to the Committee, notes the difficulty in which social workers were placed in relation to children in care, because they were unable to oblige other agencies to give to the children services they needed – and were even unable to require their own employing authority to act in the interests of these children. (Finland IR, paras. 137-8) This difficulty relates to the Committee's general observations, in relation to Article 4, about the need for different departments of state and professional disciplines to coordinate their activities (see page 65).

".... shall in accordance with their national laws ensure alternative care... such care could include, *inter alia*, foster placement, *kafalah*, adoption, or if necessary, placement in suitable institutions for the care of children"

During the drafting of article 20, the United States delegate made a proposal that States should have to "facilitate permanent adoption" of children in care. The proposal was rejected on the grounds that adoption is not the "only solution" when children cannot be cared for by their families. Even the milder proposal that children should have a right to a "stable family environment" did not survive to reach the final text. (E/1982/12/Add.1, C, pp. 56-59; Detrick, p. 299)

Adoption is unrecognized by Islamic law, which has developed instead the concept of *kafalah* – a permanent form of foster care that generally stops short of the child taking the family name or having inheritance rights. The 1986 Declaration on Social and Legal Principles relating to the Protection and Welfare of Children, with Special Reference to Foster Placement and Adoption Nationally and Internationally states in its Preamble: "Recognizing that under the principal legal systems of the world, various valuable alternative institutions exist, such as the *kafalah* of Islamic Law, which provide substitute care to children who cannot be cared for by their own parents...". Notwithstanding the non-prescriptive nature of the list of possible placements three Arab States (Brunei Darussalam, Egypt and Jordan) have entered explicit reservations to article 20 on the grounds that adoption is incompatible with the principles of Islam (CRC/C/2/Rev.5, pp. 15, 17 and 23).

The Convention on the Rights of the Child specifically addresses adoption in the next article, article 21 (page 269). As regards foster care, articles of the 1986 Declaration provide:

"6. Persons responsible for foster placement or adoption procedures should have professional or other appropriate training...

10. Foster placement of children should be regulated by law.

11. Foster family care, though temporary in nature, may continue, if necessary, until adulthood but should not preclude either prior return to the child's own parents or adoption.

12. In all matters of foster family care, the prospective foster parents and, as appropriate, the child and his or her own parents should be properly involved. A competent authority or agency should be responsible for supervision to ensure the welfare of the child."

Even though children are probably most exposed to abuse or neglect in institutions the vulnerability of children in foster care should not be underestimated. The Committee on the Rights of the Child has from time to time raised concerns, for example it recommended to Croatia that

"the system of foster care be carefully monitored in order to eliminate any possible acts of abuse against the children placed in such care." (Croatia IRCO, Add.52, para. 25)

And the Committee highly commended Iceland for introducing systematic measures for

"informing foster parents and preparing them to assume their tasks" (Iceland IRCO, Add.50, para. 7)

Those training foster caregivers and supervising foster placements should ensure that foster children are not treated as inferior to other children within the family or exploited as domestic workers.

Article 25, in relation to children placed by "competent authorities for the purposes of care, protection, or treatment of his or her physical or mental health," calls for "a periodic review of the treatment provided to the child and all other circumstances relevant to his or her placement". The task of the State is not over once a child has been placed in alternative family care or an institution. Too many children have failed to thrive, or have even suffered abuse, following such placements, so continual monitoring is essential (see page 341).

Article 3(3) also requires States Parties to ensure that "the institutions, services and facilities responsible for the care or protection of children, shall conform with the standards established by competent authorities, particularly in the areas of safety, health, in the number and suitability of their staff, as well as competent supervision" (see page 45).

Institutional care

Article 20 implies, but does not spell out, that placement in "suitable institutions for the care of children" is the last resort, second best to placement in an alternative family. The qualifier "if necessary" is used, which reflects the fact that institutional care may be the best placement for some children – for example if the child has suffered multiple foster care breakdowns, or when large families of siblings wish to remain together, or for older children nearing independence. Nonetheless the plight of large numbers of children in inappropriate institutional care has led the Committee on the Rights of the Child to refer to institutionalization as a "last resort", for example:

"...Comprehensive measures should be provided for responsible parenthood and for support for needy families, in order to assist them in their child-rearing responsibilities in the light of articles 18 and 27 of the Convention, thus limiting family disruption, reducing the numbers of institutionalized children and limiting the recourse to institutionalization to a measure of last resort." (Italy IRCO, Add.41, para. 17)

Institutional care is particularly inappropriate for younger children, whose developmental needs require a one-to-one relationship with a permanent adult caregiver. Egypt's Initial Report suggests that "stray children, orphans, children of unknown parentage, foundlings and others" are placed in custodial nurseries from the age of birth to six, then in alternative families or custodial establishments (Egypt IR, para. 170).

The numerous problems confronting children's institutions in Bulgaria

"There are numerous problems confronting the children's institutions which considerably reduce the efficiency of the care for the children and their education. The homes are incapable of compensating to a sufficient degree the absence of a family environment, and of maintaining regular contact with the parents (if the children have parents). Children placed in such homes suffer from lagging behind in the development of their personalities, disturbed communicativeness, emotional insufficiency, lack of affection for grown-ups, passiveness and mistrust. Serious deviations are observed in the intellectual and motivational spheres of the psychology of children of primary school age, as well as a proneness to improper behaviour. The inefficiency of child care for children without families is a consequence of former policies and obsolete legislation.

"Children's institutions have been situated in a very irrational manner in the country (in small towns and villages). Acute problems are encountered in financing and maintaining the specialized institutions for children. There are particularly grave problems concerning manpower: teachers have inadequate training and personal motivation, most of them have little experience (one year or less), or are beyond the retirement age; two thirds of them are women. Last but not least come the problems related to organization and legislation. There is an absence of a unified system for organization and management of the institutions. The various kinds of institutions are governed by different laws and regulations, and report to different authorities. In their current form the institutions are hardly able to conform to the requirements contained in the Convention for continuity in child care." (Bulgaria IR, paras. 129-130)

A Committee member expressed concern: "It was particularly worrying that children up to the age of six, the most important period of life, were being subjected to custodial placements. Familial fostering would be better." She suggested that the reverse provision would be preferable – that children ought to be placed in families up to age six and then in a custodial institution (Egypt SR.68, para. 51, and SR.67, para. 21).

Too many children are placed in institutions because the State has failed to put resources into keeping children with their families or finding and maintaining foster families for them. Chile, for example, notes that its "...emphasis on institutionalization in child-care policy has proved to be extremely expensive and to provide a low level of coverage in relation to care requirements; at the same time, its effects have frequently run counter to the aims of family and social reintegration" (Chile IR, para 258).

The Committee has frequently expressed concern about institutionalized children:

"The Committee wishes to express its concern about the seeming overemphasis on the resort to and use of institutional care for children in need of assistance. The Committee is of the opinion that this form of alternative care may not necessarily be the most effective, as it is reported that the assistance provided may not be of consistent quality and that insufficient attention is given to preparing children for their eventual return to their family or their integration into the community... "As regards the efforts required to reduce the recourse to institutional care for children in difficult situations, the Committee recommends that greater attention be paid to the development and use of alternative forms of care such as foster care and adoption." (Federal Republic of Yugoslavia IRCO, Add.49, paras. 15 and 34)

"...the Committee is concerned about the practice of the institutionalization in boarding schools of children who are deprived of a family environment, particularly in cases of abandonment or where children are orphaned... "The Committee recommends that alternatives to institutionalization in boarding schools, such as foster care, should be actively sought..." (Russian Federation IRCO, Add.4, paras. 11 and 19)

"The Committee is extremely concerned about the situation of children provided with care in welfare institutions. The Committee observes that the very high mortality rate in such institutions is a cause for serious alarm... "It is the opinion of the Committee that further measures should be taken by the State Party to promote the possibilities for children, particularly those who have been abandoned, to grow up in a home-like environment through, inter alia, fostering and adoption." (China IRCO, Add.56, paras. 18 and 38. See also Belarus IRCO, Add.17, para. 8; Zimbabwe IRCO, Add.55, paras. 17 and 29; Bulgaria IRCO, Add.66, para. 27)

Children's rights in Norwegian institutions

In Norway, for example, children in institutions are protected under the law so that: "Institutions shall be run in such a way that children can decide for themselves on personal matters and have whatever contact they want with other people, as long as this is commensurate with the child's age and maturity, the purpose of the stay, and the institution's responsibility for its operations, including its responsibility for security and welfare." (Norway IR, para. 99)

If children are placed in institutions, then the State must take measures to ensure that they are provided with well-trained staff, that the children's needs are met and their quality of life is good and that they are protected from abuse (see also article 3(3), page 45):

"The Committee regrets that appropriate measures have not yet been taken to effectively prevent and combat ill-treatment of children in schools or in institutions where children may be placed...

"The Committee encourages the State Party to address the situation of children in institutions, with a view to envisaging and making available possible alternatives to institutional care through, for example, guidance and counselling, foster care and education and vocational training programmes. The Committee also recommends the establishment of effective monitoring mechanism of the realization of the rights of the child placed in an institution." (Ukraine IRCO, Add.42, paras. 14 and 27)

"The Committee also recommends the further training of personnel in all institutions, such as social, legal or educational workers. An important part of such training should be to emphasize the promotion and protection of the child's sense of dignity and the issue of child neglect and maltreatment. Mechanisms to evaluate the ongoing training of personnel dealing with children are also required." (Russian Federation IRCO, Add.4, para. 19)

It is particularly important for all institutions where children are living to implement the principles of article 12. The natural way in which family members talk and listen to each other, and particularly parents listen to their children, cannot easily be replicated in more formal living institutions. Deliberate steps must be taken to ensure that staff hear and take proper account of the children's views and respect their civil rights.

Other Convention provisions, for example article 2 (protection from discrimination), article 13 (freedom of expression), article 6 (right of privacy) and article 19 (protection from mistreatment), should secure that institutions do not adopt measures that are prejudicial to the child's normal development and socialization, for example requiring the children to wear uniforms, or revealing children's personal history to their schools or other inmates, or using inappropriate controls or sanctions (such as corporal punishment, restriction of liberty, or the use of tranquillizing drugs or the deprivation of food, sleep or contact with family).

Deprivation of liberty

Article 37 addresses the rights of children deprived of their liberty, which includes "arrest, detention or imprisonment". The United Nations Rules for the Protection of Juveniles Deprived of their Liberty provides a more precise definition: "The deprivation of liberty means any form of detention or imprisonment or the placement of a person in another public or private custodial setting from which this person is not permitted to leave at will by order of any judicial, administrative or other public authority." Many children in institutions, including mental health institutions, are subjected to rules and administrative orders which prevent them from leaving the establishment, going beyond rules intended to safeguard their welfare (for example, forbidding them to go out late at night). Where children are deprived of their liberty in institutions the provisions of Article 37 and of the United Nations Rules for the Protection of Juveniles Deprived of their Liberty (endorsed by the Committee) should apply, even though these institutions operate outside the penal system.

Disabled children

Disabled children are vulnerable to abandonment by parents, either at birth or when they are older, often because the parents have inadequate support or are frightened that they will not be able to cope. Also, traditions and cultures sometimes express prejudice or hostility towards disabled people, encouraging parents to abdicate responsibility for a disabled child. Social workers may find that foster caregivers are reluctant to accept disabled children and small, home-like institutions may not have the staff or facilities to receive them. As a result such children may end up living in large or uncaring institutions (see article 23, page 293).

Rule 9(1) of the Standard Rules on the Equalization of Opportunities for Persons with Disabilities provides: "Persons with disabilities should be enabled to live with their families. States should encourage the inclusion in family counselling of appropriate modules regarding disability and its effects on family life. Respite-care and attendant-care services should be made available to families which include a person with disabilities. States should remove all unnecessary obstacles to persons who want to foster or adopt a child or adult with disabilities."

Thus States should first ensure that all measures of support have been taken to keep a disabled child within his or her family. It should perhaps be noted that expenditure on such measures is often cost-effective in the long term. The social-care services should ensure that foster caregivers are trained and encouraged to accept placements of disabled children and that small "family" institutions are equipped and staffed to receive disabled children alongside children without disabilities.

The Committee took up this issue with Ukraine:

"The Committee is concerned about the absence in Ukraine of a programme involving social work. In particular, the Committee expresses its concern at the situation of the institutionalization, treatment and protection of handicapped children. Alternatives to institutionalization are not sufficiently taken into account; support services to parents who keep their handicapped child at home are inadequate." (Ukraine IRCO, Add.42, para. 13)

Children who live and/or work on the streets

The phenomenon of "street children" (see article 2, page 31 for discussion of this term) is not addressed explicitly within the Convention on the Rights of the Child, but the number of children living or working on the streets of cities in almost all countries of the world is large and growing and is a source of great concern to the Committee on the Rights of the Child – for example:

"The Committee is concerned at the serious situation of children who, in view of increasing poverty and misery as well as of situations of abandonment or violence within the family, are forced to live and work in the streets, even at an early stage of their lives. For these reasons children often become victims of different forms of exploitation and abuse." (Peru IRCO, Add.8, para. 12)

However many such children do not, as is commonly believed, fall within the scope of article 20 because they are not in fact "deprived of their family environment". As the box describes, many "street children" in Namibia have families with whom they maintain bonds – in these cases, it is economic want that drives them on to the streets, rather than rejection or abuse within the family. In the past, damage has been done by State or non-governmental organization intervention into the lives of these children because it was assumed that any child found roaming the streets must be rescued by removal to a permanent alternative home.

Nonetheless, a significant proportion of children on city streets are there because they are orphaned (for example from conflict or famine or AIDS) or because they have been abandoned by their parents or because they have run away from physical, sexual or emotional abuse.

Today, most projects offering assistance to "street children" take a more considered and careful approach, looking both at the children's need to maintain relationships with their families and communities, and at the children's own sense of independence and self-reliance. Such projects increasingly advocate and support the principles of the Convention, which uphold children's autonomy as individuals and their civil rights (such as in articles 5, 12-16, 19, 29 and 32) and those which support the child's family (articles 5, 9, 18, 26, 27 and 30). Projects tend to be based in the locality of the child's street existence, providing practical services while supporting the child's ability to control the pace of change and encouraging rehabilitation with their families or communities.

Namibian survey of children on the streets

A Namibian survey of 515 "street children" in three urban centres "indicated that the typical street child in Namibia is black, male, poor and between 11 and 14 years of age. Almost all of the children surveyed had a family to which they returned on a regular basis, and most came from families of five or more children. About half of the children came from single-parent families, most of these being households headed by mothers, who are often more vulnerable than men to unemployment... Most of the street children surveyed were on the street to earn money for food and other necessities for themselves and their families. About half of them were school drop-outs, and many came from families with a low standard of education. However, more than 70 per cent indicated that they would like help with their schooling." (Namibia IR, paras. 190-2)

When considering solutions, due regard to be paid to "the desirability of continuity in a child's upbringing and to the child's ethnic, religious, cultural and linguistic background"

This provision relates to article 7 (right to know and be cared for by parents, see page 97) and article 8 (preservation of the child's identity, see page 111). Unfortunately a number of countries have histories of violating this right, compulsorily removing children from indigenous or minority groups and settling them with well-off childless parents. Though well-intentioned, such actions reveal a crude racism and have caused damage to many children and adults. It should be noted that this provision reflects the right of children of minority or indigenous backgrounds under article 30 generally to enjoy their culture, practice their religion and use their language (see page 407).

Continuity of upbringing implies continuity of contact, wherever possible, with parents, family and the wider community – achievable even when the child is adopted (see further discussion under article 21 page 275). Continuity of upbringing also implies finding a foster or adoptive home from the same cultural background, or ensuring that all or some members of the staff in an institution are from the same culture, and, preferably, that the institution itself is located in an appropriate community. The specifying of "linguistic background" is very important. Fluency in language is best – and often only – obtained during childhood, so every effort should be made to ensure that children learn their mother tongue even when placed with speakers of another language.

In regard to religion and culture, two caveats must be noted. First, the best interests of the child, in terms of article 3(1), may not be served by the continuity of religion or culture – for example if the child has been removed from parents because of harmful religious or cultural practices or if the child has run away from home because of a clash with parental beliefs or practices. Second, once children have sufficiently evolved capacity, their own rights to determine their religion, as well as their rights to freedom of expression and association, should be respected under articles 12 to 15.

Continuity of upbringing also implies that the State should take all measures to avoid multiple placements of children in its care. When children have suffered the trauma of losing their family they may present behavioural problems that could result in them being passed from one foster home to another, or in their spiralling downwards, through increasingly restrictive institutions, which could then lead to further behavioural problems. Care must be taken to avoid such disruption in children's lives.

Implementation Checklist

article 20

● General measures of implementation

Have appropriate general measures of implementation been taken in relation to article 20, including

☐ identification and coordination of the responsible departments and agencies at all levels of government (article 20 is relevant to the **departments of social welfare, education and health**)?

☐ identification of relevant non-governmental organizations/civil society partners?

☐ a comprehensive review to ensure that all legislation, policy and practice is compatible with the article, for all children in all parts of the jurisdiction?

☐ adoption of a strategy to secure full implementation

　　☐ which includes where necessary the identification of goals and indicators of progress?

　　☐ which does not affect any provisions which are more conducive to the rights of the child?

　　☐ which recognizes other relevant international standards?

　　☐ which involves where necessary international cooperation?

(Such measures may be part of an overall governmental strategy for implementing the Convention as a whole).

☐ budgetary analysis and allocation of necessary resources?

☐ development of mechanisms for monitoring and evaluation?

☐ making the implications of article 20 widely known to adults and children?

☐ development of appropriate training and awareness-raising (in relation to article 20 likely to include the training of **social workers, adoption agency staff, staff of institutions, foster parents, teachers and medical personnel**)?

● Specific issues in implementing article 20

☐ Are parents provided with appropriate support to avoid the need to seek alternative care for the child?

☐ When children cannot be cared for by parents, are systematic efforts made to seek a placement with members of their wider family, with appropriate support where necessary?

☐ Is there a legal obligation on the State to provide appropriate care for children deprived of their family environment?

☐ Are social services able to require assistance from health, education and other professionals in meeting the needs of children without families?

☐ Are those responsible for the placement of children without families appropriately trained?

Are the views of children obtained when

☐ alternative placements are being considered for them?

☐ alternative placements are chosen?

☐ alternative placements are being monitored?

☐ Are independent complaints systems available to protect children placed away from their family environment?

☐ Are foster parents fully investigated and authorized as appropriate before placement?

☐ Are foster parents recruited and encouraged to care for disabled children?

☐ Are foster parents trained to care for disabled children?

☐ Are foster placements regularly monitored?

☐ Are foster caregivers required to ascertain the views of the child in all matters affecting him or her and to give these views due weight?

☐ Are children placed in institutions only when necessary?

☐ Are institutional placements regularly monitored?

☐ Do all institutions caring for children have sufficient numbers of, and suitably qualified, staff?

☐ Are staff trained to secure children's rights under the Convention?

☐ Do such institutions respect children's human dignity, provide children with as normal a life as possible and take all measures to secure their integration in society?

For example, do such institutes prohibit

☐ the use of compulsory uniforms?

☐ child labour (which goes beyond normal domestic chores)?

☐ corporal punishment?

☐ restriction of liberty?

☐ the use of drugs for control purposes?

☐ deprivation of food?

☐ deprivation of sleep?

☐ deprivation of contact with families for control purposes?

☐ Are such institutions required to ascertain the views of the child in all matters affecting him or her and give these views due weight?

☐ Do all institutions, where possible, accommodate disabled children together with children without disabilities?

How to use the checklists, *see page XVII*

☐ Are changes in placements of children avoided if possible?

☐ Do projects for children living and/or working on the streets ensure that the children, where possible, maintain contact with their families and communities?

When choosing or supporting a placement, do the social-work authorities pay due regard to the desirability of continuity in the child's upbringing in relation to

☐ the child's ethnic background?

☐ the child's religious background?

☐ the child's cultural background?

☐ the child's linguistic background?

(for example, by maintaining contact with the child's family, friends and community or, where this is not possible, by making special arrangements).

Reminder : **The Convention is indivisible and its articles are interdependent. Article 20 should not be considered in isolation.**

Particular regard should be paid to:
The general principles

Article 2: all rights to be recognized for each child in jurisdiction without discrimination on any ground

Article 3(1): the best interests of the child to be a primary consideration in all actions concerning children

Article 6: right to life and maximum possible survival and development

Article 12: respect for the child's views in all matters affecting the child; opportunity to be heard in any judicial or administrative proceedings affecting the child

Closely related articles

Articles whose implementation is related to that of article 20 include:

Article 3(2) and (3): State obligations to provide protection and care and to ensure consistent standards in all placements and services for children

Article 7: right to know and be cared for by parents

Article 8: preservation of child's identity

Article 9: non-separation from parents except when necessary in best interests

Article 16: protection from arbitrary interference with privacy, family and home

Article 18: parents having primary and joint responsibility with appropriate state support

Article 21: adoption

Article 22: refugee children

Article 25: periodic review of placement

Article 30: children of minorities or indigenous peoples

Adoption

States Parties which recognize and/or permit the system of adoption shall ensure that the best interests of the child shall be the paramount consideration and they shall:

(a) Ensure that the adoption of a child is authorized only by competent authorities who determine, in accordance with applicable law and procedures and on the basis of all pertinent and reliable information, that the adoption is permissible in view of the child's status concerning parents, relatives and legal guardians and that, if required, the persons concerned have given their informed consent to the adoption on the basis of such counselling as may be necessary;

(b) Recognize that intercountry adoption may be considered as an alternative means of child's care, if the child cannot be placed in a foster or an adoptive family or cannot in any suitable manner be cared for in the child's country of origin;

(c) Ensure that the child concerned by intercountry adoption enjoys safeguards and standards equivalent to those existing in the case of national adoption;

(d) Take all appropriate measures to ensure that, in intercountry adoption, the placement does not result in improper financial gain for those involved in it;

(e) Promote, where appropriate, the objectives of the present article by concluding bilateral or multilateral arrangements or agreements, and endeavour, within this framework, to ensure that the placement of the child in another country is carried out by competent authorities or organs.

Article 21 addresses the rights of children who are adopted – in those countries which permit adoption – establishing the paramountcy of children's best interests in all adoption arrangements and detailing minimum requirements for adoption procedures. It states that intercountry adoption is only to be considered if the child cannot be suitably placed in his or her own country. The need of all young children for a family, and for a sense of security and permanency in their relationships, is recognized in most parts of the world and is celebrated in the Convention's Preamble which asserts that

Summary

the family is "...the fundamental group of society and the natural environment for the growth and well-being of all its members and particularly children" and that "the child, for the full and harmonious development of his or her personality, should grow up in a family environment, in an atmosphere of happiness, love and understanding." Adoption as the permanent solution to meet this need is, however, more controversial.

The Convention on the Rights of the Child remains neutral about the desirability of adoption even within the child's country of origin, though article 20 mentions it as one of the possible options for the care of children without families. It is clear that children's psychological need for permanency and individual attachments can be met without the formality of adoption, but where it is used it should be properly regulated by the State to safeguard children's rights. ∎

Extracts from
Committee on the Rights of the Child
Guidelines for Reports to be submitted by States Parties under the Convention

For full text of *Guidelines for Periodic Reports*, see Appendix 3, page 604.

Guidelines for Initial Reports

"Family environment and alternative care

"*Under this section, States Parties are requested to provide relevant information, including the principal legislative, judicial, administrative or other measures in force, particularly how the principles of the 'best interests of the child' and 'respect for the views of the child' are reflected therein; factors and difficulties encountered and progress achieved in implementing the relevant provisions of the Convention; and implementation priorities and specific goals for the future in respect of:...*

(g) Adoption (article 21).

In addition, States Parties are requested to provide information on the numbers of children per year within the reporting period in each of the following groups, disaggregated by age group, sex, ethnic or national background and rural or urban environment: homeless children, abused or neglected children taken into protective custody, children placed in foster care, children placed in institutional care, children placed through domestic adoption, children entering the country through intercountry adoption procedures and children leaving the country through intercountry adoption procedure

States Parties are encouraged to provide additional relevant statistical information and indicators relating to children covered in this section."

(CRC/C/5, paras. 16-18)

Guidelines for Periodic Reports

"V. FAMILY ENVIRONMENT AND ALTERNATIVE CARE

H. Adoption (Art. 21)

Please indicate the measures adopted, including of a legislative, administrative or judicial nature, to ensure that, when the State recognizes and/or permits the system of adoption, the best interests of the child shall be the paramount consideration. Information should also be provided on:

The authorities which are competent to authorize the adoption of a child;

The applicable law and procedures and the pertinent and reliable information on the basis of which adoption is determined;

The child's status concerning his or her parents, relatives and legal guardians necessary for adoption to be considered permissible;

The involvement of the persons concerned, the circumstances under which their informed consent is required and necessary counselling provided, including to allow for the consideration of the alternatives to and consequences of adoption, and the extent to which the participation of the child is ensured and his or her views are given due weight;

States Parties which "recognize and/or permit the system of adoption"

There are those who believe that adoption is the best solution for children without families. For example, the delegate from the United States in the Working Group drafting the Convention proposed a provision: "In cases where a child cannot be cared for by his parents or other members of his biological family, the competent authorities of States Parties shall take appropriate measures to facilitate permanent adoption of the child" (E/1982/12/Add.1,C., pp. 56-59, Detrick, p. 299). And the French Government, in its Initial Report, describes legislation requiring that children in care who are permanently deprived of their family environment must be put up for adoption as rapidly as possible (France IR, paras. 274 and 277).

At the other end of the spectrum of opinion are those States which operate in accordance with Islamic law and so do not recognize adoption at all. Others report negative aspects of adoption. The Bangladesh representative, for example, expressed concern during drafting of the Convention about adoptions undertaken "for reasons of proselytization" by foreign missionary agencies. (E/CN.4/1986/39, Annex IV, p. 2, Detrick, p. 312). Madagascar reported to the Committee that adoption in that country had been traditionally done "for various reasons which were not necessarily in the interests of the child. For example, the purpose of an adoption could conceivably be to create a fictitious bond of kinship between the adoptive parent who was seeking material gain or prestige or the adopted person who was an eminent person with moral or religious authority or was rich. It was a known fact that the last Malagasy Head of Government, before the arrival of the French, Prime Minister Rainilairivony, had been adopted many times." (Madagascar IR, para. 185). There are also reports of "fake adoptions" to disguise the bonded labour of children (Report of the Working Group on Contemporary Forms of Slavery, Eighteenth session, Economic and Social Council, E/CN.4/Sub.2/1993/30 p. 33; see also article 32, page 427).

Islamic law does not recognize the concept of an adoption which disguises the true parentage and blood relationships of a child. Children without families are able to live in permanent forms of foster care under *kafalah* which means in most Islamic States that they may not take the family name or have rights of inheritance. Notwithstanding the article's careful wording a number of States with Islamic populations entered a specific reservation to article 21, including Bangladesh, Brunei Darussalam, Egypt, Indonesia, Jordan, Maldives and the Syrian Arab Republic (and the Republic of Korea, for reasons unspecified). Some countries, such as Lebanon, prohibit adoption for Muslims but permit it for non-Muslims (Lebanon IR, paras. 46-47).

In addition, Canada stated: "With a view to ensuring full respect for the purposes and intent of article 20(3) and article 30 of the Convention, the Government of Canada reserves the right not to apply the provisions of article 21 to the extent that they may be inconsistent with customary forms of care among aboriginal peoples in Canada" (CRC/C/2/Rev. 5, p. 15). In discussions with the Committee, Canadian representatives indicated that a reservation had been entered to article 21 because of "custom adoption". This was explained as "an uncommon practice, which normally took place in certain indigenous communities within extended families, for example when a child was adopted by its grandparents. Such a practice might have been regarded as being at variance with the strict terms of article 21(a), and the Canadian authorities had therefore considered it appropriate to enter a reservation" (Canada SR.214, para. 59). Notwithstanding this explanation, the Committee encouraged Canada to consider withdrawing the reservation (Canada IRCO, Add.37, para. 10, see also article 30 page 410).

The best interests of the child shall be the paramount consideration

In adoption the best interests of the child must be "the paramount" consideration rather than simply "a primary" consideration as in article 3. The provision establishes that no other interests, whether economic, political, state security or those of the adopters, should take precedence over, or be considered equal to, the child's. The paramountcy principle should be clearly stated in law. Any regulation that fetters the principle could lead to a breach of the Convention – for example inflexible rules about the adoptive couples' circumstances, such as the setting of age limits, or about the child's circumstances, for example only permitting adoption in cases where the child has been legally declared abandoned. (For further discussion of "best interests" see article 3, page 40 and article 18, page 227).

"The child" is of course the child being considered for adoption, but the best interests point should not necessarily be limited to that child; other children may be affected by adoption procedures. Philippine law, for example, requires that "in cases of adoption of a child who is 10 years or older, the child's consent must first be given. Likewise, the child of the adoptive parents who is 10 years or older shall give his or her consent to the adoption" (Philippines IR para. 52). An adoption considered to be contrary to the best interests of the other children within the family would be difficult to square with the principles of the Convention.

Countries considered to have too many adoptions have been the subject of Committee concern, for example:

"The Committee notes the high number of domestic and international adoptions of Costa Rican children...
"The Committee emphasizes that the best interests of the child must be the guiding principle in the application of the Convention, especially with regard to ... adoption. In the framework of the adoption process, due consideration should be given to the provisions of article 12 as regards respect for the child."
(Costa Rica IRCO, Add.11, paras. 10 and 14)

On one occasion, the Committee has also questioned the lack of domestic adoptions:

"It is the opinion of the Committee that further measures should be taken by the State Party to promote the possibilities for children, particularly those who have been abandoned, to grow up in a home-like environment through, inter alia, fostering and adoption."
(China IRCO, Add.56, para. 38)

Adoption authorized "only by competent authorities ... in accordance with applicable law"

In all countries where adoption is allowed, the Committee has expected to see legislation regulating both its domestic and international forms.

For example

"The Committee notes that the Sri Lankan authorities have enacted new legislation on international adoption which ensures safeguards against the sale and trafficking

children. The Committee remains worried about the fact that the same measures have not been taken to regulate national adoptions. *"With regard to national adoption, .the Committee stresses the need to raise the standards to those existing for international law..."* (Sri Lanka IRCO, Add.40, paras. 17 and 35)

"The Committee also suggests that the State Party review the present legislation on adoption, in the light of the principles and provisions of the Convention, notably those of its articles 20 and 21, so as to evaluate the effectiveness of national legislation in facilitating domestic legislation." (China IRCO, Add.56, para. 38)

"With regard to adoption, despite recent changes in legislation regulating this practice, the Committee is concerned by the lack of compatibility of the current legal framework with the principles and provisions of the Convention, especially with regard to the principle of the best interests of the child (art. 3)." (Bulgaria IRCO, Add.66, para 15)

"The Committee is concerned by the existing legal framework and procedures set to regulate adoption which are not in full conformity with the principles and provisions of the Convention, especially its articles 3 and 21." (Myanmar IRCO, Add.69, para. 17)

"Competent authorities" covers the judicial and professional authorities charged with vetting the viability of the placement in terms of the best interests of the child, and with ensuring that proper consents have been obtained and all relevant information considered. Thus, both trained social workers and adjudicators should be involved in the process. The Committee recommended that, in relation to adoptions in Panama

"adequate training be provided to concerned professionals" (Panama IRCO Add.68 para 31)

Determination "on the basis of all pertinent and reliable information, that the adoption is permissible in view of the child's status concerning parents, relatives and legal guardians and that, if required, the persons concerned have given their informed consent to the adoption on the basis of such counselling as may be necessary"

While the best interests of children are the paramount consideration in an adoption process, there is a presumption within the Convention that children's best interests are served by being with

their parents wherever possible (articles 7 and 9) and that their parents have "primary responsibility" for their upbringing, a responsibility they must exercise within the framework of the child's best interests, his or her rights under the Convention and his or her evolving capacity (articles 5 and 18). An adoption can only occur if parents are unwilling or are deemed by judicial process to be unable to discharge this responsibility – any legislation that permits adoptions under less stringent conditions would probably amount to a breach of both children's and parent's rights under the Convention. The requirement for proper consent for adoption has arisen because of cases in which children have been wrongfully removed from their parents.

These safeguards do however mean that the "paramountcy" of children's best interests in adoption is in one sense circumscribed by the legal necessities of satisfying legal grounds and gaining necessary consents; if the procedures are not followed then an adoption will not proceed, regardless of the child's best interests.

The Convention's provisions mean that each potential adoption will require proper investigation with full reports by independent professionals to the authorities considering the adoption application. The question of what consents must be obtained is hedged here. "If required" leaves it up to domestic legislation – although any gross violation of either the child's or a natural parent's rights to family life would amount to a breach of this (see articles 7 and 9) and other human rights instruments. States should reconsider, for example, laws that do not permit fathers of children born outside marriage to have any potential rights in adoption procedures. Where consents are required, the Convention provides that these must be given "on the basis of such counselling as may be necessary".

The child's views

The child's views are not explicitly mentioned in the requirements relating to consent, but proper consideration of them is undoubtedly implied, as well as required under article 12 (see page 145). Children's ascertainable views must be central to any consideration of their "best interests".

In addition to taking the child's views into account, adoption legislation may also require that the child's formal consent be obtained. Some countries report that ages are set above which the child's consent is legally required for adoption (for example Nova Scotia, where consent to an adoption is needed from any child aged 12 or more (Canada IR, para. 1129), from any child aged 10 or more in Croatia (Croatia IR, para. 103)

article 21

and aged nine or more in Mongolia (Mongolia IR, paras. 135-139)). Another possibility is giving children the power to veto their own adoption. Adoption is never essential (the Islamic experience shows that permanency can be achieved without it) and is usually irrevocable. Consent to adoption therefore carries more risk, is a weightier decision, than vetoing it. Passively refraining from exercising a right of veto, rather than actively stating consent, is also less likely to place a burden of guilt on children in relation to their natural parents. It is hard to imagine in what circumstances a child of any age should be adopted against his or her expressed wishes. Even if a very young infant objected, it would seem wise to accept his or her wishes and return to the subject at a later date.

The Hague Convention on Protection and Cooperation of Children in respect of Intercountry Adoption provides that such adoptions can only take place if the authorities of the State of origin "have ensured, having regard to the age and degree of maturity of the child, that he or she has been counselled and duly informed of the effects of the adoption and of his or her consent to the adoption, where such consent is required" and that "consideration has been given to the child's wishes and opinions..." (article 4(c)). It also states that where consent is required, it must be given freely, without inducements (article 4(d)).

The Committee has emphasized the importance of the child's right under article 12 to have his or her wishes considered in relation to adoption:

"...the Committee recommends that consideration be given to extending and broadening the involvement of children in decisions affecting them in the family and in social life, including in proceedings relating to family reunification and adoption." (Germany IRCO, Add.43, para. 29)

"The Committee recommends that the State Party ensure that its adoption procedures are in conformity with the provisions of the Convention, especially its articles 3, 12 and 21..." (Honduras IRCO, Add.24, para. 26)

"In the framework of the adoption process, due consideration should be given to the provisions of article 12 of the Convention." (Mexico IRCO, Add.13, para. 18)

"Intercountry adoption may be considered as an alternative means of child's care under certain conditions"

The wording deliberately falls short of saying that countries must consider international adoption as

one of the options of care. Namibia, for example, reported to the Committee that intercountry adoption is, in effect, illegal in that country because one of the applicants for adoption of a Namibian child must also be a Namibian, or applying to become a Namibian (Namibia IR, para. 208). (The inflexibility of such a provision might however raise doubts in relation to, say, article 6, the child's right to optimum development, or article 12, respect for the child's views, in addition to any consideration of the child's best interests).

The rising number of intercountry adoptions has been the cause of much concern. Children are a highly desirable commodity in countries where low birth rates and relaxed attitudes towards illegitimacy have restricted the supply of babies for adoption. Colombia, for example, reported to the Committee that many more Colombian children are adopted by foreign couples than by Colombian couples, even though the latter are given priority over foreign applicants (Colombia IR, paras. 133-35 and p. 31). This has led an apparently increasing number of adoptions to be arranged on a commercial basis or by illicit means. Without very stringent regulation and supervision children can be trafficked for adoption or can be adopted without regard for their best interests; some children are even adopted for nefarious purposes, such as child prostitution or forms of slavery. The Committee has frequently expressed concern about the phenomenon:

"The Committee expresses its grave concern over the information brought to its attention of alleged trafficking in intercountry adoptions in violation of the provisions and principles of the Convention. It is further concerned about the absence of a normative framework in the field of intercountry adoptions, namely in the light of articles 3, 12 and 21 of the Convention." (Paraguay IRCO, Add.27, para. 11)

"... the Committee remains concerned about the sufficiency of measures taken to implement the provisions of the Convention relating to adoption, particularly intercountry adoption, and with respect to combating trafficking in children." (Nicaragua IRCO, Add.36, para. 18)

"The Committee is worried by the high rate of abandonment of children, especially newborn babies, and the lack of a comprehensive strategy to assist vulnerable families. This situation can lead to illegal intercountry adoption or other forms of trafficking and sale of children." (Ukraine IRCO, Add.42, para. 11)

"The Committee notes with concern the information provided by the State Party that an illegal adoption network has been uncovered and that the mechanisms to prevent and combat such violations of children's rights are *insufficient and ineffective."* (Guatemala IRCO, Add.58, para. 21)

Even when intercountry adoptions are regulated, the Committee has remained concerned – for example it expressed anxiety to Belarus, Costa Rica, Mexico and others about the number of international adoptions. The Committee encouraged the Danish Government, in the light of information it had received from Denmark about the poor outcome of international adoption

"to take steps to monitor more closely the situation of foreign children placed in adoptive families" (Denmark SR.201 para. 58 and IRCO, Add.33, para. 27);

and made a similar recommendation to Sweden:

"The Committee also recommends that steps should be taken to monitor more closely the situation of foreign children placed in adoptive families in Sweden." (Sweden IRCO, Add.2, para. 13)

Argentina entered a reservation to paragraphs (b),(c), (d) and (e) of article 21, but not because it was unconcerned about international adoption. On the contrary it stated that these provisions do not apply within its jurisdiction: "because, in its view, for the purpose of their implementation, a rigorous mechanism for the legal protection of the child in respect of international adoption must already be in place, in order to prevent the trafficking and sale of children" (CRC/C/2/Rev. 5, p. 12, Argentina IR (1993), para. 62). The Committee was not satisfied with this argument and recommended that it review the reservation with a view to withdrawing it (Argentina IRCO, Add.35, paras. 8 and 14).

Intercountry adoption only "if the child cannot be placed in a foster or an adoptive family or cannot in any suitable manner be cared for in the child's country of origin"

In other words intercountry adoption is clearly viewed as a solution of last resort. This was spelt out to Mexico by the Committee:

"intercountry adoption should be considered in the light of article 21, namely as a measure of last resort" (Mexico IRCO, Add.13, para. 18).
States are thus under an obligation to take active measures to ensure that all possible efforts have been made to provide suitable care for the child in his or her country of origin. This "last resort" provision is consonant with article 20(3) requiring due regard to be paid to "the desirability of continuity in a child's upbringing and to the child's ethnic, religious, cultural and linguistic

background"; with article 7, upholding the child's rights to know and be cared for by parents, and with article 8, the child's right to preserve identity. It is now confirmed in the 1993 Hague Convention on the Protection of Children and Cooperation in respect of Intercountry Adoption, which establishes the "subsidiarity principle": that an intercountry adoption should only take place "after possibilities for placement of the child within the State of origin have been given due consideration".

Duty to "ensure that the child concerned by intercountry adoption enjoys safeguards and standards equivalent to those existing in the case of national adoption"

Thus every international adoption must be authorized as being in the best interests of the child by competent authorities of the child's State, on the basis of proper investigation and information and with proper consents (with counselling, if necessary) having been obtained. While the Hague Convention lays down these ground rules and provides the details for intercountry adoption, it is, of course, up to each State to ensure that its adoption legislation, professional training and administrative mechanisms are in place. The Committee has urged any country not doing so to take immediate action, for example:

"The Committee recommends that the State Party introduce the measures necessary to monitor and supervise effectively the system of adoption of children in the light of article 21 of the Convention. It is also recommended that adequate training be provided to concerned professionals. In addition, it is recommended that the Government consider ratifying the Hague Convention on Protection of Children and Cooperation in respect of Intercountry Adoption." (Guatemala IRCO, Add.58, para. 34)

"In relation to intercountry adoption, the Committee is of the opinion that the State Party should, as soon as possible, draft and adopt legislation to regulate this activity." (Mongolia IRCO, Add.48, para. 25)

Intercountry adoption should not result in "improper financial gain"

Country reports and Committee observations highlight the widespread concern about the trafficking of children for adoption purposes. While payments by adoptive couples may be made in good faith and without harm to the child, a system that puts a price on a child's head is likely to encourage criminality, corruption and exploitation. Article 35 requires States Parties to take measures to prevent the sale of children for any purpose. Article 32 of the Hague Convention states:

"1. No one shall derive improper financial or other gain from an activity related to an intercountry adoption.

2. Only costs and expenses, including reasonable professional fees of persons involved in the adoption, may be charged or paid.

3. The directors, administrators and employees of bodies involved in an adoption shall not receive remuneration which is unreasonably high in relation to services rendered."

States that have ratified or acceded to the Hague Convention on Protection of Children and Cooperation in respect of Intercountry Adoption (as of September 1997)

Andorra	Norway
Burkina Faso	Peru
Canada	Philippines
Cyprus	Poland
Costa Rica	Romania
Denmark	Sri Lanka
Ecuador	Sweden
Finland	Venezuela
Mexico	

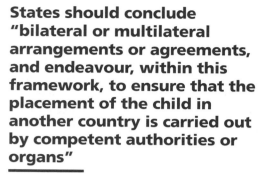

States should conclude "bilateral or multilateral arrangements or agreements, and endeavour, within this framework, to ensure that the placement of the child in another country is carried out by competent authorities or organs"

The most important treaty for States to join as parties is now the 1993 Hague Convention on Protection of Children and Cooperation in respect of Intercountry Adoption. This was drafted to meet the need for detailed, legally binding international standards, for an agreed system of supervision and for channels of communications and effective relationships between the authorities in the countries of the adopted child and the adopters. It builds upon article 21 and the rest of the Convention on the Rights of the Child and reflects the provisions of the 1986 United Nations Declaration on Social and Legal Principles relating to the Protection and Welfare of Children, with Special Reference to Foster Placement and Adoption Nationally and Internationally. The Hague Convention's first objective is "to establish safeguards to ensure that intercountry adoptions take place in the best interests of the child and with respect for his or her fundamental rights as recognized in international law" (article 1a).

The Committee has systematically taken note of the signing of this Convention, taking pains to commend those countries that have become parties (see box) and strongly encouraging those who have not yet done so. It should be noted that most of the States that have become parties have significant numbers of intercountry adoptions.

Implementation Checklist

article 21

● General measures of implementation

Have appropriate general measures of implementation been taken in relation to article 21, including

☐ identification and coordination of the responsible departments and agencies at all levels of government (article 21 is relevant to the **departments of justice, social welfare and foreign affairs**)?

☐ identification of relevant non-governmental organizations/civil society partners?

☐ a comprehensive review to ensure that all legislation, policy and practice is compatible with the article, for all children in all parts of the jurisdiction?

☐ adoption of a strategy to secure full implementation

   ☐ which includes where necessary the identification of goals and indicators of progress?

   ☐ which does not affect any provisions which are more conducive to the rights of the child?

   ☐ which recognizes other relevant international standards?

   ☐ which involves where necessary international cooperation?

(Such measures may be part of an overall governmental strategy for implementing the Convention as a whole).

☐ budgetary analysis and allocation of necessary resources?

☐ development of mechanisms for monitoring and evaluation?

☐ making the implications of article 21 widely known to adults and children?

☐ development of appropriate training and awareness-raising (in relation to article 21 likely to include the training of **social workers, judiciary, port and border control authorities, adoption agency staff and development of education for adoptive parents**)?

● Specific issues in implementing article 21

☐ Does the State recognize and/or permit a system of adoption of children?

If yes:

Does legislation and administration ensure that in all adoption proceedings (domestic and intercountry)

   ☐ the best interests of the child are the paramount consideration?

   ☐ adoptions are authorized only by competent authorities?

☐ these authorities make their decisions on the basis of all pertinent and reliable information?

☐ Does this information include the ascertainable views of the child?

☐ Are the views of the child given due weight, having regard to age and maturity?

☐ Are the views and best interests of other children affected by a proposed adoption (such as the children of the prospective adopters) considered by the competent authorities?

☐ In this process is due regard paid to the child's right to know and be cared for by his or her parents?

☐ In this process is due regard paid to preservation of the child's identity and the desirability of continuity in the child's background and to the child's ethnic, religious, cultural and linguistic background?

Before agreeing to an adoption, must the authorities be satisfied that

☐ the adoption is permissible in view of the child's status concerning parents, relatives and legal guardians?

☐ all consents required by law have been given by the persons concerned?

☐ Where consents are required by law, are the persons concerned provided with counselling?

Do children have a right to consent to an adoption

☐ at any age?

☐ at a particular age?

☐ according to age and maturity?

☐ Do all children have a right to veto their adoption?

☐ Are all adoption placements monitored and periodically reviewed by the authorities?

☐ Are intercountry adoptions only permitted if the child cannot be placed in a foster or an adoptive family or cannot be cared for in any other suitable manner within the jurisdiction?

☐ Do all children involved in intercountry adoptions (whether leaving or entering the State) enjoy safeguards and standards equivalent to those regulating domestic adoptions?

☐ Do border controls monitor the entry and exit of babies and children travelling with adults who are not their parents?

☐ Is improper financial gain from intercountry adoption prohibited by law?

☐ Has the 1993 Hague Convention on the Protection of Children and Cooperation in respect of Intercountry Adoption been ratified or acceded to?

    ☐ If yes, have all its provisions relating to law or administrative procedures been implemented?

☐ Have any other bilateral or multilateral treaties relating to adoption been concluded?

Reminder : **The Convention is indivisible and its articles are interdependent. Article 21 should not be considered in isolation.**

Particular regard should be paid to:
The general principles

Article 2: all rights to be recognized for each child in jurisdiction without discrimination on any ground

Article 3(1): the best interests of the child to be a primary consideration in all actions concerning children

Article 6: right to life and maximum possible survival and development

Article 12: respect for the child's views in all matters affecting the child; opportunity to be heard in any judicial or administrative proceedings affecting the child

Closely related articles

Articles whose implementation is related to that of article 21 include:

Article 5: parental guidance and child's evolving capacities

Article 7: child's right to know and be cared for by parents

Article 8: preservation of child's identity

Article 9: non-separation from parents except when necessary in best interests

Article 10: family reunification

Article 11: protection from illicit transfer and non-return

Article 16: protection from arbitrary interference with privacy, family and home

Article 18: parents having joint responsibility

Article 20: children deprived of their family environment

Article 25: periodic review of placement

Article 35: prevention of sale, trafficking and abduction

Refugee children

Text of Article 22

1. States Parties shall take appropriate measures to ensure that a child who is seeking refugee status or who is considered a refugee in accordance with applicable international or domestic law and procedures shall, whether unaccompanied or accompanied by his or her parents or by any other person, receive appropriate protection and humanitarian assistance in the enjoyment of applicable rights set forth in the present Convention and in other international human rights or humanitarian instruments to which the said States are Parties.

2. For this purpose, States Parties shall provide, as they consider appropriate, cooperation in any efforts by the United Nations and other competent intergovernmental organizations or non-governmental organizations cooperating with the United Nations to protect and assist such a child and to trace the parents or other members of the family of any refugee child in order to obtain information necessary for reunification with his or her family. In cases where no parents or other members of the family can be found, the child shall be accorded the same protection as any other child permanently or temporarily deprived of his or her family environment for any reason, as set forth in the present Convention.

Article 22 addresses the rights of refugee children to appropriate protection and humanitarian assistance, including tracing family members. Earlier drafts of the article emphasized that the refugee child "needs special protection and assistance". This special focus dwindled, first because the drafters recognized that the needs of these children would be met if the articles of the Convention on the Rights of the Child were properly applied to them and were fully implemented, and, second, in response to pressure from States that were cautious about according children special

rights of residence or nationality, or which did not want to bear the cost of tracing family members (E/1982/12/Add.1, pp. 64-68; Detrick, pp. 320-329).

The article must be read in conjunction with article 9 (separation from parents only when necessary in the best interests of the child), article 10 (rights to family reunification, to be dealt with in a positive, humane and expeditious manner), article 20 (protection of children without families), article 39 (recovery and rehabilitation after experience of armed conflict, torture and other forms

Summary

of abuse) and article 37 (deprivation of liberty a measure of last resort). It should also relate to the guidelines of the United Nations High Commissioner for Refugees (UNHCR), notably the 1994 *Refugee children – Guidelines on Protection and Care*, which was, as the Committee on the Rights of the Child noted

"fully inspired by the Convention and shaped in the light of its general principles. This book undeniably shows that it is possible, effective and meaningful to use the Convention as a framework for action and to foster international cooperation." (Report on the seventh session, November 1994, CRC/C/34, p. 61)

Since then UNHCR has also issued *Guidelines on Policies and Procedures in dealing with Unaccompanied Children Seeking Asylum* (1997). ∎

Extracts from
Committee on the Rights of the Child
Guidelines for Reports to be submitted by States Parties under the Convention

For full text of *Guidelines for Periodic Reports*, see Appendix 3, page 604.

Guidelines for Initial Reports

"Special protection measures

Under this section States Parties are requested to provide relevant information, including the principal legislative, judicial, administrative or other measures in force; factors and difficulties encountered and progress achieved in implementing the relevant provisions of the Convention; and implementation priorities and specific goals for the future in respect of:

(a) Children in situations of emergency

(i) Refugee children (article 22);...

Additionally, States Parties are encouraged to provide specific statistical information and indicators relevant to the children covered by paragraph 23."

(CRC/C/5 paras. 23 and 24)

Guidelines for Periodic Reports

"SPECIAL PROTECTION MEASURES

A. Children in situations of emergency

1. Refugee children (art. 22)

Please provide information on the appropriate measures adopted pursuant to article 22, paragraph 1 to ensure that a child who is seeking refugee status or who is considered a refugee in accordance with applicable international or domestic law and procedures, whether unaccompanied or accompanied by his or her parents or by any other person, receives appropriate protection and humanitarian assistance in the enjoyment of applicable rights set forth in the Convention and in other international human rights or humanitarian instruments to which the State is a party.

Reports should also indicate:

> *The international and domestic law and procedures applicable to the child who is considered a refugee or is seeking asylum;*

> *Relevant international human rights and humanitarian instruments to which the State is a party, at the multilateral, regional and bilateral levels;*

> *The domestic legislation and procedures in place, including to determine refugee status and ensure and protect the rights of asylum seeking and refugee children, as well as any safeguards established and remedies made available to the child;*

> *The protection and humanitarian assistance provided for the child in the enjoyment of his or her rights set forth in the Convention, as well as in other relevant international instruments, including civil rights and freedoms and economic, social and cultural rights;*

The measures adopted to ensure and protect the rights of the unaccompanied child or the child accompanied by his or her parents or by any other person, including in relation to temporary and long-term solutions, family tracing and family reunion;

The measures adopted to ensure respect for the general principles of the Convention, namely non-discrimination, the best interests of the child, respect for the views of the child, the right to life, and survival and development to the maximum extent possible;

The measures adopted to ensure appropriate dissemination of information and training on the rights of the child who is a refugee or is seeking asylum, particularly to the officials competent in the areas addressed by this article;

The number of asylum seeking and refugee children disaggregated inter alia *by age, gender, country of origin, nationality, accompanied or unaccompanied;*

The number of such children going to school and covered by health services;

The number of staff handling refugee children who attended training courses to understand the Convention on the Rights of the Child during the reporting period, classified by type of job.

Please also indicate the measures adopted pursuant to article 22, paragraph 2 to provide cooperation in any efforts by the United Nations and other competent intergovernmental organizations or non-governmental organizations cooperating with the United Nations to:

Protect and assist the child;

Trace the parents or other members of the family of any refugee child in order to obtain information necessary for reunification with his or her family.

In cases where no parents or other members of the family can be found, please indicate the measures adopted to ensure that the child is accorded the same protection as any other child permanently or temporarily deprived of his or her family environment for any reason, as set forth in the Convention.

Pursuant to this article, please also indicate any evaluation mechanism established to monitor the progress achieved in the implementation of the measures adopted, any difficulties encountered, as well as any priorities set for the future."

(CRC/C/58, paras. 119-122. The following paragraphs of the *Guidelines for Periodic Reports* are also relevant to reporting under this article: 25, 27, 35, 43, 49, 53, 74, and 87; for full text of *Guidelines*, see Appendix 3, page 604.)

"...a child who is seeking refugee status or who is considered a refugee in accordance with applicable international or domestic law and procedures"

The Convention relating to the Status of Refugees 1951 (as amended by the 1967 Protocol relating to the Status of Refugees) provides the international definition of refugees. The defining conditions for adults and children are, broadly speaking, that refugees must be outside their country of nationality (or without nationality) because of a well-founded fear of being persecuted for reasons of race, religion, nationality, membership in a particular social group or political opinion, and they must be unable or unwilling to return because of this fear. A child or adult who holds this refugee status cannot be forced to return to his or her country of origin, or be passed on to another country that might force such a return.

This definition has sometimes proved restrictive in its application and does not meet the needs of those having to flee a country because of famine or plague. As pressure on receiving countries mounts, so do the restrictions (for example some States have adopted prejudgements about which countries are safe or unsafe in terms of the definition). The Committee has nonetheless recommended ratification of the Convention and its Protocol to countries that have not ratified (for example, Jordan IRCO, Add. 21, para. 7; Mongolia IRCO, Add.48, para. 26; Honduras IRCO, Add.24, para. 34; Nepal IRCO, Add.57, para. 33).

Netherlands made a declaration "With regard to article 22 of the Convention, the Government of the Kingdom of the Netherlands declares:

(a) That it understands the term 'refugee' in paragraph 1 of this article as having the same meaning as in article 1 of the Convention relating to the Status of Refugees of 28 July 1951; and

(b) that it is of the opinion that the obligation imposed under the terms of this article does not prevent:

The submission of a request for admission from being made subject to certain conditions, failure to meet such conditions resulting in inadmissibility;

The referral of a request for admission to a third State, in the event that such a State is considered to be primarily responsible for dealing with the request for asylum." (CRC/C/2/Rev.5, p. 27)

The Committee has yet to consider this declaration.

"a child who is seeking refugee status"

Article 22 specifically includes within its scope children who are "seeking refugee status", which is essential to protect the needs of those children whose applications are being processed. Where there are inadequate systems for establishing refugee status the situation of children can become dire:

"The Committee is deeply concerned about administrative measures which have allegedly made it impossible for applicants from certain regions to acquire refugee status. It is reported that once refugee status is denied the applicants, including children, no longer have a legal basis for remaining in the country and consequently become vulnerable to police harassment and to the loss of social welfare entitlements." (Federal Republic of Yugoslavia IRCO, Add.49, para. 20)

Accompanied children usually, but not always, assume their parents' refugee status. Problems particularly arise with unaccompanied children who have to prove refugee status – the difficulty of establishing their status is compounded by their lack of maturity and the fact that the status may have arisen from situations or experiences of their relatives rather than issues which the children have experienced themselves. The UNHCR *Model guidelines on policies and procedures in dealing with unaccompanied children 1997* and *Refugee children – Guidelines on Protection and Care 1994* detail essential safeguards for the status determination of such children (see box) and stress that the investigative interviews and hearings should be conducted in child-friendly envir-

onments and that there should be access to appeal.

The Committee has advised:

"Information on children's rights should be made available to all refugee children in their own language." (Portugal IRCO, Add.45, para. 21)

"Upon arrival in Finland, all unaccompanied children seeking refugee status should be promptly informed in their language of their rights." (Finland IRCO, Add.53, para. 25)

"Procedures should be developed in cooperation with UNHCR in order to facilitate family reunification as well as to appoint legal representatives for unaccompanied children and to apply, when relevant, child friendly interview techniques." (Panama IRCO, Add.68, para. 34)

Refugee child's rights to "receive appropriate protection and humanitarian assistance" in relation to this Convention and any other ratified international treaty

Refugee children are among the most vulnerable groups in the world. Whatever the pressure on the receiving State its legal and moral obligations to ensure the welfare of these children are unarguable. The Committee commented, for example, on the impact of Hong Kong's refugee policy:

"The broad question of the treatment of Vietnamese children in detention centres in Hong Kong deeply concerns the Committee. It is the observation of the Committee that these children have been and continue to be the victim of a policy designed to discourage further refugees from coming into the area. While it is granted that the situation is a complex one, the policy of the continued detention of these children is incompatible with the Convention...
"With regard to the situation of Vietnamese children in detention, the Committee recommends that an evaluation of present and previous policy on this matter be undertaken, to ensure that any errors made are not repeated in the future. The Committee recommends that for the remaining children in detention a solution to their situation must be found in the light of the principles and provisions of the Convention. It is the view of the Committee, therefore, that measures must be taken immediately to ensure a marked improvement in their conditions of detention and that other measures to protect these children must be put in place." (UK dependent territory: Hong Kong IRCO, Add.63, paras. 18 and 33)

The detention of refugee children should only be used as "a measure of last resort and for the

article 22

Unaccompanied Children Seeking Asylum – UNHCR Guidelines

"Access to the territory

Because of their vulnerability, unaccompanied children seeking asylum should not be refused access to the territory.

Identification and initial action

Authorities at ports of entry should take necessary measures to ensure that unaccompanied children seeking admission to the territory are identified as such promptly and on a priority basis.

Unaccompanied children should be registered through interviews. Effective documentation of the child will help to ensure that subsequent actions are taken in the 'best interests' of the child.

A guardian or adviser should be appointed as soon as the unaccompanied child is identified. The guardian or adviser should have the necessary expertise in the field of child-caring, so as to ensure that the interests of the child are safeguarded and that his/her needs are appropriately met.

Initial interviews of unaccompanied children to collect biodata and social history information should be done immediately after arrival and in an age-appropriate manner.

It is desirable that all interviews with unaccompanied children be carried out by professionally qualified persons, specially trained in refugee and children's issues. Insofar as possible, interpreters should also be specially trained persons.

In all cases, the views and wishes of the child should be elicited and considered.

Access to asylum procedures

Children should always have access to asylum procedures, regardless of their age.

Interim care and protection of children seeking asylum

Children seeking asylum, particularly if they are unaccompanied, are entitled to special care and protection.

Children seeking asylum should not be kept in detention. This is particularly important in the case of unaccompanied children.

Refugee status determination

Considering their vulnerability and special needs, it is essential that children's refugee status applications be given priority and that every effort be made to reach a decision promptly and fairly.

Not being legally independent, an asylum-seeking child should be represented by an adult who is familiar with the child's background and who would protect his/her interests.

Interviews should be conducted by specially qualified and trained officials.

Appeals should be processed as expeditiously as possible.

In the examination of the factual elements of the claim of an unaccompanied child, particular regard should be given to the circumstances such as the child's stage of development, his/her possibly limited knowledge of the conditions in the country of origin, and their significance to the legal concept of refugee status, as well as his/her special vulnerability."

(Extracts from the Executive Summary of UNHCR *Model Guidelines on Policies and Procedures in dealing with Unaccompanied Children Seeking Asylum, 1997*)

shortest appropriate period of time" (article 37(b)). The decision to detain them should be subject both to the provisions of the Convention on the Rights of the Child and to the "Beijing Rules" (United Nations Standard Minimum Rules for the Administration of Juvenile Justice 1985); similarly, the conditions of their detention should conform to those of the Convention (article 37, page 487 and article 39, page 529) and the United Nations Rules for the Protection of Juveniles Deprived of their Liberty. The Committee suggested to Sweden:

"...that consideration be given to providing alternatives to the incarceration of children under the Aliens Act." (Sweden IRCO, Add.2, para. 12)

Even where refugee and asylum-seeking children are not in detention, their treatment may be a cause for concern to the Committee:

"The Committee emphasizes the need for further urgent efforts to improve the protection and promotion of the rights of internally displaced children." (Sudan IRCO, Add.l0, para. 24)

"The Committee is concerned about the inadequate measures taken to improve the access of displaced and refugee children to education and health services...
"In view of the general problem of displaced and refugee children, the Committee recommends that all appropriate measures be taken to ensure that those vulnerable groups have access to basic services, particularly in the fields of education, health and social rehabilitation." (Sri Lanka IRCO, Add.40, paras. 20 and 38)

"While the Committee notes that most refugees seem to be placed with host families, it expresses concern that the prevailing economic situation of these families is reported to be growing more precarious." (Federal Republic of Yugoslavia IRCO, Add.49, para. 21)

"The Committee expresses its preoccupation that the government support services to refugees and asylum seekers, including children, appear to be differentiated according to whether persons are admitted as refugees under agreement with the United Nations High Commissioner for Refugees or are present in the country as the result of an individual's application for asylum...
"...all refugee children, including asylum-seekers, coming to New Zealand outside UNHCR organized schemes, [should] be given the benefit of introduction assistance and government-delivered or funded support services." (New Zealand IRCO, Add.71, paras. 20 and 32)

Mass numbers of refugees clearly pose great challenges to receiving States. The Committee has taken pains to give credit where it is due, for example to Germany for

"...accepting comparatively large numbers of refugees and asylum-seekers, particularly from the former Yugoslavia." (Germany IRCO, Add.43, para. 9)

"The Committee acknowledges the willingness the State Party has shown for many years to accept refugees." (Pakistan IRCO, Add.18, para. 33)

"The Committee recognizes the efforts made by Canada for many years in accepting a large number of refugees and immigrants." (Canada IRCO, Add.37, para. 13, see also Sudan IRCO, Add. 10, para. 7)

And the Committee has acknowledged some of the difficulties involved:

"The presence of a very large number of refugees, particularly of Palestinian origin, constitutes a further difficulty impeding the implementation of the Convention." (Jordan IRCO, Add.21, para 7)

"Problems relating to the situation of refugees, internally displaced and 'returnees' have also arisen out of the armed conflict. In this connection, the difficult task of meeting the needs and expectations of this population which remained in or fled from the country during the period of armed conflict is recognized." (Guatemala IRCO, Add.58, para. 10)

The needs of refugee children are extensive, including ensuring that they are in safe and habitable environments and accommodated wherever possible with family and community, that their cultural and linguistic backgrounds are respected, that they have access to education and that their emotional needs are recognized, including responding to any abuse that they may have suffered. The principles of article 12 (respect for the views of the child) should always be taken into account. The UNHCR *Refugee Children – Guidelines on Protection and Care* provides much practical advice on these matters.

Family reunification

A UNHCR primary objective for refugee children, alongside ensuring their protection and healthy development, is: "To achieve durable solutions which are appropriate to the immediate and long-term developmental needs of refugee children".

Preserving and restoring the child's family unity is of the highest priority in the search for durable solutions. The principles of article 10 should apply to family reunification of refugee children; in particular that applications be dealt with in "a positive, humane and expeditious manner". This point has been made by the Committee to a number of countries, for example to Denmark:

"The Committee is also concerned about the application of the law and policy concerning children seeking asylum, particularly with regard to methods of interviewing children, including unaccompanied minors, and to ensuring that applications for the purpose of family reunification are dealt with in a positive, humane and expeditious manner." (Denmark IRCO, Add.33, para. 13. See also Spain IRCO, Add.28, para. 22; Canada IRCO, Add.37, para. 24; Belgium IRCO, Add.38, para. 19; Germany IRCO, Add.43, para. 19).

Germany was pressed heavily on its measures relating to family reunion (see article 10, page 135), and the Committee drew the attention of

article 22

Care of refugee children in Norway

"Applications from unaccompanied minors seeking asylum are treated in the same way as other applications. However, minors are not to be repatriated unless there are parents or others who can care for them in their home country. Measures in the plan are aimed at:

(a) Prompt treatment of applications for asylum;

(b) Questioning in a reassuring atmosphere;

(c) Short stays in reception centres designed especially for this group;

(d) Early settlement in municipalities;

(e) Protecting the interests and rights of the individual, for example, in connection with questions pertaining to guardians and child welfare measures;

(f) Guidance to municipalities concerning the reception of this group;

(g) Vocational training for unaccompanied minors who do not come under any ordinary education system."

In addition there are guidelines for the guardians of unaccompanied minors who seek asylum, as part of the effort to protect children's rights.

"In Norway, there are a number of refugee children who have fled their country because of war and therefore need special protection and care. A special psychosocial centre for refugees has been established as part of the University of Oslo. The centre offers instruction in child psychiatry and is also involved in the treatment of victims of torture, etc." (Norway IR, paras. 428-429)

the Federal Republic of Yugoslavia to

"the constraints that are reported to be hampering the reunification of unaccompanied refugee children with their families." (Federal Republic of Yugoslavia IRCO, Add. 49, para. 19)

The delegation from Finland was asked by a Committee member: "Were family ties taken into consideration by the authorities when deciding whether to grant residence status? How were the authorities prepared for handling cases of asylum-seeking parents? Was any attention given to the destabilizing impact on children that the prolonged uncertain status of asylum-seeking parents might have?" (Finland SR.283, para. 31).

It should, however, be noted that family reunification should not be used as a justification for acting against the child's best interests. Children may not wish to be reunited with their family or the family may reject them (for example if they have to return to the country of origin). As article 9 provides, separation from families may be necessary in the child's best interests. The Human Rights Committee states in a General Comment: "In the view of the Committee, States Parties must not expose individuals to the danger of torture or cruel, inhuman or degrading treatment or punishment upon return to another country by way of their extradition, expulsion or *refoulement*. States Parties should indicate in their reports what measures they have adopted to that end" (Human Rights Committee, General Comment 20, HRI/GEN/1/Rev.2, p. 30).

Discrimination against children refused refugee status

Article 22 covers both children with refugee status and children seeking it, but the Convention's provisions in any event cover **all** children within the country's jurisdiction (article 2), so even those children who have been refused refugee status are still protected as long as they remain in the country. The Committee told Belgium that it was

"particularly concerned that unaccompanied minors who have had their asylum request rejected, but who can remain in the country until they are 18 years old, may be deprived of an identity and denied the full enjoyment of their rights, including health care and education. Such a situation, in the view of the Committee, raises concern as to its compatibility with articles 2 and 3 of the Convention." (Belgium IRCO, Add.38, para. 9)

The point was also raised with Denmark, the Committee commenting that

"...all children who have their asylum requests rejected but who remained in the country have their rights to health, care or education provided de facto but not de jure. It is the view of the Committee that this situation is not fully compatible with the provisions and principles of articles 2 and 3 of the Convention...

"With regard to the situation of refugee children and children seeking asylum, the Committee suggests that the State Party consider

*reviewing its Alien Act as regards its compat-
ibility with the provisions and principles of the
Convention ... with regard to the provision of
health and education services to children in
asylum-seeking situations, the Committee
wishes to draw attention to the provisions of
article 2 of the Convention which state,* inter
alia, *that 'States parties shall respect and
ensure the rights set forth in the present Convention to each child within their jurisdiction."*
(Denmark IRCO, Add.33, paras. 14 and 30)

The same matter of concern was raised with
Norway, with the suggestion

*"...that the State Party consider undertaking
another comprehensive review of the policy in
relation to children seeking asylum in the
light of the principles and provisions of the
Convention..."* (Norway IRCO, Add.23, paras. 12
and 24)

The Committee was also concerned

*"at the situation of unaccompanied children
who arrive 'unexpectedly in France to obtain
refugee status' (as referred to in para. 389 of
the State Party's report). It is also concerned
about the lack of a comprehensive system of
protection involving the social and/or judicial
authorities which would apply to those children while they are subject to the jurisdiction
of the State Party, as well as in the process of
returning to their country of origin."*

The Committee asked to see new French legislation relating to the fields of nationality, entry and
residence of foreigners, refugees and asylum
seekers as well as family reunification and information on the way this legislation

*"might affect the enjoyment of the rights of
the child as recognized by the Convention, in
particular its articles 7, 9, 10 and 22 and taking into account the General Principles of the
Convention."* (France IRCO, Add.20, paras. 15
and 25)

Article 7 provides that all children are entitled to
the "right to acquire a nationality" and States Parties are particularly reminded of the importance
of this "where the child would otherwise be
stateless" (article 7, see page 102). The UNHCR
Guidelines comment: "Statelessness is often
caused by States' deliberate policies not to confer
nationality to children born to refugees. It may
also be caused by the existence of conflicting
laws regarding nationality ... All refugee children
in the country of asylum must be considered as
having, or being able to acquire, including
through naturalization, an effective nationality"
(UNHCR *Refugee Children – Guidelines on Protection and Care*, 1994, pp. 104 and 106).

The *Guidelines for Periodic Reports* asks:
"Please provide information on the measures

adopted pursuant to article 7, paragraph 2, to
ensure the child's right to acquire a nationality, in
particular where the child would otherwise be
stateless. Reference should also be made to the
implementation of this right in relation to children
born out of wedlock, and asylum-seeking and
refugee children." (para. 53)

"States Parties shall provide, as they consider appropriate, cooperation in any efforts by the United Nations and other competent intergovernmental or non-governmental organizations cooperating with the United Nations"

During the drafting of article 22, some delegates
to the Working Group were unhappy with the
idea that their countries might be obliged to cooperate with non-governmental or intergovernmental organizations, so the words "as they consider
appropriate" were added to clarify the discretionary nature of that cooperation. The requirement
that INGOs and NGOs had to be "working in
cooperation with the United Nations" was made
because, as some representatives pointed out, terrorist organizations were technically NGOs –
although others were concerned because some
valid NGOs did not work with the United Nations
(E/CN.4/1989/48, pp. 63-66; Detrick, p. 325).

The *Manual on Human Rights Reporting*, 1997
comments: "International action is naturally also
required to ensure the implementation of article
22 and generally the enjoyment of their fundamental rights by children who are refugees or
seeking refugee status. Paragraph 2 addresses this
reality in detail, stressing the importance of cooperation with United Nations bodies, intergovernmental organizations and non-governmental
organizations cooperating with the United
Nations. Their combined action is in fact essential to protect and assist the child, particularly
when there is a need to trace the parents or other
members of the child's family with a view to promote family reunification" (*Manual*, p. 471).

The unique and important work of the United
Nations High Commissioner for Refugees
(UNHCR) was stressed at all stages of drafting
the Convention. The role of the UNHCR, established by the General Assembly in 1949, is to
provide international protection to refugees under
the auspices of the United Nations and, together
with governments, to seek durable solutions
to their plight and provide them with material
assistance.

The value of UNHCR's work in relation to child refugees is emphasized by the Committee, for example:

"The Committee recommends that the Government undertake the necessary measures to introduce legislation for the protection of the rights of refugees, in line with the relevant international standards, including the Convention relating to the Status of Refugees and its Protocol. Technical assistance from UNHCR may be requested in this regard." (Honduras IRCO, Add.24, para. 34)

"Regarding the rights of refugee and asylum-seeking child, the Committee recommends that the State Party consider as a preventive measure adopting relevant legislative provisions, in consultation with the United Nations High Commissioner for Refugees." (Tunisia IRCO, Add.39, para. 16)

"...to trace parents or other members of the family of any refugee child in order to obtain information necessary for reunification"

Registration is the first step in tracing family members of refugees. It is essential that unaccompanied children are registered by a receiving State at the first possible opportunity. The International Committee of the Red Cross coordinates such efforts, but the success of tracing largely depends on the energy and commitment of the State receiving the child. When congratulating Pakistan on its willing acceptance of refugees, the Committee expressed the hope that refugee status would continue to be granted

"...as well as ensuring at the same time a comprehensive system of registration." (Pakistan IRCO, Add.18, para. 33; see also Zimbabwe IRCO, Add.55, para.13)

Myanmar has a potentially large number of internally displaced people, about whom the Committee observed:

"While welcoming the recent peace agreements between the Government and a great majority of rebel armed groups in the country, the Committee strongly recommends the State Party to prevent any occurrence of forced relocation, displacement and other types of involuntary population movements

which deeply affect families and the rights of children. The Committee also recommends that the State Party reinforce its central tracing agency to favour family reunification." (Myanmar IRCO, Add.69, para. 40)

Care has to be taken in tracing family members not inadvertently to endanger children or their families by inappropriately breaching confidentiality. Unaccompanied children and their families can be at grave risk. The Committee raised concerns about a hazardous practice of Spain:

"The Committee is worried about one aspect of the treatment of unaccompanied minors seeking refuge status which may contradict the principle that each case be dealt with on an individual basis and on its own merits. The practice of automatically informing the authorities of their country of origin may lead to their persecution, or the persecution of their relatives, for political reasons." (Spain IRCO, Add.28, para. 9)

Social work support may be needed when family reunion is achieved. Family members may not have seen each other for long periods and may have experienced very traumatizing events in the interim.

"In cases where no parents or other members of the family can be found, the child shall be accorded the same protection as any other child permanently or temporarily deprived of his or her family environment for any reason"

This provision underlines the fact that refugee and asylum seeking children are entitled to be treated the same as other children deprived of their family environment. Article 20 provides that such children are "entitled to special protection and assistance" and should be provided with alternative care, preferably family-based, if no family members are able to look after them (see page 257). Unaccompanied refugee children are, by definition, "temporarily deprived of their family environment" and States should ensure that appropriate arrangements are in place to ensure that their needs are met (see box, page 285).

Implementation Checklist

● General measures of implementation

Have appropriate general measures of implementation been taken in relation to article 22, including

☐ identification and coordination of the responsible departments and agencies at all levels of government (article 22 is relevant to the **departments of justice, foreign affairs, home affairs, social welfare, health, social security and education**)?

☐ identification of relevant non-governmental organizations/civil society partners?

☐ a comprehensive review to ensure that all legislation, policy and practice is compatible with the article, for all children in all parts of the jurisdiction?

☐ adoption of a strategy to secure full implementation

    ☐ which includes where necessary the identification of goals and indicators of progress?

    ☐ which does not affect any provisions which are more conducive to the rights of the child?

    ☐ which recognizes other relevant international standards?

    ☐ which involves where necessary international cooperation?

(Such measures may be part of an overall governmental strategy for implementing the Convention as a whole).

☐ budgetary analysis and allocation of necessary resources?

☐ development of mechanisms for monitoring and evaluation?

☐ making the implications of article 22 widely known to adults and children?

☐ development of appropriate training and awareness-raising (in relation to article 22 likely to include the training of **social workers, teachers, port and border control officers, lawyers, interpreters, child development experts, mental health personnel and child advocates**)?

● Specific issues in implementing article 22

☐ Has the State ratified the Convention relating to the Status of Refugees 1951 as amended by the 1967 Protocol relating to the Status of Refugees?

☐ Are procedures in place to determine the refugee status of children?

☐ Do the procedures for determining refugee status take into account the special needs and rights of children, particularly when the child is unaccompanied by an adult?

☐ Are the interviews and hearings conducted in a child-friendly environment?

☐ Are the child's views heard or represented in these proceedings?

Are unaccompanied children seeking asylum

    ☐ provided with legal representation?

    ☐ professional interpreters?

    ☐ decision makers experienced in child development?

    ☐ given the benefit of the doubt in relation to their claim for refugee status?

☐ Are applications by child refugees and/or their parents for the purpose of family reunion treated in a positive, humane and expeditious manner?

☐ Are unaccompanied children who are refused refugee status allowed to remain in the receiving country when to do so would be in their best interests?

☐ Are child refugees or children seeking refugee status given special assistance and protection appropriate to all their needs and in accordance with their rights under the Convention?

☐ Are children who have been refused refugee status but are nonetheless permitted to stay in the country entitled to the same assistance and facilities on the same basis as children with accredited status?

☐ Are such children informed of these rights in their own language?

☐ Are such children only deprived of their liberty as a measure of last resort and for the shortest appropriate period of time?

☐ Are they able to challenge such deprivation of liberty in a fair hearing?

☐ Are the conditions of detention humane and conducive to the health, self-respect, dignity and social integration of the child?

Are refugee and asylum seeking children:

    ☐ accommodated in safe and habitable environments, wherever possible with their family?

    ☐ in receipt of education which recognizes their culture, language and need for social integration?

    ☐ provided with appropriate support and rehabilitative care for any traumas they may have suffered?

    ☐ in receipt of all necessary health care?

☐ Does the State cooperate with non-governmental organizations or international non-governmental organizations acting in association with the United Nations in respect of refugee and asylum seeking children and in particular with the United Nations High Commissioner for Refugees and the International Committee for the Red Cross?

How to use the checklists, *see page XVII*

☐ Are all efforts made to trace family members of such children?

☐ Do such efforts ensure that the child and the child's family members are not endangered?

Reminder: **The Convention is indivisible and its articles are interdependent. Article 22 should not be considered in isolation.**

Particular regard should be paid to:
The general principles

Article 2: all rights to be recognized for each child in jurisdiction without discrimination on any ground

Article 3(1): the best interests of the child to be a primary consideration in all actions concerning children

Article 6: right to life and maximum possible survival and development

Article 12: respect for the child's views in all matters affecting the child; opportunity to be heard in any judicial or administrative proceedings affecting the child

Closely related articles

Articles whose implementation is related to that of article 22 include:

Article 7: child's right to nationality and to know and be cared for by parents

Article 8: preservation of child's identity

Article 9: non-separation from parents except when necessary in best interests

Article 10: international family reunification

Article 16: protection from arbitrary interference with privacy, family and home

Article 20: children deprived of their family environment

Article 30: children of minorities or indigenous peoples

Article 37: deprivation of liberty as a last resort

Article 38: children affected by armed conflict

Article 39: rehabilitative care for child victims

Rights of disabled children

article 23

Text of Article 23

1. States Parties recognize that a mentally or physically disabled child should enjoy a full and decent life, in conditions which ensure dignity, promote self-reliance and facilitate the child's active participation in the community.

2. States Parties recognize the right of the disabled child to special care and shall encourage and ensure the extension, subject to available resources, to the eligible child and those responsible for his or her care, of assistance for which application is made and which is appropriate to the child's condition and to the circumstances of the parents or others caring for the child.

3. Recognizing the special needs of a disabled child, assistance extended in accordance with paragraph 2 of the present article shall be provided free of charge, whenever possible, taking into account the financial resources of the parents or others caring for the child, and shall be designed to ensure that the disabled child has effective access to and receives education, training, health care services, rehabilitation services, preparation for employment and recreation opportunities in a manner conducive to the child's achieving the fullest possible social integration and individual development, including his or her cultural and spiritual development.

4. States Parties shall promote, in the spirit of international cooperation, the exchange of appropriate information in the field of preventive health care and of medical, psychological and functional treatment of disabled children, including dissemination of and access to information concerning methods of rehabilitation, education and vocational services, with the aim of enabling States Parties to improve their capabilities and skills and to widen their experience in these areas. In this regard, particular account shall be taken of the needs of developing countries.

The inclusion in the Convention of a specific article on the rights of "the disabled child" and the inclusion of disability as a specific ground for protection against discrimination under article 2 reflects growing understanding and acknowledgement of the links between disability and human rights.

Under article 2, States are required to ensure and respect all the rights set forth in the Convention on the Rights of the Child to disabled children within their jurisdiction. Article 23 provides further guidance on realizing the rights of disabled children. In its overall comments on implementation, the Committee has frequently underlined the importance of respecting the child as a subject of rights. Article 23 reemphasizes this from the perspective of the disabled child, who should be provided with conditions for living that "promote self-reliance" and facilitate "active participation in the community". Paragraphs 2 and 3 set out the right of the disabled child to "special care",

again stressing that assistance should be designed to ensure "effective access" to various services, "in a manner conducive to the child's achieving the fullest possible social integration and individual development...". Paragraph 4 promotes international cooperation to improve the capabilities and skills of States Parties. No reservations or declarations have been made with reference to article 23 by States Parties.

The Standard Rules on the Equalization of Opportunities for Persons with Disabilities, adopted by the General Assembly in 1993 (resolution 48/96, 20 December 1993), is the first detailed instrument reaffirming rights for all disabled people. It refers in its Preamble, to the Convention on the Rights of the Child "which prohibits discrimination on the basis of disability and requires special measures to ensure the rights of children with disabilities".

United Nations estimates suggest there are 500 million disabled people worldwide. ■

Extracts from
Committee on the Rights of the Child
Guidelines for Reports to be submitted by States Parties under the Convention

For full text of *Guidelines for Periodic Reports*, see Appendix 3, page 604.

Guidelines for Initial Reports

"General principles

Relevant information, including the principal legislative, judicial, administrative or other measures in force or foreseen, factors and difficulties encountered and progress achieved in implementing the provisions of the Convention, and implementation priorities and specific goals for the future should be provided in respect of:

(a) Non-discrimination (article 2). ['Disability' is included as a specific ground for discrimination in article 2]

...

In addition, States Parties are encouraged to provide relevant information on the application of these principles in the implementation of articles listed elsewhere in these guidelines."

"Basic health and welfare

Under this section States Parties are requested to provide relevant information, including the principal legislative, judicial, administrative or other measures in force; the institutional infrastructure for implementing policy in this area, particularly monitoring strategies and mechanisms; and factors and difficulties encountered and progress achieved in implementing the relevant provisions of the Convention, in respect of:

...

(b) Disabled children (article 23);
...".
(CRC/C/5, paras. 13, 14 and 19)

Guidelines for Periodic Reports

"III. GENERAL PRINCIPLES

A. Non-discrimination (art. 2)

Reports should indicate whether the principle of non-discrimination is included as a binding principle in the Constitution or in domestic legislation specifically for children and whether all the possible grounds for discrimination spelled out in article 2 of the Convention are reflected in such legal provisions. Reports should further indicate the measures adopted to ensure the rights set forth in the Convention to each child under the jurisdiction of the State without discrimination of any kind, including non-nationals, refugees and asylum-seekers.

Information should be provided on steps taken to ensure that discrimination is prevented and combated, both in law and practice, including discrimination on the basis of race, colour, sex, language, religion, political or other opinion, national, ethnic or social origin, property, disability, birth or other status of the child, his/her parents or legal guardians.

Please indicate the specific measures adopted to reduce economic, social and geographical disparities, including between rural and urban areas, to prevent discrimination against the most disadvantaged groups of children, including children belonging to minorities or indigenous communities, disabled children, children born out of wedlock, children who are non-nationals, migrants, displaced, refugees or asylum-seekers, and children who are living and/or working on the streets."

"Basic health and welfare

Disabled children (art. 23)

Please provide information on:

The situation of the mentally or physically disabled child and the measures taken to ensure:

> *The child's enjoyment of a full and decent life, in conditions which ensure the child's dignity and self-reliance;*

> *The child's enjoyment of his or her rights without discrimination of any kind and the prevention and elimination of discriminatory attitudes against him or her;*

> *The promotion of the child's active participation in the community;*

> *The child's effective access to education, training, health care and rehabilitation services, preparation for employment and recreation opportunities in a manner conducive to the child's achieving the fullest possible social integration and individual development, including his or her cultural and spiritual development;*

> *The consideration given to the inclusion of disabled children together with children without disabilities in institutions, services and facilities, including within the education system;*

> *The child's right to special care and the steps taken to ensure the extension, subject to available resources, to the eligible child and those responsible for his or her care, of assistance appropriate to the child's condition and to the circumstances of the parents or others caring for the child;*

> *That, whenever possible, assistance is provided free of charge, taking into account the financial resources of the parents or others caring for the child;*

> *The measures taken to ensure an effective evaluation of the situation of disabled children, including the development of a system of identification and tracking of disabled children, the establishment of any appropriate monitoring mechanism, the assessment of progress and of difficulties encountered, as well as any targets set for the future;*

> *The measures taken to ensure adequate training, including specialized training, for those responsible for the care of disabled children, including at the family and community levels and within relevant institutions;*

> *The measures taken to promote, in the spirit of international cooperation, the exchange of appropriate information in the field of preventive health care and of the medical, psychological and functional treatment of disabled children, including dissemination of and access to information concerning methods of rehabilitation, education and vocational services. An indication should be given of the measures taken with the aim of enabling States Parties to the Convention to improve their capabilities and skills and to widen their experience in these areas, and the consideration given to the particular needs of developing countries;*

> *The children concerned, including by type of disability, the coverage of the assistance provided, programmes and services made available, including in the fields of education, training, care, rehabilitation, employment and recreation, the financial and other resources allocated, and other relevant information, disaggregated inter alia by gender, age, rural/urban area, and social and ethnic origin."*

(CRC/C/58, paras. 25-27 and 92. The following paragraphs of the *Guidelines for Periodic Reports* are also relevant to reporting under this article: 86-87, 108; for full text of *Guidelines*, see Appendix 3, page 604.)

Recognizing the human rights of disabled people

Background to the Standard Rules

The only explicit reference to disability or handicap in the International Bill of Human Rights is in article 25 of the Universal Declaration on Human Rights, which recognizes that everyone has "the right to security in the event of unemployment, sickness, disability, widowhood, old age or other lack of livelihood in circumstances beyond his control". Disability is not mentioned in the International Covenant on Civil and Political Rights or the International Covenant on Economic, Social and Cultural Rights.

During the 1970s, the United Nations General Assembly adopted the Declaration on the Rights of Mentally Retarded People (20 December 1971) and the Declaration on the Rights of Disabled Persons (9 December 1975), which proclaimed that disabled people have the same civil and political rights as other human beings. 1981 was designated as the International Year of Disabled Persons, with the theme "Full participation and equality". In 1982 the General Assembly adopted the World Programme of Action Concerning Disabled Persons, which stressed that "More than 500 million people in the world are disabled as a consequence of mental, physical or sensory impairment. They are entitled to the same rights as all other human beings and to equal opportunities. Too often their lives are handicapped by physical and social barriers in society which hamper their full participation. Because of this, millions of children and adults in all parts of the world often face a life that is segregated and debased."

Within the United Nations Commission on Human Rights, the SubCommission on Prevention of Discrimination and Protection of Minorities adopted a recommendation that Governments give consideration to difficulties encountered by disabled persons in the enjoyment of universally proclaimed human rights, as well as to the need to strengthen procedures for them to bring allegations of violations of their human rights to a competent body vested with the authority to act on such complaints, or to the attention of the Government (Resolution 1982/1). In 1984, the Special Rapporteur on Human Rights and Disability was appointed. The final report prepared by the Special Rapporteur in 1991 notes that "In the majority of countries, at least 1 out of 10 persons has a physical, mental or sensory impairment, and at least 25 per cent of the entire population are adversely affected by the presence of disabilities ... these persons frequently live in deplorable conditions, owing to the presence of physical and social barriers which prevent their integration and full participation in the community. As a result, millions of children and adults throughout the world are segregated and deprived of virtually all their rights, and lead a wretched, marginal life." (E/CN.4/Sub.2/1991/31, para. 3)

In 1987, the Global Meeting of Experts to Review the World Programme of Action Concerning Disabled Persons at the mid-point of the United Nations Decade of Disabled Persons in Stockholm recommended that the General Assembly should convene a special conference to draft an international convention on the elimination of all forms of discrimination against persons with disabilities, to be ratified by States by the end of the Decade. A draft outline was prepared by Italy and presented to the General Assembly at its forty-second session. There were further presentations at the forty-fourth session, but no consensus could be reached: in the opinion of many representatives, existing human rights documents seemed to guarantee persons with disabilities the same rights as other persons. Following these debates in the General Assembly, the Economic and Social Council, at its first regular session in 1990, agreed to concentrate on the elaboration of an international instrument of a different kind. The Commission for Social Development was authorized to establish an ad hoc open-ended Working Group of government experts to elaborate standard rules on the equalization of opportunities for disabled children, youth and adults, in close collaboration with the specialized agencies, other inter-governmental bodies and NGOs, especially organizations of disabled persons.

The introduction to the Standard Rules on the Equalization of Opportunities for Persons with Disabilities notes that they have been developed on the basis of experience gained during the United Nations Decade of Disabled Persons: "The International Bill of Human Rights, comprising the Universal Declaration of Human Rights, the International Covenant on Economic, Social and Cultural Rights and the International Covenant on Civil and Political Rights, the Convention on the Rights of the Child and the Convention on the Elimination of All Forms of Discrimination against Women, as well as the World Programme of Action concerning Disabled Persons, constitute the political and moral foundation for the Rules."

The Standard Rules

The Standard Rules on the Equalization of Opportunities for Persons with Disabilities was adopted by the United Nations General Assembly at its forty eighth session on 20 December 1993 (for full text of Rules, see Appendix 4, page 659). The Rules upholds the principle of equal rights – "that the needs of each and every individual are of equal importance, that those needs must be made the basis for the planning of societies and that all resources must be employed in such a way as to ensure that every individual has equal opportunity for participation". The Introduction to the Rules emphasizes: "Persons with disabilities are members of society and have the right to remain within their local communities. They should receive the support they need within the ordinary structure of education, health, employment and social services." The Standard Rules has been upheld as particularly important by the Committee on Economic, Social and Cultural Rights in a General Comment on disability and the International Covenant (see below, page 298).

Most of the Standard Rules is relevant to disabled children. Various rules refer directly to children. For example:

Rule 1. Awareness-raising: "Awareness-raising should be an important part of the education of children with disabilities and in rehabilitation programmes... Awareness-raising should be part of the education of all children and should be a component of teacher-training courses and training of all professionals."

Rule 2. Medical care: "States should ensure that persons with disabilities, particularly infants and children, are provided with the same level of medical care within the same system as other members of society.... States should ensure that medical, paramedical and related personnel are adequately trained so that they do not give inappropriate advice to parents, thus restricting options for their children...."

Other rules are quoted below in relation to various elements of article 23, and throughout the *Implementation Handbook* in relation to other articles.

Definitions of "disability" and "handicap"

The introduction to the Standard Rules distinguishes between "disability" and "handicap" as follows: "The term 'disability' summarizes a great number of different functional limitations occurring in any population in any country of the world. People may be disabled by physical, intellectual or sensory impairment, medical conditions or mental illness. Such impairments, conditions or illnesses may be permanent or transitory in nature.

"The term 'handicap' means the loss or limitation of opportunities to take part in the life of the community on an equal level with others. It describes the encounter between the person with a disability and the environment. The purpose of this term is to emphasize the focus on the shortcomings in the environment and in many organized activities in society, for example information, communication and education, which prevent persons with disabilities from participating on equal terms."

The introduction goes on to explain: "The use of the two terms 'disability' and 'handicap'... should be seen in the light of modern disability history. During the 1970s, there was a strong reaction among representatives of persons with disabilities and professionals in the field of disability against the terminology of the time. The terms 'disability' and 'handicap' were often used in an unclear and confusing way, which gave poor guidance for policy-making and for political action. The terminology reflected a medical and diagnostic approach, which ignored the imperfections and deficiencies of the surrounding society."

Using a medical rather than a social definition of disability has been an important factor in building the concept of disabled people as 'different', and has resulted in the provision of specialized solutions that emphasize the differences rather than integrating them.

Monitoring the Standard Rules: the Special Rapporteur

Section IV, paragraph 2, of the Rules states that the Rules will be monitored within the framework of the sessions of the Commission for Social Development and that a Special Rapporteur with relevant and extensive experience will be appointed for a three-year term to monitor implementation of the Rules together with a Panel of Experts formed by appropriate non-governmental organizations. The Special Rapporteur is required to send out questionnaires on implementation plans for the Rules. The Special Rapporteur of the Commission for Social Development on Monitoring the Implementation of the Standard Rules was appointed in March 1994. In his December 1996 report he notes: "The recommendations in the Standard Rules are very progressive and, in the opinion of the Special Rapporteur, no country, not even among the most advanced countries, has fully implemented the Rules. Nonetheless, there is no doubt that the Rules, in the short time since their adoption, have been widely accepted and are being used as the main policy guidelines in the disability field both by Governments and non-governmental organizations." He notes that "the child aspect and the gender perspective are vague in the texts of the Rules". Both should receive more attention in future implementation efforts (A/52/56, 23 December 1996, paras. 130 and 152). The Special Rapporteur notes that there had been a very poor response to the first questionnaire circulated on implementation; a second questionnaire, transmitted in December 1995, had generated more response (A/52/56, paras. 50-65).

The Economic and Social Council adopted a resolution in 1997 on "Children with disabilities". This recognizes the need for special attention to be directed towards children with disabilities and their families or other caretakers, and requests the Special Rapporteur in his monitoring of the Rules, "to pay special attention to the situation of children with disabilities, to pursue close working relations with the Committee on the Rights of the Child in its monitoring role with respect to the Convention on the Rights of the Child, and to include in his report to the Commission for Social Development at its thirty-eighth session his findings, views, observations and recommendations on children with disabilities". The resolution also urges Governments to ensure, in accordance with rule 6 of the Standard Rules on the Equalization of Opportunities for Persons with Disabilities, that children with disabilities have equal access to education and that their education is an integral part of the educational system. UNESCO is urged to continue its programme activities aimed at the integration of children and youth with disabilities into mainstream education (E/Res/1997/20).

Committee on Economic, Social and Cultural Rights: General Comment on disability

A lengthy 1994 General Comment on "Persons with Disabilities" from the Committee on Economic, Social and Cultural Rights draws attention to the importance of addressing disability explicitly: "The absence of an explicit, disability-related provision in the Covenant [on Economic, Social and Cultural Rights] can be attributed to the lack of awareness of the importance of addressing this issue explicitly, rather than only by implication, at the time of the drafting of the Covenant over a quarter of a century ago. More recent international human rights instruments have, however, addressed the issue specifically. They include the Convention on the Rights of the Child (article 23); the African Charter on Human and Peoples' Rights (article 18(4)); and the Additional Protocol to the American Convention on Human Rights in the Area of Economic, Social and Cultural Rights (article 18). Thus it is now very widely accepted that the human rights of persons with disabilities must be protected and promoted through general, as well as specially designed, laws, policies and programmes." (Committee on Economic, Social and Cultural Rights, General Comment 5, HRI/GEN/1/Rev.2, p. 66)

The General Comment lists the instruments in which "the international community has affirmed its commitment to ensuring the full range of human rights for persons with disabilities":

- the World Programme of Action concerning Disabled Persons, providing a policy framework aimed at promoting "effective measures for prevention of disability, rehabilitation and the realization of the goals of 'full participation' of [persons with disabilities] in social life and development, and of 'equality'";

- the Guidelines for the Establishment and Development of National Coordinating Committees on Disability or Similar Bodies (adopted in 1990);

- the Principles for the Protection of Persons with Mental Illness and for the Improvement of Mental Health Care (adopted in 1991);

- the Standard Rules on the Equalization of Opportunities for Persons with Disabilities, whose purpose is to ensure that all persons with disabilities "may exercise the same rights and obligations as others" (adopted in 1993).

The Comment notes: "The Standard Rules are of major importance and constitute a particularly valuable reference guide in identifying more precisely the relevant obligations of States Parties under the Covenant."

Causes of disability

Many articles in the Convention on the Rights of the Child are related to causes of disability, and thus their implementation can help to prevent disability: for example, articles concerned with protecting the child from involvement in armed conflict and protecting the child from violence and from various forms of exploitation. Article 6 (right to life and maximum survival and development) and article 24 (right to health and health services) are relevant to the prevention of disability, as well as to respecting the right of the disabled child to special care.

A report prepared for the World Summit on Social Development suggests that major causative factors of disability include malnutrition (100 million, 20 per cent of all disabled people); accidents/trauma/war (78 million, 15.6 per cent); infectious diseases (56 million, 11.2 per cent); non-infectious diseases (100 million, 20 per cent); congenital diseases (100 million (20 per cent). But it should be noted that the figures are not straightforward. Some congenital (pre-birth) conditions are linked to malnutrition, which is preventable and fundamentally related to poverty, and many infectious and non-infectious diseases are secondary to poverty-related factors such as the drinking of polluted water (*Overcoming Obstacles to the Integration of Disabled People*, UNESCO-sponsored report as a contribution to the World Summit on Social Development, Copenhagen, March 1995, Disability Awareness in Action, London, 1995, p. 9).

The final report of the Special Rapporteur on Human Rights and Disability lists the following causes, which appeared most often in responses received from governmental and non-governmental sources, most but not all of which are causes of disability in childhood: "heredity, birth defects, lack of care during pregnancy and childbirth because of lack of coverage or ignorance, insalubrious housing, natural disasters, illiteracy and the resulting lack of information on available health services, poor sanitation and hygiene, congenital diseases, malnutrition, traffic accidents, work-related accidents and illnesses, sports accidents, the so-called diseases of 'civilization' (cardiovascular disease, mental and nervous disorders, the use of certain chemicals, change of diet and lifestyle, etc.), marriage between close relatives, accidents in the home, respiratory diseases, metabolic diseases (diabetes, kidney failure, etc.), drugs, alcohol, smoking, high blood pressure, old age, Chagas' disease, poliomyelitis, measles, etc. Non-governmental sources also place particular emphasis on factors related to the environment, air and water pollution, scientific experiments conducted without the informed consent of the victims, terrorist violence, wars, intentional physical mutilations carried out by the authorities and other attacks on the physical and mental integrity of persons, as well as violations of human rights and humanitarian law in general." (E/CN.4/Sub.2/1991/31, para. 109)

In one case, the Committee on the Rights of the Child expressed concern at the likely increase in the incidence of disability caused by inadequate supervision and care at birth:

"The Committee is concerned that only 47 per cent of births are supervised by qualified health care workers, and is alarmed at the implications this may have for increased likelihood of sickness and disability arising from preventable problems occurring during delivery..." (Bolivia IRCO, Add.1, para. 10)

The Committee has also commented on consanguineous marriages:

"The Committee suggests that further efforts should be undertaken to disseminate information about the risk of consanguineous marriages, including through the media and health education programmes." (Lebanon IRCO, Add.54, para. 38)

Poverty and disability

The World Programme of Action Concerning Disabled Persons notes that the relationship between disability and poverty has been clearly established: "While the risk of impairment is much greater for the poverty-stricken, the converse is also true. The birth of an impaired child, or the occurrence of disability in the family, often places heavy demands on the limited resources of the family and strains on its morale, thus thrusting it deeper into poverty. The combined effect of these factors results in higher proportions of disabled persons among the poorest strata of society. For this reason, the number of affected families living at the poverty level steadily increases in absolute terms. The negative impact of these trends seriously hinders the development process." (World Programme of Action, para. 41)

Armed conflict and disability

Armed conflict is a major and probably increasing cause of disability among children in many countries because of the targeting of civilians and the use of modern weapons, including, in particular, landmines (see also article 38, page 520). Such conflicts are often accompanied by a reduction or breakdown of basic health and other services. Thus the Special Rapporteur on Human Rights and Disability reports that "in the armed conflicts in Angola and Mozambique, for example, less than 10 to 20 per cent of the children received inexpensive prosthetic devices. In Nicaragua and El Salvador, only 20 per cent of children in need were provided with the necessary services."(E/CN.4/Sub.2/1991/31, para. 135)

Many disabilities are not visible. Millions of children suffer psychological trauma caused by exposure to or involvement in armed conflict. The Graça Machel study on the *Impact of Armed Conflict on Children* states that millions of children are killed by armed conflicts, "but three times as many are seriously injured or permanently disabled by it. According to WHO [World Health Organization], armed conflict and political violence are the leading causes of injury, impairment and physical disability and primarily responsible for the conditions of over 4 million children who currently live with disabilities. In Afghanistan alone, some 100,000 children have war-related disabilities, many of them caused by landmines. The lack of basic services and the destruction of health facilities during armed conflict mean that children living with disabilities get little support...." (A/51/306,1996, para. 145)

Child labour and disability

Child labour can have terrible consequences for the child's mental and physical development, and children may be particularly prone to accidents at work, causing disabilities (see article 32, page 427). The International Labour Organization has adopted a Convention and a Recommendation concerning vocational rehabilitation and employment of disabled persons (see below, page 308).

Abuse, punishment and other treatment and disability

The Special Rapporteur on Human Rights and Disability mentions some deliberately inflicted forms of punishment and other practices as causing disability: amputation as a punishment; the institutionalization of disabled people, institutional abuse, including the use of drugs; forced sterilization, castration and female circumcision (genital mutilation); and the blinding of detainees as an alternative to detention (E/CN.4/Sub.2/1991/31, para. 174). All such practices not only cause physical disabilities but also affect mental health.

The Special Rapporteur also refers to physical and psychological ill-treatment of children, both within and outside of the family, as an "extremely serious cause of disability in both developed and developing countries. The harm that can be caused in children by their parents or other persons beating, insulting, humiliating and maltreating them can be so great that in many cases it causes mental illness, social maladjustment, difficulties in school or at work, sexual impairment, etc." (E/CN.4/Sub.2/1991/31, para. 139)

The prevention of all forms of violence and exploitation, highlighted in various articles of the Convention, are relevant to prevention of disability: in particular article 19 (protection from all forms of physical or mental violence), articles 32 (economic exploitation), 34 (sexual exploitation), 36 (other forms of exploitation) and article 37 (prohibition of torture and other cruel, inhuman or degrading treatment or punishment). Special measures are required to provide safeguards for disabled children, in particular in situations where they remain in institutions or other forms of alternative care.

"...a full and decent life, in conditions which ensure dignity, promote self-reliance and facilitate the child's active participation"

Similar to the Standard Rules on the Equalization of Opportunities for Persons with Disabil-

ities, article 23 affirms the equal rights of disabled children and thus the importance of active participation, which is reflected in the other paragraphs of the article. In a report to the Commission on Human Rights SubCommission on Prevention of Discrimination and Protection of Minorities in February 1996, the Committee on the Rights of the Child summarized the general concerns that arose from its examination of States Parties' reports:

"The Committee has examined the situation of disabled children in the light of article 23 of the Convention, especially focusing on the rights of mentally and physically disabled children, with a view to ensuring their active participation in the community and respect for their dignity and the promotion of their self-reliance. The Committee is also taking into account the general principles of the Convention including article 2 (non-discrimination), article 3 (best interests of the child) and article 4.

"A first matter of concern is that some societies are not sufficiently sensitive to the needs and situation of disabled children, in the light of article 2 of the Convention. The Committee is preoccupied by the widespread discriminatory attitudes towards those children. Strategies and educational programmes, along with the adequate dissemination of information, should be undertaken to avoid certain prejudices which affect disabled children negatively...

"The Committee recognizes the prevalence of certain negative attitudes which hamper the implementation of the rights of disabled children with regard to article 23, such as isolation from the rest of society. The promotion of their rights should be further advanced through, for instance, support to parents' organizations and to community-based services and a sustained programme for moving children from institutions to a good family environment.

"The Committee is negatively impressed by the fact that some disabled children do not have adequate access to health and social care services and it expresses concern over the low number of disabled children enrolled in schools, which might reflect an insufficient attention to their specific needs. More protection should be offered them, including the possibility, through education, of integrating properly into society and participating actively in family life. Efforts for the early detection of the incidence of handicap should be made.

"Budgetary reductions have also affected disabled children who are particularly disadvantaged in their access to adequate health and educational facilities. The Committee urges countries to take all the necessary steps to minimize the negative impact of the structural

adjustment policies on the situation of disabled children. The Committee recognizes, in the light of article 4, the priority of allocating the maximum extent of the available resources to protect these children.

"International assistance and the exchange of appropriate information will also be needed to address more effectively the challenge of improving the situation of disabled children, in conformity with article 23, paragraph 4 of the Convention." (E/CN.4/Sub.2/1996/27)

General Discussion on disabled children's rights

In October 1997 the Committee held a General Discussion on "The rights of children with disabilities", from which arose detailed recommendations. The Committee decided to constitute a working group to follow these up (for details including recommendations, see box page 309).

Discrimination against disabled children

In its examination of States Parties' reports, the Committee has quite frequently listed disabled children among a number of groups of children suffering discrimination. For example:

"The Committee is concerned at the extent of discrimination on the ground of gender as well as against children born out of wedlock and children in especially difficult circumstances. It also expresses concern at the discrimination practised against children with disabilities." (Namibia IRCO, Add.14, para. 7)

"While acknowledging the State Party's commitment to evaluating the effectiveness of policy implementation for disabled children, the Committee recommends that such policy should be reviewed to ensure that it reflects the general principles of the Convention, particularly as regards preventing and combating discrimination against disabled children." (Nigeria IRCO, Add.61, para. 35)

"With regard to article 2 of the Convention, the Committee notes with concern that the principle of non-discrimination is not fully implemented for disabled children." (Slovenia IRCO, Add.65, para. 13)

It is important to note that article 2 requires that there must be no discrimination on the grounds of either the child's disability or his or her parents' or legal guardian's disability (the Standard Rules promotes the full participation of persons with disabilities in family life and has a series of provisions with this aim in rule 9):

"The Committee notes the fact that the law does not provide for protection against all the various forms of discrimination enumerated in article 2 of the Convention. As a result, it is unclear whether the law prohibits discrimina-

tion on the basis of the child's or his or her parents' or legal guardian's language, religion, political or other opinion, social origin, property, disability, birth or other status." (Sweden IRCO, Add.2, para. 7)

Non-discrimination legislation The Committee's *Guidelines for Periodic Reports* asks for information on whether "the principle of non-discrimination is included as a binding principle in the Constitution or in domestic legislation specifically for children, and whether all the possible grounds for discrimination spelled out in article 2 of the Convention are reflected in such legal provisions..." (para. 25). The Committee has indicated that it expects to see the principle of non-discrimination in national law. The Standard Rules on the Equalization of Opportunities for Persons with Disabilities provides further guidance on non-discrimination legislation in Rule 15: "States have a responsibility to create the legal bases for measures to achieve the objectives of full participation and equality for persons with disabilities.

"1. National legislation, embodying the rights and obligations of citizens, should include the rights and obligations of persons with disabilities. States are under an obligation to enable persons with disabilities to exercise their rights, including their human, civil and political rights, on an equal basis with other citizens. States must ensure that organizations of persons with disabilities are involved in the development of national legislation concerning the rights of persons with disabilities, as well as in the ongoing evaluation of that legislation.

"2. Legislative action may be needed to remove conditions that may adversely effect the lives of persons with disabilities, including harassment and victimization. Any discriminatory provisions against persons with disabilities must be eliminated. National legislation should provide for appropriate sanctions in cases of violations of the principle of non-discrimination.

"3. National legislation concerning persons with disabilities may appear in two different forms. The rights and obligations may be incorporated in general legislation or contained in special legislation. Special legislation for persons with disabilities may be established in several ways:

(a) By enacting separate legislation, dealing exclusively with disability matters;

(b) By including disability matters within legislation on particular topics;

(c) By mentioning persons with disabilities specifically in the texts that serve to interpret existing legislation.

article 23

A combination of those different approaches might be desirable. Affirmative action provisions may also be considered.

"4. States may consider establishing formal statutory complaints mechanisms in order to protect the interests of persons with disabilities."

The survey conducted by the Special Rapporteur monitoring implementation of the Standard Rules found that in 27 of the 80 countries providing information, persons with disabilities are not considered to be full-fledged citizens in a number of areas within the general legislation, including the right to vote, the right to property and the right to privacy. In 10 of the 80 countries the right to education is not guaranteed (see below, page 307); in 17, the right to marriage is not guaranteed by law; in 16, rights to parenthood/family, access to courts of law, privacy and property are not guaranteed by law; and in 14 of the countries, persons with disabilities have no political rights (A/52/56, paras. 70-71). This illustrates how far many countries still have to go in eliminating discrimination against disabled people, including disabled children, and in equalizing opportunities.

In its General Comment on disability, the Committee on Economic, Social and Cultural Rights states: "Despite some progress in terms of legislation over the past decade, the legal situation of persons with disabilities remains precarious. In order to remedy past and present discrimination, and to deter future discrimination, comprehensive anti-discrimination legislation in relation to disability would seem indispensable in virtually all States Parties. Such legislation should not only provide persons with disabilities with judicial remedies as far as possible and appropriate, but also provide for social-policy programmes which enable persons with disabilities to live an integrated, self-determined and independent life. Anti-discrimination measures should be based on the principle of equal rights for persons with disabilities and the non-disabled, which, in the words of the World Programme of Action Concerning Disabled Persons, 'implies that the needs of each and every individual are of equal importance, that these needs must be made the basis for the planning of societies, and that all resources must be employed in such a way as to ensure, for every individual, equal opportunity for participation. Disability policies should ensure the access of [persons with disabilities] to all community services...'." (Committee on Economic, Social and Cultural Rights, General Comment 5, HRI/GEN/1/Rev.2, p. 70)

As discussed in relation to article 2 (page 21), the Human Rights Committee in a General Comment has reviewed the definition of "discrimination" in human rights instruments, concluding that it believes "the term 'discrimination' as used in the Covenant [on Civil and Political Rights] should be understood to imply any distinction, exclusion, restriction or preference which is based on any ground such as race, colour, sex, language, religion, political or other opinion, national or social origin, property, birth or other status, and which has the purpose or effect of nullifying or impairing the recognition, enjoyment or exercise by all persons, on an equal footing, of all rights and freedoms" (Human Rights Committee, General Comment 18, HRI/GEN/1/Rev.2, p. 26).

This definition reinforces the need to look at implementation of every provision of the Convention from the perspective of disabled children, to determine whether they experience any distinction, exclusion, restriction or preference that has either the purpose or the effect of "nullifying or impairing" their recognition, enjoyment or exercise, on an equal footing, of all the rights and freedoms guaranteed.

In its most extreme form, discrimination against disabled children can lead to selective infanticide. The varied incidence of certain forms of disability in different regions of the world strongly suggests this. In many countries genetic testing is available, allowing the identification of certain disabilities, for example Downs Syndrome, in the womb.

In some countries where abortion is permitted, discriminatory legislation allows termination at a later stage – even up to full term – in cases of identified disability (see also article 6, page 88).

One general effect of discrimination highlighted by the Committee on the Rights of the Child is to limit the access of disabled children to basic services:

"With regard to article 2 of the Convention, the Committee notes with concern that the principle of non-discrimination is not fully implemented for girls, disabled children and

article 23

Constitutional protection

According to Paraguay's Initial Report, the National Constitution (1992) states (article 57): "Persons with special needs shall be guaranteed health care, education, recreation and vocational training to ensure their full social integration. They shall enjoy the rights granted by this Constitution to all inhabitants of the Republic on a basis of equal opportunity to offset their disadvantages." (Paraguay IR, para. 27)

illegal immigrant children, non-accompanied children and children living in rural areas, especially in the fields of education and health." (Portugal IRCO, Add.45, para. 13)

"In the light of article 2 of the Convention, the Committee also recommends that the State Party take all necessary measures ... to reinforce the access to basic services (health, education and social care) for children in rural areas and for disabled children throughout the country..." (Nepal IRCO, Add.57, para. 32)

Girls with disabilities The Platform for Action prepared by the Fourth World Conference on Women confirmed that "The girl child with disabilities faces additional barriers and needs to be ensured non-discrimination and equal enjoyment of all human rights and fundamental freedoms in accordance with the Standard Rules on the Equalization of Opportunities for Persons with Disabilities." (Platform for Action, para. 270)

The media and discrimination against disabled children The Standard Rules emphasizes that States should "encourage the portrayal of persons with disabilities by the mass media in a positive way; organizations of persons with disabilities should be consulted on this matter" (rule 1(3)). In addition, "States should encourage the media, especially television, radio and newspapers, to make their services accessible" (rule 5(9)). And in relation to promoting measures to change negative attitudes towards marriage, sexuality and parenthood of persons with disabilities, especially of girls and women with disabilities, "The media should be encouraged to play an important role in removing such negative attitudes." (rule 9(3); see also article 17, page 216)

Monitoring the situation of disabled children The *Guidelines for Periodic Reports* requires information on "measures taken to ensure an effective evaluation of the situation of disabled children, including the development of a system of identification and tracking of disabled children, the establishment of any appropriate monitoring mechanism..." (para. 92). The Standard Rules on the Equalization of Opportunities for Persons with Disabilities outlines more detailed requirements for information that should be collected and disseminated on disabled persons and research "on all aspects, including obstacles that affect the lives of persons with disabilities" (rule 13). Rule 20 sets out requirements for national monitoring and evaluation of disability programmes in the implementation of the Rules.

Research In some cases, the Committee on the Rights of the Child has called for more research, and it has also noted the importance of monitoring the situation of disabled children:

"...the Committee notes that, while the incidence of disability among the child population is low, disabled children have been the victims of abandonment and discrimination. In this regard, the Committee recommends that the State Party undertake further research on the measures required to prevent and combat discrimination on the ground of disability." (China IRCO, Add.56, para. 35)

"...Disaggregated data and appropriate indicators seem to be lacking to assess the situation of children... (including) ... abandoned, institutionalized and disabled children..." (Morocco IRCO, Add.60, para. 9)

The right of the disabled child to special care and assistance designed to promote the fullest possible social integration and individual development

Paragraphs 2 and 3 of article 23 acknowledge the need for positive action to equalize opportunities for disabled children. The words "subject to available resources" reflect the general principle found in article 4, and similar provisions in articles 26 and 27. Assistance must be requested and must be appropriate to the child's condition and to the circumstances of parents or others caring for the child. It should be provided free "whenever possible, taking into account the financial resources of the parents and others caring for the child".

The purpose of the assistance is to ensure that the child has "effective access" to a range of services (detailed below) in a manner "conducive to the child's achieving the fullest possible social

Threat of isolation

Sweden's Initial Report suggests "Perhaps the greatest threat of all to the development of disabled children is that they risk becoming isolated and cut off from the society of a family, from other children and from the rest of the community": in Sweden this has been the consideration underlying "efforts towards integration and normalization which have characterized recent decades and which to a great extent have been impelled by parents and their organizations" (Sweden IR, para. 140).

integration and individual development, including his or her cultural and spiritual development".

According priority to disabled children

The Committee has stressed that ensuring the rights of disabled children should be perceived as a priority, and it has commended Governments that have adopted such priorities:

"...In addition the Committee recommends that future development plans should accord priority to the situation of disabled children." (Sudan IRCO, Add.10, para. 23)

"The Committee also notes with satisfaction the priorities set by the Government and its serious efforts to face existing social problems, including in the fields of health and education, as well as to ensure the protection of the rights of disabled children." (Chile IRCO, Add.22, para. 8)

The Committee has suggested that insufficient attention has been paid to the implementation of article 23:

"As recognized by the State Party, the Committee is concerned that measures are lacking to implement the provisions of article 23 of the Convention relating to disabled children." (Honduras IRCO, Add.24, para. 16)

"The Committee is also concerned at the insufficient measures and programmes for the protection of the rights of the most vulnerable children, in particular ... disabled children ..." (Yemen IRCO, Add.47, para. 9. See also Argentina IRCO, Add.35, para. 11; Morocco IRCO, Add.60, para. 26)

The Standard Rules on the Equalization of Opportunities for Persons with Disabilities emphasizes that States should ensure that disability aspects are included in all relevant policy-making and national

planning and that "the needs and concerns of persons with disabilities should be incorporated into general development plans and not be treated separately" (rule 14.3), which applies equally to National Plans of Action for Children (see article 4, page 62).

Safeguarding disabled children in resource allocation

The Committee on the Rights of the Child has stated that when considering the allocation of resources to children, special attention should be paid to the needs of disabled children, among other groups. The Convention's non-discrimination principle does not prevent positive action being taken to assure the rights of such particular groups. The Standard Rules includes provisions on economic policies, noting that States have financial responsibility for national programmes and measures to create equal opportunities for persons with disabilities and suggesting that States should consider "the use of economic measures (loans, tax exemptions, earmarked grants, special funds and so on) to stimulate and support equal participation by persons with disabilities in society" (rule 16.3). Rule 8 covers income maintenance and social security, and rule 4, support services, "including assistive devices for persons with disabilities, to assist them to increase their level of independence in their daily living and to exercise their rights".

The Committee has proposed particular attention to disabled children in budgeting:

"The Committee expresses its concern that stringent budgetary measures amounting to decreases in the resources allocated for social expenditures have entailed high social costs and have adversely affected the rights of the child in Peru. Vulnerable groups of children, including children living in areas affected by the internal violence, displaced children, orphans, disabled children, children living in poverty and children living in institutions are particularly disadvantaged in their access to adequate health and educational facilities and are the primary victims of various forms of exploitation, such as child prostitution...

"...The authorities should, in the light of articles 3 and 4 of the Convention, undertake all appropriate measures to the maximum extent of their available resources to ensure that sufficient resources are allocated to children. In that regard, particular attention should be paid to the protection of ... disabled children ..." (Peru IRCO, Add.8, paras. 10 and 19)

Early identification

The Committee has maintained the importance of the early identification of a disability, to ensure necessary special care and the realization of the rights of disabled children, and it has welcomed relevant measures taken by particular States:

"The Committee welcomes specific action taken by schools and local community services to identify children's disabilities at an early stage." (Canada IRCO, Add.37, para. 7)

"...The situation of disabled children generally is an issue of concern to the Committee. The Committee requires more concrete information on the measures taken for the early identification of disabilities and the prevention of neglect or discrimination against children with disabilities." (Federal Republic of Yugoslavia IRCO, Add.49, para. 17; see also Egypt IRCO, Add.5, para. 13)

Participation rights of disabled children

Disabled children have the same rights to participation in decision-making as other children, under article 12 (see also page 152). In order to equalize their opportunities to participation, special training and strategies may be required, as well as adaptation of buildings and programmes, and the provision of appropriate technologies. The Standard Rules on the Equalization of Opportunities for Persons with Disabilities focuses on the "overall importance of accessibility in the process of the equalization of opportunities in all spheres of society. For persons with disabilities of any kind, the State should (a) introduce programmes of action to make the physical environment accessible; and (b) undertake measures to provide access to information and communication" (rule 5). The Standard Rules emphasizes throughout the importance of involving disabled persons and organizations of disabled persons "in all decision-making relating to plans and programmes concerning persons with disabilities or affecting their economic and social status" (rule 14(2)). Rule 18 expands on the role of organizations of persons with disabilities – for example "to identify needs and priorities, to participate in the planning, implementation and evaluation of services and measures concerning the lives of persons with disabilities, and to contribute to public awareness and to advocate change" (rule 18(3)).

Avoiding institutionalization

The emphasis in article 23 on "active participation in the community" and "the fullest possible social integration" implies minimizing the institutionalization of disabled children. Article 20 also supports non-institutional placements for children deprived of their family environment (see page 257), and in the light of article 2 this must apply equally to disabled children. The Committee on the Rights of the Child has questioned institutionalization and proposed that improved levels of family support should be provided to avoid it (in line with article 18, see page 225):

"Further efforts are recommended to create a better understanding among the public about the situation of children with disabilities. The promotion of their rights should be further advanced through, for instance, support to parents' organizations and a sustained programme for moving children from institutions to a good family environment." (Romania IRCO, Add.16, para. 19)

"...In particular, the Committee expresses its concern at the situation of the institutionalization, treatment and protection of handicapped children. Alternatives to institutionalization are not sufficiently taken into account; support services to parents who keep their handicapped child at home are inadequate." (Ukraine IRCO, Add.42, para. 13)

"The Committee recommends that provision be made for offering social assistance to families to help them with their child-rearing responsibilities as laid down in article 18 of the Convention as a means of reducing institutionalization of children..." (Guatemala IRCO, Add.58, para. 38)

The Initial Report of the Russian Federation acknowledges that physical installations and living conditions in boarding institutions taking orphans and children from deprived families are unsatisfactory. "There has been a recent increase in attempts by parents of large and deprived families to have their children admitted to such institutions, even going to the lengths of disowning their children (especially if they are disabled because of the high cost of looking after them). In general, there is a rapidly growing demand for boarding schools where children's upkeep is provided by the State."

During discussion on the Initial Report, a Committee member commented on the Convention's attitude to care of disabled children: "The Convention philosophized to a certain extent about the relationship between disabled children, parents and the authorities, and on the whole favoured care by parents, even though in some cases it was necessary to find a balance in the best interests of the child. Throughout the world the emphasis was shifting from institutional care to care in the family and the community, even in the poorer countries. This reflected the view held by WHO and UNICEF that the disabled child was not the problem, but society's inability to deal with such children was. The report had tended to emphasize technical measures so that the problem was presented as a technical one, but disabled children themselves would say that they were first and foremost children. Politicians the

article 23

world over needed to review their thinking on that point and to encourage the integration of disabled children into society..." (Russian Federation IR, para. 36, SR.64, para. 21)

Disabled children and alternative care
In relation to articles 9, 18 and 21 of the Convention in particular, the Standard Rules on the Equalization of Opportunities for Persons with Disabilities expects States to promote the full participation of persons with disabilities in family life, which may require special information, counselling and support measures: "They should promote their right to personal integrity and ensure that laws do not discriminate against persons with disabilities with respect to sexual relationships, marriage and parenthood. Persons with disabilities should be enabled to live with their families. States should encourage the inclusion in family counselling of appropriate modules regarding disability and its effects on family life. Respite-care and attendant-care services should be made available to families which include a person with disabilities. States should remove all unnecessary obstacles to persons who want to foster or adopt a child or adult with disabilities..." (rule 9)

Restriction of liberty of disabled children
Children who are detained because of mental illness should have the various safeguards provided by the Convention on the Rights of the Child and relevant United Nations rules and guidelines. Under article 37 of the Convention any restriction of liberty must be authorized by legislation, must not be arbitrary and must only be used as a measure of last resort and for the shortest appropriate time. Article 37(c) requires that every child deprived of liberty "shall be separated from adults unless it is considered in the child's best interest not to do so." The United Nations Rules for the Protection of Juveniles Deprived of their Liberty has a similar provision. Its rule 29 applies equally to children detained because of mental illness. The Committee on the Rights of the Child has implied that in any institutional placement, disabled children should be separated from adults, and under article 25, it has also noted the importance of the regular review of placement and treatment (see page 341):

"... Further efforts are also required to ensure the active participation of disabled children in the community in conditions which ensure their dignity and promote their self-reliance, as well as to ensure that disabled children are separated from adults suffering from mental ill-health. The Committee recommends that measures be taken to review periodically the placement and treatment of children as

required under article 25 of the Convention." (Guatemala IRCO, Add.58, para. 38)

The United Nations Rules for the Protection of Juveniles Deprived of their Liberty notes in rule 53: "A juvenile who is suffering from mental illness should be treated in a specialized institution under independent medical management. Steps should be taken, by arrangement with appropriate agencies, to ensure any necessary continuation of mental health care after release." The Rules also notes that any juvenile who "demonstrates symptoms of physical or mental difficulties, should be examined promptly by a medical officer" (rule 51).

Disabled children in the juvenile justice system
In the Convention on the Rights of the Child, article 40(2)(b)(vi) requires that any child alleged as or accused of having infringed the penal law should have the free assistance of an interpreter if the child cannot understand or speak the language used: this may require special measures for disabled children.

Disabled children and inclusive education and training
The Committee on the Rights of the Child has expressed concern about disabled children's basic right to education (article 28) and about the low proportion of disabled children enrolled in schools worldwide:

"Of special concern to the Committee has also been the situation of children in rural areas and of disabled children. In regard to the latter, the Committee expresses concern over the very low number of disabled children who are enrolled in schools, which might reflect an insufficient sensitiveness of the society to the specific needs and situation of those children." (Egypt IRCO, Add.5, para. 7)

"...The Committee particularly recommends that legislative measures be adopted with a view to ... ensuring the basic rights of all disabled children, in particular the right to education, in the light of article 23..." (Republic of Korea IRCO, Add.51, para. 22)

"[The Committee] is also concerned by the difficulties encountered by children living in rural and remote areas and disabled children in securing basic services, such as health care, social services and education." (Nepal IRCO, Add.57, para. 17)

In its examination of a number of States Parties' reports the Committee has gone beyond this general concern about the right to education to emphasize the importance of recognizing the right of disabled children to full inclusion in regular schools (and the *Guidelines for Periodic*

Reports specifically asks for information on inclusion in schools and other institutions – para. 92). In discussions with Egypt a Committee member was reported as stating: "Rather than placing disabled children in specialized institutions, efforts should be made to place them in schools attended by normal children. It was important not to favour material assistance for the disabled at the expense of human and psychological factors." (Egypt SR.67, para. 82)

In relation to various States it has recommended further inclusion:

"The Committee suggests that special programmes be developed for children with disabilities in order to define social, psychological, physical and other needs as well as to educate parents about ways of dealing with them. Further efforts are recommended to encourage schools to ensure the participation of these children in all activities." (Lebanon IRCO, Add.54, para. 39)

"With respect to improving the situation of disabled children, the Committee encourages the efforts being undertaken to integrate disabled children into regular schools, including through investment in structural changes to schools and support to the training of teachers to assist them in adjusting and adapting their teaching methods to the needs of disabled children." (UK dependent territory: Hong Kong IRCO, Add.63, para. 29)

"... The Committee is concerned, in addition, at the difficulties encountered by disabled children in gaining access to regular primary schools." (Mauritius IRCO, Add.64, para. 15)

The 1996 report of the Special Rapporteur monitoring implementation of the Standard Rules (see page 297) notes that his survey had found that disabled persons in 10 out of the 80 countries providing information are not guaranteed by law the right to education. "The right to education is denied millions of children with special educational needs, who either receive inadequate and inappropriate public education or are excluded from the public school systems. Although many developing countries have recognized the right to education, it has in many cases not been applied to persons with special educational needs." (A/52/56, paras. 71 and 110)

The Special Rapporteur refers to other surveys carried out by UNESCO: "Sixty-five countries provided information on legislation. Forty-four countries reported that general legislation applied to the children with special educational needs. Thirty-four countries reported that children with severe disabilities were excluded from education. In 18 of the 34 countries reporting exclusion, those children were excluded by law from the

public educational system. In 16 countries, the exclusion was the result of other, non-legal factors. The most common reason given for excluding some children from the public education system was the severity of the disability, lack of facilities and trained staff, long distances to schools and the fact that regular schools do not accept pupils with special educational needs. Ten countries reported that no legislation on special education exists." The Special Rapporteur tentatively concludes that "schooling for the children with special educational needs is still predominantly provided in a segregated educational system and that the rates of attendance in schools of persons with special educational needs is very low in numerous countries... In most countries integration represents an aspiration for the future." (A/52/56 paras. 111 and 113)

The Standard Rules on the Equalization of Opportunities for Persons with Disabilities identifies education as a "target area for equal participation". Under rule 6: "States should recognize the principle of equal primary, secondary and tertiary educational opportunities for children, youth and adults with disabilities, in integrated settings. They should ensure that the education of persons with disabilities is an integral part of the educational system." The rule goes on to emphasize that "education for persons with disabilities should form an integral part of national educational planning, curriculum development and school organization," to outline key elements of an inclusive system and to identify the interim role of special education and ways of meeting the communication needs of deaf and deaf/blind persons.

In 1994, following five regional seminars, a World Conference on Special Needs Education, representing 92 Governments and 26 international organizations, was held and adopted "The Salamanca Statement and Framework for Action on Special Needs Education" (more than 300 participants were brought together by UNESCO and the Government of Spain). The Statement emphasizes that "those with special educational needs must have access to regular schools which should accommodate them within a child-centred pedagogy capable of meeting those needs; regular schools with this inclusive orientation are the most effective means of combating discriminatory attitudes, creating welcoming communities, building an inclusive society and achieving education for all; moreover, they provide an effective education to the majority of children and improve the efficiency and ultimately the cost-effectiveness of the entire education system". The Statement calls on all Governments "to give the highest policy and budgetary priority to improve their education systems to enable them to include all children regardless of individual differences or difficulties." (The Salamanca Statement and Framework for Action on Special Needs Education, UNESCO ED-94/WS/18, 1994)

The Final Report of the Special Rapporteur on Human Rights and Disability (1991) notes that the World Programme of Action concerning Disabled Persons stipulates that education should, as far as possible, be provided within the ordinary school system, without any discrimination against handicapped children or adults. "However, this condition is not always met, because of the prejudices of the authorities and teachers, of the parents of other children, or even of the parents of disabled children. Consequently, in many instances where the child's disability does not constitute an obstacle in itself, discrimination prevents him from entering the ordinary school system. In some cases, it is the law itself which stipulates that disabled children must attend special schools, which is tantamount to official segregation. In other cases, the obstacle to school attendance is the lack of means of transport, both in cities and in rural areas, although the phenomenon is much more common in the latter. Shortcomings in building design have a similar effect, making access to school buildings and movement inside them difficult, and also barring access to toilets, etc., a very common phenomenon." (E/CN.4/Sub.2/1991/31, para. 186)

Among the commitments made at the World Summit for Social Development (Copenhagen, 1995) is to "Ensure equal educational opportunities at all levels for children, youth and adults with disabilities, in integrated settings, taking full account of individual differences and situations." (A/CONF.166/9, p. 19)

Health care and rehabilitation services

Disabled children have exactly the same rights to health and health care as all other children. Under the Standard Rules, States should ensure the provision of effective medical care to persons with disabilities. In particular, "States should ensure that persons with disabilities, particularly infants and children, are provided with the same level of medical care within the same system as other members of society." (rule 2.3)

As noted above, (page 300), the Committee has expressed concern about disabled children's access to basic services including health care.

Also under the Standard Rules, "States should ensure the provision of rehabilitation services to persons with disabilities in order for them to reach and sustain their optimum level of indepen-

dence and functioning"; again, the emphasis is on the provision of services to promote equalization of opportunities.

The Graça Machel study on the *Impact of Armed Conflict on Children* reports that "only 3 per cent of disabled children in developing countries receive adequate rehabilitative care, and the provision of prosthetics to children is an area that requires increased attention and financial support. In Angola and Mozambique, less than 20 per cent of children needing them received low-cost prosthetic devices; in Nicaragua and El Salvador, services were also available for only 20 per cent of the children in need. This lack of rehabilitative care is contrary to article 23 of the Convention on the Rights of the Child..." (A/51/306, para. 145)

Preparation for employment

Under the Standard Rules on the Equalization of Opportunities for Persons with Disabilities, States are asked to recognize the principle "that persons with disabilities must be empowered to exercise their human rights, particularly in the field of employment. In both rural and urban areas, they must have equal opportunities for productive and gainful employment in the labour market" (rule 7); vocational training is an essential part of seeking integration of persons with disabilities into open employment. Under article 28(1)(d) of the Convention on the Rights of the Child, States Parties are required to "Make educational and vocational information and guidance available and accessible to all children".

The International Labour Organization has adopted a Convention concerning Vocational Rehabilitation and Employment (Disabled Persons) – Convention No. 159. For the purposes of the Convention, "each Member shall consider the purpose of vocational rehabilitation as being to enable a disabled person to secure, retain and advance in suitable employment and thereby to further such person's integration or reintegration into society". Each Member is required to formulate, implement and periodically review a national policy on vocational rehabilitation and employment of disabled persons, "in accordance with national conditions, practice and possibilities". Article 4 requires the national policy to be based "on the principle of equal opportunities between disabled workers and workers generally ... Special positive measures aimed at effective equality of opportunity and treatment between disabled workers and other workers shall not be regarded as discriminating against other workers." This ILO Convention and an accompanying Recommendation (Recommendation No. 168, Recommendation concerning Vocational Rehabilitation and Employment (Disabled Persons)) were both adopted in June 1983. They have obvious implications for the preparation of disabled children for employment, and for their employment.

Recreation opportunities

The rights of the disabled child under article 31 to rest, leisure and participation in artistic and cultural life should be realized without discrimination. The Standard Rules requires States to ensure that persons with disabilities "are integrated into and can participate in cultural activities on an equal basis", and take measures to ensure "that persons with disabilities have equal opportunities for recreation and sports" (rules 10 and 11). These requirements raise issues of accessibility (rule 5) – both to the physical environment for play, recreation, culture and the arts and to information and communication. They may also demand adaptation of activities to ensure inclusion of disabled children.

The positive role of the media in promoting recreation and culture should be developed with consideration of the equal rights of disabled children. In its 1997 resolution on Children with disabilities, the Economic and Social Council called on governments "to ensure the participation of children with disabilities in recreational activities and sports" (E/Res/1997/20).

International cooperation: article 23(4)

Article 23(4) requires States Parties to promote through international cooperation the exchange of information to improve their capabilities and skills in relation to disabled children, with particular account being taken of the needs of developing countries. The Standard Rules sets out in more detail State responsibilities to cooperate. States should participate in international cooperation in order to develop common standards for national evaluation in the disability field (rule 20, para. 4). Under "Technical and economic cooperation" in rule 21, "States, both industrialized and

International cooperation for disabled children

"The aim of Swedish international assistance in the disabled sector is to integrate the disability aspect with the day-to-day development aspect. Disability aspects are taken into account both bilaterally and in cooperation with individual organizations, and also globally through UNDP [United Nations Development Programme] and other relevant organizations in the United Nations system.

"Measures for the disabled within Swedish development assistance were previously accounted for under the heading of 'health care'. For the 1992/93 fiscal year the Government has allotted a special item for support to the disabled, to underline the measures taken to improve the situation for disabled persons in the developing countries, but also to demonstrate that disability questions are not exclusively health-related." (Sweden IR, paras. 148-149)

developing, have the responsibility to cooperate in and take measures for the improvement of the living conditions of persons with disabilities in developing countries."

Measures should be integrated into general development programmes, and when planning and reviewing programmes of technical and economic cooperation, special attention should be given to the effect of such programmes on disabled people. People with disabilities and their organizations should be consulted and involved directly in the development, implementation and evaluation of development projects. Under rule 22, "International cooperation", States are encouraged to "participate actively in international cooperation concerning policies for the equalization of opportunities for persons with disabilities"; various strategies are suggested.

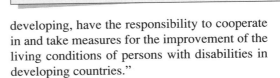

Recommendations of the Committee on the Rights of the Child General Discussion on the Rights of Children with Disabilities

On the basis of the discussions on the various issues, the following recommendations were formulated by the Chairperson of the Committee following the General Discussion held on 6 October 1997:

● In its examination of States parties reports, the Committee should commit itself to highlighting the situation of disabled children, and the need for concrete measures to ensure recognition of their rights, including in particular the right to life and maximum survival and development, the right to social inclusion and to participation; it will also emphasize that adequate monitoring of the situation of disabled children in all States must be undertaken and encourage moves to promote the collection of statistics and other information to enable constructive comparisons between regions and States;

● The possibility of drafting an early General Comment on disabled children should be considered by the Committee;

● The various bodies providing information to the Committee in the course of the reporting process should ensure that the information they provide to the Committee includes the perspective of disabled children;

● There is a need for States to review and amend persisting laws in many countries affecting disabled children which are not compatible with the principles and provisions of the Convention, for example legislation:

– which denies disabled children an equal right to life, survival and development (including in those States which allow abortion - discriminatory laws on abortion affecting disabled children, and discriminatory access to health services);

– which denies disabled children the right to education;

– which compulsorily segregates disabled children in separate institutions for care, treatment or education;

● There is a need for States to actively challenge attitudes and practices which discriminate against disabled children and deny them equal opportunities to rights guaranteed by the Convention, including infanticide, traditional practices prejudical to health and development, superstition, perception of disability as tragedy;

● In view of the appalling impact of armed conflict in causing disability of hundreds of thousands of children, States should be encouraged to ratify the Convention on the Prohibition of the Production, Use, Stockpiling and Transfer of Anti-personnel Mines and on their Destruction, due to be opened for signature in Ottawa in December 1997;

● The Committee should promote the Standard Rules on the Equalization of Opportunities for Persons with Disabilities as providing relevant standards for implementation of the Convention on the Rights of the Child and strengthen its cooperation with the Special Rapporteur on Disabilities and his Panel of Experts;

● The Committee, in cooperation with UNESCO, UNICEF and other relevant agencies, should ensure that inclusive education is included on the agendas of meetings, conferences and seminars as an integral part of education debate;

● Relevant agencies should be encouraged to develop programmes which promote alternatives to institutionalization and to develop and promote strategies to de-institutionalize children;

● The rights and interests of disabled children should be included on the agenda of multi and bilateral agencies, development agencies, donor agencies, funding organizations, such as the World Bank and regional banks as well as technical cooperation agencies;

● Research into the provision of statistics and empirical evidence should be promoted with a view to: a) promote awareness of the extent to which the right to life of disabled children is denied; b) challenge the widespread existence of superstition, prejudice, social stigma and denial of access to education in relation to disabled children; c) challenge the argument of "cost effectiveness" used to marginalize disabled children and evaluate the costs of exclusion and lost opportunities; d) encourage the prominence of the issue in the production and discussion of bio-ethical conventions;

● The development of research with disabled children should be encouraged on methods of undertaking consultation, involving them in decision-making, and giving them greater control over their lives and promote dissemination and sharing of good practices, backed up by preparation of training materials;

● Governments should be encouraged to make these materials available at community level in appropriate forms for children and disabled people - this could potentially be undertaken by one of the development agencies such as the Swedish organization of Handicapped International Aid Foundation (SHIA) or Save the Children in collaboration with some of the disabled people's organizations;

● There is a need to produce training materials on promoting participation of disabled children. In addition, the UNICEF International Child Development Centre (Innocenti Centre) should be requested to produce an edition in its series of information digests on the subject of inclusion, as its contribution to the issues raised during the General Discussion.

In view of the various contributions made and the importance of the issues considered, the Committee felt that there was a need to ensure follow-up to the general discussion. It was decided to constitute a working group on the rights of children with disabilities including members of the Committee, representatives of relevant United Nations bodies and agencies and non-governmental organizations of disabled people including disabled children, to consider further the various recommendations made and elaborate a plan of action to facilitate the concrete implementation of the various proposals. The Committee decided to further pursue the question of the mandate, composition and activities of the working group at its next session in January 1998.

Implementation Checklist

● General measures of implementation

Have appropriate general measures of implementation been taken in relation to article 23, including

☐ identification and coordination of the responsible departments and agencies at all levels of government (article 23 is relevant to **all government departments, and any coordinating agency set up to consider disability issues**)?

☐ identification of relevant non-governmental organizations/civil society partners?

☐ a comprehensive review to ensure that all legislation, policy and practice is compatible with the article, for all children in all parts of the jurisdiction?

☐ adoption of a strategy to secure full implementation

    ☐ which includes where necessary the identification of goals and indicators of progress?

    ☐ which does not affect any provisions which are more conducive to the rights of the child?

    ☐ which recognizes other relevant international standards?

    ☐ which involves where necessary international cooperation?

(Such measures may be part of an overall governmental strategy for implementing the Convention as a whole).

☐ budgetary analysis and allocation of necessary resources?

☐ development of mechanisms for monitoring and evaluation?

☐ making the implications of article 23 widely known to adults and children?

☐ development of appropriate training and awareness-raising (in relation to article 23 likely to include the training of **all those working with or for children and their families, and parenting education**)?

● Specific issues in implementing article 23

☐ Does the State have a national coordinating committee or similar body to serve as a focal point for disability matters?

☐ Has the State reviewed legislation, policy and practice in the light of the Standard Rules on the Equalization of Opportunities for Persons with Disabilities?

☐ Is there anti-discrimination legislation covering discrimination against disabled children?

☐ Does legislation in the State guarantee the disabled child enjoyment of all the rights in the Convention without discrimination?

How to use the checklists, *see page XVII*

☐ Do all disabled children have access to an independent mechanism for considering complaints relating to discrimination on the grounds of disability?

☐ Is special care and assistance available on application for all disabled children and for those caring for him/her in the State?

Is such special care and assistance provided

      ☐ free of charge in all cases?

      ☐ on a means-tested basis?

☐ Are there national and local arrangements to ensure that parents are given advice, financial assistance and practical help in bringing up a disabled child?

Do all disabled children have effective access to, and receive without discrimination in a manner conducive to the child's achieving the fullest possible social integration and individual development, including his or her cultural and spiritual development

      ☐ preschool care and education?

      ☐ education?

      ☐ training?

      ☐ health care services?

      ☐ rehabilitation services?

      ☐ recreation and play opportunities?

      ☐ cultural and artistic opportunities?

      ☐ preparation for employment?

      ☐ employment?

Are the following services provided for disabled children in an integrated setting with children without disabilities

      ☐ education ?

      ☐ training?

      ☐ alternative care including institutional care?

      ☐ play and recreation?

☐ Are special arrangements made in the State to ensure respect for disabled children's participation rights under articles 12, 13, 14 and 15?

☐ Do legislative and other measures ensure the equal right to life and maximum survival and development for the disabled child?

Are special measures taken to safeguard disabled children from all forms of violence and abuse,

      ☐ in the family?

      ☐ in alternative care?

☐ in the community?

☐ Has the State promoted the involvement of organizations of disabled children in planning, policy development and evaluation at all levels of government?

☐ Is the State involved in international cooperative exercises to exchange information and improve capacity and skills in relation to provision of services, etc. for disabled children?

Reminder: **The Convention is indivisible and its articles are interdependent. Article 23 should not be considered in isolation.**

Particular regard should be paid to:
The general principles

Article 2: all rights to be recognized for each child in jurisdiction without discrimination on any ground

Article 3(1): the best interests of the child to be a primary consideration in all actions concerning children

Article 6: right to life and maximum possible survival and development

Article 12: respect for the child's views in all matters affecting the child; opportunity to be heard in any judicial or administrative proceedings affecting the child

Closely related articles

All articles of the Convention should be considered with a view to equalizing the opportunities of disabled children to exercise their rights.

Child's right to health and health services

article 24

Text of Article 24

1. States Parties recognize the right of the child to the enjoyment of the highest attainable standard of health and to facilities for the treatment of illness and rehabilitation of health. States Parties shall strive to ensure that no child is deprived of his or her right of access to such health care services.

2. States Parties shall pursue full implementation of this right and, in particular, shall take appropriate measures:

(a) To diminish infant and child mortality;

(b) To ensure the provision of necessary medical assistance and health care to all children with emphasis on the development of primary health care;

(c) To combat disease and malnutrition, including within the framework of primary health care, through, inter alia, the application of readily available technology and through the provision of adequate nutritious foods and clean drinking water, taking into consideration the dangers and risks of environmental pollution;

(d) To ensure appropriate prenatal and postnatal health care for mothers;

(e) To ensure that all segments of society, in particular parents and children, are informed, have access to education and are supported in the use of basic knowledge of child health and nutrition, the advantages of breastfeeding, hygiene and environmental sanitation and the prevention of accidents;

(f) To develop preventive health care, guidance for parents and family planning education and services.

3. States Parties shall take all effective and appropriate measures with a view to abolishing traditional practices prejudicial to the health of children.

4. States Parties undertake to promote and encourage international cooperation with a view to achieving progressively the full realization of the right recognized in the present article. In this regard, particular account shall be taken of the needs of developing countries.

Summary

Article 24 of the Convention on the Rights of the Child builds on and develops the right to life and to survival and development to the maximum extent possible that is set out in article 6. Applying the Convention's non-discrimination principle (article 2) requires States to recognize the right of all children without discrimination to "the highest attainable standard of health" as well as to "facilities for the treatment of illness and rehabilitation of health". And States Parties must strive to ensure "that no child is deprived of his or her right of access to such health care services". Paragraph 2 provides a non-exclusive list of appropriate measures that States must take in pursuing full implementation of the right, including "to ensure the provision of necessary medical assistance and health care to all children with emphasis on the development of primary health care". The holistic nature of the Convention and the Committee's interpretation stress the obvious connections between realizing the child's health rights and the child's right to an adequate standard of living (article 27) and to education (article 28).

Respect for the views of the child needs to be built into individual health care and into the design of health services, and respect for evolving capacities (article 5, page 15) underlines the need for full consideration of adolescent health issues.

Article 24, paragraph 3, requires action with a view to abolishing traditional practices "prejudicial to the health of children", drafted because of particular concern over female genital mutilation and requiring a review of all potentially harmful practices. Paragraph 4 asserts the importance of international cooperation (reflecting the general provision found in article 4) in achieving full realization of the right to health and health care services.

The Convention's health provisions developed from provisions in the Universal Declaration of Human Rights and the two International Covenants - on Civil and Political Rights and Economic, Social and Cultural Rights, from the formulation of definitions and principles by international organizations, in particular the World Health Organization (WHO) and UNICEF. The broad definition of health adopted by the WHO in its Constitution - a state of complete physical, mental and social well-being, and not merely the absence of disease or infirmity - emphasizes again the holistic nature of the Convention and links to the broad definition of child development the Convention promotes. Healthy development of the child is of basic importance. The ability to live harmoniously in a changing total environment is essential to such development. The World Summit for Children Declaration and Plan of Action defined detailed goals for improving child health by the year 2000, derived from goals already agreed upon by UNICEF and WHO, and the World Summit for Social Development (Copenhagen, 1995) reaffirmed and added to these. The International Conference on Population and Development (Cairo, 1994), and the Fourth World Conference on Women (Beijing, 1995) have important detailed recommendations on health, including particularly adolescents' health rights. ∎

Extracts from
Committee on the Rights of the Child
Guidelines for Reports to be submitted by States Parties under the Convention

For full text of *Guidelines for Periodic Reports*, see Appendix 3, page 604.

Guidelines for Initial Reports

"Basic health and welfare

Under this section States Parties are requested to provide relevant information, including the principal legislative, judicial, administrative or other measures in force; the institutional infrastructure for implementing policy in this area, particularly monitoring strategies and mechanisms; and factors and difficulties encountered and progress achieved in implementing the relevant provisions of the Convention, in respect of:

...

(c) Health and health services (article 24);

..."

(CRC/C/5, para. 19)

Guidelines for Periodic Reports

"B. Health and health services (art. 24)

Please indicate the measures adopted pursuant to articles 6 and 24:

To recognize and ensure the right of the child to the enjoyment of the highest attainable standard of health and to facilities for treatment and rehabilitation;

To ensure that no child is deprived of his or her right of access to such health care services;

To ensure respect for the general principles of the Convention, namely non-discrimination, the best interests of the child, respect for the views of the child and the right to life, and survival and development to the maximum extent possible.

Reports should also provide information about the measures adopted to identify changes which have occurred since the submission of the State Party's previous report, their impact on the life of children, as well as the indicators used to assess the progress achieved in the implementation of this right, the difficulties encountered and any targets identified for the future, including in relation to child mortality and child morbidity, service coverage, data collection, policies and legislation, budget allocation (including in relation to the general budget), involvement of non-governmental organizations and international assistance.

Please also provide information on the measures undertaken in particular:

To diminish infant and child mortality, indicating the average rates and providing relevant disaggregated data, including by gender, age, region, rural/urban area, ethnic and social origin.

To ensure the provision of necessary medical assistance and health care to all children with emphasis on the development of primary health care, including:

The distribution of both general and primary health care services in the rural and urban areas of the country and the balance between preventative and curative health care;

Information on the children having access to and benefiting from medical assistance and health care, as well as persisting gaps, including by gender, age, ethnic and social origin, and measures adopted to reduce existing disparities;

The measures adopted to ensure a universal immunization system.

To combat disease and malnutrition, including in the framework of primary health care, through inter alia the application of readily available technology and through the provision of adequate nutritious foods and clean drinking water, taking into account the risks and dangers of environmental degradation and pollution; reports should indicate the overall situation, persisting disparities and difficulties, as well as policies to address them, including priorities identified for future action, and information should also be provided, including by gender, age, region, rural/urban, and social and ethnic origin on:

The proportion of children with low birth weight;

The nature and context of the most common diseases and their impact on children;

The proportion of the child population affected by malnutrition, including of a chronic or severe nature, and lack of clean drinking water;

The children provided with adequate nutritious food;

The risks from environmental pollution and the measures adopted to prevent and combat them.

To ensure appropriate prenatal and postnatal health care for mothers, indicating the nature of services provided, including appropriate information given, the coverage ensured, the rate of mortality and its main causes (average and disaggregated, inter alia, by age, gender, region, urban/rural area, social and ethnic origin), the proportion of pregnant women who have access to and benefit from pre- and postnatal health care, trained personnel and hospital care and delivery;

To ensure that all segments of society, in particular parents and children, are informed, have access to education and are supported in the use of basic knowledge of child health and nutrition, the advantages of breastfeeding, hygiene and environmental sanitation and the prevention of accidents; in this regard, information should also be provided on:

Campaigns, programmes, services and strategies and other relevant mechanisms developed to provide basic knowledge, information and support to the general population, in particular to parents and children;

The means used, particularly in relation to the areas of child health and nutrition, the advantages of breastfeeding and the prevention of accidents;

The availability of safe sanitation;

The measures adopted to increase food production to ensure household food security;

The measures adopted to improve the system of education and training of health personnel;

Disaggregated data, including by age, gender, region, rural/urban area, social and ethnic origin.

To develop preventive health care, guidance for parents and family planning education and services; in this regard, reports should also provide information on:

The policies and programmes developed, as well as services available;

The population covered, including in rural and urban areas, by age, gender, social and ethnic origin;

The measures adopted to prevent early pregnancy and to take into consideration the specific situation of adolescents, including provision of appropriate information and counselling;

The role played by the education system in this regard, including in the school curricula;

Disaggregated data on the incidence of children's pregnancy, including by age, region, rural/urban area, and social and ethnic origin.

Please indicate the prevalence of HIV/AIDS and the measures adopted to promote health information and education on HIV/AIDS among the general population, special groups at high risk and children, as well as:

The programmes and strategies developed to prevent HIV;

The measures adopted to assess the occurrence of HIV infection and AIDS, among both the general population and children, and its incidence inter alia by age, gender, rural/urban area;

The treatment and management provided in case of HIV infection and AIDS among children and parents, and the coverage ensured nationwide, in urban and rural areas;

The measures adopted to ensure an effective protection and assistance to children who are orphans as a result of AIDS;

The campaigns, programmes, strategies and other relevant measures adopted to prevent and combat discriminatory attitudes against children infected by HIV or with AIDS, or whose parents or family members have been infected.

Please provide information on the measures adopted pursuant to article 24, paragraph 3, with a view to abolishing all traditional practices prejudicial to the health of children, particularly girls, or otherwise contrary to the principles and provisions of the Convention (for example genital mutilation and forced marriage). Reports should also indicate any assessment made of traditional practices persisting in society that are prejudicial to children's rights.

Information should also be provided on the measures adopted pursuant to article 24, paragraph 4, to promote and encourage international cooperation with a view to achieving progressively the full realization of the right recognized in this article, and the particular consideration given to the needs of developing countries. Reports should inter alia indicate the activities and programmes developed in the framework of international cooperation, including at the bilateral and regional levels, the areas addressed, the target groups identified, the financial assistance provided and/or received and the priorities considered, as well as any evaluation made of the progress achieved and of the difficulties encountered. Mention should be made, whenever appropriate, of the involvement of United Nations organs and specialized agencies and non-governmental organizations.

(CRC/C/58, paras. 93-98. The following paragraphs of the *Guidelines for Periodic Reports* are also relevant to reporting under this article: 24, 32, 40-41, 46, 86-87, 108, 143, 166; for full text of *Guidelines*, see Appendix 3, page 604)

Background to Convention's principles

Health rights in The International Bill of Human Rights

The Universal Declaration of Human Rights includes the right to medical care as part of everyone's right to "a standard of living adequate for the health and well-being of himself and of his family", adding: "Motherhood and childhood are entitled to special care and assistance. All children, whether born in or out of wedlock, shall enjoy the same social protection" (article 25). The International Covenant on Economic, Social and Cultural Rights, in article 12, provides:

"1. The States Parties to the present Covenant recognize the right of everyone to the enjoyment of the highest attainable standard of physical and mental health.

2. The steps to be taken by the States Parties to the present Covenant to achieve the full realization of this right shall include those necessary for:

(a) The provision for the reduction of the still-birth rate and of infant mortality and for the healthy development of the child;

(b) The improvement of all aspects of environmental and industrial hygiene;

(c) The prevention, treatment and control of epidemic, endemic, occupational and other diseases;

(d) The creation of conditions which would assure to all medical service and medical attention in the event of sickness."

Both instruments also assert the right to life (for further discussion see article 6, page 85). The Convention on the Rights of the Child goes further in establishing a right of access to health care services, and providing a non-exclusive list of appropriate measures States should take.

Declaration on primary health care

The World Health Organization includes in its Charter (adopted at the International Health Conference in New York in 1946) a broad definition of "health", and the same definition was used in the "Alma Ata Declaration" on Primary Health Care – the result of the 1978 International Conference on Primary Health Care, which met in Alma Ata, Kazakstan (jointly sponsored by the WHO and UNICEF). The Declaration reaffirmed that health, "which is a state of complete physical, mental and social well-being, and not merely the absence of disease or infirmity, is a fundamental human right and that the attainment of the highest possible level of health is a most important worldwide social goal whose realization requires the action of many other social and economic sectors in addition to the health sector".

The Alma Ata Declaration defines primary health care, promoted as a priority in article 24 of the Convention on the Rights of the Child, as "essential health care based on practical, scientifically sound and socially acceptable methods and technology made universally accessible to individuals and families in the community through their full participation and at a cost that the community and country can afford to maintain at every stage of their development in the spirit of self-reliance and self-determination. It forms an integral part both of the country's health system, of which it is the central function and main focus, and of the overall social and economic development of the community. It is the first level of contact of individuals, the family and community with the national health system bringing health care as close as possible to where people live and work, and constitutes the first element of a continuing health care process" (Alma Ata Declaration, paras. I and VI; for further detail, see box on page 320).

The Declaration urges all governments to formulate national policies, strategies and plans of action to launch and sustain primary health care as part of a comprehensive national health system (Declaration of Alma Ata 1978, paras. I, VI, VII and VIII). The Declaration was endorsed by the General Assembly of the United Nations in a resolution – "Health as an integral part of development" – that reiterated WHO's appeal to the international community "to give full support to the formulation and implementation of national, regional and global strategies for achieving an acceptable level of health for all" (General Assembly resolution 34/58, 29 November 1979).

The Committee on the Rights of the Child has reinforced the Convention's emphasis on primary health care in its examination of reports from States Parties (see below, page 326).

World Summit Declaration and Plan of Action

The World Declaration on the Survival, Protection and Development of Children and the Plan of Action for implementing it, adopted at the World Summit for Children on 30 September 1990, provide both general and specific commitments for child health, related to the Convention's standards, which the Committee on the Rights of the Child has referred to in its examination of States Parties' reports. The Declaration notes under

The Alma Ata Declaration

The following is the text of the Alma Ata Declaration on Primary Health Care:

"Primary health care:

1. reflects and evolves from the economic conditions and sociocultural and political characteristics of the country and its communities and is based on the application of the relevant results of social, biomedical and health services research and public health experience;

2. addresses the main health problems of the community, providing promotive, preventive, curative and rehabilitative services accordingly;

3. includes at least: education concerning prevailing health problems and the methods of preventing and controlling them; promotion of food supply and proper nutrition; an adequate supply of safe water and basic sanitation; maternal and child health care, including family planning; immunization against the major infectious diseases; prevention and control of locally endemic diseases; appropriate treatment of common diseases and injuries; and provision of essential drugs;

4. involves, in addition to the health sector, all related sectors and aspects of national and community development, in particular agriculture, animal husbandry, food, industry, education, housing, public works, communications and other sectors; and demands the coordinated efforts of all those sectors;

5. requires and promotes maximum community and individual self-reliance and participation in the planning, organization, operation and control of primary health care, making fullest use of local, national and other available resources; and to this end develops through appropriate education the ability of communities to participate;

6. should be sustained by integrated, functional and mutually supportive referral systems, leading to the progressive improvement of comprehensive health care for all, and giving priority to those most in need;

7. relies, at local and referral levels, on health workers, including physicians, nurses, midwives, auxiliaries and community workers as applicable, as well as traditional practitioners as needed, suitably trained socially and technically to work as a health team and to respond to the expressed health needs of the community."

(Declaration of Alma Ata, 1979, para. VII)

"The challenge", that "Each day, 40,000 children die from malnutrition and disease, including acquired immunodeficiency syndrome (AIDS), from the lack of clean water and inadequate sanitation and from the effects of the drug problem". Under "The Task", the Declaration states: "Enhancement of children's health and nutrition is a first duty, and also a task for which solutions are now within reach. The lives of tens of thousands of boys and girls can be saved every day, because the causes of their death are readily preventable. Child and infant mortality is unacceptably high in many parts of the world, but can be lowered dramatically with means that are already known and easily accessible...

"Half a million mothers die each year from causes related to childbirth. Safe motherhood must be promoted in all possible ways. Emphasis must be placed on responsible planning of family size and on child spacing..." Under "The Commitment", it says: "We will work for a solid effort of national and international action to enhance children's health, to promote prenatal care and to lower infant and child mortality in all countries and among all peoples. We will promote the provision of clean water in all communities for all their children, as well as universal access to sanitation. We will work for optimal growth and development in childhood, through measures to eradicate hunger, malnutrition and famine, and thus to relieve millions of children of tragic sufferings in a world that has the means to feed all its citizens." Under "The Next Steps", the Summit participants indicated that they had decided to "adopt and implement" the Plan of Action: "We are prepared to make available the resources to meet these commitments, as part of the priorities of our national plans. We do this not only for the present generation, but for all generations to come. There can be no task nobler than giving every child a better future." (Declaration, paras. 6, 10, 14, 20, 24, 25)

Implementation Handbook for the Convention on the Rights of the Child

Health goals of the World Summit Plan of Action

The Plan of Action was developed as a guide for national programmes. It sets major goals for the survival, protection and development of children by the year 2000. These were derived from already existing goals agreed upon by WHO and UNICEF (see, for example, World Health Organization, *Development of Indicators for Monitoring Progress Towards Health for All by the Year 2000*, Geneva, 1981, pp. 124-125). The goals are intended to address the issue of equity by being applicable to all significant groups and areas within a State.

Major health goals:
Reduction of 1990 under-five child mortality rate by one third, or to a level of 70 per 1000 live births, whichever is the greater reduction;

Reduction of maternal mortality rates by half of 1990 levels;

Reduction of severe and moderate malnutrition among under-five children by one half of 1990 levels;

Universal access to safe drinking water and to sanitary means of excreta disposal.

Supporting/sectoral goals:

Women's health:
Special attention to the health and nutrition of the female child and to pregnant and lactating women;

Access by all couples to information and services to prevent pregnancies that are too early, too closely spaced, too late or too many;

Access by all pregnant women to prenatal care, trained attendants during childbirth and referral facilities for high-risk pregnancies and obstetric emergencies.

Nutrition:
Reduction in severe as well as moderate malnutrition among under-five children by half of 1990 levels;

Reduction of the rate of low birth weight (2.5 kg or less) to less than 10 per cent;

Reduction of iron deficiency anaemia in women by one third of the 1990 levels;

Virtual elimination of vitamin A deficiency and its consequences, including blindness;

Empowerment of all women to breastfeed their children exclusively for four to six months and to continue breastfeeding, with complementary food, well into the second year;

Growth promotion and its regular monitoring to be institutionalized in all countries by the end of the 1990s;

Dissemination of knowledge and supporting services to increase food production to ensure household food security.

Child health:
Global eradication of poliomyelitis by the year 2000;

Elimination of neonatal tetanus by 1995;

Reduction by 95 per cent in measles deaths and reduction by 90 per cent of measles cases compared to pre-immunization levels by 1995, as a major step towards the global eradication of measles in the longer run;

Maintenance of a high level of immunization coverage (at least 90 per cent of children under 1 year of age by the year 2000) against diphtheria, pertussis, tetanus, measles, poliomyelitis, tuberculosis and against tetanus for women of child-bearing age;

Reduction by 50 per cent in the deaths due to diarrhoea in children under the age of five years old and 25 per cent reduction in the diarrhoea incidence rate;

Reduction by one third in the deaths due to acute respiratory infections in children under five years old.

Water and sanitation:
Universal access to safe drinking water;

Universal access to sanitary means of excreta disposal;

Elimination of guinea worm disease (dracunculiasis) by the year 2000.

(Plan of Action for implementing the World Declaration on the Survival, Protection and Development of Children in the 1990s, Appendix: Goals for Children and Development in the 1990s, 30 September 1990)

The Plan of Action summarizes the current situation and specific actions required for child health and, in the appendix, provides "Goals for Children and Development in the 1990s", including more detailed goals for child health.

Progressive implementation of health rights

As with other economic, social and cultural rights, article 4 of the Convention on the Rights of the Child requires States Parties to implement article 24 "to the maximum extent of their available resources and, where needed, within the framework of international cooperation". The right to life (article 6, paragraph 1) is a principle which must be respected in all circumstances, and is included in both the Universal Declaration and the International Covenant on Civil and Political Rights (see page 87). Article 24 stresses the progressive nature of implementation: States Parties "shall strive to ensure" that no child is deprived of his or her right of access to health care ser-£vices, "shall pursue full implementation of this right" (paragraph 2), and shall promote and encourage international cooperation "with a view to achieving progressively" full realization of the right (paragraph 4).

Similarly, article 2(1) of the International Covenant on Economic, Social and Cultural Rights indicates that each State Party undertakes to take steps "to the maximum of its available resources, with a view to achieving progressively the full realization of the rights recognized in the present Covenant by all appropriate means".

The Committee on the Rights of the Child has not yet commented in detail on the interpretation of article 24 and the obligations of States Parties. But in a key General Comment on "The nature of

States Parties' obligations" under the International Covenant on Economic, Social and Cultural Rights, the Committee on Economic, Social and Cultural Rights notes that the concept of progressive realization is, on the one hand, a necessary flexibility device, reflecting the realities of the real world. "On the other hand, the phrase must be read in the light of the overall objective, indeed the *raison d'être* of the Covenant which is to establish clear obligations for States Parties in respect of the full realization of the rights in question. It thus imposes an obligation to move as expeditiously and effectively as possible towards that goal. Moreover, any deliberately retrogressive measures in that regard would require the most careful consideration and would need to be fully justified by reference to the totality of the rights provided for in the Covenant and in the context of the full use of the maximum available resources...

"... the Committee is of the view that a minimum core obligation to ensure the satisfaction of, at the very least, minimum essential levels of each of the rights is incumbent upon every State Party. Thus, for example, a State Party in which any significant number of individuals is deprived of essential foodstuffs, of essential primary health care, of basic shelter and housing, or of the most basic forms of education is, *prima facie*, failing to discharge its obligations under the Covenant ... even where the available resources are demonstrably inadequate, the obligation remains for a State Party to strive to ensure the widest possible enjoyment of the relevant rights under the prevailing circumstances. Moreover, the obligations to monitor the extent of the realization, or more especially of the non-realization, of economic, social and cultural rights, and to devise strategies and programmes for their promotion, are not in any way eliminated as a result of resource constraints." (Committee on Economic, Social and Cultural Rights, General Comment 3, HRI/GEN/1/Rev.2, p. 55; for further discussion, see article 4, page 55)

The Committee on the Rights of the Child has emphasized that effective use of resources implies a focus on primary health care (see also below, page 326):

"With a view to contributing to the most effective use of scarce resources, the Committee recommends that the State Party accord greater attention and consideration to the development of a strong primary health care system. Such a system would have the benefits of according due attention to developing a culture of nutrition, hygiene and sanitation education, transmitting health skills to

Indicators of discrimination in health

Panama's Initial Report reveals that infant mortality rates vary according to the living conditions of different regions, social classes and population groups: "Thus, infant mortality levels are three times greater than the national average among indigenous children and in regions of extreme poverty... At the national level, 24.4 per cent of children were below normal height for their age; however the percentage was 71 per cent in San Blas, 44 per cent in Bocas del Toro and 40 per cent in Darien..." (Panama IR, paras. 153 and 155)

parents, and enhancing participatory approaches to the distribution and use of resources throughout the health care system." (Federal Republic of Yugoslavia IRCO, Add.49, para. 36)

Discrimination in access to health/health care

Article 24 stresses that the State Party must recognize the right of the child to the enjoyment of the highest attainable standard of health and it must strive to ensure that no child is deprived of access to health care services. Article 24 read with article 2 requires that no child in the jurisdiction suffers discrimination in the implementation of the article – "irrespective of the child's or his or her parent's or legal guardian's race, colour, sex, language, religion, political or other opinion, national, ethnic or social origin, property, birth or other status". According to the Alma Ata Declaration: "The existing gross inequality in the health status of the people particularly between developed and developing countries as well as within countries is politically, socially and economically unacceptable and is, therefore, of common concern to all countries." (Declaration, para. II)

The Committee has linked concerns about health to discrimination issues in many cases. In particular, it has highlighted discrimination against children living in poverty, girls, disabled children, children living in rural areas and different regions of a State, ethnic groups, children of indigenous communities, asylum-seeking and refugee children and illegal immigrants (see also article 2, page 26). For example:

"... the Committee expresses its concern at the health status of children of different socio-economic groups and those belonging to ethnic minorities." (UK IRCO, Add.34, para. 13)

"With regard to article 2 of the Convention, the Committee notes with concern that the principle of non-discrimination is not fully implemented for girls, disabled children and illegal immigrant children, non-accompanied children and children living in rural areas, especially in the fields of education and health." (Portugal IRCO, Add.45, para. 13)

"The Committee wishes to express concern at the information brought to its attention which indicates that disparities exist between regions and between rural and urban areas with regard to the provision of health care to children..." (Federal Republic of Yugoslavia IRCO, Add.49, para. 17. See also, for example, China IRCO, Add.56, para. 11; Nigeria IRCO, Add.61, para. 37)

Disability

Article 23 of the Convention on the Rights of the Child requires recognition of "the right of the disabled child to special care"; assistance provided "shall be designed to ensure that the disabled child has effective access to and receives ... health care services, rehabilitation services ... in a manner conducive to the child's achieving the fullest possible social integration and individual development, including his or her cultural and spiritual development."

According to the Standard Rules on the Equalization of Opportunities for Persons with Disabilities , "States should ensure that persons with disabilities, particularly infants and children, are provided with the same level of medical care within the same system as other members of society." (rule 2.3; see article 23, page 308)

Girls

In the report of its General Discussion on the girl child (January 1995), the Committee noted that

"...The son preference, historically rooted in the patriarchal system, often manifested itself by neglect, less food and little health care. Such a situation of inferiority often favoured violence and sexual abuse within the family, as well as problems associated with early pregnancy and marriage..." (Report on the eighth session, January 1995, CRC/C/38, p. 49)

The Platform for Action of the Fourth World Conference on Women states: "Existing discrimination against the girl child in her access to nutrition and physical and mental health services endangers her current and future health. An estimated 450 million adult women in developing countries are stunted as a result of childhood protein-energy malnutrition... " (para. 266). The Platform for Action proposes that all barriers be eliminated to enable girls without exception to develop their full potential and skills through equal access to education and training, "nutrition, physical and mental health care and related information" (para. 272; see box on page 324 for details of "Strategic Objective").

Participation in relation to health rights

Article 12 requires that children's right to express their views and have them given due consideration, and to be heard in any judicial or administrative proceedings, is implemented in relation to health and health services. Consideration of participation is required both in relation to the overall planning, delivery and monitoring of health services relevant to the child, and also in relation to treatment of the individual child, and the child's right to consent or refuse consent to treatment

Eliminating discrimination against girls in health and nutrition

Strategic Objective L.5 of the Platform for Action of the Fourth World Conference on Women

Actions to be taken by Governments and international and non-governmental organizations:

(a) Provide public information on the removal of discriminatory practices against girls in food allocation, nutrition and access to health services;

(b) Sensitize the girl child, parents, teachers and society concerning good general health and nutrition and raise awareness of the health dangers and other problems connected with early pregnancies;

(c) Strengthen and reorient health education and health services, particularly primary health care programmes, including sexual and reproductive health, and design quality health programmes that meet the physical and mental needs of girls and that attend to the needs of young, expectant and nursing mothers.

(d) Establish peer education and outreach programmes with a view to strengthening individual and collective action to reduce the vulnerability of girls to HIV/AIDS and other sexually transmitted diseases, as agreed to in the Programme of Action of the International Conference on Population and Development and as established in the report of that Conference, recognizing the parental roles referred to in paragraph 267 of the Present Platform for Action [Paragraph 267 refers to the need to take into account "the responsibilities, rights and duties of parents and legal guardians to provide, in a manner consistent with the evolving capacities of the child, appropriate direction and guidance in the realization by the child of the rights recognized in the Convention on the Rights of the Child..."].

(e) Ensure education and dissemination of information to girls, especially adolescent girls, regarding the physiology of reproduction, reproductive and sexual health, as agreed to in the Programme of Action of the International Conference on Population and Development...

(f) Include health and nutritional training as an integral part of literacy programmes and school curricula starting at the primary level for the benefit of the girl child;

(g) Emphasize the role and responsibility of adolescents in sexual and reproductive health and behaviour through the provision of appropriate services and counselling...;

(h) Develop information and training programmes for health planners and implementers on the special health needs of the girl child;

(i) Take all appropriate measures with a view to abolishing traditional practices prejudicial to the health of children, as stipulated in article 24 of the Convention on the Rights of the Child."

(Platform for Action, Fourth World Conference on Women, Beijing 1995, para. 281; see also proposals on early motherhood, page 328 below.)

(see article 12, page 161 for further discussion). The *Guidelines for Periodic Reports* seeks information on any legal minimum age defined in legislation for medical counselling without parental consent and also for medical treatment or surgery without parental consent. The Convention does not support the setting of a particular age but rather requires respect for the "evolving capacities" of the child to make decisions for him or herself (see article 1, definition of a child, page 8).

"States Parties shall pursue full implementation of this right and, in particular, shall take appropriate measures...": article 24(2)

The wording indicates that the list of measures in paragraph 2 is not exclusive; other measures may be required to implement the right.

"(a) To diminish infant and child mortality"

Article 6 requires recognition that "every child has the inherent right to life"; States must ensure "to the maximum extent possible" the survival of the child (see page 85). The Committee has commended States for reducing mortality rates. The infant mortality rate is the probability of dying between birth and exactly one year of age, expressed per 1,000 live births; the term child mortality rate is often taken to mean the under-five mortality rate, which is the probability of dying between birth and exactly five years of age, expressed per 1,000 live births. But in the context of the Convention, "child" means every human being below the age of 18, and thus the concern to diminish mortality extends to 18.

As noted above (page 321) one of the World Summit for Children goals is: "...Reduction of 1990 under-five mortality rate by one third, or to 70 per 1,000 live births respectively, whichever is less". The report of the World Summit for Social Development (Copenhagen, 1995) included the goal of reducing mortality rates of infants and children under five years of age by one third of the 1990 level, or 50 to 70 per 1,000 live births, whichever is less; by the year 2015, achievement of an infant mortality rate below 35 per 1,000 live births and an under-five mortality rate below 45 per 1,000 (A/CONF.166/9, p. 51).

In 1995, under-five mortality rates varied from 320 per 1,000 live births (Niger) to 5 per 1,000 live births (Finland and Sweden). UNICEF records the world average as 89 under-five deaths per 1,000 births in 1995 (*The State of the World's Children 1997*, UNICEF, p. 80).

The Committee on the Rights of the Child has congratulated States that have made progress in reducing rates, and has expressed concern wherever rates have risen and also at situations in which rates vary in a discriminatory way:

"The considerable progress achieved by the State Party in reducing the infant and under-five mortality rates, especially through the extensive efforts focused on sustaining immunization coverage, increasing immunization rates and reducing the incidence of child malnutrition, is to be commended." (China IRCO, Add.56, para. 5)

"The Committee views the trend of rising child mortality rates as a matter of deep concern..." (Nigeria IRCO, Add.61, para. 16)

There are diverse causes of infant and child mortality, acknowledged in the World Summit for Children Declaration and other statements. A 1996 global study by the WHO and others of the cause of death of children under five provided the following breakdown:

> acute respiratory infections: 19 per cent;
> diarrhoea: 19 per cent;
> perinatal causes: 18 per cent;
> non-communicable diseases: 10 per cent:
> measles: 7 per cent;
> injuries: 6 per cent;
> malaria: 5 per cent;
> other: 16 per cent.

In terms of actual numbers, adolescents are healthy relative to infants and children under five, it is, nevertheless, still important to note the major causes of adolescent morbidity and mortality. Taken together, according to calculations of the total burden of disease among adolescents, the major causes are:

> unipolar major depression: 6.9 per cent;
> road traffic accidents: 4.9 per cent;

Lowering mortality rates

To attain the World Summit goal of reducing infant mortality rates to one third of their 1990 levels by the year 2000, China reports in its Initial Report that it has already taken various measures, "concentrating its efforts on geographically handicapped and poor regions; through the gradual establishment and bolstering of mother-and-child health care facilities and preventive measures, through widespread publicity and dissemination of information about mother-and-child health care, through training for grass roots mother-and-child health care workers and similar measures, it is actively raising the capacity for mother-and-child health care and thereby effectively raising living standards and lowering mortality rates for both women and children." (China IR, para. 43)

> falls: 4.0 per cent;
> iron deficiency anaemia: 3.7 per cent;
> war : 3.5 per cent;
> lower respiratory infections: 3.3 per cent;
> drownings: 2.8 per cent;
> self-inflicted injuries: 2.7 per cent.

While malnutrition alone accounts for just 3 per cent of under-five deaths, it plays a contributing role in more than half of all child deaths in developing countries (reported in *The Progress of Nations 1997*, UNICEF, p. 28, adapted from *The Global Burden of Disease*, WHO, The World Bank and Harvard University, 1996).

The obligations of States to respond to these causes is pursued in the following subparagraphs of article 24(2), and in other articles of the Convention on the Rights of the Child – for example to provide appropriate support for parenting (article 18) and to protect children from various forms of violence, exploitation and abuse (articles 19, 32-38).

In its *Guidelines for Periodic Reports*, the Committee acknowledges the importance of the adequate investigation of and reporting on the deaths of all children and the causes of death, and the registration of deaths and causes (para. 41). Adequate investigation is vital to inform preventive strategies to reduce infant and child mortality rates (see also article 6, page 93).

"(b) To ensure the provision of necessary medical assistance and health care to all children with emphasis on the development of primary health care"

Primary health care programmes

Panama's Initial Report describes its Maternal Health and Child Health Programmes. The main purposes of the Maternal Health Programme (targeted at pregnant women of all ages, all breastfeeding mothers, any individual capable of begetting or bearing a child, and all newborn infants from birth to discharge from hospital) are:

- to reduce maternal and perinatal morbidity and mortality rates;

- to reduce the incidence of underweight newborn infants;

- to combine in health activities preventive and curative aspects, biological and social aspects and personal and environmental aspects, and to integrate medical teams with the individual and his family;

- to conduct medical-social research, in particular on women, their families and communities.

The Child Health Programme targets children during the foetal period by means of prenatal examination, breastfed babies (neonatal examination), preschool children and adolescents. Examinations focus on growth and development, nutrition, immunological status, and psychological, social and cultural situation). Its main purposes are "to raise the standard of health of the entire population by promoting the optimum biological, psychological, and social development of children and decreasing the risks of illness and death. It promotes the education of children about preventive measures, general care, physical growth, hygiene, nutrition and early stimulation of children at their various stages of development. It promotes exclusive breastfeeding by mothers during the child's first four to six months of life." (Panama IR, paras. 127-131)

Here again, emphasis is on "all children". The Committee's general concerns have focused on a lack of priority given to primary health care, reflecting the Alma Ata Declaration (see above, page 320). For example:

"The Committee recommends that the primary health care system be improved regarding the effectiveness of, inter alia, antenatal care, health education, including sex education, family planning and immunization programmes. As regards problems relating specifically to the immunization programme, the

Committee suggests that the Government should look to international cooperation for support in the procurement and manufacturing of vaccines." (Russian Federation IRCO, Add.4, para. 20)

"The Committee is concerned to note that national health plans appear to emphasize the training of doctors rather than of nurses and other health personnel, including paramedics. Its attention has also been drawn to the apparent lack of clarity in the division of responsibilities between the provincial and federal levels for the development of a strong primary health care system...

"The Committee encourages the Government to continue taking measures to strengthen the primary health care system. The Committee would like to see greater emphasis on family education, including family planning, and encourages the training of community health care workers to assist in these tasks..." (Pakistan IRCO, Add.18, paras. 18 and 29. See also Sudan IRCO, Add.10, para. 23; Honduras IRCO, Add.24, para. 28; Madagascar IRCO, Add.26, para. 12; Jamaica IRCO, Add.32, paras. 14 and 27; Nicaragua IRCO, Add.36, para. 37)

"(c) To combat disease and malnutrition, including within the framework of primary health care, through, *inter alia*, the application of readily available technology and through the provision of adequate nutritious foods and clean drinking water, taking into consideration the dangers and risks of environmental pollution"

Again, this subparagraph emphasizes the framework of primary health care; the Committee's comments have highlighted the basic issues of nutrition and clean water, and the dangers of environmental pollution. Discrimination in provision and access to primary health care is often mentioned, particularly affecting children in rural areas and children living in poverty. For example:

"The Committee notes that the lack of provision of and access to health services and facilities, and clean water and sanitation is an extremely serious problem in rural areas. The Committee is also concerned at the prevalence of the malnutrition of children from the poorer and more disadvantaged sectors of the population, especially as regards the adverse effects of the insufficiency of nutritious food on the child's right to survival and a healthy development." (Honduras IRCO, Add.24, para. 15)

The World Summit for Children Plan of Action notes that "hunger and malnutrition in their different forms contribute to about half of the deaths of young children. More than 20 million children suffer from severe malnutrition, 150 million are under weight and 350 million women suffer from nutritional anaemia. Improved nutrition requires (a) adequate household food security, (b) healthy environment and control of infections and (c) adequate maternal and child care. With the right policies, appropriate institutional arrangements and political priority, the world is now in a position to feed all the world's children and to overcome the worst forms of malnutrition, i.e. drastically to reduce diseases that contribute to malnutrition, to halve protein-energy malnutrition, virtually to eliminate vitamin A deficiency and iodine deficiency disorders and to reduce nutritional anaemia significantly." (Plan of Action, para. 13; the relevant goals adopted by the World Summit are listed on page 321)

The Plan notes: "A major factor affecting the health of children as well as adults is the availability of clean water and safe sanitation. These are not only essential for human health and well-being, but also contribute greatly to the emancipation of women from the drudgery that has a pernicious impact on children, especially girls. Progress in child health is unlikely to be sustained if one third of the developing world's children remain without access to clean drinking water and half of them without adequate sanitary facilities."

Echoing the subparagraph's reference to "readily available technology", the Plan of Action mentions "the many innovations in simple, low-cost techniques and technologies to provide clean water and safe sanitary facilities in rural areas and urban shanty towns, it is now desirable as well as feasible, through concerted national action and international cooperation, to aim at providing all the world's children with universal access to safe drinking water and sanitary means of excreta disposal by the year 2000..." (Plan of Action, paras. 11 and 12)

Nutrition is also mentioned in subparagraph (e) of article 24(2): States should ensure dissemination of basic knowledge of nutrition, particularly to parents and children. Article 27 of the Convention (adequate standard of living) requires States Parties in cases of need to provide material assistance and support programmes, particularly with regard to nutrition, clothing and housing (see also article 27, page 355).

In the 1969 Declaration on Social Progress and Development, the "elimination of hunger and malnutrition and the guarantee of the right to proper nutrition" (article 10(6)) are listed as among the "main goals". The Universal Declaration of Human Rights states that "everyone has

the right to a standard of living adequate for the health and well-being of himself and his family, including food, clothing, housing and medical care and necessary social services..." (article 25), and the International Covenant on Economic, Social and Cultural Rights similarly recognizes the right of everyone to an adequate standard of living... "including adequate food" and the fundamental right of everyone to be free of hunger (article 11(1)). The International Conference on Nutrition (Rome, December 1992) prepared the World Declaration and Plan of Action for Nutrition, which recognizes that "access to nutritionally adequate and safe food is a right of each individual". The Declaration also affirmed "in the context of international humanitarian law that food must not be used as a tool for political pressure. Food aid must not be denied because of political affiliation, geographic location, gender, age, ethnic, tribal or religious identity." (Declaration, paras. 1 and 15)

In 1993, UNICEF published a detailed report on progress towards the World Summit goals (*Child Malnutrition: Progress Toward the World Summit for Children Goals*, UNICEF, New York, March 1993).

"(d) To ensure appropriate prenatal and postnatal health care for mothers"

The World Summit for Children Plan of Action notes: "... The causes of the high rates of infant mortality, especially neonatal mortality, are linked to untimely pregnancies, low birth weight and pre-term births, unsafe delivery, neonatal tetanus, high fertility rates, etc..." (para. 16). Almost a fifth of under-five deaths are due to perinatal causes (see page 325).

Sufficient health personnel, adequately trained and supervised, should be provided to assist all who need them. The Committee has emphasized the importance of training for everyone involved in supporting birth, including traditional birth attendants:

"The Committee is concerned that only 47 per cent of births are supervised by qualified health care workers, and is alarmed at the implications this may have for increased likelihood of sickness and disability arising from preventable problems occurring during delivery. More budgetary support is needed to correct this situation, as well as sufficient support to programmes benefiting the mental and physical development of children..." (Bolivia IRCO, Add.1, para. 10)

"Despite the considerable progress achieved in recent years in improving infant and maternal care, the Committee remains concerned about the relatively high maternal, infant and

Birth care

States Parties' Initial Reports have noted the importance of appropriate birth care. For example in Mexico, "The high mortality and morbidity rates among the child population, especially at birth, are partly attributable to unwanted pregnancies, and to premature and underweight births. The presence of other risk factors, such as lack of medical care and adverse conditions in the home, also contributes to maternal and child mortality". There is often discrimination in relation to such care. Mexico's Initial Report identifies considerable disparities in natal care between rural and urban areas: "In rural areas where services are not readily available and where there is a reluctance on the part of women to accept them for cultural reasons, traditional midwives constitute a resource of undeniable value. Thus, an improvement in mother and child care has been achieved in rural areas through the involvement of traditional midwives in institutional programmes. A Programme for Training and Monitoring Traditional Midwives has been set up for that purpose, and they have been accorded recognition and have received support through the establishment of *Posadas de Nacimiento* (Birth Hostels)." (Mexico IR, paras. 135, 148 -9)

under-five mortality rates. The Committee observes that some factors contributing to high maternal deaths may be related to the inadequacies of the training given to birth attendants and of home deliveries. It is also the view of the Committee that many problems remain with respect to the reproductive health of women, the low birth weight of children being a possible manifestation of this fact...

"...As a means of addressing the problems of maternal death and poor antenatal care and delivery services, the Committee suggests that the State Party consider introducing a more effective system training medical personnel and birth attendants. The Committee also recommends that the State Party consider requesting international cooperation from relevant international organizations to address issues relating to the reproductive health of women." (Guatemala IRCO, Add.58, paras. 22 and 35)

The Committee has noted the particular threats to mortality rates and health early motherhood poses (see further discussion under article 24(2)(f) below – family planning education and services):

"The Committee is worried by the widespread practice of early marriage and the related consequence of high child mortality rates and the negative impact on the health of girls bearing children at an early age. It is also concerned with consanguineous marriage." (Lebanon IRCO, Add.54, para. 16)

The Platform for Action adopted at the Fourth World Conference on Women highlights the problem of early motherhood: "More than 15 million girls aged 15 to 19 give birth each year. Motherhood at a very young age entails complications during pregnancy and delivery and a risk of maternal death that is much greater than average. The children of young mothers have higher levels of morbidity and mortality. Early childbearing continues to be an impediment to improvements in the educational, economic and social status of women in all parts of the world. Overall, early marriage and early motherhood can severely curtail educational and employment opportunities and are likely to have a long-term adverse impact on their and their children's quality of life." (Platform for Action, para. 268).

"(e) To ensure that all segments of society, in particular parents and children, are informed, have access to education and are supported in the use of basic knowledge of child health and nutrition, the advantages of breastfeeding, hygiene and environmental sanitation and the prevention of accidents"

This paragraph of article 24 underlines the key importance of health education and information, and support, to achieving the child's right to health and access to health care services, an idea echoed in the World Summit Declaration and Plan of Action, and the Platform for Action of the Fourth World Conference on Women. The link between health and access to basic education and achievement of literacy is acknowledged and reflected in goals in these and other plans. Under "Basic education", the Plan of Action also set as a goal: "Increased acquisition of knowledge, skills and values through all educational channels, including modern and traditional communication media, to improve the quality of life of children and families" (World Summit Plan of Action, para. 20). Article 17 of the Convention on the Rights of the Child promotes the potential role of the mass media in disseminating information of benefit to children (see article 17, page 217). Article 18 requires States to render appropriate assistance to parents in the performance of their child-rearing responsibilities, and the Committee on the Rights of the Child has frequently called for parenting and family education (see also article 18, page 228). For example:

"The Committee would like to see a stronger emphasis placed on primary health care activities which would include the development of educational programmes to cover such matters as family education, family planning, sex education and the benefits of breastfeeding. Equally, the Committee encourages the training of community health care workers to develop awareness of these subjects among the general public, including children..." (Belarus IRCO, Add.17, para. 14)

"In view of the general problems which exist with regard to the health status of the population, particularly children, the Committee suggests that the provision of primary health care be emphasized, with family planning services and knowledge of nutrition as two of its major components, and that strategies be developed to provide families with the necessary technical and other support to grow their own food." (Nicaragua IRCO, Add.36, para. 37)

Breastfeeding There are two aspects to the promotion of breastfeeding: the need for positive information, education and promotion of its advantages, and the need to challenge the negative impact of the commercial marketing of substitutes. A widely used standard for positive education is the 1989 WHO/UNICEF *Ten steps to successful breastfeeding*. These steps form the backbone of the worldwide Baby-Friendly Hospital Initiative, launched in 1991 by the WHO and UNICEF.

In 1981 the International Code of Marketing of Breastmilk Substitutes was adopted by the World Health Assembly (WHA Resolution 34.22, 1981). The Code aims "to contribute to the provision of safe and adequate nutrition for infants, by the protection and promotion of breastfeeding, and by ensuring the proper use of breastmilk substitutes, when these are necessary, on the basis of adequate information and through appropriate marketing and distribution" (Code, para. 1). In 1990, the Innocenti Declaration on the Protection, Promotion and Support of Breastfeeding included national action to implement the Code as one of its four operational targets for 1995. The World Health Assembly (WHA) has repeatedly

article
24

Promoting breastfeeding

States Parties have described in Initial Reports a variety of initiatives to promote breastfeeding, for example Argentina's Report indicates that legislation existed, but had not yet been implemented, to entitle working mothers to two breaks of half an hour per day to breastfeed (Argentina IR, para. 52). In 1991, a National Lactation Committee was set up in Chile, comprising scientific societies and civic associations, NGOs and representatives of the Ministry of Health and National Consumers' Association (Chile IR, para. 115).

China's Initial Report notes that promoting breastfeeding is "a formidable social task that requires political, legal and economic underpinnings besides energetic support from society as a whole. The Programme Outline for the 1990s sets a target of breastfeeding in 80 per cent of China's provinces by the year 2000. To reach this target, the Department of Health issued a nationwide announcement in May 1992 on the strengthening of breastfeeding, and on 7 August 1992 mounted China's first World Breastfeeding Week rally in Beijing, calling on all sectors of society to help found children's hospitals, promote compliance with the regulations on the protection of female workers, and guarantee maternity leave of at least four months... By the end of 1994, 947 children's hospitals had been established in China... To reverse the steady decline in breastfeeding in China, the State has taken steps to strengthen controls on the sale of breastmilk substitutes and restrict the marketing of such substitutes..." Manufacturers and retailers are required to conform strictly to the International Code of Marketing of Breastmilk Substitutes, and not to provide mother-and-child health care centres with substitutes free or at advantageous prices; units are forbidden to accept donations or contributions of substitutes from companies and retailers (China IR, paras. 151-153).

In Tunisia, measures to promote breastfeeding and improve the nutritional status of children include: the establishment of nutritional education units in most mother and infant health centres; daily broadcasting by the national radio of nutritional education messages directed at the public in general and mothers in particular; legislation concerning the marketing and proper utilization of mother's milk substitutes; legislation requiring every enterprise employing 50 or more women to set up a special breastfeeding room, and a circular granting to mothers employed in the public sector one hour's rest per working period for six months after the end of maternity leave. In 1992, 94.5 per cent of infants less than five months, 74.8 per cent of those aged between six and nine months, and 63.7 per cent of those aged between 10 and 12 months were breastfed (Tunisia IR, paras. 162-164).

Accidents - a primary cause of child death

Beyond the age of one, accidents are the primary cause of death in childhood in the Republic of Korea: "With the development of medicine the rate of death from diseases has decreased, but the rate of death from accidents, especially from traffic accidents, has increased..." The "Five Year Campaign to Reduce Traffic Accidents" was under way from 1992-96, and in its first year reduced child deaths by 30 per cent. The Safety Traffic Promotion Corporation, created to prevent traffic accidents, provides traffic safety education for children to the guidance teachers of schools having more than 10 classes. A "Children Protection Zone" has also been established within a radius of 500 metres of schools. (Republic of Korea IR, paras. 114-116)

reiterated its recommendation to Member States to adopt the Code and subsequent WHA resolutions in their entirety (most recently, in WHA resolution 49.15, May 1996). The Code specifies that Member States "shall communicate annually to the Director-General information on action taken to give effect to the principles and aim of the Code". The Director-General of WHO is required to report to the World Health Assembly in even years on the status of implementation of the Code, and to provide technical support on request to Member States (paras. 11.6 and 11.7).

The Committee has recognized that implementation of the Code by States Parties is a concrete measure towards the realization of parents' right to objective information on the advantages of breastfeeding and, thus, to fulfilling the obligations of article 24:

"The Committee recommends that the ban of the commercial marketing of infant formula be implemented and that breastfeeding be promoted among mothers in health facilities..." (Lebanon IRCO, Add.54, para. 34)

The Committee has addressed apparent breaches:

"The Committee is concerned about the apparent insufficiency of measures to encourage breastfeeding. The Committee notes that powdered milk for babies continues to be freely distributed in hospitals, contrary to international guidelines on this matter." (UK dependent territory: Hong Kong IRCO, Add.63, para. 16)

In a report to the Forty-fifth World Health Assembly, the Director-General reviewed infant and child nutrition and action taken to implement the International Code. An in-depth study undertaken in 14 countries reported on a wide range of problems, including *inter alia* some governments alluding to "difficulties in securing the industry's full cooperation" (A45/28).

Accident prevention Few Initial Reports have given much information on accident prevention, and there has been little comment from the Committee. Under article 3(2), States undertake to provide the protection and care necessary for children's welfare. While accident prevention is clearly part of parental responsibilities, there are aspects of it which can only be promoted adequately through State action (transport and environmental policies, provision of appropriate advice, financial support for domestic safety aids and so forth). As noted above (page 325), the Committee has stressed in its *Guidelines for Periodic Reports* the importance of investigating causes of death (para. 41). Accidents are a major cause of child death and injury in many States. Investigation is a vital part of their prevention:

"With regard to the high number of domestic or other accidents whose victims are children in Iceland, the Committee welcomes the establishment of the Accident Prevention Council in 1994." (Iceland IRCO, Add.50, para. 9)

"(f) To develop preventive health care, guidance for parents, and family planning education and services"

Programmes of preventive health care, health promotion and guidance exist in all countries and are promoted by WHO, UNICEF and other agencies.

The Committee has promoted education for parenthood, including education on health matters. The Committee's *Guidelines for Periodic Reports* asks for information on family counselling and parental education programmes, and also asks how knowledge and information on child development is transmitted to parents and other responsible adults (para. 63). Article 18 requires States to render "appropriate assistance to parents and legal guardians in the performance of their child-rearing responsibilities" and to ensure "the development of institutions, facilities and services for the care of children" (see article 18, page 232).

HIV/AIDS is threatening to reverse the progress made in reducing death and disease in many countries. Every day 1,000 children around the world die from AIDS (*The Progress of Nations 1997*, UNICEF, p. 23). Prevention demands very active information campaigns and services, targeted at all sectors of the population and particularly at adolescents. UNAIDS was formed in 1996 by six agencies: UNICEF, UNDP, UNESCO, UNFPA, WHO and The World Bank. It develops the priorities to be pursued in country programmes.

In 1997, UNAIDS published a guide to United Nations human rights machinery, summarizing the relationship between human rights and HIV/AIDS, giving a general overview of the main United Nations human rights bodies and including in an annex (annex 5(d), p. 87) "Possible issues to be addressed by the Committee on the Rights of the Child" (UNAIDS, *The UNAIDS Guide to the United Nations Human Rights Machinery*, 1997).

Immunization Immunization is one particular aspect of preventive health care. The Committee on the Rights of the Child has expressed grave concern where immunization rates have fallen and has congratulated States that have achieved significant increases in their rates. Here again, discrimination is an issue. For example:

"The Committee feels that the vaccination programmes are not adequate, both in terms of the range of vaccines offered and the groups covered, and do not correspond to the real needs, especially in rural areas." (Burkina Faso IRCO, Add.19, para. 10)

"In particular the Committee is concerned over the alarming trend that child immunization is on the decrease." (Madagascar IRCO, Add.26, para. 12)

"The Committee notes with satisfaction the successful immunization programme with 99 per cent coverage..." (Argentina IRCO, Add.35, para. 7)

Compulsory immunization

Initial Reports from some States Parties note that immunization is compulsory: for example, it is obligatory in Croatia to immunize children against tuberculosis (tuberculosis activa), diphtheria, tetanus, whooping cough (pertussis), poliomyelitis, measles, mumps, German measles and hepatitis B (Croatia IR, para. 293). In Italy, vaccination against tuberculosis is compulsory for children between 5 and 15 years of age who have a negative cuti-reaction or have been exposed to tuberculosis. The Italian Constitutional Court found the refusal of parents to allow their child to be subjected to compulsory vaccination to display "conduct prejudicial to the child". (Italy IR, para. 149)

In 1996, WHO and UNICEF jointly published *State of the world's vaccines and immunization, a review of progress, constraints and challenges;* worldwide nearly 80 per cent of the world's children under one year old are immunized, but at the same time millions of children are not fully vaccinated, especially those in remote and marginalized areas.

Family planning education and services
Some States Parties made declarations or reservations with reference to subparagraph (f) of article 24. For example, "... the Argentine Republic considers that questions relating to family planning are the exclusive concern of parents in accordance with ethical and moral principles and understands it to be a State obligation, under this article, to adopt measures providing guidance for

The Ottawa Charter on Health Promotion

In 1986, the first International Conference on Health Promotion, meeting in Ottawa, Canada, adopted a Charter on Health Promotion "for action to achieve Health for All by the year 2000 and beyond". The Charter describes health promotion "as the process of enabling people to increase control over, and to improve, their health ... Health is a positive concept emphasizing social and personal resources, as well as physical capacities. Therefore, health promotion is not just the responsibility of the health sector, but goes beyond healthy lifestyles to well-being.

"Health promotion focuses on achieving equity in health. Health promotion action aims at reducing differences in current health status and ensuring equal opportunities and resources to enable all people to achieve their full health potential. This includes a secure foundation in a supportive environment, access to information, life skills and opportunities for making healthy choices. People cannot achieve their fullest health potential unless they are able to take control of those things which determine their health. This must apply equally to women and men."

(Health Promotion - the Ottawa Charter, adopted at an International Conference on Health Promotion, November 1986, Ottawa, Canada; co-sponsored by the Canadian Public Health Association, Health and Welfare Canada, and the World Health Organization.)

School health service in Cyprus

In Cyprus, school curricula are being revised to give an emphasis "to health education in its most inclusive sense. The governmental decision for a health-promoting school programme involves all children at all levels of education. ... In the past and recent years, health and hygiene were taught and promoted as separate subjects in the school curricula. The government decision has adopted a new attitude towards health education. It is a combined effort that is incorporated not only in the whole programme of the schools but also reinforced by the involvement of the parents and the community, through parent guidance programmes, family planning education and health preventive care" (Cyprus IR, paras. 110-112).

parents and education for responsible parenthood." The Holy See's reservation states "that it interprets the phrase 'family planning education and services' in article 24(2) to mean only those methods of family planning which it considers morally acceptable, that is, the natural methods of family planning". And Poland's reservation said "With respect to article 24, paragraph 2(f), of the Convention, the Republic of Poland considers that family planning and education services for parents should be in keeping with the principles of morality" (CRC/C/2/Rev.5, pp. 12, 20, 29).

Family planning is of importance not only to prevent early or unwanted pregnancy but also to space and limit numbers of children, to enable mothers to meet the needs of existing children and to protect maternal health. Family planning issues should be of equal concern to boys and young men as to girls and young women.

The Report of the International Conference on Population and Development (Cairo, 1994) proposes as a Principle that "Reproductive health care should provide the widest range of services without any form of coercion..." (A/CONF.171/13 p. 15, Principle 8). Special emphasis should be placed on men's shared responsibility and active involvement in sexual and reproductive behaviour, including family planning, prenatal, maternal and child health, prevention of sexually transmitted diseases, including HIV and prevention of unwanted and high risk pregnancies (A/CONF.171/13 p. 30, paras. 4.26 and 4.27).

The Report also stressed that youth should be actively involved in the planning, implementation and evaluation of programmes: "This is espe-

cially important with respect to information, education and communication activities and services concerning reproductive and sexual health, including the prevention of early pregnancies, sex education and the prevention of HIV/AIDS and other sexually transmitted diseases. Access to, as well as confidentiality and privacy of, these services must be ensured with the support and guidance of their parents and in line with the Convention on the Rights of the Child. In addition, there is a need for educational programmes in favour of life planning skills, healthy lifestyles and the active discouragement of substance abuse" (para. 6.15).

The Report urges support for "integral sexual education and services for young people, with the support and guidance of their parents and in line with the Convention on the Rights of the Child, that stress responsibility of males for their own sexual health and fertility and that help them exercise those responsibilities...".

One of the agreed objectives of the Cairo Conference is to substantially reduce all adolescent pregnancies: "Recognizing the rights, duties and responsibilities of parents and other persons legally responsible for adolescents to provide, in a manner consistent with the evolving capacities of the adolescent, appropriate direction and guidance in sexual and reproductive matters, countries must ensure that the programmes and attitudes of health care providers do not restrict the access of adolescents to appropriate services and the information they need, including on sexually transmitted diseases and sexual abuse. In doing so, and in order to, *inter alia*, address sexual abuse, these services must safeguard the rights of adolescents to privacy, confidentiality, respect and informed consent, respecting cultural values and religious beliefs. In this context, countries should, where appropriate, remove legal, regulatory and social barriers to reproductive health information and care for adolescents" (A/CONF. 171/13, paras. 7.37 and 7.45) (for discussion of confidentiality, see also the child's right to privacy, article 16, page 199).

The Platform for Action of the Fourth World Conference on Women states: "More than 15 million girls aged 15 to 19 give birth each year. Motherhood at a very young age entails complications during pregnancy and delivery and a risk of maternal death that is much greater than average. The children of young mothers have higher levels of morbidity and mortality. Early child-bearing continues to be an impediment to improvements in the educational, economic and social status of women in all parts of the world..." In addition: "Sexual violence and sexu-

Targeting adolescents

Finland's Initial Report notes that it has the lowest frequency of teenage abortions in the Nordic countries and one of the lowest in the Western world. The decrease in the number of abortions coincided with the increase in the use of contraceptives: "Between 1981 and 1991, the use of the contraceptive pill by girls of 18 doubled and nearly tripled by girls of 16 ... the condom is now used more widely by young people." Since 1987, all Finnish 16-year-olds have been mailed letters containing information on AIDS and other sexually transmitted diseases, and on contraception. Every letter also contains a condom. Sexually transmitted diseases are also decreasing: syphilis is virtually non-existent in young people and only nine cases of HIV have been detected in young people between the ages of 15 and 19 from 1980 to 1992. (Finland IR, paras. 393 and 396)

Norway's Directorate of Health has drafted a plan of action to prevent unwanted pregnancies and abortions: "It is necessary to intensify the testing of methods adapted to the social and cultural affiliations of the various target groups. Special campaigns and methods will be developed for boys. Surveys show that boys take more sexual risks and have poorer knowledge of their own body and sexuality than girls. Projects and measures will be implemented in relation to the age group 13-15, aimed at enhancing their knowledge of their sexuality and enabling them to make certain choices. Efforts will also be aimed at adolescent groups who engage in high-risk behaviour." (Norway IR, para. 317)

In Hong Kong, "groups of secondary school students are trained in the knowledge and skills for health promotion in their schools and in the community. The training course takes place during the summer vacation and consists of 10 lectures and three field visits. It covers a wide range of topics including communicable diseases, HIV/AIDS, mental health, smoking, alcoholism, drug abuse and sex education. 400 and 600 secondary form student ambassadors completed the course in 1994 and 1995 respectively." (UK dependent territory: Hong Kong IR, para. 270)

ally transmitted diseases, including HIV/AIDS, have a devastating effect on children's health, and girls are more vulnerable than boys to the con-sequences of unprotected and premature sexual relations..." (Platform for Action, paras. 268 and 269)

The Committee on the Rights of the Child has frequently expressed concern at high rates of teenage pregnancy, and has proposed health education and family planning programmes, as well as counselling for teenagers, including peer counselling. It perceives teenage pregnancy as a symptom of other social problems. The Committee:

"...also notes the high number of teenage pregnancies as a result of early sexual activity, which is symptomatic of underlying social problems." (Costa Rica IRCO, Add.11, para. 10)

"The number of teenage pregnancies in Honduras is relatively high and the Committee, therefore, has serious doubts regarding the adequacy of family and sex education, particularly with regard to the general level of understanding and knowledge about family planning methods and the availability of family planning services." (Honduras IRCO, Add.24, para. 14)

"While recognizing that the Government views the problem of teenage pregnancies as a serious one, the Committee suggests that additional efforts, in the form of prevention-oriented programmes which could be part of an educational campaign, are required to reduce the number of teenage pregnancies." (UK IRCO, Add.34, para. 30. See also Colombia Prelim. Obs., Add.15, para. 15; also Colombia IRCO, Add.30, para. 21; Romania IRCO, Add.16, para. 15; Burkina Faso IRCO, Add.19, para. 8; Jamaica IRCO, Add.32, para. 24; Argentina IRCO, Add.35, para. 19)

The Committee has noted the effects of teenage pregnancy not only on health but also on educational opportunities (article 28):

"The Committee is concerned about the high rate of early pregnancy, which has negative effects on the health of the mothers and the babies, and on the mothers' enjoyment of their right to education, hampering the school attendance of the girls concerned and causing high numbers of school drop-outs....

"With regard to the high rate of early pregnancy prevailing in Uruguay, the Committee recommends that measures be adopted to provide appropriate family education and services for young people within the school and health programmes implemented in the country." (Uruguay IRCO, Add.62, paras. 12 and 22)

In relation to family planning policy, the Committee has expressed concern at the use of abortion as a method of family planning (for comments, see article 6, page 88).

"States Parties shall take all effective and appropriate measures with a view to abolishing traditional practices prejudicial to the health of children": article 24(3)

Article 24(3) – together with article 19 (which requires protection from all forms of physical or mental violence, see page 237) and the non-discrimination principle in article 2 – requires a review in all States of any traditional practices that involve violence and/or are prejudicial to the health of children.

The health risks of practices which involve some invasion of the child's bodily integrity may be intensified by their performance by people with no medical training, and in unhygienic conditions. The lack of appropriate anaesthesia intensifies the suffering of children.

Traditional practices often take place when the child is very young and unable to consent. The degree to which a mature child can, him or herself, give an informed consent to a practice that involves violence or is prejudicial to his or her own health is a distinct issue from invasive practices without consent. But article 24(3) states unequivocally that appropriate measures should be taken with a view to abolishing traditional practices prejudicial to health. Presumably, mature children should have the same rights, if any, as adults have under the law in each society to consent to practices that involve a degree of violence but are not significantly prejudicial to health.

The proposal that the Convention should protect children from traditional practices harmful to health was made by the *ad hoc* NGO group during the drafting of the Convention (E/CN.4/1986/39, pp. 10-11, Detrick, p. 350). Various country representatives proposed that the provision should refer in particular or for example to the practice of female circumcision (genital mutilation of girls and young women), which was opposed on the grounds that it would be wrong to single out one practice. One other specific practice, that of preferential care of male children, was referred to during the drafting discussions of the Working Group on the Convention (E/CN.4/1987/25, pp. 8-10, Detrick, p. 351).

Several representatives concurred that the term traditional practices would include all those outlined in the 1986 Report of the Working Group on Traditional Practices affecting the Health of Women and Children (E/CN.4/1986/42). The Report refers to female circumcision, other forms of mutilation (facial scarification), forced feeding of women, early marriage, the various taboos or practices that prevent women from controlling their own fertility, nutritional taboos and others. There was also discussion of other traditional practices, including dowries in certain regions of the world, crimes of honour and the consequences of preferential treatment for male children (E/CN/.4/1986/42, para. 18).

The Working Group decided that female circumcision, preferential treatment for male children, and traditional birth practices should be given priority consideration. It reports that in Africa alone the practice of female circumcision (more accurately described as female genital mutilation) "exists in at least 28 African countries and continues to menace the health of about 75 million women and children". The Working Group makes detailed recommendations for action, in particular, that "with a view to attaining the goal of health for all by the year 2000, national health policies should include among their priorities strategies aimed at the eradication of female circumcision in their primary health care programmes" (E/CN/.4/1986/42, para. 127).

"Son preference" is defined as "the preference of parents for male children which often manifests itself in neglect, deprivation or discriminatory treatment of girls to the detriment of their mental and physical health" (E/CN/.4/1986/42, para.143). The Working Group found the practice prevalent in many parts of the world. It notes a World Fertility Survey, which as part of its inquiry into fertility motivations, asked women to state their preference as to the sex of their next child. The results revealed that in 23 of the 39 countries studied, women showed a preference for sons ("daughter preference" was found in only two countries). The Report states that "abnormal sex ratios in infant and young child mortality rates, in nutritional status indicators and even population sex ratios show that discriminatory practices are widespread and have serious repercussions" (paras. 149, 150). When linked to neglect and discrimination towards female children, "it leads to serious health consequences which account for between 500,000 to one million deaths among female children".

The Working Group notes that the availability of amniocentesis and other techniques which enable the sex of the foetus to be determined are leading to selective abortion on grounds of gender in some areas of the world. Its Report also notes that "excess female mortality in childhood is an indicator of serious external influences against the normal biological advantages with which nature has endowed the female. Male infants have an inherently greater vulnerability than female infants for many causes of death... male mortality in childhood is higher than female mortality. The greater the proportion of deaths due to infections and malnutrition, the larger the expected difference becomes" (para. 164). Thus, the report emphasizes the importance of recording and analyzing infant and child mortality rates by gender.

The third priority for study by the Working Group is traditional birth practices, which include dietary restrictions affecting pregnant women, and unhygienic and harmful practices during labour and childbirth, including inappropriate treatment of obstructed labour, and during the period following delivery (para. 193 et seq.).

The Committee on the Elimination of All Forms of Discrimination against Women, in a General Recommendation, in 1990, expresses concern at the continuation of "the practice of female circumcision and other traditional practices harmful to the health of women", and proposes that States Parties should "take appropriate and effective measures with a view to eradicating the practice of female circumcision".

The General Recommendation also proposes that States Parties "include in their national health policies appropriate strategies aimed at eradicating female circumcision in public health care. Such strategies could include the special responsibility of health personnel including traditional birth attendants to explain the harmful consequences of female circumcision." (Committee on the Elimination of All Forms of Discrimination against Women, General Recommendation No.14, HRI/GEN/1/Rev.2, p. 108)

In 1994, the SubCommission on Prevention of Discrimination and Protection of Minorities of the Commission on Human Rights adopted the "Plan of Action for the Elimination of Harmful Traditional Practices affecting the Health of Women and Children", which arose from two regional seminars, one for African regions and one for Asian regions. The Plan of Action calls first for "a clear expression of political will and an undertaking to put an end to traditional practices affecting the health of women and girl children, particularly female circumcision". It advocates legislation, the establishment of governmental bodies and national committees, education, cooperation with religious institutions and their leaders, and the mobilization of everyone able to contribute directly or indirectly to the elimination of such practices. Included are sections on female circumcision and other traditional practices affecting health, son preference, early marriage (supporting the recommendation of the

Identified harmful practices in Nigeria

Nigeria's Initial Report records "Certain traditional practices indirectly negate the implementation of some of the provisions of the Convention. These include: discriminatory practices against girls; superstitious belief; early marriage; female circumcision; high bride price; inheritance; widowhood practices; street trading; tribal marks and tattoos." (Nigeria IR, para. 28)

Committee on the Elimination of All Forms of Discrimination against Women for 18 to be the minimum age for marriage, see article 1, page 10), child delivery practices and violence against women and girl children (E/CN.4/Sub.2/1994/10/Add.1, 22 July 1994).

A final report to the SubCommission from the Special Rapporteur on traditional practices affecting the health of women and children (1996) describes the extent of follow-up to the Plan of Action. The Rapporteur welcomes in particular a report from the Government of Niger, which included this list it had drawn up of harmful traditional practices, with a view to eliminating them: "removal of the uvula; female excision; early marriage, childbirth and weaning; dietary taboos; removing milk teeth; burning the skin; bleeding the patient; opening the lower part of the abdomen; pressing on the abdomen; pushing a [prolapsed] cervix back into place; holding the foetus in position; scarring; tattooing, piercing the earlobes, gums, lips and nose; and force-feeding". The Rapporteur's report provides further detailed recommendations (E/CN.4/Sub.2/1996/6, 14 June 1996, para. 37).

A World Health Assembly resolution on "Maternal and child health and family planning: traditional practices harmful to the health of women and children" urges all Member States to assess the extent to which such practices constitute a social and public health problem; to establish national policies and programmes that will effectively, and with suitable legal instruments, abolish female genital mutilation ... and collaborate with national NGOs in the field, where they exist, and where they do not encourage their establishment (resolution WHA 47/10, 1994).

Practices which should be reviewed in the light of the Convention's principles include:

● all forms of genital mutilation and circumcision;

- binding, scarring, burning, branding, coin-rubbing, tattooing, piercing;
- initiation ceremonies involving, for example, forced holding under water;
- deliberate discriminatory treatment of children involving violence and/or prejudicial to health – for example, preferential feeding and/or care of male children; lack of care for disabled children or children born on certain days; food taboos; etc.;
- forms of discipline which are violent and/or prejudicial to health;
- early marriage and dowries.

A member of the Committee on the Rights of the Child suggested to Sudanese Government representatives that the authorities should make it clearly understood to the population that practices such as female circumcision were prohibited: "A very positive step would be to inform young women who had just given birth to their first child in a mother and child welfare centre that female circumcision was both extremely painful for the child and prohibited by the authorities. That would be the best way of preventing that practice from being passed down from generation to generation..."

Another Committee member said that female circumcision was a serious affront to the dignity of women but was all too well rooted a practice in Africa. "People did not bring complaints because the decision to carry out female circumcision was taken within the family, often by older people, and sometimes against the will of the parents. People were often impervious to information campaigns, which, they thought, were organized by intellectuals who had little respect for tradition. The question was whether the Government was truly determined to combat the practice and to support the efforts made by non-governmental organizations. Did religious leaders take an open and strong position against the practice?" (Sudan SR.71, para. 22, SR.89, para. 22)

The Committee has expressed its concerns about traditional practices and recommended action in the Concluding Observations on Initial Reports of various States Parties. For example:

"The Committee also recommends that further efforts be undertaken to raise awareness in order to eradicate traditional practices harmful to the health of women and children. The Committee suggests that the Government and religious and community leaders take an active role in supporting efforts to eliminate the practice of female genital mutilation." (Sudan IRCO, Add.10, para. 22; see also Sudan Prelim. Obs., Add.6, para. 4)

Burkina Faso notes in its Initial Report that it has set up a National Committee to Combat Female Circumcision: "This form of violence is on the decrease, even though there are structural resistances, linked to attitudes, which make it difficult to combat." The National Committee has representatives from the country's main ministries (including Agriculture), a number of NGOs and professional associations, and "customary authorities". The Initial Report also states: "Food taboos due to persistent customary beliefs in certain regions of the country also play a part in malnutrition. Other traditional practices such as circumcision among girls, early marriage, scarring and tattooing affect maternal and child health" (Burkina Faso IR, paras. 33 and 59).

The Committee went on to note in its Concluding Observations:

"The Committee recommends that a comprehensive strategy be elaborated and effectively implemented by the Government of the State Party to eradicate the existing discrimination against girls and women. In that context, special efforts should be made to prevent existing practices of forced marriage, female circumcision and domestic violence. More attention should be paid to the wider dissemination of knowledge about modern methods of family planning." (Burkina Faso IRCO, Add.19, paras. 3, 5 and 14. See also Senegal IRCO, Add.44, paras. 18 and 24; Lebanon IRCO, Add.54, paras. 16 and 38; Cyprus IRCO, Add.59, para. 16; Nigeria IRCO, Add.61, paras. 15 and 36)

The Committee has referred to other harmful traditional practices, including early marriage and betrothals of children, consanguineous marriage and forms of child abuse within the family.

"States Parties undertake to promote and encourage international cooperation with a view to achieving progressively the full realization of the right recognized in the present article. In this regard, particular account shall be taken of the needs of developing countries": article 24(4)

WHO, UNICEF and various other United Nations and UN-related agencies are particularly engaged in promoting international cooperation. Cooperation includes aid, advice and technical assistance, collaboration on research, and so on (see also article 4, page 71).

Implementation Checklist

• *General measures of implementation*

Have appropriate general measures of implementation been taken in relation to article 24, including

☐ identification and coordination of the responsible departments and agencies at all levels of government (article 24 is particularly relevant to **departments of health, welfare, education, planning and environment**)?

☐ identification of relevant non-governmental organizations/civil society partners?

☐ a comprehensive review to ensure that all legislation, policy and practice is compatible with the article, for all children in all parts of the jurisdiction?

☐ adoption of a strategy to secure full implementation

    ☐ which includes where necessary the identification of goals and indicators of progress?

    ☐ which does not affect any provisions which are more conducive to the rights of the child?

    ☐ which recognizes other relevant international standards?

    ☐ which involves where necessary international cooperation?

(Such measures may be part of an overall governmental strategy for implementing the Convention as a whole).

☐ budgetary analysis and allocation of necessary resources?

☐ development of mechanisms for monitoring and evaluation?

☐ making the implications of article 24 widely known to adults and children?

☐ development of appropriate training and awareness-raising (in relation to article 24 likely to include the training of **health workers, social workers and teachers, and also parenting education and health promotion for children and adolescents**)?

• *Specific issues in implementing article 24*

☐ Has the State undertaken measures to implement article 24 to the maximum extent of available resources?

Does legislation in the State provide for the respect for article 12 (1) and (2) (the views of the child) in relation to

    ☐ the planning and development of all health care services?

    ☐ decision-making in relation to individual health treatment of the child?

How to use the checklists, *see page XVII*

Do all children in the jurisdiction

- ☐ have the right to enjoyment of the highest attainable standard of health?
- ☐ have access to facilities for the treatment of illness and the rehabilitation of health?

☐ Do all disabled children have the right to the same level of health care in the same system as other children?

☐ Do girls have equal rights to health care?

Is adequate information collected to ensure accuracy of

- ☐ infant mortality rates?
- ☐ under-five mortality rates?
- ☐ mortality rates for older children?
- ☐ to provide disaggregated data in order to consider issues of discrimination?

☐ Is there a consistent and continuing reduction in the infant and child mortality rates in the State?

☐ Has the State developed a definition of necessary medical assistance and health care for the child?

☐ Do all children in the jurisdiction have access to necessary medical assistance and health care?

☐ Do adolescents have access to appropriate confidential health services, including information, counselling and supplies?

☐ Is the development of primary health care adopted as a priority?

Has the State set appropriate targets for the full attainment of the child's right under article 24 in relation to

- ☐ infant, under-five, under-18 and maternal mortality rates?
- ☐ access by all women to prenatal care, trained attendants during childbirth and referral facilities for high-risk pregnancies and emergencies?
- ☐ access by all couples to information and services to ensure that pregnancies are not too early, too closely spaced, too late or too many?
- ☐ reduction of severe and moderate malnutrition among children?
- ☐ reduction of rate of low birth weight?
- ☐ reduction of iron-deficiency anaemia?
- ☐ elimination of vitamin A deficiency?
- ☐ access to safe drinking water?
- ☐ access to sanitary means of excreta disposal?
- ☐ elimination of guinea worm disease?

338

☐ protection from environmental pollution?

☐ eradication of poliomyelitis?

☐ elimination of neonatal tetanus?

☐ elimination of measles?

☐ maintenance of high levels of immunization coverage?

☐ reduction in deaths due to diarrhoea and the diarrhoea incidence rate?

☐ reduction in deaths due to acute respiratory infections?

(this list is based on World Summit Plan of Action goals)

Has the State ensured adequate access to health education, health promotion and support to the public and in particular to parents and children on

☐ child health and nutrition?

☐ advantages of breastfeeding?

☐ hygiene and environmental sanitation?

☐ prevention of accidents?

☐ preventive health care?

☐ family-planning education and services, including appropriate services for adolescents, and HIV/AIDS-related prevention education and information?

☐ Has the State taken appropriate action to ensure implementation of the International Code of Marketing of Breastmilk Substitutes?

☐ Has the State reviewed all traditional practices involving children in all sectors of the population to ensure that none is prejudicial to health or incompatible with other articles in the Convention (in particular articles 3, 6, and 19)?

☐ Has the State taken effective and appropriate measures to abolish all traditional practices prejudicial to the health of children or incompatible with other provisions of the Convention?

☐ Is the State involved in international cooperative exercises to exchange information and improve capacity and skills in relation to realizing the health rights of children?

Reminder: **The Convention is indivisible and its articles are interdependent. Article 24 should not be considered in isolation.**

Particular regard should be paid to:
The general principles

Article 2: all rights to be recognized for each child in jurisdiction without discrimination on any ground

Article 3(1): the best interests of the child to be a primary consideration in all actions concerning children

Article 6: right to life and maximum possible survival and development

Article 12: respect for the child's views in all matters affecting the child; opportunity to be heard in any judicial or administrative proceedings affecting the child

Closely related articles

Articles whose implementation is related to that of article 24 include:

Article 5: parental guidance and the child's evolving capacities

Article 17: access to appropriate information and role of the media

Article 18: parental responsibilities and State assistance

Article 19: protection from all forms of violence

Article 23: rights of disabled children

Article 25: right to periodic review of treatment

Article 27: right to adequate standard of living

Article 28: right to education

Article 29: aims of education

Articles 32-36: protection from various forms of exploitation

Article 39: recovery and reintegration for child victims

Child's right to periodic review of treatment

States Parties recognize the right of a child who has been placed by the competent authorities for the purposes of care, protection or treatment of his or her physical or mental health to a periodic review of the treatment provided to the child and all other circumstances relevant to his or her placement.

Summary

Article 25 requires periodic review of the treatment and circumstances of children who have been placed by the authorities for the purposes of care, protection or treatment of their health. This includes placements in families or institutions (private or state-run) for children deprived of their family environment (article 20), refugee children (article 22), disabled children (article 23), adopted children (article 21), sick or mentally disordered children (article 24), children being provided with rehabilitative care (article 39), children placed in residential schools (article 28), children deprived of their liberty (article 37) or in other placements for offending behaviour (article 40). Reviews should consider both the appropriateness of the placement and the progress of the treatment or care.

In its quiet way article 25 is one of children's most important rights under the Convention on the Rights of the Child, though it is largely overlooked in both country reports and Committee observations. The article is important because it provides safeguards against one of the most serious forms of child abuse – abuse by the state. Under the banner of "the best interests of the child", often sincerely believed by the authorities involved, children in all parts of the world have suffered neglect and mistreatment having been placed by State authorities in hospitals, health units, children's homes, boarding schools, detention centres, foster and adoption placements and therapeutic communities.

Article 25 is also important because it offers great potential in developing enforceable legal rights and safeguards. Regulations governing "periodic review of treatment" can establish high standards, goals and detailed practices for all professionals working with children in placements and can secure children's rights, for example to be heard, to be in touch with the outside world and to have access to an effective complaints procedure. ∎

Extracts from
Committee on the Rights of the Child
Guidelines for Reports to be submitted by States Parties under the Convention

For full text of *Guidelines for Periodic Reports*, see Appendix 3, page 604.

Guidelines for Initial Reports

"Family environment and alternative care

Under this section, States Parties are requested to provide relevant information, including the principal legislative, judicial, administrative or other measures in force, particularly how the principles of the 'best interests of the child' and 'respect for the views of the child' are reflected therein; factors and difficulties encountered and progress achieved in implementing the relevant provisions of the Convention; and implementation priorities and specific goals for the future in respect of:...

(j) Periodic review of placement (article 25)

In addition, States Parties are requested to provide information on the numbers of children per year within the reporting period in each of the following groups, disaggregated by age group, sex, ethnic or national background and rural or urban environment: homeless children, abused or neglected children taken into protective custody, children placed in foster care, children placed in institutional care, children placed through domestic adoption, children entering the country through intercountry adoption procedures and children leaving the country through intercountry adoption procedures.

States Parties are encouraged to provide additional relevant statistical information and indicators relating to children covered in this section."

(CRC/C/5, paras. 16-18)

Guidelines for Periodic Reports

"FAMILY ENVIRONMENT AND ALTERNATIVE CARE

I. Periodic review of placement (art. 25)

Please indicate the measures undertaken, including of a legislative, administrative and judicial nature, to recognize the right of the child who has been placed by the competent authorities for the purposes of care, protection or treatment of his or her physical or mental health, to a periodic review of treatment provided to the child in public and private institutions, services and facilities, as well as all other circumstances relevant to his or her placement.

Information should be provided inter alia on:

> *The authorities considered competent for such purposes, including any appropriate independent mechanism established;*

> *The circumstances taken into account in deciding on the placement of the child for his or her care, protection and treatment;*

> *The frequency of review of the placement and treatment provided;*

> *The respect ensured to the provisions and principles of the Convention, including non-discrimination, the best interests of the child and respect for the views of the child;*

> *Relevant data on the children concerned, including in situations of abandonment, disability and asylum seeking and refugees, including unaccompanied children, and in situations of conflict with the law, disaggregated inter alia by age, gender, national, ethnic and social origin, family situation and place of residence, as well as by duration of placement and frequency of its review;*

> *Progress achieved in the implementation of article 25, difficulties encountered and targets set for the future."*

(CRC/C/58, paras. 86-7. The following paragraphs of the *Guidelines for Periodic Reports* are also relevant to reporting under this article: 80 and 143; for full text of *Guidelines*, see Appendix 3, page 604.)

"...a child who has been placed by the competent authorities for the purposes of care, protection or treatment of his or her physical or mental health"

The word "competent" means that the authorities have the appropriate competence to act and is not a qualitative judgement on professional abilities – indeed this article should particularly protect children placed by **in**competent authorities.

The forms of placement falling within the scope of this article may be run by the State or privately. They include foster and adoptive families, children's homes and institutions, immigration and refugee detention centres, hospitals, health units and wards, therapeutic centres, boarding schools, detention centres and prisons. Residential schools must be included even though "education" is not mentioned among the purposes listed in article 25, since the point of a boarding placement is to secure the care of children as well as their education. "Punishment" is also not one of the purposes, but detention centres and other placements for offending behaviour under the terms of articles 37 and 40 must care for children.

Article 25 does not appear to include placements privately arranged by parents. At one stage in the drafting procedure, it was proposed that a specific exemption should be made of placements arranged by parents. Although this exemption did not appear in the final text, there was general agreement that placements by parents were not included (E/CN.4/1986/39 pp.11-13, Detrick, p.360). Exactly why privately arranged placements should not be periodically reviewed by competent authorities was not made clear, since the children concerned are, if anything, more vulnerable than those who are placed by the State.

Article 3(3) requires States to ensure standards in all institutions, services and facilities. The Committee on the Rights of the Child has encouraged States to "monitor" the rights of children in institutions, including specific mention of article 25 to Guatemala and Bulgaria:

"...Further efforts are also required to ensure the active participation of disabled children in the community in conditions which ensure their dignity and promote their self-reliance, as well as to ensure that disabled children are separated from adults suffering from mental ill-health. The Committee recommends that measures be taken to review periodically the placement and treatment of children as required under article 25 of the Convention." (Guatemala IRCO, Add.58, para 38)

"...In cases where the placement of children in institutions is necessary, measures should be adopted to ensure periodic review of the treatment provided to the child and all other circumstances relevant to his or her placement." (Bulgaria IRCO, Add.66, para. 27)

"The Committee is concerned about the adequacy of measures taken to ensure that the conditions in institutions caring for children are regularly monitored and supervised..." (Nicaragua IRCO, Add.36, para. 18)

"The Committee encourages the State Party to address the situation of children in institutions, with a view to envisaging and making available possible alternatives to institutional care and to establishing effective monitoring mechanisms of the realization of the rights of children placed in an institution." (Poland IRCO, Add.31, para. 34)

"...The Committee also recommends the establishment of effective monitoring mechanism of the realization of the rights of the child placed in an institution." (Ukraine IRCO, Add.42, para. 27)

Foster care has also been specifically mentioned:

"The Committee recommends that the system of foster care be carefully monitored in order to eliminate any possible acts of abuse against the children placed in such care." (Croatia IRCO, Add.52, para. 25)

Articles 3(3) and 25 are both about monitoring. The difference between them is that 3(3) concerns the monitoring of institutions and staff and article 25, the monitoring of the individual progress of each child in the institution.

"... a periodic review of the treatment provided to the child and all other circumstances relevant to his or her placement"

What is to be considered in the review and how often it should occur will necessarily depend on individual circumstances, but States may establish minimum requirements in their legislation. The child's "treatment" encompasses not only clinical treatment for health purposes but also all other aspects of the child's institutional experience, including, for example, measures used to control the child, the child's access to family and the outside world and how the child's education is affected. "... all other circumstances relevant to his or her placement" must essentially include the reason and justification for the placement.

In the report on its General Discussion on Juvenile Justice the Committee on the Rights of the Child commented :

article 25

"Concern was expressed at the placement of children in institutions, under a welfare pretext, without taking into due consideration the best interests of the child nor ensuring the fundamental safeguards recognized by the Convention, including the right to challenge the decision of a placement before a judicial authority, to a periodic review of the treatment provided to the child and all other circumstances relevant to the child's placement and the right to lodge complaints." (Report on tenth session, October-November 1995, CRC/C/46 para. 228)

Different sorts of review may be required:

- reviews by judicial or administrative authorities to monitor the appropriateness of compulsory placements (the Committee, for example, recommended that Bulgaria consider establishing a "guardian ad litem" system for children in institutional care (Bulgaria IRCO, Add.66, para. 27)). Where deprivation of liberty is concerned, article 37 requires that its use be "as a measure of last resort and for the shortest appropriate time" (see page ...). Rule 2 of the United Nations Rules for the Protection of Juveniles Deprived of their Liberty states that "...Deprivation of the liberty of a juvenile should be a disposition of last resort and for the minimum necessary period and should be limited to exceptional cases. The length of the sanction should be determined by the judicial authority, without precluding the possibility of his or her early release." If children are to have the possibility of early release before expiration of a determinate sentence then some form of periodic review will be necessary to determine whether such early release is possible;

- reviews by the involved professionals to assess progress of the treatment;

- reviews by independent persons as a safeguard against abuse and to check on the general welfare of the child. An essential component of the last form of review is that children should have the opportunity to speak in private about their treatment.

How often should the periodic review occur? While this is at the discretion of the State Party, it can be assumed that the more involuntary the placement is and the more extreme the treatment, the more frequently a review will be required (see box).

Implementation Checklist

● *General measures of implementation*

Have appropriate general measures of implementation been taken in relation to article 25, including

☐ identification and coordination of the responsible departments and agencies at all levels of government (article 25 is relevant to the **departments of justice, social welfare, education and health**)?

☐ identification of relevant non-governmental organizations/civil society partners?

☐ a comprehensive review to ensure that all legislation, policy and practice is compatible with the article, for all children in all parts of the jurisdiction?

☐ adoption of a strategy to secure full implementation

    ☐ which includes where necessary the identification of goals and indicators of progress?

    ☐ which does not affect any provisions which are more conducive to the rights of the child?

    ☐ which recognizes other relevant international standards?

    ☐ which involves where necessary international cooperation?

    (Such measures may be part of an overall governmental strategy for implementing the Convention as a whole).

☐ budgetary analysis and allocation of necessary resources?

☐ development of mechanisms for monitoring and evaluation?

☐ making the implications of article 25 widely known to adults and children?

☐ development of appropriate training and awareness-raising (in relation to article 25 likely to include the training of **social workers, lawyers, judiciary, child advocates, teachers, institutional staff, medical personnel (including mental health)**)

● *Specific issues in implementing article 25*

Are legal and/or administrative measures adopted to ensure the periodic review of each child who has been:

    placed for the purposes of care and protection, including

        ☐ foster care?

        ☐ adoption?

        ☐ child care institutions?

        ☐ boarding schools?

        ☐ prisons and detention centres?

and for the treatment of his or her physical or mental health, including

☐ hospitals?

☐ health units?

☐ psychiatric wards?

☐ therapeutic centres?

Are such reviews required to consider

☐ the treatment of the child (including all aspects of his or her care)?

☐ the placement of the child (including whether its continuation is necessary)?

☐ the views of the child (ascertained in private)?

☐ Are such reviews at sufficient intervals to secure the child's protection and welfare?

Reminder : **The Convention is indivisible and its articles are interdependent. Article 25 should not be considered in isolation.**

Particular regard should be paid to:
The general principles

Article 2: all rights to be recognized for each child in jurisdiction without discrimination on any ground

Article 3(1): the best interests of the child to be a primary consideration in all actions concerning children

Article 6: right to life and maximum possible survival and development

Article 12: respect for the child's views in all matters affecting the child; opportunity to be heard in any judicial or administrative proceedings affecting the child

Closely related articles

Articles whose implementation is related to that of article 25 include:

Article 20: children deprived of their family environment

Article 21: adoption

Article 22: refugee children

Article 23: disabled children

Article 24: health services

Article 28: education services

Article 37: deprivation of liberty

Article 39: rehabilitative measures

Article 40: juvenile justice systems

Child's right to benefit from social security

Text of Article 26

1. States Parties shall recognize for every child the right to benefit from social security, including social insurance, and shall take the necessary measures to achieve the full realization of this right in accordance with their national law.

2. The benefits should, where appropriate, be granted, taking into account the resources and the circumstances of the child and persons having responsibility for the maintenance of the child, as well as any other consideration relevant to an application for benefits made by or on behalf of the child.

Article 26 concerns financial support for children provided by the State. Generally, children are economically dependent upon adults. When the adults who have responsibility for children are unable to provide for them, either because they are unable to find gainful employment or because their circumstances (illness, disability, child bearing, old age and so on) prevent them from working, then the State has an obligation to ensure that the child has some form of financial support, paid directly to the child or via a responsible adult. This obligation is upheld in article 26.

Article 26 is subject to the proviso of article 4: "... With regard to economic, social and cultural rights, States Parties shall undertake such measures to the maximum extent of their available resources and, where needed, within the framework of international cooperation." During the drafting of article 26, proposals were made to make the right to social security explicitly dependent on the availability of national resources, but this was perceived to be unnecessary in view of article 4 (E/CN.4/1984/71, pp. 16-18; Detrick, pp. 364-367).

Article 9 of the International Covenant on Economic, Social and Cultural Rights provides: "The States Parties to the present Covenant recognize the right of everyone to social security, including social insurance." The Convention on the Rights of the Child alters these words in that the child has a right to "benefit from" social security rather than a right "to" social security. This reflects the fact that children's economic security is generally bound up with that of their adult caregivers. This dependence also led to the drafting of the second paragraph of article 26, making social security contingent on the caregiver's lack of resources – concerns were expressed that, otherwise, ratifying States might have to grant benefits to all children, including those of wealthy parents. The drafters did, however, agree to make clear that children could apply for benefits directly (E/CN.4/12989/48, pp. 75-78, Detrick, p. 368). ∎

Summary

Children's right "...to benefit from social security, including social insurance"

The decade spanning 1985 to 1995 saw an economic recession across the world. The recession, allied with crippling national debts and a prevailing economic philosophy calling for restraints in social security expenditure, often under aid-linked "structural adjustment" programmes, has led to many ratifying countries freezing or cutting back social security for children (see article 4, page 63). The box below describes how children in two countries have been affected.

Despite the recession and the new monetarism, some countries have protected children's access to social security. The Committee has commended a number, for example:

"The Committee notes with satisfaction that during the present period of economic recession, attention has been paid by the authorities with a view to ensuring that the budgetary resources for the social welfare of the most disadvantaged groups of the population and, among them children, will not decrease in the State Party." (Belgium IRCO, Add.38, para. 7)

(The principle of a guaranteed minimum livelihood allowance, *minimex*, was established in Belgium in 1974. Entitlement to the *minimex* is a residual right aiming to guarantee a minimum income for categories of people excluded from the social security systems; a vital minimum figure introduced to protect human dignity: "This law was considered by some to indicate that our social security system had reached perfection. It is in any case the culmination of lengthy development of social assistance in our country which led the legislature to lay down a strict definition of a genuine subjective right that can be com-

Recession and social security cutbacks – impact on children in Finland and Costa Rica

Finland

"In the 1990s Finland has suffered from the deepest recession since the Second World War... The Ministry for Social Affairs and Health has studied the effects of recession on the economic situation of households. The study reveals that, on an average, families with children have been more affected by the recession than other groups of population. Income disparities between families with children have grown larger as a result of the recession than is the case within other population groups

"This is explained by the cuts in the various benefits for families with children. These families receive a number of different benefits enjoyed simultaneously. When these benefits are all cut at once, individual families may be severely affected. The growth of income disparities between families with children is primarily a result of unemployment, which seems to increase particularly among families with children under school age. Another explanation for the deteriorating situation of families with children is that the rising prices of services are felt especially by these families, and the most by those with low incomes." (Finland IR, paras. 15 and 16)

Costa Rica

In the 1980s "External and internal imbalances forced the adoption of economic stabilization programmes which established restrictions on maintaining levels of public expenditure in the social sectors... The challenge is thus to devise a pattern of development with equity and social justice and establish a balance between economic progress and social development... In social matters, the measures adopted because of the 1980s crisis of principles have had serious consequences such as:

(a) a widening of the social gaps and the regional imbalances;

(b) changes in the organization of the family, particularly among the weaker groups, due to the need for more family members to have recourse to the labour market;

(c) a reduction in State investment in major social programmes, and

(d) the difficulty of adapting State institutions to meet the new demands and needs of the poorest groups."

The Costa Rican response is "with the help of extensive cooperation, especially from the United Nations Children's Fund (UNICEF), work has been done on the identification of methodological instruments for intersectoral intervention in priority cantons, so as to render it possible, firstly, to reach the child population in the most direct possible way; secondly, to secure a more rational use of the limited human, financial and physical resources available and, thirdly, to obtain an effective participation of local organizations and bodies in the solution of their specific problems and needs." (Costa Rica IR, paras. 3, 4 and 19)

pared to the right to social security benefits."
(Belgium IR, paras. 351-2))

"...the Committee notes with satisfaction that during this period of economic recession, which is affecting many countries, and the progression towards decentralization of social services, the budgetary resources for child welfare programmes have been increasing in the State Party. It also appreciates that a system of monitoring the policies and measures of municipalities with regard to their implementation of children's welfare programmes has been set in place through the County Governor reporting procedure." (Norway IRCO, Add.23, para. 6)

"The Committee welcomes the commitment expressed by the Delegation to adopt measures to face increasing poverty and reduce existing disparities, in spite of difficulties arising from the present economic recession. The Committee notes in this regard the establishment of the Family Support Enforcement Fund intended to help provincial and territorial governments in the field of promotion and protection of children's rights." (Canada IRCO, Add.37, para. 6)

(Canada's Child Tax Benefit represents an increase in federal government support to children and families of $2.1 billion over the period 1994-9. (Canada IR, para. 14))

"The Committee... notes with satisfaction the establishment of a national minimum guaranteed income." (Portugal IRCO, Add.45, para. 4)

"The Committee takes note with satisfaction that the Government provides a comprehensive social security system, and a wide range of welfare services for the benefit of children and their parents, particularly free health care, free education, extended pregnancy leave rights and a large day-care system." (Finland IRCO, Add.53, para. 3)

"...The Committee also welcomes the improvements to the Comprehensive Social Security Assistance Scheme, particularly with respect to benefits available in implementation of articles 26 and 27 of the Convention." (UK dependent territory: Hong Kong IRCO, Add.63, para. 7)

The Committee also noted:

"...Efforts have been made to protect the value of the child allowance." (Romania IRCO, Add.16, para. 4. See also France IRCO, Add.20, para. 20 and Germany IRCO, Add.43, para. 31)

However, a number of these commendations were qualified by the Committee's concern that, nonetheless, children from the poorest and most vulnerable sectors were falling through the social security net. Far more countries' social security systems were considered inadequate, for example

Argentina, Belarus, Bolivia, Colombia, Guatemala, Honduras, Italy, Jamaica, Mauritius, Nicaragua, Poland, Senegal, Slovenia, Sri Lanka, Ukraine and the United Kingdom. While it is undoubtedly more shameful that children in rich nations are suffering unacceptable levels of poverty, even the poorest nations have obligations under the Convention that cannot be excused, as the Committee told Nigeria:

"In view of the considerable incidence of poverty in the country and insufficiency of the minimum wage in meeting basic needs, the Committee views the absence of social support to families, including single-parent families, especially female-headed households, as a matter of serious concern...

"The Committee wishes to emphasize that the general lack of financial resources cannot be used as a justification for neglecting to establish social security programmes and social safety nets to protect the most vulnerable groups of children. Accordingly, it is the opinion of the Committee that a serious review should be undertaken to determine the consistency of the economic and social policies being developed with the State Party's obligations under the Convention, in particular articles 26 and 27, especially with respect to the establishment or improvement of social security programmes and other social protection." (Nigeria IRCO, Add.61, paras. 17 and 33)

The duty to "...take the necessary measures to achieve the full realization of this right in accordance with their national law"

Social security legislation contains many pitfalls. A common one is that it fails to target resources to those most in need. As Colombia reported to the Committee: "Social programmes and projects had previously concentrated on the provision of services, on the assumption that a satisfactory supply of services would meet the demand for services. However, this led to inequalities because it was often the sectors with the least need which benefited." (Colombia IR, para. 28)

Careful monitoring and planning is needed to surmount this difficulty (see box).

This duty also implies that States Parties must take active measures to ensure that there is full take-up of social security entitlements where appropriate for or on behalf of children. Resources should therefore be given to public information campaigns on benefit entitlements, effective administrative systems and "applicant-friendly" benefit offices, forms and procedures. Article 25 is not prescriptive as to how social security should be delivered, but States must ensure that everyone who is entitled to receive it is able to do so without discrimination or social stigma or loss of any other right and with respect for their privacy.

"... taking into account the resources and the circumstances of the child and persons having responsibility for the maintenance of the child"

The Convention underlines the financial as well as caring responsibilities of parents and others with child-rearing responsibilities, article 27(4) specifically provides for the recovery of mainte-nance by the State when necessary (see page 363).

In addition, means-testing of child social security is generally regarded as desirable, given the need to target limited resources effectively. It should, however, be noted that some degree of financial support for **all** children, regardless of their parents' circumstances, is neither unreasonable nor unviable. The State has good cause to invest in children, since they represent its future security, and families with children can be encouraged and supported by tax rebates or direct benefits. Universal benefits to all children have the added advantage of ensuring full take-up rates with very low administrative costs, since no means-testing is involved.

The World Summit for Social Development (Copenhagen 1995)

The following recommendations were made by the World Summit for enhanced social protection and reduced vulnerability:

"Social protection systems should be based on legislation and, as appropriate, strengthened and expanded, as necessary... Actions to this end should include:

(a) Strengthening and expanding programmes targeted to those in need, programmes providing universal basic protection, and social security insurance programmes, with the choice of programmes depending on national financial and administrative capacities;

(b) Developing, where necessary, a strategy for a gradual expansion of social protection programmes that provide social security for all, according to a schedule and terms and conditions related to national contexts;

(c) Ensuring that social safety nets associated with economic restructuring are considered as complementary strategies to overall poverty reduction and an increase in productive employment. Short term by nature, safety nets must protect people living in poverty and enable them to find productive employment;

(d) Designing social protection and support programmes to help people become self-sufficient as fully and quickly as possible, to assist and protect families, to reintegrate people excluded from economic activity and to prevent the social isolation or stigmatization of those who need protection;

(e) Exploring a variety of means for raising revenues to strengthen social protection programmes, and promoting efforts by the private sector and voluntary associations to provide social protection and support;

(f) Promoting the innovative efforts of self-help organizations, professional associations and other organizations of civil society in this sphere;

(g) Expanding and strengthening social protection programmes to protect working people, including the self-employed and their families, from the risk of falling into poverty, by extending coverage to as many as possible, providing benefits quickly and ensuring that entitlements continue when workers change jobs;

(h) Ensuring, through appropriate regulation, that contributory social protection plans are efficient and transparent so that the contributions of workers, employers and the State and the accumulation of resources can be monitored by the participants;

(i) Ensuring an adequate social safety net under structural adjustment programmes;

(j) Ensuring that social protection and social support programmes meet the needs of women, and especially that they take into account women's multiple roles and concerns, in particular the reintegration of women into formal work after periods of absence, support for older women, and the promotion of acceptance of women's multiple roles and responsibilities."

(World Summit for Social Development, 19 April 1995, A/CONF.166/9, pp. 52-53)

Where benefits are means-tested, great care has to be taken to ensure that the eligibility terms are non-discriminatory and non-stigmatizing to the families concerned.

Applications for benefits to be made "by or on behalf of the child"

This right emphasizes the fact that while it is important to ensure that those with legal responsibility for children are entitled to claim benefits on their behalf, it is equally important to ensure that children are directly eligible in their own right where necessary. The Netherlands entered a reservation to article 26, relating to this aspect: "The Kingdom of the Netherlands accepts the provisions of article 26 of the Convention with the reservation that these provisions shall not imply an independent entitlement of children to social security, including social insurance" (CRC/C/2/Rev 5, p. 27). The Committee has not yet considered the Netherlands' report (September 1997).

The need for an autonomous claim by the child may occur if parents are for some reason disqualified from claiming or are unable to claim. The Committee noted such a problem in Lebanon, suggesting:

"...that a health insurance card be issued for children whose parents are not entitled to social security benefits." (Lebanon IRCO, Add.54, para. 34)

Children's access to benefits need not – arguably, should not – be dependent only on their adult caregivers. Denmark, for example, places a duty on "persons in public offices or public service" to inform the relevant authorities if they believe that anybody, including children, may be in need of social assistance (Denmark IR, para. 50).

Also, children may be unable to claim because they are deemed "too old" (see article 1, definition of a child, page 5). The Committee noted with concern to New Zealand:

"...the appearance of a wide range of age cut-offs which do not appear to be necessarily

consistent under legislation administered by various government entities for eligibility for different types of government support" (New Zealand IRCO, Add.71, para. 10).

This was also an issue of concern in the United Kingdom, where many 16- and 17-year-olds are unable to claim income support even when they are not living with their families:

"The Committee notes with concern the increasing number of children living in poverty. The Committee is aware that the phenomenon of children begging and sleeping on the streets has become more visible. The Committee is concerned that the changed regulations regarding benefit entitlement to young people may have contributed to the increase in the number of young homeless people...

"...With regard to the implementation of article 4 of the Convention, the Committee would like to suggest that the General Principles of the Convention, particularly the provisions of its article 3, relating to the best interests of the child, should guide the determination of policy-making at both the central and local levels of government. This approach is of relevance to decisions taken about the allocation of resources to the social sector at the central and local governmental levels, including with regard to the allocation of benefits to children who have completed compulsory schooling and have no full-time employment..." (UK IRCO, Add.34, paras. 15 and 24)

It should also be noted that social benefit systems for adults can have unintended consequences for children, as the Committee pointed out to China:

"It is the Committee's view that inadequate measures taken in the field of social security may have led to an over-reliance on children providing future care and support to their parents. This may have contributed to the perpetuation of harmful traditional practices and attitudes such as a preference for boys, to the detriment of the protection and promotion of the right of girls and disabled children...

"It is the Committee's view that remedial measures should be sought to avoid families' over-dependence on their children, in particular providing them with care in their old age." (China IRCO, Add.56, paras. 12 and 32)

Implementation Checklist

● *General measures of implementation*

Have appropriate general measures of implementation been taken in relation to article 26, including

☐ identification and coordination of the responsible departments and agencies at all levels of government (article 26 is relevant to the **departments of social security, finance, employment, justice, housing and social welfare**)?

☐ identification of relevant non-governmental organizations/civil society partners?

☐ a comprehensive review to ensure that all legislation, policy and practice is compatible with the article, for all children in all parts of the jurisdiction?

☐ adoption of a strategy to secure full implementation

   ☐ which includes where necessary the identification of goals and indicators of progress?

   ☐ which does not affect any provisions which are more conducive to the rights of the child?

   ☐ which recognizes other relevant international standards?

   ☐ which involves where necessary international cooperation?

   (Such measures may be part of an overall governmental strategy for implementing the Convention as a whole).

☐ budgetary analysis and allocation of necessary resources?

☐ development of mechanisms for monitoring and evaluation?

☐ making the implications of article 26 widely known to adults and children?

☐ development of appropriate training and awareness-raising (in relation to article 26 likely to include the training of **benefits administrators, social workers and the judiciary**)?

● *Specific issues in implementing article 26*

☐ Does every child in need have a potential right to benefit from social security (including social insurance)?

☐ Are measures taken to ensure that legal entitlements to social security are made known to children and their families?

☐ Are measures taken to ensure that take-up of benefits is made as easy as possible (for example by automatic payments, simple application forms, accessible benefit offices and officers)?

How to use the checklists, *see page XVII*

☐ Are measures taken to ensure that the process of applying for benefits does not discriminate against any children (for example those in remote areas or of illiterate parents)?

☐ Do systems for the delivery of social security respect the child's right to privacy?

☐ Are children able to make applications for social security in their own right?

☐ Are those responsible for children's maintenance able to make applications on their behalf?

☐ Are third parties (that is, those not directly responsible for children's maintenance) able to make applications on their behalf?

Reminder: **The Convention is indivisible and its articles are interdependent. Article 26 should not be considered in isolation.**

Particular regard should be paid to:
The general principles

Article 2: all rights to be recognized for each child in jurisdiction without discrimination on any ground
Article 3(1): the best interests of the child to be a primary consideration in all actions concerning children
Article 6: right to life and maximum possible survival and development
Article 12: respect for the child's views in all matters affecting the child; opportunity to be heard in any judicial or administrative proceedings affecting the child

Closely related articles

Articles whose implementation is related to that of article 26 include:

Article 3(2): State to ensure child necessary protection and care
Article 18: parents having joint responsibility
Article 23: rights of disabled children
Article 24: right to health care services
Article 27: right to an adequate standard of living and to maintenance from parents and others
Article 28: right to education

Child's right to an adequate standard of living

article 27

1. States Parties recognize the right of every child to a standard of living adequate for the child's physical, mental, spiritual, moral and social development.

2. The parent(s) or others responsible for the child have the primary responsibility to secure, within their abilities and financial capacities, the conditions of living necessary for the child's development.

3. States Parties, in accordance with national conditions and within their means, shall take appropriate measures to assist parents and others responsible for the child to implement this right and shall in case of need provide material assistance and support programmes, particularly with regard to nutrition, clothing and housing.

4. States Parties shall take all appropriate measures to secure the recovery of maintenance for the child from the parents or other persons having financial responsibility for the child, both within the State Party and from abroad. In particular, where the person having financial responsibility for the child lives in a State different from that of the child, States Parties shall promote the accession to international agreements or the conclusion of such agreements, as well as the making of other appropriate arrangements.

Article 27 provides children with a right to an adequate standard of living for their full development. Parents have primary responsibility for securing this right; States must if necessary assist parents in doing so and in cases of need provide material supports to the child, such as food, clothing and housing. States shall also take appropriate measures to recover maintenance from parents.

Article 27 links to two essential principles of the Convention on the Rights of the Child, first the right of each child to "development", which must be to "the maximum extent" or to the "fullest potential" (articles 6 and 29(1)(a)); and second, reflected in paragraphs (2) and (4) of article 27, the primary responsibility of parents in securing this development, with the assistance of the State (articles 5, 7 and 18). Article 27 recognizes that such development cannot be

Summary

divorced from the child's conditions of living. By listing the different components of full development – physical, mental, spiritual, moral and social – article 27 makes clear that an adequate standard of living is not just limited to the basics of food, clothing and housing, important though these are. There are very few countries that have reported to the Committee to date that can claim to be using their available resources to the maximum extent possible to alleviate child need – some of the wealthiest nations of the globe have children experiencing unacceptable levels of deprivation. ■

Extracts from
Committee on the Rights of the Child
Guidelines for Reports to be submitted by States Parties under the Convention

For full text of *Guidelines for Periodic Reports*, see Appendix 3, page 604.

Guidelines for Initial Reports

"Special protection measures

● **ARTICLE 27(1)-(3)**

"Basic health and welfare

Under this section States Parties are requested to provide relevant information, including the principal legislative, judicial, administrative or other measures in force; the institutional infrastructure for implementing policy in this area, particularly monitoring strategies and mechanisms; and factors and difficulties encountered and progress achieved in implementing the relevant provisions, in respect of:

...(e) Standard of living (article 27, paras. 1-3)

In addition to information provided under paragraph 9(b) of these guidelines, States Parties are requested to specify the nature and extent of cooperation with local and national organizations of a governmental or non-governmental nature, such as institutions of social workers, concerning the implementation of this area of the Convention. States Parties are encouraged to provide additional relevant statistical information and indicators relating to children covered in this section."

(CRC/C/5, paras. 19 and 20)

● **ARTICLE 27(4)**

"Family environment and alternative care

Under this section, States parties are requested to provide relevant information, including the principal legislative, judicial, administrative or other measures in force, particularly how the principles of the "best interests of the child" and "respect for the views of the child" are reflected therein; factors and difficulties encountered and progress achieved in implementing the relevant provisions of the Convention; and implementation priorities and specific goals for the future in respect of:

...(e) Recovery of maintenance for the child (article 27, para. 4)...

States Parties are encouraged to provide additional relevant statistical information and indicators relating to children covered in this section."

(CRC/C/5, paras. 16 and 18)

Guidelines for Periodic Reports

● **ARTICLE 27(1)-(3)**

"VI. BASIC HEALTH AND WELFARE

D. Standard of living (art 27. paras. 1-3)

Please provide information on:

The measures adopted to recognize and ensure the right of every child to a standard of living adequate for the child's physical, mental, spiritual, moral and social development;

The relevant indicators used to assess such an adequate standard of living, and its incidence among the child population, including by gender, age, region, rural/urban area, social and ethnic origin, and family situation;

The criteria established to assess the ability and financial capacity of parents or others responsible for the child to secure the living conditions necessary for the child's development, as well as to identify those conditions;

All the measures taken, in accordance with national conditions and within the State Party's means, to assist parents and others responsible for the child to implement this right, including the nature of the assistance made available, its budget implications, its relation to the cost of living and its impact on the population; where relevant, the information provided should be disaggregated, inter alia by region, rural/urban area, age, gender and social and ethnic origin, the measurements adopted to provide in case of need, material assistance and support programmes, particularly with regard to nutrition, clothing and housing, indicating inter alia, the nature of such assistance and programmes, the population addressed by them, including by gender age, rural/urban area, social and ethnic origin, proportion of budget allocated, the coverage ensured, the priorities and targets identified;

Relevant measures adopted as a follow-up to the Declaration and Plan of Action adopted by the United Nations Conference on Human Settlements (Habitat II).

Reports should also provide information on the progress achieved in the implementation of these rights, difficulties encountered and targets set for the future."

(CRC/C/58, paras. 103-4)

● **ARTICLE 27(4)**

"F. Recovery of maintenance for the child

Please indicate the measures adopted (including legislative, administrative and judicial measures) and mechanisms or programmes developed to secure the recovery of maintenance for the child from the parents or other persons having financial responsibility for the child, both within the State and from abroad, including in cases of the separation or divorce of the parents. Information should also be provided on:

Measures taken to ensure the maintenance of the child in cases where parents or other persons having financial responsibility for the child evade the payment of such maintenance;

Measures adopted to ensure respect for the General Principles of the Convention, namely non-discrimination, the best interests of the child, respect for the views of the child and the right to life, survival and development to the maximum extent;

The factors and difficulties which may have affected the recovery of maintenance for the child (for example, lack of birth registration) or the enforcement of decisions concerning maintenance obligations;

The relevant international agreements the State has concluded or to which it has acceded, as well as any other appropriate arrangement it has made;

Relevant disaggregated data in this area, including by gender, age, national origin and place of residence of the child and his or her parents, or of the persons financially responsible for him or her."

(CRC/C/58, para. 79. Paragraph 66 of the *Guidelines for Periodic Reports* is also relevant to reporting under this article; for full text of *Guidelines*, see Appendix 3, page 604.)

Background

The Universal Declaration of Human Rights provides that: "Everyone has the right to a standard of living adequate for the health and well-being of himself and of his family, including food, clothing, housing and medical care and necessary social services, and the right to security in the event of unemployment, sickness, disability, widowhood, old age or other lack of livelihood in circumstances beyond his control." (article 25)

The International Covenant on Economic, Social and Cultural Rights develops this: "The States Parties to the present Covenant recognize the

right of everyone to an adequate standard of living for himself and his family, including adequate food, clothing and housing, and to the continuous improvement to living conditions. The States Parties will take appropriate steps to ensure the realization of this right, recognizing to this effect the essential importance of international cooperation based on free consent." (article 11(1))

The reporting guidelines for the Covenant, with particular reference to "the continuous improvement of living conditions", asks countries to report on whether the standard of living of all social groups has improved over time, for example over the last five or ten years. It also asks for reports on the per capita GNP of the poorest 40 per cent and for information on any "poverty line" definition, as well as for a great deal of detailed information about the "food security" of the population and the country's housing situation (*Manual on Human Rights Reporting*, 1991, pp. 60-61).

The Committee on Economic, Social and Cultural Rights has also made a significant General Comment in relation to "The nature of States Parties' obligations", quoted at length in article 4 (page 55). This accepts that not all countries will be able to meet economic and social rights in full, a fact which is explicitly recognized in the Covenants (and in the Convention on the Rights of the Child). However the goal of full implementation is set and the Covenant on Economic, Social and Cultural Rights "...imposes an obligation to move as expeditiously and effectively as possible towards that goal. Moreover, any deliberately retrogressive measures in that regard would require the most careful consideration and would need to be fully justified by reference to the totality of the rights provided for in the Covenant and in the context of the full use of the maximum available resources...

"... the Committee [on Social, Economic and Cultural Rights] is of the view that a minimum core obligation to ensure the satisfaction of, at the very least, minimum essential levels of each of the rights is incumbent upon every State Party. Thus, for example, a State Party in which any significant number of individuals is deprived of essential foodstuffs, of essential primary health care, of basic shelter and housing, or even of the most basic forms of education is, *prima facie*, failing to discharge its obligations under the Covenant..." (Committee on Economic, Social and Cultural Rights, General Comment 3, HRI/GEN/1/Rev.2, p. 55)

"... the right of every child to a standard of living adequate for the child's physical, mental, spiritual, moral and social development"

Article 6, one of the Convention's "General Principles", gives States the responsibility to "ensure to the maximum extent possible the survival and development of the child". Article 27(3) spells out three vital contributions to children's physical development – nutrition, clothing and housing. Article 24 enlarges on these, for example stressing the need for clean drinking water, health education, good hygiene and sanitation, breastfeeding, and preventive action in relation to environmental pollution, child accidents and harmful traditional practices. Articles 29 and 31 focus on children's rights to have opportunities to develop their physique, amongst other things, through sport and play – perhaps particularly important for urban children.

The civil rights of children under articles 12 to 17, the rights to enjoy their culture and religion within the security of family and community (articles 5, 7, 8, 9, 18, 20, 21 and 30) and the aims of education in article 29, all contribute to the development of children's social, moral, mental and spiritual development.

"The parent(s) or others responsible for the child have the primary responsibility to secure, within their abilities and financial capacities, the conditions of living necessary for the child's development"

The primary responsibility of parents and others responsible for the child to meet the child's needs reflects the principles stated in article 3(2), article 5 and article 18. Where provision for the child's development is concerned under article 27, parental responsibility is expressly qualified by the proviso "within their abilities and financial capacities". This is an important reminder that, where parents lack the requisite skills or resources, the State must assist the parents in meeting their responsibilities, including the provision of material assistance such as food, clothing and housing.

As discussed below, in relation to maintenance under paragraph 4 of article 27 (page 363), legislation can be very precise about what is expected from parents by defining "parental responsibility" in law in terms of meeting the child's material, emotional, developmental and intellectual needs. That such legislation might be, at the end of the day, unenforceable is not the point. Law has an important educational function as well.

"States Parties, in accordance with national conditions and within their means..."

When parents are unable to ensure an adequate standard of living for their child, the State should step in. Article 27 also puts explicit qualifications on the State's obligations – "in accordance with national conditions and within their means". These words reflect a general nervousness of governments about financial commitments and control over government expenditure (including wealthy governments – it was the United States delegate who introduced the phrase "in accordance with national conditions" and the United Kingdom delegate, "within their means" (E/CN.4/1985/64, pp. 8-10; Detrick, pp. 374-375)). However, it is doubtful whether these qualifications dilute the overarching obligation to meet the economic rights of the child "to the maximum extent of ... available resources" under article 4. "Available" surely implies "in accordance with national conditions and within... means". Certainly no country has yet argued to the Committee that the provisions of article 4 do not apply to rights under article 27.

Discussions under articles 4 and 26 highlight the Committee's frequently expressed alarm about the impact on children of structural adjustment policies in countries dependent on international aid, and of the transition to a market economy in many countries, particular in post-communist eastern Europe. The recession has also brought restraints on public expenditure everywhere. The result has been an increasing, often catastrophic impoverishment of children from population groups dependent on state aid for their survival.

Notwithstanding the Committee's deeply felt concern at the effect on children of certain policies adopted by the International Monetary Fund, the World Bank and some aid-donor nations, the Committee reminds even the most beleaguered nations of their obligations under the Convention.

The grave living conditions of the majority of Honduran children were recognized by the Committee, which noted:

"that the measures taken by the Government of Honduras to repay the external debt and to implement the structural adjustment programme have put a strain on the country's resources. The deteriorating economic situation in Honduras is causing a worsening in the living and social conditions of Hondurans, so much so that about 60 per cent of the population live in extreme poverty. It also recognizes that drought, floods and other ecological problems have had serious consequences for Honduran families, dependent on agriculture as a means of livelihood, to maintain an adequate standard of living and thus support themselves and their children.

"As almost 60 per cent of the Honduran population is under the age of 18, the country's worsening economic situation has had serious consequences for the children in Honduras. The Committee notes that the social inequalities existing in the country, including through the unequal distribution of income and land, have contributed to the considerable problems facing children in Honduras." (Honduras IRCO, Add.24, paras. 7 and 8)

During discussions with the Committee, a Honduran Government representative told the Committee: "In the past, delivery of assistance and relief activities, including food aid, had been principally concentrated in the workplace, notably in the densely populated cities; now, however, attempts were being made to decentralize distribution on the basis of national 'poverty maps' showing where the needs were greatest, and indicators provided by fieldworkers. Such reallocation of scarce resources was not without political risks as people in the cities saw their rations reduced, but it was considered necessary in order to deal with nationwide realities more effectively and equitably."

A Committee member commented that Honduras was "confronting a contradictory situation. While legislation was gradually improving, at the same time the actual situation in some spheres was steadily deteriorating.... While the discussion had been frank and open, it had not been very analytical. There had been many references to difficulties and deficiencies, but few to root causes. Unless the real causes of the problems encountered were understood, it would be impossible to overcome them. The lack of finance had been heavily stressed, but there were other shortcomings: lack of monitoring, lack of coordination, lack of measures to enforce some very good legislation and lack of awareness on the part of the public. Other difficulties stemmed from national traditions and there were also, perhaps, some elements of corruption." (Honduras SR.160, paras. 21 and 61)

In the Concluding Observations

"The Committee takes note of the initiative... to map out the poorest areas of the country

with a view to prioritizing the provision of basic services to the areas most in need... [and]... the efforts made by the State Party to provide family and social assistance programmes as well as to implement supplementary food programmes with the aid of international cooperation, including from the World Food Programme. Notwithstanding these efforts, the Committee recommends that major attention and resources must be focused on further measures to address the problems of extreme poverty affecting the majority of the population which have adversely affected the rights of the child, to, inter alia, adequate nutrition, clothing and housing."*

The Committee also recommended

"the Government consider the possibility of organizing a meeting to discuss the matter of the availability of resources for the implementation of the rights recognized in the Convention, including within the framework of international cooperation. Participants in such a meeting could include members of the Committee, the donor community, the World Bank, IMF, UNICEF, other intergovernmental organizations and non-governmental organizations." (Honduras IRCO, Add. 24, paras. 6, 29 and 22)

The Committee does not underestimate the responsibilities of the donor community, for example in relation to Bolivia:

"The Committee notes that economic factors, including a high level of external debt, have made the full application of the Convention more difficult. In this respect, the Committee notes with concern that the long-term considerations embodied in many structural adjustment policies have not adequately taken into account the needs of today's children. While the State is responsible for implementation of the Convention on the Rights of the Child, the Committee recognizes that additional international assistance will be needed to more effectively address the challenge of improving the situation of children living in poverty, particularly those from the rural areas of the country." (Bolivia IRCO, Add.1, para. 5)

Similarly, while the Committee may commend energetic action taken by richer nations to reduce poverty, it will still encourage more action, as with Canada:

"The Committee is concerned by the emerging problem of child poverty, especially among vulnerable groups. It is also worried by the increasing number of children who are brought up by single parent families, or in other problematic environments. While appreciating the programmes already set up, the Committee emphasizes the need for special programmes and services to provide the necessary care, especially in terms of education, housing and nutrition, for such children...

"While recognizing the steps already taken, the Committee notes with concern the special problems still faced by children from vulnerable and disadvantaged groups, such as aboriginal children, with regard to the enjoyment of their fundamental rights, including access to housing and education." (Canada IRCO, Add.37, paras. 12 and 17)

A main thrust of the Committee's recommendations in relation to article 27 is that countries – both rich and poor – should undertake an holistic analysis of the extent, origin and cross-relationships of all forms of child deprivation. Poverty should be mapped and its root causes identified. For example, the Committee advised Nicaragua and Germany:

"The Committee recommends that the State Party consider the possibility of focusing its attention on the organization of a more comprehensive and coordinated campaign in order to address the interrelated family and social-related problems of: the high number of family separations, the relatively high maternal mortality rate and teenage pregnancies, the number of children who are victims of violence or abuse, and the rising number of children living or begging on the street who are at risk of sexual exploitation." (Nicaragua IRCO, Add.36, para. 35)

"Taking note of the allocation of additional resources to family-related benefits and of the willingness to undertake other measures to achieve further progress in addressing the problems facing single parents, and recognizing the State Party's commitment to undertake measures to improve poorer children's access to out-of-school activities, including leisure activities, the Committee believes that greater priority should be given to an analysis of the occurrence of child poverty. Such an analysis should be undertaken from a holistic perspective, taking into account the possible linkages between such matters as housing conditions, family support to the child at home and in school, and the risk of dropping out of school. The results of this research could serve as a vehicle for discussion of these matters both in Parliament and with the relevant authorities as well as for the development of a more comprehensive and integrated approach for responding to the problems identified." (Germany IRCO, Add.43, para. 31)

"States Parties ... shall take appropriate measures to assist parents and others responsible for the child ... and shall in case of need provide material assistance and support programmes..."

The emphasis in article 27 on the State assisting parents in the exercise of their primary responsibility to secure children's living conditions, rather than directly assisting the child, is both self-protective and principled: self-protective, because the drafting nations were anxious not to be placed under duties to support the children of rich parents, or to allow parents generally to off-load their responsibilities onto the State; principled, because – as the Convention stresses – children have a right wherever possible to be cared for by their parents and kept within a family environment. Article 27 reaffirms the principle established in article 18 that while both parents have primary responsibility for their children, the State also has obligations to support parents in the role of protecting and promoting the well-being of their children.

The Committee was concerned that States might not recognize that some parents were unable to undertake their responsibilities and needed support:

"...Further steps should be taken to strengthen the system of assistance to both parents in the performance of their child-rearing responsibilities, in particular in the light of articles 18 and 27 of the Convention. It is further suggested that the problem of single parenthood be studied and that relevant programmes be established to meet the particular needs of single parents." (Poland IRCO, Add.31, para. 33)

"In view of the high rate of abandonment of children and of abortion, the Committee recommends that the State Party adopt a strategy and policy to assist vulnerable families for the support of their children. The adequacy of the current social security system and of the family planning programmes should be evaluated..." (Ukraine IRCO, Add.42, para. 26)

"The Committee encourages the State Party to adopt further measures to ensure assistance for the family to ensure its responsibilities in the upbringing and development of the child, in particular in the light of articles 18 and 27 of the Convention. Special attention should be paid to the prevention of child abandonment, as well as to the prevention of, and appropriate assistance to, child-headed families." (Republic of Korea IRCO, Add.51, para. 27)

General support for parents is discussed in greater detail under article 18 (see page 231). In addition the Committee consistently expresses concern about the group of children termed "street children", whom, following the recommendation of the Human Rights Commission (resolution 1994/93), it prefers to describe as: "Children who, in order to survive, are forced to live and/ or work on the streets". It raised the issue with Peru:

"The Committee is concerned at the serious situation of children who, in view of increasing poverty and misery as well as of situations of abandonment or violence within the family, are forced to live and work in the streets, even at an early stage of their lives. For these reasons children often become victims of different forms of exploitation and abuse." (Peru IRCO, Add.8, para. 12)

This topic is also discussed in article 20 (page 263).

"particularly with regard to nutrition"

The Committee has expressed deep concern at any evidence of child malnutrition, for example to Burkina Faso, Guatemala, Honduras, Mauritius, Nicaragua, Sri Lanka – where it cited the rate of 23 per cent of infants with low birth weight – and Uruguay. Children will fail to make any significant progress in their "physical, mental, spiritual, moral and social development" if they are malnourished, so nutrition will always be at the top of any list of priorities for children, as the World Summit Goals make clear (see page 321).

However, the Committee often subsumes malnutrition under general concerns about "poverty" and "health" in relation to impoverished groups of children (see article 24(2)(c), page 326). This may occur because no evidence has been submitted to it on child malnutrition – the country may be simply too poor to amass data on, for example, birth weight or infant undernourishment. Thus, the Committee advised Guatemala:

"...The Committee shares the concern expressed by the representative of the State party at the widespread severe malnutrition and at the inadequacies of data and statistics monitoring nutrition." (Guatemala IRCO, Add.58, para. 17)

Similarly the Committee encouraged Mauritius

"...to undertake a comprehensive study on the impact of malnutrition on child development in connection with school drop-out and child labour, and to take all appropriate measures to address this problem. International cooperation could be requested to achieve this task and consideration should be given to the strengthening of cooperation with the International Labour Organization and the United Nations Children's Fund (UNICEF)." (Mauritius IRCO, Add.64, para. 28)

Countries where children are grossly malnourished are obvious candidates for international aid – the Committee, for example, commended Honduras for the efforts it had made to

"...implement supplementary food programmes with the aid of international cooperation,

The impact of Bulgaria's transition to market economy on children's diet

"The nutrition of children during the transition to market economy is determined by two basic factors: reduced manufacture of food products and higher prices after the price liberalization of 1991. As a result the consumption of food dropped in terms of quantity and deteriorated in terms of quality. There is an increase in the consumption of carbohydrates which are cheaper, and reduced consumption of food rich in proteins and particularly of fruits and vegetables." (Bulgaria IR, para. 179)

including from the World Food Programme..." (Honduras IRCO, Add. 24, para. 29).

Goals of the World Summit for Children, in 1990, are listed in article 24 (see page 321). In addition, the World Summit for Social Development, in 1995, agreed the goal of: "Achieving food security by ensuring a safe and nutritionally adequate food supply, at both the national and international levels, a reasonable degree of stability in the supply of food, as well as physical, social and economic access to enough food for all, while reaffirming that food should not be used as a tool for political pressure" (*World Summit for Social Development*, A/CONF.166/9 p. 51).

"housing"

There are children in both wealthy and poor countries who suffer from inadequate housing or are homeless. The Committee on Economic, Social and Cultural Rights has issued a long General Comment on "the right to adequate housing" under article 11 of the Covenant, which details requirements as security of tenure, availability of basic services, affordability and accessibility of housing (Committee on Economic, Social and Cultural Rights, General Comment 4, HRI/GEN/1/Rev.2, p. 59).

General Comment 4 was endorsed by the Committee on the Rights of the Child in its Statement to the Second United Nations Conference on Human Settlements (Habitat II, in Istanbul, 1996) supporting the Habitat Agenda and the Experts' Meeting on Children and Housing (see box page 363). The Committee commented:

"The Committee believes that... the right to housing should not be interpreted in a narrow or restrictive sense, but has to be interpreted as a right to live somewhere in security, peace and dignity...

"It is important to emphasize that the rights to housing of children are interrelated to and interdependent with nearly every other right contained in the Convention. This underlines the comprehensive and holistic thrust of the Convention, as well as of its process of implementation and monitoring." (Report on the eleventh session, January 1996, CRC/C/50, pp. 77 and 79)

In this statement, the Committee specifically mentions children's right to participate in decisions relating to housing (article 12). Where children are homeless this may seem a luxurious consideration, but it is of course important that any Government undertaking to improve children's housing take into account children's views on planning and architecture. Although "housing" is singled out in article 27, any consideration of housing has to encompass the whole of the built environment – children's needs and views are equally crucial in relation to areas used primarily by them, such as schools, play areas, residential institutions, clinics and hospitals.

Habitat II declares that: "The needs of children and youth, particularly with regard to their living environment, have to be taken fully into account. Special attention needs to be paid to the participatory processes dealing with the shaping of cities, towns and neighbourhoods; this is in order to secure the living conditions of children and of youth and to make use of their insight, creativity and thoughts on the environment. Special attention must be paid to the shelter needs of vulnerable children, such as street children, refugee children and children who are victims of sexual exploitation." (United Nations Conference on Human Settlements (Habitat II), A/CONF.165/14 p. 15)

The Committee is now asking countries to report on what measures it has taken under Habitat II (see *Guidelines for Periodic Reports*, para. 103).

Detailed information by countries on the housing situation of children or detailed comment by the Committee is rare but occasionally arises, for example in relation to Croatia:

"The Committee expresses concern about the Law on Temporary Possession, according to which property may be occupied by temporary settlers in the absence of the property owners. The Committee is concerned that families affected by this law will face problems if they should return before the present occupiers have found alternative shelters...
"The Committee recommends that in the light of the best interests of the child and, when necessary, in the framework of international cooperation, the Government make special

Children's rights and housing

In February 1996, a group of experts from UNICEF, United Nations Centre for Human Settlements (UNCHS) and others met to establish the relevance of the Convention on the Rights of the Child to the goals of Habitat II. Their declaration includes the following:

"Within the home environment

- The child's need for a secure, safe, healthy environment begins in the prenatal period.
- A healthy home includes a safe and sufficient water supply, safe and accessible sanitation and waste management; also protection from traffic and other hazards, freedom from exposure to pollution, radiation and disease, and from excessive noise and overcrowding.
- The home environment should facilitate caregiving, and should meet children's basic physical, social and psychological needs.
- Children of both sexes should be provided with equal opportunities and challenges for play and learning in the home and its immediate surroundings.
- Particular attention should be given to the home-based needs of disabled and other vulnerable children.

Within the neighbourhood and community

- A supportive environment for children includes healthy, crime free, and peaceful communities. It is essential that conditions promote social justice, gender equality and participation in community life.
- Childhood and adolescence must be recognized as unique stages in human cultural development, requiring the respect and understanding of the community and society. Street children and others in difficult circumstances should not be excluded.
- Health care, education, and child-care services of high quality must be available and accessible within the community.
- It is essential that children have safe, secure, and protected environments within the community where they can play, participate and learn about their social and natural world. Adolescents, too, need places where they can be together, experience autonomy, and feel a sense of belonging.
- Children have a special interest in the creation of sustainable human settlements that will support long and fulfilling lives for themselves and future generations. They require opportunities to participate and contribute to a sustainable urban future."

Children's Rights and Habitat – Declaration and Report of the Expert Seminar, UNICEF, UNCHS/Habitat, 1996.

efforts to resolve the problem of property owners returning to their homes before their occupiers have been able to find alternative shelter." (Croatia IRCO, Add.52, paras. 15 and 26)

The child's right to maintenance: article 27(4)

The provisions of article 27(4), relating to the financial maintenance of children by parents and others legally responsible for them, are undoubtedly important for many children whose conditions of living can be greatly improved by recovery of maintenance from an absent parent (usually the father).

However, maintenance is a muddied issue – this "right of the child" can be used in a way that is not necessarily in the child's interests. For

example, fathers can use financial leverage to secure unwanted access to the child or to assert a greater right to determine the child's future; mothers can retain custody of children simply in order to secure financial support or accommodation for themselves; children of second families can sometimes be the unnoticed victims of maintenance orders. States, too, can be unscrupulous about pursuing maintenance simply as a means of reducing their public expenditure bill. Care, therefore, needs to be taken to emphasize the article 3 principle that the best interests of the child must be a primary consideration (ideally the paramount consideration) when maintenance legislation and procedures are drawn up.

Nonetheless, the maintenance of children often carries wider social benefits than simply improving the living standards of individual children. In particular it addresses the increasingly important

Namibia's maintenance laws

In Namibia "...any person who is legally entitled to maintenance needs only to make a complaint under oath to the maintenance officer at any magistrate's court; there is no need to incur the expense of obtaining legal counsel. The maintenance officer then has a duty to investigate the complaint, instituting a court enquiry if necessary. The court is empowered to make maintenance orders, to grant a judgement in the woman's favour for any money owing to her, and to punish a failure to pay with fines or imprisonment where necessary. The court also has the power to attach the man's wages if he is working. However, under the Act, a failure to make payments will not be punished where it is due to lack of means which is not the result of misconduct or unwillingness to work...There is no specific age at which a child becomes too old for maintenance payments – the test is whether or not the child is in a position to support him or herself independently." (Namibia IR, paras. 160-163)

issue of the absent father and the worldwide growth of female-headed single-parent families (both unmarried and divorced), discussed under article 18 (see page 229). Good maintenance recovery procedures can deter men from taking feckless attitudes to family planning and fatherhood and can encourage them to play a more active role in children's upbringing. Namibia, for example, a country with many challenges, including high levels of female-headed families, has taken action to ensure a simple, low-cost and effective system for mothers to pursue maintenance and reported a high volume of successful take-up by unmarried women in urban areas (see box).

Legal definitions of 'maintenance' can also be a method of spelling out parental and family responsibilities. For example the Committee was informed that parents in Argentina are under a legal duty to meet their children's needs in terms of sustenance, education, leisure, clothing, housing, assistance and expenditure on account of illness (Argentina IR, paras. 56-58). The law on the duties of parents in Bolivia goes even further, specifying responsibility to ensure that children acquire a trade or profession for the future, if necessary by covering the cost of training (Bolivia IR, para. 99). Costa Rica's legislation establishes a precedence of financial responsibility for the child within the family – parents, elder siblings, grandparents and great-grandparents, in that order (Costa Rica IR, para. 155).

Recovery of maintenance from abroad

Article 27(4) was introduced during the drafting sessions of the Convention by Finland's representative in a draft that referred only to the effective recovery of maintenance from abroad, because of difficulties both children and States had experienced in this area. The recovery of maintenance from within the State was an afterthought (E/CN.4/1988/28, p.17, Detrick, p. 378).

International conventions have established rules governing where, from whom and how children may claim maintenance in circumstances where children change their country of habitual residence and where one or both parents live or move abroad – these include the United Nations Convention on the Recovery Abroad of Maintenance (New York, 1956); and the Reciprocal Enforcement of Maintenance Orders, Hague Convention Countries Order 1993. In addition, there are a number of bilateral and regional treaties and reciprocal enforcement agreements relating to maintenance orders. In countries where there is a lot of fluidity across borders, it is particularly important for these agreements to be ratified and made easily enforceable.

Implementation Checklist

article 27

● General measures of implementation

Have appropriate general measures of implementation been taken in relation to article 27 including

☐ identification and coordination of the responsible departments and agencies at all levels of government (article 27 is relevant to the **departments of justice, home affairs, housing, social welfare and housing**)?

☐ identification of relevant non-governmental organizations/civil society partners?

☐ a comprehensive review to ensure that all legislation, policy and practice is compatible with the article, for all children in all parts of the jurisdiction?

☐ adoption of a strategy to secure full implementation

    ☐ which includes where necessary the identification of goals and indicators of progress?

    ☐ which does not affect any provisions which are more conducive to the rights of the child?

    ☐ which recognizes other relevant international standards?

    ☐ which involves where necessary international cooperation?

(Such measures may be part of an overall governmental strategy for implementing the Convention as a whole).

☐ budgetary analysis and allocation of necessary resources?

☐ development of mechanisms for monitoring and evaluation?

☐ making the implications of article 27 widely known to adults and children?

☐ development of appropriate training and awareness-raising (in relation to article 27 likely to include the training of **community developers, environmental planners, emergency aid personnel, court officers, social workers, health workers and those involved in parent education**)?

● Specific issues in implementing article 27

☐ Has the State identified the minimum standard of living necessary to secure the child's development?

Are appropriate measures taken to assist parents and others responsible for the child in securing the conditions of living necessary for the child's

    ☐ physical development?

    ☐ mental development?

    ☐ spiritual development?

- ☐ moral development?
- ☐ social development?

☐ Are measures taken to make parents fully aware of these responsibilities?

☐ Are legal or administrative criteria in place to determine whether parents have the ability and financial capacities to meet their responsibilities?

☐ Are measures and procedures taken in order to identify all children within the State who are in need because their parents are unable to secure adequate standards of living for them?

☐ Are measures adopted to analyze why children's conditions of living are insufficient for their proper development?

☐ Where children are in need, whether with their parents or otherwise, are they provided with necessary material assistance and support programmes to secure their proper development?

☐ Does the State take measures (including budgetary allocations) to ensure that every child is well-nourished?

Does the State take measures to ensure that every child is housed in accommodation that is:

- ☐ secure?
- ☐ well-serviced (particularly as regards water, sanitation and fuel)?
- ☐ safe?
- ☐ healthy?
- ☐ appropriately located (particularly as regards hospitals, schools and recreation)?
- ☐ in accordance with measures recommended by Habitat II?

☐ Are the views of children taken into account when shaping the environment in which they live?

☐ Does the State take measures to ensure that every child is adequately clothed?

☐ Where the State has insufficient resources available to secure an adequate standard of living for all children, do its economic plans include securing such standards as an explicit goal?

☐ Are appropriate applications made for international aid and technical assistance where there are insufficient resources to secure children's standard of living?

Maintenance

☐ Is legislation implemented to ensure that children can recover maintenance from both parents and from any others who have responsibility for their conditions of living?

☐ Does such legislation make the child's best interests a primary or paramount consideration?

☐ Is such legislation simple and cheap for the child or child's caregiver to enforce?

☐ Does it include measures to obtain income or assets from those who default on their maintenance responsibilities?

☐ Has the State acceded to all appropriate international or bilateral agreements and treaties relating to the recovery of maintenance abroad?

Reminder: **The Convention is indivisible and its articles are interdependent. Article 27 should not be considered in isolation.**

Particular regard should be paid to:
The general principles

Article 2: all rights to be recognized for each child in jurisdiction without discrimination on any ground

Article 3(1): the best interests of the child to be a primary consideration in all actions concerning children

Article 6: right to life and maximum possible survival and development

Article 12: respect for the child's views in all matters affecting the child; opportunity to be heard in any judicial or administrative proceedings affecting the child

Closely related articles

Articles whose implementation is related to that of article 27 include:

Article 3(2): State to ensure child necessary protection and care, taking into account parents' rights

Article 5: Parental responsibility and child's evolving capacities

Article 18: parents having joint responsibility, State support for parents

Article 24: right to health and health services

Article 26: right to social security

Child's right to education

article 28

Text of Article 28

1. States Parties recognize the right of the child to education, and with a view to achieving this right progressively and on the basis of equal opportunity, they shall, in particular:

(a) Make primary education compulsory and available free to all;

(b) Encourage the development of different forms of secondary education, including general and vocational education, make them available and accessible to every child, and take appropriate measures such as the introduction of free education and offering financial assistance in case of need;

(c) Make higher education accessible to all on the basis of capacity by every appropriate means;

(d) Make educational and vocational information and guidance available and accessible to all children;

(e) Take measures to encourage regular attendance at schools and the reduction of drop-out rates.

2. States Parties shall take all appropriate measures to ensure that school discipline is administered in a manner consistent with the child's human dignity and in conformity with the present Convention.

3. States Parties shall promote and encourage international cooperation in matters relating to education, in particular with a view to contributing to the elimination of ignorance and illiteracy throughout the world and facilitating access to scientific and technical knowledge and modern teaching methods. In this regard, particular account shall be taken of the needs of developing countries.

Summary

Article 28 of the Convention on the Rights of the Child establishes the child's right to education. Education is recognized to be essential for all children. The article stresses the right must be achieved "on the basis of equal opportunity," reflecting the fact that vast numbers of children suffer discrimination in access to education (particularly children in rural areas, girls and disabled children). Education is also expensive and not all States will be able to meet the educational needs of their children – often the right will need to be achieved "progressively". However article 28 states the core minimum: free, compulsory primary education for all, and different forms of secondary education and vocational guidance "available and accessible" to all. Higher education must be accessible "on the basis of capacity".

The article also addresses the delivery of education, in so far as States must take measures to reduce school drop-out rates and to ensure that school discipline respects the child's rights. It also encourages international cooperation on education, reflecting the fact that education can be the engine for economic growth. ■

Extracts from
Committee on the Rights of the Child
Guidelines for Reports to be submitted by States Parties under the Convention

For full text of *Guidelines for Periodic Reports*, see Appendix 3, page 604.

Guidelines for Initial Reports

"Education, leisure and cultural activities

Under this section States Parties are requested to provide relevant information, including the principal legislative, judicial, administrative or other measures in force; the institutional infrastructure for implementing policy in this area, particularly monitoring strategies and mechanisms; and factors and difficulties encountered and progress achieved in implementing the relevant provisions of the Convention, in respect of:

(a) Education, including vocational training and guidance (article 28)...

... States Parties are requested to specify the nature and extent of cooperation with local and national organizations of a governmental or non-governmental nature, such as institutions of social workers concerning the implementation of this area of the Convention. States Parties are encouraged to provide additional relevant statistical information and indicators relating to children covered in this section."

(CRC/C/5, paras. 21 and 22)

Guidelines for Periodic Reports

"VII. EDUCATION, LEISURE AND CULTURAL ACTIVITIES...

A. Education, including vocational training and guidance (art. 28)

Please indicate the measures adopted, including of a legislative, administrative and budgetary nature, to recognize and ensure the right of the child to education, and to achieve this right progressively and on the basis of equal opportunities.

In this regard, reports should indicate, inter alia:

The measures adopted to ensure respect for the general principles of the Convention, namely the best interests of the child, respect for the views of the child, the right to life, survival and development to the maximum extent possible, and non-discrimination, including with a view to reducing existing disparities;

The proportion of the overall budget (at the central, regional and local, and where appropriate at the federal and provincial levels) devoted to children and allocated to the various levels of education;

The consideration given to the real cost to the family of the child's education and the appropriate support provided;

The measures adopted to ensure that children may be taught in local, indigenous or minority languages;

Mechanisms developed to ensure the access of all children, including girls, children with special needs and children in especially difficult circumstances, to quality education adapted to the child's age and maturity;

The steps taken to ensure that there are sufficient teachers in the school system, to enhance their competence, and to ensure and assess the quality of teaching;

The measures adopted to provide adequate educational facilities, accessible to all children;

The rate of illiteracy below and over 18 years, and the rate of enrolment in literacy classes, including by age, gender, region, rural/urban area, and social and ethnic origin;

Any systems of non-formal education;

Any system or extensive initiatives by the State to provide early development and education services for young children, especially for young children from disadvantaged social groups;

The changes that have occurred in the education system (including with regard to legislation, policies, facilities, budgetary allocation, quality of education, enrolment, drop-out and literacy);

Any monitoring mechanism developed, factors and difficulties encountered and targets identified for the future;

Other relevant disaggregated data on the children concerned, including on education outcomes, inter alia by gender, age, region, rural/urban area, and national, ethnic and social origin.

Reports should also indicate the particular measures adopted:

To make primary education compulsory and available free for all, particularly children, indicating the minimum age for enrolment in primary school, the minimum and maximum ages for compulsory education, the proportion of children enrolled, who complete primary education, as well as any relevant disaggregated data including by age, gender, region, urban/rural area, national, social and ethnic origin, service coverage and budgetary allocation;

To encourage the development of different forms of secondary education, including general and vocational education, and measures adopted:

To make such forms available and accessible to every child, providing inter alia any relevant disaggregated data including by gender, age, region, rural/urban area, national, social and ethnic origin, coverage and budgetary allocation;

To introduce free secondary education and offer financial assistance in case of need, indicating the children concerned, including by gender, age, region, rural/urban area, and national, social and ethnic origin, and the budget allocated for that purpose;

To make higher education accessible to all on the basis of capacity, indicating inter alia the rate of access to higher education by age, gender and national, social and ethnic origin;

To make educational and vocational information and guidance available and accessible to all children, indicating, inter alia, the forms of such information and guidance, the mechanisms used to assess their effectiveness, the budget allocated for that purpose, as well as any relevant disaggregated data, including by age, gender, region, urban/rural area, and social and ethnic origin;

To encourage regular attendance at school and to reduce drop-out rates, including research, any mechanisms developed to assess the situation, and incentives provided to encourage school entrance, regular school attendance and school retention, any alternatives provided for children who are excluded from school, as well as other relevant data disaggregated by age, gender, region, urban/rural area, and social and ethnic origin.

Reports should also provide information on any category or group of children who do not enjoy the right to education and the circumstances in which children may be excluded from school temporarily or permanently (for example disability, deprivation of liberty, pregnancy, HIV/AIDS infection), including any arrangements made to address such situations and to ensure alternative education. Disaggregated data should be provided, including by age, gender, region, rural/urban area, and social and ethnic origin.

Please indicate all appropriate measures taken pursuant to article 28, paragraph 2, to ensure that school discipline is administered in a manner consistent with the child's human dignity and in conformity with the Convention, including:

Legislation applying to public and private schools and other education institutions and prohibiting all forms of violence, including corporal punishment, as well as any other disciplinary measures which are not consistent with the child's human dignity or in conformity with the provisions of the Convention, including articles 19, 29 and 37(a), and its general principles particularly of non-discrimination, best interests and respect for the views of the child;

article 28

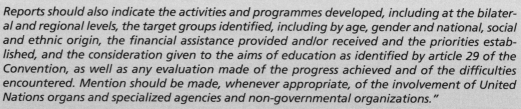

Any monitoring system of the administration of the school discipline, as well as mechanisms of reporting and complaint;

Any independent mechanism established for that purpose;

Legislation providing the opportunity for the child to participate in administrative or judicial proceedings in relation to education and affecting him or her, including those relating to the choice of school, school exclusion.

With regard to article 28, paragraph 3, please provide information on the measures adopted to promote and encourage international cooperation in matters relating to education, in particular with a view to:

Contributing to the elimination of ignorance and illiteracy throughout the world;

Facilitating access to scientific and technical knowledge and modern teaching methods;

Taking particular account of the needs of developing countries.

Reports should also indicate the activities and programmes developed, including at the bilateral and regional levels, the target groups identified, including by age, gender and national, social and ethnic origin, the financial assistance provided and/or received and the priorities established, and the consideration given to the aims of education as identified by article 29 of the Convention, as well as any evaluation made of the progress achieved and of the difficulties encountered. Mention should be made, whenever appropriate, of the involvement of United Nations organs and specialized agencies and non-governmental organizations."

(CRC/C/58, paras. 105-111. The following paragraphs of the *Guidelines for Periodic Reports* are also relevant to reporting under this article: 24, 43, 46, 57, 88, 92, 95, 118, 152 and 166; for full text of *Guidelines*, see Appendix 3, page 604.)

Background

The 1948 Universal Declaration of Human Rights states: "Everyone has the right to education. Education shall be free, at least in the elementary and fundamental stages. Elementary education shall be compulsory. Technical and professional education shall be made generally available and higher education shall be equally accessible to all on the basis of merit" (article 26).

This declaration was enhanced in the International Covenant on Economic, Social and Cultural Rights: "Primary education shall be compulsory and available free to all... Secondary education in its different forms, including technical and vocational secondary education, shall be made generally available and accessible to all by every appropriate means, and in particular by the progressive introduction of free education ... Higher education shall be made equally accessible to all, on the basis of capacity, by every appropriate means, and in particular by the progressive introduction of free education" (article 13(2)). The International Covenant goes on to provide that any ratifying State that does not provide free compulsory primary education shall undertake "within two years, to work out and adopt a detailed plan of action for the progressive implementation, within a reasonable number of years, to be fixed in the plan, of the principle of compulsory education free of charge for all" (article 14).

During the drafting of article 28 on the Convention on the Rights of the Child, concern was expressed by State representatives that the Convention should neither be weaker nor stronger than the International Covenant on Economic, Social and Cultural Rights (E/CN.4/1985/64, pp.11-15; Detrick, pp 383-386).

The 1990 World Summit for Children declares: "At present, over 100 million children are without basic schooling, and two thirds of them are girls. The provision of basic education and literacy for all are among the most important contributions that can be made to the development of the world's children" (para. 13). The World Summit sets a goal: "By the year 2000... universal access to basic education and achievement of primary education by at least 80 per cent of primary school-age children".

In the same year a World Conference on Education for All was held in Jomtien, Thailand. The resulting World Declaration on Education for All asserts that basic education "is more than an end in itself. It is the foundation for lifelong learning and human development on which countries may build, systematically, further levels and types of education and training" (article 1(4)). It states: "Every person – child, youth and adult – shall be able to benefit from educational opportunities designed to meet his basic learning needs. These needs comprise both essential learning tools (such as literacy, oral expression, numeracy, and problem solving) and the basic learning content (such as knowledge, skills, values, and attitudes) required by human beings to be able to survive, to develop their full capacities, to live and work in dignity, to improve the quality of their lives, to make informed decisions, and to continue learning. The scope of basic learning needs and how they should be met varies with individual countries and cultures, and inevitably, changes with the passage of time." (article 1(1))

During the drafting of the Convention on the Rights of the Child, members of the Working Group were keen to include the principle established in both the International Covenant on Economic, Social and Cultural Rights and the International Covenant on Civil and Political Rights that States should respect parents' rights to ensure that the education of their children is in conformity with their own religious and moral convictions. However, this was rejected on the grounds that parents' overall rights and responsibilities were dealt with elsewhere in the Convention. (E/CN.4/1985/64, pp. 11-15 and E/CN.4/1989/48, pp. 79-84; Detrick, pp. 384 and 394)

The Holy See was sufficiently concerned by this omission to enter a reservation: "That it interprets the articles of the Convention in a way which safeguards the primary and inalienable rights of parents, in particular in so far as those rights concern education (articles 13 and 28)" (CRC/C/Rev.5, p. 20). The Convention does not safeguard "primary and inalienable" rights of parents in education. These rights are subject, for example, to the best interests of the child, the evolving capacities of the child (article 5, page 75, and article 12, page 145) and the child's own rights under the Convention, including the right to an education that promotes tolerance and respect for others (article 29, page 391). Article 29 does however safeguard the rights of parents and others to establish schools outside the state system, and article 30 provides that children of minority cultures should not be denied rights to practise their language, religion and culture.

The "right of the child to education" to be achieved "progressively"

The child's basic right to education is enshrined in the first paragraph of article 28. Subparagraphs (a) to (e), which detail particular duties for States Parties in this respect, are governed by the initial statement, which provides that States Parties shall achieve the right to education "progressively and on the basis of equal opportunity."

"Education"

The definition of "education" is not limited to instruction delivered within schools (though subparagraph (e), on "school" drop-outs, and article 29(2), on private "educational institutions", imply that this will normally be the case). Article 28 mentions "vocational education", "the elimination of ... illiteracy" and "access to scientific and technical knowledge"; the broad aims of education are set out in article 29, but the Convention on the Rights of the Child does not attempt to define the detail of a basic curriculum.

However, the Eighteenth General Conference of UNESCO Recommendation Concerning Education for International Understanding, Cooperation and Peace and Education Relating to Human Rights and Fundamental Freedoms 1974 states: "The word 'education' implies the entire process of social life by means of which individuals and social groups learn to develop consciously within, and for the benefit of, the national and international communities, the whole of their personal capacities, attitudes, aptitudes and knowledge. This process is not limited to any specific activities." (article 1(a))

Nor does the Convention indicate how much time education should take up of the child's life, although the Committee raised with Madagascar a concern that:

"...In particular, the number of hours during which schools are open have been restricted." (Madagascar IRCO, Add.26, para. 13)

High illiteracy levels are often a subject of the Committee's expressed concern (see, for example, Jordan IRCO, Add.21, para. 25; Nepal IRCO, Add.57, para. 17; Guatemala IRCO, Add.58, para. 37; Mauritius IRCO, Add.64, para. 15). Otherwise, the Committee has tended to focus on the relevance of the curriculum to the child's life (as discussed in relation to subparagraph (e) below, page 381) rather than examining whether, for example, children's curricula includes adequate scientific or technical instruction. The *Guidelines for Periodic Reports* asks for details on "education outcomes" disaggregated by social groups and on the mechanisms to assess the effectiveness of educational provisions and measures to reduce school drop-out rates, all of which should focus Governments' attention on the content as well as the delivery of education (paras. 106 and 107).

"Progressively"

Some developing nations may lack the resources to ensure that secondary education, or even primary education, is accessible to all children, and even rich nations claim difficulties in ensuring that higher education is available to all young

Mexico's "Children in Solidarity" education programme

The "Children in Solidarity" Programme, part of Mexico's National Solidarity Programme to combat poverty, aims to help children living in extreme poverty who are in danger of dropping out of school. They are awarded scholarships for a 12 month period which include economic support, the provision of a monthly stock of basic food for the whole family, curative and preventive medical assistance and the monitoring of nutrition, and the promotion of recreational workshops and activities of benefit to the whole community. Children themselves contribute to the selection body for choosing beneficiaries... "The intention is to arouse the children's interest in their school and to foster an exercise that involves them in community life... The criteria applied in selection of beneficiaries are as follows: that candidates must be enrolled in school; attend school regularly; come from a family with scarce resources; and show an aptitude for collaboration and participation, both in school and within the community" (Mexico IR, paras. 321-328).

people on the basis of capacity. Nonetheless, all ratifying nations must plan for progressive provision of education, and, in line with article 4, they must ensure that this is done "to the maximum extent of available resources". The General Comment by the Committee on Economic, Social and Cultural Rights on what is meant by "progressively" is significant here (see article 4, page 55).

The *Guidelines for Periodic Reports* asks States Parties to provide information on: "The proportion of the overall budget (at the central, regional and local, and where appropriate at the federal and provincial levels) devoted to children and allocated to the various levels of education" (para. 106). What proportion of the national budget should be allocated to education has not been established by the Committee on the Rights of the Child or by United Nations' bodies. UNICEF's figures indicate that the average percentage of government expenditure on education was 4 per cent for industrialized countries, 11 per cent for developing countries and 12 per cent for the least developed countries (*The State of the World's Children 1997*, UNICEF, p. 99). Mongolia was commended by the Committee for its education provision:

"The Committee takes note with satisfaction that the Government has put children high on

its political agenda, during a difficult period of political and economic transition... by declaring 1995 the Year for Children and 1996 the Year for Education, and by allocating 20 per cent of its national budget to education." (Mongolia IRCO, Add.48, para. 3)

The Committee also welcomed Portugal's

"...increase in the budgetary allocation for education equivalent to 1 per cent of GDP until 1999" (Portugal IRCO, Add.45, para. 5).

On the other hand, Costa Rica reported to the Committee that its education budget percentage had dropped by 14 points between the 1970s and 1993, and the Committee expressed concern that this was an impact of "economic adjustment policies" (Costa Rica IRCO, Add.11, para. 8; see further discussion under article 4, page 63).

In respect of Nigeria:

"...the Committee remains concerned about the effectiveness of measures being taken to harmonize policy priorities in this area with adequate budgetary allocation" (Nigeria IRCO, Add.61, para. 18).

It can be assumed that the Committee expects to see all education budgets increasing, or at any rate not decreasing, in order to comply with the expectation inherent in the word "progressively", with the approach to implementation of social and economic rights under article 4, and in relation to other treaties, particularly the International Covenant on Economic, Social and Cultural Rights (see page 45).

The word "progressively" does not only relate to financial expenditure, it also relates to the administration of education. On a number of occasions, the Committee has found it necessary to suggest that countries take a step back and review the whole of their education systems rather than tinker with specific aspects. For example, it recommended that Jamaica undertake a thorough review of its educational system, citing:

"...The lack of adequate schooling facilities, the reduction of the educational budget, the low status of teachers, leading to a shortage of trained educators, and the insufficient measures to ensure vocational training are matters of serious concern." (Jamaica IRCO, Add.32, para. 15)

And, in respect of Honduras and Mauritius:

"...the Committee is deeply concerned at the insufficiency of measures taken ... to implement the provisions of article 28 ... especially in view of the low level of enrolment and retention of children in schools and the lack of vocational training in schools as well as the inadequacy of teacher training programmes and teaching material ... a thorough review of

the education system is urgently required."
(Honduras IRCO, Add.24, paras. 17 and 30)
"The Committee recommends that a global study on the quality of the education system be made..." (Mauritius IRCO, Add.64, para. 29)

The right to education to be achieved "on the basis of equal opportunity"

"On the basis of equal opportunity" stresses the general principle of article 2 on non-discrimination (page 19).

The foremost bar to equality of opportunity in education is, usually, the lack of resources – either in terms of a low government budget applied to education so that education is not made available to all members of the population, or in terms of families' poverty so that children have to be withheld or withdrawn from education. Governments can adopt strategies to help such families, such as Mexico's "Children in Solidarity" programme (see box opposite).

In addition, the Committee has expressed concern that specific groups of children are discriminated against in education, both in terms of the definition of the Convention against Discrimination in Education, 1960: "...Of depriving any person or group of persons of access to education of any type or at any level ... [or]... limiting any person or group of persons to education of an inferior standard" and through less direct forms of discrimination (article 1). The Committee identified various groups as suffering discrimination in education, as discussed below.

Girls

The 1990 World Summit for Children estimated that two thirds of the world's 100 million children without basic education were girls and set goals for increasing the education of female children.

These goals were endorsed by the 1995 World Conference on Women, in Beijing, which attributed the disproportionately low numbers of girls in education to "customary attitudes, child labour, early marriages, lack of funds and lack of adequate schooling facilities, teenage pregnancies and gender inequalities in society at large as well as in the family ... In some countries the shortage of women teachers can inhibit the enrolment of girls. In many cases, girls start to undertake heavy domestic chores at a very early age and are expected to manage both educational and domestic responsibilities, often resulting in poor scholastic performance and an early drop-out from schooling" (The Fourth World Conference on Women, *Platform for Action*, Beijing 1995, para. 263).

Practical help for girls in Nepal

"Various programmes have been initiated to provide equal opportunities to the girl child by reducing their work burden and providing better access to school and health facilities. These include:

- The Out-of-School Programme, under the Non-Formal Education Programme, is designed so that children, especially girls, can have access to basic education with which they can re-enter the primary school system as well as learn skills that are useful in the home;

- The Early Childhood Education and Care (ECEC) project within the Education Programme promotes home-based child care and parenting education, as well as community-based child-care centres. Child development activities help reduce the child-care burden of older girls, allowing them to attend school." (Nepal IR, para. 71)

The Conference called for full implementation of article 28 of the Convention on the Rights of the Child, including a call on Governments to "Increase enrolment and improve retention rates of girls by allocating appropriate budgetary resources and by enlisting the support of the community and parents through campaigns and flexible school schedules, incentives, scholarships, access programmes for out-of-school girls and other measures" (para. 279).

While the figures for the percentage of girls enrolling in primary and secondary education have steadily increased worldwide, in developing countries they still lag behind their male peers and, once enrolled, are much more likely to drop out of school.

The Committee points out that:
"Several States had identified persistent traditions and prejudices as a main difficulty affecting the enjoyment of girls' fundamental rights. Discrimination often arose from the way roles were traditionally distributed within the family. Girls often shared the responsibilities of the household, taking care of younger siblings and refused access to education and participation in social life...Girls below the age of 15 often do the same household work as adult women; such labour is not regarded as 'real work' and is therefore never reflected in the statistical data. To free girls from this cycle they must have equal chances and equal

treatment, with special emphasis on education." *(General discussion on the girl child, Report on the eighth session, February 1995, CRC/C/38, para. 286)*

Girls tend to be the first to be pulled out of school. Bolivia's Initial Report, for example, points out that: "Although some statistics show a high proportion of boys and girls are enrolled for basic education, defection, giving up and repetition are higher among girls because they have to carry out other duties in the family, such as looking after younger children, housework or assisting their mother in her work." (Bolivia IR, para. 174; see also Zimbabwe IRCO, Add.55, para. 19)

The Committee took up the issue of girls' education with a number of countries (see Bolivia IRCO, Add.1, para. 10; Russia IRCO, Add.4, para. 13; Jordan IRCO, Add.21, para. 25; Philippines IRCO, Add.29, para. 15; Senegal IRCO, Add.44, para. 28; Portugal IRCO, Add.45, para. 5; Zimbabwe IRCO, Add.55, para. 19; Nepal IRCO, Add.57, para. 12; Nigeria IRCO, Add.61, para. 38).

Pakistan was told:

"In line with international recommendations, the Committee wishes to emphasize the importance of focusing attention on improving the provision and quality of education, especially in view of its potential benefit for addressing various concerns, including the situation of girls and reducing the incidence of children at work, school drop-out, and illiteracy, especially of girls and women. Attention is drawn to the possibility of benefiting from the activities of women's groups to improve access to education for girls at the community level." *(Pakistan IRCO, Add.18, para. 30)*

To Egypt the Committee noted that:

"...although Egyptian laws and regulations guarantee equality between the sexes, there is in reality still a pattern of disparity between boys and girls, in particular as far as access to education is concerned." *(Egypt IRCO, Add.5, para. 6)*

Egypt analyzed the causes of this disparity as arising not only from poverty and low status of women but also "the dominant impact of customs and traditions prohibiting the teaching of girls for fear of mixing with boys" (Egypt IR, para. 238).

The Committee also linked the high rate of early pregnancy in Uruguay with low school attendance and the high drop-out rates of girls (Uruguay IRCO, Add.62, para.12).

The Committee gave special mention to China's "Spring Buds Scheme", which directed resources at the enrolment of girls in primary education, a serious issue of concern in that country where girls are the significant majority of the 2.6 million children who are not in school. Between 1989 and 1994, over 800 classes for girls were established across China, enabling 400,000 girls to go to school (China IR, paras. 187 and 178, and China IRCO, Add.56, para. 6).

It should perhaps be noted in passing that, because of changing work patterns and social attitudes, the education of boys appears likely to become one of the problems confronting both developed and developing nations in the twenty-first century, particularly as regards drop-out rates and underachievement, although the Committee has so far only noted it as an issue of concern in relation to Mongolia (Mongolia IRCO, Add.48, para. 15).

Rural children

Within the developing world there are often striking discrepancies between the education of rural and urban-based children, often commented on by the Committee (see Bolivia IRCO, Add.1, para. 10; Russia IRCO, Add.4, para. 13; Colombia IRCO, Add.30, para. 20; Philippines IRCO, Add.29, para. 15; Sri Lanka IRCO, Add.40, para. 21; Senegal IRCO, Add.44, para. 28; Mongolia IRCO, Add.48, para. 23; China IRCO, Add.56, para. 11; Nepal IRCO, Add.47, para. 17; Zimbabwe IRCO, Add.55, para. 18).

Poor educational opportunities for children in rural areas arise from a combination of factors, including the administrative cost and difficulty of servicing remote and scattered farms and villages, a dearth of teachers prepared to live in the countryside, the dependence of poor farming communities on children as labourers and the apparent irrelevance of schools and the curriculum to rural lives.

UNICEF's *The Progress of Nations 1997* identifies the massive disparity between the attendance of primary school age children in urban areas and that of children in rural areas in many developing countries. In 41 countries surveyed from 1990 to 1996: "Nearly two thirds of the countries surveyed have urban/rural gaps of at least 10 percentage points or more. In only 3 of the 41 countries – Bangladesh, Kenya and Namibia – are attendance rates in rural areas slightly higher than in urban areas." The survey also compared the disparities between boys' and girls' school attendance with the urban/rural difference and found that "In only 2 of the 41 countries – Yemen and Nepal – were gender disparities greater than urban-rural differences." It noted that disparities between regions within countries are also significant (*The Progress of Nations 1997*, UNICEF, p. 39).

Minority groups

Particular groups within populations are also liable to suffer discrimination in educational opportunities, such as children of minority cultures, indigenous peoples, gypsies, immigrants, refugees and children in armed conflict. (See, for example, Mexico IRCO, Add.13, para. 14; Madagascar IRCO, Add.26, para. 13; Philippines IRCO, Add.29, para. 15; Portugal IRCO, Add.45, para. 13).

Failure to take up educational opportunities can sometimes be attributed to the group itself, for example because they speak a minority language or pursue a nomadic lifestyle, but such forms of indirect discrimination are unacceptable to the Committee. For example it recommended the United Kingdom take "pro-active" measures to secure the education rights of children belonging to gypsy and traveller communities (UK IRCO, Add.34, para. 46) in order to accommodate their particular culture. Equality of educational opportunity can only be achieved if education is recognized as a right for all children, irrespective of their background. The Committee noted with concern, to Norway, that children who had their asylum requests rejected but remain in the country have their rights to health care and education provided *de facto* but not *de jure*, suggesting, in addition, that

"...the State Party might wish to further discuss the provision of education and health services, including with respect to all children under its jurisdiction, in order to ensure that different standards of service do not arise between municipalities" (Norway IRCO, Add.23, para. 24).

In contrast, the Committee welcomed Iceland's special programmes, set up under the auspices of the Ministry of Education, to train teachers at all levels on the education of immigrant children (Iceland IRCO, Add.50, para. 10).

The Committee recommended that Guatemala

"...focus greater efforts on... ensuring the availability of bilingual education for indigenous children... Such measures will contribute to the prevention of any form of discrimination on the basis of language with regard to the right to education." (Guatemala IRCO, Add.58, para. 37)

Inequality of educational opportunity can reflect a wider social or political discrimination towards the group. The Committee noted that Tibetan children's "quality of education is inferior" in China and suggested:

*"that a review be undertaken of measures to ensure that children in Tibet Autonomous Region and other minority areas are guaran-*teed full opportunities to develop knowledge about their own language and culture as well as to learn the Chinese language. Steps should be taken to protect these children from discrimination and to ensure their access to higher education on an equal footing" (China IRCO, Add.56, paras. 19 and 40).*

The Committee was deeply concerned, in 1996, by outright discrimination exercised in the Federal Republic of Yugoslavia:

"From the information reported to the Committee, it appears that the rejection by the population of the Government's decision to apply a uniform education system and curriculum has been followed by the summary dismissal of 18,000 teachers and other education professionals and to more than 300,000 school-age children not attending school. The subsequent development of a parallel system of education and the tensions surrounding this development in Kosovo have resulted in further detrimental effects, including the closure of schools and the harassment of teachers ... Reports of the progressive exclusion of teaching in languages other than Serbian, such as Bulgarian, are also disquieting to the Committee."

The Committee proposed:

"that the State Party give further consideration to the need to allocate greater resources to education and to reverse any trends in the education system which may perpetuate gender discrimination or stereotyping as well as to addressing other problems, including those relating to teaching in national languages" (Federal Republic of Yugoslavia IRCO, Add.49, paras. 7, 18 and 29).

Disabled children

All children, no matter how seriously disabled they are, are entitled to education that maximizes their potential. Any law or practice that limits this right, for example by deeming certain children "ineducable" or by entitling them to "health treatment" rather than "education", breaches articles 2 and 28. Moreover, the education of disabled children should be provided "in a manner conducive to the child's achieving the fullest possible social integration" (article 23(3)) which means that disabled children should, wherever possible, be educated in mainstream schools alongside children without disabilities. The Standard Rules on the Equalization of Opportunities for Persons with Disabilities addresses this issue: "In situations where the general school system does not yet adequately meet the needs of all persons with disabilities, special education may be considered. It should be aimed at preparing students for education in the general school system. The quality of such education should reflect the same

article 28

standards and ambitions as general education and should be closely linked to it. At a minimum, students with disabilities should be afforded the same portion of educational resources as students without disabilities. States should aim for the gradual integration of special education services into mainstream education. It is acknowledged that in some instances special education may currently be considered to be the most appropriate form of education for some students with disabilities.

"Owing to the particular communication needs of deaf and deaf/blind persons, their education may be more suitably provided in schools for such persons or special classes and units in mainstream schools. At the initial stage, in particular, special attention needs to be focused on culturally sensitive instruction that will result in effective communication skills and maximum independence for people who are deaf or deaf/blind." (rule 6; see also article 23, page 306)

Children in forms of detention

These children are also often denied rights to education or to appropriate education. Rules 13 and 38 to 47 of the United Nations Rules for the Protection of Juveniles Deprived of their Liberty specify in great detail high standards of education for these children, including the provision of higher, vocational, special and physical education (see article 37, page 500).

"(a) Make primary education compulsory and available free to all"

During the drafting of the Convention on the Rights of the Child there was some discussion about the word "free" (which had already appeared in other related treaties). Objections were made that cost-free education is an illusion since someone always pays, either directly or indirectly through taxes. A representative from Japan proposed that the word "free" should be interpreted to mean that education "could be made accessible to all children and not to mean that free education was a measure which States Parties were obliged to adopt" (E/CN.4/1989/48, pp. 79-84; Detrick, p. 393).

Subparagraph (a) does, however, clearly state that "free" education at the primary stage is a measure that States Parties are obliged to secure for all children, not just low-income children or other categories of children. Three countries entered reservations to this subparagraph – Samoa, Singapore and Swaziland. The Committee has yet to consider reports from these States (September 1997).

Samoa's reservation states: "The Government of Western Samoa whilst recognizing the importance of providing free primary education as specified under article 28(1)(a) of the Convention on the Rights of the Child, and being mindful of the fact that the greater proportion of schools within Western Samoa that provide primary level education are controlled by bodies outside the control of the Government ... the Government of Western Samoa thus reserves the right to allocate resources to the primary sector of education in Western Samoa in contrast to the requirement of article 28(1)(a) to provide free primary education." (CRC/C/2/Rev.5, p. 30) This reservation suggests a misunderstanding of the requirements of subparagraph (a), which does not refer to States "providing" free primary education but to them "making" it free, that is, ensuring that the provision is made but not necessarily providing it themselves. Thus, if the Samoan Government is satisfied that the "bodies outside the control of the Government" which provide primary education are providing it free of charge to all (and that the education provided is in conformity with the rest of the Convention) then the Government is not obliged to duplicate this funding.

The reservation of Swaziland is also questionable in its necessity: "The Convention on the Rights of the Child being a point of departure to guarantee child rights; taking into consideration the progressive character of the implementation of certain social, economic and cultural rights as recognized in article 4 of the Convention, the Government of the Kingdom of Swaziland would undertake the implementation of the right to free primary education to the maximum extent of available resources and expects to obtain the cooperation of the international community for its full satisfaction as soon as possible" (CRC/C/2/Rev.5, p. 32). Even if Swaziland was not able to secure free primary education for all, so long as it did genuinely deploy its available resources to the maximum extent to this end and had adopted a strategic plan for the progressive implementation of article 28, it need not enter such a reservation.

However, Singapore's reservation clearly seeks to abrogate its duty to secure free compulsory primary education for all children within the jurisdiction, and as such may fall foul of article 51(2) (which does not permit reservations "incompatible with the object and purpose of the present Convention"):

"With respect to article 28.1(a), the Republic of Singapore:

(a) does not consider itself bound by the requirement to make primary education compulsory because such a measure is unnecessary in our social context where in practice virtually all children attend primary school; and

(b) reserves the right to provide primary education free only to children who are citizens of Singapore." (CRC/C/2/Rev.5, p. 31)

The right to compulsory free primary education is so clearly stated in the Convention that any failure to meet this standard is a major source of concern to the Committee. It expressed "deep concern" that Nepal did not make primary education compulsory for all (Nepal IRCO, Add.57, para. l8). Guatemala, Jordan, Paraguay, Senegal, Yugoslavia and Zimbabwe have also been singled out for failures to provide free universal primary education. Nor is it enough to ensure that primary education is free – the Committee expressed regret that, though primary education had been made free in Ethiopia, it was not yet compulsory (Ethiopia IRCO, Add.67, para. 7). The Committee has also registered concern at the affordability of education, even if it is nominally "free"; the *Guidelines for Periodic Reports*, for example, requests information regarding "the real cost to the family of the child's education" and "incentives provided to encourage school entrance, regular school attendance and school retention" (paras. 106 and 107).

"(b) Encourage the development of different forms of secondary education, including general and vocational education, make them available and accessible to every child, and take appropriate measures such as the introduction of free education and offering financial assistance in case of need"

The wording of the right to secondary education is less absolute, and less clear, than that relating to primary education. The weaker phrasing does not reflect any doubt about the usefulness of secondary education to children but rather acknowledges that free compulsory secondary education for all is at present beyond the resources of a number of countries.

The phrase "take appropriate measures such as the introduction of free education and offering financial assistance in case of need" suggests that the availability and accessibility of education could be means-tested so that richer families pay while poor children attend free of charge or are awarded scholarships. However, such an approach can too easily lead to situations where secondary education is not "available and accessible to every child". The Committee has raised concerns about the expense of secondary education:

"The Committee takes note that concern is expressed that costs of children's education may be growing beyond the reach of certain families." (Federal Republic of Yugoslavia IRCO, Add.49, para. 18)

"The Committee is ... concerned that insufficient resources are allocated to human development projects and the emerging gaps developing between those who can afford private education ... and those who cannot ... In relation with the growing role of private educational ... institutions, the Committee recommends that a stronger emphasis be placed on public education ... by the Government with a view to ensuring that all children subject to the jurisdiction of the State Party enjoy these fundamental rights, as well as to prevent any risk of discrimination." (Lebanon IRCO, Add.54, paras. 12 and 30)

"The cost to families of secondary education are leading to an increasing drop-out rate for girls, particularly in rural areas. The Committee notes with concern the growing disparity within the education system owing to the parallel systems of private and public schools which results ultimately in racial segregation at school on the basis of the economic status of parents." (Zimbabwe IRCO, Add.55, para. 19)

"Offering financial assistance in case of need" can also be interpreted to mean giving grants to families who would otherwise depend on their children's labour as a source of income, thus withdrawing them from school. The Committee commended China's "Project Hope" scheme which is particularly targeted at children who miss schooling because of domestic poverty and which aims, by the end of the century, to make secondary education compulsory for all Chinese children (China IR, paras.181-6; China IRCO, Add.56, para. 6).

Subparagraph (b) refers to "different forms of secondary education, including general and vocational education". Education is about the development of children's fullest potential (see article 29) and the Convention recognizes that there is no set blueprint for achieving this. On the contrary there are likely to be a variety of forms of education once the basic skills of literacy and numeracy have been acquired at the primary stage.

The Convention singles out vocational education for obvious reasons. Education must have relevance to the child's current and future life; vocational and work-related training is both educational in its own right and provides a strong inducement for the child to stay in school (see "preventing drop-out" below, page 381). But the Committee has also encouraged States to develop "alternative educational programmes" (for example, Slovenia IRCO, Add.65, paras. 15 and 23, and Bulgaria IRCO, Add.66, para. 17) which suggests that countries must have flexible curricula and delivery systems to respond to the needs of the child within his or her social setting.

A secondary education with too narrow a range of options or outcomes will certainly be discriminatory; for example, the Committee informed Myanmar that:

"Of particular concern is the fact that children considered poor are channelled towards monastic Buddhist schools and are offered no alternative educational opportunity." (Myanmar IRCO, Add.69, para. 16)

At what point secondary education begins and ends is unclear; ages vary from country to country (for example "primary" education ends at age 16 under Namibian and Icelandic legislation (Namibia IR, para. 343; Iceland IR, para. 312). The Committee has tentatively suggested that basic schooling, primary and secondary together, should last for nine years:

"It is also suggested that the Government consider extending the provision of compulsory education to nine years of schooling, thereby ensuring at the same time that the age of completion of compulsory education would be harmonized with the minimum age of employment..." (Nicaragua IRCO, Add.36, para. 38)

A common age of entry to primary education is 6 years old, which implies compulsory secondary school would normally end at the age of 15. This accords with provisions relating to the minimum age for employment. Under article 2 of the Convention Concerning Minimum Age for Admission to Employment 1973 (ILO, No. 138) this minimum age: "shall not be less than the age of completion of compulsory schooling and, in any case, shall not be less than 15 years".

Failure to synchronize school-leaving age and the minimum age for employment is a frequent cause of concern, for example the Committee expressed concern over:

"...The legislative reforms setting the age of completion of education at 12 years, and the minimum age for employment at 14 years, rendering children between the ages of 12 and 14 vulnerable to the risk of economic exploitation." (Nicaragua IRCO, Add.36, para. 14)

"... the legislative discrepancy between the age for completion of mandatory education and the minimum age for admission to employment may lead to encourage adolescents to drop out from the school system." (Tunisia IRCO, Add.39, para. 9)

"...the failure to provide for an age for the completion of compulsory education as required by the Constitution of Guatemala as well as by article 2 of ILO Convention No. 138 is a matter of considerable concern to the Committee ... The Committee ... recommends that the State party set the age for completion of compulsory schooling at 15 and consider raising the minimum age of employment to 15." (Guatemala IRCO, Add.58, paras. 15 and 26) See also article 32, page 439.

"(c) Make higher education accessible to all on the basis of capacity by every appropriate means"

Although, by and large, higher education is pursued after the age of 18, the Convention correctly includes access to higher education as an integral part of children's rights, albeit one exercisable "on the basis of capacity." The Committee has not spent time considering how countries have implemented their obligations under article 28(1)(c) but has asked for detailed information under the *Guidelines for Periodic Reports*. In order to meet higher education obligations under the Convention States should at the least introduce measures enabling poor children to take entrance examinations to higher education courses and to be awarded grants or scholarships if they succeed, on the basis of equality of opportunity.

The phrase "on the basis of capacity" should not be focused solely on success in examinations, arguably a teachable skill that can lead to a distortion in favour of high-income families and private education, but should include measures of more practical and relevant capacities. It may be noted that higher education for girls may have the secondary effect of postponing early marriage and early motherhood.

"(d) Make educational and vocational information and guidance available and accessible to all children"

Again, the Committee has not focused on this right directly and, to an extent, it could be assumed that if all children are to have access to

Causes of school drop-out: an Egyptian analysis

In its Initial Report Egypt provides an analysis of the reasons why children drop out of school:

"Drop-out factors are of two kinds: internal, such as:

(a) Inappropriate school location for some pupils;

(b) Lack of sufficient interest in curricula, strict methods of instruction emphasizing memory work and dictation and neglecting individual differences, and absence from the curricula of whatever prepares children for life and the future, particularly for those for whom education ends with their completion of the basic stage;

(c) Inadequate scientific and educational teacher qualification;

(d) Lack of school services in those primary schools located in rural and poor densely-populated areas;

and external ones, which relate to the economic, social, and cultural aspects of the life of the pupils' families, including:

(a) The low income of parents which drives them to send their children to work before they complete their education for the purpose of supplementing the family economic resources. This problem has acquired a sharper edge as families have been forced to send their children to work in the fields in the absence of emigrant fathers and in view of the increase in farm worker wages;

(b) The dominant impact of customs and tradition prohibiting the teaching of girls for fear of mixing with boys;

(c) The low cultural level of rural and poor families...

Repeated failure in end-of-stage examinations, primary or preparatory, is a major reason for leaving school or for dropping out."

Negative aspects of the curricula in Egypt are identified as being:

"(a) Major curriculum orientation towards end-of-year exams;

(b) Most basic education curricula are non-functional and far removed from the life and environment of the child and do not contribute to the development of society;

(c) Rural and urban curricula are uniform and do not account for local environments."

(Egypt IR, paras. 238-9 and 247)

education and vocational training then they will be informed and guided as to what is available. Nonetheless, it is not something that should be taken for granted. Schools, communities and families may be fixed in narrow expectations about what children will do in their future lives or be poorly informed about changing opportunities and requirements in terms of vocations. Children can only develop their potential if a range of opportunities are available and they know how to obtain information about them.

"(e) Take measures to ensure regular attendance at schools and the reduction of drop-out rates"

The phenomenon of children dropping out of school is worldwide. Poverty may be the driving motivation in many societies – the child may need to work or the expense of education may be the disincentive. But even in developing countries, children drop out of school for other reasons, for example, because the curriculum is too dull, difficult or irrelevant; because the teaching is poor; because school discipline is over-punitive and disrespectful of dignity; because learning disabilities have not been identified and helped.

Subparagraph (e) is, therefore, extremely important because it extends the State's responsibilities beyond simply channelling sufficient resources into schools and passing laws compelling children to attend those schools – States must also take steps to ensure that what happens in school is sufficiently useful and attractive to keep children there.

The Committee has taken a keen interest in States' implementation of this obligation, not least because the children with the highest rates of school drop-out tend to come from the groups generally discriminated against in education – namely girls, children from rural areas, children from minority groups, children in difficult circumstances and children with disabilities. The Committee has encouraged countries to give priority to a variety of measures combating school drop-out, including comprehensive policy reviews – for example recommending that Germany initiate an analysis of child poverty:

"Such an analysis should be undertaken from a holistic perspective, taking into account the possible linkages between such matters as... support in school, and the risk of dropping out of school." (Germany IRCO, Add.43, para. 31)

Measures to combat school drop-out rates include recognizing the financial circumstances of the children. For example the Committee commented to Honduras in relation to its "high incidence of school drop out":

"...In this regard, the Committee takes note of the suggestion of the Government which has not yet been implemented to organize the school year around the agricultural seasons with a view to organizing school vacations at sowing and harvesting periods. Equally, the Committee would like to suggest that the State Party give consideration to the provision of meals and to complement the provision of health care through the schools." (Honduras IRCO, Add.24, para. 31)

Guatemala was encouraged to:

"...implement the 'Food for Education Programme' as an incentive for children to attend school."
(Guatemala IRCO, Add.58, para. 36)

The Committee agreed with Egypt's analysis (see box on previous page):

"The quality of education in schools also gives cause for concern and may be an explanation for high drop-out rates; the problem relates to pedagogical methods, curricula and the lack of adequate educational material."
(Egypt IRCO, Add.5, para. 10)

The Committee has suggested improvements to schooling to reduce drop-out rates, especially to the "appropriateness" of education:

"...greater efforts should be directed to developing low-cost but effective strategies to increase substantially the enrolment and appropriateness of education. The introduction of such measures would assist in further signalling the commitment which exists to attracting children to attend school as well as to convincing families of the value of education." (Nicaragua IRCO, Add.36, para. 38)

"...it is also suggested that an adequate adjustment of the contents of school curricula so as to incorporate vocational education, in

the light of article 28 of the Convention, might contribute to reducing the drop-out rate and prevent the entry of children into the illegal labour market or even their involvement in criminal activities." (Italy IRCO, Add.41, para. 21)

Making school more attractive is often seen in terms of better vocational education (for example, see Philippines IRCO, Add.29, para. 15, and Slovenia IRCO, Add.65, paras. 15 and 23). The Committee "notes with interest" Namibia's proposed initiative to establish more vocational training centres under a Vocational Training Bill. The Namibian Government also proposed making general secondary education more vocational: "the new junior secondary curriculum which is being introduced will include required courses from the domestic, commercial, agricultural, art or technical fields as a way to introduce students to vocational topics at this level." (Namibia IRCO, Add.14, para. 4; IR, para. 371)

Where high drop out rates are found within minority groups, solutions may need to be found through, for example, providing bilingual education for those who do not speak the majority language, or other strategies such as those adopted in Saskatchewan (see box) or the programme of mobile schools for children of nomads in Mongolia (Mongolia SR.265, para. 41). Respect for minority and indigenous cultures and languages also encourages pupils' self-esteem and thus their motivation.

As discussed above, girls often drop out of school for discriminatory reasons. The Committee has also noted the negative effect on education of teenage pregnancy:

"The Committee is concerned about the high rate of early pregnancy, which has negative effects on the health of the mothers and the babies, and on the mothers' enjoyment of their right to education, hampering the school attendance of the girls concerned and causing high numbers of school drop-outs...
"With regard to the high rate of early pregnancy prevailing in Uruguay, the Committee recommends that measures be adopted to provide appropriate family education and services for young people within the school and health programmes implemented in the country." (Uruguay IRCO, Add.62. paras. 12 and 22)

The Committee also identified the active participation of children in their schooling as a strategy to reduce high drop-out rates:

"...further steps should be taken to develop guidelines for the participation of all children in the life of the school." (Nigeria IRCO, Add.61, para. 38. See also Argentina IRCO, Add.35, para. 21; Sri Lanka IRCO, Add.40, paras. 15 and 31)

Implementation Handbook for the Convention on the Rights of the Child

As discussed under article 12 (page 159) the consideration of children's views on their education is, in any event, an obligation under the Convention, but it is also an effective method of reducing pupil disaffection.

The right to school discipline "consistent with the child's human dignity and in conformity with the present Convention"

Paragraph (2) of article 28 does not have precedent in other treaties relating to education, although of course there are provisions preventing degrading and inhuman treatment generally – principally in article 7 of the International Covenant on Civil and Political Rights: "No one shall be subjected to torture or to cruel, inhuman or degrading treatment or punishment."

The Human Rights Committee states in a General Comment: "The prohibition in article 7 relates not only to acts that cause physical pain but also to acts that cause mental suffering to the victim. In the Committee's view, moreover, the prohibition must extend to corporal punishment, including excessive chastisement ordered as punishment for a crime or as an educative or disciplinary measure. It is appropriate to emphasize in this regard that article 7 protects, in particular, children, pupils and patients in teaching and medical institutions." (Human Rights Committee, General Comment 20, HRI/GEN/I/Rev.2, p. 31)

In July 1995, for example, in comments on the fourth periodic report from the United Kingdom, the Human Rights Committee expressed concern at the continued legality of corporal punishment for some pupils in United Kingdom private schools, and formally recommended that abolition should be extended to cover all pupils (CCPR/C/79/Add.55, 27 July 1995).

The Committee on the Rights of the Child has made clear that all forms of corporal punishment, whether excessive or not, are unacceptable forms of discipline in schools or elsewhere (see discussion under article 19, page 242). The phrase in article 28 that discipline must be "in conformity with the present Convention" underlines the fact that the obligation in article 19 to protect the child from "all forms of physical or mental violence, injury or abuse" applies to schools and other educational establishments as well as the family home and child care institutions.

In addition, among the agreed aims of education under article 29 are respect for others and education "in the spirit of understanding, peace, toler-

Lowering school drop-out rates

In Saskatchewan, Canada, aboriginal students have had "tragically high" drop-out rates. "Studies in the 1980s showed close to 90 per cent were not completing grade 12. Concern about the drop-out rate was the driving force behind Education Equity, an affirmative action programme, unique to Saskatchewan, for Aboriginal students in elementary and high schools". Initiated by the Human Rights Commission, the programme includes recruiting more Aboriginal teachers, involving parents, adding culturally meaningful studies to the curriculum and providing cross-cultural training for teachers and other staff (Canada IR, paras. 582-583).

In Finland "Schools and other learning institutions have created student welfare teams with the task to intervene and to prevent further difficulties in the case of students who, for example, have problems which might lead to their leaving school without finishing. Another task for the teams is to develop cooperation between homes and the school, guidance for students and any other measures which help to create conditions conducive to successful studies." (Finland IR, para. 454)

ance, equality of sexes, and friendship among all peoples" (29(1)(d)). A member of the Committee commented to representatives from Chile:

"Repressive school discipline tended to undermine the purpose and intention of article 29, and in particular of paragraph 1(d). Teachers' associations might therefore usefully discuss article 28, paragraph 2, which the Committee interpreted to mean the use of non-violent measures. It did not believe that beating was consistent with the human dignity of the pupil or with the Convention." (Chile SR.148, para. 24)

Countries that do not ensure that corporal punishment is banned in all schools are thus likely to have the matter raised by the Committee. For example in Canada:

"Further measures seem to be needed to effectively prevent and combat all forms of corporal punishment and ill-treatment of children in schools or in institutions where children may be placed ... The Committee suggests that the State Party examine the possibility of reviewing the penal legislation allowing corporal punishment of children by parents, in schools and in institutions where

Positive school discipline in Namibia

The Namibian Educational Code of Conduct forbids corporal punishment, and protects students from verbal abuse and unjust or excessive punishment. Serious or repeated violations of school rules are dealt with by a democratically elected school board comprising parent, teacher and student (at secondary school level) representatives. The board can issue warnings, transfers, suspensions and expulsions. The Ministry of Education supports "discipline from within" and emphasizes that threats, violence and abuse of others' rights or property will not be tolerated: "as the letter and spirit of the Constitution protects the rights of all persons – teachers, students and principals – to learn and teach in safety and dignity. However, this ideal is now being approached by inviting the participation of the entire school community in formulating rules and regulations which will have widespread support. The emphasis will be on cooperation and positive incentives, but where punishment is unavoidable, it must be specific, proportionate to the offence and understood by the offender." A Committee Member congratulated Namibia on this approach: "... she hoped that, by voicing their opinions, children themselves would help to change attitudes and to enforce the new legislation against corporal punishment." (Namibia IR, paras. 373-5 and SR.109, para. 45)

children may be placed." *(Canada IRCO, Add.37, paras. 14 and 25)*

Guatemala was recommended to adopt "a campaign against corporal punishment" in schools and elsewhere (Guatemala IRCO, Add.58, para. 32). Similar concerns were raised with Nigeria (Nigeria IRCO, Add.61, para. 18) and Sri Lanka (Sri Lanka IRCO, Add.40, para. 15). Zimbabwe was informed that:

"the Committee stresses the incompatibility of corporal punishment with the provisions of ... article ... 28 paragraph 2".

The Committee recommended Zimbabwe *"...adopt appropriate legislative measures to forbid the use of any form of corporal punishment within the family and in school."* *(Zimbabwe IRCO, Add.55, paras. 18 and 32)*

The prohibition of corporal punishment does not just relate to public state-funded schools – the practice must be banned in private schools as well. The Committee raised concerns that in the United Kingdom:

"privately funded and managed schools are permitted to administer corporal punishment to children in attendance there which does not appear to be compatible with the provisions of the Convention, including those of its article 28, paragraph 2".

The Committee recommended that legislation be introduced to ban its use in private schools, a Committee member commenting: "...the British authorities should pay more attention to the provisions of articles 28 and 37 of the Convention. The right not to receive corporal punishment was a fundamental right, and one could not therefore lay down a different regime according to whether the school was public or private, all the more so as that would give rise to the question of discrimination and the application of article 2 of the Con-

vention to the education system, since whether a child was sent to a State or private school was generally linked to the family's standard of living." (United Kingdom IRCO, Add.34, para. 16 and SR.206, para. 5)

Nor is it enough to legislate against corporal punishment – measures should be taken to make sure it does not occur even when against the law, as in Syria

"The Committee ... notes with concern that disciplinary measures in schools, although it is prohibited by law, often consist of corporal punishment." *(Syrian Arab Republic IRCO, Add.70, para. 17)*

There are also other aspects of school discipline not consistent with the child's human dignity, such as public humiliation. Nor should any form of discipline breach other rights under the Convention. For example, punishments that stop children's access to their parents or friends, that deny children rest or leisure or that interfere with their right to enjoy their language or culture would be in breach of rights under the Convention and of article 28(2). The Committee reminded the Holy See that:

"... teaching methods used in schools should reflect the spirit and philosophy of the Convention." *(Holy See IRCO, Add.46, para. 12)*

Discipline should also take in the principles of article 12:

"The Committee also wishes to recommend that greater priority be accorded to the participation of children in school life, in the spirit of article 12 of the Convention, including in discussions about disciplinary measures ..." *(UK dependent territory: Hong Kong IRCO, Add.63, para. 32)*

Some countries have reported on positive rights in discipline systems, which respect children's other rights under the Convention – for example Belarus, which gives boarding pupils explicit rights to humane treatment, contact with families and their own privacy (Belarus IR, paras. 50 and 52); and Costa Rica, which provides school children with opportunities for participating in decisions relating to discipline, in line with Article 12 (Costa Rica IR, para. 90). Perhaps none has been as active on this issue as Namibia, which was congratulated by a Committee member for its approach (see box).

The promotion of international cooperation in education, particularly taking account of the needs of developing countries

Education has been shown to be one of the key components of development, both for individual children and for countries as a whole. Educational advances bring benefits to all, with positive correlations shown between educational progress and improvements to children's life chances, national economic performance, agricultural productivity and birth rates. Both UNICEF and UNESCO have invested extensive expertise, resources and energy in education: "Education requires a greater commitment than any other development activity because it is not a one-time injection but a continuous, labour-intensive process. It requires skilled, highly trained staff to dedicate year after year of patient toil. It requires quality curricula and plenty of books, slates and chalk. It requires buildings and benches." (*The Progress of Nations 1997*, UNICEF, p. 33)

A significant proportion of development aid should, therefore, be directed at assisting education programmes. In addition, countries should learn from each other how best to educate children, including the scientific know-how and modern teaching methods mentioned in paragraph (3). The *Manual on Human Rights Reporting,* 1997 advises that "programmes of international technical cooperation should therefore include in their agenda the training of teachers, their acquisition of modern pedagogic skills and the improvement of their competence. They may in fact play an instrumental role in fostering the role of education" (*Manual,* p. 465).

Implementation Checklist

article 28

● General measures of implementation

Have appropriate general measures of implementation been taken in relation to article 28, including

☐ identification and coordination of the responsible departments and agencies at all levels of government (article 28 is relevant to the **departments of education and labour**)?

☐ identification of relevant non-governmental organizations/civil society partners?

☐ a comprehensive review to ensure that all legislation, policy and practice is compatible with the article, for all children in all parts of the jurisdiction?

☐ adoption of a strategy to secure full implementation

    ☐ which includes where necessary the identification of goals and indicators of progress?

    ☐ which does not affect any provisions which are more conducive to the rights of the child?

    ☐ which recognizes other relevant international standards?

    ☐ which involves where necessary international cooperation?

(Such measures may be part of an overall governmental strategy for implementing the Convention as a whole).

☐ budgetary analysis and allocation of necessary resources?

☐ development of mechanisms for monitoring and evaluation?

☐ making the implications of article 28 widely known to adults and children?

☐ development of appropriate training and awareness-raising (in relation to article 28 likely to include the training of **teachers, education administrators and vocational guidance personnel**)?

● Specific issues in implementing article 28

☐ Do budget allocations aim for a progressive increase in education provision and a progressive development of the quality of education?

☐ Does education policy ensure progress towards maximum take-up of educational opportunities by all children (up to the age of 18)?

☐ Is there an established time-frame for achieving this policy?

☐ Has the State adopted mechanisms to measure the effectiveness of its education provision in terms of take-up and outcomes for all children within the jurisdiction?

How to use the checklists, *see page XVII*

Are active measures taken to ensure that all children have equal educational opportunities, including all

- ☐ girls?
- ☐ children from rural areas?
- ☐ children from minority cultures and indigenous groups?
- ☐ disabled children?
- ☐ sick, including hospitalized, children?
- ☐ immigrant and refugee children?
- ☐ children living away from their families?
- ☐ nomadic or gypsy children or children in temporary accommodation?
- ☐ children excluded from school?
- ☐ children in all forms of detention?
- ☐ Is primary education compulsory?
- ☐ Is primary education free to all children?
- ☐ Are all aspects of this education free (for example books, equipment or uniform (if any))?
- ☐ Are different forms of secondary education, including vocational and general education, available to every child?
- ☐ Are these free?
- ☐ If not, are measures being taken to develop the accessibility of secondary education to every child, for example by offering financial assistance to those in need?
- ☐ Are the legal ages for completion of compulsory education and admission to employment the same?
- ☐ Where this age is below 15, are steps being taken to raise this age?
- ☐ Is higher education accessible to all children on the basis of capacity?
- ☐ Is educational and vocational information and guidance made available and accessible to all children?
- ☐ What measures have been adopted to encourage school attendance and prevent school drop-out?

Do these measures take into account

- ☐ the child's home circumstances (such as a need to secure an income, to do domestic chores or to work at harvest time)?

- ☐ the appropriate geographical location of schools and their hours and times of opening?

- ☐ the relevance of the curriculum to the child's life and the provision of vocational education?

- ☐ the appropriateness of the curriculum to the child's intellectual development?

- ☐ the child's first language?

- ☐ any special needs of the child (such as disability, sickness or pregnancy)?

- ☐ respect for cultural or religious traditions and gender difference?

- ☐ respect for the child's views?

- ☐ respect for the child's dignity?

- ☐ identification of learning difficulties and help provided to avoid exam failure or forced repetition of grade years or classes?

- ☐ the need to involve the local community in the delivery of education and the need to involve schools in the life of the community?

- ☐ the effectiveness of teacher recruitment and training in preventing school disaffection?

☐ Have all appropriate measures been taken to ensure that all forms of school discipline are consistent with the child's human dignity?

☐ Is corporal punishment prohibited by law in all schools?

☐ Have all appropriate measures been taken to ensure that corporal punishment is never used?

Do all forms of school discipline conform with the Convention, including the child's right

- ☐ not to be discriminated against?

- ☐ to be treated in a manner consistent with his or her evolving capacities?

- ☐ to maintain direct contact with both parents on a regular basis (save where contrary to best interests)?

- ☐ to freedom of expression, thought, conscience and religion?

- ☐ to freedom of association (save where it is necessary to protect others)?

- ☐ to privacy?

- ☐ to protection from all forms of physical or mental violence, injury or abuse, neglect or negligent treatment, maltreatment or exploitation?

- ☐ to his or her identity, culture and language?

- ☐ to rest and leisure?

☐ to social inclusion and reintegration?

☐ Is an appropriate level of development aid sought for, or directed at, educational programmes?

Do programmes of international technical cooperation include

☐ teacher training methods?

☐ access to scientific and technical knowledge?

☐ the effective delivery of primary and secondary education?

Reminder : **The Convention is indivisible and its articles are interdependent. Article 28 should not be considered in isolation.**

Particular regard should be paid to:
The general principles

Article 2: all rights to be recognized for each child in jurisdiction without discrimination on any ground
Article 3(1): the best interests of the child to be a primary consideration in all actions concerning children
Article 6: right to life and maximum possible survival and development
Article 12: respect for the child's views in all matters affecting the child; opportunity to be heard in any judicial or administrative proceedings affecting the child

Closely related articles

Articles whose implementation is related to that of article 28 include:

Article 13: freedom of expression
Article 14: freedom of thought, conscience and religion
Article 15: freedom of association
Article 16: protection of privacy
Article 17: access to information and role of media
Article 19: protection from all forms of violence
Article 23: disabled children
Article 24: health (including health education)
Article 29: aims of education
Article 30: children of minorities or of indigenous peoples
Article 31: rest, leisure, play, recreation and culture
Article 32: child labour

The aims of education

Text of Article 29

1. States Parties agree that the education of the child shall be directed to:

(a) The development of the child's personality, talents and mental and physical abilities to their fullest potential;

(b) The development of respect for human rights and fundamental freedoms, and for the principles enshrined in the Charter of the United Nations;

(c) The development of respect for the child's parents, his or her own cultural identity, language and values, for the national values of the country in which the child is living, the country from which he or she may originate, and for civilizations different from his or her own;

(d) The preparation of the child for responsible life in a free society, in the spirit of understanding, peace, tolerance, equality of sexes, and friendship among all peoples, ethnic, national and religious groups and persons of indigenous origin;

(e) The development of respect for the natural environment.

2. No part of the present article or article 28 shall be construed so as to interfere with the liberty of individuals and bodies to establish and direct educational institutions, subject always to the observance of the principles set forth in paragraph 1 of the present article and to the requirements that the education given in such institutions shall conform to such minimum standards as may be laid down by the State.

A rticle 29 reflects a consensus of world opinion about the fundamental purposes of education. It does not detail the tools of learning (literacy, numeracy, factual knowledge, problem solving and so on) but addresses learning's basic aims: to develop children's full potential, to prepare children for "responsible life in a free society" and to enshrine the values of respect for all others and for the natural environment. The article also explicitly preserves the rights of individuals and groups to arrange their own

Summary

forms of education, so long as these fulfil the aims of education as set out in the article and any official minimum standards.

Article 26 of the Universal Declaration of Human Rights provides that: "Education shall be directed to the full development of the human personality and to the strengthening of respect for human rights and fundamental freedoms. It shall promote understanding, tolerance and friendship among all nations, racial or religious groups, and shall further the activities of the United Nations for the maintenance of peace."

Those words were adapted in the International Covenant on Economic, Social and Cultural Rights, with the italicized additions: "[States Parties] agree that education shall be directed to the full development of the human personality *and the sense of its dignity*, and shall strengthen the respect for human rights and fundamental freedoms. They further agree that *education shall enable all persons to participate effectively in a free society*, promote understanding, tolerance and friendship among all nations and all racial, *ethnic* or religious groups, and further the activ-

ities of the United Nations for the maintenance of peace" (article 13(1)).

The Convention on the Rights of the Child uses this international agreement as a starting point and significantly develops it, as discussed below. In early drafts, the aims of education were originally conceived as "the aims of education and upbringing" but this was discarded as too broad and ill-defined a concept. Several countries were concerned about the absence of explicit reference to parents' rights to choose their children's school and to ensure children's education is in conformity with the parents' religious and moral convictions, a principle set out in article 13(3) of the Covenant on Economic, Social and Cultural Rights and article 18(4) of the Covenant on Civil and Political Rights (E/CN.4/1985/64, pp.15-19; Detrick, p. 399; E/CN.4/1989/48, pp. 84-87; Detrick, pp. 405-407). As discussed in article 28 (see page 369) these rights are recognized elsewhere within the Convention (articles 5, 18 and 30) but operate within the framework of the child's own rights and freedoms. ∎

Extracts from
Committee on the Rights of the Child
Guidelines for Reports to be submitted by States Parties under the Convention

For full text of *Guidelines for Periodic Reports*, see Appendix 3, page 604.

Guidelines for Initial Reports

"Education, leisure and cultural activities

Under this section States Parties are requested to provide relevant information, including the principal legislative, judicial, administrative or other measures in force; the institutional infrastructure for implementing policy in this area, particularly monitoring strategies and mechanisms; and factors and difficulties encountered and progress achieved in implementing the relevant provisions of the Convention, in respect of:

(a) Aims of education (art. 29)...

... States Parties are requested to specify the nature and extent of cooperation with local and national organizations of a governmental or non-governmental nature, such as institutions of social workers, concerning the implementation of this area of the Convention. States Parties are encouraged to provide additional relevant statistical information and indicators relating to children covered in this section."

(CRC/C/5, paras. 21 and 22)

Guidelines for Periodic Reports

"VII. EDUCATION, LEISURE AND CULTURAL ACTIVITIES

B. Aims of education (art. 29)

Please indicate the legislative, administrative, educational and other measures adopted to ensure that the aims of education established in the State Party are consistent with the provisions of this article, in particular with regard to:

The development of respect for the child's personality, talents and mental and physical abilities to their fullest potential;

The development of respect for human rights and fundamental freedoms, and for the principles enshrined in the Charter of the United Nations, indicating whether the subject of human rights in general, and children's rights in particular, has been incorporated in the school curricula for all children and promoted in school life;

The development of respect for the child's parents, his or her own cultural identity, language and values, for the national values of the country in which the child is living, the country from which he or she originates and for civilizations different from his or her own;

The preparation of the child for responsible life in a free society, in the spirit of understanding, peace, tolerance, equality of the sexes, and friendship among all peoples, ethnic, national and religious groups and persons of indigenous origin;

The development of respect for the natural environment.

Reports should also indicate:

The training provided to teachers to prepare them to direct their teaching towards these aims;

The revision of school policies and school curricula to reflect the aims identified in article 29 at the various levels of education;

Relevant programmes and material used;

Any peer education and peer counselling promoted;

Efforts made to bring school organization in line with the Convention's principles, for example mechanisms created within schools to improve the participation of children in all decisions affecting their education and well-being.

Please indicate the measures adopted pursuant to article 29, paragraph 2, to ensure respect for the liberty of individuals and bodies to establish and direct educational institutions, subject always to the observance of the principles set forth in paragraph 1 of this article and to the requirements that the education given in such institutions conforms to such minimum standards as are laid down by the State.

Reports should also provide information on the appropriate mechanisms developed to:

Ascertain that the aims of education identified by the Convention are respected by such institutions;

Ensure respect for the general principles of the Convention, namely non-discrimination, the best interests of the child, respect for the views of the child and the right to life, survival and development to the maximum extent;

Ensure that all such institutions are conducted in conformity with standards established by competent authorities, particularly in the areas of safety, health, number and suitability of staff, as well as of competent supervision.

Reports should further provide information on the progress achieved in the implementation of this article, difficulties encountered and targets set for the future."

(CRC/C/58, paras. 112-116. The following paragraphs of the *Guidelines for Periodic Reports* are also relevant to reporting under this article: 22, 43, 44, 57, 60, 92, 95, 109, 111 and 156; for full text of *Guidelines*, see Appendix 3, page 604.)

International agreement on the aims of education

The governing phrase or *chapeau* of article 29(1) on the aims of education starts, uniquely: "States Parties agree...". Textually, this can, of course, be traced to the article's source in the International Covenant on Economic, Social and Cultural Rights, but it is significant that the phrase was retained for this Convention. The wording emphasizes that there is international consensus as to the aims of education which surmounts the often hostile boundaries of religion, nation and culture erected across so many parts of the world.

Three countries submitted reservations to article 29: Indonesia: "With reference to the provisions of

Charter of the United Nations

The text of the Preamble and Chapter 1, dealing with Purposes and Principles, of the United Nations Charter reads as follows:

Preamble:

WE THE PEOPLES OF THE UNITED NATIONS DETERMINED

• to save succeeding generations from the scourge of war, which twice in our lifetime has brought untold sorrow to mankind, and

• to reaffirm faith in fundamental human rights, in the dignity and worth of the human person, in the equal rights of men and women and of nations large and small, and

• to establish conditions under which justice and respect for the obligations arising from treaties and other sources of international law can be maintained, and

• to promote social progress and better standards of life in larger freedom,

AND FOR THESE ENDS

• to practice tolerance and live together in peace with one another as good neighbours, and

• to unite our strength to maintain international peace and security, and

• to ensure, by the acceptance of principles and the institution of methods, that armed force shall not be used, save in the common interest, and

• to employ international machinery for the promotion of the economic and social advancement of all peoples,

HAVE RESOLVED TO COMBINE OUR EFFORTS TO ACCOMPLISH THESE AIMS

Accordingly, our respective Governments, through representatives assembled in the city of San Francisco, who have exhibited their full powers found to be in good and due form, have agreed to the present Charter of the United Nations and do hereby establish an international organization to be known as the United Nations.

Chapter 1

PURPOSES AND PRINCIPLES

Article 1

The purposes of the United Nations are:

1. To maintain international peace and security, and to that end: to take effective collective measures for the prevention and removal of threats to the peace, and for the suppression of acts of aggression or other breaches of the peace, and to bring about by peaceful means, and in conformity with the principles of justice and international law, adjustment or settlement of international disputes or situations which might lead to a breach of the peace;

2. To develop friendly relations among nations based on respect for the principle of equal rights and self-determination of peoples, and to take other appropriate measures to strengthen universal peace;

3. To achieve international cooperation in solving international problems of an economic, social, cultural, or humanitarian character, and in promoting and encouraging respect for human rights and for fundamental freedoms for all without distinction as to race, sex, language, or religion; and

4. To be a centre for harmonizing the actions of nations in the attainment of these common ends...

Article 2

The Organization and its Members, in pursuit of the Purposes stated in Article 1, shall act in accordance with the following Principles.

1. The Organization is based on the principle of the sovereign equality of all its Members.

2. All Members, in order to ensure to all of them the rights and benefits resulting from membership, shall fulfil in good faith the obligations assumed by them in accordance with the present Charter.

3. All Members shall settle their international disputes by peaceful means in such a manner that international peace and security, and justice, are not endangered.

4. All Members shall refrain in their international relations from the threat or use of force against the territorial integrity or political independence of any state, or in any other manner inconsistent with the Purposes of the United Nations.

5. All Members shall give the United Nations every assistance in any action it takes in accordance with the present Charter, and shall refrain from giving assistance to any state against which the United Nations is taking preventive or enforcement action.

6. The Organization shall ensure that states which are not Members of the United Nations act in accordance with these Principles so far as may be necessary for the maintenance of international peace and security.

7. Nothing contained in the present Charter shall authorize the United Nations to intervene in matters which are essentially within the domestic jurisdiction of any state or shall require the Members to submit such matters to settlement under the present Charter; but this principle shall not prejudice the application of enforcement measures under Chapter VII.

(Charter of the United Nations, June 26, 1945)

articles... 29... the Government of the Republic of Indonesia declares that it will apply these articles in conformity with its Constitution" (CRC/C/2/Rev.5, p. 21). When Indonesia was asked to explain this reservation to the Committee, the government representative said that there were difficulties in implementing the article in view of existing legislation (Indonesia applies a national curriculum), but that it was hoped the Reservation could be withdrawn with new legislation currently in draft, which Indonesia subsequently did (Indonesia SR.79, para. 36; Indonesia IRCO, Add.25, para. 5).

Turkey: "The Republic of Turkey reserves the right to interpret and to apply the provisions of articles 17, 29 and 30 of the Convention on the Rights of the Child according to the letter and spirit of the Constitution of the Republic of Turkey and of the Treaty of Lausanne of 24 July 1923" (CRC/C/2/Rev.5, p. 33). Turkey has yet to report to the Committee so this reservation still awaits explanation (September 1997, but see article 30, page 410).

Thailand: "The application of articles 7, 22 and 29 of the Convention on the Rights of the Child shall be subject to the national laws, regulations and prevailing practices in Thailand" (CRC/C/2/Rev.5, p. 32). Thailand has also not yet reported.

In addition, a great many Islamic countries have submitted general reservations to the whole of the Convention along the lines of Iran's: "In signing this Convention the Islamic Republic of Iran is making reservation to the articles and provisions which may be contrary to the Islamic Shariah, and reserves the right to make such particular declaration, upon its ratification" (CRC/C/2/Rev.5, p. 22).

There are also those countries that have entered reservations to article 14, concerning the child's right to "freedom of thought, conscience and religion", which may be exercised under the direction of parents in a manner consistent with the child's evolving capacities – Algeria, Bangladesh, Belgium, Brunei Darussalam, Holy See, Indonesia,

Jordan, Kiribati, Malaysia, Maldives, Morocco, Netherlands, Poland, Singapore and the Syrian Arab Republic. Some (for example Belgium and the Netherlands) are concerned with putting emphasis on the child's rights, but others are concerned with either parental authority to determine the child's religious upbringing and education or with the fact that a State religion governs the education curriculum (see article 14, page 177).

However, none of these reservations necessarily leads to a breach of the principles of article 29, which in its drafting reflected agreement by countries practising all the main world religions.

"The development of the child's personality, talents and mental and physical abilities to their fullest potential"

The degree to which the education systems of States develop all children's potential depends in part upon the access and availability of education to all children on the basis of equality of opportunity, discussed under article 28 (see page 375) and the degree to which it inspires and motivates the individual child (see also article 28, in relation to school drop-out, page 381). It also vitally concerns the adequacy of special educational provision for children with disabilities and learning difficulties, discussed under article 23 (see page 306).

Article 6 requires States Parties to "ensure to the maximum extent possible the ... development of the child." Article 29(1)(a) expands on the role of education, taking it beyond just the development of children's mental abilities, traditionally perceived as the responsibility of schools. Education should also embrace children's "talents", including talents in the creative and performing arts, crafts, sports and vocational skills; their "physical abilities", ranging from basic motor coordination skills to physical activities such as swimming, gymnastics, bicycling and ball-control; and development of their "personality". This is perhaps the greatest challenge to schools and educators. How does one teach children to be kind and generous, for example, as well as literate and numerate?

Not surprisingly, the Committee has rarely been able to examine how countries fulfil these aims of education, except in terms of statistical measures such as how many children are enrolled in schools, drop out or repeat classes. The Committee has now requested States to give disaggregated information on "education outcomes" for their Periodic Reports which may produce interesting results. Current international research on comparable standards in, for example, mathematics or science shows striking variations which do not correspond to the countries' wealth or economic investment in education. Similar comparisons could be sought on the less academic aspects of education, for example the values endorsed by article 29.

A Committee member commented to Hong Kong (UK dependent territory) government representatives: "...it was difficult to reconcile quality and quantity in education ... It was inadvisable to place excessive emphasis on a type of teaching that focused primarily on accumulation of knowledge, prompting fierce competition and leading to an excessive burden of work on children, with the result that failure to pass school examinations become a tragedy. What measures were taken to foster a more human atmosphere in the school system and to allow children to develop at their own pace?" (UK dependent territory: Hong Kong SR.330, para. 46)

And the Committee raised its concern with the Republic of Korea:

"at the insufficient consideration given in the education system to the aims of education as reflected in article 29 of the Convention. The highly competitive nature of the education system risks hampering the development of the child to the fullest potential of his or her abilities and talents and the child's preparation for responsible life in a free society." (Republic of Korea IRCO Add.51 para 16)

Such a concern could be legitimately raised in relation to a number of other countries, with educational institutions and curricula narrowly focused on academic exam success, achievable by a few at the expense of many, and without concern for the aims set out in article 29.

"The development of respect for human rights and fundamental freedoms, and for

the principles enshrined in the Charter of the United Nations"

The second aim of education under subparagraph (b) includes, alongside human rights and fundamental freedoms, "the principles enshrined in the Charter of the United Nations" (see box).

The United Nations Decade for Human Rights Education, 1995-2004, was established under General Assembly Resolutions 48/127, 49/184 and 50/177. Governments and non-governmental educational agencies are being urged to establish programmes of human rights education. Human rights include rights under the Convention on the Rights of the Child and those of the general declarations and covenants, as well as those focusing on the human rights of specific population groups, such as disabled people, women and ethnic minorities. All include children in their scope.

In 1995, the United Nations Educational, Scientific and Cultural Organization (UNESCO) endorsed a Declaration and Integrated Framework of Action on Education for Peace, Human Rights and Democracy (see box opposite). The Framework sets out policies, objectives and action strategies to combat discrimination, violence and xenophobia, and to develop students' self-esteem, stressing the last as "essential to social integration...The reduction of failure must be a priority" (*Declaration and Integrated Framework of Action on Education for Peace, Human Rights and Democracy,* UNESCO 1995, para. 22).

The Committee has particularly focused its attention on whether educational curricula include the teaching of the Convention on the Rights of the Child, for example expressing the view to Hong Kong that:

"Insufficient attention appears to have been given to ... according human rights education the necessary status within the school curricula ... "The Committee recommends the incorporation of human rights education, including education about the Convention on the Rights of the Child, as a core curriculum subject in all schools. The Committee notes that this would require that sufficient time be allocated to this subject in the school timetable. The Committee also wishes to suggest that an evaluation of human rights awareness raising and education be undertaken in the future to determine its effectiveness in equipping children with tools for life and encouraging their decision-making and ability to think analytically from the perspective of human rights." (UK dependent territory: Hong Kong IRCO, Add.63, paras. 17 and 32)

A great many countries coming before the Committee have been recommended to include children's rights under the Convention in their school curricula – Belgium, Colombia, Finland, Guatemala, the Holy See (in relation to Catholic schools), Iceland, Italy, Nicaragua, Republic of Korea, Lebanon, Nigeria, Norway, Portugal, Ukraine, United Kingdom and Yemen among them. The Committee has argued that the General Assembly resolutions 48/127 and 49/184 (United Nations Decade for Human Rights Education) provide the momentum for taking this action, together with article 42 of the Convention, which requires States to "make the principles and provisions of the Convention widely known, by appropriate and active means, to adults and children alike".

Inclusion of the Convention in curricula means that knowledge of rights is a continuous process for succeeding generations of children, not just a once-only dissemination triggered by article 42, as the Committee noted to Iceland:

"While noting the steps taken to disseminate the text of the Convention among students at all school levels, the Committee notes that the inclusion of human rights in general, and of children's rights in particular, as a subject in schools and universities is still pending." (Iceland IRCO, Add.50, para. 17)

"Education" goes beyond school curricula, too, as the Committee suggested to Portugal:

"In the framework of the United Nations Decade for Human Rights Education the Committee recommends that the State Party

Education for Peace, Human Rights and Democracy

At the International Conference on Education in 1994, the following Objectives were adopted in a Declaration of the International Conference on Education for Peace, Human Rights and Democracy (endorsed by UNESCO in the following year):

"We, the Ministers of Education meeting at the 44th session of the International Conference on Education...

Strive resolutely:

• to base education on principles and methods that contribute to the development of the personality of pupils, students and adults who are respectful of their fellow human beings and determined to promote peace, human rights and democracy;

• to take suitable steps to establish in educational institutions an atmosphere contributing to the success of education for international understanding, so that they become ideal places for the exercise of tolerance, respect for human rights, the practice of democracy and learning about the diversity and wealth of cultural identities;

• to take action to eliminate all direct and indirect discrimination against girls and women in education systems and to take specific measures to ensure that they achieve their full potential;

• to pay special attention to improving curricula, the content of textbooks, and other educational materials including new technologies, with a view to educating caring and responsible citizens, open to other cultures, able to appreciate the value of freedom, respectful of human dignity and differences, and able to prevent conflicts or resolve them by non-violent means;

• to adopt measures to enhance the role and status of educators in formal and non-formal education and to give priority to pre-service and in-service training as well as the retraining of educational personnel, including planners and managers, oriented notably towards professional ethics, civic and moral education, cultural diversity, national codes and internationally recognized standards of human rights and fundamental freedoms;

• to encourage the development of innovative strategies adapted to the new challenges of educating responsible citizens committed to peace, human rights, democracy and sustainable development, and to apply appropriate measures of evaluation and assessment of these strategies;

• to prepare, as quickly as possible and taking into account the constitutional structures of each State, programmes of action for the implementation of this Declaration."

(*Declaration and Integrated Framework of Action on Education for Peace, Human Rights and Democracy*, article 2, 44th session of the International Conference on Education (Geneva 1994), endorsed by the General Conference of UNESCO at its 28th session (Paris 1995))

Education on children's rights in Argentina

The Argentine Ministry of Culture and Education has implemented the National Programme for the Educational Rights of the Child, the goal of which is the "training of educators and elaboration of educational strategies designed to help children and young people obtain knowledge, exercise the rights to which they are entitled and fulfil the responsibilities incumbent upon them". The Programme includes setting up a network of "Schools for the Rights of the Child" based on a "participation model" and teacher-training in basic concepts of human rights (Argentina IR, para. 18).

launch a permanent information campaign, both for children and adults, on the Convention." (Portugal IRCO, Add.45, para. 20)

The school curriculum is not the only way in which values are transmitted in education. The aim is not simply to teach children "human rights", in terms of the content of human rights treaties, the aim is "the development of respect for human rights". There is a hidden curriculum in the messages transmitted by the way pupils and teachers behave towards each other. Children cannot be taught respect for rights unless members of the school community practise what is preached. The administrative systems, behaviour codes and teaching methods of schools should, therefore, also reflect the principles of the Convention; children's attitudes and behaviour in the school should be appraised as carefully outside the classroom as in it.

"The development of respect for the child's parents..."

Little comment has been passed on this particular right. Allegations are sometimes made that the Convention does not support parents' rights and that it encourages children to be disrespectful of parents, so it may be useful to draw this right to the attention of those who are sceptical or suspicious of the Convention.

Children should, of course, be taught to respect everyone, including other children. Throughout history, all cultures have asserted that children are disrespectful of their parents, which is perhaps why parents are accorded special mention here. It is also true that teachers can sometimes be dismissive or scornful of parents, particularly if the parents are poorly educated or come from a minority culture. Children's identity is inevitably closely bound up with their parents', and an education which is disrespectful about pupils' parents is likely to be damaging to the children's own self-esteem.

"The development of respect for the child's ... own cultural identity, language and values, for the national values of the country in which the child is living, the country from which he or she may originate and for civilizations different from his or her own"

Many education systems actively promote patriotism in school children, sometimes at the expense of inculcating respect for different cultures, particularly minority and indigenous cultures living within the country. Occasionally, concern is expressed in some countries that teaching respect for national values has been abandoned as old-fashioned. The importance of the wording of this subparagraph is that equal weight is given to the value systems both of the ratifying State and of other States or cultures, with a particular focus on school children who are immigrants or of a minority culture. It should be noted that the word "respect" implies more than just tolerance and understanding. It means acknowledging the equal worth of peoples of all cultures, without condescension.

Education on values should permeate the whole of schooling, as the Committee commented to Lebanon:

"...the teaching of values is an important dimension that should be incorporated in the curricula at all levels of schooling. School curricula materials should be revised accordingly." (Lebanon IRCO, Add.54, para. 33)

The following subparagraph sets out some of the principles underlying the teaching of values: "the spirit of understanding, peace, tolerance ... and friendship among all peoples, ethnic, national and religious groups and persons of indigenous origin". Article 30 also protects the rights of minorities and indigenous peoples "to enjoy his or her own culture, to profess and practise his or her own religion, or to use his or her own language" (see page 407).

"The preparation of the child for responsible life in a free society..."

This is a vital aim of education, in that it emphasizes the importance of teaching the less "academic" subjects such as health and sex education, politics, budgeting, citizenship and social relationships. The Committee shared the concern of Ethiopia that

"the school curricula are divorced from cultural and social realities." (Ethiopia IRCO, Add.67, para.17)

Mauritius was urged to include sex education in its school curricula (Mauritius IRCO, Add.64, para. 29) and Lebanon was advised that in relation to school curricula

"Specific needs appear to exist in the fields of health education..." (Lebanon IRCO, Add.54, para. 18)

The Committee expressed concern to the United Kingdom about the fact that:

"...parents in England and Wales have the possibility of withdrawing their children from parts of the sex education programmes in schools".

commenting that this gave insufficient attention to the child's own rights to have his or her opinions given due weight under article 12 (UK IRCO, Add.34, para. 14). In discussions with El Salvador, a Committee member commented: "As far as sex education was concerned, while welcoming the fact that some sex education was provided, the Committee found it regrettable that girls could not take the initiative and request the necessary information." (El Salvador SR.86, para. 61)

As discussed under article 12 (page 145), "responsible life in a free society...", implies the teaching of social responsibility and active participation in the processes of democracy. This is not easily taught to children if it is not practised at the same time. As a committee member commented to representatives from China: "... the Convention's advocacy of the right of children to participate in all aspects of society and express their views demanded not just that children should be trained to act in such a way, but that adults and professionals working with children should be trained to develop participatory attitudes in children" (China SR.299, para. 33).

The *Manual on Human Rights Reporting*, 1997 calls for: "the establishment of mechanisms where children can experience and enhance their capacity for participation – either through an ongoing process of consultation and exchange within family life, by intervening in schools councils for matters relating to their education, or by influencing life at the community level through their participation in local councils" (*Manual*, p.428).

Health education: Recommendations of the International Conference on Population and Development

"Youth should be actively involved in the planning, implementation and evaluation of development activities that have a direct impact on their daily lives. This is especially important with respect to information, education and communication activities and services concerning reproductive and sexual health, including the prevention of early pregnancies, sex education and the prevention of HIV/AIDS and other sexually transmitted diseases. Access to, as well as confidentiality and privacy of, these services must be ensured with the support and guidance of their parents and in line with the Convention on the Rights of the Child. In addition, there is a need for educational programmes in favour of life planning skills, healthy lifestyles and the active discouragement of substance abuse ...

"To be most effective, education about population issues must begin in primary school and continue through all levels of formal and non-formal education, taking into account the rights and responsibilities of parents and the needs of children and adolescents. Where such programmes already exist, curricula should be reviewed, updated and broadened with a view to ensuring adequate coverage of such important concerns as gender sensitivity, reproductive choices and responsibilities, and sexually transmitted diseases, including HIV/AIDS ..."

(International Conference on Population and Development, Cairo, 1994, A/CONF/171/13, paras. 6.15 and 11.9)

The Committee suggested to France that:

"further consideration be given to ways of encouraging the expression of views by children and those views being given due weight in the decision-making processes affecting their lives, in particular within school and the local community" (France IRCO, Add.20, para. 23).

"...in the spirit of understanding ... tolerance... and friendship among all peoples, ethnic, national and religious groups and persons of indigenous origin"

Practising democracy in Spanish schools

In Spain, the Fundamental Act on the Right to Education stipulates that it is one purpose of pupils' associations: "... to express the pupils' views on everything affecting their situation in the schools". The Fundamental Law on the Organization of the Educational System lays down as principles of that system: "the development of the spirit of criticism" and "the encouragement of habits of democratic behaviour." (Spain IR, para. 117)

Confronted with countries scarred by civil conflicts and racial tensions, and with the rise in xenophobic and racist attitudes in some industrialized countries, the Committee has urged States Parties to take action under this provision. For example:

"The Committee would also like to suggest that measures to teach about children's and human rights could be used as a tool to advocate further the purposes of the European Youth Campaign, and the parallel Nordic campaign to combat racism, xenophobia, anti-Semitism and intolerance. It is also the view of the Committee that it is equally important that the teaching methods used in schools should reflect the spirit and philosophy of the Convention and the aims of education laid down in its article 29." (Denmark IRCO, Add.33, para. 29)

"It is the view of the Committee that the principle contained in article 29(1)(d) which stipulates that 'the preparation of the child for responsible life in a free society, in the spirit of understanding, peace, tolerance, equality of sexes, and friendship among all peoples, ethnic, national and religious groups and persons of indigenous origin' is an important dimension that should be integrated into curricula at all levels of schooling. School curricula materials should be developed, if they do not already exist, which aim at educating children in the spirit of tolerance of and regard for different civilizations." (Federal Republic of Yugoslavia IRCO, Add.49, para. 30)

"The Committee recommends that ... the State Party incorporate education on the rights of the child in the school curricula, paying special attention to promoting tolerance among all peoples and groups. The State Party may wish to consider requesting further international cooperation for the implementation of the measures identified for the application of the provisions of articles 28 and 29 of the Convention." (Nigeria IRCO, Add.61, para. 38. See also Croatia IRCO, Add.52, para. 19 and Guatemala IRCO, Add.58, para. 30)

"... in the spirit of ... equality of sexes"

As discussed under article 28, there is global concern about discrimination against girls in terms of access to schooling and high drop-out rates (see also article 2, page 27). The causes of this phenomenon mostly relate to social and family demands on girl children, but school life and curricula can also act as a disincentive. Once in school, it is important that the curriculum be as relevant to female life as to male life; that girls are encouraged in traditionally "male" subjects of maths, science, engineering and computing; that schools do not act in a sexist or discriminatory manner; and that the particular needs of girls are met.

The Committee's General Discussion on the girl child concluded that, as regards strategies for encouraging gender equality:

"Education was of essential importance. It allows for the harmonious and informed development of children, and gives them the necessary confidence and skills to make free choices in their lives and to act in a context of gender partnership – both at the professional and at the family level." (Report on the eighth session, January 1995, CRC/C/38, p. 50)

As the *Platform for Action* of the 1995 Beijing Fourth World Conference on Women observes: "Gender-biased educational processes, including curricula, educational materials and practices, teachers' attitudes and classroom interaction, reinforce existing gender inequalities" (para. 261). Strategic actions recommended for government include: "Develop and adopt curricula, teaching materials and textbooks to improve the self-image, lives and work opportunities of girls, particularly in areas where women have traditionally been underrepresented, such as mathematics, science and technology ...

"Encourage educational institutions and the media to adopt and project balanced and non-stereotyped images of girls and boys ...

"Promote human rights education in educational programmes and include in human rights education the fact that the human rights of women and the girl child are an inalienable, integral and indivisible part of universal human rights ...

"Develop training programmes and materials for teachers and educators, raising awareness about their own role in the educational process, with a view to providing them with effective strategies for gender-sensitive teaching ...

"Provide education and skills training to increase girls' opportunity for employment and access to decision-making processes ...

Combating sex discrimination in German schools

The German Commission for Educational Planning and the Promotion of Research of the Federation and the Lander is now focusing on comprehensive measures to eliminate sex discrimination mechanisms and outright or latent violence against girls in schools. Measures include the recognition and alteration of sexually discriminatory forms of interaction on the part of teachers; elimination of restrictive or discriminatory traditional roles in subject matter, teaching methods and teaching materials; greater acknowledgement of girls' interests, orientations and ways of learning in subject matter and teaching methods; promotion of greater self-confidence and self-determination on the part of girls; encouragement of a wider range of interests on the part of boys, especially in regard to a dual orientation toward professional work and housework. These measures are directed at teachers and parents, as well as towards boys and girls.
(Germany IR, para. 219)

"Provide education to increase girls' knowledge and skills related to the functioning of economic, financial and political systems ...

"Promote the full and equal participation of girls in extracurricular activities, such as sports, drama and cultural activities..." (Platform for Action, paras. 276-277 and 279-280)

A Committee member asked, in relation to Nicaragua's problems with discrimination "whether Nicaragua intended to make use of the school curriculum in order to change children's attitudes. Discrimination occurred as a result of the existence of different cultures, customs and attitudes. The school curriculum was a very effective means of tackling that problem." (Nicaragua SR.212, para. 58)

The Committee has recommended that:
"Measures should be taken to prevent a rise in discriminatory attitudes or prejudice towards girl children and children belonging to minority groups ... It recommends that comprehensive studies be initiated on these important issues to provide better understanding of these phenomena and facilitate the elaboration of policies and programmes to combat them effectively." (Mauritius IRCO, Add.64, para. 29)

"The Committee recommends that the inclusion of children's rights in the school curricula be pursued as a measure to ... combat paternalistic and discriminatory attitudes which, as recognized by the State party, continue to prevail in society." (Guatemala IRCO, Add.58, para. 30)

"in the spirit of ... peace"

An education delivered in the spirit of peace clearly supports the principle of non-violent methods of school discipline, as discussed under articles 19 and 28 (pages 242 and 383). Chile, for example, in 1992 established a Commission known as the School for Peace, which examined violence and ill-treatment in schools (Chile SR.146, para. 21). Education also plays a part in the objectives of articles 38 and 39, on armed conflict and rehabilitation of child victims (see pages 511 and 529).

Children are often violent towards each other, and States are just beginning to wake up to their obligations to identify and prevent bullying in schools. The United Kingdom, for example, was commended by the Committee for its anti-bullying initiatives (UK IRCO, Add.34, para. 4). Educating children in non-violence includes teaching specific skills in conflict resolution. Ontario, Canada, has introduced a "Self and Society" programme, making teachers responsible for ensuring students are able to resolve conflicts in a cooperative and non-violent manner (Canada IR, para. 818).

The Report of the Committee's General Discussion on children and armed conflict includes the following:
"General measures designed to prevent the occurrence of conflicts were discussed. Emphasis was put on the role which education can play:

(a) Education in a spirit of understanding, solidarity and peace, as reflected in article 29 of the Convention on the Rights of the Child;

(b) Education and training for the military and for groups working with and for children;

(c) Education and dissemination of information specifically for children.

Attention was also drawn to the need for creating awareness of the political grounds for the existence of conflicts; such an attitude may contribute to the consideration of solutions of mediation or conciliation designed to prevent the conflict or attenuate its effects" (Report on the second session, October 1992, CRC/C/10, para. 70).

Education to develop respect for the natural environment – examples from Chile, Namibia and Ethiopia

Chile reported that it has introduced a "national permanent environmental education programme" that aims to instil in children an awareness of and a change in attitudes towards the natural and socio-cultural environment. The programme uses training courses, publication of environmental education modules and 13 regional permanent working committees on environmental education. A "Green Network" project is planned, aiming to set up a system for the promotion, communication and coordination of environmental activities among young people from 50 secondary education schools through ecological trips; the training of 300 monitors; and the publication of simple books, posters and pamphlets. Events relating to the environment have been held, such as International Earth Day, the Month of the Sea and a national competition for "Green Action" student centres (Chile IR, para. 205).

Namibia reported that it "is in the process of implementing an innovative approach to environmental education for children. The Etosha Nature School in Etosha Game Park recently opened its doors to groups of schoolchildren for the first time. This school, which is administered by the Ministry of Wildlife, Conservation and Tourism in cooperation with the Ministry of Education and Culture, offers open air classes in ecological subjects for students from schools in the surrounding area, who can come for short field trips during school terms or for longer periods during school holidays. This nature school will ultimately be part of a network of similar schools scattered throughout the country, in order to draw on Namibia's diverse ecosystems. The life science subjects taught in the normal schools are also in the process of being redesigned to place more emphasis on ecology and environmental concerns." (Namibia IR, para. 385)

Ethiopia reported "... environmental education is carried out in selected educational institutions (basic development education centres, community skills training centres, primary and secondary schools), with Teacher Training Institutes as focal points. The general objective of EEP [the Environmental Education Project] is mainly to promote better understanding of the relationship between man and nature, promote widespread action in the protection and regeneration of the environment and ensure the relevance of education in resolving community problems like environmental degradation by taking and enhancing timely action. In the long run it is believed that EE [Environmental Education] will contribute to the overall national effort for the rational management of environmental resources in the country.

"The activities carried out in the 67 pilot centres and their achievements are impressive. Over 2,500 education staff of various levels have participated in EE seminar and workshops, 68,544 students and peasants were reached through EEP, 680,320 trees were planted and survived (between 1985 and 1991), about 75,000 copies of the EE magazine were produced and distributed to relevant institutions. Programmes on EE have been broadcast by educational radio and about 2,000 radio receivers have been distributed to schools and other centres." (Ethiopia IR, paras. 152-3)

"The development of respect for the natural environment"

This provision is unique to the Convention on the Rights of the Child and reflects the growing urgency of concern about the environment. The 1992 Rio Declaration on Environment and Development (Agenda 21) stresses that all people, including children, should be made aware of the need for sustainable development and care for the natural environment. Principle 10 provides: "Environmental issues are best handled with the participation of all concerned citizens, at the rel-

evant level", and Principal 21: "The creativity, ideals and courage of the youth of the world should be mobilized to forge a global partnership in order to achieve sustainable development and ensure a better future for all."

Agenda 21 recommendations reflect the aims of the Convention on the Rights of the Child: "Relevant authorities should ensure that every school is assisted in designing environmental activity work plans, with the participation of students and staff. Schools should involve schoolchildren in local and regional studies on environmental health, including safe drinking water, sanitation and food and ecosystems and in relevant activities, linking these studies with services and research in national parks, wildlife reserves, ecological heritage sites etc." (Chapter 36, p. 223). Agenda 21 also states: "Governments, according to their strategies, should take measures to ... establish procedures allowing for consultation and possible participation of youth of both genders, by 1993, in decision-making processes with regard to the environment, involving youth at the local, national and regional levels ... and ... establish task forces that include youth and youth non-governmental organizations to develop educational and awareness programmes specifically targeted to the youth population on critical issues pertaining to youth. These task forces should use formal and non-formal educational methods to reach a maximum audience." (Chapter 25, pp. 193-194)

The Committee recommended that Lebanon introduce teaching about the environment in schools (Lebanon IRCO, Add.54, para. 18). Chile, Namibia and Ethiopia reported interesting initiatives in this area to the Committee (see box opposite).

Freedom to establish schools outside the State system that conform to the aims of education under the Convention and any minimum standards laid down by the State

This right repeats, more or less word for word, article 13(4) of the International Covenant on Economic, Social and Cultural Rights. Despite the Committee's concern about the discriminatory impact private education may have on state education and on poor families (see article 28, page 319), the right to opt out of state education is an important one, particularly because there is no blueprint for "good education" and education systems should allow for diversity and flexibility.

The two conditions are essential fetters on this freedom – that private education should conform to the aims of education as set out in article 29(1) and that it should conform with any minimum mandatory standards. They prevent, for example, the existence of religious schooling focusing only on doctrinal texts, or schools that fail to equip children for "responsible life" by not teaching them basic skills.

The paragraph is formulated as a right of individuals rather than as an obligation of the State Party. The State Party is not required, under this article, to lay down "minimum standards". However, article 3(3) provides "States Parties shall ensure that the institutions, services and facilities responsible for the care or protection of children shall conform with standards established by competent authorities, particularly in the areas of safety, health, in the number and suitability of their staff, as well as competent supervision." This means that States do have to ensure that private schools meet such standards.

The fact that private schools are obliged to conform to the aims of education as set out in article 29(1) also implies that States have an obligation to check that they meet this obligation. The Committee told Mauritius, for example, that it was

"worried about the absence of supervision of private schools"

which suggests a duty to inspect private schools (Mauritius IRCO, Add.64, para 15). Certainly many nations do ensure that private schools are inspected in some fashion.

Implementation Checklist

article 29

● General measures of implementation

Have appropriate general measures of implementation been taken in relation to article 29, including

☐ identification and coordination of the responsible departments and agencies at all levels of government (article 29 is relevant to the **departments of education, health and the environment**)?

☐ identification of relevant non-governmental organizations/civil society partners?

☐ a comprehensive review to ensure that all legislation, policy and practice is compatible with the article, for all children in all parts of the jurisdiction?

☐ adoption of a strategy to secure full implementation

    ☐ which includes where necessary the identification of goals and indicators of progress?

    ☐ which does not affect any provisions which are more conducive to the rights of the child?

    ☐ which recognizes other relevant international standards?

    ☐ which involves where necessary international cooperation?

(Such measures may be part of an overall governmental strategy for implementing the Convention as a whole).

☐ budgetary analysis and allocation of necessary resources?

☐ development of mechanisms for monitoring and evaluation?

☐ making the implications of article 29 widely known to adults and children?

☐ development of appropriate training and awareness-raising (in relation to article 29 likely to include the training of **teachers, education administrators, vocational guidance personnel**)?

● Specific issues in implementing article 29

Do all forms of education provided for children within the country aim to

    ☐ develop their personalities to their fullest potential?

    ☐ develop their talents to their fullest potential?

    ☐ develop their mental abilities to their fullest potential?

    ☐ develop their physical abilities to their fullest potential?

☐ Is the Convention on the Rights of the Child incorporated in school curricula?

☐ Are children taught about other human rights principles?

☐ Do administrative systems in schools conform with the principles of the Convention?

How to use the checklists, *see page XVII*

☐ Do teaching methods conform with the principles of the Convention?

Do education institutions and services and educational curricula develop children's respect for

    ☐ their parents?

    ☐ their own cultural or national identity, language and values?

    ☐ the national values of the ratifying country?

    ☐ the national values of the country from which they originated?

    ☐ the national values of other civilizations?

☐ Do all forms of education aim to prepare children for responsible life in a free society?

☐ Do schools practise democratic procedures?

☐ Are children given responsibilities and opportunities to practise choice, decision-making and independence?

Are children educated about

    ☐ health promotion?

    ☐ sexuality and reproductive health?

    ☐ social relationships, including mediation and negotiation skills and non-violent conflict resolution?

    ☐ money management and budgeting?

    ☐ the law?

    ☐ responsibilities of community life and citizenship?

☐ Does education encourage understanding, tolerance and friendship among all people?

Are measures taken to combat sex discrimination in

    ☐ the curriculum?

    ☐ educational materials?

    ☐ teaching attitudes?

    ☐ school ethos?

☐ Are the children taught non-violent values in the spirit of peace?

☐ Do educational institutions prevent all expressions of violence, whether by pupils or teachers?

☐ Are measures adopted to combat bullying?

☐ Do all forms of education include strategies to develop children's respect for the natural environment?

How to use the checklists, *see page XVII*

☐ Are private schools permitted?

Do minimum standards require that private schools

    ☐ do not discriminate?

    ☐ develop their pupils' abilities to their fullest potential?

    ☐ teach and practise the values laid out in article 29(1)?

    ☐ respect the rights of the child under the Convention?

    ☐ have sufficient and appropriately skilled staff and comply with health and safety requirements?

☐ Are measures, such as inspection and regulation procedures, adopted to ensure that the education in all private schools conforms with these standards?

Reminder : **The Convention is indivisible and its articles are interdependent. Article 29 should not be considered in isolation.**

Particular regard should be paid to:
The general principles

Article 2: all rights to be recognized for each child in jurisdiction without discrimination on any ground

Article 3(1): the best interests of the child to be a primary consideration in all actions concerning children

Article 6: right to life and maximum possible survival and development

Article 12: respect for the child's views in all matters affecting the child; opportunity to be heard in any judicial or administrative proceedings affecting the child

Closely related articles

Articles whose implementation is related to that of article 29 include:

Article 13: freedom of expression

Article 14: freedom of thought, conscience and religion

Article 15: freedom of association

Article 16: protection of privacy

Article 17: access to information and role of media

Article 24: health (including health education)

Article 28: right to education

Article 30: children of minorities or of indigenous peoples

Article 31: rest, leisure, play, recreation and culture

Article 33: protection from drug abuse

Article 38: children and armed conflict

Children of minorities or of indigenous peoples

Article 30

Text of Article 30

In those States in which ethnic, religious or linguistic minorities or persons of indigenous origin exist, a child belonging to such a minority or who is indigenous shall not be denied the right, in community with other members of his or her group, to enjoy his or her own culture, to profess and practise his or her own religion, or to use his or her own language.

Article 30 protects the rights of children from minority or indigenous groups to enjoy their culture, practise their religion and use their language together with other members of their group.

It might be asked: Why is article 30 necessary? Articles 7 and 9 prevent unreasonable separation from parents; article 8 secures the right of the child "to preserve his or her identity"; article 14 safeguards children's freedom of religion with direct reference to their parents' role in this respect; article 16 prevents arbitrary or unlawful interference with the child's family; article 20 ensures that where the child is deprived of his or her family environment "due regard shall be paid to the desirability of continuity in a child's upbringing and to the child's ethnic, religious, cultural and linguistic background"; article 21 reaffirms this in respect of intercountry adoption; article 29 includes respect for the child's own culture, language and values in the aims of education and upholds the child's right to be educated outside the state system; and article 40 requires the use of interpreters if the child cannot under-

stand the language used in the administration of juvenile justice. In addition articles 10 and 22 require special measures regarding immigrant and refugee children. Overarching all, is article 2, securing all the rights of the Convention without discrimination of any kind "irrespective of the child's or his or her parent's or legal guardian's race, colour, ... language, religion, ... national, ethnic or social origin ... or other status".

Summary

In the light of this, the provisions of article 30 might seem redundant. However, the overwhelming evidence of serious and continuing discrimination against minority and indigenous populations justifies mention of their rights in a separate article.

The Convention lays proper stress on the right of children to be protected from the harmful practices of their parents, families and communities. It is equally important for the Convention to stress the right of peaceful enjoyment of practices and faiths that are not harmful, no matter how strange or alien they may seem to others. Article 30 affirms the rich diversities of cultures that are practised within a framework of human rights. ∎

Extracts from
Committee on the Rights of the Child
Guidelines for Reports to be submitted by States Parties under the Convention

For full text of *Guidelines for Periodic Reports*, see Appendix 3, page 604.

Guidelines for Initial Reports

"Special protection measures

Under this section States Parties are requested to provide relevant information, including the principal legislative, judicial, administrative or other measures in force, factors and difficulties encountered and progress achieved in implementing the relevant provisions of the Convention; and implementation priorities and specific goals for the future in respect of:

...(d) Children belonging to a minority or indigenous group (article 30)

Additionally, States Parties are encouraged to provide specific statistical information and indicators relevant to the children covered by [the previous] paragraph ..."

(CRC/C/5, paras. 23 and 24)

Guidelines for Periodic Reports

"VII. SPECIAL PROTECTION MEASURES...

D. Children belonging to a minority or an indigenous group (art. 30)

Please provide information on the measures adopted, including at the legislative, administrative, educational, budgetary and social levels, to ensure that a child belonging to an ethnic, religious or linguistic minority or who is indigenous is not denied the right, in community with other members of his or her group:

> *To enjoy his or her culture;*

> *To profess and practise his or her own religion;*

> *To use his or her own language.*

> *In this regard, reports should also indicate* inter alia:

> *The ethnic, religious or linguistic minorities or indigenous groups existing within the State Party's jurisdiction;*

> *The measures adopted to ensure the preservation of the identity of the minority or indigenous group to which the child belongs;*

> *The measures adopted to recognize and ensure the enjoyment of the rights set forth in the Convention by children belonging to a minority or who are indigenous;*

> *The measures adopted to prevent any form of discrimination and combat prejudice against those children, as well as those designed to ensure that they benefit from equal opportunities, including in relation to health care and education;*

> *The measures adopted to ensure respect for the general principles of the Convention, namely the best interests of the child, respect for the views of the child, the right to life, and survival and development to the maximum extent possible, as well as non-discrimination;*

> *The measures adopted to ensure that in the implementation of the rights recognized in article 30 due consideration is taken of other provisions of the Convention, including in the areas of civil rights, particularly in relation to the preservation of the child's identity, family environment and alternative care (for example art. 20, para. 3 and art. 21), education and the administration of juvenile justice;*

> *Relevant disaggregated data on the children concerned, including by age, gender, language, religion, and social and ethnic origin;*

> *The progress achieved and the difficulties encountered in the implementation of this article, as well as any targets set for the future."*

(CRC/C/58, paras. 165 and 166. The following paragraphs of the *Guidelines for Periodic Reports* are also relevant to reporting under this article: 22, 30, 57, 60, 81 and 106; for full text of *Guidelines*, see Appendix 3, page 604.)

Background

Article 27 of the International Covenant on Civil and Political Rights states: "In those States in which ethnic, religious or linguistic minorities exist, persons belonging to such minorities shall not be denied the right, in community with the other members of their group, to enjoy their own culture, to profess and practise their own religion, or to use their own language."

Article 30 of the Convention on the Rights of the Child thus repeats, with special reference to children, more or less word for word, the Covenant on Civil and Political Rights, save for the addition of "persons of indigenous origin." Article 30 emanated from a proposal by a non-governmental organization called the Four Directions Council, supported by Mexico, to dedicate an article of the Convention to the rights of indigenous children. The drafting Working Group quickly agreed that this should embrace the rights of all minority children and concluded that it would not be helpful to introduce wording which departed from that of the International Covenant on Civil and Political Rights (E/CN.4/1986/39, p.13; Detrick, p. 408).

The *Manual on Human Rights Reporting,* 1997 also points out that "by replacing the plural used in the Covenant '**persons** belonging to such minorities' by a reference to the **child**, it has emphasized the individual nature of the rights recognized in this article, even if they are to be enjoyed 'in community with other members' of the child's group" (*Manual*, p. 489).

These are clearly improvements that do not detract from the principles of the Covenant. In addition, it should perhaps be noted that in some countries majority populations have been denied rights (for example South Africa during apartheid) and that there are some minority groups which cannot claim to be "ethnic, religious or linguistic" (for example some "traveller" communities in western Europe) but whose rights to enjoy their culture have been unreasonably denied.

General Comment 23 by the Human Rights Committee, on article 27 of the International Covenant on Civil and Political Rights, makes the following points:

- this is a right which is conferred on individuals belonging to minority groups and which is distinct from, and additional to, all the other rights which, as individuals in common with everyone else, they are already entitled to enjoy under the Covenant;
- it is not a collective right of self-determination and does not prejudice the sovereignty and territorial integrity of a State Party. At the same time the right to enjoy culture may consist of "a way of life which is closely associated with territory and use of its resources. This may particularly be true of members of indigenous communities constituting a minority", including "such traditional activities as fishing or hunting or the right to live in reserves";
- international or domestic obligations not to discriminate, and to treat everyone equally, do not mean that minorities cannot be recognized;
- the right applies to everyone within the territory, not just citizens or people with permanent residence;
- the right to use a minority language is to be distinguished from freedom of expression and the right of accused people to an interpreter: it upholds the rights of minorities to use that language amongst themselves;
- the formulation of the right in negative terms "not to be denied the right..." nevertheless does recognize the existence of a right. This obliges the State Party to take positive measures both in terms of its own actions and against the acts of other persons in the country, in order to protect the minority group's cultural identity, language or religion;
- such positive measures must not thereby discriminate against any other group or individual or breach any other article of the Covenant;
- the aim is to ensure the survival and continual development of minorities "thus enriching the fabric of society as a whole".

(Human Rights Committee, General Comment 23, HRI/GEN/1/Rev.2, pp. 38-41)

The negative formulation of the phrase "shall not be denied the right ..." in article 27 of the Covenant (repeated in article 30 of the Convention on the Rights of the Child) was not repeated in the Declaration on the Rights of Persons Belonging to National or Ethnic, Religious and Linguistic Minorities, adopted by the General Assembly in 1992. In this text the rights of persons belonging to minorities is stated in positive rather than negative terms (for example, "States shall protect the existence and the national or ethnic, cultural, religious and linguistic identity of minorities within their respective territories...") and the obligation of States to implement these rights is also clearly stated ("... and shall encourage conditions for the promotion of that identity... States shall adopt appropriate legislative and other measures to achieve those ends") (article 1).

Because countries sometimes distinguish between the rights of citizens and those residing in the country, the ratification of the International Convention on the Protection of the Rights of All Migrant Workers and Members of their Families 1990 is also important. This Convention protects the rights of migrant workers to manifest their religion (article 12), requires ratifying States to "ensure respect for the cultural identity of migrant workers and members of their families and shall not prevent them from maintaining their cultural links with their State of origin" (article 31) and secures policies for teaching children both the local languages and their mother tongue (article 45, see page 413 below).

Reservations

Turkey and France have entered reservations in respect of article 30.

Turkey states: "The Republic of Turkey reserves the right to interpret and to apply the provisions of [articles] 17, 29 and 30 of the Convention on the Rights of the Child according to the letter and spirit of the Constitution of the Republic of Turkey and of the Treaty of Lausanne of 24 July 1923" (CRC/C/2/Rev.5, p. 33). This is said to be an oblique reference to the Kurds (Van Bueren, p. 255). Portugal has entered an objection to the reservation, but Turkey has yet (September 1997) to explain the reservation to the Committee.

France states: "The Government of the Republic declares that, in the light of article 2 of the Constitution of the French Republic, article 30 is not applicable in so far as the Republic is concerned" (CRC/C/2/Rev.5, p. 18). France's explanation of this in its Initial Report does not take the matter much further: "France entered one reservation and two interpretative declarations. The reservation concerns article 30. Having regard to article 2 of the Constitution of the French Republic ('France is a Republic, indivisible, secular, democratic and social. It shall ensure the equality of all citizens before the law without distinction of origin, race or religion. It shall respect all beliefs...'), France considers that article 30 [13 in text] is not applicable in so far as the Republic is concerned. Indeed, on the basis of these principles of equality and non-discrimination, the existence of minorities cannot be recognized in France in the sense of groups enjoying a special status. France made a similar reservation in respect of article 27 of the International Covenant on Civil and Political Rights." (France IR, Add.15, para. 47)

This explanation is difficult to understand since article 30 does not accord minority groups 'special status', it simply protects their civil rights as does the French Constitution. The General Com-

ment by the Human Rights Committee on article 27 of the Covenant addresses the French position: "The Covenant also distinguishes the rights protected under article 27 from the guarantees under articles 2(1) and 26. The entitlement, under article 2.1, to enjoy the rights under the Covenant without discrimination applies to all individuals within the territory or under the jurisdiction of the State whether or not those persons belong to a minority. In addition, there is a distinct right provided under article 26 for equality before the law, equal protection of the law, and non-discrimination in respect of rights granted and obligations imposed by the States. It governs the exercise of all rights, whether protected under the Covenant or not, which the State Party confers by law on individuals within its territory or under its jurisdiction, irrespective of whether they belong to the minorities specified in article 27 or not. Some States Parties who claim that they do not discriminate on grounds of ethnicity, language or religion, wrongly contend, on that basis alone, that they have no minorities." (Human Rights Committee, General Comment 23, HRI/GEN/1/Rev.2, p. 39)

In addition, two other countries, Canada and Venezuela, have made declarations relevant to article 30 of the Convention on the Rights of the Child.

Canada declared: "It is the understanding of the Government of Canada that, in matters relating to aboriginal peoples of Canada, the fulfilment of its responsibilities under article 4 of the Convention must take into account the provisions of article 30. In particular, in assessing what measures are appropriate to implement the rights recognized in the Convention for aboriginal children, due regard must be paid to not denying their right, in community with other members of their group, to enjoy their own culture, to profess and practise their religion and to use their own language" (CRC/C.2/Rev.5, p.15). Canada also entered a specific reservation to article 21 in relation to article 30, in so far as it allows aboriginal practices in adoption which might not be compatible with article 21, which the Committee "noted with concern" (Canada IRCO, Add.37, para. 10; see article 21, page 272). If the declaration means that Canada might give article 30 a superior status to other rights under the Convention, this must be deemed unacceptable. If it is simply a memorandum to the Canadian government to pay particular attention to the provisions of article 30, then it is harmless.

Venezuela states: "The Government of Venezuela takes the position that article 30 must be interpreted as a case in which article 2 of the Convention applies" (CRC/C.2/Rev.5, p. 35). This declaration awaits explanation, but the General

Comment by the Human Rights Committee, quoted in regard to France's reservation, is relevant.

"a child belonging to ... a minority or who is indigenous shall not be denied the right, in community with other members of his or her group, to enjoy his or her culture"

Article 30 is not about the fact that a great many minority and indigenous groups suffer from discrimination in terms of education, health and employment opportunities and from social prejudice or outright harassment. It is about cultural, religious and linguistic rights rather than about economic or political rights. Nonetheless, the entitlement "not to be denied the right ... to enjoy [their] own culture" is often disturbed by social or political forms of persecution. For example:

"The Committee suggests that the Government develop public campaigns on the rights of the child with a view to effectively addressing the problem of persisting discriminatory attitudes and practices against particular groups of children such as girl children, children belonging to a minority or indigenous group and poor children. It also suggests that further proactive measures be developed to improve the status of these groups of children." (Nicaragua IRCO, Add.36, para. 31)

"The Committee raises various points of concern with reference to the implementation of article 2 of the Convention relating to non-discrimination. It expresses grave concern about the situation of Albanian-speaking children in Kosovo, especially with regard to their health and education, as well as the degree to which this population is protected from abuse by the police ....
"The Committee strongly recommends that a solution be found to the concerns of the Committee for the situation of Albanian-speaking children in Kosovo, especially in the light of the principles and provisions of the Convention, including those of its article 3 relating to the best interests of the child. The Committee observes that the State-controlled mass media, in the interests of healing and building trust within the country, have a role and a responsibility to contribute to the efforts to foster tolerance and understanding between different groups and that the broadcasting of programmes that run counter to this objective should end. The Committee recommends that the securing and dissemination of broader and more diverse sources of information designed for children, including by broadcasting them on the mass media, would assist in ensuring further implementation of the

principles and provisions of the Convention, including those of its article 17." (Federal Republic of Yugoslavia IRCO, Add.49, paras. 7 and 28)

"The Committee ...notes that allegations continue to be made about incidents in which members of minority groups, particularly of Serbian and Muslim origin, are harassed and the perpetrators left unpunished...
" The Committee recommends that the Government devote its full efforts to actively encouraging a culture of tolerance through all possible channels, including the schools, the media and the law ..." (Croatia IRCO, Add.52, paras. 18 and 19).

What is more, the economic plight of minority and indigenous groups often leads to an erosion of their culture – across the world aboriginal or indigenous peoples, particularly, have been reduced to pitiful states as the incoming culture has dominated, corrupted and exploited these groups' culture and traditional activities.

As the Human Rights Committee pointed out (page 409) cultural rights are often bound up with survival rights of territory, fishing and hunting. Special measures may have to be taken by the State Party to ensure that health and education services are supplied without interfering with cultural practices. Costa Rica reported to the Committee, for example, that the infant mortality rate for indigenous minorities is almost three times the national average, in part because their lack of identity cards caused difficulty in claiming services of all kinds, which the Costa Rican Government is attempting to remedy (Costa Rica IR, paras. 356-9).

The Committee frequently mentions indigenous children as a group which, alongside girls and rural children, are discriminated against in relation to most articles of the Convention. Sometimes specific minority groups are singled out. For example the *talibés* of Senegal:

"The Committee is seriously worried at the difficult living conditions faced by a great number of talibés, *who are deprived of the enjoyment of their fundamental rights under the law...*
"The Committee recommends that in the implementation process of the Convention the State Party pay special attention to the situation of talibés. *Further measures should be adopted to ensure the effective enjoyment of their fundamental rights and that they are protected against any form of discrimination. Efforts should be made to ensure an effective monitoring system of their situation by the State Party, in close cooperation with religious and community leaders." (Senegal IRCO, Add.44, paras. 15 and 29)*

Or the Roma (gypsies) in Romania and in Italy:

"The Committee is concerned about the situation of children of minorities, especially within the context of articles 2, 29, 29 and 30 of the Convention. The low school attendance of the Roma (gypsy) group of children is a serious problem. In more general terms, the Committee finds that there is a need for more effective measures to combat prejudices against this minority ...

"The Government should adopt an active non-discrimination policy with respect to children of minorities. This would also, particularly in relation to the Roma (gypsy) population, require proactive measures to encourage participation and break a vicious circle of widespread prejudices resulting in hostility or neglect. The problem of low school attendance among children from the Roma minority should be urgently addressed." (Romania IRCO, Add.16, paras. 10 and 21)

"Further measures should also be taken to prevent a rise in discriminatory attitudes and prejudices towards particularly vulnerable children such as children living in poverty, children from the southern region, Roma children and foreign children. The Government should consider adopting a more active stand and coherent policy with respect to the treatment of these children and to create an environment favourable to their fullest possible integration into Italian society." (Italy IRCO, Add.41, para. 17)

The Committee's comment about integration into Italian society is an interesting one in that, although poor and southern children may well wish to integrate into the dominant Italian culture, Roma and immigrant children are, under the terms of article 30, entitled to expect to integrate on their own terms, with their cultural identity preserved, rather than to be assimilated into the majority culture.

The Committee has also encouraged general initiatives against prejudice and racism. For example, it commended Germany:

"The Committee acknowledges the determination of the State Party to prevent and combat xenophobic tendencies and manifestations of racism. The Government is to be commended for the extensive efforts undertaken to ensure the involvement of and effective cooperation between the Federal, Lander and local authorities in the implementation of a countrywide campaign to prevent and combat such phenomenon and to promote ethnic and racial harmony, in the general framework of the Youth Campaign launched by the Council of Europe." (Germany IRCO, Add.43, para. 6)

A similar campaign was proposed to Nicaragua:

"The Committee suggests that the Government develop public campaigns on the rights of the child with a view to effectively addressing the problem of persisting discriminatory attitudes and practices against particular groups of children such as girl children, children belonging to a minority or indigenous group and poor children. It is also suggested that further proactive measures be developed to improve the status of these groups of children." (Nicaragua IRCO, Add.36, para. 31)

And the Committee suggested enforceable legislation to Mexico (where there are 56 officially recorded indigenous groups and the indigenous child population is identified as one of the most vulnerable):

"Principles relating to ... the prohibition of discrimination in relation to children should be incorporated into domestic law, and it should be possible to invoke them before the courts." (Mexico IRCO, Add.13, para. 15)

In its General Discussion on Children in armed conflicts, the Committee stressed

"... the need to preserve the children's cultural environment" (Report on the second session, October 1992, CRC/C/10, p. 23).

This may be difficult when a State is receiving refugee children from a different culture to its own. However, children suffering the trauma of war and displacement particularly need the reassurance of familiar cultural practices. Securing their rights under article 30 is therefore of paramount importance.

"...to profess and practise his or her own religion"

Most minority groups are able to practise their religion without interference. In the case of Tibet, where interference has occurred, the Committee, naturally, expressed deep concern:

"In the framework of the exercise of the right to freedom of religion by children belonging to minorities, in the light of article 30 of the Convention, the Committee expresses its deep concern in connection with violations of human rights of the Tibetan religious minority. State intervention in religious principles and procedures seems to be most unfortunate for the whole generation of boys and girls among the Tibetan population ... The Committee recommends that the State Party seek a constructive response to [these] concerns." (China IRCO, Add.56, paras. 20 and 41)

In the case of Indonesia, which "officially recognizes" five religions (Islamic, Catholic,

Christian, Hindu and Buddhist), the Committee expressed its concern that

"...limiting official recognition to certain religions may give rise to practices of discrimination." (Indonesia IRCO, Add.25, para. 13)

"... to use his or her own language"

This right is about being able to speak a minority language without interference. Children's right to "use" their own language does not necessarily entitle them to be taught entirely in that language, though initially this may be necessary for refugee or immigrant children; the right may also involve positive measures to ensure that children are taught to speak their mother tongue in schools. Equally, measures may be needed to ensure that children who speak a minority language are not impeded by ignorance of the majority language.

The International Convention on the Protection of the Rights of All Migrant Workers and Members of their Families spells out such distinctions, in article 45:

"(2) States of employment shall pursue a policy, where appropriate in collaboration with the States of origin, aimed at facilitating the integration of children of migrant workers in the local school system, particularly in respect of teaching them the local language.

(3) States of employment shall endeavour to facilitate for the children of migrant workers the teaching of their mother tongue and culture and, in this regard, States of origin shall collaborate wherever appropriate.

(4) States of employment may provide special schemes of education in the mother tongue of children of migrant workers, if necessary in collaboration with the States of origin."

Thus, under this Convention, the State must take measures to integrate the children by teaching them the local language and must (if necessary) teach them their own language. In addition, it may teach them in their own language.

The Committee on the Rights of the Child has suggested States teach in minority languages:

"In the light of article 30, the Committee is concerned at the lack of measures taken to provide school education in all the existing languages and dialects." (Morocco IRCO, Add.60, para. 14)

"The Committee ... recommends that the State Party allocate resources to translate school materials into minority languages with the objective to encourage, in the appropriate regions, schools and teachers to provide edu-

cation in minority languages." (Myanmar IRCO, Add.69, para. 39)

It has also suggested the teaching of a minority language:

"The Committee also suggests that the State Party provide further support to the teaching of the Irish language in schools in Northern Ireland ..." (UK IRCO, Add.34, para. 33)

However, sometimes teaching children solely in their mother tongue may not be to their advantage. For example, the Committee raised concerns with China

"...about reports that school attendance in minority areas, including the Tibet Autonomous Region, is lagging behind, that the quality of education is inferior and that insufficient efforts have been made to develop a bilingual education system which would include adequate teaching in Chinese. These shortcomings may disadvantage Tibetan and other minority pupils applying to secondary and higher level schools ..."

The Committee suggested

"... that a review be undertaken of measures to ensure that children in the Tibet Autonomous Region and other minority areas are guaranteed full opportunities to develop knowledge about their own language and culture as well as to learn the Chinese language. Steps should be taken to protect these children from discrimination and to ensure their access to higher education on an equal footing." (China IRCO, Add.56, paras. 19 and 40)

Whichever course is adopted, teachers must be appropriately trained:

"In the light of article 30 of the Convention, [the Committee] is also worried about the insufficient number of teachers capable of working with minority children ... and encourages the relevant authorities to undertake all appropriate measures to ensure that sufficient teachers for minority children are available in all regions of the country." (Finland IRCO, Add.53, paras. 18 and 28)

Children's use of their own language is not confined to schools. The Committee noted the severe discrimination against Albanian-speaking children in the Federal Republic of Yugoslavia and recommended, amongst other things:

"...that measures should be taken to improve the activities of the mass media in imparting information for children in their own language, including Albanian." (Federal Republic of Yugoslavia IRCO, Add.49, paras. 7 and 28)

The Committee has taken particular pains to recommend that the provisions of the Convention are translated into all minority languages, for example:

"In view of the State Party's willingness to develop a culture of human rights and to change attitudes towards children in general and the indigenous population in particular, the Committee recommends that information and education about children's rights be disseminated among children and adults alike. It is also recommended that consideration be given to the translation of such information into the main indigenous languages and that appropriate measures be adopted to spread such information in such a way that it reaches groups affected by a high level of illiteracy. In the light of the considerable experience of the United Nations Children's Fund and other organizations in responding to such challenges, it is recommended that international cooperation be sought in this regard." (Guatemala

IRCO, Add.58, para. 29. See also Bolivia IRCO, Add.1, para. 18; Belgium IRCO, Add.38, para. 17; Portugal IRCO, Add.45, para. 21; and Finland IRCO, Add.53, para. 14)

The Committee has also recommended the translation of the State's Initial Report and the Committee reports (which of course include important statements relating to specific minority groups). For example:

"The Committee recommends that the report of the State party, the records of the dialogue held between itself and the State delegation and the Concluding Observations adopted by the Committee be widely disseminated throughout the nation in all minority languages as well as in Croatian..." (Croatia IRCO, Add.52, para. 28)

Implementation Checklist

● *General measures of implementation*

Have appropriate general measures of implementation been taken in relation to article 30, including

☐ identification and coordination of the responsible departments and agencies at all levels of government (article 30 is relevant to the **departments of education, home affairs, social welfare, health, media and communications**)?

☐ identification of relevant non-governmental organizations/civil society partners?

☐ a comprehensive review to ensure that all legislation, policy and practice is compatible with the article, for all children in all parts of the jurisdiction?

☐ adoption of a strategy to secure full implementation

  ☐ which includes where necessary the identification of goals and indicators of progress?

  ☐ which does not affect any provisions which are more conducive to the rights of the child?

  ☐ which recognizes other relevant international standards?

  ☐ which involves where necessary international cooperation?

(Such measures may be part of an overall governmental strategy for implementing the Convention as a whole).

☐ budgetary analysis and allocation of necessary resources?

☐ development of mechanisms for monitoring and evaluation?

☐ making the implications of article 30 widely known to adults and children?

☐ development of appropriate training and awareness-raising (in relation to article 30 likely to include the training of **teachers, social workers and police**)?

● *Specific issues in implementing article 30*

☐ Are measures taken to identify population groups of children belonging to an ethnic, religious or linguistic minority or who are of indigenous origin?

☐ Are measures taken to ensure that such children are not denied the right to enjoy their own culture in community with members of their group?

☐ Are measures taken to ensure that such children are not denied the right to profess or practise their own religion in community with members of their own group?

☐ Are measures taken to ensure that such children are not denied the right to use their own language in community with members of their group?

Do these measures include action taken

  ☐ in school?

  ☐ in the mass media?

  ☐ when children are separated for any reason from their parents, family or community?

  ☐ in legal proceedings?

☐ Where such children are taught in their mother tongue, are they also taught the majority language?

☐ Where such children are, for whatever reason, not fluent in the language used by their minority group, are measures available for teaching them this language?

☐ Are the provisions of the Convention, the Initial and Periodic Reports and all proceedings of and with the Committee on the Rights of the Child translated into all minority languages?

☐ Are children's rights against interference in their culture, religion and language under this article protected and enforceable in law?

☐ Are Government-sponsored campaigns initiated, where necessary, to combat prejudice against minorities or indigenous groups?

☐ Have children from these groups been asked whether the measures taken under this article are appropriate or sufficient?

Reminder : **The Convention is indivisible and its articles are interdependent. Article 30 should not be considered in isolation.**

Particular regard should be paid to:
The general principles

Article 2: all rights to be recognized for each child in jurisdiction without discrimination on any ground
Article 3(1): the best interests of the child to be a primary consideration in all actions concerning children
Article 6: right to life and maximum possible survival and development
Article 12: respect for the child's views in all matters affecting the child; opportunity to be heard in any judicial or administrative proceedings affecting the child

Closely related articles

Articles whose implementation is related to that of article 30 include:

Article 5: respect for responsibilities of extended family or community for the child
Article 8: right to preserve identity
Article 16: protection from arbitrary interference in family and home
Article 20: continuity of ethnic, religious, cultural and linguistic background if placed away from family
Article 21: intercountry adoption only to be considered if the child cannot be cared for in his or her own country
Article 22: special protection for refugee children
Article 24: protection from traditional practices prejudicial to health
Article 28: education to be provided on the basis of equal opportunity
Article 29: education to be directed to development of respect for all cultures and friendship between all peoples
Article 40: right to an interpreter in the juvenile justice system

Child's right to leisure, recreation and culture

article 31

Text of Article 31

1. States Parties recognize the right of the child to rest and leisure, to engage in play and recreational activities appropriate to the age of the child and to participate freely in cultural life and the arts.

2. States Parties shall respect and promote the right of the child to participate fully in cultural and artistic life and shall encourage the provision of appropriate and equal opportunities for cultural, artistic, recreational and leisure activity.

Article 31 concerns the child's rights to rest, leisure, play and recreational activities and to participate in cultural and artistic life.

The words "rest", "leisure", "play" and "recreational activities" appear on one level to be synonymous, because they are all about not working. But although not working is a unifying factor, the four words contain important differences. "Rest" includes the basic necessities of physical or mental relaxation and sleep, "leisure" is a wider term implying having the time and freedom to do as one pleases, "recreational activities" embrace the whole range of activities undertaken by choice for the purposes of pleasure (including a number which can simultaneously be termed work, such as sports, creative and performing arts, crafts and scientific, agricultural or technical pursuits) and "play" is arguably the most interesting in terms of childhood, in that it includes activities of children which are not controlled by adults and which do not necessarily conform to any rules.

Children's right to play is sometimes referred to as the "forgotten right", perhaps because it appears to the adult world as a luxury rather than a necessity of life, and because children always find ways and means of playing, even in the direst circumstances. But play is also an essential part of development and children who are unable to play, for whatever reason, may lack important social and personal skills.

Children's cultural rights include both their right of access to developmentally appropriate cultural and artistic events, and their right to undertake such activities themselves – both to join with adults in cultural and artistic pursuits and to enjoy their own. (The word "culture" in the rest of the Convention is used to refer to communities' traditions and customs; in this article the word "cultural" is used in its artistic sense). ∎

Summary

Extracts from
Committee on the Rights of the Child
Guidelines for Reports to be submitted by States Parties under the Convention

For full text of *Guidelines for Periodic Reports*, see Appendix 3, page 604.

Guidelines for Initial Reports

"Education, leisure and cultural activities

Under this section States Parties are requested to provide relevant information, including the principal legislative, judicial, administrative or other measures in force; the institutional infrastructure for implementing policy in this area, particularly monitoring strategies and mechanisms; and factors and difficulties encountered and progress achieved in implementing the relevant provisions of the Convention, in respect of:...

(c) Leisure, recreation and cultural activities (article 31)

... States Parties are requested to specify the nature and extent of cooperation with local and national organizations of a governmental or non-governmental nature, such as institutions of social workers, concerning the implementation of this area of the Convention. States Parties are encouraged to provide additional relevant statistical information and indicators relating to children covered in this section."

(CRC/C/5, paras. 21 and 22)

Guidelines for Periodic Reports

"VII. EDUCATION, LEISURE AND CULTURAL ACTIVITIES

C. Leisure, recreation and cultural activities (art. 31)

Please provide information on the measures adopted, including of a legislative nature, to recognize and ensure the right of the child to:

> *Rest and leisure;*

> *Engage in play and recreational activities appropriate to the age of the child;*

> *Participate freely in cultural life and the arts.*

In this regard, reports should also indicate:

> *The proportion of the relevant overall budget allocated (at the central, regional, local and where relevant at the federal and provincial levels) for children;*

> *The cultural, artistic, recreational and leisure activities, programmes or campaigns developed and provided at the national, regional or local, and where appropriate at the federal and provincial levels, to ensure the enjoyment of this right including in the family, in the school and in the community;*

> *The enjoyment of the rights recognized by article 31 in relation to other rights recognized by the Convention, including the right to education;*

> *The respect ensured to the general principles of the Convention, namely non-discrimination, the best interests of the child, respect for the views of the child and the right to life, survival and development to the maximum extent;*

> *Relevant data on the children concerned, including by age, gender, region, rural/urban area, and national, social and ethnic origin;*

> *Progress achieved in the implementation of article 31, difficulties encountered and targets set for the future."*

(CRC/C/58, paras. 117-118. Paragraph 92 of the *Guidelines for Periodic Reports* is also relevant to reporting under this article; for full text of *Guidelines*, see Appendix 3, page 604.)

Background

Principle 7 of the 1959 Declaration of the Rights of the Child states: "The child shall have full opportunity for play and recreation, which should be directed to the same purposes as education; society and the public authorities shall endeavour to promote the enjoyment of this right." (The "purposes of education" under the Declaration are to "promote [the child's] general culture and enable him, on a basis of equal opportunity, to develop his abilities, his individual judgement and his sense of moral and social responsibility, and to become a useful member of society" (also Principle 7)). Article 31 of the Convention on the Rights of the Child noticeably does not prescribe the purpose of play and recreation – children are as entitled as adults to play and recreation which appears purposeless (though adults have a responsibility to prevent them from engaging in leisure pursuits which are actively harmful).

The *Manual on Human Rights Reporting*, 1997 comments that the Convention's article 31 "should also be considered in combination with other relevant articles of the Convention, which will lead to recognition that the right to play and recreation should be taken into account in the framework of the right to education, thus contributing to the development of the child's abilities to their fullest potential. Similarly, in those specific circumstances, activities and ages under which children below 18 may work, in the light of article 32, the right to rest and leisure should be equally and necessarily ensured. In situations covered by article 39 relating to the recovery and social reintegration of the child victim of any form of neglect, exploitation and abuse, torture or armed conflicts, the engagement in play and recreational activities may further gain an instrumental and healing role by promoting the child's self-esteem and trust and his or her growing participation in life." The *Manual* also points out that sports activities and competitions in leisure pursuits "which may seem to be primarily designed to promote the child's well-being" should not damage the child's physical or psychological development (*Manual*, p.468; see also article 36, page 483).

Article 31 has not been the subject of much comment by the Committee, with only a few countries being reminded of their duties in relation to it, for example Hong Kong (UK dependent territory), which was told simply that

"Ways and means of ensuring fuller implementation of article 31 of the Convention also appear to deserve further study." UK dependent territory: Hong Kong IRCO, Add.63, para. 32)

Children's right to "rest and leisure"

Rest is almost as important to children's development as the basics of nutrition, housing, health care and education. Indeed, over-tired children are often unable to learn and are more susceptible to illness. A primary responsibility of ratifying States is, therefore, to ensure that children who work have adequate time for sleep and relaxation. The Night Work of Young Persons (Non-Industrial Occupations) Convention 1946, ILO No.79 and the Night Work of Young Persons (Industry) Convention (Revised) 1948, ILO No.90 protect children from working at night. The ideal principle set out in these provisions is that children under the age of 14 or in full-time education should have a consecutive period of 14 hours to rest including the period between eight o'clock in the evening and eight o'clock in the morning (article 2(1) of ILO No.79); that all children under the age of 16 should have 12 hours' rest (article 3 of No.79 and article 2 of No.90), and 16- to 18-year-olds at least seven hours (article 2 of No.90).

However, these are heavily qualified safeguards. For example, children in domestic service and children working in non-hazardous occupations with their families may be exempted entirely from these Conventions; and yet millions of children across the world work long hours in conditions of near slavery as domestic workers, and many more are forced by their family circumstances to work in family enterprises without adequate rest or education throughout most of their childhood.

The right to leisure encompasses more than just having sufficient time to sleep at night. Discussion under articles 29 and 32 explores the problems engendered by children's need to work and the complex relationship between children's work and education. Article 31 is necessary as a reminder that, in addition, children need some space for themselves between work and education (article 16, the right to privacy, also addresses this need.

In the drafting sessions Canada proposed an amendment requiring "parents, States Parties, educational institutions and others caring for children" to make "reasonable limitations on school and working hours" (E/CN.4/1983/62, Annex II; Detrick, p. 415). During discussion of El Salvador's Initial Report, a Committee member stated: "As far as the employment of children was concerned, while legislation appeared to draw a balance between work and school, access to education did not only mean school

article 31

Finland's zoning laws promote play

Finland reported to the Committee that a provision had been added to its building decrees in the early 1970s to the effect that "sufficient space for playgrounds and for free-time activities must be reserved in each city block zoned for housing. The purpose of the provision was to safeguard the best interest of children as opposed to the need for parking space for cars, a need which had been defined earlier. Also, applications for building permits should be examined with a special emphasis on the safety, health considerations and pleasantness of the spaces reserved for playgrounds or passing time. In practice, the results still leave a lot to be desired. Far too often the needs of children have to make room for roads, parking space and the efficiency of building". (Finland IR, para. 51)

attendance. It also meant ensuring that a child had the time to think about what he was learning, to do homework, and also to have the time to play and be a child." (El Salvador SR.86, para. 62)

Countries have very different legal interpretations of how many hours compulsory education should take up in a year and very different practices relating to homework (school work done at home). Some countries have customs and laws reserving one day of the week and additional religious festivals as free from work; others have regulations which ensure that children are only permitted to work for remuneration on one day of each weekend and only a portion of school holidays; others ensure that the school day has frequent rest periods. Children in compulsory schooling are, after all, already working full-time if homework is taken into account – indeed, often being forced into overtime in adult terms. If they undertake paid work in addition to schooling, they may rarely have a minute off for months on end.

Right to "engage in play and recreational activities appropriate to the age of the child"

As discussed above, play and recreational activities can be distinguished from each other in so far as play is unstructured and free from adult direction (although it may be facilitated and overseen by adults), whereas recreational activities include most aspects of a school curriculum – sports, performing and creative arts, science and technology and so forth – as well as games and spectator activities. A defining characteristic of both play and recreation is that they are not compulsory.

Few countries give adequate priority to children's right to "play". The haphazard, anarchic nature of play contributes nothing to the nation's economy or international profile. However, play does contribute a great deal to children's physical and psychological health. Many social skills, such as negotiation, sharing and self-control, are gained through unsupervised play with other children. In terms of physical development, it is essential that children spend time exercising their bodies. Medical organizations in the developed world are reporting with alarm the "coronary time bomb" arising from the new phenomenon of children spending most of their time inside schools, homes and cars, in front of televisions and computers.

Although the range of children's play is enormous and ever-changing (see, for example, the box opposite describing Madagascar's range of play activities), children's basic play needs are relatively simple. All that is required is safe, accessible space for the children's use, preferably containing possibilities for creating or changing things. Surprisingly, these are difficult to achieve in today's world (see Finnish example in the box).

The International Association for the Child's Right to Play (IPA, given consultative status with UNESCO and UNICEF) has adopted a *Declaration of the Child's Right to Play*, which states a deep concern about:

"a number of alarming trends and their negative impact on children's development:

- Society's indifference to the importance of play.
- Over-emphasis on theoretical and academic studies in schools.
- Increasing numbers of children living with inadequate provisions for survival and development.
- Inadequate environmental planning, which results in a lack of basic amenities, inappropriate housing forms, and poor traffic management.
- Increasing commercial exploitation of children, and the deterioration of cultural traditions.
- Lack of access for third world women to basic training in child care and development.
- Inadequate preparation of children to cope with life in a rapidly changing community.
- Increasing segregation of children in the community.

- The increasing numbers of working children, and their unacceptable working conditions.
- Constant exposure of children to war, violence, exploitation and destruction.
- Over-emphasis on unhealthy competition and 'winning at all costs' in children's sports."

The Declaration calls for action by five government departments: health; education, welfare, leisure and planning, for more play-oriented professionals and for fewer commercial or violent games and toys.

The Committee on the Rights of the Child observed to the Lebanon:

"The Committee believes that opportunities for the cultural development of children are critical and recommends that measures be taken to give children access to child literature and media. The need for playgrounds and child-friendly parks should be considered in city planning." (Lebanon IRCO, Add.54, para. 36)

Children's recreational activities tend to be similar to adult recreational pursuits – sports, games, films, crafts and so forth. The questions to be asked here are: do children have equal access to recreational facilities? Are resources for recreational activities equitably distributed between children and adults?

One may also ask: are some children's activities genuinely recreational? Children can be coerced into activities called recreation but which they would not choose to do if left to themselves, and give them little pleasure.

Modern agricultural methods, spiralling traffic demands and poor city planning are all the enemy of children's play. Television, though providing culture and entertainment, must also be seen as sometimes inimical to play and recreation "appropriate to the age of the child". Colombia reported that: "The disorderly urbanization that has taken place in the areas inhabited by poor families has resulted in a scarcity of community space suitable for recreation and the organization of cultural activities for children. In addition, families lack the time to devote attention to their children owing to their increasing participation in the labour market, and because of changes in family composition ... In these circumstances the principal recreational activity of children in urban areas is watching television programmes. They spend 2.1 hours of the 3 hours of free time they have in the day in front of the television screen. At weekends and on holidays they spend 4 of their 7 hours of free time in the same manner. There is thus insufficient time for cultural and sports activities." (Colombia IR, paras. 178-80) This description reflects the experiences of many countries of the world. Energetic strategies under article 31 are needed to combat the seductive allure of television.

Children's right "to participate freely in cultural life and the arts"

This right encompasses both the right of children to join with adults in their cultural and artistic pursuits and the right to child-centred culture and arts; it also includes the right of children to be both consumers and producers of arts and

Traditional and modern recreational activities in Madagascar

"Madagascar has a complex sociocultural range of traditional games. Old traditions of children's games and songs are still found in the remotest rural areas. Older boys play games that tend to be violent, while older girls' games imitate family life. As they approach maturity, and without giving up games that provide physical exercise (balls made of rags, wrestling for boys, training of oxen, boat races, etc.) children engage in traditional games with riddles, proverbs, etc. helping to develop a knowledge of popular literature (stories, legends, traditional theatre, improvised choir singing). This tradition of games and leisure activities originating in ancient customs still exists. It should not be abandoned for more 'modern' leisure activities, but should be integrated with the changes that are a result of the intense traffic passing through Madagascar: toys, imported games, collective performances by artistic groups. Such a symbiosis may be achieved within traditional communities and also through youth associations (churches, the scout movement, extracurricular and postschool activities)... However, very definite reservations have to be made about activities considered as leisure that may endanger the child's moral health and harmonious mental development: (a) In the traditional field: betting on fights between small animals (such as drugged chameleons) or cock fights ending in the death of one of the animals; (b) In the 'modern' field: pintable football, video films shown without discernment or dances held on official occasions or for popular festivals that unfortunately degenerate into drinking bouts or brawls." (Madagascar IR, paras. 233-236)

Recreational opportunities cut back for Mongolian children

"We could say that before 1990 there existed a complex system of activities for children to be involved in during their leisure time. But with the political and economic reform, the change in the administrative units of Mongolia and the reorganization of public organizations, certain changes have transpired with regard to their functions, structure and activities. With privatization, many of the cultural clubs, libraries, cinema houses, sport halls and museums were closed down over the last three years; many of the establishments designed to conduct children's activities have changed their orientation. As a result, the number of children attending leisure-time activities has necessarily been decreased. The decline in the number of children participating in these activities is closely linked to the introduction of fees for all these courses and activities. There is a new demand to conduct activities linked with production of marketable goods..." (Mongolia IR, para. 200)

Cultural opportunities opened in Mexico, Denmark, Norway, Italy and Bulgaria

Mexico described a programme initiated over a decade ago for stimulating children's access to culture, which includes drama, art, poetry and writing workshops operating in public institutions in many localities; travelling art collections and non-commercial film performances; a national exhibition of children's paintings, international cultural exchanges and a special cultural journal for children *Tiempo de Niños* (Mexico IR, paras. 221-226). The Danish Ministry of Culture has set up a special Working Group on Children and Culture to encourage initiatives such as the 'Try your own' scheme, and an experiment to open up established cultural institutions to children. The Youth and Adult Education Act 1991 gives special priority to children including the allocation of financial resources for leisure-time activities (Denmark IR, paras. 273-276). The Norwegian Council of Culture has also implemented an experimental programme called 'Try it yourself', in which children are allowed to initiate and organize their own cultural activities with a grant from the central authorities (Norway IR, para. 405). Italy reported to the Committee about a new statute requiring all local authorities to make facilities available to children for their physical exercise (Italy IR, para. 185). Bulgaria described its "National Palace for Children", offering 45 different courses in arts, sports, science and technology, for children to use in their leisure time. Four thousand children have voluntarily attended these courses. The Palace is half-funded by the State, collecting the other half from small fees, sponsorships and donations. (Bulgaria IR, para. 218)

culture. Thus, children should not be barred from adult events or performances without good reason (such as because the child might be psychologically harmed or because young infants might disrupt a performance) and, in addition, children should be given opportunities to participate in all forms of cultural and artistic activity as well as enjoy performances and exhibitions designed specifically for their pleasure.

This right obviously relates to children's rights under article 13 (freedom of expression), article 15 (freedom of association), article 17 (access to the media and to children's books) and article 30 (enjoyment of minority cultures). And given the essentially voluntary and pleasurable nature of the right, the principles of article 12 (taking account of children's views) should be given high priority.

It should be noted that children's views of what they want in recreational pursuits are often energetically sought by the commercial world for marketing purpose; these views do, indeed, determine what children get, but, unfortunately, often in terms of the lowest common denominator. However, children's more creative and stimulating participation is sought by those engaged in planning cultural activity – for example the National Canadian Children's Museum has a Children's Advisory Committee composed of children to provide it with ideas on the development and enhancement of programmes and exhibitions (Canada IR, para. 299).

States Parties' obligations to promote and encourage opportunities for children's participation in cultural, artistic, recreational and leisure activities

Because children lack both money and power, they are dependent on the adult world, including the Government, for their access to recreational, sporting and cultural opportunities. Mongolia painted a bleak picture to the Committee of the leisure activities of children in its post-communist incarnation, which highlights the need for active State measures. Other countries, however, reported exciting initiatives under article 31 (see box opposite).

Equal opportunities

Along with many of the Convention's provisions, certain categories of children need more attention and resources in order to enjoy their rights under article 31. Poor children are not necessarily deprived of leisure and culture – children from the poorest communities of the world have some of the richest lives in these terms. But poverty of environments, particularly in urban ghettos, the cost of many modern recreational activities and the need to work are obvious obstacles to the exercise of article 31 rights. State measures in this area may, therefore, have to be targeted on poorer children, as in Germany which the Committee commended for its

"... commitment to undertake measures to improve poorer children's access to out-of-school activities, including leisure activities." (Germany IRCO, Add.43, para. 31)

In addition, children with disabilities need particular assistance in gaining access to or using recreational facilities, and particular stress needs to be given to inclusive forms of recreation. Dis-

---

Culture, recreation, sport and disability

The Standard Rules on the Equalization of Opportunities for Persons with Disabilities provides:

"Rule 10 Culture

States will ensure that persons with disabilities are integrated into and can participate in cultural activities on an equal basis.

1. States should ensure that persons with disabilities have the opportunity to utilize their creative, artistic and intellectual potential, not only for their own benefit, but also for the enrichment of their community, be they in urban or rural areas. Examples of such activities are dance, music, literature, theatre, plastic arts, painting and sculpture. Particularly in developing countries, emphasis should be placed on traditional and contemporary art forms, such as puppetry, recitation and storytelling.

2. States should promote the accessibility to and availability of places for cultural performances and services, such as theatres, museums, cinemas and libraries, to persons with disabilities.

3. States should initiate the development and use of special technical arrangements to make literature, films and theatres accessible to persons with disabilities.

Rule 11 Recreation and sports

States will take measures to ensure that persons with disabilities have equal opportunities for recreation and sports.

1. States should initiate measures to make places for recreation and sports, hotels, beaches, sports arenas, gym halls, etc., accessible to persons with disabilities. Such measures should encompass support for staff in recreation and sports programmes, including projects to develop methods of accessibility, and participation, information and training programmes.

2. Tourist authorities, travel agencies, hotels, voluntary organizations and others involved in organizing recreational activities or travel opportunities should offer their services to all, taking into account the special needs of persons with disabilities. Suitable training should be provided to assist that process.

3. Sports organizations should be encouraged to develop opportunities for participation by persons with disabilities in sports activities. In some cases, accessibility measures could be enough to open up opportunities for participation. In other cases, special arrangements or special games would be needed. States should support the participation of persons with disabilities in national and international events.

4. Persons with disabilities participating in sports activities should have access to instruction and training of the same quality as other participants.

5. Organizers of sports and recreation should consult with organizations of persons with disabilities when developing their services for persons with disabilities."

---

abled children may receive special education separately from their peers, so recreation may be the only opportunity for integrated activities and is thus particularly important (see box on previous page).

Children in closed institutions, such as hospitals or forms of detention, will also require special measures. The Committee told Hong Kong that it:

"notes with appreciation the initiatives taken to make hospitals more baby and child friendly, including the measures being taken to improve paediatric ward facilities in hospitals and also to provide play areas for children in paediatric wards and areas for parents to stay with their children in hospital" (UK dependent territory: Hong Kong IRCO, Add.63, para. 7)

As regards children whose liberty has been restricted, the Committee raised the matter with Russia and expressed

"its concern as to the compatibility of juvenile justice and penitentiary institutions with article 37 of the Convention and how the rights of the child to leisure and contacts with the family and the best interests of the child are protected in such situations" (Russian Federation IRCO, Add.4, para. 14).

The United Nations Rules for the Protection of Juveniles Deprived of their Liberty is quite clear on these rights:

"18(c). Juveniles should receive and retain materials for their leisure and recreation as are compatible with the interests of the administration of justice...

"47. Every juvenile should have the right to a suitable amount of time for daily free exercise, in the open air whenever weather permits, during which time appropriate recreational and physical training should normally be provided. Adequate space, installations and equipment should be provided for these activities. Every juvenile should have additional time for daily leisure activities, part of which should be devoted, if the juvenile so wishes, to arts and crafts skill development. The detention facility should ensure that each juvenile is physically able to participate in the available programmes of physical education. Remedial physical education and therapy should be offered, under medical supervision, to juveniles needing it."

Finally, although not specifically raised by the Committee, the discrimination against girls in this area should be mentioned, since it is an almost universal phenomenon that domestic chores give girls less time to play than boys, and that where play space is available boys take up an unequal amount. Adults cooperating with children can usually remedy this, but measures are needed.

Implementation Checklist

article **31**

● *General measures of implementation*

Have appropriate general measures of implementation been taken in relation to article 31 including

☐ identification and coordination of the responsible departments and agencies at all levels of government (article 31 is relevant to the **departments of culture and sport, education, labour, health, welfare and planning**)

☐ identification of relevant non-governmental organizations/civil society partners?

☐ a comprehensive review to ensure that all legislation, policy and practice is compatible with the article, for all children in all parts of the jurisdiction?

☐ adoption of a strategy to secure full implementation

   ☐ which includes where necessary the identification of goals and indicators of progress?

   ☐ which does not affect any provisions which are more conducive to the rights of the child?

   ☐ which recognizes other relevant international standards?

   ☐ which involves where necessary international cooperation?

(Such measures may be part of an overall governmental strategy for implementing the Convention as a whole).

☐ budgetary analysis and allocation of necessary resources?

☐ development of mechanisms for monitoring and evaluation?

☐ making the implications of article 31 widely known to adults and children?

☐ development of appropriate training and awareness-raising (in relation to article 31 likely to include the training of **play workers, town and environment planners, employment inspectors, administrators of art and culture, artists, teachers and social workers**)?

● *Specific issues in implementing article 31*

☐ Are necessary measures taken to secure the right of the child to rest and leisure?

☐ Do such measures include prohibitions on children working at night or working throughout all school holiday periods?

☐ Have ILO Conventions Nos. 79 and 90 been ratified?

☐ Do compulsory school hours and homework regimes allow for rest and leisure periods?

☐ Does environmental planning take into account the play needs of children?

☐ Does this planning take account of children's views of what is needed?

☐ Are play and recreational opportunities appropriate to all ages of children (including preschoolers and teenagers) available without discrimination?

☐ Are resources allocated for sports, culture and the arts divided fairly between adults and children?

☐ Do all children have reasonable access to all cultural and artistic events?

☐ Are there any limitations on the participation of all children in cultural life and the arts?

☐ Are cultural and artistic events organized specially for children?

☐ Are children given access to cultural and artistic events through financial concessions or discounts?

☐ Do disabled children have access to integrated recreational, cultural and artistic activities?

☐ Do children in hospital have opportunities for play and recreational activities?

☐ Do children in institutions have opportunities for play, sports and recreational, artistic and cultural activities?

☐ Do children whose liberty has been restricted have opportunities for physical exercise, recreation and artistic or cultural activities?

☐ Are measures taken to ensure that girls have as equal an opportunity as boys for rest, leisure, play and recreation and to enjoy cultural and artistic activities?

Reminder : **The Convention is indivisible and its articles are interdependent. Article 31 should not be considered in isolation.**

Particular regard should be paid to:
The general principles

Article 2: all rights to be recognized for each child in jurisdiction without discrimination on any ground

Article 3(1): the best interests of the child to be a primary consideration in all actions concerning children

Article 6: right to life and maximum possible survival and development

Article 12: respect for the child's views in all matters affecting the child; opportunity to be heard in any judicial or administrative proceedings affecting the child

Closely related articles

Articles whose implementation is related to that of article 31 include:

Article 13: freedom of expression
Article 14: freedom of thought, conscience and religion
Article 15: freedom of association
Article 16: protection of privacy
Article 17: access to information, role of the media
Article 28: aims of education
Article 30: respect for minority or indigenous culture
Article 32: child labour
Article 36: protection from exploitation

Child labour

article 32

Text of Article 32

1. States Parties recognize the right of the child to be protected from economic exploitation and from performing any work that is likely to be hazardous or to interfere with the child's education, or to be harmful to the child's health or physical, mental, spiritual, moral or social development.

2. States Parties shall take legislative, administrative, social and educational measures to ensure the implementation of the present article. To this end, and having regard to the relevant provisions of other international instruments, States Parties shall in particular:

(a) Provide for a minimum age or minimum ages for admission to employment;

(b) Provide for appropriate regulation of the hours and conditions of employment;

(c) Provide for appropriate penalties or other sanctions to ensure the effective enforcement of the present article.

Article 32 recognizes the right of the child to be protected from economic exploitation; and any work that is likely

- to be hazardous, or
- to interfere with the child's education, or
- to be harmful to the child's health or physical, mental, spiritual, moral or social development.

The article requires States Parties to take legislative, administrative, social and educational measures to ensure implementation, and in particular to provide:

- a minimum age or ages for admission to employment;
- appropriate regulation of the hours and conditions of employment; and
- appropriate penalties or other sanctions to ensure effective enforcement.

States Parties must have regard "to the relevant provisions of other international instruments": the most relevant are International Labour Office Conventions and Recommendations, and the Committee on the Rights of the Child has identified among them ILO Convention No.138 on minimum ages for employment as of key importance.

The Committee on the Rights of the Child has paid particular attention to the issue of economic exploitation of children, and held a General Discussion on the issue in October 1993. ∎

Summary

Extracts from
Committee on the Rights of the Child
Guidelines for Reports to be submitted by States Parties under the Convention

For full text of *Guidelines for Periodic Reports*, see Appendix 3, page 604.

Guidelines for Initial Reports

"Special protection measures

Under this section States Parties are requested to provide relevant information, including the principal legislative, judicial, administrative or other measures in force; factors and difficulties encountered and progress achieved in implementing the relevant provisions of the Convention; and implementation priorities and specific goals for the future in respect of:

...

(c) Children in situations of exploitation including physical and psychological recovery and social reintegration (article 39)

(i) Economic exploitation, including child labour (article 32);

...".

(CRC/C/5, para. 23)

Guidelines for Periodic Reports

"VIII. SPECIAL PROTECTION MEASURES

....

C. Children in situations of exploitation, including physical and psychological recovery and social reintegration

1. Economic exploitation of children, including child labour (art. 32).

Please provide information on the measures taken, including of a legislative, administrative, social and educational nature, to recognize and ensure the right of the child to be protected from:

> *Economic exploitation;*

> *Performing any work that is likely to be hazardous or to interfere with the child's education, or to be harmful to the child's health or physical, mental, spiritual, moral or social development.*

In this regard, reports should in particular indicate:

> *Whether legislation has included a prohibition, as well as a definition, of hazardous and harmful work, and/or of the activities considered to be hazardous, harmful to the child's health or development or to interfere with the child's education;*

> *Any preventive and remedial action undertaken, including information and awareness campaigns, as well as education, in particular compulsory education, and vocational training programmes, to address the situation of child labour both in the formal and informal sector, including as domestic servants, in agriculture or within private family activities;*

> *The measures adopted to ensure respect for the general principles of the Convention, particularly non-discrimination, the best interests of the child, the right to life, and survival and development to the maximum extent possible.*

Please also indicate the appropriate measures adopted pursuant to article 32, paragraph 2, and having regard to the relevant provisions of other international instruments, including measures at the legislative and administrative levels, to provide in particular for:

> *A minimum age or minimum ages for admission to employment;*

> *Appropriate regulation of the hours and conditions of employment;*

Appropriate penalties or other sanctions to ensure the effective enforcement of this article, and any mechanism of inspection and system of complaint procedures available to the child, either directly or through a representative.

In this regard, reports should also provide information on the international conventions and other relevant instruments to which the State may be a party, including in the framework of the International Labour Organization, as well as on:

Any national policy and multidisciplinary strategy developed to prevent and combat situations of children's economic exploitation and labour;

Any coordinating and monitoring mechanism established for that purpose;

The relevant indicators identified and used;

Relevant programmes of technical cooperation and international assistance developed;

The progress achieved in the implementation of this article, benchmarks set up as well as difficulties encountered;

Relevant disaggregated data on the children concerned, including by age, gender, region, rural/urban area, and social and ethnic origin, as well as on infringements observed by inspectors and sanctions applied."

(CRC/C/58, paras. 151-154. The following paragraphs of the *Guidelines for Periodic Reports* are also relevant to reporting under this article: 24, 107, and 161; for full text of *Guidelines*, see Appendix 3, page 604.)

International instruments and standards concerning child labour

The International Labour Organization (ILO)

According to the International Labour Organization's Bureau of Statistics, there are at least 120 million working children between the ages of five and 14 (and about 250 million if those for whom work is a secondary activity are included). While a majority are in developing countries, there are pockets of child labour in many industrialized countries.

The International Labour Organization states that numerous children are still trapped in slavery in many parts of the world. "Some bondage practices are virtually indistinguishable from chattel slavery of 200 years ago, except that the markets are not so open. Children are sold outright for a sum of money. Sometimes landlords buy child workers from their tenants or, in a variant of the system, labour 'contractors' pay an advance sum to rural families in order to take their children away to work in carpet-weaving, in glass-manufacture, in prostitution... One of the most common forms of bondage is family bondage, where children work to help pay off a loan or other obligation incurred by the family... Perhaps most widespread of all are informal bondage arrangements under which impoverished parents surrender their children to outsiders simply to work in exchange for their upkeep, on the assumption that they will be better provided for as unremunerated servants in an affluent household than they could be in their own families."

Commercial sexual exploitation is a contemporary form of slavery involving millions of children – including many bought and sold across national borders by organized networks (*Child labour Targeting the intolerable*, p. 15-16).

The ILO sees priorities as the targeting of scarce resources on the most intolerable forms of child labour such as slavery, debt bondage, child prostitution and work in hazardous occupations and industries, and on the very young: "This approach has the additional advantage that policies designed to reach the children in most need are likely to benefit other working children and that focusing on the most socially repugnant examples can help maintain the necessary social commitment and consensus."

The ILO emphasizes in particular "the invisibility of endangered children. One reason why modern societies and governments have not been more active in curbing the most harmful forms of child labour is that working children are often not readily visible. It is a matter of 'out of sight, out of mind'" (*Child labour Targeting the intolerable*, p. 20).

International labour conventions

Since 1919, the International Labour Organization has adopted a number of international labour

"The single most important source of child exploitation and child abuse in the world today..."

"Numerous children work in occupations and industries which are plainly dangerous and hazardous. They are found in mines, in factories making glass bangles, matches and fireworks, in deep-sea fishing, in commercial agriculture and so on:

● Working children suffer significant growth deficits compared with children in school: they grow up shorter and lighter, and their body size continues to be small even in adulthood.

● Both anecdotal evidence and statistical surveys indicate that far too many working children are exposed to hazardous conditions which expose them to chemical and biological hazards. For example, according to one large-scale ILO national survey in the Philippines, more than 60 per cent of working children are exposed to such hazards and, of these, 40 per cent experience serious injuries or illnesses including amputations and loss of body parts.

● Large numbers of working children work under conditions which expose them to substances with long latency periods – for example, asbestos – which increases the risk of contracting chronic occupational diseases such as asbestosis or lung cancer in young adulthood...

● In rural areas, more children are believed to die of exposure to pesticide than from the most common childhood diseases put together, according to a study on occupational health in developing countries.

● Children in certain occupations are especially vulnerable to particular types of abuse. For example, many studies confirm that child domestic workers are victims of verbal and sexual abuse, beating or punishment by starvation.

Child labour is simply the single most important source of child exploitation and child abuse in the world today".

(Extracts from *Child labour Targeting the intolerable*, ILO, 1996, pp. 3-4)

article 32

Conventions concerning child labour, which are supplemented by Recommendations. The Minimum Age (Industry) Convention 1919 (No.5) prohibits children under the age of 14 from working in industrial establishments. Subsequently, nine other sectoral Conventions on the minimum age of admission to employment were adopted, applying to industry, agriculture, trimmers and stokers, maritime work, non-industrial employment, fishing and underground work. Many other ILO standards contain provisions setting minimum ages for various activities. Furthermore, general international labour Conventions regarding freedom of association, discrimination, wages and safety and health apply to all workers regardless of age. And such problems as exploitation of children through debt bondage and other "contemporary forms of slavery", such as child prostitution, are examined in the framework of the Forced Labour Convention 1930 (No.29) (applying to all "work or service which is exacted from any person under the menace of any penalty and for which the said person has not offered himself voluntarily"); by 1996, the Convention had been ratified by 139 countries.

In 1994, the ILO Committee of Experts expressed its grave concern about forced child labour and particularly about the exploitation of children for prostitution and pornography.

ILO Convention No.138 and Recommendation No.146

The most recent and comprehensive ILO instruments on child labour are the Minimum Age Convention, 1973 (No.138) and Recommendation (No.146). Convention No.138, in particular, has been upheld by the Committee on the Rights of the Child as a relevant standard, and States Parties that have not already ratified it have been urged to do so by the Committee (see below, page 438). The Minimum Age Convention is a consolidation of principles that had been gradually established in various earlier instruments and applies to all sectors of economic activity, whether the children are employed for wages or not (for details, see under "minimum ages" below, page 438). According to the ILO: "The Convention obliges ratifying States to fix a minimum age for admission to employment or work and undertake to pursue a national policy designed to ensure the effective abolition of child labour and to raise progressively the minimum age for admission to employment or work to a level consistent with the fullest physical and mental development of young persons. The Convention was not intended as a static instrument prescribing a fixed minimum standard but as a dynamic one aimed at encouraging the progressive improvement of standards and of promoting sustained action to attain the objectives. Recommendation No.146, which supplements Convention No.138, provides the broad framework and essential policy measures for both the prevention of child labour and its elimination." (*Child Labour Targeting the intolerable*, ILO, 1996, p. 24)

By 1996, 49 States had ratified Convention No. 138, but, according to the ILO, only 21 of them are developing countries, and these did not include any in Asia, where over half of all working children are found (op. cit., p. 28). The Minimum Age Recommendation (No.146) was also adopted in 1973. It provides detailed advice on implementation of Convention No.138 and emphasizes the importance of giving a high priority to the needs of children and youth in national development policies and programmes, as well as the importance of adopting measures to alleviate poverty.

Proposed ILO Convention on child labour

As part of its campaign to eliminate child labour, the ILO is currently (1997) proposing the adoption of new standards, which are likely to take the form of a new short Convention, supplemented by a Recommendation, to ban and prevent all extreme forms of child labour. In March 1996, the ILO Governing Body decided to place child labour on the agenda of the 1998 International Labour Conference with a view to the adoption of new international labour standards that place priority on immediate action to stop the intolerable exploitation of children in hazardous work and activities. In June 1996, the 83rd International Labour Conference adopted a resolution welcoming the decision to pursue new standards to put an end to the most intolerable aspects of child labour, namely the employment of children in slave-like and bonded conditions and in dangerous and hazardous work, the exploitation of very young children and the commercial sexual exploitation of children.

"The Office's proposals ... envisage a new Convention which would complement Convention No.138 and be consistent with it but which would focus on the most intolerable forms of child labour... It would apply to all children under the age of 18 and would oblige member States to suppress immediately all extreme forms of child labour including: all forms of slavery or practices similar to slavery; the sale and trafficking of children; forced or compulsory labour including debt bondage and serfdom; the use of chil-

ILO Conventions particularly relating to children

Minimum Age (Industry) Convention, 1919 (No.5);
Night Work of Young Persons (Industry) Convention, 1919 (No.6);
Minimum Age (Sea) Convention, 1920 (No.7);
Minimum Age (Agriculture) Convention, 1921 (No.10);
Minimum Age (Trimmers and Stokers) Convention, 1921 (No.15);
Forced Labour Convention, 1930 (No. 29);
Minimum Age (Non-Industrial Employment) Convention, 1932 (No.33);
Minimum Age (Sea) Convention (Revised), 1936 (No. 58);
Minimum Age (Industry) Convention (Revised), 1937 (No.59);
Minimum Age (Non-industrial Employment) Convention (Revised), 1937 (No.60);
Medical Examination of Young Persons (Industry) Convention, 1946 (No.77);
Medical Examination of Young Persons (Non-Industrial Occupations) Convention, 1946 (No.78);
Night Work of Young Persons (Non-Industrial Occupations) Convention, 1946 (No.79);
Night Work of Young Persons (Industry) Convention (Revised), 1948 (No. 90);
Minimum Age (Fishermen) Convention, 1959 (No.6 112);
Minimum Age (Underground Work) Convention, 1965 (No. 123);
Medical Examination of Young Persons (Underground Work) Convention, 1965 (No.124);
Minimum Age Convention, 1973 (No.138).

dren for prostitution; the production of pornography or pornographic performances; the production of or trafficking in drugs or other illegal activities; and the engagement of children in any type of work, which by its nature or the circumstances in which it is carried out, is likely to jeopardize their health, safety or morals..." (*Child labour Targeting the intolerable, ILO*, p. 114). A questionnaire on the content of the proposed Convention has been sent to all member States (International Labour Conference 86th Session 1998, Report VI(1): Questionnaire Child labour). International conferences are scheduled on child labour in 1997, and the proposal for new instruments is to be discussed at the 1998 International Labour Conference, with a view to adoption by the 1999 Conference.

ILO International Programme on the Elimination of Child Labour

ILO's International Programme on the Elimination of Child Labour (IPEC) is now operational in more than 25 countries. Initiated in 1992, it assists countries in elaborating and implementing comprehensive policies and targeted programmes and projects. Participating countries sign a "Memorandum of Understanding" with the ILO, under which national steering committees are established.

The ILO suggests that a national policy and programme of action needs to contain at least the following elements:

- a definition of national objectives regarding child labour;

- a description of the nature and context of the problem;

- identification of the priority target groups;

- a description of the priority target groups;

- a description of the intervention approaches to be used;

- designation of the institutional actors to be involved.

(*Child labour Targeting the intolerable*, p. 100; see also *The State of the World's Children 1997*, UNICEF, p. 19)

International Bill of Human Rights and child labour

The International Bill of Human Rights – the Universal Declaration and the two International Covenants, on Civil and Political Rights and Economic, Social and Cultural Rights – include various provisions relevant to child labour.

The Universal Declaration of Human Rights asserts: "No one shall be held in slavery or servitude; slavery and the slave trade shall be prohibited in all their forms" (article 4). Article 8 of the International Covenant on Civil and Political Rights expands on this:

"1. No one shall be held in slavery; slavery and the slave-trade in all their forms shall be prohibited.

2. No one shall be held in servitude.

3. (a) No one shall be required to perform forced or compulsory labour;

(b) Paragraph 3(a) shall not be held to preclude, in countries where imprisonment with hard labour may be imposed as a punishment for a crime, the performance of hard labour in pursuance of a sentence to such punishment by a competent court;

(c) For the purpose of this paragraph the term 'forced or compulsory labour' shall not include:

(i) Any work or service, not referred to in subparagraph (b), normally required of a person who is under detention in consequence of a lawful order of a court, or of a person during conditional release from such detention;

(ii) Any service of a military character and, in countries where conscientious objection is recognized, any national service required by law of conscientious objectors;

(iii) Any service exacted in cases of emergency or calamity threatening the life or well-being of the community;

(iv) Any work or service which forms part of normal civil obligations."

Article 23 of the Universal Declaration of Human Rights asserts the right to work:

"1. Everyone has the right to work, to free choice of employment, to just and favourable conditions of work and to protection against unemployment.

2. Everyone, without any discrimination, has the right to equal pay for equal work.

3. Everyone who works has the right to just and favourable remuneration ensuring for himself and his family an existence worthy of human dignity, and supplemented, if necessary, by other means of social protection.

4. Everyone has the right to form and to join trade unions for the protection of his interests."

The International Covenant on Economic, Social and Cultural Rights also asserts in more detail the right to work and to just and favourable conditions of work (articles 6 and 7). Paragraph 3 of article 10 of the Covenant requires "special measures of protection and assistance" for all children and young persons: "Children and young persons should be protected from economic and social exploitation. Their employment in work harmful to their morals or health or dangerous to life or likely to hamper their normal development should be punishable by law. States should also set age limits below which the paid employment of child labour should be prohibited and punishable by law."

In relation to traffic in children and child prostitution, there are various other relevant Conventions, including in particular:

- International Convention for the Suppression of the Traffic in Women and Children, 1921, as amended by Protocol approved by General Assembly of United Nations, 1947;

- Convention for the Suppression of the Traffic in Persons and of the Exploitation of the Prostitution of Others, 1949 (entered into force in 1951) requires (article 1) States to agree to punish "any person who, to gratify the passions of another: 1. Procures, entices or leads away, for purposes of prostitution, another person, even with the consent of that person; 2. Exploits the prostitution of another person, even with the consent of that person";

- Supplementary Convention on the Abolition of Slavery, the Slave Trade, and Institutions and Practices Similar to Slavery, 1956 (entered into force in 1957), article 1(d): "Any institution or practice whereby a child or young person under the age of 18 years is delivered by either or both of his natural parents or by his guardian to another person, whether for reward or not, with a view to the exploitation of the child or young person or of his labour."

World Summit Declaration and Plan of Action

In 1990, world leaders committed themselves to "work for special protection of the working child and for the abolition of illegal child labour..." (Declaration, para. 20(7)). The Plan of Action states that "More than 100 million children are engaged in employment, often heavy and hazardous and in contravention of international conventions which provide for their protection from economic exploitation and from performing work that interferes with their education and is harmful to their health and full development. With this in mind, all States should work to end such child labour practices and see how the conditions and circumstances of children in legitimate employment can be protected to provide adequate opportunity for their healthy upbringing and development." (para. 23)

Commission on Human Rights' Programme of Action

In 1993, the Commission on Human Rights adopted a Programme of Action for the Elimination of the Exploitation of Child Labour, submitted to it by the SubCommission on Prevention of Discrimination and Protection of Minorities. The Commission invited the Committee on the Rights of the Child to bear the Programme of Action in mind when examining States Parties' reports and its other activities. The Programme stresses "High priority should be given to the elimination of the most odious or degrading forms of child exploitation, in particular child prostitution, pornography, the sale of children, the employment of children in dangerous occupations or for enforced begging and debt bondage... The international community should place particular emphasis on the new phenomena of the exploitation of child labour, such as the use of children for illegal, clandestine or criminal purposes, including their implication in the narcotic drugs traffic or in armed conflicts or military activities... Action should be directed, first, towards the most dangerous forms of child labour and the elimination of work by children under 10 years of age, with a view to the total elimination of child labour as prohibited by the provisions of the relevant international instruments."

The Programme of Action highlights three particular forms of exploitation of child labour which are a flagrant crime violating the Charter of the United Nations and international instruments:

- sale and similar practices (serfdom, bond service, fake adoption, abandonment);
- child prostitution, trafficking in child pornography, and international traffic in girls and boys for immoral purposes;
- under-age maidservants in a position of servitude.

(Commission on Human Rights, Programme of Action for the Elimination of the Exploitation of Child Labour, 1993/79)

The United Nations Working Group on Contemporary Forms of Slavery has classified the sale and sexual exploitation of children as contemporary forms of slavery (see also articles 34, page 455 and 35, page 471).

Girls and economic exploitation

The Declaration and Platform for Action of the Fourth World Conference on Women (Beijing, 1995) highlights the particular discriminatory forms of child labour affecting girls: "In many cases girls start to undertake heavy domestic chores at a very early age and are expected to manage both educational and domestic responsibilities, often resulting in poor scholastic performance and an early drop-out from schooling." The Platform for Action cites child labour as one of the reasons why, of the 130 million children who in 1990 had no access to primary education, 81 million were girls. Its strategic objective L.6: "Eliminate the economic exploitation of child labour and protect young girls at work" – promotes the standards in the Convention on the Rights of the Child and ILO Conventions (Declaration and Platform for Action, paras. 263 and 282).

In a number of comments on Initial Reports, the Committee has expressed concern at these issues:

"The Committee expresses its deep concern at information it has received regarding the exploitation and abuse of girls working in the 'maquilas' (assembly factories, mainly forming part of the textile industry)." (Honduras IRCO, Add.24, para. 19)

article 32

Prevalence and causes of child labour

In Pakistan, according to the Initial Report, "In order to offset low *per capita* income, the poor are constrained to use their large family size to increase their participation in the labour force – the additional work effort coming from women and children. Among the poor, some 12 per cent of children (10-14 years) work – many in unhealthy trades for pitiful wages. There are at least 8 million working children who remain away from school... More poverty among rural households coupled with the nature of agricultural work contributes to greater child labour in rural areas...

"Quantifying child labour in Pakistan is an almost impossible task. The 1981 census reported 2.01 million children between the ages of 10 and 14 as 'working'. A small increase in this figure would be consistent with the increase in population and the decrease in the age-specific labour force participation rate reported by successive labour force surveys. There were also 3.9 million girls aged between 10 and 14 reported as 'housekeeping' in the 1981 census. This data does not cover children below the age of 10, and is also likely to underestimate children working on farms and in the urban informal sector.

"A number of laws in Pakistan in fact ban the labour of children under the age of 15 in a variety of settings and regulate conditions of employment of youths between 15 and 18 years of age. Unfortunately, in spite of this legislation, child labour is still prevalent in the country due to prevailing economic conditions. However the Governments and non-governmental organizations in the social welfare sector in collaboration with UNICEF are striving to reduce the exploitative nature of child labour. Accordingly 176 centres for children working in different trades have been set up where they receive education, health care and recreational services. The employers and parents of these children cooperate fully in this scheme." (Pakistan IR, paras. 30, 138-9)

"...The problems of the exploitation of child labour, in particular the use of young girls as domestic workers, and child prostitution also require special attention." (Morocco IRCO, Add.60, para. 15)

Children whose liberty is restricted

The United Nations Rules for the Protection of Juveniles Deprived of their Liberty requires that juveniles under arrest or awaiting trial "should be provided, where possible, with opportunities to pursue work, with remuneration, and continue education or training, but should not be required to do so. Work, education or training should not cause the continuation of the detention" (rule 18(b)). In addition, under rule 44: "All protective national and international standards applicable to child labour and young workers should apply to juveniles deprived of their liberty." Rules 45 and 46 require that juveniles deprived of their liberty should, whenever possible, be provided with the opportunity to perform remunerated work and have the right to an "equitable remuneration".

The right of the child to protection from economic exploitation

As noted in the summary to this section, the first paragraph of article 32 requires States to recognize the right of the child to be protected from economic exploitation and from performing any work which is likely to be hazardous, interfere with the child's education, or be harmful to health or physical, mental, spiritual, moral or social development.

The Committee on the Rights of the Child held a General Discussion on economic exploitation of children in October 1993. In the outline for the General Discussion, the Committee identified other articles relevant to economic exploitation in addition to article 32:

- article 33, requiring States Parties to take measures to prevent the use of children in the illicit production and trafficking of narcotic drugs;

- article 34, requiring protection against sexual exploitation;

- article 35, prevention of abduction, sale and traffic in children for any purpose;

- article 36, requiring protection against all other forms of exploitation prejudicial to any aspects of the child's welfare.

The Committee emphasized that all these articles should be read in the light of the general principles set out in articles 2, 3, 6 and 12.

The Committee has also stressed the relevance to the protection of children from economic exploitation of the child's right to education (article 28), and of measures to promote child victims' physical and psychological recovery and social reintegration (article 39).

At the conclusion of the General Discussion on economic exploitation, the Committee made a public statement and, subsequently, through a working group of its members, framed a set of recommendations (see below). The statement invited financial institutions, including the World Bank and the International Monetary Fund, to a discussion about the need to protect the rights of the child in economic reform programmes:

"When analyzing States' reports, the Committee noted that groups of children in both poor and rich countries have been victimized by sweeping measures to curb inflation and encourage economic growth. Social allocations have been cut in drastic proportion. This has caused new poverty. Groups of vulnerable children, in particular, have been made to suffer: the girl child, the disabled, minority ethnic groups, orphans, displaced and refugee children..."

Second, the Committee recommended that UNESCO take the lead in an international effort to make school education

"a real and effective alternative to exploitative child labour, including child prostitution".

And third it recommended that all Governments

"ratify promptly the International Labour Organization standards on minimum age and on conditions of employment. These international norms should also be incorporated into national legislation – and be enforced.
"The laws in many countries do not give protection against economic exploitation of children. In other cases, the legislation is consistent with international standards but is not enforced. A system for inspection of work places is needed in each country. Also, the informal sector of the economy should be systematically controlled.
"The cynicism which has made large-scale exploitation of children possible must now be effectively countered. Violations of the rights of working children should be penalized. Child prostitution must be severely criminalized; intermediaries, accomplices and 'clients' should be penalized. Child pornography should be banned." (Report on the fourth session, September-October 1993, CRC/C/20, Annex VI, pp. 57-58)

The Committee adopted "Recommendations concerning economic exploitation of children" at its fifth session in January 1994. These emphasized that the holistic approach to the human rights of children, stressed in the Convention on the Rights of the Child and in particular in the general principles of the Convention (articles 2, 3, 4 and 12),

should be used as a general framework in which to consider situations of economic exploitation of children. It called for "an adequate legal framework and necessary mechanisms of implementation", as well as periodic assessment and evaluation of progress. The Committee recommended the establishment of a national mechanism for coordinating policies and monitoring the implementation of the Convention, having specific competence in the area of protection from economic exploitation. It encouraged increasing international cooperation and stressed the essential importance of information and education to prevent situations of economic exploitation.

Specifically in the area of the protection of the child from economic exploitation, the Committee

"considers the child as a person who should be given the benefit of respect and solidarity within the family and society;

(i) In the case of sexual exploitation or exploitation through work, the Committee considers the child as a victim who should be given the benefit of special protection in terms of health, education and development.

(ii) In any event, the following must be strictly forbidden:

> *Activities jeopardizing the development of the child or contrary to human values and dignity;*
> *Activities involving cruel, inhuman or degrading treatment, the sale of children or situations of servitude;*
> *Activities that are dangerous or harmful to the child's harmonious physical, mental and spiritual development or are liable to jeopardize the future education and training of the child;*
> *Activities involving discrimination, particularly with regard to vulnerable and marginalized social groups;*
> *All activities under the minimum ages referred to in article 32, paragraph 2, of the Convention on the Rights of the Child and in particular those recommended by ILO;*
> *All activities using the child for legally punishable criminal acts, such as trafficking in drugs or prohibited goods.*

(iii) In accordance with article 32 of the Convention on the Rights of the Child, every child has the right to be protected from economic exploitation. Taking into consideration the best interests of the child, States Parties must formulate standards or revise legislation in force with a view to ensuring the legal protection of the child from any form of exploitation. States Parties are invited to take all legislative, administrative and other measures aimed at ensuring the protection of the child, taking account of all forms of employment,

Constraints on preventing child labour

Nepal's Initial Report records: "It is difficult to control and prevent child labour as the problem is rooted in poverty. Child labour is even more prevalent in the unorganized sector of the economy, and in households, where children usually work as servants. Children supplement labour in the fields and at home from an early age. Children between the ages of six and nine work about three hours a day, while children between the ages of 10 and 14 work five to six hours, with girls putting in nearly twice as many hours as boys. The girl child helps to fetch water and collect fuel and fodder.

"Activities against child labour are centred in urban areas, while the bulk of the population lives in the villages. Legislative provisions alone are not sufficient to safeguard the interests of working children. Unless there is genuine commitment of concerned agencies and individuals as well, child labour cannot be abolished.

"The growing incidence of child labour in the country is a reflection of the existing socio-economic realities... According to Child Workers in Nepal the percentage distribution of child labourers is 86 per cent in agriculture and household work, 6 per cent in services, 3 per cent in business and cottage industries, 2.4 per cent in factories, 0.6 per cent in construction, and 2 per cent in other sectors...

"Children have long been a source of income for the family. As long as families do not have alternative sources of income, child labour in one form or another will continue to be a reality. Hence, certain protective measures are to be undertaken, such as fixing basic minimum wages, providing opportunities for non-formal education and job-oriented training, basing work on the age, sex, and the physical and mental capacity of the children, and reducing working hours..." (Nepal IR, paras. 359-363 and 366)

including employment within the family and in the agricultural sector and informal employment.

(iv) States Parties must also take measures to ensure the rehabilitation of children who, as a result of economic exploitation, are exposed to serious physical and moral danger. It is essential to provide these children with the necessary social and medical assistance and to envisage social reintegration programmes for them in the light of article 39 of the Convention on the Rights of the Child." (Report on the fifth session, January 1994, CRC/C/24, pp. 38-43)

The Committee has reflected these general recommendations in its Concluding Observations on States Parties' reports. In cases where there are allegations of forced labour, the Committee has indicated the most serious concern:

"...Reports on the forced labour and slavery of children give cause for the Committee's deepest concern...
"The Committee also emphasizes the need to pay urgent and due regard to the reports of forced labour and slavery of children. The Committee believes that international cooperation, particularly technical assistance and advice, could be used to that end." (Sudan IRCO, Add.10, paras. 14 and 25; see also Sudan Prelim. Obs., Add.6, para. 12)

"The Committee is seriously alarmed at the reports of the forced labour of children, the

exploitation of child labour in the informal and agriculture sectors and the trafficking of children which has been brought to its attention." (Pakistan IRCO, Add.18, para. 21)

(See also comments on sexual exploitation, another form of forced labour: article 34, page 455).

In many cases, the Committee has expressed more general concern and made a variety of recommendations, often referring to ILO Convention No. 138 and to the possibility of States Parties seeking technical assistance from the ILO. In other cases, it has highlighted different sectors or types of employment as needing attention, for example the informal sector, child domestic servants, the fashion industry and family enterprises including agriculture. The following are examples from the many general comments and recommendations regarding article 32:

"...the Committee is concerned at the situation of children in exceptionally difficult circumstances, including the incidence of child labour, particularly on farms and in the informal sector....
"The Committee also recommends that the State Party ensures that its policy and legislation on the issue of child labour is in conformity with the provisions of the Convention on the Rights of the Child and the relevant ILO Conventions." (Namibia IRCO, Add.14, paras. 10 and 21)

"The Committee is also concerned that adequate measures are not being taken to protect children from exploitation through labour...

"In view of the significant risk of the exploitation of children through labour, particularly in the light of recent changes to national legislation, the Committee suggests that this matter be urgently addressed and that the necessary action be taken in line with the Convention and in particular its article 3 as it relates to the best interests of the child." (Belarus IRCO, Add.17, paras. 10 and 16)

"The Committee recommends that the State Party evaluate thoroughly the adequacy of measures taken to deal with issues of the exploitation of children. In the light of the legislation recently adopted in this area, namely the Employment of Children Act and the Bonded Labour System (Abolition) Act, as well as the conclusions of the Asian Regional Seminar on Children in Bondage, held in Islamabad, the Committee would like to emphasize the importance of measures to be taken for their enforcement, particularly through the establishment of complaints and inspection procedures and vigilance committees. A rehabilitation programme for children released from bonded labour is also recommended. The Committee also recommends that greater attention be given to the issues of the employment of children in the informal sector and in agriculture and that measures be taken to address these issues. The Committee believes that technical advice, particularly from ILO, may be appropriate with regard to these matters." (Pakistan IRCO, Add.18, para. 32)

"With respect to child exploitation, the Committee is concerned that child labour remains a serious problem in Nicaragua, especially in view of the high level of adult unemployment existing in the country. It is concerned about the apparent inadequacy of measures to address this issue, including for the many children working in the informal sector, including in domestic service, where no effective mechanisms appear to exist for the protection of children engaged in such work.
"It is the view of the Committee that legal reforms and a preventive campaign should be urgently introduced to address the issue of child labour. The Committee would like to suggest that the Government of Nicaragua consider requesting further technical assistance from ILO in these matters." (Nicaragua IRCO, Add.36, paras. 24 and 40. See also Madagascar IRCO, Add.26, paras. 14 and 21; Spain IRCO, Add 28, para. 24; Italy IRCO, Add.41, para. 21; Yemen IRCO, Add.47, para. 21; Guatemala IRCO, Add.58, para. 23; Nigeria IRCO, Add.61, para. 41; Mauritius IRCO, Add.64, para. 17; Bulgaria IRCO, Add.66, para. 33)

Reservations and declarations relating to article 32

Few States Parties have made reservations or declarations in relation to article 32. India made a reservation justifying progressive implementation of the article: "While fully subscribing to the objectives and purposes of the Convention, realizing that certain of the rights of the child, namely those pertaining to the economic, social and cultural rights, can only be progressively implemented in the developing countries, subject to the extent of available resources and within the framework of international cooperation; recognizing that the child has to be protected from exploitation of all forms including economic exploitation; noting that for several reasons children of different ages do work in India; having prescribed minimum ages for employment in hazardous occupations and in certain other areas; having made regulatory provisions regarding hours and conditions of employment; and being aware that it is not practical immediately to prescribe minimum ages for admission to each and every area of employment in India – the Government of India undertakes to take measures to progressively implement the provisions of article 32, particularly paragraph 2(a), in accordance with its national legislation and relevant international instruments to which it is a State Party." (CRC/C/2/Rev.5, p. 21)

New Zealand noted that it considered the rights of the child, provided for in article 32(1), "are adequately protected by its existing law. It therefore reserves the right not to legislate further or to take additional measures as may be envisaged in article 32(2)" (CRC/C/2/Rev.5, p. 28). When it examined New Zealand's Initial Report, the Committee expressed concern at

"the broad nature of the reservations made by the State Party" (New Zealand IRCO, Add.71, para. 8).

The United Kingdom indicated that its employment legislation does not treat persons under the age of 18 but over the school leaving age as children, but as "young people". "Accordingly, the United Kingdom reserves the right to continue to apply article 32 subject to such employment legislation" (CRC/C/2/Rev.5, p. 34). Here, too, the Committee expressed concern at the broad nature of the reservations made by the United Kingdom, and went on to recommend:

"Within the context of the law reform being considered with regard to matters relating to the employment of children, the Committee expresses the hope that the State Party will consider reviewing its reservation with a view to its withdrawal..." (UK IRCO, Add.34, para. 37)

Providing "a minimum age or minimum ages for admission to employment"

Article 32(2)(a) of the Convention requires that a minimum age, or minimum ages, for employment must be set; it does not prescribe any particular ages. But the Committee has indicated that such ages should be established in the light of other international instruments, and in particular ILO Convention No.138 (see full text in Appendix 4, page 633).

Basically, the ILO Convention requires:

- a commitment "to pursue a national policy designed to ensure the effective abolition of child labour and to raise progressively the minimum age for admission to employment or work to a level consistent with the fullest physical and mental development of young persons";

- a minimum age for any employment not less than the age of completion of compulsory schooling and in any event not less than 15; and

- a minimum age of 18 "for admission to any type of employment or work which by its nature or the circumstances in which it is carried out is likely to jeopardize the health, safety or morals of young persons".

But in relation to these minimum ages, the Convention allows certain limited exceptions. In relation to the minimum age for any employment or work:

- where the economy and educational facilities are insufficiently developed, a member State may, provided it has consulted with organizations of workers and employers concerned, initially specify a minimum age of 14 years (article 2);

- members that ratify may also list, after consultation, limited categories of work or employment – not hazardous – "in respect of which special and substantial problems of application arise", which are excluded from application of the Convention (article 4);

- members may initially limit the overall application of the Convention, specifying in a declaration branches of economic activity or types of undertakings to which it will be applied. The Convention must be applied as a minimum to: "mining and quarrying; manufacturing; construction; electricity, gas and water; sanitary services; transport, storage and communication; and plantations and other agricultural undertakings mainly producing for commercial purposes, but exclud-

ing family and small-scale holdings producing for local consumption and not regularly employing hired workers" (article 5);

- excluded from the Convention is work done in schools or other training institutions for general, vocational or technical education, or by persons at least 14 years of age in undertakings under specified conditions (article 6);

- national laws or regulations may permit light work by 13 to 15-year-olds (or 12 to 14 initially), which is not likely to be harmful to their health or development, and does not prejudice their attendance at school or in vocational or training programmes, "or their capacity to benefit from the instruction received" (article 7);

- national law or regulations may permit employment or work by young people who are at least 15 (or 14 initially) but have not completed their compulsory schooling, provided they meet the above conditions, and the hours and conditions of employment or work are specified;

- also after consultation, the competent authority may, by permits granted in individual cases, allow exceptions "for such purposes as participation in artistic performances"; the permits must limit hours and prescribe conditions (article 8).

In relation to hazardous work, members may initially, after consultation, set a minimum age of 16 "on condition that the health and morals of the young persons concerned are fully protected and that they have received adequate specific instruction or vocational training in the relevant branch of activity" (article 3).

The Committee on the Rights of the Child has consistently referred to the standards set by ILO Convention No.138 in relation to minimum ages for employment, and also on occasion to the proposals in ILO Recommendation No.146 (which calls on States to take as their objective the progressive raising to 16 of the minimum age of employment) and to other ILO Conventions. It has congratulated States which have already ratified Convention No.138 and urged many others to do so. For example

"...the Committee appreciates the Government's intention to ratify International Labour Convention No. 138 and other instruments relating to the minimum age for employment." (El Salvador IRCO, Add.9, para. 5. See also Egypt IRCO, Add.5, para. 15; Jordan IRCO, Add.21, para. 28; Madagascar IRCO, Add.26, para. 21; Colombia IRCO, Add.30, para. 19; Jamaica IRCO, Add.32, para. 29; Denmark IRCO, Add.33, para. 32; UK IRCO, Add.34, para. 37; Tunisia IRCO, Add.39, para. 15; Sri Lanka

IRCO, Add.40, para. 41; Portugal IRCO, Add.45, para. 22; Iceland IRCO, Add.50, para. 5; Republic of Korea IRCO, Add.51, para. 30; Finland IRCO, Add.53, para. 30; China IRCO, Add.56, para. 43; Nepal IRCO, Add.57, para. 36; Ethiopia IRCO, Add.67, para. 33; Panama IRCO, Add.68, para. 33; Syrian Arab Republic IRCO, Add.70, para. 29; New Zealand IRCO, Add.71, para. 31)

To many other States the Committee has urged conformity with the standards of the Convention and ILO Conventions. For example

"The Committee is ... concerned ... about the fact that the Code on Children and Adolescents is not completely in conformity with the relevant provisions of the Convention on the Rights of the Child and relevant Conventions of the International Labour Organization, especially with regard to minimum ages for admission to employment....

"The Committee recommends that the Code on Children and Adolescents be amended along the lines suggested by the Minister of Labour of Peru in May 1993, following comments made to that effect by the International Labour Organization." (Peru IRCO, Add.8, paras. 11 and 20)

"...the Committee recommends that appropriate measures be taken to protect children from economic exploitation and to provide for appropriate sanctions. The Committee recommends, in particular, that action be taken to ensure that the girls working in the 'maquilas' are not exploited and abused. Moreover the Committee suggests that the State Party consider the possibility of adopting adequate measures to implement ILO Convention No.169 concerning Indigenous and Tribal Peoples in Independent Countries." (Honduras IRCO, Add.24, para. 35)

"The Committee recommends that further measures be taken to implement the provisions of article 32, including in relation to the minimum age of access to employment, and that efforts be made to prevent and combat child labour in the country. Particular attention should be paid to children working in the informal sector. The Committee recommends that the State Party seek technical assistance from ILO in this area." (Philippines IRCO, Add.29, para. 26)

"The Committee notes with concern that child labour remains a problem in Uruguay and that measures taken to prevent it are insufficient. The Committee also notes with concern that the minimum age for employment in Uruguayan law is lower than the minimum age provided for in applicable international conventions, although Uruguay has ratified ILO Convention No.138." (Uruguay IRCO, Add.62, para. 15)

Work and education

Paragraph 1 of article 32 requires protection of the child from performing any work that is likely to "interfere with the child's education". As indicated above, in its general recommendations on economic exploitation, the Committee has highlighted the inter-connection between the right to education, guaranteed by article 28 (see page 369), and the exploitation in child labour. In addition, article 28 requires States to "Take measures to encourage regular attendance at schools and the reduction of drop-out rates" – for example by introducing more relevant curricula or providing grants to poor families (see article 28, page 381).

During discussion of El Salvador's Initial Report, a Committee member stated: "As far as the employment of children was concerned, while legislation appeared to draw a balance between work and school, access to education did not only mean school attendance. It also meant ensuring that a child had the time to think about what he was learning, to do homework, and also to have the time to play and to be a child..." (El Salvador SR.86, para. 62)

The Committee has indicated that some flexibility is permitted regarding "seasonal" work. During discussions with Egyptian Government representatives, a Committee member said: "It was not an intention of the Convention or the ILO Conventions to prevent children from supporting their families by doing domestic chores or helping with the harvest. But two clear aims were to ensure that all children received at least primary education and were not required to do physically or mentally hazardous work." (Egypt SR.68, para. 44)

In its Concluding Observations, the Committee commented:

"Specific concern is also expressed regarding the very large number of children between 6 and 14 years of age who are enrolled in the labour force and therefore lack, wholly or partly, the possibility to go to school. Although children may to a certain extent contribute to seasonal activities, care should always be taken that primary education is available to them and that they are not working in hazardous conditions." (Egypt IRCO, Add.5, para. 9)

In its examination of States Parties' reports, the Committee has highlighted any differences between the age for the completion of compulsory schooling and the age for admission to employment, and has proposed that they should be equalized (the *Guidelines for Periodic Reports* asks for information on the ages set for these

article 32

Awareness campaign in Sri Lanka

According to Sri Lanka's Initial Report, the Department of Probation and Child Care has launched a programme of public awareness to inform households of the current legal provisions relating to child labour and to sensitize them to the human cost of child labour. "These programmes have revealed that not all households are aware that they are violating the law in employing children under 14. In Sri Lanka families in conditions of extreme poverty may want their children to work in households in order to obtain various benefits from the arrangement; sending children as domestic servants to rich households is part of a complex patron-client relationship... Drop-out rates and absenteeism in schools may be partly due to the demand for unpaid family labour on a regular or seasonal basis in the rural areas. Children will be used during times when the demand for labour peaks as in the case of the cultivation season and the harvesting season. The possibility of adjusting school holidays to such peak demands of labour has often been discussed but there has been no definite policy decisions taken. The regular employment of children occurs mainly in the informal sector in family enterprises, both agricultural and non-agricultural, such as family farms, crafts, small trading establishments and eating houses, and repair workshops. In these enterprises the employed children also learn the skills required for these occupations. Their labour is therefore a combination of an informal apprenticeship with labour. The complex social structures which sustain child labour in these situations, both of the paid as well as the unpaid type, are not easily amenable to straightforward law enforcement..." (Sri Lanka IR, paras. 128-129)

purposes under article 1, Definition of a child, see page 9). For example:

"The legislative reforms setting the age of completion of education at 12 years, and the minimum age for employment at 14 years, rendering children between the ages of 12 and 14 vulnerable to the risk of economic exploitation, raise considerable concerns in the Committee." (Nicaragua IRCO, Add.36, para. 14)

"The Committee is concerned that the legislative discrepancy between the age for completion of mandatory education and the minimum age for admission to employment may lead to encourage adolescents to drop out from the school system." (Tunisia IRCO, Add.39, para. 9. See also Ukraine IRCO, Add.42, paras. 8 and 17; Senegal IRCO, Add.44, para. 27)

Providing "appropriate regulation of the hours and conditions of employment"

Article 32 requires detailed regulation in those instances in which children are permitted to work – above the minimum ages and where the work is not likely to be hazardous, interfere with the child's education or be harmful to the child's health or physical, mental, spiritual, moral or social development. ILO Convention No.138 indicates the exceptions permitted and also requires that hours of work and conditions be prescribed. There are also various ILO Conventions protecting children from working at night (see box, page 431; see also child's right to rest and leisure, article 31, page 419). In some cases the

Committee has expressed concern at the lack of "adequate protection." For example:

"The Committee is also concerned about the lack of adequate protection provided to child workers, in particular those employed in agriculture, domestic service and the informal sector." (Burkina Faso IRCO, Add.19, para. 13)

"In the light of the best interests of the child and other provisions of the Convention on the Rights of the Child, as well as those of ILO Convention No. 138 to which France is a party, the Committee believes that the employment of children who have not yet completed their compulsory schooling, as admitted by the legislation in the case of domestic servants and family enterprises, including in the area of agriculture, deserves reconsideration by the State Party. It also encourages the State Party to review the access by children to activities in the fashion industry in order to ensure that this only takes place on the basis of a case-by-case approach and in the light of the best interests of the child." (France IRCO, Add.20, para. 27)

During discussion of Indonesia's Initial Report, a Committee member noted that child labour had become virtually universal. "The phenomenon was also spreading, as was apparently the case in Indonesia according to the statistics. It was vital for legislation to lay down strict norms to ensure that children did not perform dangerous tasks or work that jeopardized their schooling or health. However, that was not sufficient: it was also necessary to establish economic and other conditions to permit families to comply with the law. However, there was a clear trend in many countries to disregard norms during periods of economic reform and as a result more and more children were compelled to live or to work in the street." (Indonesia SR.81, para. 40)

One important issue not dealt with explicitly in the Convention on the Rights of the Child is that of medical examinations for working children. ILO Conventions Nos. 77, 78 and 124 provide for a thorough medical examination to determine fitness for employment prior to engagement and also continued medical supervision until the age of 18; such examinations "shall not involve the child or young person, or his parents, in any expense".

Providing "appropriate penalties or other sanctions to ensure the effective enforcement of the present article"

The Committee has proposed various components of "effective enforcement" as required by article 32(2)(c), including a labour inspectorate, complaints procedure (see also article 12, page 155), and adequate penalties in cases of non-compliance. For example:

"With regard to the implementation of the provisions of the Convention concerning preventing and combating various forms of exploitation, the Committee wishes to receive further information with respect to the functioning of the labour inspectorate system and the implementation of sanctions for non-compliance with the requirements of the labour legislation." (Federal Republic of Yugoslavia IRCO, Add.49, para. 39)

"The Committee recommends that in the light of article 32 of the Convention on the Rights of the Child, further steps be taken to protect children from hazardous work, including through the adoption of stricter legislation, ratification of all relevant ILO Conventions and the appointment of a sufficient number of child labour inspectors." (Lebanon IRCO, Add.54, para. 43)

"...Child labour laws should be enforced, a system of inspection established, complaints investigated and severe penalties imposed in case of violation. Special attention should be paid to the protection of children in the informal sector, including as domestic servants. The Committee suggests that the Government consider seeking cooperation from ILO in this area." (Nepal IRCO, Add.57, para. 36)

ILO Convention No.138 requires that "all necessary measures, including the provision of appro-

priate penalties" must be taken by the competent authority to ensure effective enforcement. National laws or regulations or a competent authority must also define who is responsible for compliance with the Convention, and what registers or other documents must be kept, recording names and dates of birth ("duly certified wherever possible") of all under 18-year-olds employed or in work (article 9).

The Committee has indicated that it expects to see protection from economic exploitation reflected in detail in national legislation:

"With regard to child exploitation, the Committee is concerned at the persistence of situations of child labour, including in agriculture, domestic service and on commercial farms. It notes with particular concern the lack of a legal prohibition on child labour.
"Similar measures should be adopted to prohibit child labour below a minimum age in the light of article 32 of the Convention. In this regard, the Committee encourages the State Party to consider the recommendations made by the International Labour Organization in its mission statement of 1993 and, in particular, to prohibit the employment of young persons below 18 in hazardous activities as well as to make education free and compulsory up to the age of 15. In this connection, the Committee encourages the State Party to consider seeking assistance from the International Labour Organization." (Zimbabwe IRCO, Add.55, paras. 20 and 32; see also Indonesia IRCO, Add.25, paras. 17 and 23)

Legislation, and hence inspection and enforcement, should cover all forms of employment and work, including in the informal sector (and in the case of Myanmar the Committee expressed particular concern at economic exploitation of adopted children):

"The Committee is concerned by the fact that children working in the family environment or in family enterprises are not protected by law. The Committee is also concerned about the abuse and exploitation of adopted children, especially in the area of child labour, and at the absence of legal safeguards to protect them.
"In view to fully protect children working within their family, the Committee recommends that the State Party amend appropriately its existing legislation. The Committee also recommends that the authorities take all necessary measures to prevent and combat, by legal or any other appropriate action, the exploitation of adopted children including through labour." (Myanmar IRCO, Add.69, paras. 23 and 43)

Implementation Checklist

● General measures of implementation

Have appropriate general measures of implementation been taken in relation to article 32 including

☐ identification and coordination of the responsible departments and agencies at all levels of government (article 32 is particularly relevant to **departments of employment, industry, agriculture, social welfare, education**)?

☐ identification of relevant non-governmental organizations/civil society partners?

☐ a comprehensive review to ensure that all legislation, policy and practice is compatible with the article, for all children in all parts of the jurisdiction?

☐ adoption of a strategy to secure full implementation

☐ which includes where necessary the identification of goals and indicators of progress?

☐ which does not affect any provisions which are more conducive to the rights of the child?

☐ which recognizes other relevant international standards?

☐ which involves where necessary international cooperation?

(Such measures may be part of an overall governmental strategy for implementing the Convention as a whole).

☐ budgetary analysis and allocation of necessary resources?

☐ development of mechanisms for monitoring and evaluation?

☐ making the implications of article 32 widely known to adults and children?

☐ development of appropriate training and awareness-raising (in relation to article 32 likely to include the training of **all those responsible for inspection and enforcing employment legislation, teachers and social workers, and parenting education**)?

● Specific issues in implementing article 32

Has the State launched or promoted information campaigns

☐ for children themselves on the measures of protection they can benefit from and the risks involved in situations of economic exploitation?

☐ for the public, including training activities for professional groups working with or for children, to help achieve effective protection of children against economic exploitation?

☐ for employers and potential employers?

Does legislation, policy and practice in the State protect children from

☐ economic exploitation?

performing any work which

☐ is hazardous?

☐ interferes with the child's education?

☐ is harmful to the child's health or physical, mental, spiritual, moral or social development?

☐ involves cruel, inhuman or degrading treatment, the sale of children or servitude?

☐ involves activities in which the child is used for legally punishable criminal acts, such as trafficking in drugs or prohibited goods?

☐ is incompatible with the realization of other rights in the Convention?

Has the State

☐ ratified ILO Convention No.138 on minimum ages for admission to employment?

☐ ratified ILO Convention No.29 on forced labour?

☐ considered the implications for law, policy and practice of ILO Recommendation No.146?

☐ If not, is the State considering these actions?

☐ Has the State defined in legislation a minimum age for employment that is equal to the age of completion of compulsory education and not less than 15?

☐ Has the State considered adjusting the periods of compulsory education with any seasonal patterns of work for families?

☐ Has the State defined in legislation 18 as the minimum age for admission to any type of employment or work that by its nature or the circumstances in which it is carried out is likely to jeopardize the health, safety or morals of young persons?

☐ Has the State defined in legislation or by the decision of a competent authority the types of employment or work to which this minimum age of 18 applies?

Has the State defined in legislation limited exemptions

☐ prescribing the conditions under which children are allowed to do work in schools or other training institutions for general, vocational or technical education?

☐ enabling those aged 14 and over to do work as an integral part of a course of education or training (consistent with the conditions set out in article 6 of ILO Convention No.138)?

☐ defining any forms of "light work" which 13- to 15-year-olds are permitted to perform, which are not likely to be harmful to health or development or prejudice their education?

☐ defining hours and conditions for employment or work, if permitted, for those who are at least 15 but have not completed compulsory schooling?

☐ allowing limited employment or work for such purposes as participation in artistic performances, through a system of permits granted in individual cases (as set out in ILO Convention No. 138 article 8)?

☐ defining hours and conditions for employment of children in all cases in which employment or work is permitted?

How to use the checklists, *see page XVII*

☐ Has the State ensured adequate arrangements for medical examinations in connection with child employment?

In relation to effective enforcement of its legislation on child labour, has the State ensured through legislation and otherwise

    ☐ adequate inspection of situations of work or employment?

    ☐ adequate access for children to effective complaints procedures?

    ☐ appropriate penalties or other sanctions for non-compliance?

    ☐ adequate record-keeping and reporting in relation to any employment of children?

    ☐ the collection of adequate disaggregated data?

    ☐ that the persons responsible for compliance with provisions concerning child labour are defined?

☐ Are appropriate measures taken to reintegrate and rehabilitate victims of harmful or exploitative child labour?

Reminder: **The Convention is indivisible and its articles are interdependent. Article 32 should not be considered in isolation.**

Particular regard should be paid to:
The general principles

Article 2: all rights to be recognized for each child in jurisdiction without discrimination on any ground

Article 3(1): the best interests of the child to be a primary consideration in all actions concerning children

Article 6: right to life and maximum possible survival and development

Article 12: respect for the child's views in all matters affecting the child; opportunity to be heard in any judicial or administrative proceedings affecting the child

Closely related articles

Articles whose implementation is related to that of article 32 include:

Article 15: freedom of association (trade unions)

Article 27: adequate standard of living

Article 28: right to education

Article 31: right to leisure, play and recreation

Article 33: illicit production and trafficking in drugs

Article 34: sexual exploitation

Article 35: sale, trafficking and abduction

Article 36: other forms of harmful exploitation

Article 39: rehabilitative care for child victims

Children and drug abuse

article
33

Text of Article 33

States Parties shall take all appropriate measures, including legislative, administrative, social and educational measures, to protect children from the illicit use of narcotic drugs and psychotropic substances as defined in the relevant international treaties, and to prevent the use of children in the illicit production and trafficking of such substances.

Article 33 requires ratifying States to take all appropriate measures to:
- protect children from the illicit use of narcotic drugs and psychotropic substances as defined in the relevant international treaties;
- prevent the use of children in the production or trafficking of such drugs.

International treaties have identified scores of drugs and substances which require control, within the following broad groupings:
- opium, morphine and opium alkaloids and synthetic morphine (for example heroin);
- coca leaves and cocaine;
- cannabis products (marijuana);
- any psychotropic/psychoactive drug capable of producing a state of dependence or the abuse of

which could lead to social and public health problems warranting international control (sedatives such as barbiturates, stimulants such as amphetamines and hallucinogens such as LSD).

There are also drugs used by children that can alter their state of mind, be prejudicial to health or can be addictive such as alcohol, tobacco and solvents (such as glue) but that are not controlled by international treaties, though their use by children in many States is "illicit".

The measures to be taken by the State include legislative, administrative, social and educational ones. The emphasis of article 33 is on protection and prevention and must be read in the context of the whole Convention. ∎

Summary

Extracts from
Committee on the Rights of the Child
Guidelines for Reports to be submitted by States Parties under the Convention

For full text of *Guidelines for Periodic Reports*, see Appendix 3, page 604.

Guidelines for Initial Reports

"Special protection measures

Under this section States Parties are requested to provide relevant information, including the principal legislative, judicial, administrative or other measures in force; factors and difficulties encountered and progress achieved in implementing the relevant provisions of the Convention; and implementation priorities and specific goals for the future in respect of:...

... (ii) Drug abuse (article 33)

Additionally, States Parties are encouraged to provide specific statistical information and indicators relevant to the children covered by [the previous] paragraph."

(CRC/C/5, paras. 23 and 24)

Guidelines for Periodic Reports

"VIII. SPECIAL PROTECTION MEASURES

C. Children in situations of exploitation, including physical and psychological recovery and social reintegration...

2. Drug abuse (art. 33)

Please indicate all appropriate measures adopted, including legislative, administrative, social and educational measures, to:

> *Protect children from the illicit use of narcotic drugs and psychotropic substances, as defined in relevant international treaties;*

> *Prevent the use of children in the illicit production and trafficking of such substances.*

Reports should also indicate:

> *The relevant international conventions, including at the regional and bilateral levels, to which the State is a party;*

> *Any arrangements made and structures developed to raise awareness in the general population and amongst children, including through the school system and whenever appropriate by the consideration of this topic by the school curricula;*

> *Any measures undertaken to assist children and their families, including through counselling, advice and helplines, where appropriate of a confidential nature, and policies and strategies designed to ensure the physical and psychological recovery and social reintegration of children concerned;*

> *Any measures designed to monitor the incidence of drug abuse on children, as well as their involvement in the illicit production and trafficking of narcotic and psychotropic substances, progress achieved, difficulties encountered and targets set for the future;*

> *Any relevant disaggregated data, including by age, gender, region, rural/urban area and social and ethnic origin.*

In addition, please also provide information on legislative and other measures taken to prevent the use by children of alcohol, tobacco and other substances which may be prejudicial to their health and which may be available with or without restrictions to adults, and on any evaluation made of the effectiveness of such measures, together with relevant disaggregated data on the use by children of such substances."

(CRC/C/58, paras. 155-157. Paragraphs 24 and 159 of the *Guidelines for Periodic Reports* are also relevant to reporting under this article; for full text of *Guidelines*, see Appendix 3, page 604.)

The threat to children

In the post-war decades, children's involvement in illicit drugs was not a significant concern so the issue did not figure in the declarations and conventions of that era. Today, rising rates of drug abuse by children and young people are causing alarm worldwide, threatening both the child's development and nations' economic prosperity and social order. The issue is now high on most political agendas and was identified at the World Summit for Children (1990) as needing special attention.

The World Summit Declaration states: "We will do our best to ensure that children are not drawn into becoming victims of the scourge of illicit drugs" and the World Summit's Plan of Action said: "Drug abuse has emerged as a global menace to very large numbers of young people and, increasingly, children – including permanent damage incurred in the prenatal stages of life. Concerted action is needed by Governments and intergovernmental agencies to combat illicit production, supply, demand, trafficking and distribution of narcotic drugs and psychotropic substances to counter this tragedy. Equally important is community action and education, which are vitally needed to curb both the supply of and the demand for illicit drugs. Tobacco and alcohol abuse are also problems requiring action, especially preventive measures and education among young people." (World Summit Declaration, para. 20(7) and Plan of Action, para. 24)

Article 6 of the Convention on the Rights of the Child (children's right to life and optimum development), article 24 (children's rights to health services and health promotion) and article 29 (education to prepare children for responsible life) are also clearly relevant to this issue.

The main international treaties on drugs are the Single Convention on Narcotic Drugs 1961 as amended by the 1972 Protocol, and the Convention on Psychotropic Substances 1971 (see summary above for details of the drugs included in these treaties). In its *Guidelines for Periodic Reports* regarding this article, the Committee asks ratifying States to report on the relevant Conventions to which they are parties.

The drugs that children are particularly liable to use are the cheaper ones, so their prevalence depends in part on geography – marijuana appears in most countries, cocaine and crack in South America, opium in Asia and so forth. In addition, children in almost all countries are found to be illicitly obtaining and using alcohol and tobacco and abusing solvents, none of which is covered by international treaties. Alcohol is used in many societies and tobacco in almost all, even though they can be extremely prejudicial to health and addictive. Children's growing bodies and minds are especially vulnerable to damage from these substances and States should take all appropriate measures to protect children from their use.

Solvents are widely perceived as being the drug of childhood. Solvent abuse carries an added problem that the sale or possession of solvents, used as an ingredient in a vast range of products, is hard to regulate. Glue sniffing (the shorthand term for solvent abuse) is particularly noted as a habit of children living and working on the streets – a quick, cheap route to oblivion. Nicaragua, for example, reported to the Committee that its official figures suggested that over 2,500 children in its capital of Managua alone engage in glue-sniffing (Nicaragua SR.212, para. 19).

Drug use in the adult population is damaging enough; but when children take drugs they may irreversibly harm their mental or physical growth. Illicit drug use is also associated with criminality. Children who take drugs may often play a minor role in their production and traffic, and they may involve themselves in other crimes and forms of exploitation. As Bolivia commented: "It must be emphasized that the whole subject of the illicit use of drugs is usually linked with child exploitation and sexual exploitation, through the submergence of the children in the 'underworld', which harbours them, as in the case of the street children and working children." (Bolivia IR, para. 202)

Links with other forms of exploitation are also pointed out by the Committee:

"The Committee notes with concern the increasing crime rate among children and the vulnerability of children to sexual abuse, drug abuse and alcoholism." (Russian Federation IRCO, Add.4, para. 15)

"The Committee notes with concern the growing use and involvement of children in criminal activities and the vulnerability of children to sexual abuse, drug abuse, alcoholism, as well as torture and ill-treatment." (Poland IRCO, Add.31, para. 20)

"The issues of sexual exploitation and drug abuse as they affect children should also be addressed on an urgent basis, including with regard to the undertaking of further measures to prevent them." (UK IRCO, Add.34, para. 38. See also Belarus IRCO, Add.17, para. 10)

In the same regard, the Committee recommended firm action to Nepal, citing its

"inadequate measures taken to address the situation of children addicted to drugs ...

Young people's views on drugs in Hong Kong

"The reasons for drug abuse are varied and complex. A number of studies have shown that curiosity, identification with peers and relief of boredom are the three main reasons for initial drug use. Only a minority of drug abusers claim to have started drugs for mystical experience or self-medication. According to school surveys conducted by the Narcotics Division of the Security Branch, curiosity ranks as the most important reason for trying drugs. There has been an increase in the number of drug abusers in Chinese-speaking schools who turned to drugs for relief of boredom: 20 per cent in 1992, up from 11 per cent in 1990. The percentage of those who started drugs under peer influence also rose, from 15 per cent in 1990 to 19 per cent in 1992.

"According to the Survey on Young Drug Abusers conducted by the Narcotics Division, 13 per cent of sampled young drug abusers think heroin is not dangerous and 19 per cent think likewise about psychotropic substances. 60 per cent of sampled drug abusers think that they can control their drug-taking habit. An increasing proportion of abusers do not consider that taking psychotropic substances is dangerous and make no attempt to give up their drug-taking habit."

(UK dependent territory: Hong Kong IR, paras. 432-3)

"The Committee further recommends that firm measures be taken to ensure the right of survival of all children in Nepal, including those who live and/or work in the streets. Such measures should aim at the effective protection of children against any form of exploitation, particularly child labour, prostitution, drug-related activities and child trafficking and sale." (Nepal IRCO, Add.57, paras. 23 and 35)

Article 33 obliges States to "protect children from the illicit use of drugs...", which also includes protecting children from the effects of drug misuse by adults. Parents dependent on drugs may, for example, have babies with consequent physical or intellectual disabilities or have babies born with a drug addiction. In this respect, the Declaration on the Rights of the Child and the Preamble to the Convention on the Rights of the Child both provide that "the child, by reason of his physical and mental immaturity, needs special safeguards and care, including appropriate legal protection,

before as well as after birth". Drug abuse by parents or other family members may also result in children being neglected or harmed.

Understanding drug misuse

The problem of drug misuse by children is peculiarly alarming to the adult world because we cannot accurately map it and we do not know how best to tackle it: simply making it illegal is clearly not enough.

Establishing rates of drug use by children is obviously tricky, depending mostly on surveys of self-reported use. Some reports on the issue were made to the Committee – for example Jamaica's, where a 1988 study found that 16 per cent of 13- to 14-years-olds, 19 per cent of 15- to 16-year-olds and 25 per cent of 17- to 18-year-olds had smoked marijuana (Jamaica IR, para. 91), or Namibia's, where a 1991 survey found 19 per cent of children of 13 years or over said they used drugs (and 22 per cent said they had friends who used them) (Namibia IR, para. 475).

States are asked to report to the United Nations International Drug Control Programme (UNDCP) on activities undertaken in the field of drug abuse prevention. The reporting system at present does not allow for the evaluation of activities undertaken by countries, but the questionnaires issued by the UNDCP are currently being revised to make this possible. The United Nations Decade Against Drug Abuse 1991-2000 Political Declaration and Global Programme of Action and the Declaration of the International Conference on Drug Abuse and Illicit Trafficking and Comprehensive Multidisciplinary Outline of Future Activities in Drug Abuse Control (Resolution No. S-17/12 of 23 February 1990) lay the United Nations foundations for member States' policies and strategies in the field of drug control.

Nothing can be done about the problem without understanding it, and clearly drug misuse by children merits a high priority for research, both to describe the problem and to identify effective remedies. These include the identification of protective and risk factors and the evaluation of positive interventions. There will be differences between strategies aimed at children from communities where drugs are a significant part of the economy and those from communities where drug consumption is the problem.

The Committee's suggestion to the Federal Republic of Yugoslavia could be applied to virtually every country, since none has shown any complacency about this issue:

"Concerning the application of the provisions of article 33 of the Convention, the Committee

suggests that consideration be given, if necessary, to the further development of systems for the collection of reliable data on the problem of drug abuse and to the incorporation of a uniform drug prevention programme within the education system." (Federal Republic of Yugoslavia IRCO, Add.49, para. 40)

The criminal aspects of the issue should not obscure the fact that those involved are children, often very vulnerable children. Bolivia commented that one of the consequences of drug abuse was "poor self respect", but this can equally be identified as one of the causes. The Committee allied the high rates of drug abuse and suicide among Finnish youth, suggesting

"...additional research be undertaken in the areas of suicide and drug abuse to improve the understanding of those phenomena and generate appropriate measures to deal efficiently with them." (Finland IRCO, Add.53, para. 27)

"Legislative and administrative" measures against drugs

The Commission on Human Rights Programme of Action for the Elimination of the Exploitation of Child Labour asks countries to ensure the absolute legal prohibition of children employed in work concerned with the trafficking in and production of illicit drugs (1993/79, paras. 20 and 21) As this work is usually already illegal, countries could, perhaps, be expected to increase sentences on convicted adults if children are engaged in drug trafficking or production. Similarly, criminal codes could ensure that the selling or distribution of drugs to children is treated as a more serious offence. Canada, for example, reported that it was proposing to introduce legislation that would treat drug dealing in and around schools or involving children as an "aggravating factor" in the commission of drug offences (Canada IR, para. 363). Legal measures are also needed in respect of solvent abuse, in order to fetter the access by children to solvents – for example by attaching criminal penalties to the sale of solvents to children without authorization by parents or others, or making it an offence to supply solvents to children who are likely to abuse them.

States can also take measures to combat economic dependence on drugs, for example by encouraging farmers to cultivate crops other than drug crops by special subsidies or tax exemptions (see, for example, Viet Nam IR, para. 252).

However, it should be noted that article 33 is concerned with the "protection" of children from drug abuse. Placing harsh custodial penalties on children for drug use is an ineffective form of protection. The custodial experience may remove children from temptation, but cannot teach them how to cope with the temptation once back on the streets; moreover prisons or detention centres may expose these children to more serious forms of drug abuse or serve to introduce them to the drug underworld. It is perhaps more constructive to vest legal powers to intervene in cases of child drug abuse in the welfare offices rather the criminal justice offices of government.

"Social and educational" measures

The Council of Europe's recommendations of 1984 relating to children and drug abuse (see

Prevention of drug abuse in Ecuador

The highest prevalence of drug abuse in Ecuador is found among youths between the ages of 17 and 25. But drug consumption starts much earlier in the country, particularly among children in especially difficult circumstances. In Ecuador, some 100,000 children work on the street and in the informal sector; in the cities of Quito and Guayaquil alone, 5,000 children are institutionalized and 5,500 work or live in the streets. A 1988 study indicates that 90 per cent of the children entering institutional care have drug-consumption histories.

A project called the Ecuadorian Centre for Training of Street Educators has amended its curriculum to include drug abuse. Through contact and through distance learning methods street educators, social workers, coordinators and administrators of projects have been trained in basic counselling, preventive education strategies and the implementation of drug abuse prevention programmes, including the close monitoring of drug abuse among children. At the same time, local monitoring and training networks have been established in 12 cities, which organize three training events a year in each target city. The Centre also provides technical support to institutions in the formulation, administration and implementation of drug abuse preventive education programmes. The project has also elaborated and implemented innovative training strategies and models in drug abuse prevention based on research and lessons learned from practice.

(Information provided by the United Nations International Drug Control Programme)

article 33

Recommendations for measures against drug abuse by children

The Council of Europe's Recommendation on the Fight against Drug Abuse and Trafficking 1984 includes recommendations for general measures relating to international cooperation over drug offences. In relation to children, its recommendations include:

- forbidding the sale of solvents to minors without parental permission;

- accompanying drug policies with "long-term positive strategies, preparing young people to play a constructive and creative role in democratic society and encouraging the continued cultural development of adults";

- improving health promotion and education, including integrating drugs education in the curriculum "the focus of the information being to make young people aware of their responsibility for their own well-being, but also the penal consequences resulting from it";

- developing professional training schemes to ensure cross-disciplinary coordination – "a situation which does not at present exist between teachers and families, judges and doctors, police and the social services";

- aiming public information at reducing tolerance of drug abuse and increasing recognition of early symptoms of drug abuse, particularly among children;

- developing therapeutic communities "where young people receive help from teams with sufficient training to do an all-round job, encompassing health, psychological and social requirements and capable of listening to young people in difficulties, since these latter frequently reject traditional institutions, such as psychiatric centres, for example";

- finding a middle way between compulsory treatment and reliance on voluntary attendance by under-18 year-olds (e.g. by suspending criminal sentences if the offender agrees to drug treatment).

(Council of Europe's European Recommendation 989 on the Fight against Drug Abuse and Trafficking 1984)

box) stand up well, over a decade later. Their emphasis is on recognition of the problem, and on strong but non-punitive forms of intervention that look to the broader picture and to long-term solutions. Unfortunately, many are still unimplemented in European countries. Indeed which country can confidently assert that there is effective cross-disciplinary coordination in regard to drugs and the young?

Not all children have drugs education on their school curricula, and where it is, it may often be ineffective or even counter-productive (containing dangerous misinformation or inadvertently glamorizing drug taking). Anti-drug strategies should take account of the views of children themselves. Some countries have given drug education a high priority (for example Canada, which makes drug education a mandatory part of the school curriculum from grade one and is piloting intensive drug education and counselling for any drug-related incidents (Canada IR, para. 841) and also Chile, which uses peer education in its drug education programmes in secondary schools (Chile IR, para. 197)).

The media have a clear part to play. The United Nations Guidelines for the Prevention of Juvenile Delinquency (the "Riyadh Guidelines") states: "The mass media should be aware of its extensive social role and responsibility, as well as its influence, in communications relating to youthful drug and alcohol abuse. It should use its power for drug abuse prevention by relaying consistent messages through a balanced approach. Effective drug awareness campaigns at all levels should be promoted." (para. 44)

Health services also need to be oriented to drug misuse by children. In many countries the paediatric systems are not competent to handle drug abuse by children and adult treatment centres do not accept under-age clients or patients. Therapeutic rehabilitative services specifically tailored for children and young people are urgently needed.

Implementation Checklist

● *General measures of implementation*

Have appropriate general measures of implementation been taken in relation to article 33, including

☐ identification and coordination of the responsible departments and agencies at all levels of government (article 33 is relevant to the **departments of justice, home affairs, social welfare, education, health, media and public relations**)?

☐ identification of relevant non-governmental organizations/civil society partners?

☐ a comprehensive review to ensure that all legislation, policy and practice is compatible with the article, for all children in all parts of the jurisdiction?

☐ adoption of a strategy to secure full implementation

> ☐ which includes where necessary the identification of goals and indicators of progress?

> ☐ which does not affect any provisions which are more conducive to the rights of the child?

> ☐ which recognizes other relevant international standards?

> ☐ which involves where necessary international cooperation?

(Such measures may be part of an overall governmental strategy for implementing the Convention as a whole).

☐ budgetary analysis and allocation of necessary resources?

☐ development of mechanisms for monitoring and evaluation?

☐ making the implications of article 33 widely known to adults and children?

☐ development of appropriate training and awareness-raising (in relation to article 33 likely to include the training of **community and street workers, youth workers, social workers, teachers, police, judiciary, medical and psychological professionals and parent education**)?

● *Specific issues in implementing article 33*

Has the State ratified:

> ☐ the 1961 Single Convention on Narcotic Drugs with its 1972 amending Protocol?

> ☐ the 1971 Convention on Psychotropic Drugs?

☐ Do laws clearly prohibit the use of illicit narcotic drugs and psychotropic substances?

☐ Do laws clearly prohibit the production and trafficking of these drugs and substances?

☐ Does the law attach any additional penalties for drug offences committed by adults where children have been sold or given these drugs and substances or where children have been used for their production or trafficking?

☐ Does the law prevent the sale of solvents to children without appropriate authorization from parents or other adults?

☐ Have any surveys been undertaken to assess the scale of drug misuse among children?

Has research been undertaken in relation to drug abuse and children to

    ☐ identify risk factors?

    ☐ identify preventive strategies?

    ☐ identify rehabilitative strategies?

Is drug education a part of

    ☐ primary education currricula?

    ☐ secondary education curricula?

    ☐ youth and community work?

    ☐ parenting education?

☐ Are treatment therapies and rehabilitative services, specifically tailored for children who abuse drugs, available in the health or social welfare sectors?

☐ Are rehabilitative interventions, based on the best interests of the children concerned, available to parents and other family members who abuse drugs?

☐ Are the views of children taken into account when anti-drug policies and strategies are devised?

☐ Do legal interventions aim at rehabilitating rather than punishing children who become involved in drugs?

☐ Do professionals and judiciary in the juvenile justice system coordinate with professionals in the health, education and social work sectors in responding to drug offences by children?

☐ Are measures taken to protect young people in closed or locked institutions from exposure to drugs?

☐ Are there public campaigns to discourage the use of drugs by the young?

☐ Are such campaigns evaluated?

☐ Are parents and other adults informed about the early symptoms of drug abuse in children and about sources of help?

Reminder : **The Convention is indivisible and its articles are interdependent. Article 33 should not be considered in isolation.**

Particular regard should be paid to:
The general principles

Article 2: all rights to be recognized for each child in jurisdiction without discrimination on any ground

Article 3(1): the best interests of the child to be a primary consideration in all actions concerning children

Article 6: right to life and maximum possible survival and development

Article 12: respect for the child's views in all matters affecting the child; opportunity to be heard in any judicial or administrative proceedings affecting the child

Closely related articles

Articles whose implementation is related to that of article 33 include:

Article 17: mass media, dissemination of information

Article 19: protection from all forms of maltreatment by parents and other carers

Article 24: health and health services

Article 29: education to prepare children for responsible life in a free society

Article 32: protection from hazardous or exploitative work

Article 37: protection for children deprived of liberty

Article 39: rehabilitative care

Sexual exploitation of children

Text of Article 34

States Parties undertake to protect the child from all forms of sexual exploitation and sexual abuse. For these purposes, States Parties shall in particular take all appropriate national, bilateral and multilateral measures to prevent:

(a) The inducement or coercion of a child to engage in any unlawful sexual activity;

(b) The exploitative use of children in prostitution or other unlawful sexual practices;

(c) The exploitative use of children in pornographic performances and materials.

Article 34 provides obligations to protect children from "all forms of sexual exploitation and sexual abuse", requiring national, bilateral and multilateral measures to protect children from three particular (and often linked) forms of exploitation set out in paragraphs (a), (b) and (c). Article 19 more generally covers protection from "all forms of physical or mental violence" and specifically mentions sexual abuse (see page 241). The exploitative use of children in prostitution and pornography, which States Parties are required to take all appropriate measures to prevent, is linked to the sale of and traffic in children (see article 35, page 474).

While sexual exploitation of children has only received international attention relatively recently, it has been highlighted extensively within the United Nations system during the 1990s, with the appointment of a Special Rapporteur on the sale of children, child prostitution and child pornography, the adoption of Programmes of Action by the Commission on Human Rights, the proposal for an optional protocol to the Convention on the sale of children, child prostitution and child pornography (regarded as unnecessary by the Committee and some involved non-governmental organizations), and the World Congress against Commercial Exploitation of Children, held in Stockholm in 1996 (see below, page 461). ■

Summary

Extracts from
Committee on the Rights of the Child
Guidelines for Reports to be submitted by States Parties under the Convention

For full text of *Guidelines for Periodic Reports*, see Appendix 3, page 604.

Guidelines for Initial Reports

"Special protection measures

Under this section States Parties are requested to provide relevant information, including the principal legislative, judicial, administrative or other measures in force; factors and difficulties encountered and progress achieved in implementing the relevant provisions of the Convention; and implementation priorities and specific goals for the future in respect of:

...

(c) Children in situations of exploitation, including physical and psychological recovery and social reintegration (article 39)

...

(iii) Sexual exploitation and sexual abuse (article 34);

...

Additionally, States Parties are encouraged to provide specific statistical information and indicators relevant to the children covered by paragraph 23."

(CRC/C/5, paras. 23 and 24)

Guidelines for Periodic Reports

"VIII. SPECIAL PROTECTION MEASURES

....

C. Children in situations of exploitation, including physical and psychological recovery and social reintegration;

...

3. Sexual exploitation and sexual abuse (art.34).

Please indicate the measures adopted, including of a legislative, educational and social nature, to protect the child from all forms of sexual exploitation and sexual abuse. Reports should in particular provide information on all national, bilateral and multilateral measures taken to prevent:

    (a) the inducement or coercion of a child to engage in any unlawful sexual activity;

    (b) the exploitative use of children in prostitution or other unlawful sexual practices;

    (c) the exploitative use of children in pornographic performances and materials.

Reports should also indicate, inter alia:

    Information, awareness and education campaigns to prevent any form of sexual exploitation or abuse of the child, including campaigns undertaken in cooperation with the media;

    Any national and multidisciplinary strategy developed to ensure protection of children below the age of 18 against all forms of sexual exploitation and abuse, including within the family;

    Any coordinating and monitoring mechanism established for that purpose;

    The relevant indicators identified and used;

    Legislation developed to ensure effective protection of child victims, including through access to legal and other appropriate assistance and support services;

    Whether sexual exploitation and abuse of children, child prostitution and child pornography, including the possession of child pornography, and the use of children in other unlawful sexual practices are considered criminal offences;

    Whether the principle of extraterritoriality has been incorporated in the legislation to criminalize the sexual exploitation of children by nationals and residents of the State Party when committed in other countries;

    Whether special units of law enforcement officials and police liaison officers have been appointed to deal with children who have been sexually exploited or abused, and whether appropriate training has been provided to them;

Relevant bilateral, regional and multilateral agreements concluded or to which the State Party may have acceded to foster the prevention of all forms of sexual abuse and exploitation and to ensure the effective protection of child victims, including in the areas of judicial cooperation and cooperation among law enforcement officials;

Relevant programmes of technical cooperation and international assistance developed with United Nations bodies and other international organizations, as well as with other competent bodies, including INTERPOL, and non-governmental organizations;

*Relevant activities and programmes developed, including of a multidisciplinary nature, to ensure the recovery and reintegration of the child victim of sexual exploitation or abuse, in the light of **article 39** of the Convention;*

The measures adopted to ensure respect for the general principles of the Convention, namely non-discrimination, the best interests of the child, respect for the views of the child, the right to life, and survival and development to the maximum extent possible;

Relevant disaggregated data on the children concerned by the implementation of article 34, including by age, gender, region, rural/urban area, and national, social and ethnic origin. Such data should include ... the number of cases of commercial sexual exploitation, sexual abuse... reported during this period;

The progress achieved in the implementation of article 34, difficulties encountered and targets set."

(CRC/C/58, paras. 158-159. The following paragraphs of the *Guidelines for Periodic Reports* are also relevant to reporting under this article: 24, 88-89 and 161; for full text of *Guidelines*, see Appendix 3, page 604.)

General framework for consideration of sexual exploitation

Following its General Discussion on economic exploitation of children in October 1993, the Committee on the Rights of the Child issued a statement that included comment on sexual exploitation:

"Child prostitution must be severely criminalized; intermediaries, accomplices and 'clients' should be penalized. Child pornography should be banned." (Report on the fourth session, September-October 1993, CRC/C/20, p. 58)

During its sixth session (April 1994), the Committee adopted a formal statement on "Cooperation with United Nations bodies – Sale of children, child prostitution and child pornography", in which it emphasized the important framework established by the Convention to deal with such situations and stressed
"that the child affected by situations of sale, prostitution and pornography should be considered mainly as a victim and that all measures adopted should ensure full respect for his or her human dignity, as well as special protection and support within the family and society" (Report on the sixth session, April 1994, CRC/C/29, p. 4; see also Report on the tenth session, October-November 1995, CRC/C/46, paras. 220 and 226).

The Committee has made further detailed comments to the open-ended Working Group established by the Commission on Human Rights to consider a draft optional protocol to the Convention on the Rights of the Child, which stress the overall framework provided by the Convention in which the issues of sexual exploitation should be considered. In its approach to the question of an optional protocol, the Committee has consistently emphasized the importance of strengthening existing international standards (for further discussion and details of draft optional protocol, see below, page 467).

In a 1996 statement to the Working Group, the Committee pointed out that the Convention not only provides specific provisions on sexual exploitation, but that it also

"set up a holistic approach for the consideration of the human rights of children. In the light of such an approach, all rights are recognized as inherent to the human dignity of the child, and the implementation of one right will only be effective when taking into consideration the implementation of, and respect for, all the other rights of the child. In a word, the Convention reaffirms the indivisibility and interdependence of human rights.

"The protection of the child from all forms of exploitation, including from sale, prostitution or pornography, should therefore not be seen simply in isolation but in the broader context of the realization of children's rights and taking in due consideration the international obligations arising from the Convention."

The Committee went on to say that the Convention calls on States *"to take action ... to prevent such situations... to reinforce the system of children's rights protection, and to ensure the physical and psychological recovery and social reintegration of child victims of any such form of exploitation... Legal reform, awareness and information campaigns, education and training activities on children's rights, as well as the establishment of a monitoring mechanism based on a systematic data collection and evaluation, are some essential measures in this regard."*

The Committee also noted that other important legal instruments had been adopted relevant to the protection of the child against exploitation, mentioning the Convention on the Elimination of All Forms of Discrimination against Women, the Convention on the Suppression of Traffic in Persons and of the Exploitation of the Prostitution of Others, and the ILO Convention on Forced Labour (ILO Convention No. 29),

"which are in reality used by the Committee on the Rights of the Child within the framework of its monitoring functions" (Report on the eleventh session, January 1996, CRC/C/50, p. 46).

The Committee's examination of States Parties' reports

The Committee has paid consistent attention to the issue of sexual exploitation during its examination of Initial Reports from States Parties. On occasion, the Committee has noted a lack of information and has stressed the importance of establishing a monitoring mechanism. For example

"... there seems to be a lack of information on children who are victims of sexual exploitation, including incest" (Sweden IRCO, Add.2, para. 9).

The Committee's *Guidelines for Periodic Reports* seeks detailed information on implementation, including disaggregated data (para. 159).

The Committee has proposed the study of the "root causes" and has suggested that Governments should work closely with NGOs, including children's groups (the Agenda for Action adopted by the 1996 World Congress against Commercial Sexual Exploitation includes a section on child participation; see article 12, page 157):

"The Committee recommends that the State intensify its action against all violence directed at and ill-treatment of children, in particular sexual abuse. An increased number of programmes should aim at the prevention of sexual misbehaviour towards children. The deep causes of the phenomenon should be

seriously looked at. The Committee also recommends the active participation of non-governmental organizations as well as children and youth groups in changing and influencing attitudes in that regard." (Philippines IRCO, Add.29, para. 24)

"Further information and research findings on the causes of sexual exploitation and abuse would be welcomed by the Committee. The Committee also suggests that the State Party consider the possibility of reviewing its legislation in relation to the age of sexual consent in the light of concerns raised on this matter by the Committee. It is also the view of the Committee that serious consideration should be given to the possibility of allocating further resources for programmes for the prevention of sexual abuse and exploitation and the rehabilitation of victims, including training of and support to the professionals dealing with these issues and the development of an integrated and coordinated approach to assist both the victims and the perpetrators of such abuse. In connection with this point, the Committee wishes to encourage the State Party to consider greater use of the media in relation to awareness-raising and education on the dangers of sexual exploitation and abuse and the issues of HIV/AIDS and other sexually transmitted diseases." (Federal Republic of Yugoslavia IRCO, Add.49, para. 41)

Often, the Committee simply notes the occurrence of the problem, sometimes linked to other forms of exploitation, and the lack of sufficient measures to prevent sexual exploitation. For example:

"...The Committee is also concerned [at] ... the appearance of the problem of the sexual exploitation of children and the problem of drug abuse." (Belarus IRCO, Add.17, para. 10)

"The Committee is concerned that insufficient measures have been taken to protect children against sexual abuse and exploitation. "The Committee encourages the State Party to take all appropriate measures to prevent and combat sexual abuse and sexual exploitation of children, and to ensure their physical and psychological recovery and rehabilitation in the light of article 39 of the Convention." (Panama IRCO, Add.68, paras. 10 and 35. See also Denmark IRCO, Add.33, para. 15; UK IRCO, Add.34, para. 38; Ukraine IRCO, Add.42, para. 14; Mongolia IRCO, Add.48, para. 16; China IRCO, Add.56, para. 23; Morocco IRCO, Add.60, para. 15; Nigeria IRCO, Add.61, para. 42)

The Committee has noted links with drug abuse and with other criminal activities:

"The Committee notes with concern the increasing crime rate among children and the vulnerability of children to sexual abuse, drug abuse and alcoholism.

"The Committee emphasizes that more determined steps need to be taken to combat child prostitution; for example, the police forces should accord high priority to the investigation of such cases and the development of programmes to implement the provisions contained in article 39 of the Convention." (Russian Federation IRCO, Add.4, paras. 15 and 24)

"The Committee notes with concern the growing use and involvement of children in criminal activities and the vulnerability of children to sexual abuse, drug abuse, alcoholism, as well as torture and ill-treatment." (Poland IRCO, Add.31, para. 20)

The Committee has also noted links between transnational trafficking and sexual exploitation:

"Furthermore, the Committee expresses its regret that insufficient measures are being taken to address the problems of child abuse, including sexual abuse, and the sale and trafficking of children, child prostitution and child pornography. It is especially concerned by the fact that a significant amount of girls, and sometimes boys, are victims of transnational trafficking to be sexually exploited in brothels across the border.

"The Committee ... recommends that the State Party takes all appropriate measures to prevent and combat child abuse, including sexual abuse, and the sale and trafficking of children, child prostitution and child pornography. The Committee is encouraging the establishment of bilateral agreements between concerned parties to prevent and combat transnational trafficking and sale of children for sexual exploitation." (Myanmar IRCO, Add.69, paras. 24 and 44)

Groups particularly vulnerable to sexual exploitation

The Committee has identified certain groups of children as being at particular risk of sexual exploitation:

"Vulnerable groups of children, including girl children, indigenous children and children living in poverty, are particularly disadvantaged in their access to adequate health and educational facilities and are the primary victims of such abuses as sale and trafficking, child labour and sexual and other forms of exploitation..." (Bolivia IRCO, Add.1, para. 9)

"The growing number of children living and/or working on the street, child prostitution and pornography are also matters of concern..." (Viet Nam IRCO, Add.3, para. 6)

"The Committee expresses its grave concern that an increasing number of children who make a living by selling and begging on the streets are especially vulnerable to sexual exploitation." (Nicaragua IRCO, Add.36, para. 25)

"The Committee is concerned by the increasing phenomenon of child prostitution that affects in particular children belonging to the lower castes. It is worried about the absence of measures to combat this phenomenon and the lack of rehabilitation measures..." (Nepal IRCO, Add.57, para. 23)

"The Committee is concerned by the recent incidence of prostitution which affects particularly non-Cypriot children..." (Cyprus IRCO, Add.59, para. 18)

Girls

The Platform for Action of the Fourth World Conference on Women notes: "Sexual violence and sexually transmitted diseases, including HIV/AIDS, have a devastating effect on children's health, and girls are more vulnerable than boys to the consequences of unprotected and premature sexual relations. Girls often face pressures to engage in sexual activity. Due to such factors as their youth, social pressures, lack of protective laws, or failure to enforce laws, girls are more vulnerable to all kinds of violence, particularly sexual violence, including rape, sexual abuse, sexual exploitation, trafficking..." (Platform for Action, para. 269). Proposed actions include the elimination of child pornography, child prostitution, sexual abuse, rape and incest (paras. 277 (b) and (d)).

Child domestic workers are particularly prone to sexual exploitation. *The State of the World's Children 1997* suggests: "Sexual abuse is often regarded by the employer as part of the employment terms" (p. 33).

Disabled children

Difficulties of communication and the institutionalization of many disabled children may make them particularly prone to sexual exploitation and abuse (see article 23, page 300). The Standard Rules on the Equalization of Opportunities for Persons with Disabilities notes: "Persons with disabilities and their families need to be fully informed about taking precautions against sexual and other forms of abuse. Persons with disabilities are particularly vulnerable to abuse in the family, community and institutions and need to be educated on how to avoid the occurrence of abuse, recognize when abuse has occurred and report on such acts." (rule 9(4))

Armed conflict

The study on the *Impact of Armed Conflict on Children* suggests: "Rape is not incidental to conflict. It can occur on a random and uncontrolled basis due to the general disruption of social boundaries and the license granted to soldiers and

article 34

Sexual exploitation and armed conflict

In her study on the *Impact of Armed Conflict on Children,* Ms Graça Machel submits the following specific recommendations regarding sexual exploitation and gender-based violence:

(a) All humanitarian responses in conflict situations must emphasize the special reproductive health needs of women and girls including access to family planning services, pregnancy as a result of rape, sexual mutilation, childbirth at an early age or infection with sexually transmitted diseases, including HIV/AIDS. Equally important are the psychosocial needs of mothers who have been subjected to gender-based violence and who need help in order to foster the conditions necessary for the healthy development of their children;

(b) All military personnel, including peacekeeping personnel, should receive instruction on their responsibilities towards civilian communities and particularly towards women and children as part of their training;

(c) Clear and easily accessible systems should be established for reporting on sexual abuse within both military and civilian populations;

(d) The treatment of rape as a war crime must be clarified, pursued within military and civilian populations, and punished accordingly. Appropriate legal and rehabilitative remedies must be made available to reflect the nature of the crime and its harm;

(e) Refugee and displaced persons camps should be so designed as to improve security for women and girls. Women should also be involved in all aspects of camp administration but especially in organizing distribution and security systems. Increased numbers of female personnel should be deployed to the field as protection officers and counsellors;

(f) In every conflict, support programmes should be established for victims of sexual abuse and gender-based violence. These should offer confidential counselling on a wide range of issues, including the rights of victims. They should also provide educational activities and skills training.

(*Impact of Armed Conflict on Children,* A/51/306, para. 110)

militias. More often, however, it functions like other forms of torture and is used as a tactical weapon of war to humiliate and weaken the morale of the perceived enemy. During armed conflict, rape is used to terrorize populations or to force civilians to flee."

Twelve country studies on sexual exploitation of children in situations of armed conflict were prepared for the report, which show that women and girls are particularly at risk; children affected by gender-based violence also include those who have witnessed the rape of a family member and those who are ostracized because of an assault on a mother. The studies illustrate how poverty, hunger and desperation may force women and girls into prostitution and how children have been trafficked from conflict situations to work in brothels in other countries. Sexual exploitation has a devastating effect on physical and emotional development; unwanted and unsafe sex is likely to lead to sexually transmitted diseases and HIV/AIDS, which not only affect immediate health but also future sexual and reproductive health and mortality. The report provides specific recommendations on the subject of sexual exploitation and gender-based violence (*Impact of Armed Conflict on Children,* A/51/306, paras. 91 et seq., and 110).

The Special Rapporteur of the Commission on Human Rights, on the situation of systematic rape, sexual slavery and slavery-like practices during periods of armed conflict, has also drawn attention to the particular threat of sexual violence faced by young girls in situations of armed conflict (E/CN.4/Sub.2/1996/26, 16 July 1996).

Detailed relevant practical advice for conflict situations is provided in *Guidelines for HIV Interventions in Emergency Settings,* a joint publication of UNHCR, WHO and UNAIDS, which emphasizes that "HIV spreads fastest in conditions of poverty, powerlessness and social instability – conditions that are often at their most extreme during emergencies" (UNAIDS – Joint United Nations Programme on HIV/AIDS, 1996, p. 2).

Refugees

The Office of the United Nations High Commissioner for Refugees points out that refugees, in particular unaccompanied children, are especially vulnerable to sexual exploitation and abuse. UNHCR published *Sexual Violence against Refugees: Guidelines on Prevention and Response* in 1995. The report states: "Sexual violence against refugees is widespread. Women and young girls – and, less frequently, men and boys

– are vulnerable to attack, both during their flight and while in exile. They are vulnerable from many quarters and in every case, the physical and psychological trauma that results can only add to the pain of displacement and the bitterness of exile". It provides a detailed background, preventive measures and practical measures to be taken in response to incidents of sexual violence. Among categories of refugees identified as being most at risk of sexual violence are unaccompanied children, children in foster care arrangements and those in detention or detention-like situations (*Sexual Violence against Refugees, Guidelines on Prevention and Response, UNHCR 1995*, para. 1.2).

Legislative and other measures

The Committee on the Rights of the Child has placed a particular emphasis on the need for legislation as a basis for protection against sexual exploitation. The *Guidelines for Periodic Reports* requests information on "legislative, educational and social" measures to protect the child from all forms of sexual exploitation and sexual abuse. The Committee has noted the need for specific legislation, and the *Guidelines* asks in particular "whether sexual exploitation and abuse of children, child prostitution and child pornography, including the possession of child pornography, and the use of children in other unlawful sexual practices are considered criminal offences" (para. 158). The *Guidelines* also asks about criminalizing sexual exploitation by nationals in other countries (see below, page 463). In addition, it seeks information on the legal minimum age for sexual consent (para. 24; see below, page 462 and article 1, page 9).

The Committee's comments reflect the need for "specific and appropriate" legislation and programmes:

"... the Committee is concerned by the recent rise in child prostitution and the production

---

World Congress declaration

The World Congress against Commercial Sexual Exploitation of Children (Stockholm, 1996) in its Declaration calls on States, in cooperation with national and international organizations and civil society, to:

- accord high priority to action against the commercial sexual exploitation of children and allocate adequate resources for this purpose;

- promote stronger cooperation between States and all sectors of society to prevent children from entering the sex trade and to strengthen the role of families in protecting children against commercial sexual exploitation;

- criminalize the commercial sexual exploitation of children, as well as other forms of sexual exploitation of children, and condemn and penalize all those offenders involved, whether local or foreign, while ensuring that the child victims of this practice are not penalized;

- review and revise, where appropriate, laws, policies, programmes and practices to eliminate the commercial sexual exploitation of children;

- enforce laws, policies and programmes to protect children from commercial sexual exploitation and strengthen communication and cooperation between law enforcement authorities;

- promote adoption, implementation and dissemination of laws, policies, and programmes supported by relevant regional, national and local mechanisms against the commercial sexual exploitation of children;

- develop and implement comprehensive gender-sensitive plans and programmes to prevent the commercial sexual exploitation of children, to protect and assist the child victims and to facilitate their recovery and reintegration into society;

- create a climate through education, social mobilization, and development activities to ensure that parents and others legally responsible for children are able to fulfil their rights, duties and responsibilities to protect children from commercial sexual exploitation;

- mobilize political and other partners, national and international communities, including intergovernmental organizations and non-governmental organizations, to assist countries in eliminating the commercial sexual exploitation of children; and

- enhance the role of popular participation, including that of children, in preventing and eliminating the commercial sexual exploitation of children.

The Agenda for Action provides detailed proposals under the headings: "Coordination and cooperation; Prevention; Protection; Recovery and Reintegration; and Child participation" (A/51/385).

and dissemination of pornographic materials involving children. In this regard, the fact that no specific and appropriate legislation and programmes exist to prevent and combat sexual abuse and exploitation is a serious concern to the Committee.

"The Committee suggests ... that appropriate legal measures be taken to combat sexual abuse and exploitation of children. Cases of abuse should be properly investigated, sanctions applied to perpetrators and publicity given to the decisions taken in those cases..." (Bulgaria IRCO, Add.66, paras. 14 and 30)

The Committee has proposed that legal reform should include making the use of child prostitutes and the possession of child pornography, as well as the publication and distribution of child pornography, an offence:

"The Committee is deeply concerned that appropriate, in particular legislative, measures have not yet been taken to forbid the possession of child pornography and the purchasing of sexual services from child prostitutes. It is also seriously concerned at the existence of sex telephone services accessible by children...
"In the process of reforming the Penal Code, the Committee strongly recommends that the possession of child pornography materials and the purchase of sexual services from child prostitutes be made illegal...".

The Committee went on to recommend in addition:

"... that the State Party take all appropriate measures to protect children from accessing sex telephone services and from the risk of being sexually exploited by paedophiles through these telephone services that can be accessed by anyone..." (Finland IRCO, Add.53, paras. 19 and 29)

"The Committee is concerned that the provisions of the Penal Code relating to protection against sexual abuse, which provide no safeguard for the protection of boy victims, are inconsistent with the principles and provisions of the Convention.
"...The Committee also recommends that the penal law be amended so that adults having sexual intercourse with boys under 16 be considered as a criminal act..." (Mauritius IRCO, Add.64, paras. 16 and 32)

The Committee has stressed the importance of adopting a non-punitive approach to child victims of sexual exploitation; this approach is echoed in the Stockholm World Congress against Commercial Sexual Exploitation Agenda for Action, proposing that particular care should be taken to ensure that judicial procedures do not aggravate the trauma already experienced by the child and that the response of the system be cou-

pled with legal aid assistance, when appropriate, and the provision of judicial remedies to the child victims.

Age of sexual consent

The Committee's *Guidelines* for both Initial and Periodic Reports seek information on the age of sexual consent (under "Definition of a child"; see article 1, page 9). Most countries define the age at which children are to be judged as able to consent to sexual activity; it varies widely, between the ages of 12 and 18. The *Guidelines* also seeks information on the age for marriage, and the Committee has expressed concern at low ages, and at discrimination between the marriage ages for girls and for boys (it appears that ability to consent to sexual activities is assumed at marriage age in all States). The definition of sexual abuse of children covers more than non-consensual activities, including sexual activities with children below the age of consent, whether or not they appeared willing or even initiating partners. In most societies, sexual interference or assault without consent or involving any form of coercion are prohibited, whatever the age or status of the participants (although the criminalizing of rape within marriage may not yet have occurred in all societies).

During the drafting of what became article 34 of the Convention on the Rights of the Child, representatives from France and the Netherlands, who had proposed inclusion of an article on protection of children from exploitation, including, in particular, sexual exploitation, stated that the purpose was not to regulate the sexual life of children but rather to combat the sexual exploitation of children. During the drafting there was an unsuccessful attempt to delete the word "unlawful" from paragraph (a), which would have implied, according to the Convention's definition of a child, that all sexual activity with under-18-year-olds was to be prevented (E/CN.4/1987/25, pp. 15-24; Detrick, p. 434).

Aside from the bar on discrimination in article 2, the Convention is not prescriptive about the age at which the child is to be given the right to consent to sexual activity. Such limits need to be judged against the overall principles of respect for the child's evolving capacities, and for his or her best interests and health and maximum development. Sexual exploitation of children may well continue beyond any set age of consent, and the protection of article 34 exists up to the age of 18.

The Committee has not proposed a particular age of consent, but it has in the case of some States Parties proposed that the age should be raised.

From the Philippines Initial Report it appears that the age of consent is 12 (Philippines IR, para. 30). The Committee recommended:

"Serious consideration should be given to raising the age limit for sexual consent..." (Philippines IRCO, Add.29, para. 18)

The Committee has pointed out inadequate definition:

"...The Committee also expresses its concern that the age of sexual maturity has not been fixed, which threatens the protection of children from possible exploitation in the use of pornographic materials...

"...The Committee suggests that the Government should reassess the effectiveness of present regulations regarding the exploitation of children in pornographic materials." (Sweden IRCO, Add.2, paras. 8 and 11)

"The Committee also suggests that the State Party consider the possibility of reviewing its legislation in relation to the age of sexual consent in the light of the concerns raised on this matter by the Committee." (Federal Republic of Yugoslavia IRCO, Add.49, para. 41)

In some countries a minimum age at which a child is permitted to consent to sexual activities is specified, and in addition a higher age when the sexual relationship is with a person in a position of trust or authority over the child (relation, teacher, caregiver, and so on). Thus for example, Canada's Initial Report states: "According to the Criminal Code it is a criminal offence to have sex with someone under the age of 14 years, with an exception where the younger partner is at least 12 years of age, where the age difference between the two partners is less than two years, and where the older youth is not in a position of trust or authority over the younger one, nor is the latter his or her dependant." (Canada IR, para. 45)

During discussions with the Committee, a Finnish representative indicated: "... Finnish law provided two age limits with regard to sexual relations. The first, which applied to relations between minors, was 14 years of age, and the second, which covered relations between adults and minors, was 16 years of age. Legislation in that area was currently under review and a limit of 15 years of age for both categories of relations had been proposed. Advocates of that view put forward three arguments: young people were maturing more quickly than in the past; other European countries had set the limit at 15 years; and studies showed that one third of Finnish youth had had sexual relations before the age of 15."

A Committee member commented that Finland should perhaps consider setting different ages for sexual consent between young people and between children and adults, in order to protect children from the potentially exploitative influence of adults. The Finnish representative responded that the Committee's comments were reflected in new proposed changes to the Penal Code: "When the age and the level of emotional and social maturity of sexual partners were close together, the sexual act would not be considered a crime. In cases where an individual took advantage of his greater age or status to influence a younger individual, the age of protection would be 18. Legislation currently in force set a higher age of consent for homosexual than for heterosexual relations; under the revised legislation, that age would be the same." (Finland SR.283, paras. 11 and 21)

In some countries, there are different ages of consent for girls and for boys, and for different forms of sexuality – heterosexuality and homosexuality. These differences, like the common gender differences in minimum age for marriage, appear to breach article 2 of the Convention.

Sex tourism – the principle of "extraterritoriality"

The Committee has expressed concern about countries where "sex tourism" involving children has been identified. It has also noted that children working as domestic servants are particularly at risk of sexual exploitation. For example:

"The Committee expresses its grave concern about the substantial number of children working as domestic servants and who are often subjected to sexual abuse. It is also deeply worried about the increasing number of children exploited sexually, especially young boys forced into prostitution, both locally and in international sex tourism.

"The Committee expresses its deep concern about the development of sexual exploitation of children, especially of boys, through sex tourism. The Committee suggests that the authorities engage a prevention campaign on the HIV virus and strengthen its procedures to supervise tourist areas where the problem prevails." (Sri Lanka IRCO, Add.40, paras. 23 and 42)

"The Committee encourages the State Party to take all appropriate measures to prevent and combat ... sexual exploitation of children, including victims of sexual tourism." (Mauritius IRCO, Add.64, para. 31)

The *Guidelines for Periodic Reports* asks for information on legal developments in this area: "whether the principle of extraterritoriality has been incorporated in the legislation to criminalize the sexual exploitation of children by nationals and residents of the State Party when committed in other countries" (para. 159). Equally important is enforcement of legislation in the country in which the sexual exploitation takes place.

The Committee has welcomed legislative developments in States Parties:

"...the Committee particularly welcomes the adoption of ... a recent law which extends the national jurisdiction in cases of child prostitution and pornography and allows the State to prosecute any person accused of 'sex tourism'..." (Belgium IRCO, Add.38, para. 5)

"...the Committee notes with satisfaction that the Criminal Law has been extended to make sexual abuse of children abroad a criminal offence. In addition, note is taken of the recent measures to make the possession of pornographic materials featuring children a punishable offence." (Germany IRCO, Add.43, para. 10)

In 1985, the World Tourism Organization adopted a Tourism Bill of Rights and Tourist Code that reminds States of the need to prevent any possibility of using tourism to exploit others for prostitution purposes, asks those involved in organizing tourism to refrain from encouraging the use of tourism for all forms of exploitation and asks tourists themselves to "refrain from exploiting others for prostitution purposes" (see E/CN.4/Sub.2/1993/31, para. 81).

Complaints procedures

In the report of its General Discussion on juvenile justice, the Committee noted that children were often denied the right to lodge complaints when they were victims of violation of their fundamental rights, including in cases of ill-treatment and sexual abuse. The need for children to have access to effective complaints procedures has been a consistent concern of the Committee (Report on the tenth session, October-November 1995, CRC/C/46, paras. 220 and 226; see also article 12, page 155, and article 19, page 250). Children in institutions are especially vulnerable, often isolated from independent adults; disabled children may also be particularly vulnerable, because of communication and other difficulties.

Children's complaints, and their evidence when cases come to court, must be taken seriously, in line with the Convention. Difficulties for children in challenging exploitation in court and having their evidence taken seriously have concerned the Committee:

"In addition, the Committee is of the opinion that other legislation in force in Paraguay relating to the definition of the child with regard to ... the non-validity of children's statements in cases of alleged sexual abuse also raises concern as to its compatibility with the spirit and purpose of the Convention,

especially in ensuring that the best interests of the child shall be a primary consideration in all actions concerning children." (Paraguay Prelim. Obs., Add.27, para. 7)

In one case the Committee was concerned to ensure protection for professionals who report sexual abuse:

"...Finally, the Committee recommends that measures be taken fully to protect professionals who report evidence of sexual abuse to the relevant authorities." (Finland IRCO, Add.53, para. 29)

Other measures

Many other rights guaranteed in the Convention are relevant to the prevention of sexual exploitation. The Agenda for Action of the Stockholm World Congress against Commercial Sexual Exploitation highlights, for example:

- access to education to improve the status of children;
- improvement of access to all services and providing a supportive environment for families and children vulnerable to commercial sexual exploitation;
- maximize education on the rights of the child; promote children's rights in family education and family development assistance;
- identify or establish peer education programmes and monitoring networks to combat commercial sexual exploitation;
- formulate or strengthen and implement gender-sensitive national social and economic policies and programmes to assist vulnerable children, and families and communities in resisting acts which can lead to commercial sexual exploitation, "with special attention to family abuse, harmful traditional practices and their impact on girls, and to promoting the value of children as human beings rather than commodities; and reduce poverty by promoting gainful employment, income generation and other supports";
- mobilize the business sector, including the tourist industry, against the use of its networks and establishments for commercial sexual exploitation;
- encourage media professionals to develop strategies which strengthen the role of the media in providing information of the highest quality, reliability and ethical standards concerning all aspects of commercial sexual exploitation;
- target those involved with commercial sexual exploitation of children with information, education and outreach campaigns and pro-

grammes to promote behavioural changes to counter the practice.

(A/51/385)

Recovery and reintegration

Article 39 (see page 529) requires States Parties to take all appropriate measures to promote physical and psychological recovery and social reintegration of child victims of any form of abuse, exploitation and so forth. The Committee has emphasized the importance of adopting a non-punitive approach to child victims of sexual exploitation (see above, page 457). The Agenda for Action of the Stockholm World Congress suggests that social, medical and psychological counselling and other support should be provided to child victims and their families; that there should be gender-sensitive training of medical personnel, teachers, social workers, non-governmental organizations and others working to help child victims; that social stigmatization of victims should be prevented and their recovery and reintegration in communities and families should be facilitated; and that where institutionalization is necessary, it should be for the shortest possible period.

Bilateral and multilateral measures

One reason why the importance of international cooperation to prevent and combat sexual exploitation of children is recognized is because many forms of exploitation have become transnational, for example sex tourism, trafficking in child prostitutes, and dissemination of child pornography including through the Internet. The Committee's *Guidelines for Periodic Reports* seeks information on "bilateral, regional and multilateral agreements", including judicial cooperation and cooperation among law enforcement officials. The Agenda for Action, adopted at the Stockholm World Congress in 1996, promoted "better cooperation between countries and international organizations, including regional organizations, and other catalysts which have a key role in eliminating the commercial sexual exploitation of children, including the Committee on the Rights of the Child, UNICEF, ILO, UNESCO, UNDP, WHO, UNAIDS, UNHCR, IOM, the World Bank/IMF, INTERPOL, United Nations Crime Prevention and Criminal Justice Division, UNFPA, the World Tourism Organization, the United Nations Commissioner for Human Rights, the United Nations Centre for Human Rights, the United Nations Commission on Human Rights and its Special Rapporteur on the Sale of Children, and the Working Group on Contemporary Forms of Slavery, each taking guidance from the Agenda for Action in their activities in accordance with their respective mandates..." (A/51/385, p. 5)

One important example of international cooperation is INTERPOL's Standing Working Party on Offences Committed against Minors (1993).

Other international instruments and standards

In its "Human Rights Studies Series", the Centre for Human Rights published in 1996 *Sexual exploitation of children* (by Vitit Muntarbhorn, former Special Rapporteur of the Commission on Human Rights on the sale of children, child prostitution and child pornography), which summarizes United Nations and other international initiatives. Papers prepared for the Stockholm World Congress include a detailed summary of "The International Legal Framework and Current National Legislative and Enforcement Responses", submitted by End Child Prostitution in Asian Tourism (ECPAT).

The International Bill of Human Rights and other Conventions

The Universal Declaration of Human Rights (article 4) requires generally that: "No one shall be held in slavery or servitude; slavery and the slave trade shall be prohibited in all their forms." This is repeated in article 8 of the International Covenant on Civil and Political Rights, which also covers "forced and compulsory labour" (see article 32, page 427). The Human Rights Committee, in a General Comment on article 24 of the International Covenant (which recognizes children's right to protection), notes the need to protect children "from being exploited by means of forced labour or prostitution" (Human Rights Committee, General Comment 17, HRI/GEN/1/Rev.2, p. 23).

The 1949 Convention for the Suppression of the Traffic in Persons and of the Exploitation of the Prostitution of Others targets procurers and exploiters of prostitutes (General Assembly Resolution 317(IV), 2 December 1949, annex); the 1956 Supplementary Convention on the Abolition of Slavery, the Slave Trade and Institutions and Practices Similar to Slavery requires States to "take all practicable and necessary legislative and other measures to bring about progressively and as soon as possible the complete abolition or abandonment of", *inter alia*, "any institution or practice whereby a child or young person under the age of 18 years, is delivered by either or both of his natural parents or by his guardian to another person, whether for reward or not, with a view to the exploitation of the child or young person or of his labour". The 1979 Convention on the Elimination of All Forms of Discrimination against Women requires States Parties in article 6 to "take all appropriate measures, including legislation, to suppress all forms of traffic in women and exploitation of prostitution of women".

The Committee on the Elimination of Discrimination against Women issued a General Recommendation in 1991 on Violence against women which notes in commenting on article 6 that: "Poverty and unemployment force many women, including young girls, into prostitution. Prostitutes are especially vulnerable to violence because their status, which may be unlawful, tends to marginalize them. They need the equal protection of laws against rape and other forms of violence." (Committee on the Elimination of Discrimination against Women, General Recommendation No. 19, HRI/GEN/1/Rev.2, p. 112)

The Fourth World Conference on Women proposed that such instruments needed to be "reviewed and strengthened" (para. 122).

Other international initiatives

Following the adoption of the Convention on the Rights of the Child in 1989, increasing attention has been paid through various United Nations bodies and other international initiatives, to the sexual exploitation of children.

World Summit
The 1990 World Summit Declaration on the Survival, Protection and Development of Children included a commitment to work for the millions of children "who live under especially difficult circumstances ... the abused, the socially disadvantaged and the exploited..." and to tackle the root causes leading to such situations (Declaration, para. 20). And in 1993 the Vienna Declaration and Programme of Action adopted by the World Conference on Human Rights also highlighted children in especially difficult circumstances including child victims of sexual exploitation (A/CONF.157/24 (Part I), chap. III, paras. 21 and 48).

Commission on Human Rights' Special Rapporteurs and Programmes of Action
In 1990, the Commission on Human Rights appointed a Special Rapporteur on the sale of children, child prostitution and child pornography, who prepares annual reports for the Commission, carries out field visits and prepares country-specific reports; communicates with Governments where there are allegations of violations of children's rights; and promotes international cooperation. (For further discussion of sale of and trafficking in children, see article 35, page 471).

The successive reports of the Rapporteurs provide detailed discussion and recommendations for action. In an interim report prepared for the fifty-first session of the United Nations General Assembly (October 1996) the Special Rapporteur asserted that certain characteristics typified most commercial sexual exploitation of children:

"(a) It is invisible. Children drawn into the net of prostitution are for the most part hidden from public scrutiny, either physically (they are not placed on display as are their adult counterparts), or under the guise of being of age, through falsification of identification papers;

(b) It is mobile. The invisible nature of the phenomenon necessitates not only deviation from the usual place of operation like brothels, hotels, bars, and the like, but also frequent changes in the areas of operation;

(c) It is global. While the gravity of the situation for children may vary from region to region or from country to country, reports show that this kind of child abuse exists in practically all corners of the world. The contagious nature of the phenomenon causes the blurring of lines between sending and receiving countries. Some countries that used to be considered supply countries are becoming demand countries as well. Likewise, children of countries heretofore considered to be on the demand side, are starting to be victimized in their own country or elsewhere;

(d) It is escalating. Fear of AIDS and other sexually transmitted diseases, *inter alia*, leads to a greater demand for younger sexual partners. Children used to be substitutes for adult prostitutes; now, however, there is marked increase of preference for children over adults, pushing up the worth of children in the sex market;

(e) It is a highly profitable business. This is borne out by the fact that it involves not only ad hoc or individual 'entrepreneurs', it is often conducted by international profiteers using systematic methods of recruitment within a highly organized syndicated network, which is often also involved in other criminal activities such as drug dealing." (A/51/456, 7 October 1996) The report provides detailed recommendations for further action.

In a report submitted to the Commission on Human Rights in February 1997, the Rapporteur summarized recommendations for national and international action, and suggested follow-up to the World Congress (E/CN.4/1997/95, 7 February 1997).

Two other Special Rapporteurs – on violence against women (appointed by Commission on Human Rights resolution 1994/45) and on situations of systematic rape, sexual slavery, and slavery-like practices during periods of armed conflict (appointed by the SubCommission on Prevention of Discrimination and Protection of Minorities) – have presented reports and recommendations relevant to the protection of children from sexual exploitation (for example, see E/CN.4/1996/53, and E/CN.4/Sub.2/1996/26).

In a 1992 resolution, the Commission on Human Rights adopted Programmes of action for the prevention of the sale of children, child prostitution and child pornography (Commission on Human Rights resolution 1992/74, 5 March 1992, annex). States were invited to consider the Programme of Action in relation to the Plan of Action for implementing the World Declaration on the Survival, Protection and Development of Children in the 1990s and to the implementation of the Convention on the Rights of the Child.

Possible draft optional protocol

In 1994, the Committee on the Rights of the Child noted the adoption by the Commission on Human Rights of a further resolution on the need to adopt effective international measures for the prevention and eradication of the sale of children, child prostitution and child pornography (resolution 1994/90, 9 March 1994), and the decision of the Commission to establish an open-ended Working Group to prepare guidelines for a possible draft optional protocol to the Convention on the sale of children, child prostitution and child pornography, as well as basic measures needed for their prevention and eradication. During its sixth session (April 1994) the Committee adopted a formal statement on "Cooperation with United Nations bodies – Sale of children, child prostitution and child pornography", in which it stressed the important framework established by the Convention to deal with such situations, quoted above (page 457).

The Committee concluded:

"... it is the firm belief of the Committee that the priority should now lie with the strengthening of the implementation of such existing international standards."
(E/CN.4/1994/WG.14/2/Add.1, p. 8)

In a subsequent statement to the open-ended Working Group in 1996, the Committee reiterated that it believed that priority should lay with strengthening the implementation of existing standards (Report on the eleventh session, January 1996, CRC/C/50, p. 43). The Working Group met in February 1997, and a report of this session includes the drafts of texts that were considered and debated (E/CN.4/1997/97).

The World Congress against Commercial Sexual Exploitation of Children

The World Congress, held in Stockholm in August 1996, included government representatives from 122 countries together with United Nations agencies and NGOs, which committed themselves to a "global partnership against the commercial sexual exploitation of children" and produced a detailed Declaration and Agenda for Action rooted in the Convention: "The commercial sexual exploitation of children is a fundamental violation of children's rights. It comprises sexual abuse by the adult and remuneration in cash or kind to the child or to a third person or persons. The child is treated as a sexual object and as a commercial object. The commercial sexual exploitation of children constitutes a form of coercion and violence against children, and amounts to forced labour and a contemporary form of slavery." (Declaration, A/51/385, para. 5)

The Agenda for Action identified the Committee on the Rights of the Child as a catalyst, with a key role in eliminating commercial sexual exploitation.

The Agenda provides detailed recommendations for legislative, social and educational measures, many of them quoted above. It urges States to prepare national agendas for action and indicators of progress, with set goals and a time frame for implementation by the year 2000.

Implementation Checklist

article
34

● General measures of implementation

Have appropriate general measures of implementation been taken in relation to article 34, including

☐ identification and coordination of the responsible departments and agencies at all levels of government (article 34 is relevant to **departments of justice, law enforcement, health, social welfare, and education**)?

☐ identification of relevant non-governmental organizations/civil society partners?

☐ a comprehensive review to ensure that all legislation, policy and practice is compatible with the article, for all children in all parts of the jurisdiction?

☐ adoption of a strategy to secure full implementation

    ☐ which includes where necessary the identification of goals and indicators of progress?

    ☐ which does not affect any provisions which are more conducive to the rights of the child?

    ☐ which recognizes other relevant international standards?

    ☐ which involves where necessary international cooperation?

(Such measures may be part of an overall governmental strategy for implementing the Convention as a whole).

☐ budgetary analysis and allocation of necessary resources?

☐ development of mechanisms for monitoring and evaluation?

☐ making the implications of article 34 widely known to adults and children?

☐ development of appropriate training and awareness-raising (in relation to article 34 likely to include the training of **all those working with children and their families, teachers, social and community workers, health workers, police, judges and court officials, and parenting education**)?

● Specific issues in implementing article 34

Has the State considered the implications for law, policy and practice of

    ☐ the Programme of Action of the Human Rights Commission for the Prevention of the Sale of Children, Child Prostitution and Child Pornography?

    ☐ the Declaration and Agenda for Action of the 1996 World Congress against Commercial Sexual Exploitation of Children and developed a national agenda for action?

☐ Has the State carried out and/or promoted education and information strategies against sexual exploitation of children?

☐ Has the State ensured the dissemination of appropriate sex education and other information for children?

article
34

How to use the checklists, *see page XVII*

☐ Has the State established an age or ages below which the child is deemed to be unable to consent to sexual activities?

☐ Has the State defined unlawful sexual activity involving children?

☐ Has the State introduced appropriate legislative, educational and social measures to prevent the inducement or coercion of a child to engage in any unlawful sexual activity?

☐ Has the State ensured that the child victim of such coercion, inducement or exploitative use is not criminalized?

☐ Has the State reviewed all measures to protect children from sexual exploitation to ensure that measures do not further abuse the child in the process of investigation and intervention?

Has the State introduced appropriate legislation and/or other measures to prevent the exploitative use of children

       ☐ in prostitution or other unlawful sexual practices?

       ☐ in pornographic performances and materials?

       ☐ through access to "sex telephones"?

☐ Has the State established appropriate procedures to give children effective access to complaints procedures and to the courts in cases involving sexual abuse and exploitation, including within their family?

Has the State ensured appropriate measures to protect particularly vulnerable groups, including

       ☐ disabled children?

       ☐ domestic servants?

       ☐ children in institutions, including those whose liberty is restricted?

☐ Has the State introduced legislative and/or other measures to provide child witnesses in cases involving sexual exploitation with appropriate support and protection?

In relation to child pornography, is it an offence to

       ☐ possess it?

       ☐ produce it?

       ☐ disseminate it?

☐ Has the State reviewed law, policy and practice to ensure appropriate control of child pornography produced and/or disseminated through the Internet and other modern technological means?

☐ Has the State introduced legislation and/or other appropriate measures to ensure that its nationals can be prosecuted for unlawful sexual exploitation of children in other countries?

☐ Is there sufficient recording and reporting of disaggregated data, and other information concerning sexual exploitation of children, to provide an accurate situation analysis?

☐ Has the State acceded to and promoted bilateral and multilateral measures to protect the child from sexual abuse and sexual exploitation?

SEXUAL EXPLOITATION

469

Particular regard should be paid to:
The general principles

Article 2: all rights to be recognized for each child in jurisdiction without discrimination on any ground

Article 3(1): the best interests of the child to be a primary consideration in all actions concerning children

Article 6: right to life and maximum possible survival and development

Article 12: respect for the child's views in all matters affecting the child; opportunity to be heard in any judicial or administrative proceedings affecting the child

Closely related articles

Articles whose implementation is related to that of article 34 include:

Article 18: parental responsibilities
Article 19: protection from all forms of violence
Article 20: alternative care
Article 22: refugee children
Article 23: disabled children
Article 24: health and health care
Article 27: adequate standard of living
Article 28: right to education
Article 32: child labour
Article 33: drug abuse
Article 35: sale, trafficking and abduction
Article 38: armed conflict
Article 39: rehabilitative care for child victims

Prevention of abduction, sale and trafficking

article 35

Text of Article 35

States Parties shall take all appropriate national, bilateral and multilateral measures to prevent the abduction of, the sale of or traffic in children for any purpose or in any form.

Article 35 acts as a fail-safe protection for children at risk of abduction, sale or trafficking. Article 11 protects against the illicit "transfer or non-return of children abroad" (usually undertaken by relatives, not for profit); article 21 provides that international adoption must not involve "im-proper financial gain"; article 32 protects children against exploitative or harmful work, article 33, from involvement in drug trafficking, article 34 from their use in the sex trade and article 36, from all other forms of exploitation. Article 35 is a safety net to ensure that children are safe from being abducted or procured for these purposes or for any other purpose ■

Summary

Extracts from
Committee on the Rights of the Child
Guidelines for Reports to be submitted by States Parties under the Convention

For full text of *Guidelines for Periodic Reports*, see Appendix 3, page 604.

Guidelines for Initial Reports

"Special protection measures

Under this section States Parties are requested to provide relevant information, including the principal legislative, judicial, administrative or other measures in force; factors and difficulties encountered and progress achieved in implementing the relevant provisions of the Convention; and implementation priorities and specific goals for the future in respect of: ...

...(v) Sale, trafficking and abduction (article 35)...

Additionally, States Parties are encouraged to provide specific statistical information and indicators relevant to the children covered by [the previous] paragraph."
(CRC/C/5, paras. 23 and 24)

Guidelines for Periodic Reports

"VIII. SPECIAL PROTECTION MEASURES

C. Children in situations of exploitation, including physical and psychological recovery and social reintegration ...

4. Sale, trafficking and abduction (art. 35)

Please provide information on all measures adopted, including of a legislative, administrative, educational and budgetary nature, at the national, bilateral and multilateral levels, to prevent the abduction of, the sale of or traffic in children for any purpose or in any form.

In this regard, reports should indicate inter alia:

The legislation adopted to ensure effective protection of children against abduction, sale and trafficking, including through the consideration of these acts as criminal offences;

Awareness and information campaigns to prevent their occurrence, including campaigns undertaken in cooperation with the media;

The allocation of appropriate resources for the development and implementation of relevant policies and programmes;

Any national strategy developed to prevent and suppress such acts;

Any coordinating and monitoring mechanism established for that purpose;

The relevant indicators identified and used;

Whether special units have been created among law enforcement officials to deal with these acts;

Relevant training activities provided to the competent authorities;

Structures and programmes developed to provide support services to the children concerned and to promote their physical and psychological recovery and social reintegration, in the light of **article 39;**

The measures adopted to ensure that in the implementation of article 35 due consideration is taken of other provisions of the Convention, including in the areas of civil rights, particularly in relation to the preservation of the identity of the child, adoption and prevention of any form of exploitation of children, including child labour and sexual exploitation;

The measures adopted to ensure respect for the general principles of the Convention, including non-discrimination, the best interests of the child, respect for the views of the child, the right to life, and survival and development to the maximum extent possible.

Reports should also indicate the relevant bilateral and multilateral agreements concluded by the State Party, or to which it may have acceded, to prevent the sale and abduction of and trafficking in children, including in the areas of international cooperation between judicial authorities and law enforcement officials, inter alia on any existing system of collection and exchange of information on perpetrators of such acts as well as on the child victims. Relevant disaggregated information should also be provided on the children concerned by the implementation of article 35, including by age, gender, region, rural/urban area, and social and ethnic origin, as well as on the progress achieved in

Background

In the initial phases of drafting the Convention on the Rights of the Child, articles 34, 35 and 36 were condensed into one, but the Working Group agreed it would be more useful to tease out the separate strands of child exploitation. Article 35 was introduced because the sale or trafficking of children was wider in scope than that of article 34, which relates to prostitution and child pornography (E/CN.4/1987/25, pp. 15-24; Detrick, p. 429).

How does the "abduction of, the sale of or traffic in children" manifest itself? Children can be unlawfully abducted by their natural parents or relatives in disputes over custody. Article 11 addresses such incidents where children are taken across borders (see page 139), but article 35 also requires measures to deal with internal abductions within the jurisdiction. In addition, children in poor countries can be sold into the equivalent of slavery, through bonded labour or debt repayment, and they can be trafficked for the purposes of begging. Article 32 protects children from economic exploitation (see page 427). In conditions of war, children can be forced to become soldiers or servants to armed forces (see article 38, page 511). Children can also be trafficked for the purposes of sex – into prostitution or the production of pornography or, less overtly, through forced marriages or traditional practices such as *Ngosi* in Zimbabwe (see article 34, page 455). Children, particularly babies, are a desirable commodity for adoption: article 21 requires measures to ensure that intercountry adoption "does not result in improper financial gain for those involved in it" (see page 274). There is also a strong suspicion that children's bodies are being used to provide organs for transplants, in breach of article 6.

Thus, with article 35, the Convention provides a double protection for children: the main forms of child trafficking are dealt with in those different articles, but blanket action on abduction, sale or traffic "for any purpose or in any form" is also required by this article.

The Committee on the Rights of the Child has participated in consideration of a possible Optional Protocol on the sale of children, child prostitution and child pornography, and reasonably concluded:

"The Convention has defined the legal framework in this field. It was later meaningfully complemented by the two programmes of action adopted by the Commission on Human Rights, for the prevention of the Sale of Children, Child Prostitution and Child Pornography and for the Elimination of the Exploitation of Child Labour... In view of this reality, it is the firm belief of the Committee that priority should now lie with the strengthening of the implementation of such existing international standards." (E/CN.4/1994/WG.14.2/Add.1, p. 9, paras. 36 and 39)

Trafficking and child labour

The Committee has raised concern about the trafficking of children for the purposes of labour:

"The Committee is seriously alarmed at the reports of the forced labour of children, the exploitation of child labour in the informal and agriculture sectors and the trafficking of children which has been brought to its attention." (Pakistan IRCO, Add.18, para. 21)

"In view of the scale of the problem of sale and trafficking of children, especially girls, the Committee is deeply concerned about the absence of a specific law and policy to combat this phenomenon.
"The Committee further recommends that firm measures be taken to ensure the right of survival of all children in Nepal, including those who live and/or work in the streets. Such measures should aim at the effective protection of children against any form of exploitation, particularly child labour, prostitution, drug-related activities and child trafficking and sale.
"In order to effectively combat intercountry trafficking and sale of children, the Committee strongly suggests that Nepal take all appropriate measures, including legislative and administrative ones, and encourages the State Party to consider adopting bilateral measures to prevent and eliminate such phenomena. Awareness campaigns should be developed at the community level and a thorough monitoring system should be established." (Nepal IRCO, Add.57, paras. 22, 35 and 37)

The eighteenth session of the Working Group on Contemporary Forms of Slavery under the Commission of Human Rights heard evidence of bonded labour in Nepal under the system of *kamaiyas*, a one year contract whereby the whole family is the labour unit, estimated to be as many as 100,000 families in bondage; and in Pakistan where children were effectively enslaved in certain industries – carpet and textiles, coal mining, brick-making and camel racing – although the Commission was also informed of recent Pakistani legislation freeing all bonded labourers and penalizing the practice (E/CN.4/Sub.2/1993/30, paras. 51-59).

These are only two examples. In many parts of the developing world, children are effectively sold into slavery, often as domestic servants. Children are also used to beg, sometimes having been deliberately deformed. Colombia reported that its legislation punishes "begging with the aid of a child" with stiffer penalties "if the child is below the age of 12 years or has physical or mental deficiencies which tend to produce feelings of pity, repulsion or the like" (Colombia IR, para. 139). There is also evidence that exploiting children for the purposes of begging is undertaken as a mass commercial enterprise, for example the exporting of children from the Indian subcontinent to Mecca.

The Programme of Action for the Elimination of the Exploitation of Child Labour focuses on remedying underlying causes of child labour but also calls for "energetic repressive action" in relation to the trafficking of children, citing in particular serfdom, bond service, fake adoption, abandonment, child prostitution, enforced begging, trafficking in child pornography and children for immoral purposes and under-age maidservants in a position of servitude. Where bonded labour is concerned, legislation is needed that nullifies the debts and obligations owed by the family as well as which prohibits such bondage. (Commission on Human Rights, 1993/79, paras. 3 and 14)

Trafficking and adoption
As discussed under article 21, the Hague Convention on the Protection of Children and Cooperation in respect of Intercountry Adoption is now the main international tool for preventing the international trafficking of children for the purposes of adoption. It prohibits improper financial gain from intercountry adoption, specifying that "only costs and expenses, including reasonable professional fees ... may be charged or paid" (article 32). The Hague Convention was only open for ratification in 1993 so its effectiveness has yet to be tested. There are still reports of intercountry adoption sales, particularly in South and Central America and Eastern Europe, as buyers from the Western world place a premium on Caucasian children; but it is a global phenomenon because in normal circumstances the number of hopeful adoptive couples tend to exceed the number of healthy babies available for adop-

tion. And, although intercountry adoptions are the prime source of profit, the clandestine selling of children for adoption also operates internally within many jurisdictions.

Some countries have taken steps to prohibit intercountry adoptions (see box opposite) or curtail them to cases of abandoned or institutionalized children only (see, for example, Sale of Children, Report submitted by Mr. Vitit Muntarbhorn, Special Rapporteur appointed in accordance with Commission resolution 1990/68, E/CN.4/ 1992/55, paras. 56-63). However, such measures, though designed to prevent trafficking and to uphold the child's rights under articles 7, 8 and 10 (to know and be cared for by parents, to preservation of identity and not to be separated from parents), appear to be a less flexible means of securing the best interests of individual children than those provided by the Hague Convention.

The Committee raised concerns about trafficking through adoption with the Ukraine:

"The Committee is worried by the high rate of abandonment of children, especially newborn babies, and the lack of a comprehensive strategy to assist vulnerable families. This situation can lead to illegal intercountry adoption or other forms of trafficking and sale of children. In this context the Committee is also concerned about the absence of any law prohibiting the sale and trafficking of children, and the fact that the right of the child to have his/her identity preserved is not guaranteed by the law ...

"With regard to the sale and trafficking of children, the Committee encourages the Government to clearly prohibit this illegal activity and to ensure that the right of the child to have his/her identity preserved is fully endorsed ..." (Ukraine IRCO, Add.42, paras. 11 and 28)

The Committee commended Sri Lanka for having

"...enacted new legislation on international adoption which ensures safeguards against the sale and trafficking of children." (Sri Lanka IRCO, Add.40, para. 17)

Trafficking and sexual exploitation
Article 34 addresses children's right to protection from all forms of sexual exploitation, including prostitution or the use of children in pornography (see page 455). Both of these activities have commercial motives as well as sexual ones: child prostitution and child pornography are increasingly profitable businesses in many parts of the world. Naturally this is a concern of the Committee, for example:

"In the light of articles 34 and 35 of the Convention, the Committee encourages the State Party in its efforts to follow up at both the national and regional levels on the measures

required to prevent and combat the sexual exploitation of children." (Nigeria IRCO, Add.61, para. 42)

"The Committee shares the State Party's concern that there has been an upsurge in recent years of kidnapping and abduction of children. In this connection, the Committee wishes to express its serious concern about the apparent inadequacy of measures taken to prevent and combat the problems of the sale, trafficking and sexual exploitation of children. "The State Party is urged to take further action for the maintenance of strong and comprehensive measures to combat the abandonment and infanticide of girls as well as the trafficking, sale and kidnapping or abduction of girls." (China IRCO, Add.56, paras. 23 and 36).

The Committee suggested to Sweden: "Recognizing that the ratification of other international human rights instruments has a favourable influence on the promotion of the rights of the child, the State Party might consider ratifying the Convention for the Suppression of the Traffic in Persons and of the Exploitation of the Prostitution of Others." (Sweden IRCO, Add.2, para. 13)

The Commission on Human Rights, in its 1992 Programmes of Action for the prevention of the sale of children, child prostitution and child pornography, tackles these issues comprehensively, making recommendations on public awareness, social support and education as well as encouraging measures directly impacting on the perpetrators and victims of child trafficking.

The Programmes recommend that legislation should be reviewed to ensure that all forms of knowingly trafficking in children (including by parents) are penalized and that intergovernmental cooperation should be pursued, both in terms of ratification of relevant treaties (in particular the Convention on the Abolition of Slavery, the Slave Trade and Institutions and Practices Similar to Slavery, of 1956, and the Convention for the Suppression of the Traffic in Persons and of the Exploitation of the Prostitution of Others of 1949). They recommend practical forms of cooperation between law enforcement agencies: "States should establish their own data bases, improve their reporting at all levels, exchange information and report to the International Criminal Police Organization to enable a special data bank on suspects involved in cross-border trafficking, sale or sexual exploitation of children to be set up. The experience gained in international police cooperation in combating drug traffic should be used to prevent international traffic in and sexual exploitation of children."

The Federal Republic of Yugoslavia's measures against trafficking through adoption

"In order to avoid the possibility of trafficking in children separated from their parents or war orphans in the former Yugoslavia through adoption, the stand has been taken that until the end of the war international adoptions shall not be permitted. However, within the framework of cooperation with the International Social Service, cases have been reported of mothers going abroad to give birth to their children in foreign hospitals and authorizing the adoption of their newborns, which gives rise to suspicions of child trafficking. This practice calls for greater bilateral cooperation within the framework of the Convention Concerning the Powers of Authorities and the Law Applicable in respect of the Protection of Infants, irrespective of the fact that the Federal Republic of Yugoslavia has not yet signed this Convention."

(Federal Republic of Yugoslavia IR, para. 420)

The Programmes also recommend the establishment of special intergovernmental tasks forces to promote measures in alliance with appropriate non-governmental organizations (Commission on Human Rights, 1992/74, paras. 35-36). An interim report on this issue to the General Assembly in 1996 made further recommendations – for example for synchronizing legislation between countries and coordinating registries of missing children (Interim Report to the General Assembly, Sale of children, child prostitution and child pornography, A/51/456, October 1996, para. 87(d)-(g)).

The issue of sex tourism received intensive scrutiny at the 1996 Stockholm World Congress against Commercial Sexual Exploitation of Children, which called for States:

● "to develop or strengthen and implement laws to criminalize the acts of the nationals of the countries of origin when committed against children in the countries of destination ('extraterritorial criminal laws');

● to promote extradition and other arrangements to ensure that a person who exploits a child for sexual purposes in another country ('the destination country') is prosecuted either in the country of origin or the destination country;

Assistance to Nepalese girls who have been the victims of trafficking

"UNICEF, in coordination with local NGOs, is preparing a national-level campaign to promote awareness of the trafficking of girls from Nepal to India. Activities will include advocacy at the ministerial level to strengthen the laws regarding human trafficking, and working with the police to generate commitment to stronger enforcement of laws. The programme intends to generate microlevel interventions in the districts most affected by girl child trafficking. Since poverty is one of the major causes that have forced girls into prostitution, a major focus will be on income-generating skills. Literacy will be another focus. In a study of some 400-500 Nepalese prostitutes in Bombay, an NGO, the Women's Rehabilitation Centre (WOREC), found that most were illiterate..."

(Nepal IR, para. 390)

- to strengthen laws and law enforcement, including confiscation and seizure of assets and profits, and other sanctions, against those who commit sexual crimes against children in destination countries;

- to share relevant data."

(Declaration and Agenda For Action, World Congress against Commercial Sexual Exploitation of Children, 1996, A/51/385, para. 4(d))

Trafficking and organ transplants

Evidence of the trafficking of children's organs for medical purposes appears to be largely anecdotal. A systematic investigation of the alleged cases around the world has not yet been undertaken. But given the urgent demand within wealthy nations for children's organs for transplants and the total vulnerability of many children in developing nations, the likelihood of such a trade must be high.

The Special Rapporteur on the sale of children, child prostitution and child pornography reported to the Commission on Human Rights: "The issue of children sold for organ transplantation remains the most sensitive aspect of the Special Rapporteur's mandate. While evidence abounds concerning a trade in adult organs in various parts of the globe, the search for proof concerning a trade in children's organs poses greater difficulties. It should be noted that during the Special Rapporteur's mission to Nepal in 1993, Nepali police informed him of a recent case concerning

children trafficked into India for this illicit purpose. There is thus mounting evidence of a market for children's organs." (E/CN.4/1994/84, para. 100)

A representative of the International Association of Democratic Lawyers made a statement to the fourth meeting of the Commission on Human Rights Sub-commission on Prevention of Discrimination and Protection of Minorities Working Group on Contemporary Forms of Slavery (18th session) that: "it appeared that the traffic [in human organs], particularly involving children, was worsening. It was thought to be thriving in Argentina, Colombia, Honduras, Mexico and Peru, while there was considered to be evidence of traffic in children's organs in Albania, Greece and Italy. She underlined that children, victims of that traffic, were usually killed by the traffickers." (E/CN.4/Sub.2/ 1993/30, para. 65)

The World Health Organization (WHO) has examined this issue, commenting: "The use of unrelated living donors raises the possibility of the poor especially in developing countries, where potential unrelated donors are subject to temptation to sell their organs ... While organ and tissue donation for altruism or love may be ethically acceptable, the donation for profit should be deprecated." (Human Organ Transplantation: A report on developments under the auspices of the World Health Organization, 1987-1991). The WHO Guiding Principles on Human Organ Transplantation recommends that "no organ shall be removed from the body of a living minor for the purpose of transplantation. Exceptions may be made under national law in the case of regenerative tissue" (Principle 4). This exception would allow for transplants of bone marrow, but would preclude, for example, a child donating one of his kidneys or lungs to a sibling (although under Principle 3, adults are permitted to donate organs to genetically related recipients). Principle 5 prohibits commercial transactions in relation to organ transplants.

Trafficking and armed conflict

Article 38 of the Convention on the Rights of the Child covers armed conflict and children (page 511). While some of the world's "child soldiers" are volunteers, many are reluctant or forced recruits, a serious form of abduction. Such acts may be perpetrated by guerrilla forces, in which case the ratifying State can do little to intervene. Sometimes the Government compulsorily conscripts children, in which case a clear breach of article 35 occurs since such an act constitutes an abduction, even if the child is above the minimum age for recruitment set at 15 by article 38.

Victims, not criminals

When adopting or strengthening laws to penalize the trafficking of children, it is obviously important not to criminalize children themselves. They are the victims not the criminals. Similarly where children are trafficked, particularly when they find themselves in an unfamiliar country, it is important that first priority is given to treating them humanely. Article 39 of the Convention on the Rights of the Child requires States to take all appropriate measures to promote the recovery and social reintegration of child victims (page 529).

A 1994 report to the General Assembly on Sale of Children, child prostitution and child pornography recommends: "Where children are trafficked across frontiers, the General Assembly should encourage States and national and international organizations to ensure that the true age of the children is ascertained by independent and objective assessment, preferably with the cooperation of the non-governmental sector. If they are to be returned to the country of origin, their safety must be guaranteed by independent monitoring and follow-up. Pending their return to the country of origin, they should not be treated as illegal migrants by the receiving countries, but should be dealt with humanely as special cases of humanitarian concern. Upon the children's return, the country of origin should treat them with respect and in accordance with international human rights principles, backed up by adequate family-based and community-based rehabilitation measures." (Provisional report to the General Assembly on Sale of children, child prostitution and child pornography, A/49/478, October 1994, para. 31)

Furthermore, the 1996 Stockholm World Congress against Commercial Sexual Exploitation of Children recommends promoting the participation of children and others who are potential helpers of children so that they are able to express their views and act as advocates of children's rights (Declaration and Agenda for Action, World Congress against Commercial Sexual Exploitation of Children, 1996, para. 6).

Implementation Checklist

article 35

● General measures of implementation

Have appropriate general measures of implementation been taken in relation to article 35, including

☐ identification and coordination of the responsible departments and agencies at all levels of government (article 35 is relevant to **departments of justice, foreign affairs, home affairs, labour, education, social welfare and health**)?

☐ identification of relevant non-governmental organizations/civil society partners?

☐ a comprehensive review to ensure that all legislation, policy and practice is compatible with the article, for all children in all parts of the jurisdiction?

☐ adoption of a strategy to secure full implementation

    ☐ which includes where necessary the identification of goals and indicators of progress?

    ☐ which does not affect any provisions which are more conducive to the rights of the child?

    ☐ which recognizes other relevant international standards?

    ☐ which involves where necessary international cooperation?

(Such measures may be part of an overall governmental strategy for implementing the Convention as a whole).

☐ budgetary analysis and allocation of necessary resources?

☐ development of mechanisms for monitoring and evaluation?

☐ making the implications of article 35 widely known to adults and children?

☐ development of appropriate training and awareness-raising (in relation to article 35 likely to include the training of **police, social workers, adoption agencies staff and health personnel**)?

● Specific issues in implementing article 35

☐ Have legal and administrative measures been adopted to ensure that children abducted within the jurisdiction are found as speedily as possible and returned?

☐ Are all forms of the sale or trafficking of children illegal, including when perpetrated by parents?

☐ Have legal and administrative measures been adopted to ensure that children cannot be sold into any form of bonded labour?

How to use the checklists, *see page XVII*

☐ When bonded labour is being abolished, are measures taken to nullify any debts that have led to children entering such labour?

☐ Is the use of children for the purpose of begging an unlawful activity?

Has the State ratified or acceded to

    ☐ The Hague Convention on the Protection of Children and Cooperation in respect of Intercountry Adoption?

    ☐ The Hague Convention on Civil Aspects of International Child Abduction?

    ☐ The Convention for the Suppression of the Traffic in Persons and of the Exploitation of the Prostitution of Others 1949?

    ☐ The Convention on the Abolition of Slavery, the Slave Trade and Institutions and Practices Similar to Slavery 1956?

☐ Does the law prohibit any form of improper financial gain from intercountry adoption?

☐ Do all relevant State agencies, in particular the police and welfare services, cooperate internationally in identifying and tracing all forms of cross-border trafficking in children?

☐ Are measures taken to ensure that children who are victims of cross-border trafficking can return safely and lawfully to their country of origin?

☐ Is there a national data base of both missing children and known offenders in child trafficking?

☐ Are measures adopted to assist the prosecution of those engaged in child trafficking outside the jurisdiction?

☐ Does the law prohibit the sale of organs from any living child (save for regenerative tissue)?

☐ Is it unlawful to compulsorily conscript a child (under 18 years of age) into the armed services?

☐ Are child victims of abduction, sale or trafficking treated humanely as victims, not criminals, and provided with all appropriate forms of support and assistance?

☐ Are children's views on the most appropriate measures for preventing their abduction, sale and traffic given due weight?

Reminder : **The Convention is indivisible and its articles are interdependent. Article 35 should not be considered in isolation.**

Particular regard should be paid to:
The general principles

Article 2: all rights to be recognized for each child in jurisdiction without discrimination on any ground

Article 3(1): the best interests of the child to be a primary consideration in all actions concerning children

Article 6: right to life and maximum possible survival and development

Article 12: respect for the child's views in all matters affecting the child; opportunity to be heard in any judicial or administrative proceedings affecting the child

Closely related articles

Articles whose implementation is related to that of article 35 include:

Article 8: preservation of child's identity

Article 11: protection from illicit transfer and non-return

Article 16: protection from arbitrary interference in privacy, family and home

Article 20: children without families

Article 21: adoption

Article 32: child labour

Article 33: drug abuse and trafficking

Article 34: sexual exploitation

Article 36: other forms of exploitation

Article 39: rehabilitative care

Protection from other forms of exploitation

Text of Article 36

States Parties shall protect the child against all other forms of exploitation prejudicial to any aspects of the child's welfare.

Summary

In drafting the Convention, article 36 was introduced to ensure that the "social" exploitation of children was recognized, along with their sexual and economic exploitation, but examples of what was meant by social exploitation were not given (E/CN.4/1987/25, pp. 15-24; Detrick, p. 452). The Committee has not as yet raised any specific concerns under this article. Forms of exploitation not addressed under other articles include the exploitation of gifted children, the exploitation of children by the media and the exploitation of children by researchers or for the purposes of medical or scientific experimentation. ∎

Extracts from
Committee on the Rights of the Child
Guidelines for Reports to be submitted by States Parties under the Convention

For full text of *Guidelines for Periodic Reports*, see Appendix 3, page 604.

Guidelines for Initial Reports

"Special protection measures

Under this section, States Parties are requested to provide relevant information, including the principal legislative, judicial, administrative or other measures in force; factors and difficulties encountered and progress achieved in implementing the relevant provisions of the Convention; and implementation priorities and specific goals for the future in respect of:...

... (c) Children in situations of exploitation ...

...(iv) Other forms of exploitation (article 36)...

Additionally, States Parties are encouraged to provide specific statistical information and indicators relevant to the children covered by [the previous] paragraph..."

(CRC/C/5, paras. 23 and 24)

Guidelines for Periodic Reports

"VIII. SPECIAL PROTECTION MEASURES

C. Children in situations of exploitation, including physical and psychological recovery and social reintegration

5. Other forms of exploitation (art. 36)

Please provide information on all measures adopted, including of a legislative, administrative, educational, budgetary and social nature, to protect the child against all forms of exploitation prejudicial to any aspects of his or her welfare.

Reports should also indicate, inter alia:

> *The prevalence of any form of exploitation prejudicial to the child's welfare;*

> *Awareness and information campaigns launched, including for children, families and the public at large, as well as the involvement of the media;*

> *Training activities developed for professional groups working with and for children;*

> *Any national strategy developed to ensure protection to the child and the targets set for the future;*

> *Any mechanism established to monitor the situation of the child, the progress achieved in the implementation of this article and any difficulties encountered;*

> *The relevant indicators used;*

> *Measures adopted to ensure the physical and psychological recovery, as well as the social reintegration, of the child victim of exploitation prejudicial to any aspects of his or her welfare;*

> *Relevant measures adopted to ensure respect for the general principles of the Convention, namely non-discrimination, the best interests of the child, respect for the views of the child, the right to life and survival and development to the maximum extent possible;*

> *The measures adopted to ensure that the implementation of this article takes into due consideration other relevant provisions of the Convention;*

> *Relevant disaggregated data on the children concerned by the implementation of this article, including by age, gender, region, rural/urban area, and national, social and ethnic origin."*

(CRC/C/58, paras. 163 and 164)

Examples of "other forms of exploitation"

Articles 11 (illicit transfer and non-return of children), 21 (adoption), 32 (employment), 33 (drug trafficking), 34 (sexual exploitation), 35 (abduction, sale and trafficking) and 38 (armed conflict) address the many ways in which children are exploited by adults. Article 36 is a safety net protection to cover "all other forms of exploitation", including social exploitation.

Gifted children

For example, children with talents in competitive sports, games, performing arts and so forth can have these talents developed by families, the media, businesses and state authorities at the expense of their overall physical and mental development. Regulations relating to child labour often exclude "voluntary" activities such as these and therefore may not be monitored by child welfare agencies.

The media

As discussed in relation to articles 16 (page 201) and 17 (page 219), children can be exploited by the media, for example by identifying child victims or child offenders, or by securing performances by children without their informed consent which are potentially harmful to their development. The Committee commented, in relation to its General Discussion on the Child and the Media:

"In their reporting, the media give an 'image' of the child; they reflect and influence perceptions about who children are and how they behave. This image could create and convey respect for young people; however, it could also spread prejudices and stereotypes which may have a negative influence on public opinion and politicians. Nuanced and well-informed reporting is to the benefit of the rights of the child.

"It is important that the media themselves do not abuse children. The integrity of the child should be protected in reporting about, for instance, involvement in criminal activities, sexual abuse and family problems. Fortunately, the media in some countries have voluntarily agreed to respect guidelines which offer such protection of the privacy of the child; however, such ethical standards are not always adhered to." (Report on the eleventh session, January 1996, CRC/C/50, p. 80)

Research and experimentation

Children can also be exploited by researchers or experimenters, for example by breaches of their privacy or by requiring them to undertake tasks that breach their rights or are disrespectful of their human dignity. Article 7 of the International Covenant on Civil and Political Rights expressly prohibits medical or scientific experimentation without free consent. As discussed under article 37 (page 494) the Human Rights Committee states in a General Comment that this was particularly important to anyone "not capable of giving a valid consent" or who was in any form of detention or imprisonment (Human Rights Committee, General Comment 20, HRI/GEN/1/Rev.2, p. 31).

The Convention does not address this issue, although the question of the "free consent" of children to research or medical or social experimentation is even more problematic than that of adults. It would be wrong to outlaw all forms of experimentation on children, since some experimental forms of treatment may offer children their only hope of cure and, in any event, it is argued that medical experimentation is a necessary part of medical progress. The Council for International Organizations of Medical Sciences has issued *International Ethical Guidelines for Biomedical Research Involving Human Subjects* which includes guidelines on when and how children may be the subject of research.

Where older children are involved, the issue also relates to their civil rights under the Convention, for example to be heard, to freedom of expression and of association, and to respect for their "evolving capacities". The Committee asks States to report on any minimum legal age for "medical counselling", and for "medical treatment or surgery without parental consent" (*Guidelines for Periodic Reports*, para. 24). It is reasonable to assume that children competent to determine medical treatment or surgery will also be competent to consent to participation in research or medical experimentation. States should ensure that all research and experimentation involving children conforms to a mandatory ethical code underpinned by statute.

States should also take measures for the rehabilitation of children harmed by any of these "other" forms of exploitation, in accordance with article 39.

Implementation Checklist

article 36

● General measures of implementation

Have appropriate general measures of implementation been taken in relation to article 36, including

☐ identification and coordination of the responsible departments and agencies at all levels of government (article 36 is likely to involve **departments of health, social welfare, labour, media and education**)?

☐ identification of relevant non-governmental organizations/civil society partners?

☐ a comprehensive review to ensure that all legislation, policy and practice is compatible with the article, for all children in all parts of the jurisdiction?

☐ adoption of a strategy to secure full implementation

    ☐ which includes where necessary the identification of goals and indicators of progress?

    ☐ which does not affect any provisions which are more conducive to the rights of the child?

    ☐ which recognizes other relevant international standards?

    ☐ which involves where necessary international cooperation?

(Such measures may be part of an overall governmental strategy for implementing the Convention as a whole).

☐ budgetary analysis and allocation of necessary resources?

☐ development of mechanisms for monitoring and evaluation?

☐ making the implications of article 36 widely known to adults and children?

☐ development of appropriate training and awareness-raising (in relation to article 36 likely to include the training of **media producers, employment officers, social workers, researchers, medical personnel and scientists**)?

● Specific issues in implementing article 36

☐ Are legal and administrative mechanisms in place to ensure that children are protected from all forms of exploitation?

☐ Are welfare agencies empowered to intervene when there is concern that children are undertaking activities, for whatever reason, which impair their overall physical, mental, emotional, spiritual, moral and social development?

☐ Do measures prevent the exploitation of children by the media?

□ Do measures prevent the use of children for all forms of research, including medical or scientific experimentation, unless appropriate consents have been obtained from the child and/or child's parents or legal guardians?

□ Is all research and experimentation involving children regulated by a mandatory code of ethical practice?

□ Are measures taken to provide rehabilitative services for children who have suffered from any form of exploitation covered by this article?

Reminder : **The Convention is indivisible and its articles are interdependent. Article 36 should not be considered in isolation.**

Particular regard should be paid to:
The general principles

Article 2: all rights to be recognized for each child in jurisdiction without discrimination on any ground
Article 3(1): the best interests of the child to be a primary consideration in all actions concerning children
Article 6: right to life and maximum possible survival and development
Article 12: respect for the child's views in all matters affecting the child; opportunity to be heard in any judicial or administrative proceedings affecting the child

Closely related articles

Articles whose implementation is related to that of article 36 include:

Article 16: protection from arbitrary interference in privacy, family and home
Article 17: responsibilities of the media
Article 32: child labour
Article 34: sexual exploitation of children
Article 35: abduction, sale and trafficking of children
Article 39: rehabilitative care

Torture, degrading treatment and deprivation of liberty

article 37

States Parties shall ensure that:

(a) No child shall be subjected to torture or other cruel, inhuman or degrading treatment or punishment. Neither capital punishment nor life imprisonment without possibility of release shall be imposed for offences committed by persons below eighteen years of age;

(b) No child shall be deprived of his or her liberty unlawfully or arbitrarily. The arrest, detention or imprisonment of a child shall be in conformity with the law and shall be used only as a measure of last resort and for the shortest appropriate period of time;

(c) Every child deprived of liberty shall be treated with humanity and respect for the inherent dignity of the human person, and in a manner which takes into account the needs of persons of his or her age. In particular, every child deprived of liberty shall be separated from adults unless it is considered in the child's best interest not to do so and shall have the right to maintain contact with his or her family through correspondence and visits, save in exceptional circumstances;

(d) Every child deprived of his or her liberty shall have the right to prompt access to legal and other appropriate assistance, as well as the right to challenge the legality of the deprivation of his or her liberty before a court or other competent, independent and impartial authority, and to a prompt decision on any such action.

Article 37 provides the child with the right to be protected from
- torture;
- other cruel, inhuman or degrading treatment or punishment;
- capital punishment;
- life imprisonment without possibility of release;
- unlawful or arbitrary deprivation of liberty.

The article sets out conditions for any arrest, detention or imprisonment of the child, which shall be
- in conformity with the law
- used only as a measure of last resort; and
- for the shortest possible time.

Summary

And the article sets out further conditions for the treatment of any child deprived of liberty
- to be treated with humanity and respect for the inherent dignity of the human person;
- in a manner which takes into account the needs of persons of his or her age;
- to be separated from adults unless it is considered in the child's best interest not to do so;
- to maintain contact with his or her family, through correspondence and visits, save in exceptional circumstances;
- to have the right to prompt access to legal and other appropriate assistance;
- to have the right to challenge the legality of the deprivation of liberty before a court or other competent, independent and impartial authority;
- to have the right to a prompt decision on such action.

Article 37, together with article 40 (administration of juvenile justice) and article 39 (rehabilitation and reintegration), are the Convention's specific provisions relating to children in trouble with the law. But the provisions on protection from torture and cruel, inhuman or degrading treatment or punishment, and all the provisions relating to the restriction of liberty, do not just cover children in trouble with the law (in many States restriction of the liberty of children is permitted for reasons not related to criminal offences – "welfare", mental health and in relation to asylum-seeking and immigration). Article 39 provides an obligation to promote the recovery and reintegration of child victims of torture and other cruel, inhuman or degrading treatment or punishment (see page 529). ∎

Extracts from
Committee on the Rights of the Child
Guidelines for Reports to be submitted by States Parties under the Convention

For full text of *Guidelines for Periodic Reports*, see Appendix 3, page 604.

Guidelines for Initial Reports

"Civil rights and freedoms

Under this section, States Parties are requested to provide relevant information, including the principal legislative, judicial, administrative or other measures in force; factors and difficulties encountered and progress achieved in implementing the relevant provisions of the Convention; and implementation priorities and specific goals for the future in respect of:

....

(h) The right not to be subjected to torture or other cruel, inhuman or degrading treatment or punishment (article 37(a)).

...

"Special protection measures

Under this section States Parties are requested to provide relevant information, including the principal legislative, judicial, administrative or other measures in force; factors and difficulties encountered and progress achieved in implementing the relevant provisions of the Convention; and implementation priorities and specific goals for the future in respect of:

...

(b) Children in conflict with the law...

(ii) Children deprived of their liberty, including any form of detention, imprisonment or placement in custodial settings (article 37(b), (c) and (d));

(iii) The sentencing of juveniles, in particular the prohibition of capital punishment and life imprisonment (article 37(a));

... "

Additionally, States Parties are encouraged to provide specific statistical information and indicators relevant to the children covered by paragraph 23".

(CRC/C/5, paras. 15, 23-24)

Guidelines for Periodic Reports

IV. CIVIL RIGHTS AND FREEDOMS (arts. 7, 8, 13-17 and 37(a))

Under this section, States Parties are requested to provide information on the measures adopted to ensure that the civil rights and freedoms of children set forth in the Convention, in particular those covered by articles 7, 8, 13-17 and 37(a), are recognized by law specifically in relation to children and implemented in practice, including by administrative and judicial bodies, at the national, regional and local levels, and where appropriate at the federal and provincial levels.

...

"H. The right not to be subjected to torture or other cruel, inhuman or degrading treatment or punishment (art.37(a))

Please indicate whether torture or other cruel, inhuman or degrading treatment or punishment of children is punished by the criminal law, and whether complaint procedures have been established and remedies made available to the child. Please also provide information on:

> *Awareness campaigns launched to prevent torture or other cruel, inhuman or degrading treatment or punishment of children;*
>
> *Educative and training activities developed, particularly with personnel in institutions, services and facilities working with and for children, aimed at preventing any form of ill-treatment;*
>
> *Any cases where children have been victims of any such acts;*
>
> *Measures adopted to prevent the impunity of perpetrators, including by investigating such cases and punishing those found responsible;*
>
> *Measures adopted to ensure the physical and psychological recovery and reintegration of children who have been tortured or otherwise ill-treated;*
>
> *Any independent monitoring system established."*

"VIII. SPECIAL PROTECTION MEASURES (arts. 22, 38, 39, 40, 37 (b)-(d), 32-36)

...

B. Children involved with the system of administration of juvenile justice

...

2. Children deprived of their liberty, including any form of detention, imprisonment or placement in custodial settings (art. 37(b)-(d))

Please indicate the legislative and other measures adopted pursuant to **article 37(b)** *to ensure that:*

> *No child is deprived of his or her liberty unlawfully or arbitrarily (note: According to the United Nations Rules for the Protection of Juveniles Deprived of their Liberty, deprivation of liberty means any form of detention or imprisonment or the placement of a person in another public or private custodial setting from which this person is not permitted to leave at will by order of any judicial, administrative or other public authority (rule 11(b)).*
>
> *The arrest detention or imprisonment of a child is in conformity with the law and is used only as a measure of last resort and for the shortest appropriate period of time;*
>
> *The general principles of the Convention are respected, namely non-discrimination, the best interests of the child, respect for the views of the child, the right to life, and survival and development to the maximum extent possible.*

Reports should also indicate the existing alternatives to deprivation of liberty, the frequency with which they are used and the children concerned, including by age, gender, region, rural/urban area, and social and ethnic origin.

Information should also be given on the measures and mechanisms established to:

> *Prevent the deprivation of liberty of children, including through arrest, detention and imprisonment, inter alia in relation to asylum seekers and refugees;*
>
> *Prevent the imposition of indeterminate sentences, including through their legal prohibition;*
>
> *Monitor the situation of the children concerned, including through an independent mechanism;*
>
> *Monitor progress, identify difficulties and set goals for the future.*

In this regard, information should further be provided on the number of children deprived of liberty unlawfully, arbitrarily and within the law, as well as on the period of deprivation of liberty, including data disaggregated by gender, age, region, rural/urban area, and national, social and ethnic origin, and the reasons for such deprivation of liberty.

Please indicate the legislative and other measures adopted pursuant to **article 37(c)** *to ensure that any child deprived of liberty is treated:*

With humanity and respect for the inherent humanity of the human person;

In a manner which takes into account the needs of persons of his or her age.

Reports should also provide information on the measures adopted and arrangements made to ensure that:

The child deprived of liberty is separated from adults unless it is considered in the best interests of the child not to do so;

The child has the right to maintain contact with his or her family through correspondence and visits (indicating the number of such contacts), save in exceptional circumstances, those circumstances being specified in the report;

The conditions in institutions in which children are placed are supervised and monitored, including by an independent mechanism;

Complaint procedures are made available to the child;

A periodic review is made of the situation of the child and of the circumstances relevant to his/her placement;

Education and health services are provided to the child;

The general principles of the Convention are respected, namely non-discrimination, the best interests of the child, respect for the views of the child, right to life, and survival and development to the maximum extent possible.

*Please indicate the measures adopted pursuant to **article 37 (d)** to ensure that every child deprived of liberty has the right to:*

Prompt access to legal and other appropriate assistance, indicating inter alia *whether there is any legal time-limit for such access to assistance and what other appropriate assistance may be made available to the child;*

Challenge the legality of the deprivation of his or her liberty before a court or other competent, independent and impartial authority;

A prompt decision on any such action, indicating inter alia *whether there is any legal time-limit for such a decision to be taken.*

Information should also be provided on the overall situation, as well as on the percentage of cases where legal or other assistance has been provided, and where the legality of the deprivation of liberty has been confirmed, including disaggregated data on the children concerned, including by age, gender, region, rural/urban area, and social and ethnic origin.

Reports should also indicate the progress achieved in the implementation of article 37 (b) to (d), difficulties encountered and targets set for the future.

3. The sentencing of children, with particular reference to the prohibition of capital punishment and life imprisonment (art. 37(a))

Please provide information on the measures adopted, at the legislative and other levels, to ensure that neither capital punishment nor life imprisonment without possibility of release is imposed for offences committed by persons below 18 years of age.

Please also indicate the progress achieved in the implementation of article 37(a), difficulties encountered and targets set for the future."

(CRC/C/58, paras. 48, 61, 138-148; The following paragraphs of the *Guidelines for Periodic Reports* are also relevant to reporting under this article: 24, 35, 43, 59, 86-87, 109 and 149-150; for full text of *Guidelines*, see Appendix 3, page 604.)

United Nations rules and guidelines on juvenile justice

The Committee, in its examination of States Parties' reports and in other comments, has indicated that it regards the United Nations rules and guidelines relating to juvenile justice as providing relevant detailed standards for the implementation of article 37 (the United Nations Standard Minimum Rules for the Administration of Juvenile Justice, the "Beijing Rules", the United Nations Rules for the Protection of Juveniles Deprived of their Liberty, and the United Nations Guidelines for the Prevention of Juvenile Delinquency, the "Riyadh Guidelines"):

"...the Convention called for the implementation of the most conducive provisions for the realization of the rights of the child, and had therefore to be considered in conjunction with other relevant instruments, namely the Beijing Rules, the Riyadh Guidelines and the Rules for the Protection of Juveniles Deprived

*of their Liberty. Those instruments comple-
mented and provided guidance for the implementation of the rights recognized by the
Convention and confirmed that there was no
possible conflict between human rights and
juvenile justice." (Report on General Discussion
on administration of juvenile justice, Report on the
tenth session, October-November 1995, CRC/C/46,
para. 214)*

The Committee has stated that the Convention,
and these rules and guidelines taken together

*"call for the adoption of a child-oriented
system, that recognizes the child as a subject
of fundamental rights and freedoms and
stresses the need for all actions concerning
children to be guided by the best interests of
the child as a primary consideration." (Outline
for General Discussion on the Administration of
Juvenile Justice, Report on the ninth session,
May-June 1995, CRC/C/43, Annex VIII, p. 64)*

"No child shall be subjected to torture or other cruel, inhuman or degrading treatment or punishment"

Paragraph (a) of article 37 emphasizes that the
absolute prohibition on torture, and cruel, inhuman or degrading treatment or punishment,
upheld for everyone in the Universal Declaration
of Human Rights (article 5) and the International
Covenant on Civil and Political Rights (article 7),
applies equally to children. And it should be
underlined that this prohibition applies to all
children wherever they are. As the *Manual on
Human Rights Reporting*, 1997, states: "By presenting it as a general and absolute right, the Convention shows that any of the forms of treatment
or punishment covered by this article should be
prevented and combated at all moments and in
all circumstances, including within family life or
in the school system." (*Manual*, p.440)

In 1975, the General Assembly adopted the De-
claration on the Protection of All Persons from
Being Subjected to Torture and Other Cruel,
Inhuman or Degrading Treatment or Punishment
(General Assembly Resolution 3452 (XXX), 9
December 1975, Annex). The provisions of the
Declaration formed the basis for the Convention
against Torture and Other Cruel, Inhuman or
Degrading Treatment or Punishment (adopted by
General Assembly Resolution 39/46, 10 December 1984). It defines torture, for its purposes, as
meaning "any act by which severe pain or suffering, whether physical or mental, is intentionally
inflicted by or at the instigation of a public official on a person for such purposes as obtaining
from him or a third person information or a con-

fession, punishing him for an act he or a third person has committed or is suspected of having committed, or intimidating or coercing him or a third
person, or for any reason based on discrimination
of any kind, when such pain or suffering is inflicted by or at the instigation of or with the consent
or acquiescence of a public official or other
person acting in an official capacity. It does
not include pain or suffering arising only from,
inherent in or incidental to lawful sanctions"
(article 1).

The Convention established the Committee
against Torture, which oversees implementation
of the Convention, and seeks to resolve cases of
alleged torture brought to its notice. In addition,
the Commission on Human Rights has appointed
a Special Rapporteur on Torture, who acts in individual cases and reports to the Commission.

The Human Rights Committee has made two
General Comments on article 7 of the International Covenant on Civil and Political Rights:
first in 1982 (Human Rights Committee, General Comment 7, HRI/GEN/1/Rev.2, p. 7) and then
in 1992, a Comment that "replaces General Comment 7, reflecting and further developing it". In
it, the Committee emphasizes: "The aim of the
provisions of article 7 ... is to protect both the dignity and the physical and mental integrity of the
individual. It is the duty of the State Party to
afford everyone protection through legislative
and other measures as may be necessary, against
the acts prohibited by article 7, whether inflicted
by people acting in their official capacity, outside
their official capacity or in a private capacity...
The text of article 7 allows of no limitation. The
Committee also reaffirms that, even in situations
of public emergency ... no derogation from the
provision of article 7 is allowed and its provisions
must remain in force. The Committee likewise
observes that no justification or extenuating circumstances may be invoked to excuse a violation
of article 7 for any reasons, including those
based on an order from a superior officer or public authority." (The Geneva Conventions and
Additional Protocols include provisions on
restriction of liberty of persons affected by armed
conflict, but do not of course undermine the fundamental principles of human rights, see article
38, page 511)

The Human Rights Committee notes that the
Covenant does not contain any definition of the
concepts covered by article 7, "nor does the Committee consider it necessary to draw up a list of
prohibited acts or to establish sharp distinctions
between the different kinds of punishment or
treatment; the distinctions depend on the nature,
purpose and severity of the treatment applied..."

The Committee has also noted that "it is not sufficient for the implementation of article 7 to prohibit such treatment or punishment or to make it a crime. States Parties should inform the Committee of the legislative, administrative, judicial and other measures they take to prevent and punish acts of torture and cruel, inhuman and degrading treatment in any territory under their jurisdiction." In addition, "In the view of the Committee, States Parties must not expose individuals to the danger of torture or cruel, inhuman or degrading treatment or punishment upon return to another country by way of their extradition, expulsion or *refoulement*. States Parties should indicate in their reports what measures they have adopted to that end." (Human Rights Committee, General Comment 20, HRI/GEN/1/Rev.2, p. 30)

In 1993, the General Assembly adopted a Declaration on the Protection of All Persons from Enforced Disappearances (A/RES/47/133), noting that any act of enforced disappearance is an offence of human dignity and constitutes a violation of the rules of international law, including "the right not to be subjected to torture and other cruel, inhuman or degrading treatment or punishment. It also violates or constitutes a grave threat to the right to life" (article 1). Article 20 of the Declaration covers the prevention of the abduction of children of parents subjected to enforced disappearance and of children born during their mother's enforced disappearance.

The Committee on the Rights of the Child requires article 37(a) of the Convention on the Rights of the Child to be reflected in national legislation as applying to children. In its *Guidelines for Periodic Reports*, the Committee requests information on "whether torture or other cruel, inhuman or degrading treatment or punishment of children is punished by the criminal law" (para. 61). The Committee has referred states to the definition of torture in article 1 of the Convention against Torture (see above, page 491):

"The Committee would like to suggest that the State Party consider in its legislation the implications of article 37(a) of the Convention on the Rights of the Child and, in this connection, that it also pays attention to the definition of torture provided for in article 1 of the Convention against Torture and Other Cruel, Inhuman or Degrading Treatment or Punishment, to which Norway is also a party." (Norway IRCO, Add.23, para. 15)

The Committee noted to Nepal that:

"... It is concerned, inter alia, about ... the provision of the Muluki Ain No.2 that allows mentally ill children to be put in jail and chained, and the legal definition of torture which is not in compliance with article 37(a)

of the Convention." (Nepal IRCO, Add.57, para. 24)

And to Panama:

"... measures must be undertaken to ensure the conformity of national legislation with the provisions of article 37(a) of the Convention." (Panama IRCO, Add.68, para. 22)

The Committee has proposed accession to the Convention against Torture:

"The Committee encourages the Government of Bolivia to consider the possibility of acceding to the Convention against Torture and Other Cruel, Inhuman or Degrading Treatment or Punishment." (Bolivia IRCO, Add.1, para. 15)

And in the case of one State Party, China, the Committee has referred to the observations of the Committee against Torture:

"The Committee concurs with the contents of the observations adopted by the Committee against Torture where the points raised are relevant to the situation of children below the age of 18." (China IRCO, Add.56, para. 42)

The Committee has proposed formal investigations of any allegations of torture and that perpetrators should be brought to trial (by civilian courts) and if found guilty, punished:

"The Committee recommends that investigations be conducted into cases of extrajudicial executions, disappearances and torture which are carried out in the context of the internal violence prevailing in several parts of the country. Those accused of such abuses should be tried, and when found guilty punished. Furthermore, special measures should be taken to ensure that children are protected against the occurrence of such human rights violations and that they benefit from recovery and reintegration programmes in an environment which fosters the dignity and the self-confidence of the child." (Peru IRCO, Add.8, para. 16)

"The Committee recommends that the State Party should intensify its action against all violence resulting in cases of ill-treatment of children, in particular when committed by members of the police forces and security services and the military. The State Party should ensure that cases of crimes committed against children by members of the armed forces or the police are tried before civilian courts." (Mexico IRCO, Add.13, para. 17. See also Indonesia Prelim. Obs., Add.7, para. 17; Indonesia IRCO, Add.25, para. 24)

The Committee has stressed the importance of complaints procedures (see *Guidelines for Periodic Reports*, para. 61; see also article 12, page 155), in particular for children in institutions:

Implementation Handbook for the Convention on the Rights of the Child

"The State party should ensure that adequate procedures and mechanisms be developed to deal with complaints of the ill-treatment of children, and that cases of violations of children's rights be duly investigated." (Jamaica IRCO, Add.32, para. 26)

"... The Committee further suggests that the setting up of an independent monitoring body to receive and consider complaints of children involved with the administration of juvenile justice be duly considered by the Syrian authorities." (Syrian Arab Republic IRCO, Add.70, para. 30. See also Federal Republic of Yugoslavia IRCO, Add.49, para. 22; Nigeria IRCO, Add.61, para. 23)

In the report of its General Discussion on juvenile justice, the Committee on the Rights of the Child noted the importance of periodic visits and independent monitoring of institutions, and also noted the current efforts of the Commission on Human Rights aimed at introducing a system of periodic visits to places of detention through an optional protocol to the Convention against Torture and Other Cruel, Inhuman or Degrading Treatment or Punishment. (Report on the tenth session, October-November 1995, CRC/C/46, para. 229)

Corporal punishment

In its General Comment on article 7 of the International Covenant on Civil and Political Rights, the Human Rights Committee indicates that the prohibition on torture and cruel, inhuman or degrading treatment or punishment extends to corporal punishment: "The prohibition in article 7 relates not only to acts that cause physical pain but also to acts that cause mental suffering to the victim. In the Committee's view, moreover, the prohibition must extend to corporal punishment, including excessive chastisement ordered as punishment for a crime or as an educative or disciplinary measure. It is appropriate to emphasize in this regard that article 7 protects, in particular, children, pupils and patients in teaching and medical institutions." (Human Rights Committee, General Comment 20, HRI/GEN/1/Rev.2, p. 30)

The Committee on the Rights of the Child has gone beyond condemnation of "excessive" chastisement, and noted in its Concluding Observations on States Parties' reports and in other comments that any corporal punishment of children is incompatible with the Convention on the Rights of the Child, citing, in particular, article 19, which requires protection of children "from all forms of physical or mental violence", and in relation to school discipline, article 28(2), in addition to article 37. For example, in the report on its seventh session in November 1994, the Committee stated:

"In the framework of its mandate, the Committee has paid particular attention to the child's right to physical integrity. In the same spirit, it has stressed that corporal punishment of children is incompatible with the Convention and has often proposed the revision of existing legislation, as well as the development of awareness and educational campaigns, to prevent child abuse and the physical punishment of children." (Report on seventh session, September-October 1994, Annex IV, p. 63)

The Committee has in particular criticized legal provisions in States Parties that attempt to draw a line between acceptable and unacceptable forms of corporal punishment. In many Concluding Observations on States Parties' Initial Reports, the Committee has called for a clear prohibition of all corporal punishment – in the family, in other forms of care, in schools and in the penal system. For example:

"The Committee expresses its concern at the acceptance in the legislation of the use of corporal punishment in school, as well as within the family. It stresses the incompatibility of corporal punishment, as well as any other form of violence, injury, neglect, abuse or degrading treatment, with the provisions of the Convention, in particular articles 19, 28 paragraph 2 and 37." (Zimbabwe IRCO, Add.55, para. 18)

The Committee's *Guidelines for Periodic Reports* asks "whether legislation (criminal and/or family law) includes a prohibition of all forms of physical and mental violence, including corporal punishment, deliberate humiliation, injury, abuse, neglect or exploitation, *inter alia* within the family, in foster and other forms of care, and in public or private institutions, such as penal institutions and schools" (para. 88; for detailed discussion and further comments of Committee, see article 19, page 246).

The Committee's examination of States Parties' Initial Reports has found that corporal punishment persists for juveniles in some countries as a sentence of the courts. This raises an issue under article 37 as well as article 19, and conflicts with the United Nations rules and guidelines relating to juvenile justice, which the Committee has consistently promoted as providing relevant standards:

- the "Beijing Rules": rule 17.3 (Guiding Principles in Adjudication and Disposition) states that "Juveniles shall not be subject to corporal punishment".

- the United Nations Rules for the Protection of Juveniles Deprived of their Liberty: rule 67 states that "all disciplinary measures constituting cruel, inhuman or degrading treatment shall be strictly prohibited, including corporal punishment..."

- the "Riyadh Guidelines": para. 21(h) states that education systems should devote particular attention to "avoidance of harsh disciplinary measures, particularly corporal punishment"; para. 54 says "No child or young person should be subjected to harsh or degrading correction or punishment measures at home, in schools or in any other institutions".

Examples of the Committee's comments follow:

"The Committee expresses the hope that the review of child-related laws will result in the total abolition of flogging." (Sudan IRCO. Add.10, para. 17)

"The Committee is concerned at the present system of juvenile justice, including the lack of a clear legal prohibition of capital punishment, life imprisonment without possibility of release and indeterminate sentencing, as well as at the recourse to whipping as a disciplinary measure for boys." (Zimbabwe IRCO, Add.55, para. 21. See also Pakistan IRCO, Add.18, paras. 12 and 23; Ethiopia IRCO, Add.67, para. 20)

The Committee against Torture, which oversees the Convention against Torture and Other Cruel, Inhuman or Degrading Treatment or Punishment, has also noted that corporal punishment "could constitute in itself a violation of the Convention." (see, for example, Report of the Committee against Torture, General Assembly Official Records, 50th session, Supplement No.44, (A/50/44), paras. 169 and 177)

The Commission on Crime Prevention and Criminal Justice adopted a resolution in April 1994 specifically stressing the importance of article 19 of the Convention, and calling on States to take all possible steps to eliminate violence against children in accordance with the Convention (Report on the seventh session, CRC/C/34, 8 November 1994, p. 63).

Solitary confinement or isolation of children

The Human Rights Committee, in its General Comment on article 7 of the International Covenant on Civil and Political Rights, notes that "prolonged solitary confinement of the detained or imprisoned person may amount to acts prohibited by article 7" (Human Rights Committee, General Comment 20, HRI/GEN/1/Rev.2, p. 31). Thus, placing a child in isolation or solitary confinement raises a further issue under article 37(a) of the Convention, in addition to the issues relating to the restriction of liberty involved.

In one case, the Committee on the Rights of the Child has commented on isolation of children in pre-trial detention:

"...The Committee is also concerned that ... children may be kept in prison for a period of 15 days and be kept in isolation." (Belgium IRCO, Add.38, para. 11)

Article 7 of the International Covenant on Civil and Political Rights has an additional provision, not repeated in article 37, which expressly prohibits medical or scientific experimentation without free consent, and the Human Rights Committee in its General Comment notes that reports of States Parties generally give little information on this point: "More attention should be given to the need and means to ensure observance of this provision. The Committee also observes that special protection in regard to such experiments is necessary in the case of persons not capable of giving valid consent, and in particular those under any form of detention or imprisonment. Such persons should not be subjected to any medical or scientific experimentation that may be detrimental to their health" (Human Rights Committee, General Comment 20, HRI/GEN/1/Rev.2, p. 31). There is no equivalent provision relating to children in the Convention on the Rights of the Child; but article 36 protects the child from "all other forms of exploitation prejudicial to any aspects of the child's welfare" (page 483).

"Neither capital punishment nor life imprisonment without possibility of release shall be imposed for offences committed by persons below eighteen years of age"

Article 37(a) of the Convention on the Rights of the Child prohibits the death penalty for offences committed by persons below 18; article 6, providing all children with the right to life and maximum survival and development, has the same effect. As noted under article 6 (page 89) the International Covenant on Civil and Political Rights also states (in its article 6): "Sentence of death shall not be imposed for crimes committed by persons below eighteen years of age and shall not be carried out on pregnant women" (para 5). (A Second Optional Protocol to the Covenant, adopted by the General Assembly in 1989, aims at abolition of the death penalty: under its article 1, no one within the jurisdiction of a State Party to the Protocol may be executed.)

The Committee on the Rights of the Child has raised the issue with a number of States Parties and emphasized that it is not enough that the death penalty is not applied to children. Its prohibition must be confirmed in legislation. In addition paragraph (a) prohibits sentences of life imprisonment without possibility of release for offences committed before the age of 18, and it should be noted here that paragraph (b) requires that any detention or imprisonment must be used "only as a measure of last resort and for the shortest appropriate period".

The Committee has often found both capital punishment and life imprisonment without possibility of release in a State Party's system applying to juveniles:

"...The hope is also expressed that ... the State Party will take into account the Committee's concerns, particularly its recommendations with regard to the abolition of flogging and capital punishment for children under the age of 18, and that deprivation of liberty should only be used as a measure of last resort and for the shortest period of time..." (Pakistan IRCO, Add.18, para. 23)

"The Committee expresses its concern about the possibility of relinquishment of jurisdiction provided for in article 38 of the Young Persons' Protection Act which allows for young persons between 16 and 18 to be tried as adults and thereby face the imposition of a death sentence or a sentence of life imprisonment..." (Belgium IRCO, Add.38, para. 11)

"The Committee remains concerned that national legislation appears to allow children between the ages of 16 and 18 to be sentenced to death with a two-year suspension of execution. It is the opinion of the Committee that the imposition of suspended death sentences on children constitutes cruel, inhuman or degrading treatment or punishment. Further, it is noted that under the Penal Code a juvenile offender aged between 14 and 18 may legally be sentenced to life imprisonment for a particularly serious crime. Although the sentence of life imprisonment may be reduced on the grounds of 'repentance' or 'merit' and judicial experience in China shows that sentences to life imprisonment can benefit from a mitigation, the Committee wishes to stress that the Convention prescribes that neither capital punishment nor life imprisonment without the possibility of release shall be imposed for offences committed by persons below the age of 18. It is the Committee's view that the aforementioned provisions of national law are incompatible with the principles and provisions of the Convention, notably those of its article 37(a)." (China IRCO, Add.56, para. 21. See also Zimbabwe IRCO, Add.55, para. 21; Guatemala IRCO, Add.58, para. 15; Nigeria IRCO, Add.61, para. 20)

The Committee has expressed concern at "extrajudicial executions":

"The Committee recommends that investigations be conducted into cases of extrajudicial executions, disappearances and torture which are carried out in the context of the internal violence prevailing in several parts of the country..." (Peru IRCO, Add.8, para. 16)

A 1989 resolution of the Economic and Social Committee of the United Nations proposes Principles on the Effective Prevention and Investigation of Extra-Legal, Arbitrary and Summary Executions. (ECOSOC Resolution 1989/65, 24 May 1989)

The Committee has expressed concern at "indeterminate sentences" as well as sentences of life imprisonment without the possibility of release:

"The Committee is concerned at the present system of juvenile justice, including the lack of a clear legal prohibition of capital punishment, life imprisonment without possibility of release and indeterminate sentencing..." (Zimbabwe IRCO, Add.55, para. 21)

"No child shall be deprived of his or her liberty unlawfully or arbitrarily. The arrest, detention or imprisonment of a child shall be in conformity with the law and shall be used only as a measure of last resort and for the shortest appropriate period of time"

In relation to deprivation of liberty by official or public bodies, the Committee has adopted the definition of restriction of liberty in the United Nations Rules for the Protection of Juveniles Deprived of their Liberty: "The deprivation of liberty means any form of detention or imprisonment or the placement of a person in another public or private custodial setting from which this person is not permitted to leave at will by order of any judicial, administrative or other public authority" (see *Guidelines for Periodic Reports*, para. 137, note).

Paragraph (1) of article 9 of the International Covenant on Civil and Political Rights states: "1. Everyone has the right to liberty and security of person. No one shall be subjected to arbitrary arrest or detention. No one shall be deprived of his liberty except on such grounds and in accordance with such procedures as are established by law." In a General Comment, the Human Rights Committee points out "that paragraph 1 is applicable to all deprivations of liberty, whether in criminal cases or in other cases such as, for example, mental illness, vagrancy, drug addiction, educational purposes, immigration control, etc." (Human Rights Committee, General Comment 8, HRI/GEN/1/Rev.2, p. 8)

During its examination of States Parties' Initial Reports, the Committee on the Rights of the Child has found there are various routes, in various systems, to children's liberty being restricted, in welfare, health, and immigration as well as penal systems.

"Arrest", "detention" and "imprisonment" have been defined in the Body of Principles for the Protection of All Persons under Any Form of Detention or Imprisonment: "arrest" is the act of "apprehending a person for the alleged commission of an offence"; "detention" is any deprivation of liberty, except as the result of a conviction for an offence; and "imprisonment" refers to deprivation of liberty arising from a conviction.

Paragraph 4 of article 9 of the International Covenant on Civil and Political Rights states: "Anyone who is deprived of his liberty by arrest or detention shall be entitled to take proceedings before a court, in order that that court may decide without delay on the lawfulness of his detention and order his release if the detention is not lawful."

Article 37(b) of the Convention requires that any restriction of liberty of children, whether part of the juvenile justice system or otherwise, must not be arbitrary and must be authorized in legislation. The wording of paragraph (b), strongly supported by the relevant United Nations rules and guidelines, emphasizes that restriction of liberty for under 18-year-olds should be exceptional – a last resort and always "for the shortest appropriate time".

During discussion of Pakistan's Initial Report, a Committee member "pointed out that the expression 'as a last resort' in article 37 of the Convention was often misunderstood as referring to children guilty of serious crimes; in fact, it meant that prison could be resorted to only if there was no other way of giving the child the protection it needed. The phrase 'for the shortest appropriate period of time' implied that other measures than prison sentences should be sought..." (Pakistan SR.323, para. 56)

In addition, in relation to the juvenile justice system, article 40 emphasizes the overall aim of promoting the child's sense of dignity and worth and his or her reintegration, and the particular desirability of avoiding, when appropriate, resorting to judicial proceedings and of promoting alternatives to institutional care (see page 539).

The "Beijing Rules" in rule 17 sets detailed "Guiding principles in adjudication and disposition":

"(b) Restrictions on the personal liberty of the juvenile shall be imposed only after careful con-sideration and shall be limited to the possible minimum.

(c) Deprivation of personal liberty shall not be imposed unless the juvenile is adjudicated of a serious act involving violence against another person or of persistence in committing other serious offences and unless there is no other appropriate response.

(d) The well-being of the juvenile shall be the guiding factor in the consideration of her or his case..."

The United Nations General Assembly resolution adopting the United Nations Rules for the Protection of Juveniles Deprived of their Liberty (resolution 45/113, 14 December 1990, and Annex) notes that "juveniles deprived of their liberty are highly vulnerable to abuse, victimization and the violation of their rights", and affirms that "the placement of a juvenile in an institution should always be a disposition of last resort and for the minimum necessary period". Rule 2 states that "Deprivation of the liberty of a juvenile should be a disposition of last resort and for the minimum necessary period and should be limited to exceptional cases. The length of the sanction should be determined by the judicial authority, without precluding the possibility of his or her early release."

The United Nations Standard Minimum Rules for Non-custodial Measures (the "Tokyo Rules") were adopted in 1990 to provide a set of basic principles to promote the use of non-custodial measures generally, as well as minimum safeguards for persons subject to alternatives to imprisonment. The Rules notes that there should be no discrimination in their application on grounds of age (rule 2.2).

The Committee on the Rights of the Child has expressed concern at the use of the restriction of liberty for young children and has emphasized that a minimum age for any restriction of liberty should be defined in legislation. In its *Guidelines for Periodic Reports*, the Committee seeks information under article 1 (definition of a child) on any legal minimum age defined in national legislation for the deprivation of liberty, "including by arrest, detention and imprisonment, *inter alia* in the areas of administration of justice, asylum-seeking and placement of children in welfare and health institutions" (para. 24). In relation to the Initial Report of the Syrian Arab Republic, the Committee

"...notes in particular that children may be deprived of liberty at a very low age and that sufficient attention has not been paid to date to find alternatives to institutional care of children." (Syrian Arab Republic IRCO, Add.70, para. 19)

"...the apparent absence in national legislation of minimum ages below which a child may not be deprived of liberty or considered criminally responsible causes deep concern to the Committee...

"... the Committee recommends that the State Party defines in its legislation a minimum age below which children may not be deprived of their liberty..." (Panama IRCO, Add.68, paras. 21 and 22; see also UK IRCO, Add.34, para. 10, quoted below)

The Committee has expressed concern at the length of restriction of liberty of children on arrest and during investigation (pre-trial detention), as well as the length of sentences, both generally and in specific circumstances. It should be noted that article 37(d) provides the right to challenge the legality of any deprivation of liberty before a court or other appropriate body "and to a prompt decision on any such action".

In some cases, its concern has been general:

"...Deprivation of liberty should always be envisaged as the very last resort, and particular attention should be paid to rehabilitation measures, psychological recovery and social reintegration..." (Egypt IRCO, Add.5, para. 14)

"Particular attention should be paid to deprivation of liberty only as a measure of last resort and for the shortest possible period of time..." (Myanmar IRCO, Add.69, para. 46; see also Bulgaria IRCO, Add.66, para. 19)

Arrest, pre-trial detention

In relation to arrest, the Human Rights Committee states in its General Comment on article 9 of the Covenant on Civil and Political Rights that "in criminal cases any person arrested or detained has to be brought 'promptly' before a judge or other officer authorized by law to exercise judicial power. More precise time limits are fixed by law in most States Parties and, in the view of the Committee, delays must not exceed a few days..." The Human Rights Committee goes on to state that "pre-trial detention should be an exception and as short as possible." (Human Rights Committee, General Comment 8, HRI/GEN/1/Rev.2, p. 8)

The Human Rights Committee has also indicated that it disapproves of pre-trial detention for juveniles. Members of the Committee expressed concern regarding one State where there was no minimum age for pre-trial detention and where juveniles between 12 and 18 years old could be detained by the juvenile courts before trial. (Official Records of the General Assembly, Forty-sixth session, Supplement No.40 A/46/40, paras. 66, 69 and 99 *in fine* (Canada); quoted in *Human rights and pre-trial detention*, Centre for Human Rights Crime Prevention and Crimi-

nal Justice Branch, Professional Training Series No.3, 1994)

The "Beijing Rules" notes (rule 10(2)) that following the apprehension of a juvenile, "A judge or other competent official or body shall, without delay, consider the issue of release". The Rules also states: "Detention pending trial shall be used only as a measure of last resort and for the shortest possible period of time. Whenever possible, detention pending trial shall be replaced by alternative measures, such as close supervision, intensive care or placement within a family or in an educational setting or home" (rule 13). The United Nations Rules for the Protection of Juveniles Deprived of their Liberty states that: "... Detention before trial shall be avoided to the extent possible and limited to exceptional circumstances. Therefore all efforts shall be made to apply alternative measures. When preventive detention is nevertheless used, juvenile courts and investigative bodies shall give the highest priority to the most expeditious processing of such cases to ensure the shortest possible duration of detention..." (rule 17)

The Committee on the Rights of the Child has frequently expressed concern at the length of pre-trial detention permitted in States Parties. In relation to Bolivia, it noted its concern that:

"... a child may remain in custody for the excessively long period of 45 days before the legality of his or her detention is decided upon." (Bolivia IRCO, Add.1, para. 11. See also Belgium IRCO, Add.38, para. 11; Madagascar IRCO, Add.26, para. 16; Jamaica IRCO, Add.32, para. 17; Slovenia IRCO, Add.65, paras. 19 and 27)

In relation to the impact of emergency legislation in Northern Ireland, which is part of the United Kingdom, the Committee was concerned at the detention without charge of very young children for periods of up to seven days:

"...The Committee is concerned about the absence of effective safeguards to prevent the ill-treatment of children under the emergency legislation. In this connection, the Committee observes that under the same legislation it is possible to hold children as young as 10 for 7 days without charge. It is also noted that the emergency legislation which gives the police and army the power to stop, question and search people on the street has led to complaints of children being badly treated. The Committee is concerned about this situation which may lead to a lack of confidence in the system of investigation and action on such complaints." (UK IRCO, Add.34, para. 10)

Imprisonment

In relation to sentences for criminal offences, the Committee has expressed concern at custodial sentences for young children and also at lengthy and indeterminate sentences:

"The Committee notes that long periods of imprisonment for delinquent children set forth in national penal legislation are not in conformity with the provisions of article 37 of the Convention..." (Viet Nam IRCO, Add.3, para. 6)

"The Committee notes that the sanctions set forth in the legislation as regards juvenile offenders, especially in cases carrying the death penalty or life imprisonment, reduced respectively to life imprisonment or to 20 years imprisonment, are excessively high. Harsh sentences, as well as the occurrence of arbitrary detention of juveniles and the admittedly very difficult conditions of detention, are not in conformity with the provisions of articles 37 and 40 of the Convention." (Burkina Faso IRCO, Add.19, para. 11)

In relation to the United Kingdom, the Committee expressed concern at the introduction of "secure training orders" authorizing custody for 12 to 14-year-olds, and other increases in custodial sentences:

"... The Committee also recommends the introduction of careful monitoring of the new Criminal Justice and Public Order Act 1994 with a view to ensuring full respect for the Convention on the Rights of the Child. In particular, the provisions of the Act which allow for, inter alia, placement of secure training orders on children aged between 12 and 14, indeterminate detention, and the doubling of sentences which may be imposed on 15 to 17-year-old children should be reviewed with respect to their compatibility with the principles and provisions of the Convention." (UK IRCO, Add.34, para. 36)

"...The Committee is also concerned that the provisions of national legislation by which a child may be detained 'at Her Majesty's Pleasure' may permit the indiscriminate sentencing of children for indeterminate periods...

"...Finally, the Committee wishes to emphasize that the Convention requires that detention be a measure of last resort and for the shortest appropriate period of time. The institutionalization and detention of children must be avoided as much as possible and alternatives to such practices must be developed and implemented..." (Nigeria IRCO, Add.61, paras. 21 and 40)

"The Committee is deeply concerned at the present system of juvenile justice, which is not in conformity with articles 37, 39 and 40 of the Convention. It is particularly concerned about the age of criminal responsibility at nine years and that as from the age of 15 years children are treated as adults. In this regard, the Committee regrets that it has not been made clear during the discussion wheth-

er the latter meant that children above 15 years of age may be sentenced to life imprisonment or detained together with adults..." (Ethiopia IRCO, Add.67, para. 20)

The Committee has also raised the issue of non-discrimination (article 2) in relation to sentencing:

"With regard to articles 37 and 40, the Committee is concerned that there are not adequate safeguards to ensure non-discrimination in the implementation of these provisions of the Convention. The Committee is concerned about the present discretionary procedure of considering the 'personality' of the child as a criteria for passing sentences. This practice, in its actual application, may often be discriminatory against children living in poverty..." (Bolivia IRCO, Add.1, para. 11)

Detention outside the juvenile justice system

As illustrated above (page 496) the Committee has pointed out that the provisions limiting restriction of liberty under article 37 apply to all instances of restriction of liberty, including, for example, in health and welfare institutions and in relation to asylum-seekers and refugee children. The limitations on restriction of liberty in paragraph (b) and the safeguards in paragraphs (c) and (d) must be applied equally, as must the standards set out in the relevant United Nations rules and guidelines.

Detention of children in relation to asylum-seeking and immigration: The policy of the United Nations High Commissioner for Refugees is that refugee children should not be detained. The UNHCR *Refugee Children – Guidelines on Protection and Care* states: "Unfortunately, refugee children are sometimes detained or threatened with detention because of their own, or their parents', illegal entry into a country of asylum. Because detention can be very harmful to refugee children, it must be 'used only as a measure of last resort and for the shortest appropriate period of time'". The *Guidelines* emphasizes the need for special arrangements: "Strong efforts must be made to have them released from detention and placed in other accommodation. Families must be kept together at all times, which includes their stay in detention as well as being released together." Detention must be in conformity with the State's law, and "a distinction must be made between refugees/asylum seekers and other aliens". International standards including those of the Convention and the relevant United Nations rules must be complied with (*Guidelines*, pp. 86-88). (UNHCR Executive Conclusion No.44 (1986) discusses the limited circumstances in which asylum-seekers can be detained and sets out basic standards for their treatment)

The UNHCR Policy on Refugee Children requires UNHCR staff to specifically pursue the protection of refugee children at risk from detention (UNHCR Policy on Refugee Children, UNHCR Executive Committee, EC/SCP/82, para. 27).

The Committee on the Rights of the Child has expressed concern at detention affecting asylum-seeking children and aliens:

"The Committee is also concerned at the practice of taking foreign children into custody under the Aliens Act and notes that this practice is discriminatory in so far as Swedish children generally cannot be placed in custody until after the age of 18...

"... The Committee also suggests that consideration be given to providing alternatives to the incarceration of children under the Aliens Act and that a public defence counsel be appointed for children in conflict with the law." (Sweden IRCO, Add.2, paras. 9 and 12)

During discussion of Canada's Initial Report, a Committee member noted "that arrangements made to detain children in immigration or asylum cases might not fully take into account their particular needs even when they were detained in comfortable surroundings such as hotels. Such detention was still a deprivation of liberty under article 37(b) of the Convention, according to which such a measure should only be a last resort and for the shortest possible period of time. According to some reports, children had been detained in Canada for a year or more..."

The Committee member went on to note that "under article 37(d) of the Convention, any child deprived of his or her liberty should have 'the right to prompt access to legal and other appropriate assistance, as well as the right to challenge the legality of the deprivation of his or her liberty before a court or other competent, independent and impartial authority'. It was not entirely clear that arrangements in Canada, where such decisions were made by the immigration authorities, met those criteria. Clarification was also needed on whether children in such situations enjoyed the right of *habeas corpus*, which was a crucial legal safeguard... the Committee took very seriously the obligations of States Parties under article 37(b) concerning the deprivation of liberty. Such an experience was often extremely traumatic to children in a foreign environment, even when they were detained in comfortable surroundings. Were alternative measures being sought?" (Canada SR.216, paras. 86-88)

The Concluding Observations stated:

"Deprivation of liberty of children, particularly unaccompanied children, for security or other purposes should only be used as a measure of last resort in accordance with article 37(b) of the Convention." (Canada IRCO, Add.37, para. 24; see also: UK dependent territory: Hong Kong IRCO, Add.63, para. 33)

Deprivation of liberty for children in need of protection: The Committee has noted that it does not accept that deprivation of liberty should be used for children in need of protection. Chile's Initial Report indicates that "children under the age of 18 who have been abandoned, ill-treated and/or present behavioural problems, may be deprived of their liberty or have their liberty restricted", initially in a centre for observation and diagnosis and subsequently, when a juvenile magistrate decides to apply a protective measure, which can include internment in specialized educational establishments (Chile IR, paras. 54-55). The Initial Report notes that while the State has no right to impose penalties on children regarded as not responsible for criminal actions, "the correctional and rehabilitation measures which may be applied by the juvenile judge can extend to custodial measures which in fact are felt by the minor to be a penalty" (Chile IR, para. 236). During discussion, a Committee member stated: "Deprivation of liberty was unacceptable in the case of children in need of protection because they had been abandoned or subjected to ill-treatment. Such children had committed no offence against the law... To deprive children of 16 or 17 years of age of their liberty for 15 days or more while awaiting a decision on their capacity for discernment, could affect them adversely and was contrary to the provisions of article 37 of the Convention, especially as it seemed that such detention could take place among convicted offenders." Another Committee member noted that "if children in need of protection were placed in a position where they were deprived of their liberty, they were in fact being deprived of the protection of the law." (Chile SR.148, paras. 34-35 and 38)

Other Committee comments include:

"... Furthermore, the Committee is worried about the provisions of national legislation which provide for the detention of children assessed to be 'beyond parental control'. The possibility that abandoned children or children living and/or working on the street would have such measures applied against them is of special concern to the Committee. It is the view of the Committee that these legislative measures do not appear to be compatible with the provisions of article 37(b) of the Convention, which lays down that the arrest,

detention or imprisonment of a child shall only be used as a measure of last resort and for the shortest appropriate period of time. Equally, the Committee is concerned about the application in practice of the provisions of section 3 of the Children and Persons Law [which] may lead to the arbitrary detention of children, which is incompatible with the provisions and principles of the Convention." (Nigeria IRCO, Add.61, para. 21)

The Committee has also noted that mentally ill children should never be detained in prison:

"The law permitting the placement of mentally disturbed children in jails should be reviewed as a matter of urgency." (Nepal IRCO, Add.57, para. 38)

"Every child deprived of liberty shall be treated with humanity and respect for the inherent dignity of the human person, and in a manner which takes into account the needs of persons of his or her age"

This provision of article 37 stresses that children deprived of their liberty should not lose their fundamental rights, and that their treatment must take account of their age and child development. The United Nations Rules for the Protection of Juveniles Deprived of their Liberty states in rule 13: "Juveniles deprived of their liberty shall not for any reason related to their status be denied the civil, economic, political, social or cultural rights to which they are entitled under national or international law, and which are compatible with the deprivation of liberty, such as social security rights and benefits, freedom of association and, upon reaching the minimum age established by law, the right to marry."

The Committee has often expressed concern at the conditions in detention institutions and places where children's liberty is restricted. It has proposed that the detailed standards in the "Beijing Rules" and the United Nations Rules for the Protection of Juveniles Deprived of their Liberty should be applied to all situations, and indicated that the Convention requires effective monitoring, inspection and complaints procedures, as well as appropriate training of all personnel:

"... The Committee is also concerned by the serious conditions in the correctional facilities which, as recognized by the delegation, may adversely affect the fulfilment of the State Party's obligations under the Convention and other international human rights standards." (Madagascar IRCO, Add.26, para. 16)

"The Committee is very much alarmed at the reports it has received of the ill-treatment of children in detention centres. In view of the seriousness of such alleged violations, the Committee is concerned about the insufficient training provided to law enforcement officials and personnel of detention centres on the provisions and principles of the Convention and other relevant international instruments such as the 'Beijing Rules', the 'Riyadh Guidelines' and the United Nations Rules for the Protection of Children Deprived of their Liberty." (Paraguay Prelim. Obs., Add.27, para. 13. See also Myanmar IRCO, Add.69, para. 46; Colombia IRCO, Add.30, para. 18)

The Committee has noted the importance of registering all children deprived of their liberty, and the *Guidelines for Periodic Reports* asks for detailed information on the numbers of children deprived of liberty "unlawfully, arbitrarily and within the law", the reasons and periods of deprivation of liberty, and that data should be disaggregated (para. 141).

The fact that deprivation of liberty occurs in "institutions" rather than prisons does not lessen the need for strict conditions, monitoring, etc. Article 3(3) of the Convention requires States to ensure that all institutions conform with standards established by competent authorities (see page 45). During discussion with the Committee, Government representatives from Egypt indicated that under–18-year-olds "were not required to serve prison sentences but could be placed in specialized institutions". A Committee member commented on the sometimes unclear distinction between imprisonment and placement in an institution: "Were the conditions in the latter really different, particularly if a minor was required to remain there for some 10 years? Could the conditions in an institution be considered to resemble more closely the normal environment in which a child could expect to find himself or did they resemble a prison environment? The importance of reviewing a juvenile's situation must be emphasized; a child should be offered some prospect of a better future if he demonstrated a willingness or capacity to change and a greater maturity." Another Committee member pointed out that "there was a small proportion of young offenders who might be difficult to handle in institutions and whose situation must be constantly monitored. There was always a risk that, when minors were not subject to normal court hearings and sentences, their treatment might not be more lenient or humane and might indeed become quite arbitrary." (Egypt SR.68, paras. 24, 30 and 33)

In its Concluding Observations, the Committee recommended:

"...Deprivation of liberty should always be envisaged as the very last resort, and particular attention should be paid to rehabilitation measures, psychological recovery and social reintegration. Furthermore, deprivation of liberty in social care institutions should be regularly monitored by a judge or independent body." (Egypt IRCO, Add.5, para. 14)

"In particular, every child deprived of liberty shall be separated from adults unless it is considered in the child's best interest not to do so"

The principle in article 37(c) that every child deprived of liberty shall be separated from adults is qualified – "unless it is considered in the child's best interest not to do so". In the International Covenant on Civil and Political Rights, article 10(2)(b) requires: "Accused juvenile persons shall be separated from adults and brought as speedily as possible for adjudication." Similarly, in the Standard Minimum Rules for the Treatment of Prisoners, rule 8(d) requires: "Young prisoners shall be kept separate from adults." In a General Comment on article 10 of the Covenant on Civil and Political Rights, the Human Rights Committee states: "Subparagraph 2(b) calls, *inter alia*, for accused juvenile persons to be separated from adults. The information in reports shows that a number of States are not taking sufficient account of the fact that this is an unconditional requirement of the Covenant. It is the Committee's opinion that, as is clear from the text of the Covenant, deviation from States Parties' obligations under subparagraph 2(b) cannot be justified by any consideration whatsoever." (Human Rights Committee, General Comment 9, HRI/GEN/1/Rev.2, p. 10)

Several States Parties made reservations or declarations concerning this provision of article 37. For example, Australia notes: "... In relation to the second sentence of paragraph (c), the obligation to separate children from adults in prison is accepted only to the extent that such imprisonment is considered by the responsible authorities to be feasible and consistent with the obligation that children be able to maintain contact with their families, having regard to the geography and demography of Australia. Australia, therefore, ratifies the Convention to the extent that it is unable to comply with the obligations imposed by article 37(c)". Canada "accepts the general principle of article 37(c) of the Convention, but reserves the right not to detain children separately from adults where this is not appropriate or feasible". Iceland

Separation and best interests

Finland ratified the Convention on the Rights of the Child without reservations. But its Initial Report indicates that "The most difficult problem was considered to be the obligation in article 37(c) to separate a child deprived of liberty from adults. There were neither at the time nor are there now enough units for children only. When the Convention was ratified, the Ministry of Justice took the view that, because of the small number of child prisoners in Finland, the placement of a child in a unit accommodating only minors is not necessarily even in the best interest of the child. For those below 18 years to be separated from adults they have to be concentrated in a very few units. This leads to the disconnection of their social ties. If, on the other hand, a child is placed in a unit for adults, located not too far from his or her home, the obligation to separate him from adults means that he cannot eat, exercise outdoors or participate in the various activities with the other prisoners, thus effectively isolating him or her from human contact. An added factor is that the criminal subcultures of young people may only be reinforced in units designed solely for young offenders." (Finland IR, paras. 19-20)

notes that separation is not obligatory under Icelandic law, but that the law provided for age to be taken into account when deciding placement: "... it is expected that decisions on the imprisonment of juveniles will always take account of the juvenile's best interest".

New Zealand reserved the right not to apply article 37(c) "where the shortage of suitable facilities makes the mixing of juveniles and adults unavoidable; and further reserves the right not to apply article 37(c) where the interests of other juveniles in an establishment require the removal of a particular juvenile offender or where mixing is considered to be of benefit to the persons concerned." And the United Kingdom states: "Where at any time there is a lack of suitable accommodation or adequate facilities for a particular individual in any institution in which young offenders are detained, or where the mixing of adults and children is deemed to be mutually beneficial, the United Kingdom reserves the right not to apply article 37(c) in so far as those provisions require children who are detained to be accommodated separately from adults." (CRC/C/2/Rev.5, pp. 13, 15, 21, 28 and 34)

The Committee on the Rights of the Child has expressed concern at these reservations and welcomed commitments from States Parties to review them with a view to withdrawal (see, for example, Canada IRCO, Add.37, para. 10; Iceland IRCO, Add.50, para. 4; New Zealand IRCO, Add.71, para. 8; UK IRCO, Add.34, para. 7).

The Committee has commented on instances of non-separation. For example:

"In regard to children in conflict with the law, the Committee suggests that further consideration should be given to ensuring that children in detention are separated from adults, taking into account the best interests of the child and alternatives to institutional care. In this connection, the State Party may wish to study the situation in those countries where arrangements for liaison between juveniles and the police force have been established..." (Sweden IRCO, Add.2, para. 12)

"Problems appear to exist in relation to ... non-separation of children from adult detainees..." (Lebanon IRCO, Add.54, para. 19)

The Committee has also noted that separation from adults applies to all situations of restriction of liberty, including in psychiatric institutions:

"The Committee is worried by the State Party's current shortage of facilities for the psychiatric treatment of children. This shortage may result in the non-separation of children from adults in psychiatric establishments...
"The Committee recommends the State Party take all appropriate measures to prevent mentally-ill children being institutionalized in the same facilities as adults..." (Finland IRCO, Add.53, paras. 16 and 27)

Separation of pre-trial detainees from other children deprived of liberty

The International Covenant on Civil and Political Rights requires that "Accused persons shall, save in exceptional circumstances, be segregated from convicted persons and shall be subject to separate treatment appropriate to their status as unconvicted persons" (article 10(2)(a)). Also the Standard Minimum Rules for Prisoners states that: "Untried prisoners shall be kept separate from convicted prisoners" (rule 8(b)). And the United Nations Rules for the Protection of Juveniles Deprived of their Liberty says: "... Untried detainees should be separated from convicted juveniles" (rule 17).

The Committee on the Rights of the Child has confirmed that pre-trial detainees should be separated from convicted detainees. The Committee

"...also deplores the fact that children taken into custody though not convicted of any criminal offence, may nevertheless be kept in detention in the same premises as convicted persons" (Jordan IRCO, Add.21, para. 16).

"...and shall have the right to maintain contact with his or her family through correspondence and visits, save in exceptional circumstances"

Paragraph (c) of article 37 requires that every child deprived of liberty shall "have the right to maintain contact with his or her family through correspondence and visits, save in exceptional circumstances". Such circumstances would have to be justified in the context of the Convention's principles, including in particular the child's best interests:

"The Committee expresses its concern as to the compatibility of juvenile justice and penitentiary institutions with article 37 of the Convention and how the rights of the child to leisure and contact with the family and the best interests of the child are protected in such situations. The Committee also expresses concern at the present organization of the system of administration of justice and its compatibility with article 37 of the Convention and other standards relating to juvenile justice." (Russian Federation IRCO, Add.4, para. 14)

"Moreover, the Committee is seriously concerned about the conditions in place of detention for children, especially with regard to children's access to their parents, the medical services and educational programmes offered and the services in place to facilitate the recovery and rehabilitation of children..." (Nigeria IRCO, Add.61, para. 23)

"Every child deprived of his or her liberty shall have the right to prompt access to legal and other appropriate assistance, as well as the right to challenge the legality of the deprivation of his or her liberty before a court or other competent, independent and impartial authority, and to a prompt decision on any such action"

Article 40 provides further detail of the safeguards that must be provided in relation to the administration of juvenile justice, as does the "Beijing Rules" (the United Nations Standard Minimum Rules for the Administration of Juvenile Justice) and other instruments (for full discussion, see article 40, page 539).

The right to challenge the legality of any deprivation of liberty and to a prompt decision is guaranteed by article 8 of the Universal Declaration on Human Rights: "Everyone has the right to an effective remedy by the competent national tribunals for acts violating the fundamental rights granted him by the constitution or by law"; and article 9(4) of the International Covenant on Civil and Political Rights says: "Anyone who is deprived of his liberty by arrest or detention shall be entitled to take proceedings before a court, in order that that court may decide without delay on the lawfulness of his detention and order his release if the detention is not lawful." The Human Rights Committee has provided comments on what constitutes a "court" for this purpose and also notes that article 9(4) of the Covenant applies to all cases of detention, including those ordered by an administrative body or authority. (see Antti Vuolanne v Finland (265/1987) (7 April 1989), Official Records of the General Assembly, Forty-fourth session, Supplement No. 40 A/44/40, annex X, sect. J etc., quoted in *Human Rights and Pre-trial Detention*, p. 40)

The Body of Principles for the Protection of All Persons under Any form of Detention or Imprisonment (General Assembly resolution 43/173, 9 December 1988, annex) provides in principle 32: "1. A detained person or his counsel shall be entitled at any time to take proceedings according to domestic law before a judicial or other authority to challenge the lawfulness of his detention in order to obtain his release without delay, if it is unlawful. 2. The proceedings ... shall be simple and expeditious and at no cost for detained persons without adequate means. The detaining authority shall produce without unreasonable delay the detained person before the reviewing authority". In 1992, a Commission of Human Rights resolution (1992/35) urged States that had not already done so to establish such procedures.

The Committee on the Rights of the Child has commented on the lack of appropriate legal assistance. Under article 1 (definition of a child), the Committee seeks information on any legal age defined in legislation for "legal ... counselling without parental consent" (*Guidelines for Periodic Reports*, para. 24). In one case it noted

"...The age for legal counselling without parental consent is unclear and practices in this regard may not be in conformity with article 37(d) of the Convention." (Bolivia IRCO, Add.1, para. 11)

The Committee has emphasized that the safeguards apply to all forms of deprivation of liberty, not only those in the system of juvenile justice (and it should be noted that rule 3 of the "Beijing Rules" encourages the extension of the principles of the Rules to cover all juveniles dealt with in

care and welfare proceedings). In the report following its General Discussion on juvenile justice the Committee noted:

"Concern was expressed at the placement of children in institutions, under a welfare pretext, without taking into due consideration the best interests of the child nor ensuring the fundamental safeguards recognized by the Convention, including the right to challenge the decision of placement before a judicial authority, to a periodic review of the treatment provided to the child and all other circumstances relevant to the child's placement and the right to lodge complaints." (Report on the tenth session, October-November 1995, CRC/C/46, para. 228)

Other comments in relation to individual States Parties include:

"...Furthermore, deprivation of liberty in social care institutions should be regularly monitored by a judge or an independent body." (Egypt IRCO, Add.5, para. 14)

"...the Committee wishes to emphasize that the legal safeguards provided for in the relevant principles and provisions of the Convention, including those of article 40, must be provided to all children, whether the deprivation of their liberty results from the application of a welfare or a criminal procedure." (Nigeria IRCO, Add.61, para. 39)

Complaints procedures

The Committee has interpreted article 12 of the Convention as requiring the provision of complaints procedures for children (see page 155) and has highlighted the particular need for complaints procedures for children whose liberty is restricted.

The report on the Committee's General Discussion on juvenile justice notes that children involved with the juvenile justice system

"were ... often denied the right to lodge complaints when they were victims of violation of their fundamental rights, including in cases of ill-treatment and sexual abuse..." (Report on the tenth session, October-November 1995, CRC/C/46, para. 220)

Rule 24 of the United Nations Rules for the Protection of Juveniles Deprived of their Liberty requires that "On admission, all juveniles shall be given a copy of the rules governing the detention facility and a written description of their rights and obligations in a language they can understand, together with the address of the authorities competent to receive complaints, as well as the address of public or private agencies and organizations which provide legal assistance. For those juveniles who are illiterate or who cannot understand the language in the written form, the information should be conveyed in a manner enabling full comprehension."

Rule 25 says "All juveniles should be helped to understand the regulations governing the internal organization of the facility, the goals and methodology of the care provided, the disciplinary requirements and procedures, other authorized methods of seeking information and of making complaints, and all such other matters as are necessary to enable them to understand fully their rights and obligations during detention."

In addition, rules 75 to 78 require that juveniles have the opportunity to make requests or complaints to the direction of the detention facility and his or her authorized representative, to the central administration, the judicial authority or other proper authorities through approved channels. "Efforts should be made to establish an independent office (ombudsman) to receive and investigate complaints made by juveniles deprived of their liberty and to assist in the achievement of equitable settlements" (rule 77). "Every juvenile should have the right to request assistance from family members, legal counsellors, humanitarian groups or others where possible, in order to make a complaint. Illiterate juveniles should be provided with assistance should they need to use the services of public or private agencies and organizations which provide legal counsel or which are competent to receive complaints." (rule 78)

In relation to Nigeria's Initial Report, the Committee stated:

"...It is equally concerned about the inappropriateness and ineffectiveness of measures for the supervision and monitoring of the situation of children in detention, including for dealing with children's complaints of abuse or ill-treatment, and the lack of measures to ensure that these complaints are addressed in a serious and expeditious manner." (Nigeria IRCO, Add.61, para. 23)

Training

The Committee has consistently recommended that all those involved in any form of restriction of liberty of children, and in the administration of juvenile justice systems should receive training in the principles and provisions of the Convention and of the relevant United Nations rules and guidelines (see article 40, page 544 for a full list of references to the Committee's comments relating to juvenile justice).

Implementation Checklist

article 37

● General measures of implementation

Have appropriate general measures of implementation been taken in relation to article 37, including

☐ identification and coordination of the responsible departments and agencies at all levels of government (article 37 is relevant to **departments of justice, home affairs, social welfare, immigration**)?

☐ identification of relevant non-governmental organizations/civil society partners?

☐ a comprehensive review to ensure that all legislation, policy and practice is compatible with the article, for all children in all parts of the jurisdiction?

☐ adoption of a strategy to secure full implementation

    ☐ which includes where necessary the identification of goals and indicators of progress?

    ☐ which does not affect any provisions which are more conducive to the rights of the child?

    ☐ which recognizes other relevant international standards?

    ☐ which involves where necessary international cooperation?

(Such measures may be part of an overall governmental strategy for implementing the Convention as a whole).

☐ budgetary analysis and allocation of necessary resources?

☐ development of mechanisms for monitoring and evaluation?

☐ making the implications of article 37 widely known to adults and children?

☐ development of appropriate training and awareness-raising (in relation to article 37 likely to include training for **the judiciary, lawyers, police, all those working in the juvenile justice system and institutional care including detention, and any other forms of restriction of liberty**)?

● Specific issues in implementing article 37

☐ Is the prohibition of torture and all other cruel, inhuman or degrading treatment or punishment included in legislation specifically applying to all children in the jurisdiction?

☐ Is torture defined in this legislation?

☐ Are there no exceptions allowed to this legislation under any circumstances?

☐ Is capital punishment prohibited in legislation for offences committed by children below the age of 18?

☐ Is life imprisonment without the possibility of release not available in any circumstances for under-18-year-olds?

☐ Are indefinite or indeterminate sentences not available in any circumstances for under-18-year-olds?

Is any form of corporal punishment prohibited in legislation and not used for under-18-year-olds

 ☐ as a sentence of the courts or a punishment in penal institutions?

 ☐ as a punishment in schools?

 ☐ as a punishment in any other institutions including children?

 ☐ as a punishment in any forms of alternative care?

 ☐ as a punishment within the family?

☐ Is solitary confinement of children prohibited under all circumstances?

☐ Has the State initiated or promoted awareness-raising and information campaigns to protect children from torture and other cruel, inhuman or degrading treatment?

☐ Has the State ratified the Convention against Torture and Other Cruel, Inhuman or Degrading Treatment or Punishment?

Arrest

☐ Are all under-18-year-olds treated as children within the justice system?

Does legislation, policy and practice ensure that arrest of children is used

 ☐ only as a measure of last resort?

 ☐ for the shortest appropriate period of time?

Is there a minimum age below which a child

 ☐ cannot be arrested?

 ☐ cannot be detained prior to arrest by police or other authorities?

Do legislation and other measures in the State ensure that any detention of a juvenile prior to arrest is

 ☐ only used as a measure of last resort?

 ☐ for the shortest appropriate period of time?

Deprivation of liberty following arrest

☐ Is there a defined maximum period for detention of a child following arrest without a court hearing at which the detention can be challenged?

☐ Is there a minimum age below which a child cannot be detained following arrest and prior to a court hearing?

How to use the checklists, *see page XVII*

Does legislation ensure that any detention of a juvenile following arrest is

- ☐ a measure of last resort?
- ☐ for the shortest appropriate time?

Pre-trial deprivation of liberty

Does legislation ensure that any pre-trial detention of a child is

- ☐ a measure of last resort?
- ☐ for the shortest appropriate time?

☐ Is there a minimum age below which a child cannot be detained prior to a trial?

☐ Does legislation ensure that children detained pre-trial are separated from convicted children?

☐ Are alternative measures available to prevent pre-trial detention of children whenever possible?

Deprivation of liberty as a sentence of the courts

☐ Is there a minimum age at which a sentence of imprisonment may be imposed on a child?

☐ Are there no other arrangements that allow for the restriction of liberty of children who are alleged as, accused of or recognized as having committed certain crimes below this minimum age?

Do safeguards exist to ensure that sentences of imprisonment, or sentences that involve the restriction of liberty of a child, are used only

- ☐ as a measure of last resort?
- ☐ for the shortest appropriate time?

Restriction of liberty other than as a sentence of the courts

Is all other legislation permitting the restriction of liberty of under-18-year-olds consistent with article 37 and other articles, wherever such restriction occurs, including

- ☐ in the criminal/juvenile justice system?
- ☐ in the welfare system?
- ☐ in the education system?
- ☐ in the health system including mental health?
- ☐ in relation to asylum-seeking and immigration?
- ☐ in any other circumstances whatsoever?

☐ In each case, does the legislation define a minimum age below which no child (boy/girl) may have his or her liberty restricted?

TORTURE, DEPRIVATION OF LIBERTY

How to use the checklists, *see page XVII*

In each case, does the legislation ensure that any detention outside the penal system is

☐ a measure of last resort?

☐ for the shortest appropriate period of time?

☐ not for an indeterminate period?

☐ Is there restriction of liberty of children in circumstances not set out in legislation?

Does legislation exist to prevent arbitrary restriction of liberty of children in

☐ State-provided institutions and services?

☐ other institutions and services?

☐ Does legislation exist to limit deprivation of liberty of children by parents/guardians/foster parents, and so forth?

Conditions in detention

(see also the detailed standards in the United Nations Rules for the Protection of Juveniles Deprived of their Liberty)

☐ Have the United Nations Rules for the Protection of Juveniles Deprived of their Liberty been incorporated into legislation applying to all situations of deprivation of liberty?

☐ Is there effective inspection and monitoring of all institutions in which children may be deprived of their liberty?

☐ Is the right of the child deprived of liberty to a periodic review of his or her situation and treatment set out in legislation?

☐ Are the details of any restriction of liberty of any child appropriately registered, reported and recorded?

☐ Is disaggregated data available on all children deprived of liberty?

☐ Do all children deprived of liberty have access to effective complaints procedures concerning all aspects of their treatment?

Separation from adults

Are children always separated from adults in detention unless it is considered not to be in the child's best interest

☐ prior to arrest?

☐ following arrest?

☐ pre-trial?

☐ following sentence by a court?

☐ in the health, including mental health, system?

☐ in the welfare system?

☐ in relation to asylum-seeking and immigration?

☐ in any other situation?

Contacts with family while detained

☐ Is the right of the child deprived of liberty to maintain contact with his or her family through correspondence and visits set out in legislation?

☐ Are any restrictions on this right limited to exceptional circumstances?

☐ In case of any restrictions, does the child concerned have a right of appeal to an independent body?

Access to legal and other assistance

Does the child deprived of liberty have the right to prompt legal and other appropriate assistance

☐ when detained prior to arrest?

☐ on arrest?

☐ when detained pre-trial?

☐ when detained following a sentence of the courts?

☐ when deprived of liberty in any other circumstances?

Arrangements to challenge restriction of liberty

Does every child deprived of liberty have the right to challenge the deprivation of liberty before a court or some other competent authority

☐ when detained before arrest?

☐ when detained following arrest?

☐ when sentenced to be detained?

☐ when their liberty is restricted in other circumstances?

☐ In the case of such challenges of restriction of liberty, does legislation guarantee the child a prompt decision, within a defined period of time?

Reminder : **The Convention is indivisible and its articles are interdependent. Article 37 should not be considered in isolation.**

Particular regard should be paid to:
The general principles

Article 2: all rights to be recognized for each child in jurisdiction without discrimination on any ground

Article 3(1): the best interests of the child to be a primary consideration in all actions concerning children

Article 6: right to life and maximum possible survival and development
Article 12: respect for the child's views in all matters affecting the child; opportunity to be heard in any judicial or administrative proceedings affecting the child

Closely related articles

Articles whose implementation is related to that of article 37 include:

Article 19: protection from all forms of violence
Article 20: alternative care
Article 22: refugee children
Article 24: restriction of liberty in health service
Article 25: periodic review of placement/treatment
Article 34: protection from sexual exploitation
Article 38: armed conflict
Article 39: rehabilitative care for victims of torture, etc.
Article 40: juvenile justice

Protection of children affected by armed conflict

article 38

Text of Article 38

1. States Parties undertake to respect and to ensure respect for rules of international humanitarian law applicable to them in armed conflicts which are relevant to the child.

2. States Parties shall take all feasible measures to ensure that persons who have not attained the age of fifteen years do not take a direct part in hostilities.

3. States Parties shall refrain from recruiting any person who has not attained the age of fifteen years into their armed forces. In recruiting among those persons who have attained the age of fifteen years but who have not attained the age of eighteen years, States Parties shall endeavour to give priority to those who are oldest.

4. In accordance with their obligations under international humanitarian law to protect the civilian population in armed conflicts, States Parties shall take all feasible measures to ensure protection and care of children who are affected by an armed conflict.

Summary

Under article 38, States Parties are required to
- respect and ensure respect for rules of international humanitarian law applicable to them in armed conflicts (principally, the four Geneva Conventions and two additional Protocols);
- take all feasible measures to ensure that under-15-year-olds do not take a direct part in hostilities;
- refrain from recruiting under-15-year-olds into armed forces;
- give priority to the oldest in recruiting any 15- to 18-year-olds;
- take all feasible measures to ensure protection and care of children affected by an armed conflict.

The Committee on the Rights of the Child has emphasized that the effects of armed conflict on children should be considered in the framework of all the articles of the Convention on the Rights of the Child; that States should take measures to ensure the realization of the rights of all children in their jurisdiction in times of armed conflict; and that the principles of the Convention are not subject to derogation in times of armed conflict. In particular, it has stressed that it believes, in the light of the definition of the child and the principle of the best interests of the child, that no child under the age of 18 should be allowed to be involved in hostilities, either directly or indirectly, and that no child under 18 should be recruited into armed forces, either through conscription or voluntary enlistment.

In 1994, the Commission on Human Rights, encouraged by the Committee on the Rights of the Child, established a Working Group to draft an Optional Protocol to the Convention, in particular to raise the minimum age of involvement in hostilities and recruitment into armed forces to 18 years old (drafting is still proceeding in September 1997).

In 1996 a major study, proposed by the Committee, on the *Impact of Armed Conflict on Children*, by Ms Graça Machel, was presented to the General Assembly.

In its examination of States Parties' reports, the Committee has expressed grave concern to many States at the effects of armed conflict on children. ■

Extracts from
Committee on the Rights of the Child
Guidelines for Reports to be submitted by States Parties under the Convention

For full text of *Guidelines for Periodic Reports*, see Appendix 3, page 604.

Guidelines for Initial Reports

"Special protection measures

Under this section States Parties are requested to provide relevant information, including the principal legislative, judicial, administrative or other measures in force; factors and difficulties encountered and progress achieved in implementing the relevant provisions of the Convention; and implementation priorities and specific goals for the future in respect of:

Children in situations of emergency

...

(ii) Children in armed conflicts (article 38, including physical and psychological recovery and social reintegration (article 39);...".

(CRC/C/5, para. 23)

Guidelines for Periodic Reports

"VIII. SPECIAL PROTECTION MEASURES (arts. 22, 38, 39, 40, 37(b) - (d), 32-36)

A. Children in situations of emergency

2. Children in armed conflicts (art.38) including physical and psychological recovery and social reintegration (art.39)

*Please provide information on the measures adopted pursuant to **article 38**, including of a legislative, administrative and educational nature, to respect and ensure respect for the rules of international humanitarian law applicable to the State in armed conflicts which are relevant to the child. In this regard, reports should identify the relevant international conventions, instruments and other rules of humanitarian law applicable to the State and the measures adopted to enforce them, as well as to ensure their effective dissemination and appropriate training for professionals concerned.*

Please indicate all the measures taken pursuant to article 38, paragraph 2, including of a legislative, administrative or other nature, to ensure that persons who have not attained the age of 15 years do not take a direct part in hostilities. In this regard, reports should also indicate the measures adopted to ensure and protect the rights of the child during hostilities. Information should also be provided on any mechanism established to monitor this situation. When relevant, indication should also be given of the proportion of children participating in hostilities, including by age, gender and social and ethnic origin.

Please indicate the measures adopted pursuant to article 38, paragraph 3, including of a legislative and administrative nature, to ensure that no person who has not attained the age of 15 years is recruited into the armed forces, as well as to ensure that, in recruiting among those persons who have attained the age of 15 years but who have not attained the age of 18 years, priority is given to those who are oldest. In this regard, reports should also indicate any mechanisms established to monitor this situation, as well as the proportion of children being recruited or voluntarily enlisted into armed forces, including by age, gender, and social and ethnic origin.

Please provide information on all the measures adopted pursuant to article 38, paragraph 4, and in accordance with the State's obligations under international humanitarian law to protect the civilian population in armed conflicts, including measures of a legislative, administrative, budgetary and other nature, to ensure the protection and care of children who are affected by an armed conflict.

In this regard, please indicate the relevant international humanitarian law applicable to the State, the criteria used to assess the feasibility of the measures adopted, the steps taken to identify and address the specific situation of children within the civilian population and to ensure respect for and protection of their rights, the measures adopted to ensure that humanitarian assistance and relief programmes are promoted and put in place, including through the negotiation of special arrangements such as corridors of peace and days of tranquillity, as well as any relevant disaggregated data on the children concerned, including by age, gender, and national, social and ethnic origin. Where relevant, please also indicate the number of child casualties due to armed conflict, as well as the number of children displaced because of armed conflict.

When providing information on the implementation of article 38, please further indicate the respect ensured to the general principles of the Convention, namely non-discrimination, the best interests of the child, respect for the views of the child and the right to life, development and survival to the maximum extent.

*Please indicate all measures adopted pursuant to **article 39** to:*

Promote physical and psychological recovery and social reintegration of child victims of armed conflicts;

Ensure that such recovery and reintegration takes place in an environment which fosters the health, self-respect and dignity of the child.

In this regard, reports should provide information inter alia on:

The policies and programmes developed, including at the family and community levels, to address the physical and psychological effects of conflicts on children and to promote their reintegration in society;

The steps taken to ensure the demobilization of child soldiers and to prepare them to participate actively and responsibly in society;

The role played by education and vocational training;

The surveys and research undertaken;

The budget allocated for them (at the national, regional, local and where appropriate at the federal and provincial levels);

The number of children who received physical and/or psychological treatment as a consequence of armed conflict.

Information should also be provided on the progress achieved on the implementation of articles 38 and 39, on any difficulties encountered and targets set for the future."

(CRC/C/58, paras. 123-131. The following paragraphs of the *Guidelines for Periodic Reports* are also relevant to reporting under this article: 24, 119-122; for full text of *Guidelines*, see Appendix 3, page 604.)

International humanitarian law

The Committee has indicated that the relevant international humanitarian law, referred to in paragraphs 1 and 4 of article 38, includes the four Geneva Conventions, the two Additional Protocols, the Declaration on the Protection of Women and Children in Emergency and Armed Conflict, the Declaration on the Rights of the Child (in which Principle 8 states: "The child shall in all circumstances be among the first to receive protection and relief"), and the Convention on the Rights of the Child. Mention was also made of other United Nations standards, such as the International Covenant on Civil and Political Rights, and General Comment 17, adopted by the Human Rights Committee on article 24 of that Covenant, which recognizes the right of children to necessary protection. In its General Comment the Human Rights Committee emphasizes that "as individuals children benefit from all of the civil rights enunciated in the Covenant". It also "wishes to draw the attention of States Parties to the need to include in their reports information on measures adopted to ensure that children do not take a direct part in armed conflicts". It goes on to note that while the Covenant does not set an age at which a child attains majority, "... a State

Party cannot absolve itself from its obligations under the Covenant regarding persons under the age of 18, notwithstanding that they have reached the age of majority under domestic law." (Human Rights Committee, General Comment 17, HRI/GEN/1/Rev.2, p. 23)

During the drafting of the Convention on the Rights of the Child, there was a strong move both to ensure that its provisions did not in any way undermine existing standards in international humanitarian law (in line with General Assembly resolution 41/120, which urges member States, in developing new international standards, to give due consideration to the established international legal framework) and to extend protection up to the age of 18. The final version of article 38 was a compromise, and several representatives in the Working Group indicated that they could not join the consensus in adopting it because, while it was consistent with Additional Protocol I to the Geneva Conventions, it failed to extend to children in internal conflicts a level of protection equal to that recognized in Additional Protocol II (see opposite) and might thus be said to undermine existing standards of humanitarian law. But the chairman ruled that the text had been adopted by consensus (E/CN.4/1989/ 48, pp. 110-116, Detrick, p. 515; also E/CN.4/ 1989/48, pp. 5-8, Detrick, p. 630).

The study on the *Impact of Armed Conflict on Children* (see below, page 526) notes that the International Committee of the Red Cross, the International Federation for the Red Cross and the Red Crescent Societies and the National Societies have adopted the following as a full definition of international humanitarian law: "international rules, established by treaties or custom, which are specifically intended to solve humanitarian problems directly arising from international or non-international armed conflicts and which, for humanitarian reasons, limit the right of parties to a conflict to use the methods and means of warfare of their choice or protect persons and property that are, or may be, affected by conflict". The report notes that the Convention on the Rights of the Child provides "the most comprehensive and specific protection for children". It also mentions the relevance of the two International Covenants, and the Convention on the Elimination of All Forms of Discrimination against Women, and other specialist treaties covering such issues as torture, genocide and racial discrimination. The 1951 Convention relating to the Status of Refugees and its Protocol of 1967 (see article 22, page 281) provide basic standards for the protection of refugees in countries of asylum. Beyond this, there are various regional

instruments (A/51/306, paras. 211 (note 40), 226 et seq., and 222-225).

The Geneva Conventions and Additional Protocols

The four Geneva Conventions were adopted in 1949 at the Geneva Diplomatic Conference, sponsored by the International Red Cross: Geneva Convention No.1 for the Amelioration of the Condition of the Wounded and Sick in Armed Forces in the Field, 1949; Geneva Convention No.2 for the Amelioration of the Condition of Wounded, Sick and Shipwrecked Members of Armed Forces at Sea, 1949; Geneva Convention No.3 Relative to the Treatment of Prisoners of War, 1949; and Geneva Convention No.4 Relative to the Protection of Civilian Persons in Time of War, 1949.

Convention No.4 offers general protection to children as civilians and has been ratified, almost as universally as the Convention on the Rights of the Child, by 186 states (*Impact of Armed Conflict on Children*, A/51/306, para. 212). Article 3, common to all four Conventions, covers "armed conflict not of an international character occurring in the territory of one of the High Contracting Parties." Persons "taking no active part in the hostilities" must in all circumstances be treated humanely, and be protected from "violence to life and person", in particular from murder of all kinds, mutilation, cruel treatment and torture, hostage-taking, humiliating and degrading treatment, and so forth. The Conventions do not contain any minimum age for child participation in hostilities. Also under the Convention No. 4, children and pregnant women are among those for whom the Parties should endeavour to conclude local agreements to remove them from "besieged or encircled areas" (article 17); each State must allow the free passage of relief intended for children under the age of 15 and maternity cases (article 23); children under the age of 15 and mothers of children under 7 are among those who can be received into the hospital or safety zones established by the parties in an international armed conflict (article 38(5)); an occupying power must facilitate the proper working of institutions devoted to the care of children in occupied territories (article 50). (Other provisions relating to children are in articles 81 and 89).

In 1977, two Protocols Additional to the Conventions were adopted. Protocol I (ratified by 144 states by 1996), covering international armed conflicts, requires that the fighting parties distinguish at all times between combatants and civilians and that the only legal targets of attack should be military in nature. It covers all civilians, but two articles also offer specific protection to children. Article 77 – Protection of children – states:

"1. Children shall be the object of special respect and shall be protected from any form of indecent assault. The Parties to the conflict shall provide them with the care and aid they require, whether because of their age or for any other reason.

2. The Parties to the conflict shall take all feasible measures in order that children who have not attained the age of fifteen years do not take a direct part in hostilities and, in particular, they shall refrain from recruiting them into their armed forces. In recruiting among those persons who have attained the age of fifteen years but who have not attained the age of eighteen years, the Parties to the conflict shall endeavour to give priority to those who are oldest.

3. If, in exceptional cases, despite the provisions of paragraph 2, children who have not attained the age of fifteen years take a direct part in hostilities and fall into the power of an adverse Party, they shall continue to benefit from the special protection accorded by this Article, whether or not they are prisoners of war.

4. If arrested, detained or interned for reasons related to the armed conflict, children shall be held in quarters separate from the quarters of adults, except where families are accommodated as family units as provided in Article 75, paragraph 5.

5. The death penalty for an offence related to the armed conflict shall not be executed on persons who had not attained the age of eighteen years at the time the offence was committed."

Article 78 of Protocol 1 deals with the evacuation of children to another country; this should not take place except for compelling reasons, and the article establishes some of the terms under which any evacuation should take place (in relation to internal conflicts, evacuation of children is covered in Protocol II, article 4(3)(e) – see below).

Also in Protocol I, newborn babies and maternity cases are categorized with "wounded" and "sick", in need of respect and protection (article 8 (a)).

Article 4 of Protocol II (ratified by 136 states by 1996), which applies to non-international – that is internal – armed conflicts, includes a paragraph on protection of children, which requires that:

"3. Children shall be provided with the care and aid they require, and in particular:

(a) they shall receive an education, including religious and moral education, in keeping with

the wishes of their parents, or in the absence of parents, of those responsible for their care;

(b) all appropriate steps shall be taken to facilitate the reunion of families temporarily separated;

(c) children who have not attained the age of fifteen years shall neither be recruited in the armed forces or groups nor allowed to take part in hostilities;

(d) the special protection provided by this Article to children who have not attained the age of fifteen years shall remain applicable to them if they take a direct part in hostilities despite the provisions of subparagraph (c) and are captured;

(e) measures shall be taken, if necessary, and whenever possible with the consent of their parents or persons who by law or custom are primarily responsible for their care, to remove children temporarily from the area in which hostilities are taking place to a safer area within the country and ensure that they are accompanied by persons responsible for their safety and well-being."

Declaration on the Protection of Women and Children in Emergency and Armed Conflict

In 1974, the United Nations General Assembly adopted the Declaration on the Protection of Women and Children in Emergency and Armed Conflict (Res. 3318 (XXIX)). In its Preamble the General Assembly expresses its "deep concern over the sufferings of women and children belonging to the civilian population who in periods of emergency and armed conflict in the struggle for peace, self-determination, national liberation and independence are too often the victims of inhuman acts and consequently suffer serious harm..." The General Assembly is "conscious of its responsibility for the destiny of the rising generation and for the destiny of mothers, who play an important role in society, in the family and particularly in the upbringing of children. Bearing in mind the need to provide special protection of women and children belonging to the civilian population..." it called for strict observance of principles covering: protection from attacks and bombing and the use of chemical and bacteriological weapons; fulfilment of the Geneva Conventions and other international instruments; all efforts to spare women and children from the ravages of war; considering criminal all forms of repression and cruel and inhuman treatment of women and children; and that women and children finding themselves in circumstances of emergency or armed conflict must not be deprived of shelter, food, medical aid or other inalienable rights.

Committee's General Discussion on Children in armed conflicts

At its first session, September-October 1991, the Committee on the Rights of the Child decided to hold its first General Discussion on "Children in armed conflicts", enabling the Committee to make various comments that aid interpretation of article 38 and of the rest of the Convention in relation to armed conflict. In the Report on its second session, following the General Discussion, the Committee drew attention to the fact that

"in recent years, a growing number of conflicts are occurring (more than 150 since the Second World War) using more sophisticated and brutal weapons and fighting methods, affecting a growing number of civilians, particularly children".

The Committee went on to stress:

"the need to underline the complexity of the question of children in armed conflicts, which should not be simply reduced to the consideration of a single provision of the Convention, namely article 38",
and
"the need to ensure an effective protection of children in a period of armed conflict, in the overall framework of the realization of all the rights of the child, inherent to his or her dignity and essential to the full and harmonious development of his or her personality"
(Report on the second session, September-October 1992, CRC/C/10, pp. 20-21).

The Committee noted the various provisions that make up international humanitarian law relating to children in armed conflicts and the need always to apply norms most conducive to the realization of the rights of the child:

"It was pointed out that there are some situations in which children did not benefit from the protection of existing standards, as was very often the case in internal strife. There was therefore a need to consider a set of minimum humanitarian standards to be applicable in all situations to all children, without discrimination, in a period of armed conflict, thus filling any possible existing gaps.
"When basing the consideration of the question of children in armed conflict on the Convention itself, it was recalled that States Parties have undertaken to respect and ensure all the rights set forth therein to all children within their jurisdiction (art.2). States Parties have also made a commitment to adopt all appropriate measures in order to achieve such a purpose (art.4), and that, in all actions taken, the best interests of the child shall be a primary consideration (art.3). None of these

general provisions admits a derogation in time or war or emergency.

"It was further recalled that the Convention, under its article 41, invites States Parties to always apply the norms which are more conducive to the realization of the rights of the child, contained either in applicable international law or in national legislation. Finally, attention was drawn to the fact that States Parties may also make declarations when ratifying or acceding to the Convention, expressing their commitment before the international community to apply more conducive standards than those directly deriving from the Convention, namely by not recruiting children under 18 years of age into the armed forces."

The report went on to review general measures to prevent conflict, emphasizing education:

"...(a) Education in a spirit of understanding, solidarity and peace, as a general and continuous process, as reflected in article 29 of the Convention on the Rights of the Child;

(b) Education and training for the military and for groups working with and for children;

(c) Education and dissemination of information specifically for children.

"Attention was also drawn to the need for creating awareness of the political grounds for the existence of conflicts; such an attitude may contribute to the consideration of solutions of mediation or conciliation designed to prevent the conflict or attenuate its effects.

"Importance was also given to the question of arms expenditure, the sale of arms and the advisability of considering an adequate monitoring mechanism of this reality. As a general preventive measure, reference was also made to the prevention of child abuse and neglect, which could contribute to the prevention of future use of violence.

"Specific preventive measures designed to prevent the involvement of children in armed conflicts were also discussed: mention was made of the interdiction of recruitment into the armed forces under a certain age, as well as of the adoption of measures ensuring that children will not take part in hostilities or suffer their effects."

In relation to effective protection for children in situations of armed conflict, the report recalls the overall framework of the realization of the rights of the child, which should be ensured. Special reference was made in the Discussion to

"protecting the family environment; ensuring the provision of essential care and assistance; ensuring access to health, food and education; prohibiting torture, abuse or neglect; prohibiting the death penalty; and the need to preserve the children's cultural environment, as well as the need of protection in situations of

deprivation of liberty. Particular emphasis was also put on the need to ensure humanitarian assistance and relief and humanitarian access to children in situations of armed conflict. In this respect, special attention was paid to important measures, such as days of tranquillity and corridors of peace."

The Committee agreed on measures it could take and established a Working Group of members to consider:

- drafting more specific guidelines for the implementation of articles 38 and 39;
- the possibility of a preliminary general comment;
- drafting a set of recommendations;
- realization of general studies on some aspects of the problem;
- preliminary drafting of a future Optional Protocol to raise the age of recruitment to 18.

The Committee also proposed, in examining States Parties' reports, that it could:

- welcome declarations made by some States Parties that they would not recruit under-18-year-olds;
- emphasize the need for information on the legislation and practice of States Parties on the application of article 38;
- seek information under article 41 on whether the most conducive norms are applied, or encourage development of more protective provisions in national law;
- encourage States that allow recruitment under 18 to consider how this situation takes the best interests of the child as the primary consideration;
- emphasize and encourage all States to consider in continuous monitoring whether all necessary and appropriate measures have been adopted to ensure the full realization of the rights of the child to all children under their jurisdiction.

(Report on the second session, September-October 1992, CRC/C/10, para. 61 et seq.)

Recruitment of under-18-year-olds

The Committee is of the opinion that the Convention requires protection of all children under 18 from direct or indirect involvement in hostilities and that no under-18-year-olds should be recruited into armed forces, and it has proposed an Optional Protocol to the Convention to this effect (see below, page 523). As indicated previously (page 514), a dispute over the language of

Children "zones of peace"

In the Philippines, "the Special Protection Act declares children as 'Zones of peace'. This Act provides that children shall not be the object of attack, and shall be the object of special respect... Children are not to be recruited into the Armed Forces of the Philippines or into any armed group, not allowed to take part in the fighting and not to be used as guides, couriers or spies. In any *barangay* where armed conflict occurs, the *barangay* chairperson shall submit to the municipal social welfare and development officer the names of all children residing in the *barangay* within 24 hours of the start of the conflict. Delivery of basic social services is to be kept unhampered and the safety of service-providers ensured. Public infrastructures, such as schools and health facilities, are not to be utilized for military purposes.

"During any evacuation resulting from armed conflict, children are to be given priority... Measures shall be taken to ensure that children who are evacuated are accompanied by persons responsible for their safety and well-being. Wherever possible, members of the same family are to be housed in the same premises.

"In any case where a child is arrested for reasons related to armed conflict, he or she shall be entitled to separate detention from adults, immediate full legal assistance, immediate notice of arrest to the child's parents or guardians, and release on recognizance to the Department of Social Welfare and Development or any responsible member of the community within 24 hours..." (Philippines IR, paras. 201-203)

article 38 and the protection afforded to 15- to 18-year-olds took place in the Working Group which drafted the Convention.

Article 38 refers to recruitment rather than to conscription. Article 38, as drafted, permits the recruitment of under-18-year-olds, but conscription is not mentioned and should not form part of State law or practice. Compelling children, at any age, to join the armed forces would amount to a breach of article 35 (abduction) and article 32 (forced labour).

A number of States Parties made declarations on ratifying which expressed concern that article 38 did not prohibit the involvement in hostilities and the recruitment into armed forces of all under-18-year-olds. For example:

"The Principality of Andorra deplores the fact that the Convention on the Rights of the Child does not prohibit the use of children in armed conflicts. It also disagrees with the provisions of article 38, paragraphs 2 and 3, concerning the participation and recruitment of children from the age of 15."

"Concerning article 38 of the Convention, the Argentine Republic declares that it would have liked the Convention categorically to prohibit the use of children in armed conflicts; such a prohibition exists in its domestic law which, by virtue of article 41 of the Convention, it shall continue to apply in this regard."

"Austria will not make any use of the possibility provided for in article 38, paragraph 2, to determine an age limit of 15 years for taking part in hostilities as this rule is incompatible with article 3, paragraph 1, which determines that the best interests of the child shall be a primary consideration..." (also declarations from Colombia, Germany, Netherlands, Poland, Spain, Uruguay - CRC/C/2/Rev.5, pp. 11-34)

The Committee has welcomed such declarations:

"The Committee notes with satisfaction the declaration made by Spain at the time of its ratification of the Convention with regard to the provisions of paragraphs 2 and 3 of article 38 and the commitment of the State Party not to permit the recruitment and participation in armed conflict of persons below the age of 18 years." (Spain IRCO, Add.28, para. 3. See also Argentina IRCO, Add.35, para. 3; Germany IRCO, Add.43, para. 4; Uruguay IRCO, Add.62, para. 3)

The Committee has also applauded States' intention to improve protection in recruitment:

"... note is taken of the ... proposal to make military service voluntary as well as ensuring that it does not take place before the age of 18..." (Honduras IRCO, Add.24, para. 3)

The recruitment of child soldiers has been severely condemned by the Committee:

*"Of ... grave concern to the Committee are the numerous reported cases of forced and underage recruitment of child-soldiers...
"The Committee strongly recommends that the army of the State Party should fully refrain from recruiting underaged children, in the light of existing international human rights and humanitarian standards. Forced recruitment of children should also be in all cases abolished as well as their involvement in forced labour." (Myanmar IRCO, Add.69, paras. 22 and 42)*

In one other case in which it appeared under-18-year-olds could be recruited, it expressed concern:

"The Committee expresses its concern over the lack of clarity and apparent discrepancies contained in the law with regard to the definition of the child. The Committee notes that, although persons under 18 in Sweden do not enjoy full legal capacity, they may yet be subjected to military service and that a person aged 15 or over can be accepted in the Home Guard defence...

"With respect to the definition of the child, the Committee recommends that the State Party consider an approach which is more coherent and more closely reflects the general principles and the provisions of the Convention. In recognition of the spirit of article 38 of the Convention, steps might be taken to close the gap in the law which at present allows for the possibility of conscripting children under the age of 18 into the armed forces..." (Sweden IRCO, Add.2, paras. 8 and 11)

The *Guidelines for Periodic Reports* asks for information on "The steps taken to ensure the demobilization of child soldiers and to prepare them to participate actively and responsibly in society" (para. 130; see article 39, page 534).

The study on the *Impact of Armed Conflict on Children* notes that adults are increasingly recruiting children as soldiers. Children also serve armies in supporting roles, as cooks, porters, messengers and spies. Most are adolescents, though many child soldiers are 10 years old or younger: "While the majority are boys, girls also are recruited. The children most likely to become soldiers are those from impoverished and marginalized backgrounds and those who have become separated from their families." (paras. 34-35; the report provides a detailed commentary and proposals to end recruitment of child soldiers)

Principles concerning recruitment:
A seminar on prevention of recruitment of children into the armed forces and demobilization and social reintegration of child soldiers in Africa produced a set of principles in 1997 (the "Cape Town principles", adopted by participants in a seminar organized by UNICEF and the NGO Subgroup of the NGO Working Group on the Convention on the Rights of the Child). These propose (see box) that 18 should be the minimum age for any participation in hostilities and for all forms of recruitment into all armed forces and armed groups, and that the Optional Protocol to the Convention (see page 253) should be supported and ratified.

Training

In its Concluding Observations, the Committee has frequently recommended training for military

Proposals for the prevention of child recruitment

The following proposals arose from a 1997 seminar in Cape Town:

"Recruitment encompasses compulsory, forced and voluntary recruitment into any kind of regular or irregular armed force or armed group.

1. Establish 18 as the minimum age for any participation in hostilities and for all forms of recruitment into all armed forces and armed groups.

2. Governments should adopt and ratify the Optional Protocol to the Convention on the Rights of the Child, raising the minimum age from 15 to 18.

3. Governments should ratify and implement pertinent regional and international treaties and incorporate them into national law.

4. Governments should adopt national legislation on voluntary and compulsory recruitment with a minimum age of 18 years and should establish proper recruitment procedures and the means to enforce them. Those responsible for illegally recruiting children should be brought to justice.

5. A permanent International Criminal Court should be established whose jurisdiction would cover, *inter alia*, the illegal recruitment of children.

6. Written agreements between or with all parties to the conflict which include a commitment on the minimum age of recruitment should be concluded.

7. Monitoring, documentation and advocacy are fundamental to eliminating child recruitment and to informing programmes to this end. Community efforts to prevent recruitment should be developed and supported.

8. Programmes to prevent recruitment of children should be developed in response to the expressed needs and aspirations of the children.

9. In programmes for children, particular attention should be paid to those most at risk of recruitment: children in conflict zones, children (especially adolescents) separated from or without families, including children in institutions; other marginalized groups (e.g. street children, certain minorities, refugees and the internally displaced); economically and socially deprived children.

10. All efforts should be made to keep or reunite children with their families or to place them within a family structure.

11. Ensure birth registration, including for refugees and internally displaced children, and the provision of identity documents to all children, particularly those most at risk of recruitment.

12. Access to education, including secondary education and vocational training, should be promoted for *all* children, including refugee and internally displaced children.

13. Special protection measures are needed to prevent recruitment of children in camps for refugees and internally displaced persons.

14. The international community should recognize that children who leave their country of origin to avoid illegal recruitment or participation in hostilities are in need of international protection. Children who are not nationals of the country in which they are fighting are also in need of international protection.

15. Controls should be imposed on the manufacture and transfer of arms, especially small arms. No arms should be supplied to parties to an armed conflict who are recruiting children or allowing them to take part in hostilities."

A further section of the Principles covers "Demobilization" and "Return to family and community life".

Cape Town Principles on the prevention of recruitment of children into the armed forces and demobilization and social reintegration of child soldiers in Africa, adopted by participants in the Symposium organized by UNICEF in cooperation with the NGO Subgroup of the NGO Working Group on the Convention on the Rights of the Child, Cape Town, 30 April 1997.

personnel, including United Nations peace-keeping forces, among others, in the principles and provisions of the Convention:

"Similarly, training about the Convention should be incorporated into the curricula of professionals working with or for children, including teachers, social workers, law enforcement officials, judicial personnel and personnel of the Italian contingents of the United Nations peace-keeping forces." (Italy IRCO, Add.41, para. 15)

Prosecution for war crimes

In one case, the Committee has welcomed the intention of a State Party government to prosecute those involved in crimes against the civilian population during armed conflict:

"The Committee welcomes the intentions expressed by the Government to prosecute people who committed crimes against the civilian population, including children, during and after 'Operation Storm' in August 1995 in the Krajina area and to provide safe conditions for returnees." (Croatia IRCO, Add.52, para. 9)

Various relevant international agencies, including the International Committee for the Red Cross, have proposed that the recruitment of under-15-year-olds should be termed an offence against international humanitarian law (the International Committee has compiled a list of offences that could fall under the jurisdiction of the proposed International Criminal Court).

Anti-personnel mines

The Committee and other bodies have noted the devastating effects that anti-personnel landmines have had on children, and congratulated States that have aided the international campaign against them:

"The Committee also notes the significant contribution being made by the State Party to the international campaign addressing the issue of the hazardous impact of anti-personnel landmines on the civilian population and, in particular, on children." (France IRCO, Add.20, para. 10)

Committee members have frequently questioned States Parties on whether they have taken action to prevent the production, export and use of landmines. For example, it was raised during consideration of Belgium's Initial Report. A Government representative responded: "A moratorium existed on the export of landmines. The European Union had recently informed the United Nations that it would also adopt a moratorium on the export of such weapons. Belgian legislation

was at the forefront because it prohibited the production and export of mines." (Belgium SR.224, para. 61)

The study on the *Impact of Armed Conflict on Children* supports a total ban on anti-personnel mines. It indicates that the use of landmines is regulated by Protocol II of the Convention on Prohibitions or Restrictions on the Use of Certain Conventional Weapons Which May Be Deemed to Be Excessively Injurious or to Have Indiscriminate Effects; Protocol II was reviewed during 1994-1996. In the view of the study, current legal protection "falls far short of even the bare minimum needed to protect children and their families." The study notes that: "Many legal experts believe that landmines are already an illegal weapon under international law and should be prohibited because they counter two basic principles of humanitarian law. First, the principle of distinction holds that attacks may only be directed against military objectives. Landmines do not distinguish between military and civilian targets. Second, the principle of unnecessary suffering holds that, even if an attack is directed against a legitimate military objective, the attack is not lawful if it can result in excessive injury or suffering to civilians. Thus, the military utility of a weapon must outweigh its impact on civil society, and the long destructive life of a landmine is clearly greater than any immediate utility. These principles apply to all States as part of customary international law".

The study states: "Children in at least 68 countries live amid the contamination of more than 110 million landmines. Added to this number are millions of items of unexploded ordnance, bombs, shells and grenades that failed to detonate on impact. Like landmines, unexploded ordnance are weapons deemed to have indiscriminate effects, triggered by innocent and unsuspecting passers-by." More than 40 countries have now stated that they are in favour of banning landmines: "Some have already taken concrete steps to ban the use, production and trade of the weapons and have begun to destroy their stocks. The expert urges that all States follow the lead of countries like Belgium and enact comprehensive national legislation to ban landmines."

Among the study's recommendations are that Governments should immediately enact comprehensive national legislation to ban the production, use, trade and stockpiling of landmines. Governments should support the campaign for a worldwide ban, at the very least on anti-personnel mines, at the next review conference for the Convention on Conventional Weapons in 2001. And in reports to the Committee on the Rights of the Child, States Parties, where relevant, should report on progress in enacting comprehensive legislation, on measures being taken in mine clearance and in programmes to promote children's awareness of landmines and to rehabilitate those who have been injured (A/51/306, para. 126).

In October 1996, the Canadian Government initiated what has been labelled "The Ottawa process", at an international conference in Ottawa, inviting all Governments to return to Ottawa in December 1997 to sign a legally binding treaty banning anti-personnel landmines.

Preparatory meetings were held in Vienna, Bonn and Brussels during the Spring of 1997, and at a diplomatic conference in Oslo in September 1997, 89 Governments agreed on a draft Convention - "Convention on the Prohibition of the Use, Stockpiling, Production and Transfer of Anti-personnel Mines and on their Destruction."

The Treaty opens for signature in Ottawa on 3 December 1997. Over 100 Governments had by October 1997 indicated their willingness to accept the Convention, which enters into force after 40 ratifications. The draft Convention's most significant provisions are:

● a complete prohibition on the use, stockpiling, production and transfer of anti-personnel mines (APMs);

● an exception for the continued use of anti-vehicle mines equipped with anti-handling devices;

● an exception for the continued use and stockpiling of APMs for training in mine clearance and related activities;

● stockpiled APMs to be destroyed within four years of entry into force;

● APMs within minefields to be cleared within 10 years of entry into force (States Parties may, however, be granted an extension of the time period, with an additional 10 years);

● an obligation to report total numbers of stockpiled APMs, location of minefields, etc.;

● States Parties in a position to do so to provide assistance with mine clearance, rehabilitation of mine victims, etc.;

● a simple verification procedure, including the possibility of sending out fact-finding missions in cases of suspected violations of the Convention."

In December 1996, the United Nations General Assembly adopted a resolution with 156 countries supporting, none against and 10 abstentions, urging Governments to "pursue vigorously" an international agreement to ban anti-personnel landmines (A/C.1/51/L.46).

Results of armed conflict

During its examination of States Parties' reports, the Committee has frequently had cause to comment at the direct and indirect effects of armed conflict on children. For example:

"The Committee expresses concern as to the effects of armed conflict on children, including the provision of humanitarian assistance and relief and protection of children in situations of armed conflict. In emergency situations, all parties involved should do their utmost to facilitate humanitarian assistance to protect the lives of children...

"The Committee recognizes that natural and man-made disasters have had a negative impact on efforts by the State Party to ensure full implementation of the Convention. In this regard, the Committee notes the problems caused by civil war in the south of the Sudan and that the different groups involved in this conflict have often disregarded the best interests of the child." (Sudan Prelim. Obs., Add.6, para. 9 and Sudan IRCO, Add.10, para. 8)

"The Committee notes that political violence and terrorism have had a considerable negative impact on the situation of children in Peru. Many children have been subjected to various forms of violations and have been obliged to flee areas affected by such violence.

"The Committee expresses its deep concern at the continued violence which has already caused thousands of killings, disappearances and displacements of children and parents. It is therefore necessary that the Peruvian Government and Peruvian society adopt an urgent, effective and fair response to protect the rights of the child." (Peru IRCO, Add.8, paras. 5 and 7)

"The Committee is alarmed at the large number of children who have been abandoned, displaced or who have become orphans as a result of the armed conflict, as well as those who, in order to survive, are forced to live and work in the street...

"In relation to the adverse impact of the internal conflict on children who live in exceptionally difficult situations, the Committee wishes to receive precise information with regard to rehabilitation programmes for affected children and the progress of such programmes, as well as statistical data with regard to displaced children within the country." (El Salvador IRCO, Add.9, paras. 11 and 16)

"The Committee further recognizes the difficulties arising from political instability in a period of democratization, including the adverse effects of the armed conflict on children." (Philippines IRCO, Add.29, para. 6)

article 38

The reality of war

Lebanon's Initial Report, following a detailed description of legislative protection of the "sacred" right to life and maximum survival and development, comments: "In effect, all the laws pertaining to the protection of the child and his/her survival were not able to protect children from bullets, rockets and bombs that killed, maimed, orphaned and traumatized many of them for a period of 16 years."

The Initial Report indicates that the war "has left many social ills that are overwhelming. The housing situation, the electricity cuts, the shortage of water supply, the lack of schools, the high inflation rate, the displacement of families, the high rate of pollution, the lack of town planning that does not leave any breathing or playing space for children, the archaic curricula that overburden children, and many other social ills could be considered forms of exploitation..." (Lebanon IR, paras. 22 and 150)

Yemen's Initial Report catalogues the effects on children of armed conflict, noting the "extremely costly" loss of life and equipment, and the use of public funds for military purposes, "which should have been spent on development and on repairing the economic infrastructure". Particular adverse effects of the internal conflict included:

- an increase in the number of injured and disabled children;
- a rise in the number of beggars and homeless persons;
- a rise in the number of school drop-outs in order to meet basic needs;
- a rise in the number of child deaths;
- an increase in the number of children employed before adulthood. (Yemen IR, para. 41)

"The Committee takes note of the difficult economic and social situation of Sri Lanka, particularly due to the adverse effects of structural adjustment measures and the ongoing civil armed conflict in the north and east regions of the country which drains national resources. Eight of the 25 provinces of the country are affected by the conflict which during the last 12 years has taken the lives of 30,000 people and currently has an impact on over half a million children.

"The Committee is seriously preoccupied by the large number of children affected by the armed conflict and especially those who have been displaced and those who have become orphans as a result of the war. The Committee is also worried about the hazardous provision of health services in areas affected by the armed conflict. The Committee notes with regret that the Initial Report of Sri Lanka did not give comprehensive information on the effect of armed conflict on children, their involvement in the armed forces and the way the authorities handle child soldiers prisoners of war.

"With regard to the traumatic impact on children of the civil armed conflict in Sri Lanka, the Committee recommends that, in the light of article 44, paragraph 4, of the Convention, additional information be submitted to the Committee within two years about the effects of the armed conflict on children, their participation in combat and the way authorities handle child soldiers prisoners of war." (Sri Lanka IRCO, Add.40, paras. 6, 24 and 44)

"Although the State Party has not been the theatre of war, the consequences of hostilities in the neighbouring territories has had a severe impact on the population.

"Such consequences of the war on the territory of the former Yugoslavia, combined with the realities of sanctions seem to have led to a worsening of the indicators of the health and education situation of the children of the Federal Republic, including lower immunization coverage, more nutrition-related disorders and illnesses, and an increase in the number of children suffering from mild and serious mental disorders. The sanctions against the Federal Republic may have led to the isolation of professionals dealing with the rights of the child." (Federal Republic of Yugoslavia IRCO, Add.49, paras. 3 and 5)

"The Committee also notes the major problems experienced as a consequence of war, which has borne a severe impact on the population, including children, leading to heavy casualties, long-lasting physical, emotional and psychological effects, as well as the disruption of some basic services. It takes special note of an unknown number of children who have suffered the most fundamental violations of their right to life, and the existence of a large population of refugees and displaced persons, exceeding a half million, who are being attended to by international aid." (Croatia IRCO, Add.52, para. 11)

"The Committee recommends that relevant international agencies and institutions, as well as other Governments, develop cooperation with Lebanese authorities and voluntary organizations, in the reconstruction effort after the many years of war devastation. Displaced persons and refugees should be given priority in such international cooperation." (Lebanon IRCO, Add.54, para. 45)

"Over 30 years of armed conflict in the country have left a legacy of human rights violations, impunity and a climate of fear and intimidation which hampers the confidence of the population in the ability of procedures and mechanisms to ensure respect for human rights." (Guatemala IRCO, Add.58, para. 7)

Armed conflicts cause population movements. People flee in large numbers, becoming refugees or internally displaced people. The study on the *Impact of Armed Conflict on Children* suggests that "at least half of all refugees and displaced people are children. At a crucial and vulnerable time in their lives, they have been brutally uprooted and exposed to danger and insecurity. In the course of displacement, millions of children have been separated from their families, physically abused, exploited and abducted into military groups, or they have perished from hunger and disease" (A/51/306, paras. 63-66). Article 22 of the Convention covers the particular rights of refugee children (see page 281).

Children affected by armed conflict are often also victims of sexual abuse and exploitation: "Rape poses a continual threat to women and girls during armed conflict, as do other forms of gender-based violence, including prostitution, sexual humiliation and mutilation, trafficking and domestic violence..." (A/51/306, para. 91, et seq.; the study also provides detailed recommendations for preventing sexual exploitation and gender-based violence; for further discussion see article 34, page 460).

The Special Rapporteur of the Commission on Human Rights on the situation of systematic rape, sexual slavery and slavery-like practices during periods of armed conflict has also drawn attention to the particular threat of sexual violence faced by young girls in situations of armed conflict (E/CN.4/Sub.2/1996/26, 16 July 1996).

Optional Protocol to the Convention on involvement of children in armed conflicts

In its third session in January 1993 the Committee agreed to prepare a preliminary draft of an Optional Protocol to the Convention, raising to 18 the age mentioned in article 38 of the Convention:

"In this framework, the Committee encouraged States Parties to give consideration to the adoption of possible measures aimed at raising the age mentioned in article 38 to 18 years."

The preliminary draft begins: "Article 1: States Parties shall take all feasible measures to ensure that persons who have not attained the age of eighteen years do not take part in hostilities; Article 2: States Parties shall refrain from recruiting any person who has not attained the age of eighteen years into their armed forces". The draft substitutes these provisions for paragraphs 2 and 3 of article 38 (Report on the third session, January 1993, CRC/C/16, Preliminary Draft Optional Protocol on Involvement of Children in Armed Conflicts, Annex VII, p. 59).

During its sixth session, the Committee welcomed the decision of the Commission on Human Rights to establish an open-ended Working Group to elaborate as a matter of priority the draft Optional Protocol, using the Committee's preliminary draft as a basis for discussions (Report on the sixth session, April 1994, CRC/C/29, p. 3). The Committee submitted further comments to the Working Group in January 1996. The Committee noted that the recent International Conference of the Red Cross and Red Crescent Movement had recommended by consensus that parties to conflicts refrain from arming children under the age of 18 and take every feasible step to ensure that children under the age of 18 do not take part in hostilities.

The Committee commented:

"In the view of the Committee, the involvement in hostilities of persons who have not attained the age of 18 is harmful for them physically and psychologically, and affects the full enjoyment of their fundamental rights. For this reason, it is the belief of the Committee that persons below 18 should never be involved in hostilities. In fact, participation in armed conflicts, either of a direct or indirect nature, raises serious risks for the life of children and hampers their harmonious development and the realization of the rights which are inherent to their human dignity including the rights to a family environment, to education and health, to a nationality, or not to be subject to ill-treatment or exploitation. It is important to recognize that in a situation of emergency, it is very difficult to draw the line between what is to be considered direct and indirect participation. Risks encountered and fundamental rights denied are similar in both cases, and any situation undermining respect for the rights of the child should be clearly avoided. For this reason, we are convinced that a clear prohibition of participation in hostilities of persons below the age of 18, either directly or indirectly, should be reflected in the Optional Protocol.

"The Committee also believes that, in order to ensure the full realization of children's rights as recognized by the Convention, States Parties should not recruit into their armed forces persons below the age of 18. The same rule

should apply as a matter of principle to voluntary enlistment. Reality shows that emergency situations often pave the way for the instrumentalization of children, and lead to great risks for them. For this reason, voluntary enlistment in the armed forces should never be used as an excuse to allow for the possible direct or indirect participation in hostilities of persons below the age of 18. Even in those areas where voluntary enlistment would be accepted by States, the training of such persons should incorporate and pay due regard to education on humanitarian and human rights, in the light of the Convention on the Rights of the Child and in particular of the provisions of articles 28, 29 and 42.

"In the same spirit, in relation to situations where recruitment, enrolment or enlistment of children below 18 would be made by armed groups, it might be preferable to have a child-centred approach stressing that no child should be used or allowed to participate directly or indirectly in hostilities..." (Report on the eleventh session, January 1996, CRC/C/50, pp. 42-43)

The Committee continued to press these points in subsequent comments to the Working Group (see, for example, E/CN.4/1997/WG.13/2/Add.1, p. 3).

In her study on the *Impact of Armed Conflict on Children*, Ms Graça Machel states: "While the Convention on the Rights of the Child offers comprehensive protection to children, it needs strengthening with respect to the participation of children in armed conflict. The Committee on the Rights of the Child has recognized the importance of raising the minimum age of recruitment to 18 years..." The report notes that the scope of the draft text of the Optional Protocol has been significantly broadened from the preliminary draft prepared by the Committee "to include articles on non-state entities, on rehabilitation and social reintegration of child victims of armed conflicts, and on a procedure of confidential enquiries by the Committee on the Rights of the Child. Despite the progress that has been made, there continues to be resistance on the issue of voluntary recruitment and on distinguishing between direct and indirect participation. The argument that the age of recruitment is merely a technical matter to be decided by individual Governments fails to take into account the fact that effective protection of children from the impact of armed conflict requires an unqualified legal and moral commitment which acknowledges that children have no part in armed conflict." (A/51/306, para. 231)

The report of the January 1997 meeting of the Working Group provides statements made by members of the Committee on the Rights of the Child on behalf of the Committee:

"... the Committee reiterated that it attached particular importance to the exercise of drafting an Optional Protocol to the Convention on the Rights of the Child on the involvement of children in armed conflicts, in view of the decisive impact such a Protocol would have on the protection of children's rights contained in the Convention... The Committee took the opportunity to reaffirm its position in relation to the different draft provisions under discussion by the working group and emphasized what it considered to be the most important elements. These were: that persons below the age of 18 years should never be allowed to be involved in hostilities, either directly or indirectly, as such involvement was physically and psychologically harmful to children and affected the full enjoyment of their fundamental rights; that persons below the age of 18 should neither be recruited on an involuntary basis nor allowed to enlist as volunteers into the armed forces of States Parties or non-governmental armed groups; that even in situations where voluntary enlistment would be accepted by States, training of such persons should incorporate and pay due regard to education on human rights and humanitarian law; and that the Optional Protocol should not admit any reservations in view of its aim, which was to allow States Parties to the Convention on the Rights of the Child which were in a position to do so, to clearly commit themselves not to recruit children below 18 years of age or allow their participation in hostilities."

The report of the Working Group indicates that clarification was sought about the Committee's comments on the importance of including in the Optional Protocol an article on recruitment of minors by non-governmental armed groups. Another question was directed at the Committee about the situation of children attending military schools:

"In answer, it was stated that in some 28 ongoing situations of armed conflict, persons below the age of 18 were being used heavily by non-governmental groups in hostilities, both directly and indirectly. It was, therefore, most important that the Optional Protocol should address the issue, obliging States Parties to take all possible steps to prevent the recruitment of children by such insurgent groups in their territory. It was also recommended that the terminology of the Optional Protocol should not go beyond that contained in the Protocol II Additional to the 1949 Geneva Conventions. With regard to military schools, the Committee felt that such institutions should be supervised by the Ministry of Education rather than by the Ministry of Defence, and that provisions protecting stu-

dents below the age of 18 from being used as tools in armed conflict should be included in the new instrument. In any case, the Committee warned that in emergency situations there was often a temptation to use students as soldiers." (ECN.4/1997/WG.13/CRP.1/Rev.1)

The training of children in military schools is a part of their education and should therefore adhere to the aims for education set out in article 29, including "The preparation of the child for responsible life in a free society, in the spirit of understanding, peace, tolerance, equality of sexes, and friendship among all peoples..." (see article 29, page 391) There is a risk that education in military schools could be a brutalising experience: such institutions must respect all the principles and provisions of the Convention, ensuring that the child is protected from all forms of physical and mental violence.

World Summit for Children

World leaders at the World Summit for Children (New York, 1990) committed themselves to "...work carefully to protect children from the scourge of war and to take measures to prevent further armed conflicts, in order to give children everywhere a peaceful and secure future. We will promote the values of peace, understanding and dialogue in the education of children. The essential needs of children must be protected even in times of war and in violence-ridden areas. We ask that periods of tranquillity and special relief cor-

ridors be observed for the benefit of children, where war and violence are still taking place." (The World Summit Declaration, para. 20(8))

In its Plan of Action, one of the major goals for survival, protection and development of children by the year 2000 is: "(g) Protection of children in especially difficult circumstances, particularly in situations of armed conflict." The Plan promotes measures like "days of tranquillity" and "corridors of peace", and concludes that "To build the foundation for a peaceful world where violence and war will cease to be acceptable means for settling disputes and conflicts, children's education should inculcate the values of peace, tolerance, understanding and dialogue." (Plan of Action, paras. 5 and 25)

World Conference on Human Rights:

The Committee on the Rights of the Child, in its third session, proposed a resolution, for consideration at the World Conference on Human Rights (held in Vienna in June 1993), to urge all States and all parties involved in armed conflicts to take all necessary measures to ensure that children are adequately protected from all kinds of negative effects of armed conflicts and can effectively enjoy their rights. (Report on the third session, January 1993, CRC/C/16, recommendation to the General Assembly, Annex V, p. 56)

The Vienna Declaration and Programme of Action, which resulted from the Conference, strongly supported the proposal for a special study to improve the protection of children in armed conflicts: "Humanitarian norms should be

---

The Graça Machel study: a "comprehensive agenda for action"

A message from the United Nations Secretary General, introducing the study, states: "In the study, the expert proposes the elements of a comprehensive agenda for action by Member States and the international community to improve the protection and care of children in conflict situations, and to prevent these conflicts from occurring. The study demonstrates the centrality of these issues to the international human rights, peace and security and development agendas, and should serve to promote urgent and resolute action on the part of the international community to redress the plight of children affected by armed conflicts."

In its introduction, the study outlines "The attack on children". During 1995, 30 major armed conflicts raged in different locations, all of them within States, between factions split along ethnic, religious or cultural lines. "In the past decade, an estimated two million children have been killed in armed conflict. Three times as many have been seriously injured or permanently disabled, many of them maimed by landmines. Countless others have been forced to witness or even to take part in horrifying acts of violence. These statistics are shocking enough, but more chilling is the conclusion to be drawn from them: more and more of the world is being sucked into a desolate moral vacuum. This is a space devoid of the most basic human values; a space in which children are slaughtered, raped and maimed; a space in which children are exploited as soldiers; a space in which children are starved and exposed to extreme brutality. Such unregulated terror and violence speak of deliberate victimization. There are few further depths to which humanity can sink." (A/51/306, paras. 2 and 3)

implemented and measures taken in order to protect and facilitate assistance to children in war zones. Measures should include protection for children against indiscriminate use of all weapons of war, especially anti-personnel mines. The need for aftercare and rehabilitation of children traumatized by war must be addressed urgently. The Conference calls on the Committee on the Rights of the Child to study the question of raising the minimum age of recruitment into armed forces." (A/CONF.157/23, para. 50)

Study on Impact of Armed Conflict on Children

In its third session, the Committee recommended to the General Assembly that it should request the Secretary General to undertake a study "on ways and means of improving the protection of children from the adverse affect of armed conflicts" (Report on the third Session, January 1993, CRC/C/16, p. 4, and Annex VI, p. 58). It was this proposal that led to the appointment by the Secretary-General of Ms. Graça Machel to carry out the study (pursuant to General Assembly resolution 48/157).

The study was published in August 1996 and presented to the fifty-first session of the General Assembly.

In September 1997 the Secretary-General of the United Nations appointed as his Special Representative for children and armed conflict Mr. Olara Otunnu for a period of three years. He is mandated to work closely with the Committee on the Rights of the Child, and to report annually to the General Assembly and the Commission on Human Rights.

The study and its annexes provide detailed discussion and recommendations on "Mitigating the impact of armed conflict on children"; "Relevance and adequacy of existing standards for the protection of children"; "Reconstruction and reconciliation"; "Conflict prevention" and "Implementation mechanisms".

In relation to implementation of international standards, the study proposes:

- that all States that have not done so should become Parties to the Convention on the Rights of the Child immediately;

- all Governments should adopt measures to effectively implement the Convention, the Geneva Conventions and their Additional Protocols and the 1951 Convention relating to the Status of Refugees and its Protocol;

- Governments must train and educate the judiciary, police, security personnel and armed forces, especially those participating in peacekeeping operations, in humanitarian and human rights law;

- humanitarian organizations should similarly train their staff. All international bodies working in conflict zones should establish procedures for prompt, confidential and objective reporting of violations that come to their attention;

- humanitarian organizations should assist Governments in educating children about their rights;

- humanitarian agencies and organizations should seek to reach signed agreements with non-state entities, committing them to abide by humanitarian and human rights law;

- civil society should actively disseminate humanitarian and human rights law and engage in advocacy, reporting and monitoring of infringements of children's rights;

- building on existing guidelines, UNICEF should develop more comprehensive guidelines on the protection and care of children in conflict situations;

- the Committee on the Rights of the Child should be encouraged to include in its report to the General Assembly specific information on the measures adopted by States Parties to protect children in situations of armed conflict.

(A/51/306, para. 240)

Implementation Checklist

article **38**

● *General measures of implementation*

Have appropriate general measures of implementation been taken in relation to article 38, including

☐ identification and coordination of the responsible departments and agencies at all levels of government (article 38 is relevant to **departments of defence, foreign affairs, home affairs, education, social welfare**)?

☐ identification of relevant non-governmental organizations/civil society partners?

☐ a comprehensive review to ensure that all legislation, policy and practice is compatible with the article, for all children in all parts of the jurisdiction?

☐ adoption of a strategy to secure full implementation

   ☐ which includes where necessary the identification of goals and indicators of progress?

   ☐ which does not affect any provisions which are more conducive to the rights of the child?

   ☐ which recognizes other relevant international standards?

☐ which involves where necessary international cooperation?
(Such measures may be part of an overall governmental strategy for implementing the Convention as a whole).

☐ budgetary analysis and allocation of necessary resources?

☐ development of mechanisms for monitoring and evaluation?

☐ making the implications of article 38 widely known to adults and children?

☐ development of appropriate training and awareness-raising (in relation to article 38 likely to include training for **all members of armed forces, including peacekeeping forces, social workers, aid workers, psychologists and health workers**)?

● *Specific issues in implementing article 38*

Has the State ratified/acceded to

   ☐ the four Geneva Conventions of 1949?

   ☐ Additional Protocol I?

   ☐ Additional Protocol II?

   ☐ Other international instruments relevant to the protection of children affected by armed conflict?

☐ Has the State taken appropriate steps to ensure that children under the age of 15 do not take a direct part in hostilities?

☐ Has the State taken appropriate steps to ensure that children under the age of 18 do not take a direct or indirect part in hostilities?

☐ Has the State ensured that no child under the age of 18 is conscripted into the armed forces?

Has the State adopted legislation and other appropriate measures

   ☐ to prevent the recruitment of children who have not attained the age of 15 into the armed forces?

☐ to give priority to the oldest in recruiting any child under the age of 18?

☐ to prevent the recruitment of any child under 18 into the armed forces?

☐ Has the State taken measures to prohibit and prevent the recruitment of any child under the age of 18 by non-government forces?

☐ Has the State ensured that military schools do not recruit students below the age of 18?

☐ Has the State ensured that any military schools which do recruit students below the age of 18 are supervised by the ministry of education rather than of defence?

☐ Has the State ensured that military schools respect the aims for education set out in article 29 of the Convention?

☐ Has the State taken all feasible measures to ensure protection and care of all children affected by armed conflict?

☐ Has the State reviewed and taken appropriate action on the recommendations of the study on the *Impact of Armed Conflict on Children?*

☐ In relation to article 38(4) of the Convention, has the State taken national, bilateral and international action to protect children from anti-personnel mines?

☐ Has the State signified its intention to ratify the Optional Protocol to the Convention on involvement of children in armed conflicts?

Reminder : **The Convention is indivisible and its articles are interdependent. Article 38 should not be considered in isolation.**

Particular regard should be paid to:
The general principles

Article 2: all rights to be recognized for each child in jurisdiction without discrimination on any ground

Article 3(1): the best interests of the child to be a primary consideration in all actions concerning children

Article 6: right to life and maximum possible survival and development

Article 12: respect for the child's views in all matters affecting the child; opportunity to be heard in any judicial or administrative proceedings affecting the child

Closely related articles

Articles whose implementation is related to that of article 38 include:

Article 19: protection from all forms of violence

Article 22: refugee children

Article 29: aims of education

Article 34: protection from sexual exploitation

Article 35: abduction and trafficking

Article 37: protection from torture, cruel inhuman or degrading treatment or punishment

Article 39: rehabilitative care for victims of armed conflict

Rehabilitation of child victims

Text of Article 39

States Parties shall take all appropriate measures to promote physical and psychological recovery and social reintegration of a child victim of: any form of neglect, exploitation, or abuse; torture or any other form of cruel, inhuman or degrading treatment or punishment; or armed conflicts. Such recovery and reintegration shall take place in an environment which fosters the health, self-respect and dignity of the child.

Summary

Article 39 requires measures to help child victims of

● any form of violence, neglect, exploitation or abuse (for example, as detailed in articles 19, 32, 33, 34, 35, 36);

● torture or any other form of cruel, inhuman or degrading treatment or punishment (article 37);

● armed conflicts (article 38).

The article provides that recovery and reintegration must take place in an environment that fosters the health, self-respect and dignity of the child. The general principles of the Convention on the Rights of the Child require that such measures must be available without discrimination to all child victims; the best interests of the child must be a primary consideration; the maximum survival and development of the child must be ensured; and the views of the child should be respected – for example in planning and implementing programmes, including in individual cases. Other rights in the Convention, to health and health care services (article 24), to education (article 28) and to an adequate standard of living (article 27) are relevant to this article's implementation, as is the obligation under article 20 to provide special care and assistance to children temporarily or permanently deprived of their family environment.

In Concluding Observations on States Parties' reports, the Committee has frequently grouped article 39 with articles 37 and 40. It has indicated that measures are required under article 39 for all children who are victims of the treatment or punishment prohibited in article 37 whether it occurs within the family, in institutions or the community. Article 40(1) requires that all children who come within the scope of the juvenile justice system ("alleged as, accused of, or recognized as having infringed the penal law") must be treated in a manner consistent with "promoting the child's reintegration and the child's assuming a constructive role in society". Article 19, requiring the protection of children from all forms of physical or mental violence, also mentions treatment and follow-up. Article 25 provides children who have been placed for care, protection or treatment – including for purposes of rehabilitation – with a right to a periodic review.

In its comments on States Parties' Initial Reports, the Committee has indicated that the wording of article 39 requires consideration of a wide range of potential child victims. In addition to the situations specifically mentioned in article 39, the Committee has referred to issues such as victims of violence, refugee children (article 22), child labour and forced labour (article 32), drug abuse and trafficking (article 33), family conflict and the sale and trafficking of children (article 35), and children involved in the system of juvenile justice (articles 37 and 40). ∎

Extracts from
Committee on the Rights of the Child
Guidelines for Reports to be submitted by States Parties under the Convention

For full text of *Guidelines for Periodic Reports*, see Appendix 3, page 604.

Guidelines for Initial Reports

"Special protection measures

Under this section, States Parties are requested to provide relevant information, including the principal legislative, judicial, administrative or other measures in force; factors and difficulties encountered and progress achieved in implementing the relevant provisions of the Convention; and implementation priorities and specific goals for the future in respect of:

(a) Children in situations of emergency;

    (i) Refugee children (article 22);

    (ii) Children in armed conflicts (article 38), including physical and psychological recovery and social reintegration (article 39);

    ...".

(b) Children in conflict with the law.

    ...

    (iv) Physical and psychological recovery and social integration (article 39).

(c) Children in situations of exploitation including physical and psychological recovery and social reintegration (article 39)

    (i) Economic exploitation, including child labour (article 32);

    (ii) Drug abuse (article 33);

    (iii) Sexual exploitation and sexual abuse (article 34);

    (iv) Other forms of exploitation (article 36);

    (v) Sale, trafficking and abduction (article 35).

    ...

Additionally, States Parties are encouraged to provide specific statistical information and indicators relevant to the children covered by paragraph 23.

(CRC/C/5, paras. 23-24)

Guidelines for Periodic Reports

"VIII. SPECIAL PROTECTION MEASURES (arts. 22, 38, 39, 40, 37(b)-(d), 32-36)

Physical and psychological recovery and social reintegration of the child (art. 39)

Please provide information on all measures taken pursuant to article 39 and in the light of article 40, paragraph 1, to promote the physical and psychological recovery and social reintegration of the child involved with the system of the administration of juvenile justice, and to ensure that such recovery and reintegration take place in an environment which fosters the health, self-respect and dignity of the child.

Reports should also identify, inter alia, the mechanisms established and the programmes and activities developed for that purpose, as well as the education and vocational training

Rehabilitating child victims

The Committee on the Rights of the Child has frequently commented on the lack of adequate measures to rehabilitate child victims. For example:

"... special programmes should be set up to promote physical and psychological recovery and social reintegration of children victims of any form of neglect, abuse, exploitation, torture or ill-treatment in an environment which fosters the health, self-respect and dignity of the child." (Poland IRCO, Add.31, para. 30)

"The Committee is of the view that the implementation of the provisions of article 39 of the Convention deserves greater attention. Programmes and strategies should be developed to ensure that measures are in place to promote the physical and psychological recovery and social reintegration of a child victim of, inter alia, neglect, sexual exploitation, abuse, family conflict, violence, drug abuse, as well as of children in the system of administration of justice. Such measures should be applied within the national context but also within the framework of international cooperation." (UK IRCO, Add.34, para. 39)

"The Committee recommends that all necessary measures be taken by the State Party to fully implement article 39 of the Convention, especially to promote the physical and psychological recovery and social reintegration of children victims of armed conflict, abuse and neglect, any form of violence, including rape, child labour and forced labour, sexual exploitation and trafficking and sale. The Committee would like to suggest that the State Party consider seeking international assistance in this area of reintegration from appropriate UN bodies including UNICEF." (Myanmar IRCO, Add.69, para. 45. See also Denmark IRCO, Add.33, para. 32; Ukraine IRCO, Add.42, para. 29; Nigeria IRCO, Add.61, para. 43; Bulgaria IRCO, Add.66, para. 30)

The Committee has raised the issue of compensation of child victims:

"The Committee urges that the State Party take all necessary measures to prevent disappearances, torture, ill-treatment, and illegal or arbitrary detention of minors; that all such cases be systematically investigated in order to bring those suspected of having committed such acts before the courts; and that those found guilty be punished and that the victims be compensated." (Indonesia IRCO, Add.25, para. 24)

Child victims of neglect, exploitation or abuse

Various articles of the Convention provide protective rights, requiring States to take a range of actions to prevent violence, neglect and exploitation of children. The purpose of article 39 is to require appropriate action for those who still fall victim.

The Programme of Action for the Prevention of the Sale of Children, Child Prostitution and Child Pornography, adopted by the Commission on Human Rights, proposes:

"34. Rehabilitation and reintegration programmes using an interdisciplinary approach should be established to assist children who have been victims of trafficking, sale or sexual exploitation and their families. Agencies implementing such programmes, whether public or non-governmental, should be established, or strengthened by being provided with the necessary support and funding. They should be encouraged to request technical assistance, evaluational assistance, information on new methods of self-funding schemes, etc., from United Nations bodies and from public or private, national or international sources with relevant competence." (Commission of Human Rights Resolution 1992/74, 5 March 1992, annex)

In October 1996, the Special Rapporteur on the sale of children, child prostitution and child pornography, in a report to the General Assembly, noted that recovery and rehabilitation were "the most difficult aspects of the entire process, both for the victims and for those helping them. The most efficient rescue programmes would be of little value unless coupled with some structure that would assist in the healing process of the child, physically, mentally and psychologically." The Special Rapporteur noted that recovery and reintegration are both time-consuming and very expensive. A wide range of programmes need to be included: food and shelter, placement in schools, skills training, medical and psychological help, and possible placement in foster families. While it was appealing to talk of a hope of reintegration into the family, especially in the case of child sex workers, there were various complications. For those children who have been sexually abused by a parent, step-parent or relative, or have been sold by their own families, it is difficult to contemplate a return. Ostracism from families and communities was an added factor. "There is generally a lack of awareness regarding the imperative need for treatment and recovery of victims. They are therefore invariably left to themselves, especially after the termination of the case. In instances where the prosecution of the case results in conviction of the offender, the victim is deemed to have received redress. Very often efforts at rehabilitation are concentrated on the offender rather than on the child victim." (A/51/456, paras. 71 and 72)

The Agenda for Action adopted by the World Congress against Commercial Sexual Exploitation of Children includes a section on "Recovery and Reintegration", emphasizing that a non-punitive approach should be adopted to child victims of commercial sexual exploitation and proposing:

- victims and their families should receive social, medical and psychological counselling and other support;

- medical personnel, teachers, social workers and relevant NGOs helping child victims should receive gender-sensitive training;

- effective action to prevent and remove social stigmatization of child victims and their families;

- the facilitation of recovery and reintegration whenever possible in families and communities;

- promotion of alternative means of livelihood for child victims and their families so as to prevent further commercial sexual exploitation. (A/51/385, para. 5)

The Committee has noted the particular need for rehabilitation for child victims of all forms of abuse and exploitation:

"...Moreover, the Committee notes the insufficient measures taken to address the issue of ill-treatment and abuse, including sexual abuse, within the family, as well as the issues of physical and psychological recovery and social reintegration of child victims of such ill-treatment or abuse....

"...It further recommends that appropriate mechanisms be established to ensure the physical and psychological recovery and social reintegration of child victims of such ill-treatment and abuse, in the light of article 39 of the Convention." (New Zealand IRCO, Add.71, paras. 16 and 29. See also Russian Federation IRCO, Add.4, para. 24; Belarus IRCO, Add.17, para. 14; Italy IRCO, Add.41, para. 12; Nepal IRCO, Add.57, para. 19; Panama IRCO, Add.68, para. 35)

In relation to drug abuse, a need for rehabilitative services tailored specifically for children exists in many countries where there are inadequate services for adults or children; see article 33, page 445.

The Committee has noted the importance of respect for the child victim's right to privacy, in particular in cases involving abuse including sexual exploitation, and the role of the media in respecting privacy (for discussion, see article 16, page 201 and article 17, page 219):

"With respect to child abuse, including sexual abuse, the Committee is seriously alarmed by the prevalence of this type of abuse. The Committee is worried about the fact that no specific rehabilitation measures exist for abused children and that they are treated like delinquents....

"The Committee suggest that rehabilitation measures be taken for abused children and that the Government prohibits the publication by the media of the names of the victims." (Sri Lanka IRCO, Add.40, paras. 15 and 36)

Child victims of economic exploitation

Following its General Discussion on the economic exploitation of children, the Committee on the Rights of the Child produced a series of recommendations. These recognized that all rights in the Convention are indivisible and interrelated and that action to prevent and combat economic exploitation of children must take place within the framework of the Convention's general principles (articles 2, 3, 4 and 12). An adequate legal framework and necessary measures of implementation must be developed in conformity with the principles and provisions (see also article 32, page 427):

"Such measures will strengthen the prevention of situations of economic exploitation and of their detrimental effects on the lives of children, should be aimed at reinforcing the system of children's protection and will promote the physical and psychological recovery and social reintegration of children victims of any form of economic exploitation, in an environment which fosters the health, self-respect and dignity of the child."

In particular, the Committee recommended:

"States Parties must also take measures to ensure the rehabilitation of children who, as a result of economic exploitation, are exposed to serious physical and moral danger. It is essential to provide these children with the necessary social and medical assistance and to envisage social reintegration programmes for them in the light of article 39 of the Convention on the Rights of the Child." (Report on the fifth session, January 1994, CRC/C/24, pp. 39 and 43)

The International Labour Organization (ILO), in its handbook *Child labour Targeting the intolerable*, suggests: "A child's withdrawal from work should be accompanied by a whole range of supportive measures. This is especially important if children have been stunted in their development because they were bonded, have worked practically since they were toddlers, have been prostituted or have been living and working on the streets without their families or without any stable social environment. In addition to education, training, health services and nutrition, these children need to be provided with intensive counselling, a safe environment, and often legal aid. To this end, a number of action programmes for these children have set up drop-in centres where they can stay and recuperate.

"The evidence has shown that these children need a range of professional services, from social workers and family or child therapists to psychiatrists. Volunteers or community workers also play an important part, but their work is very taxing. There is a very high turnover of field workers, and therefore they need special training and guidance. Cooperation with the police is often required, too, so that 'rehabilitated' children are not stigmatized or persecuted. Agencies have also tried with some success to reunite children with their families. In such cases, support has to be extended to the families as well. Comprehensive rehabilitation measures are badly needed and should be provided even if their cost is very high." The ILO also highlights the severe short- and long-term physical and psychological effects of child labour, including in particular hazardous work and forms of forced labour, among them commercial sexual exploitation, requiring specialist and long-term support and rehabilitation (*Child labour Targeting the intolerable*, pp. 9 et seq., 107).

In the Programme of Action for the Elimination of the Exploitation of Child Labour of the Commission on Human Rights, the need to offer an alternative to take children out of the circle of poverty and exploitation is emphasized: "Urgent measures could be taken on behalf of children who are subjected to high physical and moral risks. It is important to give them protection and assistance, including social and medical assistance, while at the same time pursuing the objective of the elimination of child labour. These urgent measures should be backed up by programmes of social rehabilitation." (Commission on Human Rights, resolution 1993/79, para. 12)

Children involved with system of juvenile justice

The *Guidelines for Periodic Reports* asks for information on "all measures taken pursuant to article 39 and paragraph 1 of article 40 to promote the physical and psychological recovery and social reintegration of the child involved with the system of the administration of juvenile justice, and to ensure that such recovery and reintegration takes place in an environment which fosters the health, self-respect and dignity of the child" (para. 149). This underlines that such children should be recognized as victims, as well as perpetrators of offences.

The Committee on the Rights of the Child has promoted the United Nations rules and guidelines relating to juvenile justice as providing relevant standards for the implementation of the Convention, and in particular the implementation of articles 37, 39 and 40. In many cases, it has asked States Parties generally to review their juvenile justice system in the light of articles 37, 39 and 40, and of the rules and guidelines. For example:

"The Committee recommends that the State Party envisage undertaking a comprehensive reform of the system of juvenile justice and that the Convention and other international standards in this field, such as the 'Beijing Rules', the 'Riyadh Guidelines' and the United Nations Rules for the Protection of Juveniles Deprived of their Liberty, be seen as a guide in this revision. Attention should also be paid to measures for rehabilitation and social reintegration, in line with article 39 of the Convention." (Jordan IRCO, Add.21, para. 27; for a list of similar recommendations, see article 40, page 539)

The "Riyadh Guidelines" on the Prevention of Juvenile Delinquency proposes that comprehensive development plans should include victim compensation and assistance programmes, with full participation by young people (para. 9). The Guidelines also notes that schools can usefully serve as resource and referral centres for the provision of medical, counselling and other services to young persons, "particularly those with special needs and suffering from abuse, neglect, victimization and exploitation" (para. 26). Communities should provide, or strengthen where they exist, "a wide range of community-based support measures for young persons, including community development centres, recreational facilities and services to respond to the special problems of children who are at social risk... Special facilities should be set up to provide adequate shelter for young persons who are no longer able to live at home or who do not have homes to live in... Government agencies should take special responsibility and provide necessary services for homeless or street children; information about local facilities, accommodation, employment and other forms and sources of help should be made readily available to young persons." (paras. 33, 34 and 38)

The United Nations Rules for the Protection of Juveniles Deprived of their Liberty include a section on "Return to the community": "All juveniles should benefit from arrangements designed to assist them in returning to society, family life, education or employment after release. Procedures, including early release, and special courses should be devised to this end" (rule 79). "Competent authorities should provide or ensure services to assist juveniles in reestablishing themselves in society and to lessen prejudice against such juveniles. These services should ensure, to the extent possible, that the juvenile is provided with suitable residence, employment, clothing and sufficient means to maintain himself or herself upon release in order to facilitate successful reintegration. The representatives of agencies providing such services should be consulted and should have access to juveniles while detained, with a view to assisting them in their return to the community." (rule 80)

Child victims of torture, inhuman or degrading treatment or punishment

The occurrence of practices breaching the prohibition in article 37 on torture and other forms of cruel, inhuman or degrading treatment and punishment was raised in the Committee's General Discussion on juvenile justice, and the Committee noted that in States Parties

"insufficient attention was paid to the need for the promotion of an effective system of physical and psychological recovery and social reintegration of the child, in an environment that fostered his or her health, self-respect and dignity." (Report on the tenth session, October-November 1995, CRC/C/46, para. 221)

Article 14 of the Convention against Torture and Other Cruel, Inhuman or Degrading Treatment £or Punishment states: "1. Each State Party shall ensure in its legal system that the victim of an act of torture obtains redress and has an enforceable right to fair and adequate compensation, including the means for as full rehabilitation as possible. In the event of the death of the victim as a result of an act of torture, his dependants shall be entitled to compensation.

"2. Nothing in this article shall affect any right of the victim or other persons to compensation which may exist under national law."

The United Nations General Assembly in 1985 adopted the Declaration of Basic Principles of Justice for Victims of Crime and Abuse of Power. It calls on States to provide remedies, including restitution and/or compensation, and necessary material, medical, psychological and social assistance to victims of official abuse, and to provide them with justice – to the extent to which such abuse is a violation of national law (General Assembly Resolution 40/34, 29 November 1985, Annex).

In the case of various States Parties, the Committee has expressed concern about child victims of torture and other inhuman or degrading treatment or punishment (see also article 37, page 487):

"The Committee recommends that the State Party undertake a comprehensive reform of the system of juvenile justice and that the Convention and other international standards in this field, such as the 'Beijing Rules', the 'Riyadh Guidelines' and the United Nations Rules for the Protection of Juveniles Deprived of their Liberty, be seen as a guide in this revision. Attention should also be paid to measures for rehabilitation and social reintegration, in line with article 39 of the Convention." (Indonesia IRCO, Add.25, para. 20)

"...special measures should be taken to ensure that children are protected against the occurrence of such human rights violations and that they benefit from recovery and reintegration programmes in an environment which fosters the dignity and the self-confidence of the child." (Peru IRCO, Add.8, para. 16)

Child victims of armed conflict

Following its General Discussion on Children in armed conflicts, the Committee noted:

"Consideration was particularly given to article 39 of the Convention: different experiences and programmes were brought to the attention of the Committee, underlying the need for resources and goods (namely, food and medicine). Moreover, emphasis was put on the need to consider a coherent plan for recovery and reintegration, to be planned and implemented in a combined effort by United Nations bodies and non-governmental organizations. Attention should be paid to (a) the implementation and monitoring of adequate strategies and (b) the need to reinforce the involvement of the family and the local community in this process." (Report on the second session, September-October 1992, CRC/C/10, para. 74)

Protective provisions in the Geneva Conventions and the two Additional Protocols are relevant to the implementation of article 39 for child victims of armed conflict (see article 38, page 514).

The Committee has on occasion requested further information:

"In relation to the adverse impact of the internal conflict on children who live in exceptionally difficult situations, the Committee wishes to receive precise information with regard to rehabilitation programmes for affected children and the progress of such programmes, ₤as well as statistical data with regard to displaced children within the country."
(El Salvador IRCO, Add.9, para. 16)

The Committee has made some specific recommendations:

"In connection with the implementation of article 39 of the Convention, the Committee suggests that the State Party consider as a matter of priority the further development of rehabilitative programmes. In this regard, the problem of the apparent scarcity and inadequacy of programmes for the treatment of post-traumatic stress disorders, identified primarily in refugee children, needs to be adequately addressed.
"...It is also the view of the Committee that serious consideration should be given to the possibility of allocating further resources for programmes for the prevention of sexual abuse and exploitation and the rehabilitation of victims, including training of and support to the professionals dealing with these issues and the development of an integrated and coordinated approach to assist both the victims and the perpetrators of such abuse."
(Federal Republic of Yugoslavia IRCO, Add.49, paras. 37 and 41)

"The Committee recommends that the State Party give careful consideration to placing greater emphasis on psycho-social recovery and reintegration of 'passive victims' of violence and the armed conflict in Lebanon."
(Lebanon IRCO, Add.54, para. 42)

"The problems of children traumatized by the effects of armed conflict and violence in society are, in the Committee's view, a matter of serious concern. In this connection, the Com-

Alleviating negative effects of war

Lebanon's Initial Report notes "There are attempts in the country, initiated by NGOs and supported by the Government and international organizations, to alleviate the negative effects of war. The programmes are varied and comprise different age groups. They include structural classroom discussion, drama, puppetry, summer camps, day camps, publications, conferences, seminars, exchange programmes with other countries, extra-curricular activities in schools and many others. The programmes, although varied, have the ultimate aim of healing the psyches of the young and recapturing the magic of childhood of which they were robbed at an early age. Children whose early years were turbulent and whose development was disrupted by acts of violence and hate need very special attention. The results so far are encouraging, but the years ahead can only tell if the aims will be fulfilled." (Lebanon IR, para. 113)

mittee recommends that the State Party give consideration to the implementation of specific projects for children, to be carried out in an environment which fosters the health, self-respect and dignity of the child." (Guatemala IRCO, Add.58, para. 39)

The Committee has also suggested that refugee children should be regarded as victims for the purpose of article 39:

"In view of the general problem of displaced and refugee children, the Committee recommends that all appropriate measures be taken to ensure that those vulnerable groups have access to basic services, particularly in the fields of education, health and social rehabilitation." (Sri Lanka IRCO, Add.40, para. 38)

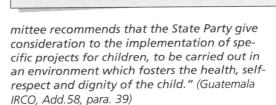

Implementation Checklist

article 39

● General measures of implementation

Have appropriate general measures of implementation been taken in relation to article 39, including

☐ identification and coordination of the responsible departments and agencies at all levels of government (article 39 is relevant to **departments of social welfare, health, employment, justice, defence, foreign affairs**)?

☐ identification of relevant non-governmental organizations/civil society partners?

☐ a comprehensive review to ensure that all legislation, policy and practice is compatible with the article, for all children in all parts of the jurisdiction?

☐ adoption of a strategy to secure full implementation

    ☐ which includes where necessary the identification of goals and indicators of progress?

    ☐ which does not affect any provisions which are more conducive to the rights of the child?

    ☐ which recognizes other relevant international standards?

    ☐ which involves where necessary international cooperation?

(Such measures may be part of an overall governmental strategy for implementing the Convention as a whole).

☐ budgetary analysis and allocation of necessary resources?

☐ development of mechanisms for monitoring and evaluation?

☐ making the implications of article 39 widely known to adults and children?

☐ development of appropriate training and awareness-raising (in relation to article 39 likely to include the training of **all those responsible for child protection, teachers, social workers and health workers**)?

● Specific issues in implementing article 39

Does the State ensure that appropriate rehabilitative measures, consistent with article 39, are taken to promote physical and psychological recovery and social reintegration of all children within its jurisdiction who are victims of

    ☐ any form of neglect?

    ☐ violence or abuse?

    ☐ sexual abuse?

    ☐ sexual exploitation?

    ☐ drug abuse?

    ☐ economic exploitation?

    ☐ sale or trafficking?

    ☐ torture?

☐ any other form of cruel, inhuman or degrading treatment or punishment?

☐ armed conflicts?

☐ Does the State ensure appropriate recovery and social reintegration for children involved in the juvenile justice system?

☐ Has the State taken appropriate measures to ensure that compensation is available for child victims?

☐ Has the State reviewed the environment in which such recovery and reintegration takes place in each case to ensure that it fosters the health, self-respect and dignity of the child?

☐ Has the State ensured that there is respect for the views of the child victims in planning and implementing programmes for recovery and reintegration, including in individual cases?

Reminder : **The Convention is indivisible and its articles are interdependent. Article 39 should not be considered in isolation.**

Particular regard should be paid to:
The general principles

Article 2: all rights to be recognized for each child in jurisdiction without discrimination on any ground

Article 3(1): the best interests of the child to be a primary consideration in all actions concerning children

Article 6: right to life and maximum possible survival and development

Article 12: respect for the child's views in all matters affecting the child; opportunity to be heard in any judicial or administrative proceedings affecting the child

Closely related articles

Articles whose implementation is related to that of article 39 include:

Article 19: protection from all forms of violence

Article 22: refugee children

Article 32: child labour

Article 33: drug abuse

Article 34: sexual exploitation

Article 35: sale, trafficking and abduction

Article 36: other forms of exploitation

Article 37: torture or any other cruel, inhuman or degrading treatment or punishment

Article 38: armed conflict

Article 40: juvenile justice

Administration of juvenile justice

Text of Article 40

1. States Parties recognize the right of every child alleged as, accused of, or recognized as having infringed the penal law to be treated in a manner consistent with the promotion of the child's sense of dignity and worth, which reinforces the child's respect for the human rights and fundamental freedoms of others and which takes into account the child's age and the desirability of promoting the child's reintegration and the child's assuming a constructive role in society.

2. To this end, and having regard to the relevant provisions of international instruments, States Parties shall, in particular, ensure that:

(a) No child shall be alleged as, be accused of, or recognized as having infringed the penal law by reason of acts or omissions that were not prohibited by national or international law at the time they were committed;

(b) Every child alleged as or accused of having infringed the penal law has at least the following guarantees:

(i)   To be presumed innocent until proven guilty according to law;

(ii)   To be informed promptly and directly of the charges against him or her, and, if appropriate through his or her parents or legal guardians, and to have legal or other appropriate assistance in the preparation and presentation of his or her defence;

(iii)   To have the matter determined without delay by a competent, independent and impartial authority or judicial body in a fair hearing according to law, in the presence of legal or other appropriate assistance and, unless it is considered not to be in the best interest of the child, in particular, taking into account his or her age or situation, his or her parents or legal guardians;

(iv)   Not to be compelled to give testimony or to confess guilt; to examine or have examined adverse witnesses and to obtain the participation and examination of witnesses on his or her behalf under conditions of equality;

(v)   If considered to have infringed the penal law, to have this decision and any measures imposed in consequence thereof reviewed by a higher competent, independent and impartial authority or judicial body according to law;

(vi)   To have the free assistance of an interpreter if the child cannot understand or speak the language used;

(vii)   To have his or her privacy fully respected at all stages of the proceedings.

3. States Parties shall seek to promote the establishment of laws, procedures, authorities and institutions specifically applicable to children alleged as, accused of, or recognized as having infringed the penal law, and, in particular:

(a)   the establishment of a minimum age below which children shall be presumed not to have the capacity to infringe the penal law;

(b)   whenever appropriate and desirable, measures for dealing with such children without resorting to judicial proceedings, providing that human rights and legal safeguards are fully respected.

4. A variety of dispositions, such as care, guidance and supervision orders; counselling; probation; foster care; education and vocational training programmes and other alternatives to institutional care shall be available to ensure that children are dealt with in a manner appropriate to their well being and proportionate both to their circumstances and the offence.

Summary

Article 40 of the Convention on the Rights of the Child covers the rights of all children alleged as, accused of or recognized as having infringed the penal law. Thus, it covers treatment from the moment an allegation is made, through investigation, arrest, charge, any pre-trial period, trial and sentence. The article requires States to promote a distinctive system of juvenile justice for children (i.e., in the light of article 1, up to 18 or the age of majority) with specific positive rather than punitive aims set out in paragraph 1. Article 40 details a list of minimum guarantees for the child and it requires States Parties to set a minimum age of criminal responsibility, to provide measures for dealing with children who may have infringed the penal law without resorting to judicial proceedings and to provide a variety of alternative dispositions to institutional care. In addi-

tion, article 37 (page 487) bars the death penalty and life imprisonment without possibility of release and insists that any restriction of liberty must be used as a last resort and for the shortest appropriate period of time. Article 39 requires measures to promote physical and psychological recovery and reintegration of child victims (page 529). Also, to be noted, is that the Committee on the Rights of the Child has commended the United Nations rules and guidelines on juvenile justice as providing relevant standards for the implementation of the Convention on the Rights of the Child.

In the outline for its 1995 General Discussion on the administration of juvenile justice, the Committee stated that the Convention, together with the United Nations rules and guidelines on juvenile justice, "call for the adoption of a child-oriented system". ∎

Extracts from
Committee on the Rights of the Child
Guidelines for Reports to be submitted by States Parties under the Convention

For full text of *Guidelines for Periodic Reports*, see Appendix 3, page 604.

Guidelines for Initial Reports

"Special protection measures
"Under this section, States Parties are requested to provide relevant information, including the principal legislative, judicial, administrative or other measures in force; factors and difficulties encountered and progress achieved in implementing the relevant provisions of the Convention; and implementation priorities and specific goals for the future in respect of:

...

(b) Children in conflict with the law
(i) The administration of juvenile justice (article 40)

....
(CRC/C/5, para. 23)

Guidelines for Periodic Reports

VIII. SPECIAL PROTECTION MEASURES (arts. 22, 38, 39, 40, 37(b)-(d), 32-36)

B. Children involved with the system of administration of juvenile justice

1. The administration of juvenile justice (art.40)

Please provide information on the legislative and other measures taken to recognize and ensure the right of every child involved with the system of the administration of juvenile justice (alleged as, accused of, or recognized as having infringed the penal law) to be treated in a manner:

Consistent with the promotion of the child's sense of dignity and worth;

Which reinforces the child's respect for the human rights and fundamental freedoms of others;

Which takes into account the child's age and the desirability of promoting the child's reintegration and the child's assuming a constructive role in society;

Which ensures respect for the general principles of the Convention, namely non-discrimination, the best interests of the child, respect for the views of the child and the right to life, survival and development to the maximum extent.

With respect to article 40, paragraph 2, please indicate the relevant international instruments applicable in the area of the administration of juvenile justice, including at the multilateral, regional or bilateral levels, as well as legislative and other appropriate measures adopted to ensure in particular that:

No child shall be alleged as, accused of or recognized as having infringed the penal law by reason of acts or omissions that were not prohibited by national or international law at the time they were committed;

Every child alleged as or accused of having infringed the penal law has at least the following guarantees, indicating, where relevant, additional guarantees provided to the child:

To be presumed innocent until proven guilty according to law;

To be informed promptly (indicating any time-limit fixed by law) and directly of the charges against him or her and, if appropriate, through his or her legal guardians, and to have legal or other appropriate assistance in the preparation and presentation of his or her defence; in this regard, please indicate what other appropriate assistance may be made available to the child;

To have the matter determined without delay (indicating any time-limit fixed by law) by a competent, independent and impartial authority or judicial body in a fair hearing according to law, in the presence of legal or other appropriate assistance (indicating what other appropriate assistance may be made available to the child) and, unless it is considered not to be in the best interests of the child, in particular taking into account his or her age or situation, in the presence of his or her parents or legal guardians;

Not to be compelled to give testimony or to confess guilt; to examine or have examined adverse witnesses and to obtain the participation and examination of witnesses on his or her behalf under conditions of equality;

If considered to have infringed the penal law, to have this decision and any measures imposed in consequence thereof reviewed by a higher competent, independent and impartial authority or judicial body according to law;

To have the free assistance of an interpreter if the child cannot understand or speak the language used;

To have his or her privacy respected at all stages of the proceedings.

Please indicate the measures adopted pursuant to article 40, paragraph 3, to promote the establishment of laws, procedures, authorities and institutions specially applicable to children alleged as, accused of, or recognized as having infringed the penal law, providing information inter alia on the areas addressed by legislation and procedures, as well as the functions, number and distribution throughout the country. Reports should in particular indicate the measures adopted to ensure a child-orientated system, including:

The establishment of a minimum age below which children shall be presumed not to have the capacity to infringe the penal law:

Measures taken for dealing with such children without resorting to judicial proceedings, and to ensure that in such cases human rights and legal safeguards are fully respected, indicating the situations in which such a system applies and relevant procedures established for that purpose.

Please indicate the variety of dispositions made available pursuant to article 40, paragraph 4, including care, guidance and supervision orders, counselling, probation, foster care, education and vocational training programmes and other alternatives to institutional care, to ensure that children are dealt with in a manner appropriate to their well-being and proportionate both to their circumstances and the offence.

Reports should further indicate the training activities developed for all professionals involved with the system of juvenile justice, including judges, prosecutors, lawyers, law enforcement officials, immigration officers and social workers, on the provisions of the Convention and other relevant international instruments in the field of juvenile justice, including the 'Beijing Rules', the 'Riyadh Guidelines' and the United Nations Rules for the Protection of Juveniles Deprived of their Liberty.

Relevant information should also be provided on the progress achieved in the implementation of article 40, any difficulties encountered and targets set for the future, as well as disaggregated data on the children concerned, inter alia by age, gender, region, rural/urban area, national, social and ethnic origin, offence and disposition made available.

(CRC/C/58, paras. 132-137. The following paragraphs of the *Guidelines for Periodic Reports* are also relevant to reporting under this article: 24, 35, 43, 46, 59, 86-87, 88, 138-150 and 166; for full text of *Guidelines*, see Appendix 3, page 604.)

United Nations rules and guidelines on juvenile justice

The Committee, in its examination of States Parties' reports and in other comments, has indicated consistently that it regards the United Nations rules and guidelines relating to juvenile justice as providing relevant detailed standards for the implementation of article 40 and the administration of juvenile justice: the United Nations Standard Minimum Rules for the Administration of Juvenile Justice – the "Beijing Rules"; the United Nations Rules for the Protection of Juveniles Deprived of their Liberty; and the United Nations Guidelines for the Prevention of Juvenile Delinquency – the "Riyadh

Guidelines": see Appendix 4, page 636, for full text).

It should be noted that the "Beijing Rules" defines "juvenile" as a child or young person who, under the respective legal systems, may be dealt with for an offence in a manner which is different from an adult. The provisions on juvenile justice in the Convention on the Rights of the Child apply to "children", defined for the purposes of the Convention as everyone below the age of 18, unless under national law majority is attained earlier. The Committee has indicated that States Parties should not reduce the protection available to under-18-year-olds simply because majority is reached earlier (see also Human Rights Committee General Comment 17,

HRI/GEN/1/Rev.2, p. 24, quoted on page 4). Thus, the Committee on the Rights of the Child believes that the standards in the rules and guidelines should be applied to all aged under 18.

The "Beijing Rules" proposes that they should be applied beyond the criminal justice system for juveniles. Its rule 3 states:

"(1) The relevant provisions of the Rules shall be applied not only to juvenile offenders but also to juveniles who may be proceeded against for any specific behaviour that would not be punishable if committed by an adult.

(2) Efforts should be made to extend the principles embodied in the Rules to all juveniles who are dealt with in welfare and care proceedings.

(3) Efforts shall also be made to extend the principles embodied in the Rules to young adult offenders."

The official commentary on the "Beijing Rules" indicates that rule 3(1) applies to "the so-called 'status offences' prescribed in various national legal systems where the range of behaviour considered to be an offence is wider for juveniles than it is for adults (for example, truancy, school and family disobedience, public drunkenness, etc.)."

General concerns of the Committee

As noted in the summary above, the Committee has stated that the Convention and the United Nations rules and guidelines together

"call for the adoption of a child-oriented system, that recognizes the child as a subject of fundamental rights and freedoms and stresses the need for all actions concerning children to be guided by the best interests of the child as a primary consideration." (Report on the ninth session, May-June 1995, CRC/C/43, Annex VIII, p. 64)

This call for "a child-oriented system" has been repeated in Concluding Observations on States Parties' reports (for example, see Senegal IRCO, Add.44, para. 26; UK IRCO, Add.34, para. 35).

In the report of its General Discussion on juvenile justice, the Committee noted that States Parties' reports

"were usually limited to a general description of legal provisions, rarely addressing social factors leading to the involvement of juveniles with the system of administration of justice or the social consequences of the decisions taken in that context..." (Report on the tenth session, October-November 1995, CRC/C/46, para. 217)

The Committee has often pointed out the social roots of juvenile crime and violence in its com-

ments and discussions with States Parties. For example, a Committee member noted during discussion of Jamaica's juvenile justice system that "... young offenders should be seen as both perpetrators and victims; the criminality of children was a measure of violence in the broader society..." (Jamaica SR.197, para. 89)

The "Beijing Rules" requires that in all cases involving criminal offences, except minor offences, "before the competent authority renders a final disposition prior to sentencing, the background and circumstances in which the juvenile is living or the conditions under which the offence has been committed shall be properly investigated so as to facilitate judicious adjudication of the case by the competent authority" (rule 16).

In the case of many States Parties, the Committee has expressed concern that the system of justice for juveniles is not compatible with the principles and provisions of the Convention, in particular articles 37, 39 and 40, and of other international instruments, citing in particular the United Nations rules and guidelines. In some cases, it picks up specific issues within the overall system. It has paid particular attention to the need to develop a distinct system for juvenile justice; to the age of criminal responsibility, which in many cases it believes is set too low (see page 550); and to the importance of training focused on children's rights (see page 546).

For example:

"As regards legislative reform in the area of the administration of juvenile justice, the Committee wishes to emphasize that any new legislative measures to be introduced in the State Party must be guided by the principles and provisions of the Convention on the Rights of the Child and other relevant international instruments, in particular, the 'Beijing Rules', the 'Riyadh Guidelines' and the United Nations Rules for the Protection of Juveniles Deprived of their Liberty. In this regard, the Committee urges the Government to ensure that the age of criminal responsibility is not reduced. The Committee also wishes to recommend, in particular, that the system of the administration of juvenile justice must be adequately supported to function appropriately. This requires, inter alia, that juvenile judges be trained and function in all areas or 'departments' of Honduras. Equally, the Committee recommends that the systems for the supervision of and visits to places of juvenile detention must be adequately provided for. It also recommends that the State Party further strengthen measures to reduce the period of custody of juveniles to ensure that a juvenile's deprivation of liberty is used only as a

article 40

measure of last resort." (Honduras IRCO, Add.24, para. 32)

Similar general recommendations have been made to many States, among them: Viet Nam IRCO, Add.3, para. 8; Russian Federation IRCO, Add.4, para. 22; Egypt IRCO, Add.5, para. 14; Sudan IRCO, Add.10, paras. 15 and 26; Costa Rica IRCO, Add.11, para. 15; Namibia IRCO, Add.14, para. 20; Colombia Prelim. Obs., Add.15, para. 14; Romania IRCO, Add.16, para. 20; Belarus IRCO, Add.17, para. 10; Pakistan IRCO, Add.18, paras. 20 and 31; Burkina Faso IRCO, Add.19, para. 17; Jordan IRCO, Add.21, para. 27; Chile IRCO, Add.22, para. 17; Indonesia IRCO, Add.25, para. 20; Madagascar IRCO, Add.26, para. 22; Philippines IRCO, Add.29, paras. 17 and 27; Poland IRCO, Add.31, paras. 19 and 32; Jamaica IRCO, Add.32, para. 30; Nicaragua IRCO, Add.36, para. 39; Ukraine IRCO, Add.42, paras. 16 and 31; Senegal IRCO, Add.44, para. 26; Portugal IRCO, Add.45, paras. 18 and 25; Yemen IRCO, Add.47, para. 10; Mongolia IRCO, Add.48, para. 29; Republic of Korea IRCO, Add.51, paras. 18 and 31; Lebanon IRCO, Add.54, para. 44; Nepal IRCO, Add.57, paras. 24 and 38; Guatemala IRCO, Add.58, para. 40; Cyprus IRCO, Add.59, para. 19; Morocco IRCO, Add.60, paras. 16 and 28; Uruguay IRCO, Add.62, para. 24; Mauritius IRCO, Add.64, paras. 20 and 32; Bulgaria IRCO, Add.66, para. 34; Ethiopia IRCO, Add.67, para. 34; Panama IRCO, Add.68, para. 35; Myanmar IRCO, Add.69, para. 46; Syrian Arab Republic IRCO, Add.70, para. 30.

The holistic nature of the Convention and the central importance of the general principles in articles 2, 3 and 12 is particularly stressed in the Report of the Committee's General Discussion on juvenile justice as the context for planning juvenile justice systems:

"It was particularly felt that the general principles of the Convention had not been adequately reflected in national legislation or practice..." (Report on the tenth session, October-November 1995, CRC/C/46, para. 218).

The Committee's *Guidelines for Periodic Reports* seeks information on legislative and other measures taken to ensure the right of every child involved with the juvenile justice system to be treated in a manner "which ensures respect for the general principles of the Convention, namely non-discrimination, the best interests of the child, respect for the views of the child and the right to life, survival and development to the maximum extent" (para. 132).

Non-discrimination

In relation to non-discrimination, the report of the General Discussion states

"...particular concern was expressed about instances where criteria of a subjective and arbitrary nature (such as with regard to the attainment of puberty, the age of discernment or the personality of the child) still prevailed in the assessment of the criminal responsibility of children and in deciding upon the measures applicable to them..." (Report on the tenth session, October-November 1995, CRC/C/46, para. 218)

The Committee has noted, for example, discrimination or potential discrimination against economically and socially disadvantaged children:

"The Committee recommends that the State Party undertake to ensure that adequate protection is afforded to economically and socially disadvantaged children in conflict with the law and that alternatives to institutional care are available, as provided for under article 40, paragraphs 3 and 4, of the Convention." *(Bolivia IRCO, Add.1, para. 16)*

The Committee has also expressed concern at exceptions that are discriminatory. For example:

"The Committee deplores that, under Decree-Law No. 25564, children between 15 and 18 years of age who are suspected of being involved in terrorist activities do not benefit from safeguards and guarantees afforded by the system of administration of juvenile justice under normal circumstances...
"The Committee also recommends that the provisions of Decree-Law No. 25564 dealing with the liability of children suspected of being involved in terrorist activities be repealed or amended in order for children below 18 years of age to enjoy fully the rights set forth in articles 37, 39 and 40 of the Convention." (Peru IRCO, Add.8, paras. 9 and 18)

The Committee noted discriminatory, or arbitrary, sentencing in Ethiopia:

"...the Committee expresses concern at the possibility ... provided for in article 172 of the Penal Code to sentence children to corporal punishment, at the sole discretion of the judge, in particular with regard to the 'bad or good character' of the child, in determining the penalty to be applied to the child, and at the possible limitations of the right to legal counsel." (Ethiopia IRCO, Add.67, para. 20)

The "Beijing Rules" includes a non-discrimination principle: "The following Standard Minimum Rules shall be applied to juvenile offenders impartially, without distinction of any kind, for example as to race, colour, sex, language, religion, political or other opinions, national or social origin, property, birth or other status." (rule 2(1))

Best interests

Consistent with the best interests principle in article 3 of the Convention on the Rights of the

Child, the "Beijing Rules" requires that Member States seek "to further the well-being of the juvenile and her or his family" (rule 1(1)); and that "The juvenile justice system shall emphasize the well-being of the juvenile..." (rule 5(1)). Also proceedings "shall be conducive to the best interests of the juvenile..." (rule 14(2)); and "The well-being of the juvenile shall be the guiding factor in the consideration of her or his case." (rule 17(1)(d))

The Committee stated in the report of its General Discussion:

"The principle of the best interests of the child was reaffirmed by the Convention in the context of the administration of juvenile justice, particularly when it stressed that the child should be treated in a manner consistent with the promotion of his or her sense of dignity and worth which reinforced respect for the child's human rights and fundamental freedoms and took into account the child's age and special needs. However, reports revealed that special juvenile justice systems were often non-existent, that judges, lawyers, social workers or personnel in institutions were not given any special training and that information on fundamental rights and legal safeguards were not provided to children..." (Report on the tenth session, October-November 1995, CRC/C/46, para. 219)

A Committee member stated in discussions with Mongolia that in revising the penal code, "the rehabilitation of offenders should be the primary objective, not the third, following the protection of society and the punishment of the child in the interest of society, as appeared to be the case" (Mongolia SR.266, para. 38).

Participation

Article 12 of the Convention on the Rights of the Child requires that a child capable of expressing views must have the right to express those views freely in all matters affecting the child and that the child's views must be given due weight (paragraph 1); in particular, the child must have an opportunity to be heard in any judicial and administrative proceedings affecting him or her (paragraph 2; see page 150). In order to exercise these participatory rights, the child must have access to appropriate information. Thus, children should be involved in the planning and implementation of the justice system affecting children and have a right to be heard and have their views taken seriously in all aspects of the system and all procedures. Article 37 specifically provides children with the right to appropriate legal and other assistance and to challenge any deprivation of liberty before a court or similar body. Article 40 requires that the child is informed promptly and directly of the charges against him or her, has access to legal and other appropriate assistance and is entitled to play a full part in the proceedings (with the assistance of an interpreter, if needed). Equally important in relation to formal proceedings, the child has the right to remain silent (see below, page 548). The "Beijing Rules" requires that proceedings shall be conducted "... in an atmosphere of understanding, which shall allow the juvenile to participate therein and to express herself or himself freely" (rule 14(2)).

On occasions, the Committee has specifically noted the lack of consideration of article 12 in juvenile justice. For example:

"The Committee expresses its concern regarding the implementation of article 12 of the Convention. The views of the child are not sufficiently taken into account, especially within the family, the school and the juvenile justice system." (Sri Lanka IRCO, Add.40, para. 13)

The "Riyadh Guidelines" in particular emphasizes the importance of participation in prevention as well as planning and implementation: "For the purposes of the interpretation of these guidelines, a child-centred orientation should be pursued. Young persons should have an active role and partnership within society and should not be considered as mere objects of socialization or control" (para. 3). For example, as part of the "comprehensive prevention plans" proposed for every level of government, there should be "Youth participation in delinquency prevention policies and processes, including recourse to community resources, youth self-help, and victim compensation and assistance programmes" (para. 9(h)). In the community, "youth organizations should be created or strengthened at the local level and given full participatory status in the management of community affairs. These organizations should encourage youth to organize collective and voluntary projects, particularly projects aimed at helping young persons in need of assistance" (para. 37). In preparing plans and policies for young people "... Young persons themselves should be involved in their formulation, development and implementation." (para. 50)

The report of the Committee's General Discussion on juvenile justice indicated that

"Similarly, in relation to the right of the child to participate in proceeding affecting him or her, States Parties' reports had indicated that children were seldom made sufficiently aware of their rights, including the right to assistance from a legal counsel or of the circumstances surrounding the case or of the measures decided." (Report on the tenth session, October-November 1995, CRC/C/46, para. 220)

Public perceptions of teenage offenders

During discussion of Spain's Initial Report, a government representative commented on the public alarm caused by juvenile offending: "The social perception that minors were responsible for a large proportion of offences seemed to some extent to derive from the impression given by teenage behaviour, which could be regarded as arrogant and in some cases destructive. The media gave very widespread coverage to offences committed by minors, and that tended to distort and exaggerate the problem. There were in fact no more than three or four cases a year of manslaughter by children under the age of 13, for example, and the situation was not therefore as dramatic as was sometimes portrayed. To offset such a trend facts must be publicized to show the true situation. It was important to avoid exaggeration by the media and to make every effort to ensure that young people found their place in society and on the labour market." (Spain SR.173, para. 50)

Effect of public opinion on juvenile justice

The Committee also noted in the report of its General Discussion that

"...the increasing trend for juvenile justice to become the subject of social and emotional pressure was a matter of particular concern, since it created opportunities to undermine respect for the best interests of the child" (Report on the tenth session, October-November 1995, CRC/C/46, para. 220).

This was borne out during discussions between the Committee and Chilean Government representatives, one of whom stated that criminal legislation was the most difficult area in which to introduce new legislation respecting children's rights:

"Since 1991, there had been a growing feeling, not in fact borne out by the relevant statistics among the general public in Chile that there had been a sharp increase in delinquency. The present climate of public opinion was therefore not conducive to the adoption of laws guaranteeing protection to offenders." (Chile SR.146, para. 33)

The "Beijing Rules" notes in "Fundamental perspectives" that "Juvenile justice shall be conceived as an integral part of the national development process of each country, within a compre-

hensive framework of social justice for all juveniles, thus, at the same time, contributing to the protection of the young and the maintenance of a peaceful order in society." (rule 1(4))

Training for juvenile justice

The Committee has consistently recommended that all those involved with children in the juvenile justice system, both in its planning and administration and in its institutions and programmes, should receive adequate training with a particular focus on the principles and provisions of the Convention and the relevant United Nations rules and guidelines. For example:

"The Committee suggests that a larger part of the education and training of law enforcement personnel, judges and other administration of justice officials be devoted to an understanding of international standards on juvenile justice..." (Argentina IRCO, Add.35, para. 18)

"The Committee is further concerned about the lack of specialized training of professionals working in the field of juvenile justice, which hampers efforts to ensure the independence of the judiciary and the capacity of the system to effectively investigate crimes committed against children and undermines measures to eradicate impunity." (Guatemala IRCO, Add.58, para. 24. See also Bulgaria IRCO, Add.66, para. 34; Myanmar IRCO, Add.69, para. 46)

Prevention of offending

The Convention on the Rights of the Child does not specifically address prevention of offending, but as indicated above, the Committee on the Rights of the Child has emphasized the social roots of offending, and it has also consistently proposed that the "Riyadh Guidelines" on Prevention of Juvenile Delinquency should be regarded as providing relevant standards for implementation. The Guidelines requires "comprehensive prevention plans" to be instituted at every level of government and proposes that they should be implemented within the framework of the Convention and other international instruments. The Committee has suggested measures in line with the Guidelines:

"...The Committee also wishes to recommend that the State Party take the necessary measures to prevent juvenile delinquency as set down in the Convention and complemented by the 'Riyadh Guidelines'." (UK IRCO, Add.34, para. 35)

"...the right of every child .... to be treated in a manner consistent with the promotion of the child's sense of dignity and worth, which reinforces the child's respect for the

human rights and fundamental freedoms of others and which takes into account the child's age and the desirability of promoting the child's reintegration and the child's assuming a constructive role in society": article 40(1)

Paragraph 1 of article 40 of the Convention upholds the positive, rehabilitative aims of the juvenile justice system, which have been underlined by the Committee in the wider context of the best interests of the child (see above, page 543). The paragraph links to the provisions in paragraphs 3 and 4 of the same article, which stress the importance of at least excluding younger children from criminal responsibility, avoiding judicial proceedings and developing a variety of dispositions including in particular alternatives to institutional care (see below, pages 551). It also echoes the aims of education set out in article 29 (see page 391), which include development of respect for human rights, and preparation of the child for responsible life in a free society.

In relation to criminal justice systems, the International Covenant on Civil and Political Rights requires "In the case of juvenile persons, the procedure shall be such as will take account of their age and the desirability of promoting their rehabilitation" (article 14(4)).

"To this end, and having regard to relevant provisions of international instruments, States Parties shall, in particular, ensure that:
"(a) No child shall be alleged as, be accused of, or recognized as having infringed the penal law by reason of acts or omissions that were not prohibited by national or international law at the time they were committed": article 40(2)(a)

These words reflect the principle that offences must have been defined in the criminal law at the time they were committed. See, for example, the Universal Declaration of Human Rights, article 11(2), and the International Covenant on Civil and Political Rights, article 15. In addition, the Covenant states "... Nor shall a heavier penalty be imposed than the one that was applicable at the

time when the criminal offence was committed. If, subsequent to the commission of the offence, provision is made by law for the imposition of a lighter penalty, the offender shall benefit thereby."

"(b) Every child alleged as or accused of having infringed the penal law has at least the following guarantees: ..."

Thus, paragraph 2(b) of article 40 sets out a minimum list of guarantees that must be available to children alleged as or accused of criminal acts. Some reflect principles already established for everyone including children under other international instruments, but some are applicable specifically to children. The "Beijing Rules" states: "Basic procedural safeguards such as the presumption of innocence, the right to be notified of the charges, the right to remain silent, the right to counsel, the right to the presence of a parent or guardian, the right to confront and cross-examine witnesses and the right to appeal to a higher authority shall be guaranteed at all stages of proceedings" (rule 7(1)). The commentary to the Rules notes: "Rule 7(1) emphasizes some important points that represent essential elements for a fair and just trial and that are internationally recognized in existing human rights instruments... Rules 14 et seq. of these Standard Minimum Rules specify issues that are important for proceedings in juvenile cases, in particular, while rule 7(1) affirms the most basic procedural safeguards in a general way." Rule 14 states: "14(1) Where the case of a juvenile offender has not been diverted (under rule 11), she or he shall be dealt with by the competent authority (court, tribunal, board, council, etc.) according to the principles of a fair and just trial. 14(2) The proceedings shall be conducive to the best interests of the juvenile and shall be conducted in an atmosphere of understanding, which shall allow the juvenile to participate therein and to express herself or himself freely."

"...(i) To be presumed innocent until proven guilty according to law"
This reflects provisions in the Universal Declaration of Human Rights, article 11, and the International Covenant on Civil and Political Rights, article 14(2).

The Committee on the Rights of the Child has noted with concern legislation that enables silence to be interpreted as supporting a finding of guilt (also relating to the right not to be compelled to give testimony or to confess guilt – article 40(2)(b)(iv)):

"The Committee is also concerned that The Criminal Evidence (N.I.) Order 1988 appears to be incompatible with article 40 of the Convention, in particular with the right to presumption of innocence and the right not to be compelled to give testimony or confess guilt. It is noted that silence in response to police questioning can be used to support a finding of guilt against a child over 10 years of age in Northern Ireland. Silence at trial can be similarly used against children over 14 years of age...

"The Committee recommends that the emergency and other legislation, including in relation to the system of administration of juvenile justice, at present in operation in Northern Ireland should be reviewed to ensure its consistency with the principles and provisions of the Convention." (UK IRCO, Add.34, paras. 20 and 34)

"...(ii) To be informed promptly and directly of the charges against him or her, and, if appropriate, through his or her parents or legal guardians, and to have legal or other appropriate assistance in the preparation and presentation of his or her defence"

Article 9(2) of the International Covenant on Civil and Political Rights requires that anyone who is arrested shall be informed, at the time of arrest, of the reasons for it "and shall be promptly informed of any charges against him". Article 14(3)(a) requires that everyone charged with a criminal offence shall be "informed promptly and in detail in a language which he understands of the nature and cause of the charge against him." The Convention adds the requirement to inform the child "if appropriate, through his or her parents or legal guardians" – presumably this requirement is to be decided in the light of the child's best interests.

The "Beijing Rules" expands on the right to legal assistance: "Throughout the proceedings the juvenile shall have the right to be represented by a legal adviser or to apply for free legal aid where there is provision for such aid in the country." (rule 15(1))

In addition, the Covenant on Civil and Political Rights provides that everyone charged with a criminal offence should have "adequate time and facilities for the preparation of his defence and to communicate with counsel of his own choosing" (article 14(2)(b)) and "to be tried in his presence, and to defend himself in person or through legal assistance of his own choosing; to be informed, if he does not have legal assistance, of this right; and to have legal assistance assigned to him, in any case where the interests of justice so require, and without payment by him in any such case if he

does not have sufficient means to pay for it" (article 14(2)(d)).

On ratification of the Convention on the Rights of the Child, Germany made a reservation reflecting one made in relation to the International Covenant on Civil and Political Rights, in respect of article 40(2)(b)(ii) and (iv), stating that "these provisions shall be applied in such a way that, in the case of minor infringement of the penal law, there shall not in each and every case exist:

(a) A right to have 'legal or other appropriate assistance' in the preparation and presentation of the defence, and/or

(b) An obligation to have a sentence not calling for imprisonment reviewed by a higher competent authority or judicial body." (CRC/C/2/Rev.5, p. 19)

When it examined Germany's Initial Report, the Committee commented:

"With regard to matters relating to juvenile justice, the Committee expresses its concern about the declaration [in fact, a reservation] made by the State Party to article 40(2)(b)(ii) which appears to limit the child's rights to access to justice and to a fair hearing as well as the right to legal assistance and defence...
"Note is taken of the Government's intention to reform the system of juvenile justice, including with regard to considering strengthening the services and the development of child-friendly proceedings for dealing with child victims and witnesses ... Additionally within this framework, the Committee expresses the hope that the declarations made by the State Party to article 40(2)(b)(ii) and (v) will be reviewed with a view to their possible withdrawal." (Germany IRCO, Add.43, paras. 20 and 34)

"(iii) To have the matter determined without delay by a competent, independent and impartial authority or judicial body in a fair hearing according to law, in the presence of legal or other appropriate assistance and, unless it is considered not to be in the best interest of the child, in particular, taking into account his or her age or situation, his or her parents or legal guardians"

There are similar provisions in the Universal Declaration of Human Rights, article 10, and the International Covenant on Civil and Political Rights, article 14. The Covenant requires trial without "undue" delay; the Convention on the Rights of the Child removes that qualification "undue" in the case of children. Article 40 of the Convention does not refer to pre-trial detention because article 37 requires that restriction of liberty in any circumstances may only be used as a measure of last resort and for the shortest appropriate period (see article 37, page 495 for discussion and for the Committee's, and other, comments).

Article 40 adds to the child's established right to legal and other appropriate assistance, the principle that the child's parents or legal guardians should be present, "unless it is considered not to be in the best interest of the child". The article implies that parents or legal guardians can be required to be present, and can be excluded in certain cases. The "Beijing Rules" emphasizes this: "The parents or the guardian shall be entitled to participate in the proceedings and may be required by the competent authority to attend them in the interest of the juvenile. They may, however, be denied participation by the competent authority if there are reasons to assume that such exclusion is necessary in the interest of the juvenile." (rule 15(2))

The Committee has stressed that

"...Particular attention should be paid to the right of children to prompt access to legal assistance..." (Bulgaria IRCO, Add.66, para. 34)

"(iv) Not to be compelled to give testimony or to confess guilt; to examine or have examined adverse witnesses and to obtain the participation and examination of witnesses on his or her behalf under conditions of equality"

See the Universal Declaration of Human Rights, article 11 and the International Covenant on Civil and Political Rights, article 14, which requires that in the determination of a criminal charge, everyone shall be entitled "not to be compelled to testify against himself or to confess guilt" (article 14(3)(g)). (See also, the Committee's comments quoted under article 40(2)(b)(i), above, page 547.)

"(v) If considered to have infringed the penal law, to have this decision and any measures imposed in consequence thereof reviewed by a higher competent, independent and impartial authority or judicial body according to law"

Article 14(5) of the International Covenant on Civil and Political Rights requires: "Everyone convicted of a crime shall have the right to his conviction and sentence being reviewed by a higher tribunal according to law".

When it ratified the Convention, Denmark made a reservation relating to article 40(2)(b)(v): "It is a fundamental principle in the Danish Adminis-

tration of Justice Act that everybody shall be entitled to have any penal measures imposed on him or her by a court of first instance reviewed by a higher court. There are, however, some provisions limiting this right in certain cases, for instance verdicts returned by a jury on the question of guilt, which have not been reversed by the legally trained judges of the court" (CRC/C/2/Rev.5, p. 17; Norway also made a reservation, but withdrew it in 1995: CRC/C/2/Rev.5, p. 35). The Committee commented:

"The Committee notes with concern that the State Party made a reservation to article 40(2)(b)(v) of the Convention, but also notes that the Government may reconsider this reservation....
"The Committee wishes to encourage the State Party to consider the possibility of withdrawing its reservation to the Convention, and would like to be kept informed of developments on this matter." (Denmark IRCO, Add.33, paras. 8 and 16)

(See also Committee's comments on Germany's reservation to this subparagraph, discussed under article 40(2)(b)(ii) above).

"(vi) To have the free assistance of an interpreter if the child cannot understand or speak the language used"

The International Covenant on Civil and Political Rights, article 14(3)(f), guarantees the same right. This is important not only to children who speak a different language, but also to disabled children.

"(vii) To have his or her privacy fully respected at all stages of the proceedings"

Article 14(1) of the International Covenant on Civil and Political Rights provides general rules requiring public hearings, indicating limited circumstances in which the press and public may be excluded: "... any judgment rendered in a criminal case or in a suit at law shall be made public except where the interest of juvenile persons otherwise requires or the proceedings concern matrimonial disputes or the guardianship of children."

The "Beijing Rules" expands on the provision in article 40 of the Convention: "The juvenile's right to privacy shall be respected at all stages in order to avoid harm being caused to her or him by undue publicity or by the process of labelling. In principle, no information that may lead to the identification of a juvenile offender shall be published." (rule 8(1) and (2))

The official commentary on the Rules explains: "Rule 8 stresses the importance of the protection

Three stages defined by juvenile justice legislation

In the Syrian Arab Republic, the Juvenile Delinquents Act divides childhood into the following three stages:

"(a) The first stage of childhood, from birth to seven years of age. During this stage, the child bears no criminal responsibility...

(b) The second stage of childhood, covering adolescents from seven to 15 years of age. During this stage, although some legal proceedings may be instituted against them, the court cannot sentence them to any penalty whatsoever.

(c) The third stage of childhood, covering juveniles from 15 to 18 years of age..."

(Syrian Arab Republic IR, para. 236)

of the juvenile's right to privacy. Young persons are particularly susceptible to stigmatization. Criminological research into labelling processes has provided evidence of the detrimental effects (of different kinds) resulting from the permanent identification of young persons as 'delinquent' or 'criminal'.

"Rule 8 also stresses the importance of protecting the juvenile from the adverse effects that may result from the publication in the mass media of information about the case (for example the names of young offenders, alleged or convicted). The interest of the individual should be protected and upheld, at least in principle."

In line with the Rules, in the report of its General Discussion on juvenile justice the Committee stated:

"The privacy of the child should be fully respected in all stages of the proceedings, including in relation to criminal records and possible reporting by the media." (Report on the tenth session, October-November 1995, CRC/C/46, para. 227; see also article 16, the child's right to privacy, page 201; and article 17, the role of the mass media, page 219)

"3. States Parties shall seek to promote the establishment of laws, procedures, authorities and institutions specifically applicable to children alleged as, accused of, or recognized as having infringed the penal law...": article 40(3)

The Committee has consistently proposed a distinct system of juvenile justice for all under-18-year-olds. The "Beijing Rules" also emphasizes: "Efforts should be made to establish, in each national jurisdiction, a set of laws, rules and provisions specifically applicable to juvenile offenders and institutions and bodies entrusted with the functions of the administration of juvenile justice and designed:

(a) To meet the varying needs of juvenile offenders, while protecting their basic rights;

(b) To meet the needs of society;

(c) To implement the following rules thoroughly and fairly." (rule 2(3))

The Committee has made various relevant specific recommendations. For example, the Committee

"... notes with particular concern that in the majority of departments in the State Party juvenile judges have not been appointed and that there is a lack of training programmes for juvenile judges..." (Honduras IRCO, Add.24, para. 18)

"The Committee also recommends that juvenile courts be set up in all provinces." (Argentina IRCO, Add.35, para. 18)

"... specialized courts should be established as a priority matter..." (Bulgaria IRCO, Add.66, para. 34)

Furthermore, it has welcomed the introduction of specific legislation:

"The Committee welcomes the recent adoption and entry into force of the new juvenile code, which represents significant progress towards harmonizing legislation and policy with the provisions of the Convention and thereby providing a legal framework for its implementation." (Bolivia IRCO, Add.1, para. 4)

Concern has been expressed when provisions are not in the "spirit" of article 40(3):

"The Committee suggests that the State Party consider reviewing its juvenile justice system in order to ensure that proceedings against persons under 18 years of age are fully compatible with the spirit of article 40, paragraph 3, of the Convention." (Norway IRCO, Add.23, para. 25)

"(a) the establishment of a minimum age below which children shall be presumed not to have the capacity to infringe the penal law"

The Committee's *Guidelines for Periodic Reports* asks under article 1 (definition of a child) for information on the minimum legal age defined in legislation for criminal responsibility (para. 24). Under article 40 the *Guidelines* requests information on "The establishment of a minimum age below which children shall be presumed not to have the capacity to infringe the penal law" (para. 134). The "Beijing Rules" requires in rule 4: "In those legal systems recognizing the concept of the age of criminal responsibility for juveniles, the beginning of that age shall not be fixed at too low an age level, bearing in mind the facts of emotional, mental and intellectual maturity."

The commentary to rule 4 states: "The minimum age of criminal responsibility differs widely owing to history and culture. The modern approach would be to consider whether a child can live up to the moral and psychological components of criminal responsibility; that is, whether a child, by virtue of her or his individual discernment and understanding, can be held responsible for essentially anti-social behaviour. If the age of criminal responsibility is fixed too low or if there is no lower age limit at all, the notion of responsibility would become meaningless. In general, there is a close relationship between the notion of responsibility for delinquent or criminal behaviour and other social rights and responsibilities (such as marital status, civil majority etc.). Efforts should therefore be made to agree on a reasonable lowest age limit that is applicable internationally."

The Committee has expressed particular concern when it appears no age has been fixed in law:

"...The lack of a minimum age below which children are presumed not to have the capacity to infringe penal law is also noted with concern." (Senegal IRCO, Add.44, para. 11. See also Guatemala IRCO, Add.58, paras. 15 and 26; Panama IRCO, Add.68, para. 21)

A balance must be found between protection and responsibility, particularly with regard to the minimum age for criminal majority, a Committee member was reported as commenting during discussion of Senegal's Initial Report: "...she was concerned that children's judges were given the possibility of considering that a child could be criminally responsible on the basis of his personality. However, if there was a minimum age below which the law recognized that no child could infringe the criminal law, then there could be no possibility for differences of interpretation." (Senegal SR.248, para. 26)

Some States Parties' reports have indicated confusion over the definition of the age of criminal responsibility, in some cases setting a different, and lower, age for serious offences. For example, in Belarus, criminal responsibility commences at 16, except that it may commence at 14 "when a particularly serious crime has been committed: attempted murder of a militia officer in the execution of his duty; rape; deliberate acts which

may cause a train crash; robbery with violence; robbery or threat of violence, whether or not endangering human life; theft of weapons, ammunition or narcotic substances; and some other offences" (Belarus IR, para. 105). The Committee stated that the situation in relation to the administration of juvenile justice was a matter of general concern (Belarus IRCO, Add.17, para. 10).

In relation to Jordan's report, the Committee noted:

"In the field of the administration of juvenile justice, the Committee is concerned about the application of article 92 of the Penal Code, in accordance with which, although no one under 18 years of age may be held criminally responsible, criminal proceedings may be brought against children over 7 years of age..." (Jordan IRCO, Add.21, para. 16)

The Committee has frequently expressed concern when the age is set too low, but does not prescribe a particular age. During discussions on the Initial Report of UK dependent territory: Hong Kong, a Committee member stated that in his view the age of criminal responsibility set by Hong Kong (seven) was too low. "Although it was stated that, for children between 7 and 11, there would be an assessment of whether the crime committed was understood by the child to be seriously wrong, that was an unsatisfactory solution. The mere fact of having to go through such an assessment procedure was burdensome for a child of such a young age. Even cases where the child was aware that its action was wrong might well reflect the fact that it was not in full control of its situation. Very young child offenders should be seen more as victims than as culprits, since statistics showed that almost all came from difficult family backgrounds. It was misleading to speak of a 'voluntary intention' to commit crime in a child of that age. The overwhelming majority of countries had set the age of criminal responsibility much higher, and even 14 was considered low..." (UK dependent territory: Hong Kong, SR.329, para. 79).

Similar comments have been made to other States:

"More specifically, the Committee recommends that serious consideration be given to raising the age of criminal responsibility throughout the areas of the United Kingdom." (UK IRCO, Add.34, para. 36)

The Committee "is deeply concerned by the low age of criminal responsibility (8 years old) and the status of children between 16 and 18 years old who are considered by penal law as adults. Those children are examined by adult courts....
"It is suggested that due attention be paid to the best interest of the child, to his or her right to be heard, and that deprivation of

liberty be considered as a measure of last resort and for the minimum period possible. In this regard the Committee recommends that the criminal age be raised and that persons aged between 16 and 18 be considered as children." (Sri Lanka IRCO, Add.40, paras. 22 and 40)

"...the age of criminal responsibility should not be set at too low an age and it should be ensured that below such an age, children are presumed not to have the capacity to infringe the penal law, in the light of article 40, paragraph 3(a), of the Convention." (Yemen IRCO, Add.47, para. 14. See also Cyprus IRCO, Add.59, para. 10; Nigeria IRCO, Add.61, para. 22; UK dependent territory: Hong Kong IRCO, Add.63, paras. 19 and 34; Ethiopia IRCO, Add.67, para. 20)

There must be no discrimination in the age, for example between girls and boys, or between different regions of the country: a Committee member said in discussions with Mexico: "It appeared that the minimum legal age for criminal responsibility was generally 18 years but lower in some parts of Mexico. It was difficult to see how children could be treated equally if their status in that respect depended on their place of residence. Article 40, paragraph 3(a), of the Convention clearly did not allow for different ages of criminal responsibility..." (Mexico SR.106, para. 37)

The Committee has welcomed a proposal to set the age at 18:

"... The Committee welcomes the information provided by the State Party that the new draft children's decree will set the age limit for criminal responsibility at 18." (Nigeria IRCO, Add.61, para. 39)

"(b) whenever appropriate and desirable, measures for dealing with such children without resorting to judicial proceedings, providing that human rights and legal safeguards are fully respected"

The "Beijing Rules" expands on the encouragement of diversion from judicial proceedings in rule 11:

"(1) Consideration shall be given, wherever appropriate, to dealing with juvenile offenders without resorting to formal trial by the competent authority, referred to in rule 14(1) below.

(2) The police, the prosecution or other agencies dealing with juvenile cases shall be empowered to dispose of such cases, at their discretion, without recourse to formal hearings, in accordance with the criteria laid down for that purpose in the respective legal system and also in accordance with the principles contained in these Rules.

(3) Any diversion involving referral to appropriate community or other services shall require the consent of the juvenile, or her or his parents or guardian, provided that such decision to refer a case shall be subject to review by a competent authority, upon application.

(4) In order to facilitate the discretionary disposition of juvenile cases, efforts shall be made to provide for community programmes, such as temporary supervision, and guidance, restitution, and compensation of victims."

The official commentary on the "Beijing Rules" notes that: "Diversion, involving removal from criminal justice processing and, frequently, redirection to community support services, is commonly practised on a formal and informal basis in many legal systems. This practice serves to hinder the negative effects of subsequent proceedings in juvenile justice administration (for example the stigma of conviction and sentence). In many cases, non-intervention would be the best response. Thus, diversion at the outset and without referral to alternative (social) services may be the optimal response. This is especially the case where the offence is of a non-serious nature and where the family, the school or other informal social control institutions have already reacted, or are likely to react, in an appropriate and constructive manner.

"As stated in rule 11(2), diversion may be used at any point of decision-making – by the police, the prosecution or other agencies such as the courts, tribunals, boards or councils. It may be exercised by one authority or several or all authorities, according to the rules and policies of the respective systems and in line with the present Rules. It may not necessarily be limited to petty cases, thus rendering diversion an important instrument.

"Rule 11(3) stresses the important requirement of securing the consent of the young offender (or the parent or guardian) to the recommended diversionary measure(s). (Diversion to community service without such consent would contradict the Abolition of Forced Labour Convention). However, this consent should not be left unchallengeable, since it might sometimes be given out of sheer desperation on the part of the juvenile. The rule underlines that care should be taken to minimize the potential for coercion and intimidation at all levels in the diversion process. Juveniles should not feel pressured (for example in order to avoid court appearance) or be pressured into consenting to diversion programmes. Thus, it is advocated that provision should be made for an objective appraisal of the appropriateness of dispositions involving young offenders by a 'competent authority upon application'.

"Rule 11(4) recommends the provision of viable alternatives to juvenile justice processing in the form of community-based diversion. Programmes that involve settlement by victim restitution and those that seek to avoid future conflict with the law through temporary supervision and guidance are especially commended. The merits of individual cases would make diversion appropriate, even when more serious offences have been committed (for example first offence, the act having been committed under peer pressure, etc.)."

The United Nations Standard Minimum Rules for Non-custodial Measures (the "Tokyo Rules") are also relevant to this provision of article 40 of the Convention and the following provision. The Rules do not refer specifically to juveniles, but state that they should be applied without discrimination based on age. They provide minimum safeguards for persons subject to alternatives to imprisonment.

"4. A variety of dispositions such as care, guidance and supervision orders; counselling; probation; foster care; education and vocational training programmes and other alternatives to institutional care shall be available to ensure that children are dealt with in a manner appropriate to their well-being and proportionate both to their cir- cumstances and the offence": article 40(4)

In addition to this provision, article 37 emphasizes that restriction of liberty of children must only be used as a last resort and for the shortest appropriate period, and it bars capital punishment, life imprisonment without possibility of release, and any cruel, inhuman or degrading treatment or punishment (see article 37, page 487).

Paragraph 4 of article 40 requires that alternatives to institutional care must be available, to ensure that sentencing is consistent with the aims of juvenile justice and the general principles of the Convention.

The "Beijing Rules" sets more detailed "Guiding principles in adjudication and disposition" (rule 17):

"(1) The disposition of the competent authority shall be guided by the following principles:

   (a) The reaction taken shall always be in proportion not only to the circumstances and the gravity of the offence but also to the circumstances and the needs of the juvenile as well as to the needs of the society...

   ...

   (d) The well-being of the juvenile shall be the guiding factor in the consideration of her or his case..."

(The remaining principles in rule 17 relate to restriction of liberty, capital punishment and corporal punishment; see article 37, page 487).

Implementation Checklist

article 40

● *General measures of implementation*

Have appropriate general measures of implementation been taken in relation to article 40, including

☐ identification and coordination of the responsible departments and agencies at all levels of government (article 40 is relevant to **departments of justice, home affairs, social welfare, education, health**)?

☐ identification of relevant non-governmental organizations/civil society partners?

☐ a comprehensive review to ensure that all legislation, policy and practice is compatible with the article, for all children in all parts of the jurisdiction?

☐ adoption of a strategy to secure full implementation

    ☐ which includes where necessary the identification of goals and indicators of progress?

    ☐ which does not affect any provisions which are more conducive to the rights of the child?

    ☐ which recognizes other relevant international standards?

    ☐ which involves where necessary international cooperation?

    (Such measures may be part of an overall governmental strategy for implementing the Convention as a whole).

☐ budgetary analysis and allocation of necessary resources?

☐ development of mechanisms for monitoring and evaluation?

☐ making the implications of article 40 widely known to adults and children?

☐ development of appropriate training and awareness-raising (in relation to article 40 likely to include the training of the **judiciary, lawyers, police, and all others working in the juvenile justice system, and in support of systems of diversion and prevention**)?

● *Specific issues in implementing article 40*

Does legislation, policy and practice in the State uphold the right of every child in the jurisdiction alleged as, accused of or recognized as having infringed the penal law to be treated in a manner which

    ☐ is consistent with the promotion of the child's sense of dignity and worth?

    ☐ reinforces the child's respect for fundamental human rights and for the fundamental freedoms of others?

    ☐ takes into account the child's age?

    ☐ takes into account the desirability of promoting the child's reintegration?

Implementation Handbook for the Convention on the Rights of the Child

How to use the checklists, *see page XVII*

□ takes into account the desirability of the child assuming a constructive role in society?

□ In planning its system of juvenile justice, has the State had regard to the relevant United Nations rules and guidelines and to other relevant international instruments?

□ Does legislation ensure that children cannot come into the criminal justice system because of acts or omissions that were not prohibited by national or international law at the time they were committed?

Does legislation, policy and practice in the State guarantee to any child alleged as or accused of having infringed the penal law the right

□ to be presumed innocent until proved guilty according to the law?

to be informed of the charges against him or her

□ promptly?

□ directly?

□ if appropriate through parents and guardians?

in the preparation and presentation of his defence, to have appropriate

□ legal assistance?

□ other assistance?

to have the matter determined

□ without delay?

□ by a competent and impartial authority or judicial body?

□ in a fair hearing (according to international instruments, including the "Beijing Rules")?

□ in the presence of legal and other appropriate assistance?

□ in the presence – unless judged not to be in the child's best interest, and taking account of the child's age or situation – of parents or legal guardians?

□ in the child's own presence?

not to be compelled

□ to give testimony?

□ to confess guilt?

to be able

□ to examine or have examined adverse witnesses?

□ to obtain the participation and examination of witnesses on his or her behalf under conditions of equality?

if considered to have infringed the criminal law, to have a review by a higher, competent, independent and impartial authority or judicial body according to law,

How to use the checklists, *see page XVII*

of
- ☐ the decision?
- ☐ any measures imposed in consequence thereof?
- ☐ to have the free assistance of an interpreter if the child cannot understand or speak the language used?
- ☐ to have his or her privacy fully respected at all stages of the proceedings?

Are hearings involving children open to
- ☐ the public?
- ☐ representatives of the press?

☐ Are there appropriate limits on press reporting of such hearings and their results?

☐ Does legislation ensure that there are no circumstances in which the identity of a child alleged as, accused of or recognized as having infringed the penal law can be disclosed?

☐ Is there a system of juvenile justice in the State distinctive from that relating to adults?

☐ Are all children up to 18 years of age alleged as, accused of or recognized as having infringed the penal law in the jurisdiction, without exception, dealt with through the system of juvenile justice?

Does the juvenile justice system include, specifically for such children, distinct
- ☐ laws?
- ☐ procedures?
- ☐ authorities?
- ☐ institutions?
- ☐ disposals?

☐ Is a minimum age defined in law below which children are presumed not to have the capacity to infringe the criminal law?

☐ If such an age is defined, are there no circumstances in which a child below that age can be alleged as, accused of or recognized as having infringed the criminal law?

☐ Does legislation, policy and practice provide measures for dealing with children alleged as, accused of or recognized as having infringed the penal law without resorting to judicial proceedings?

☐ If so, do safeguards exist for the child who believes him/herself to be innocent?

Are a variety of dispositions available, such as
- ☐ care orders?
- ☐ guidance and supervision orders?
- ☐ diversion to mental health treatment?
- ☐ victim reparation/restitution?

How to use the checklists, *see page XVII*

- ☐ counselling?
- ☐ probation?
- ☐ foster care?
- ☐ education?
- ☐ vocational training courses?
- ☐ any other alternatives to institutional care?

Does legislation, policy and practice ensure that children are dealt with

- ☐ in a manner appropriate to their well-being?

proportionate to
- ☐ their circumstances?
- ☐ the offence?

Reminder : **The Convention is indivisible and its articles are interdependent. Article 40 should not be considered in isolation.**

Particular regard should be paid to:
The general principles

Article 2: all rights to be recognized for each child in jurisdiction without discrimination on any ground
Article 3(1): the best interests of the child to be a primary consideration in all actions concerning children
Article 6: right to life and maximum possible survival and development
Article 12: respect for the child's views in all matters affecting the child; opportunity to be heard in any judicial or administrative proceedings affecting the child

Closely related articles

Articles whose implementation is related to that of article 40 include:

Article 16: right to privacy
Article 19: protection from all forms of violence
Article 20: alternative care
Article 25: periodic review of placement/treatment
Article 37: prohibition of death sentence and life imprisonment; limits on restriction of liberty, etc.
Article 38: armed conflict
Article 39: rehabilitative care for victims

Respect for existing human rights standards

Text of Article 41

Nothing in the present Convention shall affect any provisions which are more conducive to the realization of the rights of the child and which may be contained in:

(a) The law of a State Party; or

(b) International law in force for that State.

Article 41 ensures that the Convention's standards do not undermine any provisions "more conducive to the realization of the rights of the child" that are in a State Party's law or in international law in force in a particular State. ∎

Summary

Extracts from

Committee on the Rights of the Child

Guidelines for Reports to be submitted by States Parties under the Convention

For full text of *Guidelines for Periodic Reports*, see Appendix 3, page 604.

Guidelines for Periodic Reports

"I. GENERAL MEASURES OF IMPLEMENTATION (arts. 4, 42, and 44, paragraph 6)

...

In the light of article 41 of the Convention, please indicate any provisions of the national legislation which are more conducive to the realization of the rights of the child..."
(CRC/C/58, para. 14)

Protecting existing standards

During the drafting of the Convention on the Rights of the Child, article 41 evolved from a suggestion that there should be an article relating to the applicability of provisions of other international instruments, in particular the International Covenants on Civil and Political Rights and on Economic, Social and Cultural Rights. During the drafting process it was broadened to cover "international law in force", and the discussion indicated that "international law" was to be given broad interpretation, covering customary international law (E/CN.4/1989/48, pp. 116-119 etc.; see Detrick, pp. 521 et seq.).

A key 1986 United Nations General Assembly resolution (resolution 41/120) includes guidelines relating to the elaboration of new international instruments. It urges member States, when developing new international human rights standards, to give due consideration to the established international legal framework, to avoid undermining existing standards in any way.

The Vienna Declaration and Programme of Action, adopted at the World Conference on Human Rights in 1993, recalls this resolution, and "recognizing the need to maintain consistency with the high quality of existing international standards and to avoid proliferation of human rights instruments ... calls on the United Nations human rights bodies, when considering the elaboration of new international standards, to keep those guidelines in mind, to consult with human rights treaty bodies on the necessity for drafting new standards and to request the Secretariat to carry out technical reviews of proposed new instruments." (A/CONF.157/23, p.14)

One example of the Committee on the Rights of the Child making reference to article 41 occurred in the report of its General Discussion on armed conflict, when it reminded States that article 41

"invites States Parties to always apply the norms which are more conducive to the realization of the rights of the child, contained either in applicable international law or in national legislation." (Report on the second session, September-October 1992, CRC/C/10, para. 68)

In this particular case, the Committee was encouraging States to refrain from recruiting children under 18 into armed forces (see also article 38, page 514 for further discussion: there was a dispute during the drafting of article 38 that it undermined existing standards of protection).

Implementation Checklist

☐ Has there been a review of national legislation to consider whether it includes or could include provisions more conducive to the rights of the child than those of the Convention?

☐ Has there been a review of applicable international law to consider whether it includes provisions more conducive to the rights of the child than those of the Convention?

Making Convention widely known

article 42

Text of Article 42

States Parties undertake to make the principles and provisions of the Convention widely known, by appropriate and active means, to adults and children alike.

Summary

Rights are of little use to individuals unless individuals are aware of them. Article 42 confirms the obligation States Parties assume to make the Convention on the Rights of the Child known "by appropriate and active means" to adults and children. The Committee on the Rights of the Child has underlined the importance of disseminating the Convention's principles and provisions to all sectors of the population. In addition, it has suggested that the Convention should be incorporated into school curricula and into the training of those who work with or for children. ∎

Extracts from
Committee on the Rights of the Child
Guidelines for Reports to be submitted by States Parties under the Convention

For full text of *Guidelines for Periodic Reports*, see Appendix 3, page 604.

Guidelines for Initial Reports

"General measures of implementation

...

In addition, States Parties are requested to describe the measures that have been taken or are foreseen, pursuant to article 42 of the Convention, to make the principles and provisions of the Convention widely known, by appropriate and active means, to adults and children alike."
(CRC/C/5, para. 10)

Guidelines for Periodic Reports

"GENERAL MEASURES OF IMPLEMENTATION...

*...In addition, States are requested to describe the measures that have been taken or are foreseen, pursuant to **article 42** of the Convention, to make the principles and provisions of the Convention widely known, by appropriate and active means, to adults and children alike. In this regard, reports should also indicate:*

> *The extent to which the Convention has been translated into the national, local, minority or indigenous languages. In this connection, an indication should be given of the number of languages into which the Convention has been translated and the number of copies translated into the minority languages during the reporting period;*

> *Whether the Convention has been translated and has been made available in the languages spoken by the larger refugee and immigrant groups in the country concerned;*

> *The measures adopted to publicize the Convention and create widespread awareness of its principles and provisions. In this connection, an indication should be given of the number of meetings (such as parliamentary or governmental conferences, workshops, seminars) held, the number of programmes broadcast on radio or television and the number of publications issued explaining the Convention on the Rights of the Child during the reporting period;*

> *The specific steps taken to make the Convention widely known to children and the extent to which it has been reflected in the school curricula and considered in parents' education campaigns. An indication should be given of the number of copies of the Convention distributed in the educational system and to the public at large during the reporting period;*

> *The measures adopted to provide education on the Convention to public officials, as well as to train professional groups working with and for children, such as teachers, law enforcement officials, including police, immigration officers, judges, prosecutors, lawyers, defence forces, medical doctors, health workers and social workers;*

> *The extent to which the principles and provisions of the Convention have been incorporated in professional training curricula and codes of conduct or regulations;*

> *The steps taken to promote understanding of the principles and provisions of the Convention by the mass media and by information and publishing agencies;*

> *The involvement of non-governmental organizations in awareness and advocacy campaigns on the Convention, as well as any support provided to them. In this connection, an indication should be given of the number of non-governmental organizations who participated in such events during the reporting period;*

> *The participation of children in any of these activities."*

(CRC/C/58, para. 22. In addition, there are many references in the *Guidelines for Periodic Reports* to training activities related to the Convention: see box, page 604.)

A "comprehensive strategy" for dissemination

In its *Guidelines* for Initial and Periodic Reports, the Committee on the Rights of the Child has included the implications of article 42 under "General Measures of Implementation", linking it to article 4. In addition, under article 44(6) the Committee emphasizes the importance of widely publicizing at country-level States Parties' Initial and Periodic Reports, reports of discussions with the Committee and the Committee's Concluding Observations (see article 44(6), page 582).

In its comments on Initial Reports, the Committee has emphasized that dissemination can achieve a variety of purposes:

- ensuring the visibility of children;
- enhancing respect for children;
- reaffirming the value of children's fundamental rights;
- enhancing democratic institutions;
- achieving national reconciliation;
- encouraging the protection of the rights of children belonging to minority groups;
- changing negative attitudes towards children;
- combating and eradicating existing prejudices against vulnerable groups of children and harmful cultural practices.

The Committee has stressed in various comments the need for a "comprehensive strategy" for dissemination, an "ongoing and systematic approach", a "permanent information campaign", and "systematic and continuous steps". To one State Party it proposed that an interministerial group should plan dissemination (Iceland IRCO, Add.50, para. 8). In others, it has encouraged recourse to international cooperation and the help of bodies such as the High Commissioner for Human Rights/Centre for Human Rights and UNICEF:

"In order to effectively combat persisting discriminatory attitudes and negative traditions affecting girls, the Committee encourages the State Party to launch a comprehensive and integrated public information campaign aimed at promoting children's rights within the society, and particularly within the family. The Committee also recommends that the State Party ensure specific training on the Convention for professional groups working with and for children, including teachers, social workers, health personnel, judges and law enforcement officials. International cooperation with, inter alia, the Centre for Human Rights and the United Nations Children's Fund could be sought to this effect...

"Get to know children"

Spain's Initial Report describes a campaign launched through the mass media: "The main object of the initiative in its first phase is to put over the idea of the importance for society of overall and specific knowledge of the world of childhood and the fact that the child is a developing being inside a society undergoing continuous change. The campaign is centred basically on the needs of the child in two main directions: the need for protection and, in turn, the need for autonomy: the need for protection is determined by the level of development of the child and the need for autonomy is understood as a need to assign the child an active, participatory and creative role in the milieu in which he or she is developing, as an essential condition for growth... Video copies have been made of the television publicity spot used in the campaign and these have been disseminated free of charge for use in public places and training activities. The central slogan of the whole campaign can be summarized in the words: 'Listen to them!'. The complementary message is 'You don't know what you're losing by not listening to your children'." (Spain IR, paras. 23, 24 and 26)

"The Committee is of the opinion that greater efforts are required to make the provisions and principles of the Convention widely known and understood by adults and children alike, in the light of articles 12 and 42 of the Convention. It encourages the State Party to further increase public awareness of the participatory rights of children, as well as to consider incorporating the Convention in the school curriculum." (Nepal IRCO, Add.57, paras. 26 and 27)

The Committee has proposed that the text of the Convention should be widely circulated, as well as information on, and explanations of, the Convention. It should be available in all languages, and the Committee has emphasized the importance of ensuring it reaches the general public and the entire population, including for instance those living in remote rural areas (for example, see Honduras IRCO, Add.24, para. 23).

The Committee has urged the use of the media for dissemination (see also article 17, page 213). The *Guidelines for Periodic Reports* also asks for information on steps taken to promote understanding of the principles and provisions of the Convention by the mass media and by information and publishing agencies (para. 22). The

Training proposed in the Committee's Guidelines for Periodic Reports

The *Guidelines for Periodic Reports* prepared by the Committee on the Rights of the Child underlines repeatedly the importance of training as a strategy for implementation of the Convention. The *Guidelines* requests information on training programmes and the content of training in relation to the following:

Article 3   The extent to which the principle of the "best interests of the child" is included in the training of professionals dealing with children's rights. (para. 39)

Article 4   Measures taken to provide education on the Convention to public officials, as well as to train professional groups working with and for children, such as teachers, law enforcement officials, including police, immigration officers, judges, prosecutors, lawyers, defence forces, medical doctors, health workers and social workers.

The extent to which the principles and provisions of the Convention have been included in professional training curricula and codes of conduct or regulations. (para. 22)

Article 5   Parental education programmes and training activities provided to relevant professional groups (for example social workers), including information on any evaluation of effectiveness.

Measures to convey knowledge and information about child development and the evolving capacities of the child to parents or other persons responsible for the child. (para. 63)

Article 7   Measures taken to provide adequate training to personnel working on registration of births. (para. 50)

Article 12   Measures to train professionals working with children to encourage children to exercise their right to express their views, and to give children's views due weight.

Details of child development courses provided for: judges in general, family court judges, juvenile court judges, probation officers, police officers, prison officers, teachers, health workers and other professionals

Details of the number of courses about the Convention included in the curricula of: law schools, teacher training schools, medical schools and institutions, nursing schools, social work schools, psychology departments and sociology departments. (para. 46)

Article 19   Special training provided for relevant professionals in the protection of the child from all forms of violence, abuse, neglect, etc. (para. 89)

Article 22   Training courses for staff working with refugee children. (para. 120)

Article 23   Measures taken to ensure adequate training, including specialized training, for those responsible for the care of disabled children, including at the family and community levels and within relevant institutions. (para. 92)

Article 24   Campaigns, programmes, etc., developed to provide basic knowledge, information and support to the general population, including in particular parents and children, on child health, nutrition, the advantages of breastfeeding, hygiene and environmental sanitation and the prevention of accidents.

Measures adopted to improve the system of education and training of health personnel. (para. 95)

Article 28   Steps taken to enhance the competence of teachers and to ensure quality of teaching. (para. 106)

Article 29   Training provided to teachers to prepare them to direct teaching to the aims of education set out in article 29. (para. 113)

Article 34   Appropriate training for special units of law enforcement officials and police liaison officers dealing with children who have been sexually abused or exploited. (para. 159)

Article 35   Relevant training activities provided to competent authorities concerned with abduction, sale or traffic in children. (para. 161)

Article 36   Training activities for professional groups working with or for children on forms of exploitation prejudicial to the child's welfare. (para. 164)

Article 37(a)   Educative and training activities developed, particularly with personnel in institutions, services and facilities working with and for children, aimed at preventing any form of ill-treatment. (para. 61)

Article 38   Appropriate training for professionals concerned with the protection of children affected by armed conflict, including the rules of international humanitarian law. (para. 123)

Article 40   Training activities for all professionals involved with the system of juvenile justice, including judges, prosecutors, lawyers, law enforcement officials, immigration officers and social workers, on the provisions of the Convention and the United Nations Rules and Guidelines in the field of juvenile justice. (para. 136)

(CRC/C/58)

Committee strongly encourages the involvement of civil society, including NGOs and children's groups, as well as close cooperation with community and religious leaders. The final sentence in the relevant section of the *Guidelines for Periodic Reports* asks for information on "the participation of children in any of these activities" (para. 22).

During discussion of Slovenia's Initial Report, a Committee member was reported as noting that the Convention "was addressed not only to all levels of government and society as a whole, but also to children themselves. Although most countries reporting to the Committee claimed that sufficient information was provided to children, schools and teacher training institutions to create awareness of the Convention and provided documentation in support of those claims, members of the Committee in their travels had found that, in general, the majority of children they met were unaware of the rights of the child or of the text of the Convention." (Slovenia SR.337, para. 20)

The Committee has proposed that the Convention should be incorporated into school and university curricula and appropriate measures taken *"to facilitate access by children to information produced for them"* (Mauritius IRCO, Add.64, para. 27).

The Committee perceives this process as an appropriate response to the United Nations Decade for Human Rights Education (see also article 29, page 396). The *Guidelines for Periodic Reports* also asks whether the Convention has been incorporated into the education of parents (para. 22).

Training concerning Convention

The Committee has proposed specific training courses (both initial training and in-service retraining) for those working with children, mentioning in a variety of recommendations the following groups as targets for such training: judges, lawyers, law enforcement officials, personnel in detention/correctional facilities, immigration officers, United Nations peace-keeping forces and military personnel, teachers, social workers, those providing psychological support to families and children, personnel and professionals working with or for children, those working in institutions for children, including welfare institutions, doctors, health and family-planning workers, government officials and decision makers, personnel entrusted with data collection under the Convention, and so forth. The *Guidelines for Periodic Reports* refers to incorporating the Convention in "professional training curricula, codes of conduct or regulations".

The following are examples of comments and recommendations made by the Committee during its examination of States Parties' Initial Reports:

"The text of the Convention should be disseminated as widely as possible among the public at large and, in particular, among judges, teachers and members of other professions working with children. Furthermore, specific training courses should be organized for law enforcement personnel and the personnel in correctional facilities as well as for those working with families with psychological problems." (Egypt IRCO, Add.5, para. 16)

"The Committee is of the opinion that greater efforts are required to make the principles and provisions of the Convention widely known to and understood by adults and children alike, including article 12 of the Convention relating to the right of the child to express his or her views and have them taken into account. The Committee would like to suggest that a comprehensive strategy be worked out and put into operation as quickly as possible to realize this objective. It is important that such information should be prepared in the languages of children belonging to minorities or indigenous groups and should reach the people living in the remoter rural areas. Training material and programmes about the rights of the child should also be prepared and provided to personnel and professionals working with children, including judges, teachers, those working in institutions for children and law enforcement officials." (Honduras IRCO, Add.24, para. 23)

"The Committee suggests that serious consideration be given to training in the rights of the child of professional groups working with or for children, including teachers, judges and defensores de familia y de menores. The Committee believes that a new attitude and approach should be developed, particularly as regards the police and the military, in order to enhance respect for all children, regardless of their social, economic or other background, and to reaffirm the value of their fundamental rights. In this connection, information and training programmes should be strengthened." (Colombia IRCO, Add.30, para. 22)

"The Committee encourages the State Party to pursue and develop its policy aimed at disseminating information and increasing public awareness of the Convention. It recommends that a nationwide education campaign be launched, in the framework of the United Nations Decade for Human Rights Education, to sensitize the population at large – including children themselves – to the principles and provisions of the Convention, and that consideration be given to incorporating the rights of

Making the Convention widely known in Nepal: the letterhead campaign

Nepal describes in its Initial Report "Essay, poetry and poster competitions have been organized regularly by NGOs and by the Government. On the international organization side, UNICEF has played a significant role in advocating the rights of the child. Brochures, music tapes, photo panels and radio and TV shows have been produced to promote the Convention. The most recent and unique effort has been the letterhead campaign, in which NGOs, different professional groups and even commercial companies have been requested by UNICEF to print an article from the Convention at the bottom of their letterheads. It is estimated that more than a million such copies have already been printed. Some commercial companies have also decided to print Convention messages on their products. Furthermore, some post offices have agreed to stamp the Convention's articles on all incoming and outgoing mail..." (Nepal IR, para. 46)

the child in the school curricula. At the same time, the State Party should integrate the Convention into the training curricula for professional groups dealing with children, especially judges, lawyers, immigration officers,

peace-keepers and teachers." (Canada IRCO, Add.37, para. 19. See also Denmark IRCO, Add.33, paras. 22 and 23; Belgium IRCO, Add.38, para. 17; Ukraine IRCO, Add.42, para. 21; Germany IRCO, Add.43, paras. 15 and 26; Senegal IRCO, Add.44, para. 9; Croatia IRCO, Add.52, para. 24; UK dependent territory: Hong Kong IRCO, Add.63, para. 23; Mauritius IRCO, Add.64, para. 27)

The Committee has also proposed surveys to review the degree of awareness of sectors of the population about the Convention and its implications (for example, UK dependent territory: Hong Kong IRCO, Add.63, para. 23).

Human Rights Committee General Comment

The Human Rights Committee, in a General Comment on "Implementation at the national level" of the International Covenant on Civil and Political Rights, states: "... it is very important that individuals should know what their rights under the Covenant (and the Optional Protocol, as the case may be) are and also that all administrative and judicial authorities should be aware of the obligations which the State Party has assumed under the Covenant. To this end, the Covenant should be publicized in all official languages of the State and steps should be taken to familiarize the authorities concerned with its contents as part of their training. It is desirable also to give publicity to the State Party's cooperation with the Committee." (Human Rights Committee, General Comment 3, HRI/GEN/1/Rev.2, p. 4)

Implementation Checklist

article
42

● *General measures of implementation*

Have appropriate general measures of implementation been taken in relation to article 42, including

☐ identification and coordination of the responsible departments and agencies at all levels of government (article 42 is relevant in particular to the **departments of education, social welfare, justice – but all departments should be involved**)?

☐ identification of relevant non-governmental organizations/civil society partners?

☐ a comprehensive review to ensure that all legislation, policy and practice is compatible with the article, for all children in all parts of the jurisdiction?

☐ adoption of a strategy to secure full implementation

    ☐ which includes where necessary the identification of goals and indicators of progress?

    ☐ which does not affect any provisions which are more conducive to the rights of the child?

    ☐ which recognizes other relevant international standards?

    ☐ which involves where necessary international cooperation?

(Such measures may be part of an overall governmental strategy for implementing the Convention as a whole).

☐ budgetary analysis and allocation of necessary resources?

☐ development of mechanisms for monitoring and evaluation?

● *Specific issues in implementing article 42*

Has the State taken active steps to make the provisions and principles of the Convention widely known throughout the population

    ☐ to adults?

    ☐ to children?

☐ Has the Convention, and information about its implications, been translated into all languages in use throughout the jurisdiction and appropriately disseminated?

☐ Has the Convention, and information about its implications, been disseminated in appropriate media for disabled children and adults?

Has the Convention and information about its implications been incorporated into the curriculum of

    ☐ all schools?

☐ all other educational institutions?

training courses – both initial and in-service – for those working with or for children, including

    ☐ judges?

    ☐ lawyers?

    ☐ law enforcement officials?

    ☐ personnel in detention/correctional facilities?

    ☐ immigration officers?

    ☐ military personnel and United Nations peacekeeping forces?

    ☐ teachers?

    ☐ social workers?

    ☐ those providing psychological support to families and children?

    ☐ those working in institutions for children, including welfare institutions?

    ☐ doctors, health and family planning workers?

    ☐ government officials and decision makers?

    ☐ personnel entrusted with data collection under the Convention?

    ☐ other personnel and professionals working with or for children?

Have programmes for dissemination of the Convention and its principles and provisions involved

    ☐ the mass media?

    ☐ appropriate NGOs and civil society?

    ☐ children's groups?

☐ Have steps been taken to encourage the understanding of the principles and provisions of the Convention by the mass media and by information and publishing agencies?

Has the State undertaken or commissioned research into awareness of the Convention and its principles and provisions among

    ☐ the general public?

    ☐ those working with or for children?

    ☐ children?

Reminder : **The Convention is indivisible and its articles are interdependent. Article 42 should not be considered in isolation. Article 42 requires dissemination of information to adults and children alike about <u>all</u> the principles and provisions of the Convention, in the light of the non-discrimination principle in article 2.**

The Committee on the Rights of the Child

Article 43

Text of Article 43

1. For the purpose of examining the progress made by States Parties in achieving the realization of the obligations undertaken in the present Convention, there shall be established a Committee on the Rights of the Child, which shall carry out the functions hereinafter provided.

2. The Committee shall consist of 10 experts of high moral standing and recognized competence in the field covered by this Convention. The members of the Committee shall be elected by States Parties from among their nationals and shall serve in their personal capacity, consideration being given to equitable geographical distribution, as well as to the principal legal systems.

3. The members of the Committee shall be elected by secret ballot from a list of persons nominated by States Parties. Each State Party may nominate one person from among its own nationals.

4. The initial election to the Committee shall be held no later than six months after the date of the entry into force of the present Convention and thereafter every second year. At least four months before the date of each election, the Secretary-General of the United Nations shall address a letter to States Parties inviting them to submit their nominations within two months. The Secretary-General shall subsequently prepare a list in alphabetical order of all persons thus nominated, indicating States Parties which have nominated them, and shall submit it to the States Parties to the present Convention.

5. The elections shall be held at meetings of States Parties convened by the Secretary-General at United Nations Headquarters. At those meetings, for which two thirds of States Parties shall constitute a quorum, the persons elected to the Committee shall be those who obtain the largest number of votes and an absolute majority of the votes of the representatives of States Parties present and voting.

6. The members of the Committee shall be elected for a term of four years. They shall be eligible for re-election if renominated. The term of five of the members elected at the first election shall expire at the end of two years; immediately after the first election, the names of these five members shall be chosen by lot by the Chairman of the meeting.

7. If a member of the Committee dies or resigns or declares that for any other cause he or she can no longer perform the duties of the Committee, the State Party which nominated the member shall appoint another expert from among its nationals to serve for the remainder of the term, subject to the approval of the Committee.

8. The Committee shall establish its own rules of procedure.

9. The Committee shall elect its officers for a period of two years.

10. The meetings of the Committee shall normally be held at United Nations Headquarters or at any other convenient place as determined by the Committee. The Committee shall normally meet annually. The duration of the meetings of the Committee shall be determined, and reviewed, if necessary, by a meeting of the States Parties to the present Convention, subject to the approval of the General Assembly.

11. The Secretary-General of the United Nations shall provide the necessary staff and facilities for the effective performance of the functions of the Committee under the present Convention.

12. With the approval of the General Assembly, the members of the Committee established under the present Convention shall receive emoluments from the United Nations resources on such terms and conditions as the Assembly may decide.

The Committee in 1997

The members of the Committee, as at September 1997, with their terms of office, are as follows:

Name of member	Nominating State	First elected	Current Term of office
Ms. Sandra P. Mason, Chair	Barbados	1991	1995 - 1999
Ms. Judith Karp, Vice-Chair	Israel	1995	1995 - 1999
Mr. Yuri M. Kolosov, Vice-Chair	Russian Federation	1991	1995 - 1999
Mr. Ghassan Salim Rabah, Vice-Chair	Lebanon	1997	1997 - 2001
Ms. Nafsiah Mboi, Rapporteur	Indonesia	1997	1997 - 2001
Mr. Francesco Paolo Fulci	Italy	1997	1997 - 2001
Ms. E. M. Queen Mokhuane	South Africa	1997	1997 - 2001
Ms. Awa N'Deye Ouedraogo	Burkina Faso	1997	1997 - 1999
Ms. Lisbet Palme	Sweden	1997	1997 - 1999
Ms. Marilia Sardenberg	Brazil	1991	1997 - 2001

Article 43 sets out the monitoring role of the Committee on the Rights of the Child, the procedures for electing its members and for its meetings. ■

....

Role of the Committee

The function of the Committee on the Rights of the Child is to provide an international mechanism for monitoring progress on implementation of the Convention on the Rights of the Child – in the words of the Convention: "For the purpose of examining the progress made by States Parties in achieving the realization of the obligations undertaken in the ... Convention" (article 43(1)). Its major tasks are to examine the Initial and Periodic Reports submitted to it by States Parties under article 44 of the Convention, and working with other Treaty Bodies, United Nations agencies and other bodies to promote the Convention and the realization of the rights of the child.

The Committee is considered the highest international authority for interpreting the Convention.

Committee membership and election

The Committee comprises 10 "experts of high moral standing and recognized competence in the field covered by this Convention". Members are elected to serve for a period of four years and are eligible for re-election if they are nominated again at the expiry of their term. Each State Party is entitled to nominate one of its nationals to stand for election. Elections are held every second year. At least four months prior to an election, the Secretary-General invites each State Party to nominate one person from among its nationals within two months. A list is prepared of all those nominated and an election by secret ballot is held at a meeting of States Parties convened by the Secretary-General at United Nations Headquarters. The Convention requires that consideration be given in the elections to "equitable geographical distribution, as well as to the principal legal systems" (article 43(2)).

A proposal to increase the size of the Committee from 10 to 18 members, initiated by Costa Rica, was adopted by consensus at a conference of States Parties on 12 December 1995, and endorsed by the General Assembly (resolution 50/155, 21 December 1995). It requires formal acceptance by two thirds of States Parties before it will come into force. By September 1997,

46 States Parties had notified their acceptance; 120 acceptances are required for the proposal to come into force.

Members serve in a personal capacity. They do not represent their State or any organization. In the report of its second session, Committee members noted the importance of the independence of the elected experts:

"They recalled the provision of the Convention which states that members shall serve in their personal capacity; they reaffirmed that the mandate derives from the provisions and principles of the Convention on the Rights of the Child and that the Committee members are solely accountable to the children of the world. It was pointed out that, although elected by States Parties' representatives, members do not represent their country, Government or any other organization to which they may belong. In view of the relevance of this consideration, and in order to ensure the principle of impartiality, the members of the Committee reiterated the desirability of not participating in the Committee's discussions during the examination of the reports submitted by their own Governments. They also recognized that, when acting in the framework of the rights of the child, there is a need to clearly distinguish between their personal or professional role and their role as members of the Committee." (Report on the second session, September-October 1992, CRC/C/10, p. 33)

When a member joins the Committee he or she makes the following declaration: "I solemnly declare that I will perform my duties and exercise my powers as a member of the Committee on the Rights of the Child honourably, faithfully, impartially and conscientiously."

If a member fails for whatever reason to complete a term of office, the State Party that nominated the member appoints another expert from among its nationals – subject to the approval of the Committee – to serve for the remainder of the term.

Rules of Procedure and officers

The Committee is responsible for establishing its own rules of procedure, and elects its officers for two years. According to the Rules of Procedure adopted by the Committee at its 22nd

The NGO Group for the Convention on the Rights of the Child

The NGO Group for the Convention on the Rights of the Child promotes the involvement of non-governmental organizations in the reporting process to the Committee on the Rights of the Child, encouraging the development of NGO coalitions at national level. The NGO Group has produced a resource guide outlining the reporting process. It is intended to assist NGOs in understanding and using the process to further the implementation of the Convention at national level. The NPO Group can be contacted at:

NGO Group for the Convention on the Rights of the Child
c/o Defence for Children International (DCI)
P.O. Box 88, CH-1211 Geneva 20, Switzerland
ph. (41) 22 734 0558; fax (41) 22 740 1145
e-mail: dci-ngo.group@pinguet.ch

meeting on 15 October 1991 (A/47/41, Annex IV, p. 20) the officers to be elected are a chairperson, three vice-chairpersons and a rapporteur.

Meetings of the Committee

Currently, in 1997, the Committee meets three times a year, each session being of three weeks duration (in January, May/June and September/October) at the Palais des Nations in Geneva, Switzerland. At these sessions it examines States Parties' reports in discussion with government representatives and conducts any other formal business (including, for example, General Discussions). The Committee presently devotes an average of three three-hour periods over a period of two days to the public examination of each report, usually examining six reports at each session. At the end of the session it prepares "Concluding Observations" on each State Party report (for details of the reporting process, see article 44, page 575).

In addition, the Committee has held informal regional meetings – for example for Latin America in 1992 and the South East Asian region in Bangkok in 1993, organized by UNICEF with support and assistance from the Centre for Human Rights, other United Nations agencies and bodies.

Pre-sessional Working Group

Immediately following each formal session, there is a one-week meeting of a Working Group of Committee members (the "Pre-sessional Working Group") to prepare for the following session; in practice, not all Committee members attend.

The Committee has emphasized in particular the crucial role that non-governmental organizations (NGOs) from the State concerned play in providing expert advice to it during the meetings of the Pre-sessional Working Group. Other United Nations agencies, including UNICEF, ILO, WHO, UNHCR and UNESCO, and sometimes international NGOs, brief the Committee. (For detailed description, see article 44, page 580)

The outcome of the Pre-sessional Working Group is a "List of Issues" to be raised with the States Parties whose reports are to be examined at the next session.

General Discussions

The Committee included in its Rules of Procedure the ability to devote meetings during its regular session to General Discussions on one specific article of the Convention or a related subject. At its first session it agreed that the first General Discussion should be on the topic "Children in armed conflicts" (held on 5 October 1992).

The purpose is for the Committee to explore in depth with United Nations agencies, NGOs and individual experts particular issues, to improve its work in monitoring implementation, and to provide recommendations for States Parties and others.

Other General Discussions have been held on:

- Economic exploitation of the child (4 October 1993)
- The role of the family in the promotion of the rights of the child (10 October 1994)
- The girl child (23 January 1995)
- Administration of juvenile justice (9 October 1995)
- The child and the media (7 October 1996)
- The rights of children with disabilities (6 October 1997)

General comments

As with other Treaty Bodies, the Committee's Rules of Procedure allow it to make General Comments "based on the articles and provisions of the Convention with a view to promoting its further implementation and assisting States Parties in fulfilling their reporting obligations". As of September 1997, the Committee has not issued any General Comments. It may also make general recommendations based on information received during the reporting process or from other sources.

Documentation of activities

The Office of the High Commissioner for Human Rights is the Secretariat for the Committee on behalf of the Secretary-General. Summary

572

Implementation Handbook for the Convention on the Rights of the Child

records are prepared for all public and some private meetings of the Committee (all meetings are held in public unless the Committee decides otherwise). The Initial and Periodic Reports of States Parties, Concluding Observations of the Committee, summary records and reports on the Committee's sessions are generally made available in the Committee's three working languages (English, French and Spanish; although summary records are not generally translated into Spanish); in addition the Committee may decide to make particular documents available in one or more of the other "official" languages of the Convention (Arabic, Chinese and Russian).

The Committee's official documents are available from:

Secretariat to the Committee on the Rights of the Child, Office of the High Commissioner for Human Rights, Room D.205, Palais des Nations, 8-14 Avenue de la Paix, 1211 Geneva 10, Switzerland (ph. 00 41 22 917 1234; fax 00 41 22 917 0123). They are available electronically:

http://www.unhchr.ch

Also from the Distribution and Sales Section, Palais des Nations, 8-14 Avenue de la Paix, 1211 Geneva 10, Switzerland.

Reporting obligations of States Parties

article **44**

Article 44 sets out the obligations of States Parties to the Convention on the Rights of the Child to report to the Committee on the Rights of the Child, within two years of ratification, and then every five years. The Committee may request further information. The Committee reports on its activities every two years to the General Assembly, through the Economic and Social Council. States Parties are required to make their reports widely available to the public in their own countries. ■

Summary

Extracts from
Committee on the Rights of the Child
Guidelines for Reports to be submitted by States Parties under the Convention

For full text of *Guidelines for Periodic Reports*, see Appendix 3, page 604.
For text of *Guidelines* on paragraph 6 of article 44, see below, page 583.

Guidelines for Initial Reports

"Introduction

Article 44, paragraph 1, of the Convention on the Rights of the Child provides that "States Parties undertake to submit to the Committee, through the Secretary-General of the United Nations, reports on the measures they have adopted which give effect to the rights recognized therein and on the progress made in the enjoyment of those rights:

(a) Within two years of the entry into force of the Convention for the State Party concerned,

(b) Thereafter every five years.

Article 44 of the Convention further provides, in paragraph 2, that reports submitted to the Committee on the Rights of the Child shall indicate factors and difficulties, if any, affecting the fulfilment of the obligations under the Convention and shall also contain sufficient information to provide the Committee with a comprehensive understanding of the implementation of the Convention in the country concerned.

The Committee believes that the process of preparing a report for submission to the Committee offers an important occasion for conducting a comprehensive review of the various measures undertaken to harmonize national law and policy with the Convention and to monitor progress made in the enjoyment of the rights set forth in the Convention. Additionally, the process should be one that encourages and facilitates popular participation and public scrutiny of government policies.

The Committee considers that the reporting process entails an ongoing reaffirmation by States Parties of their commitment to respect and ensure observance of the rights set forth in the Convention and serves as the essential vehicle for the establishment of a meaningful dialogue between the States Parties and the Committee.

The general part of States Parties' reports, relating to matters that are of interest to monitoring bodies under various human rights instruments, should be prepared in accordance with the "Consolidated guidelines for the initial part of the reports of States Parties", as contained in document HRI/1991/1. The present guidelines, which were adopted by the Committee on the Rights of the Child at its 22nd meeting (first session), held on 15 October 1991, should be followed in the preparation of the Initial Reports of States Parties relating to the implementation of the Convention on the Rights of the Child.

The Committee intends to formulate guidelines for the preparation of periodic reports that are to be submitted pursuant to article 44, paragraph 1(b), of the Convention in due course.

Reports should be accompanied by copies of the principal legislative and other texts as well as detailed statistical information and indicators referred to therein, which will be made available to members of the Committee. It should be noted, however, that for reasons of economy they will not be translated or reproduced for general distribution. It is desirable, therefore, that when a text is not actually quoted in or annexed to the report itself, the report should contain sufficient information to be understood without reference to those texts.

The provisions of the Convention have been grouped under different sections, equal importance being attached to all the rights recognized by the Convention."

(CRC/C/5, paras. 1-8)

Guidelines for Periodic Reports

(The Guidelines for Periodic Reports *contain similar introductory paragraphs to those in the* Guidelines for Initial Reports. *For full text, see Appendix 3, page 604.)*
"Introduction

...

Periodic reports on the implementation of the Convention should provide information with respect to the period covered by the report on:

The measures adopted by the State Party, including the conclusion of and accession to bilateral and multilateral agreements in the field of children's rights, and changes which have occurred in legislation and practice at the national, regional and local levels, and where appropriate at the federal and provincial levels, such as:

> *Mechanisms and structures to coordinate and monitor efforts to implement the Convention;*
>
> *Overall or sectoral policies, programmes and services developed to implement the Convention.*

The progress achieved in the enjoyment of children's rights;

The factors and difficulties encountered in the full implementation of the rights set forth in the Convention and on steps taken to overcome them;

The plans envisaged to improve further the realization of the rights of the child.

Periodic reports should include information on the consideration given to the Concluding Observations adopted by the Committee in relation to the previous report, including on:

> **The areas of concern identified by the Committee, as well as difficulties which may have affected the realization of such suggestions and recommendations;**
>
> **The measures adopted as a follow-up to the suggestions and recommendations addressed by the Committee to the State Party upon examination of its previous report. Steps taken to implement should be identified in relation to each suggestion and recommendation and all relevant action taken should be specified including in relation to legislation, policy, mechanisms, structures and allocation of resources;**
>
> **The difficulties which may have affected the realization of such suggestions and recommendations;**
>
> **The steps taken to widely disseminate the previous report, as well as the Concluding Observations adopted by the Committee.**

Reports should be accompanied by copies of the principal legislative texts and judicial decisions, as well as detailed statistical information, indicators referred to therein and relevant research. This accompanying material will be made available to the members of the Committee. Quantitative information should indicate variations between various areas of the country and within areas and between groups of children and include:

> *Changes in the status of children;*
>
> *Variations by age, gender, region, rural/urban area, and social and ethnic group;*
>
> *Changes in community systems serving children;*
>
> *Changes in budget allocation and expenditure for sectors serving children;*
>
> *Changes in the extent of international cooperation received or contributed for the realization of children's rights.*

It should be noted, however, that for reasons of economy, these documents will not be translated or reproduced for general distribution. It is desirable, therefore, that when a text is not actually quoted in or annexed to the report itself, the report should contain sufficient information to be clearly understood without reference to those texts.

IN THE LIGHT OF ARTICLE 44, PARAGRAPH 3, OF THE CONVENTION, WHEN A STATE PARTY HAS SUBMITTED A COMPREHENSIVE INITIAL REPORT TO THE COMMITTEE OR HAS PREVIOUSLY PROVIDED DETAILED INFORMATION TO THE COMMITTEE, IT NEED NOT REPEAT SUCH BASIC INFORMATION IN ITS SUBSEQUENT REPORTS. IT SHOULD, HOWEVER, CLEARLY REFERENCE THE INFORMATION PREVIOUSLY TRANSMITTED, AND INDICATE THE CHANGES THAT HAVE OCCURRED DURING THE REPORTING PERIOD.

In the present guidelines the provisions of the Convention have been grouped in clusters with a view to assisting States Parties in the preparation of their reports. This approach reflects the Convention's holistic perspective of children's rights: that they are indivisible and interrelated, and that equal importance should be attached to each and every right recognized therein.

Information provided in States Parties' reports on the various sections identified by the Committee should closely follow the present guidelines with regard to content."

(CRC/C/58, paras. 5-10)

Initial Reports and Periodic Reports

The Convention comes into force in a State Party on the thirtieth day after the State has formally adopted the Convention (deposited its instrument of ratification or accession with the Secretary-General of the United Nations). The State Party then acquires obligations to report to the Committee:

● within two years of the entry into force of the Convention (Initial Report);

● thereafter every five years (Periodic Reports) (article 44(1)(a) and (b)).

Periodic Reports become due five years after the due date for delivery of the Initial Report; delay in submitting an Initial Report, or delay in the examination of the Report by the Committee, does not alter the date on which the next Report is due. Reports should cover measures adopted to give effect to the rights recognized in the Convention, "and on the progress made on the enjoyment of those rights". Reports must indicate factors and difficulties affecting implementation: "Reports should also contain sufficient information to provide the Committee with a comprehensive understanding of the implementation of the Convention in the country concerned." (para. 1)

The Committee can request States Parties to provide further information "relevant to the implementation of the Convention." (article 44(4)) Where a State Party has submitted a comprehensive Initial Report, in subsequent Periodic Reports it need not repeat basic information already provided. The Committee has indicated that it will, if necessary, take urgent action to seek to prevent serious violations of the Convention. The Committee sees its "urgent action procedure" as part of the reporting process under article 44, and it may request additional information from a State Party on a particular situation or issue and also propose a visit to the State. If urgent actions arise that are relevant to the sphere of competence of another Treaty Body, the Committee will inform the other body (Report on the second session, September-October 1992, CRC/C/10, paras. 54-58; Report on the fourth session, September-October 1993, CRC/C/20, paras. 155-6). It appears that as of September 1997, the Committee has initiated urgent actions in only a small number of cases.

Reporting guidelines

The Committee has drafted *General Guidelines regarding the form and contents of Initial Reports* (CRC/C/5) and *General Guidelines regarding the form and contents of Periodic Reports*

(CRC/C/58). In this *Handbook*, relevant extracts from the *Guidelines* are quoted under each article. The full text of the *Guidelines for Periodic Reports* is in Appendix 3, page 604. In the Guidelines, the Committee has grouped the provisions of the Convention in clusters, to assist States Parties in the preparation of their reports. "This approach reflects the Convention's holistic perspective of children's rights: that they are indivisible and interrelated, and that equal importance should be attached to each and every right recognized therein" (CRC/C/58, para. 9; see box for details of clusters).

In addition, States Parties are sent the *Consolidated Guidelines for the initial part of the reports of States Parties* (HRI/1991/1). This was agreed on by the various supervisory bodies established under the United Nations human rights treaties, to avoid duplication of general reporting obligations by States Parties to the various Covenants and Conventions.

Reports of the Committee

Under article 44(5), the Committee is required to submit reports on its activities to the General Assembly, through the Economic and Social Council, every two years. For details of documentation of the Committee's activities, see page 573.

Committee's "overview" of the reporting process

The Committee adopted an "overview" of the reporting procedures at its seventh session in October 1994, intended

"to make the current procedures more transparent and readily accessible to States Parties and others interested in the implementation of the Convention, including United Nations agencies and other competent bodies such as non-governmental organizations".

The overview describes the process of examination of States Parties' reports, and procedures for follow-up and for overdue reports (see box on page 580 for extracts). "The Committee strongly recommends all States Parties to report to it in accordance with the guidelines and in a thorough and timely manner."

The Committee requested the Secretariat to record details of its requests to States Parties for specific follow-up information after examining an Initial Report. The list of these follow-up requests is published periodically (see, for example, CRC/C/27/Rev.8, 13 March 1997).

Guide to the Committee's Guidelines

In its *Guidelines* for Initial Reports and Periodic Reports, the Committee on the Rights of the Child has grouped the provisions of the Convention in clusters: "This approach reflects the Convention's holistic perspective of children's rights: that they are indivisible and interrelated, and that equal importance should be attached to each and every right recognized therein." (CRC/C/58, para. 9).

The following are the clusters:

I General measures of implementation
Article 4: implementation obligations; article 42: making Convention widely known; article 44(6): making reports widely available (in *Guidelines for Periodic Reports*, also covers article 41: respect for existing standards*).*

II Definition of the child
Article 1.

III General principles
Article 2: non-discrimination; article 3(1): best interests to be a primary consideration; (the *Guidelines for Periodic Reports* also covers article 3(2): the State's obligation to ensure necessary care and protection; and article 3(3): standards for institutions, services and facilities); article 6: the right to life, survival and development (see also, VI, below); article 12: respect for the views of the child.

IV Civil rights and freedoms
Article 7: right to name, nationality and to know and be cared for by parents; article 8: preservation of child's identity; article 13: freedom of expression; article 14: freedom of thought, conscience and religion; article 15: freedom of association and peaceful assembly; article 16: protection of privacy; article 17: child's access to information, and role of mass media; article 37(a): right not to be subjected to torture or other cruel, inhuman or degrading treatment or punishment. (The *Guidelines for Periodic Reports* indicate (para. 48) that these are not the only provisions in the Convention which constitute civil rights and freedoms).

V Family environment and alternative care
Article 5: parental guidance and child's evolving capacities; article 18(1) and (2): parental responsibilities and State's assistance; article 9: separation from parents; article 10: family reunification; article 11: illicit transfer and non-return; article 27(4): recovery of maintenance for the child; article 20: children deprived of their family environment; article 21: adoption; article 25: periodic review of placement and treatment; article 19: protection from all forms of violence; article 39: rehabilitation and reintegration of victims of violence (see also VIII below).

VI Basic health and welfare
Article 6: right to life, survival and development (see also, III above); article 18(3): support for working parents; article 23: rights of disabled children; article 24: right to health and health services; article 26: right to social security; article 27(1)-(3): right to adequate standard of living.

VII Education, leisure and cultural activities
Article 28: right to education; article 29: aims of education; article 31: right to leisure, play and participation in cultural and artistic activities.

VIII Special protection measures

A Children in situations of emergency
Article 22: refugee children; article 38: children and armed conflict; article 39: rehabilitation of child victims (see also V above);

B Children involved with the system of administration of juvenile justice
Article 40: administration of juvenile justice; article 37(a): prohibition of capital punishment and life imprisonment; article 37(b)-(d): restriction of liberty; article 39: rehabilitation and reintegration of child victims (see also V above).

C Children in situations of exploitation
Article 32: child labour; article 33: drug abuse; article 34: sexual exploitation; article 35: sale, trafficking and abduction; article 36: other forms of exploitation.

D Children belonging to a minority or an indigenous group
Article 30.

Committee on the Rights of the Child: "Overview of the Reporting Procedures" – extracts

"B. Examination of States Parties' reports
Work of the Pre-sessional Working Group

Discussions of a State Party report with government representatives are prepared by a Working Group. The Working Group normally meets immediately after one session of the Committee to prepare for the next one. All Committee members are invited to the pre-sessional meeting. These meetings are not open to the public and there are no formal records. Any decisions taken by the Working Group are reported to the Committee at its next plenary session.

The principal purpose of the Working Group is to identify in advance the most important issues to be discussed with the representatives of the States. The intent is to give advance notice to the States Parties of the principal issues which might arise in the examination of their reports. The Convention on the Rights of the Child is wide-ranging, comprehensive and complex; the possibility for government representatives to prepare in advance their answers to some of the principal questions is likely to make the discussion more constructive.

The Secretariat prepares country files for the Pre-sessional Working Group, containing information relevant to each of the reports to be examined For this purpose the Committee invites relevant United Nations bodies and specialized agencies, non-governmental organizations and other competent bodies to submit appropriate documentation to the Secretariat. Some of the information is included in the country analysis documents, other information is placed in files which are available to Committee members during the sessions.

A special emphasis is placed on receiving relevant documentation from bodies and agencies within the United Nations system, such as UNICEF, ILO, WHO, UNHCR, UNESCO, UNDP and the World Bank, as well as from other human rights treaty bodies and mechanisms, and from non-governmental organizations, both domestic and international. Such contributions are also of importance in regard to discussions about technical advice and assistance in the light of article 45(b) of the Convention.

Representatives of the United Nations bodies and agencies take part in the meetings of the Working Group and give expert advice. The working group may also invite representatives of other competent bodies, including non-governmental organizations, to provide information.

The Working Group draws up a List of Issues which is sent to the respective Government through diplomatic channels. In order to facilitate the efficiency of the dialogue, the Committee requests the State Party to provide the answers to its List of Issues in writing and in advance of the session, in time for them to be translated into the working languages of the Committee.

An invitation to a forthcoming session of the Committee is also sent to the State Party, indicating the date, time and venue for the planned discussion.

Presentation of the report

The State Party report will be discussed in open and public meetings of the Committee, during which both the State representatives and Committee members take the floor. Relevant United Nations bodies and agencies are represented. Summary records of the meetings are issued and the United Nations Department of Public Information is invited to cover the proceedings for the purpose of their Press Releases. Other journalists are free to attend, as are representatives of non-governmental organizations and any interested individual.

With the factual situation largely clarified in writing, there should be room in the discussions to analyze 'progress achieved' and 'factors and difficulties encountered' in the implementation of the Convention. As the purpose of the whole process is constructive, sufficient time should be given to discussions about 'implementation priorities' and 'future goals'. For these reasons, the Committee welcomes the representation of the State Party to be a delegation with concrete involvement in strategic decisions relating to the rights of the child. When delegations are headed by someone with governmental responsibility, the discussions are likely to be more fruitful and have more impact on policy-making and implementation activities.

After a brief introduction of the report, the State delegation is asked to provide information on subjects covered by the List of Issues, starting with the first section of the guidelines, i.e. general measures of implementation. Then the dialogue starts. Committee members may want to ask further questions or make comments on the written or oral answers, and the delegation may respond. The discussion moves step by step through the next group of issues according to the guidelines.

States Parties which have made reservations to the Convention may be asked about the implications of that position in the light of article 51, paragraph 2, of the Convention, which stipulates that reservations incompatible with the object and purpose of the Convention shall not be permitted. Another point of reference is the recommendation by the 1993 World Conference on Human Rights that reservations should be formulated as precisely and narrowly as possible and that States should regularly review any reservations with a view to withdrawing them.

Towards the end of the discussion, Committee members summarize their observations on the report and the discussion itself and may also make suggestions and recommendations. Lastly, the State delegation is invited to make a final statement. Afterwards, the Committee will, in a closed meeting, agree on written Concluding Observations which include suggestions and recommendations. If it is deemed that the information submitted is insufficient, or that there is a need to clarify a number of issues further, and it is agreed that the discussion about the report should continue at a later session, the observations will be preliminary and the State Party will be informed accordingly.

The Concluding Observations usually contain the following aspects: introduction; positive aspects (including progress achieved); factors and difficulties impeding the implementation; principal subjects for concern; suggestions and recommendations addressed to the State Party. The Preliminary Observations usually have a similar structure, but it is made clear that they are not final.

The Committee may in its observations request additional information from the State Party, in accordance with article 44 of the Convention, in order to be able to better assess the situation in the State Party. A deadline for submission of such written material will be determined.

The Concluding Observations are made public on the last day of a Committee session during the adoption of the report, of which they form a part. Once adopted, they are made available to the States Parties concerned, and also issued as official documents of the Committee. In accordance with article 44, paragraph 5, of the Convention, the Committee's reports are submitted to the United Nations General Assembly, through the Economic and Social Council, for its consideration, every two years.

In the spirit of article 44, paragraph 6, it is important that the Concluding Observations are made widely available in the State Party concerned. If it so wishes, the State Party may address any of the observations in the context of any additional information that it provides to the Committee.

C. Procedures for follow-up action

It is assumed that concerns expressed by the Committee in its Concluding Observations will be addressed in a detailed manner by the State Party in its next report. The Committee may mention in its observations some specific issues on which it is particularly interested to receive detailed information.

In cases where the Committee has asked for additional information in accordance with article 44, paragraph 4, such information will be on the agenda at a future session.

When the discussion of a State Party report ends with Preliminary Observations by the Committee, the dialogue will continue at a future session. The Preliminary Observations outline the issues to be discussed at the next stage and specify what further information the Committee requests, in advance and in writing.

The Committee may, in accordance with article 45(b), transmit to relevant agencies and bodies, including the Centre for Human Rights, any reports from States Parties containing a request or indicating a need for technical advice or assistance, along with the Committee's observations and suggestions. This refers to needs both in relation to the reporting process and to implementation programmes.

States can request support from the Programme of Advisory Services and Technical Assistance of the Centre for Human Rights. Such requests could concern reviews required for ratification or accession and preparation of the report, as well as training seminars and other activities to make the principles and provisions of the Convention known and incorporated into national legislation and action plans.

The Concluding Observations of the Committee are disseminated to all relevant United Nations bodies and agencies, as well as other competent bodies, and might serve as a basis for discussions on international cooperation. The Committee may also, in its observations, make particular reference to the need for and possibilities of such cooperation.

D. Procedure in relation to overdue reports

The Convention makes reporting in time an obligation in itself. The Committee emphasizes the importance of timely reports.

Records are kept on the submission of reports, specifying which ones are overdue. The Committee issues regular reminders to States.

With such communications, information is also given about the possibility for States to request technical assistance and advisory services from the United Nations Centre for Human Rights.

In a case of persistent non-reporting by a State Party, the Committee may decide to consider the situation in the country in the absence of a report, but on the basis of all available information. The State party will be notified about such a decision in advance of the event."

(CRC/C/33)

Making reports under the Convention widely available: article 44(6)

The Committee on the Rights of the Child in its Concluding Observations has invariably urged each State Party to ensure wide availability of its Initial Report, any additional information submitted to the Committee, the summary records of discussions with the Committee and the Committee's Concluding Observations. Paragraph 6 of article 44 requires States Parties to "make their reports widely available to the public in their own countries". The Committee has urged States Parties to ensure translation into appropriate languages and to ensure that reports are the subject of parliamentary debate and consideration by non-governmental organizations.

For example:

"The Committee recommends that the State Party's report to the Committee, the summary records of the discussion of the report and the Concluding Observations adopted by the Committee be widely disseminated in the country with a view to promoting wider awareness of children's rights, including at the Land and local levels, among the authorities, non-governmental organizations, relevant professional groups and the community at large, including children." (Germany IRCO, Add.43, para. 36)

"The Committee encourages the State Party to disseminate widely the State Party report, the summary records of the discussion of the report in the Committee and the Concluding Observations adopted by the Committee following its consideration of the report. The Committee would like to suggest that these documents be brought to the attention of Parliament and that the suggestions and recommendations for action contained therein be followed up in close cooperation with the non-governmental society." (Finland IRCO, Add.53, para. 31)

Implementation Checklist

● *article* 44 (6)

Has the State made widely available
- ☐ its Initial Report, and any Periodic Reports?
- ☐ any additional information submitted to the Committee on the Rights of the Child?
- ☐ the summary records of discussions of the Initial and Periodic Reports?
- ☐ the Committee's Concluding Observations on the Initial Report and Periodic Reports?

Have these reports
- ☐ been translated and disseminated in national, local, minority or indigenous languages?
- ☐ been debated in Parliament?
- ☐ been the subject of discussion and debate with appropriate non-governmental organizations?

Cooperation with United Nations agencies and other bodies

article 45

Text of Article 45

In order to foster the effective implementation of the Convention and to encourage international cooperation in the field covered by the Convention:

(a) The specialized agencies, the United Nations Children's Fund and other United Nations organs shall be entitled to be represented at the consideration of the implementation of such provisions of the present Convention as fall within the scope of their mandate. The Committee may invite the specialized agencies, the United Nations Children's Fund and other competent bodies as it may consider appropriate to provide expert advice on the implementation of the Convention in areas falling within the scope of their respective mandates. The Committee may invite the specialized agencies, the United Nations Children's Fund and other United Nations organs to submit reports on the implementation of the Convention in areas falling within the scope of their activities;

(b) The Committee shall transmit, as it may consider appropriate, to the specialized agencies, the United Nations Children's Fund and other competent bodies, any reports from States Parties that contain a request, or indicate a need, for technical advice or assistance, along with the Committee's observations and suggestions, if any, on these requests or indications;

(c) The Committee may recommend to the General Assembly to request the Secretary-General to undertake on its behalf studies on specific issues relating to the rights of the child;

(d) The Committee may make suggestions and general recommendations based on information received pursuant to articles 44 and 45 of the present Convention. Such suggestions and general recommendations shall be transmitted to any State Party concerned and reported to the General Assembly, together with comments, if any, from States Parties.

Article 45 sets out arrangements intended to foster effective implementation of the Convention and to encourage international cooperation. It outlines the role for specialized agencies, UNICEF and other United Nations organs; they are entitled to be represented when implementation of aspects of the Convention which come within their mandate are being considered. The Committee can invite these bodies, and "other competent bodies" (interpreted as including appropriate non-governmental organizations) to provide expert advice and to submit reports (article 45(a); brief details of related United Nations and United Nations-related bodies are given in Appendix 1, page 591).

Article 45(b) requires the Committee to submit to specialized agencies, UNICEF and "other competent bodies" any reports from States Parties that include a request, or indicate a need, for technical advice or assistance. At its third session the Committee decided that when appropriate it would indicate a possible need for technical assistance in its Concluding Observations on States Parties' reports. Where the need for a specific programme of technical advice or assistance is identified, the Committee indicated it would encourage a meeting between the governmental delegation from the State Party and the relevant United Nations or other competent body. (Report on the fourth session, January 1993, CRC/C/16, paras. 139-145)

Article 45(c) enables the Committee to recommend that the General Assembly requests the Secretary General to undertake, on behalf of the Assembly, studies on specific issues relating to the rights of the child. It was, for example, a proposal from the Committee which led to the major study on the *Impact of Armed Conflict on Children* by Ms Graça Machel (CRC/C/16, p. 4; see also article 38, page 526).

Article 45(d) entitles the Committee to make suggestions and general recommendations, to be transmitted to any States Parties concerned and reported to the General Assembly, along with any comments from States Parties.

The Committee noted in the report of its second session that it could play the role of catalyst in developing the agenda for research and study on the rights of the child at the international level (Report on the second session, September-October 1992, CRC/C/10, para. 60).

Article 4 of the Convention stresses the importance of international cooperation in implementing the Convention, and there are specific references to international cooperation in articles 17(b), 23(4), 24(4) and 28(3). ∎

Miscellaneous provisions concerning the Convention

articles 46-54

(for full text of these articles, see Appendix 2, pages 602 to 603)

Signature, ratification, accession, coming into force

These articles cover arrangements for signature, ratification and accession to the Convention, and for its coming into force. The Convention comes into force in a State on the thirtieth day following deposit of the State's instrument of ratification or accession. Once in force, the State acquires obligations under international law to respect and ensure the rights contained in the Convention.

Amendments to the Convention

Any State Party may propose an amendment to the Convention, which is filed with the Secretary-General, who sends it to States Parties. If, within four months, at least a third of the States Parties favour a conference to consider and vote on the proposal, the Secretary-General convenes a conference. Any amendment adopted by a majority of States Parties present and voting at the conference is submitted to the General Assembly for approval. Once approved by the General Assembly and accepted by a two-thirds majority of States Parties, the amendment enters into force. It becomes binding on those States Parties which have accepted it.

Reservations

Reservations made by States Parties at the time of ratification or accession are deposited with the Secretary-General, and circulated to all States.

Paragraph 2 of article 51 emphasizes that: "A reservation incompatible with the object and purpose of the present Convention shall not be permitted". Reservations can be withdrawn at any time by notification to the Secretary-General, who then informs other States.

Article 2 of the Vienna Convention on the Law of Treaties defines "reservation" as a "unilateral statement, however phrased or named, made by a State, when signing, ratifying, accepting, approving or acceding to a treaty, whereby it purports to exclude or to modify the legal effect of certain provisions of the treaty in their application to that State".

Some States make "declarations", which are intended simply to clarify their interpretation of a particular phrase, but if the declaration appears to "exclude or to modify the legal effect of certain provisions" of the Convention, it will be treated as a reservation.

In its *Guidelines for Periodic Reports* the Committee on the Rights of the Child notes that the World Conference on Human Rights encourages States to consider reviewing any reservation with a view to withdrawing it (A/CONF.157/23, II, paras. 5 and 46).

The *Guidelines* asks for information on whether "the Government considers it necessary to maintain the reservations it has made, if any, or has the intention of withdrawing them." (para. 11)

Denouncing the Convention

A State Party can denounce the Convention at any time by written notification to the Secretary-General; denunciation becomes effective one year later.

Depositary of the Convention

The Secretary General is designated as the depositary of the Convention.

Official languages

The original text of the Convention in Arabic, Chinese, English, French, Russian and Spanish – all to be regarded as equally authentic – are deposited with the Secretary-General.

Appendices

Guide to United Nations and United Nations-related agencies

This appendix gives brief directory information about other agencies and bodies within the United Nations system which are relevant to the Convention on the Rights of the Child and its implementation

General Assembly

The General Assembly consists of all members of the United Nations (as at September 1997 there were 185 members). It may discuss any questions or matters within the scope of the United Nations Charter, or relating to the powers and functions of any organ provided for in the Charter. The General Assembly normally meets once a year in September at United Nations headquarters in New York, but special sessions, and emergency special sessions may also be called. It receives and considers reports from other organs. The Committee on the Rights of the Child is required to report on its activities to the General Assembly, through the Economic and Social Council, every two years (article 44(5)).

• *United Nations Headquarters, New York, NY 10017, USA*
ph. (1) 212 963 1234
fax (1) 212 963 4879
World Wide Web Site:
http://www.un.org/ga/index.html

Economic and Social Council

The United Nations Charter charges the United Nations to promote within the social and economic fields: higher standards of living, full employment, and conditions of social and economic progress and development; solutions of international economic, social, health and related problems, and international cultural and educational cooperation, and universal respect for and observance of human rights and fundamental freedoms for all without distinctions to race, sex, language or religion.

The 54-member Economic and Social Council (ECOSOC) is elected by the General Assembly. It makes or initiates studies and reports with respect to international economic, social, cultural, educational, health and related matters. It makes recommendations to the General Assembly, to the members of the United Nations, and to the specialized agencies concerned. It also makes recommendations for the purpose of promoting respect for, and observance of human rights. It prepares draft conventions for submission to the Assembly within its competence and calls international conferences on such matters. It enters into agreements with specialized agencies and makes arrangements for consultation with non-governmental organizations.

ECOSOC now holds one session a year between May and July, alternately in New York and Geneva.

ECOSOC has set up various commissions in economic and social fields and for the promotion of human rights, described below.

• *ECOSOC Secretariat, c/o United Nations Headquarters, DPCSD Room 2963J, New York, NY 10017, USA*
ph. (1) 212 963 1234
fax (1) 212 963 4879
World Wide Web Site: http://www.un.org/overview/organs/ecosoc.html

Commission for Social Development (CSD)

Established to advise ECOSOC on social policies of a general character, and in particular on matters in the social field not covered by the specialized intergovernmental agencies. Meets biennially in New York.

Centre for International Crime Prevention (CICP)

Provides policy guidance to member States, develops the United Nations crime prevention programme, etc. Membership elected by ECOSOC. Meets annually in Vienna.

• *Centre for International Crime Prevention, UN Office in Vienna, Vienna International Centre, Wagramer Strasse 5, P.O. Box 500, 1400 Vienna, Austria*
ph. (43) 1 21345
fax (43) 1 209 2599
World Wide Web Site:
http://www.ifs.univie.ac.at/~uncjin/uncjin.html

Commission on Human Rights

Established in 1946, by resolution of ECOSOC, with mandate to prepare recommendations and reports regarding an international bill of rights, international declarations or conventions and any other matters concerning human rights. Membership elected by ECOSOC. Meets annually in Geneva.

• *Palais des Nations, 8-14 Avenue de la Paix, 1211 Geneva 10, Switzerland*
ph. (41) 22 917 3456
fax (41) 22 917 0214
World Wide Web Site: http://www.unhchr.ch

Has various mechanisms and Working Groups, some specifically relevant to children's rights:

- **Working Group on Draft Optional Protocol to the Convention on the Rights of the Child on the Involvement of Children in Armed Conflict:** established by resolution of Commission on Human Rights in 1994.
- **Working Group on Draft Optional Protocol to the Convention on the Rights of the Child on the Sale of Children, Child Prostitution and Child Pornography:** established by resolution of the Commission in 1994.

There are other current Working Groups on the right to development, and enforced or involuntary disappearances.

- **Special Rapporteur on the Sale of Children, Child Prostitution and Child Pornography** established in 1990 to fulfil the mandate of assessing the situation of the sale of children, child prostitution and child pornography worldwide.

There are other thematic Special Rapporteurs, as well as those with country-specific mandates. Examples of other thematic Rapporteurs include the following:
- **Special Rapporteur on Torture and other cruel, inhuman, or degrading treatment or punishment**
- **Special Rapporteur on violence against women, its causes and consequences**
- **Special Rapporteur on situations of systematic rape, sexual slavery, and slavery-like practices during periods of armed conflict**

Sub-Commission on Prevention of Discrimination and Protection of Minorities
Established by Commission on Human Rights to undertake studies and make recommendations to the Commission concerning the prevention of discrimination of any kind relating to human rights and fundamental freedoms and the protection of racial, national, religious and linguistic minorities, and to carry out other functions for ECOSOC or the Commission. Members nominated by Governments and elected by Commission. Meets annually in Geneva. The Sub-Commission has established various Working Groups, including on Contemporary Forms of Slavery (which focuses on issues such as child labour, child prostitution, illegal adoption and early marriage), and on indigenous populations.
* *c/o Commission on Human Rights, Palais des Nations 8-14 Av. de la Paix, 1211 Geneva 10, Switzerland*
ph. (41) 22 917 3456
fax (41) 22 917 0123
World Wide Web Site: http://www.unhchr.ch

Commission on Narcotic Drugs
Established by ECOSOC in 1946 to advise the Council and prepare draft international agreements on all matters relating to the control of narcotic drugs. Members elected by ECOSOC. Meets annually in Vienna.
* *Vienna International Centre, Wagramer Strasse 5, P.O. Box 500, 1400 Vienna, Austria*
ph. (43) 1 21345 5885
fax (43) 1 21345 5866
World Wide Web Site:
http://www.undcp.org/cnd.html

Commission on Population and Development
Established by ECOSOC to study and advise the Council on population changes, including migration, and their effect on economic and social conditions. Current name was adopted following 1994 International Conference on Population and Development (ICPD), when it was charged with monitoring, reviewing and assessing implementation of the ICPD Programme of Action at national, regional and international levels. Members elected by ECOSOC. Meets annually in New York.
* *c/o ECOSOC Secretariat, United Nations Headquarters, DPCSD Room 2963J, New York, NY 10017, USA,*
ph. (1) 212 963 1234
fax (1) 212 963 4879
World Wide Web Site: http://www.un.org/ overview/organs/ecosoc.html

Commission on the Status of Women
Established by ECOSOC to prepare reports on matters concerning the promotion of women's rights in the political, economic, social and educational fields, and to make recommendations concerning women's rights. Members elected by ECOSOC. Meets annually in New York and has established various working groups.
* *c/o ECOSOC Secretariat, United Nations Headquarters, DPCSD Room 2963J, New York, NY 10017, USA,*
ph. (1) 212 963 1234
fax (1) 212 963 4879
World Wide Web Site: http://www.un.org/ overview/organs/ecosoc.html

Commission on Human Settlements (Habitat)
A Standing Committee of ECOSOC, established by General Assembly resolution in 1977; provides overall direction to the United Nations Centre for Human Settlements (Habitat) which serves as the Commission's secretariat, and provides a focal point for human settlements action and the coordination of action within the United Nations system. Members elected by ECOSOC. Meets biennially.
* *United Nations Office at Nairobi, P.O. Box 30030, Nairobi, Kenya*
ph. (254) 2 621-234
fax (254) 2 624 266

There are various other Commissions established by ECOSOC, including the Commission on Science and Technology for Development, the Commission on Sustainable Development, the Statistical Commission. There are also Regional Economic or Economic and Social Commissions. Other Standing Committees include the Committee for Programme and Coordination, and the Committee on Non-governmental Organizations (to report on consultative relationship between the Council and NGOs, and on what action the Council should take on submissions from NGOs). There are also "Expert Committees" established by ECOSOC (among them the Committee on Economic, Social and Cultural Rights, which oversees implementation of the International Covenant on Economic, Social and Cultural Rights; see below, page 629).

International Court of Justice
The principal judicial organ of the United Nations, functioning according to its statute which is part of the United Nations Charter. Its main purpose is to decide, in accordance with international law, such cases as are submitted to it by States. It is directed to apply international conventions establishing rules expressly recognized by the contesting States; international custom, as evidence of a general practice accepted as law; the general principles of law recognized by civilized nations; judicial decisions and the teachings of the most highly qualified jurists of the various nations, as subsidiary means for the determination of the rules of law. Gives advisory opinions on legal questions to the General Assembly and to other organs of the United Nations and specialized agencies, when authorized to do so. Members elected by General Assembly and Security Council.

* *Peace Palace, Carnegieplein 2, 2517KL The Hague, The Netherlands*
ph. (31) 70 302 2323
fax (31) 70 364 9928
World Wide Web:http://www.icj-cij.org

Human Rights Treaty Bodies
The Treaty Bodies are the Committees established to monitor the implementation of various human rights treaties, and to receive and consider reports from States Parties to those treaties:

Committee against Torture (CAT)
The Convention Against Torture and Other Cruel, Inhuman or Degrading Treatment or Punishment entered into force in 1987, and establishes an expert committee of 10, elected by States Parties to the Convention. It considers reports, makes general comments and where a State has accepted its competence may make inquiries about individual States Parties, and also about applications from individuals claiming to be victims of a violation of the Convention.
* *Palais des Nations, 8-14 Avenue de la Paix, 1211 Geneva 10, Switzerland*
ph. (41) 22 9173456
fax (41) 22 917 0123
World Wide Web Site: http://www.unhchr.ch

Committee on the Elimination of Discrimination against Women (CEDAW)
The Convention on the Elimination of All Forms of Discrimination against Women entered into force in 1981 and establishes an expert committee of 23, elected by States Parties. It considers progress made in implementation, including considering reports submitted by States Parties.
* *Division for the Advancement of Women, Department of Policy Coordination and Sustainable Development, United Nations Headquarters, New York, NY 10017, USA*
ph. (1) 212 963 1151
fax (1) 212 963 3463
World Wide Web Site:
http://www.un.org/dpcsd/daw/cedaw.html

Committee on the Elimination of Racial Discrimination (CERD)
The International Convention on the Elimination of All Forms of Racial Discrimination entered into force in 1969 and establishes a Committee of 18 experts elected by States Parties. The Committee examines reports from States Parties, and where a State has accepted its competence, may consider communications from individuals or groups of individuals claiming to be victims of a violation of the Convention.
* *Palais des Nations, 8-14 Avenue de la Paix, 1211 Geneva 10, Switzerland*
ph. (41) 22 917 3456
fax (41) 22 917 0123
World Wide Web Site: http://www.unhchr.ch

Committee on the Rights of the Child
For detailed description of mandate and role, see article 43, page 569.
* *Secretariat to the Committee on the Rights of the Child, Office of the High Commissioner for Human Rights, Room D.205, Palais des Nations, 8-14 Avenue de la Paix, 1211 Geneva 10, Switzerland*
ph. (41) 22 917 3456
fax (41) 22 917 0123
World Wide Web Site: http://www.unhchr.ch

Human Rights Committee

The International Covenant on Civil and Political Rights entered into force in 1976, and establishes an expert committee of 18. The Human Rights Committee considers reports from States Parties. Under the First Optional Protocol to the Covenant, States may recognize the competence of the Committee to consider communications from individuals alleging violations of human rights. A Second Optional Protocol, aimed at abolition of the death penalty, came into force in 1991.

• *Palais des Nations, 8-14 Avenue de la Paix, 1211 Geneva 10, Switzerland*
ph. (41) 22 9173456
fax (41) 22 917 0123
World Wide Web Site: http://www.unhchr.ch

Committee on Economic, Social and Cultural Rights

The International Covenant on Economic, Social and Cultural Rights entered into force in 1976. The Economic and Social Council of the General Assembly (ECOSOC) at first established a working group on implementation, to assist it with consideration of reports. In 1985, ECOSOC, by resolution 1985/17, renamed the Working Group the Committee on Economic, Social and Cultural Rights, to be composed of 18 experts elected by States Parties. It considers States Parties' reports, and reports to ECOSOC.

• *Palais des Nations, 8-14 Avenue de la Paix, 1211 Geneva 10, Switzerland*
ph. (41) 22 9173456
fax (41) 22 917 0123
World Wide Web Site: http://www.unhchr.ch

OTHER BODIES SUBSIDIARY TO OR RELATED TO THE UN

International Research and Training Institute for the Advancement of Women (INSTRAW)

Established by ECOSOC resolution 1998 (LX) in 1976, INSTRAW is an autonomous institute within the United Nations system. The Institute undertakes research, training and information activities towards developing new methods for enhancing women's economic and political empowerment and heir contribution to sustainable development and for making the overall development process more attuned to the needs and concerns of women. INSTRAW incorporates a life-cycle approach in its research and training activities, thereby extending its work to include elderly and young women, and the girl child (para. 334, Beijing Platform for Action). The Institute's work is concentrated in four main areas: economic and political empowerment; environment and sustainable development; communications and media; statistics and indicators on gender issues.

• *INSTRAW Headquarters, Calle César Nicolás Pensón 102-A, Santo Domingo, Dominican Republic*
ph. (809) 685 2111
fax (809) 685 2117
e-mail: instraw.hq.sd@codetel.net.do

• *INSTRAW Liaison Office, Room DC1-1106 One United Nations Plaza, New York, New York 10017, USA*
ph. (1) 212 963 5684
fax (1) 212 963 2978
World Wide Web Site: http://www.un.org/instraw

Office of the UN High Commissioner for Human Rights

The UN General Assembly created the post of High Commissioner for Human Rights in 1993 to promote and protect the effective enjoyment by all of all civil, cultural, economic, political and social rights, including the right to development (Assembly resolution 48/141 1993). The High Commissioner functions as the United Nations official with principal responsibility for UN human rights activities. The Office, formerly known as the United Nations Centre for Human Rights, provides secretariat and substantive services to the United Nations Human Rights bodies, including the Committee on the Rights of the Child. In 1997, as part of the High Commissioner's Plan of Action for the strengthening of the implementation of the Convention on the Rights of the Child, a Support Team was appointed to reinforce the substantive servicing of the Committee on the Rights of the Child. The Office conducts research and studies on human rights, coordinates liaison with NGOs, prepares publications, collects and disseminates information. The Office also provides, upon request from governments, advisory services and technical assistance. For details see *Advisory Services and technical cooperation in the field of human rights*, Human Rights Fact Sheet No.3 (rev.1), Centre for Human Rights, 1996.

• *Palais des Nations, 8-14 Avenue de la Paix, 1211 Geneva 10, Switzerland*
ph. (41) 22 917 3456
fax (41) 22 917 0123
World Wide Web Site: http://www.unhchr.ch

Office of the UN High Commissioner for Refugees (UNHCR)

UNHCR's mandate is to provide international protection to refugees and others of concern to UNHCR, and to seek durable solutions to their plight. Activities in fulfilment of this mandate include provision of material assistance, legal advice and assistance, and cooperation with other agencies. UNHCR has developed specific policies, practices and guidelines relating to refugee children. It seeks to promote the standards contained in the Convention on the Rights of the Child and to provide protection, promotion and implementation of durable solutions for refugee children which are in their best interests.

• *UNHCR, Senior Coordinator for Refugee Children, 94 rue de Montbrillant, Case Postale 2500, 1211 Geneva 2, Switzerland*
ph. (41) 22 739 8111
fax (41) 22 731 9546
World Wide Web Site: http://www.unhcr.ch

UN Conference on Trade and Development (UNCTAD)

The General Assembly established UNCTAD in 1964; it meets every four years. Its principal function is the promotion of international trade, with a view to maximising the trade and development opportunities of developing countries.

• *Palais des Nations, 8-14 Avenue de la Paix, 1211 Geneva 10, Switzerland*
ph. (41) 22 907 1234
fax (41) 22 907 0057
World Wide Web Site: http://www.unicc.org/unctad

UN Development Fund for Women (UNIFEM)

In 1984 the General Assembly decided that the activities of the Voluntary Fund for the UN Decade for Women should be continued by establishing a separate entity - UNIFEM - in autonomous association with the UN Development Programme (UNDP - see below). Its aims are to serve as a catalyst with the goal of ensuring the appropriate involvement of women in mainstream development activities, promoting the human rights of women and supporting innovative and experimental activities benefiting women in line with national and regional priorities.

• *304 East 45th Street, 6th Floor, New York, NY 10017, USA*
ph. (1) 212 906 6400
fax (1) 212 906 6705
World Wide Web Site: http://www.unifem.undp.org

UN Institute for Training and Research (UNITAR)

Established by General Assembly resolution, UNITAR became operational in 1966. Its purpose is to enhance the effectiveness of the UN in achieving its major objectives, in particular the maintenance of international peace and security and promotion of economic and social development. It provides training to persons, particularly from developing countries, for assignments with the UN or specialized agencies or related to their work. It also conducts research and study related to the functions and objectives of the UN (later resolutions affirmed that it should focus on providing training programmes and research related to training).

• *Palais des Nations, 8-14 Avenue de la Paix, 1211 Geneva 10, Switzerland*
ph. (41) 22 798 5850
fax (41) 22 733 1383
e-mail: headoffice@unitar.org
World Wide Web Site: http://www.unitar.org

UN Interregional Crime and Justice Research Institute (UNICRI)

Established in 1968 to undertake and promote policy-oriented research, training and technical cooperation activities in crime prevention and criminal justice. UNICRI has implemented, *inter alia*, a study on child abuse, the compilation and analysis of an international bibliography on violence in the family, a comparative study on Romani youth and the juvenile justice system. It plans to implement a project on children in difficult circumstances in South East Asia, and a study on the interactions between youths from migrant families and drug trafficking and consumption.

• *Via Giulia 52, 00186 Rome, Italy*
ph. (39) 6 6877437
fax (39) 6 6892638
e-mail: unicri@unicri.it
World Wide Web Site: http://www.unicri.it

UN Research Institute for Social Development (UNRISD)

An autonomous agency engaging in multidisciplinary research on the social dimensions of contemporary development problems. Its work is guided by the conviction that, for effective development policies to be formulated, an understanding of the social and political context is crucial. The Institute attempts to provide governments, development agencies, grassroots organizations and scholars with a better understanding of how development policies and processes of economic, social and environmental change affect different social groups. Working through an extensive network of national research centres, UNRISD aims to promote original research and strengthen research capacity in developing countries.

• *Programme Information Officer, UNRISD*
Palais des Nations, 8-14 Avenue de la Paix,
1211 Geneva 10, Switzerland
ph. (41) 22 798 58 50
fax (41) 22 740 0791
e-mail: info@unrisd.org
World Wide Web Site: http://www.unrisd.org

RECOGNIZED FUNDS AND PROGRAMMES OF THE UN

UN Children's Fund (UNICEF)

In 1946 the General Assembly established the UN International Children's Emergency Fund as a temporary body to provide emergency assistance to children in war-ravaged countries. By resolution in 1953 it placed the Fund on a permanent footing, changing the name but retaining the acronym.

UNICEF is mandated by the United Nations General Assembly to advocate for the protection of children's rights, to help meet their basic needs and to expand their opportunities to reach their full potential. UNICEF focusses its attention on implementing the rights contained in the Convention on the Rights of the Child, using them as a blueprint for its programmes. UNICEF programmes seek to combine strategies for improving access to and quality of basic social services together with legal, policy, and public education initiatives that promote and protect children's rights. UNICEF assists governments in revising policies and institutions and in making and enforcing laws that uphold the best interests of children. An integral part of UNICEF's approach is to create opportunities for children to express their views on issues affecting their lives and to actively participate in decision-making processes.

• *Three United Nations Plaza, New York,*
NY 10017, USA
ph. (1) 212 326 7000
fax (1) 212 888 7465
World Wide Web Site: http://www.unicef.org

UN Development Fund (UNDP)

The UNDP administers and coordinates most of the technical assistance provided through the UN system. It was formed by General Assembly resolution which combined the UN Expanded Programme of Technical Assistance with the Special Fund. The current Mission Statement endorsed in 1996 states that the mission is to help countries in their efforts to achieve sustainable human development by assisting them to build their capacity to design and carry out development programmes in poverty eradication, employment creation and sustainable livelihoods, the empowerment of women and the protection and regeneration of the environment, giving first priority to poverty eradication. Special attention is paid to the needs of the least developed countries.

• *One United Nations Plaza, New York,*
NY 10017, USA
ph. (1) 212 906 5000
fax (1) 212 826 2057
World Wide Web Site: http://www.undp.org

UN Environment Programme (UNEP)

Following the 1972 UN Conference on the Human Environment, the General Assembly established the United Nations Environment Programme, with a Governing Council, Secretariat and an Environment Fund with a detailed mandate of functions and responsibilities. On 4 April 1997, the resumed 19th session of the Governing Council established a High-Level Committee of Ministers and Officials as a subsidiary organ of the Council, consisting of 36 members elected from among members of the United Nations and its specialized agencies. The new Committee will have the mandate to consider the international environmental agenda and to make reforms and policy recommendations to the Governing Council.

• *P.O. Box 30552, United Nations Avenue,*
Gigiri, Nairobi, Kenya
ph. (254) 2 621234
fax (254) 2 226 886
World Wide Web Site: http://www.unep.org

UN International Drug Control Programme (UNDCP)

Established in 1991, following General Assembly resolution (41/179, 21 December 1990). UNDCP's work is guided by the three United Nations drug abuse control Conventions. UNDCP acts as the focal point for the coordination of international drug abuse control activities within the UN system. UNDCP provides substantial services to the Commission on Narcotic Drugs. UNDCP addresses all aspects of the drug problem, including prevention, treatment and rehabilitation of drug addicts.

UNDCP promotes programmes and interventions aiming at reducing drug abuse among young people and particularly out-of-school youth, street children and working children. UNDCP cooperates with other United Nations agencies in the definition of comprehensive programmes addressing health and education of youth at risk.

• *Demand Reduction Section, UNDCP*
P.O. Box 500, A-1400 Vienna, Austria
ph. (43) 1 21345 5474
fax (43) 1 21345 5866
World Wide Web Site: http://www.undcp.org

UN Population Fund (UNFPA)

In 1969 the United Nations Trust Fund for Population Activities was established. In 1987, it was renamed the United Nations Population Fund. Shares Executive Board with UN Development Programme. Three main areas of work are: to help ensure universal access to reproductive health, including family planning and sexual health, to all couples and individuals, by the year 2015; to support population and development strategies that enable capacity-building in population programming; to promote awareness of population and development issues and to advocate for the mobilization of the resources and political will necessary to accomplish its areas of work.

UNFPA is guided by, and promotes, the principles of the Programme of Action of the International Conference on Population and Development (1994). In particular UNFPA affirms its commitment to reproductive rights, gender equality and male responsibility, and to the autonomy and empowerment of women everywhere.

• *Technical and Evaluation Division,*
220 East 42nd Street, New York, NY 10017,
USA
ph. (1) 212 297 5211
fax (1) 212 297 4915
World Wide Web: http://www.unfpa.org

World Food Programme (WFP)

The World Food Programme is the food aid arm of the United Nations system.

Established by parallel resolutions of the General Assembly and the Food and Agriculture Organization (FAO) in 1961, it provides approximately one quarter of global food aid to combat hunger and to save the lives of victims of natural and other disasters. WFP's mission is threefold: to meet refugee and other emergency and protracted relief food needs, and to provide the associated logistic support; to improve the nutrition and quality of life of needy people at critical times in their lives, in such a way that they can fully realize their human potential; and to help the hungry poor become self-reliant and build assets such as roads and schools in their communities.

WFP concentrates its efforts and resources on assisting the most vulnerable: women, children and the elderly. It provides food aid primarily to least-developed and low-income, food-deficit countries, with the aim of eradicating hunger and promoting food security. The ultimate objective of food aid is the elimination of the need for food aid.

WFP also administers the International Emergency Food Reserve created by the General Assembly.

• *Via Cristoforo Colombo 426, 00145 Rome,*
Italy
ph. (39) 6 522821
fax (39) 6 5960 2348/5228 2111
World Wide Web Site: http://www.wfp.org

SPECIALIZED AGENCIES

These are separate autonomous organisations, "established by intergovernmental agreement and having wide international responsibilities, as defined in their basic instruments, in economic, social, cultural, educational, health and related fields", and which have "been brought into relationship with the United Nations". In some cases their activities are coordinated by ECOSOC.

International Labour Organization (ILO)

Established in 1919; became a specialized agency of the United Nations in 1946. ILO seeks to improve working and living conditions through the adoption of international labour conventions and recommendations setting standards in such fields as wages, hours of work, conditions of employment and social security. It conducts research and technical cooperation activities with the aim of promoting democracy and human rights, alleviating unemployment and poverty, and protecting working people. ILO has a tripartite structure, representing governments, employers and workers. The International Labour Conference meets each year.

ILO aims to establish national policies to eliminate child labour effectively, and to raise the minimum age for work to a level consistent with the development of children. In addition, ILO is in the process of establishing a new instrument in 1998-1999 that focuses on eliminating the most exploitative forms of child labour. In the field of technical cooperation, ILO has operated the IPEC Programme since 1992 to strengthen national capacities and to create a worldwide movement against child labour. The Programme is operating in 26 countries and there is preparatory work in a further 15 countries.

• *Application of Standards Branch, ILO*
4 Route des Morillons, 1211 Geneva 22,
Switzerland
ph. (41) 22 799 7062/799 7502
fax (41) 22 799 6771
World Wide Web Site: http://www.ilo.org

Food and Agriculture Organization (FAO)

Established in 1945. Its aims are to raise levels of nutrition and standards of living, securing improvements in the efficiency of the production and distribution of all food and agricultural products; bettering the condition of rural populations; and thus contributing towards an expanding world economy and ensuring humanity's freedom from hunger. The conference meets every two years, and elects a Council with delegated powers.

In November 1996, heads of state and government and government ministers from 186 countries attended the World Food Summit at FAO in Rome at which they pledged to reduce food hunger by at least half by 2015. In the Rome Declaration on World Food Security and Plan of Action, they promised to "give special attention to promoting and protecting the interests and needs of the child, particularly the girl child, in food security programmes, consistent with the ... Convention on the Rights of the Child". FAO targets rural women through projects to improve their access to credit, training, land and agricultural inputs, as a way of also improving child nutrition.

• *Viale Delle Terme di Caracalla, 00100 Rome,*
Italy
ph. (39) 6 57051
fax (39) 6 5705 3152
World Wide Web Site: http://www.fao.org

UN Educational, Scientific and Cultural Organization (UNESCO)

Established in 1945, the central purpose of UNESCO is to contribute to peace, security and development through education and intellectual cooperation. Because of its mandate for education and human rights teaching, a significant part of the Organization's work has always been in the service of children's rights. A major effort of the Organization since its foundation has been to ensure the child's right to education. In working with its Member States to achieve education for all, UNESCO has been concerned to promote not just literacy or instruction in the sciences, but an education that promotes tolerance and respect for others. In addition, support is provided for the Convention's non-discrimination principle, by working actively for the education of girls and other marginalized groups, such as children with special needs, street children, children speaking minority languages, children in armed conflict.

Other major programmes within UNESCO are its communications and culture programmes. The communications programme promotes active measures to assist the protection and participation of children in the media. With Gothenburg University, Sweden, an International Clearing House for Children and Violence on the Screen has been established.

• *Early Childhood and Family Education Section, Social and Human Sciences Section Humanistic, Cultural and International Education Section*
7 Place de Fontenoy, 75700 Paris, France
ph. (33) 1 45 68 10 00
fax (33) 1 45 67 16 90
World Wide Web Site: http://www.unesco.org

World Health Organization (WHO)

The World Health Organization, established in 1948, has its headquarters in Geneva, Switzerland, with Regional Offices in Alexandria; Copenhagen; Brazzaville; Manila; New Delhi and Washington. The work of WHO towards its main objective of the attainment by all peoples of the highest possible level of mental and physical health includes many activities aimed at children. These activities contribute to assuring the right of all children to health and health care. Specific examples include Integrated Management of Childhood Illness (IMCI), a strategy jointly developed with UNICEF to address the major killers of children: pneumonia, diarrhoea, measles, malaria and malnutrition through a combination of preventive and treatment interventions. WHO's Expanded Programme on Immunization aims to ensure that children everywhere receive protection against common diseases for which vaccines exist. Promotion of better nutrition, including breastfeeding and the prevention of injury, are other examples of how WHO is working to protect children's rights in the area of health. The Organization also has an initiative addressed to school children and an adolescent health programme targeting the special needs and rights of this group of children. The World Health Assembly is held annually.

• *20 Avenue Appia, 1211 Geneva 27, Switzerland*
ph. (41) 22 791 2111
fax (41) 22 791 0746
World Wide Web Site:http://www.who.org

World Bank Group

The World Bank Group includes **the International Bank for Reconstruction and Development (IBRD); the International Development Association (IDA); and the International Finance Corporation (IFC).** The **IBRD** was established to promote the international flow of capital for productive purposes and to assist in financing the rebuilding of nations devastated by the Second World War. Its main objective now is lending for productive projects or to finance reform programmes which will lead to economic growth in its less developed member countries. The **IDA**'s purpose is to promote economic development by providing finance to the less developed regions of the world on much more concessionary terms than those of conventional loans. The **IFC**'s particular purpose is to promote the growth of the private sector and to assist productive private enterprises in its developing member countries, where such enterprises can advance economic development.

• *1818 H Street NW, Washington DC 20433,*
USA
ph. (1) 202 477 1234
fax (1) 202 477 6391
World Wide Web Site: http://www.worldbank.org

International Monetary Fund (IMF)

The purposes of the IMF are to promote international monetary cooperation through consultation and collaboration; facilitate the expansion and balanced growth of international trade, and to contribute thereby to the promotion and maintenance of high levels of employment and real income; promote exchange stability and orderly exchange arrangements; assist in the establishment of a multilateral system of payments and the elimination of foreign exchange restrictions; assist members through the temporary provision of financial resources to correct maladjustments in their balance of payments.

• *700 19th Street NW, Washington DC 20431,*
USA
ph. (1) 202 623 7090
fax (1) 202 623 6220
World Wide Web Site: http://www.imf.org/

International Narcotics Control Board (INCB)

INCB was established pursuant to the Single Convention on Narcotic Drugs of 1961. The Board's task is to monitor international and domestic movement of narcotic drugs and psychotropic substances used for medical and scientific needs and precursor chemicals which can be used in the illicit manufacture of drugs and to promote overall compliance by governments with the various international drug control treaties.

• *Vienna International Centre, Wagramer Strasse 5, P.O. Box 500, 1400 Vienna, Austria*
ph. (43) 1 213450
fax (43) 1 21345-5867
World Wide Web Site:
http://undcp.org/incb_hp.html

World Trade Organization (WTO)

WTO is the legal and institutional foundation of the multilateral trading system. It provides the principal contractual obligations determining how governments frame and implement trade policy. It is also the platform on which trade relations among States evolve through collective debate, negotiation and adjudication. Its principal functions are to administer and implement multilateral and plurilateral trade agreements, to act as a forum for multilateral trade negotiations, seek to resolve trade disputes and examine national trade policies. WTO is the successor to the 1947 General Agreement on Tariffs and Trade (GATT).

• *Centre William Rappard, 154 Rue de Lausanne, 1211 Geneva 21, Switzerland*
ph. (41) 22 739 5019
fax: (41) 22 739 5458
World Wide Web Site: http://www.intracen.org

Joint United Nations Programme on HIV/AIDS (UNAIDS)
The Joint United Nations Programme on HIV/AIDS (UNAIDS) was established in January 1996. UNAIDS is a co-sponsored programme that brings together the United Nations Children's Fund (UNICEF), the United Nations Development Programme (UNDP), the United Nations Population Fund (UNFPA), the United Nations Educational, Scientific and Cultural Organization (UNESCO), the World Health Organization (WHO) and the World Bank in a common effort against the epidemic. It is the first programme of its kind in the UN system: a small programme with a large outreach and the potential to lever significant resources and action through the creation of strategic partnerships. UNAIDS strives to prevent the spread of HIV/AIDS amongst children and youth and to reduce the vulnerablity of children, families and communities to its impact.

• *20 Avenue Appia, 1211 Geneva 27, Switzerland*
ph.: (41) 22 791 3666
fax: (41) 22 791 4187
e-mail: unaids@unaids.org
World Wide Web Site: http://www.unaids.org

Convention on the Rights of the Child

Adopted by the General Assembly of the United Nations on 20 Novembrer 1989

Preamble

The States Parties to the present Convention,

Considering that, in accordance with the principles proclaimed in the Charter of the United Nations, recognition of the inherent dignity and of the equal and inalienable rights of all members of the human family is the foundation of freedom, justice and peace in the world,

Bearing in mind that the peoples of the United Nations have, in the Charter, reaffirmed their faith in fundamental human rights and in the dignity and worth of the human person, and have determined to promote social progress and better standards of life in larger freedom,

Recognizing that the United Nations has, in the Universal Declaration of Human Rights and in the International Covenants on Human Rights, proclaimed and agreed that everyone is entitled to all the rights and freedoms set forth therein, without distinction of any kind, such as race, colour, sex, language, religion, political or other opinion, national or social origin, property, birth or other status,

Recalling that, in the Universal Declaration of Human Rights, the United Nations has proclaimed that childhood is entitled to special care and assistance,

Convinced that the family, as the fundamental group of society and the natural environment for the growth and well-being of all its members and particularly children, should be afforded the necessary protection and assistance so that it can fully assume its responsibilities within the community,

Recognizing that the child, for the full and harmonious development of his or her personality, should grow up in a family environment, in an atmosphere of happiness, love and understanding,

Considering that the child should be fully prepared to live an individual life in society, and brought up in the spirit of the ideals proclaimed in the Charter of the United Nations, and in particular in the spirit of peace, dignity, tolerance, freedom, equality and solidarity,

Bearing in mind that the need to extend particular care to the child has been stated in the Geneva Declaration of the Rights of the Child of 1924 and in the Declaration of the Rights of the Child adopted by the United Nations on 20 November 1959 and recognized in the Universal Declaration of Human Rights, in the International Covenant on Civil and Political Rights (in particular in articles 23 and 24), in the International Covenant on Economic, Social and Cultural Rights (in particular in article ten) and in the statutes and relevant instruments of specialized agencies and international organizations concerned with the welfare of children,

Bearing in mind that, as indicated in the Declaration of the Rights of the Child, "the child, by reason of his physical and mental immaturity, needs special safeguards and care, including appropriate legal protection, before as well as after birth,"

Recalling the provisions of the Declaration on Social and Legal Principles relating to the Protection and Welfare of Children, with Special Reference to Foster Placement and Adoption Nationally and Internationally; the United Nations Standard Minimum Rules for the Administration of Juvenile Justice ("The Beijing Rules"); and the Declaration on the Protection of Women and Children in Emergency and Armed Conflict,

Recognizing that, in all countries in the world, there are children living in exceptionally difficult conditions, and that such children need special consideration,

Taking due account of the importance of the traditions and cultural values of each people for the protection and harmonious development of the child,

Recognizing the importance of international cooperation for improving the living conditions of children in every country, in particular in the developing countries,

Have agreed as follows:

Part I

Article 1

For the purposes of the present Convention, a child means every human being below the age of 18 years unless, under the law applicable to the child, majority is attained earlier.

Article 2

1. States Parties shall respect and ensure the rights set forth in the present Convention to each child within their jurisdiction without discrimination of any kind, irrespective of the child's or his or her parent's or legal guardian's race, colour, sex, language, religion, political or other opinion, national, ethnic or social origin, property, disability, birth or other status.
2. States Parties shall take all appropriate measures to ensure that the child is protected against all forms of discrimination or punishment on the basis of the status, activities, expressed opinions, or beliefs of the child's parents, legal guardians, or family members.

Article 3

1. In all actions concerning children, whether undertaken by public or private social welfare institutions, courts of law, administrative authorities or legislative bodies, the best interests of the child shall be a primary consideration.
2. States Parties undertake to ensure the child such protection and care as is necessary for his or her well-being, taking into account the rights and duties of his or her parents, legal guardians, or other individuals legally responsible for him or her, and, to this end, shall take all appropriate legislative and administrative measures.
3. States Parties shall ensure that the institutions, services and facilities responsible for the care or protection of children shall conform with the standards established by competent authorities, particularly in the areas of safety, health, in the number and suitability of their staff, as well as competent supervision.

Article 4

States Parties shall undertake all appropriate legislative, administrative, and other measures for the implementation of the rights recognized in the present Convention. With regard to economic, social and cultural rights, States Parties shall undertake such measures to the maximum extent of their available resources and, where needed, within the framework of international cooperation.

Article 5

States Parties shall respect the responsibilities, rights and duties of parents or, where applicable, the members of the extended family or community as provided for by local custom, legal guardians or other persons legally responsible for the child, to provide, in a manner consistent with the evolving capacities of the child, appropriate direction and guidance in the exercise by the child of the rights recognized in the present Convention.

Article 6

1. States Parties recognize that every child has the inherent right to life.
2. States Parties shall ensure to the maximum extent possible the survival and development of the child.

Article 7

1. The child shall be registered immediately after birth and shall have the right from birth to a name, the right to acquire a nationality and, as far as possible, the right to know and be cared for by his or her parents.
2. States Parties shall ensure the implementation of these rights in accordance with their national law and their obligations under the relevant international instruments in this field, in particular where the child would otherwise be stateless.

Article 8

1. States Parties undertake to respect the right of the child to preserve his or her identity, including nationality, name and family relations as recognized by law without unlawful interference.
2. Where a child is illegally deprived of some or all of the elements of his or her identity, States Parties shall provide appropriate assistance and protection, with a view to speedily re-establishing his or her identity.

Article 9

1. States Parties shall ensure that a child shall not be separated from his or her parents against their will, except when competent authorities subject to judicial review determine, in accordance with applicable law and procedures, that such separation is necessary for the best interests of the child. Such determination may be necessary in a particular case such as one involving abuse or neglect of the child by the parents, or one where the parents are living separately and a decision must be made as to the child's place of residence.
2. In any proceedings pursuant to paragraph 1 of the present article, all interested parties shall be given an opportunity to participate in the proceedings and make their views known.
3. States Parties shall respect the right of the child who is separated from one or both parents to maintain personal relations and direct contact with both parents on a regular basis, except if it is contrary to the child's best interests.
4. Where such separation results from any action initiated by a State Party, such as the detention, imprisonment, exile, deportation or death (including death arising from any cause while the person is in the custody of the State) of one or both parents or of the child, that State Party shall, upon request, provide the parents, the child or, if appropriate, another member of the family with the essential information concerning the whereabouts of the absent member(s) of the family unless the provision of the information would be detrimental to the well-being of the child. States Parties shall further ensure that the submission of such a request shall of itself entail no adverse consequences for the person(s) concerned.

Article 10

1. In accordance with the obligation of States Parties under article 9, paragraph 1, applications by a child or his or her parents to enter or leave a State Party for the purpose of family reunification shall be dealt with by States Parties in a positive, humane and expeditious manner. States Parties shall further ensure that the submission of such a request shall entail no adverse consequences for the applicants and for the members of their family.
2. A child whose parents reside in different States shall have the right to maintain on a regular basis, save in exceptional circumstances personal relations and direct contacts with both parents. Towards that end and in accordance with the obligation of States Parties under article 9, paragraph 1, States Parties shall respect the right of the child and his or her parents to leave any country, including their own, and to enter their own country. The right to leave any country shall be subject only to such restrictions as are prescribed by law and which are necessary to protect the national security, public order (*ordre public*), public health or morals or the rights and freedoms of others and are consistent with the other rights recognized in the present Convention.

Article 11

1. States Parties shall take measures to combat the illicit transfer and non-return of children abroad.
2. To this end, States Parties shall promote the conclusion of bilateral or multilateral agreements or accession to existing agreements.

Article 12

1. States Parties shall assure to the child who is capable of forming his or her own views the right to express those views freely in all matters affecting the child, the views of the child being given due weight in accordance with the age and maturity of the child.
2. For this purpose, the child shall in particular be provided the opportunity to be heard in any judicial and administrative proceedings affecting the child, either directly, or through a representative or an appropriate body, in a manner consistent with the procedural rules of national law.

Article 13

1. The child shall have the right to freedom of expression; this right shall include freedom to seek, receive and impart information and ideas of all kinds, regardless of frontiers, either orally, in writing or in print, in the form of art, or through any other media of the child's choice.
2. The exercise of this right may be subject to certain restrictions, but these shall only be such as are provided by law and are necessary:
   (a) For respect of the rights or reputations of others; or
   (b) For the protection of national security or of public order (*ordre public*), or of public health or morals.

Article 14

1. States Parties shall respect the right of the child to freedom of thought, conscience and religion.

2. States Parties shall respect the rights and duties of the parents and, when applicable, legal guardians, to provide direction to the child in the exercise of his or her right in a manner consistent with the evolving capacities of the child.

3. Freedom to manifest one's religion or beliefs may be subject only to such limitations as are prescribed by law and are necessary to protect public safety, order, health or morals, or the fundamental rights and freedoms of others.

● Article 15

1. States Parties recognize the rights of the child to freedom of association and to freedom of peaceful assembly.

2. No restrictions may be placed on the exercise of these rights other than those imposed in conformity with the law and which are necessary in a democratic society in the interests of national security or public safety, public order (*ordre public*), the protection of public health or morals or the protection of the rights and freedoms of others.

● Article 16

1. No child shall be subjected to arbitrary or unlawful interference with his or her privacy, family, home or correspondence, nor to unlawful attacks on his or her honour and reputation.

2. The child has the right to the protection of the law against such interference or attacks.

● Article 17

States Parties recognize the important function performed by the mass media and shall ensure that the child has access to information and material from a diversity of national and international sources, especially those aimed at the promotion of his or her social, spiritual and moral well-being and physical and mental health. To this end, States Parties shall:

(a) Encourage the mass media to disseminate information and material of social and cultural benefit to the child and in accordance with the spirit of article 29;

(b) Encourage international cooperation in the production, exchange and dissemination of such information and material from a diversity of cultural, national and international sources;

(c) Encourage the production and dissemination of children's books;

(d) Encourage the mass media to have particular regard to the linguistic needs of the child who belongs to a minority group or who is indigenous;

(e) Encourage the development of appropriate guidelines for the protection of the child from information and material injurious to his or her well-being, bearing in mind the provisions of articles 13 and 18.

● Article 18

1. States Parties shall use their best efforts to ensure recognition of the principle that both parents have common responsibilities for the upbringing and development of the child. Parents or, as the case may be, legal guardians, have the primary responsibility for the upbringing and development of the child. The best

interests of the child will be their basic concern.

2. For the purpose of guaranteeing and promoting the rights set forth in the present Convention, States Parties shall render appropriate assistance to parents and legal guardians in the performance of their child-rearing responsibilities and shall ensure the development of institutions, facilities and services for the care of children.

3. States Parties shall take all appropriate measures to ensure that children of working parents have the right to benefit from child-care services and facilities for which they are eligible.

● Article 19

1. States Parties shall take all appropriate legislative, administrative, social and educational measures to protect the child from all forms of physical or mental violence, injury or abuse, neglect or negligent treatment, maltreatment or exploitation, including sexual abuse, while in the care of parent(s), legal guardian(s) or any other person who has the care of the child.

2. Such protective measures should, as appropriate, include effective procedures for the establishment of social programmes to provide necessary support for the child and for those who have the care of the child, as well as for other forms of prevention and for identification, reporting, referral, investigation, treatment and follow-up of instances of child maltreatment described heretofore, and, as appropriate, for judicial involvement.

● Article 20

1. A child temporarily or permanently deprived of his or her family environment, or in whose own best interests cannot be allowed to remain in that environment, shall be entitled to special protection and assistance provided by the State.

2. States Parties shall in accordance with their national laws ensure alternative care for such a child.

3. Such care could include, *inter alia*, foster placement, *Kafalah* of Islamic law, adoption, or if necessary placement in suitable institutions for the care of children. When considering solutions, due regard shall be paid to the desirability of continuity in a child's upbringing and to the child's ethnic, religious, cultural and linguistic background.

● Article 21

States Parties that recognize and/or permit the system of adoption shall ensure that the best interests of the child shall be the paramount consideration and they shall:

(a) Ensure that the adoption of a child is authorized only by competent authorities who determine, in accordance with applicable law and procedures and on the basis of all pertinent and reliable information, that the adoption is permissible in view of the child's status concerning parents, relatives and legal guardians and that, if required, the persons concerned have given their informed consent to the adoption on the basis of such counselling as may be necessary;

(b) Recognize that intercountry adoption may be considered as an alternative means of child's care, if the child cannot be placed in a foster or an adoptive family or cannot in any suitable manner be cared for in the child's country of origin;

(c) Ensure that the child concerned by intercountry adoption enjoys safeguards and standards equivalent to those existing in the case of national adoption;

(d) Take all appropriate measures to ensure that, in intercountry adoption, the placement does not result in improper financial gain for those involved in it;

(e) Promote, where appropriate, the objectives of the present article by concluding bilateral or multilateral arrangements or agreements, and endeavour, within this framework, to ensure that the placement of the child in another country is carried out by competent authorities or organs.

● Article 22

1. States Parties shall take appropriate measures to ensure that a child who is seeking refugee status or who is considered a refugee in accordance with applicable international or domestic law and procedures shall, whether unaccompanied or accompanied by his or her parents or by any other person, receive appropriate protection and humanitarian assistance in the enjoyment of applicable rights set forth in the present Convention and in other international human rights or humanitarian instruments to which the said States are Parties.

2. For this purpose, States Parties shall provide, as they consider appropriate, cooperation in any efforts by the United Nations and other competent intergovernmental organizations or non-governmental organizations cooperating with the United Nations to protect and assist such a child and to trace the parents or other members of the family of any refugee child in order to obtain information necessary for reunification with his or her family. In cases where no parents or other members of the family can be found, the child shall be accorded the same protection as any other child permanently or temporarily deprived of his or her family environment for any reason, as set forth in the present Convention.

● Article 23

1. States Parties recognize that a mentally or physically disabled child should enjoy a full and decent life, in conditions which ensure dignity, promote self-reliance, and facilitate the child's active participation in the community.

2. States Parties recognize the right of the disabled child to special care and shall encourage and ensure the extension, subject to available resources, to the eligible child and those responsible for his or her care, of assistance for which application is made and which is appropriate to the child's condition and to the circumstances of the parents or others caring for the child.

3. Recognizing the special needs of a disabled child, assistance extended in accordance with paragraph 2 of the present article shall be provided free of charge, whenever possible, taking

into account the financial resources of the parents or others caring for the child, and shall be designed to ensure that the disabled child has effective access to and receives education, training, health care services, rehabilitation services, preparation for employment and recreation opportunities in a manner conducive to the child's achieving the fullest possible social integration and individual development, including his or her cultural and spiritual development.

4. States Parties shall promote, in the spirit of international cooperation, the exchange of appropriate information in the field of preventive health care and of medical, psychological and functional treatment of disabled children, including dissemination of and access to information concerning methods of rehabilitation, education and vocational services, with the aim of enabling States Parties to improve their capabilities and skills and to widen their experience in these areas. In this regard, particular account shall be taken of the needs of developing countries.

Article 24

1. States Parties recognize the right of the child to the enjoyment of the highest attainable standard of health and to facilities for the treatment of illness and rehabilitation of health. States Parties shall strive to ensure that no child is deprived of his or her right of access to such health care services.

2. States Parties shall pursue full implementation of this right and, in particular, shall take appropriate measures:

(a) To diminish infant and child mortality;
(b) To ensure the provision of necessary medical assistance and health care to all children with emphasis on the development of primary health care;
(c) To combat disease and malnutrition including within the framework of primary health care, through *inter alia* the application of readily available technology and through the provision of adequate nutritious foods and clean drinking water, taking into consideration the dangers and risks of environmental pollution;
(d) To ensure appropriate pre-natal and post-natal health care for mothers;
(e) To ensure that all segments of society, in particular parents and children, are informed, have access to education and are supported in the use of basic knowledge of child health and nutrition, the advantages of breast-feeding, hygiene and environmental sanitation and the prevention of accidents;
(f) To develop preventive health care, guidance for parents and family planning education and services.

3. States Parties shall take all effective and appropriate measures with a view to abolishing traditional practices prejudicial to the health of children.

4. States Parties undertake to promote and encourage international cooperation with a view to achieving progressively the full realization of the right recognized in the present article. In this regard, particular account shall be taken of the needs of developing countries.

Article 25

States Parties recognize the right of a child who has been placed by the competent authorities for the purposes of care, protection or treatment of his or her physical or mental health, to a periodic review of the treatment provided to the child and all other circumstances relevant to his or her placement.

Article 26

1. States Parties shall recognize for every child the right to benefit from social security, including social insurance, and shall take the necessary measures to achieve the full realization of this right in accordance with their national law.

2. The benefits should, where appropriate, be granted, taking into account the resources and the circumstances of the child and persons having responsibility for the maintenance of the child, as well as any other consideration relevant to an application for benefits made by or on behalf of the child.

Article 27

1. States Parties recognize the right of every child to a standard of living adequate for the child's physical, mental, spiritual, moral and social development.

2. The parent(s) or others responsible for the child have the primary responsibility to secure, within their abilities and financial capacities, the conditions of living necessary for the child's development.

3. States Parties, in accordance with national conditions and within their means, shall take appropriate measures to assist parents and others responsible for the child to implement this right and shall in case of need provide material assistance and support programmes, particularly with regard to nutrition, clothing and housing.

4. States Parties shall take all appropriate measures to secure the recovery of maintenance for the child from the parents or other persons having financial responsibility for the child, both within the State Party and from abroad. In particular, where the person having financial responsibility for the child lives in a State different from that of the child, States Parties shall promote the accession to international agreements or the conclusion of such agreements, as well as the making of other appropriate arrangements.

Article 28

1. States Parties recognize the right of the child to education, and with a view to achieving this right progressively and on the basis of equal opportunity, they shall, in particular:

(a) Make primary education compulsory and available free to all;
(b) Encourage the development of different forms of secondary education, including general and vocational education, make them available and accessible to every child, and take appropriate measures such as the introduction of free education and offering financial assistance in case of need;
(c) Make higher education accessible to all on the basis of capacity by every appropriate means;
(d) Make educational and vocational information and guidance available and accessible to all children;
(e) Take measures to encourage regular attendance at schools and the reduction of drop-out rates.

2. States Parties shall take all appropriate measures to ensure that school discipline is administered in a manner consistent with the child's human dignity and in conformity with the present Convention.

3. States Parties shall promote and encourage international cooperation in matters relating to education, in particular with a view to contributing to the elimination of ignorance and illiteracy throughout the world and facilitating access to scientific and technical knowledge and modern teaching methods. In this regard, particular account shall be taken of the needs of developing countries.

Article 29

1. States Parties agree that the education of the child shall be directed to:

(a) The development of the child's personality, talents and mental and physical abilities to their fullest potential;
(b) The development of respect for human rights and fundamental freedoms, and for the principles enshrined in the Charter of the United Nations;
(c) The development of respect for the child's parents, his or her own cultural identity, language and values, for the national values of the country in which the child is living, the country from which he or she may originate, and for civilizations different from his or her own;
(d) The preparation of the child for responsible life in a free society, in the spirit of understanding, peace, tolerance, equality of sexes, and friendship among all peoples, ethnic, national and religious groups and persons of indigenous origin;
(e) The development of respect for the natural environment.

2. No part of the present article or article 28 shall be construed so as to interfere with the liberty of individuals and bodies to establish and direct educational institutions, subject always to the observance of the principles set forth in paragraph 1 of the present article and to the requirements that the education given in such institutions shall conform to such minimum standards as may be laid down by the State.

Article 30

In those States in which ethnic, religious or linguistic minorities or persons of indigenous origin exist, a child belonging to such a minority or who is indigenous shall not be denied the right, in community with other members of his or her group, to enjoy his or her own culture, to profess and practise his or her own religion, or to use his or her own language.

Article 31

1. States Parties recognize the right of the child to rest and leisure, to engage in play and recreational activities appropriate to the age of the child and to participate freely in cultural life and the arts.

2. States Parties shall respect and promote the right of the child to participate fully in cultural and artistic life and shall encourage the provision of appropriate and equal opportunities for cultural, artistic, recreational and leisure activity.

Article 32

1. States Parties recognize the right of the child to be protected from economic exploitation and from performing any work that is likely to be hazardous or to interfere with the child's education, or to be harmful to the child's health or physical, mental, spiritual, moral or social development.

2. States Parties shall take legislative, administrative, social and educational measures to ensure the implementation of the present article. To this end, and having regard to the relevant provisions of other international instruments, States Parties shall in particular:

(a) Provide for a minimum age or minimum ages for admissions to employment;

(b) Provide for appropriate regulation of the hours and conditions of employment;

(c) Provide for appropriate penalties or other sanctions to ensure the effective enforcement of the present article.

Article 33

States Parties shall take all appropriate measures, including legislative, administrative, social and educational measures, to protect children from the illicit use of narcotic drugs and psychotropic substances as defined in the relevant international treaties, and to prevent the use of children in the illicit production and trafficking of such substances.

Article 34

States Parties undertake to protect the child from all forms of sexual exploitation and sexual abuse. For these purposes, States Parties shall in particular take all appropriate national, bilateral and multilateral measures to prevent:

(a) The inducement or coercion of a child to engage in any unlawful sexual activity;

(b) The exploitative use of children in prostitution or other unlawful sexual practises;

(c) The exploitative use of children in pornographic performances and materials.

Article 35

States Parties shall take all appropriate national, bilateral and multilateral measures to prevent the abduction of, the sale of or traffic in children for any purpose or in any form.

Article 36

States Parties shall protect the child against all other forms of exploitation prejudicial to any aspects of the child's welfare.

Article 37

States Parties shall ensure that:

(a) No child shall be subjected to torture or other cruel, inhuman or degrading treatment or punishment. Neither capital punishment nor life imprisonment without possibility of release shall be imposed for offences committed by persons below 18 years of age;

(b) No child shall be deprived of his or her liberty unlawfully or arbitrarily. The arrest, detention or imprisonment of a child shall be in conformity with the law and shall be used only as a measure of last resort and for the shortest appropriate period of time;

(c) Every child deprived of liberty shall be treated with humanity and respect for the inherent dignity of the human person, and in a manner which takes into account the needs of persons of his or her age. In particular every child deprived of liberty shall be separated from adults unless it is considered in the child's best interest not to do so and shall have the right to maintain contact with his or her family through correspondence and visits, save in exceptional circumstances;

(d) Every child deprived of his or her liberty shall have the right to prompt access to legal and other appropriate assistance, as well as the right to challenge the legality of the deprivation of his or her liberty before a court or other competent, independent and impartial authority, and to a prompt decision on any such action.

Article 38

1. States Parties undertake to respect and to ensure respect for rules of international humanitarian law applicable to them in armed conflicts which are relevant to the child.

2. States Parties shall take all feasible measures to ensure that persons who have not attained the age of 15 years do not take a direct part in hostilities.

3. States Parties shall refrain from recruiting any person who has not attained the age of 15 years into their armed forces. In recruiting among those persons who have attained the age of 15 years but who have not attained the age of 18 years, States Parties shall endeavour to give priority to those who are oldest.

4. In accordance with their obligations under international humanitarian law to protect the civilian population in armed conflicts, States Parties shall take all feasible measures to ensure protection and care of children who are affected by an armed conflict.

Article 39

States Parties shall take all appropriate measures to promote physical and psychological recovery and social reintegration of a child victim of: any form of neglect, exploitation, or abuse; torture or any other form of cruel, inhuman or degrading treatment or punishment; or armed conflicts. Such recovery and reintegration shall take place in an environment which fosters the health, self-respect and dignity of the child.

Article 40

1. States Parties recognize the right of every child alleged as, accused of, or recognized as having infringed the penal law to be treated in a manner consistent with the promotion of the child's sense of dignity and worth, which reinforces the child's respect for the human rights and fundamental freedoms of others and which takes into account the child's age and the desirability of promoting the child's reintegration and the child's assuming a constructive role in society.

2. To this end, and having regard to the relevant provisions of international instruments, States Parties shall, in particular, ensure that:

(a) No child shall be alleged as, be accused of, or recognized as having infringed the penal law by reason of acts or omissions that were not prohibited by national or international law at the time they were committed;

(b) Every child alleged as or accused of having infringed the penal law has at least the following guarantees:

(i) To be presumed innocent until proven guilty according to law;

(ii) To be informed promptly and directly of the charges against him or her, and, if appropriate, through his or her parents or legal guardians, and to have legal or other appropriate assistance in the preparation and presentation of his or her defence;

(iii) To have the matter determined without delay by a competent, independent and impartial authority or judicial body in a fair hearing according to law, in the presence of legal or other appropriate assistance and, unless it is considered not to be in the best interest of the child, in particular, taking into account his or her age or situation, his or her parents or legal guardians;

(iv) Not to be compelled to give testimony or to confess guilt; to examine or have examined adverse witnesses and to obtain the participation and examination of witnesses on his or her behalf under conditions of equality;

(v) If considered to have infringed the penal law, to have this decision and any measures imposed in consequence thereof reviewed by a higher competent, independent and impartial authority or judicial body according to law;

(vi) To have the free assistance of an interpreter if the child cannot understand or speak the language used;

(vii) To have his or her privacy fully respected at all stages of the proceedings.

3. States Parties shall seek to promote the establishment of laws, procedures, authorities and institutions specifically applicable to children alleged as, accused of, or recognized as having infringed the penal law, and, in particular:

(a) the establishment of a minimum age below which children shall be presumed not to have the capacity to infringe the penal law;

(b) whenever appropriate and desirable, measures for dealing with such children without resorting to judicial proceedings, providing that human rights and legal safeguards are fully respected.

4. A variety of dispositions, such as care, guidance and supervision orders; counselling; probation; foster care; education and vocational training programmes and other alternatives to institutional care shall be available to ensure that children are dealt with in a manner appropriate to their well-being and proportionate both to their circumstances and the offence.

● Article 41

Nothing in the present Convention shall affect any provisions which are more conducive to the realization of the rights of the child and which may be contained in:

(a) The law of a State Party; or

(b) International law in force for that State.

Part II

● Article 42

States Parties undertake to make the principles and provisions of the Convention widely known, by appropriate and active means, to adults and children alike.

● Article 43

1. For the purpose of examining the progress made by States Parties in achieving the realization of the obligations undertaken in the present Convention, there shall be established a Committee on the Rights of the Child, which shall carry out the functions hereinafter provided.

2. The Committee shall consist of ten experts of high moral standing and recognized competence in the field covered by this Convention. The members of the Committee shall be elected by States Parties from among their nationals and shall serve in their personal capacity, consideration being given to equitable geographical distribution, as well as to the principal legal systems.

3. The members of the Committee shall be elected by secret ballot from a list of persons nominated by States Parties. Each State Party may nominate one person from among its own nationals.

4. The initial election to the Committee shall be held no later than six months after the date of the entry into force of the present Convention and thereafter every second year. At least four months before the date of each election, the Secretary-General of the United Nations shall address a letter to States Parties inviting them to submit their nominations within two months. The Secretary-General shall subsequently prepare a list in alphabetical order of all persons thus nominated, indicating States Parties which have nominated them, and shall submit it to the States Parties to the present Convention.

5. The elections shall be held at meetings of States Parties convened by the Secretary-General at United Nations Headquarters. At those meetings, for which two thirds of States Parties shall constitute a quorum, the persons elected to the Committee shall be those who obtain the largest number of votes and an absolute majority of the votes of the representatives of States Parties present and voting.

6. The members of the Committee shall be elected for a term of four years. They shall be eligible for re-election if renominated. The term of five of the members elected at the first election shall expire at the end of two years; immediately after the first election, the names of these five members shall be chosen by lot by the Chairman of the meeting.

7. If a member of the Committee dies or resigns or declares that for any other cause he or she can no longer perform the duties of the Committee, the State Party which nominated the member shall appoint another expert from among its nationals to serve for the remainder of the term, subject to the approval of the Committee.

8. The Committee shall establish its own rules of procedure.

9. The Committee shall elect its officers for a period of two years.

10. The meetings of the Committee shall normally be held at United Nations Headquarters or at any other convenient place as determined by the Committee. The Committee shall normally meet annually. The duration of the meetings of the Committee shall be determined, and reviewed, if necessary, by a meeting of the States Parties to the present Convention, subject to the approval of the General Assembly.

11. The Secretary-General of the United Nations shall provide the necessary staff and facilities for the effective performance of the functions of the Committee under the present Convention.

12. With the approval of the General Assembly, the members of the Committee established under the present Convention shall receive emoluments from the United Nations resources on such terms and conditions as the Assembly may decide.

● Article 44

1. States Parties undertake to submit to the Committee, through the Secretary-General of the United Nations, reports on the measures they have adopted which give effect to the rights recognized herein and on the progress made on the enjoyment of those rights:

(a) Within two years of the entry into force of the Convention for the State Party concerned,

(b) Thereafter every five years.

2. Reports made under the present article shall indicate factors and difficulties, if any, affecting the degree of fulfilment of the obligations under the present Convention. Reports shall also contain sufficient information to provide the Committee with a comprehensive understanding of the implementation of the Convention in the country concerned.

3. A State Party which has submitted a comprehensive initial report to the Committee need not

in its subsequent reports submitted in accordance with paragraph 1(b) of the present article repeat basic information previously provided.

4. The Committee may request from States Parties further information relevant to the implementation of the Convention.

5. The Committee shall submit to the General Assembly, through the Economic and Social Council, every two years, reports on its activities.

6. States Parties shall make their reports widely available to the public in their own countries.

● Article 45

In order to foster the effective implementation of the Convention and to encourage international cooperation in the field covered by the Convention:

(a) The specialized agencies, the United Nations Children's Fund and other United Nations organs shall be entitled to be represented at the consideration of the implementation of such provisions of the present Convention as fall within the scope of their mandate. The Committee may invite the specialized agencies, the United Nations Children's Fund and other competent bodies as it may consider appropriate to provide expert advice on the implementation of the Convention in areas falling within the scope of their respective mandates. The Committee may invite the specialized agencies, the United Nations Children's Fund and other United Nations organs to submit reports on the implementation of the Convention in areas falling within the scope of their activities;

(b) The Committee shall transmit, as it may consider appropriate, to the specialized agencies, the United Nations Children's Fund and other competent bodies, any reports from States Parties that contain a request, or indicate a need, for technical advice or assistance, along with the Committee's observations and suggestions, if any, on these requests or indications;

(c) The Committee may recommend to the General Assembly to request the Secretary-General to undertake on its behalf studies on specific issues relating to the rights of the child;

(d) The Committee may make suggestions and general recommendations based on information received pursuant to articles 44 and 45 of the present Convention. Such suggestions and general recommendations shall be transmitted to any State Party concerned and reported to the General Assembly, together with comments, if any, from States Parties.

Part III

● Article 46

The present Convention shall be open for signature by all States.

● Article 47

The present Convention is subject to ratification. Instruments of ratification shall be with the Secretary-General of the United Nations.

● Article 48

The present Convention shall remain open for accession by any State. The instruments of accession shall be deposited with the Secretary-General of the United Nations.

● Article 49

1. The present Convention shall enter into force on the thirtieth day following the date of deposit with the Secretary-General of the United Nations of the twentieth instrument of ratification or accession.

2. For each State ratifying or acceding to the Convention after the deposit of the twentieth instrument of ratification or accession, the Convention shall enter into force on the thirtieth day after the deposit by such State of its instrument of ratification or accession.

● Article 50

1. Any State Party may propose an amendment and file it with the Secretary-General of the United Nations. The Secretary-General shall thereupon communicate the proposed amendment to States Parties, with a request that they indicate whether they favour a conference of States Parties for the purpose of considering and voting upon the proposals. In the event that, within four months from the date of such communication, at least one third of the States Parties favour such a conference, the Secretary-General shall convene the conference under the auspices of the United Nations. Any amendment adopted by a majority of States Parties present and voting at the conference shall be submitted to the General Assembly for approval.

2. An amendment adopted in accordance with paragraph 1 of the present article shall enter into force when it has been approved by the General Assembly of the United Nations and accepted by a two-thirds majority of States Parties.

3. When an amendment enters into force, it shall be binding on those States Parties which have accepted it, other States Parties still being bound by the provisions of the present Convention and any earlier amendments which they have accepted.

● Article 51

1. The Secretary-General of the United Nations shall receive and circulate to all States the text of reservations made by States at the time of ratification or accession.

2. A reservation incompatible with the object and purpose of the present Convention shall not be permitted.

3. Reservations may be withdrawn at any time by notification to that effect addressed to the Secretary-General of the United Nations, who shall then inform all States. Such notification shall take effect on the date on which it is received by the Secretary-General.

● Article 52

A State Party may denounce the present Convention by written notification to the Secretary-General of the United Nations. Denunciation becomes effective one year after the date of receipt of the notification by the Secretary-General.

● Article 53

The Secretary-General of the United Nations is designated as the depositary of the present Convention.

● Article 54

The original of the present Convention, of which the Arabic, Chinese, English, French, Russian and Spanish texts are equally authentic, shall be deposited with the Secretary-General of the United Nations.

In witness thereof the undersigned plenipotentiaries, being duly authorized thereto by their respective Governments, have signed the present Convention.

Reporting Guidelines to Governments

General Guidelines Regarding the Form and Contents of Periodic Reports to Be Submitted by States Parties Under Article 44, Paragraph 1 (B), of the Convention

Adopted by the Committee on the Rights of the Child at its 343rd meeting (thirteenth session) on 11 October 1996

I ntroduction

1. Pursuant to article 44, paragraph 1 of the Convention on the Rights of the Child, States Parties undertake to submit to the Committee, through the Secretary-General of the United Nations, reports on the implementation of the Convention:

(a) Within two years of the entry into force of the Convention for the State Party concerned;

(b) Thereafter every five years.

Reports should provide information on the measures adopted by the State Party to give effect to the rights set forth in the Convention and on the progress made in the enjoyment of those rights and should indicate the factors and difficulties, if any, affecting the degree of fulfilment of the obligations under the Convention. The Committee, in providing these guidelines, wishes to emphasize its supportive role in fostering effective implementation of the Convention and in encouraging international cooperation, as called for in article 45. Reports should also contain sufficient information to provide the Committee with a comprehensive understanding of the implementation of the Convention in the country concerned.

2. The Committee may, in the light of article 44, paragraph 4 of the Convention, request from States Parties further information relevant to the implementation of the Convention.

3. The Committee believes that the process of preparing a report for submission to the Committee provides an important opportunity to conduct a comprehensive review of the various measures undertaken to harmonize law and policy with the Convention and to monitor progress made in the enjoyment of the rights set forth in the Convention. Such a process should encourage and facilitate popular participation and public scrutiny of government policies.

4. The Committee considers that the reporting process entails an ongoing reaffirmation by States Parties of their commitment to respect and ensure observance of the rights enshrined in the Convention and serves as the essential vehicle for the establishment of a meaningful dialogue between the Committee and the States Parties.

5. Periodic reports on the implementation of the Convention should provide information with respect to the period covered by the report on:

The measures adopted by the State Party, including the conclusion of and accession to bilateral and multilateral agreements in the field of children's rights, and changes which have occurred in legislation and practice at the national, regional and local levels, and where appropriate at the federal and provincial levels, such as:

Mechanisms and structures to coordinate and monitor efforts to implement the Convention;

Overall or sectoral policies, programmes and services developed to implement the Convention.

The progress achieved in the enjoyment of children's rights;

The factors and difficulties encountered in the full implementation of the rights set forth in the Convention and on steps taken to overcome them;

The plans envisaged to improve further the realization of the rights of the child.

6. Periodic reports should include information on the consideration given to the concluding observations adopted by the Committee in relation to the previous report, including on:

The areas of concern identified by the Committee, as well as difficulties which may have affected the realization of such suggestions and recommendations;

The measures adopted as a follow-up to the suggestions and recommendations addressed by the Committee to the State Party upon examination of its previous report. Steps taken to implement should be identified in relation to each suggestion and recommendation and all relevant action taken should be specified including in relation to legislation, policy, mechanisms, structures and allocation of resources;

The difficulties which may have affected the realization of such suggestions and recommendations;

The steps taken to widely disseminate the previous report, as well as the concluding observations adopted by the Committee.

7. Reports should be accompanied by copies of the principal legislative texts and judicial decisions, as well as detailed statistical information, indicators referred to therein and relevant research. This accompanying material will be made available to the members of the Committee. Quantitative information should indicate variations between various areas of the country and within areas and between groups of children and include:

Changes in the status of children;

Variations by age, gender, region, rural/urban area, and social and ethnic group;

Changes in community systems serving children;

Changes in budget allocation and expenditure for sectors serving children;

Changes in the extent of international cooperation received or contributed for the realization of children's rights.

It should be noted, however, that for reasons of economy, these documents will not be translated or reproduced for general distribution. It is desirable, therefore, that when a text is not actually quoted in or annexed to the report itself, the report should contain sufficient information to be clearly understood without reference to those texts.

8. IN THE LIGHT OF ARTICLE 44, PARAGRAPH 3, OF THE CONVENTION, WHEN A STATE PARTY HAS SUBMITTED A COMPREHENSIVE INITIAL REPORT TO THE COMMITTEE OR HAS PREVIOUSLY PROVIDED DETAILED INFORMATION TO THE COMMITTEE, IT NEED NOT REPEAT SUCH BASIC INFORMATION IN ITS SUBSEQUENT REPORTS. IT SHOULD, HOWEVER, CLEARLY REFERENCE THE INFORMATION PREVIOUSLY TRANSMITTED, AND INDICATE THE CHANGES THAT HAVE OCCURRED DURING THE REPORTING PERIOD.

9. In the present guidelines the provisions of the Convention have been grouped in clusters with a view to assisting States Parties in the preparation of their reports. This approach reflects the Convention's holistic perspective of children's rights: that they are indivisible and interrelated, and that equal importance should be attached to each and every right recognized therein.

10. Information provided in States Parties' reports on the various sections identified by the Committee should closely follow the present guidelines with regard to content.

I. GENERAL MEASURES OF IMPLEMENTATION
(arts. 4; 42 and 44, paragraph 6 of the Convention)
SEE PARAGRAPH 8 ABOVE

11. In the spirit of the World Conference on Human Rights, which encouraged States to consider reviewing any reservation with a view to withdrawing it (see A/CONF.157/23, II, paras. 5 and 46), please indicate whether the Government considers it necessary to maintain the reservations it has made, if any, or has the intention of withdrawing them.

12. States Parties are requested to provide relevant information pursuant to article 4 of the Convention, including information on the measures adopted to bring national legislation and practice into full conformity with the principles and provisions of the Convention, together with details of:

Any comprehensive review of the domestic legislation to ensure compliance with the Convention;

Any new laws or codes adopted, as well as amendments introduced into domestic legislation to ensure implementation of the Convention.

13. Please indicate the status of the Convention in domestic law:

With respect to recognition in the Constitution or other national legislation of the rights set forth in the Convention;

With respect to the possibility for the provisions of the Convention to be directly invoked before the courts and applied by the national authorities;

In the event of a conflict with national legislation.

14. In the light of article 41 of the Convention, please indicate any provisions of the national legislation which are more conducive to the realization of the rights of the child.

15. Please provide information on judicial decisions applying the principles and provisions of the Convention.

16. Please provide information on remedies available in cases of violation of the rights recognized by the Convention.

17. Please indicate any steps taken or envisaged to adopt a comprehensive national strategy for children in the framework of the Convention, such as a national plan of action on children's rights and relevant goals established.

18. Please provide information on existing or planned mechanisms at the national, regional and local levels, and when relevant at the federal and provincial levels, for ensuring implementation of the Convention, for coordinating policies relevant to children and for monitoring progress achieved, including information on:

The governmental departments competent in the areas covered by the Convention, the steps taken to ensure the effective coordination of their activities, as well as to monitor the progress made by them;

The steps taken to ensure effective coordination of activities between central, regional and local authorities, and where relevant between federal and provincial authorities;

Any governmental institutions created to promote the rights of the child and monitor implementation, and how they relate to non-governmental organizations;

Any independent body established to promote and protect the rights of the child, such as an Ombudsperson or a Commissioner;

The measures taken to ensure the systematic gathering of data on children and their fundamental rights and to assess existing trends at the national, regional and local levels, and where appropriate at the federal and provincial levels, as well as the steps taken to develop mechanisms for the identification and gathering of appropriate indicators, statistics, relevant research and other relevant information as a basis for policy-making in the field of children's rights;

The steps taken to ensure a periodic evaluation of progress in the implementation of the Convention at the national, regional and local levels, and where appropriate at the federal and provincial levels, including through the preparation of any periodic report by the Government to the Parliament.

19. Please indicate any initiatives taken in cooperation with the civil society (for example, professional groups, non-governmental organizations) and any mechanisms developed to evaluate progress achieved.

20. Using indicators or target figures where necessary, please indicate the measures undertaken to ensure the implementation at the national, regional and local levels, and where relevant at the federal and provincial levels, of the economic, social and cultural rights of children to the maximum extent of available resources, including:

The steps undertaken to ensure coordination between economic and social policies;

The proportion of the budget devoted to social expenditures for children, including health, welfare and education, at the central, regional and local levels, and where appropriate at the federal and provincial levels;

The budget trends over the period covered by the report;

Arrangements for budgetary analysis enabling the amount and proportion spent on children to be clearly identified;

The steps taken to ensure that all competent national, regional and local authorities are guided by the best interests of the child in their budgetary decisions and evaluate the priority given to children in their policy-making;

The measures taken to ensure that disparities between different regions and groups of children are bridged in relation to the provision of social services;

The measures taken to ensure that children, particularly those belonging to the most disadvantaged groups, are protected against the adverse effects of economic policies, including the reduction of budgetary allocations in the social sector.

21. Please indicate the extent to which international cooperation relevant to the State Party is designed to foster the implementation of the Convention, including economic, social and cultural rights of children. Please indicate the proportion of international aid at the multilateral and bilateral levels allocated to programmes for children and the promotion of their rights and, where appropriate, the assistance received from regional and international financial institutions. Please also indicate the percentage of international cooperation contributed during the reporting period in the total government budget, as well as the percentages of such cooperation respectively allocated to the health sector, to the education sector, to the social sector and to other sectors. Please further indicate any relevant measures adopted as a follow-up to the Declaration and Programme of Action of the World Summit for Social Development.

22. In addition, States are requested to describe the measures that have been taken or are foreseen, pursuant to article 42 of the Convention, to make the principles and provisions of the Convention widely known, by appropriate and active means, to adults and children alike. In this regard, reports should also indicate:

The extent to which the Convention has been translated into the national, local, minority or indigenous languages. In this connection, an indication should be given of the number of languages into which the Convention has been translated and the number of copies translated into the minority languages during the reporting period;

Whether the Convention has been translated and has been made available in the languages spoken by the larger refugee and immigrant groups in the country concerned;

The measures adopted to publicize the Convention and create widespread awareness of its principles and provisions. In this connection, an indication should be given of the number of meetings (such as parliamentary or governmental conferences, workshops, seminars) held, the number of programmes broadcast on radio or television and the number of publications issued explaining the Convention on the Rights of the Child during the reporting period;

The specific steps taken to make the Convention widely known to children and the extent to which it has been reflected in the school curricula and considered in parents' education campaigns. An indication should be given of the number of copies of the Convention distributed in the educational system and to the public at large during the reporting period;

The measures adopted to provide education on the Convention to public officials, as well as to train professional groups working with and for children, such as teachers, law enforcement officials, including police, immigration officers, judges, prosecutors, lawyers, defence forces, medical doctors, health workers and social workers;

The extent to which the principles and provisions of the Convention have been incorporated in professional training curricula and codes of conduct or regulations;

The steps taken to promote understanding of the principles and provisions of the Convention by the mass media and by information and publishing agencies;

The involvement of non-governmental organizations in awareness and advocacy campaigns on the Convention, as well as any support provided to them. In this connection, an indication should be given of the number of non-governmental organizations who participated in such events during the reporting period;

The participation of children in any of these activities.

23. States are also requested to describe the measures undertaken or foreseen, pursuant to article 44, paragraph 6, to make their reports widely available to the public at large in their own countries. In this regard, please indicate:

The process of preparation of the present report, in particular the extent to which governmental departments, at the central, regional and local levels, and where appropriate, at the federal and provincial levels, participated, and non-governmental organizations were involved. An indication should also be given of the number of non-governmental organizations which participated in the preparation of the report;

The steps taken to publicize the report, to translate and disseminate it in the national, local, minority or indigenous languages. An indication should be given of the number of meetings (such as parliamentary and governmental conferences, workshops, seminars)

held, the number of programmes broadcast on radio or television, the number of publications issued explaining the report and the number of non-governmental organizations which participated in such events during the reporting period;

The measures adopted or foreseen to ensure wide dissemination and consideration of the summary records and the concluding observations adopted by the Committee in relation to the State Party's report, including any parliamentary hearing or media coverage. Please indicate the events undertaken to publicize the concluding observations and summary records of the previous report, including the number of meetings (such as parliamentary or governmental conferences, workshops, seminars) held, the number of programmes broadcast on radio or television, the number of publications issued explaining the concluding observations and summary records, and the number of non-governmental organizations which participated in such events during the reporting period.

II. DEFINITION OF THE CHILD (art. 1)
SEE PARAGRAPH 8 ABOVE

24. Under this section, States Parties are requested to provide relevant information with respect to article 1 of the Convention, including on:

Any differences between national legislation and the Convention on the definition of the child;

The minimum legal age defined by the national legislation for the following:

Legal and medical counselling without parental consent;

Medical treatment or surgery without parental consent;

End of compulsory education;

Admission to employment or work, including hazardous work, part-time and full-time work;

Marriage;

Sexual consent;

Voluntary enlistment in the armed forces;

Conscription into the armed forces;

Participation in hostilities;

Criminal responsibility;

Deprivation of liberty, including by arrest, detention and imprisonment, *inter alia* in the areas of administration of justice, asylum-seeking and placement of children in welfare and health institutions;

Capital punishment and life imprisonment;

Giving testimony in court, in civil and criminal cases;

Lodging complaints and seeking redress before a court or other relevant authority without parental consent;

Participating in administrative and judicial proceedings affecting the child;

Giving consent to change of identity, including change of name, modification of family relations, adoption, guardianship;

Having access to information concerning the biological family;

Legal capacity to inherit, to conduct property transactions;

To create or join associations;

Choosing a religion or attending religious school teaching;

Consumption of alcohol and other controlled substances;

How the minimum age for employment relates to the age of completion of compulsory schooling, how it affects the right of the child to education and how relevant international instruments are taken into account;

In cases where there is a difference in the legislation between girls and boys, including in relation to marriage and sexual consent, the extent to which article 2 of the Convention has been given consideration;

In cases where the criteria of puberty is used under criminal law, the extent to which this provision is differently applied to girls and boys, and whether the principles and provisions of the Convention are taken into consideration.

III. GENERAL PRINCIPLES
SEE PARAGRAPH 8 ABOVE

A. Non-discrimination (art. 2)

25. Reports should indicate whether the principle of non-discrimination is included as a binding principle in the Constitution or in domestic legislation specifically for children and whether all the possible grounds for discrimination spelled out in article 2 of the Convention are reflected in such legal provisions. Reports should further indicate the measures adopted to ensure the rights set forth in the Convention to each child under the jurisdiction of the State without discrimination of any kind, including non-nationals, refugees and asylum-seekers.

26. Information should be provided on steps taken to ensure that discrimination is prevented and combated, both in law and practice, including discrimination on the basis of race, colour, sex, language, religion, political or other opinion, national, ethnic or social origin, property, disability, birth or other status of the child, his/her parents or legal guardians.

27. Please indicate the specific measures adopted to reduce economic, social and geographical disparities, including between rural and urban areas, to prevent discrimination against the most disadvantaged groups of children, including children belonging to minorities or indigenous communities, disabled children, children born out of wedlock, children who are non-nationals, migrants, displaced, refugees or asylum-seekers, and children who are living and/or working on the streets.

28. Please provide information on the specific measures taken to eliminate discrimination against girls and when appropriate indicate measures adopted as a follow-up to the Fourth World Conference on Women.

29. Please indicate measures taken to collect disaggregated data for the various groups of children mentioned above.

30. What measures have been taken to prevent and eliminate attitudes to and prejudice against children contributing to social or ethnic tension, racism and xenophobia?

31. Information should also be provided on the measures pursuant to article 2, paragraph 2 taken to ensure that the child is protected against all forms of discrimination or punishment on the basis of the status, activities, expressed opinions or beliefs of the child's parents, legal guardians or family members.

32. Please indicate major problems encountered in implementing the provisions of article 2 and plans to solve these problems, as well as any evaluation of progress in preventing and combating all forms of discrimination, including those arising from negative traditional practices.

B. Best interests of the child (art. 3)

33. Reports should indicate whether the principle of the best interests of the child and the need for it to be a primary consideration in all actions concerning children is reflected in the Constitution and relevant national legislation and regulations.

34. Please provide information on the consideration given to this principle by courts of law, administrative authorities or legislative bodies, as well as by public or private social welfare agencies.

35. Please provide information on how the best interests of the child have been given primary consideration in family life, school life, social life and in areas such as:
Budgetary allocations, including at the central, regional and local levels, and where appropriate at the federal and provincial levels, and within governmental departments;
Planning and development policies, including housing, transport and environmental policies;
Adoption;
Immigration, asylum-seeking and refugee procedures;
The administration of juvenile justice;
The placement and care of children in institutions;
Social security.

36. Information should be included on the measures taken in the light of article 3, paragraph 2, including of a legislative and administrative nature, to ensure children such protection and care as is necessary for their well-being.

37. Information should also be provided on the steps taken pursuant to article 3, paragraph 3, to establish appropriate standards for all public and private institutions, services and facilities responsible for the care and protection of children and to ensure that they conform with such standards, particularly in the areas of safety, health, number and suitability of their staff, as well as competent supervision.

38. In the light of the legislative and administrative measures taken to ensure the consideration of the best interests of the child, please indicate the main problems remaining in this respect.

39. Please indicate in what ways the principle of the best interests of the child is made part of the training of professionals dealing with children's rights.

C. The right to life, survival and development (art. 6)

40. Please describe specific measures taken to guarantee the child's right to life and to create an environment conducive to ensuring to the maximum extent possible the survival and development of the child, including physical, mental, spiritual, moral, psychological and social development, in a manner compatible with human dignity, and to prepare the child for an individual life in a free society.

41. Information should also be provided on the measures taken to ensure the registration of the deaths of children, the causes of death and, where appropriate, investigation and reporting on such deaths, as well as on the measures adopted to prevent children's suicide and monitor its incidence and to ensure the survival of children at all ages, including adolescents, and the prevention of risks to which that group may be particularly exposed (for example, sexually transmitted diseases, street violence). Please provide relevant disaggregated data, including on the number of suicides among children.

D. Respect for the views of the child (art. 12)

42. Reports should indicate how the right of the child to express views freely on all matters affecting him or her, and provision for those views to be given due weight have been incorporated in legislation.

43. Please provide information on legislative and other measures taken to ensure the right of the child to express views in a manner consistent with his or her evolving capacities, including in:
Family life;
School life;
The administration of juvenile justice;
Placement and life in institutional and other forms of care;
Asylum-seeking procedures.

44. Please indicate the opportunities provided for the child to be heard in judicial and administrative proceedings affecting him or her, as well as the situations in which the child can intervene directly or through a representative or an appropriate body (see also para. 34 above).

45. Please provide information on any bodies or instances where the child has a right to participate in decision-making, such as schools or local councils.

46. Please indicate what measures have been taken to raise the awareness of families and the public in general of the need to encourage children to exercise their right to express their views, and to train professionals working with children to encourage children to do so, and to give their views due weight. An indication should be given of the number of hours of child development courses provided for the following staff:
Judges in general;
Family court judges;
Juvenile court judges;
Probation officers;
Police officers;
Prison officers;
Teachers;
Health workers;
Other professionals.
An indication should also be provided of the number of courses about the Convention included in the curriculum of:
Law schools;
Teachers training schools;
Medical schools and institutions;
Nursing schools;
Social work schools;
Psychology departments;
Sociology departments.

47. Please indicate how the views of the child obtained through public opinion, consultations and assessment of complaints are taken into consideration in the legal provisions, and in policy or judicial decisions.

IV. CIVIL RIGHTS AND FREEDOMS (arts. 7; 8; 13-17 and 37 (a))
SEE PARAGRAPH 8 ABOVE

48. Under this section, States Parties are requested to provide information on the measures adopted to ensure that the civil rights and freedoms of children set forth in the Convention, in particular those covered by articles 7, 8, 13 to 17 and 37 (a), are recognized by law specifically in relation to children and implemented in practice, including by administrative and judicial bodies, at the national, regional and local levels, and where appropriate at the federal and provincial levels.

A. Name and nationality (art. 7)

49. Please indicate the measures taken or envisaged to ensure that every child is registered immediately after birth. Please also indicate the steps undertaken to prevent the non-registration of children immediately after birth, including in view of possible social or cultural obstacles, *inter alia* in rural or remote areas, in relation to nomadic groups, displaced persons, as well as asylum-seeking and refugee children.

50. Please provide information on the measures taken to sensitize and mobilize public opinion on the need for birth registration of children, and to provide adequate training to registry personnel.

51. Please also provide information on the elements of the child's identity included in the birth registration and the measures adopted to prevent any kind of stigmatization or discrimination of the child.

52. Please indicate the measures adopted to ensure the child's right to know and be cared for by his or her parents.

53. Please provide information on the measures adopted pursuant to article 7, paragraph 2, to ensure the child's right to acquire a nationality, in particular where the child would otherwise be stateless. Reference should also be made to the implementation of this right in relation to children born out of wedlock, and asylum-seeking and refugee children. Please indicate the criteria applied for the acquisition of nationality and whether the child is allowed to acquire the nationality of both parents.

B. Preservation of identity (art. 8)

54. Please indicate the measures adopted to preserve the child's identity and to prevent any unlawful interference. In the case of the illegal deprivation of some or all of the elements of the child's identity, reports should also indicate the measures adopted to provide appropriate assistance and protection to the child and ensure the speedy re-establishment of his or her identity.

C. Freedom of expression (art. 13)

55. Please provide information on the measures adopted to ensure the child's right to freedom of expression, including to seek, receive and impart information and ideas regardless of frontiers. Reports should also indicate the restrictions to which the exercise of this right may be subject in conformity with article 13, paragraph 2.

D. Freedom of thought, conscience and religion (art. 14)

56. Please provide information on the exercise of the right to freedom of thought, conscience and religion by children, and the extent to which the child's evolving capacities are taken into consideration.

57. Please indicate the measures adopted to ensure the child's freedom to manifest his or her religion or beliefs, including with regard to minorities or indigenous groups. Information should also be provided on measures to ensure respect for the child's rights in relation to any religious teaching in public schools or institutions, as well as on any limitations to which this freedom may be subject in conformity with article 14, paragraph 3.

E. Freedom of association and peaceful assembly (art. 15)

58. Please indicate the measures adopted to ensure the child's right to freedom of association and peaceful assembly, including any specific legislation enacted to establish the conditions under which children are allowed to create or join associations. Please also indicate any restriction that may be placed on the exercise of these rights, in conformity with article 15, paragraph 2. Information should also be provided on existing children's associations and the role they play in the promotion of children's rights.

F. Protection of privacy (art. 16)

59. Please indicate the measures adopted to prevent any arbitrary or unlawful interference with the child's privacy, family, home or correspondence, as well as any attack on his or her honour and reputation. Please provide information on the protection provided by the law against such interference or attacks, and the remedies made available to the child. Information should also be provided on specific measures adopted for children placed in institutions for treatment, care or protection, including in judicial or administrative proceedings.

G. Access to appropriate information (art. 17)

60. Please provide information on the measures adopted to ensure that children have access from a diversity of national and inter-national sources to information and material aimed at the promotion of the child's social, spiritual and moral well-being and physical and mental health. Please also indicate the measures adopted to encourage:

The production and dissemination of children's books, and the dissemination by the mass media of information and material of social and cultural benefit to the child, with particular regard to the linguistic needs of children belonging to a minority group or who are indigenous;

International cooperation in the production, exchange and dissemination of such information and material of social and cultural benefit for the child, in accordance with the spirit of article 29 of the Convention on the aims of education, including any international agreements concluded for that purpose;

The development of appropriate guidelines for the protection of the child from information and material injurious to his or her well-being, as well as from harmful exposure in the mass media, bearing in mind the provisions of articles 13 and 18.

H. The right not to be subjected to torture or other cruel, inhuman or degrading treatment or punishment (art. 37 (a))

61. Please indicate whether torture or other cruel, inhuman or degrading treatment or punishment of children is punished by the criminal law, and whether complaint procedures have been established and remedies made available to the child. Please also provide information on:

Awareness campaigns launched to prevent torture or other cruel, inhuman or degrading treatment or punishment of children;

Educative and training activities developed, particularly with personnel in institutions, services and facilities working with and for children, aimed at preventing any form of ill-treatment;

Any cases where children have been victims of any such acts;

Measures adopted to prevent the impunity of perpetrators, including by investigating such cases and punishing those found responsible;

Measures adopted to ensure the physical and psychological recovery and reintegration of children who have been tortured or otherwise ill-treated;

Any independent monitoring system established.

V. FAMILY ENVIRONMENT AND ALTERNATIVE CARE
(arts. 5; 18, paras. 1-2; 9-11; 19-21; 25; 27, para. 4; and 39)
SEE PARAGRAPH 8 ABOVE

A. Parental guidance (art. 5)

62. Please provide information on family structures within the society and indicate the measures adopted to ensure respect for the responsibilities, rights and duties of parents or where applicable the members of the extended family or community as provided for by local custom, legal guardians or other per-sons legally responsible for the child, to provide appropriate direction and guidance to the child, further indicating how such direction and guidance are consistent with the child's evolving capacities.

63. Please indicate any family counselling services or parental education programmes available, as well as awareness campaigns for parents and children on the rights of the child within family life, and training activities provided to relevant professional groups (for example, social workers) and indicate if any evaluation has been made of their effectiveness. Please also indicate how knowledge and information about child development and the evolving capacities of the child are conveyed to parents or other persons responsible for the child.

64. Information should also be provided on the measures adopted to ensure respect for the principles of the Convention, namely non-discrimination, the best interests of the child, respect for the views of the child, the right to life, and survival and development to the maximum extent possible, as well as on the progress achieved in the implementation of article 5, any difficulties encountered and the indicators used.

B. Parental responsibilities (art. 18, paras. 1-2)

65. Please provide information on the consideration given by law to parental responsibility, including the recognition of the common responsibilities of both parents in the upbringing and development of the child and, that the best interests of the child will be their basic concern. Also indicate how the principles of non-discrimination, respect for the views of the child and the development of the child to the maximum extent, as provided for by the Convention, are taken into account.

66. Please provide information on the measures adopted to render appropriate assistance to parents and legal guardians in the performance of their child-rearing responsibilities, as well as on the institutions, facilities and services developed for the care of children. Information should also be provided on specific measures adopted for children from single-parent families and belonging to the most disadvantaged groups, including those living in extreme poverty.

67. Relevant disaggregated information (for example, by gender, age, region, rural/urban areas and social and ethnic origin) should be given on children having benefited from any of these measures and resources allocated to them (at the national, regional and local levels, and where appropriate at the federal and provincial levels). Information should also be provided on progress achieved and difficulties encountered in the implementation of article 18, as well as on the targets set for the future.

C. Separation from parents (art. 9)

68. Please indicate the measures adopted, including of a legislative and judicial nature, to ensure that the child is not separated from his or her parents except when such separation is necessary for the best interests of the child,

as in cases of abuse or neglect of the child or when the parents live separately and a decision must be made as to the child's place of residence. Please identify the competent authorities intervening in these decisions, the applicable law and procedure and the role of judicial review.

69. Please provide information on the measures taken pursuant to article 9, paragraph 2 to ensure to all interested parties, including the child, an opportunity to participate in any proceedings and to make their views known.

70. Please indicate the measures adopted, including of a legislative, judicial and administrative nature, to ensure that the child who is separated from one or both parents has the right to maintain personal relations and direct contacts with both parents on a regular basis, except if it is contrary to the best interests of the child. Please further indicate the extent to which the views of the child are taken into consideration in this regard.

71. Please indicate the measures adopted pursuant to article 9, paragraph 4 to ensure that in the case of the childs separation from one or both of his or her parents as a result of any action initiated by the State, essential information on the whereabouts of the absent member(s) of the family is provided, upon request, to the child, to the parents or, if appropriate, to another member of the family, unless the provision of the information would be detrimental to the well-being of the child. Also indicate the measures undertaken to ensure that the submission of such a request entails no adverse consequences for the person(s) concerned.

72. Relevant disaggregated information (for example, by age, gender and national, ethnic and social origin) should be provided *inter alia* in relation to situations of detention, imprisonment, exile, deportation or death, together with an assessment of progress achieved in the implementation of article 9, difficulties encountered and targets set for the future.

D. Family reunification (art. 10)

73. Please provide information on the measures adopted to ensure that applications by a child or his or her parents to enter or leave a country for the purpose of family reunification are dealt with by the State in a positive, humane and expeditious manner and that the submission of such a request entails no adverse consequences for the applicants and the members of their family.

74. Please also indicate how such applications are considered in the light of the Convention and in particular of its general principles of non-discrimination, the best interests of the child, respect for the views of the child, the right to life, and survival and development to the maximum extent possible, including in the case of unaccompanied and asylum seeking children. Disaggregated information should also be provided, including by gender, age, and national and ethnic origin.

75. Please indicate the measures undertaken to ensure the right of a child whose parents reside in different States to maintain on a regular basis personal relations and direct contacts with both parents. Please also indicate any exceptions and their compatibility with the provisions and principles of the Convention.

76. Information should be provided on the steps taken to ensure respect for the right of the child and his or her parents to leave any country, including their own, and to enter their own country. They should indicate any restrictions imposed on the right to leave the country, how they are prescribed by law, necessary to protect national security, public order (*ordre public*), public health or morals or the rights and freedoms of others and the extent to which they are consistent with the other rights recognized in the Convention, including the principles of non-discrimination, the best interests of the child, respect for the views of the child, the right to life, and survival and development to the maximum extent possible.

77. Reports should also provide information on the progress achieved in the implementation of article 10, difficulties encountered and targets set for the future.

E. Illicit transfer and non-return (art. 11)

78. Please provide information on:

The steps taken to prevent and combat the illicit transfer and non-return of children abroad, including legislative, administrative or judicial measures, as well as mechanisms established to monitor such situations;

Any bilateral or multilateral agreement on this subject concluded by the State Party or to which it may have acceded and the impact they have had;

Progress achieved and the difficulties met with in countering such situations, together with relevant data on the children concerned, including by gender, age, national origin, place of residence, family status and relationship with the perpetrator of the illicit transfer.

F. Recovery of maintenance for the child (art. 27, para. 4)

79. Please indicate the measures adopted (including legislative, administrative and judicial measures) and mechanisms or programmes developed to secure the recovery of maintenance for the child from the parents or other persons having financial responsibility for the child, both within the State and from abroad, including in cases of the separation or divorce of the parents. Information should also be provided on:

Measures taken to ensure the maintenance of the child in cases where parents or other persons having financial responsibility for the child evade the payment of such maintenance;

Measures adopted to ensure respect for the general principles of the Convention, namely non-discrimination, the best interests of the child, respect for the views of the child and the right to life, survival and development to the maximum extent;

The factors and difficulties which may have affected the recovery of maintenance for the child (for example, lack of birth registration) or the enforcement of decisions concerning maintenance obligations;

The relevant international agreements the State has concluded or to which it has acceded, as well as any other appropriate arrangement it has made;

Relevant disaggregated data in this area, including by gender, age, national origin and place of residence of the child and his or her parents, or of the persons financially responsible for him or her.

G. Children deprived of their family environment (art. 20)

80. Please indicate the measures adopted to ensure:

Special protection and assistance to the child who is temporarily or permanently deprived of his or her family environment or in whose own best interests cannot be allowed to remain in that environment;

Alternative care for such a child, specifying the available forms of such care (*inter alia* foster placement, kafalah of Islamic law, adoption or if necessary placement in suitable institutions for the care of the child);

That the placement of such a child in suitable institutions will only be used if really necessary;

Monitoring of the situation of children placed in alternative care;

Respect for the general principles of the Convention, namely non-discrimination, the best interests of the child, respect for the views of the child and the right to life, survival and development to the maximum extent.

81. Reports should also indicate the extent to which, when such solutions are being considered, due regard is paid to the desirability of continuity in the childs upbringing and to the childs ethnic, religious, cultural and linguistic background. Disaggregated information should be provided on the children concerned by all such measures, including by gender, age, national, social or ethnic origin, language, religion, and by the nature of the measure of alternative care applied.

82. Reports should also provide information on the progress achieved in the implementation of this article, any difficulties encountered or on targets set for the future.

H. Adoption (art. 21)

83. Please indicate the measures adopted, including of a legislative, administrative or judicial nature, to ensure that, when the State recognizes and/or permits the system of adoption, the best interests of the child shall be the paramount consideration. Information should also be provided on:

The authorities which are competent to authorize the adoption of a child;

The applicable law and procedures and the pertinent and reliable information on the basis of which adoption is determined;

The child's status concerning his or her parents, relatives and legal guardians necessary for adoption to be considered permissible;

The involvement of the persons concerned, the circumstances under which their informed consent is required and necessary counselling provided, including to allow for the consideration of the alternatives to and consequences of adoption, and the extent to which the participation of the child is ensured and his or her views are given due weight;

Existing safeguards to protect the child, including any monitoring mechanism put in place;

The effects of adoption on the rights of the child, particularly his or her civil rights, including the child's identity and the right of the child to know his or her biological parents.

84. In the case of intercountry adoption, please indicate the measures undertaken to ensure that:

Such a solution is only considered as an alternative means of care for the child if he or she cannot be placed in a foster or an adoptive family or cannot in any suitable manner be cared for in the childs country of origin;

The child involved in intercountry adoption enjoys safeguards and standards equivalent to those existing in the case of national adoption;

Placement by intercountry adoption does not result in improper financial gain for those involved in it;

Appropriate mechanisms have been established to monitor the situation of the child, including following his or her placement through intercountry adoption, and to ensure that his or her best interests prevail as a paramount consideration.

85. Reports should also indicate:

Any bilateral or multilateral arrangements or agreements concluded by the State to promote the objectives of article 21 (for example, the Hague Convention of May 1993 on Protection of Children and Cooperation in respect of Intercountry Adoption);

Within this framework, the measures adopted to ensure that the placement of a child in another country is carried out by competent authorities or organs;

Relevant disaggregated data on the children involved in intercountry adoption, including by age, gender, status of the child, situation of the child's family of origin and of adoption, as well as country of origin and of adoption;

Progress achieved in the implementation of article 21, difficulties encountered and targets set for the future.

I. Periodic review of placement (art. 25)

86. Please indicate the measures undertaken, including of a legislative, administrative and judicial nature, to recognize the right of the child who has been placed by the competent authorities for the purposes of care, protection or treatment of his or her physical and mental health, to a periodic review of the treatment provided to the child in public and private institutions, services and facilities, as well as all other circumstances relevant to his or her placement.

87. Information should be provided *inter alia* on:

The authorities considered competent for such purposes, including any appropriate independent mechanism established;

The circumstances taken into account in deciding on the placement of the child for his or her care, protection and treatment;

The frequency of review of the placement and treatment provided;

The respect ensured to the provisions and principles of the Convention, including non-discrimination, the best interests of the child and respect for the views of the child;

Relevant data on the children concerned, including in situations of abandonment, disability and asylum seeking and refugees, including unaccompanied children, and in situations of conflict with the law, disaggregated *inter alia* by age, gender, national, ethnic and social origin, family situation and place of residence, as well as by duration of placement and frequency of its review;

Progress achieved in the implementation of article 25, difficulties encountered and targets set for the future.

J. Abuse and neglect (art. 19), including physical and psychological recovery and social reintegration (art. 39)

88. Please indicate all appropriate legislative, administrative, social and educational measures taken pursuant to article 19 to protect the child from all forms of physical or mental violence, injury or abuse, neglect or negligent treatment, maltreatment or exploitation, including sexual abuse while in the care of parent(s), legal guardian(s) or any other person who has the care of the child. Reports should indicate in particular:

Whether legislation (criminal and/or family law) includes a prohibition of all forms of physical and mental violence, including corporal punishment, deliberate humiliation, injury, abuse, neglect or exploitation, *inter alia* within the family, in foster and other forms of care, and in public or private institutions, such as penal institutions and schools;

Other existing legal safeguards relevant to the protection of the child as required by article 19;

Whether complaint procedures have been foreseen and the child can lodge complaints, either directly or through a representative, as well as remedies available (for example, compensation);

The procedures developed for intervention by the authorities in cases where the child requires protection from any form of violence, abuse or negligence, as required by article 19;

The educational and other measures adopted to promote positive and non-violent forms of discipline, care and treatment of the child;

Any information and awareness-raising campaigns to prevent situations of violence, abuse or negligence and to strengthen the system for the child's protection;

Any mechanisms established to monitor the extent of the forms of violence, injury or abuse, neglect, maltreatment or exploitation considered by article 19, including within the family, in institutional or other care, of a welfare, educational or penal nature, and the

social and other factors contributing thereto, as well as any evaluation made of the effectiveness of the measures adopted; in this regard disaggregated data should be provided on the children concerned, including by age, gender, family situation, rural/urban, social and ethnic origin.

89. With respect to article 19, paragraph 2, reports should also provide information *inter alia* on:

Effective procedures developed for the establishment of social programmes to provide necessary support for the child and those who have the care of the child, including rehabilitation mechanisms;

Any other forms of prevention;

Effective measures adopted for the identification, reporting, referral, investigation, treatment and follow-up of instances of maltreatment covered by article 19, as well as for judicial involvement;

The existence of any system of mandatory reporting for professional groups working with and for children (for example teachers, medical doctors);

The existence of confidential help lines, advice or counselling for child victims of violence, abuse or neglect or any other form considered by article 19;

The special training provided for relevant professionals. (See also para. 34 above).

90. Please also indicate the measures adopted pursuant to article 39 to ensure the physical and psychological recovery and social reintegration of the child victim of any form of neglect, exploitation or abuse referred to in article 19, in an environment which fosters the health, self-respect and dignity of the child. Information should also be provided on the progress achieved, any difficulties encountered and on the targets set for the future.

91. Reports should also provide information on the progress achieved in the implementation of these articles, difficulties encountered and targets set for the future.

VI. BASIC HEALTH AND WELFARE (arts. 6; 18, para. 3; 23; 24; 26; 27, paras. 1-3)

SEE PARAGRAPH 8 ABOVE

A. Disabled children (art. 23)

92. Please provide information on:

The situation of the mentally or physically disabled child and the measures taken to ensure:

The child's enjoyment of a full and decent life, in conditions which ensure the child's dignity and self-reliance;

The child's enjoyment of his or her rights without discrimination of any kind and the prevention and elimination of discriminatory attitudes against him or her;

The promotion of the child's active participation in the community;

The child's effective access to education, training, health care and rehabilitation services, preparation for employment and recreation opportunities in a manner conducive to the child's achieving the fullest possible social integration and individual development, including his or her cultural and spiritual development;

The consideration given to the inclusion of disabled children together with children without disabilities in institutions, services and facilities, including within the education system;

The child's right to special care and the steps taken to ensure the extension, subject to available resources, to the eligible child and those responsible for his or her care, of assistance appropriate to the child's condition and to the circumstances of the parents or others caring for the child;

That, whenever possible, assistance is provided free of charge, taking into account the financial resources of the parents or others caring for the child;

The measures taken to ensure an effective evaluation of the situation of disabled children, including the development of a system of identification and tracking of disabled children, the establishment of any appropriate monitoring mechanism, the assessment of progress and of difficulties encountered, as well as any targets set for the future;

The measures taken to ensure adequate training, including specialized training, for those responsible for the care of disabled children, including at the family and community levels and within relevant institutions;

The measures taken to promote, in the spirit of international cooperation, the exchange of appropriate information in the field of preventive health care and of the medical, psychological and functional treatment of disabled children, including dissemination of and access to information concerning methods of rehabilitation, education and vocational services. An indication should be given of the measures taken with the aim of enabling States Parties to the Convention to improve their capabilities and skills and to widen their experience in these areas, and the consideration given to the particular needs of developing countries;

The children concerned, including by type of disability, the coverage of the assistance provided, programmes and services made available, including in the fields of education, training, care, rehabilitation, employment and recreation, the financial and other resources allocated, and other relevant information, disaggregated *inter alia* by gender, age, rural/urban area, and social and ethnic origin.

B. Health and health services (art. 24)

93. Please indicate the measures adopted pursuant to articles 6 and 24:

To recognize and ensure the right of the child to the enjoyment of the highest attainable standard of health and to facilities for treatment and rehabilitation;

To ensure that no child is deprived of his or her right of access to such health care services;

To ensure respect for the general principles of the Convention, namely non-discrimination, the best interests of the child, respect for the views of the child and the right to life, and survival and development to the maximum extent possible.

94. Reports should also provide information about the measures adopted to identify changes which have occurred since the submission of the State Parties previous report, their impact on the life of children, as well as the indicators used to assess the progress achieved in the implementation of this right, the difficulties encountered and any targets identified for the future, including in relation to child mortality and child morbidity, service coverage, data collection, policies and legislation, budget allocation (including in relation to the general budget), involvement of non-governmental organizations and international assistance.

95. Please also provide information on the measures undertaken in particular:

To diminish infant and child mortality, indicating the average rates and providing relevant disaggregated data, including by gender, age, region, rural/urban area, ethnic and social origin.

To ensure the provision of necessary medical assistance and health care to all children with emphasis on the development of primary health care, including:

The distribution of both general and primary health care services in the rural and urban areas of the country and the balance between preventive and curative health care;

Information on the children having access to and benefiting from medical assistance and health care, as well as persisting gaps, including by gender, age, ethnic and social origin, and measures adopted to reduce existing disparities;

The measures adopted to ensure a universal immunization system.

To combat disease and malnutrition, including in the framework of primary health care, through *inter alia* the application of readily available technology and through the provision of adequate nutritious foods and clean drinking water, taking into account the risks and dangers of environmental degradation and pollution; reports should indicate the overall situation, persisting disparities and difficulties, as well as policies to address them, including priorities identified for future action, and information should also be provided, including by gender, age, region, rural/urban area, and social and ethnic origin on:

The proportion of children with low birth weight;

The nature and context of the most common diseases and their impact on children;

The proportion of the child population affected by malnutrition, including of a chronic or severe nature, and lack of clean drinking water;

The children provided with adequate nutritious food;

The risks from environmental pollution and the measures adopted to prevent and combat them.

To ensure appropriate prenatal and post-natal health care for mothers, indicating the nature of services provided, including appropriate information given, the coverage ensured, the rate of mortality and its main causes (average

and disaggregated, *inter alia*, by age, gender, region, urban/rural area, social and ethnic origin), the proportion of pregnant women who have access to and benefit from pre- and post-natal health care, trained personnel and hospital care and delivery;

To ensure that all segments of society, in particular parents and children, are informed, have access to education and are supported in the use of basic knowledge of child health and nutrition, the advantages of breast-feeding, hygiene and environmental sanitation and the prevention of accidents; in this regard, information should also be provided on:

Campaigns, programmes, services and strategies and other relevant mechanisms developed to provide basic knowledge, information and support to the general population, in particular to parents and children;

The means used, particularly in relation to the areas of child health and nutrition, the advantages of breast-feeding and the prevention of accidents;

The availability of safe sanitation;

The measures adopted to increase food production to ensure household food security;

The measures adopted to improve the system of education and training of health personnel;

Disaggregated data, including by age, gender, region, rural/urban area, social and ethnic origin.

To develop preventive health care, guidance for parents and family planning education and services; in this regard, reports should also provide information on:

The policies and programmes developed, as well as services available;

The population covered, including in rural and urban areas, by age, gender, social and ethnic origin;

The measures adopted to prevent early pregnancy and to take into consideration the specific situation of adolescents, including provision of appropriate information and counselling;

The role played by the education system in this regard, including in the school curricula;

Disaggregated data on the incidence of children's pregnancy, including by age, region, rural/urban area, and social and ethnic origin.

96. Please indicate the prevalence of HIV/AIDS and the measures adopted to promote health information and education on HIV/AIDS among the general population, special groups at high risk and children, as well as:

The programmes and strategies developed to prevent HIV;

The measures adopted to assess the occurrence of HIV infection and AIDS, among both the general population and children, and its incidence *inter alia* by age, gender, rural/urban area;

The treatment and management provided in case of HIV infection and AIDS among children and parents, and the coverage ensured nationwide, in urban and rural areas;

The measures adopted to ensure an effective protection and assistance to children who are orphans as a result of AIDS;

The campaigns, programmes, strategies and other relevant measures adopted to prevent and combat discriminatory attitudes against children infected by HIV or with AIDS, or whose parents or family members have been infected.

97. Please provide information on the measures adopted pursuant to article 24, paragraph 3, with a view to abolishing all traditional practices prejudicial to the health of children, particularly girls, or otherwise contrary to the principles and provisions of the Convention (for example, genital mutilation and forced marriage). Reports should also indicate any assessment made of traditional practices persisting in society that are prejudicial to children's rights.

98. Information should also be provided on the measures adopted pursuant to article 24, paragraph 4, to promote and encourage international cooperation with a view to achieving progressively the full realization of the right recognized in this article, and the particular consideration given to the needs of developing countries. Reports should *inter alia* indicate the activities and programmes developed in the framework of international cooperation, including at the bilateral and regional levels, the areas addressed, the target groups identified, the financial assistance provided and/or received and the priorities considered, as well as any evaluation made of the progress achieved and of the difficulties encountered. Mention should be made, whenever appropriate, of the involvement of United Nations organs and specialized agencies and non-governmental organizations.

C. Social security and child care services and facilities
(arts. 26 and 18, para. 3)

99. With respect to article 26, please provide information on:

The measures adopted to recognize for every child the right to benefit from social security, including social insurance;

The necessary measures taken to achieve the full realization of this right in accordance with the national law;

The manner in which the benefits granted take into account the resources and the circumstances of the child and of the persons having responsibility for his or her maintenance, as well as any other considerations relevant to an application for benefits made by or on behalf of the child.

100. Reports should also indicate the legal provisions relevant to the implementation of this right, the circumstances under which children themselves are allowed to apply for social security measures, either directly or through a representative, the criteria taken into account to grant the benefits, as well as any relevant disaggregated information concerning the coverage and financial implications of such measures, its incidence by age, gender, number of children per family, civil status of the parents, the situation of single parents, and the relationship of social security to unemployment.

101. Please indicate the measures adopted pursuant to article 18, paragraph 3, and taking into account the provisions of articles 3, 6 and 12 of the Convention, to ensure that children of working parents have the right to benefit from child-care services and facilities for which they are eligible. In this regard, reports should *inter alia* provide information on the legislation adopted to recognize this right and ensure its realization, as well as on the coverage with regard to services and facilities, by region and by urban and rural areas, as well as on their financial implications and on the children benefiting from such measures, including by age, gender and national, social and ethnic origin.

102. Reports should also provide information on the progress achieved in the implementation of these rights, the difficulties encountered and any targets identified for the future.

D. Standard of living (art. 27, paras. 1-3)
103. Please provide information on:

The measures adopted to recognize and ensure the right of every child to a standard of living adequate for the child's physical, mental, spiritual, moral and social development;

The relevant indicators used to assess such an adequate standard of living, and its incidence among the child population, including by gender, age, region, rural/urban area, social and ethnic origin, and family situation;

The criteria established to assess the ability and financial capacity of parents or others responsible for the child to secure the living conditions necessary for the child's development, as well as to identify those conditions;

All the measures taken, in accordance with national conditions and within the State Party's means, to assist parents and others responsible for the child to implement this right, including the nature of the assistance made available, its budget implications, its relation to the cost of living and its impact on the population; where relevant, the information provided should be disaggregated, *inter alia* by region, rural/urban area, age, gender and social and ethnic origin;

The measures adopted to provide, in case of need, material assistance and support programmes, particularly with regard to nutrition, clothing and housing, indicating, *inter alia*, the nature of such assistance and programmes, the population addressed by them, including by gender, age, rural/urban area, social and ethnic origin, the proportion of budget allocated, the coverage ensured, the priorities and targets identified;

Relevant measures adopted as a follow-up to the Declaration and Plan of Action adopted by the United Nations Conference on Human Settlements (Habitat II).

104. Reports should also provide information on the progress achieved in the implementation of these rights, difficulties encountered and targets set for the future.

VII. EDUCATION, LEISURE AND CULTURAL ACTIVITIES
(arts. 28; 29; 31)
SEE PARAGRAPH 8 ABOVE

A. Education, including vocational training and guidance (art. 28)

105. Please indicate the measures adopted, including of a legislative, administrative and budgetary nature, to recognize and ensure the right of the child to education, and to achieve this right progressively and on the basis of equal opportunities.

106. In this regard, reports should indicate, *inter alia*:

The measures adopted to ensure respect for the general principles of the Convention, namely the best interests of the child, respect for the views of the child, the right to life, survival and development to the maximum extent possible, and non-discrimination, including with a view to reducing existing disparities;

The proportion of the overall budget (at the central, regional and local, and where appropriate at the federal and provincial levels) devoted to children and allocated to the various levels of education;

The consideration given to the real cost to the family of the child's education and the appropriate support provided;

The measures adopted to ensure that children may be taught in local, indigenous or minority languages;

Mechanisms developed to ensure the access of all children, including girls, children with special needs and children in especially difficult circumstances, to quality education adapted to the child's age and maturity;

The steps taken to ensure that there are sufficient teachers in the school system, to enhance their competence, and to ensure and assess the quality of teaching;

The measures adopted to provide adequate educational facilities, accessible to all children;

The rate of illiteracy below and over 18 years, and the rate of enrolment in literacy classes, including by age, gender, region, rural/urban area, and social and ethnic origin;

Any systems of non-formal education;

Any system or extensive initiatives by the State to provide early development and education services for young children, especially for young children from disadvantaged social groups;

The changes that have occurred in the education system (including with regard to legislation, policies, facilities, budgetary allocation, quality of education, enrolment, drop-out and literacy);

Any monitoring mechanism developed, factors and difficulties encountered and targets identified for the future;

Other relevant disaggregated data on the children concerned, including on education outcomes, *inter alia* by gender, age, region, rural/urban area, and national, ethnic and social origin.

107. Reports should also indicate the particular measures adopted:

To make primary education compulsory and available free for all, particularly children, indicating the minimum age for enrolment in primary school, the minimum and maximum ages for compulsory education, the proportion of children enrolled who complete primary education, as well as any relevant disaggregated data including by age, gender, region, urban/rural area, national, social and ethnic origin, service coverage and budgetary allocation;

To encourage the development of different forms of secondary education, including general and vocational education, and measures adopted:

To make such forms available and accessible to every child, providing *inter alia* any relevant disaggregated data including by gender, age, region, rural/urban area, national, social and ethnic origin, coverage and budgetary allocation;

To introduce free secondary education and offer financial assistance in case of need, indicating the children concerned, including by gender, age, region, rural/urban area, and national, social and ethnic origin, and the budget allocated for that purpose;

To make higher education accessible to all on the basis of capacity, indicating *inter alia* the rate of access to higher education by age, gender and national, social and ethnic origin;

To make educational and vocational information and guidance available and accessible to all children, indicating, *inter alia*, the forms of such information and guidance, the mechanisms used to assess their effectiveness, the budget allocated for that purpose, as well as any relevant disaggregated data, including by age, gender, region, urban/rural area, and social and ethnic origin;

To encourage regular attendance at school and to reduce drop-out rates, including research, any mechanisms developed to assess the situation, and incentives provided to encourage school entrance, regular school attendance and school retention, any alternatives provided for children who are excluded from school, as well as other relevant data disaggregated by age, gender, region, urban/rural area, and social and ethnic origin.

108. Reports should also provide information on any category or group of children who do not enjoy the right to education and the circumstances in which children may be excluded from school temporarily or permanently (for example disability, deprivation of liberty, pregnancy, HIV/AIDS infection), including any arrangements made to address such situations and to ensure alternative education. Disaggregated data should be provided, including by age, gender, region, rural/urban area, and social and ethnic origin.

109. Please indicate all appropriate measures taken pursuant to article 28, paragraph 2, to ensure that school discipline is administered in a manner consistent with the child's human dignity and in conformity with the Convention, including:

Legislation applying to public and private schools and other education institutions and prohibiting all forms of violence, including corporal punishment, as well as any other disciplinary measures which are not consistent with the child's human dignity or in conformity with the provisions of the Convention, including articles 19, 29 and 37 (a), and its general principles particularly of non-discrimination, best interests and respect for the views of the child;

Any monitoring system of the administration of the school discipline, as well as mechanisms of reporting and complaint;

Any independent mechanism established for that purpose;

Legislation providing the opportunity for the child to participate in administrative or judicial proceedings relating to education and affecting him or her, including those relating to the choice of school, school exclusion.

110. With regard to article 28, paragraph 3, please provide information on the measures adopted to promote and encourage international cooperation in matters relating to education, in particular with a view to:

Contributing to the elimination of ignorance and illiteracy throughout the world;

Facilitating access to scientific and technical knowledge and modern teaching methods;

Taking particular account of the needs of developing countries.

111. Reports should also indicate the activities and programmes developed, including at the bilateral and regional levels, the target groups identified, including by age, gender and national, social and ethnic origin, the financial assistance provided and/or received and the priorities established, and the consideration given to the aims of education as identified by article 29 of the Convention, as well as any evaluation made of the progress achieved and of the difficulties encountered. Mention should be made, whenever appropriate, of the involvement of United Nations organs and specialized agencies and non-governmental organizations.

B. Aims of education (art. 29)

112. Please indicate the legislative, administrative, educational and other measures adopted to ensure that the aims of education established in the State Party are consistent with the provisions of this article, in particular with regard to:

The development of respect for the child's personality, talents and mental and physical abilities to their fullest potential;

The development of respect for human rights and fundamental freedoms, and for the principles enshrined in the Charter of the United Nations, indicating whether the subject of human rights in general, and children's rights in particular, has been incorporated in the school curricula for all children and promoted in school life;

The development of respect for the child's parents, his or her own cultural identity, language and values, for the national values of the country in which the child is living, the country from which he or she originates and for civilizations different from his or her own;

The preparation of the child for responsible life in a free society, in the spirit of understanding, peace, tolerance, equality of the sexes, and friendship among all peoples, ethnic, national and religious groups and persons of indigenous origin;

The development of respect for the natural environment.

113. Reports should also indicate:

The training provided to teachers to prepare them to direct their teaching towards these aims;

The revision of school policies and school curricula to reflect the aims identified in article 29 at the various levels of education;

Relevant programmes and material used;

Any peer education and peer counselling promoted;

Efforts made to bring school organization in line with the Convention's principles, for example mechanisms created within schools to improve the participation of children in all decisions affecting their education and well-being.

114. Please indicate the measures adopted pursuant to article 29, paragraph 2, to ensure respect for the liberty of individuals and bodies to establish and direct educational institutions, subject always to the observance of the principles set forth in paragraph 1 of this article and to the requirements that the education given in such institutions conforms to such minimum standards as are laid down by the State.

115. Reports should also provide information on the appropriate mechanisms developed to:

Ascertain that the aims of education identified by the Convention are respected by such institutions;

Ensure respect for the general principles of the Convention, namely non-discrimination, the best interests of the child, respect for the views of the child and the right to life, survival and development to the maximum extent;

Ensure that all such institutions are conducted in conformity with standards established by competent authorities, particularly in the areas of safety, health, number and suitability of staff, as well as of competent supervision.

116. Reports should further provide information on the progress achieved in the implementation of this article, difficulties encountered and targets set for the future.

C. Leisure, recreation and cultural activities (art. 31)

117. Please provide information on the measures adopted, including of a legislative nature, to recognize and ensure the right of the child to:

Rest and leisure;

Engage in play and recreational activities appropriate to the age of the child;

Participate freely in cultural life and the arts.

118. In this regard, reports should also indicate:

The proportion of the relevant overall budget allocated (at the central, regional, local and where relevant at the federal and provincial levels) for children;

The cultural, artistic, recreational and leisure activities, programmes or campaigns developed and provided at the national, regional or local, and where appropriate at the federal and provincial levels, to ensure the enjoyment of this right including in the family, in the school and in the community;

The enjoyment of the rights recognized by article 31 in relation to other rights recognized by the Convention, including the right to education;

The respect ensured to the general principles of the Convention, namely non-discrimination, the best interests of the child, respect for the views of the child and the right to life, survival and development to the maximum extent;

Relevant data on the children concerned, including by age, gender, region, rural/urban area, and national, social and ethnic origin;

Progress achieved in the implementation of article 31, difficulties encountered and targets set for the future.

VIII. SPECIAL PROTECTION MEASURES (arts. 22; 38; 39; 40; 37 (b)-(d); 32-36)

SEE PARAGRAPH 8 ABOVE

A. Children in situations of emergency
1. Refugee children (art. 22)

119. Please provide information on the appropriate measures adopted pursuant to article 22, paragraph 1 to ensure that a child who is seeking refugee status or who is considered a refugee in accordance with applicable international or domestic law and procedures, whether unaccompanied or accompanied by his or her parents or by any other person, receives appropriate protection and humanitarian assistance in the enjoyment of applicable rights set forth in the Convention and in other international human rights or humanitarian instruments to which the State is a Party.

120. Reports should also indicate:

The international and domestic law and procedures applicable to the child who is considered a refugee or is seeking asylum;

Relevant international human rights and humanitarian instruments to which the State is a Party, at the multilateral, regional and bilateral levels;

The domestic legislation and procedures in place, including to determine refugee status and ensure and protect the rights of asylum seeking and refugee children, as well as any safeguards established and remedies made available to the child;

The protection and humanitarian assistance provided to the child in the enjoyment of his or her rights set forth in the Convention, as well as in other relevant international instruments, including civil rights and freedoms and economic, social and cultural rights;

The measures adopted to ensure and protect the rights of the unaccompanied child or of the child accompanied by his or her parents or by any other person, including in relation to temporary and long-term solutions, family tracing and family reunion;

The measures adopted to ensure respect for the general principles of the Convention, namely non-discrimination, the best interests of the child, respect for the views of the child, the right to life, and survival and development to the maximum extent possible;

The measures adopted to ensure appropriate dissemination of information and training on

the rights of the child who is a refugee or is seeking asylum, particularly to the officials competent in the areas addressed by this article;

The number of asylum seeking and refugee children disaggregated *inter alia* by age, gender, country of origin, nationality, accompanied or unaccompanied;

The number of such children going to school and covered by health services;

The number of staff handling refugee children who attended training courses to understand the Convention on the Rights of the Child during the reporting period, classified by type of job.

121. Please also indicate the measures adopted pursuant to article 22, paragraph 2 to provide cooperation in any efforts by the United Nations and other competent intergovernmental organizations or non-governmental organizations cooperating with the United Nations to: Protect and assist the child;

Trace the parents or other members of the family of any refugee child in order to obtain information necessary for reunification with his or her family.

In cases where no parents or other members of the family can be found, please indicate the measures adopted to ensure that the child is accorded the same protection as any other child permanently or temporarily deprived of his or her family environment for any reason, as set forth in the Convention.

122. Pursuant to this article, please also indicate any evaluation mechanism established to monitor the progress achieved in the implementation of the measures adopted, any difficulties encountered, as well as any priorities set for the future.

2. Children in armed conflicts (art. 38), including physical and psychological recovery and social reintegration (art. 39)

123. Please provide information on the measures adopted pursuant to article 38, including of a legislative, administrative and educational nature, to respect and ensure respect for the rules of international humanitarian law applicable to the State in armed conflicts which are relevant to the child. In this regard, reports should identify the relevant international conventions, instruments and other rules of humanitarian law applicable to the State and the measures adopted to enforce them, as well as to ensure their effective dissemination and appropriate training for professionals concerned.

124. Please indicate all the measures taken pursuant to article 38, paragraph 2, including of a legislative, administrative or other nature, to ensure that persons who have not attained the age of 15 years do not take a direct part in hostilities. In this regard, reports should also indicate the measures adopted to ensure and protect the rights of the child during hostilities. Information should also be provided on any mechanism established to monitor this situation. When relevant, indication should also be given of the proportion of children participating in hostilities, including by age, gender and social and ethnic origin.

125. Please indicate the measures adopted pursuant to article 38, paragraph 3, including of a legislative and administrative nature, to ensure that no person who has not attained the age of 15 years is recruited into the armed forces, as well as to ensure that, in recruiting among those persons who have attained the age of 15 years but who have not attained the age of 18 years, priority is given to those who are oldest. In this regard, reports should also indicate any mechanisms established to monitor this situation, as well as the proportion of children being recruited or voluntarily enlisted into armed forces, including by age, gender, and social and ethnic origin.

126. Please provide information on all the measures adopted pursuant to article 38, paragraph 4, and in accordance with the State's obligations under international humanitarian law to protect the civilian population in armed conflicts, including measures of a legislative, administrative, budgetary and other nature, to ensure the protection and care of children who are affected by an armed conflict.

127. In this regard, please indicate the relevant international humanitarian law applicable to the State, the criteria used to assess the feasibility of the measures adopted, the steps taken to identify and address the specific situation of children within the civilian population and to ensure respect for and protection of their rights, the measures adopted to ensure that humanitarian assistance and relief programmes are promoted and put in place, including through the negotiation of special arrangements such as corridors of peace and days of tranquillity, as well as any relevant disaggregated data on the children concerned, including by age, gender, and national, social and ethnic origin. Where relevant, please also indicate the number of child casualties due to armed conflict, as well as the number of children displaced because of armed conflict.

128. When providing information on the implementation of the provisions of article 38, please further indicate the respect ensure to the general principles of the Convention, namely non-discrimination, the best interests of the child, respect for the views of the child and the right to life, development and survival to the maximum extent.

129. Please indicate all measures adopted pursuant to article 39 to:

Promote physical and psychological recovery and social reintegration of child victims of armed conflicts;

Ensure that such recovery and reintegration takes place in an environment which fosters the health, self-respect and dignity of the child.

130. In this regard, reports should provide information *inter alia* on:

The policies and programmes developed, including at the family and community levels, to address the physical and psychological effects of conflicts on children and to promote their reintegration in society;

The steps taken to ensure the demobilization of child soldiers and to prepare them to participate actively and responsibly in society;

The role played by education and vocational training;

The surveys and research undertaken;

The budget allocated for them (at the national, regional, local and where appropriate at the federal and provincial levels);

The number of children who received physical and/or psychological treatment as a consequence of armed conflict.

131. Information should also be provided on the progress achieved on the implementation of articles 38 and 39, on any difficulties encountered and targets set for the future.

B. Children involved with the system of administration of juvenile justice

1. The administration of juvenile justice (art. 40)

132. Please provide information on the legislative and other measures taken to recognize and ensure the right of every child involved with the system of the administration of juvenile justice (alleged as, accused of, or recognized as having infringed the penal law) to be treated in a manner:

Consistent with the promotion of the child's sense of dignity and worth;

Which reinforces the child's respect for the human rights and fundamental freedoms of others;

Which takes into account the child's age and the desirability of promoting the child's reintegration and the child's assuming a constructive role in society;

Which ensures respect for the general principles of the Convention, namely non-discrimination, the best interests of the child, respect for the views of the child and the right to life, survival and development to the maximum extent.

133. With respect to article 40, paragraph 2, please indicate the relevant international instruments applicable in the area of the administration of juvenile justice, including at the multilateral, regional or bilateral levels, as well as legislative and other appropriate measures adopted to ensure in particular that:

No child shall be alleged as, accused of or recognized as having infringed the penal law by reason of acts or omissions that were not prohibited by national or international law at the time they were committed;

Every child alleged as or accused of having infringed the penal law has at least the following guarantees, indicating, where relevant, additional guarantees provided to the child:

To be presumed innocent until proven guilty according to law;

To be informed promptly (indicating any time-limit fixed by law) and directly of the charges against him or her and, if appropriate, through his or her legal guardians, and to have legal or other appropriate assistance in the preparation and presentation of his or her defence; in this regard, please indicate what other appropriate assistance may be made available to the child;

To have the matter determined without delay (indicating any time-limit fixed by law) by a competent, independent and impartial authority or judicial body in a fair hearing according

to law, in the presence of legal or other appropriate assistance (indicating what other appropriate assistance may be made available to the child) and, unless it is considered not to be in the best interests of the child, in particular taking into account his or her age or situation, in the presence of his or her parents or legal guardians;

Not to be compelled to give testimony or to confess guilt; to examine or have examined adverse witnesses and to obtain the participation and examination of witnesses on his or her behalf under conditions of equality;

If considered to have infringed the penal law, to have this decision and any measures imposed in consequence thereof reviewed by a higher competent, independent and impartial authority or judicial body according to law;

To have the free assistance of an interpreter if the child cannot understand or speak the language used;

To have his or her privacy respected at all stages of the proceedings.

134. Please indicate the measures adopted pursuant to article 40, paragraph 3 to promote the establishment of laws, procedures, authorities and institutions specially applicable to children alleged as, accused of, or recognized as having infringed the penal law, providing information *inter alia* on the areas addressed by legislation and procedures, as well as the functions, number and distribution throughout the country. Reports should in particular indicate the measures adopted to ensure a child-oriented system, including:

The establishment of a minimum age below which children shall be presumed not to have the capacity to infringe the penal law;

Measures taken for dealing with such children without resorting to judicial proceedings, and to ensure that in such cases human rights and legal safeguards are fully respected, indicating the situations in which such a system applies and relevant procedures established for that purpose.

135. Please indicate the variety of dispositions made available pursuant to article 40, paragraph 4, including care, guidance and supervision orders, counselling, probation, foster care, education and vocational training programmes and other alternatives to institutional care, to ensure that children are dealt with in a manner appropriate to their well-being and proportionate both to their circumstances and the offence.

136. Reports should further indicate the training activities developed for all professionals involved with the system of juvenile justice, including judges, prosecutors, lawyers, law enforcement officials, immigration officers and social workers, on the provisions of the Convention and other relevant international instruments in the field of juvenile justice, including the Beijing Rules, the Riyadh Guidelines and the United Nations Rules for the Protection of Juveniles Deprived of their Liberty.

137. Relevant information should also be provided on the progress achieved in the implementation of article 40, any difficulties encountered and targets set for the future, as well as disaggregated data on the children concerned,

inter alia by age, gender, region, rural/urban area, national, social and ethnic origin, offence and disposition made available.

2. Children deprived of their liberty, including any form of detention, imprisonment or placement in custodial settings (art. 37 (b)-(d))

138. Please indicate the legislative and other measures adopted pursuant to article 37 (b) to ensure that:

No child is deprived of his or her liberty unlawfully or arbitrarily; /According to the United Nations Rules for the Protection of Juveniles Deprived of their Liberty, deprivation of liberty means any form of detention or imprisonment or the placement of a person in another public or private custodial setting from which this person is not permitted to leave at will by order of any judicial, administrative or other public authority (rule 11 (b))./

The arrest, detention or imprisonment of a child is in conformity with the law and is used only as a measure of last resort and for the shortest appropriate period of time;

The general principles of the Convention are respected, namely non-discrimination, the best interests of the child, respect for the views of the child, the right to life, and survival and development to the maximum extent possible.

139. Reports should also indicate the existing alternatives to deprivation of liberty, the frequency with which they are used and the children concerned, including by age, gender, region, rural/urban area, and social and ethnic origin.

140. Information should also be given on the measures and mechanisms established to:

Prevent the deprivation of liberty of children, including through arrest, detention and imprisonment, *inter alia* in relation to asylum seekers and refugees;

Prevent the imposition of indeterminate sentences, including through their legal prohibition;

Monitor the situation of the children concerned, including through an independent mechanism;

Monitor progress, identify difficulties and set goals for the future.

141. In this regard, information should further be provided on the number of children deprived of liberty, unlawfully, arbitrarily and within the law, as well as on the period of deprivation of liberty, including data disaggregated by gender, age, region, rural/urban area, and national, social and ethnic origin, and the reasons for such deprivation of liberty.

142. Please indicate the legislative and other measures adopted pursuant to article 37 (c) to ensure that any child deprived of liberty is treated:

With humanity and respect for the inherent humanity of the human person;

In a manner which takes into account the needs of persons of his or her age.

143. Reports should also provide information on the measures adopted and arrangements made to ensure that:

The child deprived of liberty is separated from adults unless it is considered in the best interests of the child not to do so;

The child has the right to maintain contact with his or her family through correspondence and visits (indicating the number of such contacts), save in exceptional circumstances, those circumstances being specified in the report;

The conditions in institutions in which children are placed are supervised and monitored, including by an independent mechanism;

Complaint procedures are made available to the child;

A periodic review is made of the situation of the child and of the circumstances relevant to his/her placement;

Education and health services are provided to the child;

The general principles of the Convention are respected, namely non-discrimination, the best interests of the child, respect for the views of the child, the right to life, and survival and development to the maximum extent possible.

144. Please indicate the measures adopted pursuant to article 37 (d) to ensure that every child deprived of liberty has the right to:

Prompt access to legal and other appropriate assistance, indicating *inter alia* whether there is any legal time-limit for such access to assistance and what other appropriate assistance may be made available to the child;

Challenge the legality of the deprivation of his or her liberty before a court or other competent, independent and impartial authority;

A prompt decision on any such action, indicating *inter alia* whether there is any legal time-limit for such a decision to be taken.

145. Information should also be provided on the overall situation, as well as on the percentage of cases where legal or other assistance has been provided, and where the legality of the deprivation of liberty has been confirmed, including disaggregated data on the children concerned, including by age, gender, region, rural/urban area, and social and ethnic origin.

146. Reports should also indicate the progress achieved in the implementation of article 37 (b) to (d), difficulties encountered and targets set for the future.

3. The sentencing of children, with particular reference to the prohibition of capital punishment and life imprisonment (art. 37 (a))

147. Please provide information on the measures adopted, at the legislative and other levels, to ensure that neither capital punishment nor life imprisonment without possibility of release is imposed for offences committed by persons below 18 years of age.

148. Please also indicate the progress achieved in the implementation of article 37 (a), difficulties encountered and targets set for the future.

4. Physical and psychological recovery and social reintegration of the child (art. 39)

149. Please provide information on all measures taken pursuant to article 39 and in the light of article 40, paragraph 1, to promote the physical and psychological recovery and social reintegration of the child involved with the system of the administration of juvenile justice, and to ensure that such recovery and reintegration take place in an environment which fosters the health, self-respect and dignity of the child.

150. Reports should also identify, *inter alia*, the mechanisms established and the programmes and activities developed for that purpose, as well as the education and vocational training provided, and indicate relevant disaggregated data on the children concerned, including by age, gender, region, rural/urban area, and social and ethnic origin. They should further indicate the progress achieved in the implementation of article 39, difficulties encountered and targets set for the future.

C. Children in situations of exploitation, including physical and psychological recovery and social reintegration

1. Economic exploitation of children, including child labour (art. 32)

151. Please provide information on the measures taken, including of a legislative, administrative, social and educational nature, to recognize and ensure the right of the child to be protected from:

Economic exploitation;

Performing any work that is likely to be hazardous or to interfere with the child's education, or to be harmful to the child's health or physical, mental, spiritual, moral or social development.

152. In this regard, reports should in particular indicate:

Whether legislation has included a prohibition, as well as a definition, of hazardous and harmful work, and/or of the activities considered to be hazardous, harmful to the child's health or development or to interfere with the child's education;

Any preventive and remedial action undertaken, including information and awareness campaigns, as well as education, in particular compulsory education, and vocational training programmes, to address the situation of child labour both in the formal and informal sector, including as domestic servants, in agriculture or within private family activities;

The measures adopted to ensure respect for the general principles of the Convention, particularly non-discrimination, the best interests of the child, the right to life, and survival and development to the maximum extent possible.

153. Please also indicate the appropriate measures adopted pursuant to article 32, paragraph 2, and having regard to the relevant provisions of other international instruments, including measures at the legislative and administrative levels, to provide in particular for:

A minimum age or minimum ages for admission to employment;

Appropriate regulation of the hours and conditions of employment;

Appropriate penalties or other sanctions to ensure the effective enforcement of this article, and any mechanism of inspection and system of complaint procedures available to the child, either directly or through a representative.

154. In this regard, reports should also provide information on the international conventions and other relevant instruments to which the State may be a Party, including in the framework of the International Labour Organization, as well as on:

Any national policy and multidisciplinary strategy developed to prevent and combat situations of children's economic exploitation and labour;

Any coordinating and monitoring mechanism established for that purpose;

The relevant indicators identified and used;

Relevant programmes of technical cooperation and international assistance developed;

The progress achieved in the implementation of this article, benchmarks set up as well as difficulties encountered;

Relevant disaggregated data on the children concerned, including by age, gender, region, rural/urban area, and social and ethnic origin, as well as on infringements observed by inspectors and sanctions applied.

2. Drug abuse (art. 33)

155. Please indicate all appropriate measures adopted, including legislative, administrative, social and educational measures, to:

Protect children from the illicit use of narcotic drugs and psychotropic substances, as defined in relevant international treaties;

Prevent the use of children in the illicit production and trafficking of such substances.

156. Reports should also indicate:

The relevant international conventions, including at the regional and bilateral levels, to which the State is a party;

Any arrangements made and structures developed to raise awareness in the general population and amongst children, including through the school system and whenever appropriate by the consideration of this topic by the school curricula;

Any measures undertaken to assist children and their families, including through counselling, advice and helpliness, where appropriate of a confidential nature, and policies and strategies designed to ensure the physical and psychological recovery and social reintegration of children concerned;

Any measures designed to monitor the incidence of drug abuse on children, as well as their involvement in the illicit production and trafficking of narcotic and psychotropic substances, progress achieved, difficulties encountered and targets set for the future;

Any relevant disaggregated data, including by age, gender, region, rural/urban area, and social and ethnic origin.

157. In addition, please also provide information on legislative and other measures taken to prevent the use by children of alcohol, tobacco and other substances which may be prejudicial to their health and which may be available with or without restrictions to adults, and on any evaluation made of the effectiveness of such measures, together with relevant disaggregated data on the use by children of such substances.

3. Sexual exploitation and sexual abuse (art. 34)

158. Please indicate the measures adopted, including of a legislative, educational and social nature, to protect the child from all

forms of sexual exploitation and sexual abuse. Reports should in particular provide information on all national, bilateral and multilateral measures taken to prevent:

(a) the inducement or coercion of a child to engage in any unlawful sexual activity;

(b) the exploitative use of children in prostitution or other unlawful sexual practices;

(c) the exploitative use of children in pornographic performances and materials.

159. Reports should also indicate, *inter alia*:

Information, awareness and education campaigns to prevent any form of sexual exploitation or abuse of the child, including campaigns undertaken in cooperation with the media;

Any national and multidisciplinary strategy developed to ensure protection of children below the age of 18 against all forms of sexual exploitation and abuse, including within the family;

Any coordinating and monitoring mechanism established for that purpose;

The relevant indicators identified and used;

Legislation developed to ensure effective protection of child victims, including through access to legal and other appropriate assistance and support services;

Whether sexual exploitation and abuse of children, child prostitution and child pornography, including the possession of child pornography, and the use of children in other unlawful sexual practices are considered criminal offences;

Whether the principle of extraterritoriality has been incorporated in the legislation to criminalize the sexual exploitation of children by nationals and residents of the State Party when committed in other countries;

Whether special units of law enforcement officials and police liaison officers have been appointed to deal with children who have been sexually exploited or abused, and whether appropriate training has been provided to them;

Relevant bilateral, regional and multilateral agreements concluded or to which the State Party may have acceded to foster the prevention of all forms of sexual abuse and exploitation and to ensure the effective protection of child victims, including in the areas of judicial cooperation and cooperation among law enforcement officials;

Relevant programmes of technical cooperation and international assistance developed with United Nations bodies and other international organizations, as well as with other competent bodies, including INTERPOL, and non-governmental organizations;

Relevant activities and programmes developed, including of a multidisciplinary nature, to ensure the recovery and reintegration of the child victim of sexual exploitation or abuse, in the light of article 39 of the Convention;

The measures adopted to ensure respect for the general principles of the Convention, namely non-discrimination, the best interests of the child, respect for the views of the child, the right to life, and survival and development to the maximum extent possible;

Relevant disaggregated data on the children concerned by the implementation of article 34,

including by age, gender, region, rural/urban area, and national, social and ethnic origin. Such data should include the number of cases in which a child was used in drug trafficking during the reporting period; the minimum penalty in the law for using children in drug trafficking; and the number of cases of commercial sexual exploitation, sexual abuse, sale of children, abduction of children and violence against children reported during this period;

The progress achieved in the implementation of article 34, difficulties encountered and targets set.

4. Sale, trafficking and abduction (art. 35)

160. Please provide information on all measures adopted, including of a legislative, administrative, educational and budgetary nature, at the national, bilateral and multilateral levels, to prevent the abduction of, the sale of or traffic in children for any purpose or in any form.

161. In this regard, reports should indicate *inter alia*:

The legislation adopted to ensure effective protection of children against abduction, sale and trafficking, including through the consideration of these acts as criminal offences;

Awareness and information campaigns to prevent their occurrence, including campaigns undertaken in cooperation with the media;

The allocation of appropriate resources for the development and implementation of relevant policies and programmes;

Any national strategy developed to prevent and suppress such acts;

Any coordinating and monitoring mechanism established for that purpose;

The relevant indicators identified and used;

Whether special units have been created among law enforcement officials to deal with these acts;

Relevant training activities provided to the competent authorities;

Structures and programmes developed to provide support services to the children concerned and to promote their physical and psychological recovery and social reintegration, in the light of article 39;

The measures adopted to ensure that in the implementation of article 35 due consideration is taken of other provisions of the Convention, including in the areas of civil rights, particularly in relation to the preservation of the identity of the child, adoption and prevention of any form of exploitation of children, including child labour and sexual exploitation;

The measures adopted to ensure respect for the general principles of the Convention, including non-discrimination, the best interests of the child, respect for the views of the child, the right to life, and survival and development to the maximum extent possible.

162. Reports should also indicate the relevant bilateral and multilateral agreements concluded by the State Party, or to which it may have acceded, to prevent the sale and abduction of and trafficking in children, including in the areas of international cooperation between judicial authorities and law enforcement officials, *inter alia* on any existing system of collection and exchange of information on perpe-

trators of such acts as well as on the child victims. Relevant disaggregated information should also be provided on the children concerned by the implementation of article 35, including by age, gender, region, rural/urban area, and social and ethnic origin, as well as on the progress achieved in the implementation of this article, the difficulties encountered and the targets set for the future.

5. Other forms of exploitation (art. 36)

163. Please provide information on all measures adopted, including of a legislative, administrative, educational, budgetary and social nature, to protect the child against all forms of exploitation prejudicial to any aspects of his or her welfare.

164. Reports should also indicate, *inter alia*:

The prevalence of any form of exploitation prejudicial to the child's welfare;

Awareness and information campaigns launched, including for children, families and the public at large, as well as the involvement of the media;

Training activities developed for professional groups working with and for children;

Any national strategy developed to ensure protection to the child and the targets set for the future;

Any mechanism established to monitor the situation of the child, the progress achieved in the implementation of this article and any difficulties encountered;

The relevant indicators used;

Measures adopted to ensure the physical and psychological recovery, as well as the social reintegration, of the child victim of exploitation prejudicial to any aspects of his or her welfare;

Relevant measures adopted to ensure respect for the general principles of the Convention, namely non-discrimination, the best interests of the child, respect for the views of the child, the right to life and survival and development to the maximum extent possible;

The measures adopted to ensure that the implementation of this article takes into due consideration other relevant provisions of the Convention;

Relevant disaggregated data on the children concerned by the implementation of this article, including by age, gender, region, rural/urban area, and national, social and ethnic origin.

D. Children belonging to a minority or an indigenous group (art. 30)

165. Please provide information on the measures adopted, including at the legislative, administrative, educational, budgetary and social levels, to ensure that a child belonging to an ethnic, religious or linguistic minority or who is indigenous is not denied the right, in community with other members of his or her group:

To enjoy his or her culture;

To profess and practise his or her own religion;

To use his or her own language.

166. In this regard, reports should also indicate *inter alia*:

The ethnic, religious or linguistic minorities or indigenous groups existing within the State Party's jurisdiction;

The measures adopted to ensure the preservation of the identity of the minority or indigenous group to which the child belongs;

The measures adopted to recognize and ensure the enjoyment of the rights set forth in the Convention by children belonging to a minority or who are indigenous;

The measures adopted to prevent any form of discrimination and combat prejudice against those children, as well as those designed to ensure that they benefit from equal opportunities, including in relation to health care and education;

The measures adopted to ensure respect for the general principles of the Convention, namely the best interests of the child, respect for the views of the child, the right to life, and survival and development to the maximum extent possible, as well as non-discrimination;

The measures adopted to ensure that in the implementation of the rights recognized in article 30 due consideration is taken of other provisions of the Convention, including in the areas of civil rights, particularly in relation to the preservation of the child's identity, family environment and alternative care (for example art. 20, para. 3 and art. 21), education and the administration of juvenile justice;

Relevant disaggregated data on the children concerned, including by age, gender, language, religion, and social and ethnic origin;

The progress achieved and the difficulties encountered in the implementation of this article, as well as any targets set for the future.

Universal Declaration of Human Rights

Adopted and proclaimed by General Assembly resolution 217 A (III) of 10 December 1948

Preamble

Whereas recognition of the inherent dignity and of the equal and inalienable rights of all members of the human family is the foundation of freedom, justice and peace in the world,

Whereas disregard and contempt for human rights have resulted in barbarous acts which have outraged the conscience of mankind, and the advent of a world in which human beings shall enjoy freedom of speech and belief and freedom from fear and want has been proclaimed as the highest aspiration of the common people,

Whereas it is essential, if man is not to be compelled to have recourse, as a last resort, to rebellion against tyranny and oppression, that human rights should be protected by the rule of law,

Whereas it is essential to promote the development of friendly relations between nations,

Whereas the peoples of the United Nations have in the Charter reaffirmed their faith in fundamental human rights, in the dignity and worth of the human person and in the equal rights of men and women and have determined to promote social progress and better standards of life in larger freedom,

Whereas Member States have pledged themselves to achieve, in cooperation with the United Nations, the promotion of universal respect for and observance of human rights and fundamental freedoms,

Whereas a common understanding of these rights and freedoms is of the greatest importance for the full realization of this pledge,

Now, therefore,

The General Assembly,

Proclaims this Universal Declaration of Human Rights as a common standard of achievement for all peoples and ali nations, to the end that every individual and every organ of society, keeping this Declaration constantly in mind, shall strive by teaching and education to promote respect for these rights and freedoms and by progressive measures, national and international, to secure their universal and effective recognition and observance, both among the peoples of Member States themselves and among the peoples of territories under their jurisdiction.

● Article 1

All human beings are born free and equal in dignity and rights. They are endowed with reason and conscience and should act towards one another in a spirit of brotherhood.

● Article 2

Everyone is entitled to all the rights and freedoms set forth in this Declaration, without distinction of any kind, such as race, colour, sex, language, religion, political or other opinion, national or social origin, property, birth or other status.

Furthermore, no distinction shall be made on the basis of the political, jurisdictional or international status of the country or territory to which a person belongs, whether it be independent, trust, non-self-governing or under any other limitation of sovereignty.

● Article 3

Everyone has the right to life, liberty and security of person.

● Article 4

No one shall be held in slavery or servitude; slavery and the slave trade shall be prohibited in all their forms.

● Article 5

No one shall be subjected to torture or to cruel, inhuman or degrading treatment or punishment.

● Article 6

Everyone has the right to recognition everywhere as a person before the law.

Article 7

All are equal before the law and are entitled without any discrimination to equal protection of the law. All are entitled to equal protection against any discrimination in violation of this Declaration and against any incitement to such discrimination.

Article 8

Everyone has the right to an effective remedy by the competent national tribunals for acts violating the fundamental rights granted him by the constitution or by law.

Article 9

No one shall be subjected to arbitrary arrest, detention or exile.

Article 10

Everyone is entitled in full equality to a fair and public hearing by an independent and impartial tribunal, in the determination of his rights and obligations and of any criminal charge against him.

Article 11

Everyone charged with a penal offence has the right to be presumed innocent until proved guilty according to law in a public trial at which he has had all the guarantees necessary for his defence.

No one shall be held guilty of any penal offence on account of any act or omission which did not constitute a penal offence, under national or international law, at the time when it was committed. Nor shall a heavier penalty be imposed than the one that was applicable at the time the penal offence was committed.

Article 12

No one shall be subjected to arbitrary interference with his privacy, family, home or correspondence, nor to attacks upon his honour and reputation. Everyone has the right to the protection of the law against such interference or attacks.

Article 13

Everyone has the right to freedom of movement and residence within the borders of each State. Everyone has the right to leave any country, including his own, and to return to his country.

Article 14

Everyone has the right to seek and to enjoy in other countries asylum from persecution.

This right may not be invoked in the case of prosecutions genuinely arising from non-political crimes or from acts contrary to the purposes and principles of the United Nations.

Article 15

Everyone has the right to a nationality.

No one shall be arbitrarily deprived of his nationality nor denied the right to change his nationality.

Article 16

Men and women of full age, without any limitation due to race, nationality or religion, have the right to marry and to found a family. They are entitled to equal rights as to marriage, during marriage and at its dissolution.

Marriage shall be entered into only with the free and full consent of the intending spouses.

The family is the natural and fundamental group unit of society and is entitled to protection by society and the State.

Article 17

Everyone has the right to own property alone as well as in association with others.

No one shall be arbitrarily deprived of his property.

Article 18

Everyone has the right to freedom of thought, conscience and religion; this right includes freedom to change his religion or belief, and freedom, either alone or in community with others and in public or private, to manifest his religion or belief in teaching, practice, worship and observance

Article 19

Everyone has the right to freedom of opinion and expression; this right includes freedom to hold opinions without interference and to seek, receive and impart information and ideas through any media and regardless of frontiers.

Article 20

Everyone has the right to freedom of peaceful assembly and association.

No one may be compelled to belong to an association.

Article 21

Everyone has the right to take part in the government of his country, directly or through freely chosen representatives.

Everyone has the right to equal access to public service in his country.

The will of the people shall be the basis of the authority of government; this will shall be expressed in periodic and genuine elections which shall be by universal and equal suffrage and shall be held by secret vote or by equivalent free voting procedures.

Article 22

Everyone, as a member of society, has the right to social security and is entitled to realization, through national effort and international co-operation and in accordance with the organization and resources of each State, of the economic, social and cultural rights indispensable for his dignity and the free development of his personality.

Article 23

Everyone has the right to work, to free choice of employment, to just and favourable conditions of work and to protection against unemployment.

Everyone, without any discrimination, has the right to equal pay for equal work.

Everyone who works has the right to just and favourable remuneration ensuring for himself and his family an existence worthy of human dignity, and supplemented, if necessary, by other means of social protection.

Everyone has the right to form and to join trade unions for the protection of his interests.

Article 24

Everyone has the right to rest and leisure, including reasonable limitation of working hours and periodic holidays with pay.

Article 25

Everyone has the right to a standard of living adequate for the health and well-being of himself and of his family, including food, clothing, housing and medical care and necessary social services, and the right to security in the event of unemployment, sickness, disability, widowhood, old age or other lack of livelihood in circumstances beyond his control.

Motherhood and childhood are entitled to special care and assistance. All children, whether born in or out of wedlock, shall enjoy the same social protection.

Article 26

Everyone has the right to education. Education shall be free, at least in the elementary and fundamental stages. Elementary education shall be compulsory. Technical and professional education shall be made generally available and higher education shall be equally accessible to all on the basis of merit.

Education shall be directed to the full development of the human personality and to the strengthening of respect for human rights and fundamental freedoms. It shall promote understanding, tolerance and friendship among all nations, racial or religious groups, and shall further the activities of the United Nations for the maintenance of peace.

Parents have a prior right to choose the kind of education that shall be given to their children.

Article 27

Everyone has the right freely to participate in the cultural life of the community, to enjoy the arts and to share in scientific advancement and its benefits.

Everyone has the right to the protection of the moral and material interests resulting from any scientific, literary or artistic production of which he is the author.

Article 28

Everyone is entitled to a social and international order in which the rights and freedoms set forth in this Declaration can be fully realized.

Article 29

Everyone has duties to the community in which alone the free and full development of his personality is possible.

In the exercise of his rights and freedoms, everyone shall be subject only to such limitations as are determined by law solely for the purpose of securing due recognition and respect for the rights and freedoms of others and of meeting the just requirements of morality, public order and the general welfare in a democratic society.

These rights and freedoms may in no case be exercised contrary to the purposes and principles of the United Nations.

Article 30

Nothing in this Declaration may be interpreted as implying for any State, group or person any right to engage in any activity or to perform any act aimed at the destruction of any of the rights and freedoms set forth herein.

Declaration of the Rights of the Child

Proclaimed by
General Assembly resolution 1386(XIV)
of 20 November 1959

Preamble

Whereas the peoples of the United Nations have, in the Charter, reaffirmed their faith in fundamental human rights and in the dignity and worth of the human person, and have determined to promote social progress and better standards of life in larger freedom,

Whereas the United Nations has, in the Universal Declaration of Human Rights, proclaimed that everyone is entitled to all the rights and freedoms set forth therein, without distinction of any kind, such as race, colour, sex, language, religion, political or other opinion, national or social origin, property, birth or other status,

Whereas the child, by reason of his physical and mental immaturity, needs special safeguards and care, including appropriate legal protection, before as well as after birth,

Whereas the need for such special safeguards has been stated in the Geneva Declaration of the Rights of the Child of 1924, and recognized in the Universal Declaration of Human Rights and in the statutes of specialized agencies and international organizations concerned with the welfare of children,

Whereas mankind owes to the child the best it has to give,

Now therefore,

The General Assembly

Proclaims this Declaration of the Rights of the Child to the end that he may have a happy childhood and enjoy for his own good and for the good of society the rights and freedoms herein set forth, and calls upon parents, upon men and women as individuals, and upon voluntary organizations, local authorities and national Governments to recognize these rights and strive for their observance by legislative and other measures progressively taken in accordance with the following principles:

● Principle 1

The child shall enjoy all the rights set forth in this Declaration. Every child, without any exception whatsoever, shall be entitled to these rights, without distinction or discrimination on account of race, colour, sex, language, religion, political or other opinion, national or social origin, property, birth or other status, whether of himself or of his family.

● Principle 2

The child shall enjoy special protection, and shall be given opportunities and facilities, by law and by other means, to enable him to develop physically, mentally, morally, spiritually and socially in a healthy and normal manner and in conditions of freedom and dignity. In the enactment of laws for this purpose, the best interests of the child shall be the paramount consideration.

● Principle 3

The child shall be entitled from his birth to a name and a nationality.

● Principle 4

The child shall enjoy the benefits of social security. He shall be entitled to grow and develop in health; to this end, special care and protection shall be provided both to him and to his mother, including adequate pre-natal and post-natal care. The child shall have the right to adequate nutrition, housing, recreation and medical services.

● Principle 5

The child who is physically, mentally or socially handicapped shall be given the special treatment, education and care required by his particular condition.

● Principle 6

The child, for the full and harmonious development of his personality, needs love and understanding. He shall, wherever possible, grow up in the care and under the responsibility of his parents, and, in any case, in an atmosphere of affection and of moral and material security; a child of tender years shall not, save in exceptional circumstances, be separated from his mother. Society and the public authorities shall have the duty to extend particular care to children without a family and to those without adequate means of support. Payment of State and other assistance towards the maintenance of children of large families is desirable.

● Principle 7

The child is entitled to receive education, which shall be free and compulsory, at least in the elementary stages. He shall be given an education which will promote his general culture and enable him, on a basis of equal opportunity, to develop his abilities, his indi-vidual judgement, and his sense of moral and social responsibility, and to become a useful member of society.

The best interests of the child shall be the guiding principle of those responsible for his education and guidance; that responsibility lies in the first place with his parents.

The child shall have full opportunity for play and recreation, which should be directed to the same purposes as education; society and the public authorities shall endeavour to promote the enjoyment of this right.

● Principle 8

The child shall in all circumstances be among the first to receive protection and relief.

● Principle 9

The child shall be protected against all forms of neglect, cruelty and exploitation.

He shall not be the subject of traffic, in any form.

The child shall not be admitted to employment before an appropriate minimum age; he shall in no case be caused or permitted to engage in any occupation or employment which would prejudice his health or education, or interfere with his physical, mental or moral development.

● Principle 10

The child shall be protected from practices which may foster racial, religious and any other form of discrimination. He shall be brought up in a spirit of understanding, tolerance, friendship among peoples, peace and universal brotherhood, and in full consciousness that his energy and talents should be devoted to the service of his fellow men.

International Covenant on Civil and Political Rights

Adopted and opened for signature, ratification and accession by General Assembly resolution 2200A (XXI) of 16 December 1966

Preamble

The States Parties to the present Covenant,

Considering that, in accordance with the principles proclaimed in the Charter of the United Nations, recognition of the inherent dignity and of the equal and inalienable rights of all members of the human family is the foundation of freedom, justice and peace in the world,

Recognizing that these rights derive from the inherent dignity of the human person,

Recognizing that, in accordance with the Universal Declaration of Human Rights, the ideal of free human beings enjoying civil and political freedom and freedom from fear and want can only be achieved if conditions are created whereby everyone may enjoy his civil and political rights, as well as his economic, social and cultural rights,

Considering the obligation of States under the Charter of the United Nations to promote universal respect for, and observance of, human rights and freedoms,

Realizing that the individual, having duties to other individuals and to the community to which he belongs, is under a responsibility to strive for the promotion and observance of the rights recognized in the present Covenant,

Agree upon the following articles:

PART I

● Article 1

1. All peoples have the right of self-determination. By virtue of that right they freely determine their political status and freely pursue their economic, social and cultural development.

2. All peoples may, for their own ends, freely dispose of their natural wealth and resources without prejudice to any obligations arising out of international economic co-operation, based upon the principle of mutual benefit, and international law. In no case may a people be deprived of its own means of subsistence.

3. The States Parties to the present Covenant, including those having responsibility for the administration of Non-Self-Governing and Trust Territories, shall promote the realization of the right of self-determination, and shall respect that right, in conformity with the provisions of the Charter of the United Nations.

PART II

● Article 2

1. Each State Party to the present Covenant undertakes to respect and to ensure to all individuals within its territory and subject to its jurisdiction the rights recognized in the present Covenant, without distinction of any kind, such as race, colour, sex, language, religion, political or other opinion, national or social origin, property, birth or other status.

2. Where not already provided for by existing legislative or other measures, each State Party to the present Covenant undertakes to take the necessary steps, in accordance with its constitutional processes and with the provisions of the present Covenant, to adopt such laws or other measures as may be necessary to give effect to the rights recognized in the present Covenant.

3. Each State Party to the present Covenant undertakes:

(a) To ensure that any person whose rights or freedoms as herein recognized are violated shall have an effective remedy, notwithstanding that the violation has been committed by persons acting in an official capacity;

(b) To ensure that any person claiming such a remedy shall have his right thereto determined by competent judicial, administrative or legislative authorities, or by any other competent authority provided for by the legal system of the State, and to develop the possibilities of judicial remedy;

(c) To ensure that the competent authorities shall enforce such remedies when granted.

Article 3

The States Parties to the present Covenant undertake to ensure the equal right of men and women to the enjoyment of all civil and political rights set forth in the present Covenant.

Article 4

1 . In time of public emergency which threatens the life of the nation and the existence of which is officially proclaimed, the States Parties to the present Covenant may take measures derogating from their obligations under the present Covenant to the extent strictly required by the exigencies of the situation, provided that such measures are not inconsistent with their other obligations under international law and do not involve discrimination solely on the ground of race, colour, sex, language, religion or social origin.

2. No derogation from articles 6, 7, 8 (paragraphs 1 and 2), 11, 15, 16 and 18 may be made under this provision.

3. Any State Party to the present Covenant availing itself of the right of derogation shall immediately inform the other States Parties to the present Covenant, through the intermediary of the Secretary-General of the United Nations, of the provisions from which it has derogated and of the reasons by which it was actuated. A further communication shall be made, through the same intermediary, on the date on which it terminates such derogation.

Article 5

1. Nothing in the present Covenant may be interpreted as implying for any State, group or person any right to engage in any activity or perform any act aimed at the destruction of any of the rights and freedoms recognized herein or at their limitation to a greater extent than is provided for in the present Covenant.

2. There shall be no restriction upon or derogation from any of the fundamental human rights recognized or existing in any State Party to the present Covenant pursuant to law, conventions, regulations or custom on the pretext that the present Covenant does not recognize such rights or that it recognizes them to a lesser extent.

PART III

Article 6

1. Every human being has the inherent right to life. This right shall be protected by law. No one shall be arbitrarily deprived of his life.

2. In countries which have not abolished the death penalty, sentence of death may be imposed only for the most serious crimes in accordance with the law in force at the time of the commission of the crime and not contrary to the provisions of the present Covenant and to the Convention on the Prevention and Punishment of the Crime of Genocide. This penalty can only be carried out pursuant to a final judgement rendered by a competent court.

3. When deprivation of life constitutes the crime of genocide, it is understood that nothing in this article shall authorize any State

Party to the present Covenant to derogate in any way from any obligation assumed under the provisions of the Convention on the Prevention and Punishment of the Crime of Genocide.

4. Anyone sentenced to death shall have the right to seek pardon or commutation of the sentence. Amnesty, pardon or commutation of the sentence of death may be granted in all cases.

5. Sentence of death shall not be imposed for crimes committed by persons below eighteen years of age and shall not be carried out on pregnant women.

6. Nothing in this article shall be invoked to delay or to prevent the abolition of capital punishment by any State Party to the present Covenant.

Article 7

No one shall be subjected to torture or to cruel, inhuman or degrading treatment or punishment. In particular, no one shall be subjected without his free consent to medical or scientific experimentation.

Article 8

1. No one shall be held in slavery; slavery and the slave-trade in all their forms shall be prohibited.

2. No one shall be held in servitude.

3. (a) No one shall be required to perform forced or compulsory labour;

(b) Paragraph 3 (a) shall not be held to preclude, in countries where imprisonment with hard labour may be imposed as a punishment for a crime, the performance of hard labour in pursuance of a sentence to such punishment by a competent court;

(c) For the purpose of this paragraph the term "forced or compulsory labour" shall not include:

(i) Any work or service, not referred to in subparagraph (b), normally required of a person who is under detention in consequence of a lawful order of a court, or of a person during conditional release from such detention;

(ii) Any service of a military character and, in countries where conscientious objection is recognized, any national service required by law of conscientious objectors;

(iii) Any service exacted in cases of emergency or calamity threatening the life or well-being of the community;

(iv) Any work or service which forms part of normal civil obligations.

Article 9

1. Everyone has the right to liberty and security of person. No one shall be subjected to arbitrary arrest or detention. No one shall be deprived of his liberty except on such grounds and in accordance with such procedure as are established by law.

2. Anyone who is arrested shall be informed, at the time of arrest, of the reasons for his arrest and shall be promptly informed of any charges against him.

3. Anyone arrested or detained on a criminal charge shall be brought promptly before a judge or other officer authorized by law to exercise judicial power and shall be entitled to trial within a reasonable time or to release. It shall not be the general rule that persons awaiting trial shall be detained in custody, but release may be subject to guarantees to appear for trial, at any other stage of the judicial proceedings, and, should occasion arise, for execution of the judgement.

4. Anyone who is deprived of his liberty by arrest or detention shall be entitled to take proceedings before a court, in order that court may decide without delay on the lawfulness of his detention and order his release if the detention is not lawful.

5. Anyone who has been the victim of unlawful arrest or detention shall have an enforceable right to compensation.

Article 10

1. All persons deprived of their liberty shall be treated with humanity and with respect for the inherent dignity of the human person.

2. (a) Accused persons shall, save in exceptional circumstances, be segregated from convicted persons and shall be subject to separate treatment appropriate to their status as unconvicted persons;

(b) Accused juvenile persons shall be separated from adults and brought as speedily as possible for adjudication.

3. The penitentiary system shall comprise treatment of prisoners the essential aim of which shall be their reformation and social rehabilitation. Juvenile offenders shall be segregated from adults and be accorded treatment appropriate to their age and legal status.

Article 11

No one shall be imprisoned merely on the ground of inability to fulfil a contractual obligation.

Article 12

1. Everyone lawfully within the territory of a State shall, within that territory, have the right to liberty of movement and freedom to choose his residence.

2. Everyone shall be free to leave any country, including his own.

3. The above-mentioned rights shall not be subject to any restrictions except those which are provided by law, are necessary to protect national security, public order (ordre public), public health or morals or the rights and freedoms of others, and are consistent with the other rights recognized in the present Covenant.

4. No one shall be arbitrarily deprived of the right to enter his own country.

Article 13

An alien lawfully in the territory of a State Party to the present Covenant may be expelled therefrom only in pursuance of a decision reached in accordance with law and shall, except where compelling reasons of national security otherwise require, be allowed to submit the reasons against his expulsion and to have his case reviewed by, and be represented for the purpose before, the competent authority or a person or persons especially designated by the competent authority.

● Article 14

1. All persons shall be equal before the courts and tribunals. In the determination of any criminal charge against him, or of his rights and obligations in a suit at law, everyone shall be entitled to a fair and public hearing by a competent, independent and impartial tribunal established by law. The press and the public may be excluded from all or part of a trial for reasons of morals, public order (*ordre public*) or national security in a democratic society, or when the interest of the private lives of the parties so requires, or to the extent strictly necessary in the opinion of the court in special circumstances where publicity would prejudice the interests of justice; but any judgement rendered in a criminal case or in a suit at law shall be made public except where the interest of juvenile persons otherwise requires or the proceedings concern matrimonial disputes or the guardianship of children.

2. Everyone charged with a criminal offence shall have the right to be presumed innocent until proved guilty according to law.

3. In the determination of any criminal charge against him, everyone shall be entitled to the following minimum guarantees, in full equality:

(a) To be informed promptly and in detail in a language which he understands of the nature and cause of the charge against him;

(b) To have adequate time and facilities for the preparation of his defence and to communicate with counsel of his own choosing;

(c) To be tried without undue delay;

(d) To be tried in his presence, and to defend himself in person or through legal assistance of his own choosing; to be informed, if he does not have legal assistance, of this right; and to have legal assistance assigned to him, in any case where the interests of justice so require, and without payment by him in any such case if he does not have sufficient means to pay for it;

(e) To examine, or have examined, the witnesses against him and to obtain the attendance and examination of witnesses on his behalf under the same conditions as witnesses against him;

(f) To have the free assistance of an interpreter if he cannot understand or speak the language used in court;

(g) Not to be compelled to testify against himself or to confess guilt.

4. In the case of juvenile persons, the procedure shall be such as will take account of their age and the desirability of promoting their rehabilitation.

5. Everyone convicted of a crime shall have the right to his conviction and sentence being reviewed by a higher tribunal according to law.

6. When a person has by a final decision been convicted of a criminal offence and when subsequently his conviction has been reversed or he has been pardoned on the ground that a new or newly discovered fact shows conclusively that there has been a miscarriage of justice, the person who has suffered punishment as a result of such conviction shall be compensated according to law, unless it is proved that the non-disclosure of the unknown fact in time is wholly or partly attributable to him.

7. No one shall be liable to be tried or punished again for an offence for which he has already been finally convicted or acquitted in accordance with the law and penal procedure of each country.

● Article 15

1 . No one shall be held guilty of any criminal offence on account of any act or omission which did not constitute a criminal offence, under national or international law, at the time when it was committed. Nor shall a heavier penalty be imposed than the one that was applicable at the time when the criminal offence was committed. If, subsequent to the commission of the offence, provision is made by law for the imposition of the lighter penalty, the offender shall benefit thereby.

2. Nothing in this article shall prejudice the trial and punishment of any person for any act or omission which, at the time when it was committed, was criminal according to the general principles of law recognized by the community of nations.

● Article 16

Everyone shall have the right to recognition everywhere as a person before the law.

● Article 17

1. No one shall be subjected to arbitrary or unlawful interference with his privacy, family, home or correspondence, nor to unlawful attacks on his honour and reputation.

2. Everyone has the right to the protection of the law against such interference or attacks.

● Article 18

1. Everyone shall have the right to freedom of thought, conscience and religion. This right shall include freedom to have or to adopt a religion or belief of his choice, and freedom, either individually or in community with others and in public or private, to manifest his religion or belief in worship, observance, practice and teaching.

2. No one shall be subject to coercion which would impair his freedom to have or to adopt a religion or belief of his choice.

3. Freedom to manifest one's religion or beliefs may be subject only to such limitations as are prescribed by law and are necessary to protect public safety, order, health, or morals or the fundamental rights and freedoms of others.

4. The States Parties to the present Covenant undertake to have respect for the liberty of parents and, when applicable, legal guardians to ensure the religious and moral education of their children in conformity with their own convictions.

● Article 19

1. Everyone shall have the right to hold opinions without interference.

2. Everyone shall have the right to freedom of expression; this right shall include freedom to seek, receive and impart information and ideas of all kinds, regardless of frontiers, either orally, in writing or in print, in the form of art, or through any other media of his choice.

3. The exercise of the rights provided for in paragraph 2 of this article carries with it special duties and responsibilities. It may therefore be subject to certain restrictions, but these shall only be such as are provided by law and are necessary:

(a) For respect of the rights or reputations of others;

(b) For the protection of national security or of public order (*ordre public*), or of public health or morals.

● Article 20

1. Any propaganda for war shall be prohibited by law.

2. Any advocacy of national, racial or religious hatred that constitutes incitement to discrimination, hostility or violence shall be prohibited by law.

● Article 21

The right of peaceful assembly shall be recognized. No restrictions may be placed on the exercise of this right other than those imposed in conformity with the law and which are necessary in a democratic society in the interests of national security or public safety, public order (*ordre public*), the protection of public health or morals or the protection of the rights and freedoms of others.

● Article 22

1. Everyone shall have the right to freedom of association with others, including the right to form and join trade unions for the protection of his interests.

2. No restrictions may be placed on the exercise of this right other than those which are prescribed by law and which are necessary in a democratic society in the interests of national security or public safety, public order (*ordre public*), the protection of public health or morals or the protection of the rights and freedoms of others. This article shall not prevent the imposition of lawful restrictions on members of the armed forces and of the police in their exercise of this right.

3. Nothing in this article shall authorize States Parties to the International Labour Organization Convention of 1948 concerning Freedom of Association and Protection of the Right to Organize to take legislative measures which would prejudice, or to apply the law in such a manner as to prejudice, the guarantees provided for in that Convention.

● Article 23

1. The family is the natural and fundamental group unit of society and is entitled to protection by society and the State.

2. The right of men and women of marriageable age to marry and to found a family shall be recognized.

3. No marriage shall be entered into without the free and full consent of the intending spouses.

4. States Parties to the present Covenant shall take appropriate steps to ensure equality of rights and responsibilities of spouses as to marriage, during marriage and at its dissolution. In the case of dissolution, provision shall be made for the necessary protection of any children.

● Article 24

1. Every child shall have, without any discrimination as to race, colour, sex, language, religion, national or social origin, property or birth, the right to such measures of protection as are required by his status as a minor, on the part of his family, society and the State.

2. Every child shall be registered immediately after birth and shall have a name.

3. Every child has the right to acquire a nationality.

● Article 25

Every citizen shall have the right and the opportunity, without any of the distinctions mentioned in article 2 and without unreasonable restrictions:

(a) To take part in the conduct of public affairs, directly or through freely chosen representatives;

(b) To vote and to be elected at genuine periodic elections which shall be by universal and equal suffrage and shall be held by secret ballot, guaranteeing the free expression of the will of the electors;

(c) To have access, on general terms of equality, to public service in his country.

● Article 26

All persons are equal before the law and are entitled without any discrimination to the equal protection of the law. In this respect, the law shall prohibit any discrimination and guarantee to all persons equal and effective protection against discrimination on any ground such as race, colour, sex, language, religion, political or other opinion, national or social origin, property, birth or other status.

● Article 27

In those States in which ethnic, religious or linguistic minorities exist, persons belonging to such minorities shall not be denied the right, in community with the other members of their group, to enjoy their own culture, to profess and practise their own religion, or to use their own language.

PART IV

● Article 28

1. There shall be established a Human Rights Committee (hereafter referred to in the present Covenant as the Committee). It shall consist of eighteen members and shall carry out the functions hereinafter provided.

2. The Committee shall be composed of nationals of the States Parties to the present Covenant who shall be persons of high moral character and recognized competence in the field of human rights, consideration being given to the usefulness of the participation of some persons having legal experience.

3. The members of the Committee shall be elected and shall serve in their personal capacity.

● Article 29

1 . The members of the Committee shall be elected by secret ballot from a list of persons possessing the qualifications prescribed in article 28 and nominated for the purpose by the States Parties to the present Covenant.

2. Each State Party to the present Covenant may nominate not more than two persons. These persons shall be nationals of the nominating State.

3. A person shall be eligible for renomination.

● Article 30

1. The initial election shall be held no later than six months after the date of the entry into force of the present Covenant.

2. At least four months before the date of each election to the Committee, other than an election to fill a vacancy declared in accordance with article 34, the Secretary-General of the United Nations shall address a written invitation to the States Parties to the present Covenant to submit their nominations for membership of the Committee within three months.

3. The Secretary-General of the United Nations shall prepare a list in alphabetical order of all the persons thus nominated, with an indication of the States Parties which have nominated them, and shall submit it to the States Parties to the present Covenant no later than one month before the date of each election.

4. Elections of the members of the Committee shall be held at a meeting of the States Parties to the present Covenant convened by the Secretary General of the United Nations at the Headquarters of the United Nations. At that meeting, for which two thirds of the States Parties to the present Covenant shall constitute a quorum, the persons elected to the Committee shall be those nominees who obtain the largest number of votes and an absolute majority of the votes of the representatives of States Parties present and voting.

● Article 31

1. The Committee may not include more than one national of the same State.

2. In the election of the Committee, consideration shall be given to equitable geographical distribution of membership and to the representation of the different forms of civilization and of the principal legal systems.

● Article 32

1. The members of the Committee shall be elected for a term of four years. They shall be eligible for re-election if renominated. However, the terms of nine of the members elected at the first election shall expire at the end of two years; immediately after the first election, the names of these nine members shall be chosen by lot by the Chairman of the meeting referred to in article 30, paragraph 4.

2. Elections at the expiry of office shall be held in accordance with the preceding articles of this part of the present Covenant.

● Article 33

1. If, in the unanimous opinion of the other members, a member of the Committee has ceased to carry out his functions for any cause other than absence of a temporary character, the Chairman of the Committee shall notify the Secretary-General of the United Nations, who shall then declare the seat of that member to be vacant.

2. In the event of the death or the resignation of a member of the Committee, the Chairman shall immediately notify the Secretary-General of the United Nations, who shall declare the seat vacant from the date of death or the date on which the resignation takes effect.

● Article 34

1. When a vacancy is declared in accordance with article 33 and if the term of office of the member to be replaced does not expire within six months of the declaration of the vacancy, the Secretary-General of the United Nations shall notify each of the States Parties to the present Covenant, which may within two months submit nominations in accordance with article 29 for the purpose of filling the vacancy.

2. The Secretary-General of the United Nations shall prepare a list in alphabetical order of the persons thus nominated and shall submit it to the States Parties to the present Covenant. The election to fill the vacancy shall then take place in accordance with the relevant provisions of this part of the present Covenant.

3. A member of the Committee elected to fill a vacancy declared in accordance with article 33 shall hold office for the remainder of the term of the member who vacated the seat on the Committee under the provisions of that article.

● Article 35

The members of the Committee shall, with the approval of the General Assembly of the United Nations, receive emoluments from United Nations resources on such terms and conditions as the General Assembly may decide, having regard to the importance of the Committee's responsibilities.

● Article 36

The Secretary-General of the United Nations shall provide the necessary staff and facilities for the effective performance of the functions of the Committee under the present Covenant.

● Article 37

1. The Secretary-General of the United Nations shall convene the initial meeting of the Committee at the Headquarters of the United Nations.

2. After its initial meeting, the Committee shall meet at such times as shall be provided in its rules of procedure.

3. The Committee shall normally meet at the Headquarters of the United Nations or at the United Nations Office at Geneva.

Article 38

Every member of the Committee shall, before taking up his duties, make a solemn declaration in open committee that he will perform his functions impartially and conscientiously.

Article 39

1. The Committee shall elect its officers for a term of two years. They may be re-elected.

2. The Committee shall establish its own rules of procedure, but these rules shall provide, *inter alia*, that:

(a) Twelve members shall constitute a quorum;

(b) Decisions of the Committee shall be made by a majority vote of the members present.

Article 40

1. The States Parties to the present Covenant undertake to submit reports on the measures they have adopted which give effect to the rights recognized herein and on the progress made in the enjoyment of those rights:

(a) Within one year of the entry into force of the present Covenant for the States Parties concerned;

(b) Thereafter whenever the Committee so requests.

2. All reports shall be submitted to the Secretary-General of the United Nations, who shall transmit them to the Committee for consideration. Reports shall indicate the factors and difficulties, if any, affecting the implementation of the present Covenant.

3. The Secretary-General of the United Nations may, after consultation with the Committee, transmit to the specialized agencies concerned copies of such parts of the reports as may fall within their field of competence.

4. The Committee shall study the reports submitted by the States Parties to the present Covenant. It shall transmit its reports, and such general comments as it may consider appropriate, to the States Parties. The Committee may also transmit to the Economic and Social Council these comments along with the copies of the reports it has received from States Parties to the present Covenant.

5. The States Parties to the present Covenant may submit to the Committee observations on any comments that may be made in accordance with paragraph 4 of this article.

Article 41

1. A State Party to the present Covenant may at any time declare under this article that it recognizes the competence of the Committee to receive and consider communications to the effect that a State Party claims that another State Party is not fulfilling its obligations under the present Covenant. Communications under this article may be received and considered only if submitted by a State Party which has made a declaration recognizing in regard to itself the competence of the Committee. No communication shall be received by the Committee if it concerns a State Party which has not made such a declaration. Communications received under this article shall be dealt with in accordance with the following procedure:

(a) If a State Party to the present Covenant considers that another State Party is not giving effect to the provisions of the present Covenant, it may, by written communication, bring the matter to the attention of that State Party. Within three months after the receipt of the communication the receiving State shall afford the State which sent the communication an explanation, or any other statement in writing clarifying the matter which should include, to the extent possible and pertinent, reference to domestic procedures and remedies taken, pending, or available in the matter;

(b) If the matter is not adjusted to the satisfaction of both States Parties concerned within six months after the receipt by the receiving State of the initial communication, either State shall have the right to refer the matter to the Committee, by notice given to the Committee and to the other State;

(c) The Committee shall deal with a matter referred to it only after it has ascertained that all available domestic remedies have been invoked and exhausted in the matter, in conformity with the generally recognized principles of international law. This shall not be the rule where the application of the remedies is unreasonably prolonged;

(d) The Committee shall hold closed meetings when examining communications under this article;

(e) Subject to the provisions of subparagraph (c), the Committee shall make available its good offices to the States Parties concerned with a view to a friendly solution of the matter on the basis of respect for human rights and fundamental freedoms as recognized in the present Covenant;

(f) In any matter referred to it, the Committee may call upon the States Parties concerned, referred to in subparagraph (b), to supply any relevant information;

(g) The States Parties concerned, referred to in subparagraph (b), shall have the right to be represented when the matter is being considered in the Committee and to make submissions orally and/or in writing;

(h) The Committee shall, within twelve months after the date of receipt of notice under subparagraph (b), submit a report:

(i) If a solution within the terms of subparagraph (e) is reached, the Committee shall confine its report to a brief statement of the facts and of the solution reached;

(ii) If a solution within the terms of subparagraph (e) is not reached, the Committee shall confine its report to a brief statement of the facts; the written submissions and record of the oral submissions made by the States Parties concerned shall be attached to the report. In every matter, the report shall be communicated to the States Parties concerned.

2. The provisions of this article shall come into force when ten States Parties to the present Covenant have made declarations under paragraph I of this article. Such declarations shall be deposited by the States Parties with the Secretary-General of the United Nations, who shall transmit copies thereof to the other States Parties. A declaration may be withdrawn at any time by notification to the Secretary-General. Such a withdrawal shall not prejudice the consideration of any matter which is the subject of a communication already transmitted under this article; no further communication by any State Party shall be received after the notification of withdrawal of the declaration has been received by the Secretary-General, unless the State Party concerned has made a new declaration.

Article 42

1. (a) If a matter referred to the Committee in accordance with article 41 is not resolved to the satisfaction of the States Parties concerned, the Committee may, with the prior consent of the States Parties concerned, appoint an ad hoc Conciliation Commission (hereinafter referred to as the Commission). The good offices of the Commission shall be made available to the States Parties concerned with a view to an amicable solution of the matter on the basis of respect for the present Covenant;

(b) The Commission shall consist of five persons acceptable to the States Parties concerned. If the States Parties concerned fail to reach agreement within three months on all or part of the composition of the Commission, the members of the Commission concerning whom no agreement has been reached shall be elected by secret ballot by a two-thirds majority vote of the Committee from among its members.

2. The members of the Commission shall serve in their personal capacity. They shall not be nationals of the States Parties concerned, or of a State not Party to the present Covenant, or of a State Party which has not made a declaration under article 41.

3. The Commission shall elect its own Chairman and adopt its own rules of procedure.

4. The meetings of the Commission shall normally be held at the Headquarters of the United Nations or at the United Nations Office at Geneva. However, they may be held at such other convenient places as the Commission may determine in consultation with the Secretary-General of the United Nations and the States Parties concerned.

5. The secretariat provided in accordance with article 36 shall also service the commissions appointed under this article.

6. The information received and collated by the Committee shall be made available to the Commission and the Commission may call upon the States Parties concerned to supply any other relevant information.

7. When the Commission has fully considered the matter, but in any event not later than twelve months after having been seized of the matter, it shall submit to the Chairman of the

Committee a report for communication to the States Parties concerned:

(a) If the Commission is unable to complete its consideration of the matter within twelve months, it shall confine its report to a brief statement of the status of its consideration of the matter;

(b) If an amicable solution to the matter on tie basis of respect for human rights as recognized in the present Covenant is reached, the Commission shall confine its report to a brief statement of the facts and of the solution reached;

(c) If a solution within the terms of subparagraph (b) is not reached, the Commission's report shall embody its findings on all questions of fact relevant to the issues between the States Parties concerned, and its views on the possibilities of an amicable solution of the matter. This report shall also contain the written submissions and a record of the oral submissions made by the States Parties concerned;

(d) If the Commission's report is submitted under subparagraph (c), the States Parties concerned shall, within three months of the receipt of the report, notify the Chairman of the Committee whether or not they accept the contents of the report of the Commission.

8. The provisions of this article are without prejudice to the responsibilities of the Committee under article 41.

9. The States Parties concerned shall share equally all the expenses of the members of the Commission in accordance with estimates to be provided by the Secretary-General of the United Nations.

10. The Secretary-General of the United Nations shall be empowered to pay the expenses of the members of the Commission, if necessary, before reimbursement by the States Parties concerned, in accordance with paragraph 9 of this article.

● Article 43

The members of the Committee, and of the ad hoc conciliation commissions which may be appointed under article 42, shall be entitled to the facilities, privileges and immunities of experts on mission for the United Nations as laid down in the relevant sections of the Convention on the Privileges and Immunities of the United Nations.

● Article 44

The provisions for the implementation of the present Covenant shall apply without prejudice to the procedures prescribed in the field of human rights by or under the constituent instruments and the conventions of the United Nations and of the specialized agencies and shall not prevent the States Parties to the present Covenant from having recourse to other procedures for settling a dispute in accordance with general or special international agreements in force between them.

● Article 45

The Committee shall submit to the General Assembly of the United Nations, through the Economic and Social Council, an annual report on its activities.

PART V

● Article 46

Nothing in the present Covenant shall be interpreted as impairing the provisions of the Charter of the United Nations and of the constitutions of the specialized agencies which define the respective responsibilities of the various organs of the United Nations and of the specialized agencies in regard to the matters dealt with in the present Covenant.

● Article 47

Nothing in the present Covenant shall be interpreted as impairing the inherent right of all peoples to enjoy and utilize fully and freely their natural wealth and resources.

PART VI

● Article 48

1. The present Covenant is open for signature by any State Member of the United Nations or member of any of its specialized agencies, by any State Party to the Statute of the International Court of Justice, and by any other State which has been invited by the General Assembly of the United Nations to become a Party to the present Covenant.

2. The present Covenant is subject to ratification. Instruments of ratification shall be deposited with the Secretary-General of the United Nations.

3. The present Covenant shall be open to accession by any State referred to in paragraph 1 of this article.

4. Accession shall be effected by the deposit of an instrument of accession with the Secretary-General of the United Nations.

5. The Secretary-General of the United Nations shall inform all States which have signed this Covenant or acceded to it of the deposit of each instrument of ratification or accession.

● Article 49

1. The present Covenant shall enter into force three months after the date of the deposit with the Secretary-General of the United Nations of the thirty-fifth instrument of ratification or instrument of accession.

2. For each State ratifying the present Covenant or acceding to it after the deposit of the thirty-fifth instrument of ratification or instrument of accession, the present Covenant shall enter into force three months after the date of the deposit of its own instrument of ratification or instrument of accession.

● Article 50

The provisions of the present Covenant shall extend to all parts of federal States without any limitations or exceptions.

● Article 51

1. Any State Party to the present Covenant may propose an amendment and file it with the Secretary-General of the United Nations. The Secretary-General of the United Nations shall thereupon communicate any proposed amendments to the States Parties to the present Covenant with a request that they notify him whether they favour a conference of States Parties for the purpose of considering and voting upon the proposals. In the event that at least one third of the States Parties favours such a conference, the Secretary-General shall convene the conference under the auspices of the United Nations. Any amendment adopted by a majority of the States Parties present and voting at the conference shall be submitted to the General Assembly of the United Nations for approval.

2. Amendments shall come into force when they have been approved by the General Assembly of the United Nations and accepted by a two-thirds majority of the States Parties to the present Covenant in accordance with their respective constitutional processes. 3. When amendments come into force, they shall be binding on those States Parties which have accepted them, other States Parties still being bound by the provisions of the present Covenant and any earlier amendment which they have accepted.

● Article 52

Irrespective of the notifications made under article 48, paragraph 5, the Secretary-General of the United Nations shall inform all States referred to in paragraph I of the same article of the following particulars:

(a) Signatures, ratifications and accessions under article 48;

(b) The date of the entry into force of the present Covenant under article 49 and the date of the entry into force of any amendments under article 51.

● Article 53

1. The present Covenant, of which the Chinese, English, French, Russian and Spanish texts are equally authentic, shall be deposited in the archives of the United Nations.

2. The Secretary-General of the United Nations shall transmit certified copies of the present Covenant to all States referred to in article 48.

International Covenant on Economic, Social and Cultural Rights

Adopted and opened for signature, ratification and accession by General Assembly resolution 2200A (XXI) of 16 December 1966

Preamble

*T*he States Parties to the present Covenant,

Considering that, in accordance with the principles proclaimed in the Charter of the United Nations, recognition of the inherent dignity and of the equal and inalienable rights of all members of the human family is the foundation of freedom, justice and peace in the world,

Recognizing that these rights derive from the inherent dignity of the human person,

Recognizing that, in accordance with the Universal Declaration of Human Rights, the ideal of free human beings enjoying civil and political freedom and freedom from fear and want can only be achieved if conditions are created whereby everyone may enjoy his civil and political rights, as well as his economic, social and cultural rights,

Considering the obligation of States under the Charter of the United Nations to promote universal respect for, and observance of, human rights and freedoms,

Realizing that the individual, having duties to other individuals and to the community to which he belongs, is under a responsibility to strive for the promotion and observance of the rights recognized in the present Covenant,

Agree upon the following articles:

PART I

● Article 1

1. All peoples have the right of self-determination. By virtue of that right they freely determine their political status and freely pursue their economic, social and cultural development.

2. All peoples may, for their own ends, freely dispose of their natural wealth and resources without prejudice to any obligations arising out of international economic co-operation, based upon the principle of mutual benefit, and international law. In no case may a people be deprived of its own means of subsistence.

3. The States Parties to the present Covenant, including those having responsibility for the administration of Non-Self-Governing and Trust Territories, shall promote the realization of the right of self-determination, and shall respect that right, in conformity with the provisions of the Charter of the United Nations.

PART II

● Article 2

1. Each State Party to the present Covenant undertakes to take steps, individually and through international assistance and cooperation, especially economic and technical, to the maximum of its available resources, with a view to achieving progressively the full realization of the rights recognized in the present Covenant by all appropriate means, including particularly the adoption of legislative measures.

2. The States Parties to the present Covenant undertake to guarantee that the rights enunciated in the present Covenant will be exercised without discrimination of any kind as to race, colour, sex, language, religion, political or other opinion, national or social origin, property, birth or other status.

3. Developing countries, with due regard to human rights and their national economy, may determine to what extent they would guarantee the economic rights recognized in the present Covenant to non-nationals.

● Article 3

The States Parties to the present Covenant undertake to ensure the equal right of men and women to the enjoyment of all economic, social and cultural rights set forth in the present Covenant.

● Article 4

The States Parties to the present Covenant recognize that, in the enjoyment of those rights provided by the State in conformity with the present Covenant, the State may subject such rights only to such limitations as are determined by law only in so far as this may be compatible with the nature of these rights and solely for the purpose of promoting the general welfare in a democratic society.

● Article 5

1. Nothing in the present Covenant may be interpreted as implying for any State, group or person any right to engage in any activity or to perform any act aimed at the destruction of any of the rights or freedoms recognized herein, or at their limitation to a greater extent than is provided for in the present Covenant.

2. No restriction upon or derogation from any of the fundamental human rights recognized or existing in any country in virtue of law, conventions, regulations or custom shall be admitted on the pretext that the present Covenant does not recognize such rights or that it recognizes them to a lesser extent.

PART III

● Article 6

1. The States Parties to the present Covenant recognize the right to work, which includes the right of everyone to the opportunity to gain his living by work which he freely chooses or accepts, and will take appropriate steps to safeguard this right.

2. The steps to be taken by a State Party to the present Covenant to achieve the full realization of this right shall include technical and vocational guidance and training programmes, policies and techniques to achieve steady economic, social and cultural development and full and productive employment under conditions safeguarding fundamental political and economic freedoms to the individual.

● Article 7

The States Parties to the present Covenant recognize the right of everyone to the enjoyment of just and favourable conditions of work which ensure, in particular:

(a) Remuneration which provides all workers, as a minimum, with:

(i) Fair wages and equal remuneration for work of equal value without distinction of any kind, in particular women being guaranteed conditions of work not inferior to those enjoyed by men, with equal pay for equal work;

(ii) A decent living for themselves and their families in accordance with the provisions of the present Covenant;

(b) Safe and healthy working conditions;

(c) Equal opportunity for everyone to be promoted in his employment to an appropriate higher level, subject to no considerations other than those of seniority and competence;

(d) Rest, leisure and reasonable limitation of working hours and periodic holidays with pay, as well as remuneration for public holidays

● Article 8

1. The States Parties to the present Covenant undertake to ensure:

(a) The right of everyone to form trade unions and join the trade union of his choice, subject only to the rules of the organization concerned, for the promotion and protection of his economic and social interests. No restrictions may be placed on the exercise of this right other than those prescribed by law and which are necessary in a democratic society in the interests of national security or public order or for the protection of the rights and freedoms of others;

(b) The right of trade unions to establish national federations or confederations and the right of the latter to form or join international trade-union organizations;

(c) The right of trade unions to function freely subject to no limitations other than those prescribed by law and which are necessary in a democratic society in the interests of national security or public order or for the protection of the rights and freedoms of others;

(d) The right to strike, provided that it is exercised in conformity with the laws of the particular country.

2. This article shall not prevent the imposition of lawful restrictions on the exercise of these rights by members of the armed forces or of the police or of the administration of the State.

3. Nothing in this article shall authorize States Parties to the International Labour Organization Convention of 1948 concerning Freedom of Association and Protection of the Right to Organize to take legislative measures which would prejudice, or apply the law in such a manner as would prejudice, the guarantees provided for in that Convention.

● Article 9

The States Parties to the present Covenant recognize the right of everyone to social security, including social insurance.

● Article 10

The States Parties to the present Covenant recognize that:

1. The widest possible protection and assistance should be accorded to the family, which is the natural and fundamental group unit of society, particularly for its establishment and while it is responsible for the care and education of dependent children. Marriage must be entered into with the free consent of the intending spouses.

2. Special protection should be accorded to mothers during a reasonable period before and after childbirth. During such period working mothers should be accorded paid leave or leave with adequate social security benefits.

3. Special measures of protection and assistance should be taken on behalf of all children and young persons without any discrimination for reasons of parentage or other conditions. Children and young persons should be protected from economic and social exploitation. Their employment in work harmful to their morals or health or dangerous to life or likely to hamper their normal development should be punishable by law. States should also set age limits

below which the paid employment of child labour should be prohibited and punishable by law.

● Article 11

1. The States Parties to the present Covenant recognize the right of everyone to an adequate standard of living for himself and his family, including adequate food, clothing and housing, and to the continuous improvement of living conditions. The States Parties will take appropriate steps to ensure the realization of this right, recognizing to this effect the essential importance of international cooperation based on free consent.

2. The States Parties to the present Covenant, recognizing the fundamental right of everyone to be free from hunger, shall take, individually and through international co-operation, the measures, including specific programmes, which are needed:

(a) To improve methods of production, conservation and distribution of food by making full use of technical and scientific knowledge, by disseminating knowledge of the principles of nutrition and by developing or reforming agrarian systems in such a way as to achieve the most efficient development and utilization of natural resources;

(b) Taking into account the problems of both food-importing and food-exporting countries, to ensure an equitable distribution of world food supplies in relation to need.

● Article 12

1. The States Parties to the present Covenant recognize the right of everyone to the enjoyment of the highest attainable standard of physical and mental health.

2. The steps to be taken by the States Parties to the present Covenant to achieve the full realization of this right shall include those necessary for:

(a) The provision for the reduction of the stillbirth-rate and of infant mortality and for the healthy development of the child;

(b) The improvement of all aspects of environmental and industrial hygiene;

(c) The prevention, treatment and control of epidemic, endemic, occupational and other diseases;

(d) The creation of conditions which would assure to all medical service and medical attention in the event of sickness.

● Article 13

1. The States Parties to the present Covenant recognize the right of everyone to education. They agree that education shall be directed to the full development of the human personality and the sense of its dignity, and shall strengthen the respect for human rights and fundamental freedoms. They further agree that education shall enable all persons to participate effectively in a free society, promote understanding, tolerance and friendship among all nations and all racial, ethnic or religious groups, and further the activities of the United Nations for the maintenance of peace.

2. The States Parties to the present Covenant recognize that, with a view to achieving the full realization of this right:

(a) Primary education shall be compulsory and available free to all;

(b) Secondary education in its different forms, including technical and vocational secondary education, shall be made generally available and accessible to all by every appropriate means, and in particular by the progressive introduction of free education;

(c) Higher education shall be made equally accessible to all, on the basis of capacity, by every appropriate means, and in particular by the progressive introduction of free education;

(d) Fundamental education shall be encouraged or intensified as far as possible for those persons who have not received or completed the whole period of their primary education;

(e) The development of a system of schools at all levels shall be actively pursued, an adequate fellowship system shall be established, and the material conditions of teaching staff shall be continuously improved.

3. The States Parties to the present Covenant undertake to have respect for the liberty of parents and, when applicable, legal guardians to choose for their children schools, other than those established by the public authorities, which conform to such minimum educational standards as may be laid down or approved by the State and to ensure the religious and moral education of their children in conformity with their own convictions.

4. No part of this article shall be construed so as to interfere with the liberty of individuals and bodies to establish and direct educational institutions, subject always to the observance of the principles set forth in paragraph I of this article and to the requirement that the education given in such institutions shall conform to such minimum standards as may be laid down by the State.

● **Article 14**

Each State Party to the present Covenant which, at the time of becoming a Party, has not been able to secure in its metropolitan territory or other territories under its jurisdiction compulsory primary education, free of charge, undertakes, within two years, to work out and adopt a detailed plan of action for the progressive implementation, within a reasonable number of years, to be fixed in the plan, of the principle of compulsory education free of charge for all.

● **Article 15**

1. The States Parties to the present Covenant recognize the right of everyone:

(a) To take part in cultural life;

(b) To enjoy the benefits of scientific progress and its applications;

(c) To benefit from the protection of the moral and material interests resulting from any scientific, literary or artistic production of which he is the author.

2. The steps to be taken by the States Parties to the present Covenant to achieve the full realization of this right shall include those necessary for the conservation, the development and the diffusion of science and culture.

3. The States Parties to the present Covenant undertake to respect the freedom indispensable for scientific research and creative activity.

4. The States Parties to the present Covenant recognize the benefits to be derived from the encouragement and development of international contacts and cooperation in the scientific and cultural fields.

PART IV

● **Article 16**

1. The States Parties to the present Covenant undertake to submit in conformity with this part of the Covenant reports on the measures which they have adopted and the progress made in achieving the observance of the rights recognized herein.

2. (a) All reports shall be submitted to the Secretary-General of the United Nations, who shall transmit copies to the Economic and Social Council for consideration in accordance with the provisions of the present Covenant;

(b) The Secretary-General of the United Nations shall also transmit to the specialized agencies copies of the reports, or any relevant parts therefrom, from States Parties to the present Covenant which are also members of these specialized agencies in so far as these reports, or parts therefrom, relate to any matters which fall within the responsibilities of the said agencies in accordance with their constitutional instruments.

● **Article 17**

1. The States Parties to the present Covenant shall furnish their reports in stages, in accordance with a programme to be established by the Economic and Social Council within one year of the entry into force of the present Covenant after consultation with the States Parties and the specialized agencies concerned.

2. Reports may indicate factors and difficulties affecting the degree of fulfilment of obligations under the present Covenant.

3. Where relevant information has previously been furnished to the United Nations or to any specialized agency by any State Party to the present Covenant, it will not be necessary to reproduce that information, but a precise reference to the information so furnished will suffice.

● **Article 18**

Pursuant to its responsibilities under the Charter of the United Nations in the field of human rights and fundamental freedoms, the Economic and Social Council may make arrangements with the specialized agencies in respect of their reporting to it on the progress made in achieving the observance of the provisions of the present Covenant falling within the scope of their activities. These reports may include particulars of decisions and recommendations on

such implementation adopted by their competent organs.

● **Article 19**

The Economic and Social Council may transmit to the Commission on Human Rights for study and general recommendation or, as appropriate, for information the reports concerning human rights submitted by States in accordance with articles 16 and 17, and those concerning human rights submitted by the specialized agencies in accordance with article 18.

● **Article 20**

The States Parties to the present Covenant and the specialized agencies concerned may submit comments to the Economic and Social Council on any general recommendation under article 19 or reference to such general recommendation in any report of the Commission on Human Rights or any documentation referred to therein.

● **Article 21**

The Economic and Social Council may submit from time to time to the General Assembly reports with recommendations of a general nature and a summary of the information received from the States Parties to the present Covenant and the specialized agencies on the measures taken and the progress made in achieving general observance of the rights recognized in the present Covenant.

● **Article 22**

The Economic and Social Council may bring to the attention of other organs of the United Nations, their subsidiary organs and specialized agencies concerned with furnishing technical assistance any matters arising out of the reports referred to in this part of the present Covenant which may assist such bodies in deciding, each within its field of competence, on the advisability of international measures likely to contribute to the effective progressive implementation of the present Covenant.

● **Article 23**

The States Parties to the present Covenant agree that international action for the achievement of the rights recognized in the present Covenant includes such methods as the conclusion of conventions, the adoption of recommendations, the furnishing of technical assistance and the holding of regional meetings and technical meetings for the purpose of consultation and study organized in conjunction with the Governments concerned.

● **Article 24**

Nothing in the present Covenant shall be interpreted as impairing the provisions of the Charter of the United Nations and of the constitutions of the specialized agencies which define the respective responsibilities of the various organs of the United Nations and of the specialized agencies in regard to the matters dealt with in the present Covenant.

● **Article 25**

Nothing in the present Covenant shall be interpreted as impairing the inherent right of all peoples to enjoy and utilize fully and freely their natural wealth and resources.

PART V

● Article 26

1. The present Covenant is open for signature by any State Member of the United Nations or member of any of its specialized agencies, by any State Party to the Statute of the International Court of Justice, and by any other State which has been invited by the General Assembly of the United Nations to become a party to the present Covenant.

2. The present Covenant is subject to ratification. Instruments of ratification shall be deposited with the Secretary-General of the United Nations.

3. The present Covenant shall be open to accession by any State referred to in paragraph 1 of this article.

4. Accession shall be effected by the deposit of an instrument of accession with the Secretary-General of the United Nations.

5. The Secretary-General of the United Nations shall inform all States which have signed the present Covenant or acceded to it of the deposit of each instrument of ratification or accession.

● Article 27

1. The present Covenant shall enter into force three months after the date of the deposit with the Secretary-General of the United Nations of the thirty-fifth instrument of ratification or instrument of accession.

2. For each State ratifying the present Covenant or acceding to it after the deposit of the thirty-fifth instrument of ratification or instrument of accession, the present Covenant shall enter into force three months after the date of the deposit of its own instrument of ratification or instrument of accession.

● Article 28

The provisions of the present Covenant shall extend to all parts of federal States without any limitations or exceptions.

● Article 29

1. Any State Party to the present Covenant may propose an amendment and file it with the Secretary-General of the United Nations. The Secretary-General shall thereupon communicate any proposed amendments to the States Parties to the present Covenant with a request that they notify him whether they favour a conference of States Parties for the purpose of considering and voting upon the proposals. In the event that at least one third of the States Parties favours such a conference, the Secretary-General shall convene the conference under the auspices of the United Nations. Any amendment adopted by a majority of the States Parties present and voting at the conference shall be submitted to the General Assembly of the United Nations for approval.

2. Amendments shall come into force when they have been approved by the General Assembly of the United Nations and accepted by a two-thirds majority of the States Parties to the present Covenant in accordance with their respective constitutional processes.

3. When amendments come into force they shall be binding on those States Parties which have accepted them, other States Parties still being bound by the provisions of the present Covenant and any earlier amendment which they have accepted.

● Article 30

Irrespective of the notifications made under article 26, paragraph 5, the Secretary-General of the United Nations shall inform all States referred to in paragraph I of the same article of the following particulars:

(a) Signatures, ratifications and accessions under article 26;

(b) The date of the entry into force of the present Covenant under article 27 and the date of the entry into force of any amendments under article 29.

● Article 31

1. The present Covenant, of which the Chinese, English, French, Russian and Spanish texts are equally authentic, shall be deposited in the archives of the United Nations.

2. The Secretary-General of the United Nations shall transmit certified copies of the present Covenant to all States referred to in article 26.

ILO Convention concerning Minimum Age for Admission to Employment

Adopted by the Governing Body of the International Labour Office on 26 June 1973

Preamble

The General Conference of the International Labour Organisation,

Having been convened at Geneva by the Governing Body of the International Labour Office, and having met in its Fifty-eighth Session on 6 June 1973, and

Having decided upon the adoption of certain proposals with regard to minimum age for admission to employment, which is the fourth item on the agenda of the session, and

Noting the terms of the Minimum Age (Industry) Convention, 1919, the Minimum Age (Sea) Convention, 1920, the Minimum Age (Agriculture) Convention, 1921, the Minimum Age (Trimmers and Stokers) Convention, 1921, the Minimum Age (Non-Industrial Employment) Convention, 1932, the Minimum Age (Sea) Convention (Revised), 1936, the Minimum Age (Industry) Convention (Revised), 1937, the Minimum Age (Non-Industrial Employment) Convention (Revised), 1937, the Minimum Age (Fishermen) Convention, 1959, and the Minimum Age (Underground Work) Convention, 1965, and

Considering that the time has come to establish a general instrument on the subject, which would gradually replace the existing ones applicable to limited economic sectors, with a view to achieving the total abolition of child labour, and

Having determined that these proposals shall take the form of an international Convention,

Adopts the twenty-sixth day of June of the year one thousand nine hundred and seventy-three, the following Convention, which may be cited as the Minimum Age Convention, 1973:

● Article 1

Each Member for which this Convention is in force undertakes to pursue a national policy designed to ensure the effective abolition of child labour and to raise progressively the minimum age for admission to employment or work to a level consistent with the fullest physical and mental development of young persons.

● Article 2

1. Each Member which ratifies this Convention shall specify, in a declaration appended to its ratification, a minimum age for admission to employment or work within its territory and on means of transport registered in its territory; subject to Articles 4 to 8 of this Conven-tion, no one under that age shall be admitted to employment or work in any occupation.
2. Each Member which has ratified this Convention may subsequently notify the Director-General of the International Labour Office, by further declarations, that it specifies a minimum age higher than that previously specified.
3. The minimum age specified in pursuance of paragraph 1 of this Article shall not be less than the age of completion of compulsory schooling and, in any case, shall not be less than 15 years.
4. Notwithstanding the provisions of paragraph 3 of this Article, a Member whose economy and educational facilities are insufficiently developed may, after consultation with the organisations of employers and workers concerned, where such exist, initially specify a minimum age of 14 years.
5. Each Member which has specified a minimum age of 14 years in pursuance of the provisions of the preceding paragraph shall include in its reports on the application of this Convention submitted under article 22 of the Constitution of the International Labour Organisation a statement—
(a) that its reason for doing so subsists; or
(b) that it renounces its right to avail itself of the provisions in question as from a stated date.

● Article 3

1. The minimum age for admission to any type of employment or work which by its nature or

the circumstances in which it is carried out is likely to jeopardise the health, safety or morals of young persons shall not be less than 18 years.

2. The types of employment or work to which paragraph 1 of this Article applies shall be determined by national laws or regulations or by the competent authority, after consultation with the organisations of employers and workers concerned, where such exist.

3. Notwithstanding the provisions of paragraph 1 of this Article, national laws or regulations or the competent authority may, after consultation with the organisations of employers and workers concerned, where such exist, authorise employment or work as from the age of 16 years on condition that the health, safety and morals of the young persons concerned are fully protected and that the young persons have received adequate specific instruction or vocational training in the relevant branch of activity.

● Article 4

1. In so far as necessary, the competent authority, after consultation with the organisations of employers and workers concerned, where such exist, may exclude from the application of this Convention limited categories of employment or work in respect of which special and substantial problems of application arise.

2. Each Member which ratifies this Convention shall list in its first report
on the application of the Convention submitted under article 22 of the Constitution of the International Labour Organisation any categories which may have been excluded in pursuance of paragraph 1 of this Article, giving the reasons for such exclusion, and shall state in subsequent reports the position of its law and practice in respect of the categories excluded and the extent to which effect has been given or is proposed to be given to the Convention in respect of such categories.

3. Employment or work covered by Article 3 of this Convention shall not be excluded from the application of the Convention in pursuance of this Article.

● Article 5

1. A Member whose economy and administrative facilities are insufficiently developed may, after consultation with the organisations of employers and workers concerned, where such exist, initially limit the scope of application of this Convention.

2. Each Member which avails itself of the provisions of paragraph 1 of this Article shall specify, in a declaration appended to its ratification, the branches of economic activity or types of undertakings to which it will apply the provisions of the Convention.

3. The provisions of the Convention shall be applicable as a minimum to the following: mining and quarrying; manufacturing; construction; electricity, gas and water; sanitary services; transport, storage and communication; and plantations and other agricultural undertakings mainly producing for commercial

purposes, but excluding family and small-scale holdings producing for local consumption and not regularly employing hired workers.

4. Any Member which has limited the scope of application of this Convention in pursuance of this Article—

(a) shall indicate in its reports under article 22 of the Constitution of the International Labour Organisation the general position as regards the employment or work of young persons and children in the branches of activity which are excluded from the scope of application of this Convention and any progress which may have been made towards wider application of the provisions of the Convention;

(b) may at any time formally extend the scope of application by a declaration addressed to the Director-General of the International Labour Office.

● Article 6

This Convention does not apply to work done by children and young persons in schools for general, vocational or technical education or in other training institutions, or to work done by persons at least 14 years of age in undertakings, where such work is carried out in accordance with conditions prescribed by the competent authority, after consultation with the organizations of employers and workers concerned, where such exist, and is an integral part of—

(a) a course of education or training for which a school or training institution is primarily responsible;

(b) a programme of training mainly or entirely in an undertaking, which programme has been approved by the competent authority; or

(c) a programme of guidance or orientation designed to facilitate the choice of an occupation or of a line of training.

● Article 7

1. National laws or regulations may permit the employment or work of persons 13 to 15 years of age on light work which is—

(a) not likely to be harmful to their health or development; and

(b) not such as to prejudice their attendance at school, their participation in vocational orientation or training programmes approved by the competent authority or their capacity to benefit from the instruction received.

2. National laws or regulations may also permit the employment or work of persons who are at least 15 years of age but have not yet completed their compulsory schooling on work which meets the requirements set forth in sub-paragraphs (a) and (b) of paragraph 1 of this Article.

3. The competent authority shall determine the activities in which employment or work may be permitted under paragraphs 1 and 2 of this Article and shall prescribe the number of hours during which and the conditions in which such employment or work may be undertaken.

4. Notwithstanding the provisions of paragraphs 1 and 2 of this Article, a Member which has availed itself of the provisions of paragraph 4 of Article 2 may, for as long as it continues to do so, substitute the ages 12 and 14 for the ages 13 and 15 in paragraph 1 and the age 14 for the age 15 in paragraph 2 of this Article.

● Article 8

1. After consultation with the organisations of employers and workers concerned, where such exist, the competent authority may, by permits granted in individual cases, allow exceptions to the prohibition of employment or work provided for in Article 2 of this Convention, for such purposes as participation in artistic performances.

2. Permits so granted shall limit the number of hours during which and prescribe the conditions in which employment or work is allowed.

● Article 9

1. All necessary measures, including the provision of appropriate penalties, shall be taken by the competent authority to ensure the effective enforcement of the provisions of this Convention.

2. National laws or regulations or the competent authority shall define the persons responsible for compliance with the provisions giving effect to the Convention.

3. National laws or regulations or the competent authority shall prescribe the registers or other documents which shall be kept and made available by the employer; such registers or documents shall contain the names and ages or dates of birth, duly certified wherever possible, of persons whom he employs or who work for him and who are less than 18 years of age.

● Article 10

1. This Convention revises, on the terms set forth in this Article, the Minimum Age (Industry) Convention, 1919, the Minimum Age (Sea) Convention, 1920, the Minimum Age (Agriculture) Convention, 1921, the Minimum Age (Trimmers and Stokers) Convention, 1921, the Minimum Age (Non-Industrial Employment) Convention, 1932, the Minimum Age (Sea) Convention (Revised), 1936, the Minimum Age (Industry) Convention (Revised), 1937, the Minimum Age (Non-Industrial Employment) Convention (Revised), 1937, the Minimum Age (Fishermen) Convention, 1959, and the Minimum Age (Underground Work) Convention, 1965.

2. The coming into force of this Convention shall not close the Minimum Age (Sea) Convention (Revised), 1936, the Minimum Age (Industry) Convention (Revised), 1937, the Minimum Age (Non-Industrial Employment) Convention (Revised), 1937, the Minimum Age (Fishermen) Convention, 1959, or the Minimum Age (Underground Work) Convention, 1965, to further ratification.

3. The Minimum Age (Industry) Convention, 1919, the Minimum Age (Sea) Convention, 1920, the Minimum Age (Agriculture) Convention, 1921, and the Minimum Age (Trimmers

and Stokers) Convention, 1921, shall be closed to further ratification when all the parties thereto have consented to such closing by ratification of this Convention or by a declaration communicated to the Director-General of the International Labour Office.

4. When the obligations of this Convention are accepted—

(a) by a Member which is a party to the Minimum Age (Industry) Convention (Revised), 1937, and a minimum age of not less than 15 years is specified in pursuance of Article 2 of this Convention, this shall *ipso jure* involve the immediate denunciation of that Convention,

(b) in respect of non-industrial employment as defined in the Minimum Age (Non-Industrial Employment) Convention, 1932, by a Member which is a party to that Convention, this shall *ipso jure* involve the immediate denunciation of that Convention,

(c) in respect of non-industrial employment as defined in the Minimum Age (Non-Industrial Employment) Convention (Revised), 1937, by a Member which is a party to that Convention, and a minimum age of not less than 15 years is specified in pursuance of Article 2 of this Convention, this shall *ipso jure* involve the immediate denunciation of that Convention,

(d) in respect of maritime employment, by a Member which is a party to the Minimum Age (Sea) Convention (Revised), 1936, and a minimum age of not less than 15 years is specified in pursuance of Article 2 of this Convention or the Member specifies that Article 3 of this Convention applies to maritime employment, this shall *ipso jure* involve the immediate denunciation of that Convention,

(e) in respect of employment in maritime fishing, by a Member which is a party to the Minimum Age (Fishermen) Convention, 1959, and a minimum age of not less than 15 years is specified in pursuance of Article 2 of this Convention or the Member specifies that Article 3 of this Convention applies to employment in maritime fishing, this shall *ipso jure* involve the immediate denunciation of that Convention,

(f) by a Member which is a party to the Minimum Age (Underground Work) Convention, 1965, and a minimum age of not less than the age specified in pursuance of that Convention is specified in pursuance of Article 2 of this Convention or the Member specifies that such an age applies to employment underground in mines in vir-

tue of Article 3 of this Convention, this shall *ipso jure* involve the immediate denunciation of that Convention, if and when this Convention shall have come into force.

5. Acceptance of the obligations of this Convention

(a) shall involve the denunciation of the Minimum Age (Industry) Convention, 1919, in accordance with Article 12 thereof,

(b) in respect of agriculture shall involve the denunciation of the Minimum Age (Agriculture) Convention, 1921, in accordance with Article 9 thereof,

(c) in respect of maritime employment shall involve the denunciation of the Minimum Age (Sea) Convention, 1920, in accordance with Article 10 thereof, and of the Minimum Age (Trimmers and Stokers) Convention, 1921, in accordance with Article 12 thereof, if and when this Convention shall have come into force.

● Article 11

The formal ratifications of this Convention shall be communicated to the Director-General of the International Labour Office for registration.

● Article 12

1. This Convention shall be binding only upon those Members of the International Labour Organisation whose ratifications have been registered with the Director-General.

2. It shall come into force twelve months after the date on which the ratifications of two Members have been registered with the Director-General.

3. Thereafter, this Convention shall come into force for any Member twelve months after the date on which its ratifications has been registered.

● Article 13

1. A Member which has ratified this Convention may denounce it after the expiration of ten years from the date on which the Convention first comes into force, by an Act communicated to the Director-General of the International Labour Office for registration. Such denunciation should not take effect until one year after the date on which it is registered.

2. Each Member which has ratified this Convention and which does not, within the year following the expiration of the period of ten years mentioned in the preceding paragraph, exercise the right of denunciation provided for in this Article, will be bound for another period of ten years and, thereafter, may denounce this Convention at the expiration of each peri-

od of ten years under the terms provided for in this Article.

● Article 14

1. The Director-General of the International Labour Office shall notify all Members of the International Labour Organisation of the registration of all ratifications and denunciations communicated to him by the Members of the Organisation.

2. When notifying the Members of the Organisation of the registration of the second ratification communicated to him, the Director-General shall draw the attention of the Members of the Organisation to the date upon which the Convention will come into force.

● Article 15

The Director-General of the International Labour Office shall communicate to the Secretary-General of the United Nations for registration in accordance with Article 102 of the Charter of the United Nations full particulars of all ratifications and acts of denunciation registered by him in accordance with the provisions of the preceding Articles.

● Article 16

At such times as may consider necessary the Governing Body of the International Labour Office shall present to the General Conference a report on the working of this Convention and shall examine the desirability of placing on the agenda of the Conference the question of its revision in whole or in part.

● Article 17

1. Should the Conference adopt a new Convention revising this Convention in whole or in part, then, unless the new Convention otherwise provides:

a) the ratification by a Member of the new revising Convention shall *ipso jure* involve the immediate denunciation of this Convention, notwithstanding the provisions of Article 13 above, if and when the new revising Convention shall have come into force;

b) as from the date when the new revising Convention comes into force this Convention shall cease to be open to ratification by the Members.

2. This Convention shall in any case remain in force in its actual form and content for those Members which have ratified it but have not ratified the revising Convention.

● Article 18

The English and French versions of the text of this Convention are equally authoritative.

United Nations Standard Minimum Rules for the Administration of Juvenile Justice

(The Beijing Rules)

Adopted by General Assembly resolution 40/33
of 29 November 1985

Preamble

he General Assembly,

Bearing in mind the Universal Declaration of Human Rights, the International Covenant on Civil and Political Rights and the International Covenant on Economic, Social and Cultural Rights, as well as other international human rights instruments pertaining to the rights of young persons,

Also bearing in mind that 1985 was designated the International Youth Year: Participation, Development, Peace and that the international community has placed importance on the protection and promotion of the rights of the young, as witnessed by the significance attached to the Declaration of the Rights of the Child,

Recalling solution 4 adopted by the Sixth United Nations congress on the Prevention of Crime and the treatment of Offenders, which called fore the development of standard minimum rules for the administration of juvenile justice and the care of juveniles, which could serve as a model for Member States,

Recalling also Economic and Social Council decision 1984/153 of 25 May 1984, by which the draft rules were forwarded to the Seventh United Nations Congress on the Prevention of Crime and the Treatment of Offenders, held at Milan, Italy, from 26 August to 6 September 1985, through the Interregional Preparatory Meeting, held at Beijing from 14 to 18 May 1984,

Recognizing that the young, owing to their early stage of human development, require particular care and assistance with regard to physical, mental and social development, and require legal protection in conditions of peace, freedom, dignity and security,

Considering that existing national legislation, policies and practices may well require review and the rules,

Considering further that, although such standards may seem difficult to achieve at present in view of existing social, economic, cultural, political and legal conditions, they are nevertheless intended to be attainable as a policy minimum,

1. *Notes* with appreciation the work carried out by the Committee on Crime Prevention and Control, the Secretary-General , the United Nations Asia and Far East Institute for the Prevention of Crime and Treatment of Offenders and other United Nations institutes in the development of the Standard Minimum Rules for the Administration of Juvenile Justice;

2. *Takes note* with appreciation of the report of the Secretary-General on the draft Standard Minimum Rules for the Administration of Juvenile Justice;

3. *Commends* the Interregional Preparatory Meeting held at Beijing for having finalized the text of the rules submitted to the Seventh United Nations Congress on the Prevention of Crime and Treatment of Offenders for consideration and final action;

4. *Adopts* the United Nations Standard Minimum Rules for the Administration of Juvenile Justice recommended by the Seventh Congress, contained in the annex to the present resolution, and approves the recommendations of the Seventh Congress that the Rules should be known as "Beijing Rules";

Invites Member States to adapt, wherever this is necessary, their national legislation, policies and practice, particularly in training juvenile justice personnel, to the Beijing Rules and to bring the Rules to the attention of relevant authorities and the public in general;

6. *Calls upon* the Committee on Crime Prevention and Control to formulate measures for the effective implementation of the Beijing Rules, with the assistance of the United Nations institutes on the prevention of Crime and the treatment of offenders.

7. *Invites* Member States to inform the Secretary-General on the implementation of the Beijing Rules and to report regularly to the Committee on Crime Prevention and Control on the results achieved;

8. *Requests* Member States and the Secretary-General to undertake research and to develop a data base with respect to effective policies and practices in the administration of juvenile justice;

9. *Requests* the Secretary-General and invites Member States to ensure the widest possible dissemination of the text of the Beijing Rules in all of the official languages of the United Nations, including the intensification of information activities in the field of juvenile justice;

10. *Requests* the Secretary-General to develop pilot projects on the implementation of the Beijing Rules;

11. *Requests* the Secretary-General and Member States to provide the necessary resources to ensure the successful implementation of the Beijing Rules, in particular in the areas of recruitment, training and exchange of personnel, research and evaluation, and the development of new alternatives to institutionalization

12. *Requests* the Eighth United Nations Congress on the Prevention of Crime and the Treatment of Offenders to review the progress made in the implementation of the Beijing Rules and of the recommendations contained in the present resolution, under a separate agenda item on juvenile justice;

13. *Urges* all relevant organs of the United Nations system, in particular the regional commissions and specialized agencies, the United Nations institutes for the prevention of crime and the treatment of offenders, other intergovernmental organizations and non-governmental organizations to collaborate with the Secretariat and to take the necessary measures to ensure a concerted and sustained effort, within their respective fields of technical competence, to implement the principles contained in the Beijing Rules.

PART ONE
GENERAL PRINCIPLES

1. Fundamental perspectives

1.1 Member States shall seek, in conformity with their respective general interests, to further the well-being of the juvenile and her or his family.

1.2 Member States shall endeavour to develop conditions that will ensure for the juvenile a meaningful life in the community, which, during that period in life when she or he is most susceptible to deviant behaviour, will foster a process of personal development and education that is as free from crime and delinquency as possible.

1.3 Sufficient attention shall be given to positive measures that involve the full mobilization of all possible resources, including the family, volunteers and other community groups, as well as schools and other community institutions, for the purpose of promoting the well-being of the juvenile, with a view to reducing the need for intervention under the law, and of effectively, fairly and humanely dealing with the juvenile in conflict with the law.

1.4 Juvenile justice shall be conceived as an integral part of the national development process of each country, within a comprehensive framework of social justice for all juveniles, thus, at the same time, contributing to the protection of the young and the maintenance of a peaceful order in society.

1.5 These Rules shall be implemented in the context of economic, social and cultural conditions prevailing in each Member State.

1.6 Juvenile justice services shall be systematically developed and coordinated with a view to improving and sustaining the competence of personnel involved in the services, including their methods, approaches and attitudes.

Commentary

These broad fundamental perspectives refer to comprehensive social policy in general and aim at promoting juvenile welfare to the greatest possible extent, which will minimize the necessity of intervention by the juvenile justice system, and in turn, will reduce the harm that may be caused by any intervention. Such care measures for the young, before the onset of delinquency, are basic policy requisites designed to obviate the need for the application of the Rules.

Rules 1.1 to 1.3 point to the important role that a constructive social policy for juveniles will play, *inter alia*, in the prevention of juvenile crime and delinquency. Rule 1.4 defines juvenile justice as an integral part of social justice for juveniles, while rule 1.6 refers to the necessity of constantly improving juvenile justice, without falling behind the development of progressive social policy for juveniles in general and bearing in mind the need for consistent improvement of staff services.

Rule 1.5 seeks to take account of existing conditions in Member States which would cause the manner of implementation of particular rules necessarily to be different from the manner adopted in other States.

2. Scope of the Rules and definitions used

2.1 The following Standard Minimum Rules shall be applied to juvenile offenders impartially, without distinction of any kind, for example as to race, colour, sex, language, religion, political or other opinions, national or social origin, property, birth or other status.

2.2 For purposes of these Rules, the following definitions shall be applied by Member States in a manner which is compatible with their respective legal systems and concepts:

(a) A juvenile is a child or young person who, under the respective legal systems, may be dealt with for an offence in a manner which is different from an adult;

(b) An offence is any behaviour (act or omission) that is punishable by law under the respective legal systems;

(c) A juvenile offender is a child or young person who is alleged to have committed or who has been found to have committed an offence.

2.3 Efforts shall be made to establish, in each national jurisdiction, a set of laws, rules and provisions specifically applicable to juvenile offenders and institutions and bodies entrusted with the functions of the administration of juvenile justice and designed:

(a) To meet the varying needs of juvenile offenders, while protecting their basic rights;

(b) To meet the needs of society;

(c) To implement the following rules thoroughly and fairly.

Commentary

The Standard Minimum Rules are deliberately formulated so as to be applicable within different legal systems and, at the same time, to set some minimum standards for the handling of juvenile offenders under any definition of a juvenile and under any system of dealing with juvenile offenders. The Rules are always to be applied impartially and without distinction of any kind.

Rule 2.1 therefore stresses the importance of the Rules always being applied impartially and without distinction of any kind. The rule follows the formulation of principle 2 of the Declaration of the Rights of the Child. Rule 2.2 defines "juvenile" and "offence" as the components of the notion of the "juvenile offender", who is the main subject of these Standard Minimum Rules (see, however, also rules 3 and 4). It should be noted that age limits will depend on, and are explicitly made dependent on, each respective legal system, thus fully respecting the economic, social, political, cultural and legal systems of Member States. This makes for a wide variety of ages coming under the definition of "juvenile", ranging from 7 years to 18 years or above. Such a variety seems inevitable in view of the different national legal systems and does not diminish the impact of these Standard Minimum Rules.

Rule 2.3 is addressed to the necessity of specific national legislation for the optimal implementation of these Standard Minimum Rules, both legally and practically.

3. Extension of the Rules

3.1 The relevant provisions of the Rules shall be applied not only to juvenile offenders but also to juveniles who may be proceeded against for any specific behaviour that would not be punishable if committed by an adult.
3.2 Efforts shall be made to extend the principles embodied in the Rules to all juveniles who are dealt with in welfare and care proceedings.
3.3 Efforts shall also be made to extend the principles embodied in the Rules to young adult offenders.

Commentary

Rule 3 extends the protection afforded by the Standard Minimum Rules for the Administration of Juvenile Justice to cover:

(a) The so-called "status offences" prescribed in various national legal systems where the range of behaviour considered to be an offence is wider for juveniles than it is for adults (for example, truancy, school and family disobedience, public drunkenness, etc.) (rule 3.1);

(b) Juvenile welfare and care proceedings (rule 3.2);

(c) Proceedings dealing with young adult offenders, depending of course on each given age limit (rule 3.3).

The extension of the Rules to cover these three areas seems to be justified. Rule 3.1 provides minimum guarantees in those fields, and rule 3.2 is considered a desirable step in the direction of more fair, equitable and humane justice for all juveniles in conflict with the law.

4. Age of criminal responsibility

4.1 In those legal systems recognizing the concept of the age of criminal responsibility for juveniles, the beginning of that age shall not be fixed at too low an age level, bearing in mind the facts of emotional, mental and intellectual maturity.

Commentary

The minimum age of criminal responsibility differs widely owing to history and culture. The modern approach would be to consider whether a child can live up to the moral and psychological components of criminal responsibility; that is, whether a child, by virtue of her or his individual discernment and understanding, can be held responsible for essentially antisocial behaviour. If the age of criminal responsibility is fixed too low or if there is no lower age limit at all, the notion of responsibility would become meaningless. In general, there is a close relationship between the notion of responsibility for delinquent or criminal behaviour and other social rights and responsibilities (such as marital status, civil majority, etc.).

Efforts should therefore be made to agree on a reasonable lowest age limit that is applicable internationally.

5. Aims of juvenile justice

5.1 The juvenile justice system shall emphasize the well-being of the juvenile and shall ensure that any reaction to juvenile offenders shall always be in proportion to the circumstances of both the offenders and the offence.

Commentary

Rule 5 refers to two of the most important objectives of juvenile justice. The first objective is the promotion of the well-being of the juvenile. This is the main focus of those legal systems in which juvenile offenders are dealt with by family courts or administrative authorities, but the well-being of the juvenile should also be emphasized in legal systems that follow the criminal court model, thus contributing to the avoidance of merely punitive sanctions. (See also rule 14.)

The second objective is "the principle of proportionality". This principle is well-known as an instrument for curbing punitive sanctions, mostly expressed in terms of just deserts in relation to the gravity of the offence. The response to young offenders should be based on the consideration not only of the gravity of the offence but also of personal circumstances. The individual circumstances of the offender (for example social status, family situation, the harm caused by the offence or other factors affecting personal circumstances) should influence the proportionality of the reactions (for example by having regard to the offender's endeavour to indemnify the victim or to her or his willingness to turn to wholesome and useful life).

By the same token, reactions aiming to ensure the welfare of the young offender may go beyond necessity and therefore infringe upon the fundamental rights of the young individual, as has been observed in some juvenile justice systems. Here, too, the proportionality of the reaction to the circumstances of both the offender and the offence, including the victim, should be safeguarded.

In essence, rule 5 calls for no less and no more than a fair reaction in any given cases of juvenile delinquency and crime. The issues combined in the rule may help to stimulate development in both regards: new and innovative types of reactions are as desirable as precautions against any undue widening of the net of formal social control over juveniles.

6. Scope of discretion

6.1 In view of the varying special needs of juveniles as well as the variety of measures available, appropriate scope for discretion shall be allowed at all stages of proceedings and at the different levels of juvenile justice administration, including investigation, prosecution, adjudication and the follow-up of dispositions.
6.2 Efforts shall be made, however, to ensure sufficient accountability at all stages and levels in the exercise of any such discretion.
6.3 Those who exercise discretion shall be specially qualified or trained to exercise it judiciously and in accordance with their functions and mandates.

Commentary

Rules 6.1, 6.2 and 6.3 combine several important features of effective, fair and humane juvenile justice administration: the need to permit the exercise of discretionary power at all significant levels of processing so that those who make determinations can take the actions deemed to be most appropriate in each individual case; and the need to provide checks and balances in order to curb any abuses of discretionary power and to safeguard the rights of the young offender. Accountability and professionalism are instruments best apt to curb broad discretion. Thus, professional qualifications and expert training are emphasized here as a valuable means of ensuring the judicious exercise of discretion in matters of juvenile offenders. (See also rules 1.6 and 2.2.) The formulation of specific guidelines on the exercise of discretion and the provision of systems of review, appeal and the like in order to permit scrutiny of decisions and accountability are emphasized in this context. Such mechanisms are not specified here, as they do not easily lend themselves to incorporation into international standard minimum rules, which cannot possibly cover all differences in justice systems.

7. Rights of juveniles

7.1 Basic procedural safeguards such as the presumption of innocence, the right to be notified of the charges, the right to remain silent, the right to counsel, the right to the presence of a parent or guardian, the right to confront and cross-examine witnesses and the right to appeal to a higher authority shall be guaranteed at all stages of proceedings.

Commentary

Rule 7.1 emphasizes some important points that represent essential elements for a fair and just trial and that are internationally recognized in existing human rights instruments (See also rule 14.). The presumption of innocence, for instance, is also to be found in article 11 of the Universal Declaration of Human Rights and in article 14, paragraph 2, of the International Covenant on Civil and Political Rights. Rules 14 seq. of these Standard Minimum Rules specify issues that are important for proceedings in juvenile cases, in particular, while rule 7.1 affirms the most basic procedural safeguards in a general way.

8. Protection of privacy

8.1 The juvenile's right to privacy shall be respected at all stages in order to avoid harm being caused to her or him by undue publicity or by the process of labelling.

8.2 In principle, no information that may lead to the identification of a juvenile offender shall be published.

Commentary

Rule 8 stresses the importance of the protection of the juvenile's right to privacy. Young persons are particularly susceptible to stigmatization. Criminological research into labelling processes has provided evidence of the detrimental effects (of different kinds) resulting from the permanent identification of young persons as "delinquent" or "criminal".

Rule 8 stresses the importance of protecting the juvenile from the adverse effects that may result from the publication in the mass media of information about the case (for example the names of young offenders, alleged or convicted). The interest of the individual should be protected and upheld, at least in principle (The general contents of rule 8 are further specified in rule 21.1.).

9. Saving clause

9.1 Nothing in these Rules shall be interpreted as precluding the application of the Standard Minimum Rules for the Treatment of Prisoners adopted by the United Nations and other human rights instruments and standards recognized by the international community that relate to the care and protection of the young.

Commentary

Rule 9 is meant to avoid any misunderstanding in interpreting and implementing the present Rules in conformity with principles contained in relevant existing or emerging international human rights instruments and standards-such as the Universal Declaration of Human Rights, the International Covenant on Economic, Social and Cultural Rights and the International Covenant on Civil and Political Rights, and the Declaration of the Rights of the Child and the draft convention on the rights of the child. It should be understood that the application of the present Rules is without prejudice to any such international instruments which may contain provisions of wider application (See also rule 27.).

PART TWO
INVESTIGATION AND PROSECUTION

10. Initial contact

10.1 Upon the apprehension of a juvenile, her or his parents or guardian shall be immediately notified of such apprehension, and, where such immediate notification is not possible, the parents or guardian shall be notified within the shortest possible time thereafter.

10.2 A judge or other competent official or body shall, without delay, consider the issue of release.

10.3 Contacts between the law enforcement agencies and a juvenile offender shall be managed in such a way as to respect the legal status of the juvenile, promote the well-being of the juvenile and avoid harm to her or him, with due regard to the circumstances of the case.

Commentary

Rule 10.1 is in principle contained in rule 92 of the Standard Minimum Rules for the Treatment of Prisoners.

The question of release (rule 10.2) shall be considered without delay by a judge or other competent official. The latter refers to any person or institution in the broadest sense of the term, including community boards or police authorities having power to release an arrested person. (See also the International Covenant on Civil and Political Rights, article 9, paragraph 3.)

Rule 10.3 deals with some fundamental aspects of the procedures and behaviour on the part of the police and other law enforcement officials in cases of juvenile crime. To "avoid harm" admittedly is flexible wording and covers many features of possible interaction (for example the use of harsh language, physical violence or exposure to the environment). Involvement in juvenile justice processes in itself can be "harmful" to juveniles; the term "avoid harm" should be broadly interpreted, therefore, as doing the least harm possible to the juvenile in the first instance, as well as any additional or undue harm. This is especially important in the initial contact with law enforcement agencies, which might profoundly influence the juvenile's attitude towards the State and society. Moreover, the success of any further intervention is largely dependent on such initial contacts. Compassion and kind firmness are important in these situations.

11. Diversion

11.1 Consideration shall be given, wherever appropriate, to dealing with juvenile offenders without resorting to formal trial by the competent authority, referred to in rule 14.1 below.

11.2 The police, the prosecution or other agencies dealing with juvenile cases shall be empowered to dispose of such cases, at their discretion, without recourse to formal hearings, in accordance with the criteria laid down for that purpose in the respective legal system and also in accordance with the principles contained in these Rules.

11.3 Any diversion involving referral to appropriate community or other services shall require the consent of the juvenile, or her or his parents or guardian, provided that such decision to refer a case shall be subject to review by a competent authority, upon application.

11.4 In order to facilitate the discretionary disposition of juvenile cases, efforts shall be made to provide for community programmes, such as temporary supervision and guidance, restitution, and compensation of victims.

Commentary

Diversion, involving removal from criminal justice processing and, frequently, redirection to community support services, is commonly practised on a formal and informal basis in many legal systems. This practice serves to hinder the negative effects of subsequent proceedings in juvenile justice administration (for example the stigma of conviction and sentence). In many cases, non-intervention would be the best response. Thus, diversion at the outset and without referral to alternative (social) services may be the optimal response. This is especially the case where the offence is of a non-serious nature and where the family, the school or other informal social control institutions have already reacted, or are likely to react, in an appropriate and constructive manner.

As stated in rule 11.2, diversion may be used at any point of decision-making by the police, the prosecution or other agencies such as the courts, tribunals, boards or councils. It may be exercised by one authority or several or all authorities, according to the rules and policies of the respective systems and in line with the present Rules. It need not necessarily be limited to petty cases, thus rendering diversion an important instrument.

Rule 11.3 stresses the important requirement of securing the consent of the young offender (or the parent or guardian) to the recommended diversionary measure(s). (Diversion to community service without such consent would contradict the Abolition of Forced Labour Convention.) However, this consent should not be left unchallengeable, since it might sometimes be given out of sheer desperation on the part of the juvenile. The rule underlines that care should be taken to minimize the potential for coercion and intimidation at all levels in the diversion process. Juveniles should not feel pressured (for example in order to avoid court appearance) or be pressured into consenting to diversion programmes. Thus, it is advocated that provision should be made for an objective appraisal of the appropriateness of dispositions involving young offenders by a "competent authority upon application". (The "competent authority", may be different from that referred to in rule 14.)

Rule 11.4 recommends the provision of viable alternatives to juvenile justice processing in the form of community-based diversion. Programmes that involve settlement by victim restitution and those that seek to avoid future conflict with the law through temporary supervision and guidance are especially commended. The merits of individual cases would make diversion appropriate, even when more serious offences have been committed (for example first offence, the act having been committed under peer pressure, etc.).

12. Specialization within the police

12.1 In order to best fulfil their functions, police officers who frequently or exclusively deal with juveniles or who are primarily engaged in the prevention of juvenile crime shall be specially instructed and trained. In large cities, special police units should be established for that purpose.

Commentary

Rule 12 draws attention to the need for specialized training for all law enforcement officials who are involved in the administration of juvenile justice. As police are the first point of contact with the juvenile justice system, it is most important that they act in an informed and appropriate manner.

While the relationship between urbanization and crime is clearly complex, an increase in juvenile crime has been associated with the growth of large cities, particularly with rapid and unplanned growth. Specialized police units would therefore be indispensable, not only in the interest of implementing specific principles contained in the present instrument (such as rule 1.6) but more generally for improving the prevention and control of juvenile crime and the handling of juvenile offenders.

13. Detention pending trial

13.1 Detention pending trial shall be used only as a measure of last resort and for the shortest possible period of time.

13.2 Whenever possible, detention pending trial shall be replaced by alternative measures, such as close supervision, intensive care or placement with a family or in an educational setting or home.

13.3 Juveniles under detention pending trial shall be entitled to all rights and guarantees of the Standard Minimum Rules for the Treatment of Prisoners adopted by the United Nations.

13.4 Juveniles under detention pending trial shall be kept separate from adults and shall be detained in a separate institution or in a separate part of an institution also holding adults.

13.5 While in custody, juveniles shall receive care, protection and all necessary individual assistance - social, educational, vocational, psychological, medical and physical-that they may require in view of their age, sex and personality.

Commentary

The danger to juveniles of "criminal contamination" while in detention pending trial must not be underestimated. It is therefore important to stress the need for alternative measures. By doing so, rule 13.1 encourages the devising of new and innovative measures to avoid such detention in the interest of the well-being of the juvenile. Juveniles under detention pending trial are entitled to all the rights and guarantees of the Standard Minimum Rules for the Treatment of Prisoners as well as the International Covenant on Civil and Political Rights, especially article 9 and article 10, paragraphs 2 (b) and 3.

Rule 13.4 does not prevent States from taking other measures against the negative influences of adult offenders which are at least as effective as the measures mentioned in the rule.

Different forms of assistance that may become necessary have been enumerated to draw attention to the broad range of particular needs of young detainees to be addressed (for example females or males, drug addicts, alcoholics, mentally ill juveniles, young persons suffering from the trauma, for example, of arrest, etc.).

Varying physical and psychological characteristics of young detainees may warrant classification measures by which some are kept separate while in detention pending trial, thus contributing to the avoidance of victimization and rendering more appropriate assistance.

The Sixth United Nations Congress on the Prevention of Crime and the Treatment of Offenders, in its resolution 4 on juvenile justice standards, specified that the Rules, *inter alia*, should reflect the basic principle that pre-trial detention should be used only as a last resort, that no minors should be held in a facility where they are vulnerable to the negative influences of adult detainees and that account should always be taken of the needs particular to their stage of development.

PART THREE

ADJUDICATION AND DISPOSITION

14. Competent authority to adjudicate

14.1 Where the case of a juvenile offender has not been diverted (under rule 11), she or he shall be dealt with by the competent authority (court, tribunal, board, council, etc.) according to the principles of a fair and just trial.

14.2 The proceedings shall be conducive to the best interests of the juvenile and shall be conducted in an atmosphere of understanding, which shall allow the juvenile to participate therein and to express herself or himself freely.

Commentary

It is difficult to formulate a definition of the competent body or person that would universally describe an adjudicating authority. "Competent authority" is meant to include those who preside over courts or tribunals (composed of a single judge or of several members), including professional and lay magistrates as well as administrative boards (for example the Scottish and Scandinavian systems) or other more informal community and conflict resolution agencies of an adjudicatory nature.

The procedure for dealing with juvenile offenders shall in any case follow the minimum standards that are applied almost universally for any criminal defendant under the procedure known as "due process of law". In accordance with due process, a "fair and just trial" includes such basic safeguards as the presumption of innocence, the presentation and examination of witnesses, the common legal defences, the right to remain silent, the right to have the last word in a hearing, the right to appeal, etc. (See also rule 7.1.)

15. Legal counsel, parents and guardians

15.1 Throughout the proceedings the juvenile shall have the right to be represented by a legal adviser or to apply for free legal aid where there is provision for such aid in the country.

15.2 The parents or the guardian shall be entitled to participate in the proceedings and may be required by the competent authority to attend them in the interest of the juvenile. They may, however, be denied participation by the competent authority if there are reasons to assume that such exclusion is necessary in the interest of the juvenile.

Commentary

Rule 15.1 uses terminology similar to that found in rule 93 of the Standard Minimum

Rules for the Treatment of Prisoners. Whereas legal counsel and free legal aid are needed to assure the juvenile legal assistance, the right of the parents or guardian to participate as stated in rule 15.2 should be viewed as general psychological and emotional assistance to the juvenile - a function extending throughout the procedure.

The competent authority's search for an adequate disposition of the case may profit, in particular, from the cooperation of the legal representatives of the juvenile (or, for that matter, some other personal assistant who the juvenile can and does really trust). Such concern can be thwarted if the presence of parents or guardians at the hearings plays a negative role, for instance, if they display a hostile attitude towards the juvenile, hence, the possibility of their exclusion must be provided for.

16. Social inquiry reports

16.1 In all cases except those involving minor offences, before the competent authority renders a final disposition prior to sentencing, the background and circumstances in which the juvenile is living or the conditions under which the offence has been committed shall be properly investigated so as to facilitate judicious adjudication of the case by the competent authority.

Commentary

Social inquiry reports (social reports or presentence reports) are an indispensable aid in most legal proceedings involving juveniles. The competent authority should be informed of relevant facts about the juvenile, such as social and family background, school career, educational experiences, etc. For this purpose, some jurisdictions use special social services or personnel attached to the court or board. Other personnel, including probation officers, may serve the same function. The rule therefore requires that adequate social services should be available to deliver social inquiry reports of a qualified nature.

17. Guiding principles in adjudication and disposition

17.1 The disposition of the competent authority shall be guided by the following principles:

(a) The reaction taken shall always be in proportion not only to the circumstances and the gravity of the offence but also to the circumstances and the needs of the juvenile as well as to the needs of the society;

(b) Restrictions on the personal liberty of the juvenile shall be imposed only after careful consideration and shall be limited to the possible minimum;

(c) Deprivation of personal liberty shall not be imposed unless the juvenile is adjudicated of a serious act involving violence against another person or of persistence in committing other serious offences and unless there is no other appropriate response;

(d) The well-being of the juvenile shall be the guiding factor in the consideration of her or his case.

17.2 Capital punishment shall not be imposed for any crime committed by juveniles.

17.3 Juveniles shall not be subject to corporal punishment.

17.4 The competent authority shall have the power to discontinue the proceedings at any time.

Commentary

The main difficulty in formulating guidelines for the adjudication of young persons stems from the fact that there are unresolved conflicts of a philosophical nature, such as the following:

(a) Rehabilitation versus just desert;

(b) Assistance versus repression and punishment;

(c) Reaction according to the singular merits of an individual case versus reaction according to the protection of society in general;

(d) General deterrence versus individual incapacitation.

The conflict between these approaches is more pronounced in juvenile cases than in adult cases. With the variety of causes and reactions characterizing juvenile cases, these alternatives become intricately interwoven.

It is not the function of the Standard Minimum Rules for the Administration of Juvenile Justice to prescribe which approach is to be followed but rather to identify one that is most closely in consonance with internationally accepted principles. Therefore the essential elements as laid down in rule 17.1 , in particular in subparagraphs (a) and (c), are mainly to be understood as practical guidelines that should ensure a common starting point; if heeded by the concerned authorities (see also rule 5), they could contribute considerably to ensuring that the fundamental rights of juvenile offenders are protected, especially the fundamental rights of personal development and education.

Rule 17.1 (b) implies that strictly punitive approaches are not appropriate. Whereas in adult cases, and possibly also in cases of severe offences by juveniles, just desert and retributive sanctions might be considered to have some merit, in juvenile cases such considerations should always be outweighed by the interest of safeguarding the well-being and the future of the young person.

In line with resolution 8 of the Sixth United Nations Congress, rule 17.1 (b) encourages the use of alternatives to institutionalization to the maximum extent possible, bearing in mind the need to respond to the specific requirements of the young. Thus, full use should be made of the range of existing alternative sanctions and new alternative sanctions should be developed, bearing the public safety in mind. Probation should be granted to the greatest possible extent via suspended sentences, conditional sentences, board orders and other dispositions.

Rule 17.1 (c) corresponds to one of the guiding principles in resolution 4 of the Sixth Congress which aims at avoiding incarceration in the case of juveniles unless there is no other appropriate response that will protect the public safety.

The provision prohibiting capital punishment in rule 17.2 is in accordance with article 6, paragraph 5, of the International Covenant on Civil and Political Rights.

The provision against corporal punishment is in line with article 7 of the International Covenant on Civil and Political Rights and the Declaration on the Protection of All Persons from Being Subjected to Torture and Other Cruel, Inhuman or Degrading Treatment or Punishment, as well as the Convention against Torture and Other Cruel, Inhuman or Degrading Treatment or Punishment and the draft convention on the rights of the child.

The power to discontinue the proceedings at any time (rule 17.4) is a characteristic inherent in the handling of juvenile offenders as opposed to adults. At any time, circumstances may become known to the competent authority which would make a complete cessation of the intervention appear to be the best disposition of the case.

18. Various disposition measures

18.1 A large variety of disposition measures shall be made available to the competent authority, allowing for flexibility so as to avoid institutionalization to the greatest extent possible. Such measures, some of which may be combined, include:

(a) Care, guidance and supervision orders;

(b) Probation;

(c) Community service orders;

(d) Financial penalties, compensation and restitution;

(e) Intermediate treatment and other treatment orders;

(f) Orders to participate in group counselling and similar activities;

(g) Orders concerning foster care, living communities or other educational settings;

(h) Other relevant orders.

18.2 No juvenile shall be removed from parental supervision, whether partly or entirely, unless the circumstances of her or his case make this necessary.

Commentary

Rule 18.1 attempts to enumerate some of the important reactions and sanctions that have been practised and proved successful thus far, in different legal systems. On the whole they represent promising opinions that deserve replication and further development. The rule does not enumerate staffing requirements because of possible shortages of adequate staff in some regions; in those regions measures requiring less staff may be tried or developed.

The examples given in rule 18.1 have in common, above all, a reliance on and an appeal to the community for the effective implementation of alternative dispositions. Community-based correction is a traditional measure that has taken on many aspects. On that basis, relevant authorities should be encouraged to offer community-based services.

Rule 18.2 points to the importance of the family which, according to article 10, paragraph 1, of the International Covenant on Economic, Social and Cultural Rights, is "the natural and fundamental group unit of society". Within the

family, the parents have not only the right but also the responsibility to care for and supervise their children. Rule 18.2, therefore, requires that the separation of children from their parents is a measure of last resort. It may be resorted to only when the facts of the case clearly warrant this grave step (for example child abuse).

19. Least possible use of institutionalization

19.1 The placement of a juvenile in an institution shall always be a disposition of last resort and for the minimum necessary period.

Commentary

Progressive criminology advocates the use of non-institutional over institutional treatment. Little or no difference has been found in terms of the success of institutionalization as compared to non-institutionalization. The many adverse influences on an individual that seem unavoidable within any institutional setting evidently cannot be outbalanced by treatment efforts. This is especially the case for juveniles, who are vulnerable to negative influences. Moreover, the negative effects, not only of loss of liberty but also of separation from the usual social environment, are certainly more acute for juveniles than for adults because of their early stage of development.

Rule 19 aims at restricting institutionalization in two regards: in quantity ("last resort") and in time ("minimum necessary period"). Rule 19 reflects one of the basic guiding principles of resolution 4 of the Sixth United Nations Congress: a juvenile offender should not be incarcerated unless there is no other appropriate response. The rule, therefore, makes the appeal that if a juvenile must be institutionalized, the loss of liberty should be restricted to the least possible degree, with special institutional arrangements for confinement and bearing in mind the differences in kinds of offenders, offences and institutions. In fact, priority should be given to "open" over "closed" institutions. Furthermore, any facility should be of a correctional or educational rather than of a prison type.

20. Avoidance of unnecessary delay

20.1 Each case shall from the outset be handled expeditiously, without any unnecessary delay.

Commentary

The speedy conduct of formal procedures in juvenile cases is a paramount concern. Otherwise whatever good may be achieved by the procedure and the disposition is at risk. As time passes, the juvenile will find it increasingly difficult, if not impossible, to relate the procedure and disposition to the offence, both intellectually and psychologically.

21. Records

21.1 Records of juvenile offenders shall be kept strictly confidential and closed to third parties. Access to such records shall be limited to persons directly concerned with the disposition of the case at hand or other duly authorized persons.

21.2 Records of juvenile offenders shall not be used in adult proceedings in subsequent cases involving the same offender.

Commentary

The rule attempts to achieve a balance between conflicting interests connected with records or files: those of the police, prosecution and other authorities in improving control versus the interests of the juvenile offender. (See also rule 8.) "Other duly authorized persons" would generally include among others, researchers.

22. Need for professionalism and training

22.1 Professional education, in-service training, refresher courses and other appropriate modes of instruction shall be utilized to establish and maintain the necessary professional competence of all personnel dealing with juvenile cases.

22.2 Juvenile justice personnel shall reflect the diversity of juveniles who come into contact with the juvenile justice system. Efforts shall be made to ensure the fair representation of women and minorities in juvenile justice agencies.

Commentary

The authorities competent for disposition may be persons with very different backgrounds (magistrates in the United Kingdom of Great Britain and Northern Ireland and in regions influenced by the common law system; legally trained judges in countries using Roman law and in regions influenced by them; and elsewhere elected or appointed laymen or jurists, members of community-based boards, etc.). For all these authorities, a minimum training in law, sociology, psychology, criminology and behavioural sciences would be required. This is considered as important as the organizational specialization and independence of the competent authority.

For social workers and probation officers, it might not be feasible to require professional specialization as a prerequisite for taking over any function dealing with juvenile offenders. Thus, professional on-the-job instruction would be minimum qualifications.

Professional qualifications are an essential element in ensuring the impartial and effective administration of juvenile justice. Accordingly, it is necessary to improve the recruitment, advancement and professional training of personnel and to provide them with the necessary means to enable them to properly fulfil their functions.

All political, social, sexual, racial, religious, cultural or any other kind of discrimination in the selection, appointment and advancement of juvenile justice personnel should be avoided in order to achieve impartiality in the administration of juvenile justice. This was recommended by the Sixth Congress. Furthermore, the Sixth Congress called on Member States to ensure the fair and equal treatment of women as criminal justice personnel and recommended that special measures should be taken to recruit, train and facilitate the advancement of female personnel in juvenile justice administration.

PART FOUR

NON-INSTITUTIONAL TREATMENT

23. Effective implementation of disposition

23.1 Appropriate provisions shall be made for the implementation of orders of the competent authority, as referred to in rule 14.1 above, by that authority itself or by some other authority as circumstances may require

23.2 Such provisions shall include the power to modify the orders as the competent authority may deem necessary from time to time, provided that such modification shall be determined in accordance with the principles contained in these Rules.

Commentary

Disposition in juvenile cases, more so than in adult cases, tends to influence the offender's life for a long period of time. Thus, it is important that the competent authority or an independent body (parole board, probation office, youth welfare institutions or others) with qualifications equal to those of the competent authority that originally disposed of the case should monitor the implementation of the disposition. In some countries, a *juge de l'exécution des peines* has been installed for this purpose.

The composition, powers and functions of the authority must be flexible; they are described in general terms in rule 23 in order to ensure wide acceptability.

24. Provision of needed assistance

24.1 Efforts shall be made to provide juveniles, at all stages of the proceedings, with necessary assistance such as lodging, education or vocational training, employment or any other assistance, helpful and practical, in order to facilitate the rehabilitative process.

Commentary

The promotion of the well-being of the juvenile is of paramount consideration. Thus, rule 24 emphasizes the importance of providing requisite facilities, services and other necessary assistance as may further the best interests of the juvenile throughout the rehabilitative process.

25. Mobilization of volunteers and other community services

25.1 Volunteers, voluntary organizations, local institutions and other community resources shall be called upon to contribute effectively to the rehabilitation of the juvenile in a community setting and, as far as possible, within the family unit.

Commentary

This rule reflects the need for a rehabilitative orientation of all work with juvenile offenders. Cooperation with the community is indispensable if the directives of the competent authority are to be carried out effectively. Volunteers and voluntary services, in particular, have proved to be valuable resources but are at present underutilized. In some instances, the cooperation of ex-offenders (including ex-addicts) can be of considerable assistance.

Rule 25 emanates from the principles laid down in rules 1.1 to 1.6 and follows the relevant provisions of the International Covenant on Civil and Political Rights.

PART FIVE

INSTITUTIONAL TREATMENT

26. Objectives of institutional treatment

26.1 The objective of training and treatment of juveniles placed in institutions is to provide care, protection, education and vocational skills, with a view to assisting them to assume socially constructive and productive roles in society.

26.2 Juveniles in institutions shall receive care, protection and all necessary assistance - social, educational, vocational, psychological, medical and physical - that they may require because of their age, sex, and personality and in the interest of their wholesome development.

26.3 Juveniles in institutions shall be kept separate from adults and shall be detained in a separate institution or in a separate part of an institution also holding adults.

26.4 Young female offenders placed in an institution deserve special attention as to their personal needs and problems. They shall by no means receive less care, protection, assistance, treatment and training than young male offenders. Their fair treatment shall be ensured.

26.5 In the interest and well-being of the institutionalized juvenile, the parents or guardians shall have a right of access.

26.6 Interministerial and interdepartmental cooperation shall be fostered for the purpose of providing adequate academic or, as appropriate, vocational training to institutionalized juveniles, with a view to ensuring that they do no leave the institution at an educational disadvantage.

Commentary

The objectives of institutional treatment as stipulated in rules 26.1 and 26.2 would be acceptable to any system and culture. However, they have not yet been attained everywhere, and much more has to be done in this respect. Medical and psychological assistance, in particular, are extremely important for institutionalized drug addicts, violent and mentally ill young persons.

The avoidance of negative influences through adult offenders and the safeguarding of the well-being of juveniles in an institutional setting, as stipulated in rule 26.3, are in line with one of the basic guiding principles of the Rules, as set out by the Sixth Congress in its resolution 4. The rule does not prevent States from taking other measures against the negative influences of adult offenders, which are at least as effective as the measures mentioned in the rule. (See also rule 13.4)

Rule 26.4 addresses the fact that female offenders normally receive less attention than their male counterparts, as pointed out by the Sixth Congress. In particular, resolution 9 of the Sixth Congress calls for the fair treatment of female offenders at every stage of criminal justice processes and for special attention to their particular problems and needs while in custody. Moreover, this rule should also be considered in the light of the Caracas Declaration of the Sixth Congress, which, *inter alia*, calls for equal treatment in criminal justice administration, and against the background of the Declaration on the Elimination of Discrimination against Women and the Convention on the Elimination of All Forms of Discrimination against Women.

The right of access (rule 26.5) follows from the provisions of rules 7.1, 10.1, 15.2 and 18.2. Interministerial and interdepartmental cooperation (rule 26.6) are of particular importance in the interest of generally enhancing the quality of institutional treatment and training.

27. Application of the Standard Minimum Rules for the Treatment of Prisoners adopted by the United Nations

27.1 The Standard Minimum Rules for the Treatment of Prisoners and related recommendations shall be applicable as far as relevant to the treatment of juvenile offenders in institutions, including those in detention pending adjudication.

27.2 Efforts shall be made to implement the relevant principles laid down in the Standard Minimum Rules for the Treatment of Prisoners to the largest possible extent so as to meet the varying needs of juveniles specific to their age, sex and personality.

Commentary

The Standard Minimum Rules for the Treatment of Prisoners were among the first instruments of this kind to be promulgated by the United Nations. It is generally agreed that they have had a world-wide impact. Although there are still countries where implementation is more an aspiration than a fact, those Standard Minimum Rules continue to be an important influence in the humane and equitable administration of correctional institutions.

Some essential protections covering juvenile offenders in institutions are contained in the Standard Minimum Rules for the Treatment of Prisoners (accommodation, architecture, bedding, clothing, complaints and requests, contact with the outside world, food, medical care, religious service, separation of ages, staffing, work, etc.) as are provisions concerning punishment and discipline, and restraint for dangerous offenders. It would not be appropriate to modify those Standard Minimum Rules according to the particular characteristics of institutions for juvenile offenders within the scope of the Standard Minimum Rules for the Administration of Juvenile Justice.

Rule 27 focuses on the necessary requirements for juveniles in institutions (rule 27.1) as well as on the varying needs specific to their age, sex and personality (rule 27.2). Thus, the objectives and content of the rule interrelate to the relevant provisions of the Standard Minimum Rules for the Treatment of Prisoners.

28. Frequent and early recourse to conditional release

28.1 Conditional release from an institution shall be used by the appropriate authority to the greatest possible extent, and shall be granted at the earliest possible time.

28.2 Juveniles released conditionally from an institution shall be assisted and supervised by an appropriate authority and shall receive full support by the community.

Commentary

The power to order conditional release may rest with the competent authority, as mentioned in rule 14.1 or with some other authority. In view of this, it is adequate to refer here to the "appropriate", rather than to the "competent" authority.

Circumstances permitting, conditional release shall be preferred to serving a full sentence. Upon evidence of satisfactory progress towards rehabilitation, even offenders who had been deemed dangerous at the time of their institutionalization can be conditionally released whenever feasible. Like probation, such release may be conditional on the satisfactory fulfilment of the requirements specified by the relevant authorities for a period of time established in the decision, for example relating to "good behaviour" of the offender, attendance in community programmes, residence in half-way houses, etc.

In the case of offenders conditionally released from an institution, assistance and supervision by a probation or other officer (particularly where probation has not yet been adopted) should be provided and community support should be encouraged.

29. Semi-institutional arrangements

29.1 Efforts shall be made to provide semi-institutional arrangements, such as half-way houses, educational homes, day-time training centres and other such appropriate arrangements that may assist juveniles in their proper reintegration into society.

Commentary

The importance of care following a period of institutionalization should not be underestimated. This rule emphasizes the necessity of forming a net of semi-institutional arrangements.

This rule also emphasizes the need for a diverse range of facilities and services designed to meet the different needs of young offenders re-entering the community and to provide guidance and structural support as an important step towards successful reintegration into society.

PART SIX

RESEARCH, PLANNING, POLICY FORMULATION AND EVALUATION

30. Research as a basis for planning, policy formulation and evaluation

30.1 Efforts shall be made to organize and promote necessary research as a basis for effective planning and policy formulation.

30.2 Efforts shall be made to review and appraise periodically the trends, problems and causes of juvenile delinquency and crime as well as the varying particular needs of juveniles in custody.

30.3 Efforts shall be made to establish a regular evaluative research mechanism built into the system of juvenile justice administration and to collect and analyse relevant data and information for appropriate assessment and future improvement and reform of the administration.

30.4 The delivery of services in juvenile justice administration shall be systematically planned and implemented as an integral part of national development efforts.

Commentary

The utilization of research as a basis for an informed juvenile justice policy is widely acknowledged as an important mechanism for keeping practices abreast of advances in knowledge and the continuing development and improvement of the juvenile justice system. The mutual feedback between research and policy is especially important in juvenile justice. With rapid and often drastic changes in the life-styles of the young and in the forms and dimensions of juvenile crime, the societal and justice responses to juvenile crime and delinquency quickly become outmoded and inadequate.

Rule 30 thus establishes standards for integrating research into the process of policy formulation and application in juvenile justice administration. The rule draws particular attention to the need for regular review and evaluation of existing programmes and measures and for planning within the broader context of overall development objectives.

A constant appraisal of the needs of juveniles, as well as the trends and problems of delinquency, is a prerequisite for improving the methods of formulating appropriate policies and establishing adequate interventions, at both formal and informal levels. In this context, research by independent persons and bodies should be facilitated by responsible agencies, and it may be valuable to obtain and to take into account the views of juveniles themselves, not only those who come into contact with the system.

The process of planning must particularly emphasize a more effective and equitable system for the delivery of necessary services. Towards that end, there should be a comprehensive and regular assessment of the wide-ranging, particular needs and problems of juveniles and an identification of clear-cut priorities. In that connection, there should also be a coordination in the use of existing resources, including alternatives and community support that would be suitable in setting up specific procedures designed to implement and monitor established programmes.

United Nations Guidelines for the Prevention of Juvenile Delinquency

(The Riyadh Guidelines)

Adopted and proclaimed by General Assembly resolution 45/112 of 14 December 1990

The General Assembly,

Bearing in mind the Universal Declaration of Human Rights, the International Covenant on Economic, Social and Cultural Rights and the International Covenant on Civil and Political Rights, as well as other international instruments pertaining to the rights and well-being of young persons, including relevant standards established by the International Labour Organization,

Bearing in mind also the Declaration of the Rights of the Child*, the Convention on the Rights of the Child, and the United Nations Standard Minimum Rules for the Administration of juvenile justice (The Beijing Rules),

Recalling General Assembly resolution 40/33 of 29 November 1983, in which the Assembly adopted the United Nations Standard Minimum Rules for the Administration of Juvenile Justice recommended by the Seventh United Nations Congress on the Prevention of Crime and the Treatment of Offenders,

Recalling also that the General Assembly, in its resolution 40/35 of 29 November 1985, called for the development of standards for the prevention of juvenile delinquency which would assist Member States in formulating and implementing specialized programmes and policies, emphasizing assistance, care and community involvement, and called upon the Economic And Social Council to report to the Eighth United Nations Congress on the Prevention of Crime and the Treatment of Offenders on the progress achieved with respect to the standards, for review and action,

Recalling further that the Economic and Social Council, in resolution 1986/10 of 21 May 1986, requested the Eighth Congress

to consider the standards for the prevention of juvenile delinquency, with the view to adoption,

Recognizing the need to develop national, regional and international approaches and strategies for the prevention of juvenile delinquency,

Affirming that every child has basic human rights, including, in particular, access to free education,

Mindful of the large number of young persons who may or may not be in conflict with law but who are abandoned, neglected, abused, exposed to drug abuse, in marginal circumstances, and who are in general at social risk,

Taking into account the benefits of progressive policies for the prevention of delinquency and the welfare of the community,

1. *Notes* with satisfaction the substantive work accomplished by the Committee on Crime Prevention and Control and the Secretary-General in the formulation of the guidelines for the prevention of juvenile delinquency;

2. *Expresses* appreciation for the valuable collaboration of the Security Studies and Training Centre at Riyadh, in hosting International Meeting of Experts on Juvenile Delinquency, held at Riyadh from 28 February to 1 March 1988, in cooperation with the United Nations Office at Vienna;

3. *Adopts* the United Nations Guidelines for the Prevention of Delinquency contained in the annex to the present resolution, to be called the Riyadh Guidelines

4. *Calls upon* Member States, in their comprehensive crime prevention plans, to apply the Guidelines in national law, policy and practice and bring the Guidelines to the attention of the relevant authorities, including policy makers, juvenile justi-

ce ersonnel, educators, the mass media, practitioners and scholars;

5. *Requests* the Secretary-General and invites Member States to ensure the widest possible dissemination of the text of the Guidelines in all official languages of the United Nations;

6. *Further requests* the Secretary-General and invites all relevant United Nations offices and interested institutions, in particular, the United Nations Children's Fund, as well as individual experts, to make a concerted effort to promote the application of the Guidelines;

7. *Also requests* the Secretary-General to intensify research on particular situations of social risk and on the exploitation of children, including the use of children as instruments of criminality, with a view to developing comprehensive countermeasures and to report thereon to the Ninth United Nations Congress on the Prevention of Crime and the Treatment of Offenders;

8. *Further requests* the Secretary-General to issue a composite manual on juvenile justice standards, containing the United Nations Standard Minimum Rules Guidelines on the Prevention of Juvenile Delinquency (The Riyadh Guideline), and the United Nations Rules for the Protection of Juveniles Deprived of their Liberty*, and a set of full commentaries on their provisions;

9. *Urges* all relevant bodies within the United Nations system to collaborate with the Secretary-General in taking appro-

priate measures to ensure the implementation of the present resolutions;

10. *Invites* the Sub-Commission on Prevention of Discrimination and Protection of Minorities of the Commission on Human Rights to consider this new international instrument with a view to promoting the application of its provisions;

11. *Invites* Member States to support strongly the organization of technical and scientific workshops, and pilot and demonstration projects on practical issues and policy matters relating to the application of the provisions of the Guidelines and to the establishment of concrete matters for community-based services designed to respond to the special needs, problems and concerns of young persons, and requests the Secretary-General to co-ordinate efforts in this respect;

12. *Also invites* Member States to inform the Secretary-General on theimplementation of the Guidelines and to report regularly to the Committee on Crime Prevention and Control on the results achieved;

13. *Recommends* that the Committee on Crime Prevention and Control request the Ninth Congress to review the progress made in the promotion and application of the Riyadh Guidelines and the recommendations contained in the present resolution, under separate agenda item on juvenile justice and keep the matter under constant review.

I. FUNDAMENTAL PRINCIPLES

1. The prevention of juvenile delinquency is an essential part of crime prevention in society. By engaging in lawful, socially useful activities and adopting a humanistic orientation towards society and outlook on life, young persons can develop non-criminogenic attitudes.

2. The successful prevention of juvenile delinquency requires efforts on the part of the entire society to ensure the harmonious development of adolescents, with respect for and promotion of their personality from early childhood.

3. For the purposes of the interpretation of the present Guidelines, a child-centred orientation should be pursued. Young persons should have an active role and partnership within society and should not be considered as mere objects of socialization or control.

4. In the implementation of the present Guidelines, in accordance with national legal systems, the well-being of young persons from their early childhood should be the focus of any preventive programme.

5. The need for and importance of progressive delinquency prevention policies and the systematic study and the elaboration of measures should be recognized. These should avoid criminalizing and penalizing a child for behaviour that does not cause serious damage to the development of the child or harm to others. Such policies and measures should involve:

(a) The provision of opportunities, in particular educational opportunities, to meet the varying needs of young persons and to serve as a supportive framework for safeguarding the personal development of all young persons, particularly those who are demonstrably endangered or at social risk and are in need of special care and protection;

(b) Specialized philosophies and approaches for delinquency prevention, on the basis of laws, processes, institutions, facilities and a service delivery network aimed at reducing the motivation, need and opportunity for, or conditions giving rise to, the commission of infractions;

(c) Official intervention to be pursued primarily in the overall interest of the young person and guided by fairness and equity;

(d) Safeguarding the well-being, development, rights and interests of all young persons;

(e) Consideration that youthful behaviour or conduct that does not conform to overall social norms and values is often part of the maturation and growth process and tends to disappear spontaneously in most individuals with the transition to adulthood;

(f) Awareness that, in the predominant opinion of experts, labelling a young person as "deviant", "delinquent" or "predelinquent" often contributes to the development of a consistent pattern of undesirable behaviour by young persons.

6. Community-based services and programmes should be developed for the prevention of juvenile delinquency, particularly where no agencies have yet been established. Formal agencies of social control should only be utilized as a means of last resort.

II. SCOPE OF THE GUIDELINES

7. The present Guidelines should be interpreted and implemented within the broad framework of the Universal Declaration of Human Rights, the International Covenant on Economic, Social and Cultural Rights, the International Covenant on Civil and Political Rights, the Declaration of the Rights of the Child and the Convention on the Rights of the Child, and in the context of the United Nations Standard Minimum Rules for the Administration of Juvenile Justice (The Beijing Rules), as well as other instruments and norms relating to the rights, interests and well-being of all children and young persons.

8. The present Guidelines should also be implemented in the context of the economic, social and cultural conditions prevailing in each Member State.

III. GENERAL PREVENTION

9. Comprehensive prevention plans should be instituted at every level of Government and include the following:

(a) In-depth analyses of the problem and inventories of programmes, services, facilities and resources available;

(b) Well-defined responsibilities for the qualified agencies, institutions and personnel involved in preventive efforts;

(c) Mechanisms for the appropriate coordination of prevention efforts between governmental and non-governmental agencies;

(d) Policies, programmes and strategies based on prognostic studies to be continuously monitored and carefully evaluated in the course of implementation;

(e) Methods for effectively reducing the opportunity to commit delinquent acts;

(f) Community involvement through a wide range of services and programmes;

(g) Close interdisciplinary cooperation between national, State, provincial and local governments, with the involvement of the private sector representative citizens of the community to be served, and labour, child-care, health education, social, law enforcement and judicial agencies in taking concerted action to prevent juvenile delinquency and youth crime;

(h) Youth participation in delinquency prevention policies and processes, including recourse to community resources, youth self-help, and victim compensation and assistance programmes;

(i) Specialized personnel at all levels.

IV. SOCIALIZATION PROCESSES

10. Emphasis should be placed on preventive policies facilitating the successful socialization and integration of all children and young persons, in particular through the family, the community, peer groups, schools, vocational training and the world of work, as well as through voluntary organizations. Due respect should be given to the proper personal development of children and young persons, and they should be accepted as full and equal partners in socialization and integration processes.

A. Family

11. Every society should place a high priority on the needs and well-being of the family and of all its members.

12. Since the family is the central unit responsible for the primary socialization of children, governmental and social efforts to preserve the integrity of the family, including the extended family, should be pursued. The society has a responsibility to assist the family in providing care and protection and in ensuring the physical and mental well-being of children. Adequate arrangements including day-care should be provided.

13. Governments should establish policies that are conducive to the bringing up of children in stable and settled family environments. Families in need of assistance in the resolution of conditions of instability or conflict should be provided with requisite services.

14. Where a stable and settled family environment is lacking and when community efforts to assist parents in this regard have failed and the extended family cannot fulfil this role, alternative placements, including foster care and adoption, should be considered. Such placements should replicate, to the extent possible, a stable and settled family environment, while, at the same time, establishing a sense of permanency for children, thus avoiding problems associated with "foster drift".

15. Special attention should be given to children of families affected by problems brought about by rapid and uneven economic, social and cultural change, in particular the children of indigenous, migrant and refugee families. As such changes may disrupt the social capacity of the family to secure the traditional rearing and nurturing of children, often as a result of role and culture conflict, innovative and socially constructive modalities for the socialization of children have to be designed.

16. Measures should be taken and programmes developed to provide families with the opportunity to learn about parental roles and obligations as regards child development and child care, promoting positive parent-child relationships, sensitizing parents to the problems of children and young persons and encouraging their involvement in family and community-based activities.

17. Governments should take measures to promote family cohesion and harmony and to discourage the separation of children from their parents, unless circumstances affecting the welfare and future of the child leave no viable alternative.

18. It is important to emphasize the socialization function of the family and extended family; it is also equally important to recognize the future role, responsibilities, participation and partnership of young persons in society.

19. In ensuring the right of the child to proper socialization, Governments and other agencies should rely on existing social and legal agencies, but, whenever traditional institutions and customs are no longer effective, they should also provide and allow for innovative measures.

B. Education

20. Governments are under an obligation to make public education accessible to all young persons.

21. Education systems should, in addition to their academic and vocational training activities, devote particular attention to the following:

(a) Teaching of basic values and developing respect for the child's own cultural identity and patterns, for the social values of the country in which the child is living, for civilizations different from the child's own and for human rights and fundamental freedoms;

(b) Promotion and development of the personality, talents and mental and physical abilities of young people to their fullest potential;

(c) Involvement of young persons as active and effective participants in, rather than mere objects of, the educational process;

(d) Undertaking activities that foster a sense of identity with and of belonging to the school and the community;

(e) Encouragement of young persons to understand and respect diverse views and opinions, as well as cultural and other differences;

(f) Provision of information and guidance regarding vocational training, employment opportunities and career development;

(g) Provision of positive emotional support to young persons and the avoidance of psychological maltreatment;

(h) Avoidance of harsh disciplinary measures, particularly corporal punishment.

22. Educational systems should seek to work together with parents, community organizations and agencies concerned with the activities of young persons.

23. Young persons and their families should be informed about the law and their rights and responsibilities under the law, as well as the universal value system, including United Nations instruments.

24. Educational systems should extend particular care and attention to young persons who are at social risk. Specialized prevention programmes and educational materials, curricula, approaches and tools should be developed and fully utilized.

25. Special attention should be given to comprehensive policies and strategies for the prevention of alcohol, drug and other substance abuse by young persons. Teachers and other professionals should be equipped and trained to prevent and deal with these problems. Information on the use and abuse of drugs, including alcohol, should be made available to the student body.

26. Schools should serve as resource and referral centres for the provision of medical, counselling and other services to young persons, particularly those with special needs and suffering from abuse, neglect, victimization and exploitation.

27. Through a variety of educational programmes, teachers and other adults and the student body should be sensitized to the problems, needs and perceptions of young persons, particularly those belonging to underprivileged, disadvantaged, ethnic or other minority and low-income groups.

28. School systems should attempt to meet and promote the highest professional and educational standards with respect to curricula, teaching and learning methods and approaches, and the recruitment and training of qualified teachers. Regular monitoring and assessment of performance by the appropriate professional organizations and authorities should be ensured.

29. School systems should plan, develop and implement extracurricular activities of interest to young persons, in co-operation with community groups.

30. Special assistance should be given to children and young persons who find it difficult to comply with attendance codes, and to "drop-outs".

31. Schools should promote policies and rules that are fair and just; students should be represented in bodies formulating school policy, including policy on discipline, and decision-making.

C. Community

32. Community-based services and programmes which respond to the special needs, problems,

interests and concerns of young persons and which offer appropriate counselling and guidance to young persons and their families should be developed, or strengthened where they exist.

33. Communities should provide, or strengthen where they exist, a wide range of community-based support measures for young persons, including community development centres, recreational facilities and services to respond to the special problems of children who are at social risk. In providing these helping measures, respect for individual rights should be ensured.

34. Special facilities should be set up to provide adequate shelter for young persons who are no longer able to live at home or who do not have homes to live in.

35. A range of services and helping measures should be provided to deal with the difficulties experienced by young persons in the transition to adulthood. Such services should include special programmes for young drug abusers which emphasize care, counselling, assistance and therapy-oriented interventions.

36. Voluntary organizations providing services for young persons should be given financial and other support by Governments and other institutions.

37. Youth organizations should be created or strengthened at the local level and given full participatory status in the management of community affairs. These organizations should encourage youth to organize collective and voluntary projects, particularly projects aimed at helping young persons in need of assistance.

38. Government agencies should take special responsibility and provide necessary services for homeless or street children; information about local facilities, accommodation, employment and other forms and sources of help should be made readily available to young persons.

39. A wide range of recreational facilities and services of particular interest to young persons should be established and made easily accessible to them.

D. Mass media

40. The mass media should be encouraged to ensure that young persons have access to information and material from a diversity of national and international sources.

41. The mass media should be encouraged to portray the positive contribution of young persons to society.

42. The mass media should be encouraged to disseminate information on the existence of services, facilities and opportunities for young persons in society.

43. The mass media generally, and the television and film media in particular, should be encouraged to minimize the level of pornography, drugs and violence portrayed and to display violence and exploitation disfavourably, as well as to avoid demeaning and degrading presentations, especially of children, women and interpersonal relations, and to promote egalitarian principles and roles.

44. The mass media should be aware of its extensive social role and responsibility, as well as its influence, in communications relating to youthful drug and alcohol abuse. It should use its power for drug abuse prevention by relaying consistent messages through a balanced approach. Effective drug awareness campaigns at all levels should be promoted.

V. SOCIAL POLICY

45. Government agencies should give high priority to plans and programmes for young persons and should provide sufficient funds and other resources for the effective delivery of services, facilities and staff for adequate medical and mental health care, nutrition, housing and other relevant services, including drug and alcohol abuse prevention and treatment, ensuring that such resources reach and actually benefit young persons.

46. The institutionalization of young persons should be a measure of last resort and for the minimum necessary period, and the best interests of the young person should be of paramount importance. Criteria authorizing formal intervention of this type should be strictly defined and limited to the following situations: (a) where the child or young person has suffered harm that has been inflicted by the parents or guardians; (b) where the child or young person has been sexually, physically or emotionally abused by the parents or guardians; (c) where the child or young person has been neglected, abandoned or exploited by the parents or guardians; (d) where the child or young person is threatened by physical or moral danger due to the behaviour of the parents or guardians; and (e) where a serious physical or psychological danger to the child or young person has manifested itself in his or her own behaviour and neither the parents, the guardians, the juvenile himself or herself nor non-residential community services can meet the danger by means other than institutionalization.

47. Government agencies should provide young persons with the opportunity of continuing in full-time education, funded by the State where parents or guardians are unable to support the young persons, and of receiving work experience.

48. Programmes to prevent delinquency should be planned and developed on the basis of reliable, scientific research findings, and periodically monitored, evaluated and adjusted accordingly.

49. Scientific information should be disseminated to the professional community and to the public at large about the sort of behaviour or situation which indicates or may result in physical and psychological victimization, harm and abuse, as well as exploitation, of young persons.

50. Generally, participation in plans and programmes should be voluntary. Young persons themselves should be involved in their formulation, development and implementation.

51. Government should begin or continue to explore, develop and implement policies, measures and strategies within and outside the criminal justice system to prevent domestic violence against and affecting young persons and to ensure fair treatment to these victims of domestic violence.

VI. LEGISLATION AND JUVENILE JUSTICE ADMINISTRATION

52. Governments should enact and enforce specific laws and procedures to promote and protect the rights and well-being of all young persons.

53. Legislation preventing the victimization, abuse, exploitation and the use for criminal activities of children and young persons should be enacted and enforced.

54. No child or young person should be subjected to harsh or degrading correction or punishment measures at home, in schools or in any other institutions.

55. Legislation and enforcement aimed at restricting and controlling accessibility of weapons of any sort to children and young persons should be pursued.

56. In order to prevent further stigmatization, victimization and criminalization of young persons, legislation should be enacted to ensure that any conduct not considered an offence or not penalized if committed by an adult is not considered an offence and not penalized if committed by a young person.

57. Consideration should be given to the establishment of an office of ombudsman or similar independent organ, which would ensure that the status, rights and interests of young persons are upheld and that proper referral to available services is made. The ombudsman or other organ designated would also supervise the implementation of the Riyadh Guidelines, the Beijing Rules and the Rules for the Protection of Juveniles Deprived of their Liberty. The ombudsman or other organ would, at regular intervals, publish a report on the progress made and on the difficulties encountered in the implementation of the instrument. Child advocacy services should also be established.

58. Law enforcement and other relevant personnel, of both sexes, should be trained to respond to the special needs of young persons and should be familiar with and use, to the maximum extent possible, programmes and referral possibilities for the diversion of young persons from the justice system.

59. Legislation should be enacted and strictly enforced to protect children and young persons from drug abuse and drug traffickers.

VII. RESEARCH, POLICY DEVELOPMENT AND COORDINATION

60. Efforts should be made and appropriate mechanisms established to promote, on both a multidisciplinary and an intradisciplinary basis, interaction and coordination between economic, social, education and health agencies and services, the justice system, youth, community and development agencies and other relevant institutions.

61. The exchange of information, experience and expertise gained through projects, programmes, practices and initiatives relating to youth crime, delinquency prevention and juve-

nile justice should be intensified at the national, regional and international levels.

62. Regional and international cooperation on matters of youth crime, delinquency prevention and juvenile justice involving practitioners, experts and decision makers should be further developed and strengthened.

63. Technical and scientific cooperation on practical and policy-related matters, particularly in training, pilot and demonstration projects, and on specific issues concerning the prevention of youth crime and juvenile delin- quency should be strongly supported by all Governments, the United Nations system and other concerned organizations.

64. Collaboration should be encouraged in undertaking scientific research with respect to effective modalities for youth crime and juvenile delinquency prevention and the findings of such research should be widely disseminated and evaluated.

65. Appropriate United Nations bodies, institutes, agencies and offices should pursue close collaboration and coordination on various questions related to children juvenile justice and youth crime and juvenile delinquency prevention.

66. On the basis of the present Guidelines, the United Nations Secretariat, in cooperation with interested institutions, should play an active role in the conduct of research, scientific collaboration, the formulation of policy options and the review and monitoring of their implementation, and should serve as a source of reliable information on effective modalities for delinquency prevention.

United Nations Rules for the Protection of Juveniles Deprived of their Liberty

Adopted by General Assembly resolution 45/113 of 14 December 1990

Preamble

The General Assembly,

Bearing in mind the Universal Declaration of Human Rights, the Convention against Torture and Other Cruel, Inhuman or Degrading Treatment or Punishment and the Convention on the Rights of the Child, as well as other international instruments relating to the protection of the rights and well-being of young persons,

Bearing in mind also the Standard Minimum Rules for the Treatment of Prisoners adopted by the First United Nations Congress on the Prevention of Crime and Treatment of Offenders,

Bearing in mind further the Body of Principles for the Protection of All Persons under Any Form of Detention or Imprisonment, approved by the General Assembly by its resolution 43/173 of 9 December 1988 and contained in the annex thereto,

Recalling the United Nations Standard Minimum Rules for the Administration of Juvenile Justice (The Beijing Rules),

Recalling also resolution 21 of the Seventh United Nations Congress on the Prevention of Crime and the Treatment of Offenders, in which the Congress called for the development of rules for the protection of juveniles deprived of their liberty,

Recalling further that the economic and Social Council, in section II of its resolution 1986/10 of 21 May 1986, requested the Secretary-General to report on progress achieved in the development of the rules to the Committee on Crime Prevention and Control at its tenth session and requested the Eighth United Nations Congress on the Prevention of Crime

and the Treatment of Offenders to consider the proposed rules with a view to their adoption,

Alarmed at the conditions and circumstances under which juveniles are being deprived of their liberty world wide,

Aware that juveniles deprived of their liberty are highly vulnerable to abuse, victimization and the violation of their rights,

Concerned that many systems do not differentiate between adults and juveniles at various of stages of the administration of justice and that juveniles are therefore being held in jails and facilities with adults,

1. *Affirms* that the placement of a juvenile in an institution should always be a disposition of last resort and for the minimum necessary period;

2. *Recognizes* that, because of their high vulnerability, juveniles deprived of their liberty require special attention and protection and that their rights and well-being should be guaranteed during and after the period when they are deprived of their liberty;

3. *Notes with appreciation* the valuable work of the Secretariat and the collaboration which has been established between the Secretariat and experts, practitioners, intergovernmental organizations, the non-governmental community, particularly Amnesty International, Defense for Children International and Rädda Barnen International (Swedish Save the Children Federation), and scientific institutions concerned with the rights of children and juvenile justice in the development of United Nations draft Rules for the Protection of Juveniles Deprived of their Liberty;

4. *Adopts* the United Nations Rules for the Protection of Juveniles Deprived of their Liberty contained in the annex to the present resolution;

5. *Calls upon* the Committee on Crime Prevention and Control to formulate measures for the effective implementation of the Rules, with the assistance of the United Nations institutes on the prevention of crime and the treatment of offenders;

6. *Invites* Member States to adapt, wherever necessary, their national legislation, policies and practices, particularly in the training of all categories of juvenile justice personnel, to the spirit of the Rules, and to bring them to the attention of relevant authorities and the public in general;

7. *Also invites* Member States to inform the Secretary-General of their efforts to apply the Rules in law, policy and practice and to report regularly to the Committee on Crime Prevention and Control on the results achieved in their implementation;

8. *Requests* the Secretary-General and invites Member States to ensure the widest possible dissemination of the text of the Rules in all of the official languages of the United Nations;

9. *Requests* the Secretary-General to conduct comparative research, pursue the requisite collaboration and devise strategies to deal with the different categories of serious and persistent young offenders, and to prepare a policy-oriented report thereon for submission to the Ninth United Nations Congress on the Prevention of Crime and the Treatment of Offenders;

10. *Also requests* the Secretary-General and urges Member States to allocate the necessary resources to ensure the successful application and implementation of the Rules, in particular in the areas of recruitment, training and exchange of all categories of juvenile justice personnel;

11. *Urges* all relevant bodies of the United Nations system, in particular the United Nations Children's Fund, the regional commissions and specialized agencies, the United Nations institutes for the prevention of crime and the treatment of offenders and all concerned intergovernmental and non-governmental organization, to collaborate with the Secretary-General and to take the necessary measures to ensure a concerted and sustained effort within their respective fields of technical competence to promote the application of the Rules;

12. *Invites* the Sub-Commission on Prevention of Discrimination and Protection of Minorities of the Commission on Human Rights to consider this new international instrument, with a view to promoting the application of its provisions;

13. *Requests* the Ninth Congress to review the progress made on the promotion and application of the Rules and on the recommendations contained in the present resolution, under a separate agenda item on juvenile justice.

I. FUNDAMENTAL PERSPECTIVES

1. The juvenile justice system should uphold the rights and safety and promote the physical and mental well-being of juveniles. Imprisonment should be used as a last resort.

2. Juveniles should only be deprived of their liberty in accordance with the principles and procedures set forth in these Rules and in the United Nations Standard Minimum Rules for the Administration of Juvenile Justice (The Beijing Rules). Deprivation of the liberty of a juvenile should be a disposition of last resort and for the minimum necessary period and should be limited to exceptional cases. The length of the sanction should be determined by the judicial authority, without precluding the possibility of his or her early release.

3. The Rules are intended to establish minimum standards accepted by the United Nations for the protection of juveniles deprived of their liberty in all forms, consistent with human rights and fundamental freedoms, and with a view to counteracting the detrimental effects of all types of detention and to fostering integration in society.

4. The Rules should be applied impartially, without discrimination of any kind as to race, colour, sex, age, language, religion, nationality, political or other opinion, cultural beliefs or practices, property, birth or family status, ethnic or social origin, and disability. The religious and cultural beliefs, practices and moral concepts of the juvenile should be respected.

5. The Rules are designed to serve as convenient standards of reference and to provide encouragement and guidance to professionals involved in the management of the juvenile justice system.

6. The Rules should be made readily available to juvenile justice personnel in their national languages. Juveniles who are not fluent in the language spoken by the personnel of the detention facility should have the right to the services of an interpreter free of charge whenever necessary, in particular during medical examinations and disciplinary proceedings.

7. Where appropriate, States should incorporate the Rules into their legislation or amend it accordingly and provide effective remedies for their breach, including compensation when injuries are inflicted on juveniles. States should also monitor the application of the Rules.

8. The competent authorities should constantly seek to increase the awareness of the public that the care of detained juveniles and preparation for their return to society is a social service of great importance, and to this end active steps should be taken to foster open contacts between the juveniles and the local community.

9. Nothing in the Rules should be interpreted as precluding the application of the relevant United Nations and human rights instruments and standards, recognized by the international community, that are more conducive to ensuring the rights, care and protection of juveniles, children and all young persons.

10. In the event that the practical application of particular Rules contained in sections II to V, inclusive, presents any conflict with the Rules contained in the present section, compliance with the latter shall be regarded as the predominant requirement.

II. SCOPE AND APPLICATION OF THE RULES

11. For the purposes of the Rules, the following definitions should apply:

(a) A juvenile is every person under the age of 18. The age limit below which it should not be permitted to deprive a child of his or her liberty should be determined by law;

(b) The deprivation of liberty means any form of detention or imprisonment or the placement of a person in a public or private custodial setting, from which this person is not permitted to leave at will, by order of any judicial, administrative or other public authority.

12. The deprivation of liberty should be effected in conditions and circumstances which ensure respect for the human rights of juveniles. Juveniles detained in facilities should be guaranteed the benefit of meaningful activities and programmes which would serve to promote and sustain their health and self-respect, to foster their sense of responsibility and encourage those attitudes and skills that will assist them in developing their potential as members of society.

13. Juveniles deprived of their liberty shall not for any reason related to their status be denied the civil, economic, political, social or cultural rights to which they are entitled under national or international law, and which are compatible with the deprivation of liberty.

14. The protection of the individual rights of juveniles with special regard to the legality of the execution of the detention measures shall be ensured by the competent authority, while the objectives of social integration should be secured by regular inspections and other means of control carried out, according to international standards, national laws and regulations, by a duly constituted body authorized to visit the juveniles and not belonging to the detention facility.

15. The Rules apply to all types and forms of detention facilities in which juveniles are deprived of their liberty. Sections I, II, IV and V of the Rules apply to all detention facilities and institutional settings in which juveniles are detained, and section III applies specifically to juveniles under arrest or awaiting trial.

16. The Rules shall be implemented in the context of the economic, social and cultural conditions prevailing in each Member State.

III. JUVENILES UNDER ARREST OR AWAITING TRAIL

17. Juveniles who are detained under arrest or awaiting trial ("untried") are presumed innocent and shall be treated as such. Detention before trial shall be avoided to the extent possible and limited to exceptional circumstances. Therefore, all efforts shall be made to apply alternative measures. When preventive detention is nevertheless used, juvenile courts and investigative bodies shall give the highest priority to the most expeditious processing of such cases to ensure the shortest possible duration of detention. Untried detainees should be separated from convicted juveniles.

18. The conditions under which an untried juvenile is detained should be consistent with the rules set out below, with additional specific provisions as are necessary and appropriate, given the requirements of the presumption of innocence, the duration of the detention and the legal status and circumstances of the juvenile. These provisions would include, but not necessarily be restricted to, the following:

(a) Juveniles should have the right of legal counsel and be enabled to apply for free legal aid, where such aid is available, and to communicate regularly with their legal advisers. Privacy and confidentiality shall be ensured for such communications;

(b) Juveniles should be provided, where possible, with opportunities to pursue work, with remuneration, and continue education or training, but should not be required to do so. Work, education or training should not cause the continuation of the detention;

(c) Juveniles should receive and retain materials for their leisure and recreation as are compatible with the interests of the administration of justice.

IV. THE MANAGEMENT OF JUVENILE FACILITIES

A. Records

19. All reports, including legal records, medical records and records of disciplinary proceedings, and all other documents relating to the form, content and details of treatment, should be placed in a confidential individual file, which should be kept up to date, accessible only to authorized persons and classified in such a way as to be easily understood. Where possible, every juvenile should have the right to contest any fact or opinion contained in his or her file so as to permit rectification of inaccurate, unfounded or unfair statements. In order to exercise this right, there should be procedures that allow an appropriate third party to have access to and to consult the file on request. Upon release, the records of juveniles shall be sealed, and, at an appropriate time, expunged.

20. No juvenile should be received in any detention facility without a valid commitment order of a judicial, administrative or other public authority. The details of this order should be immediately entered in the register. No juvenile should be detained in any facility where there is no such register.

B. Admission, registration, movement and transfer

21. In every place where juveniles are detained, a complete and secure record of the following information should be kept concerning each juvenile received:

(a) Information on the identity of the juvenile;

(b) The fact of and reasons for commitment and the authority therefor;

(c) The day and hour of admission, transfer and release;

(d) Details of the notifications to parents and guardians on every admission, transfer or release of the juvenile in their care at the time of commitment;

(e) Details of known physical and mental health problems, including drug and alcohol abuse.

22. The information on admission, place, transfer and release should be provided without delay to the parents and guardians or closest relative of the juvenile concerned.

23. As soon as possible after reception, full reports and relevant information on the personal situation and circumstances of each juvenile should be drawn up and submitted to the administration.

24. On admission, all juveniles shall be given a copy of the rules governing the detention facility and a written description of their rights and obligations in a language they can understand, together with the address of the authorities competent to receive complaints, as well as the address of public or private agencies and organizations which provide legal assistance. For those juveniles who are illiterate or who cannot understand the language in the written form, the information should be conveyed in a manner enabling full comprehension.

25. All juveniles should be helped to understand the regulations governing the internal organization of the facility, the goals and methodology of the care provided, the disciplinary requirements and procedures, other authorized methods of seeking information and of making complaints and all such other matters as are necessary to enable them to understand fully their rights and obligations during detention.

26. The transport of juveniles should be carried out at the expense of the administration in conveyances with adequate ventilation and light, in conditions that should in no way subject them to hardship or indignity. Juveniles should not be transferred from one facility to another arbitrarily.

C. Classification and placement

27. As soon as possible after the moment of admission, each juvenile should be interviewed, and a psychological and social report identifying any factors relevant to the specific type and level of care and programme required by the juvenile should be prepared. This report, together with the report prepared by a medical officer who has examined the juvenile upon admission, should be forwarded to the director for purposes of determining the most appropriate placement for the juvenile within the facility and the specific type and level of care and programme required and to be pursued. When special rehabilitative treatment is required, and the length of stay in the facility permits, trained personnel of the facility should prepare a written, individualized treatment plan specifying treatment objectives and time-frame and the means, stages and delays with which the objectives should be approached.

28. The detention of juveniles should only take place under conditions that take full account of their particular needs, status and special requirements according to their age, personality, sex and type of offence, as well as mental and physical health, and which ensure their protection from harmful influences and risk situations. The principal criterion for the separation of different categories of juveniles deprived of their liberty should be the provision of the type of care best suited to the particular needs of the individuals concerned and the protection of their physical, mental and moral integrity and well-being.

29. In all detention facilities juveniles should be separated from adults, unless they are members of the same family. Under controlled conditions, juveniles may be brought together with carefully selected adults as part of a special programme that has been shown to be beneficial for the juveniles concerned.

30. Open detention facilities for juveniles should be established. Open detention facilities are those with no or minimal security measures. The population in such detention facilities should be as small as possible. The number of juveniles detained in closed facilities should be small enough to enable individualized treatment. Detention facilities for juveniles should be decentralized and of such size as to facilitate access and contact between the juveniles and their families. Small-scale

detention facilities should be established and integrated into the social, economic and cultural environment of the community.

D. Physical environment and accommodation
31. Juveniles deprived of their liberty have the right to facilities and services that meet all the requirements of health and human dignity.
32. The design of detention facilities for juveniles and the physical environment should be in keeping with the rehabilitative aim of residential treatment, with due regard to the need of the juvenile for privacy, sensory stimuli, opportunities for association with peers and participation in sports, physical exercise and leisure-time activities. The design and structure of juvenile detention facilities should be such as to minimize the risk of fire and to ensure safe evacuation from the premises. There should be an effective alarm system in case of fire, as well as formal and drilled procedures to ensure the safety of the juveniles. Detention facilities should not be located in areas where there are known health or other hazards or risks.
33. Sleeping accommodation should normally consist of small group dormitories or individual bedrooms, while bearing in mind local standards. During sleeping hours there should be regular, unobtrusive supervision of all sleeping areas, including individual rooms and group dormitories, in order to ensure the protection of each juvenile. Every juvenile should, in accordance with local or national standards, be provided with separate and sufficient bedding, which should be clean when issued, kept in good order and changed often enough to ensure cleanliness.
34. Sanitary installations should be so located and of a sufficient standard to enable every juvenile to comply, as required, with their physical needs in privacy and in a clean and decent manner.
35. The possession of personal effects is a basic element of the right to privacy and essential to the psychological well-being of the juvenile. The right of every juvenile to possess personal effects and to have adequate storage facilities for them should be fully recognized and respected. Personal effects that the juvenile does not choose to retain or that are confiscated should be placed in safe custody. An inventory thereof should be signed by the juvenile. Steps should be taken to keep them in good condition. All such articles and money should be returned to the juvenile on release, except in so far as he or she has been authorized to spend money or send such property out of the facility. If a juvenile receives or is found in possession of any medicine, the medical officer should decide what use should be made of it.
36. To the extent possible juveniles should have the right to use their own clothing. Detention facilities should ensure that each juvenile has personal clothing suitable for the climate and adequate to ensure good health, and which should in no manner be degrading or humiliating. Juveniles removed from or leaving a facility for any purpose should be allowed to wear their own clothing.
37. Every detention facility shall ensure that every juvenile receives food that is suitably prepared and presented at normal meal times and of a quality and quantity to satisfy the standards of dietetics, hygiene and health and, as far as possible, religious and cultural requirements. Clean drinking water should be available to every juvenile at any time.

E. Education, vocational training and work
38. Every juvenile of compulsory school age has the right to education suited to his or her needs and abilities and designed to prepare him or her for return to society. Such education should be provided outside the detention facility in community schools wherever possible and, in any case, by qualified teachers through programmes integrated with the education system of the country so that, after release, juveniles may continue their education without difficulty. Special attention should be given by the administration of the detention facilities to the education of juveniles of foreign origin or with particular cultural or ethnic needs. Juveniles who are illiterate or have cognitive or learning difficulties should have the right to special education.
39. Juveniles above compulsory school age who wish to continue their education should be permitted and encouraged to do so, and every effort should be made to provide them with access to appropriate educational programmes.
40. Diplomas or educational certificates awarded to juveniles while in detention should not indicate in any way that the juvenile has been institutionalized.
41. Every detention facility should provide access to a library that is adequately stocked with both instructional and recreational books and periodicals suitable for the juveniles, who should be encouraged and enabled to make full use of it.
42. Every juvenile should have the right to receive vocational training in occupations likely to prepare him or her for future employment.
43. With due regard to proper vocational selection and to the requirements of institutional administration, juveniles should be able to choose the type of work they wish to perform.
44. All protective national and international standards applicable to child labour and young workers should apply to juveniles deprived of their liberty.
45. Wherever possible, juveniles should be provided with the opportunity to perform remunerated labour, if possible within the local community, as a complement to the vocational training provided in order to enhance the possibility of finding suitable employment when they return to their communities. The type of work should be such as to provide appropriate training that will be of benefit to the juveniles following release. The organization and methods of work offered in detention facilities should resemble as closely as possible those of similar work in the community, so as to prepare juveniles for the conditions of normal occupational life.
46. Every juvenile who performs work should have the right to an equitable remuneration. The interests of the juveniles and of their vocational training should not be subordinated to the purpose of making a profit for the detention facility or a third party. Part of the earnings of a juvenile should normally be set aside to constitute a savings fund to be handed over to the juvenile on release. The juvenile should have the right to use the remainder of those earnings to purchase articles for his or her own use or to indemnify the victim injured by his or her offence or to send it to his or her family or other persons outside the detention facility.

F. Recreation
47. Every juvenile should have the right to a suitable amount of time for daily free exercise, in the open air whenever weather permits, during which time appropriate recreational and physical training should normally be provided. Adequate space, installations and equipment should be provided for these activities. Every juvenile should have additional time for daily leisure activities, part of which should be devoted, if the juvenile so wishes, to arts and crafts skill development. The detention facility should ensure that each juvenile is physically able to participate in the available programmes of physical education. Remedial physical education and therapy should be offered, under medical supervision, to juveniles needing it.

G. Religion
48. Every juvenile should be allowed to satisfy the needs of his or her religious and spiritual life, in particular by attending the services or meetings provided in the detention facility or by conducting his or her own services and having possession of the necessary books or items of religious observance and instruction of his or her denomination. If a detention facility contains a sufficient number of juveniles of a given religion, one or more qualified representatives of that religion should be appointed or approved and allowed to hold regular services and to pay pastoral visits in private to juveniles at their request. Every juvenile should have the right to receive visits from a qualified representative of any religion of his or her choice, as well as the right not to participate in religious services and freely to decline religious education, counselling or indoctrination.

H. Medical care
49. Every juvenile shall receive adequate medical care, both preventive and remedial, including dental, ophthalmological and mental health care, as well as pharmaceutical products and special diets as medically indicated. All such medical care should, where possible, be provided to detained juveniles through the appropriate health facilities and services of the community in which the detention facility is located, in order to prevent stigmatization of the juvenile and promote self-respect and integration into the community.
50. Every juvenile has a right to be examined by a physician immediately upon admission to a detention facility, for the purpose of recording any evidence of prior ill-treatment and

identifying any physical or mental condition requiring medical attention.

51. The medical services provided to juveniles should seek to detect and should treat any physical or mental illness, substance abuse or other condition that may hinder the integration of the juvenile into society. Every detention facility for juveniles should have immediate access to adequate medical facilities and equipment appropriate to the number and requirements of its residents and staff trained in preventive health care and the handling of medical emergencies. Every juvenile who is ill, who complains of illness or who demonstrates symptoms of physical or mental difficulties, should be examined promptly by a medical officer.

52. Any medical officer who has reason to believe that the physical or mental health of a juvenile has been or will be injuriously affected by continued detention, a hunger strike or any condition of detention should report this fact immediately to the director of the detention facility in question and to the independent authority responsible for safeguarding the well-being of the juvenile.

53. A juvenile who is suffering from mental illness should be treated in a specialized institution under independent medical management. Steps should be taken, by arrangement with appropriate agencies, to ensure any necessary continuation of mental health care after release.

54. Juvenile detention facilities should adopt specialized drug abuse prevention and rehabilitation programmes administered by qualified personnel. These programmes should be adapted to the age, sex and other requirements of the juveniles concerned, and detoxification facilities and services staffed by trained personnel should be available to drug- or alcohol-dependent juveniles.

55. Medicines should be administered only for necessary treatment on medical grounds and, when possible, after having obtained the informed consent of the juvenile concerned. In particular, they must not be administered with a view to eliciting information or a confession, as a punishment or as a means of restraint. Juveniles shall never be testers in the experimental use of drugs and treatment. The administration of any drug should always be authorized and carried out by qualified medical personnel.

I. Notification of illness, injury and death

56. The family or guardian of a juvenile and any other person designated by the juvenile have the right to be informed of the state of health of the juvenile on request and in the event of any important changes in the health of the juvenile. The director of the detention facility should notify immediately the family or guardian of the juvenile concerned, or other designated person, in case of death, illness requiring transfer of the juvenile to an outside medical facility, or a condition requiring clinical care within the detention facility for more than 48 hours. Notification should also be given to the consular authorities of the State of which a foreign juvenile is a citizen.

57. Upon the death of a juvenile during the period of deprivation of liberty, the nearest relative should have the right to inspect the death certificate, see the body and determine the method of disposal of the body. Upon the death of a juvenile in detention, there should be an independent inquiry into the causes of death, the report of which should be made accessible to the nearest relative. This inquiry should also be made when the death of a juvenile occurs within six months from the date of his or her release from the detention facility and there is reason to believe that the death is related to the period of detention.

58. A juvenile should be informed at the earliest possible time of the death, serious illness or injury of any immediate family member and should be provided with the opportunity to attend the funeral of the deceased or go to the bedside of a critically ill relative.

J. Contacts with the wider community

59. Every means should be provided to ensure that juveniles have adequate communication with the outside world, which is an integral part of the right to fair and humane treatment and is essential to the preparation of juveniles for their return to society. Juveniles should be allowed to communicate with their families, friends and other persons or representatives of reputable outside organizations, to leave detention facilities for a visit to their home and family and to receive special permission to leave the detention facility for educational, vocational or other important reasons. Should the juvenile be serving a sentence, the time spent outside a detention facility should be counted as part of the period of sentence.

60. Every juvenile should have the right to receive regular and frequent visits, in principle once a week and not less than once a month, in circumstances that respect the need of the juvenile for privacy, contact and unrestricted communication with the family and the defence counsel.

61. Every juvenile should have the right to communicate in writing or by telephone at least twice a week with the person of his or her choice, unless legally restricted, and should be assisted as necessary in order effectively to enjoy this right. Every juvenile should have the right to receive correspondence.

62. Juveniles should have the opportunity to keep themselves informed regularly of the news by reading newspapers, periodicals and other publications, through access to radio and television programmes and motion pictures, and through the visits of the representatives of any lawful club or organization in which the juvenile is interested.

K. Limitations of physical restraint and the use of force

63. Recourse to instruments of restraint and to force for any purpose should be prohibited, except as set forth in rule 64 below.

64. Instruments of restraint and force can only be used in exceptional cases, where all other control methods have been exhausted and failed, and only as explicitly authorized and specified by law and regulation. They should not cause humiliation or degradation, and should be used restrictively and only for the shortest possible period of time. By order of the director of the administration, such instruments might be resorted to in order to prevent the juvenile from inflicting self-injury, injuries to others or serious destruction of property. In such instances, the director should at once consult medical and other relevant personnel and report to the higher administrative authority.

65. The carrying and use of weapons by personnel should be prohibited in any facility where juveniles are detained.

L. Disciplinary procedures

66. Any disciplinary measures and procedures should maintain the interest of safety and an ordered community life and should be consistent with the upholding of the inherent dignity of the juvenile and the fundamental objective of institutional care, namely, instilling a sense of justice, self-respect and respect for the basic rights of every person.

67. All disciplinary measures constituting cruel, inhuman or degrading treatment shall be strictly prohibited, including corporal punishment, placement in a dark cell, closed or solitary confinement or any other punishment that may compromise the physical or mental health of the juvenile concerned. The reduction of diet and the restriction or denial of contact with family members should be prohibited for any purpose. Labour should always be viewed as an educational tool and a means of promoting the self-respect of the juvenile in preparing him or her for return to the community and should not be imposed as a disciplinary sanction. No juvenile should be sanctioned more than once for the same disciplinary infraction. Collective sanctions should be prohibited.

68. Legislation or regulations adopted by the competent administrative authority should establish norms concerning the following, taking full account of the fundamental characteristics, needs and rights of juveniles:

(a) Conduct constituting a disciplinary offence;

(b) Type and duration of disciplinary sanctions that may be inflicted;

(c) The authority competent to impose such sanctions;

(d) The authority competent to consider appeals.

69. A report of misconduct should be presented promptly to the competent authority, which should decide on it without undue delay. The competent authority should conduct a thorough examination of the case.

70. No juvenile should be disciplinarily sanctioned except in strict accordance with the terms of the law and regulations in force. No juvenile should be sanctioned unless he or she has been informed of the alleged infraction in a manner appropriate to the full understanding of the juvenile, and given a proper opportunity of presenting his or her defence, including the right of appeal to a competent impartial

authority. Complete records should be kept of all disciplinary proceedings.

71. No juveniles should be responsible for disciplinary functions except in the supervision of specified social, educational or sports activities or in self-government programmes.

M. Inspection and complaints

72. Qualified inspectors or an equivalent duly constituted authority not belonging to the administration of the facility should be empowered to conduct inspections on a regular basis and to undertake unannounced inspections on their own initiative, and should enjoy full guarantees of independence in the exercise of this function. Inspectors should have unrestricted access to all persons employed by or working in any facility where juveniles are or may be deprived of their liberty, to all juveniles and to all records of such facilities.

73. Qualified medical officers attached to the inspecting authority or the public health service should participate in the inspections, evaluating compliance with the rules concerning the physical environment, hygiene, accommodation, food, exercise and medical services, as well as any other aspect or conditions of institutional life that affect the physical and mental health of juveniles. Every juvenile should have the right to talk in confidence to any inspecting officer.

74. After completing the inspection, the inspector should be required to submit a report on the findings. The report should include an evaluation of the compliance of the detention facilities with the present rules and relevant provisions of national law, and recommendations regarding any steps considered necessary to ensure compliance with them. Any facts discovered by an inspector that appear to indicate that a violation of legal provisions concerning the rights of juveniles or the operation of a juvenile detention facility has occurred should be communicated to the competent authorities for investigation and prosecution.

75. Every juvenile should have the opportunity of making requests or complaints to the director of the detention facility and to his or her authorized representative.

76. Every juvenile should have the right to make a request or complaint, without censorship as to substance, to the central administration, the judicial authority or other proper authorities through approved channels, and to be informed of the response without delay.

77. Efforts should be made to establish an independent office (ombudsman) to receive and investigate complaints made by juveniles deprived of their liberty and to assist in the achievement of equitable settlements.

78. Every juvenile should have the right to request assistance from family members, legal counsellors, humanitarian groups or others where possible, in order to make a complaint. Illiterate juveniles should be provided with assistance should they need to use the services of public or private agencies and organizations which provide legal counsel or which are competent to receive complaints.

N. Return to the community

79. All juveniles should benefit from arrangements designed to assist them in returning to society, family life, education or employment after release. Procedures, including early release, and special courses should be devised to this end.

80. Competent authorities should provide or ensure services to assist juveniles in re-establishing themselves in society and to lessen prejudice against such juveniles. These services should ensure', to the extent possible, that the juvenile is provided with suitable residence, employment, clothing, and sufficient means to maintain himself or herself upon release in order to facilitate successful reintegration. The representatives of agencies providing such services should be consulted and should have access to juveniles while detained, with a view to assisting them in their return to the community.

V. Personnel

81. Personnel should be qualified and include a sufficient number of specialists such as educators, vocational instructors, counsellors, social workers, psychiatrists and psychologists. These and other specialist staff should normally be employed on a permanent basis. This should not preclude part-time or volunteer workers when the level of support and training they can provide is appropriate and beneficial. Detention facilities should make use of all remedial, educational, moral, spiritual, and other resources and forms of assistance that are appropriate and available in the community, according to the individual needs and problems of detained juveniles.

82. The administration should provide for the careful selection and recruitment of every grade and type of personnel, since the proper management of detention facilities depends on their integrity, humanity, ability and professional capacity to deal with juveniles, as well as personal suitability for the work.

83. To secure the foregoing ends, personnel should be appointed as professional officers with adequate remuneration to attract and retain suitable women and men. The personnel of juvenile detention facilities should be continually encouraged to fulfil their duties and obligations in a humane, committed, professional, fair and efficient manner, to conduct themselves at all times in such a way as to deserve and gain the respect of the juveniles, and to provide juveniles with a positive role model and perspective.

84. The administration should introduce forms of organization and management that facilitate communications between different categories of staff in each detention facility so as to enhance cooperation between the various services engaged in the care of juveniles, as well as between staff and the administration, with a view to ensuring that staff directly in contact with juveniles are able to function in conditions favourable to the efficient fulfilment of their duties.

85. The personnel should receive such training as will enable them to carry out their responsibilities effectively, in particular training in child psychology, child welfare and international standards and norms of human rights and the rights of the child, including the present Rules. The personnel should maintain and improve their knowledge and professional capacity by attending courses of in-service training, to be organized at suitable intervals throughout their career.

86. The director of a facility should be adequately qualified for his or her task, with administrative ability and suitable training and experience, and should carry out his or her duties on a full-time basis.

87. In the performance of their duties, personnel of detention facilities should respect and protect the human dignity and fundamental human rights of all juveniles, in particular, as follows:

(a) No member of the detention facility or institutional personnel may inflict, instigate or tolerate any act of torture or any form of harsh, cruel, inhuman or degrading treatment, punishment, correction or discipline under any pretext or circumstance whatsoever;

(b) All personnel should rigorously oppose and combat any act of corruption, reporting it without delay to the competent authorities;

(c) All personnel should respect the present Rules. Personnel who have reason to believe that a serious violation of the present Rules has occurred or is about to occur should report the matter to their superior authorities or organs vested with reviewing or remedial power;

(d) All personnel should ensure the full protection of the physical and mental health of juveniles, including protection from physical, sexual and emotional abuse and exploitation, and should take immediate action to secure medical attention whenever required;

(e) All personnel should respect the right of the juvenile to privacy, and, in particular, should safeguard all confidential matters concerning juveniles or their families learned as a result of their professional capacity;

(f) All personnel should seek to minimize any differences between life inside and outside the detention facility which tend to lessen due respect for the dignity of juveniles as human beings.

Hague Convention on the Protection of Children and Cooperation in Respect of Intercountry Adoption

Hague Conference on Private International Law,
The Hague, 29 May 1993

Preamble

The States signatory
to the present Convention,

Recognizing that the child, for the full and harmonious development of his or her personality, should grow up in a family environment, in an atmosphere of happiness, love and understanding,

Recalling that each State should take, as a matter of priority, appropriate measures to enable the child to remain in the care of his or her family of origin,

Recognizing that intercountry adoption may offer the advantage of a permanent family to a child for whom a suitable family cannot be found in his or her State of origin,

Convinced of the necessity to take measures to ensure that intercountry adoptions are made in the best interests of the child and with respect for his or her fundamental rights, and to prevent the abduction, the sale of, or traffic in children,

Desiring to establish common provisions to this effect, taking into account the principles set forth in international instruments, in particular the United Nations Convention on the Rights of the Child, of 20 November 1989, and the United Nations Declaration on Social and Legal Principles relating to the Protection and Welfare of Children, with Special Reference to Foster Placement and Adoption Nationally and Internationally (General Assembly Resolution 41/85, of 3 December 1986),

Have agreed upon the following provisions:

Chapter I

Scope of the Convention

● Article 1

The objects of the present Convention are-
(a) to establish safeguards to ensure that intercountry adoptions take place in the best interests of the child and with respect for his or her fundamental rights as recognized in international law;
(b) to establish a system of cooperation amongst Contracting States to ensure that those safeguards are respected and thereby prevent the abduction, the sale of, or traffic in children;
(c) to secure the recognition in Contracting States of adoptions made in accordance with the Convention.

● Article 2

(1) The Convention shall apply where a child habitually resident in one Contracting State ("the State of origin") has been, is being, or is to be moved to another Contracting State ("the receiving State") either after his or her adoption in the State of origin by spouses or a person habitually resident in the receiving State, or for the purposes of such an adoption in the receiving State or in the State of origin.

(2) The Convention covers only adoptions which create a permanent parent-child relationship.

● Article 3

The Convention ceases to apply if the agreements mentioned in Article 17, sub-paragraph c, have not been given before the child attains the age of eighteen years.

Chapter II

Requirement for Intercountry Adoptions

● Article 4

An adoption within the scope of the Convention shall take place only if the competent authorities of the State of origin
(a) have established that the child is adoptable;
(b) have determined, after possibilities for placement of the child within the State of origin have been given due consideration, that an intercountry adoption is in the child's best interests;
(c) have ensured that
(1) the persons, institutions and authorities whose consent is necessary for adoption, have

been counselled as may be necessary and duly informed of the effects of their consent, in particular whether or not an adoption will result in the termination of the legal relationship between the child and his or her family of origin,

(2) such persons, institutions and authorities have given their consent freely, in the required legal form, and expressed or evidenced in writing,

(3) the consents have not been induced by payment or compensation of any kind and have not been withdrawn, and

(4) the consent of the mother, where required, has been given only after the birth of the child; and

(d) have ensured, having regard to the age and degree of maturity of the child, that

(1) he or she has been counselled and duly informed of the effects of the adoption and of his or her consent to the adoption, where such consent is required,

(2) consideration has been given to the child's wishes and opinions,

(3) the child's consent to the adoption, where such consent is required, has been given freely, in the required legal form, and expressed or evidenced in writing, and

(4) such consent has not been induced by payment or compensation of any kind.

Article 5

An adoption within the scope of the Convention shall take place only if the competent authorities of the receiving State

(a) have determined that the prospective adoptive parents are eligible and suited to adopt;

(b) have ensured that the prospective adoptive parents have been counselled as may be necessary; and

(c) have determined that the child is or will be authorized to enter and reside permanently in that State.

Chapter III
Central Authorities and Accredited Bodies

Article 6

(1) A Contracting State shall designate a Central Authority to discharge the duties which are imposed by the Convention upon such authorities.

(2) Federal States, States with more than one system of law or States having autonomous territorial units shall be free to appoint more than one Central Authority and to specify the territorial or personal extent of their functions. Where a State has appointed more than one Central Authority, it shall designate the Central Authority to which any communication may be addressed for transmission to the appropriate Central Authority within that State.

Article 7

(1) Central Authorities shall cooperate with each other and promote cooperation amongst the competent authorities in their States to protect children and to achieve the other objects of the Convention.

(2) They shall take directly all appropriate measures to—

(a) provide information as to the laws of their States concerning adoption and other general information, such as statistics and standard forms;

(b) keep one another informed about the operation of the Convention and, as far as possible, eliminate any obstacles to its application.

Article 8

Central Authorities shall take, directly or through public authorities, all appropriate measures to prevent improper financial or other gain in connection with an adoption and to deter all practices contrary to the objects of the Convention.

Article 9

Central Authorities shall take, directly or through public authorities or other bodies duly accredited in their State, all appropriate measures, in particular to

(a) facilitate, follow and expedite proceedings with a view to obtaining the adoption;

(c) promote the development of adoption counselling and postadoption services in their States;

(d) provide each other with general evaluation reports about experience with intercountry adoption;

(e) reply, in so far as is permitted by the law of their State, to justified requests from other Central Authorities or public authorities for information about a particular adoption situation.

Article 10

Accreditation shall only be granted to and maintained by bodies demonstrating their competence to carry out properly the tasks with which they may be entrusted.

Article 11

An accredited body shall

(a) pursue only non-profit objectives according to such conditions and within such limits as may be established by the competent authorities of the State of accreditation;

(b) be directed and staffed by persons qualified by their ethical standards and by training or experience to work in the field of intercountry adoption; and

(c) be subject to supervision by competent authorities of that State as to its composition, operation and financial situation.

Article 12

A body accredited in one Contracting State may act in another Contracting State only if the competent authorities of both States have authorized it to do so.

Article 13

The designation of the Central Authorities and, where appropriate, the extent of their functions, as well as the names and addresses of the accredited bodies shall be communicated by each Contracting State to the Permanent Bureau of the Hague Conference on Private International Law.

Chapter IV
Procedural Requirements in Intercountry Adoption

Article 14

Persons habitually resident in a Contracting State, who wish to adopt a child habitually resident in another Contracting State, shall apply to the Central Authority in the State of their habitual residence.

Article 15

(1) If the Central Authority of the receiving State is satisfied that the applicants are eligible and suited to adopt, it shall prepare a report including information about their identity, eligibility and suitability to adopt, background, family and medical history, social environment, reasons for adoption, ability to undertake an intercountry adoption, as well as the characteristics of the children for whom they would be qualified to care.

(2) It shall transmit the report to the Central Authority of the State of origin.

Article 16

(1) If the Central Authority of the State of origin is satisfied that the child is adoptable, it shall

(a) prepare a report including information about his or her identity, adoptability, background, social environment, family history, medical history including that of the child's family, and any special needs of the child;

(b) give due consideration to the child's upbringing and to his or her ethnic, religious and cultural background;

(c) ensure that consents have been obtained in accordance with Article 4; and

(d) determine, on the basis in particular of the reports relating to the child and the prospective adoptive parents, whether envisaged placement is in the best interests of the child.

(2) It shall transmit to the Central Authority of the receiving State its report on the child, proof that the necessary consents have been obtained and the reasons for its determination on the placement, taking care not to reveal the identity of the mother and the father if, in the State of origin, these identities may not be disclosed.

Article 17

Any decision in the State or origin that a child should be entrusted to prospective adoptive parents may only be made if

(a) the Central Authority of that State has ensured that the prospective adoptive parents agree;

(b) the Central Authority of the receiving State has approved such decision, where such approval is required by the law of that State or by the Central Authority of the State of origin;

(c) the Central Authorities of both States have agreed that the adoption may proceed; and

(d) it has been determined, in accordance with Article 5, that the prospective adoptive parents are eligible and suited to adopt and that the child is or will be authorized to enter and reside permanently in the receiving State.

Article 18

The Central Authorities of both States shall take all necessary steps to obtain permission for the child to leave the State of origin and to enter and reside permanently in the receiving State.

Article 19

(1) The transfer of the child to the receiving State may only be carried out if the requirements of Article 17 have been satisfied.

(2) The Central Authorities of both States shall ensure that this transfer takes place in secure and appropriate circumstances and, if possible, in the company of the adoptive or prospective adoptive parents.

(3) If the transfer of the child does not take place, the reports referred to in Articles 15 and 16 are to be sent back to the authorities who forwarded them.

Article 20

The Central Authorities shall keep each other informed about the adoption process and the measures taken to complete it, as well as about the progress of the placement if a probationary period is required.

Article 21

(1) Where the adoption is to take place after the transfer of the child to the receiving State and it appears to the Central Authority of that State and the continued placement of the child with the prospective adoptive parents is not in the childs best interests, such Central Authority shall take the measures necessary to protect the child, in particular

(a) to cause the child to be withdrawn from the prospective adoptive parents and to arrange temporary care;

(b) in consultation with the Central Authority of the State or origin, to arrange without delay a new placement of the child with a view to adoption or, if this is not appropriate, to arrange alternative long-term care; an adoption shall not take place until the Central Authority of the State of origin has been duly informed concerning the new prospective adoptive parents;

(c) as a last resort, to arrange the return of the child, if his or her interests so require.

(2) Having regard in particular to the age and degree of maturity of the child, he or she shall be consulted and, where appropriate, his or her consent obtained in relation to measures to be taken under this Article.

Article 22

(1) The functions of a Central Authority under this Chapter may be performed by public authorities or by bodies accredited under Chapter III, to the extent permitted by the law of its State.

(2) Any Contracting State may declare to the depository of the Convention that the functions of the Central Authority under Articles 15 and 21 may be performed in that State, to the extent permitted by the law and subject to the supervision of the competent authorities of that State, also by bodies or persons who

(a) meet the requirements of integrity, professional competence, experience and accountability of that State; and

(b) are qualified by their ethical standards and by training or experience to work in the field of intercountry adoption.

(3) A Contracting State which makes the declaration provided for in paragraph 2 shall keep the Permanent Bureau of the Hague Conference on Private International Law informed of the names and addresses of these bodies and persons.

(4) Any Contracting State may declare to the depository of the Convention that adoptions of children habitually resident in its territory may only take place if the functions of the Central Authorities are performed in accordance with paragraph 1.

(5) Notwithstanding any declaration made under paragraph 2, the reports provided for in Articles 15 and 16 shall, in every case, be prepared under the responsibility of the Central Authority or other authorities or bodies in accordance with paragraph 1.

Chapter V
Recognitions and Effects of the Adoption

Article 23

(1) An adoption certified by the competent authority of the State of the adoption as having been made in accordance with the Convention shall be recognized by operation of law in the other Contracting States. The certificate shall specify when and by whom the agreements under Article 17, sub-paragraph c, were given.

(2) Each Contracting State shall, at the time of signature, ratification, acceptance, approval or accession, notify the depository of the Convention of the identity and the functions of the authority or the authorities which, in that State, are competent to make the certification. It shall also notify the depository of any modification in the designation of these authorities

Article 24

The recognition of an adoption may be refused in a Contracting State only if the adoption is manifestly contrary to its public policy, taking into account the best interests of the child.

Article 25

Any Contracting State may declare to the depository of the Convention that it will not be bound under this Convention to recognize adoptions made in accordance with an agreement concluded by application of Article 39, paragraph 2.

Article 26

(1) The recognition of an adoption includes recognition of

(a) the legal parent-child relationship between the child and his or her adoptive parents;

(b) parental responsibility of the adoptive parents for the child;

(c) the termination of a pre-existing legal relationship between the child and his or her mother and father, if the adoption has this effect in the Contracting State where it was made.

(2) In the case of an adoption having the effect of terminating a pre-existing legal parent-child relationship, the child shall enjoy in the receiving State, and in any other Contracting State where the adoption is recognized, rights equivalent to those resulting from adoptions having this effect in each such State.

(3) The preceding paragraphs shall not prejudice the application of any provision more favourable for the child, in force in the Contracting State which recognizes the adoption.

Article 27

(1) Where an adoption granted in the State of origin does not have the effect of terminating a pre-existing legal parent-child relationship, it may, in the receiving State which recognizes the adoption under the Convention, be converted into an adoption having such an effect

(a) if the law of the receiving State so permits; and

(b) if the consents referred to in Article 4, sub-paragraphs c and d, have been or are given for the purpose of such an adoption.

(2) Article 23 applies to the decision converting the adoption.

Chapter VI
General Provisions

Article 28

The Convention does not affect any law of a State of origin which requires that the adoption of a child habitually resident within that State take place in that State or which prohibits the child's placement in, or transfer to, the receiving State prior to adoption.

Article 29

There shall be no contact between the prospective adoptive parents and the child's parents or any other person who has care of the child until the requirements of Article 4, sub-paragraphs a to c, and Article 5, sub-paragraph a, have been met, unless the adoption takes place within a family or unless the contact is in compliance with the conditions established by the competent authority of the State of origin.

Article 30

(1) The competent authorities of a Contracting State shall ensure that information held by them concerning the child's origin, in particular information concerning the identity of his or her parents, as well as the medical history, is preserved.

(2) They shall ensure that the child or his or her representative has access to such information, under appropriate guidance, in so far as is permitted by the law of that State.

Article 31

Without prejudice to Article 30, personal data gathered or transmitted under the Convention, especially data referred to in Articles 15 and 16, shall be used only for the purposes for which they were gathered or transmitted.

Article 32

(1) No one shall derive improper financial or other gain from an activity related to an inter-country adoption.

(2) Only costs and expenses, including reasonable professional fees of persons involved in the adoption, may be charged or paid.

(3) The directors, administrators and employees of bodies involved in an adoption shall not receive remuneration which is unreasonably high in relation to services rendered.

Article 33

A competent authority which finds that any provision of the Convention has not been respected or that there is a serious risk that it may not be respected, shall immediately inform the Central Authority of its State. This Central Authority shall be responsible for ensuring that appropriate measures are taken.

Article 34

If the competent authority of the State of destination of a document so requests, a translation certified as being in conformity with the original must be furnished. Unless otherwise provided, the costs of such translation are to be borne by the prospective adoptive parents.

Article 35

The competent authorities of the Contracting States shall act expeditiously in the process of adoption.

Article 36

In relation to a State which has two or more systems of law with regard to adoption applicable in different territorial units

(a) any reference to habitual residence in that State shall be construed as referring to habitual residence in a territorial unit of that State;

(b) any reference to the law of that State shall be construed as referring to the law in force in the relevant territorial unit;

(c) any reference to the competent authorities or to the public authorities of that State shall be construed as referring to those authorized to act in the relevant territorial unit;

(d) any reference to the accredited bodies of that State shall be construed as referring to bodies accredited in the relevant territorial unit.

Article 37

In relation to a State which with regard to adoption has two or more systems of law applicable to different categories of persons, any reference to the law of that State shall be construed as referring to the legal system specified by the law of that State.

Article 38

A State within which different territorial units have their own rules of law in respect of adoption shall not be bound to apply the Convention where a State with a unified system of law would not be bound to do so.

Article 39

(1) The Convention does not affect any international instrument to which Contracting States are Parties and which contains provisions on matters governed by the Convention, unless a contrary declaration is made by the States Parties to such instrument.

(2) Any Contracting State may enter into agreements with one or more other Contracting States, with a view to improving the application of the Convention in their mutual relations. These agreements may derogate only from the provisions of Articles 165 to 16 and 18 to 21. The States which have concluded such an agreement shall transmit a copy to the depository of the Convention.

Article 40

No reservation to the Convention shall be permitted.

Article 41

The Convention shall apply in every case where an application pursuant to Article 14 has been received after the Convention has entered into force in the receiving State and the State or origin.

Article 42

The Secretary General of the Hague Conference on Private International Law shall at regular intervals convene a Special Commission in order to review the practical operation of the Convention.

Chapter VII
Final Clauses

Article 43

(1) The Convention shall be open for signature by the States which were Members of the Hague Conference on Private International Law at the time of its Seventeenth Session and by the other States which participated in that Session.

(2) It shall be ratified, accepted or approved and the instruments of ratification, acceptance or approval shall be deposited with the Ministry of Foreign Affairs of the Kingdom of the Netherlands, depository of the Convention.

Article 44

(1) Any other State may accede to the Convention after it has entered into force in accordance with Article 46, paragraph 1.

(2) The instrument of accession shall be deposited with the depository.

(3) Such accession shall have effect only as regards the relations between the acceding State and those Contracting States which have not raised an objection to its accession in the six months after the receipt of the notification referred to in sub-paragraph b of Article 48. Such an objection may also be raised by States at the time when they ratify, accept or approve the Convention after an accession. Any such objection shall be notified to the depository.

Article 45

(1) If a State has two or more territorial units in which different systems of law are applicable in relation to matters dealt with in the Convention, it may at the time of signature, ratification, acceptance, approval or accession declare that this Convention shall extend to all its territorial units or only to one or more of them and may modify this declaration by submitting another declaration at any time.

(2) Any such declaration shall be notified to the depository and shall state expressly the territorial units to which the Convention applies.

(3) If a State makes no declaration under this Article, the Convention is to extend to all territorial units of that State.

Article 46

(1) The Convention shall enter into force on the first day of the month following the expiration of three months after the deposit of the third instrument of ratification, acceptance or approval referred to in Article 43.

(2) Thereafter the Convention shall enter into force—

(a) for each State ratifying, accepting or approving it subsequently, or acceding to it, on the first day of the month following the expiration of three months after the deposit of its instrument of ratification, acceptance, approval or accession;

(b) for a territorial unit to which the Convention has been extended in conformity with Article 45, on the first day of the month following the expiration of three months after the notification referred to in that Article.

Article 47

(1) A State Party to the Convention may denounce it by a notification in writing addressed to the depository.

(2) The denunciation takes effect on the first day of the month following the expiration of twelve months after the notification is received by the depository. Where a longer period for the denunciation to take effect is specified in the notification, the denunciation takes effect upon the expiration of such longer period after the notification is received by the depository.

Article 48

The depository shall notify the States Members of the Hague Conference on Private International Law, the other States which participated in the Seventeenth Session and the States which have acceded in accordance with Article 44, of the following-

(a) the signatures, ratifications, acceptances and approvals referred to in Article 43;

(b) the accessions and objections raised to accessions referred to in Article 44;

(c) the date on which the Convention enters into force in accordance with Article 46;

(d) the declarations and designations referred to in Articles 22, 23, 25 and 45;

(e) the agreements referred to in Article 39;

(f) the denunciations referred to in Article 47.

In witness whereof the undersigned, being duly authorized thereto, have signed this Convention. Done at The Hague, on the 29th day of May 1993, in the English and French languages, both texts being equally authentic, in a single copy which shall be deposited in the archives of the Government of the Kingdom of the Netherlands, and of which a certified copy shall be sent, through diplomatic channels, to each of the States Members of the Hague Conference on Private International Law at the date of its Seventeenth Session and to each of the other States which participated in that Session.

Standard Rules on the Equalization of Opportunities for Persons with Disabilities

**Resolution Adopted by the General Assembly
on the Report of the Third Committee (A/48/627)
on 20 December 1993**

he General Assembly,

Recalling Economic and Social Council resolution 1990/26 of 24 May 1990, in which the Council authorized the Commission for Social Development to consider, at its thirty-second session, the establishment of an ad hoc open-ended working group of government experts, funded by voluntary contributions, to elaborate standard rules on the equalization of opportunities for disabled children, youth and adults, in close collaboration with the specialized agencies, other intergovernmental bodies and non-governmental organizations, especially organizations of disabled persons, and requested the Commission, should it establish such a working group, to finalize the text of those rules for consideration by the Council in 1993 and for submission to the General Assembly at its forty-eighth session,

Also recalling that in its resolution 32/2 of 20 February 1991 the Commission for Social Development decided to establish an ad hoc open-ended working group of government experts in accordance with Economic and Social Council resolution 1990/26,

Noting with appreciation the participation of many States, specialized agencies, intergovernmental bodies and non-governmental organizations, especially organizations of disabled persons, in the deliberations of the working group,

Also noting with appreciation the generous financial contributions of Member States to the working group,

Welcoming the fact that the working group was able to fulfil its mandate within three sessions of five working days each,

Acknowledging with appreciation the report of the ad hoc open-ended working group to elaborate standard rules on the equalization of opportunities for persons with disabilities,

Taking note of the discussion in the Commission for Social Development at its thirty-third session on the draft standard rules contained in the report of the working group,

1. *Adopts* the Standard Rules on the Equalization of Opportunities for Persons with Disabilities, set forth in the annex to the present resolution;

2. *Requests* Member States to apply the Rules in developing national disability programmes;

3. *Urges* Member States to meet the requests of the Special Rapporteur for information on the implementation of the Rules;

4. *Requests* the Secretary-General to promote the implementation of the Rules and to report thereon to the General Assembly at its fiftieth session;

5. *Urges* Member States to support, financially and other-wise, the implementation of the Rules.

INTRODUCTION

Background and current needs

1. There are persons with disabilities in all parts of the world and at all levels in every society. The number of persons with disabilities in the world is large and is growing.

2. Both the causes and the consequences of disability vary throughout the world. Those variations are the result of different socio-economic circumstances and of the different provisions that States make for the well-being of their citizens.

3. Present disability policy is the result of developments over the past 200 years. In many ways it reflects the general living conditions and social and economic policies of different times. In the disability field, however, there are also many specific circumstances that have influenced the living conditions of persons with disabilities. Ignorance, neglect,

superstition and fear are social factors that throughout the history of disability have isolated persons with disabilities and delayed their development.

4. Over the years disability policy developed from elementary care at institutions to education for children with disabilities and rehabilitation for persons who became disabled during adult life. Through education and rehabilitation, persons with disabilities became more active and a driving force in the further development of disability policy. Organizations of persons with disabilities, their families and advocates were formed, which advocated better conditions for persons with disabilities. After the Second World War the concepts of integration and normalization were introduced, which reflected a growing awareness of the capabilities of persons with disabilities.

5. Towards the end of the 1960s organizations of persons with disabilities in some countries started to formulate a new concept of disability. That new concept indicated the close connection between the limitation experienced by individuals with disabilities, the design and structure of their environments and the attitude of the general population. At the same time the problems of disability in developing countries were more and more highlighted. In some of those countries the percentage of the population with disabilities was estimated to be very high and, for the most part, persons with disabilities were extremely poor.

Previous international action

6. The rights of persons with disabilities have been the subject of much attention in the United Nations and other international organizations over a long period of time. The most important outcome of the International Year of Disabled Persons, 1981, was the World Programme of Action concerning Disabled Persons, adopted by the General Assembly by its resolution 37/52 of 3 December 1982. The Year and the World Programme of Action provided a strong impetus for progress in the field. They both emphasized the right of persons with disabilities to the same opportunities as other citizens and to an equal share in the improvements in living conditions resulting from economic and social development. There also, for the first time, handicap was defined as a function of the relationship between persons with disabilities and their environment.

7. The Global Meeting of Experts to Review the Implementation of the WorldProgramme of Action concerning Disabled Persons at the Mid-Point of the United Nations Decade of Disabled Persons was held at Stockholm in 1987. It was suggested at the Meeting that a guiding philosophy should be developed to indicate the priorities for action in the years ahead. The basis of that philosophy should be the recognition of the rights of persons with disabilities.

8. Consequently, the Meeting recommended that the General Assembly convened a special conference to draft an international convention on the elimination of all forms of discrimination against persons with disabilities, to be ratified by States by the end of the Decade.

9. A draft outline of the convention was prepared by Italy and presented to the General Assembly at its forty-second session. Further presentations concerning a draft convention were made by Sweden at the forty-fourth session of the Assembly. However, on both occasions, no consensus could be reached on the suitability of such a convention. In the opinion of many representatives, existing human rights documents seemed to guarantee persons with disabilities the same rights as other persons.

Towards standard rules

10. Guided by the deliberations in the General Assembly, the Economic and Social Council, at its first regular session of 1990, finally agreed to concentrate on the elaboration of an international instrument of a different kind. By its resolution 1990/26 of 24 May 1990, the Council authorized the Commission for Social Development to consider, at its thirty-second session, the establishment of an ad hoc open-ended working group of government experts, funded by voluntary contributions, to elaborate standard rules on the equalization of opportunities for disabled children, youth and adults, in close collaboration with the specialized agencies, other intergovernmental bodies and non-governmental organizations, especially organizations of disabled persons. The Council also requested the Commission to finalize the text of those rules for consideration in 1993 and for submission to the General Assembly at its forty-eighth session.

11. The subsequent discussions in the Third Committee of the General Assembly at the forty-fifth session showed that there was wide support for the new initiative to elaborate standard rules on the equalization of opportunities for persons with disabilities.

12. At the thirty-second session of the Commission for Social Development, the initiative for standard rules received the support of a large number of representatives and discussions led to the adoption of resolution 32/2 of 20 February 1991, in which the Commission decided to establish an ad hoc open-ended working group in accordance with Economic and Social Council resolution 1990/26.

Purpose and content of the Standard Rules on the Equalization of Opportunities for Persons with Disabilities

13. The Standard Rules on the Equalization of Opportunities for Persons with Disabilities have been developed on the basis of the experience gained during the United Nations Decade of Disabled Persons (1983-1992). The International Bill of Human Rights, comprising the Universal Declaration of Human Rights, the International Covenant on Economic, Social and Cultural Rights and the International Covenant on Civil and Political Rights, the Convention on the Rights of the Child and the Convention on the Elimination of All Forms of Discrimination against Women, as well as the World Programme of Action concerning Disabled Persons, constitute the political and moral foundation for the Rules.

14. Although the Rules are not compulsory, they can become international customary rules when they are applied by a great number of States with the intention of respecting a rule in international law. They imply a strong moral and political commitment on behalf of States to take action for the equalization of opportunities for persons with disabilities. Important principles for responsibility, action and cooperation are indicated. Areas of decisive importance for the quality of life and for the achievement of full participation and equality are pointed out. The Rules offer an instrument for policy-making and action to persons with disabilities and their organizations. They provide a basis for technical and economic cooperation among States, the United Nations and other international organizations.

15. The purpose of the Rules is to ensure that girls, boys, women and men with disabilities, as members of their societies, may exercise the same rights and obligations as others. In all societies of the world there are still obstacles preventing persons with disabilities from exercising their rights and freedoms and making it difficult for them to participate fully in the activities of their societies. It is the responsibility of States to take appropriate action to remove such obstacles. Persons with disabilities and their organizations should play an active role as partners in this process. The equalization of opportunities for persons with disabilities is an essential contribution in the general and worldwide effort to mobilize human resources. Special attention may need to be directed towards groups such as women, children, the elderly, the poor, migrant workers, persons with dual or multiple disabilities, indigenous people and ethnic minorities. In addition, there are a large number of refugees with disabilities who have special needs requiring attention.

Fundamental concepts in disability policy

16. The concepts set out below appear throughout the Rules. They are essentially built on the concepts in the World Programme of Action concerning Disabled Persons. In some cases they reflect the development that has taken place during the United Nations Decade of Disabled Persons.

Disability and handicap

17. The term "disability" summarizes a great number of different functional limitations occurring in any population in any country of the world. People may be disabled by physical, intellectual or sensory impairment, medical conditions or mental illness. Such impairments, conditions or illnesses may be permanent or transitory in nature.

18. The term "handicap" means the loss or limitation of opportunities to take part in the life of the community on an equal level with others. It describes the encounter between the person with a disability and the environment. The purpose of this term is to emphasize the focus on the shortcomings in the environment and in many organized activities in society, for example, information, communication and edu-

cation, which prevent persons with disabilities from participating on equal terms.

19. The use of the two terms "disability" and "handicap", as defined in paragraphs 17 and 18 above, should be seen in the light of modern disability history. During the 1970s there was a strong reaction among representatives of organizations of persons with disabilities and professionals in the field of disability against the terminology of the time. The terms "disability" and "handicap" were often used in an unclear and confusing way, which gave poor guidance for policy-making and for political action. The terminology reflected a medical and diagnostic approach, which ignored the imperfections and deficiencies of the surrounding society.

20. In 1980, the World Health Organization adopted an international classification of impairments, disabilities and handicaps, which suggested a more precise and at the same time relativistic approach. The International Classification of Impairments, Disabilities, and Handicaps makes a clear distinction between "impairment", "disability" and "handicap". It has been extensively used in areas such as rehabilitation, education, statistics, policy, legislation, demography, sociology, economics and anthropology. Some users have expressed concern that the Classification, in its definition of the term "handicap", may still be considered too medical and too centred on the individual, and may not adequately clarify the interaction between societal conditions or expectations and the abilities of the individual. Those concerns, and others expressed by users during the 12 years since its publication, will be addressed in forthcoming revisions of the Classification.

21. As a result of experience gained in the implementation of the World Programme of Action and of the general discussion that took place during the United Nations Decade of Disabled Persons, there was a deepening of knowledge and extension of understanding concerning disability issues and the terminology used. Current terminology recognizes the necessity of addressing both the individual needs (such as rehabilitation and technical aids) and the shortcomings of the society (various obstacles for participation).

Prevention

22. The term "prevention" means action aimed at preventing the occurrence of physical, intellectual, psychiatric or sensory impairments (primary prevention) or at preventing impairments from causing a permanent functional limitation or disability (secondary prevention). Prevention may include many different types of action, such as primary health care, prenatal and postnatal care, education in nutrition, immunization campaigns against communicable diseases, measures to control endemic diseases, safety regulations, programmes for the prevention of accidents in different environments, including adaptation of workplaces to prevent occupational disabilities and diseases, and prevention of disability resulting from pollution of the environment or armed conflict.

Rehabilitation

23. The term "rehabilitation" refers to a process aimed at enabling persons with disabilities to reach and maintain their optimal physical, sensory, intellectual, psychiatric and/or social functional levels, thus providing them with the tools to change their lives towards a higher level of independence. Rehabilitation may include measures to provide and/or restore functions, or compensate for the loss or absence of a function or for a functional limitation. The rehabilitation process does not involve initial medical care. It includes a wide range of measures and activities from more basic and general rehabilitation to goal-oriented activities, for instance vocational rehabilitation.

Equalization of opportunities

24. The term "equalization of opportunities" means the process through which the various systems of society and the environment, such as services, activities, information and documentation, are made available to all, particularly to persons with disabilities.

25. The principle of equal rights implies that the needs of each and every individual are of equal importance, that those needs must be made the basis for the planning of societies and that all resources must be employed in such a way as to ensure that every individual has equal opportunity for participation.

26. Persons with disabilities are members of society and have the right to remain within their local communities. They should receive the support they need within the ordinary structures of education, health, employment and social services.

27. As persons with disabilities achieve equal rights, they should also have equal obligations. As those rights are being achieved, societies should raise their expectations of persons with disabilities. As part of the process of equal opportunities, provision should be made to assist persons with disabilities to assume their full responsibility as members of society.

PREAMBLE

States,

Mindful of the pledge made, under the Charter of the United Nations, to take joint and separate action in cooperation with the Organization to promote higher standards of living, full employment, and conditions of economic and social progress and development,

Reaffirming the commitment to human rights and fundamental freedoms, social justice and the dignity and worth of the human person proclaimed in the Charter,

Recalling in particular the international standards on human rights, which have been laid down in the Universal Declaration of Human Rights, the International Covenant on Economic, Social and Cultural Rights and the International Covenant on Civil and Political Rights,

Underlining that those instruments proclaim that the rights recognized therein should be ensured equally to all individuals without discrimination,

Recalling the Convention on the Rights of the Child, which prohibits discrimination on the basis of disability and requires special measures to ensure the rights of children with disabilities, and the International Convention on the Protection of the Rights of All Migrant Workers and Members of Their Families, which provides for some protective measures against disability,

Recalling also the provisions in the Convention on the Elimination of All Forms of Discrimination against Women to ensure the rights of girls and women with disabilities, Having regard to the Declaration on the Rights of Disabled Persons, the Declaration on the Rights of Mentally Retarded Persons, the Declaration on Social Progress and Development, the Principles for the Protection of Persons with Mental Illness and for the Improvement of Mental Health Care and other relevant instruments adopted by the General Assembly,

Also having regard to the relevant conventions and recommendations adopted by the International Labour Organisation, with particular reference to participation in employment without discrimination for persons with disabilities,

Mindful of the relevant recommendations and work of the United Nations Educational, Scientific and Cultural Organization, in particular the World Declaration on Education for All, the World Health Organization, the United Nations Children's Fund and other concerned organizations,

Having regard to the commitment made by States concerning the protection of the environment,

Mindful of the devastation caused by armed conflict and deploring the use of scarce resources in the production of weapons,

Recognizing that the World Programme of Action concerning Disabled Persons and the definition therein of equalization of opportunities represent earnest ambitions on the part of the international community to render those various international instruments and recommendations of practical and concrete significance,

Acknowledging that the objective of the United Nations Decade of Disabled Persons (1983-1992) to implement the World Programme of Action is still valid and requires urgent and continued action,

Recalling that the World Programme of Action is based on concepts that are equally valid in developing and industrialized countries,

Convinced that intensified efforts are needed to achieve the full and equal enjoyment of human rights and participation in society by persons with disabilities,

Re-emphasizing that persons with disabilities, and their parents, guardians, advocates and organizations, must be active partners with States in the planning and implementation of all measures affecting their civil, political, economic, social and cultural rights,

In pursuance of Economic and Social Council resolution 1990/26, and basing themselves on the specific measures required for the attainment by persons with disabilities of equality with others, enumerated in detail in the World Programme of Action,

Have adopted the Standard Rules on the Equalization of Opportunities for Persons with Disabilities outlined below, in order:

(a) To stress that all action in the field of disability presupposes adequate knowledge and experience of the conditions and special needs of persons with disabilities;

(b) To emphasize that the process through which every aspect of societal organization is made accessible to all is a basic objective of socio-economic development;

(c) To outline crucial aspects of social policies in the field of disability, including, as appropriate, the active encouragement of technical and economic cooperation;

(d) To provide models for the political decision-making process required for the attainment of equal opportunities, bearing in mind the widely differing technical and economic levels, the fact that the process must reflect keen understanding of the cultural context within which it takes place and the crucial role of persons with disabilities in it;

(e) To propose national mechanisms for close collaboration among States, the organs of the United Nations system, other intergovernmental bodies and organizations of persons with disabilities;

(f) To propose an effective machinery for monitoring the process by which States seek to attain the equalization of opportunities for persons with disabilities.

I. PRECONDITIONS FOR EQUAL PARTICIPATION

Rule 1. Awareness-raising

States should take action to raise awareness in society about persons with disabilities, their rights, their needs, their potential and their contribution.

1. States should ensure that responsible authorities distribute up-to-date information on available programmes and services to persons with disabilities, their families, professionals in the field and the general public. Information to persons with disabilities should be presented in accessible form.

2. States should initiate and support information campaigns concerning persons with disabilities and disability policies, conveying the message that persons with disabilities are citizens with the same rights and obligations as others, thus justifying measures to remove all obstacles to full participation.

3. States should encourage the portrayal of persons with disabilities by the mass media in a positive way; organizations of persons with disabilities should be consulted on this matter.

4. States should ensure that public education programmes reflect in all their aspects the principle of full participation and equality.

5. States should invite persons with disabilities and their families and organizations to participate in public education programmes concerning disability matters.

6. States should encourage enterprises in the private sector to include disability issues in all aspects of their activity.

7. States should initiate and promote programmes aimed at raising the level of awareness of persons with disabilities concerning their rights and potential. Increased self-reliance and empowerment will assist persons with disabilities to take advantage of the opportunities available to them.

8. Awareness-raising should be an important part of the education of children with disabilities and in rehabilitation programmes. Persons with disabilities could also assist one another in awareness-raising through the activities of their own organizations.

9. Awareness-raising should be part of the education of all children and should be a component of teacher-training courses and training of all professionals.

Rule 2. Medical care

States should ensure the provision of effective medical care to persons with disabilities.

1. States should work towards the provision of programmes run by multidisciplinary teams of professionals for early detection, assessment and treatment of impairment. This could prevent, reduce or eliminate disabling effects. Such programmes should ensure the full participation of persons with disabilities and their families at the individual level, and of organizations of persons with disabilities at the planning and evaluation level.

2. Local community workers should be trained to participate in areas such as early detection of impairments, the provision of primary assistance and referral to appropriate services.

3. States should ensure that persons with disabilities, particularly infants and children, are provided with the same level of medical care within the same system as other members of society.

4. States should ensure that all medical and paramedical personnel are adequately trained and equipped to give medical care to persons with disabilities and that they have access to relevant treatment methods and technology.

5. States should ensure that medical, paramedical and related personnel are adequately trained so that they do not give inappropriate advice to parents, thus restricting options for their children. This training should be an ongoing process and should be based on the latest information available.

6. States should ensure that persons with disabilities are provided with any regular treatment and medicines they may need to preserve or improve their level of functioning.

Rule 3. Rehabilitation*

*Rehabilitation is a fundamental concept in disability policy and is defined above in paragraph 23 of the introduction.

States should ensure the provision of rehabilitation services to persons with disabilities in order for them to reach and sustain their optimum level of independence and functioning.

1. States should develop national rehabilitation programmes for all groups of persons with disabilities. Such programmes should be based on the actual individual needs of persons with disabilities and on the principles of full participation and equality.

2. Such programmes should include a wide range of activities, such as basic skills training to improve or compensate for an affected function, counselling of persons with disabilities and their families, developing self-reliance, and occasional services such as assessment and guidance.

3. All persons with disabilities, including persons with severe and/or multiple disabilities, who require rehabilitation should have access to it.

4. Persons with disabilities and their families should be able to participate in the design and organization of rehabilitation services concerning themselves.

5. All rehabilitation services should be available in the local community where the person with disabilities lives. However, in some instances, in order to attain a certain training objective, special time-limited rehabilitation courses may be organized, where appropriate, in residential form.

6. Persons with disabilities and their families should be encouraged to involve themselves in rehabilitation, for instance as trained teachers, instructors or counsellors.

7. States should draw upon the expertise of organizations of persons with disabilities when formulating or evaluating rehabilitation programmes.

Rule 4. Support services

States should ensure the development and supply of support services, including assistive devices for persons with disabilities, to assist them to increase their level of independence in their daily living and to exercise their rights.

1. States should ensure the provision of assistive devices and equipment, personal assistance and interpreter services, according to the needs of persons with disabilities, as important measures to achieve the equalization of opportunities.

2. States should support the development, production, distribution and servicing of assistive devices and equipment and the dissemination of knowledge about them.

3. To achieve this, generally available technical know-how should be utilized. In States where high-technology industry is available, it should be fully utilized to improve the standard and effectiveness of assistive devices and equipment. It is important to stimulate the development and production of simple and inexpensive devices, using local material and local production facilities when possible. Persons with disabilities themselves could be involved in the production of those devices.

4. States should recognize that all persons with disabilities who need assistive devices should have access to them as appropriate, including financial accessibility. This may mean that assistive devices and equipment should be provided free of charge or at such a low price that persons with disabilities or their families can afford to buy them.

5. In rehabilitation programmes for the provision of assistive devices and equipment, States should consider the special requirements of girls and boys with disabilities concerning the

design, durability and age-appropriateness of assistive devices and equipment.

6. States should support the development and provision of personal assistance programmes and interpretation services, especially for persons with severe and/or multiple disabilities. Such programmes would increase the level of participation of persons with disabilities in everyday life at home, at work, in school and during leisure-time activities.

7. Personal assistance programmes should be designed in such a way that the persons with disabilities using the programmes have a decisive influence on the way in which the programmes are delivered.

II. TARGET AREAS FOR EQUAL PARTICIPATION

Rule 5. Accessibility

States should recognize the overall importance of accessibility in the process of the equalization of opportunities in all spheres of society. For persons with disabilities of any kind, States should (a) introduce programmes of action to make the physical environment accessible; and (b) undertake measures to provide access to information and communication.

(a) Access to the physical environment

1. States should initiate measures to remove the obstacles to participation in the physical environment. Such measures should be to develop standards and guidelines and to consider enacting legislation to ensure accessibility to various areas in society, such as housing, buildings, public transport services and other means of transportation, streets and other outdoor environments.

2. States should ensure that architects, construction engineers and others who are professionally involved in the design and construction of the physical environment have access to adequate information on disability policy and measures to achieve accessibility.

3. Accessibility requirements should be included in the design and
construction of the physical environment from the beginning of the designing process.

4. Organizations of persons with disabilities should be consulted when standards and norms for accessibility are being developed. They should also be involved locally from the initial planning stage when public construction projects are being designed, thus ensuring maximum accessibility.

(b) Access to information and communication

5. Persons with disabilities and, where appropriate, their families and advocates should have access to full information on diagnosis, rights and available services and programmes, at all stages. Such information should be presented in forms accessible to persons with disabilities.

6. States should develop strategies to make information services and documentation accessible for different groups of persons with disabilities. Braille, tape services, large print and other appropriate technologies should be used to provide access to written information and documentation for persons with visual impairments. Similarly, appropriate technologies should be used to provide access to spoken information for persons with auditory impairments or comprehension difficulties.

7. Consideration should be given to the use of sign language in the education of deaf children, in their families and communities. Sign language interpretation services should also be provided to facilitate the communication between deaf persons and others.

8. Consideration should also be given to the needs of people with other communication disabilities.

9. States should encourage the media, especially television, radio and newspapers, to make their services accessible.

10. States should ensure that new computerized information and service systems offered to the general public are either made initially accessible or are adapted to be made accessible to persons with disabilities.

11. Organizations of persons with disabilities should be consulted when measures to make information services accessible are being developed.

Rule 6. Education

States should recognize the principle of equal primary, secondary and tertiary educational opportunities for children, youth and adults with disabilities, in integrated settings. They should ensure that the education of persons with disabilities is an integral part of the educational system.

1. General educational authorities are responsible for the education of persons with disabilities in integrated settings. Education for persons with disabilities should form an integral part of national educational planning curriculum development and school organization.

2. Education in mainstream schools presupposes the provision of interpreter and other appropriate support services. Adequate accessibility and support services, designed to meet the needs of persons with different disabilities, should be provided.

3. Parent groups and organizations of persons with disabilities should be involved in the education process at all levels.

4. In States where education is compulsory it should be provided to girl and boys with all kinds and all levels of disabilities, including the most severe.

5. Special attention should be given in the following areas:

(a) Very young children with disabilities;

(b) Pre-school children with disabilities;

(c) Adults with disabilities, particularly women.

6. To accommodate educational provisions for persons with disabilities in the mainstream, States should:

(a) Have a clearly stated policy, understood and accepted at the school level and by the wider community;

(b) Allow for curriculum flexibility, addition and adaptation;

(c) Provide for quality materials, ongoing teacher training and support teachers.

7. Integrated education and community-based programmes should be seen as complementary approaches in providing cost-effective education and training for persons with disabilities. National community-based programmes should encourage communities to use and develop their resources to provide local education to persons with disabilities.

8. In situations where the general school system does not yet adequately meet the needs of all persons with disabilities, special education may be considered. It should be aimed at preparing students for education in the general school system. The quality of such education should reflect the same standards and ambitions as general education and should be closely linked to it. At a minimum, students with disabilities should be afforded the same portion of educational resources as students without disabilities. States should aim for the gradual integration of special education services into mainstream education. It is acknowledged that in some instances special education may currently be considered to be the most appropriate form of education for some students with disabilities.

9. Owing to the particular communication needs of deaf and deaf/blind persons, their education may be more suitably provided in schools for such persons or special classes and units in mainstream schools. At the initial stage, in particular, special attention needs to be focused on culturally sensitive instruction that will result in effective communication skills and maximum independence for people who are deaf or deaf/blind.

Rule 7. Employment

States should recognize the principle that persons with disabilities must be empowered to exercise their human rights, particularly in the field of employment. In both rural and urban areas they must have equal opportunities for productive and gainful employment in the labour market.

1. Laws and regulations in the employment field must not discriminate against persons with disabilities and must not raise obstacles to their employment.

2. States should actively support the integration of persons with disabilities into open employment. This active support could occur through a variety of measures, such as vocational training, incentive-oriented quota schemes, reserved or designated employment, loans or grants for small business, exclusive contracts or priority production rights, tax concessions, contract compliance or other technical or financial assistance to enterprises employing workers with disabilities. States should also encourage employers to make reasonable adjustments to accommodate persons with disabilities.

3. States' action programmes should include:

(a) Measures to design and adapt workplaces and work premises in such a way that they become accessible to persons with different disabilities;

(b) Support for the use of new technologies and the development and production of assistive devices, tools and equipment and measures to facilitate access to such devices and equipment for persons with disabilities to enable them to gain and maintain employment;

(c) Provision of appropriate training and placement and ongoing support such as personal assistance and interpreter services.

4. States should initiate and support public awareness-raising campaigns designed to overcome negative attitudes and prejudices concerning workers with disabilities.

5. In their capacity as employers, States should create favourable conditions for the employment of persons with disabilities in the public sector.

6. States, workers' organizations and employers should cooperate to ensure equitable recruitment and promotion policies, employment conditions, rates of pay, measures to improve the work environment in order to prevent injuries and impairments and measures for the rehabilitation of employees who have sustained employment-related injuries.

7. The aim should always be for persons with disabilities to obtain employment in the open labour market. For persons with disabilities whose needs cannot be met in open employment, small units of sheltered or supported employment may be an alternative. It is important that the quality of such programmes be assessed in terms of their relevance and sufficiency in providing opportunities for persons with disabilities to gain employment in the labour market.

8. Measures should be taken to include persons with disabilities in training and employment programmes in the private and informal sectors.

9. States, workers' organizations and employers should cooperate with organizations of persons with disabilities concerning all measures to create training and employment opportunities, including flexible hours, part-time work, job-sharing, self-employment and attendant care for persons with disabilities.

Rule 8. Income maintenance and social security

States are responsible for the provision of social security and income maintenance for persons with disabilities.

1. States should ensure the provision of adequate income support to persons with disabilities who, owing to disability or disability-related factors, have temporarily lost or received a reduction in their income or have been denied employment opportunities. States should ensure that the provision of support takes into account the costs frequently incurred by persons with disabilities and their families as a result of the disability.

2. In countries where social security, social insurance or other social welfare schemes exist or are being developed for the general population, States should ensure that such systems do not exclude or discriminate against persons with disabilities.

3. States should also ensure the provision of income support and social security protection to individuals who undertake the care of a person with a disability.

4. Social security systems should include incentives to restore the income-earning capacity of persons with disabilities. Such systems should provide or contribute to the organization, development and financing of vocational training. They should also assist with placement services.

5. Social security programmes should also provide incentives for persons with disabilities to seek employment in order to establish or re-establish their income-earning capacity.

6. Income support should be maintained as long as the disabling conditions remain in a manner that does not discourage persons with disabilities from seeking employment. It should only be reduced or terminated when persons with disabilities achieve adequate and secure income.

7. States, in countries where social security is to a large extent provided by the private sector, should encourage local communities, welfare organizations and families to develop self-help measures and incentives for employment or employment-related activities for persons with disabilities.

Rule 9. Family life and personal integrity

States should promote the full participation of persons with disabilities in family life. They should promote their right to personal integrity and ensure that laws do not discriminate against persons with disabilities with respect to sexual relationships, marriage and parenthood.

1. Persons with disabilities should be enabled to live with their families. States should encourage the inclusion in family counselling of appropriate modules regarding disability and its effects on family life. Respite-care and attendant-care services should be made available to families which include a person with disabilities. States should remove all unnecessary obstacles to persons who want to foster or adopt a child or adult with disabilities.

2. Persons with disabilities must not be denied the opportunity to experience their sexuality, have sexual relationships and experience parenthood. Taking into account that persons with disabilities may experience difficulties in getting married and setting up a family, States should encourage the availability of appropriate counselling. Persons with disabilities must have the same access as others to family-planning methods, as well as to information in accessible form on the sexual functioning of their bodies.

3. States should promote measures to change negative attitudes towards marriage, sexuality and parenthood of persons with disabilities, especially of girls and women with disabilities, which still prevail in society. The media should be encouraged to play an important role in removing such negative attitudes.

4. Persons with disabilities and their families need to be fully informed about taking precautions against sexual and other forms of abuse. Persons with disabilities are particularly vulnerable to abuse in the family, community or institutions and need to be educated on how to avoid the occurrence of abuse, recognize when abuse has occurred and report on such acts.

Rule 10. Culture

States will ensure that persons with disabilities are integrated into and can participate in cultural activities on an equal basis.

1. States should ensure that persons with disabilities have the opportunity to utilize their creative, artistic and intellectual potential, not only for their own benefit, but also for the enrichment of their community, be they in urban or rural areas. Examples of such activities are dance, music, literature, theatre, plastic arts, painting and sculpture. Particularly in developing countries, emphasis should be placed on traditional and contemporary art forms, such as puppetry, recitation and story-telling.

2. States should promote the accessibility to and availability of places for cultural performances and services, such as theatres, museums, cinemas and libraries, to persons with disabilities.

3. States should initiate the development and use of special technical arrangements to make literature, films and theatre accessible to persons with disabilities.

Rule 11. Recreation and sports

States will take measures to ensure that persons with disabilities have equal opportunities for recreation and sports.

1. States should initiate measures to make places for recreation and sports, hotels, beaches, sports arenas, gym halls, etc., accessible to persons with disabilities. Such measures should encompass support for staff in recreation and sports programmes, including projects to develop methods of accessibility, and participation, information and training programmes.

2. Tourist authorities, travel agencies, hotels, voluntary organizations and others involved in organizing recreational activities or travel opportunities should offer their services to all, taking into account the special needs of persons with disabilities. Suitable training should be provided to assist that process.

3. Sports organizations should be encouraged to develop opportunities for participation by persons with disabilities in sports activities. In some cases, accessibility measures could be enough to open up opportunities for participation. In other cases, special arrangements or special games would be needed. States should support the participation of persons with disabilities in national and international events.

4. Persons with disabilities participating in sports activities should have access to instruction and training of the same quality as other participants.

5. Organizers of sports and recreation should consult with organizations of persons with disabilities when developing their services for persons with disabilities.

Rule 12. Religion

States will encourage measures for equal participation by persons with disabilities in the religious life of their communities.

1. States should encourage, in consultation with religious authorities, measures to eliminate discrimination and make religious activities accessible to persons with disabilities.

2. States should encourage the distribution of information on disability matters to religious institutions and organizations. States should also encourage religious authorities to include information on disability policies in the training for religious professions, as well as in religious education programmes.

3. They should also encourage the accessibility of religious literature to persons with sensory impairments.

4. States and/or religious organizations should consult with organizations of persons with disabilities when developing measures for equal participation in religious activities.

III. IMPLEMENTATION MEASURES

Rule 13. Information and research

States assume the ultimate responsibility for the collection and dissemination of information on the living conditions of persons with disabilities and promote comprehensive research on all aspects, including obstacles that affect the lives of persons with disabilities.

1. States should, at regular intervals, collect gender-specific statistics and other information concerning the living conditions of persons with disabilities. Such data collection could be conducted in conjunction with national censuses and household surveys and could be undertaken in close collaboration, *inter alia*, with universities, research institutes and organizations of persons with disabilities. The data collection should include questions on programmes and services and their use.

2. States should consider establishing a data bank on disability, which would include statistics on available services and programmes as well as on the different groups of persons with disabilities. They should bear in mind the need to protect individual privacy and personal integrity.

3. States should initiate and support programmes of research on social, economic and participation issues that affect the lives of persons with disabilities and their families. Such research should include studies on the causes, types and frequencies of disabilities, the availability and efficacy of existing programmes and the need for development and evaluation of services and support measures.

4. States should develop and adopt terminology and criteria for the conduct of national surveys, in cooperation with organizations of persons with disabilities.

5. States should facilitate the participation of persons with disabilities in data collection and research. To undertake such research States should particularly encourage the recruitment of qualified persons with disabilities.

6. States should support the exchange of research findings and experiences.

7. States should take measures to disseminate information and knowledge on disability to all political and administration levels within national, regional and local spheres.

Rule 14. Policy-making and planning

States will ensure that disability aspects are included in all relevant policy-making and national planning.

1. States should initiate and plan adequate policies for persons with disabilities at the national level, and stimulate and support action at regional and local levels.

2. States should involve organizations of persons with disabilities in all decision-making relating to plans and programmes concerning persons with disabilities or affecting their economic and social status.

3. The needs and concerns of persons with disabilities should be incorporated into general development plans and not be treated separately.

4. The ultimate responsibility of States for the situation of persons with disabilities does not relieve others of their responsibility. Anyone in charge of services, activities or the provision of information in society should be encouraged to accept responsibility for making such programmes available to persons with disabilities.

5. States should facilitate the development by local communities of programmes and measures for persons with disabilities. One way of doing this could be to develop manuals or check-lists and provide training programmes for local staff.

Rule 15. Legislation

States have a responsibility to create the legal bases for measures to achieve the objectives of full participation and equality for persons with disabilities.

1. National legislation, embodying the rights and obligations of citizens, should include the rights and obligations of persons with disabilities. States are under an obligation to enable persons with disabilities to exercise their rights, including their human, civil and political rights, on an equal basis with other citizens. States must ensure that organizations of persons with disabilities are involved in the development of national legislation concerning the rights of persons with disabilities, as well as in the ongoing evaluation of that legislation.

2. Legislative action may be needed to remove conditions that may adversely affect the lives of persons with disabilities, including harassment and victimization. Any discriminatory provisions against persons with disabilities must be eliminated. National legislation should provide for appropriate sanctions in case of violations of the principles of non-discrimination.

3. National legislation concerning persons with disabilities may appear in two different forms. The rights and obligations may be incorporated in general legislation or contained in special legislation. Special legislation for persons with disabilities may be established in several ways:

(a) By enacting separate legislation, dealing exclusively with disability matters;

(b) By including disability matters within legislation on particular topics;

(c) By mentioning persons with disabilities specifically in the texts that serve to interpret existing legislation.

A combination of those different approaches might be desirable. Affirmative action provisions may also be considered.

4. States may consider establishing formal statutory complaints mechanisms in order to protect the interests of persons with disabilities.

Rule 16. Economic policies

States have the financial responsibility for national programmes and measures to create equal opportunities for persons with disabilities.

1. States should include disability matters in the regular budgets of all national, regional and local government bodies.

2. States, non-governmental organizations and other interested bodies should interact to determine the most effective ways of supporting projects and measures relevant to persons with disabilities.

3. States should consider the use of economic measures (loans, tax exemptions, earmarked grants, special funds, and so on) to stimulate and support equal participation by persons with disabilities in society.

4. In many States it may be advisable to establish a disability development fund, which could support various pilot projects and self-help programmes at the grass-roots level.

Rule 17. Coordination of work

States are responsible for the establishment and strengthening of national coordinating committees, or similar bodies, to serve as a national focal point on disability matters.

1. The national coordinating committee or similar bodies should be permanent and based on legal as well as appropriate administrative regulation.

2. A combination of representatives of private and public organizations is most likely to achieve an intersectoral and multidisciplinary composition. Representatives could be drawn from concerned government ministries, organizations of persons with disabilities and non-governmental organizations.

3. Organizations of persons with disabilities should have considerable influence in the national coordinating committee in order to ensure proper feedback of their concerns.

4. The national coordinating committee should be provided with sufficient autonomy and resources to fulfil its responsibilities in relation to its decision-making capacities. It should report to the highest governmental level.

Rule 18. Organizations of persons with disabilities

States should recognize the right of the organizations of persons with disabilities to represent persons with disabilities at national, regional and local levels. States should also recognize the advisory role of organizations of persons with disabilities in decision-making on disability matters.

1. States should encourage and support economically and in other ways the formation and strengthening of organizations of persons with disabilities, family members and/or advocates. States should recognize that those organiza-

tions have a role to play in the development of disability policy.

2. States should establish ongoing communication with organizations of persons with disabilities and ensure their participation in the development of government policies.

3. The role of organizations of persons with disabilities could be to identify needs and priorities, to participate in the planning, implementation and evaluation of services and measures concerning the lives of persons with disabilities, and to contribute to public awareness and to advocate change.

4. As instruments of self-help, organizations of persons with disabilities provide and promote opportunities for the development of skills in various fields, mutual support among members and information sharing.

5. Organizations of persons with disabilities could perform their advisory role in many different ways such as having permanent representation on boards of government-funded agencies, serving on public commissions and providing expert knowledge on different projects.

6. The advisory role of organizations of persons with disabilities should be ongoing in order to develop and deepen the exchange of views and information between the State and the organizations.

7. Organizations should be permanently represented on the national coordinating committee or similar bodies.

8. The role of local organizations of persons with disabilities should be developed and strengthened to ensure that they influence matters at the community level.

Rule 19. Personnel training

States are responsible for ensuring the adequate training of personnel, at all levels, involved in the planning and provision of programmes and services concerning persons with disabilities.

1. States should ensure that all authorities providing services in the disability field give adequate training to their personnel.

2. In the training of professionals in the disability field, as well as in the provision of information on disability in general training programmes, the principle of full participation and equality should be appropriately reflected.

3. States should develop training programmes in consultation with organizations of persons with disabilities, and persons with disabilities should be involved as teachers, instructors or advisers in staff training programmes.

4. The training of community workers is of great strategic importance, particularly in developing countries. It should involve persons with disabilities and include the development of appropriate values, competence and technologies as well as skills which can be practised by persons with disabilities, their parents, families and members of the community.

Rule 20. National monitoring and evaluation of disability programmes in the implementation of he Rules

States are responsible for the continuous monitoring and evaluation of the implementation of national programmes and services concern-

ing the equalization of opportunities for persons with disabilities.

1. States should periodically and systematically evaluate national disability programmes and disseminate both the bases and the results of the evaluations.

2. States should develop and adopt terminology and criteria for the evaluation of disability-related programmes and services.

3. Such criteria and terminology should be developed in close cooperation with organizations of persons with disabilities from the earliest conceptual and planning stages.

4. States should participate in international cooperation in order to develop common standards for national evaluation in the disability field. States should encourage national coordinating committees to participate also.

5. The evaluation of various programmes in the disability field should be built in at the planning stage, so that the overall efficacy in fulfilling their policy objectives can be evaluated.

Rule 21. Technical and economic cooperation

States, both industrialized and developing, have the responsibility to cooperate in and take measures for the improvement of the living conditions of persons with disabilities in developing countries.

1. Measures to achieve the equalization of opportunities of persons with disabilities, including refugees with disabilities, should be integrated into general development programmes.

2. Such measures must be integrated into all forms of technical and economic cooperation, bilateral and multilateral, governmental and non-governmental. States should bring up disability issues in discussions on such cooperation with their counterparts.

3. When planning and reviewing programmes of technical and economic cooperation, special attention should be given to the effects of such programmes on the situation of persons with disabilities. It is of the utmost importance that persons with disabilities and their organizations are consulted on any development projects designed for persons with disabilities. They should be directly involved in the development, implementation and evaluation of such projects.

4. Priority areas for technical and economic cooperation should include:

(a) The development of human resources through the development of skills, abilities and potentials of persons with disabilities and the initiation of employment-generating activities for and of persons with disabilities;

(b) The development and dissemination of appropriate disability-related technologies and know-how.

5. States are also encouraged to support the formation and strengthening of organizations of persons with disabilities.

6. States should take measures to improve the knowledge of disability issues among staff involved at all levels in the administration

of technical and economic cooperation programmes.

Rule 22. International cooperation

States will participate actively in international cooperation concerning policies for the equalization of opportunities for persons with disabilities.

1. Within the United Nations, the specialized agencies and other concerned intergovernmental organizations, States should participate in the development of disability policy.

2. Whenever appropriate, States should introduce disability aspects in general negotiations concerning standards, information exchange, development programmes, etc.

3. States should encourage and support the exchange of knowledge and experience among:

(a) Non-governmental organizations concerned with disability issues;

(b) Research institutions and individual researchers involved in disability issues;

(c) Representatives of field programmes and of professional groups in the disability field;

(d) Organizations of persons with disabilities;

(e) National coordinating committees.

4. States should ensure that the United Nations and the specialized agencies, as well as all intergovernmental and interparliamentary bodies, at global and regional levels, include in their work the global and regional organizations of persons with disabilities.

IV. MONITORING MECHANISM

1. The purpose of a monitoring mechanism is to further the effective implementation of the Rules. It will assist each State in assessing its level of implementation of the Rules and in measuring its progress. The monitoring should identify obstacles and suggest suitable measures that would contribute to the successful implementation of the Rules. The monitoring mechanism will recognize the economic, social and cultural features existing in individual States. An important element should also be the provision of advisory services and the exchange of experience and information between States.

2. The Rules shall be monitored within the framework of the sessions of the Commission for Social Development. A Special Rapporteur with relevant and extensive experience in disability issues and international organizations shall be appointed, if necessary, funded by extrabudgetary resources, for three years to monitor the implementation of the Rules.

3. International organizations of persons with disabilities having consultative status with the Economic and Social Council and organizations representing persons with disabilities who have not yet formed their own organizations should be invited to create among themselves a panel of experts, on which organizations of persons with disabilities shall have a majority, taking into account the different kinds of disabilities and necessary equitable geographical distribution, to be consulted by the Special Rapporteur and, when appropriate, by the Secretariat.

4. The panel of experts will be encouraged by the Special Rapporteur to review, advise and provide feedback and suggestions on the promotion, implementation and monitoring of the Rules.

5. The Special Rapporteur shall send a set of questions to States, entities within the United Nations system, and intergovernmental' and non-governmental organizations, including organizations of persons with disabilities. The set of questions should address implementation plans for the Rules in States. The questions should be selective in nature and cover a number of specific rules for in-depth evaluation. In preparing the questions the Special Rapporteur should consult with the panel of experts and the Secretariat.

6. The Special Rapporteur shall seek to establish a direct dialogue not only with States but also with local non-governmental organizations, seeking their views and comments on any information intended to be included in the reports. The Special Rapporteur shall provide advisory services on the implementation and monitoring of the Rules and assistance in the preparation of replies to the sets of questions.

7. The Department for Policy Coordination and Sustainable Development of the Secretariat, as the United Nations focal point on disability issues, the United Nations Development Pro-gramme and other entities and mechanisms within the United Nations system, such as the regional commissions and specialized agencies and inter-agency meetings, shall cooperate with the Special Rapporteur in the implementation and monitoring of the Rules at the national level.

8. The Special Rapporteur, assisted by the Secretariat, shall prepare reports for submission to the Commission for Social Development at its thirty-fourth and thirty-fifth sessions. In preparing such reports, the Rapporteur should consult with the panel of experts.

9. States should encourage national coordinating committees or similar bodies to participate in implementation and monitoring. As the focal points on disability matters at the national level, they should be encouraged to establish procedures to coordinate the monitoring of the Rules. Organizations of persons with disabilities should be encouraged to be actively involved in the monitoring of the process at all levels.

10. Should extrabudgetary resources be identified, one or more positions of interregional adviser on the Rules should be created to provide direct services to States, including:

(a) The organization of national and regional training seminars on the content of the Rules;

(b) The development of guidelines to assist in strategies for implementation of the Rules;

(c) Dissemination of information about best practices concerning implementation of the Rules.

11. At its thirty-fourth session, the Commission for Social Development should establish an open-ended working group to examine the Special Rapporteur's report and make recommendations on how to improve the application of the Rules. In examining the Special Rapporteur's report, the Commission, through its open-ended working group, shall consult international organizations of persons with disabilities and specialized agencies, in accordance with rules 71 and 76 of the rules of procedure of the functional commissions of the Economic and Social Council.

12. At its session following the end of the Special Rapporteur's mandate, the Commission should examine the possibility of either renewing that mandate, appointing a new Special Rapporteur or considering another monitoring mechanism, and should make appropriate recommendations to the Economic and Social Council.

13. States should be encouraged to contribute to the United Nations Voluntary Fund on Disability in order to further the implementation of the Rules.

Bibliography

RTICLE 1

● Instruments:

League of Nations Declaration of the Rights of the Child (1924)

Universal Declaration of Human Rights (1948)

Declaration of the Rights of the Child (1959)

Convention on Consent to Marriage, Minimum Age for Marriage and Registration of Marriages (1962)

Recommendation on Consent to Marriage, Minimum Age for Marriage and Registration of Marriages (1965)

United Nations Standard Minimum Rules for the Administration of Juvenile Justice (the "Beijing Rules") (1985)

● Other sources:

Committee on the Elimination of Discrimination against Women, General Recommendation 21, "Equality in marriage and family relations", 1993, in *Compilation of General Comments and General Recommendations Adopted by Human Rights Treaty Bodies*, HR1/GEN/1/Rev.2, 29 March 1996

Committee on the Rights of the Child, *General Guidelines Regarding the Form and Contents of Initial Reports to be submitted by States Parties Under Article 44, Paragraph 1(a), of the Convention on the Rights of the Child*, CRC/C/5, 15 October 1991

Committee on the Rights of the Child, *General Guidelines Regarding the Form and Contents of Periodic Reports to be submitted by States Parties under Article 44, Paragraph 1(b), of the Convention on the Rights of the Child*, CRC/C/58, 20 November 1996

"The Convention on the Rights of the Child", by Marta Santos Pais, in *Manual on Human Rights Reporting under six major international human rights instruments,* Office of the High Commissioner for Human Rights, Geneva; United Nations Institute for Training and Research (UNITAR), United Nations Staff College Project, Turin, United Nations, Geneva, 1997

Committee on the Rights of the Child, *Reservations, Declarations and Objections Relating to the Convention on the Rights of the Child*, CRC/C/2/Rev.5, 30 July 1996

The United Nations Convention on the Rights of the Child A Guide to the "Travaux Préparatoires", compiled and edited by Sharon Detrick, contributors Jaap Doek, Nigel Cantwell, Martinus Nijhoff Publishers, The Netherlands, 1992

ARTICLE 2

● Instruments:

International Convention on the Elimination of All Forms of Racial Discrimination (1965)

International Covenant on Civil and Political Rights (1966)

International Covenant on Economic, Social and Cultural Rights (1966)

Convention on the Elimination of All Forms of Discrimination against Women (1979)

● Other sources:

Bulletin of Human Rights 91/2: The Rights of the Child, Alston, P., "The legal framework of the Convention on the Rights of the Child", United Nations, 1991

Commission on Human Rights, "The plight of street children", resolution 1994/93, 9 March 1994

Commission on Human Rights, "Special Rapporteur on violence against women preliminary report", E/CN.4/1995/42,22 November 1994

Committee on the Rights of the Child, *General Guidelines Regarding the Form and Contents of Initial Reports to be submitted by States Parties Under Article 44, Paragraph 1 (a), of the Convention on the Rights of the Child*, CRC/C/5, 15 October 1991

Committee on the Rights of the Child, *General Guidelines Regarding the Form and Contents of Periodic Reports to be submitted by States Parties under Article 44, Paragraph 1(b), of the Convention on the Rights of the Child*, CRC/C/58, 20 November 1996

Fourth World Conference on Women, Beijing, China, 4-15 September 1995, *Platform for Action and the Beijing Declaration*, Department of Public Information, United Nations, New York, 1996

Human Rights Committee, General Comment 18, "Non-discrimination", 1989,in *Compilation of General Comments and General Recommendations Adopted by Human Rights Treaty Bodies*", HR1/GEN/1/Rev.2, 29 March 1996

International Conference on Population and Development, Cairo, 1994, "Report of the International Conference on Population and Development", A/CONF.171/13, 18 October 1994

World Summit for Children, "World Declaration on the Survival, Protection and Development of Children and Plan of Action for Implementing the World Declaration on the Survival, Protection and Development of Children in the 1990s", CF/WSC/1990/WS-001, United Nations, New York, 30 September 1990

ARTICLE 3

● **Instruments:**

Declaration of the Rights of the Child (1959)

Convention on the Elimination of All Forms of Discrimination against Women (1979)

Declaration on Social and Legal Principles relating to the Protection and Welfare of Children, with Special Reference to Foster Placement and Adoption Nationally and Internationally (1986)

● **Other sources:**

Bulletin of Human Rights 91/2, The Rights of the Child, Alston, P., "The legal framework of the Convention on the Rights of the Child", United Nations, 1991

Committee on the Rights of the Child, *General Guidelines Regarding the Form and Contents of Initial Reports to be submitted by States Parties Under Article 44, Paragraph 1(a), of the Convention on the Rights of the Child,* CRC/C/5, 15 October 1991

Committee on the Rights of the Child, *General Guidelines Regarding the Form and Contents of Periodic Reports to be submitted by States Parties under Article 44, Paragraph 1(b), of the Convention on the Rights of the Child,* CRC/C/58, 20 November 1996

Human Rights Committee, General Comment 17, "Article 24", 1989; Human Rights Committee, General Comment 19, "Article 23", 1990, in *Compilation of General Comments and General Recommendations Adopted by Human Rights Treaty Bodies,* HR1/GEN/1/Rev.2, 29 March 1996

The United Nations Convention on the Rights of the Child A Guide to the "Travaux Préparatoires", compiled and edited by Sharon Detrick, contributors Jaap Doek, Nigel Cantwell, Martinus Nijhoff Publishers, The Netherlands, 1992

ARTICLE 4

● **Instruments:**

International Covenant on Civil and Political Rights (1966)

International Covenant on Economic, Social and Cultural Rights (1966)

● **Other sources:**

Committee on Economic, Social and Cultural Rights, General Comment 3, "The nature of States Parties' Obligations", 1990, in *Compilation of General Comments and General Recommendations Adopted by Human Rights Treaty Bodies,* HR1/GEN/1/Rev.2, 29 March 1996

Committee on the Rights of the Child, *General Guidelines Regarding the Form and Contents of Initial Reports to be submitted by States Parties Under Article 44, Paragraph 1(a), of the Convention on the Rights of the Child,* CRC/C/5, 15 October 1991

Committee on the Rights of the Child, *General Guidelines Regarding the Form and Contents of Periodic Reports to be submitted by States Parties under Article 44, Paragraph 1(b), of the Convention on the Rights of the Child,* CRC/C/58, 20 November 1996

Human Rights Committee, General Comment 3, "Article 2, Implementation at the national level", 1981, in *Compilation of General Comments and General Recommendations Adopted by Human Rights Treaty Bodies,* HR1/GEN/1/Rev.2, 29 March 1996

Implementing the Convention on the Rights of the Child: Resource Mobilization in Low-income Countries, edited by James R. Himes, UNICEF International Child Development Centre, Martinus Nijhoff, 1995

The United Nations Convention on the Rights of the Child A Guide to the "Travaux Préparatoires", compiled and edited by Sharon Detrick, contributors Jaap Doek, Nigel Cantwell, Martinus Nijhoff Publishers, The Netherlands, 1992

United Nations Development Programme, *Human Development Report 1994,* "20/20 Initiatives: from 1994 United Nations Development Programme (UNDP)", Oxford University Press, New York, Oxford, 1994

World Conference on Human Rights, Vienna, 14-25 June 1993, "Vienna Declaration and Programme of Action", A/CONF.157/23, 12 July 1993

World Summit for Children, "World Declaration on the Survival, Protection and Development of Children and Plan of Action for Implementing the World Declaration on the Survival, Protection and Development of Children in the 1990s", CF/WSC/1990/WS-001, United Nations, New York, 30 September 1990

World Summit for Social Development, Copenhagen, Denmark, 6-12 March 1995, "Report of the World Summit for Social Development", A/CONF.166/9, 19 April 1995

ARTICLE 5

● **Instruments:**

International Covenant on Civil and Political Rights (1966)

United Nations Standard Minimum Rules for the Administration of Juvenile Justice (the "Beijing Rules") (1985)

United Nations Guidelines for the Prevention of Juvenile Delinquency (the "Riyadh Guidelines") (1990)

● **Other sources:**

Committee on the Rights of the Child, *General Guidelines Regarding the Form and Contents of Initial Reports to be submitted by States Parties Under Article 44, Paragraph 1(a), of the Convention on the Rights of the Child,* CRC/C/5, 15 October 1991

Committee on the Rights of the Child, *General Guidelines Regarding the Form and Contents of Periodic Reports to be submitted by States Parties under Article 44, Paragraph 1(b), of the Convention on the Rights of the Child,* CRC/C/58, 20 November 1996

Committee on the Rights of the Child, *Reservations, Declarations and Objections Relating to the Convention on the Rights of the Child,* CRC/C/2/Rev.5, 30 July 1996

Human Rights Committee, General Comment 17, "Article 24", 1989; Human Rights Committee, General Comment 19, "Article 23",

1990, in *Compilation of General Comments and General Recommendations Adopted by Human Rights Treaty Bodies,* HR1/GEN/1/Rev.2, 29 March 1996

"The Convention on the Rights of the Child", by Marta Santos Pais, in *Manual on Human Rights Reporting under six major international human rights instruments,* Office of the High Commissioner for Human Rights, Geneva; United Nations Institute for Training and Research (UNITAR), United Nations Staff College Project, Turin, United Nations, Geneva, 1997

ARTICLE 6

● **Instruments:**

Universal Declaration of Human Rights (1948)

International Covenant on Civil and Political Rights (1966)

Second Optional Protocol to the International Covenant on Civil and Political Rights, aiming at the abolition of the death penalty (1989)

United Nations Rules for the Protection of Juveniles Deprived of their Liberty (1990)

Standard Rules on the Equalization of Opportunities for Persons with Disabilities (1993)

Declaration on the Protection of All Persons from Enforced Disappearances (1993)

● **Other sources:**

Fourth World Conference on Women, Beijing, China, 4-15 September 1995, *Platform for Action and the Beijing Declaration,* Department of Public Information, United Nations, New York, 1996

Commission on Human Rights, "Report of the Working Group on Traditional Practices affecting the health of Women and Children", E/CN.4/1986/42, February 1986

Committee on the Rights of the Child, *General Guidelines Regarding the Form and Contents of Initial Reports to be submitted by States Parties Under Article 44, Paragraph 1(a), of the Convention on the Rights of the Child,* CRC/C/5, 15 October 1991

Committee on the Rights of the Child, *General Guidelines Regarding the Form and Contents of Periodic Reports to be submitted by States Parties under Article 44, Paragraph 1(b), of the Convention on the Rights of the Child,* CRC/C/58, 20 November 1996

Human Rights Committee, General Comment 6, "Article 6", 1982; Human Rights Committee, General Comment 14, "Article 6", 1984, in *Compilation of General Comments and General Recommendations Adopted by Human Rights Treaty Bodies,* HR1/GEN/1/Rev.2, 29 March 1996

"The Convention on the Rights of the Child", by Marta Santos Pais, in *Manual on Human Rights Reporting under six major international human rights instruments,* Office of the High Commissioner for Human Rights, Geneva; United Nations Institute for Training and Research (UNITAR), United Nations Staff College Project, Turin, United Nations, Geneva, 1997

The United Nations Convention on the Rights of the Child A Guide to the "Travaux Préparatoires", compiled and edited by Sharon

Detrick, contributors Jaap Doek, Nigel Cantwell, Martinus Nijhoff Publishers, The Netherlands, 1992

United Nations Children's Fund, *The Progress of Nations: The nations of the world ranked according to their achievements in child health, nutrition, education, water and sanitation, and progress for women, 1996,* UNICEF, New York, 1996

World Summit for Children, "World Declaration on the Survival, Protection and Development of Children and Plan of Action for Implementing the World Declaration on the Survival, Protection and Development of Children in the 1990s", CF/WSC/1990/WS-001, United Nations, New York, 30 September 1990

World Summit for Social Development, Copenhagen, Denmark, 6-12 March 1995, "Report of the World Summit for Social Development", A/CONF.166/9, 19 April 1995

ARTICLE 7

● **Instruments:**

Declaration of the Rights of the Child (1959)

International Covenant on Civil and Political Rights (1966)

Declaration on Social and Legal Principles relating to the Protection and Welfare of Children, with Special Reference to Foster Placement and Adoption Nationally and Internationally (1986)

Hague Convention on Protection of Children and Cooperation in respect of intercountry Adoption (1993)

● **Other sources:**

Committee on the Rights of the Child, *General Guidelines Regarding the Form and Contents of Initial Reports to be submitted by States Parties Under Article 44, Paragraph 1(a), of the Convention on the Rights of the Child,* CRC/C/5, October 15 1991

Committee on the Rights of the Child, *General Guidelines Regarding the Form and Contents of Periodic Reports to be submitted by States Parties under Article 44, Paragraph 1(b), of the Convention on the Rights of the Child,* CRC/C/58, 20 November 1996

Committee on the Rights of the Child, *Reservations, Declarations and Objections Relating to the Convention on the Rights of the Child,* CRC/C/2/Rev.5, 30 July 1996

Human Rights Committee, General Comment 17, "Article 24", 1989, in *Compilation of General Comments and General Recommendations Adopted by Human Rights Treaty Bodies,* HR1/GEN/1/Rev.2, 29 March 1996

"The Convention on the Rights of the Child", by Marta Santos Pais, in *Manual on Human Rights Reporting under six major international human rights instruments,* Office of the High Commissioner for Human Rights, Geneva; United Nations Institute for Training and Research (UNITAR), United Nations Staff College Project, Turin, United Nations, Geneva, 1997

The United Nations Convention on the Rights of the Child A Guide to the "Travaux Préparatoires", compiled and edited by Sharon

Detrick, contributors Jaap Doek, Nigel Cantwell, Martinus Nijhoff Publishers, The Netherlands, 1992

ARTICLE 8

● **Instruments:**

Declaration on the Protection of All Persons from Enforced Disappearances (1993)

Additional Protocol I to the Geneva Conventions of 12 August 1949, Geneva 1977

● **Other sources:**

Committee on the Rights of the Child, *General Guidelines Regarding the Form and Contents of Initial Reports to be submitted by States Parties Under Article 44, Paragraph 1(a), of the Convention on the Rights of the Child,* CRC/C/5, 15 October 1991

Committee on the Rights of the Child, *General Guidelines Regarding the Form and Contents of Periodic Reports to be submitted by States Parties under Article 44, Paragraph 1(b), of the Convention on the Rights of the Child,* CRC/C/58, 20 November 1996

"The Convention on the Rights of the Child", by Marta Santos Pais, in *Manual on Human Rights Reporting under six major international human rights instruments,* Office of the High Commissioner for Human Rights, Geneva; United Nations Institute for Training and Research (UNITAR), United Nations Staff College Project, Turin, United Nations, Geneva, 1997

The United Nations Convention on the Rights of the Child A Guide to the "Travaux Préparatoires", compiled and edited by Sharon Detrick, contributors Jaap Doek, Nigel Cantwell, Martinus Nijhoff Publishers, The Netherlands, 1992

ARTICLE 9

● **Instruments:**

Declaration of the Rights of the Child (1959)

International Covenant on Civil and Political Rights (1966)

International Covenant on Economic, Social and Cultural Rights (1966)

United Nations Standard Minimum Rules for the Administration of Juvenile Justice (the "Beijing Rules"), (1985)

● **Other sources:**

Committee on the Rights of the Child, *General Guidelines Regarding the Form and Contents of Initial Reports to be submitted by States Parties Under Article 44, Paragraph 1(a), of the Convention on the Rights of the Child,* CRC/C/5, October 15 1991

Committee on the Rights of the Child, *General Guidelines Regarding the Form and Contents of Periodic Reports to be submitted by States Parties under Article 44, Paragraph 1(b), of the Convention on the Rights of the Child,* CRC/C/58, 20 November 1996

Committee on the Rights of the Child, *Reservations, Declarations and Objections Relating to the Convention on the Rights of the Child,* CRC/C/2/Rev.5, 30 July 1996

The United Nations Convention on the Rights of the Child A Guide to the "Travaux Préparatoires", compiled and edited by Sharon Detrick, contributors Jaap Doek, Nigel Cantwell, Martinus Nijhoff Publishers, The Netherlands, 1992

ARTICLE 10

● **Instruments:**

International Covenant on Civil and Political Rights (1966)

Hague Convention on the Civil Aspects of International Child Abduction (1980)

International Convention on the Protection of the Rights of All Migrant Workers and Members of Their Families (1990)

● **Other sources:**

Committee on the Rights of the Child, *General Guidelines Regarding the Form and Contents of Initial Reports to be submitted by States Parties Under Article 44, Paragraph 1(a), of the Convention on the Rights of the Child,* CRC/C/5, 15 October 1991

Committee on the Rights of the Child, *General Guidelines Regarding the Form and Contents of Periodic Reports to be submitted by States Parties under Article 44, Paragraph 1(b), of the Convention on the Rights of the Child,* CRC/C/58, 20 November 1996

Committee on the Rights of the Child, *Reservations, Declarations and Objections Relating to the Convention on the Rights of the Child,* CRC/C/2/Rev.5, 30 July 1996

The United Nations Convention on the Rights of the Child A Guide to the "Travaux Préparatoires", compiled and edited by Sharon Detrick, contributors Jaap Doek, Nigel Cantwell, Martinus Nijhoff Publishers, The Netherlands, 1992

ARTICLE 11

● **Instruments:**

European Convention on the Recognition and Enforcement of Decisions Concerning Custody of Children and on Restoration of Custody of Children (1980)

Hague Convention on the Civil Aspects of International Child Abduction (1980)

Inter-American Convention on the International Return of Children (1989)

● **Other sources:**

Committee on the Rights of the Child, *General Guidelines Regarding the Form and Contents of Initial Reports to be submitted by States Parties Under Article 44, Paragraph 1(a), of the Convention on the Rights of the Child,* CRC/C/5, 15 October 1991

Committee on the Rights of the Child, *General Guidelines Regarding the Form and Contents of Periodic Reports to be submitted by States Parties under Article 44, Paragraph 1(b), of the Convention on the Rights of the Child,* CRC/C/58, 20 November 1996

"The Convention on the Rights of the Child", by Marta Santos Pais, in *Manual on Human Rights Reporting under six major international human rights instruments,* Office of the High Commissioner for Human Rights, Geneva;

United Nations Institute for Training and Research (UNITAR), United Nations Staff College Project, Turin, United Nations, Geneva, 1997

ARTICLE 12

● **Instruments:**

Universal Declaration of Human Rights (1948)

International Covenant on Civil and Political Rights (1966)

Hague Convention on the Civil Aspects of International Child Abduction (1980)

United Nations Guidelines for the Prevention of Juvenile Delinquency (the "Riyadh Guidelines") (1990)

United Nations Rules for the Protection of Juveniles Deprived of their Liberty (1990)

Standard Rules on the Equalization of Opportunities for Persons with Disabilities (1993)

● **Other sources:**

Building the Smallest Democracy at the Heart of Society, United Nations Centre for Social Development and Humanitarian Affairs, Vienna, 1991

Earth Summit '92: The United Nations Conference on Environment and Development, Rio de Janeiro 1992, The Regency Press Corporation Ltd., UK, 1992

Fourth World Conference on Women, Beijing, China, 4-15 September 1995, *Platform for Action and the Beijing Declaration,* Department of Public Information, United Nations, New York, 1996

Committee on the Rights of the Child, *General Guidelines Regarding the Form and Contents of Initial Reports to be submitted by States Parties Under Article 44, Paragraph 1(a), of the Convention on the Rights of the Child,* CRC/C/5, 15 October 1991

Committee on the Rights of the Child, *General Guidelines Regarding the Form and Contents of Periodic Reports to be submitted by States Parties under Article 44, Paragraph 1(b), of the Convention on the Rights of the Child,* CRC/C/58, 20 November 1996

Committee on the Rights of the Child, *Reservations, Declarations and Objections Relating to the Convention on the Rights of the Child,* CRC/C/2/Rev.5, 30 July 1996

Refugee Children: Guidelines on Protection and Care, UNHCR, Geneva, 1994

"The Convention on the Rights of the Child", by Marta Santos Pais, in *Manual on Human Rights Reporting under six major international human rights instruments,* Office of the High Commissioner for Human Rights, Geneva; United Nations Institute for Training and Research (UNITAR), United Nations Staff College Project, Turin, United Nations, Geneva, 1997

The United Nations Convention on the Rights of the Child A Guide to the "Travaux Préparatoires", compiled and edited by Sharon Detrick, contributors Jaap Doek, Nigel Cantwell, Martinus Nijhoff Publishers, The Netherlands, 1992

United Nations Conference on Human Settlements (Habitat 11), "Report of the United Nations Conference on Human Settlements (Habitat 11)", A/CONF.165/14, 7 August 1996

World Congress against Commercial Sexual Exploitation of Children, "Declaration and Agenda for Action", Stockholm, August 1996, A/51/385, 1996

World Summit for Children, "World Declaration on the Survival, Protection and Development of Children and Plan of Action for Implementing the World Declaration on the Survival, Protection and Development of Children in the 1990s", CF/WSC/1990/WS-001, United Nations, New York, 30 September 1990

ARTICLE 13

● **Instruments:**

Universal Declaration of Human Rights (1948)

International Covenant on Civil and Political Rights (1966)

United Nations Rules for the Protection of Juveniles Deprived of their Liberty (1990)

Standard Rules on the Equalization of Opportunities for Persons with Disabilities (1993)

● **Other sources:**

Committee on the Rights of the Child, *General Guidelines Regarding the Form and Contents of Initial Reports to be submitted by States Parties Under Article 44, Paragraph 1(a), of the Convention on the Rights of the Child,* CRC/C/5, 15 October 1991

Committee on the Rights of the Child, *General Guidelines Regarding the Form and Contents of Periodic Reports to be submitted by States Parties under Article 44, Paragraph 1(b), of the Convention on the Rights of the Child,* CRC/C/58, 20 November 1996

Committee on the Rights of the Child, *Reservations, Declarations and Objections Relating to the Convention on the Rights of the Child,* CRC/C/2/Rev.5, 30 July 1996

Human Rights Committee, General Comment 10, "Article 19", 1983; General Comment 17, "Article 24", 1989, in *Compilation of General Comments and General Recommendations Adopted by Human Rights Treaty Bodies,* HR1/GEN/1/Rev.2, 29 March 1996

"The Convention on the Rights of the Child", by Marta Santos Pais, in *Manual on Human Rights Reporting under six major international human rights instruments,* Office of the High Commissioner for Human Rights, Geneva; United Nations Institute for Training and Research (UNITAR), United Nations Staff College Project, Turin, United Nations, Geneva, 1997

The United Nations Convention on the Rights of the Child A Guide to the "Travaux Préparatoires", compiled and edited by Sharon Detrick, contributors Jaap Doek, Nigel Cantwell, Martinus Nijhoff Publishers, The Netherlands, 1992

ARTICLE 14

● **Instruments:**

Universal Declaration of Human Rights (1948)

International Covenant on Civil and Political Rights (1966)

United Nations Rules for the Protection of Juveniles Deprived of their Liberty (1990)

Standard Rules on the Equalization of Opportunities for Persons with Disabilities (1993)

● **Other sources:**

Committee on the Rights of the Child, *General Guidelines Regarding the Form and Contents of Initial Reports to be submitted by States Parties Under Article 44, Paragraph 1(a), of the Convention on the Rights of the Child,* CRC/C/5, 15 October 1991

Committee on the Rights of the Child, *General Guidelines Regarding the Form and Contents of Periodic Reports to be submitted by States Parties under Article 44, Paragraph 1(b), of the Convention on the Rights of the Child,* CRC/C/58, 20 November 1996

Committee on the Rights of the Child, *Reservations, Declarations and Objections Relating to the Convention on the Rights of the Child,* CRC/C/2/Rev.5, 30 July 1996

Human Rights Commission, "Respect for conscientious objection to military service", resolution 1987/46, E/CN.4/1987/60, 1987

Human Rights Committee, General Comment 22, "Article 18", 1993, in *Compilation of General Comments and General Recommendations Adopted by Human Rights Treaty Bodies,* HR1/GEN/1/Rev.2, 29 March 1996

Manual on Human Rights Reporting under six major international human rights instruments, HR/PUB/91/1, United Nations Centre for Human Rights, Geneva and United Nations Institute for Training and Research (UNITAR), Geneva, United Nations, New York, 1991

ARTICLE 15

● **Instruments:**

Universal Declaration of Human Rights (1948)

International Covenant on Civil and Political Rights (1966)

United Nations Rules for the Protection of Juveniles Deprived of their Liberty (1990)

Standard Rules on the Equalization of Opportunities for Persons with Disabilities (1993)

● **Other sources:**

General Assembly, "World Programme of Action Concerning Disabled Persons", United Nations Decade of Disabled Persons, 1983-1992, United Nations, New York, 1983

Committee on the Rights of the Child, *General Guidelines Regarding the Form and Contents of Initial Reports to be submitted by States Parties Under Article 44, Paragraph 1(a), of the Convention on the Rights of the Child,* CRC/C/5, 15 October 1991

Committee on the Rights of the Child, *General Guidelines Regarding the Form and Contents of Periodic Reports to be submitted by States Parties under Article 44, Paragraph 1(b), of the Convention on the Rights of the Child,* CRC/C/58, 20 November 1996

ARTICLE 16

● **Instruments:**

Universal Declaration of Human Rights (1948)

International Covenant on Civil and Political Rights (1966)

United Nations Standard Minimum Rules for the Administration of Juvenile Justice (the "Beijing Rules"), (1985)

United Nations Rules for the Protection of Juveniles Deprived of their Liberty (1990)

● **Other sources:**

Committee on the Rights of the Child, *General Guidelines Regarding the Form and Contents of Initial Reports to be submitted by States Parties Under Article 44, Paragraph 1(a), of the Convention on the Rights of the Child*, CRC/C/5, 15 October 1995

Committee on the Rights of the Child, *General Guidelines Regarding the Form and Contents of Periodic Reports to be submitted by States Parties under Article 44, Paragraph 1(b), of the Convention on the Rights of the Child*, CRC/C/58, 20 November 1996

Human Rights Committee, General Comment 16, "Article 17", 1988, in *Compilation of General Comments and General Recommendations Adopted by Human Rights Treaty Bodies*, HR1/GEN/1/Rev.2, 29 March 1996

The United Nations Convention on the Rights of the Child A Guide to the "Travaux Préparatoires", compiled and edited by Sharon Detrick, contributors Jaap Doek, Nigel Cantwell, Martinus Nijhoff Publishers, The Netherlands, 1992

ARTICLE 17

● **Instruments:**

Declaration on Fundamental Principles concerning the Contribution of the Mass Media to Strengthening Peace and International Understanding, to the Promotion of Human Rights and to Countering Racialism, Apartheid and Incitement to War (UNESCO, 1978)

United Nations Guidelines for the Prevention of Juvenile Delinquency (the "Riyadh Guidelines") (1990)

United Nations Rules for the Protection of Juveniles Deprived of their Liberty (1990)

Standard Rules on the Equalization of Opportunities for Persons with Disabilities (1993)

● **Other sources:**

Children, the UN Convention and the Media, paper for Committee on the Rights of the Child General Discussion, Thomas Hammarberg, 7 October 1996

Fourth World Conference on Women, Beijing, China, 4-15 September 1995, *Platform for Action and the Beijing Declaration,* Department of Public Information, United Nations, New York, 1996

Committee on the Rights of the Child, *General Guidelines Regarding the Form and Contents of Initial Reports to be submitted by States Parties Under Article 44, Paragraph 1(a), of the Convention on the Rights of the Child,* CRC/C/5, 15 October 1991

Committee on the Rights of the Child, *General Guidelines Regarding the Form and Contents of Periodic Reports to be submitted by States Parties under Article 44, Paragraph 1(b), of the Convention on the Rights of the Child,* CRC/C/58, 20 November 1996

"Impact of Armed Conflict on Children", Report of the expert of the Secretary-General, Ms. Graça Machel, A/51/306, 26 August 1996

The United Nations Convention on the Rights

of the Child A Guide to the "Travaux Préparatoires", compiled and edited by Sharon Detrick, contributors Jaap Doek, Nigel Cantwell, Martinus Nijhoff Publishers, The Netherlands, 1992

"Working Group on Children and the Media", Report to the Committee on the Rights of the Child, High Commissioner for Human Rights/Centre for Human Rights, May 1997

World Congress against Commercial Sexual Exploitation of Children, "Declaration and Agenda for Action", A/51/385, Stockholm, 1996

ARTICLE 18

● **Instruments:**

International Covenant on Civil and Political Rights (1966)

United Nations Guidelines for the Prevention of Juvenile Delinquency (the "Riyadh Guidelines") (1990)

● **Other sources:**

Committee on Economic, Social and Cultural Rights, General Comment 5, "Persons with disabilities", 1989, in *Compilation of General Comments and General Recommendations Adopted by Human Rights Treaty Bodies*, HR1/GEN/1/Rev.2, 29 March 1996

Committee on the Rights of the Child, *General Guidelines Regarding the Form and Contents of Initial Reports to be submitted by States Parties Under Article 44, Paragraph 1(a), of the Convention on the Rights of the Child*, CRC/C/5, 15 October 1991

Committee on the Rights of the Child, *General Guidelines Regarding the Form and Contents of Periodic Reports to be submitted by States Parties under Article 44, Paragraph 1(b), of the Convention on the Rights of the Child*, CRC/C/58, 20 November 1996

Committee on the Rights of the Child, *Reservations, Declarations and Objections Relating to the Convention on the Rights of the Child*, CRC/C/2/Rev.5, 30 July 1996

Human Rights Committee, General Comment 17, "Article 24", 1989; Human Rights Committee, General Comment 19, "Article 23", 1990, in *Compilation of General Comments and General Recommendations Adopted by Human Rights Treaty Bodies,* HR1/GEN/1/Rev.2, 29 March 1996

International Conference on Population and Development, Cairo, 1994, "Report of the International Conference on Population and Development", A/CONF.171/13, 18 October 1994

The United Nations Convention on the Rights of the Child A Guide to the "Travaux Préparatoires", compiled and edited by Sharon Detrick, contributors Jaap Doek, Nigel Cantwell, Martinus Nijhoff Publishers, The Netherlands, 1992

World Summit for Children, "World Declaration on the Survival, Protection and Development of Children and Plan of Action for Implementing the World Declaration on the Survival, Protection and Development of Children in the 1990s", CF/WSC/1990/WS-001, United

Nations, New York, 30 September 1990

ARTICLE 19

● **Instruments:**

United Nations Standard Minimum Rules for the Administration of Juvenile Justice (the "Beijing Rules") (1985)

United Nations Guidelines for the Prevention of Juvenile Delinquency (the "Riyadh Guidelines") (1990)

United Nations Rules for the Protection of Juveniles Deprived of their Liberty (1990)

Standard Rules on the Equalization of Opportunities for Persons with Disabilities (1993)

● **Other sources:**

Commission on Crime Prevention and Criminal Justice, resolution 3/1, April 1994

Commission on Human Rights, "Question of the human rights of all persons subjected to any form of detention or imprisonment; Expert group meeting on children and juveniles in detention: application of human rights standards (Vienna, 30 October - 4 November 1994)", E/CN.4/1995/100, 16 December 1994

Committee on the Rights of the Child, *General Guidelines Regarding the Form and Contents of Initial Reports to be submitted by States Parties Under Article 44, Paragraph 1(a), of the Convention on the Rights of the Child,* CRC/C/5, 15 October 1991

Committee on the Rights of the Child, *General Guidelines Regarding the Form and Contents of Periodic Reports to be submitted by States Parties under Article 44, Paragraph 1(b), of the Convention on the Rights of the Child,* CRC/C/58, 20 November 1996

Human Rights Committee, General Comment 7, "Article 7", 1982; General Comment 20, "Article 7", 1992, in *Compilation of General Comments and General Recommendations Adopted by Human Rights Treaty Bodies,* HR1/GEN/1/Rev.2, 29 March 1996

World Health Organization, *Protocol for the Study of Interpersonal Physical Abuse of Children,* WHO, Geneva, 1994

ARTICLE 20

● **Instruments:**

Declaration on Social and Legal Principles relating to the Protection and Welfare of Children, with Special Reference to Foster Placement and Adoption Nationally and Internationally (1986)

United Nations Rules for the Protection of Juveniles Deprived of their Liberty (1990)

Standard Rules on the Equalization of Opportunities for Persons with Disabilities (1993)

● **Other sources:**

Centre for Human Rights, Professional Training Series No.1, *Human Rights and Social Work: A Manual for Schools of Social Work and the Social Work Profession,* United Nations, New York and Geneva, 1994

Committee on the Rights of the Child, *General Guidelines Regarding the Form and Contents of Initial Reports to be submitted by States Parties Under Article 44, Paragraph 1(a), of the*

Convention on the Rights of the Child, CRC/C/5, 15 October 1991

Committee on the Rights of the Child, *General Guidelines Regarding the Form and Contents of Periodic Reports to be submitted by States Parties under Article 44, Paragraph 1(b), of the Convention on the Rights of the Child,* CRC/C/58, 20 November 1996

Committee on the Rights of the Child, *Reservations, Declarations and Objections Relating to the Convention on the Rights of the Child,* CRC/C/2/Rev.5, 30 July 1996

The United Nations Convention on the Rights of the Child A Guide to the "Travaux Préparatoires", compiled and edited by Sharon Detrick, contributors Jaap Doek, Nigel Cantwell, Martinus Nijhoff Publishers, The Netherlands, 1992

ARTICLE 21

● **Instruments:**

Declaration on Social and Legal Principles relating to the Protection and Welfare of Children, with Special Reference to Foster Placement and Adoption Nationally and Internationally (1986)

Hague Convention on Protection of Children and Cooperation in respect of Intercountry Adoption (1993)

● **Other sources:**

Economic and Social Council, "Report of the Working Group on Contemporary Forms of Slavery", eighteenth session, E/CN.4/Sub.2/1993/30, 23 June 1993

Committee on the Rights of the Child, *General Guidelines Regarding the Form and Contents of Initial Reports to be submitted by States Parties Under Article 44, Paragraph 1(a), of the Convention on the Rights of the Child,* CRC/C/5, 15 October 1991

Committee on the Rights of the Child, *General Guidelines Regarding the Form and Contents of Periodic Reports to be submitted by States Parties under Article 44, Paragraph 1(b), of the Convention on the Rights of the Child,* CRC/C/58, 20 November 1996

Committee on the Rights of the Child, *Reservations, Declarations and Objections Relating to the Convention on the Rights of the Child,* CRC/C/2/Rev.5, 30 July 1996

The United Nations Convention on the Rights of the Child A Guide to the "Travaux Préparatoires", compiled and edited by Sharon Detrick, contributors Jaap Doek, Nigel Cantwell, Martinus Nijhoff Publishers, The Netherlands, 1992

ARTICLE 22

● **Instruments:**

Convention relating to the Status of Refugees (1951), as amended by the *Protocol relating to the Status of Refugees (1967)*

United Nations Standard Minimum Rules for the Administration of Juvenile Justice (the "Beijing Rules") (1985)

United Nations Rules for the Protection of Juveniles Deprived of their Liberty (1990)

● **Other sources:**

Committee on the Rights of the Child, *General Guidelines Regarding the Form and Contents of Initial Reports to be submitted by States Parties Under Article 44, Paragraph 1(a), of the Convention on the Rights of the Child,* CRC/C/5, 15 October 1991

Committee on the Rights of the Child, *General Guidelines Regarding the Form and Contents of Periodic Reports to be submitted by States Parties under Article 44, Paragraph 1(b), of the Convention on the Rights of the Child,* CRC/C/58, 20 November 1996

Committee on the Rights of the Child, *Reservations, Declarations and Objections Relating to the Convention on the Rights of the Child,* CRC/C/2/Rev.5, 30 July 1996

Human Rights Committee, General Comment 20, "Article 7", 1992, in *Compilation of General Comments and General Recommendations Adopted by Human Rights Treaty Bodies,* HR1/GEN/1/Rev.2, 29 March 1996

"The Convention on the Rights of the Child", by Marta Santos Pais, in *Manual on Human Rights Reporting under six major international human rights instruments,* Office of the High Commissioner for Human Rights, Geneva; United Nations Institute for Training and Research (UNITAR), United Nations Staff College Project, Turin, United Nations, Geneva, 1997

The United Nations Convention on the Rights of the Child A Guide to the "Travaux Préparatoires", compiled and edited by Sharon Detrick, contributors Jaap Doek, Nigel Cantwell, Martinus Nijhoff Publishers, The Netherlands, 1992

United Nations High Commissioner for Refugees (UNHCR), *Refugee Children: Guidelines on Protection and Care,* UNHCR, Geneva, 1994

United Nations High Commissioner for Refugees (UNHCR), "Model Guidelines on Policies and Procedures in dealing with Unaccompanied Children Seeking Asylum", UNHCR, 1997

ARTICLE 23

● **Instruments:**

Universal Declaration of Human Rights (1948)

International Covenant on Civil and Political Rights (1966)

International Covenant on Economic, Social and Cultural Rights (1966)

Declaration on the Rights of Mentally Retarded People (1971)

Declaration on the Rights of Disabled Persons (1975)

Convention on the Elimination of All Forms of Discrimination against Women (1979)

ILO Convention No.159, concerning Vocational Rehabilitation and Employment (Disabled Persons), International Labour Organization (1983)

International Convention on the Protection of the Rights of All Migrant Workers and Members of Their Families (1990)

United Nations Rules for the Protection of Juveniles Deprived of their Liberty (1990)

Standard Rules on the Equalization of Opportunities for Persons with Disabilities (1993)

● **Other sources:**

Commission for Social Development, "Report of the Special Rapporteur on Monitoring the implementation of the Standard Rules on the Equalization of Opportunities for Persons with Disabilities", A/52/56, 23 December 1996

Commission on Human Rights, Sub-commission on Prevention of Discrimination and Protection of Minorities, resolution 1982/1, 1982

Committee on Economic, Social and Cultural Rights, General Comment 5, "Persons with disabilities", 1994, in *Compilation of General Comments and General Recommendations Adopted by Human Rights Treaty Bodies,* HR1/GEN/1/Rev.2, 29 March 1996

Committee on the Rights of the Child, *General Guidelines Regarding the Form and Contents of Initial Reports to be submitted by States Parties Under Article 44, Paragraph 1(a), of the Convention on the Rights of the Child,* CRC/C/5, 15 October 1991

Committee on the Rights of the Child, *General Guidelines Regarding the Form and Contents of Periodic Reports to be submitted by States Parties under Article 44, Paragraph 1(b), of the Convention on the Rights of the Child,* CRC/C/58, 20 November 1996

Economic and Social Council, "Human Rights and Disability; Final Report prepared by Mr. Leadro Despouy, Special Rapporteur", E/CN.4/Sub.2/1991/31, 12 July 1991

Economic and Social Council, "Report of the Secretary-General prepared pursuant to Sub-Commission resolution 1995/17", E/CN.4/Sub.2/1996/27, 2 July 1996

Economic and Social Council, resolution on "Children with disabilities", E/1997/L.23, 1997

Fourth World Conference on Women, Beijing, China, 4-15 September 1995, *Platform for Action and the Beijing Declaration,* Department of Public Information, United Nations, New York, 1996

General Assembly, "Principles for the Protection of Persons with Mental Illness and for the Improvement of Mental Health Care", resolution 46/119, 17 December 1991

General Assembly, "World Programme of Action Concerning Disabled Persons", United Nations Decade of Disabled Persons, 1983-1992, United Nations, New York, 1983

"Guidelines for the Establishment and Development of National Coordinating Committees on Disability or Similar Bodies", A/C.3/46/4, annex I, 1990

Human Rights Committee, General Comment 18, "Non-discrimination", 1989, in *Compilation of General Comments and General Recommendations Adopted by Human Rights Treaty Bodies,* HR1/GEN/1/Rev.2, 29 March 1996

"Impact of Armed Conflict on Children, Report of the expert of the Secretary-General, Ms Graça Machel", A/51/306, 26 August 1996

ILO Recommendation No. 168, concerning Vocational Rehabilitation and Employment (Disabled Persons), International Labour Organization, June 1983

Overcoming Obstacles to the Integration of Disabled People, UNESCO sponsored report as a contribution to The World Summit on Social Development, Copenhagen, Denmark, March 1995, Disability Awareness in Action, London, UK, 1995

World Conference on Special Needs Education, "The Salamanca Statement and Framework for Action on Special Needs Education", UNESCO, ED-94/WS/18, 1994

World Summit for Social Development, Copenhagen, 6-12 March 1995, "Report of the World Summit for Social Development", A/CONF.166/9, 19 April 1995

ARTICLE 24

● **Instruments:**

Universal Declaration of Human Rights (1948)
International Covenant on Civil and Political Rights (1966)
International Covenant on Economic, Social and Cultural Rights (1966)
Declaration on Social Progress and Development (1969)
Standard Rules on the Equalization of Opportunities for Persons with Disabilities (1993)

● **Other sources:**

Committee on Economic, Social and Cultural Rights, General Comment 3, "The nature of States Parties' obligations", 1990, in *Compilation of General Comments and General Recommendations Adopted by Human Rights Treaty Bodies,* HR1/GEN/1/Rev.2, 29 March 1996

Committee on the Elimination of Discrimination against Women, General Comment 14, "Female circumcision", 1990, in *Compilation of General Comments and General Recommendations Adopted by Human Rights Treaty Bodies,* HR1/GEN/1/Rev.2, 29 March 1996

Committee on the Rights of the Child, *General Guidelines Regarding the Form and Contents of Initial Reports to be submitted by States Parties Under Article 44, Paragraph 1(a), of the Convention on the Rights of the Child,* CRC/C/5, 15 October 1991

Committee on the Rights of the Child, *General Guidelines Regarding the Form and Contents of Periodic Reports to be submitted by States Parties under Article 44, Paragraph 1(b), of the Convention on the Rights of the Child,* CRC/C/58, 20 November 1996

Estimates of the Burden of Disease among adolescents, youth and young people, C. Murray and C. Michaud, unpublished, 1996

Fourth World Conference on Women, Beijing, China, 4-15 September 1995, *Platform for Action and the Beijing Declaration,* Department of Public Information, United Nations, New York, 1996

General Assembly, "Health as an integral part of development", resolution 34/58, 29 November 1979

Innocenti Declaration on the Protection, Promotion and Support of Breastfeeding, 1990

International Conference on Health Promotion, Ottawa, Canada, 1986, "Health Promotion - The Ottawa Charter", co-sponsored by World Health Organization, Canadian Public Health Association, Health and Welfare Canada, November 1986

International Conference on Nutrition, "World Declaration and Plan of Action for Nutrition", Food and Agriculture Organization/World Health Organization, Rome, 1992

International Conference on Population and Development, Cairo 1994, "Report of the International Conference on Population and Development", A/CONF.171/13, 18 October 1994

"Report of the Working Group on Traditional Practices affecting the Health of Women and Children", E/CN.4/1986/42, February 1986

Sub-commission on Prevention of Discrimination and Protection of Minorities of the Commission on Human Rights, "Final report from the Special Rapporteur on traditional practices affecting the health of women and children", E/CN.4/Sub.2/1996/6, 14 June 1996

Sub-commission on Prevention of Discrimination and Protection of Minorities of the Commission on Human Rights, "Plan of action for the elimination of harmful traditional practices affecting the health of women and children", E/CN.4/Sub.2/1994/10/Add.1, 22 July 1994

The United Nations Convention on the Rights of the Child A Guide to the "Travaux Préparatoires", compiled and edited by Sharon Detrick, contributors Jaap Doek, Nigel Cantwell, Martinus Nijhoff Publishers, The Netherlands, 1992

UNAIDS, *The UNAIDS Guide to the United Nations Human Rights Machinery,* UNAIDS, Geneva, 1997

UNICEF/WHO, *State of the World's Vaccines and Immunization, a review of progress, constraints and challenges,* UNICEF/WHO, 1996

United Nations Children's Fund, *Child malnutrition: Progress towards the World Summit for Children Goals,* UNICEF, New York, March 1993

United Nations Children's Fund, *The Progress of Nations: The nations of the world ranked according to their achievements in child health, nutrition, education, water and sanitation, and progress for women, 1997,* UNICEF, New York, 1997

United Nations Children's Fund, *The State of the World's Children 1997,* Oxford University Press for UNICEF, Oxford and New York, 1997

WHO and UNICEF, International Declaration on Primary Health Care (Alma Ata Declaration), 1978

WHO/UNICEF, *Ten steps to successful breastfeeding,* 1989

World Health Organization, International Code of Marketing Breast-milk Substitutes, 1981

World Health Organization Constitution, adopted at International Health Conference, New York, 19 June 1946, as amended, WHO, Geneva 1989

World Summit for Children, "World Declaration on the Survival, Protection and Development of Children and Plan of Action for Implementing the World Declaration on the Survival, Protection and Development of Children in the 1990s", CF/WSC/1990/WS-001, United Nations, New York, 30 September 1990

World Summit for Social Development, Copenhagen, 6-12 March 1995, "Report of the World Summit for Social Development", A/CONF.166/9, 19 April 1995

World Health Assembly, Report of Director General, A45/28 1992

World Health Assembly resolution: "Maternal and child health and family planning: traditional practices harmful to the health of women and children", WHA 47/10, 1994

ARTICLE 25

● **Instruments:**

United Nations Rules for the Protection of Juveniles Deprived of their Liberty (1990)

● **Other sources:**

Committee on the Rights of the Child, *General Guidelines Regarding the Form and Contents of Initial Reports to be submitted by States Parties Under Article 44, Paragraph 1(a), of the Convention on the Rights of the Child,* CRC/C/5, 15 October 1991

Committee on the Rights of the Child, *General Guidelines Regarding the Form and Contents of Periodic Reports to be submitted by States Parties under Article 44, Paragraph 1(b), of the Convention on the Rights of the Child,* CRC/C/58, 20 November 1996

Committee on the Rights of the Child, *Reservations, Declarations and Objections Relating to the Convention on the Rights of the Child,* CRC/C/2/Rev.5, 30 July 1996

The United Nations Convention on the Rights of the Child A Guide to the "Travaux Préparatoires", compiled and edited by Sharon Detrick, contributors Jaap Doek, Nigel Cantwell, Martinus Nijhoff Publishers, The Netherlands, 1992

ARTICLE 26

● **Instruments:**

International Covenant on Economic, Social and Cultural Rights (1966)

● **Other sources:**

Committee on the Rights of the Child, *General Guidelines Regarding the Form and Contents of Initial Reports to be submitted by States Parties Under Article 44, Paragraph 1(a), of the Convention on the Rights of the Child,* CRC/C/5, 15 October 1991

Committee on the Rights of the Child, *General Guidelines Regarding the Form and Contents of Periodic Reports to be submitted by States Parties under Article 44, Paragraph 1(b), of the Convention on the Rights of the Child,* CRC/C/58, 20 November 1996

The United Nations Convention on the Rights of the Child A Guide to the "Travaux Préparatoires", compiled and edited by Sharon Detrick, contributors Jaap Doek, Nigel Cantwell, Martinus Nijhoff Publishers, The Netherlands, 1992

World Summit for Social Development, Copenhagen, 6-12 March 1995, "Report of the World Summit for Social Development", A/CONF.166/9, 19 April 1995

ARTICLE 27

● **Instruments:**

Universal Declaration of Human Rights (1948)

Unitd Nations Convention on the Recovery Abroad of Maintenance (1956)

International Covenant on Economic, Social and Cultural Rights (1966)

Reciprocal Enforcement of Maintenance Orders, Hague Convention Countries, Order (1993)

● **Other sources:**

Children's Rights and Habitat - Housing Neighbourhood & Settlement, Declaration and Report of the Expert Seminar Prepcom 111 Edition 1996, Children's Environments Research Group, Human Settlements Commission, Urban Section UNICEF, New York, 1996

Commission on Human Rights, "The Plight of street children", resolution 1994/93, 9 March 1994

Committee on Economic, Social and Cultural Rights, General Comment 3, "The nature of States Parties' obligations", 1990, in *Compilation of General Comments and General Recommendations Adopted by Human Rights Treaty Bodies,* HR1/GEN/1/Rev.2, 29 March 1996

Committee on the Rights of the Child, *General Guidelines Regarding the Form and Contents of Initial Reports to be submitted by States Parties Under Article 44, Paragraph 1(a), of the Convention on the Rights of the Child,* CRC/C/5, 15 October 1991

Committee on the Rights of the Child, *General Guidelines Regarding the Form and Contents of Periodic Reports to be submitted by States Parties under Article 44, Paragraph 1(b), of the Convention on the Rights of the Child,* CRC/C/58, 20 November 1996

Manual on Human Rights Reporting Under Six Major International Human Rights Instruments, United Nations Centre for Human Rights, Geneva and United Nations Institute for Training and Research (UNITAR) Geneva United Nations, HR/PUB/91/1, New York, 1991

The United Nations Convention on the Rights of the Child A Guide to the "Travaux Préparatoires", compiled and edited by Sharon Detrick, contributors Jaap Doek, Nigel Cantwell, Martinus Nijhoff Publishers, The Netherlands, 1992

United Nations Conference on Human Settlements (Habitat II), "Report of the United Nations Conference on Human Settlements (Habitat II)", A/CONF.165/14, 7 August 1996

World Summit for Children, "World Declaration on the Survival, Protection and Development of Children and Plan of Action for Implementing the World Declaration on the Survival, Protection and Development of Children in the 1990s", CF/WSC/1990/WS-001, United Nations, New York, 30 September 1990

World Summit for Social Development, Copenhagen, 6-12 March 1995, "Report of the World Summit for Social Development", A/CONF.166/9, 19 April 1995

ARTICLE 28

● **Instruments:**

Universal Declaration of Human Rights (1948)

International Covenant on Economic, Social and Cultural Rights (1966)

International Covenant on Civil and Political Rights (1966)

ILO Convention No.138 "Concerning Minimum Age for Admission to Employment" (1973)

Recommendation Concerning Education for International Understanding, Cooperation and Peace and Education Relating to Human Rights and Fundamental Freedoms (UNESCO) (1974)

Convention against Discrimination in Education (1960)

United Nations Rules for the Protection of Juveniles Deprived of their Liberty (1990)

Standard Rules on the Equalization of Opportunities for Persons with Disabilities (1993)

● **Other sources:**

Committee on the Rights of the Child, *General Guidelines Regarding the Form and Contents of Initial Reports to be submitted by States Parties Under Article 44, Paragraph 1(a), of the Convention on the Rights of the Child,* CRC/C/5, 15 October 1991

Committee on the Rights of the Child, *General Guidelines Regarding the Form and Contents of Periodic Reports to be submitted by States Parties under Article 44, Paragraph 1(b), of the Convention on the Rights of the Child,* CRC/C/58, 20 November 1996

Committee on the Rights of the Child, *Reservations, Declarations and Objections Relating to the Convention on the Rights of the Child,* CRC/C/2/Rev.5, 30 July 1996

Fourth World Conference on Women, Beijing, China 4-15 September 1995, *Platform for Action and the Beijing Declaration,* Department of Public Information, United Nations, New York, 1996

Human Rights Committee, examination of Fourth Periodic Report of the United Kingdom, CCPR/C/79/Add.55, 27 July 1995

Human Rights Committee, General Comment 20, "Article 7", 1992, in *Compilation of General Comments and General Recommendations Adopted by Human Rights Treaty Bodies,* HR1/GEN/1/Rev.2, 29 March 1996

"The Convention on the Rights of the Child", by Marta Santos Pais, in *Manual on Human Rights Reporting under six major international human rights instruments,* Office of the High Commissioner for Human Rights, Geneva; United Nations Institute for Training and Research (UNITAR), United Nations Staff College Project, Turin, United Nations, Geneva, 1997

The United Nations Convention on the Rights of the Child A Guide to the "Travaux Préparatoires", compiled and edited by Sharon Detrick, contributors Jaap Doek, Nigel

Cantwell, Martinus Nijhoff Publishers, The Netherlands, 1992

United Nations Children's Fund, *The Progress of Nations: The nations of the world ranked according to their achievements in child health, nutrition, education, water and sanitation, and progress for women, 1997,* UNICEF, New York, 1997

United Nations Children's Fund, *The State of the World's Children 1997,* Oxford University Press for UNICEF, Oxford and New York, 1997

World Conference on Education for All, Jomtien, Thailand, "World Declaration on Education for All and Framework for Action Meeting Basic Learning Needs", 5-9 March 1990

World Summit for Children, "World Declaration on the Survival, Protection and Development of Children and Plan of Action for Implementing the World Declaration on the Survival, Protection and Development of Children in the 1990s", CF/WSC/1990/WS-001, United Nations, New York, 30 September 1990

ARTICLE 29

● **Instruments:**

Universal Declaration of Human Rights (1948)

International Covenant on Civil and Political Rights (1966)

International Covenant on Economic, Social and Cultural Rights (1966)

Declaration and Integrated Framework of Action on Education for Peace, Human Rights and Democracy (UNESCO) (1995)

● **Other sources:**

Charter of the United Nations and Statute of the International Court of Justice, Department of Public Information, United Nations, September 1995

Committee on the Rights of the Child, *General Guidelines Regarding the Form and Contents of Initial Reports to be submitted by States Parties Under Article 44, Paragraph 1(a), of the Convention on the Rights of the Child,* CRC/C/5, 15 October 1991

Committee on the Rights of the Child, *General Guidelines Regarding the Form and Contents of Periodic Reports to be submitted by States Parties under Article 44, Paragraph 1(b), of the Convention on the Rights of the Child,* CRC/C/58, 20 November 1996

Committee on the Rights of the Child, *Reservations, Declarations and Objections Relating to the Convention on the Rights of the Child,* CRC/C/2/Rev.5, 30 July 1996

Earth Summit '92: The United Nations Conference on Environment and Development Rio de Janeiro 1992, The Regency Press Corporation Ltd., UK, 1992

Fourth World Conference on Women, Beijing, China, 4-15 September 1995, *Platform for Action and the Beijing Declaration,* Department of Public Information, United Nations, New York, 1996

General Assembly, "United Nations Decade for Human Rights Education", Resolutions 48/127, 1993; 49/184, 1994 and 50/177, 1995

International Conference on Population and Development, Cairo 1994, "Report of the International Conference on Population and Development", A/CONF.171/13, 18 October 1994

"The Convention on the Rights of the Child", by Marta Santos Pais, in *Manual on Human Rights Reporting under six major international human rights instruments*, Office of the High Commissioner for Human Rights, Geneva; United Nations Institute for Training and Research (UNITAR), United Nations Staff College Project, Turin, United Nations, Geneva, 1997

The United Nations Convention on the Rights of the Child A Guide to the "Travaux Préparatoires", compiled and edited by Sharon Detrick, contributors Jaap Doek, Nigel Cantwell, Martinus Nijhoff Publishers, The Netherlands, 1992

ARTICLE 30

● **Instruments:**

International Covenant on Civil and Political Rights (1966)

International Convention on the Protection of the Rights of All Migrant Workers and Members of their Families (1990)

Declaration on the Rights of Persons Belonging to National or Ethnic, Religious and Linguistic Minorities (1992)

● **Other sources:**

Committee on the Rights of the Child, *General Guidelines Regarding the Form and Contents of Initial Reports to be submitted by States Parties Under Article 44, Paragraph 1(a), of the Convention on the Rights of the Child*, CRC/C/5, 15 October 1991

Committee on the Rights of the Child, *General Guidelines Regarding the Form and Contents of Periodic Reports to be submitted by States Parties under Article 44, Paragraph 1(b), of the Convention on the Rights of the Child*, CRC/C/58, 20 November 1996

Committee on the Rights of the Child, *Reservations, Declarations and Objections Relating to the Convention on the Rights of the Child*, CRC/C/2/Rev.5, 30 July 1996

Human Rights Committee, General Comment 23, "Article 27", 1994, in *Compilation of General Comments and General Recommendations Adopted by Human Rights Treaty Bodies*, HR1/GEN/1/Rev.2, 29 March 1996

"The Convention on the Rights of the Child", by Marta Santos Pais, in *Manual on Human Rights Reporting under six major international human rights instruments*, Office of the High Commissioner for Human Rights, Geneva; United Nations Institute for Training and Research (UNITAR), United Nations Staff College Project, Turin, United Nations, Geneva, 1997

The International Law on the Rights of the Child, Geraldine Van Bueren, Save the Children, Martinus Nijhoff, 1995

The United Nations Convention on the Rights of the Child A Guide to the "Travaux Préparatoires", compiled and edited by Shar-

on Detrick, contributors Jaap Doek, Nigel Cantwell, Martinus Nijhoff Publishers, The Netherlands, 1992

ARTICLE 31

● **Instruments:**

ILO Convention No.79, Night Work of Young Persons (Non Industrial Occupations) (1946)

ILO Convention (Revised) No.90, Night Work of Young Persons (Industry) (1948)

Declaration of the Rights of the Child (1959)

United Nations Rules for the Protection of Juveniles Deprived of their Liberty (1990)

Standard Rules on the Equalization of Opportunities for Persons with Disabilities (1993)

● **Other sources:**

Committee on the Rights of the Child, *General Guidelines Regarding the Form and Contents of Initial Reports to be submitted by States Parties Under Article 44, Paragraph 1(a), of the Convention on the Rights of the Child*, CRC/C/5, 15 October 1991

Committee on the Rights of the Child, *General Guidelines Regarding the Form and Contents of Periodic Reports to be submitted by States Parties under Article 44, Paragraph 1(b), of the Convention on the Rights of the Child*, CRC/C/58, 20 November 1996

International Association for the Child's Right to Play, *IPA Declaration of the Child's Right to Play*, November 1988 and 1989

"The Convention on the Rights of the Child", by Marta Santos Pais, in *Manual on Human Rights Reporting under six major international human rights instruments*, Office of the High Commissioner for Human Rights, Geneva; United Nations Institute for Training and Research (UNITAR), United Nations Staff College Project, Turin, United Nations, Geneva, 1997

The United Nations Convention on the Rights of the Child A Guide to the "Travaux Préparatoires", compiled and edited by Sharon Detrick, contributors Jaap Doek, Nigel Cantwell, Martinus Nijhoff Publishers, The Netherlands, 1992

ARTICLE 32

● **Instruments:**

ILO Convention No.5, Minimum Age (Industry) (1919)

ILO Convention No.29, Forced Labour (1930)

ILO Convention No.77, Medical Examination of Young Persons (Industry) (1946)

ILO Convention No.78, Medical Examination of Young Persons (Non-Industrial Occupations) (1946)

International Convention for the Suppression of the Traffic in Women and Children (1921), as amended by Protocol (1947)

Universal Declaration of Human Rights (1948)

Convention for the Suppression of the Traffic in Persons and of the Exploitation of the Prostitution of Others (1949)

Supplementary Convention on the Abolition of Slavery, the Slave Trade, and Institutions and Practices Similar to Slavery (1956)

ILO Convention No.124, Medical Examination of Young Persons (Underground Work) (1965)

International Covenant on Civil and Political Rights (1966)

International Covenant on Economic, Social and Cultural Rights (1966)

ILO Convention No.138, Concerning Minimum Age for Admission to Employment (1973)

United Nations Rules for the Protection of Juveniles Deprived of their Liberty (1990)

● **Other sources:**

Commission on Human Rights, "Programme of Action for the Elimination of the Exploitation of Child Labour", 1993/79, 10 March 1993

Committee on the Rights of the Child, *General Guidelines Regarding the Form and Contents of Initial Reports to be submitted by States Parties Under Article 44, Paragraph 1(a), of the Convention on the Rights of the Child*, CRC/C/5, 15 October 1991

Committee on the Rights of the Child, *General Guidelines Regarding the Form and Contents of Periodic Reports to be submitted by States Parties under Article 44, Paragraph 1(b), of the Convention on the Rights of the Child*, CRC/C/58, 20 November 1996

Committee on the Rights of the Child, *Reservations, Declarations and Objections Relating to the Convention on the Rights of the Child*, CRC/C/2/Rev.5, 30 July 1996

Economic and Social Council, "Contemporary Forms of Slavery: Report of the Working Group on its eighteenth session", E/CN.4/Sub.2/1993/30, 23 June 1993

Fourth World Conference on Women, Beijing, China, 4-15 September 1995, *Platform for Action and the Beijing Declaration*, Department of Public Information, United Nations, New York, 1996

International Labour Conference, 86th Session 1998, *Child Labour Report V1 (1): Questionnaire*, International Labour Office, Geneva, 1996

International Labour Organization, *Classified Guide to International Labour Standards (Including instruments adopted up to the 83rd Session of the International Labour Conference, 1996)*, Appl.10, ILO, Geneva, 1996

ILO Recommendation No.146, concerning Minimum Age for Admission to Employment, (1973)

International Labour Organization, *Child labour Targeting the intolerable*, International Labour Organization, Geneva, 1996

United Nations Children's Fund, *The State of the World's Children 1997*, Oxford University Press for UNICEF, Oxford and New York, 1997

World Summit for Children, "World Declaration on the Survival, Protection and Development of Children and Plan of Action for Implementing the World Declaration on the Survival, Protection and Development of Children in the 1990s", CF/WSC/1990/WS-001, United Nations, New York, 30 September 1990

ARTICLE 33

● **Instruments:**

Single Convention on Narcotic Drugs (1961), as amended by Protocol (1972)

Convention on Psychotropic Substances (1971)
United Nations Guidelines for the Prevention of Juvenile Delinquency (the "Riyadh Guidelines") (1990)

● **Other sources:**

Commission on Human Rights, "Programme of Action for the Elimination of the Exploitation of Child Labour", 1993/79, 10 March 1993

Committee on the Rights of the Child, *General Guidelines Regarding the Form and Contents of Initial Reports to be submitted by States Parties Under Article 44, Paragraph 1(a), of the Convention on the Rights of the Child*, CRC/C/5, 15 October 1991

Committee on the Rights of the Child, *General Guidelines Regarding the Form and Contents of Periodic Reports to be submitted by States Parties under Article 44, Paragraph 1(b), of the Convention on the Rights of the Child*, CRC/C/58, 20 November 1996

Council of Europe Recommendation 989 on the Fight Against Drug Abuse and Trafficking (1984)

United Nations Decade against Drug Abuse 1991-2000, Political Declaration and Global Programme of Action, and resolution S-17/2, 23 February 1990

Declaration of the International Conference on Drug Abuse and Illicit Trafficking and Comprehensive Multidisciplinary Outline of Future Activities in Drug Abuse Control,

World Summit for Children, "World Declaration on the Survival, Protection and Development of Children and Plan of Action for Implementing the World Declaration on the Survival, Protection and Development of Children in the 1990s", CF/WSC/1990/WS-001, United Nations, New York, 30 September 1990

ARTICLE 34

● **Instruments:**

ILO Convention No.29, Forced Labour (1930)
Universal Declaration of Human Rights (1948)
Convention for the Suppression of the Traffic in Persons and of the Exploitation of the Prostitution of Others (1949)
Supplementary Convention on the Abolition of Slavery, the Slave Trade, and Institutions and Practices Similar to Slavery (1956)
International Covenant on Civil and Political Rights (1966)
Convention on the Elimination of All Forms of Discrimination Against Women (1979)
Standard Rules on the Equalization of Opportunities for Persons with Disabilities (1993)

● **Other sources:**

Centre for Human Rights, Muntarbhorn, Vitit, former Special Rapporteur of the Commission on Human Rights, Human Rights Study Series 8, *Sexual Exploitation of Children, on the sale of children, child prostitution and child pornography,* Geneva, 1996

Commission on Human Rights, "Interim report of the Special Rapporteur on the sale of children, child prostitution and pornography", E/CN.4/1997/95, 7 February 1997

Commission on Human Rights, "Programmes of action for the prevention of the sale of children, child prostitution and child pornog-

raphy and the elimination of the exploitation of child labour", resolution 1992/74, 5 March 1992

Commission on Human Rights, "Question of a draft optional protocol to the Convention on the Rights of the Child on the sale of children, child prostitution and child pornography, as well as basic measures needed for their eradication", E/CN.4/1997/97, 2 April 1997

Commission on Human Rights, Report of the Special Rapporteur on violence against women, its causes and consequences, Ms. Radhika Coomaraswamy, submitted in accordance with Commission on Human Rights resolution 1995/85, E/CN.4/1996/3, 5 February 1996

Commission on Human Rights, resolution on "Need to adopt effective international measures for the prevention and eradication of the sale of children, child prostitution and child pornography", resolution 1994/90, 9 March 1994

Commission on Human Rights, "Special Rapporteur on situations of systematic rape, sexual slavery, and slavery-like practices during periods of armed conflict'", E/CN.4/Sub.2/1996/26, 16 July 1996

Committee on the Elimination of Discrimination against Women, General Recommendation No. 19, "Violence against women", 1992, in *Compilation of General Comments and General Recommendations Adopted by Human Rights Treaty Bodies,* HR1/GEN/1/Rev.2, 29 March 1996

Committee on the Rights of the Child, *General Guidelines Regarding the Form and Contents of Initial Reports to be submitted by States Parties Under Article 44, Paragraph 1(a), of the Convention on the Rights of the Child,* CRC/C/5, 15 October 1991

Committee on the Rights of the Child, *General Guidelines Regarding the Form and Contents of Periodic Reports to be submitted by States Parties under Article 44, Paragraph 1(b), of the Convention on the Rights of the Child,* CRC/C/58, 20 November 1996

End Child Prostitution in Asian Tourism (ECPAT), "The International Legal Framework and Current National Legislative and Enforcement Responses", submission to the World Congress against Commercial Sexual Exploitation of Children, 1996

Fourth World Conference on Women, Beijing, China 4-15 September 1995, *Platform for Action and the Beijing Declaration,* Department of Public Information, United Nations, New York, 1996

General Assembly, "Promotion and Protection of the Rights of the Child: Sale of children, child prostitution and child pornography", A/49/478, 5 October 1994

General Assembly, "Promotion and Protection of the Rights of the Child: Sale of children, child prostitution and child pornography, interim report of Ms Ofelia Calcetas-Santos, Special Rapporteur of the Commission on Human Rights on the sale of children, child

prostitution and child pornography", A/51/456, 7 October 1996

Human Rights Committee, General Comment 17, "Article 24", 1989, in *Compilation of General Comments and General Recommendations Adopted by Human Rights Treaty Bodies,* HR1/GEN/1/Rev.2, 29 March 1996

"Impact of Armed Conflict on Children", Report of the expert of the Secretary-General, Ms Graça Machel', A/51/306, 26 August 1996

INTERPOL, Report of the Standing Working Party on Offences Committed against Minors, Lyon, 1993

The United Nations Convention on the Rights of the Child A Guide to the "Travaux Préparatoires", compiled and edited by Sharon Detrick, contributors Jaap Doek, Nigel Cantwell, Martinus Nijhoff Publishers, The Netherlands, 1992

World Tourism Organization, *Tourism Bill of Rights and Tourist Code,* 1985

UNHCR, WHO and UNAIDS, *Guidelines for HIV Interventions in Emergency Settings,* UNAIDS - Joint United Nations Programme on HIV/AIDS, 1996

UNHCR, *Sexual violence against refugees, Guidelines on Prevention and Response,* UNHCR, Geneva, 1995

United Nations Children's Fund, *The State of the World's Children 1997,* Oxford University Press for UNICEF, Oxford and New York, 1997

World Conference on Human Rights, Vienna Declaration and Programme of Action, A/CONF.157/24, 1993

World Congress against Commercial Sexual Exploitation of Children, "Declaration and Agenda for Action", A/51/385, Stockholm 1996

World Summit for Children, "World Declaration on the Survival, Protection and Development of Children and Plan of Action for Implementing the World Declaration on the Survival, Protection and Development of Children in the 1990s", CF/WSC/1990/WS-001, United Nations, New York, 30 September 1990

ARTICLE 35

● **Instruments:**

Convention for the Suppression of the Traffic in Persons and of the Explpoitation of the Prostitution of Others (1949)
Convention on the Abolition of Slavery, the Slave Trade and Institutions and Practices Similar to Slavery (1956)
Hague Convention on the Protection of Children and Cooperation in respect of Intercountry Adoption (1993)

● **Other sources:**

Commission on Human Rights, "Programme of Action for the Elimination of the Exploitation of Child Labour", 1993/79, 10 March 1993

Commission on Human Rights, Programmes of Action for the prevention of the sale of children, child prostitution and child pornography and for the elimination of the exploitation of child labour, 1992/74, 5 March 1992

Commission on Human Rights, "Rights of the Child, Sale of Children, Report submitted by

Mr Vitit Muntarbhorn, Special Rapporteur appointed in accordance with Commission resolution 1990/68", E/CN.4/1992/55, 22 January 1992

Commission on Human Rights, "Rights of the Child, Sale of children, child prostituion and child pornography, Report submitted by Mr Vitit Muntarbhorn, Special Rapporteur appointed in accordance with Commission resolution 1993/82", E/CN.4/1994/84, 14 January 1994

Commission on Human Rights, Sub-Commission on the Prevention of Discrimination and Protection of Minorities, Working Group on contemporary forms of slavery, E/CN.4/Sub.2/1993/30, 1993

Committee on the Rights of the Child, *General Guidelines Regarding the Form and Contents of Initial Reports to be submitted by States Parties Under Article 44, Paragraph 1(a), of the Convention on the Rights of the Child*, CRC/C/5, 15 October 1991

Committee on the Rights of the Child, *General Guidelines Regarding the Form and Contents of Periodic Reports to be submitted by States Parties under Article 44, Paragraph 1(b), of the Convention on the Rights of the Child*, CRC/C/58, 20 November 1996

General Assembly, "Promotion and Protection of the Rights of Children, Sale of children, child prostitution and child pornography, provisional report prepared by Mr Vitit Muntarbhorn, Special Rapporteur of the Commission on Human Rights on the sale of children, child prostitution and child pornography", A/49/478, 5 October 1994

General Assembly, "Promotion and Protection of the Rights of Children, Sale of children, child prostitution and child pornography, interim report by Ms. Ofelia Calcetas-Santos, Special Rapporteur of the Commission on Human Rights on the sale of children, child prostitution and child pornography", A/51/456, 7 October 1996

The United Nations Convention on the Rights of the Child A Guide to the "Travaux Préparatoires", compiled and edited by Sharon Detrick, contributors Jaap Doek, Nigel Cantwell, Martinus Nijhoff Publishers, The Netherlands, 1992

Working Group on a draft optional protocol to the Convention on the Rights of the Child on the sale of children, child prostitution and child pornography, E/CN.4/1994/WG.14/Add.1

World Congress against Commercial Sexual Exploitation of Children, "Declaration and Agenda for Action", Stockholm, August 1996, A/51/385, 1996

World Health Organization, Guiding Principles on Human Organ Transplantation, 1991

Human Organ Transplantation: A report on developments under the auspices of the World Health Organization 1987-1991, International Digest of Health Legislation 1991: 42, 389-413, pp. 26-28.

ARTICLE 36
● Instruments:

International Covenant on Civil and Political Rights (1966)

● Other sources:

Committee on the Rights of the Child, *General Guidelines Regarding the Form and Contents of Initial Reports to be submitted by States Parties Under Article 44, Paragraph 1(a), of the Convention on the Rights of the Child*, CRC/C/5, 15 October 1991

Committee on the Rights of the Child, *General Guidelines Regarding the Form and Contents of Periodic Reports to be submitted by States Parties under Article 44, Paragraph 1(b), of the Convention on the Rights of the Child*, CRC/C/58, 20 November 1996

Human Rights Committee, General Comment 20, "Article 7", 1992, in *Compilation of General Comments and General Recommendations Adopted by Human Rights Treaty Bodies*, HR1/GEN/1/Rev.2, 29 March 1996

The United Nations Convention on the Rights of the Child A Guide to the "Travaux Préparatoires", compiled and edited by Sharon Detrick, contributors Jaap Doek, Nigel Cantwell, Martinus Nijhoff Publishers, The Netherlands, 1992

Council for International Organizations of Medical Sciences, *International Ethical Guidelines for Biomedical Research Involving Human Subjects*, Geneva 1993

ARTICLE 37
● Instruments:

Universal Declaration of Human Rights (1948)

International Covenant on Civil and Political Rights (1966)

Second Optional Protocol to the International Covenant on Civil and Political Rights (1989)

Declaration on the Potection of All Persons from Being Subjected to Torture and Other Cruel, Inhuman or Degrading Treatment or Punishment (1975)

Convention against Torture and Other Cruel, Inhuman or Degrading Treatment or Punishment (1984)

Standard Minimum Rules for the Treatment of Prisoners (1984)

United Nations Standard Minimum Rules for the Administration of Juvenile Justice (the "Beijing Rules") (1985)

Body of Principles for the Protection of All Persons under Any form of Detention or Imprisonment (1988)

Principles on the Effective Prevention and Investigation of Extra-Legal, Arbitrary and Summary Executions (1989)

United Nations Guidelines for the Prevention of Juvenile Delinquency (the "Riyadh Guidelines") (1990)

United Nations Rules for the Protection of Juveniles Deprived of their Liberty (1990)

United Nations Standard Minimum Rules for Non-custodial Measures (the "Tokyo Rules") (1990)

Declaration on the Protection of All Persons from Enforced Disappearances (1993)

● Other sources:

Centre for Human Rights, Crime Prevention and Criminal Justice Branch *Human Rights and Pre-trial Detention*, Professional Training Series No.3, United Nations, New York and Geneva, 1994

Commission on Crime Prevention and Criminal Justice, resolution 3/1, April 1994

Commission on Human Rights, resolution 1992/35, "Habeas Corpus", 28 February 1992

Committee on the Rights of the Child, *General Guidelines Regarding the Form and Contents of Initial Reports to be submitted by States Parties Under Article 44, Paragraph 1(a), of the Convention on the Rights of the Child*, CRC/C/5, 15 October 1991

Committee on the Rights of the Child, *General Guidelines Regarding the Form and Contents of Periodic Reports to be submitted by States Parties under Article 44, Paragraph 1(b), of the Convention on the Rights of the Child*, CRC/C/58, 20 November 1996

General Assembly, "Official Records of the General Assembly, Forty-fourth session, Supplement No.40", A/44/40, 1989

General Assembly, "Official Records of the General Assembly, Forty-sixth session, Supplement No 40", A/46/40, 1991

General Assembly, "Report of the Committee Against Torture", 50th Session, Supplement No 44, A/50/44, 1995

General Assembly, "United Nations Rules for the Protection of Juveniles Deprived of their Liberty", resolution 45/113, 14 December 1990

Human Rights Committee, General Comment 7, "Article 7", 1982; General Comment 8, "Article 9", 1982; General Comment 9, "Article 10", 1982; General Comment 20, "Article 7", 1992, in *Compilation of General Comments and General Recommendations Adopted by Human Rights Treaty Bodies*, HR1/GEN/1/Rev.2, 29 March 1996

United Nations High Commissioner for Refugees (UNHCR), *Refugee Children: Guidelines on Protection and Care*, UNHCR, Geneva, 1994

UNHCR, Executive Conclusion No. 44, 1986

UNHCR Policy on Refugee Children, UNHCR Executive Committee EC/SCP/82, 1993

ARTICLE 38
● Instruments:

Geneva Convention for the Amelioration of the Condition of the Wounded and Sick in Armed Forces in the Field (1949)

Geneva Convention for the Amelioration of the Condition of Wounded, Sick and Shipwrecked Members of Armed Forces at Sea (1949)

Geneva Convention Relative to the Treatment of Prisoners of War (1949)

Geneva Convention Relative to the Protection of Civilian Persons in Time of War (1949)

Convention relating to the Status of Refugees (1951), as amended by the *Protocol relating to the Status of Refugees (1967)*

Declaration of the Rights of the Child (1959)

International Covenant on Civil and Political Rights (1966)

Declaration on the Protection of Women and Children in Emergency and Armed Conflict (1974)

Protocol Additional to the Geneva Conventions of 12 August 1949 and relating to the Protection of the Victims of International Armed Conflicts (Protocol I) (1977)

Protocol Additional to the Geneva Conventions of 12 August 1949 and relating to the Protection of Victims of Non-International Armed Conflicts (Protocol II) (1977)

Convention on the Elimination of All Forms of Discrimination against Women (1979)

Convention on Prohibitions or Restrictions on the Use of Certain Conventional Weapons Which May Be Deemed to Be Excessively Injurious or to Have Indiscriminate Effects (1983); Protocol II on Prohibitions or Restrictions on the use of Mines, Booby-traps and other devices, as amended 1996 (not yet in force; September 1997)

● **Other sources:**

Commission on Human Rights, "Inter-sessional open-ended working group on a draft optional protocol to the Convention on the Rights of the Child on involvement of children in armed conflicts, Comments on the report of the working group", E/CN.4/1997/WG.13/2/Add.1, 27 December 1996

Commission on Human Rights, Report of the working group on a draft optional protocol to the Convention on the Rights of the Child on involvement of children in armed conflicts", E/CN.4/1996/102, 21 March 1996,

Commission of Human Rights, "Special Rapporteur on situations of systematic rape, sexual slavery, and slavery-like practices during periods of armed conflict", E/CN.4/Sub.2/1996/26, 16 July 1996

Committee on the Rights of the Child, *General Guidelines Regarding the Form and Contents of Initial Reports to be submitted by States Parties Under Article 44, Paragraph 1(a), of the Convention on the Rights of the Child,* CRC/C/5, 15 October 1991

Committee on the Rights of the Child, *General Guidelines Regarding the Form and Contents of Periodic Reports to be submitted by States Parties under Article 44, Paragraph 1(b), of the Convention on the Rights of the Child,* CRC/C/58, 20 November 1996

Committee on the Rights of the Child, *Reservations, Declarations and Objections Relating to the Convention on the Rights of the Child,* CRC/C/2/Rev.5, 30 July 1996

Draft Convention on the Prohibition of the Use, Stockpiling, Production and Transfer of Anti-Personnel Mines and on their Destruction, Diplomatic Conference, Oslo, September 1997

General Assembly, "An international agreement to ban anti-personnel landmines", resolution A/RES/51/45/5, 10 December 1996

Human Rights Committee, General Comment 17, "Article 24", 1989 in *Compilation of General Comments and General Recommendations Adopted by Human Rights Treaty Bodies,* HRI/GEN/1/Rev.2, 29 March 1996

"Impact of Armed Conflict on Children", Report of the expert of the Secretary-General, Ms Graça Machel, A/51/306, 26 August 1996

Symposium organised by UNICEF in Cooperation with NGO sub-group of the NGO Working Group on the Convention on the Rights of the Child, "Cape Town Principles on the prevention of recruitment into the armed forces and demobilization and social reintegration of child soldiers in Africa", adopted by participants, Cape Town, 30 April 1997

The United Nations Convention on the Rights of the Child A Guide to the "Travaux Préparatoires", compiled and edited by Sharon Detrick, contributors Jaap Doek, Nigel Cantwell, Martinus Nijhoff Publishers, The Netherlands, 1992

World Conference on Human Rights, Vienna, 1993, "Vienna Declaration and Programme of Action", A/CONF.157/23, 1993

World Summit for Children, "World Declaration on the Survival, Protection and Development of Children and Plan of Action for Implementing the World Declaration on the Survival, Protection and Development of Children in the 1990s", CF/WSC/1990/WS-001, United Nations, New York, 30 September 1990

ARTICLE 39

● **Instruments:**

Geneva Convention No.1 for the Amelioration of the Condition of the Wounded and Sick in Armed Forces in the Field (1949)

Geneva Convention No.2 for the Amelioration of the Condition of Wounded, Sick and Shipwrecked Members of Armed Forces at Sea (1949)

Geneva Convention No.3 Relative to the Treatment of Prisoners of War (1949)

Geneva Convention No.4 Relative to the Protection of Civilian Persons in Time of War (1949)

Protocol Additional to the Geneva Conventions of 12 August 1949 and relating to the Protection of the Victims of International Armed Conflicts (Protocol I) (1977)

Protocol Additional to the Geneva Conventions of 12 August 1949 and relating to the Protection of Victims of Non-International Armed Conflicts (Protocol II) (1977)

Convention against Torture and Other Cruel, Inhuman or Degrading Treatment or Punishment (1984)

United Nations Standard Minimum Rules for the Administration of Juvenile Justice (the "Beijing Rules") (1985)

Declaration of Basic Principles of Justice for Victims of Crime and Abuse of Power (1985)

United Nations Guidelines for the Prevention of Juvenile Delinquency (the "Riyadh Guidelines") (1990)

United Nations Rules for the Protection of Juveniles Deprived of their Liberty (1990)

● **Other sources:**

Commission on Human Rights, "Programme of Action for the Elimination of the Exploitation of Child Labour", 1993/79, 10 March 1993

Commission on Human Rights, "Programmes of action for the prevention of the sale of children, child prostitution and child pornography and the elimination of the exploitation of child labour", resolution 1992/74, annex, 5 March 1992

Committee on the Rights of the Child, *General Guidelines Regarding the Form and Contents of Initial Reports to be submitted by States Parties Under Article 44, Paragraph 1(a), of the Convention on the Rights of the Child,* CRC/C/5, 15 October 1991

Committee on the Rights of the Child, *General Guidelines Regarding the Form and Contents of Periodic Reports to be submitted by States Parties under Article 44, Paragraph 1(b), of the Convention on the Rights of the Child,* CRC/C/58, 20 November 1996

General Assembly, "Promotion and Protection of the Rights of the Child: Sale of children, child prostitution and child pornography, interim report of Ms Ofelia Calcetas-Santos, Special Rapporteur of the Commission on Human Rights on the sale of children, child prostitution and child pornography", A/51/456, 7 October 1996

International Labour Organization, *Child labour Targeting the intolerable,* ILO, Geneva, 1996

World Congress against Commercial Sexual Exploitation of Children, "Declaration and Agenda for Action", A/51/385, Stockholm 1996

ARTICLE 40

● **Instruments:**

ILO Convention No.29, Forced Labour (1930)

Universal Declaration of Human Rights (1948)

International Covenant on Civil and Political Rights (1966)

United Nations Standard Minimum Rules for the Administration of Juvenile Justice (the "Beijing Rules") (1985)

United Nations Guidelines for the Prevention of Juvenile Delinquency (the "Riyadh Guidelines") (1990)

United Nations Rules for the Protection of Juveniles Deprived of their Liberty (1990)

United Nations Standard Minimum Rules for Non-custodial Measures (the "Tokyo Rules") (1990)

● **Other sources:**

Committee on the Rights of the Child, *General Guidelines Regarding the Form and Contents of Initial Reports to be submitted by States Parties Under Article 44, Paragraph 1(a), of the Convention on the Rights of the Child,* CRC/C/5, 15 October 1991

Committee on the Rights of the Child, *General Guidelines Regarding the Form and Contents of Periodic Reports to be submitted by States Parties under Article 44, Paragraph 1(b), of the Convention on the Rights of the Child,* CRC/C/58, 20 November 1996

Committee on the Rights of the Child, *Reservations, Declarations and Objections Relating to the Convention on the Rights of the Child,* CRC/C/2/Rev.5, 30 July 1996

Human Rights Committee, General Comment 17, "Article 24", 1989, in *Compilation of General Comments and General Recommendations*

Adopted by Human Rights Treaty Bodies, HR1/GEN/1/Rev.2, 29 March 1996

ARTICLE 41

● **Instruments:**

International Covenant on Civil and Political Rights (1966)

International Covenant on Economic, Social and Cultural Rights (1966)

● **Other sources:**

Committee on the Rights of the Child, *General Guidelines Regarding the Form and Contents of Periodic Reports to be submitted by States Parties under Article 44, Paragraph 1(b), of the Convention on the Rights of the Child,* CRC/C/58, 20 November 1996

The United Nations Convention on the Rights of the Child A Guide to the "Travaux Pré-paratoires", compiled and edited by Sharon Detrick, contributors Jaap Doek, Nigel Cantwell, Martinus Nijhoff Publishers, The Netherlands, 1992

General Assembly resolution 41/120, Setting International Standards in the field of human rights, 1986, World Conference on Human Rights, Vienna, 1993, "Vienna Declaration and Programme of Action", A/CONF.157/23, 1993

ARTICLE 42

● **Instruments:**

International Covenant on Civil and Political Rights (1966)

● **Other sources:**

Committee on the Rights of the Child, *General Guidelines Regarding the Form and Contents of Initial Reports to be submitted by States Parties Under Article 44, Paragraph 1(a), of the Convention on the Rights of the Child,* CRC/C/5, 15 October 1991

Committee on the Rights of the Child, *General Guidelines Regarding the Form and Contents of Periodic Reports to be submitted by States Parties under Article 44, Paragraph 1(b), of the Convention on the Rights of the Child,* CRC/C/58, 20 November 1996

Human Rights Committee, General Comment 3, "Article 2 Implementation at the national level", 1981, in *Compilation of General Comments and General Recommendations Adopted by Human Rights Treaty Bodies,* HR1/GEN/1/Rev.2, 29 March 1996

ACRONYMS

For explanation of abbreviations used in references - IRCO, SR, etc., see page XVIII

AIDS	acquired immunodeficiency syndrome
CAT	Committee against Torture
CEDC	Children in especially difficult circumstances
CEDAW	Committee on the Elimination of Discrimination against Women
CERD	Committee on the Elimination of Racial Discrimination
CRC	Committee on the Rights of the Child
CSD	Commission for Social Development
ECOSOC	Economic and Social Council of the United Nations
FAO	Food and Agriculture Organization of the United Nations
HIV	human immunodeficiency virus
HRC	Human Rights Committee
IBRD	International Bank for Reconstruction and Development
ICDC	International Child Development Centre
ICPD	International Conference on Population and Development
IDA	International Development Association
IFC	International Finance Corporation
ILO	International Labour Organization
IMF	International Monetary Fund
INCB	International Narcotics Control Board
INGO	international non-governmental organization
INSTRAW	International Research and Training Institute for the Advancement of Women
INTERPOL	International Criminal Police Organization
IPA	International Association for the Child's Rights to Play
IPEC	International Programme on the Elimination of Child Labour
NGO	non-governmental organization
UNAIDS	Joint United Nations Programme on HIV/AIDS
UNCHS	United Nations Centre for Human Settlements (Habitat)
UNCTAD	United Nations Conference on Trade and Development
UNDCP	United Nations International Drug Control Programme
UNDP	United Nations Development Programme
UNEP	United Nations Environment Programme
UNESCO	United Nations Educational, Scientific and Cultural Organization
UNFPA	United Nations Population Fund
UNHCR	United Nations High Commissioner for Refugees
UNICEF	United Nations Children's Fund
UNICRI	United Nations Interregional Crime and Justice Research Institute
UNIFEM	United Nations Development Fund for Women
UNITAR	United Nations Institute for Training and Research
UNRISD	United Nations Research Institute for Social Development
WFP	World Food Programme
WHA	World Health Assembly
WHO	World Health Organization
WSC	World Summit for Children
WTO	World Trade Organization